WEST'S PARALEGAL TODAY
THE LEGAL TEAM AT WORK
Second Edition

The West Legal Studies Series

Your options keep growing with West Legal Studies

Each year our list continues to offer you more options for every area of the law to meet your course or on-the-job reference requirements. We now have over 140 titles from which to choose in the following areas:

- Administrative Law
- Alternative Dispute Resolution
- Bankruptcy
- Business Organizations/Corporations
- Civil Litigation and Procedure
- CLA Exam Preparation
- Client Accounting
- Computer in the Law Office
- Constitutional Law
- Contract Law
- Criminal Law and Procedure
- Document Preparation
- Environmental Law
- Ethics
- Family Law
- Federal Taxation
- Intellectual Property
- Introduction to Law
- Introduction to Paralegalism
- Law Office Management
- Law Office Procedures
- Legal Research, Writing, and Analysis
- Legal Terminology
- Paralegal Employment
- Real Estate Law
- Reference Materials
- Torts and Personal Injury Law
- Will, Trusts, and Estate Administration

You will find unparalleled, practical support

Each book is augmented by instructor and student supplements to ensure the best learning experience possible. We also offer custom publishing and other benefits such as West's Student Achievement Award. In addition, our sales representatives are ready to provide you with dependable service.

We want to hear from you

Our best contributions for improving the quality of our books and instructional materials is feedback from the people who use them. If you have a question, concern, or observation about any of our materials, or you have a product proposal or manuscript, we want to hear from you. Please contact your local representative or write us at the following address:

West Legal Studies, 3 Columbia Circle, P.O. Box 15015, Albany, NY 12212-5015

For additional information point your browser at
www.westlegalstudies.com

WEST'S PARALEGAL TODAY
THE LEGAL TEAM AT WORK

Second Edition

ROGER LeROY MILLER
Institute for University Studies
Arlington, Texas

&

MARY MEINZINGER URISKO
Madonna University, Michigan
Assistant Dean, Paralegal Program

WEST LEGAL STUDIES
Thomson Learning™

Africa • Australia • Canada • Denmark • Japan • Mexico • New Zealand • Philippines
Puerto Rico • Singapore • Spain • United Kingdom • United States

NOTICE TO THE READER

Publisher does not warrant or guarantee any of the products described herein or perform any independent analysis in connection with any of the product information contained herein. Publisher does not assume, and expressly disclaims, any obligation to obtain and include information other than that provided to it by the manufacturer.

The reader is expressly warned to consider and adopt all safety precautions that might be indicated by the activities herein and to avoid all potential hazards. By following the instructions contained herein, the reader willingly assumes all risks in connection with such instructions.

The Publisher makes no representation or warranties of any kind, including but not limited to, the warranties of fitness for particular purpose or merchantability, nor are any such representations implied with respect to the material set forth herein, and the publisher takes no responsibility with respect to such material. The publisher shall not be liable for any special, consequential, or exemplary damages resulting, in whole or part, from the readers' use of, or reliance upon, this material.

West Legal Studies Staff:

Business Unit Director: Susan Simpfenderfer
Executive Editor: Marlene McHugh Pratt
Acquisitions Editor: Joan Gill
Developmental Editor: Rhonda Dearborn
Editorial Assistant: Lisa Flatley
Executive Marketing Manager: Donna Lewis
Executive Production Manager: Wendy Troeger
Production Editor: Laurie A. Boyce
Production Service and Design: Ann Borman
Composition: Parkwood Composition Services, Inc.
Copyediting: Suzie Franklin DeFazio and Lavina Miller
Index: Bob Marsh
Cover Images: Photodisc

COPYRIGHT © 2000
West Legal Studies is an imprint of Delmar, a division of Thomson Learning.
The Thomson Learning logo is a registered trademark used herein under license.

Printed in the United States of America
3 4 5 6 7 8 9 10 XXX 05 04 03 02 01 00

For more information, contact:
Delmar, 3 Columbia Circle, PO Box 15015, Albany, NY 12212-0515;
or find us on the World Wide Web at http://www.westlegalstudies.com

All rights reserved. Thomson Learning © 2000. The text of this publication, or any part thereof, may not be reproduced or transmitted in any form or by any means, electronics or mechanical, including photocopying, recording, storage in an information retrieval system, or otherwise, without prior permission of the publisher.

You can request permission to use material from this text through the following phone and fax numbers: Phone: 1-800-730-2214; Fax 1-800-730-2215; or visit our Web site at http://www.thomsonrights.com

Library of Congress Cataloging-in-Publication Data
Miller, Roger LeRoy
    West's paralegal today : the legal team at work / Roger LeRoy Miller, Mary S. Urisko.—2nd ed.
      p. cm.
    ISBN 0-7668-1009-7
    1. Legal assistants—United States. I. Urisko, Mary S.
II. Title
KF320.L4M556 1999
340'.023'73—dc21

99-29176
CIP

DEDICATION

To Leslie and Phil,

for a long history together,

and an even longer future.

Thanks.

R.L.M.

To John Koestner,

marty meinzinger,

jerry meinzinger,

For your friendship.

M.M.U.

Contents in Brief

Preface   xxviii

Introduction to the Student   xlv

Part 1: The Paralegal Profession   1

Chapter 1
Today's Professional Paralegal   2

Chapter 2
Careers in the Legal Community   27

Chapter 3
Ethics and Professional Responsibility   71

Chapter 4
The Legal Workplace   116

Part 2: Introduction to Law   147

Chapter 5
Sources of American Law   148

Chapter 6
The Court System and Alternative Dispute Resolution   178

Chapter 7
Substantive Law I   214

Chapter 8
Substantive Law II   258

Chapter 9
Administrative Law and Government Regulation 289

Part 3:
Legal Procedures and Paralegal Skills 329

Chapter 10
Civil Litigation—Before the Trial 330
Chapter 11
Trial Procedures 382
Chapter 12
Criminal Law and Procedures 414
Chapter 13
Conducting Interviews and Investigations 452
Chapter 14
Legal Research 487
Chapter 15
Computer-Assisted Legal Research 540
Chapter 16
Legal Analysis and Writing 582

Appendix A
NALA's Code of Ethics and Professional Responsibility 635
Appendix B
NALA's Model Standards and Guidelines for the Utilization of Legal Assistants 637

APPENDIX C
NFPA's Model Code of Ethics and Professional Responsibility and Guidelines for Enforcement 641

APPENDIX D
The ABA's Model Guidelines for the Utilization of Legal Assistant Services 651

APPENDIX E
Paralegal Ethics and Regulation: How to Find State-Specific Information 663

APPENDIX F
Paralegal Associations 667

APPENDIX G
State and Major Local Bar Associations 673

APPENDIX H
Information on NALA's CLA and CLAS Examinations 679

APPENDIX I
Information on NFPA's PACE Examination 687

APPENDIX J
The Constitution of the United States 691

APPENDIX K
Spanish Equivalents for Important Legal Terms in English 707

Glossary 713

Index 729

Contents

Preface xxviii

Introduction to the Student xlv

PART 1: THE PARALEGAL PROFESSION 1

CHAPTER 1
Today's Professional Paralegal 2

Ethical Concern: Paralegal Expertise and Legal Advice 5

Ethical Concern: Ethics and the Effective Utilization of Paralegals 9

Developing Paralegal Skills: Preparing for the CLA Exam 12

Technology and Today's Paralegal: The Changing Paralegal Workplace 15

Featured Guest: Wendy B. Edson, Ten Tips for Effective Communication 16

Developing Paralegal Skills: Interviewing a Client 18

Paralegal Profile: Trusts and Estates Paralegal 20

Today's Professional Paralegal: A Winning Combination 22

INTRODUCTION 3
WHAT IS A PARALEGAL? 3
WHAT DO PARALEGALS DO? 5
HISTORY OF THE PARALEGAL PROFESSION 6
  Paralegal Associations and Professional Growth 7
  Economics and the Paralegal Profession 8
PARALEGAL EDUCATION 8
  Educational Options 9
  Curriculum—A Blend of Substantive and Procedural Law 10
  The ABA's Role in Paralegal Education 10
  Certification 11
  Continuing Legal Education 12
PARALEGAL SKILLS 13
  Organizational Skills 13
  Analytical Skills 14
  Computer Skills 14
  Interpersonal Skills 14
  Communication Skills 15
PERSONAL ATTRIBUTES OF THE PROFESSIONAL PARALEGAL 19
  Responsibility and Reliability 19
  Commitment 19
  Objectivity 20
  The Ability to Keep Confidences 21
  Other Attributes 21
THE FUTURE OF THE PROFESSION 21

Chapter 2
Careers in the Legal Community 27

Introduction 28
Where Paralegals Work 28
  Law Firms 28
  Corporations and Other Business Organizations 31
  Government 32
  Legal Aid Offices 33
  Freelance Paralegals 33
Paralegal Specialties 34
  Litigation Assistance 34
  Personal-Injury Law 35
  Criminal Law 35
  Corporate Law 36
  Bankruptcy Law 37
  Employment and Labor Law 37
  Estate Planning and Probate Administration 39
  Intellectual-Property Law 40
  Environmental Law 41
  Real-Estate Law 42
  Family Law 42
  Emerging Specialty Areas 44
Paralegal Compensation 45
  Compensation Surveys 45
  Job Benefits 46
  Salaries versus Hourly Wages 46
  Federal Law and Overtime Pay 47
Planning Your Career 48
  Defining Your Long-Term Goals 48
  Short-Term Goals and Job Realities 48
Locating Potential Employers 49
  Networking 49
  Finding Available Jobs 49
  Identifying Possible Employers 50
Job-Placement Services 50
Marketing Your Skills 53
  The Application Process 54
  The Interview 59
  The Follow-Up Letter 62
  Maintain Job-Hunting Files 62
  Salary Negotiations 63
Reevaluating Your Career 65
  Career Paths 65
  Creating Opportunities 65
  Other Options 67

Developing Paralegal Skills: Contracts Administrator 32

Developing Paralegal Skills: Working for a Public Defender 36

Ethical Concern: Serving the Interests of Bereaved Clients 40

Paralegal Profile: Real-Estate Paralegal 43

Ethical Concern: Questions about Child Custody 44

Technology and Today's Paralegal: Online Job Searching 51

Featured Guest: Denise Templeton, Paralegal Career Planning and Development 52

Developing Paralegal Skills: A Career Plan 54

Ethical Concern: "Gilding the Lily" 60

Today's Professional Paralegal: Conducting a Title Exam 66

Chapter 3
Ethics and Professional Responsibility 71

Ethical Concern: Missed Deadlines 79

Developing Paralegal Skills: Inadequate Supervision 80

Developing Paralegal Skills: Client Intends to Commit a Crime 82

Ethical Concern: Social Events and Confidentiality 83

Technology and Today's Paralegal: Is E-Mail "Confidential"? 84

Ethical Concern: Personal versus Professional Ethics 85

Developing Paralegal Skills: Building an Ethical Wall 88

Featured Guest: Michael A. Pener, Ten Tips for Ethics and the Paralegal 90

Developing Paralegal Skills: Avoiding UPL Problems 101

Paralegal Profile: Freelance Paralegal 102

Ethical Concern: Saying "If I were you . . . " and the UPL 105

Today's Professional Paralegal: Working for the Attorney Discipline Board 109

INTRODUCTION 72
THE REGULATION OF ATTORNEYS 72
   Who Are the Regulators? 73
   Licensing Requirements 74
   Ethical Codes and Rules 74
   Sanctions for Violations 75
ATTORNEY ETHICS AND PARALEGAL PRACTICE 77
   The Duty of Competence 77
   Confidentiality of Information 79
   Confidentiality and the Attorney-Client Privilege 83
   Conflict of Interest 86
THE INDIRECT REGULATION OF PARALEGALS 89
   Paralegal Ethical Codes 89
   Guidelines for the Utilization of Paralegals 91
   The Increasing Scope of Paralegal Responsibilities 96
THE UNAUTHORIZED PRACTICE OF LAW 98
   Giving Legal Opinions and Advice 99
   Representing Clients in Court 100
   Disclosure of Paralegal Status 100
   Paralegals Freelancing for Attorneys 101
   Independent Paralegals and the UPL 103
SHOULD PARALEGALS BE LICENSED? 105
   General versus Limited Licensing 105
   Direct Regulation—The Pros and Cons 106
   Other Considerations 108
A FINAL NOTE 108

Chapter 4
The Legal Workplace 116

Paralegal Profile: Legal Support Supervisor 120

INTRODUCTION 117
THE ORGANIZATIONAL STRUCTURE OF LAW FIRMS 117
   Sole Proprietorships 117
   Partnerships 118
   Professional Corporations 118
LAW-OFFICE MANAGEMENT AND PERSONNEL 118

Developing Paralegal Skills: Client File Confidentiality 124

Featured Guest: Kathleen Mercer Reed, Ten Tips for Creating and Maintaining an Efficient File System 126

Ethical Concern: Handling Clients' Questions about Fees 130

Ethical Concern: Trust Accounts 132

Developing Paralegal Skills: Creating a Trust Account 133

Ethical Concern: Back Up Your Work 136

Developing Paralegal Skills: A Client Complains about a Bill 137

Technology and Today's Paralegal: Cyberspace Communications 138

Today's Professional Paralegal: Managing Conflict in the Legal Workplace 139

EMPLOYMENT POLICIES 121
Performance Evaluations 121
Employment Termination 122
Employment Discrimination 122

FILING PROCEDURES 123
Client Files 123
Work-Product Files and Reference Materials 127
Forms Files 128

FINANCIAL PROCEDURES 128
Fee Arrangements 128
Client Trust Accounts 131
The Prohibition against Fee Splitting 132
Billing and Timekeeping Procedures 132
Ethics and Client Billing Practices 136

COMMUNICATING WITH CLIENTS 137

LAW-OFFICE CULTURE AND POLITICS 140

PART 2: INTRODUCTION TO LAW 147

CHAPTER 5
Sources of American Law 148

Developing Paralegal Skills: State versus Federal Legislation 152

Paralegal Profile: Legal Assistant in a General Law Practice 154

Ethical Concern: Legal Research and *Stare Decisis* 158

INTRODUCTION 149
WHAT IS LAW? 149
CONSTITUTIONAL LAW 149
The Federal Constitution 149
State Constitutions 151
Substantive Law Concept Summary: Constitutional Law 151
Constitutional Law and the Paralegal 151
STATUTORY LAW 152
The Expanding Scope of Statutory Law 152

CONTENTS   XV

Developing Paralegal Skills: Analyzing a Case for Specific Performance   161

Ethical Concern: the Statute of Limitations and the Duty of Competence   162

Ethical Concern: What to Do When Someone Asks You about Remedies   164

Developing Paralegal Skills: Following Up with a Client   166

Technology and Today's Paralegal: Finding Information on Other Nations' Laws   167

Featured Guest: Daniel F. Hinkel, *Pro Bono* for Paralegals   168

Today's Professional Paralegal: Legal and Paralegal Practice in England   172

Substantive Law Concept Summary: Statutory Law   153
Statutory Law and the Paralegal   153
ADMINISTRATIVE LAW   153
Agency Creation and Function   155
Substantive Law Concept Summary: Administrative Law   155
Administrative Law and the Paralegal   155
CASE LAW AND THE COMMON LAW TRADITION   156
Early English Courts of Law   156
The Doctrine of *Stare Decisis*   157
Remedies at Law versus Remedies in Equity   159
The Common Law Today   162
Statutory Law and the Common Law   162
The Terminology of Case Law   163
Substantive Law Concept Summary: Case Law and the Common Law Tradition   165
Common Law and the Paralegal   166
NATIONAL AND INTERNATIONAL LAW   167
National Law   168
International Law   170
Substantive Law Concept Summary: National and International Law   170
International Law and the Paralegal   171

CHAPTER 6

The Court System and Alternative Dispute Resolution   178

Developing Paralegal Skills: Choice of Courts: State or Federal?   183

Ethical Concern: Meeting Procedural Deadlines   186

Developing Paralegal Skills: Trial Emergency   188

Developing Paralegal Skills: Federal Court Jurisdiction   194

Technology and Today's Paralegal: Filing Court Documents Electronically   195

INTRODUCTION   179
THE AMERICAN SYSTEM OF JUSTICE   179
Types of Jurisdiction   179
Jurisdiction of the Federal Courts   181
Venue   182
Standing to Sue   183
Judicial Procedures   184
The American System of Justice and the Paralegal   184
Procedural Law Concept Summary: The American System of Justice   185
STATE COURT SYSTEMS   186
Trial Courts   186
Courts of Appeals   188
Procedural Law Concept Summary: State Court Systems   189
State Court Systems and the Paralegal   189

Featured Guest: Andrea Nager Chasen, Mediation and the Paralegal 198

Ethical Concern: Potential Arbitration Problems 201

Ethical Concern: Private Justice 203

Today's Professional Paralegal: Arbitrating Commercial Contracts 205

Paralegal Profile: Litigation Paralegal 206

The Federal Court System 190
- U.S. District Courts 190
- U.S. Courts of Appeals 191
- The United States Supreme Court 192
- The Federal Court System and the Paralegal 192
- *Procedural Law Concept Summary:* The Federal Court System 193

Alternative Dispute Resolution 194
- Negotiation 194
- Mediation 196
- Arbitration 200
- Other ADR Forms 202
- Court-Referred ADR 202
- Providers of ADR Services 203
- *Procedural Law Concept Summary:* Alternative Dispute Resolution 204
- ADR and the Paralegal 205

Chapter 7
Substantive Law I 214

Ethical Concern: Malpractice Suits 218

Developing Paralegal Skills: Product-Liability Paralegals 219

Featured Guest: John DeLeo, J.D., The Paralegal's Relationship to the Law 222

Developing Paralegal Skills: Contract Review 227

Technology and Today's Paralegal: Contract Forms 230

Ethical Concern: Real-Estate Sales and the Duties of Competence and Diligence 233

Ethical Concern: Accurate Paperwork and the Sale of Real Estate 239

Paralegal Profile: Real-Estate Paralegal 241

Introduction 215
Torts 215
- Intentional Torts 215
- Negligence 216
- Strict Liability 218
- Tort Law and the Paralegal 219
- *Substantive Law Concept Summary:* Torts 220

Contracts 221
- Contract Requirements 222
- Defenses to Contract Enforceability 224
- Sales Contracts and Warranties 225
- Remedies for Breach of Contract 226
- Contract Law and the Paralegal 227
- *Substantive Law Concept Summary:* Contract Law 228

Real Property 230
- Ownership Rights in Property 231
- The Transfer and Sale of Real Property 232
- Leases 239
- Property Law and the Paralegal 240

Wills, Trusts, and Estates 243
- Wills 244
- *Substantive Law Concept Summary:* Property Law 244
- Trusts 246
- Other Estate-Planning Devices 248

CONTENTS xvii

Developing Paralegal Skills: Reviewing the Closing Package 243

Developing Paralegal Skills: Drafting a Client's Will 246

Today's Professional Paralegal: Relocation Assistance 250

Estate Administration 248
Wills, Trusts, and Estates and the Paralegal 248
Substantive Law Concept Summary: Wills, Trusts, and Estates 249

CHAPTER 8
Substantive Law II 258

Ethical Concern: The Paralegal as Agent and Subagent 260

Developing Paralegal Skills: A Case of *Respondeat Superior* 262

Ethical Concern: The Paralegal as an Apparent Partner 265

Developing Paralegal Skills: Reserving a Corporate Name 270

Featured Guest: Lloyd G. Pearcy, The Paralegal and Projects Involving Business Organizations 274

Ethical Concern: Meeting Federal Court Deadlines 278

Paralegal Profile: Debtor/Creditor and Real-Estate Paralegal 279

Technology and Today's Paralegal: The Expanding World of Intellectual Property 281

Today's Professional Paralegal: Preparing Articles of Incorporation 282

INTRODUCTION 259
AGENCY LAW 259
  Fiduciary Duties 259
  Agency Relationships and Third Parties 259
  Agency Law and the Paralegal 260
  Substantive Law Concept Summary: The Law of Agency 261
FORMS OF BUSINESS ORGANIZATION 261
  Sole Proprietorships 261
  Partnerships 263
  Corporations 266
  Limited Liability Companies and Partnerships 273
  Business Organizations and the Paralegal 276
  Substantive Law Concept Summary: Forms of Business Organization 277
INTELLECTUAL PROPERTY 278
  Forms of Intellectual Property 280
  Substantive Law Concept Summary: Intellectual Property 280
  Intellectual Property and the Paralegal 283

CONTENTS

Chapter 9
Administrative Law and Government Regulation 289

Featured Guest: Judy A. Long, Paralegal Positions in Government 292

Ethical Concern: Putting the Client's Interests First 295

Paralegal Profile: Immigration Paralegal 296

Developing Paralegal Skills: Preparing for an Administrative Hearing 297

Ethical Concern: Decorum before Agency Hearings 298

Developing Paralegal Skills: Approval to Practice before the IRS 299

Ethical Concern: Confidentiality and Administrative Practice 301

Technology and Today's Paralegal: Consumer Protection against Internet Fraud 304

Developing Paralegal Skills: Discharged for Garnishment 307

Developing Paralegal Skills: Monitoring the *Federal Register* 314

Today's Professional Paralegal: Developing a Policy on Sexual Harassment 321

INTRODUCTION 290
ADMINISTRATIVE LAW 290
   Types of Administrative Agencies 290
   Agency Powers 293
   Administrative Process 295
   State Administrative Agencies 298
   Paralegal Practice before Administrative Agencies 299
   Administrative Law and the Paralegal 300
   Substantive Law Concept Summary: Administrative Law 300
CONSUMER LAW 301
   Deceptive Advertising 302
   Labeling and Packaging Laws 303
   Sales Transactions 303
   Consumer Health and Safety 304
   Consumer Credit Protection 305
   Consumer Law and the Paralegal 307
   Substantive Law Concept Summary: Consumer Law 308
ENVIRONMENTAL LAW 309
   Common Law Actions 309
   Federal Regulation of the Environment 309
   Air Pollution 310
   Water Pollution 310
   Toxic Chemicals 312
   State and Local Regulation 313
   Environmental Law and the Paralegal 314
   Substantive Law Concept Summary: Environmental Law 315
EMPLOYMENT RELATIONSHIPS 316
   Employment at Will 316
   Labor Laws 316
   Family and Medical Leave 317
   State Workers' Compensation Laws 318
   Employment Discrimination 318
   Substantive Law Concept Summary: Employment Relationships 320
   Employment Relationships and the Paralegal 320

Part 3:
Legal Procedures and Paralegal Skills 329

Chapter 10
Civil Litigation—Before the Trial 330

Ethical Concern:
The Unauthorized Practice of Law 334

Developing Paralegal Skills:
File Work-Up 335

Developing Paralegal Skills:
Federal Court Rules—Creating a Complaint Checklist 342

Ethical Concern:
Deadlines and the Duty of Competence 354

Paralegal Profile: Litigation Paralegal 356

Ethical Concern:
Keeping Client Information Confidential 357

Featured Guest: James W. H. McCord, Ten Tips for Drafting Interrogatories 358

Developing Paralegal Skills:
Deposition Summaries 368

Technology and Today's Paralegal: Indexing the Deposition Transcript 371

Today's Professional Paralegal: Witness Coordination 375

INTRODUCTION 331
CIVIL LITIGATION—A BIRD'S EYE VIEW 331
  Pretrial Settlements 331
  Procedural Requirements 332
  A Hypothetical Lawsuit 332
THE PRELIMINARIES 333
  The Initial Client Interview 333
  Preliminary Investigation 334
  Creating the Litigation File 334
THE PLEADINGS 335
  Drafting the Complaint 337
  Filing the Complaint 341
  Service of Process 343
  Notice and Waiver of Service—FRCP 4(d) 346
  The Defendant's Response 349
  Amending the Pleadings 353
PRETRIAL MOTIONS 353
  Motion for Judgment on the Pleadings 353
  Motion for Summary Judgment 354
TRADITIONAL DISCOVERY TOOLS 356
  Interrogatories 357
  Depositions 360
  Other Discovery Requests 370
REVISED DISCOVERY PROCEDURES UNDER FRCP 26 371
  Initial Disclosures 372
  Discovery Plan 373
  Subsequent Disclosures 373

Chapter 11
Trial Procedures 382

Developing Paralegal Skills:
Locating Expert Witnesses 386

INTRODUCTION 383
PREPARING FOR TRIAL 383
  Contacting and Preparing Witnesses 383

Ethical Concern: Why Subpoena Friendly Witnesses? 386

Technology and Today's Paralegal: Presentation Technology 388

Developing Paralegal Skills: Trial Support 389

Featured Guest: Vitorio F. San Juan, Ten Tips for Preparing a Trial Notebook 390

Ethical Concern: Should You Tell Your Supervising Attorney What You Know about a Prospective Juror? 393

Paralegal Profile: Litigation Paralegal 394

Ethical Concern: Communicating with Jurors 401

Developing Paralegal Skills: Locating Assets 406

Today's Professional Paralegal: Drafting *Voir Dire* Questions Like a Pro 407

Exhibits and Displays 387
The Trial Notebook 387
PRETRIAL CONFERENCE 388
JURY SELECTION 389
  Voir Dire 390
  Challenges during *Voir Dire* 392
THE TRIAL 394
  Opening Statements 396
  The Plaintiff's Case 396
  Motion for a Directed Verdict
    (Motion for Judgment as a Matter of Law) 399
  The Defendant's Case 399
  Closing Arguments 399
  Jury Instructions 401
  The Verdict 401
POSTTRIAL MOTIONS AND PROCEDURES 402
  Posttrial Motions 402
  Appealing the Verdict 403
ENFORCING THE JUDGMENT 405

CHAPTER 12
Criminal Law and Procedures 414

Technology and Today's Paralegal: Keeping Up with Cyber Crimes 418

Paralegal Profile: Criminal Law Paralegal 420

Developing Paralegal Skills: Year-and-a-Day Defense 422

Featured Guest: Pamela Poole Weber, Paralegals and Criminal Litigation 424

Ethical Concern: The Ethics of Plea Bargaining 437

Developing Paralegal Skills: The Prosecutor's Office—Warrant Division 441

INTRODUCTION 415
WHAT IS A CRIME? 415
  Classifications of Crimes 416
  The Variety of Criminal Acts 417
ELEMENTS OF CRIMINAL LIABILITY 417
  The Criminal Act 417
  State of Mind 418
  Defenses to Criminal Liability 419
CONSTITUTIONAL SAFEGUARDS 421
  The *Miranda* Rule 422
  The Erosion of the *Miranda* Rule 423
CRIMINAL PROCEDURES PRIOR TO PROSECUTION 426
  Arrest 426
  Booking 430
  Investigation after the Arrest 431
THE PROSECUTION BEGINS 432

CONTENTS xxi

Ethical Concern: Preparing Exhibits for Trial 442
Developing Paralegal Skills: Discovery in the Criminal Case 443
Ethical Concern: The Benefits of Good Record Keeping 444
Today's Professional Paralegal: Working for the District Court 445

Filing the Complaint 432
Initial Appearance 433
Preliminary Hearing 434
Grand Jury Review 434
Arraignment 435
Pretrial Motions 436
Discovery 437
THE TRIAL 437
Special Features of Criminal Trials 439
Sentencing 444
Appeal 446

CHAPTER 13
Conducting Interviews and Investigations 452

Developing Paralegal Skills: The Tape-Recorded Interview 456
Featured Guest: Anna Durham Boling, Ten Tips for More Effective Interviewing 462
Ethical Concern: Handling Client Documents 464
Ethical Concern: The Unauthorized Practice of Law 465
Ethical Concern: Keeping the Client Informed 466
Developing Paralegal Skills: Keeping an Evidence Log 472
Technology and Today's Paralegal: Online Medical Research 474
Paralegal Profile: Insurance Paralegal 476
Developing Paralegal Skills: Accessing Government Information 478
Today's Professional Paralegal: Interviewing a Client 480

INTRODUCTION 453
PLANNING THE INTERVIEW 453
  Know What Information You Want to Obtain 453
  Recording the Interview 453
INTERVIEWING SKILLS 456
  Interpersonal Skills 457
  Questioning Skills 457
  Listening Skills 459
INTERVIEWING CLIENTS 460
  The Initial Client Interview 460
  Subsequent Client Interviews 460
  The Informational Interview 462
  Summarizing the Interview 464
INTERVIEWING WITNESSES 464
  Types of Witnesses 465
  Questioning Witnesses 467
  Checking the Witness's Qualifications 467
  Witness Statements 468
PLANNING AND CONDUCTING INVESTIGATIONS 468
  Where Do You Start? 469
  Creating an Investigation Plan 470
  Locating Witnesses 474
  Accessing Government Information 475
  Investigation and the Rules of Evidence 477
  Summarizing Your Results 481

CONTENTS

Chapter 14
Legal Research 487

Ethical Concern: Efficiency in Research 489

Developing Paralegal Skills: Defining the Issues to be Researched 491

Paralegal Profile: Litigation Paralegal 500

Featured Guest: E. J. Yera, Ten Tips for Effective Legal Research 509

Ethical Concern: Avoiding Plagiarism 511

Technology and Today's Paralegal: Looking Ahead 512

Developing Paralegal Skills: Understanding Case Citations 518

Ethical Concern: Citing Sources 519

Developing Paralegal Skills: Researching the *U.S.C.A.* 524

Ethical Concern: The Importance of Finding Current Law 532

Today's Professional Paralegal: Mapping Out a Research Strategy 533

INTRODUCTION 488
PRIMARY AND SECONDARY SOURCES 488
RESEARCHING CASE LAW—THE PRELIMINARY STEPS 489
  Defining the Issue 489
  Determining Your Research Goals 490
SECONDARY SOURCES OF CASE LAW 492
  Legal Encyclopedias 492
  Case Digests 495
  Annotations: *American Law Reports* 501
  Treatises 503
  Restatements of the Law 503
  Legal Periodicals 506
THE CASE REPORTING SYSTEM 511
  State Court Decisions 511
  Federal Court Decisions 514
  United States Supreme Court Decisions 514
RESEARCHING STATUTORY LAW 519
  The Publication of Federal Statutes 519
  The *United States Code* 520
  Unofficial Versions of the Federal Code 521
  Interpreting Statutory Law 523
  Researching Legislative History 523
  State Codes 525
RESEARCHING ADMINISTRATIVE LAW 525
  The *Code of Federal Regulations* 526
  Publication of the *C.F.R.* 526
  Finding Tools for Administrative Law 526
FINDING CONSTITUTIONAL LAW 526
UPDATING THE LAW—LEARNING TO USE CITATORS 529
  Case Law 529
  Statutory and Constitutional Law 530
  Administrative Regulations 530
  Legal Periodicals 532
  Online Citators 532

Chapter 15
Computer-Assisted Legal Research 540

Developing Paralegal Skills: Cite Checking on Westlaw® 545

INTRODUCTION 541
CD-ROMS AND LEGAL RESEARCH 541
  Advantages of Using CD-ROMs 541
  Disadvantages of Using CD-ROMs 542

Ethical Concern:
Cutting the Cost of Legal Research 546

Developing Paralegal Skills:
Conducting Legal Research on the Internet 555

Developing Paralegal Skills:
Medical Research on the Internet 558

Technology and Today's Paralegal: Creative Online Searching 561

Ethical Concern:
Surfing the Web 562

Paralegal Profile: Litigation Paralegal and Web Site Designer 566

Featured Guest: Jan Richmond, Keeping Current on Computer Technology 569

Ethical Concern:
Finding Ethical Opinions on the Web 572

Today's Professional Paralegal: Locating Guardians and Wards 577

WESTLAW® AND LEXIS® 542
  Accessing Westlaw® or Lexis® 543
  Retrieving a Document by Citation 544
  Checking a Citation 544
  Selecting a Database 544
  Searching a Database 545
  Browser Enhancements 547

GOING ONLINE—INTERNET BASICS 548
  What Is the Internet? 548
  Internet Tools 548
  Accessing the Internet 550
  Navigating the Internet 551

CONDUCTING ONLINE RESEARCH 553
  A Threshold Question: Is the Internet The Right Research Tool for Your Project? 554
  Plan Ahead—Analyze the Facts and Identify the Issues 557

STARTING POINTS 558
  Discovering What Resources Are Available 560
  Browsing the Links 562
  Narrowing Your Focus 562
  Evaluating What You Find 563
  Updating Your Results 564

LOCATING PEOPLE AND INVESTIGATING COMPANIES 565
  Finding People 565
  Investigating Companies 567

SOME OF THE BEST LEGAL-RESOURCE SITES ON THE INTERNET 568
  Basic Resources 571
  University Sites 573
  Government Sites 574
  Sites for Associations and Organizations 574
  Free Commercial Sites 575

CHAPTER 16
Legal Analysis and Writing 582

Developing Paralegal Skills: Interpreting Statutes 596

Technology and Today's Paralegal: Online "Plain English" Guidelines 600

Ethical Concern:
Ethics and Time Management 603

INTRODUCTION 583
ANALYZING CASE LAW 583
  The Components of a Case 583
  Analyzing Cases 589
  Summarizing and Briefing Cases 589
  Synthesizing Your Research Results 590

ANALYZING STATUTORY LAW 592
  Reading Statutory Law 592
  Interpreting Statutory Law 594

Featured Guest: Richard M. Terry, Ten Tips for Effective Legal Writing   605

Ethical Concern: "Confidential" Correspondence   608

Developing Paralegal Skills: Writing to Clients   611

Ethical Concern: Letters and the Unauthorized Practice of Law   613

Paralegal Profile: Litigation Paralegal   615

Ethical Concern: Objectivity and the Legal Memorandum   619

Today's Professional Paralegal: Preparing the Internal Memorandum   629

LEGAL WRITING—THE PRELIMINARIES   595
   Understanding the Assignment   595
   Time Constraints and Flexibility   596
   Writing Approaches   597

THE IMPORTANCE OF GOOD WRITING SKILLS   597
   Organize and Outline Your Presentation   597
   Write to Your Audience   598
   Avoid Legalese   599
   Be Brief and to the Point   599
   Writing Basics: Sentences   600
   Writing Basics: Paragraphs and Transitions   601
   Be Alert for Sexist Language   602
   Proofread and Revise Your Document   603

PLEADINGS AND DISCOVERY   604

GENERAL LEGAL CORRESPONDENCE   604
   General Format for Legal Correspondence   604
   Types of Legal Letters   609

THE INTERNAL MEMORANDUM   613
   Heading   614
   Statement of the Facts   614
   Questions Presented   616
   Brief Conclusions   616
   Discussion and Analysis   617
   Conclusion   619

THE APPELLATE BRIEF   620
   Types of Appellate Briefs   621
   Writing an Effective Appellate Brief   621

APPENDIX A
NALA's Code of Ethics and Professional Responsibility   635

APPENDIX B
NALA's Model Standards and Guidelines for the Utilization of Legal Assistants   637

Appendix C
NFPA's Model Code of Ethics and Professional Responsibility and Guidelines for Enforcement 641

Appendix D
The ABA's Model Guidelines for the Utilization of Legal Assistant Services 651

Appendix E
Paralegal Ethics and Regulation: How to Find State-Specific Information 663

Appendix F
Paralegal Associations 667

Appendix G
State and Major Local Bar Associations 673

Appendix H
Information on NALA's CLA and CLAS Examinations 679

Appendix I
Information on NFPA's PACE Examination 687

Appendix J
The Constitution of the United States 691

Appendix K
Spanish Equivalents for Important Legal Terms in English 707

Glossary 713

Index 729

PREFACE

One of the fastest-growing occupations in America today is that of the paralegal, or legal assistant. It seems fitting, then, that you and your students should have a new textbook that reflects the excitement surrounding paralegal studies today. *West's Paralegal Today: The Legal Team at Work*, Second Edition, we believe, imparts this excitement to your students. They will find paralegal studies accessible and interesting. This book is modern, colorful, and visually attractive, which encourages learning. We are certain that you and your students will find this text extremely effective.

West's Paralegal Today, Second Edition, makes the paralegal field come alive for the student. We use real-world examples, present numerous boxed-in features, and support the text with the most extensive supplements package ever offered for an introductory paralegal textbook.

Thomson Learning and West Group have been providing authoritative materials to the entire legal field for over 120 years. *West's Paralegal Today*, Second Edition, draws on the expertise of publishers that have had a long history of encouraging excellence in legal education.

All of the basic areas of paralegal studies are covered in *West's Paralegal Today*, Second Edition. These include careers, ethics and professional responsibility, pretrial preparation, trial procedures, criminal law, legal interviewing and investigation, legal research, computer-assisted legal research, and legal analysis and writing. In addition, there are a number of key features, which we describe in this preface.

A Practical, Realistic Approach

There sometimes exists an enormous gulf between classroom learning and on-the-job realities. We have tried to bridge this gulf in *West's Paralegal Today*, Second Edition, by offering a text full of practical advice and "hands-on" activities. Exercises at the end of each chapter provide opportunities for your students to apply the concepts and skills discussed in the chapter. Many of the book's other key features, which you will read about shortly, were designed specifically to give your students a glimpse of the types of situations and demands that they may encounter on the job as professional paralegals. A special introduction to the student, which appears just before Chapter 1, contains practical advice and tips on how to master the legal concepts and procedures presented in this text—advice and tips that your students can also apply later, on the job.

West's Paralegal Today, Second Edition, also realistically portrays paralegal working environments and on-the-job challenges. Ethical dimensions of the practice of law frame paralegals' work experiences to a significant extent. Because of this, we have made a special effort to show how seemingly abstract ethical rules affect the day-to-day tasks performed by attorneys and paralegals in the legal workplace.

TECHNOLOGY

We have attempted to make sure that *West's Paralegal Today*, Second Edition, is the most modern and up-to-date text available in today's marketplace. To that end, we have included in the Second Edition a number of new features and materials indicating how the latest developments in technology are affecting the law, the legal workplace, and paralegal tasks. Among other things, these features and materials will help your students learn how to take advantage of technology, including the Internet, to enhance their efficiency and productivity as paralegals.

A New Chapter on CALR

An entirely new chapter on computer-assisted legal research (Chapter 15) shows students how they can do legal research and investigation using CD-ROMs, the legal databases provided by Westlaw® and Lexis®, and online information available at various Web sites.

A New Feature Focusing on Technology

A new feature, titled *Technology and Today's Paralegal*, has been added for the Second Edition. Each of these boxed-in features, which appear throughout the text, focuses on how technology is affecting a specific aspect of paralegal work or on how paralegals can use technology to their benefit. For example, in Chapter 2 (Careers in the Legal Community) we have included a feature discussing "Online Job Searching." The feature offers guidelines to students on how they can find employment opportunities using the Internet. Titles of other features include the following:

- Is E-Mail "Confidential"? (Chapter 3).
- Filing Court Documents Electronically (Chapter 6).

From Chapter 1 . . .

TECHNOLOGY AND TODAY'S PARALEGAL
The Changing Paralegal Workplace

In many ways, technology has simplified the work of legal assistants. Documents can be easily drafted and revised on the computer. Mistakes can be eliminated with the stroke of a key, and changes can be made in a matter of just seconds. Computerized forms make generating the paperwork for routine legal transactions, such as bankruptcy filings or divorce petitions, a relatively simple matter. Database management systems allow paralegals to track or analyze hundreds—if not thousands—of documents without having to search through boxes filled with documents. E-mail messages can be created and sent in a fraction of the time it takes to create, reproduce, and distribute hard-copy memos or letters. Online databases have made it possible to conduct legal research and find information relevant to a legal investigation without leaving the office.

Indeed, it would seem that technology, by making legal work faster and easier to accomplish, might reduce the need for paralegals. That, however, is not true. Indeed, the opposite is occurring—technology is opening the door to new positions for paralegals. For example, some of today's paralegals are carving out a niche for themselves as Internet specialists. A paralegal who can conduct research efficiently, using online resources, is a valuable asset to any firm or agency. In a law office, efficient research saves time and money—for the firm and clients alike. Other paralegals are becoming experts in electronic evidence, encoding documents relating to a particular legal matter so that those documents can easily be retrieved in the event of a lawsuit.

Another emerging field in which paralegals may play a significant role has to do with the types of documents that should be entered into, or retained on, electronic systems. Even documents that have been previously deleted from a hard drive may be retrieved and used as evidence in a lawsuit, and companies that want to prevent future problems with electronic evidence increasingly are turning to their lawyers for advice on this issue. A paralegal knowledgeable in this area is a valuable member of the legal team in such situations.

Finally, technology has made it possible for some paralegals to perform at least some of their work at home. The virtual workplace, made feasible by telephones, faxes, and modems, is now becoming a reality.

We cannot predict what the future may hold, but one thing seems certain: as technology advances, there will be an increasing need for creative adaptations of technology to the field of legal work. High-tech paralegals who can fill this need will very likely be the highest paid—and the most valued—legal assistants in the future.

PREFACE

- Indexing the Deposition Transcript (Chapter 10).
- Presentation Technology (Chapter 11).
- Keeping Up with Cyber Crimes (Chapter 12).
- Online "Plain English" Guidelines (Chapter 16).

Margin Web Sites

In every chapter, we have added several features titled *On the Web* in the margins. These features offer Web sites that students can access for further information on the topic being discussed in the text.

From Chapter 1 . . .

Chapter-Ending Internet Exercises

To help your students learn how to navigate the Web and find various types of information online, we have included at the end of each chapter one or more Internet exercises in a section titled *Using Internet Resources*. Each exercise directs the student to a specific Web site and asks a series of questions about the materials available at that site.

From Chapter 9 . . .

USING INTERNET RESOURCES

1. Many paralegals, at one time or another, are asked to assist in cases dealing with employment discrimination. For that reason, it is a good idea to become familiar with the agency that administers federal laws prohibiting various forms of employment discrimination, the Equal Employment Opportunity Commission (EEOC). This exercise will help you learn more about this agency and its activities. First, access the EEOC's Web site at www.eeoc.gov. Browse through the site, and then find answers to the following questions:
   a. What federal law (enabling legislation) established the EEOC? What federal acts does it enforce?
   b. Within how many days after a discriminatory action must an employee file a charge (claim) with the EEOC? Can employees first file a charge with a state or local agency that implements state and local laws?
   c. How many claims of discrimination were filed with the EEOC in the most recent year listed? What percentage of the total annual claims dealt with each of the following types of discrimination: sexual harassment, disability-based discrimination, and race-based discrimination?
   d. Give the titles of two recent "Enforcement Guidelines" issued by the EEOC.

2. The Federal Trade Commission (FTC) provides information on consumer law issues through its Web site, located at www.ftc.gov. Go to this Web site, follow the directions given below, and then answer these questions:
   a. Select "Who We Are & How We Serve You." What are the vision, mission, and goals of the FTC?
   b. Click on "How the FTC Brings an Action." Summarize in two paragraphs how the FTC brings an action.
   c. Click on "Privacy Policy." What is the FTC's privacy policy regarding those who visit its Web site?
   d. Click on "Where to Go for More Information." Make a list of the offices, including their names and addresses, to contact for additional information, along with any other sources included.
   e. Go back to the home page and select "Consumer Protection." What areas of consumer protection does the FTC regulate?
   f. From the home page, access "Current News Releases." Do any of these news releases deal with false advertising? Prepare a one-paragraph summary of one of the news releases.

West's Paralegal Online Resource Center

The West Legal Studies Web site, at www.westlegalstudies.com continues to offer numerous resources for paralegal professionals, instructors, and students. At this site, you and your students will find over 220 links to legal and paralegal information sites. This site also hosts a page dedicated to *West's Paralegal Today*, Second Edition, where you and your students can find text updates, hot links, and other resources.

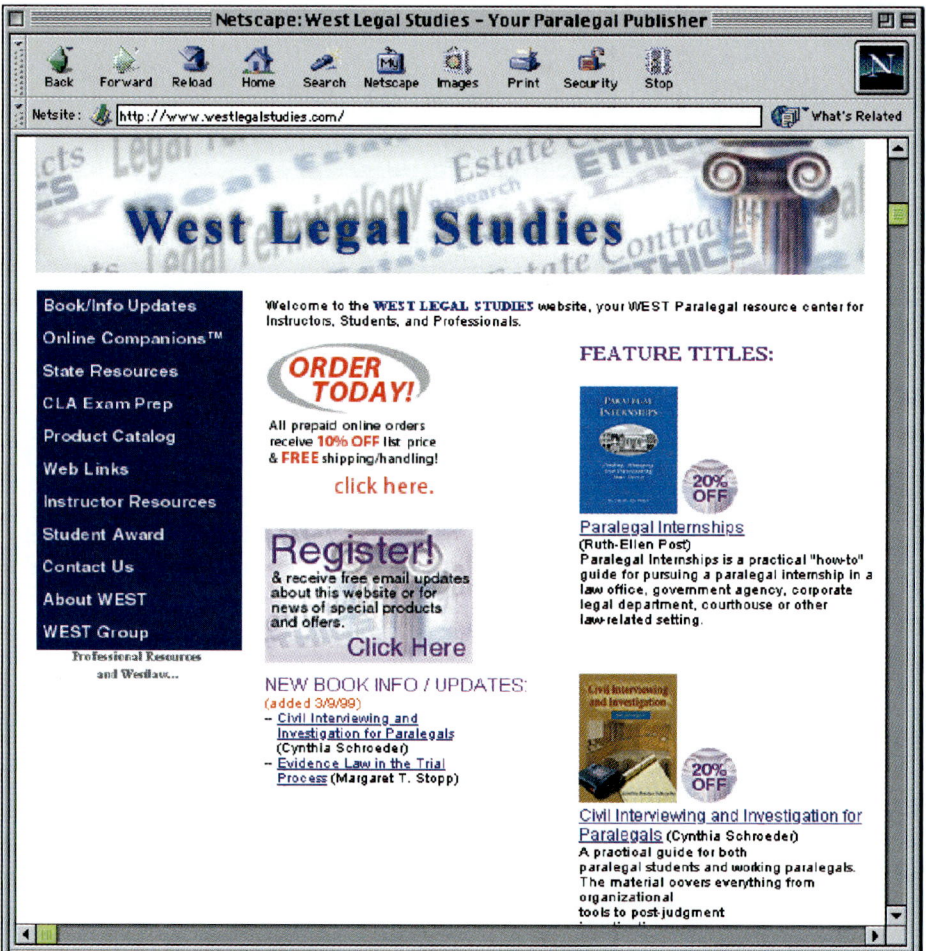

The Organization of this Textbook

As every paralegal instructor knows, ideally materials should be presented in such a way that students can build their skills and knowledge bases block by block. This is difficult because, no matter where you begin, you will need to refer to some information that has not yet been presented to the student. For example, if you try to explain what paralegals do on the first or second day of class, you will necessarily have to mention terms that may be unfamiliar to the students, such as *litigation* or *substantive law* or *procedural law*. In writing this text, the authors have attempted, whenever possible, to organize the topics covered in such a way that the student is never mystified by terms and concepts not yet discussed.

We realize that no one way of organizing the coverage of topics in a paralegal text will be suitable for all instructors, but we have attempted to accommodate your needs as much as possible by organizing the text into three basic parts. Part 1 (Chapters 1–4) focuses primarily on the paralegal profession—its origins and development, the wide array of paralegal careers, the threshold ethical responsibilities of the profession, and the requirements and procedures that students can expect to find in the legal workplace. Part 2 (Chapters 5–9) focuses on substantive law, including basic legal concepts in such areas as tort law and contract law, and also covers administrative law and government regulation. Part 3 (Chapters 10–16) looks in detail at legal procedures and paralegal skills. The student learns about the basic procedural requirements in civil and criminal litigation, and the skills involved in conducting interviews and investigations, legal research, and legal writing and analysis.

It is our hope that this organization of the materials will allow the greatest flexibility for instructors. Although to a certain extent each chapter in this text "builds" on information contained in previous chapters, the chapters and parts can also be used independently. In other words, those instructors who wish to alter the presentation of topics to fit their course outlines, or who wish to use selected chapters or parts only, will find it relatively easy to do so.

KEY FEATURES

In addition to the new *Technology and Today's Paralegal* features, which we have already discussed, every chapter in this text has the following features. Each feature is set apart and used both to instruct and to pique the interest of your paralegal students.

Developing Paralegal Skills

These boxed-in features present hypothetical examples of paralegals at work to help your students develop crucial paralegal skills. For the Second Edition, these features have been revised to include checklists and practical tips. Some examples are the following:

- Building an Ethical Wall (Chapter 3).
- Federal Court Rules—Creating a Complaint Checklist (Chapter 10).
- The Prosecutor's Office—Warrant Division (Chapter 12).
- Keeping an Evidence Log (Chapter 13).
- Medical Research on the Internet (Chapter 14).

From Chapter 3 . . .

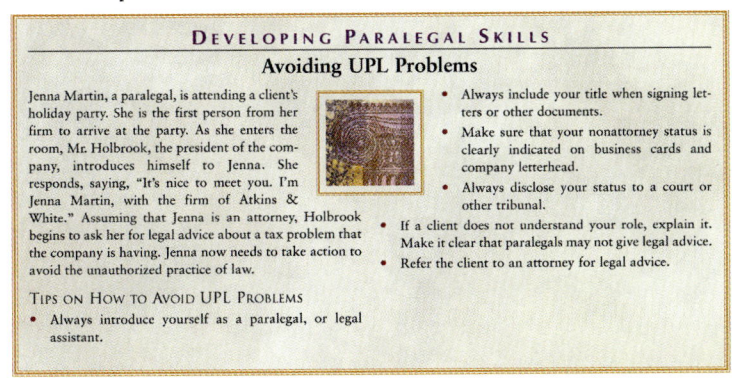

Ethical Concerns

Every chapter presents three or more *Ethical Concerns*. These features typically take a student into a hypothetical situation that clearly presents an ethical problem. When possible, students are told what they should and should not do in particular situations being discussed. Some examples are the following:

- Saying "If I were you . . ." and the UPL (Chapter 3).
- Confidentiality and Administrative Practice (Chapter 9).
- Deadlines and the Duty of Competence (Chapter 10).
- Ethics and Time Management (Chapter 16).

From Chapter 1 . . .

ETHICAL CONCERN
Paralegal Expertise and Legal Advice

Paralegals often become very knowledgeable in a specific area of the law. If you specialize in environmental law, for example, you will become very knowledgeable about environmental claims. In working with a client on a matter involving an environmental agency, you might therefore be tempted to advise the client on which type of action would be most favorable to him or her. Never do so. As will be discussed in detail in Chapter 3, only attorneys may give legal advice, and paralegals who give legal advice risk penalties for the unauthorized practice of law. Whatever legal advice is given to the client must come either directly from the attorney or, if from you, must reflect exactly (or nearly exactly) what the attorney said with no embellishment on your part. After consulting with your supervising attorney, for example, you can say to the client that Mr. X (the attorney) "advises that you do all that you can to settle the claim as soon as possible."

From Chapter 2 . . .

PARALEGAL PROFILE
Real-Estate Paralegal

DORA DYE has been a real estate/corporate paralegal since 1986. She has worked at several major San Francisco law firms and has transferred her skills to the corporate environment. She is currently the Dispositions Closing Coordinator at the RREEF Funds.

Dye was the president of the San Francisco Paralegal Association (SFPA) in 1993 and 1994 and currently serves on the Education Committee of both SFPA and the National Federation of Paralegal Associations, Inc. (NFPA). She is an active member of the NFPA's PACE Development Committee and co-authored the chapter, "Factual and Legal Research" in the Paralegal Advanced Competency Exam Study Manual with her husband, David Dye.

Dye also teaches legal writing, legal-assisting work experience, and commercial law via distance learning at City College of San Francisco's Paralegal/Legal Studies Program and is an associate professor of the paralegal program at California State University, Hayward.

Dye earned a bachelor of arts degree in Spanish, with distinction in general scholarship, and a master of arts degree in Spanish from the University of California, Berkeley. In addition, Dye received a master of business administration degree in International Business, with distinction, from Armstrong University.

What do you like best about your work?
"I enjoy the field of real estate, because I am able to bring in all of my experiences from the past to my current position. While working at various law firms, I became a senior paralegal specializing in multimillion-dollar real estate closings. That experience has allowed me to transfer my knowledge and skills in real estate, business, and the law to a corporate environment and to work more effectively with internal and external legal counsel. Becoming a part-time paralegal instructor has enabled me to share my knowledge and skills with future paralegals. I have even used my Spanish skills when doing pro bono work."

"Bringing to your position all experiences that you have had will add to your value as a paralegal."

What is the greatest challenge that you face in your area of work?
"Satisfying the twin goals of cost efficiency and the generation of a superior work product represents the greatest challenge. To meet these goals, it is important to 'get it right' the first time. Today, paralegals have a more personal relationship with clients. Clients call paralegals directly to handle issues that require the attorney's attention, thus improving the quality of legal services being delivered and keeping costs down."

What advice do you have for would-be paralegals in your area of work?
"Be as detail oriented as possible, and be the best that you can be in all things that you do. Bringing to your position all experiences that you have had will add to your value as a paralegal.

Paralegal students should get work experience. Without work experience, students do not have an idea of office culture and environment, which are important aspects of a job."

What are some tips for success as a paralegal in your area of work?
"A successful paralegal knows what needs to be done and does it before he or she is asked. If you anticipate the needs of your attorneys and your clients, you will always be prepared to deal with matters more efficiently and effectively."

Paralegal Profiles

Every chapter has a profile of a paralegal who is currently working in a specific area of law. These profiles open with a short biography of the paralegal and then present the paralegal's own answers to questions asked by the interviewer. The paralegal tells of his or her greatest challenges on the job, gives suggestions about what he or she thinks students should concentrate on when studying to become a paralegal, and offers tips for being a successful paralegal in his or her line of work. This feature gives your students insights into various legal specialties and the diversity of paralegal working environments.

PREFACE xxxiii

Featured-Guest Articles

Each chapter has a contributed article written by an educator or an expert in the field. These articles offer your students practical tips on some aspect of paralegal work relating to the topic covered in the chapter. Some examples are the following:

- "Paralegal Career Planning and Development," by Denise Templeton, president and chief executive officer of Templeton & Associates, a legal-support services firm, and one of the founders of the Minnesota Association of Legal Assistants, the American Association for Paralegal Education, and the National Federation of Paralegal Associations (Chapter 2).
- "Ten Tips on Ethics and the Paralegal," by Michael A. Pener, professor at Johnson County Community College, Overland Park, Kansas (Chapter 3).
- "Ten Tips for Drafting Interrogatories," by James W. H. McCord, director of paralegal programs at Eastern Kentucky University, Richmond, Kentucky (Chapter 10).
- "Keeping Current on Computer Technology," by Jan Richmond, instructor at St. Louis Community College, St. Louis, Missouri (Chapter 15).

From Chapter 1 . . .

FEATURED GUEST: WENDY B. EDSON
Ten Tips for Effective Communication

BIOGRAPHICAL NOTE

Wendy B. Edson received her master's degree in library science (M.L.S.) from the University of Rhode Island and served as law librarian at the Buffalo, New York, firm of Phillips, Lytle, Hitchcock, Blain and Huber. In 1978, she joined the Paralegal Studies faculty at Hilbert College, in Hamburg, New York, and helped to develop an ABA-approved bachelor's degree program in 1992. She teaches paralegalism and legal ethics, legal research and writing, law and literature, volunteerism, and alternate dispute resolution. She also developed and coordinates the internship program. Edson reviews and publishes on the topics of paralegal education, legal research and writing, and community service. She has lectured to legal professionals on legal research, teaching skills, internships, community service, environmental law, and ADR. Professor Edson is an AAfPE member and has presented papers at its national conferences and chaired model syllabi projects.

Words! They are the building blocks of human communication. Whether words are exchanged face-to-face—or by e-mail, phone, fax, or letter—communication is a two-way street. But how do we become skilled at maneuvering the *two-way* traffic of interpersonal communication? As in driving, we need to follow the "rules of the road." The rules of the road in regard to communication traffic are embodied in the following ten tips.

1. Establish Communication Equality. Communication equality does not require that individuals hold equal status in an office or organization but requires that each party believe in *equal rights* to speak and listen. Observe someone whom you consider to be a good communicator. You will note that he or she demonstrates equality by actively listening and responding appropriately to whoever is speaking. Workplace problems often reflect communication ailments rooted in inequality. A firm belief in communication equality, despite job titles, will help to create a cooperative, productive working environment.

2. Plan for Time and Space. Effective communication requires *time*. Imagine your reaction to a request to work overtime if your supervising attorney took thirty seconds to order you to do the work versus taking two minutes to explain the reason for the request and listening to your response. In the first situation, the attorney saved one and a half minutes but scored "zero" in terms of communication skills. In today's rushed world, it is easy to overlook the importance of communication skills in morale building and creating a cooperative, efficient work force.

Effective communicators are aware of how the physical environment in which a conversation takes place can affect the communication process. Communication is always enhanced when the parties have reasonable privacy and are not continually interrupted. Another important factor is physical comfort. Choosing an inappropriate time and place for communication denies the importance of the matters being discussed and may send the wrong message to both the speaker and the listener.

3. Set the Agenda. Skilled communicators prepare an *agenda*—whether written or mental—of matters to be discussed in order of their priority. Frequently, both parties bring their respective agendas to a discussion, which means that priorities may need to be negotiated. A subordinate who brings up the topic of desired vacation time when the supervisor is preoccupied with a major project clearly demonstrates that his or her priorities are different from those of the supervisor.

Successful communication requires that the parties first negotiate a *common agenda*—that is, determine jointly the agenda for a particular discussion or meeting and what topics should take priority. Then, the topics can be dealt with one by one, in terms of their relative importance, to the satisfaction of both parties. *Agenda awareness* prevents parties from jumping from topic to topic without successfully resolving anything.

4. Fine-Tune Your Speaking Skills. Observe an individual whom you consider to be a good speaker, whether

Continued on next page

FEATURED GUEST, Continued

before a group of persons or on a one-on-one basis. What skills does that individual demonstrate? Effective speakers work hard to express thoughts clearly; sometimes, they refer to notes or lists to refresh their memories. Skilled speakers also try to communicate accurately and to talk about matters that they know will interest their listeners. They cultivate *communication empathy*—the sincere effort to put themselves in their listeners' shoes. As you speak to others, pause occasionally and ask yourself, "Would I enjoy listening to what I am saying and how I am saying it?"

5. Cultivate Listening Skills. Listening is not just refraining from speaking while another person is talking but an *active* process—the other half of the communication partnership. An active listener does not interrupt the speaker. If you sense that the speaker is engaging in a monologue, responsive behavior—including body language, attentiveness, and appropriate remarks—can steer the conversation back to a dialogue without cutting off the speaker.

An active listener realizes that listening is an investment in effective communication. By truly responding to what is being said, rather than regarding listening time as insignificant or time to plan his or her own remarks, the skilled listener establishes a bond of trust with the speaker. Active listeners avoid preconceived ideas about topics being discussed and assume that they do not know all the answers.

6. Watch for Body Language. Body language is nonverbal communication that reflects our emotional state. Physical positions, such as leaning forward or away from the speaker while listening, can reinforce or negate our spoken responses. Body attitudes, whether relaxed (comfortable posture, leaning forward, uncrossed arms and legs, relaxed neck and shoulders) or tense (stiff posture, backing away, crossed arms and legs, rigid neck and shoulders) vividly illustrate our responses before we utter a word. Eye contact is one of the most important tools in the body language tool kit for communication. Interviewers, social workers, and police officers have learned that steady and responsive eye contact means sincerity and credibility.

7. Put Note Taking in Perspective. Over involvement in note taking detracts from the communication process because opportunities to listen actively, speak responsively, and be sensitive to body language are reduced. The speaker may ramble while the listener records the ramblings in extensive notes.

When it is necessary to take notes, it is helpful to establish some rapport with the speaker or listener before launching the note-taking process. Alternatively, follow-up notes can be a workable solution to the problem. The note taker can devote the interview time to communication and, after the interview, record his or her general impressions of the interview and identify specific issues that need to be discussed further.

8. Recognize the Role of Criticism. *Constructive criticism* focuses on specific actions or behaviors rather than personalities. It is objective rather than subjective. Criticism that is stated calmly and objectively ("We need to rewrite the section on holo-

> "Eye contact is one of the most important tools in the body language tool kit for communication."

graphic wills.") is much more palatable for the person being criticized than is criticism in the form of a personal attack ("You did a terrible job"). By placing emphasis on actions instead of personalities, the parties can more easily work toward a satisfactory solution. If both the critic and the person being criticized can remain calm and can separate actions from personalities, then criticism will usually produce the desired result and *mutual* satisfaction.

9. Aim for Satisfactory Closure. Closure means "wrapping up" the communication. Successful communicators know that handling closure properly can leave a participant with a good feeling even if the solution was not exactly what he or she initially desired. Summarizing the discussion and checking for agreement or a need for further discussion will encourage all participants to follow the tenth tip.

10. Commit to Communicate. Excellent speakers and listeners have positive, self-confident attitudes that problems can be solved if the "rules of the road" are followed. Skilled communicators cultivate open minds, self-knowledge, and the ability to tolerate differences and empathize with others. They are committed to exercising their rights and responsibilities as speakers and listeners in the communication process.

Today's Professional Paralegal

Near the end of every chapter we have included a special feature entitled *Today's Professional Paralegal*. This important feature exposes your students to situations that they are likely to encounter on the job and offers guidance on how certain types of problems can be resolved. Some examples are the following:

- Managing Conflict (Chapter 4).
- Relocation Assistance (Chapter 7).
- Drafting *Voir Dire* Questions Like a Pro (Chapter 10).
- Accessing Government Information (Chapter 13).

From Chapter 1 . . .

> **TODAY'S PROFESSIONAL PARALEGAL**
> ### A Winning Combination
>
> Susan Latham is a legal secretary for Melinda Oakwood, a real-estate attorney who is a partner in the law firm of Morris, Crowther, Oakwood & Miller. The law firm is one of the largest in the state, employing over 300 attorneys, 75 paralegals, 130 secretaries, and many support staff members. Susan, who has become more of a legal assistant than a secretary to Melinda, has decided, at the age of forty, to return to the local university to obtain a paralegal degree. This way, Susan can be rewarded (in the form of higher wages) for the work that she actually does already and can seek advancement in the firm.
>
> Susan has worked for Melinda for eleven years. She has been given increased responsibility because she has shown Melinda that she is dependable and reliable in handling her work assignments. Her work is always turned in on time, and it is always accurate.
>
> **LEARNING ON THE JOB**
> Susan was very lucky to have Melinda as a supervising attorney. Melinda, who had been a teacher for ten years before she went to law school, liked to teach Susan how to undertake new work assignments. When Susan had a new type of document to prepare at work, Melinda would give her a sample document and very good instructions. Now that Susan is studying to be a paralegal, Melinda has started assisting Susan with her school assignments by giving her sample documents and copies of the laws that require those documents. Melinda also points out the differences between the class assignments and the sample documents and discusses with Susan why the differences matter from a legal perspective.
>
> Additionally, Melinda encourages Susan to ask questions about school assignments and to take her time completing them so that when they are turned in, they are accurate. Susan has a strong sense of commitment, so she always sees a project through even if it seems to take forever.
>
>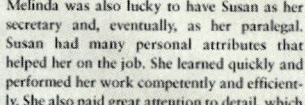
>
> **USING PERSONAL ATTRIBUTES**
> Melinda was also lucky to have Susan as her secretary and, eventually, as her paralegal. Susan had many personal attributes that helped her on the job. She learned quickly and performed her work competently and efficiently. She also paid great attention to detail, which was one of the reasons Melinda encouraged Susan to get a paralegal degree. Unlike Melinda's former paralegal, who would send out letters and fail to include the documents that should have been enclosed, Susan was meticulous. And Melinda could always count on Susan to keep client information confidential.
>
> Susan already had good computer and organizational skills when Melinda hired her. She did need to improve her analytical and listening skills, though. Susan's analytical skills are already improving as a result of a course she is taking in legal research, which requires case analysis. Over time, Susan learned to listen to Melinda's instructions and to question Melinda when Susan was not exactly certain about what Melinda wanted her to do.
>
> **THE RESULT: A WINNING TEAM**
> Melinda and Susan have developed a solid working relationship. It took time for Susan to develop some of the skills that she needed, but Melinda was a good and patient teacher. It also took time to develop a trusting relationship, but now Melinda can confidently delegate significant assignments to Susan, knowing that Susan will complete them accurately. Now that Susan is in a paralegal program, Melinda can also delegate more challenging work to Susan, and Susan can eventually be promoted to paralegal status. Melinda and Susan work productively and efficiently together. They like and rely on each other and enjoy their work. Theirs is a winning combination of talents and skills.

OTHER SPECIAL PEDAGOGICAL FEATURES

We have included in *West's Paralegal Today*, Second Edition, a number of additional pedagogical features, including those discussed below.

Chapter Outlines

On every chapter-opening page, a *Chapter Outline* lists the first-level headings within the chapter. These outlines allow you and your students to tell at a glance what topics are covered in the chapters.

Chapter Objectives

In every chapter, just following the *Chapter Outline*, we list five or six chapter objectives. Your students will know immediately what is expected of them as they read each chapter.

Margin Web Sites

As already mentioned, *On the Web* features appear in the page margins throughout the text. These features direct students to specific Web sites for further information on the topics being discussed.

Vocabulary and Margin Definitions

Legal terminology is often a major challenge for beginning paralegal students. We have used an important pedagogical device—margin definitions—to help your students understand legal terms. Whenever an important term is introduced, it is done so in boldface type and defined. In addition, the term is listed and defined in the margin of the page, alongside the paragraph in which the boldfaced term appears.

At the end of each chapter, all terms that have been boldfaced within the chapter are listed in alphabetical order in a section called *Key Terms and Concepts*. The page on which the term is defined is given after each term. Your students can briefly examine this list to make sure that they understand all of the important terms introduced in the chapter. If they do not understand a term completely, they can immediately refer to the page number given and review the term.

All boldfaced terms are again listed and defined in the *Glossary* at the end of the text. Spanish equivalents to many important legal terms in English are provided in a separate glossary.

Estate Administration
The process in which a decedent's personal representative settles the affairs of the decedent's estate (collects assets, pays debts and taxes, and distributes the remaining assets to heirs); the process is usually overseen by a probate court.

Joint Tenancy
The joint ownership of property by two or more co-owners in which each co-owner owns an undivided portion of the property. On the death of one of the joint tenants, his or her interest automatically passes to the surviving joint tenant or tenants.

Concept Summaries

We have added special summaries of legal concepts in those chapters that focus on substantive law (Chapters 5, 7, 8, and 9) and on the court system (Chapter 6). These summaries allow the student to review essential legal concepts in various

From Chapter 6 . . .

PROCEDURAL LAW CONCEPT SUMMARY
The Federal Court System

U.S. District Courts	The federal district court is the equivalent of the state trial court. The district court exercises general jurisdiction over claims arising under federal law or based on diversity of citizenship. Federal courts of limited jurisdiction include bankruptcy courts and the other courts listed on the lowest tier of Exhibit 6.3.
U.S. Courts of Appeals	There are thirteen intermediate courts of appeals (or circuit courts of appeals) in the federal court system. Of those circuit courts, twelve hear appeals from the district courts within their circuits. The thirteenth circuit court has national appellate jurisdiction over certain types of cases, such as cases involving patent law (see Chapter 8) and cases in which the U.S. government is a defendant.
United States Supreme Court	The United States Supreme Court is the highest court in the federal court system and the final arbiter of the Constitution and federal law. Although the Supreme Court has original jurisdiction in some cases, it functions primarily as an appellate court. If the Supreme Court decides to review a case, it will issue a writ of *certiorari*, an order to a lower court requiring the latter to send it the record of the case for review.
Federal Court Judges and Justices	Judges and justices in the federal court system are appointed by the president of the United States and confirmed by the Senate. Federal court judges and justices receive lifetime appointments.

areas of the law. For example, Chapter 7 introduces the student to the laws governing torts, contracts, real property, and wills, trusts, and estates. To help the student review and retain the legal concepts and principles involved in these areas of law, we present a concept summary for each area.

Exhibits and Forms

When appropriate, we present exhibits illustrating important forms or concepts relating to paralegal work. Many exhibits are filled in with hypothetical data. Exhibits and forms in *West's Paralegal Today*, Second Edition, include those listed below:

- A Sample Retainer Agreement (Chapter 4).
- A Sample Complaint (Chapter 10).
- Major Procedural Steps in a Criminal Case (Chapter 12).
- An Investigation Plan (Chapter 13).

In Chapter 16, we present a special *fold-out exhibit* (Exhibit 16.1), which shows the major components of a court case, including excerpts from the court's opinion. Important sections, terms, and phrases in the sample case are defined or discussed in margin annotations.

CHAPTER-ENDING MATERIALS FOR REVIEW AND STUDY

Every chapter contains numerous chapter-ending pedagogical materials. These materials are designed to provide a wide variety of assignments for your students. The chapter-ending pedagogy begins with the *Key Terms and Concepts*, which we have already mentioned. Next are the materials described below.

Chapter Summary

Every chapter ends with a series of numbered paragraphs that summarize the major points made in the chapter. These summaries can be used by students to review and test their knowledge of the topics covered in the chapter.

Questions for Review

In every chapter, following the *Chapter Summary*, are ten relatively straightforward questions for review. These questions are designed to test the student's knowledge of the basic concepts discussed in the chapter.

Ethical Questions

Because of the importance of ethical issues in paralegal training, we have also included at the end of each chapter two or more ethical questions. Each question presents a hypothetical situation, which is followed by one or two questions about what the paralegal should do to solve the dilemma.

Practice Questions and Assignments

The "hands-on" approach to learning paralegal skills is emphasized in the practice questions and assignments. There are several of these questions and assignments at the end of each chapter. A particular situation is presented, and the student is asked to actually carry out an assignment.

Questions for Critical Analysis

Every chapter has several questions for critical analysis. These questions are designed to elicit critical analysis and discussion of issues relating to the topics covered in the chapter.

Projects

There are two or more projects at the end of every chapter. These are specific work tasks that your students can carry out. Often, these projects involve obtaining information from sources that paralegals may deal with on the job, such as a library, a court, a prosecutor's office, or a police department.

Using Internet Resources

As already mentioned, concluding the chapter-ending materials in each chapter is a section titled *Using Internet Resources*. The Internet exercises presented in these sections are designed to familiarize students with useful Web sites and with the extensive array of resources now available online.

APPENDICES

To make this text a reference source for your students, we have included the appendices listed below:

A	NALA's Code of Ethics and Professional Responsibility
B	NALA's Model Standards and Guidelines for the Utilization of Legal Assistants, Annotated
C	NFPA's Model Code of Ethics and Professional Responsibility and Guidelines for Enforcement
D	The ABA's Model Guidelines for the Utilization of Legal Assistant Services
E	Paralegal Ethics and Regulation: How to Find State-Specific Information
F	Paralegal Associations
G	State and Major Local Bar Associations
H	Information on NALA's CLA and CLAS Examinations
I	Information on NFPA's PACE Examination
J	The Constitution of the United States
K	Spanish Equivalents for Important Legal Terms in English

NEW CHAPTERS AND SIGNIFICANT CHANGES TO THE SECOND EDITION

The authors have made a number of significant changes and additions to *West's Paralegal Today* for the Second Edition. We think that we have improved the text greatly, thanks in part to the many suggestions we have received from users of the First Edition as well as from other paralegal educators and legal professionals.

New Chapters, Features, and Other Changes

Generally, all elements in the book—including the text, exhibits, features, and end-of-chapter pedagogy—have been updated as necessary. Significant additions and changes to the Second Edition include the following:

- **An entirely new chapter on computer-assisted legal research (CALR)**—This chapter introduces the student to legal research using CD-ROMs, legal-research services such as Westlaw® and Lexis®, and the Internet.
- *Technology and Today's Paralegal*—This new feature, which appears in every chapter, explores ways in which paralegals can take advantage of new technology to simplify their tasks and enhance their efficiency.
- *On the Web*—This new feature, which appears in the page margins, highlights Web sites that are relevant to the topics being discussed and that students can access to obtain more information.
- *Using Internet Resources*—The Second Edition includes, at the end of every chapter, one or more Internet exercises to familiarize students with how to access and evaluate information available on the Web.
- New *Paralegal Profiles*—Most of these profiles are new to this edition.
- The *Developing Paralegal Skills* **features have been modified**—These features now include practical tips and checklists on the topics covered in the features.
- **NFPA's PACE examination and NALA's Online Campus**—These two recent developments are discussed in Chapter 1.
- **More information on paralegal practice areas**—Chapter 2 now includes descriptions of legal aid offices; freelance paralegals; and a number of emerging specialty areas, such as elder law and legal nurse consulting.
- **Coverage of the regulatory developments in New Jersey, Utah, and other states**—These developments are mentioned in Chapter 1 and discussed in more detail in Chapter 3.
- **Wills, trusts, and estates**—A discussion of wills, trusts, and estates has been added to Chapter 7.
- **Limited liability companies and partnerships**—These relatively new types of business organizations are described in Chapter 8.
- **Environmental law**—A new section on environmental law has been added for this edition (see Chapter 9).
- **New and updated appendices**—All appendices have been updated as necessary, and an entirely new appendix on NFPA's PACE examination has been added.

For Users of the First Edition

Those of you who have used the First Edition of this text will probably want to know of some other changes that have been made for the Second Edition. In addition to the changes and additions just mentioned, we have made the following changes to *West's Paralegal Today* for this edition:

- **Chapter 1** (Today's Professional Paralegal)—The chapter now includes a completely rewritten section on the definition of a paralegal and also includes the AAfPE's definition of a paralegal. Additionally, the AAfPE's role in paralegal education has been stressed, as has the growing importance of computer technology, including online communications, in the legal workplace.
- **Chapter 2** (Careers in the Legal Community)—The discussion of areas of paralegal practice now includes legal aid offices; freelance paralegals; and a number of emerging specialty areas, such as elder law and legal nurse consulting. The chapter also includes a section—and a special feature—on online job searching.
- **Chapter 3** (Ethics and Professional Responsibility)—This chapter combines, updates, and streamlines the coverage of the materials presented in Chapters 3 and 4 of the First Edition.

PREFACE

- **Chapters 7, 8, and 9** (Substantive Law I, Substantive Law II, and Administrative Law and Government Regulation, respectively)—Chapters 7 and 8 of the First Edition have been expanded into three chapters; additionally, the First Edition's coverage of administrative law has been reduced and is now included in Chapter 9.
- **Chapter 13** (Conducting Interviews and Investigations)—The chapter integrates the materials presented in Chapters 14 and 15 of the First Edition.
- **Appendix A of the First Edition**—The appendix formerly entitled "Mastering *West's Paralegal Today*: How to Study Legal Concepts and Procedures" has been moved to the front of the book. It now appears as an "Introduction to the Student" just before Chapter 1. A section entitled "Going Online" has been added to this introduction.

SUPPLEMENTAL TEACHING/LEARNING MATERIALS

West's Paralegal Today, Second Edition, is accompanied by what is arguably the largest number of teaching and learning supplements available for any text of its kind. We understand that instructors face a difficult task in finding the time necessary to teach the materials that they wish to cover during each term. In conjunction with a number of our colleagues, we have developed supplementary teaching materials that we believe are the best obtainable today. Each component of the supplements package is described below.

Instructor's Manual

Written by the authors of the text, the *Instructor's Manual* contains the following:

- A sample course syllabus.
- Chapter/lecture outlines.
- Teaching suggestions.
- Test Bank.
- Answers to text exercises and questions.
- Transparency masters.
- PowerPoint presentation slides.

Study Guide

Prepared by Celia Elwell of the University of Oklahoma, the *Study Guide* includes the following features:

- Chapter objectives are presented in checklist form so that students can review systematically the topics they have learned and determine which areas need more study.
- Chapter outlines provide succinct, easy-to-read summaries of the chapters and help students review the material. Study suggestions are included within the outlines, including tips on how to remember key information.
- Review questions in true-false, fill-in-the-blank, and multiple-choice formats provide students with an extensive review of the terminology and concepts presented in each chapter of the text. There are between thirty and fifty review questions for each chapter.
- Additional practice questions, questions for critical analysis, and ethical questions reinforce the concepts and procedures presented in the chapters.

Computerized Test Bank

The Test Bank found in the *Instructor's Manual* is also available in a computerized format on CD-ROM. The platforms supported include Windows™ 3.1 and 95, Windows™ NT, and Macintosh. Features include:

- Multiple methods of question selection.
- Multiple outputs—that is, print, ASCII, RTF.
- Graphic support (black and white).
- Random questioning output.
- Special character support.

State-Specific Supplements

State-specific supplements are available for California, Florida, New York, and Texas. These supplements are keyed to each chapter in the text and point out state-specific information when it differs from the text's discussion. These supplements will be made available online as a downloadable electronic supplement.

Citation-At-A-Glance

This handy reference card provides a quick, portable reference to the basic rules of citation for the most commonly cited legal sources, including judicial opinions, statutes, and secondary sources, such as legal encyclopedias and legal periodicals. *Citation-At-A-Glance* uses the rules set forth in *The Bluebook: A Uniform System of Citation*. A free copy of this valuable supplement is included with every student text.

Web Page

Come visit our Web site at **www.Westlegalstudies.com**, where you will find valuable information specific to this book and other West Legal Studies texts.

Strategies for Paralegal Educators

Strategies and Tips for Paralegal Educators, a pamphlet by Anita Tebbe of Johnson County Community College, provides teaching strategies specifically designed for paralegal educators. It concentrates on how to teach and is organized in three parts: the WHO of paralegal education—students and teachers; the WHAT of paralegal education—goals and objectives; and the HOW of paralegal education—methods of instruction, methods of evaluation, and other aspects of teaching. A copy of this pamphlet is available to each adopter. Quantities for distribution to adjunct instructors are available for purchase at a minimal price. A coupon in the pamphlet provides ordering information.

Westlaw®

West's online computerized legal-research system offers students "hands-on" experience with a system commonly used in law offices. Qualified adopters can receive ten free hours of Westlaw®. Westlaw® can be accessed with Macintosh and IBM PCs and compatibles. A modem is required.

PREFACE

Acknowledgments

In creating the Second Edition of *West's Paralegal Today*, a number of professionals offered us penetrating criticisms, comments, and suggestions for improving the text. While we haven't been able to comply with every request, each of the reviewers listed below will see that many of his or her suggestions have been taken to heart.

Laura Barnard
Lakeland Community College, OH

Linda S. Cioffredi
Woodbury College, VT

Arlene A. Cleveland
Pellissippi State Technical Community College, TN

Lynne D. Dahlborg
Suffolk University, MA

Kevin R. Derr
Pennsylvania College of Technology, PA

Wendy B. Edson
Hilbert College, NY

Paul D. Guymon
William Rainey Harper College, IL

Sharon Halford
Community College of Aurura, CO

Melinda Hess
College of Saint Mary, NE

Susan J. Howery
Yavapai College, AZ

Melissa M. Jones
Samford University, AL

Constance Ford Mungle
Oklahoma City University, OK

Martha G. Nielson
University of Calif., San Diego, CA

Anthony Piazza
David N. Myers College, OH

Loretta Thornhill
Hagerstown Community College, MD

Julia Tryk
Cuyahoga Community College, OH

Numerous careful and conscientious individuals have helped us in this undertaking from the beginning. We continue to be indebted to those whose contributions helped to make the First Edition of *West's Paralegal Today* a valuable teaching/learning text. We particularly thank the following paralegal educators for their insightful criticisms and comments:

Laura Barnard
Lakeland Community College, OH

Jeptha Clemens
Northwest Mississippi Community College

Donna Hamblin Donathan
Marshall University Community College, OH

Susan Howery
Davenport College, MI

Wendy Edson
Hilbert College, NY

Pamela Faller
College of the Sequoias, CA

Gary Glascom
Cedar Crest College, PA

Dolores Grissom
Samford University, AL

Jean A. Hellman
Loyola University, Chicago, IL

Marlene L. Hoover
El Camino College, CA

Jennifer Allen Labosky
Davidson County Community College, NC

Dora J. Lew
California State University, Hayward

Mary Hatfield Lowe
Westark Community College, AZ

Gerald A. Loy
Broome Community College, NY

Linda Mort
Kellogg Community College, MI

H. Margaret Nickerson
William Woods College, MO

Martha Nielsen
University of California, San Diego

Elizabeth L. Nobis
Lansing Community College, MI

Joy D. O'Donnell
Pima Community College, AZ

Francis D. Polk
Ocean County College, NJ

Ruth-Ellen Post
Rivier College, NH

Elizabeth Raulerson
Indian River Community College, FL

Kathleen Mercer Reed
University of Toledo, Ohio

Lynn Retzak
Lakeshore Technical Institute, Wisconsin

Evelyn L. Riyhani
University of California, Irvine

Melanie A. P. Rowand
California State University, Hayward

Vitonio F. San Juan
University of La Verne, California

Susan F. Schulz
Southern Career Institute, Florida

We also are grateful to the following paralegal educators, our featured guests in *West's Paralegal Today*, Second Edition, for enhancing the quality of our book with their tips and illuminating insights into paralegal practice:

Anna Durham Boling
Athens Area Technical Institute, GA

Andrea Nager Chasen
Private Law Practice

John DeLeo
Central Pennsylvania Business School, PA

Wendy B. Edson
Hilbert College, NY

Daniel F. Hinkel
National Center for Paralegal Training, GA

Judy A. Long
Rio Hondo College, CA

James W. H. McCord
Eastern Kentucky University, KY

Lloyd Pearcy
Private Law Practice, CO

Michael A. Pener
Johnson County Community College, KS

Kathleen Mercer Reed
University of Toledo's Community and Technical College, OH

Jan Richmond
St. Louis Community College, MO

Vitonio F. San Juan
University of La Verne, CA

Denise Templeton
President and Chief Executive Officer of Templeton & Associates

Richard M. Terry
Baltimore City Community College, MD

Pamela Poole Weber
Seminole Community College, FL

E. J. Yera
Holmes Regional Medical Center, FL

Additionally, we extend our gratitude to those on-the-job paralegals who agreed to appear in the *Paralegal Profiles* of *West's Paralegal Today*, Second Edition.

In preparing *West's Paralegal Today*, Second Edition, we were also the beneficiaries of the expertise brought to the project by the editorial and production staff of the West Legal Studies program. Our editor, Joan Gill, successfully guided the project through each phase and put together a supplements package that is without parallel in the teaching and learning of paralegal skills. Rhonda Dearborn, our developmental editor, was also incredibly helpful in putting together the teaching/learning package. We sincerely appreciate the efforts of our project editor, Ann Borman, who designed what we feel is the most visually attractive paralegal text on the market, and of the production supervisor on the project, Bill Stryker. We also wish to thank our production manager, Wendy Troeger, and production editor, Laurie Boyce, for their assistance throughout the production process.

A number of other individuals contributed significantly to the quality of *West's Paralegal Today*, Second Edition. We wish to thank William Eric Hollowell for his assistance in creating what we believe is the best chapter on computer-assisted legal research in any paralegal text on the market today. We also thank Lavina Leed Miller and Roxie Lee for their help in coordinating the authors' work on the project and for their research and proofreading efforts. We are grateful to Suzie Franklin Defazio, whose copyediting and proofreading skills will not go unnoticed, and to Suzanne Jasin for her assistance.

We know that we are not perfect. If you or your students have suggestions on how we can improve this book, write to us. That way, we can make *West's Paralegal Today*, Second Edition, an even better book in the future. We promise to answer every single letter that we receive.

Roger LeRoy Miller
Mary Meinzinger Urisko

Introduction to the Student

The law sometimes is considered a difficult subject because it uses a specialized vocabulary and requires substantial time and effort to learn. Those who work with and teach law believe that the subject matter is exciting and definitely worth your efforts. Everything in *West's Paralegal Today: The Legal Team at Work*, Second Edition, has been written for the precise purpose of helping you learn the most important aspects of law and legal procedures.

Learning is a lifelong process. Your learning of legal concepts and procedures will not end when you finish your paralegal studies. On the contrary, the end of your paralegal studies marks the beginning of your learning process in regard to law and legal procedures. Just as valuable to you as the knowledge base you can acquire from mastering the legal concepts and terms in *West's Paralegal Today*, Second Edition, is a knowledge of *how to learn* those legal concepts and terms. The focus in this introduction, therefore, is on developing learning skills that you can apply to any subject matter and at any time throughout your career.

The suggestions and study tips offered in this introduction can help you "learn how to learn" law and procedures and maximize your chances of success as a paralegal student. They can also help you build lifelong learning habits that you can use in other classes and throughout your career as a paralegal.

Mastering Your Text

A mistake commonly made by students is the assumption that the best way to understand the content of written material is to read and reread that material. True, if you read through a chapter ten times, you probably have acquired a knowledge of its contents, but think of the time you have spent in the process. What you want to strive for is using your time *effectively*. We offer here some suggestions on how to study the chapters of *West's Paralegal Today* most effectively.

Read One Section at a Time

A piano student once said to her teacher, "This piece is so complicated. How can I possibly learn it?" The teacher responded, "It's simple: measure by measure." That advice can be applied to any challenging task. As a paralegal student, you are faced with the task of learning complicated legal concepts and procedures. By dividing up your work into manageable units, you will find that before long, you have achieved your goal. Each chapter in *West's Paralegal Today,* Second Edition, is divided into several major sections. By concentrating on sections, rather than chapters, you will find it easier to master the chapter's contents.

Assume, for example, that you have been assigned to read Chapter 7 of *West's Paralegal Today,* Second Edition. That chapter covers basic concepts and principles involving various bodies of substantive law, including contract law, torts, property law, and wills, trusts, and estates. Mastering each of these topics requires you to learn a number of different legal concepts and terms. You will find it easier to master all of these topics if you concentrate on just one topic at a time. For example, you might begin with the section on contract law and focus only on that section.

Once you have read through a section, do not stop there. Go back through the section again and organize the material in your mind. Outlining the section is one way to mentally organize what you have read.

Make an Outline

An outline is simply a method for organizing information. The reason an outline can be helpful is that it illustrates visually how concepts relate to each other. Outlining can be done as part of your reading of each section, but your outline will be more accurate (and more helpful later on) if you have already read through a section and have a general understanding of the topics covered within that section.

THE BENEFITS OF OUTLINING. Although you may not believe that you need to outline, our experience has been that the act of *physically* writing an outline for a chapter helps most students to improve greatly their ability to retain and master the material being studied. Even if you make an outline that is no more than the headings in the text, you will be studying more efficiently than you otherwise would be.

Outlining is also a paralegal skill. As a paralegal, you will need to present legal concepts and fact patterns in an outline format. For example, paralegals frequently create legal memoranda to summarize their research results. The legal memorandum is usually presented in an outline format, which indicates how the topics covered in the memo relate to one another logically or sequentially. There is no better time to master the skill of outlining than the present, while you are a student. You can learn this skill by outlining sections and chapters of *West's Paralegal Today,* Second Edition.

IDENTIFY THE MAIN CONCEPTS IN EACH SECTION. You can use the chapter outlines at the beginning of each chapter as a starting point on your outlines for each section and chapter. The chapter-opening outlines include the headings of each major section within the chapter. You use these headings as a guide when creating a more thorough and detailed outline of each section. Be careful, though. To make an effective outline you have to be selective. Outlines that contain all the information in the text are not very useful. Your objective in outlining is to identify main concepts and to arrange more detailed concepts under those main concepts. Therefore, in outlining, your first goal is to *identify the main concepts in each section.* Often the large, first-level headings within your textbook and in the chapter-opening outlines are sufficient as identifiers of the major concepts within each section. You may decide, however, that you want to phrase an identifier in a way that is more meaningful to you.

OUTLINE FORMAT. Your outline should consist of several levels written in a standard outline format. The most important concepts are assigned an upper-case roman numeral; the second most important, a capital letter; the third most important, numbers; the fourth most important, lower-case letters; and the fifth most important, lower-case roman numerals. The number of levels you use in an outline varies, of course, with the complexity of the subject matter. In some outlines, or portions of outlines, you may need to use only two levels. In others, you may need as many as five or more levels.

As an example of how to use numerals and letters in an outline, we present below a partial outline of the contracts section in Chapter 7 of *West's Paralegal Today,* Second Edition.

FUNDAMENTAL LEGAL CONCEPTS: CONTRACTS

I. Definition of a contract
   A. General definition: An exchange of promises that can be enforced in court.
   B. Specific definition: An oral or written agreement formed by two or more parties who promise to perform or refrain from performing some act now or in the future.
II. Breach of contract: Occurs when a party to a contract fails to perform as promised.
III. Requirements of a valid contract
   A. Agreement—divided into two events:
      1. The offer—one party (offeror) makes an offer to another party (offeree) to form a contract.
         a. Requirements of the offer
            i. Must reflect a serious and objective intent on part of offeror to form a contract.
            ii. Must contain sufficiently definite terms so that if accepted, the contract's terms will be clear to a court if a dispute arises.
         b. Offeror may normally revoke (take back) offer at any time prior to acceptance.
      2. Acceptance
         a. Acceptance by offeree creates binding contract (if other requirements for a valid contract are also met).
         b. Acceptance can only be made by offeree, not a third party.
         c. Acceptance must be timely—within time period designated by offeror or within a "reasonable time."
   B. Consideration . . .

Consider Marking Your Text

From kindergarten through high school, you typically did not own your own textbooks. They were made available by the school system. You were told not to mark in them. Now that you own your own text for a course, your learning can be greatly improved by marking your text. There is a trade-off here. The more you mark up your textbook, the less you will receive from the bookstore when you sell it back at the end of the semester. The benefit is a better understanding of the subject matter, and the cost is the reduction in the price you receive for the resale of the text. Additionally, if you want a text that you can mark with your own notations, you necessarily have to buy a new one or a used one that has no markings. Both carry a higher price tag than a used textbook with markings.

THE BENEFITS OF MARKING.   Marking is helpful because it assists you to become an *active* participant in the mastery of the material. Researchers have shown that the physical act of marking, just like the physical act of outlining, helps you better retain the material. The better the material is organized in your mind, the more you will remember. There are two types of readers—passive and active. The active reader outlines and/or marks. Active readers typically do better on exams. Perhaps one of the reasons that active readers retain more is because the physical act of outlining and/or marking requires greater concentration. It is through greater concentration that more is remembered.

DIFFERENT WAYS OF MARKING. The most commonly used form of marking is to underline important points. The second most commonly used method is to use a felt-tipped highlighter, or marker, in yellow or some other transparent color. Marking also includes circling, numbering, using arrows, making brief notes, or any other method that allows you to locate things when you go back to skim the pages in your textbook prior to an exam—or when creating your outline, if you mark your text first and then outline it.

POINTS TO REMEMBER WHEN MARKING. Here are two important points to remember when marking your text:

1. *Read through the entire section before you begin marking.* You cannot mark a section until you know what is important, and you cannot know what is important until you read through the whole section.

2. *Do not mark too extensively.* You should mark your text selectively. If you fill up each page with arrows, asterisks, circles, and underlines, marking will be of little use. When you go back to review the material, you will not be able to find what was important. The key is *selective* activity. Mark each page in a way that allows you to see the most important points at a glance.

Memory Devices

During the course of your study of *West's Paralegal Today,* Second Edition, you will encounter numerous legal terms that are most likely new to you. Your challenge will be to remember these terms and incorporate them into your own "working" vocabulary. You will also need to remember legal concepts and principles. We look here at some techniques for learning and retaining legal terms and concepts.

FLASH CARDS. Using flash cards is a remarkably effective method of learning new terms or concepts. Through sheer repetition, or drilling, flash cards force you to recall certain ideas and repeat them. Although published flash cards are available in many bookstores, you should try to create your own by writing terms or concepts on index cards. Write the key term or concept on one side and the definition, process, or description on the other side.

There are several advantages to creating your own flash cards. First, the exercise of actually writing the information will help you insert the term into your permanent memory. Second, you do not need flash cards for terms that you already know or that you will not need to know for your particular course. Third, you can phrase the answer in a meaningful way, with unique cues that are designed just for your purposes. This personalizes the flash card, making the information easier to remember. Finally, you can modify the definition, if need be, so that it matches more closely the particular definition preferred by your instructor.

It is helpful to create your flash cards consistently and routinely at a given point in the learning process. One good moment is when you are reading or outlining your text. Make a flash card for each boldfaced term and write the margin definition on the flash card. Also include pronunciation instructions, if appropriate, on the card.

Take your flash cards with you everywhere. Review them at lunch, while you wait in line, or when you ride on the bus. When a flash card contains a term that is difficult to pronounce, say the term aloud, if possible, as often as you can. When you have a term memorized, set that card aside but save it as an exam-review device for later in the term. Prepare new cards as you cover new terms or concepts in class.

MNEMONICS. One method that students commonly employ to remember legal concepts and principles is the use of mnemonic (pronounced "nee-*mahn*-ick") devices. Mnemonic devices are merely aids to memory. A mnemonic device can be a word, a formula, or a rhyme. As an aid to remembering the elements of a cause of action in negligence (see Chapter 7), for example, you might use the mnemonic ABCD, in which the letters represent the following concepts:

A represents "A duty of care."
B represents "Breach of the duty of care."
C represents "Causation (the breach must cause an injury)."
D represents "Damage (injury or harm)."

Similarly, to remember the basic activities that paralegals may not legally undertake (see Chapter 3), you might use the mnemonic FACt, in which the letters represent the following concepts:

F represents "fees"—paralegals may not set legal fees.
A represents "advice"—paralegals may not give legal advice.
Ct represents "court"—paralegals, with some exceptions, may not represent clients in court.

Whenever you want to memorize various components of a legal doctrine or concept, consider devising a mnemonic. Mnemonics need not make sense in themselves. The point is, if they help you remember something, then use them. Any association you can make with a difficult term to help you pronounce it, spell it, or define it more easily is a useful learning tool.

Identify What You Do Not Understand

One of the most important things you can do prior to class is clarify in your mind which terms, concepts, or procedures you *do not* understand. You can do this when marking your text by placing check marks or question marks by material that you find difficult to comprehend. Similarly, you can include queries in your outline. For example, in the sample partial outline of contracts presented earlier in this introduction, you might add a query following the subsection on acceptance that reads, "What is considered to be a 'reasonable time'"?

Once you have outlined and marked your text, go back to any problem areas that you have encountered and *think about them.* You will find that it is very exciting to figure out difficult material on your own. If you still do not understand a concept thoroughly, make a note to follow up on this topic later in the classroom. Perhaps the instructor's lecture will clarify the issue. If not, make a point of asking for clarification.

As a paralegal, you may be frequently asked to undertake preliminary investigations of legal claims. Identifying what facts are *not known* is the starting point for any investigation and focuses investigatory efforts. As a student, you might think about class time as an opportunity to "investigate" further the subject matter of your course. Identifying before class what you do not know about a topic allows you to focus your "investigative" efforts, particularly your listening efforts, during class and to maximize classroom opportunities for learning.

LEARNING IN THE CLASSROOM

The classroom is the heart of your learning experience as a paralegal student. Each instructor develops an overall plan for a course that includes many elements, which are integrated, or brought together, during class sessions. A major element in your instructor's course plan will be, of course, the material presented in your textbook, *West's Paralegal Today*, Second Edition. As discussed in the preceding section, reading your textbook assignments thoroughly, before class, is one way to enhance your chances of truly mastering the subject matter of the course. Equally important to this goal, though, are listening carefully to your instructor and taking good notes.

Be an Active Listener

The ability to listen actively is a learned skill and one that will benefit you throughout your career as a paralegal. When your supervising attorney gives instructions, for example, it is crucial that you understand those instructions clearly. If you do not, you will need to ask the attorney to further clarify the instructions until you know exactly what your assignment is. Similarly, when you are interviewing clients or witnesses, you will need to be constantly interacting, mentally, with the information the client or witness is giving you so that you can follow up, immediately if necessary, on that information with further questions or actions.

As a paralegal student, you can practice listening skills in the classroom that you will need to exercise later on the job. The more immediate benefit of listening actively is, of course, a better chance of obtaining an excellent course grade.

In a nutshell, active listening as a student requires you to do the following:

1. *Listen attentively.* For anything to be communicated verbally by one person to another, the listener has to pay attention or no communication will take place. If you find your attention wandering in the classroom, make a conscious effort to become alert and focus on what is being said.

2. *Mentally interact with what is being said.* Active listening involves mentally "acting" on the information being conveyed by the speaker (your instructor). For example, if your instructor is discussing the elements required for a cause of action in negligence, you do not want simply to write down, word for word, what the instructor is saying. Rather, you first make sure that you *understand* the meaning of what is being said. This requires you to think about what is being said in the context of what else you know about the topic. Does the information make sense within that context? Does what you are hearing raise further questions in your mind? If so, make a note of them.

3. *Ask for clarification.* If you do not understand what the instructor is saying or if something is confusing, ask for clarification. How you do this will depend to some extent on the size of your class and the degree of classroom formality. In some classes, you might feel comfortable raising your hand and questioning the instructor at that point during the lecture or discussion. In other classes, you might make a note to talk to the instructor about the topic after class or later, during the instructor's office hours.

Take Good Notes

The ability to take good notes is another skill that will help you excel both in your paralegal studies and on the job as a paralegal. Ideally, you will understand clearly everything that is being said in the classroom, and note taking will simply consist of jotting down, in your own words, brief phrases and sentences to remind you of what was stated. Often, however, you may not understand fully what the instructor is talking about, or it may take half of the class period before it becomes clear to you where your instructor is going with a certain idea or topic. In the meantime, should you take notes?

The best answer to this question is, of course, "Ask for clarification." But in some situations, interrupting a lecturer may be awkward or perceived as discourteous. In these circumstances, the wiser choice might be to take notes. Write down, to the extent possible, what the instructor is saying, including brief summaries of any examples the instructor is presenting. Later, when you have more knowledge of the subject, what the instructor said during that period may fall into place. If not, find an opportunity to ask for clarification.

Two other suggestions for taking good notes and making effective use of them are the following: (1) develop and use a shorthand system and (2) review and summarize your notes as soon as possible after class.

DEVELOP AND USE A SHORTHAND SYSTEM. There may be times during a lecture when you want to take extensive notes. For example, your instructor may be discussing a hypothetical scenario to illustrate a legal concept. Because you know that hypothetical examples are very useful in understanding (and later reviewing) legal concepts, you want to include a description of the hypothetical example in your notes. Using abbreviations and symbols can help you include more information in your notes in less time.

In taking notes of a hypothetical example, consider designating a single letter as representative of each person or entity involved in the example. This eliminates the need to write and rewrite the names of each person or entity as they are used. For example, if a hypothetical involves three business firms, you could designate each firm by a letter: *A* could stand for Abel Electronics, *B* for Brentwood Manufacturing, and *C* for Crandall Industries.

Certain symbols and abbreviations, including those listed below, are fairly widely used as a kind of "shorthand" by legal professionals and others to designate certain concepts, parties, or procedures:

Δ	defendant
π	plaintiff
≈	similar to
≠	not equal to, not the same as
∴	therefore
a/k/a	also known as
atty	attorney
b/c or **b/cz**	because
b/p	burden of proof
cert	*certiorari*
dely	delivery
dep	deposition
disc	discovery
JML	judgment as a matter of law
JNOV	judgment *non obstante veredicto* (notwithstanding the verdict)
JOP	judgment on the pleadings

juris	jurisdiction
K	contract
mtg	mortgage
n/a	not applicable
neg	negligence
PL	paralegal
Q	as a consequence, consequently
re	regarding
§ or sec	section
s/b	should be
S/F	Statute of Frauds
S/L	statute of limitations

You will want to expand on this short list by creating and using other symbols or abbreviations. Once you develop a workable shorthand system, routinely use it in the classroom and then carry it over to your job. Most firms or corporations you will work for will also commonly use symbols and abbreviations, which you can add to your shorthand system later. It may also be helpful to become familiar with proofing symbols, which are listed under "proofreading" in the dictionary.

REVIEW AND REVISE YOUR NOTES AFTER EACH CLASS. An excellent habit to form is reviewing and revising your class notes as soon as possible after the class period ends. Often, at the moment you write certain notes, you are not sure of how they fit in the overall design of the lecture. After class, however, you usually have a better perspective and know how the "pieces of the puzzle" fit together. Reviewing and summarizing your notes while the topic is still fresh in your mind—at the end of each day, for example—gives you the opportunity to reorganize them in a logical manner.

If you have a computer available, consider also typing up your notes. That way, when you want to review them, you will be able to read them quickly. Using a basic outline format when typing your notes (or rewriting them, if you do not have a computer available) will be particularly helpful later. You can tell at a glance the logical relationships between the various statements made in class.

Although reviewing and summarizing your notes each day or at other frequent intervals may seem overly time consuming, in the long run it pays off. First, as with outlining and marking a text, reviewing your notes after class allows you to learn actively—you can think about what was covered during the class period, place various concepts in perspective, and decide what you do or do not understand after you complete your review. Second, you have probably already learned that memory is fickle. Even though we think we will not forget something we learned, in fact, we often do. When preparing for an exam, for example, you will want to remember what the instructor said in class about a particular topic. But, if you are like most people, your memory of that day and that class period may be rather fuzzy several weeks later. If you have taken good notes and summarized them legibly and logically, you will be able to review the topic quickly and effectively.

Networking in the Classroom

Several times in *West's Paralegal Today*, Second Edition, the authors, the featured-guest authors, and the paralegals profiled have all mentioned the importance of networking. The best time to begin networking is in the classroom. Consciously make an effort to get to know your instructor. Let him or her come to know you and your interests. Later, when looking for a job, you may want to ask that instructor for a reference.

Similarly, make an effort to become acquainted with other students in your class. Compared to students who are taking other college courses, such as math courses and history courses, there is a greater likelihood those of you in paralegal studies will be working in the same geographic area and may eventually belong to the same paralegal associations. Establishing connections with your classmates now may lead to networking possibilities later on the job, which offers many benefits for paralegals. One good way to establish long-term relationships with other students is by forming a study group.

Forming and Organizing a Study Group

Many paralegal students join together in study groups to exchange ideas, to share the task of outlining subjects, to prepare for examinations, and to lend support to each other generally. If you want to start a study group, a good way to find potential members is to observe your classmates and decide which students participate actively and frequently in class. Then approach those individuals with your idea of forming a study group. The number of participants in a study group can vary. Ordinarily, three to five members is sufficient for a good discussion. A study group with more than six members may defeat the goal of having each member actively participate, to the greatest extent possible, in group discussions.

Some paralegal students form study groups that meet on an "as needed" basis. For example, any member could call a meeting when there is an upcoming exam or difficult subject matter to be learned. Other students establish ongoing study groups that meet throughout the year (and sometimes for the entire paralegal program). The group works as a team and as such is an excellent preparatory device for working as part of a legal team in a law firm. Study groups can also continue on after course work is completed to prepare for certification exams as paralegals. These groups are also a great way to build relationships with other future paralegals with whom you may want to network later, on the job.

Meeting Times and Places. It is helpful to set up a regular meeting time and hold that time sacred. The members must be committed to the meeting times and to completing their assignments, or the group will not serve its purpose. Study groups can meet anywhere. You might meet in a classroom, another school room, a member's home, a park, or a restaurant. Many paralegal schools and colleges have multipurpose rooms or study areas available to students who wish to meet in small groups. Some rooms are equipped with easels or drawing boards, which help facilitate discussions. Audiovisual equipment may also be available for the group's use, such as a television with a VCR for viewing videotaped lectures. The group should select a meeting place that has limited distractions and sufficient space to accommodate each member's opened books, notes, and other materials.

Work Allocation. Teamwork is very important in the paralegal profession. Study groups can help you learn to function as a member of a team by distributing the workload among the group. Work (such as outlining chapters) should be allocated among the group members. It is important to define clearly who will be doing what work. It may be a good idea at the close of each meeting to have each member state out loud what work he or she will be responsible for completing prior to the next meeting. Whatever work one member does, he or she should make copies to distribute to the other members at the meeting.

EVALUATING YOUR GROUP. You should realize from the outset that your study group will be of little help if you are doing most of the work. You need to make sure that everyone who joins the group is as committed to learning the material as you are and that you make this concern known to the others. The teamwork approach is only effective if everybody does his or her share. Teamwork involves trust and reliance. If you cannot trust one of the members to form an accurate outline of a topic, you will not be able to rely on that outline. You will end up doing the work yourself, just as a precaution. Therefore, be very selective about whom you invite to join the group. If you joined an already existing group, leave it if it turns out to be a waste of your time.

ORGANIZING YOUR WORK PRODUCT

A part of the learning experience takes place through special homework assignments, research projects, and possibly study-group meetings. For example, if you are studying pretrial litigation procedures, you will read about these procedures in Chapter 10 of *West's Paralegal Today*, Second Edition. Your instructor will also likely devote class time to a discussion of these procedures. Additionally, you may be asked to create a sample complaint or to check your state's rules governing the filing of complaints in state courts. You also might have notes on a study-group discussion of these procedures.

How can you best organize all the materials generated during the coverage of a given topic? Here are a few suggestions that you might find useful. If you follow these suggestions, you will find that reviewing your work prior to exams is relatively easy—most of the work will already have been done.

CONSIDER USING A THREE-RING BINDER. An excellent way to integrate what you have learned is by using a three-ring binder and divider sheets with tabs for the different topics you cover. As you begin studying *West's Paralegal Today*, Second Edition, for example, consider having a different section in your binder for each chapter. Within that section, you can place your chapter outline (formed while reading the text), notes taken in the classroom or during other reading assignments, samples of projects you have done relating to topics in that chapter, and so on.

INTEGRATE YOUR NOTES INTO ONE DOCUMENT, IF POSSIBLE. If you have used a computer to key in your chapter outlines and class notes, consider incorporating everything you have learned about a topic into one document—a master, detailed outline of the topic. This can be done relatively easily by using the "cut and paste" feature of word-processing programs. The result will be a comprehensive outline of a particular topic that will make reviewing the topic prior to an exam (and perhaps later, on the job) a simple matter.

THE BENEFITS OF USING A COMPUTER

Many of the paralegals profiled in *West's Paralegal Today*, Second Edition, mentioned that if they were students again, they would spend more time developing computer skills. You should consider acquiring a personal computer, if possible. If not, see if you can arrange with someone else to use his or her personal computer on a routine basis. If your school or college has computers available in the library or some other place for student use, you might also use one of those computers.

Find out when there is usually a computer available—such as early in the morning—and use the computer routinely at this time.

Using a computer provides many benefits. First, you can practice your keyboarding and word-processing skills (essential paralegal skills) simultaneously as you take notes or work on research or other class projects. Second, if you have a computer available, you can type up and better organize your notes. Such time is well spent because it not only increases your knowledge of the topics but also makes it easy to review what you have learned prior to exams.

Finally, a key benefit of using a computer is the quality of any work product or homework assignment that you submit to your instructor. The editing and formatting features of word-processing programs allow you to correct misspelled words, reorganize your presentation, and generally revise your document with little effort. The spell-checker and grammar-checker features help you avoid glaring errors. The formatting features allow you to present your document in an attractive format. You can change margins and use different fonts (such as italics or boldface) to emphasize certain words or phrases. As a paralegal, you will be using a computer and a word-processing system to generate your work. You will also be expected to know how to use computers to create quality work products. The more you can learn about computers and word processing as a student, the easier it will be for you to perform your job as a paralegal.

GOING ONLINE

Another benefit of using a computer is, of course, the ability to go "online"—that is, connect to the Internet—and access the vast resources available on that worldwide computer network. In Chapter 15 of *West's Paralegal Today,* Second Edition, you will learn what the Internet is and how it can be used by legal professionals to obtain information on a variety of topics. A large number of colleges and universities offer free Internet access to their students. If you do not have a personal computer, check with your library to see if you can go online using one of the computers the library makes available to students.

You can obtain information online about most of the topics covered in this text. To help you learn how to find and evaluate specific online information, every chapter in this book ends with one or more Internet exercises in a section titled *Using Internet Resources.* Additionally, we have provided Internet addresses for numerous Web sites in the margins of the pages. If you go to these Web sites, you will find additional information about the topic being discussed in the text. In the *Technology and Today's Paralegal* features throughout this text, we have provided other Web sites when appropriate, and a good portion of Chapter 15 (titled "Computer-Assisted Legal Research") contains numerous references to specific Web sites that offer useful information for paralegals and other legal professionals.

Realize that Internet sites tend to come and go, and there is no guarantee that a site referred to in this text will be there by the time this book is in print. We have tried, though, to include sites that so far have proved to be fairly stable. If you do have difficulty reaching a site (that is, if your destination is "Not Found" or has "No DNS Entry"), do not immediately assume that the site does not exist. First, recheck the Web site address (Uniform Resource Locator, or URL) shown in your browser. Remember you have to type the URL exactly as written: upper case and lower case are important. If it appears that the URL has been keyed in correctly, then try the following technique: delete all of the information to the right of the forward slash that is farthest to the right and press enter.

For example, suppose that you are trying to reach the following Web site: **lawlib.wuacc.edu/washlaw/washlaw.html.** First, check the URL as you keyed it in. Then try deleting the final "washlaw.html" from the URL and press enter. If you still have problems, delete "washlaw," which is now the farthest to the right. Eventually, you will get back to the home page and can again start your search.

PREPARING FOR EXAMS

Being prepared for exams is crucial to doing well as a paralegal student. If you have followed the study tips and suggestions given in the preceding pages of this introduction, you will have little problem preparing for an exam. You will have at your fingertips detailed outlines of the topics covered, a marked textbook that allows you to review major concepts quickly and easily, and class notes. If you have integrated your outlines and class notes in one comprehensive, detailed outline, you will have an even easier task when it comes time to prepare for an examination.

In addition to mastering the material in *West's Paralegal Today*, Second Edition, and in the classroom, if you want to do well on an exam, you should develop an exam-taking strategy. For example, prior to any exam, you should find answers to the following questions:

- What type of exam are you going to take—essay, objective, or both?
- What reading materials and lectures will be covered on the exam?
- What materials should you bring to the exam? Will you need paper to write on, or will paper be provided?
- Will you be allowed to refer to your text or notes during the exam (as in an open-book exam)?
- Will the exam be computerized? If so, you will probably need to bring several number 2 pencils to the exam.
- How much time will be allowed for the exam?

The more you can find out in advance about an exam, the better you can prepare for it. For example, if you learn that there will an essay question on the exam, one way to prepare for the question is to practice writing timed essays. In other words, find out in advance how much time you will have for each essay question, say fifteen minutes, and then practice writing an answer to a sample essay question during a fifteen-minute time period. This is the only way you will develop the skills needed to pace yourself for an essay exam. Because most essay exams are "closed book," do your timed essay practice without using the book.

Usually, you can anticipate certain essay exam questions. You do this by going over the major concept headings, either in your lecture notes or in your text. Search for the themes that tie the materials together, and then think about questions that your instructor might ask you. You might even list possible essay questions as a review device. Then write a short outline for each of the questions that will most likely be asked. Some instructors give their students a list of questions from which the essay questions on the exam will be drawn. This gives you an opportunity to prepare answers for each of the questions in advance. Even though you cannot take your sample essays to class and copy them there, you will have organized the material in your mind.

Taking Exams

There are several strategies you can employ while taking exams to improve your grade, including those discussed below.

Following Instructions

Students are often in such a hurry to start an exam that they take little time to read the instructions. The instructions can be critical, however. In a multiple-choice exam, for example, if there is no indication that there is a penalty for guessing, then you should never leave a question unanswered. Even if there are only a few minutes remaining at the end of the exam, you should guess at the answers for those questions about which you are uncertain.

You also need to make sure that you are following the specific procedures required for the exam. Some exams require that you use a number 2 lead pencil to fill in the dots on a machine-graded answer sheet. Other exams require underlining or circling. In short, you have to look at the instructions carefully.

Finally, check to make sure that you have all the pages of the examination. If you are uncertain, ask the instructor or the exam proctor. It is hard to justify not having done your exam correctly because you failed to answer all of the questions. Simply stating that you did not have them will pose a problem for both you and your instructor. Do not take a chance. Double-check to make sure.

Use Exam Time Effectively

Examinations are often timed. This can make an otherwise straightforward question more difficult because of the *time pressure* that the student faces. Timed examinations require that a question or cluster of questions be answered within a specified period of time. If you must complete thirty multiple-choice questions in one hour, then you have two minutes to work on each individual question. If you finish fifteen of those questions in one minute instead of two, then you will have banked fifteen minutes that can be spent elsewhere on the examination or used to double-check your answers.

Consider the following example. Assume that you have ninety minutes for the entire exam: thirty minutes to answer the multiple-choice questions, fifteen minutes to answer the true-false questions, and forty-five minutes to answer a long essay question. If you could shave ten minutes off the time it takes to answer the multiple-choice section and five minutes off the time it takes to answer the true-false questions, you will have fifteen additional minutes to complete the long essay question.

Taking Objective Examinations

The most important point to discover initially with any objective test is if there is a penalty for guessing. If there is none, you have nothing to lose by guessing. In contrast, if a point or portion of a point will be subtracted for each incorrect answer, then you probably should not answer any question for which you are purely guessing.

Students usually commit one of two errors when they read objective-exam questions: (1) they read things into the questions that do not exist, or (2) they skip over certain words or phrases.

Most test questions include key words such as:

all
always
never
only

If you miss these key words you will be missing the "trick" part of the question. Also, you must look for questions that are only *partly* correct, particularly if you are answering true-false questions.

Never answer a question without reading all of the alternatives. More than one of them may be correct. If more than one of them seems correct, make sure you select the answer that seems the *most* correct.

Whenever the answer to an objective question is not obvious, start with the process of elimination. Throw out the answers that are clearly incorrect. Even with objective exams in which there is a penalty for guessing, if you can throw out several obviously incorrect answers, then you may wish to guess among the remaining ones because your probability of choosing the correct answer is relatively high. Typically, the easiest way to eliminate incorrect answers is to look for those that are meaningless, illogical, or inconsistent. Often, test authors put in choices that make perfect sense and are indeed true, but they are not the answer to the question you are to answer.

Writing Essay Exams

As with objective exams, you need to read the directions to the essay questions carefully. It is best to write out a brief outline *before* you start answering the question. The outline should present your conclusion in one or two sentences, then your supporting argument. You should take care not to include in your essay information that is irrelevant, even if you think it is interesting. It is important to stay on the subject. We can tell you from firsthand experience that no instructor likes to read answers to unasked questions.

Finally, write as legibly as possible. The authors can tell you that it is easier to be favorably inclined to a student's essay if we do not have to reread it several times to decipher the handwriting.

PART I
THE PARALEGAL PROFESSION

CHAPTER 1
Today's Professional Paralegal

CHAPTER 2
Careers in the Legal Community

CHAPTER 3
Ethics and Professional Responsibility

CHAPTER 4
The Legal Workplace

CHAPTER 1

Today's Professional Paralegal

Chapter Outline
❖ Introduction ❖ What Is a Paralegal? ❖ What Do Paralegals Do?
❖ History of the Paralegal Profession ❖ Paralegal Education
❖ Paralegal Skills ❖ Personal Attributes of the Professional Paralegal
❖ The Future of the Profession

After completing this chapter, you will know:
- What a paralegal is and does.
- How and why the paralegal profession developed.
- The professional organizations that exist for paralegals and the benefits of membership in them.
- The education and training available to paralegals.
- The skills that are useful for a paralegal to have.
- Some important personal attributes of the professional paralegal.

INTRODUCTION

If you are considering a career as a paralegal, be prepared to be part of an exciting profession. Among other things, you will find that paralegal work encompasses much, much more than drafting documents full of fine print and memorizing relevant legal procedures. As a paralegal, you will deal with real people and real problems. Even when you are doing legal research, the real world is not too far away. When locating and analyzing court cases, for example, you will find that each case tells a story of its own, involving specific people and circumstances. Generally, through your legal work you will learn much about human nature, the law, and how the law applies to real-life problems.

You will also find that the paralegal field offers a wide variety of opportunities for both personal and professional development. In the next chapter, you will read about career opportunities available for paralegals—and there are many. In fact, the paralegal profession is now one of the fastest-growing occupations in the United States. Jobs are available not only in law firms, large and small, but also in corporate enterprises, government offices and courts, real-estate firms, and numerous other organizations that use legal services, including public utilities, health insurers, and banks.

What is a paralegal? What do paralegals do? What kinds of educational training, job skills, and personal qualities must one have to become a successful paralegal? If you are contemplating a career as a professional paralegal, you will want to know the answers to these questions. In this introductory chapter, we provide those answers, as well as general background information on the evolution of the paralegal profession.

WHAT IS A PARALEGAL?

One of the challenges of describing any emerging profession is defining with some precision what the members of that profession do. Certainly, since its beginnings in the 1960s and 1970s, it has been challenging to come up with a definition of the paralegal profession that is both broad enough to include the diverse types of services that paralegals perform and narrow enough to identify with some specificity who is and is not a member of this profession. As you will read in Chapter 3, if paralegal professionals are to be regulated—by licensing requirements, for example—then how paralegals are defined becomes a crucial issue and one with serious implications for the profession.

Generally, we can say that a **paralegal**, or a **legal assistant**, is a person sufficiently trained in law and legal procedures to assist attorneys in the delivery of legal services to the public or to perform legal work as otherwise authorized by law. If you aspire to be a paralegal, however, you will want to become familiar with the more specific definitions of a paralegal given by legal professionals. Look at Exhibit 1.1 on the next page. There we show the definitions of a paralegal given by the **American Bar Association (ABA)**, a national association of attorneys, and the two leading national paralegal associations, the **National Association of Legal Assistants (NALA)** and the **National Federation of Paralegal Associations (NFPA)**, both of which will be discussed in more detail shortly. The final definition in the exhibit is that given by the **American Association for Paralegal Education (AAfPE)**, an organization that plays a major role in developing paralegal educational programs and curriculum across the nation.

When reading through these definitions, note how the terms *paralegal* and *legal assistant* are used in the first three definitions (the definition given by AAfPE refers only to "paralegals"). The definitions given by the ABA and NFPA (usually

Paralegal (or Legal Assistant)
A person sufficiently trained or experienced in the law and legal procedures to assist attorneys in the delivery of legal services to the public or to perform legal work as otherwise authorized by law.

American Bar Association (ABA)
A voluntary national association of attorneys. The ABA plays an active role in developing educational and ethical standards for attorneys and in pursuing improvements in the administration of justice.

National Association of Legal Assistants (NALA)
One of the two largest national paralegal associations in the United States; formed in 1975. NALA is actively involved in paralegal professional development.

National Federation of Paralegal Associations (NFPA)
One of the two largest national paralegal associations in the United States; formed in 1974. NFPA is actively involved in paralegal professional development.

American Association for Paralegal Education (AAfPE)
A national organization of paralegal educators; the AAfPE was established in 1981 to promote high standards for paralegal education.

EXHIBIT 1.1
Four Definitions of a Paralegal, or Legal Assistant

The American Bar Association's definition:	The National Association of Legal Assistants' definition:	The National Federation of Paralegal Associations' definition:	The American Association for Paralegal Education's definition:
A legal assistant or paralegal is a person, qualified by education, training or work experience, who is employed or retained by a lawyer, law office, corporation, governmental agency or other entity and who performs specifically delegated substantive legal work for which a lawyer is responsible.	Legal assistants, also known as paralegals, are a distinguishable group of persons who assist attorneys in the delivery of legal services. Through formal education, training and experience, legal assistants have knowledge and expertise regarding the legal system and substantive and procedural law which qualify them to do work of a legal nature under the supervision of an attorney.	A paralegal/legal assistant is a person qualified through education, training or work experience to perform substantive legal work that requires knowledge of legal concepts and that is customarily, but not exclusively, performed by a lawyer. This person may be retained or employed by a lawyer, law office, governmental agency or other entity or may be authorized by administrative, statutory or court authority to perform this work.	Paralegals perform substantive and procedural legal work as authorized by law, which work, in the absence of the paralegal, would be performed by an attorney. Paralegals have knowledge of the law gained through education, or education and work experience, which qualifies them to perform legal work. Paralegals adhere to recognized ethical standards and rules of professional responsibility.

pronounced *nif*pah) imply that the terms may be used interchangeably. In this book, we follow this practice (as many attorneys do) and use the terms as if they were synonymous. NALA's definition, however, which states that legal assistants are "also known as paralegals," does not necessarily imply that the terms are interchangeable. In fact, NALA members generally prefer the term *legal assistant* over *paralegal* because it is more restrictive. Legal assistants work under the supervision of attorneys, whereas not all those who call themselves paralegals do so. As you will learn in Chapter 2, some paralegals—known as "independent paralegals" or "legal technicians"—work independently and provide certain types of legal help (such as obtaining or filling out legal forms for bankruptcy filings or other legal transactions) directly to the public.

Note also how the definitions use slightly different wording with respect to paralegal qualifications. Particularly notice how the terms *and* and *or* affect the definitions. For example, both the ABA and NFPA state that a paralegal (or legal assistant) is a person qualified by "education, training *or* work experience," whereas NALA uses the phrase "formal education, training *and* experience" and the AAfPE states that a paralegal's knowledge of the law is gained through "education, *or* education *and* work experience." [Emphasis added.] By using *and* instead of *or* before the word "experience," the latter two definitions place greater emphasis on education as a paralegal qualification.

Significantly, both the ABA and NALA define legal assistants, or paralegals, as those who do work "for which a lawyer is responsible" (see the ABA's definition) or "under the supervision of an attorney" (see NALA's definition). In contrast, NFPA's broad definition does not mention attorney supervision, and the AAfPE states that paralegals perform legal work "as authorized by law." All of these organizations, however, emphasize that there are certain types of legal work

On the Web
For more information on the definitions of a paralegal, or legal assistant, given by the ABA, NALA, NFPA, and AAfPE, go to the following Web sites:
ABA: www.abanet.org
NALA: www.nala.org
NFPA: www.paralegals.org
AAfPE: www.aafpe.org

> ## ETHICAL CONCERN
> ### Paralegal Expertise and Legal Advice
>
> Paralegals often become very knowledgeable in a specific area of the law. If you specialize in environmental law, for example, you will become very knowledgeable about environmental claims. In working with a client on a matter involving an environmental agency, you might therefore be tempted to advise the client on which type of action would be most favorable to him or her. Never do so. As will be discussed in detail in Chapter 3, only attorneys may give legal advice, and paralegals who give legal advice risk penalties for the unauthorized practice of law. Whatever legal advice is given to the client must come either directly from the attorney or, if from you, must reflect exactly (or nearly exactly) what the attorney said with no embellishment on your part. After consulting with your supervising attorney, for example, you can say to the client that Mr. X (the attorney) "advises that you do all that you can to settle the claim as soon as possible."

that paralegals by law may not undertake. For example, a paralegal may not give legal advice, set legal fees, or (with rare exceptions) represent a client in court (see Chapter 3).

Finally, all four definitions indicate that paralegals perform "substantive" legal work. This is an important element of these definitions because it indicates that paralegals, although they are not attorneys, often perform work that was traditionally undertaken only by attorneys.

What Do Paralegals Do?

Throughout this book, you will read about the different ways in which paralegals assist attorneys; it is impossible to list them all in this brief space. The following list is just a sampling of some of the tasks that paralegals typically perform in a traditional paralegal setting—a law office. Bear in mind, though, that today an increasing number of paralegals are finding work in nontraditional (non-law-office) settings, including corporations, government agencies, courts, insurance companies, real-estate firms, and virtually any other entity that uses legal services.

- *Draft legal documents*—such as legal correspondence, documents to be filed with the court, and interoffice memoranda.
- *Calendar and track important deadlines*—such as the dates when certain documents must be filed with the court.
- *Assist attorneys in preparing for trial*—by preparing exhibits, documents, and trial notebooks that the attorney will need to have on hand at trial. Some paralegals also assist attorneys during trials.
- *Interview clients and witnesses*—to gather relevant facts and information about a lawsuit, for example.
- *Conduct legal investigations*—to gather facts about cases by interviewing clients and witnesses and obtaining relevant records (such as medical records or the police report of an accident).
- *Organize and maintain client files*—or (as is often the situation) supervise the organization and maintenance of client files.

- *Conduct legal research*—to find, analyze, and summarize court decisions, statutes, or regulations applicable to a client's case.
- *Use computers and technology*—to carry out the above tasks.

The specific kinds of tasks that paralegals perform vary, of course, from office to office. If you work in a one-attorney office, for example, you will probably not have much secretarial or clerical assistance. In other words, your job might overlap to some extent with that of the legal secretary. Your tasks might range from conducting sophisticated legal research and investigations to performing nonbillable clerical activities, such as photocopying documents and answering the telephone while the secretary is out to lunch.

If you work in a larger law firm, you will have more support staff (secretaries, file clerks, and others) to whom you can delegate tasks. Your work might also be more specialized. Instead of dealing with a number of cases relating to different areas of the law, you might concentrate solely on certain types of cases. If you work in a law firm's real-estate department, for example, you will deal only with legal matters relating to that area of the law.

Typically, today's paralegal performs many tasks using various types of legal software, electronic communications systems, and online databases. For example, trial preparation (see Chapter 10) increasingly involves using document management systems to track and make readily accessible the various materials needed for trial. Also, when conducting legal investigations and research, paralegals can now access online much of the information that they need (see Chapters 13 and 15).

HISTORY OF THE PARALEGAL PROFESSION

The paralegal profession initially developed in response to the need for a legal professional to fill a position somewhere between that of an attorney and that of a legal secretary—so that legal services could be provided to the public at lower cost. The need for greater access to legal services, which became a significant issue in the 1960s, continues to propel developments in the legal arena, including the increased use of paralegals to make legal services more affordable.

Law Clerk
In the context of law-office work, a law student who works as an apprentice, during the summer or part-time during the school year, with an attorney or a law firm to gain practical legal experience.

Staff Attorney
An attorney who is hired by a law firm as an employee and who has no ownership rights in the firm.

To some extent, law clerks fill this need. A **law clerk** is a law student who gains practical experience in the law by working for a law firm. Law clerks are often hired on a temporary basis (for the summer, for example, when they are not attending school, or to assist on a specific project).[1]

The problem faced by law firms is that if they require permanent, full-time legal assistance, hiring a law student on a temporary or part-time basis will not fill this need. Another option is, of course, to hire a law-school graduate as a **staff attorney** (a hired attorney who, unlike a partner in a partnership, has no ownership rights in a firm) on a full-time basis; this, however, might be too great an expense for the firm.

Competent and experienced legal secretaries began to fill the need faced by many law firms to have full-time assistance at a lower cost. The first paralegals were legal secretaries who had become, through on-the-job experience, extremely competent and skilled in legal procedures. They learned how to do legal research and investigation, draft documents to be filed with the court, and perform other tasks that today's paralegals are trained to undertake. Eventually, legal assistants succeeded in defining themselves as a distinct professional group within the field of law. Paralegal professional associations and paralegal education programs fur-

---

1. The term *law clerk* is also used to designate an attorney who does legal research and writing for a judge or a justice.

ther advanced the professional status of paralegals. Today, individuals who want to become legal assistants can enter a paralegal program and receive specialized training.

In 1968, the ABA recognized, for the first time, the professional status of paralegals. In that same year, the ABA formed a special committee, now known as the ABA's Standing Committee on Legal Assistants, to study and discuss how lawyers could most effectively use nonlawyers in their practices. In the last thirty years, the committee has worked closely with paralegal organizations and other groups to achieve its goal of making legal services more affordable to the public by integrating legal assistants into the legal services delivery team. The ABA has played a significant role in approving paralegal education programs. The ABA has also created an "Associate Member" category for legal assistants. Membership allows legal assistants to become involved in the activities of the ABA and enhances the working relationship between lawyers and paralegals.

Paralegal Associations and Professional Growth

One feature that distinguishes a profession from other occupations is that the members of a profession form professional associations for the following purposes:

- To establish a forum (place) in which issues relating to their profession can be discussed, experiences can be shared, and communication networks can be established.
- To establish guidelines to regulate their activities, such as ethical codes of conduct.
- To determine the level of skills or educational preparation necessary to the type of work performed by the members of the profession.
- To establish or sponsor educational programs to train potential professional practitioners or provide continuing education for those members who are already practicing their profession.

The evolution of the *paralegal profession* is thus directly related to the formation of paralegal associations. The earliest paralegal associations were formed at the state and local levels. The formation of national paralegal associations in the mid-1970s significantly furthered the professional interests and goals of paralegals.

STATE AND LOCAL PARALEGAL ASSOCIATIONS. By the early 1970s, there were numerous local paralegal associations. If you look at Appendix F at the end of this book, you will see that today every state has a paralegal association, and several states have many regional or local organizations within their borders. Practicing paralegals typically belong to their local (and/or state) paralegal association, as well as one of the national paralegal associations discussed below. Most **state bar associations**—associations of attorneys at the state level—also allow paralegals to become associate members of their organizations.

THE NATIONAL FEDERATION OF PARALEGAL ASSOCIATIONS (NFPA). The National Federation of Paralegal Associations (NFPA), which was founded in 1974, was created to represent paralegals at U.S. Senate hearings that were considering the question of whether paralegals should be regulated. NFPA represented the few local paralegal organizations that existed in 1974. As of 1999, its membership consisted of about sixty paralegal associations from around the country, encompassing over 17,000 legal assistants. The member associations of NFPA are referred to as affiliated associations, or **affiliates**, of NFPA.

On the Web
The Web site for the ABA's Standing Committee on Legal Assistants is: **www.abanet.org/legalassts/approval.html**. (*Note:* No Web address ever ends in a comma, period, or semicolon. Consequently, you should ignore phrase-ending punctuation (commas or semicolons) and sentence-ending punctuation (periods) when using the Web addresses cited in this book.)

State Bar Association
An association of attorneys within a state. Membership in the state bar association is mandatory in over two-thirds of the states—that is, before an attorney can practice law in a state, he or she must be admitted to that state's bar association.

Affiliate
An entity that is connected (or affiliated) with another entity. State and local branches of national or regional paralegal associations are often referred to as affiliates.

On the Web
You can find a detailed listing of national paralegal associations at the Web site of West Legal Studies, the West paralegal resource center. Go to www.WestLegalStudies.com.

THE NATIONAL ASSOCIATION OF LEGAL ASSISTANTS (NALA). The National Association of Legal Assistants (NALA) was formed in 1975. Unlike NFPA, NALA has individual members. As of 1999, NALA and its ninety affiliated associations reached over 18,000 legal assistants nationwide. While both NALA and NFPA encourage the growth of the profession, they differ on the direction that the profession should take, as you will learn in Chapter 3.

OTHER NATIONAL PARALEGAL ASSOCIATIONS. As the profession developed, other national professional organizations were formed. Professional Legal Assistants, Inc. (PLA), was chartered in 1985. Other national paralegal professional associations include the Legal Assistant Management Association, the American Paralegal Association, and the National Association for Independent Paralegals. The names and addresses of these and other paralegal associations, including state associations, are given in Appendix F.

BENEFITS OF PROFESSIONAL MEMBERSHIP. As a paralegal, you will find that membership in a paralegal association offers numerous benefits. Among other things, membership offers the following kinds of opportunities:

- To meet and network with others in your profession.
- To receive professional publications or access online databases that keep you up to date on the latest laws, court cases, and bar association opinions that affect the paralegal profession.
- To participate in meetings to develop policy relating to emerging issues concerning the profession.
- To continue your training and education through seminars, workshops, and other programs, including online Continuing Legal Education (CLE) programs.
- Depending on the association you join, to have access to group insurance plans or other special products and services offered by the association.

Economics and the Paralegal Profession

In the modern competitive environment for legal services, clients shop around, and the cost of those services is an important factor in determining which lawyer or law firm will be hired. Lawyers can provide lower-cost legal services to their clients when they use paralegals because they can bill their clients at lower rates for paralegal work. As you will read in Chapter 4, in which this topic is explored more fully, the billable rate for a paralegal (the hourly rate charged to clients for work done on their behalf) is substantially less than that for an attorney.

Clients, then, benefit from the use of paralegals because the clients pay less for legal services. Lawyers who delegate substantive legal work to paralegals also benefit because it frees up their time and allows them to concentrate on the areas of legal work that demand their expertise. They can also take on more clients and thus increase the firm's profits.

PARALEGAL EDUCATION

One of the reasons for the growth of the paralegal profession has been the development of paralegal educational programs by paralegal educators. As mentioned earlier, the American Association for Paralegal Education (AAfPE) has played a leading role in this arena. The AAfPE develops standards and competencies appropriate for paralegal training and promotes quality education programs generally.

> ## ETHICAL CONCERN
> ### Ethics and the Effective Utilization of Paralegals
>
> As you will read in Chapter 3, the ethical codes and guidelines regulating attorneys urge attorneys to use paralegals effectively—because the effective use of paralegals in legal representation benefits the public by providing quality legal services at lower cost. Paralegal ethical codes and guidelines also reflect this commitment. As a paralegal, you will share in this ethical responsibility.
>
> What can you do to promote the effective use of paralegal services? One thing you can do is to join a paralegal association and work together with other association members toward this goal. Another step you can take is to encourage your supervising attorney to delegate substantive work to you. For example, you might volunteer to take on certain tasks so that you can display your competence. Some attorneys do not yet realize how many tasks paralegals can competently perform and how beneficial it is for them (freeing up their time for other work and lowering clients' bills) to delegate substantive work to paralegals.

Although no law—as yet—requires paralegals to meet specific educational requirements, such laws may be just around the corner. In 1998, the New Jersey Supreme Court Committee on Paralegal Education and Regulation recommended that paralegals in the state of New Jersey be subject to a system of licensure. If the committee's recommendations are adopted by the New Jersey Supreme Court, paralegals in New Jersey will have to obtain licenses to practice their profession—and such licensing will involve educational requirements. Utah is also currently considering a proposal that paralegals be subject to licensing requirements, and a number of other states are evaluating similar plans. You will read more about this issue, which is of vital concern for paralegals, in Chapter 3.

Even in the absence of licensing requirements, however, you will find that the job market demands a certain amount of education and training. You will have difficulty finding employment as a paralegal without having completed a paralegal training course or having received a degree in the field. Depending on your educational background and experience, you can spend anywhere from several months to several years obtaining a paralegal certificate or a degree.

On the Web
You can download the entire one-hundred-page report submitted by the New Jersey Supreme Court Committee on Paralegal Education and Regulation from the following Web site: **www.state.nj.us/ judiciary/index.html**.

Educational Options

Educational options for paralegals include certificate programs and degree programs. These are available through colleges and universities, community colleges, business schools, and trade schools.

CERTIFICATE PROGRAMS. Many paralegals choose the certificate program. Depending on the student's educational background, certificate programs can take up to eighteen months to complete. A student who already has a bachelor's degree can attend a program offered through a college or university. Normally, this type of program takes one year to finish. The certificate that is awarded to the student who successfully completes this type of program is referred to as a **post-degree certificate.**

Another option is to attend a certificate program offered by a private, for-profit business school, trade school, or college. Typically, this type of program

Post-Degree Certificate
A certificate awarded by a college or university to an individual who, having already completed an associate's degree or bachelor's degree program, successfully completes a paralegal program of study.

requires a high school diploma for admission. The length of time to complete such a program ranges from three to eighteen months. After the program is completed, the student receives a **paralegal certificate.**

Paralegal Certificate
A certificate awarded to an individual with a high school diploma or its equivalent who has successfully completed a paralegal program of study at a private, for-profit business school, trade school, or college.

DEGREE PROGRAMS. Degree options include an associate's degree or a bachelor's degree. The **associate's degree,** which normally is obtained from a community college, requires the completion of approximately sixty semester hours. The degree requirements are typically split evenly between general education courses (such as English, math, science, history, and social sciences) and law courses.

A **bachelor's degree** requires the completion of about 120 semester hours. From fifty to sixty of these hours are spent in general education courses similar to those required for the associate's degree. In addition, students take courses in their major area—legal-assistant studies—and may select a minor field (not all bachelor's programs require a minor). Minors that complement a legal-assistant major include computer information systems, business administration, communications, and public administration. These minors are helpful because they provide paralegals with useful skills and information relating to computer technology, business firms, and government agencies. Certain minors, particularly minors in environmental studies and computer information systems, help to boost the legal assistant's desirability in today's job market, which increasingly requires knowledge and skills in these areas. Additionally, paralegals who combine a bachelor's degree in a field such as nursing with a paralegal certificate are highly sought after.

Associate's Degree
An academic degree signifying the completion of a two-year course of study, normally at a community college.

Bachelor's Degree
An academic degree signifying the completion of a four-year course of study at a college or university.

ADVANCED DEGREES. In addition to the degree programs discussed above, graduate programs offer degrees that may advance your career opportunities. For example, if you are interested in management or administration, a master's degree in business administration (MBA) or in legal administration would be of great help in attaining your career goals. A master's degree normally requires, at a minimum, an additional year of course work beyond the bachelor's degree.

A law degree, which all attorneys must obtain, requires extensive educational preparation. As you will read in Chapter 3, prospective attorneys must normally obtain a bachelor's degree from a four-year college or university and then attend law school for an additional three years.

On the Web
Information on paralegal education programs is available on both the NALA and NFPA Web sites (www.nala.org and www.paralegals.org, respectively).

Curriculum—A Blend of Substantive and Procedural Law

A legal assistant's education includes the study of both substantive law and procedural law. **Substantive law** includes all laws that define, describe, regulate, and create legal rights and obligations. For example, a law prohibiting employment discrimination on the basis of age falls into the category of substantive law. **Procedural law** establishes the methods of enforcing the rights established by substantive law. Questions about what documents need to be filed to begin a lawsuit, when the documents should be filed, which court will hear the case, which witnesses will be called, and so on are all questions of procedural law. In brief, substantive law defines our legal rights and obligations; procedural law specifies what methods, or procedures, must be employed to enforce those rights and obligations.

Substantive Law
Law that defines the rights and duties of individuals with respect to each other, as opposed to procedural law, which defines the manner in which these rights and duties may be enforced.

Procedural Law
Rules that define the manner in which the rights and duties of individuals may be enforced.

The ABA's Role in Paralegal Education

The ABA has played an active role in paralegal educational programs since the early 1970s. By 1973, the ABA had drafted and formally adopted a set of educational standards for paralegal training programs. Programs that meet these standards and that are approved by the ABA are usually referred to as **ABA-approved programs.** Today, the ABA approval commission consists of members of the ABA as well as representatives from NALA, NFPA, and the American Association for Paralegal Education. Of the paralegal education programs in existence today (about 650), the ABA has approved 218. Paralegal schools are not required to be ABA approved. ABA approval is a voluntary process that gives extra credibility to those schools that successfully apply for it.

ABA-Approved Program
A legal or paralegal educational program that satisfies the standards for paralegal training set forth by the American Bar Association.

Certification

Certification involves recognition by a private professional group or a state agency that an individual has met specified standards of proficiency. Note that certification, as used here, is not the same as receiving a paralegal certificate. A paralegal certificate means that the paralegal has successfully completed a specific course of studies. A *certified paralegal,* in contrast, is one who has demonstrated his or her knowledge and competence in the field by taking and passing an examination administered by a private professional group or a state agency.

Certification
Formal recognition by a private group or a state agency that an individual has satisfied the group's standards of proficiency, knowledge, and competence; ordinarily accomplished through the taking of an examination.

NALA'S CERTIFICATION PROGRAM. NALA's certification program for paralegals is called the **Certified Legal Assistant (CLA) Certification Program.** Paralegals who wish to become certified by NALA may apply to take the CLA exam. The CLA exam provides recognition of the legal assistant's abilities and competence. This voluntary, comprehensive, two-day exam is given three times a year. The exam covers basic areas, such as communication skills (verbal and written), judgment and analytical skills, ethics, and human relations, as well as legal research and legal terminology. It also covers substantive and procedural law. Each person taking the exam must pass a section on the U.S. legal system, as well as four other areas of substantive law. The legal assistant can choose from nine sections: litigation, estate planning and probate, real estate, criminal law, bankruptcy, contracts, business organizations and corporations, administrative law, and family law.

On the Web
You can learn about upcoming CLAS exams on the NALA Web site at **www.nala.org/educ.htm.** For more information on NFPA's PACE program, go to **www.paralegals.org/ PACE/home.html.**

In addition to the CLA exam, NALA offers exams for those who wish to become certified by NALA as specialists in certain areas of practice. To become a **Certified Legal Assistant Specialist (CLAS),** a legal assistant must demonstrate special competence in a particular field. Specialty exams are offered in the following areas: bankruptcy, civil litigation, probate and estate planning, corporate and business law, criminal law and procedure, real estate, and intellectual property. Appendix H offers further information on NALA certification procedures and requirements.

Certified Legal Assistant (CLA)
A legal assistant whose legal competency has been certified by the National Association of Legal Assistants (NALA) following an examination that tests the legal assistant's knowledge and skills.

NFPA'S CERTIFICATION PROGRAM. In 1994, the members of NFPA voted to establish a certification program called the Paralegal Advanced Competency Exam, or PACE, which was implemented in 1996. This certification program is offered to paralegals who have a minimum of two years' experience and who meet specific educational requirements. The PACE is a four-hour, computer-generated examination designed to test the competency level of experienced paralegals. The exam has two tiers; each tier addresses different areas. The first tier deals with general legal issues, ethics, and state-specific laws. The second tier addresses specialty sections. A paralegal who passes the PACE exam may be designated as a "PACE-Registered Paralegal," or, more simply, an "RP." Information on NFPA's PACE program is included in Appendix I of this book.

Certified Legal Assistant Specialist (CLAS)
A legal assistant whose competency in a legal specialty has been certified by the National Association of Legal Assistants (NALA) following an examination of the legal assistant's knowledge and skills in the specialty area.

DEVELOPING PARALEGAL SKILLS

Preparing for the CLA Exam

Rita Barron received her paralegal certificate over a year ago and has been working in a law office since graduation. She plans to take the Certified Legal Assistant (CLA) exam in a few months. Rita consults with Jill Sanderson, a CLA, about taking the exam. Jill advises Rita that forming a study group helped her to study for the test, when she was a student. Jill's group divided up topics, then met once a week to share outlines. It was a lot of work, but their efforts paid off; the entire group passed the exam with flying colors.

STUDY GROUP TIPS
- Select committed group members.
- Devise a plan for sharing the work.
- Clearly assign topics to be outlined.
- Share outlines and assignments regularly.
- Evaluate the group members' efforts.
- Consult online resources or a CLA review guide.

STATE CERTIFICATION. Many states are now considering the development of state-administered or statewide voluntary certification programs, and some states are beginning to implement such programs. In 1994, for example, the Texas Bar Association Board of Legal Specialization established a voluntary certification program that permits paralegals in Texas to become certified as specialists in the following three areas: civil trial law, personal-injury law, and family law. To become certified paralegal specialists in these areas, paralegals must meet minimum standards for certification.

In July 1994, the California Alliance of Paralegal Associations (CAPA) and NALA formally agreed to develop and administer a voluntary statewide certification program for paralegals in California. Under the program, launched in 1995, a paralegal may become certified as a California Advanced Specialist (CAS) in several specialty practice areas. These areas include civil litigation, business organizations and business law, real estate, estates and trusts, and family law. Other states, including Florida and Louisiana, have also implemented voluntary certification programs.

Keep in mind that certification is a *voluntary* procedure. Whether paralegals, like attorneys, should be regulated by state law through mandatory licensing requirements—which would involve meeting certain educational standards, just as certification does—is a separate issue. As mentioned earlier, New Jersey is in the process of evaluating whether to license paralegals in that state. In Utah, the state bar association has recommended a licensing program that includes passing the CLA exam. Other states are also considering some form of licensing procedures. We will discuss this issue further in Chapter 3, in the context of the regulation of legal professionals.

Continuing Legal Education

Paralegals can—and often do—extend their formal education after they begin employment through Continuing Legal Education (CLE) programs. CLE courses, which are offered by state bar associations and paralegal associations, often take the form of special seminars and workshops that focus on specific topics or areas.

Through CLE, attorneys and paralegals can learn more about specialized areas of law or keep up to date on the latest developments in the law and in technology. For example, if you work as a litigation paralegal, you might want to attend a seminar on computerized litigation support, or you might want to learn more about the rules of evidence or about how medical records can be used as litigation tools. Clearly, the more you learn about these or other topics relating to litigation, the more valuable you will become to your employer. For this reason, many employers today encourage their paralegals to take CLE courses and often pay some or all of the costs involved.

In most states, attorneys are required to take a specific number of hours of CLE each year to maintain their licenses to practice law. Some paralegal associations impose similar requirements on their members as a condition of membership renewal with full membership rights (including voting rights) in their organizations. Both NALA and NFPA require paralegals who are certified through their certification programs to take a designated number of CLE hours per year to maintain their status as certified paralegals. Each of these organizations now offers online CLE courses (see their Web sites for more information).

On the Web
NALA is implementing an online campus for continuing legal education (CLE) at www.nalacampus.com. For information on NFPA's online CLE offerings, go to www.paralegals.org/CLE/home.html.

Paralegal Skills

Paralegals need and use a variety of skills on the job. Depending on your personality traits, some skills will be easier than others for you to learn. For example, if you tend to be an organized person, you will have little difficulty in acquiring and applying the required organizational skills. Throughout this book, you will read in detail about the specific skills that you will need in your work as a paralegal. Here, we describe the general types of skills that this profession requires.

Organizational Skills

Being a well-organized person is a plus for a legal assistant. Law offices are busy places. There are phone calls to be answered and returned, witnesses to get to court and on the witness stand on time, documents to be filed, and checklists and procedures to be followed. If you are able to organize files, create procedures and checklists, and keep things running smoothly, you will be doing a great service to the legal team and to clients.

If you work in a nontraditional setting, such as for a corporation or for the government, you will similarly find that good organizational skills are the key to success in your job. No matter where you work, you will need to organize files, certain types of data, and—most important—your time.

If organization comes naturally to you, you are ahead of the game. If not, now is the time to learn and practice organizational skills. You will find plenty of opportunities to do this as a paralegal student—by organizing your notebooks, devising an efficient tracking system for homework assignments, creating a study or work schedule and following it, and so on. Other suggestions for organizing your time and work, both as a student and as a paralegal on the job, are included at the beginning of this book. You will also find in any university or public library an abundance of books that offer guidelines on how to organize efficiently your work, your use of time, and your life generally.

Analytical Skills

Legal assistants also need analytical skills, especially when engaging in tasks relating to trials, legal investigations, legal research and writing, and certain other assignments. *Analysis* is usually defined as the separation of a whole into its parts. Legal professionals need to be able to take complex theories and fact patterns and break them down into smaller, more easily understandable components. As you will read in Chapter 16, an important aspect of legal research and writing involves analysis. Analysis is used to decipher the meaning of the law as set forth in the decisions handed down by the courts and in statutes passed by legislatures.

Analysis also involves, to some extent, the ability to synthesize—or put together—facts and legal concepts in such a way that they form a single unit, or "picture." For example, if you are conducting a legal investigation, you will uncover numerous facts and opinions about a certain event, such as an automobile accident. You will learn how the client believed the accident occurred, how any available witnesses described it, and what facts are indicated or implied by medical records or police reports. As a paralegal, you will want to discern how the facts and opinions you have gathered fit together into patterns or sequences. Further, you will want to determine how the facts fit into the legal strategy that your supervising attorney plans to pursue.

In any working environment, paralegals may be responsible for gathering and analyzing certain types of data. A corporate paralegal, for example, may be required to analyze new government regulations to see how they will affect the corporation. A paralegal working for the federal Environmental Protection Agency may be responsible for collecting and analyzing data on toxic waste disposal and drafting a memo setting forth his or her conclusions on the matter.

Computer Skills

In any workplace today, computer skills are essential. Advances in technology are virtually transforming the way in which law firms and other organizations operate. At a minimum, you will be expected to have experience with word processing (generating and revising documents using a computer) and to have some data-entry skills. Realize, though, that paralegals who are well versed in computer technology will increasingly have an edge over those who are not in the paralegal job market. Already, some of the best-paying paralegal positions are held by paralegal specialists who know how to use sophisticated computer equipment and software, such as database management systems, and how to adapt new technology to their workplace needs to improve efficiency.

We cannot stress enough that to become a successful paralegal, the best thing you can do during your paralegal training is to become as knowledgeable as possible about computer technology, including online communications. Throughout this book, you will read about how technology is now being applied to all areas of legal practice. You will also learn how you can use technology, particularly the Internet, to perform various paralegal tasks and to keep up to date on the law.

As computer technology continues to advance, high-tech paralegals will increasingly be in demand. (See this chapter's feature *Technology and Today's Paralegal: The Changing Paralegal Workplace* for a glimpse at how technology is not only transforming the paralegal workplace but also creating new types of paralegal positions.)

Interpersonal Skills

The ability to communicate and interact effectively with other people is an important asset for the paralegal. Paralegals work closely with their supervising attor-

TECHNOLOGY AND TODAY'S PARALEGAL

The Changing Paralegal Workplace

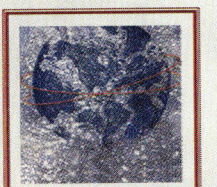

In many ways, technology has simplified the work of legal assistants. Documents can be easily drafted and revised on the computer. Mistakes can be eliminated with the stroke of a key, and changes can be made in a matter of just seconds. Computerized forms make generating the paperwork for routine legal transactions, such as bankruptcy filings or divorce petitions, a relatively simple matter. Database management systems allow paralegals to track or analyze hundreds—if not thousands—of documents without having to search through boxes filled with documents. E-mail messages can be created and sent in a fraction of the time it takes to create, reproduce, and distribute hard-copy memos or letters. Online databases have made it possible to conduct legal research and find information relevant to a legal investigation without leaving the office.

Indeed, it would seem that technology, by making legal work faster and easier to accomplish, might reduce the need for paralegals. That, however, is not true. Indeed, the opposite is occurring—technology is opening the door to new positions for paralegals. For example, some of today's paralegals are carving out a niche for themselves as Internet specialists. A paralegal who can conduct research efficiently, using online resources, is a valuable asset to any firm or agency. In a law office, efficient research saves time and money—for the firm and clients alike. Other paralegals are becoming experts in electronic evidence—encoding documents relating to a particular legal matter so that those documents can easily be retrieved in the event of a lawsuit.

Another emerging field in which paralegals may play a significant role has to do with the types of documents that should be entered into, or retained on, electronic systems. Even documents that have been previously deleted from a hard drive may be retrieved and used as evidence in a lawsuit, and companies that want to prevent future problems with electronic evidence increasingly are turning to their lawyers for advice on this issue. A paralegal knowledgeable in this area is a valuable member of the legal team in such situations.

Finally, technology has made it possible for some paralegals to perform at least some of their work at home. The virtual workplace, made feasible by telephones, faxes, and modems, is now becoming a reality.

We cannot predict what the future may hold, but one thing seems certain: as technology advances, there will be an increasing need for creative adaptations of technology to the field of legal work. High-tech paralegals who can fill this need will very likely be the highest-paid—and the most valued—legal assistants in the future.

---

neys, and the capacity to cultivate a positive working relationship helps get tasks done more efficiently. Paralegals also work with legal secretaries and other support staff in the law office, with attorneys and paralegals from other firms, with court personnel, and with numerous other people. Paralegals frequently interview clients and witnesses. As you will read in Chapter 13, if you can relate well to the person whom you are interviewing, your chances of obtaining useful information are increased.

There may be times when you will have to deal with clients who are experiencing difficulties in their lives, such as divorce or the death of a loved one. These people will need to be handled with sensitivity, tact, understanding, and courtesy. There will also be times when you will have to deal with people in your office who are under a great deal of stress or who for some other reason are demanding and less than courteous to you. You will need to know how to respond to these people in ways that promote positive working relationships.

Communication Skills

Good communication skills are critical when working in the legal area. In fact, it is sometimes said that the legal profession is a "communications profession" because effective legal representation depends to a great extent on how well a legal

Featured Guest: Wendy B. Edson
Ten Tips for Effective Communication

BIOGRAPHICAL NOTE

Wendy B. Edson received her master's degree in library science (M.L.S.) from the University of Rhode Island and served as law librarian at the Buffalo, New York, firm of Phillips, Lytle, Hitchcock, Blain and Huber. In 1978, she joined the Paralegal Studies faculty at Hilbert College, in Hamburg, New York, and helped to develop an ABA-approved bachelor's degree program in 1992. She teaches paralegalism and legal ethics, legal research and writing, law and literature, volunteerism, and alternative dispute resolution (ADR). She also developed and coordinates the internship program. Edson reviews and publishes on the topics of paralegal education, legal research and writing, and community service. She has lectured to legal professionals on legal research, teaching skills, internships, community service, environmental law, and ADR. Professor Edson is an AAfPE member and has presented papers at its national conferences and chaired model syllabi projects.

Words! They are the building blocks of human communication. Whether words are exchanged face to face—or by e-mail, phone, fax, or letter—communication is a two-way street. But how do we become skilled at maneuvering the *two-way* traffic of interpersonal communication? As in driving, we need to follow the "rules of the road." The rules of the road in regard to communication traffic are embodied in the following ten tips.

1. Establish Communication Equality. Communication equality does not require that individuals hold equal status in an office or organization but requires that each party believe in *equal rights* to speak and listen. Observe someone whom you consider to be a good communicator. You will note that he or she demonstrates equality by actively listening and responding appropriately to whoever is speaking. Workplace problems often reflect communication ailments rooted in inequality. A firm belief in communication equality, despite job titles, will help to create a cooperative, productive working environment.

2. Plan for Time and Space. Effective communication requires *time*. Imagine your reaction to a request to work overtime if your supervising attorney took thirty seconds to order you to do the work versus taking two minutes to explain the reason for the request and listening to your response. In the first situation, the attorney saved one and a half minutes but scored "zero" in terms of communication skills. In today's rushed world, it is easy to overlook the importance of communication skills in morale building and creating a cooperative, efficient work force.

Effective communicators are aware of how the physical environment in which a conversation takes place can affect the communication process. Communication is always enhanced when the parties have reasonable privacy and are not continually interrupted. Another important factor is physical comfort.

Choosing an inappropriate time and place for communication denies the importance of the matters being discussed and may send the wrong message to both the speaker and the listener.

3. Set the Agenda. Skilled communicators prepare an *agenda*—whether written or mental—of matters to be discussed in order of their priority. Frequently, both parties bring their respective agendas to a discussion, which means that priorities may need to be negotiated. A subordinate who brings up the topic of desired vacation time when the supervisor is preoccupied with a major project clearly demonstrates that his or her priorities are different from those of the supervisor.

Successful communication requires that the parties first negotiate a *common agenda*—that is, determine jointly the agenda for a particular discussion or meeting and what topics should take priority. Then, the topics can be dealt with one by one, in terms of their relative importance, to the satisfaction of both parties. *Agenda awareness* prevents parties from jumping from topic to topic without successfully resolving anything.

4. Fine-Tune Your Speaking Skills. Observe an individual whom you consider to be a good speaker, whether before a group of persons or on a one-on-one basis. What skills does that individual demonstrate? Effective

FEATURED GUEST, Continued

speakers work hard to express thoughts clearly; sometimes, they refer to notes or lists to refresh their memories. Skilled speakers also try to communicate accurately and to talk about matters that they know will interest their listeners. They cultivate *communication empathy*—the sincere effort to put themselves in their listeners' shoes. As you speak to others, pause occasionally and ask yourself: "Would I enjoy listening to what I am saying and how I am saying it?"

5. **Cultivate Listening Skills.** Listening is not just refraining from speaking while another person is talking but an *active* process—the other half of the communication partnership. An active listener does not interrupt the speaker. If you sense that the speaker is engaging in a monologue, responsive behavior—including body language, attentiveness, and appropriate remarks—can steer the conversation back to a dialogue without cutting off the speaker.

An active listener realizes that listening is an investment in effective communication. By truly responding to what is being said, rather than regarding listening time as insignificant or time to plan his or her own remarks, the skilled listener establishes a bond of trust with the speaker. Active listeners avoid preconceived ideas about topics being discussed and assume that they do not know all the answers.

6. **Watch for Body Language.** Body language is nonverbal communication that reflects our emotional state. Physical positions, such as leaning forward or away from the speaker while listening, can reinforce or negate our spoken responses.

Body attitudes, whether relaxed (comfortable posture, leaning forward, uncrossed arms and legs, relaxed neck and shoulders) or tense (stiff posture, backing away, crossed arms and legs, rigid neck and shoulders) vividly illustrate our responses before we utter a word. Eye contact is one of the most important tools in the body language tool kit for communication. Interviewers, social workers, and police officers have learned that steady and responsive eye contact means sincerity and credibility.

7. **Put Note Taking in Perspective.** Overinvolvement in note taking detracts from the communication process because opportunities to listen actively, speak responsively, and be sensitive to body language are reduced. The speaker may ramble while the listener records the ramblings in extensive notes.

When it is necessary to take notes, it is helpful to establish some rapport with the speaker or listener before launching the note-taking process. Alternatively, follow-up notes can be a workable solution to the problem. The note taker can devote the interview time to communication and, after the interview, record his or her general impressions of the interview and identify specific issues that need to be discussed further.

8. **Recognize the Role of Criticism.** *Constructive criticism* focuses on specific actions or behaviors rather than personalities. It is objective rather than subjective. Criticism that is stated calmly and objectively ("We need to rewrite the section on holographic wills.") is much more palatable for the person being criticized than is criticism in the form of a personal attack ("You did a terrible job."). By placing emphasis on actions instead of personalities, the parties can more easily work toward a satisfactory solution. If both the critic and the person being criticized can remain calm and can separate actions from personalities, then criticism will usually produce the desired result and *mutual* satisfaction.

> "Eye contact is one of the most important tools in the body language tool kit for communication."

9. **Aim for Satisfactory Closure.** Closure means "wrapping up" the communication. Successful communicators know that handling closure properly can leave a participant with a good feeling even if the solution was not exactly what he or she initially desired. Summarizing the discussion and checking for agreement or a need for further discussion will encourage all participants to follow the tenth tip.

10. **Commit to Communicate.** Excellent speakers and listeners have positive, self-confident attitudes that problems can be solved if the "rules of the road" are followed. Skilled communicators cultivate open minds, self-knowledge, and the ability to tolerate differences and empathize with others. They are committed to exercising their rights and responsibilities as speakers and listeners in the communication process.

DEVELOPING PARALEGAL SKILLS

Interviewing a Client

Brenda Lundquist is a paralegal in a one-attorney firm. Brenda has multiple responsibilities, including interviewing prospective divorce clients. Using a standard set of forms, Brenda meets with the prospective client and obtains information about the reasons for the divorce, finances and assets, and desired custody arrangements. This information is needed to assist her supervising attorney in determining whether she will take the case. The information also will help Brenda in preparing the documents to be filed with the court should the attorney decide to represent the client. Brenda enjoys the work because she likes helping people, and often people who are getting divorced need both emotional and legal support.

CHECKLIST FOR CLIENT INTERVIEWS
- Plan the interview in advance.
- Print out forms and checklists to use during the interview.
- Introduce yourself as a legal assistant.
- Explain the purpose of the interview to the client.
- Communicate your questions precisely.
- Listen carefully and be supportive, as necessary.
- Summarize the client's major concerns.
- Give the client a "time line" for what will happen next in the legal proceedings.

---

professional can communicate with clients, witnesses, court judges and juries, opposing attorneys, and others. Poor communication can damage a case, destroy a client relationship, and harm the legal professional's reputation. Good communication, in contrast, wins cases, clients, and sometimes promotions.

Communication skills include reading skills, speaking skills, listening skills, and writing skills. We look briefly at each of these skills here.

Although we focus on communication skills in the law-office setting, realize that good communication skills are essential to success in any work environment.

READING SKILLS. Reading skills involve more than just being able to decipher the meaning of written letters and words. Reading skills also involve understanding the *meaning* of a sentence, paragraph, section, or page. As a legal professional, you will need to be able to read and understand many different types of written materials, including statutes and court decisions. You will therefore need to become familiar with legal terminology and concepts so that you grasp the meaning of these legal writings. You will also need to develop the ability to read documents *carefully* so that you do not miss important distinctions, such as the difference in meaning that can result from the use of *and* instead of *or*.

SPEAKING SKILLS. Paralegals must also be able to speak well. In addition to using correct grammar, legal assistants need to be precise and clear in communicating ideas or facts to others. For example, when you discuss facts learned in an investigation with your supervising attorney, your oral report must communicate exactly what you found, or it could mislead the attorney. A miscommunication in this context could have serious consequences if it leads the attorney to take an action detrimental to the client's interests. Oral communication also has a nonverbal dimension—that is, we communicate our thoughts and feelings through gestures, facial expressions, and other "body language" as well as through words.

LISTENING SKILLS. Good listening skills are extremely important in the context of paralegal work. Paralegals must follow instructions meticulously. To understand the instructions that you receive, you must listen carefully. Asking follow-up questions will help you to clarify anything that you do not understand. Also, repeating the instructions will not only ensure that you understand them but also give the attorney a chance to add anything that he or she may have forgotten to tell you initially. Listening skills are particularly important in the interviewing context. In Chapter 13, you will read in greater detail about different types of listening skills and techniques that will help you conduct effective interviews with clients or witnesses.

WRITING SKILLS.   Finally, it is important for paralegals to have excellent writing skills. Legal assistants draft letters, memoranda, and a variety of legal documents. Letters to clients, witnesses, court clerks, and others must be clear and well organized and must follow the rules of grammar and punctuation. Legal documents must also be free of errors. Lawyers are generally scrupulously attentive to detail in their work, and they expect legal assistants to be equally so. Remember, you represent your supervising attorney when you write. You will learn more about writing skills in Chapter 16.

PERSONAL ATTRIBUTES OF THE PROFESSIONAL PARALEGAL

There are many different attributes that help paralegals succeed in their careers. The paralegal who is responsible, reliable, committed to hard work, objective, ethical, and generally considerate of others will have an easy time meeting the challenges presented by his or her work. These attributes define an individual's personality and character, and they are also important in paralegal practice.

Responsibility and Reliability

The paralegal must be responsible and reliable. The practice of law involves helping people with their legal problems. A paralegal's mistake, such as faxing a document to the wrong party or missing a deadline for filing a certain document with the court, could cause a client to lose his or her legal rights (and possibly cause a lawsuit to be brought against the attorney).

Attorneys frequently mention how they *rely* on their paralegals to perform certain tasks for them. The responsible paralegal is reliable. He or she completes tasks accurately and on time. Paralegals often mention how important trust is to efficient teamwork in the legal office. Each team member must be able to trust the other members of the legal team to do their share of the work—or the team effort may fail.

Commitment

Being committed to your work and the goals of your employer is important, too. Many tasks can take hours, days, weeks, or even months to perform, and you must be dedicated to giving your best effort until the job is completed. Commitment to your work involves persistence.

For example, if you are attempting to track down heirs to a will and you are having difficulty locating them, you must try everything possible to find them before you give up the search. You will need to review county birth and marriage records to try to locate them through their siblings and spouses. If that does not work, you will need to contact state agencies, such as the motor vehicle department, to try to obtain addresses from their driver's licenses or vehicle registration

Paralegal Profile

SUSAN J. MARTIN *is a paralegal in the Trusts and Estates department of Devine, Millimet & Branch, a large law firm, and has offices in the firm's Manchester, New Hampshire, and Andover, Massachusetts, locations. She has been in the legal profession for over twenty-two years. She worked for nine years as a legal secretary before becoming a paralegal and has worked in both large and small law firms in New Hampshire, Maine, Florida, Colorado, and Montana. She has a certificate from the National Association of Legal Secretaries, a certificate in paralegal studies from the University of New Hampshire, and an associate's degree from Franklin Pierce College in New Hampshire, where she is currently a bachelor's degree candidate. Martin is a member of the PACE Development Committee of the National Federation of Paralegal Associations (NFPA) and was an item writer/content area expert for the PACE exam. She is president of the Paralegal Association of New Hampshire (1998–1999) and chairs its Committee on Paralegal Education; is editor of the association's bimonthly newsletter,* The Annotator; *and is also an adjunct member of the Delivery of Legal Services Committee of the New Hampshire Bar Association and a member of the bar association's Technology Section.*

Trusts and Estates Paralegal

What do you like best about your work?
"One of the benefits of working in the trusts and estates field is that you are not involved in contentious lawsuits in which, in many cases, there is no winner and everyone is unhappy. Although estate clients are frequently dealing with grief and loss, they are not openly hostile or defensive. For the most part, clients view the trusts and estates team in a very positive way, and this makes the job very enjoyable."

What is the greatest challenge that you face in your area of work?
"Probably the greatest challenge of my job is keeping informed about the changes in federal and state tax law. The Internal Revenue Code is complex and convoluted, and new rules and regulations are promulgated daily. Also, it is not unusual to have an estate that is subject not only to federal tax laws but also to the tax laws of several states. Sorting out tax obligations and coordinating the timely filing of several tax returns can sometimes be a very difficult task."

What advice do you have for would-be paralegals in your area of work?
"To function well as a paralegal in the trusts and estates field, you must have a broad general knowledge of many other fields of law, including real estate, corporations, family law, and even civil litigation. You must also have some knowledge of basic accounting principles. People who function well as paralegals in this field usually have excellent quantitative skills, are extremely organized, are able to manage numerous files and deadlines simultaneously, can exercise sound independent judgment, and can work with a minimum of supervision. You must be computer literate and have proficient keyboarding skills."

> "To be successful in this field, you must be bright and articulate, and have a passion for detail."

What are some tips for success as a paralegal in your area of work?
"To be successful in this field, you must be bright and articulate, and have a passion for detail. You should love working with people. Working with the elderly requires compassion, humility, and resourcefulness. In this field in particular, you will meet clients from every social strata, ethnic background, and cultural association, and that requires patience, tolerance, and good humor."

---

records. You might also have to advertise in newspapers. Being diligent in your search means that you keep going until you have exhausted virtually every possible information source.

Objectivity

Another personal attribute of professional behavior is objectivity. To the extent that personal emotions or biases interfere with the goal of serving the client's interest, the paralegal must set these emotions or biases aside. For example, your sympathy for a client's plight should not prevent you from acknowledging factual evidence that is harmful to the client's position.

Lawyers and paralegals sometimes find themselves working on behalf of clients whom, for one reason or another, they dislike or do not respect. You may dislike having to deal with one of your firm's overly aggressive business clients, for example, or with a criminal defendant charged with spousal abuse, which you find extremely offensive. But these feelings should not affect the quality of the services you render. The job of the attorney and the paralegal is to see that the client's interests are not harmed by their personal views or assumptions.

The Ability to Keep Confidences

One of the requirements of being a paralegal is the ability to keep client information confidential. The word *requirement* is used here because being able to keep confidences is not just a desirable attribute in a paralegal, but a mandatory one. As you will read in Chapter 3, attorneys are ethically and legally obligated to keep all information relating to the representation of a client strictly confidential unless the client consents to the disclosure of the information.[2] The attorney may disclose this information only to people who are also working on behalf of the client and who therefore need to know it. Paralegals share in this duty imposed on all attorneys. If a paralegal reveals confidential client information to anyone outside the group working on the client's case, the lawyer (and the paralegal) may face legal consequences (including being sued by the client) if the client suffers harm as a result.

Keeping client information confidential means that you, as a paralegal, cannot divulge such information even to your spouse, family members, or closest friends. You should not talk about a client's case in hallways, elevators, or other areas in which others may overhear your conversation. Keeping work-related information confidential is an important part of being a responsible and reliable paralegal.

Other Attributes

Other attributes of the professional paralegal include accuracy, efficiency, attentiveness to detail, discretion, diplomacy, and the ability to work under pressure. Each of these attributes is considered appropriate in a law office because it enhances the firm's ability to serve the client's needs most effectively.

When deadlines approach and the pace of office work becomes somewhat frantic, it may be difficult to meet the challenge of acting professionally. For example, you may have to complete a brief (a document filed with a court to support an attorney's argument) by noon. It is 11 A.M., and you still have a considerable portion of the brief to finish. When the pressure is on, it is important to remain calm and focus on completing your task quickly and accurately to ensure quality work.

THE FUTURE OF THE PROFESSION

Since its beginnings over thirty years ago, the paralegal profession has been in a state of constant change, and by all indications, it will continue to evolve as we enter the new century. Legal services are costly, and the public is demanding access to more affordable legal services. This means that the role of the paralegal in delivering lower-cost legal services will most likely continue to expand. According to

---

2. Exceptions to the confidentiality rule are made in certain circumstances, as will be discussed in Chapter 3.

Today's Professional Paralegal

A Winning Combination

Susan Latham is a legal secretary for Melinda Oakwood, a real-estate attorney who is a partner in the law firm of Morris, Crowther, Oakwood & Miller. The law firm is one of the largest in the state, employing over 300 attorneys, 75 paralegals, 130 secretaries, and many support staff members. Susan, who has become more of a legal assistant than a secretary to Melinda, has decided, at the age of forty, to return to the local university to obtain a paralegal degree. This way, Susan can be rewarded (in the form of higher wages) for the work that she actually does already and can seek advancement in the firm.

Susan has worked for Melinda for eleven years. She has been given increased responsibility because she has shown Melinda that she is dependable and reliable in handling her work assignments. Her work is always turned in on time, and it is always accurate.

Learning on the Job

Susan was very lucky to have Melinda as a supervising attorney. Melinda, who had been a teacher for ten years before she went to law school, liked to teach Susan how to undertake new work assignments. When Susan had a new type of document to prepare at work, Melinda would give her a sample document and very good instructions. Now that Susan is studying to be a paralegal, Melinda has started assisting Susan with her school assignments by giving her sample documents and copies of the laws that require those documents. Melinda also points out the differences between the class assignments and the sample documents and discusses with Susan why the differences matter from a legal perspective.

Additionally, Melinda encourages Susan to ask questions about school assignments and to take her time completing them so that when they are turned in, they are accurate. Susan has a strong sense of commitment, so she always sees a project through even if it seems to take forever.

Using Personal Attributes

Melinda was also lucky to have Susan as her secretary and, eventually, as her paralegal. Susan had many personal attributes that helped her on the job. She learned quickly and performed her work competently and efficiently.

She also paid great attention to detail, which was one of the reasons Melinda encouraged Susan to get a paralegal degree. Unlike Melinda's former paralegal, who would send out letters and fail to include the documents that should have been enclosed, Susan was meticulous. And Melinda could always count on Susan to keep client information confidential.

Susan already had good computer and organizational skills when Melinda hired her. She did need to improve her analytical and listening skills, though. Susan's analytical skills are already improving as a result of a course she is taking in legal research, which requires case analysis. Over time, Susan learned to listen to Melinda's instructions and to question Melinda when Susan was not exactly certain about what Melinda wanted her to do.

The Result: A Winning Team

Melinda and Susan have developed a solid working relationship. It took time for Susan to develop some of the skills that she needed, but Melinda was a good and patient teacher. It also took time to develop a trusting relationship, but now Melinda can confidently delegate significant assignments to Susan, knowing that Susan will complete them accurately. Now that Susan is in a paralegal program, Melinda can also delegate more challenging work to Susan, and Susan can eventually be promoted to paralegal status. Melinda and Susan work productively and efficiently together. They like and rely on each other and enjoy their work. Theirs is a winning combination of talents and skills.

the U.S. Department of Labor's Bureau of Labor Statistics, paralegal employment is expected to grow much faster than the average for all occupations through the year 2005.

The paralegal profession is a dynamic, changing, and growing field within the legal arena. Although legal assistants initially worked only in the law-firm context, as mentioned, today's job opportunities for paralegals include working for corporations, government agencies, and other organizations. Those who enter the profession today will find not only a variety of career options but also the opportunity to help chart the course the profession will take in the future.

KEY TERMS AND CONCEPTS

ABA-approved program   11
affiliate   7
American Association for Paralegal Education (AAfPE)   3
American Bar Association (ABA)   3
associate's degree   10
bachelor's degree   10
certification   11

Certified Legal Assistant (CLA)   11
Certified Legal Assistant Specialist (CLAS)   11
law clerk   6
legal assistant   3
National Association of Legal Assistants (NALA)   3
National Federation of Paralegal Associations (NFPA)   3

paralegal   3
paralegal certificate   10
post-degree certificate   9
procedural law   10
staff attorney   6
state bar association   7
substantive law   10

CHAPTER SUMMARY

1. Many legal professionals use the terms *paralegal* and *legal assistant* interchangeably. A paralegal, or a legal assistant, can be defined as a person sufficiently trained in law and legal procedures to assist attorneys in the delivery of legal services to the public or to perform legal work as otherwise authorized by law. Paralegal expertise may be attained through on-the-job experience or through paralegal training programs, but paralegal training programs are increasingly important to success in the paralegal field (and may be required for paralegal practice in the future in states that adopt paralegal licensing programs). Paralegals are not attorneys but attorneys' assistants. Attorneys supervise paralegal work and assume ultimate responsibility for it. Paralegals perform many of the tasks involved in legal representation that have traditionally been handled by attorneys. Certain tasks, however (such as giving legal advice, setting fees for legal services, and representing clients in court), can only be handled by attorneys.

2. Typical tasks performed by paralegals who work in law offices include drafting legal documents, calendaring and tracking important deadlines, assisting attorneys in trial preparation and at trial, interviewing clients and witnesses, organizing and maintaining client files, conducting legal investigations, and conducting legal research.

3. The first paralegals were legal secretaries who, through on-the-job experience, developed the skills and expertise now taught in paralegal training programs. The paralegal profession evolved rapidly because paralegals filled the growing need for lower-cost, permanent, and competent legal assistance. In 1968, the American Bar Association recognized the professional status of paralegals.

4. The formation of paralegal associations was a significant step in the growth of the paralegal profession. By the early 1970s, numerous local paralegal organizations were in existence. By the mid-1970s, the National Federation of Paralegal Associations (NFPA) and the National Association of Legal

Assistants (NALA)—the two leading national paralegal associations—had been formed.

5. Paralegal professional associations provide a forum in which professional issues can be discussed, establish guidelines to regulate professional conduct, determine skill levels and educational requirements, and in some cases establish or sponsor educational programs. Professional membership provides numerous opportunities for paralegals.

6. The curriculum in paralegal programs focuses on both procedural law and substantive law. Paralegal educational options include certificate programs and degree programs. A person who has a bachelor's degree can receive a post-degree certificate by completing a program offered by a college or university, which usually takes one year. Paralegal certificates can be obtained through programs of varying lengths, offered by business schools, trade schools, and other for-profit occupational training centers. Degree options include an associate's degree and a bachelor's degree.

7. The American Bar Association has played an active role in paralegal education programs since the early 1970s. Paralegal programs that meet standards established by the ABA (currently, about one-third of all paralegal programs) are called ABA-approved programs.

8. Certification involves recognition by a private professional group or a state agency that a person has met specified standards of proficiency. The National Association of Legal Assistants (NALA) has developed a certification program for paralegals. After meeting specified requirements (including passing an examination), a paralegal can become certified by NALA as a Certified Legal Assistant (CLA) or a Certified Legal Assistant Specialist (CLAS). More recently, the National Federation of Paralegal Associations (NFPA) has developed a certification program called the Paralegal Advanced Competency Exam, or PACE. State certification programs now exist in several states, including Texas, California, Louisiana, and Florida.

9. Paralegals need to have a variety of skills. It is especially important for paralegals to have good organizational, analytical, computer, interpersonal, and communication skills.

10. Certain personal attributes are also important in paralegal practice. These attributes include responsibility, reliability, commitment to hard work, objectivity, the ability to keep confidences, accuracy, efficiency, attentiveness to detail, discretion, diplomacy, and the ability to work under pressure.

Questions for Review

1. What is a paralegal? What are some of the key elements in the four definitions of a legal assistant, or paralegal, given in Exhibit 1.1? Is there any difference between a paralegal and a legal assistant?

2. What kinds of tasks do paralegals perform?

3. Why did the paralegal profession evolve? What needs within the legal profession do paralegals meet? When and by which organization was the paralegal profession first recognized as a profession?

4. Name the two largest national paralegal associations in the United States. When and why were they formed? What are the benefits of belonging to a paralegal association?

5. What type of educational programs and training are available to paralegals? Must a person meet specific educational requirements to work as a paralegal?

6. What role does the American Bar Association play in paralegal education?

7. What does *certification* mean? What is a CLA? What is a CLAS? What does PACE stand for?

8. Name some states that have certification programs. Is state certification mandatory in those states?

9. List and describe the skills that are useful in paralegal practice. Do you have these skills?

10. List and describe some of the personal attributes of a professional paralegal. Do you feel that persons who do not have these attributes can cultivate them? If so, how?

ETHICAL QUESTIONS

1. Richard attends a six-month paralegal course and earns a certificate. In the West Coast city where he lives, certified paralegals—those with a CLA designation—are in great demand in the job market. Richard responds to a newspaper advertisement for a certified paralegal, indicating that he is one. Has Richard done anything unethical? What is the difference between a certificate and certification?

2. Paula Abrams works as a paralegal for a small law firm that specializes in tax law. Recently, Paula purchased some new tax-return software and was trained in how to use it. Last week, Paula used the software to prepare tax returns for the Benedetto family. Paula saved the forms on a disk. She then retrieved the Benedetto forms and used them for the Marshalls' tax return. Paula entered much of the Marshalls' tax information into the computer. Mr. Marshall had not provided the children's Social Security numbers to Paula, though, so she only keyed in the information that she had available and decided to add the Social Security numbers later.

   In the tax-season rush, Paula inadvertently neglected to enter the children's Social Security numbers on the Marshalls' tax return. Several months later, the Marshalls received a letter from the Internal Revenue Service stating that their exemptions were denied because their children's Social Security numbers were claimed on someone else's tax return. How might this situation be resolved? What other kinds of ethical problems might result from using computer-generated forms?

PRACTICE QUESTIONS AND ASSIGNMENTS

1. Refer to Appendix F and Appendix G at the end of this book (or, if you have access to the Internet, you can go to **www.findlaw.com** and find the answers to the following questions:
   a. What is the street address, e-mail address, and telephone number of the state bar association in your state?
   b. Is there an affiliate of the National Association of Legal Assistants or the National Federation of Paralegal Associations in your city? Where is the nearest affiliate of either of these organizations located?
   c. Are there any regional or local paralegal associations in your area? If so, what are their names, street and e-mail addresses, and phone numbers?

2. Using the material on paralegal skills presented in the chapter, which of the following are skills that a paralegal should have? Explain why.
   a. Reading skills.
   b. Interpersonal skills.
   c. Marketing skills.
   d. Oral communication skills.
   e. Math skills.
   f. Computer skills.
   g. Management skills.

3. Which of the following personal attributes, presented in the chapter, are helpful to a paralegal? Why?
   a. Insensitivity.
   b. Commitment.
   c. Integrity.
   d. Unreliability.
   e. Objectivity.
   f. Inaccuracy.

QUESTIONS FOR CRITICAL ANALYSIS

1. Tom, Sandy, and Barbara are having coffee after their first paralegal class. The instructor discussed the meanings of the terms *paralegal* and *legal assistant* as defined by NALA and NFPA, the two national paralegal associations, as well as the American Bar Association and the American Association for Paralegal Education. The students are not sure that they understand the differences among the definitions or whether the differences are significant. What is your opinion of the definitions? How would you explain the definitions and how they differ to a group of your classmates? Given the differences in the definitions, would you prefer to belong to one paralegal organization over another? Why?

2. Joan McMahon is meeting with an adviser at her local college to discuss the possibility of enrolling in

the school's legal-assistant program. Joan has completed two years of college-level courses in general education, which she could transfer, but she has had no legal-assistant classes. The adviser explains that there are three different degree options at the college: an associate's degree, a bachelor's degree, and a post-degree certificate. Other for-profit business schools in the area offer certificate programs as well. How would you explain the differences in the degree and certificate options to Joan? Which options would Joan most likely favor? Why?

Projects

1. Write or telephone the National Association of Legal Assistants and the National Federation of Paralegal Associations (see Appendix F for the addresses and telephone numbers of these associations). See if they have affiliates in your area. Also, see if there are any state or local paralegal organizations in your area. Contact them for membership information. Do they accept student members?

2. Arrange an interview with an experienced paralegal, such as a graduate of your program or another paralegal that you may know. Ask the paralegal what he or she thinks are the most important skills and characteristics that paralegals should have.

Using Internet Resources

Browse through the materials on the Web sites of the National Association of Legal Assistants, or NALA (at www.nala.org), and the National Federation of Paralegal Associations, or NFPA (at www.paralegals.org). Then do the following:

1. Look closely at the benefits of membership listed by each of these organizations. How do they compare? Are there any significant differences?

2. Examine the information that is included on each site about the organization's certification program. For each program, summarize the requirements that a paralegal must meet to become certified.

3. Select an article about a current development or issue in the paralegal profession from either NALA's "News & Updates" or NFPA's "What's New?" pages. Write a one-paragraph summary of the article, indicating what the article is about and why the topic treated is significant.

4. Go to "What is a paralegal/legal assistant?" at the NALA web site (at www.nala.org). Which of the following tasks might legal assistants perform, according to the information provided there?

   a. Draft legal documents.
   b. Try cases in court.
   c. Locate witnesses.
   d. Give legal advice.
   e. Set legal fees.
   f. Interview clients.
   g. Perform legal investigations.

CHAPTER 2

Careers in the Legal Community

Chapter Outline

▪ Introduction ▪ Where Paralegals Work ▪ Paralegal Specialties
▪ Paralegal Compensation ▪ Planning Your Career
▪ Locating Potential Employers ▪ Job-Placement Services
▪ Marketing Your Skills ▪ Reevaluating Your Career

After completing this chapter, you will know:

- What types of firms and organizations hire paralegals.
- Some areas of law in which paralegals specialize.
- How much paralegals can expect to earn.
- How paralegals are compensated for overtime work.
- How to prepare a career plan and pursue it.
- What is involved in a job search and how to go about it.

On the Web
For helpful information on all aspects of paralegal careers, go to the National Association of Legal Assistants' Web site at **www.nala.org** and the National Federation of Paralegal Associations' Web site at **www.paralegals.org**.

INTRODUCTION

As a paralegal, you will enjoy a broad spectrum of employment opportunities. In the past two decades, attorneys have begun to realize how the use of paralegals in the law office can help them achieve the goal of providing quality legal services at lower cost to clients. Paralegals perform a number of tasks that in the past only attorneys handled. By turning over these tasks to paralegals, whose hourly fees are lower than those of attorneys, law firms can represent more clients, and clients pay less for their services.

The fact that you are entering a growth profession presents further opportunities. As mentioned in Chapter 1, the first paralegals were legal secretaries who had acquired, through experience, the necessary skills and abilities to assist attorneys in substantive legal work within the law-firm environment. As the paralegal profession developed, so did opportunities for paralegals in other employment settings. Corporations began to realize how paralegals could be used effectively in their legal departments. Government agencies created positions for paralegals. Banks, insurance companies, and other firms and institutions began to hire paralegals to assist with work that required legal training. Today, most paralegals continue to work for law firms, as will be discussed shortly, but they are increasingly assuming greater responsibilities as attorneys realize the benefits of delegating substantive legal work to paralegals.

This chapter provides a point of departure for your career planning. In the pages that follow, you will read about where paralegals work, some special areas of paralegal practice, and how paralegals are compensated. You will also learn about the essential steps involved in planning for a successful career and how to go about finding a job.

WHERE PARALEGALS WORK

Paralegal employers fall into a number of categories. This section describes the general characteristics of each of the major types of working environments.

Law Firms

When paralegals first established themselves within the legal community in the 1960s, they assisted lawyers in a law-firm setting. Today, as indicated in Exhibit 2.1, law firms continue to hire more paralegals than do any other organizations. Law firms vary in size from the small, one-attorney office to the huge "megafirm" with hundreds of attorneys. As you can see in Exhibit 2.2, the majority of paralegals working for law firms are employed by firms having fewer than twenty attorneys, and over half (56 percent) are employed by firms having ten or fewer attorneys.[1]

WORKING FOR A SMALL FIRM. Many paralegals begin their careers working for small law practices, such as one-attorney firms or firms with just a few attorneys. To some extent, this is because of the greater number of small law firms, relative to large ones. It may also be due to geographic location. For example, a

On the Web
You can obtain a host of information on specific law firms by going to their Web pages. For one example, go to Hale & Dorr's Web site at **www.haledorr.com**. (To find Web sites for law firms, check one of the legal directories discussed later in this chapter.)

---

1. One of the difficulties in describing law-firm environments is that the terms *small law firm* and *large law firm* mean different things to different people. In a large metropolitan city, for example, a firm with fifteen attorneys might qualify as a small law firm. In a smaller, more rural community, however, a firm with fifteen attorneys would be considered a very large law firm. In this text, we refer to law firms with fifteen or fewer attorneys as small law firms and firms with over fifteen attorneys as large firms.

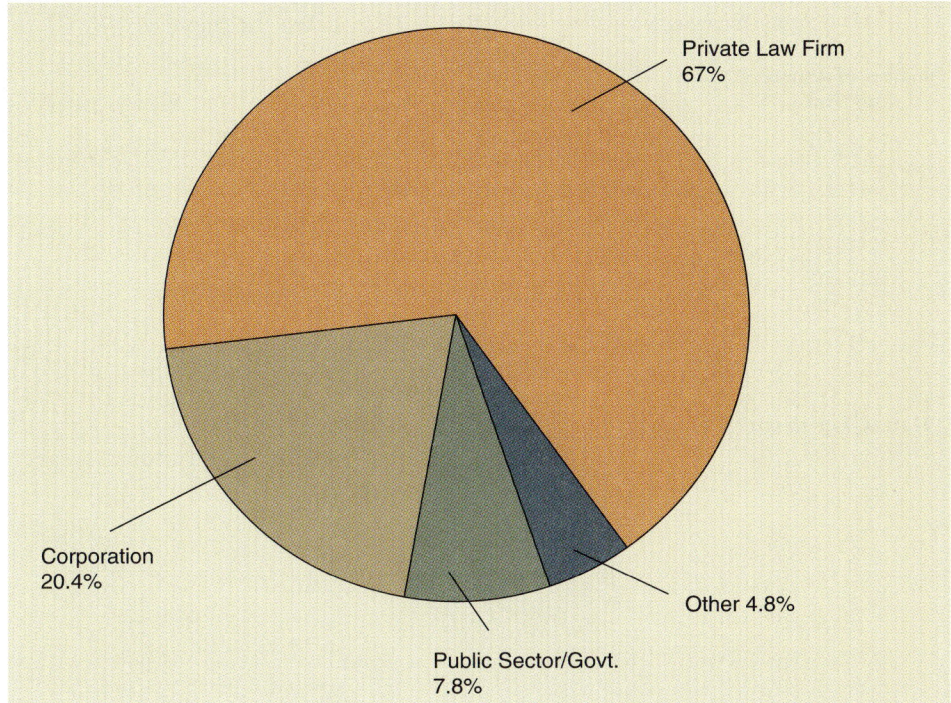

EXHIBIT 2.1
Where Paralegals Work

© 1999 James Publishing, Inc. Reprinted courtesy of *Legal Assistant Today* magazine. For subscription information call (800) 394-2626.

Source: "Are They Paying You What You're Worth? Legal Assistant Today's 1998–99 Salary survey Results," *Legal Assistant Today,* January/February 1999, pp. 53–57.

paralegal who lives in a relatively rural environment, such as a small community, may find that his or her only option is to work for a small legal practice.

Working for a small firm offers many advantages to the beginning paralegal, and you should be aware of them. If the firm is a general law practice, you will have the opportunity to gain experience in many different areas of the law. You will be able to learn whether you enjoy working in one area (such as family law) more than another area (such as personal-injury law) in the event that you later decide to specialize. Some paralegals also prefer the often more personal and less formal environment of the small law office, as well as the variety of tasks and greater flexibility that frequently characterize this setting.

A characteristic of small firms that may prove challenging to you has to do with compensation. Small firms pay, on average, lower salaries than larger firms

NUMBER OF ATTORNEYS IN FIRM	PERCENTAGE OF ALL LAW FIRM PARALEGALS EMPLOYED BY FIRM
0–5	40%
6–10	16%
11–20	15%
21–30	7%
31–40	4%
41–50	2%
Over 50	16%

EXHIBIT 2.2
Paralegal Employment in Law Firms by Size of Firm

© 1999 James Publishing, Inc. Reprinted courtesy of *Legal Assistant Today* magazine. For subscription information call (800) 394-2626.

Source: "Legal Assistant Today's 1997–98 Salary Survey Results," *Legal Assistant Today,* March/April 1998, pp. 72–77. (These data were not included in the 1998–1999 salary survey results reported in *Legal Assistant Today,* January/February 1999, pp. 53–57.)

EXHIBIT 2.3
Paralegal Compensation

© 1999 James Publishing, Inc. Reprinted courtesy of *Legal Assistant Today* magazine. For subscription information call (800) 394-2626.

By Firm Size		By Type of Employer	
Number of Attorneys in Firm	Average Salary	Employer	Average Salary
1	$32,212	Private Law Firm	$33,880
2–5	$33,800	Corporation	$42,050
6–10	$34,109	Government	$31,370
11–25	$37,227		
26–50	$36,770		
51–100	$41,664		
101 plus	$41,232		

By Years of Experience			
Years of Experience	Salary		
	No Degree	Associate's Degree	Bachelor's Degree
Less than 1	$21,859	$23,640	$26,773
1–3	$30,505	$27,270	$31,328
3–5	$29,208	$30,319	$34,867
5–7	$38,325	$36,561	$32,765
7–10	$37,003	$35,786	$38,341
10–15	$37,209	$38,552	$38,577
15–20	$41,325	$45,301	$42,026
20 plus	$42,325	$44,550	$44,983

By Specialty			
Specialty	Average Salary	Specialty	Average Salary
Intellectual Property	$44,436	Employment	$33,445
Corporate	$39,758	Real Estate	$32,500
Environmental	$37,479	Family	$31,923
Litigation	$37,240	Personal Injury	$31,671
Bankruptcy	$35,884	Criminal	$31,645
Insurance Defense	$34,909	General	$29,169
Estate/Probate	$34,858	Workers' Compensation	$25,145
Regulatory	$33,890		

Source: "Are They Paying You What You're Worth? Legal Assistant Today's 1998–99 Salary Survey Results," *Legal Assistant Today,* January/February 1999, pp. 53–57.

do. As Exhibit 2.3 indicates, paralegal income is closely related to firm size. Generally, the larger the firm, the higher the paralegal salaries. Small firms also find it hard to afford the employee benefits packages, including insurance and pension plans, that large firms often provide for their employees.

Paralegals who work for small firms may also have less support staff to assist them. This means that if you work in a small law office, your job may involve a substantial amount of secretarial or clerical work.

WORKING FOR A LARGE FIRM. In contrast to the (typically) more casual environment of the small law office, larger law firms usually are more formal. If you work for a larger firm, your responsibilities will probably be limited to specific, more well-defined types of tasks. For example, you may work for a department that handles (or for an attorney who handles) only certain types of cases, such as real-estate transactions. Office procedures and employment policies will also be more clearly defined and may be set forth in a written employment manual.

The advantages of the large firm include greater opportunities for promotions and career advancement, higher salaries and (typically) better benefits packages, more support staff for paralegals, and (often) more sophisticated computer technology and greater access to research resources.

You may view certain characteristics of large law firms as either advantages or disadvantages, depending on your personality and preferences. For example, if you favor the more specialized work and more formal working environment of the large law firm, then you will view these characteristics as advantages. If you prefer to handle a greater variety of tasks and enjoy the more personal, informal atmosphere of the small law office, then you might view the specialization and formality of the large law firm as disadvantages.

Corporations and Other Business Organizations

Over the past three decades, as mentioned earlier, paralegals have been given opportunities to work in business environments outside of law firms. Many of these businesses (such as insurance companies and banks) engage in activities that are highly regulated by government. Others (such as title insurance companies, law-book publishers, legal-software companies, and law schools) are in some way related to the practice of law. In addition, a vast number of businesses that need legal assistance hire paralegals.

An increasing number of paralegals work for corporate legal departments. Most major corporations hire in-house attorneys to handle corporate legal affairs. Some extremely large corporations have hundreds of attorneys on their payrolls. Paralegals who work for corporations ordinarily work under the supervision of in-house attorneys and assist them in such tasks as the following:

- Scheduling corporate meetings; drafting meeting notices, agendas, and minutes; and assembling documents necessary for meetings.
- Preparing case files, drafting documents, and doing other work related to lawsuits in which the corporation is involved.
- Collecting and interpreting technical information for corporate reports to a regulatory agency (such as the Environmental Protection Agency).
- Drafting documents necessary to register for patent, trademark, or copyright protection for a corporate product.
- Researching laws and regulations that might affect corporate actions or policies.
- Preparing and reviewing corporate contracts. (In large firms, some paralegals specialize in the area of contract analysis.)
- Working with outside counsel.

As noted in Exhibit 2.1 on page 29, over 20 percent of paralegals are now working in corporate environments. On average, paralegals working for corporations receive higher salaries than those working for law firms, as indicated earlier in Exhibit 2.3. Paralegals who work for corporations normally work more regular hours and experience less stress than paralegals who work for law firms. For example, unlike in law firms, in the corporate environment paralegals are not required to generate a specific number of "billable hours" per year (hours billed to clients for paralegal services performed—discussed in Chapter 4) because there are no clients to bill—the corporation is the client.

DEVELOPING PARALEGAL SKILLS

Contracts Administrator

Martha Parnell, a legal assistant, works as a contracts administrator for the Best Engines Corporation. Martha's job is to take calls from buyers who want to negotiate contracts with Best Engines. The corporation uses preprinted forms containing provisions that Best Engines prefers to have in its contracts, terms that are advantageous to Best Engines. Some customers buy large quantities of engines to use in factories or to pump oil out of oil wells or through pipelines. These companies usually want to negotiate contract terms that provide them with more rights.

Martha has just received a telephone call from a buyer who wants to negotiate an indemnity provision, which in the preprinted form contract requires the buyer to pay Best Engines for any losses arising under the contract.

She discusses alternative indemnity provisions, such as splitting the indemnity or leaving it out entirely, with the buyer. Martha then arranges to call the buyer back after discussing the various proposals with the general counsel (the attorney who heads the legal department).

TIPS FOR WORKING WITH CONTRACTS
- Know who—buyer or seller—holds the strongest bargaining position.
- Understand what the contract terms mean.
- Discuss all proposals with your client.
- Understand which terms your client will likely agree to and why.
- Determine which contract terms will be "deal busters."
- Set a timetable for finalizing the contract.

Government

A growing number of paralegals (around 8 percent) are employed by the government.

ADMINISTRATIVE AGENCIES. Most paralegals who work for the government work for administrative agencies, such as the federal Environmental Protection Agency or a state environmental resources department. Paralegals who work for government agencies may be engaged in administrative appeals work (see Chapter 9), general or specialized legal research, welfare eligibility and claims, disability claims, the examination of documents (such as loan applications), and many other types of tasks. Your best source of information about employment positions in a particular administrative agency is the agency itself. You can find the names and telephone numbers of federal agencies, as well as a description of their functions, in the *United States Government Manual,* available in your public or college library. See also the featured-guest article in Chapter 9 entitled "Paralegal Positions in Government."

Paralegals who work for government agencies normally work regular hours, tend to work fewer total hours per year (have more vacation time) than paralegals in other environments, and, like paralegals who work for corporations, do not have to worry about billable hours. Additionally, paralegals who work for the government usually enjoy comprehensive employment benefits. Salaries, however, are on average lower than those offered by traditional law firms and other employers in the private sector, as indicated earlier in Exhibit 2.3.

On the Web
You can locate information on government agencies at numerous Web sites, including that of FindLaw at www.findlaw.com.

LEGISLATIVE OFFICES. Legislators in the U.S. Congress and in several state legislatures typically have staff members to help them with their various duties. These duties often include legal research and writing, and paralegals sometimes perform such services. For example, a senator who plans to propose an amendment to a law may ask a paralegal on his or her staff to research the legislative history of that law carefully (to discern the legislature's intention when passing the law—see Chapter 14) and write up a summary of that history.

LAW ENFORCEMENT OFFICES AND COURTS. Many paralegals also work for government law enforcement offices and institutions. As you will read in Chapter 12, which discusses criminal law and procedures in detail, a person accused of a crime is prosecuted by a *public prosecutor*. Public prosecutors (such as district attorneys, state attorneys general, or U.S. attorneys) are government officials who are paid by the government. Accused persons may be defended by private attorneys, or, if they cannot afford to hire a lawyer, by *public defenders*—attorneys paid for by the state to ensure that criminal defendants are not deprived of their constitutional right to counsel. Both public prosecutors and public defenders rely on paralegals to handle much of their legal work. (See Chapter 12 for a discussion of legal work relating to criminal law and procedures.)

Paralegals also find work in other government environments, such as federal or state court administrative offices. Court administrative work ranges from recording and filing court documents (such as the documents filed during a lawsuit—see Chapters 10 and 11) to handling collections for a regional tax authority for a local small claims court (courts that handle claims below a specified threshold amount—see Chapter 6). Paralegals may also work for bankruptcy courts (see page 37 for a discussion of bankruptcy law).

Legal Aid Offices

Legal aid offices provide legal services to those who find it difficult to pay for legal representation. During President Lyndon Johnson's "War on Poverty" in the 1960s, the government began to set aside funds for legal services organizations around the country to help less advantaged groups obtain needed legal assistance at low or no cost. Most legal aid continues to be government funded, although some support comes from private legal foundations.

Many paralegals who work in this type of setting find their jobs rewarding, even though they often receive lower salaries than they would in other areas. In part, this is because of the nature of the work—helping needy individuals. Additionally, paralegals in legal aid offices generally assume a wider array of responsibilities than they would in a traditional law office or one of the other environments described earlier. For example, some federal and state administrative agencies, including the Social Security Administration at the federal level, allow paralegals to represent clients in agency hearings and judicial proceedings. As you will read in Chapter 3, paralegals normally are not allowed to represent clients—only attorneys can do so. Exceptions to this rule exist when a court or agency permits nonlawyers to represent others in court or before administrative agency hearings.

Freelance Paralegals

A growing number of paralegals operate as freelancers. **Freelance paralegals** (also called *independent contractors* or *contract paralegals*) own their own businesses and perform specified types of legal work for attorneys on a contract basis.

Freelance Paralegal
A paralegal who operates his or her own business and provides services to attorneys on a contractual basis. A freelance paralegal works under the supervision of an attorney, who assumes responsibility for the paralegal's work product.

Attorneys who need temporary legal assistance sometimes contract with freelance paralegals to work on particular projects. Attorneys who need legal assistance but cannot afford to hire full-time paralegals might hire freelancers to work on a part-time basis. (The suggestions offered later in this chapter on how you can find work as a paralegal apply to freelance jobs as well.)

One of the benefits freelance paralegals enjoy about their services is the flexibility it gives them. Depending on the nature of the project, they may work at home or in an attorney's office. Some types of legal work, such as online legal research, can easily be conducted from a home office. Others, such as handling litigation documents or interviewing clients, require the paralegal to work in the attorney's office.

Realize that freelance paralegals work under attorney supervision. Freelancers are not to be confused with **independent paralegals**—often called *legal technicians,* who do *not* work under the supervision of an attorney and who provide (sell) legal services directly to the public. These services include helping members of the public obtain and fill out forms for certain types of legal transactions, such as bankruptcy filings and divorce petitions. As you will read in Chapter 3, independent paralegals run the risk of violating state statutes prohibiting the unauthorized practice of law.

Independent Paralegal
A paralegal who offers services directly to the public, normally for a fee, without attorney supervision. Independent paralegals assist consumers by supplying them with forms and procedural knowledge relating to simple or routine legal procedures.

Paralegal Specialties

While many paralegals work for small firms that offer a wide range of legal services, other paralegals have found it useful and satisfying to specialize in one area of law. There are numerous opportunities for the paralegal who wishes to concentrate his or her efforts on a particular area and become a specialist. Here we discuss just a few of these specialty areas.

Litigation Assistance

Working a lawsuit through the court system is called **litigation.** Paralegals who specialize in assisting attorneys in the litigation process are called **litigation paralegals.** Litigation paralegals work in general law practices, small litigation firms, litigation departments of larger law firms, or corporate legal departments. Litigation paralegals often specialize in a certain type of litigation, such as personal-injury litigation (which will be discussed shortly) or product-liability cases (which involve injuries caused by defective products). Some litigation paralegals may also work primarily on behalf of **plaintiffs** (those who bring lawsuits) or on behalf of **defendants** (those against whom lawsuits are brought). Lawyers in a personal-injury practice, for example, often represent plaintiffs. Lawyers in a criminal law practice represent criminal defendants—those accused of crimes.

You will read in detail about litigation procedures and the important role played by paralegals in the litigation process in Chapters 10 and 11. We indicate below just a sampling of the kinds of work that a paralegal might perform during the litigation process:

Litigation
The process of working a lawsuit through the court system.

Litigation Paralegals
Paralegals who specialize in assisting attorneys in the litigation process.

Plaintiff
A party who initiates a lawsuit.

Defendant
A party against whom a lawsuit is brought.

- Interview a client to obtain detailed information about a case.
- Locate and interview witnesses.
- Contact relevant medical personnel and institutions, employers, or other sources of factual information relating to a case. Prepare medical releases.
- Prepare documents to initiate (or defend against) a lawsuit and file them with the court, draft interrogatories (written questions to be answered under oath

by the opposing party), attend depositions (recorded question-and-answer sessions in which an attorney questions a party or a witness), and summarize deposition transcripts.
- Prepare exhibits for trial, arrange to have all needed equipment and supplies in the courtroom at the time of the trial, create a trial notebook for the attorney to refer to during the trial, and prepare the client and witnesses for trial.
- Assist at trial and in any posttrial procedures, such as those required for appealing the case to a higher court.

Personal-Injury Law

Much litigation involves claims brought by persons who have been injured in automobile accidents or other incidents as a result of the negligence of others. *Negligence* is a *tort*, or civil wrong, and someone who has been injured as a result of another's negligence is entitled under tort law to obtain compensation from the wrongdoer. (Tort law, including negligence, will be discussed in Chapter 7.)

Paralegals who specialize in the area of personal-injury litigation often work for law firms that concentrate their efforts on this domain. Personal-injury paralegals are also hired by insurance companies to investigate claims. Defendants in personal-injury cases are typically insured by automobile or other insurance, and a defendant's insurance company will therefore have an interest in the outcome of the litigation.

A paralegal working on a personal-injury case would typically perform the following types of tasks:

- Interview a client (plaintiff) to obtain details about an accident and the injuries sustained by the client.
- Interview witnesses to the accident to gather as much information about the accident as possible.
- Obtain medical reports from physicians and hospitals describing the plaintiff's injuries.
- Obtain employment data to verify the amount of lost wages that should be claimed as damages—if the client's current or future employment is affected by the injury.
- Obtain a copy of the police report, and, if necessary, consult with police officers and investigators who worked on the case.
- Generally, provide litigation assistance.

Criminal Law

Law is sometimes classified into the two categories of civil law and criminal law. **Civil law** is concerned with the duties that exist between persons or between citizens and their governments, excluding the duty not to commit crimes. Contract law, for example, is part of civil law. The whole body of tort law, which has to do with the infringement by one person of the legally recognized rights of another (see Chapter 7), is an area of civil law.

Criminal law, in contrast, is concerned with wrongs committed against the public as a whole. Criminal acts are prohibited by federal, state, or local statutes. In a criminal case, the government seeks to impose a penalty on a person who has committed a crime. In a civil case, one party tries to make the other party comply with a duty or pay for the damage caused by the failure to so comply.

Civil Law
The branch of law dealing with the definition and enforcement of all private or public rights, as opposed to criminal matters.

Criminal Law
The branch of law that governs and defines those actions that are crimes and that subjects persons convicted of crimes to punishment imposed by the government.

DEVELOPING PARALEGAL SKILLS
Working for a Public Defender

Michele Sanchez works as a paralegal for the public defender's office in her county. Today, she has been assigned to go to the county jail to meet with a new client. The client has been jailed for child abuse and is very upset. She demands to be released from jail immediately. Michele notes her concerns and informs the client of the scheduling of the bail hearings.

TIPS FOR MEETING WITH A NEW CLIENT
- Review the case before meeting with the client.
- Listen carefully and supportively.
- Communicate with empathy.
- Minimize note taking.
- Do not appear to judge the client.

Paralegals who specialize in the area of criminal law may work for public prosecutors, public defenders, or criminal defense attorneys. Criminal litigation is similar to civil litigation in many respects, and the kinds of work performed by litigation paralegals (described previously) also apply in the criminal law context. In addition to providing general litigation assistance, a paralegal working in the area of criminal law might perform the following tasks:

- As a public prosecutor's legal assistant, draft search warrants, which authorize law enforcement officers to search a person or place.
- As a public prosecutor's legal assistant, draft arrest warrants, which authorize law enforcement officers to arrest and take into custody a criminal suspect.
- As a public prosecutor's legal assistant, act as a liaison between the police department and the public prosecutor's office.
- As a defense attorney's legal assistant, assist a criminal defendant in making arrangements to post bail (so that the defendant can be released from custody until further proceedings are held—see Chapter 12).
- Generally, help to make sure that a criminal defendant's constitutional rights are not violated by any action undertaken by police officers or attorneys handling the case.

On the Web
You can gain insight into criminal law and procedures by looking at some of the famous criminal law cases included on Court TV's Web site. Go to www.courttv.com/index.html.

Corporate Law

Corporate law consists of the laws that govern the formation, financing, merger and acquisition, and termination of corporations, as well as the rights and duties of those who own and run the corporation. You will read in detail about the meaning of these terms in Chapter 8.

Paralegals who specialize in corporate law may work for a corporation, in its legal department, or for a law firm that specializes in corporate law. The demand for paralegals who are experienced in the area of corporate law is expanding. If you refer back to Exhibit 2.3 on paralegal compensation, you will see that paralegals specializing in this area also receive, on average, higher salaries or wages than paralegals in most other specialty areas.

Here are just a few of the tasks that a paralegal working in the area of corporate law might be asked to undertake:

- Prepare articles of incorporation and file them with the appropriate state office (usually the secretary of state's office).
- Draft corporate bylaws (rules that govern the internal affairs of the corporation).

Corporate Law
Law that governs the formation, financing, merger and acquisition, and termination of corporations, as well as the rights and duties of those who own and run the corporation.

- Prepare minutes of corporate meetings and maintain a minutes binder.
- Draft shareholder proposals.
- Review or prepare documents relating to the sale of corporate securities (stocks and bonds); assist a supervising attorney in making sure that federal and state requirements relating to the sale of corporate securities are met.
- Assist with legal work relating to corporate mergers and acquisitions, such as researching a corporation's financial status.
- File the papers necessary to terminate a corporation's legal existence.

Bankruptcy Law

Bankruptcy law is a body of law that allows debtors to obtain relief from their debts. Bankruptcy law is federal law, and bankruptcy proceedings take place in federal courts (see the discussion of the federal court system in Chapter 6). The twin goals of bankruptcy law are (1) to protect a debtor by giving him or her a fresh start, free from creditors' claims; and (2) to ensure that creditors who are competing for a debtor's assets are treated fairly. Bankruptcy law provides for several types of relief, and both individuals and business firms may petition for bankruptcy.

Both large and small law firms practice bankruptcy law. A corporation undergoing bankruptcy proceedings (often in the form of a "reorganization," as provided for under bankruptcy law) may hire, on a temporary basis, a paralegal experienced in bankruptcy law to assist in the process. If you are working on behalf of a debtor who seeks bankruptcy relief, you might perform the following types of tasks:

- Interview the debtor (which may be an individual or a corporate representative) to obtain information relating to the debtor's income, debts, and assets.
- Review creditors' claims and verify their validity.
- Prepare the necessary documents for submission to the bankruptcy court.
- Attend bankruptcy proceedings.
- Assist in defending the debtor against any legal actions concerning the bankruptcy proceedings.

Bankruptcy Law
The body of federal law that governs bankruptcy proceedings. The twin goals of bankruptcy law are (1) to protect a debtor by giving him or her a fresh start, free from creditors' claims; and (2) to ensure that creditors who are competing for a debtor's assets are treated fairly.

On the Web
If you are interested in bankruptcy law, a good site for learning about current bankruptcy issues is that of the American Bankruptcy Institute at **www.abiworld.org**.

Employment and Labor Law

As will be discussed in Chapter 9, laws governing employment relationships are referred to collectively as *employment and labor law*. Employment and labor law includes laws governing health and safety in the workplace, labor unions and union-management relations, employment discrimination, wrongful employment termination, pension plans, retirement and disability income (Social Security), employee privacy rights, the minimum wage that must be paid, and overtime wages.

Paralegals who are experienced in one or more of these areas of employment and labor law may work for law firms, corporations and other business entities, or government agencies. Often, paralegals specialize in just one area of employment law. For example, many paralegals work in the area of workers' compensation. Under state **workers' compensation statutes,** employees who are injured on the job are compensated from state funds (obtained from taxes paid by employers). Paralegals working in this area of employment law assist persons injured on the job in obtaining compensation from the state workers' compensation board. As mentioned earlier, some government agencies allow paralegals to represent clients during agency hearings, which are conducted by agencies to settle disputes,

Workers' Compensation Statutes
State laws establishing an administrative procedure for compensating workers for injuries that arise in the course of their employment.

On the Web
Several law firms that specialize in labor and employment issues have posted their newsletters on the Web. One such firm is Arent Fox, which you can access at www.arentfox.com.

or during negotiations with the agencies. Many state workers' compensation boards allow paralegals to represent clients in such hearings.

Numerous other areas of employment and labor law are regulated by administrative agencies, and paralegals working in those areas need to be familiar with the relevant agency's requirements and procedures. Here are just a few agencies involved in regulating the workplace and with which employment-law paralegals should be familiar:

- *National Labor Relations Board (NLRB)*—A federal agency that implements federal laws governing union organizational activities, union elections, and labor-management relations generally.
- *Occupational Safety and Health Administration (OSHA)*—A federal agency that implements federal laws governing safety in the workplace. OSHA establishes safety standards that employers must follow. State agencies also establish safety and health standards.
- *Equal Employment Opportunity Commission (EEOC)*—A federal agency that administers and enforces federal laws prohibiting employment discrimination on the basis of race, color, national origin, gender, religion, age, or disability. Before an employee can sue an employer for discrimination in violation of these federal laws, the employee must comply with EEOC procedures for handling such complaints.
- *Labor Management Services Administration (LMSA)*—A federal agency that implements the provisions of the federal Employee Retirement Income Security Act (ERISA), which imposes certain requirements on employers in regard to pension funds.

Paralegals working in the area of employment and labor law often have extensive contact with these and other administrative agencies. If you work as a paralegal in the law-firm or corporate environment, you might undertake the following types of tasks, each of which may involve rules and procedures established by government agencies:

- Conduct research on labor law to determine how the law applies to a labor-management contract or dispute.
- Draft a contract setting forth the terms of a labor-management agreement.
- Assist in informal negotiations to settle a dispute between an employee and an employer or between a labor union and a firm's managers.
- Assist in formal dispute-settlement proceedings before one of the above-mentioned government agencies.
- Act as a mediator to help parties involved in labor or employment conflicts settle their disputes out of court (see Chapter 6 for further information on mediation and other forms of alternative dispute resolution, or ADR).
- Inform a client of the procedures involved in submitting a claim of employment discrimination to the EEOC and assist the client in preparing the necessary documents.
- Prepare the documents needed to initiate (or defend against) a lawsuit for employment discrimination in violation of federal or state law and generally assist in the litigation process.
- Contact and work with the state workers' compensation board on behalf of a client who is seeking compensation for injuries incurred during the course of employment.

- Draft employment policies to make sure that a business client (or a corporate employer) complies with federal and state laws prohibiting discrimination in the workplace.
- Assist a business client (or a corporate employer) in benefits planning to ensure compliance with the requirements of ERISA and any other laws regulating employee benefits, such as health, life, or disability insurance.

Estate Planning and Probate Administration

Estate planning and probate administration both have to do with the transfer of an owner's property, or *estate*, on the owner's death. Through **estate planning**, the owner decides, *before* death, how his or her property will be transferred to others. The owner may make a **will**, for example, to designate the persons to whom his or her property shall be transferred. The formal requirements for a valid will are set forth in state statutes, and because these requirements may differ from state to state, paralegals working in this area should be familiar with their state's law governing wills. If the property passes by will, depending on the size of the estate and other factors, the genuineness of the will may have to be proved (**probated**) in **probate court** (a county or other court that handles probate procedures). Probate administration thus involves the procedures relating to the transfer of property *after* the owner's death.

The process of probate may take many months and, in some cases, more than a year. The *personal representative* (a person named in the will to handle the affairs of the deceased after his or her death) or an *administrator* (a person appointed by the court if no personal representative is named in the will) satisfies all obligations (pays debts, taxes, and so on) of the deceased. The personal representative or administrator also arranges to have the deceased's property distributed among the heirs in accordance with the will's provisions. Because the probate process can be time consuming, many people arrange to have at least some of their property transferred in ways other than by will.

One estate-planning possibility involves the establishment of a **trust**, a legal arrangement in which the property owner transfers legal title to his or her property to a *trustee*. The trustee (which may be a relative or trusted friend of the property owner, an attorney, a law firm, or a banking institution) has a duty imposed by law to hold the property for the use or benefit of another (the *beneficiary* of the trust). A trust created during the owner's life is called a living trust. A trust provided for in a will comes into existence on the owner's death. Estate planning often involves life insurance. A person who wants to provide for a spouse and children after his or her death, for example, may obtain a life insurance policy listing the spouse and children as beneficiaries. On the death of the insured person, the beneficiaries receive the amount specified in the policy.

Paralegals who specialize in the area of estate planning and probate frequently work for law firms, but they may also be employed by other firms or agencies, such as banks, as well as by probate courts. If you work in this area, these are some of the tasks that you might perform:

- Interview clients to obtain information relating to their assets, how and to whom they want to transfer their property on death, and what arrangements they want to have made for the guardianship of minor children.
- Draft wills and other documents required to set up a trust fund.

Estate Planning
Making arrangements, during a person's lifetime, for the transfer of that person's property or obligations to others on the person's death. Estate planning often involves executing a will, establishing a trust fund, or taking out a life insurance policy to provide for others, such as a spouse or children, on one's death.

Will
A document directing how and to whom the maker's property and obligations are to be transferred on his or her death.

Probate
The process of "proving" the validity of a will and ensuring that the instructions in a valid will are carried out.

Probate Court
A court that probates wills; usually a county court.

Trust
An arrangement in which title to property is held by one person (a trustee) for the benefit of another (a beneficiary).

On the Web
To find the wills of famous people (John Lennon, Jacqueline Kennedy Onassis, Elvis Presley, and dozens of others), go to www.ca-probate.com/wills.htm.

> ## ETHICAL CONCERN
> ### Serving the Interests of Bereaved Clients
>
> One of the hardest events to cope with is the loss of a loved one, yet it is precisely at this time that bereaved persons must also cope with funeral arrangements and legal formalities. These formalities may include checking with an attorney, locating a will if one was made, tending to the decedent's financial affairs, and so on. Undertaking these activities can be costly, and financial needs may cause further stress.
>
> These are factors that paralegals should keep in mind when dealing with clients during the probate process. Probate proceedings always take time, but the duration may be reduced by the paralegal who files the necessary forms in a timely fashion and follows up on the status of the proceedings to make sure that there are no unnecessary delays. Your kind or sympathetic words may be appreciated by a bereaved client; but you can best serve his or her interests by doing your job efficiently and responsibly and by undertaking any action you can to speed up the probate process.

- Make sure that all procedural requirements are met during the probate process—that the proper documents are submitted to the court in a timely fashion, for example.
- Gather information relating to the debts and assets of the deceased, and assist in settling all financial and other obligations of the deceased.
- Locate heirs, if necessary.
- Explain probate procedures to family members or other heirs of the deceased and keep them informed of the status of the proceedings.

Intellectual-Property Law

Intellectual Property
Property that results from intellectual, creative processes. Copyrights, patents, and trademarks are examples of intellectual property.

Intellectual property consists of the products of individuals' minds—products that result from intellectual, creative processes. Those who create intellectual property acquire certain rights over the use of that property, and these rights are protected by law. Literary and artistic works are protected by *copyright law. Trademark law* protects business firms' distinctive marks or mottos. Inventions are protected by *patent law.*

Although it is an abstract term for an abstract concept, intellectual property is nonetheless wholly familiar to virtually everyone. The book you are reading is copyrighted. Undoubtedly, the personal computer you use is trademarked and patented. The software you use on that computer might be copyrighted. The primary benefit of intellectual-property rights to the owner is that he or she controls the commercial use of the property. The owner, for example, may sell the intellectual-property rights to another, may collect royalties on the use of the property (such as a popular song) by others, and may prevent all but one publisher from reproducing the property (such as a novel). In Chapter 8, you will read in greater detail about laws governing intellectual property.

Many law firms (or special departments of large law firms) specialize in intellectual-property law, such as patent law, while other firms provide a spectrum of legal services to their clients, of which intellectual-property law is only a part. Corporate legal departments may be responsible for registering copyrights, patents, or trademarks with the federal government.[2] Paralegal specialists in the area of intellectual property frequently undertake the following kinds of work:

- Interview clients who want to register for copyright, trademark, or patent protection of certain intellectual property, such as a new computer program, a product name, or an invention.
- Conduct research to find out whether someone has already applied for patent or trademark protection of an invention or product that the firm's client (or a corporate employer) wants to develop or register.
- Draft the documents that are necessary to apply for patent, trademark, or copyright protection.
- Draft contracts or licensing agreements that provide for another's authorized use of a copyrighted, patented, or trademarked product.
- In the corporate environment, monitor others' uses of the corporation's intellectual property and others' compliance with licensing agreements.
- Assist in litigation resulting from the *infringement* (unlawful use of) copyright, trademark, or patent rights.

On the Web
If you are interested in how cyberspace is affecting the laws governing intellectual property, a good general site covering current issues is that offered by the Bureau of National Affairs at www.bna.com/e-law.

Environmental Law

Environmental law consists of all laws that have been created to protect the environment. Environmental law involves the regulation of air and water pollution, natural resource management, endangered species protection, hazardous waste disposal and the clean-up of hazardous waste sites, pesticide control, and nuclear power regulation.

Employers of paralegal specialists in environmental law include administrative agencies (such as the federal Environmental Protection Agency, the state's natural resource department, and the local zoning board), environmental law departments of large law firms, law firms that specialize in environmental law, and corporations. Corporations with legal departments often employ environmental specialists. For example, a corporation may employ a paralegal as an *environmental coordinator* to assist the corporation in proper compliance with environmental regulations.

Here are some of the types of tasks that paralegal specialists in the area of environmental law frequently perform:

- Coordinate a corporate employer's environmental programs and policies and ensure that the corporation is complying properly with environmental regulations.
- Obtain permits from local, state, or federal environmental agencies to use land in certain ways (such as clearing trees or filling wetlands).
- Prepare forms and documents relating to the disposal of hazardous waste created by a corporate client's (or corporate employer's) manufacturing plants.
- Assist in litigation or other legal actions relating to violations of environmental laws. Paralegals play an important role in coordinating different aspects of the litigation (which may involve multiple violators) and in managing case files, which are often voluminous.

Environmental Law
All state and federal laws or regulations enacted or issued to protect the environment and preserve environmental resources.

On the Web
For news articles on environmental topics and links to other sites that deal with environmental issues, go to the Environmental Law page of Law Journal EXTRA! at www.ljx.com/practice/environment/index.html.

---

2. Copyrights are registered with the U.S. Copyright Office, Library of Congress, Washington, DC 20559. Patents and trademarks are registered with the Patent and Trademark Office, U.S. Department of Commerce, Washington, DC 20231.

- Attend conferences with administrative agency personnel or hearings conducted by an agency to assist in the settlement of a dispute.
- As an environmental agency employee, investigate and process claims of violations and assist in settling claims.

Real-Estate Law

Real Estate
Land and things permanently attached to the land, such as houses, buildings, and trees and foliage.

Real estate, or *real property,* consists of land and all things permanently attached to the land, such as houses, buildings, and trees and foliage. Because of the value of real estate (for most people, a home is the most expensive purchase they will ever make), attorneys frequently assist persons or business firms that buy or sell real property to make sure that nothing important is overlooked. Paralegals who specialize in the area of real estate may find employment in a number of environments, including small law firms that specialize in real-estate transactions, real-estate departments in large law firms, corporations or other business firms that frequently buy or sell real property, banking institutions (which finance real-estate purchases), title companies, or real-estate agencies. You will read in greater detail about real-property law in Chapter 7. Here we list just a few of the tasks that paralegals working in this area might perform:

- Interview clients who want to buy or sell real property.
- Draft contracts for the sale of real estate.
- Conduct *title* examinations. (The title to real property represents the right to own and possess the property, and title examinations are conducted to see if there are any defects in the title.)
- Review title abstracts, which summarize the ownership history of real property.
- Draft mortgage agreements.
- Provide information to banking institutions involved in financing clients' real-estate purchases.
- Prepare *deeds* (a deed is a written document that transfers title from one person to another).
- Make sure that property transfers are recorded in the appropriate public office (usually the county register of deeds office).
- Schedule *closings* (the closing is the final step in the purchase of real estate—see Chapter 7).
- Attend closings (when permitted by state law to do so).

Family Law

Family Law
Law relating to family matters, such as marriage, divorce, child support, and child custody.

Family law, as the term implies, deals with family matters, such as marriage, divorce, alimony, child support, and child custody. Family law is governed primarily by state statutes. If you specialize in this area, you will need to become familiar with your state's requirements concerning marriage and divorce procedures, child support, and related issues.

As a family-law specialist, you might work for a small family-law practice, a family-law department in a large law firm, or with a state or local agency, such as a community services agency, that assists persons who need help with family-related problems. As a paralegal working in the area of family law, you might perform such tasks as the following:

- Interview a divorcing client to obtain information relating to the couple's assets and liabilities.

Paralegal Profile

DORA DYE earned a bachelor of arts degree in Spanish, with distinction in general scholarship, and a master of arts degree in Spanish from the University of California, Berkeley. In addition, Dye received a master of business administration degree in International Business, with distinction, from Armstrong University.

Dye has been a real-estate and corporate paralegal since 1986. She has worked at several major San Francisco law firms and has transferred her skills in large real-estate and corporate transactions to the corporate environment. She is currently the Dispositions Closing Coordinator at the RREEF Funds.

Dye is a member of the San Francisco Paralegal Association (SFPA) and the National Federation of Paralegal Associations, Inc. (NFPA). She is an active member of the NFPA's PACE Development Committee and has taught the legal research and writing component of the PACE Review Seminar, as well as co-authored the chapter, "Factual and Legal Research" in the Paralegal Advanced Competency Exam Study Manual with her husband, David Dye.

Dye also teaches various courses in paralegal programs at the City College of San Francisco and California State University, Hayward. She has worked with members of the American Association for Paralegal Education to prepare model syllabi for real-estate law and introduction-to-paralegalism courses.

Real-Estate Paralegal

What do you like best about your work?
"I enjoy the field of real estate, because I am able to bring all of my experiences from the past to my current position. While working at various law firms, I became a senior paralegal specializing in multimillion-dollar real-estate closings. That experience has allowed me to transfer my knowledge and skills in real estate, business, and the law to a corporate environment and to work more effectively with internal and external legal counsel. Becoming a part-time paralegal instructor has enabled me to share my knowledge and skills with future paralegals. I have even used my Spanish skills when doing *pro bono* work."

What is the greatest challenge that you face in your area of work?
"Satisfying the twin goals of cost efficiency and the generation of a superior work product represents the greatest challenge. To meet these goals, it is important to 'get it right' the first time. Today, paralegals have a more personal relationship with clients. Clients call paralegals directly to handle issues that require the attorney's attention, thus improving the quality of legal services being delivered and keeping costs down."

What advice do you have for would-be paralegals in your area of work?
"Be as detail oriented as possible, and be the best that you can be in all things that you do. Bringing to your position all of the experiences that you have had will add to your value as a paralegal. Paralegal students should get work experience. Without work experience, students do not have an idea of office culture and environment, which are important aspects of a job."

What are some tips for success as a paralegal in your area of work?
"A successful paralegal knows what needs to be done and does it before he or she is asked. If you anticipate the needs of your attorneys and your clients, you will always be prepared to deal with matters more efficiently and effectively."

> "A successful paralegal knows what needs to be done and does it before he or she is asked."

> ### ETHICAL CONCERN
> ## Questions about Child Custody
>
> Divorcing clients frequently ask whether they can take their children out of the state while the mediation or divorce proceedings are under way. For example, suppose that Kerry Lynn, a paralegal, receives a call from a client who wants to know if it would be all right to take her children to her mother's home in another state over the weekend. Kerry tells the client that there is no problem with that.
>
> Normally, there would be no problem, but what Kerry doesn't know is that in this case, just two days ago, the court ordered that the children could not leave the state. The client, relying on Kerry's answer, violates the order. Kerry has both given legal advice to a client (which only attorneys may do) and has caused the client to suffer adverse legal consequences as a result of that advice.
>
> In your work as a paralegal, you may face similar questions from divorcing parents. You should always let the client know that as a paralegal, you cannot give legal advice, which you would be doing if you answered such questions.

- Research state laws governing child custody and assist in making child-custody arrangements for a divorcing couple.
- Draft a settlement (separation) agreement.
- Prepare the necessary documents to be filed with the court in a divorce action and assist in the litigation process.
- Prepare a client for divorce proceedings.
- Assist a client—particularly a spouse who has never handled household financial affairs—in financial planning.
- Assist clients in adoption proceedings.
- Interact with mediators (see Chapter 6) and counselors who are dealing with family problems.

Emerging Specialty Areas

The above listing of specialty areas is by no means exhaustive. In addition to these domains, there are several emerging areas that offer opportunities for paralegals who wish to specialize. For example, as the U.S. population ages, more and more attorneys are focusing on servicing the needs of older clients. **Elder law** is the term used to describe this broad specialty. Paralegals who work in this practice area may be asked to assist in a variety of tasks, including those relating to estate planning (discussed earlier), age-discrimination claims, financial arrangements for long-term care, abuse suffered by elderly persons, and the visitation rights of grandparents.

An increasing number of paralegals are also finding work in the area of **immigration law.** In the 1990s, immigration rates climbed significantly from those of previous decades. As the number of immigrants increased, so did the need for legal services among immigrant groups. Today, a number of law firms specialize in immigration law, particularly in California, New York, and other states with large immigrant populations. If you specialize in this area, you might assist clients who need help in filling out applications for work permits or visas, or who need

Elder Law
A term used to describe a relatively new legal specialty that involves servicing the needs of older clients, such as estate planning and making arrangements for long-term care.

Immigration Law
All laws that set forth the requirements that persons must meet if they wish to visit or immigrate to the United States.

information on how to become U.S. citizens. You may help clients contact foreign government offices about their immigration status or assist clients who are involved in deportation proceedings.

Over the past decade, many nurses have found profitable and challenging work as paralegals. A paralegal who is also a trained nurse is particularly well equipped to evaluate legal claims involving injuries, such as those involved in personal-injury, medical malpractice, or product-liability lawsuits. A relatively new specialty area among nurses—and within the legal profession—is that of the **legal nurse consultant (LNC)**. An LNC consults with legal professionals and others on medical aspects of legal claims or issues. LNCs usually work independently (offering their services on a contract basis) and are typically well paid for their services—up to $200 per hour, in some cases. The American Association of Legal Nurse Consultants now offers a certification program in which nurses who meet the eligibility criteria (including appropriate educational credentials and sufficient experience as a legal nurse) and pass an examination may become certified as LNCs.

As mentioned in the *Technology and Today's Paralegal* feature in Chapter 1, developments in technology are transforming the legal workplace. These developments are also opening doors to possible areas of specialization for paralegals. Paralegals who acquire expertise in high-tech equipment and software applications can perform valuable services for their employers and command high salaries.

Legal Nurse Consultant (LNC)
A nurse who consults with legal professionals and others about medical aspects of legal claims or issues. Legal nurse consultants normally must have at least a bachelor's degree in nursing and a significant amount of nursing experience.

On the Web
To learn more about the American Association of Legal Nurse Consultants and its certification programs, go to www.aalnc.org.

PARALEGAL COMPENSATION

What do paralegals earn? This is an important question for anyone contemplating a career as a paralegal. You can get some idea of what paralegals make, on average, from paralegal compensation surveys. Following a discussion of these surveys, we look at some other components of paralegal compensation, including job benefits and how paralegals are compensated for overtime work.

Compensation Surveys

If you refer back to Exhibit 2.3, you can see that paralegal income is affected by a number of factors. We have already mentioned how the average income of paralegals is affected by firm size (smaller or larger) and the type of employer (law firm, corporation, or government). Other income-determining factors include years of experience working as a paralegal, as well as the area of practice. Note that the average salary of a paralegal working in the area of intellectual-property law is $44,436, approximately $19,291 more than that of a paralegal working in the area of workers' compensation. Average salaries are also affected by location.

Exhibit 2.3 indicates *national* averages. To have a clearer picture of what your potential future income will be, you need to look at the average paralegal income in the state where you live or plan to work. As you can see in Exhibit 2.4 on the next page, paralegals working in California earn, on average, over $16,706 more than paralegals working in Nebraska.

Keep in mind that salary statistics do not tell the whole story. Although paralegals earn more in California than in a midwestern state such as Nebraska, the cost of living is higher in California than in Nebraska. This means that your real income—the amount of goods and services that you can purchase with your income—may, in fact, be the same in both states despite the differences in salary. Salary statistics also do not reveal another important component of compensation—job benefits.

EXHIBIT 2.4
Paralegal Compensation by State

© 1999 James Publishing, Inc. Reprinted courtesy of *Legal Assistant Today* magazine. For subscription information call (800) 394-2626.

State	Average Salary	State	Average Salary
Alabama	$36,225	Montana*	$26,742
Alaska	$26,800	Nebraska*	$24,440
Arizona	$37,268	Nevada*	$36,980
Arkansas	$33,592	New Hampshire*	$31,000
California	$41,146	New Jersey	$36,576
Colorado	$32,457	New Mexico*	$25,307
Connecticut	$37,364	New York	$39,123
Delaware	$39,500	North Carolina	$28,691
District of Columbia*	$39,750	North Dakota*	$33,491
Florida	$40,229	Ohio	$34,542
Georgia	$37,465	Oklahoma*	$32,400
Hawaii*	$39,400	Oregon	$38,196
Idaho*	$29,000	Pennsylvania	$35,557
Illinois	$31,851	Rhode Island*	$30,417
Indiana*	$29,674	South Carolina	$30,900
Iowa	$34,450	South Dakota*	$30,000
Kansas*	$30,840	Tennessee	$29,619
Kentucky	$27,183	Texas	$37,004
Louisiana*	$29,250	Utah*	$34,200
Maine*	$29,250	Vermont*	$32,750
Maryland*	$30,902	Virginia	$32,648
Massachusetts	$43,200	Washington	$33,851
Michigan	$34,651	West Virginia*	$33,500
Minnesota	$34,080	Wisconsin	$33,538
Mississippi*	$34,440	Wyoming*	$25,875
Missouri	$29,452		

*Based on less than ten verifiable submissions. This means that the salaries included here may not be representative of paralegal salaries in your state.

Source: "Are They Paying You What You're Worth? Legal Assistant Today's 1998–99 Salary Survey Results," *Legal Assistant Today,* January/February 1999, pp. 53–57.

Job Benefits

Part of your total compensation package as an employee will consist of various job benefits. These benefits may include paid holidays, sick leave, group insurance coverage (life, disability, medical, dental), pension plans, and possibly others. Benefits packages vary from firm to firm. For example, one employer may pay the entire premium for your life and health insurance, while another employer may require you to contribute part of the cost of the insurance. Usually, the larger the firm, the greater the value of the benefits package.

> **When evaluating any job offer, you need to consider the benefits that you will receive and what these benefits are worth to you.**

You will read more about the importance of job benefits later in this chapter, in the context of evaluating a job offer.

Salaries versus Hourly Wages

Most paralegals are salaried employees. In other words, they receive a specified annual salary regardless of the number of hours they actually work. Other paralegals are paid an hourly wage rate for every hour worked. Paralegals are frequently asked to work overtime, and how they are compensated for overtime work usually depends on whether they are salaried employees or are paid hourly wages. Many firms compensate their salaried paralegals for overtime work through year-end **bonuses,** which are special payments made to employees in recognition of their devotion to the firm and the high quality of their work. Paralegals often receive annual bonuses ranging from $1,200 to nearly $3,000, depending on years of experience, firm size, and so on. Some firms allow salaried employees to take compensatory time off work (for example, an hour off for every hour worked beyond usual working hours). Employees who are paid an hourly wage rate are normally paid overtime wages.

Bonus
An end-of-the-year payment to a salaried employee in appreciation for that employee's overtime work, work quality, diligence, or dedication to the firm.

Federal Law and Overtime Pay

A major issue in the paralegal profession in regard to compensation has to do with overtime pay. Some paralegals who receive year-end bonuses question whether their bonuses sufficiently compensate them for the amount of overtime they have worked. The debate over overtime pay is complicated by the fact that the Fair Labor Standards Act (Wage-Hour Law) of 1938 requires employers to pay employees **overtime wages**—one and a half times their normal hourly rate for all hours worked beyond forty hours per week. The act exempts certain types of employees from this overtime-pay requirement, however. *Exempt employees* include those who qualify under the terms of the act as holding "administrative," "executive," or "professional" positions.

Overtime Wages
Wages paid to workers who are paid an hourly wage rate to compensate them for overtime work (hours worked beyond forty hours per week). Under federal law, overtime wages are at least one and a half times the regular hourly wage rate.

The issue, then, is whether paralegals are exempt or nonexempt employees under the Fair Labor Standards Act. If they are exempt, they need not be paid an hourly overtime rate. If they are nonexempt, by law they must be paid overtime wages. Many firms argue that their paralegals are professionals and thus exempt from the act. Other firms, fearing possible liability for unfair labor practices, are beginning to pay overtime wages to their paralegals. Paralegals seem to be split fairly evenly on the issue, as are their employers. According to the 1998–99 paralegal compensation survey conducted by the National Association of Legal Assistants (NALA), 56.1 percent of paralegals are classified by their employers as exempt employees, while 43.9 percent are classified as nonexempt.[3]

In early 1994, a federal court addressed this issue for the first time. The case arose when twenty-three paralegals who worked for Page & Addison, a law firm in Dallas, Texas, sought $40,000 in back wages for overtime hours that they had worked. The Department of Labor, which enforces the Fair Labor Standards Act, had concluded that the paralegals were nonexempt employees and thus subject to the act's overtime provisions. The federal court, however, disagreed, finding that paralegals could be classified as exempt (or professional) employees because they perform important work and exercise discretion and independent judgment.[4] Although the court decision in the *Page & Addison* case is significant, it does not mean that all paralegals are now classified as exempt employees. Rather, the issue is decided on the basis of the specific facts of a given case. The question of how paralegals should be classified for labor-law purposes continues to divide the profession.

---

3. *Legal Assistant Today,* January/February, 1999, p. 55.
4. *U.S. Department of Labor v. Page & Addison, P.C.,* U.S. District Court, Dallas, Texas, No. 91-2655, March 15, 1994.

PLANNING YOUR CAREER

Career planning involves essentially three steps. The first step is defining your long-term goals. The second step involves devising short-term goals and adjusting these goals to meet the realities of the job market. We look at these two steps of career planning in this section. Later in this chapter, we discuss the third step: reevaluating your career after you have had some on-the-job experience as a paralegal.

Defining Your Long-Term Goals

From the outset, you will want to define, as clearly as possible, your career goals, and this requires some personal reflection and self-assessment. What are you looking for in a career? Why do you want to become a paralegal? Is income the most important factor? Is job satisfaction (doing the kind of work you like) the most important factor? Is the environment in which you work the most important factor? What profession could best utilize your special talents or skills? Asking yourself these and other broad questions about your personal preferences and values will help you define more clearly your overall professional goals.

Do not be surprised to find that your long-term goals change over time. As you gain more experience as a paralegal and your life circumstances change, you may decide that your former long-term goals are no longer appropriate. For example, you may desire a level of career involvement as a single person that may not be appropriate to your situation should you marry and have children. Similarly, later in life, when your children leave home and you are faced with an "empty nest," you may have different goals with respect to your work.

Also, at the outset of your career, you cannot know what opportunities might present themselves in the future. Career planning is an ongoing challenge for paralegals, just as it is for everyone. Throughout your career as a paralegal, you will probably meet other paralegals who have made career changes. A high percentage of paralegals in today's work force, for example, decided to become paralegals after several years of working in another profession, such as nursing, law enforcement, business administration, or accounting. Changes within the profession, your own experiences, and new opportunities constantly affect the career choices before you. The realities you face during your career may play a significant role in modifying your long-term goals.

Short-Term Goals and Job Realities

Long-term goals are just that—goals that we hope to achieve over the long run. It may take many years or even a lifetime to attain certain long-term goals that we set for ourselves. Short-term goals are the steps that we take to realize our long-term goals. As an entry-level paralegal, one of your short-term goals is simply to find a job.

Ideally, you will find a job that provides you with a salary commensurate with your training and abilities, a level of responsibility that is comfortable (or challenging) for you, and excellent job benefits. The realities of the job market are not always what we wish them to be, however. You should be prepared for the possibility that you might not find the "right" employer or the "perfect" job for you when you first start your job search. You may be lucky from the outset, but then again, it may take several attempts before you find the employer and the job that best suits your needs, skills, and talents. Remember, though, that even if you do not find the perfect job right away, you can gain valuable skills and experience in *any* job environment—skills and experience that can help you achieve long-term goals in the future. In fact, you might want to "try on" jobs at different-sized firms and in different specialty areas to see how they "fit" with your particular needs.

LOCATING POTENTIAL EMPLOYERS

Looking for a job is time consuming and requires attention to detail, persistence, and creativity. Your paralegal education is preparing you, among other things, to do investigative research. The investigative skills that you will use on the job as a paralegal are the ones that you should apply when looking for a job.

Where do you begin your investigation? How can you find out what paralegal jobs are available in your area or elsewhere? How do you know which law firms practice the type of law that interests you? The following suggestions will help you find answers to all of these questions.

Networking

Career opportunities often go unpublished. Many firms post notices within their own organizations before publishing online or in the "Help Wanted" section of a newspaper or periodical. This opens doors to their own employees before the general public. It also spares employers from having to wade through hundreds of employment applications for a vacant position. If you have connections within an organization, you may be told that a position is opening before other candidates are aware that an opportunity exists.

Paralegals looking for jobs often learn of available positions through networking. For paralegals, **networking** is the process of making personal connections with other paralegals, paralegal instructors, attorneys, and others who are involved in (or who know someone who is involved in) the paralegal or legal profession. You should begin networking while you are still attending your paralegal program. Cultivate relationships with your instructors. Let them know your career interests, and ask them for their advice. See if your local paralegal association allows students to be members. If it does, attend meetings and become acquainted with other paralegals, who may know of job opportunities.

Cultivate connections during your internship as a paralegal, as well. One of the benefits of internships or of working part-time in a law firm while studying to be a paralegal is that it allows you to establish connections that may be useful in your job search, and the firm itself may offer you a full-time job when you graduate. According to the 1998–99 survey of paralegal compensation conducted by the National Association of Legal Assistants (NALA), over 28 percent of paralegals found entry-level jobs or new jobs through networking.[5] Throughout your career, you will find that networking can provide valuable job leads.

Networking
Making personal connections and cultivating relationships with people in a certain field, profession, or area of interest.

Finding Available Jobs

Your next effort should be to locate sources that list paralegal job openings. A good place to start is with the classified ads in your local newspaper. **Trade journals** and similar publications, such as your local or state bar association's

Trade Journal
A newsletter, magazine, or other periodical that provides a certain trade or profession with information (products, trends, or developments) relating to that trade or profession.

---
5. "Are They Paying You What You're Worth? Legal Assistant Today's 1998–99 Salary Survey Results," *Legal Assistant Today,* January/February 1999, pp. 53–57.

journal or newsletters, usually list openings for legal professionals, including paralegals. Increasingly, employers advertise job openings in online publications and turn to online databases to find prospective employees. In fact, today probably the best starting point when launching your job search is the Internet. (For more information on how you can use the Internet to search for jobs, see the feature *Technology and Today's Paralegal: Online Job Searching*.)

Identifying Possible Employers

You should also identify firms and organizations for which you might like to work and submit an employment application to them. In a well-organized job search, you will locate and contact those organizations that offer the benefits, salary, opportunities for advancement, work environment, and legal specialty of your choice. Even though one of these organizations may not have vacancies in your field at the moment, you want your job application to be immediately available to the potential employer when an opening does occur. Most firms, if they are interested in your qualifications, will keep your application on file for six months or so and may contact you if a position becomes available.

It is a good idea to begin compiling employer information for your job search while you are still completing your paralegal studies. Many of the resources you will need are available at the college or university that you attend or through your paralegal program (or, increasingly, online).

On the Web
You can search the Yellow Pages online at a number of Web sites, including Yahoo's Yellow Pages at **yp.yahoo.com.**

THE YELLOW PAGES. An obvious source of information is the Yellow Pages of your local telephone directory. Look under "Attorneys" for the names of attorneys and law firms in your locale. If you want to work in a special area, such as real estate, you might look under other listings, such as "Title Companies." Many libraries have the Yellow Pages for major cities across the country, which allows you to broaden the geographic scope of your search. You may be able to find similar information in online "Yellow Pages" listings.

LEGAL DIRECTORIES. There are numerous legal directories that provide lists of attorneys, their locations, and their areas of practice. The *Martindale-Hubbel Law Directory*, which you can find at most law libraries (or online at **www.martindale.com**), lists the names, addresses, telephone numbers, areas of legal practice, and other data for many lawyers and law firms throughout the United States. It is an excellent resource for paralegals interested in working for law firms or corporate legal departments. *West's Legal Directory* is another valuable source of information. It is now on the Internet at **www.wld.com.** The directory contains a detailed listing of U.S. and Canadian attorneys and law firms, state and federal attorneys and offices, and corporate legal departments and general counsel. You can find links to more than one hundred other directories listing attorneys and legal professionals at the following government Web site: **www.house.gov.**

On the Web
If you are looking for a job in a corporate legal department, CompanyLink offers information on more than 45,000 U.S. companies. Go to **www.companylink.com.** Hoovers Online offers 10,000 "company capsules" and links to even more Web sites at **www.hoovers.com.**

JOB-PLACEMENT SERVICES

Throughout your job search, make full use of your school's placement service. Many paralegal programs provide job-placement services, and ABA-approved schools are required to provide ongoing placement services for students. Placement offices are staffed with personnel trained to assist you in finding a job, as well as in preparing job-search tools, such as your résumé and a list of potential employers.

TECHNOLOGY AND TODAY'S PARALEGAL
Online Job Searching

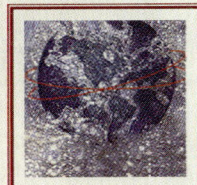

Given how the Internet has affected all aspects of business and professional life, it is not surprising that it has also become an invaluable device for both employers looking for job candidates and those seeking jobs. Today's paralegal can take advantage of this tool to make job searches much easier than in the past.

ONLINE EMPLOYMENT ADS

Paralegals looking for employment can access an increasing number of online sources to find out what positions are available in their field. A good starting point is the Hieros Gamos Employment Center's Web site (at www.hg.org/employment.html), which calls itself "the largest source of jobs on the Internet." At this site, in addition to finding job vacancies in your field, you can indicate the type of position you are interested in and ask to be notified by e-mail when a position in that area is posted. If you go to jobs.findlaw.com, you will find a state-by-state list of job openings for paralegals.

A site sponsored by Cornell University and *Human Resource Executive* magazine (at www.workindex.com) allows you to search for listings in your area and also provides links to numerous other job-information sites and search engines. You can find links to multiple state employment offices, federal jobs, and employment ads from publications in various areas of the country at Job Bank USA's site (go to www.jobbankusa.com/jobs.html).

Many states now publish job openings for state government positions on their Web pages, and some include application forms on their sites as well. For example, Vermont publishes its biweekly job notices on its Web site (at www.state.vt.us/pers/recruit/bulletin.htm).

These sites and the links they offer will help get you started on your job search. To find other sites, check with your paralegal program director, your school's placement office, or your local paralegal association. All of these sources will have information on current Web sites that you can access for job information. You might also check NFPA's Internet marketing page (at www.paralegals.org/Marketing/Internet.html) to obtain information on how you can include your ad or résumé on its site.

POST YOUR RÉSUMÉ ONLINE

Increasingly, employers are recruiting new employees by using online résumé banks. These sites allow employers to search through databases of job seekers to find job candidates whose skills and qualifications most closely correlate with the employers' needs. In a sense, résumé banks are the online world's version of the traditional "Positions Wanted" ads in newspapers. A key difference for job seekers is that, unlike ads in newspapers and other publications, there is little or no cost involved in posting a résumé online—or keeping it there for some time.

One of the oldest résumé sites is that offered by LAWMATCH (at www.lawmatch.com). LAWMATCH, like many other sites now offering such services, has both public and confidential sections. In a public listing, the identity of the candidate is revealed online. In a confidential listing, the identity of the candidate is not revealed; rather, interested employers are directed to call LAWMATCH, which then notifies the candidate of the employment opportunity. Confidential listings typically are sought by people who may not want their current employers to know that they are interested in other employment. This kind of site may be useful to you later in your career, when you are looking for greater opportunities. The Legal Employment Search Site (at www.legalemploy.com) has links to numerous sites where you can post your résumé online; this site also gives helpful suggestions on how to use the Internet in your job search.

WEB HOME PAGES

Virtually all large firms (and increasingly, many small firms) have Web pages, as do federal and state government agencies. Once you have the name of a firm or agency that interests you, you can go online to see if that organization has a Web page. The Web page of a firm or agency may contain much useful information for job seekers, including, in some cases, available positions and the name of the person you should contact about employment.

To find home pages of law firms, a good starting point is FindLaw's site at www.findlaw.com/14firms/index.html. Just keying in the name of the firm on a search engine may lead you to the firm's home page. You can locate the home pages for federal government agencies by accessing Federal World's site at www.fedworld.gov. To locate information on state governments, including state agencies, try www.law.cornell.edu/states/index.html and www.findlaw.com/11stategov/index.html.

Featured Guest: Denise Templeton

Paralegal Career Planning and Development

Biographical Note

Denise Templeton is the president and chief executive officer of Templeton & Associates, a legal support services firm based in Minneapolis, Minnesota. She has been involved with the paralegal profession since she graduated from the Institute for Paralegal Training in Philadelphia in 1972. Her professional career has included work as a legal assistant in both the public and private sectors, as well as seven years as the director of the legal assistant program at the University of Minnesota. In 1985, she founded the Minnesota Legal Assistant Institute, a private, postsecondary certificate program. Templeton is also a founder of the Minnesota Association of Legal Assistants, the American Association for Paralegal Education, and the National Federation of Paralegal Associations (NFPA). She is currently on the NFPA Advisory Council.

In the early 1970s, the paralegal field was just beginning to be officially recognized, and its parameters were undefined. The larger law firms and corporate legal departments were the first to grasp the concept that legal assistants could free busy attorneys by taking over the more routine legal tasks. This enabled law firms to get more work done in the same amount of time and at a constant level of quality. Because paralegals were a less expensive resource than attorneys, clients were able to pay less for legal services without sacrificing quality.

Then, as now, the majority of paralegals were employed in the litigation area [relating to lawsuits]. Over time, more specialty areas have opened up, and today's paralegal can be involved in anything from real estate to environmental law. Many opportunities are available now, and many more will be created in the future. People are entering the paralegal field in greater numbers each year. The successful legal assistant knows the importance of adopting a career-development strategy. My strategy includes six basic components: (1) self-awareness, (2) knowledge of the field, (3) openness to opportunity, (4) professional development, (5) support systems, and (6) periodic review.

Self-Awareness

Self-awareness involves creating a vision. You must envision what you want and expect from a paralegal career based on your knowledge of yourself and what is important to you in your work. As you develop your career path, think about where you want to start and where you want to be in the long run. There are many possibilities in terms of both work environments and types of work. As a beginner, you may seek a large, structured office and a position that is clearly defined. One of the larger law firms or a corporate legal department may provide you with this framework. You may, however, sense that a smaller, less structured environment would be more comfortable for you. Your duties may be more varied. In any event, analyze your previous experience and prioritize your goals. Decide which goal is most important for you.

Knowledge of the Field

In tandem with self-assessment, consider the realities of the paralegal field itself. Again, because of the many options available in terms of legal specialties and work environments, the paralegal field can accommodate many types of people.

Another option is to contact a local paralegal association (or the state bar association's paralegal division, if one exists) to learn the names of any legal-placement services in your area. (The names and addresses of paralegal associations and bar associations in each state are listed in Appendix F and Appendix G, respectively, at the end of this book.) If you use the services of a legal-placement agency, be sure that you make it clear to the agency that you are looking for work as a paralegal, not as a legal secretary. Also, find out whether you or the employer will pay the agency's placement fee. In some agencies and for some jobs, you may be required to pay part or all of the fee.

FEATURED GUEST, Continued

Some areas of law require more intensity, time, and dedication than others. If you are already juggling the demands of a job and a family, for example, overtime may be a serious problem. Talk to people working in the area that interests you. Learn about the advantages and disadvantages of working in that area. The more you learn about that area, the more accurate and complete will be your picture of what to expect and how the position fits in with your vision.

OPENNESS TO OPPORTUNITY

By keeping an open mind and being aware of changing interests, you will be able to create new opportunities for yourself and take advantage of opportunities that arise as your career develops. Even if you have already created your vision of the ideal paralegal career path, stay open to possibilities that may present themselves. If you are trained in probate practice (which deals with the transfer of property on a person's death), for example, you may find that real estate is a compatible specialty. By making your interest in real-estate practice known to your supervisor, you demonstrate a willingness to expand your legal knowledge. Ultimately, you may work for a corporation in its real-estate management or development division. The idea of cross-training becomes increasingly more acceptable as firms develop a more flexible work force. When the economy takes a turn for the worse, those who have multiple skills can be reassigned rather than laid off.

PROFESSIONAL DEVELOPMENT

Closely aligned with openness to opportunity is staying aware of developments in your profession. Developing and maintaining professional contacts and reading paralegal publications regularly are great ways to keep up with trends in your field. This knowledge can help you decide when and how to make turns in your career path. Also, the critical skill of networking plays an important role for any professional, including the paralegal. From the beginning, keep a current list of the people you meet and the areas in which they work. Become an active member of your local paralegal association. If there is no paralegal association in your community, then start one. Read the periodicals published by national paralegal associations and bar associations, and read materials that will keep you up to date on what is happening locally and nationally with paralegals. Ask paralegals and attorneys what they read, and attend continuing-education seminars to expand your knowledge base.

SUPPORT SYSTEMS

The value of having people give you encouragement and constructive crit-

> "Today's paralegal can be involved in anything from real estate to environmental law."

icism cannot be overstated. When you share ideas and concerns with others involved in your work, you will have a more balanced perspective on your work. Balance is an important ingredient in life. When you are working in a very intense, deadline-oriented atmosphere, balance can be painfully elusive. That is why having friends and participating in activities both inside and outside the legal profession is important to your well-being. Promise yourself that you will take regular vacations with family and friends and keep yourself healthy, happy, and productive.

PERIODIC REVIEW

Remember, change is the only constant in life. Many opportunities exist now that were not possible when the paralegal field was new. Many new opportunities will arise in the future. By taking the time periodically to take stock of your own changing needs and desires, as well as the evolution of the field, you can decide which career step to take next and when to take it. For those paralegals who take charge of their own destinies, there are many ways to grow and prosper as legal professionals.

MARKETING YOUR SKILLS

Once you have located potential employers, the next step in your job search is to market your skills and yourself effectively to those employers. Marketing your skills involves three stages: the application process, interviewing for jobs, and following up on job interviews.

You should keep in mind throughout your job search that each personal contact you make, whether it results in employment or not, has potential for your future. A firm may not hire you today, for example, because you lack experience.

DEVELOPING PARALEGAL SKILLS

A Career Plan

Rob Johnson, a paralegal student who is working toward a bachelor's degree with a major in legal assistance, needs to find a job for the internship class that is required for graduation. Rob, however, does not want to take just any job. Rob wants his internship to be the springboard for his career as a paralegal. Rob thus begins to implement some career-planning strategies.

CHECKLIST FOR CAREER PLANNING
- Establish long-term goals.
- Review the current job market and establish short-term goals.
- Locate available jobs and employers.
- Network.
- Reevaluate your job every few years.

But it may hire you a year from now if by then you have the experience that it is seeking. Therefore, always keep track of the contacts you make during your search, be patient, and be professional. You may be surprised how many doors will open for you, if not today, then tomorrow.

The Application Process

As a paralegal looking for professional employment, you will need to assemble and present professional application materials. The basic materials you should create are a résumé, a cover letter, a list of professional references, and a portfolio. The following discussion explains each of these documents and gives some practical tips on how to create them.

THE RÉSUMÉ. For almost all job applications, you must submit a personal *résumé*, which summarizes your employment and educational background. Your résumé is an advertisement, and you should invest the time to make that advertisement effective. Because personnel officers in law firms, corporations, and government agencies may receive a hundred or more résumés for each position they advertise, your résumé should create the best possible impression if you want to gain a competitive edge over other job seekers.

Either generate your résumé yourself, using a computer and a laser printer, or have a professional résumé-preparation service do it for you. Format each page so that the reader is able to scan it quickly and catch the highlights. You might vary the type size, but never use a type size or style that is difficult to read.

What to Include in Your Résumé. Your name, address, telephone number, e-mail address, and fax number belong at the beginning of your résumé. The résumé should be simple, brief, and clear. As a general rule, it should contain only information that is relevant to the job that you are seeking. A one-page résumé is usually sufficient, unless two pages are required to list relevant educational background and work experience. Exhibit 2.5 shows a sample résumé. Note that you should avoid placing your name and address in the upper left-hand corner, as this area is often stapled.

Divide your résumé into logical sections with headings, such as those shown in Exhibit 2.5. Whenever you list dates, such as educational and employment

> **EXHIBIT 2.5**
> **A Sample Résumé**

ELENA LOPEZ

1131 North Shore Drive
Nita City, NI 48804
Telephone: (616) 555-0102 • Fax: (616) 555-2103 • E-mail: elopez@nitanet.net

---

EMPLOYMENT OBJECTIVE
A position as a paralegal in a private law firm that specializes in personal-injury practice.

EDUCATION

1998 Postbaccalaureate Certificate
  Midwestern Professional School for Paralegals, Green Bay, WI
  Focus: Litigation Procedures; Legal Investigation, Research, Writing.
  GPA 3.8.

1993 Bachelor of Arts degree
  University of Wisconsin, Madison, WI 53706.
  Political Science major. GPA 3.5.

PARALEGAL EXPERIENCE

- Paralegal with the Caldwell Legal Clinic,
  3189 Plainview, Nita City, Nita 48801. June 1998 to the present.
  Responsibilities: General legal research and writing, and trial preparation in personal-injury cases.

- Paralegal with the Free Legal Aid Society,
  122 W. Fourth St., Green Bay, WI 54311. June 1997 to May 1998.
  Responsibilities: Part-time assistance to legal-aid attorneys in their representation of indigent clients in matters such as divorce, abuse, child custody, paternity, and landlord/tenant disputes.

- Research Assistant,
  Political Science Department, University of Wisconsin. January 1994 to May 1997.
  Responsibilities: Research on the effectiveness of federal welfare programs in reducing poverty in the United States.

AFFILIATIONS
Paralegal Association of Wisconsin
National Association of Legal Assistants

---

dates, list them chronologically, in reverse order. In other words, list your most recent educational or work history first. When discussing your education, list the names, cities, and states of the colleges or universities that you have attended and the degrees that you have received. You may want to indicate your major and minor concentrations and those courses that are most related to your professional goal, such as "Major: Paralegal Studies" or "Minor: Political Science." When listing your work experience, specify what your responsibilities have been in each position that you have held. Also, include any volunteer work that you have done.

Scholarships or honors should also be indicated. If you have a high grade point average (GPA), you should include it in your résumé. Under the heading "Selected Accomplishments," you might indicate your ability to speak a foreign language or other special skill, such as online research skills.

What if you are an entry-level paralegal and have no work experience to list? What can you include on your résumé to fill out the page? If you are facing this situation, add more information on your educational background and experience. You can list specific courses that you took, particular skills—such as computer skills—that you acquired during your paralegal training, and student affiliations.

Do Not Include Personal Data. Avoid including personal data (such as age, marital status, number of children, gender, or hobbies) in your résumé. Employers are prohibited by law from discriminating against employees or job candidates on the basis of race, color, gender, national origin, religion, age, or disability. You can help them fulfill this legal obligation by not including in your résumé any information that could serve as a basis for discrimination. For the same reason, you would be wise not to include a photograph of yourself with your résumé. Also, most prospective employers are not interested in such information as personal preferences, pastimes, or hobbies.

Proofread Your Results. Carefully proofread your résumé. Use the spelling checker and grammar checker on your computer, but do not rely on them totally. Have a friend or teacher review your résumé for punctuation, syntax, grammar, spelling, and content. If you find an error, you need to fix it, even if it means having new résumés printed. A mistake on your résumé tells the potential employer that you are a careless worker, and this message may ruin your chances of landing a job.

THE COVER LETTER. To encourage the recruiter to review your résumé, you need to capture his or her attention with a *cover letter* that accompanies the résumé. Because the cover letter often represents your first contact with an employer, it should be written carefully and precisely. It should be brief, perhaps only two or three paragraphs in length. Exhibit 2.6 shows a sample cover letter. Whenever possible, you should learn the name of the individual in charge of hiring (by phone or e-mail, if necessary) and direct your letter to that person. If you do not know the name of the individual responsible for reviewing résumés, use a generic title, such as "Human Resources Manager" or "Legal Assistant Manager."

Your cover letter should point out a few things about yourself and your qualifications for the position that might persuade a recruiter to examine your résumé. As a recently graduated paralegal, for example, you might draw attention to your high academic standing at school, your eagerness to specialize in the same area of law as the employer (perhaps listing some courses relating to that specialty), and your willingness to relocate to the employer's city. Your job is to convince the recruiter that you are a close match to the mental picture that he or she has of the perfect candidate for the job. Make sure that the reader knows when and where you can be reached. Often this is best indicated in the closing paragraph of the letter, as shown in Exhibit 2.6.

As with your résumé, you should read through your letter several times and have someone else read it also to make sure that it is free from mistakes and easily understood. You should use the same type of paper for your cover letter as you use for your résumé.

EXHIBIT 2.6
A Sample Cover Letter

ELENA LOPEZ

1131 North Shore Drive
Nita City, NI 48804
Telephone: (616) 555-0102 • Fax: (616) 555-2103 • E-mail: elopez@nitanet.net

August 22, 1999

Mr. Allen P. Gilmore
Jeffers, Gilmore & Dunn
553 Fifth Avenue, Suite 101
Nita City, NI 48801

Dear Mr. Gilmore:

I am responding to your advertisement in the *University of Nita Law Journal* for a paralegal to assist you in personal-injury litigation.

My bachelor of arts degree is from the University of Nita. I am a recent graduate of the Midwestern Professional School for Paralegals. My paralegal courses included litigation procedures, legal research, legal investigation, and legal writing. I hope to specialize in the area of personal-injury law.

I would like very much to meet with you or your representative to learn more about the position that you have available. I am enclosing a copy of my résumé and a list of professional references.

If you wish to contact me, I can be reached at the telephone number and e-mail address given above.

Sincerely yours,

Elena Lopez

Elena Lopez

Enclosures

What about e-mailing your cover letter and résumé to prospective employers? This is a difficult question. On the one hand, e-mail is much faster than regular mail or express delivery services. On the other hand, an e-mail résumé does not look as nice. Furthermore, while some firms are accustomed to receiving applications by e-mail, others are not. Generally, you need to use your own judgment. If the job you are applying for was advertised online or if the employer provided an e-mail address for interested job candidates to use, then e-mail is probably appropriate. Job candidates who submit applications via e-mail should also send, via regular mail, printed copies of their letters and résumés as well.

LIST OF PROFESSIONAL REFERENCES.   If a firm is interested in your application, you will probably be asked to provide a list of references—people whom the firm can contact to obtain information about you and your abilities. A paralegal instructor who has worked closely with you on an academic project, an internship supervisor who has firsthand knowledge of your work, or a past employer who has observed your problem-solving ability would all make excellent references. You should have at least three professionally relevant references, but no more than five references are necessary (if an interviewer needs additional references, he or she will ask for them). Never include the names of family members, friends, or others who will be clearly biased in your favor.

You should list your references on a separate sheet of paper, making sure to include your name, address, telephone number, and so on at the top of the page, in the same format as on your résumé. For each person included on your list of references, include his or her current institutional affiliation or business firm, address, telephone number, fax number, and, if you know it, e-mail address. Generally, try to make it easy for prospective employers to contact and communicate with your references.

When creating your list of references, always remember the following rule:

> **Never list a person's name as a reference unless you have first obtained that person's permission to do so.**

After all, it will not help you win the position if one of your references is surprised by the call or is unavailable, such as a paralegal instructor who is out of the country for the year. Such events raise a red flag to the interviewer and indicate that you are not concerned with details.

Obtaining permission from legal professionals to use their names as references also gives you an opportunity to discuss your plans and goals with them, and they may be able to advise you and assist you in your networking. Additionally, it gives you a chance to discuss with them the kinds of experience and skills in which a prospective employer may be interested.

Professional Portfolio
A job applicant's collection of selected personal documents (such as school transcripts, writing samples, and certificates) for presentation to a potential employer.

YOUR PROFESSIONAL PORTFOLIO.   When a potential employer asks you for an interview, have your **professional portfolio** of selected documents ready to give to the interviewer. The professional portfolio should contain another copy of your résumé, a list of references, letters of recommendation written by previous employers or instructors, samples of legal documents that you have composed, college or university transcripts, and any other relevant professional information, such as proof of professional certification or achievement. This collection of documents should be well organized and professionally presented. Depending on the size of your portfolio, a cover sheet, a table of contents, and a commercial binder may be appropriate.

The interviewer may be very interested in your research and writing skills. Therefore, your professional portfolio should contain several brief samples of legal writing. If you are looking for your first legal position, go through your paralegal drafting assignments and pull out those that reflect your best work and that relate to the job skills you wish to demonstrate. Then, working with an instructor or other mentor, revise and improve those samples for inclusion in the portfolio. Documents that you have drafted while an intern or when working as a part-time or full-time paralegal might also be used. These documents make excellent writing samples because they involve real-life circumstances. Be careful, however, and always remember to do the following:

 On any sample document, completely blacken out (or "white out") any identifying reference to the client unless you have the client's permission to disclose his or her identity or the information is not confidential.

Always include a résumé, as well as a list of references, in your professional portfolio, even though you already sent your résumé to the prospective employer with your cover letter. Interviewers may not have the résumé at hand at the time of the interview, and providing a second copy with your professional portfolio is a thoughtful gesture on your part.

Some interviewers may examine your professional portfolio carefully. Others may retain it to examine later, after the interview has concluded. Still others may not be interested in it at all. If there is a particular item in your portfolio that you would like the interviewer to see, make sure you point this out before leaving the interview.

The Interview

Interviews with potential employers may be the most challenging (and most stressful) aspect of your search for employment. The interview ordinarily takes place after the employer has reviewed your cover letter and résumé. Often, if the employer is interested in your application, a secretary or legal assistant will contact you to schedule an interview.

Every interview will be a unique experience. Some interviews will go very well, but you may still lose out to another candidate. Nonetheless, you have made a good contact, and you may be able to use this interviewer as a resource for information about other jobs. Remember what went right about the interview, and try to use that information at the next one. Other interviews may go poorly. There are good lessons to be learned from poor interviews, however.

You will also find that some interviewers are more skilled at interviewing than others. Some have a talent for getting applicants to open up and discuss candidly their work and backgrounds. Others are confrontational and put the already nervous candidate on the defensive. Still others may be unprepared for the interview. They may not have had time to check the job requirements, for example, or when the position is available. Unfortunately, as the person being interviewed, you have no control over who will interview you. The following discussion will help you prepare for a first paralegal job interview and will also serve as a refresher for you when seeking a career change.

BEFORE THE INTERVIEW. You can do many things prior to the interview to enhance your chances of getting the job. First of all, you should do your "homework." Learn as much about the employer as possible. Check with your instructors or other legal professionals to find out if they are familiar with the firm or the interviewer. Check the employer's Web site, if there is one, and consult relevant directories, such as legal and company directories, as well as business publications, to see what you can learn about the firm and its members. When you are called for an interview, learn the full name of the interviewer, so that you will be able to address him or her by name during the interview and properly address a follow-up letter. During the interview, use Mr. or Ms. unless directed by the interviewer to be less formal.

> ## ETHICAL CONCERN
> ### "Gilding the Lily"
>
> When applying and interviewing for a job, be honest about your skills and job qualifications. Even though you are trying to impress a prospective employer, never succumb to the temptation to "gild the lily" by exaggerating your experience and qualifications.
>
> Suppose that you are interviewing for a job and the interviewer asks you about your GPA. Wanting to impress the interviewer, you say that your GPA was 3.8 when in fact it was 3.4. This "little white lie" may cost you the job. Prospective employers usually check your credentials, including your transcripts. Any misrepresentation, no matter how minor it may seem, will create a negative impression. Professional responsibility requires, among other things, that you be honest and pay scrupulous attention to detail—not only on the job but also during the job-application process.

Anticipate and review in your mind the possible questions that you might be asked during the interview. Then prepare (and possibly rehearse with a friend) your answers to these questions. For example, if you did not graduate from high school with your class but later fulfilled the requirements to graduate and received a general equivalency diploma (GED), you might well be asked why you dropped out of school. If you have already prepared an answer for this question, it may save you the embarrassment of having to decide, on the spot, how to reduce a complicated story to a brief sentence or two.

You should also prepare yourself to be interviewed by a "team" of legal professionals, such as an attorney and another paralegal or perhaps two or more attorneys and/or paralegals. Many prospective employers today invite others who will be working with a new paralegal to participate in the interviewing process.

Promptness is an extremely important factor. When preparing for an interview, you should therefore do the following:

- **Arrive for the interview at least ten minutes early and allow plenty of extra time to get there. If the firm is located in an area that is unfamiliar to you, make sure that you know how to get there, how long it will take, and, if you are driving, whether parking space is available nearby.**

Appearance is also important. Wear a relatively conservative suit or dress to the interview, and limit your use of jewelry or other flashy accents. You can find further tips on how to prepare for a job interview by checking online career sites or by looking at books dealing with careers and job hunting at a local bookstore or the library.

AT THE INTERVIEW. During the interview, pay attention and listen closely to the interviewer's questions, observations, and comments. The interviewer asks questions to learn whether the candidate will fit comfortably into the firm, whether the candidate is organized and competent and will satisfactorily perform the job, and whether the candidate is reliable and will apply himself or herself to mastering the tasks presented. Your answers should be directly related to the questions, and you should not stray from the point. If you are unsure of what the interviewer means by a certain question, ask for clarification.

EXHIBIT 2.7
Objectionable or Illegal Questions

> **Q. Are you married?**
>
> **A.** If you are concerned about my social life interfering with work, I can assure you that I keep the two very distinct.
>
> **Q. Do you have any children yet?**
>
> **A.** That question leads me to believe that you would be concerned about my ability to prioritize my job and other responsibilities. Is that something that you are worried about?
>
> **Q. Are you or your husband a member of the Republican Party?**
>
> **A.** That is a private matter. Please realize that my family and political life will not interfere with my ability to do excellent work for your firm.
>
> **Q. You're quite a bit more mature than other applicants. Will you be thinking of retiring in the next ten years?**
>
> **A.** I don't understand how my age relates to my ability to perform this job.

Interviewers use certain question formats to elicit certain types of responses. Four typical formats for questions are the following:

- *Closed-ended questions*—to elicit simple "Yes" or "No" answers.
- *Open-ended questions*—which invite you to discuss, in some detail, a specific topic or experience.
- *Hypothetical questions*—to learn how you might respond to situations that could arise during the course of your employment.
- *Pressure questions*—to see how you deal with uncomfortable situations or unpleasant discussions.

You will learn more about these question formats in Chapter 13, when we discuss some techniques that paralegals use when interviewing clients.

Be aware that certain types of questions are illegal, or at least objectionable. These include questions directed at your marital status, family, religion, race, color, national origin, age, health or disability, or arrest record. You do not have to answer such questions unless you choose to do so. Exhibit 2.7 above shows some examples of how you might respond to these types of questions.

As odd as it may seem, one of the most difficult moments is when the interviewer turns the questioning around by asking, "Now then, do you have any questions?" Be prepared for this query. Before the interview, take time to list your concerns. Bring the list to the interview with you. Questioning the interviewer gives you an opportunity to learn more about the firm and how it uses paralegal services. Questioning the interviewer also may also give the interviewer an opportunity to see how you might interview a client on behalf of the firm. Exhibit 2.8 on the next page lists some sample questions that you might ask the interviewer. Note that you should not raise the issue of salary at the first interview unless you are offered the job.

AFTER THE INTERVIEW. You should not expect to be hired as the result of a single interview, although occasionally this does happen. Often, two and maybe three interviews take place before you are offered a job. After leaving the interview, jot down a few notes to provide a refresher for your memory should you be called back for a second (or third) interview. You will impress the interviewer if

EXHIBIT 2.8
Questioning the Interviewer

> **Questions that you might want to ask the interviewer include the following:**
>
> - What is the method by which the firm assigns duties to paralegals?
> - How do paralegals function within the organization?
> - What clerical support staff is available for paralegals?
> - Does the job involve travel? How will travel expenses be covered?
> - What computer technology is used by the firm?
> - Does the firm support paralegal continuing-education and training programs?
> - Will client contact be direct or indirect?
> - Does the firm have an in-house library and access to computerized research services that paralegals can use?
> - Will the paralegal be assigned work in a given specialty, such as real-estate or family law?
> - When does the job begin?
> - What method is used to review and evaluate paralegal performance?
> - How are paralegals supervised and by whom?
> - Are paralegals classified as exempt employees by this firm?

you are able to "pick up where you left off" from a discussion initiated several weeks earlier. Also, list the names and positions of the people you met during the interview or just before or after it.

The Follow-Up Letter

A day or two after the interview, but not longer than a week later, you should send a *follow-up letter* to the interviewer. In this brief letter, you can reiterate your availability and interest in the position, thank the interviewer for his or her time in interviewing you, and perhaps refer to a discussion that took place during the interview.

You may have left the interview with the impression that the meeting went poorly. But the interviewer may have a different sense of what happened at the meeting. Interviewers have different styles, and what you interpreted to be a bad interview may just have been a reflection of that interviewer's particular approach or style. You simply have no way of being certain, so follow through and make yourself available for the job or at least for another meeting. For an example of a follow-up letter, see Exhibit 2.9.

Maintain Job-Hunting Files

In addition to keeping your professional portfolio materials up to date, you need to create a filing system to stay abreast of your job-search activities. You should create a separate file for each potential employer and keep copies of your letters, including e-mail messages, and any responses to that employer in your file. You might also want to keep lists or notes on addresses, telephone numbers, e-mail addresses, dates of contacts, advantages and disadvantages of employment with the various firms that you have contacted or by which you have been interviewed, topics discussed at interviews, and so on. Then, when you are called for an interview, you will have information on the firm at your fingertips. Always keep in mind that when looking for paralegal employment, your "job" is finding work as a paralegal—and it pays to be efficient.

> **EXHIBIT 2.9**
> A Sample Follow-Up Letter

ELENA LOPEZ

1131 North Shore Drive
Nita City, NI 48804
Telephone: (616) 555-0102 • Fax: (616) 555-2103 • E-mail: elopez@nitanet.net

---

September 3, 1999

Mr. Allen P. Gilmore
Jeffers, Gilmore & Dunn
553 Fifth Avenue, Suite 101
Nita City, NI 48801

Dear Mr. Gilmore:

Thank you for taking time out of your busy schedule to meet with me last Thursday about your firm's entry-level paralegal position. I very much enjoyed our discussion, as well as the opportunity to meet some of your firm's employees.

I am extremely interested in the possibility of becoming a member of your legal team and look forward to the prospect of meeting with you again in the near future.

Sincerely yours,

Elena Lopez

Elena Lopez

Your files will also provide you with an excellent resource for networking even after you have a permanent position. The files may also provide useful information for a career change in the future.

Salary Negotiations

Sometimes a firm states a salary or a salary range in its advertisement for a paralegal. During a first interview, a prospective employer may offer that information as well. In other situations, an applicant does not know what the salary for a certain position will be until he or she is offered the job.

When you are offered a job, be prepared for the prospective employer to indicate a salary figure and ask you if that figure is acceptable to you. If it is acceptable, then you have no problem. If you think it is too low, then the situation becomes more delicate. If you have no other job offer and really need a job, you may not want to foreclose this job opportunity by saying that the salary is too low. You might instead tell the prospective employer that the job interests you and that

BENEFITS

What benefits are included? • Will the benefits package include medical insurance? • Life insurance? • Disability insurance? • Dental insurance? • What portion, if any, of the insurance premium will be deducted from your wages? • Is there an employee pension plan? • How many paid vacation days will you have? • Will the firm cover your paralegal association fees? • Will the firm assist you in tuition and other costs associated with continuing paralegal education? • Will the firm assist in day-care arrangements and/or costs? • Will you have access to a company automobile? • Does the firm help with parking expenses (important in major cities)?

CAREER OPPORTUNITIES

Does the position offer you opportunities for advancement? You may be willing to accept a lower salary now if you know that it will increase as you move up the career ladder.

COMPENSATION

Will you receive an annual salary or be paid by the hour? • If you will receive an annual salary, will you receive annual bonuses? • How are bonuses determined? • Is the salary negotiable? (In some large firms and in government agencies, it may not be.)

COMPETITION

How stiff is the competition for this job? If you really want the job and are competing with numerous other candidates for the position, you might want to accept a lower salary just to land the job.

JOB DESCRIPTION

What are the paralegal's duties within the organization? Do you have sufficient training and experience to handle these duties? • Are you under- or overqualified for the job? • Will your skills as a paralegal be utilized effectively? • How hard will you be expected to work? • How much overtime work will likely be required? • How stressful will the job be?

JOB FLEXIBILITY

How flexible are the working hours? • If you work eight hours overtime one week, can you take a (paid) day off the following week? • Can you take time off during periods when the workload is less?

LOCATION

Do you want to live in this community? • What is the cost of living in this area? Remember, a $40,000 salary in New York City, where housing and taxes are very expensive, may not give you as much real income as a $30,000 salary in a smaller, midsized community in the Midwest.

PERMANENCE

Is the job a permanent or temporary position? Usually, hourly rates for temporary assistance are higher than for permanent employees.

TRAVEL

Will you be required to travel? • If so, how often or extensively? • How will travel expenses be handled? Will you pay them up front and then be reimbursed by the employer?

EXHIBIT 2.10
Salary Negotiations:
What Is This Job Worth to You?

you will consider the offer seriously. Also, remember that salary is just one factor in deciding what a job is worth to you. In addition to salary, you need to consider job benefits and other factors, including those listed in Exhibit 2.10 above.

Some prospective employers do not suggest a salary or a salary range but rather ask the job applicant what kind of salary he or she had in mind. You should be prepared for this question and should have researched paralegal salaries in the area.

 Unless you are already familiar with the firm's salary structure, you should research the compensation given to paralegals in similar job situations in your community before you discuss salary with a prospective employer.

You can find information on salaries by checking local, state, and national paralegal compensation surveys. Check first with your local paralegal association to see if it has collected data on local paralegal salaries. You might also find helpful information in your school's placement office.

Suppose that you have found in your research that paralegals in the community usually start at $29,000 but that many with your education and training start at $33,000. If you ask for an annual salary of $35,000, then you may be unrealistically expensive—and the job offer may be lost. If you ask for $33,000, then you are still "in the ballpark"—and you may win the job.

Negotiating salaries can be difficult. On the one hand, you want to obtain a good salary and do not want to underprice your services. On the other hand, overpricing your services may extinguish an employment opportunity or eliminate the possibility of working for an otherwise suitable employer. Your best option might be to state a salary range that is acceptable to you. That way, you are not pinned down to a specific figure. Note, though, that if you indicate an acceptable salary range, you invite an offer of the lowest salary—so the low end of the salary range should be the threshold amount that you will accept.

REEVALUATING YOUR CAREER

Once you have gained experience working as a paralegal, you can undertake the third step in career planning: reevaluation. Assume that you have worked for a long enough period (two to four years, for example) to have acquired experience in certain types of paralegal work. At this point, you should reevaluate your career goals and reassess your abilities based on your accumulated experience.

Paralegals who want to advance in their careers normally have three options: (1) being promoted or transferring to another department or branch office of the firm, (2) moving to another firm—and perhaps another specialty, and (3) going back to school for additional education.

Career Paths

Larger firms often provide career paths for their paralegal employees. Moving from the entry-level position of *legal-assistant clerk* to the position of *legal-assistant manager*, for example, may be one career track within a large law firm. A career track with a state government agency might begin at a *legal-technician* level and advance to a *legal-specialist* level.

Creating Opportunities

Smaller firms, in contrast, usually have no predetermined career path or opportunities for promotion and career advancement. If you are the only paralegal in a small law firm, there will be no specified career path within the firm for you to follow. If you find yourself in this situation, you might consider staying with the firm and creating your own position or career ladder. Moving up the ladder is often a matter of bringing in someone new to assist you with your paralegal responsibilities. Are you prevented from taking on more complicated tasks (which you are capable of performing) because of your heavy workload, much of which could be handled by a paralegal with less experience? Suggest a plan to your employer that shows how you can provide more complex legal services if you delegate many of your existing responsibilities to a new paralegal employee. One of the advantages of working for a small firm is the lack of any set, formal structure for promotions. If the firm is expanding, the paralegal may have significant input into how and to whom responsibilities will be assigned as new people are hired.

You can also create opportunities by acquiring additional education. If you are interested in a particular specialty area, course work in that area, in addition

Today's Professional Paralegal

Conducting a Title Exam

Kim Murphy is a paralegal working for the real-estate law firm of Clark & Clark. Today, Kim is going to the Winston County Register of Deeds office to examine the title to the Spartan Shopping Center, located in Winston County. The owner of the shopping center, one of Clark & Clark's clients, has received an offer to sell the center, which has recently become very valuable. Kim's supervising attorney must prepare an abstract of title, which is a history of who owned the property, when past transfers were made, and other significant events. The abstract will be used to assure the buyer that he or she will receive clear and marketable title to the property.

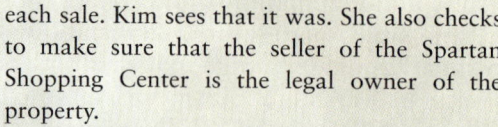

Kim arrives at the county offices. She takes the elevator to the third floor, where the Register of Deeds Office is located. As Kim approaches the counter, a clerk asks her, "What do you need today?" Kim recognizes the clerk, Sam McGrath, who has worked there for as long as Kim has worked for Clark & Clark. He often assists Kim and is very helpful.

"Sam, I need to run a title search and then I need copies of the deeds for the Spartan Shopping Center," responds Kim. "Okay, fill out this form, and I'll run the title search for you on the computer," says Sam. Kim writes down the name and address of the shopping center and hands the form to Sam.

Examining Ownership Records

Sam leaves the counter and goes to a room behind it, which contains computers. He runs the search through the computer that contains all of the records that were originally held in a book called the *Liber*. This is where all of the deeds, liens, and other documents affecting title to real estate are filed. Sam returns with a computerized list and copies of the deeds that show who has owned the property.

Kim thanks Sam and sits down at a nearby table to review the information that Sam has given her. Kim reads through each deed. She checks to see that each deed contains the same description of the property—to ensure that the entire parcel of land was conveyed (transferred) with each sale. Kim sees that it was. She also checks to make sure that the seller of the Spartan Shopping Center is the legal owner of the property.

Checking for Liens

Next, Kim reviews the computer printout for any *liens* (rights of creditors against the property for payment of debts) that might have been filed against the property. Kim notes the mortgage lien, which is normal and expected. Typically, when the purchase of real property is financed by a mortgage loan, the lending institution places a lien on the property until the buyer has made all payments due under the terms of the loan contract. She also notes that the Internal Revenue Service (IRS) has placed a tax lien on the property. A tax lien means that the current owner is behind in the payment of taxes and that the IRS has the right to *foreclose on* (take temporary ownership of) the shopping center and sell it, using the proceeds to pay the overdue taxes. Any remaining proceeds would be returned to the shopping center's owner. If the IRS is not paid at the time of the new mortgage, the IRS will have priority over the new lender. Most lenders will not grant a loan under these circumstances.

The Consequences of the Tax Lien for the Client

Kim realizes that the tax lien creates serious problems for Clark & Clark's client. Once the abstract is prepared, the buyer's attorney will learn about the lien and warn the buyer of the obvious risk. This tax lien must be resolved before Clark & Clark's client can sell the property.

Kim makes a copy of the computer printout and walks over to the cashier to pay for the title search and the copies of the deeds. The cost is $5.00 for the title search and $1.00 for each deed. She makes certain to get a receipt so that she can be reimbursed by the firm for the expense. Kim then returns to the office to inform her supervising attorney of the tax lien.

---

to your existing paralegal training and experience, may help land a job that can advance your career ambitions. Alternatively, you might decide to work toward an advanced degree, such as a master's in business administration (MBA), to create new career opportunities. Some paralegals opt to go to law school and become attorneys.

Other Options

There are many other alternatives. You may apply for a job with another firm that offers you a better position or more advancement opportunities. You might apply for a position that has become available in a branch office of your firm. You might volunteer to speak to paralegal classes and seminars and, in so doing, establish new contacts and contribute to paralegal professional development. Researching and writing law-related articles for your paralegal association's newsletter or trade magazine improves your professional stature in the legal community as well. Any of these activities will increase your visibility both inside and outside the firm. In a broad sense, these activities are part of networking. The people you meet when engaging in these activities may offer you employment opportunities that you did not even know existed but that are perfect for you.

KEY TERMS AND CONCEPTS

bankruptcy law 37
bonus 47
civil law 35
corporate law 36
criminal law 35
defendant 34
elder law 44
environmental law 41
estate planning 39
family law 42
freelance paralegal 33
immigration law 44
independent paralegal 34
intellectual property 40
legal nurse consultant (LNC) 45
litigation 34
litigation paralegal 34
networking 49
overtime wages 47
plaintiff 34
professional portfolio 58
probate 39
probate court 39
real estate 42
trade journal 49
trust 39
will 39
workers' compensation statutes 37

CHAPTER SUMMARY

1. The job opportunities available in today's paralegal employment market are extraordinarily varied. Traditionally, paralegals worked for law firms, and most paralegals continue to work in the law-firm environment. Increasingly, however, paralegals are finding employment in corporate legal departments, as well as other business institutions, such as banks and insurance companies. A growing number of paralegals work for government agencies at the federal or state level. Paralegals also work in law enforcement offices, in courts, in legal aid offices, or in their own businesses, as freelancers.

2. Paralegals often specialize in particular areas of law, including the following areas: litigation assistance, personal-injury law, criminal law, corporate law, bankruptcy law, employment and labor law, estate planning and probate administration, intellectual-property law, environmental law, real-estate law, and family law. Emerging specialty areas include elder law, immigration law, and legal nurse consulting.

3. Salaries and wage rates for paralegal employees vary substantially. Factors affecting compensation include geographical location, firm size, and type of employer (law firm, corporation, or government agency). Many paralegals are salaried—that is, they are paid a specified amount per year, regardless of the number of hours worked. Overtime work is compensated through year-end bonuses or in some other way, such as equivalent time off work. Other paralegals are paid hourly wages for all regular hours worked and overtime wages for all hours worked exceeding forty hours per week.

4. Career planning involves three steps: defining your long-term career goals, devising short-term goals and adjusting those goals to fit job realities, and reevaluating your career and career goals after you have had some on-the-job experience.

5. When looking for employment, you should apply the investigative skills that you learned in your paralegal training. Many paralegals learn of jobs through networking with other professionals. You can begin networking while you are still a paralegal student. You can locate potential employers by reviewing published and posted information about law firms and other possible employers, including information contained in legal trade journals, newspapers, and directories. Using Internet resources is increasingly an efficient means of finding useful information about prospective employers. You should also stay in contact with your school's placement service.

6. In marketing your skills as a paralegal, you will need to submit an application to potential employers. The application documents you create should include a résumé, a cover letter, a list of professional references, and a professional portfolio. The résumé presents a clear and concise summary of your employment and educational history. The cover letter briefly mentions some of your most important qualifications and draws attention to the résumé. The professional portfolio, which you provide at the job interview, contains an additional copy of the résumé, letters of recommendation, brief samples of legal writing, transcripts, and other relevant documents.

7. In preparing for a job interview, you should learn as much about the firm as possible. You should also anticipate questions that might be asked and prepare answers in advance. Make sure that you know how to get to the prospective employer's office, and arrive about ten minutes early. During the interview, listen closely to the questions that are asked. Illegal questions need not be answered, but you should phrase your responses carefully. After the interview, send a follow-up letter to the interviewer. The letter should thank the interviewer for his or her time and reaffirm your interest in the position.

8. Career goals change over time, as do job opportunities. Advancing in your career may mean educating your employer about your abilities so that you can take on more responsibility, looking for a job in a different department or branch office of the same firm or with another firm, or acquiring further education. Active participation in paralegal professional organizations or in paralegal education is a way to achieve higher visibility in the profession and to learn of new professional opportunities.

Questions for Review

1. Name and describe five types of organizations that hire paralegals. What percentage of paralegals work in law firms?

2. From your perspective, what would be the advantages and disadvantages of working for each of the following organizations?
   a. A small law firm.
   b. A large law firm.
   c. A corporation.
   d. A government agency or organization.

3. List and briefly describe each of the paralegal specialties discussed in this chapter. Which specialty area or areas interest you the most? Why?

4. How are paralegals compensated? What is the average paralegal salary in your state? On average, in what specialty area do paralegals receive the highest salaries?

5. What are the advantages of being paid a salary? List some advantages of being paid an hourly wage. What are the disadvantages of each type of paralegal compensation?

6. How can paralegals locate potential employers? Of the methods suggested in this chapter for locating potential employers, which method do you think would be most effective in finding a job? Why?

7. List and describe the materials that are needed for the job-application process.

8. What should you do before a job interview? What types of questions may be asked during a job interview? What steps should you take after a job interview?

9. When are salary arrangements discussed during the job-application process? What factors other than salary should you consider when determining what a job is worth?

10. What are some ways in which you can advance in your paralegal career?

ETHICAL QUESTIONS

1. Tom Brown is a legal assistant in a busy litigation firm. As Tom is walking in the door at 8:30 A.M., he passes Mike Walker, his supervising attorney, who is on his way to court to begin a trial. As they pass, Mike says to Tom, "I need a motion and a brief for the *Jones* case. I've left the file on your desk." Mike walks out the door and down the street to court. Tom becomes very anxious because he knows very little about the case and the law involved. Can Tom competently prepare the motion and brief? Why or why not? What should Tom do?

2. Laura Bronson has just started her first job with the firm of Thompson & Smith, a general law practice. Laura is asked to prepare articles of incorporation for one of the firm's corporate clients. Laura did not take corporate law while studying to be a paralegal and has never prepared articles of incorporation before. Should Laura accept the assignment? If she does accept it, what obligations does she have?

3. Dennis Walker works at a very busy law firm. On each side of his desk, there are one-foot-high stacks of work, leaving only enough room for a small work space in the center of the desk and a spot for the telephone. His floor is likewise stacked high with legal documents. Dennis constantly misses deadlines and is often in trouble for turning work in late or doing work incorrectly. Dennis has tried to get organized but feels that it is impossible to do so because he has such a heavy workload. What are Dennis's ethical obligations in this situation?

PRACTICE QUESTIONS AND ASSIGNMENTS

1. Outside of the traditional law firm, for what types of employers do paralegals work?

2. Using Exhibit 2.5, *A Sample Résumé* prepare a résumé. If access to word-processing software with a variety of fonts and graphics is available, try creating a highly professional résumé using this type of software or other technology that is available.

3. Which of the following factors affect paralegal compensation?

   a. Geographical location.
   b. Job-interview preparation.
   c. Type of employer.
   d. Short-term goals.
   e. Firm size.

QUESTIONS FOR CRITICAL ANALYSIS

1. Do you think that the way paralegals are paid (by annual salary or by hourly wages) affects their attitudes about their work? Would you prefer one of these options over the other? If so, why? Draft a one-page memo to your supervising attorney requesting a change from hourly wages to an annual salary, supporting the request with reasons that will benefit both of you.

2. What are your long-term career goals? Do your short-term goals relate logically to the attainment of your long-term goals? Why or why not? Write one to two paragraphs explaining your long-term goals and how your short-term goals relate to them. Write these paragraphs to a potential employer.

PROJECTS

1. Locate the *Martindale-Hubbel Law Directory* in your school's library or your local law library. Find three law firms in your locale that practice areas of law in which you are interested. Write down the

names and addresses of the firms. Also, try to find the name of the hiring partners or human resources managers whom you could contact about a job in the future. Start your job file today!

2. Find out if your school has a placement office. If so, does it offer professional assistance or workshops in résumé preparation and interviewing? Find out at what point in your education you may use these services. Make a note of this information and keep it in your job file.

3. Ask your program director if your school has a legal-assistant student club and how you can get involved in it. Network with other students, and consider how the club may be used to network on a broader scale—that is, to network with graduates, attorneys, and potential employers.

Using Internet Resources

1. Go on the Internet and access LAWMATCH at www.lawmatch.com, an online résumé bank. How do you use it? Would you post your résumé there? Why or why not? If you are currently looking for a position, try posting your résumé on that site.

2. Visit the Web site of CareerPath at www.careerpath.com. Browse through the site and write a one-page description of its offerings with respect to paralegal careers. Next, click on the box titled "Find Jobs by Newspaper." Conduct a search for jobs in the "legal" category (entering "paralegal" as a key word) that were listed in the most recent Sunday editions of three newspapers in your region. Then answer the following questions:

   a. What were the names and dates of the three newspapers you selected? How many ads for paralegals did you find in these papers?

   b. Were any of the ads for entry-level positions?

   c. What percentage of the ads were for work in law offices? List the other types of firms or organizations that advertised job openings, if there were any.

   d. Select two of the ads that most interest you and write a brief summary of the paralegal responsibilities involved in each job.

   e. Generally, how were interested paralegals directed to respond to the ads? Did any firms invite responses by e-mail?

CHAPTER 3

Ethics and Professional Responsibility

Chapter Outline

◼ Introduction ◼ The Regulation of Attorneys ◼ Attorney Ethics and Paralegal Practice ◼ The Indirect Regulation of Paralegals ◼ The Unauthorized Practice of Law ◼ Should Paralegals Be Licensed? ◼ A Final Note

After completing this chapter, you will know:

- Why and how legal professionals are regulated.
- Some important ethical rules governing the conduct of attorneys.
- How the rules governing attorneys affect paralegal practice.
- The kinds of activities that paralegals are and are not legally permitted to perform.
- Some of the pros and cons of regulation, including the debate over paralegal licensing.

Introduction

As discussed in the previous chapter, paralegals preparing for a career in today's legal arena have a variety of career options. Regardless of which career path you choose to follow, you should have a firm grasp of your state's ethical rules governing the legal profession. When you work under the supervision of an attorney, as most paralegals do, you and the attorney become team members. You will work together on behalf of clients and share in the ethical and legal responsibilities arising as a result of the attorney-client relationship.

In preparing for a career as a paralegal, you must know what these responsibilities are, why they exist, and how they affect you. The first part of this chapter is devoted to the regulation of attorneys because the ethical duties imposed on attorneys by state law affect paralegals as well. If a paralegal violates one of the rules governing attorneys, that violation may result in serious consequences for the client, for the attorney, and for the paralegal. As you read through the rules governing attorney conduct that are discussed in this chapter, keep in mind that these rules also govern paralegal practice, if indirectly.

Although attorneys are subject to direct regulation by the state, paralegals are not—although they may be in the near future, in the form of licensing requirements. Paralegals are regulated indirectly, however, both by attorney ethical codes and by state laws that prohibit nonlawyers from practicing law.[1] As the paralegal profession develops, professional paralegal organizations, the American Bar Association, and state bar associations of attorneys continue to issue guidelines that also serve to indirectly regulate paralegals.

The Regulation of Attorneys

The term *regulate* derives from the Latin term *regula*, meaning "rule." According to Webster's dictionary, to regulate means "to control or direct in agreement with a rule." To a significant extent, attorneys engage in **self-regulation** because they themselves establish the majority of the rules governing their profession. One of the hallmarks of a profession is the establishment of minimum standards and levels of competence that its members should follow. The accounting profession, for example, has established such standards, as have physicians, engineers, and members of virtually every other profession.

Attorneys are also regulated externally by the state, because the rules of behavior established by the legal profession are adopted and enforced by state authorities. The purpose of regulating attorney behavior is to protect the public interest. By establishing educational and licensing requirements, state authorities ensure that anyone practicing law is competent to do so. Second, by defining specific ethical requirements for attorneys, the states protect the public against unethical attorney behavior that may affect clients' welfare. We will discuss these requirements and rules shortly. First, however, you should know how these rules are created and enforced.

Self-Regulation
The regulation of the conduct of a professional group by members of the group themselves. Self-regulation usually involves the establishment of ethical or professional standards of behavior with which members of the group must comply.

---

1. Some legal professionals maintain that statutes that prohibit nonlawyers from practicing law constitute a form of direct regulation, because paralegals who violate such statutes may be directly sanctioned (in the form of criminal penalties) under those laws. In this chapter, we use the term *direct regulation* to mean state regulation of a specified professional group, particularly through state licensing requirements.

Who Are the Regulators?

Key participants in determining what rules should govern attorneys and the practice of law, as well as how these rules should be enforced, are bar associations, state supreme courts, state legislatures, and, in some cases, the United States Supreme Court. Procedures for regulating attorneys vary, of course, from state to state. What follows is a general discussion of some of the possible regulators.

BAR ASSOCIATIONS.   Lawyers themselves determine the requirements for entering the legal profession and the rules of conduct they will follow. Traditionally, lawyers have joined together in professional groups, or bar associations, at the local, state, and national levels to discuss issues affecting the legal profession and to decide on standards of professional conduct.

Although membership in local and national bar associations is always voluntary, membership in the state bar association is mandatory in over two-thirds of the states. In these states, before an attorney can practice law, he or she must be admitted to the state's bar association. Approximately half of the lawyers in the United States are members of the American Bar Association (ABA), the voluntary national bar association discussed in Chapter 1. As you will read shortly, the ABA plays a key regulatory role by proposing model (uniform) codes, or rules of conduct, for adoption by the various states.

On the Web
You can access information on state bar associations, legislatures, and courts, including the United States Supreme Court, at www.findlaw.com. The American Bar Association is online at www.abanet.org.

STATE SUPREME COURTS.   Typically, the state's highest court, often called the state supreme court, is the ultimate regulatory authority in that state.[2] The court's judges decide what conditions (such as licensing requirements, discussed below) must be met before an attorney can practice law within the state and under what conditions that privilege will be suspended or revoked. In many states, the state supreme court works closely with the state bar association. The state bar association may recommend rules and requirements to the court. If the court so orders, these rules and requirements become state law. Under the authority of the courts, state bar associations often perform routine regulatory functions, including the initiation of disciplinary proceedings against attorneys who fail to comply with professional requirements.

STATE LEGISLATURES.   State legislatures regulate the legal profession by enacting legislation affecting attorneys—statutes prohibiting the unauthorized practice of law, for example. In a few states, the states' highest courts delegate significant regulatory responsibilities to the state legislatures, which may include the power to bring disciplinary proceedings against attorneys.

THE UNITED STATES SUPREME COURT.   Occasionally, the United States Supreme Court decides issues relating to attorney conduct. For example, until a few decades ago, state ethical codes, or rules governing attorney conduct, prohibited lawyers from advertising their services to the public. These restrictions on advertising were challenged as an unconstitutional limitation on attorneys' rights to free speech, and ultimately, the United States Supreme Court decided the issue. In a case decided in 1977, *Bates v. State Bar of Arizona,*[3] the Supreme Court ruled that truthful advertising of the availability and price of routine legal services was protected speech

---

2. There are exceptions, however. In some states, a lower state appellate court performs this function.
3. 433 U.S. 350, 97 S.Ct. 2691, 53 L.Ed.2d 810 (1977). (See Chapter 14 for a discussion of how to read case citations.)

under the First Amendment to the U.S. Constitution and that provisions of state ethical codes forbidding such advertising were therefore unconstitutional.

Licensing Requirements

Licensing
A government's official act of granting permission to an individual, such as an attorney, to do something that would be illegal in the absence of such permission.

The **licensing** of attorneys, which gives them the right to practice law, is accomplished at the state level. Each state has different requirements that individuals must meet before they are allowed to practice law and give legal advice. Generally, however, there are three basic requirements:

1. In most states, prospective attorneys must have obtained a bachelor's degree from a university or college[4] and must have graduated from an accredited law school (in many states, the school must be accredited by the ABA), which requires an additional three years of study.
2. In all states, a prospective attorney must pass a state bar examination—a very rigorous and thorough examination that tests the candidate's knowledge of the law and (in some states) the state's ethical rules governing attorneys. The examination covers both state law (law applicable to the particular state in which the attorney is taking the exam and wishes to practice) and multistate law (law applicable in most states, including federal law).[5]
3. The candidate must pass an extensive personal background investigation to verify that he or she is a responsible individual and otherwise qualifies to engage in an ethical profession. An illegal act committed by the candidate in the past, for example, might disqualify the individual from being permitted to practice law.

Only when these requirements have been met can an individual be admitted to the state bar and legally practice law within the state.

Licensing requirements for attorneys are the result of a long history of attempts to restrict entry into the legal profession. The earliest of these restrictions date to the colonial era. During the 1700s, local bar associations began to form agreements to restrict membership to those who fulfilled certain educational and apprenticeship requirements. At the same time, to curb unnecessary litigation and the detrimental effects of incompetent legal practitioners, courts began to require that individuals representing clients in court proceedings had to be licensed by the court to do so.

Beginning in the mid-1850s, restrictions on who could (or could not) practice law were given statewide effect by state statutes prohibiting the **unauthorized practice of law (UPL)**. Court decisions relating to unauthorized legal practice also date to this period. By the 1930s, virtually all states had enacted legislation prohibiting anyone but licensed attorneys from practicing law. As you will see in subsequent sections, many of the regulatory issues facing the legal profession—and particularly paralegals—are directly related to these UPL statutes.

Unauthorized Practice of Law (UPL)
The act of engaging in actions defined by a legal authority, such as a state legislature, as constituting the "practice of law" without legal authorization to do so.

Ethical Codes and Rules

The legal profession is also regulated through ethical codes and rules adopted by each state—in most states, by order of the state supreme court. These codes of pro-

---

4. In some states, including Vermont, one need not have completed a bachelor's degree but must have completed a specified number of credits toward a degree.
5. Note that a few states allow individuals who have not attended law school but who have undertaken a form of independent study and practice (usually as paralegals) to take the bar exam and be admitted to the practice of law.

fessional conduct—the names of the codes vary from state to state—evolved over a long period of time. A major step toward ethical regulation was taken in 1908, when the ABA approved the Canons of Ethics, which consisted of thirty-two ethical principles. In the following decades, various states adopted these canons as law.

Today's state ethical codes are based, for the most part, on two subsequent revisions of the ABA canons: the Model Code of Professional Responsibility (published in 1969) and the Model Rules of Professional Conduct (published in 1983 to replace the Model Code). Although most of the states have now adopted the 1983 revision, the 1969 code is still in effect in some states, so you should be familiar with the basic format and content of both the Model Code and the Model Rules.

On the Web
To find out which code of ethics your state has adopted, go to www.legalethics.com/states.htm.

THE MODEL CODE OF PROFESSIONAL RESPONSIBILITY. The ABA Model Code of Professional Responsibility, often referred to simply as the Model Code, consists of nine canons. In the Model Code, each canon is followed by sections entitled "Ethical Considerations" (ECs) and "Disciplinary Rules" (DRs). The ethical considerations are "aspirational" in character—that is, they suggest ideal conduct, not behavior that is necessarily required by law. For example, Canon 6 ("A lawyer should represent a client competently") is followed by EC 6–1, which states (in part) that a lawyer "should strive to become and remain proficient in his practice." In contrast, disciplinary rules are mandatory in character—an attorney may be subject to disciplinary action for breaking one of the rules. For example, DR 6–101 (which follows Canon 6) states that a lawyer "shall not . . . [n]eglect a legal matter entrusted to him."

THE MODEL RULES OF PROFESSIONAL CONDUCT. The 1983 revision of the Model Code—referred to as the Model Rules of Professional Conduct or, more simply, as the Model Rules—represented a thorough revamping of the code. The Model Rules replaced the canons, ethical considerations, and disciplinary rules of the Model Code with a set of rules organized under eight general headings, as outlined in Exhibit 3.1 on the next page. Each rule is followed by comments shedding additional light on the rule's application and how it compares with the Model Code's treatment of the same issue.

Sanctions for Violations

Attorneys who violate the rules governing professional conduct are subject to disciplinary proceedings brought by the state bar association, state supreme court, or state legislature—depending on the state's regulatory scheme. In most states, unethical attorney actions are reported (by clients, legal professionals, or others) to the ethics committee of the state bar association, which is obligated to investigate each complaint thoroughly. For serious violations, the state bar association or the court initiates disciplinary proceedings against the attorney.

Sanctions range from a **reprimand** (a formal "scolding" of the attorney—the mildest sanction[6]) to **suspension** (a more serious sanction by which the attorney is prohibited from practicing law in the state for a given period of time, such as one month or one year, or for an indefinite period of time) to **disbarment** (revocation of the attorney's license to practice law in the state—the most serious sanction).

Reprimand
A disciplinary sanction in which an attorney is rebuked for his or her misbehavior. Although a reprimand is the mildest sanction for attorney misconduct, it is nonetheless a serious one and may significantly damage the attorney's reputation in the legal community.

Suspension
A serious disciplinary sanction in which an attorney who has violated an ethical rule or a law is prohibited from practicing law in the state for a specified or an indefinite period of time.

Disbarment
A severe disciplinary sanction in which an attorney's license to practice law in the state is revoked because of unethical or illegal conduct.

---

6. Even this mildest sanction can seriously damage an attorney's reputation within the legal community. In some states, state bar associations publish in their monthly journals the names of violators and details of the violations for all members of the bar to read (see the discussion of attorney disciplinary proceedings in the feature *Today's Professional Paralegal* at the end of this chapter).

EXHIBIT 3.1
The ABA Model Rules of Professional Conduct (Headings Only)

CLIENT-LAWYER RELATIONSHIP

1.1	Competence
1.2	Scope of Representation
1.3	Diligence
1.4	Communication
1.5	Fees
1.6	Confidentiality of Information
1.7	Conflict of Interest: General Rule
1.8	Conflict of Interest: Prohibited Transactions
1.9	Conflict of Interest: Former Client
1.10	Imputed Disqualification: General Rule
1.11	Successive Government and Private Employment
1.12	Former Judge or Arbitrator
1.13	Organization as Client
1.14	Client under a Disability
1.15	Safekeeping Property
1.16	Declining or Terminating Representation

COUNSELOR

2.1	Advisor
2.2	Intermediary
2.3	Evaluation for Use by Third Persons

ADVOCATE

3.1	Meritorious Claims and Contentions
3.2	Expediting Litigation
3.3	Candor toward the Tribunal
3.4	Fairness to Opposing Party and Counsel
3.5	Impartiality and Decorum of the Tribunal
3.6	Trial Publicity
3.7	Lawyer as Witness
3.8	Special Responsibilities of a Prosecutor
3.9	Advocate in Nonadjudicative Proceedings

TRANSACTIONS WITH PERSONS OTHER THAN CLIENTS

4.1	Truthfulness in Statement to Others
4.2	Communication with Person Represented by Counsel
4.3	Dealing with Unrepresented Person
4.4	Respect for Rights of Third Persons

LAW FIRMS AND ASSOCIATIONS

5.1	Responsibilities of a Partner or Supervisory Lawyer
5.2	Responsibilities of a Subordinate Lawyer
5.3	Responsibilities Regarding Nonlawyer Assistants
5.4	Professional Independence of a Lawyer
5.5	Unauthorized Practice of Law
5.6	Restrictions on Right to Practice

PUBLIC SERVICE

6.1	*Pro Bono Publico* Service
6.2	Accepting Appointments
6.3	Membership in Legal Services Organization
6.4	Law Reform Activities Affecting Client Interests

INFORMATION ABOUT LEGAL SERVICES

7.1	Communications Concerning a Lawyer's Services
7.2	Advertising
7.3	Direct Contact with Prospective Clients
7.4	Communication of Fields of Practice
7.5	Firm Names and Letterheads

MAINTAINING THE INTEGRITY OF THE PROFESSION

8.1	Bar Admission and Disciplinary Matters
8.2	Judicial and Legal Officials
8.3	Reporting Professional Misconduct
8.4	Misconduct
8.5	Jurisdiction

© 1999. Reprinted by permission of the American Bar Association. Copies of the ABA Model Rules of Professional Conduct (1999) are available from Service Center, American Bar Association, 750 North Lake Shore Drive, Chicago, IL 60611, 312-988-5522. Courtesy: National Federation of Paralegal Associations, Inc.

In addition to these sanctions, attorneys may be subject to civil liability for negligence. As will be discussed in Chapter 7, *negligence* (called **malpractice** when committed by a professional, such as an attorney) is a tort (a wrongful act) that is committed when an individual fails to perform a legally recognized duty. Tort law allows one who is injured by another's wrongful or careless act to bring a civil lawsuit against the wrongdoer for **damages** (compensation in the form of money). Of course, a client is permitted to bring a lawsuit against an attorney only if the client has suffered harm because of the attorney's failure to perform a legal duty.

If a paralegal's breach of a professional duty causes a client to suffer substantial harm, the client may sue not only the attorney but also the paralegal. Although law firms' liability insurance policies typically cover paralegals as well as attorneys, if the paralegal is working on a contract (freelance) basis, he or she will not be covered under a liability policy covering the firm's employees. Just one lawsuit could ruin a freelance paralegal financially—as well as destroy that paralegal's reputation in the legal community. (Note that liability insurance is especially important for independent paralegals, or legal technicians, as well.)

Attorneys and paralegals are also subject to potential criminal liability under criminal statutes prohibiting fraud, theft, and other crimes.

Malpractice
Professional misconduct or negligence—the failure to exercise due care—on the part of a professional, such as an attorney or a physician.

Damages
Money sought as a remedy for a civil wrong, such as a breach of contract or a tortious act.

ATTORNEY ETHICS AND PARALEGAL PRACTICE

The state ethical codes are fairly uniform because they are patterned after either the Model Code or the Model Rules (except in California and Florida, whose codes depart significantly from the ABA's models). Because most state codes are guided by the Model Rules of Professional Conduct, the rules discussed in this section are drawn from the Model Rules. Keep in mind, though, the following important guideline:

 Your own state's code of conduct is the governing authority on attorney conduct in your state.

As a paralegal, one of your foremost professional responsibilities is to meticulously follow the rules set forth in your state's ethical code. You will thus want to obtain a copy of your state's ethical code and become familiar with its contents. A good practice is to keep the code near at hand in your office (or on your desk).

Professional duties—and the possibility of violating them—are involved in virtually every task you will perform as a paralegal. Even if you memorize every one of the rules governing the legal profession, you can still quite easily unintentionally violate a rule (you should realize that paralegals rarely breach professional duties intentionally). To minimize the chances that you will unintentionally violate a rule, you need to know not only what the rules are but also how they apply to the day-to-day realities of your job.

The rules relating to competence, confidentiality, and conflict of interest deserve special attention here because they pose particularly difficult ethical problems for paralegals. Other important rules that affect paralegal performance—including the duty to charge reasonable fees, the duty to protect clients' property, and the duty to keep the client reasonably informed—will be discussed elsewhere in this text as they relate to special topics.

The Duty of Competence

The first of the Model Rules states one of the most fundamental duties of attorneys—the duty of competence. Rule 1.1 of the Model Rules reads as follows:

A lawyer shall provide competent representation to a client. Competent representation requires the legal knowledge, skill, thoroughness and preparation reasonably necessary for representation.

Competent legal representation is a basic requirement of the profession, and **breaching** (failing to perform) this duty may subject attorneys to one or more of the sanctions discussed earlier. As a paralegal, you should realize that when you undertake work on an attorney's behalf, you share in this duty. If your supervising attorney asks you to research a particular legal issue for a client, for example, you must make sure that your research is careful and thorough—because the attorney's reputation (and the client's welfare) may depend on your performance. You should also realize that careless conduct of the research, if it results in substantial injury to the client's interests, may subject you personally to liability for negligence, not to mention the loss of a job or career opportunities.

Breach
To violate a legal duty by an act or a failure to act.

HOW THE DUTY OF COMPETENCE CAN BE BREACHED. Most breaches of the duty of competence are inadvertent. Often, breaches of the duty of competence have to do with missed deadlines. Paralegals frequently work on several cases simultaneously, and keeping track of every deadline in every case can be challenging—especially for paralegals who are pressed for time.

Organization is the key to making sure that all deadlines are met. All important dates relating to every case or client should be entered on a calendar. Larger firms typically use computerized calendaring and "tickler" (reminder) systems. Even the smallest firm normally has calendaring procedures and tickler systems in place. In addition to making sure that all deadlines are entered into the appropriate systems, you may want to have your own personal calendar for tracking dates that are relevant to the cases on which you are working—and then make sure that you consistently use it. You should develop a habit of checking your calendar every morning when you arrive at work or some other convenient time. Also, you should check frequently with your attorney about deadlines that he or she may not have mentioned to you.

On the Web
The Web sites of the two national paralegal associations, the National Association of Legal Assistants (NALA) and the National Federation of Paralegal Associations (NFPA), are good sources for information on the ethical responsibilities of paralegals, including new, technology-related ethical challenges. You can access NALA's site at **www.nala.org**. The URL for NFPA'S site is **www.paralegals.org**.

The duty of competence can also be breached in numerous other ways. For example, erroneous information might be included (or crucial information omitted) in a legal document to be filed with the court. If the attorney fails to notice the error before signing the document, and the document is delivered to the court containing the erroneous information, a breach of the duty of competence has occurred. Depending on its legal effect, this breach may expose the attorney and the paralegal to liability for negligence. To prevent these kinds of violations, you need to be especially careful in drafting and proofreading documents.

Generally, if you are ever unsure about what to include in a document, when it must be completed or filed with the court, how extensively you should research a legal issue, or any other aspect of an assignment, you should ask your supervising attorney for special instructions. You should also make sure that your work is adequately overseen by your attorney, to reduce the chances that it will contain costly mistakes or errors.

INADEQUATE SUPERVISION. Rule 5.3 of the Model Rules defines the responsibilities of attorneys in regard to nonlawyer assistants. This rule states, in part, that "A lawyer should give . . . assistants appropriate instruction and supervision. . . . The measures employed in supervising nonlawyers should take account of the fact that they do not have legal training and are not subject to professional discipline." The rule also states that "a lawyer shall be responsible for the conduct of [a nonlawyer] that would be a violation of the rules of professional conduct if engaged in by a lawyer."

> # ETHICAL CONCERN
> ## Missed Deadlines
>
> As a paralegal, you will find that one of your most useful allies is a calendar. Consistently entering important deadlines on a calendaring system (computerized or otherwise) will help to ensure that you and your supervising attorney do not breach the duty of competence simply because a document was not filed with the court on time. For example, if a *complaint* (the document that initiates a lawsuit—see Chapter 10) is served on one of your firm's clients, you must file with the court the client's *answer* to the complaint within a specified number of days. If you fail to file the answer during that time period, the court could enter a judgment in favor of the party bringing the lawsuit. As you might imagine, the consequences of this judgment—called a *default judgment*—can be extremely detrimental to the client. As a paralegal, you need to be aware of the seriousness of the consequences of missed deadlines for your clients, especially the consequences of failing to file an answer on time.

Because attorneys have a duty to supervise nonlawyer assistants and are held legally responsible for their assistants' work, it may seem logical to assume that attorneys will take time to direct that work carefully. In fact, paralegals may find it difficult to ensure that their work is adequately supervised. For one thing, most paralegals are kept very busy, and making sure that all their tasks are properly overseen can be time consuming. Similarly, an attorney often does not want to take the time to read through every document drafted by his or her paralegal—particularly if the attorney knows that the paralegal is competent. Nonetheless, as a paralegal, you have a duty to assist your supervising attorney in fulfilling his or her ethical obligations, including the attorney's obligation to supervise your work.

If you ever feel that your attorney is not adequately supervising your work, there are several things you can do. You can try to improve communications with the attorney—generally, the more you communicate with your supervising attorney, the more likely it is that the attorney will take an active role in directing your activities. You can also ask the attorney for feedback on your work. Sometimes, it helps to place reminders on your personal calendar to discuss particular issues or questions with the attorney. Then, when an opportunity to talk to him or her arises, these issues or questions will be fresh in your mind. Another tactic is to attach a note to a document that you have prepared for the attorney, requesting him or her to review the document (or revised sections of the document) carefully before signing it.

Confidentiality of Information

Rule 1.6 of the Model Rules concerns attorney-client confidentiality. The rule of confidentiality is one of the oldest and most important rules of the legal profession, primarily because it would be difficult for a lawyer to properly represent a client without such a rule. A client must be able to confide in his or her attorney so that the attorney can best represent the client's interest. Because confidentiality is one of the easiest rules to violate, a thorough understanding of the rule is essential.

The general rule of confidentiality, as stated in the first paragraph of Rule 1.6, is that all information relating to the representation of a client must be kept confidential

Developing Paralegal Skills

Inadequate Supervision

Michael Patton is a paralegal in a small, busy, general practice law firm. His supervising attorney, Muriel Chapman, answers his question about the amount of temporary alimony to be inserted into the judgment of divorce that he is preparing. She tells Michael that the $5,000 figure is the total amount, not the annual amount. Next, Michael requests that Muriel review the judgment before it is signed by the parties and filed with the court. Muriel tells Michael that she does not need to review his work—she is confident that he has prepared the document correctly because he always asks questions when he is uncertain. Michael remembers the adequate supervision rule and asks Muriel again to review his work. She finally agrees, stating, "You know, Michael, you are rather persistent in making me do 'the right thing.'"

Tips for Obtaining Adequate Supervision

- Request your supervising attorney to review your work.
- Use notes or ticklers as reminders to ask for a review.
- Make the review as convenient as possible for your supervising attorney.
- Discuss your ethical concerns with the attorney.
- Be persistent.

---

unless the client consents to disclosure. Note that the rule does not make any qualifications about what kind of information is confidential. It simply states that a lawyer may not reveal "information relating to representation of a client."

Does this mean that if a client tells you that he is the president of a local company, you have to keep that information confidential, even when the whole community knows that fact? For example, could you tell your spouse, "Mr. X is the president of XYZ Corporation"? It may seem permissible, because that fact is, after all, public knowledge. But in so doing, you must not indicate, by words or conduct, that Mr. X is a client of your firm. In such a situation, it is hard to know just what assumptions might be made based on what you have said. Consider another example. Suppose that one evening at dinner you told your spouse that you had met Mr. X that day. Your spouse might reasonably assume that your firm was handling some legal matter involving Mr. X. Because it may be difficult to decide what information is or is not confidential, a good rule of thumb is the following:

 Paralegals should regard all information about a client or a client's case as confidential information.

EXCEPTIONS TO THE RULE. Rule 1.6 provides for certain exceptions, each of which we look at here.

Client Consents to the Disclosure. Paragraph (a) of the rule indicates that an attorney may reveal confidential information if the client consents to the disclosure. For example, suppose that an attorney is drawing up a will for a client, and the client is making his only son the sole beneficiary under the will and leaving nothing to his daughter. The daughter calls and wants to know how her father's will reads. The attorney cannot divulge this confidential information to the daughter because the client has not consented to such disclosure. Now suppose that the client told the attorney that if his daughter calls the attorney to find out if she inherited anything under the will, the attorney is to "go ahead and tell her that she gets nothing." In this situation, the attorney could disclose the information because the client consented to the disclosure.

Impliedly Authorized Disclosures. Paragraph (a) of Rule 1.6 also states that an attorney may make "disclosures that are impliedly authorized in order to carry out the representation." The latter exception is clearly necessary. Legal representation of clients necessarily involves the attorney's assistants, and they must have access to the confidential information to do their jobs. If a paralegal is working on the client's case, for example, he or she must know what the client told the attorney about the legal matter and must have access to information in the client's file concerning the case.

Client Intends a Harmful Act. Paragraph (b) of Rule 1.6 provides for two other exceptions. The first exception applies when a client reveals that he or she intends to commit a criminal act that may cause bodily harm or death to another. In this situation, the policy underlying the rule of confidentiality (protection of the client's legal rights) is outweighed by the policy of protecting another from imminent bodily harm or death.

The problem with this exception is that it is sometimes difficult to determine whether the client really intends to do what he or she threatens. Also, it is not always clear whether a client's intended behavior is in fact a criminal act that will result in bodily harm or death to another. If you are ever confronted with a situation in which you suspect that a client is about to harm another, discuss the matter immediately with your supervising attorney; he or she will decide what should be done.

Defending against a Client's Legal Action. The second exception in paragraph (b) of Rule 1.6 is particularly important for attorneys and paralegals. The classic example of this exception is a client's malpractice suit against an attorney. In this situation, it is essential for the lawyer to reveal confidential information to prove that he or she was not negligent. Note, though, that the attorney is permitted to disclose confidential information only to the extent that it is essential to defend against the lawsuit.

VIOLATIONS OF THE CONFIDENTIALITY RULE. Paralegals, like other professionals, spend a good part of their lives engaged in their work. Naturally, they are tempted to discuss their work at home, with spouses and family members, or with others, such as co-workers and good friends. As a paralegal, perhaps one of the greatest temptations you will face is the desire to discuss a particularly interesting case, or some aspect of a case, with someone you know. You can deal with this temptation in two ways: you can decide, as a matter of policy, never to discuss anything concerning your work; or you can limit your discussion to issues and comments that will not reveal the identity of your client. The latter approach is, for many paralegals, a more realistic solution, but it requires great care. Something you say may reveal a client's identity, even though you are not aware of it.

Conversations Overheard by Others. Violations of the confidentiality rule may happen simply by oversight. For example, suppose that you and the legal secretary in your office are both working on the same case and continue, as you walk down the hallway toward the elevator, a conversation about the case that you started in the office. You pause in front of the elevator, not realizing that your

Developing Paralegal Skills
Client Intends to Commit a Crime

Samantha Serles, a legal assistant with a degree in psychology, is meeting with a client whom her firm is defending. The client, Jim Storming, has been charged with the murder of his mother-in-law. Samantha's job is to assess the client's mental state and consider whether he needs further evaluation. Samantha begins talking to Jim. She asks him how things are going and how he feels. He rolls his eyes at her questions and says, "How do you think I feel, being locked up in this place?" She decides to try to talk to him about the crime. "Jim," she says, "have you thought any more about how your mother-in-law died and about what happened that night?" "Yeah," he says. "I've thought about it plenty. I killed her, you know. But they aren't going to be able prove that I did it."

Samantha just listens as he continues. "I hated her. She talked my wife into divorcing me, and then she and  my ex-wife turned my kids against me. I'm going to get even with my ex-wife for that, too. I've been talking to some guys in here. They told me how I can have her taken care of while I'm in here. Then I won't have to take the rap for that one either." Samantha has seen enough to know that Jim needs psychiatric evaluation.

CHECKLIST FOR DETERMINING WHETHER A CLIENT INTENDS A HARMFUL ACT
- Is the threat one of a criminal act?
- If so, is it one that would cause bodily harm or death to another?
- Is the threat real?
- Always inform your supervising attorney of the threat.

Third Parties
Persons or entities that are not directly involved in an agreement (such as a contract), legal proceeding (such as a lawsuit), or relationship (such as an attorney-client relationship).

conversation is being overheard by someone around the corner from you. You have no way of knowing the person is there, and you have no way of knowing whether the confidential information that you inadvertently revealed will have any adverse effect on your client's interests. One way to avoid the possibility of unwittingly revealing confidential information to **third parties** is to follow this rule of thumb:

 Never discuss confidential information when you are in a common area, such as a hallway, an elevator, or a cafeteria, where a conversation might be overheard.

Electronic Communications and Confidentiality. Whenever you talk to or about a client on the telephone, make sure that your conversation will not be overheard by a third party. You may be sitting in your private office, but if your door is open, someone may overhear the conversation. Paralegals should take special care when using cellular phones. Cellular phones are not secure; conversations on such phones can be picked up by anyone in the vicinity with a scanner. As a precaution, you should thus never disclose confidential information when talking on a cellular phone. Because of the widespread use of mobile phones, paralegals today often, as a routine precaution, ask a client who is calling whether he or she is calling from a mobile unit. If the client is using a mobile phone, the paralegal can caution the client that confidential information should not be discussed.

Even such a simple operation as sending a fax can pose ethical pitfalls. Generally, you should exercise great care to make sure that you (1) send the fax to the right person (for example, when a letter is addressed to an opposing party in a lawsuit but is supposed to be sent to the client for his or her approval) and (2) dial the correct fax number.

> ### ETHICAL CONCERN
> ### Social Events and Confidentiality
>
> Assume that you are at a party with some other paralegals. You tell a paralegal whom you know quite well of some startling news—that a client of your firm, a prominent city official, is being investigated for drug dealing. Although your friend promises to keep this information strictly confidential, she nonetheless relays it to her husband, who in turn tells a co-worker, who in turn tells a friend, and so on. Within a few days, the news has reached the press, and the resulting media coverage results in irreparable harm to the official's reputation and standing in the community. If it can be proved that the harm is the direct result of your breach of the duty of confidentiality, the official could sue both you and the attorney for whom you work for damages.

You also need to be cautious when sending e-mail messages. For example, suppose that you are asked by your supervising attorney to send an e-mail message to a client and to attach a document containing the attorney's analysis of confidential information submitted by the client. The client's e-mail address is in your e-mail "address book," along with other numbers. You click on the client's name, type a brief message, attach the document, and click "send." Too late, you realize that you accidentally clicked on the opposing counsel's name instead of your client's. By a click of the mouse, you have disclosed important confidential information. To avoid this kind of problem, before you click "send," you should take a minute to review not only the message—grammar, sentence structure, and spelling—but also to verify the recipient's name and/or address. (For a further discussion of confidentiality problems posed by the use of e-mail, see the feature *Technology and Today's Paralegal: Is E-Mail "Confidential"?*)

Other Ways of Violating the Confidentiality Rule. There are numerous other ways in which you can reveal confidential information without intending to do so. A file or document sitting on your desk, if observed by a third party, may reveal the identity of a client or enough information to suggest the client's identity. A computer screen, if visible to those passing by your desk, could convey information to someone who is not authorized to know that information.

Confidentiality and the Attorney-Client Privilege

All information relating to a client's representation is considered confidential information. Some confidential information also qualifies as privileged information, or information subject to the **attorney-client privilege**.

The attorney-client privilege can be vitally important during the litigation process. As you will read in Chapter 10, prior to a trial each attorney is permitted to obtain information relating to the case from the opposing attorney and other persons, such as witnesses. This means that attorneys must exchange a certain amount of information relating to their clients. An attorney need not divulge privileged information, however—unless the client consents to the disclosure or a court orders the disclosure. Similarly, if an attorney is called to the witness stand

On the Web
A good site for updates on how technology affects the responsibilities of legal professionals is the Web site of Law Journal EXTRA! at www.ljx.com/practice/ professionalresponsibility.

Attorney-Client Privilege
A rule of evidence requiring that confidential communications between a client and his or her attorney (relating to their professional relationship) be kept confidential, unless the client consents to disclosure.

TECHNOLOGY AND TODAY'S PARALEGAL
Is E-Mail "Confidential"?

The widespread use of the Internet by lawyers and paralegals has raised a host of ethical issues, many of which you will read about in later chapters of this book. Here we look at a question of particular importance to all legal professionals, including paralegals: Does communicating with a client via e-mail constitute a violation of the confidentiality rule?

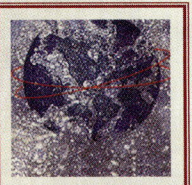

Although the courts have not yet addressed this question, bar associations in several states have rendered ethical opinions on the subject. Among the first to do so was South Carolina, which concluded in 1994 that lawyers should not use e-mail for sensitive client communications because it is possible for e-mail to be intercepted. For the next few years, there seemed to be a growing consensus that only encrypted communications (encoded messages, using encryption software) with clients could be considered confidential.

Since 1997, however, several states have reached the opposite conclusion. For example, when the Vermont state bar's ethics panel considered the issue recently, it reasoned that since "(a) e-mail privacy is no less to be expected than in ordinary phone calls, and (b) unauthorized interception is illegal, a lawyer does not violate [the confidentiality rule] by communicating with a client by e-mail . . . without encryption." The panel went on to say that in various instances "of a very sensitive nature, encryption might be prudent, in which case ordinary phone calls would obviously be deemed inadequate." This reasoning is typical of state bar ethics committees in some other states, including Illinois, Arizona, and even South Carolina—which reversed its earlier opinion when it revisited the issue in 1997.

Despite this trend toward acknowledging e-mail as a confidential medium, as a paralegal you should be very cautious when communicating with clients over the Internet. In one of its two cyberspace ethics opinions, the National Federation of Paralegal Associations (NFPA) advised paralegals that the best way to avoid possible confidentiality problems is to simply not put any confidential information on the Internet. NFPA also suggested that legal professionals take other steps, such as considering encryption for e-mail with clients, establishing procedures and policies on the topic for all office personnel to follow, and using disclaimers in e-mail messages to indicate that the communications may not be secure.

---

during a trial, the attorney may not disclose privileged information unless the court orders him or her to do so.

WHAT KIND OF INFORMATION IS PRIVILEGED? State statutes and court cases define what constitutes privileged information. Generally, any communications concerning a client's legal rights or problem fall under the attorney-client privilege. For example, suppose that an attorney's client is a criminal defendant. The client tells the attorney that she was actually in the vicinity of the crime site at the time of the crime, but to her knowledge, no one noticed her presence there. This is privileged information that the attorney may only disclose with the client's consent or on a court's order to do so.

Other types of information, although confidential, are not necessarily privileged. For example, information relating to a client's identity is usually not privileged. Nor, as a rule, is information concerning client fees. Furthermore, information concerning the client's personal or business affairs is not privileged unless it is related to the legal claim. For example, suppose that a client who is bringing a malpractice suit against a physician mentions to the attorney that he is divorcing his wife. Unless the client's divorce is related in some way to the malpractice suit being handled by the attorney, the information about the divorce normally is not considered privileged.

ETHICAL CONCERN
Personal versus Professional Ethics

What happens when a paralegal's personal ethical standards come into conflict with a professional duty, such as the duty of confidentiality? When this dilemma faced Merrell Williams, a paralegal with the Kentucky law firm of Wyatt, Tarrant & Combs, he decided to violate the duty of confidentiality to satisfy his conscience. From 1988 to 1992, he took over 4,000 pages of confidential documents belonging to his firm's client, tobacco manufacturer Brown & Williamson (B&W), and gave them to the press and others. The documents immediately became a "smoking gun" for antismoking forces involved in litigation against the tobacco industry.

To some, Williams is a hero. After all, he sacrificed his job and faced a lawsuit by his former employer (which was settled in 1997) to help protect the public against the dangers of smoking. To others, Williams's actions were wrongful. Essentially, the question boils down to this: Is it ever in the public interest for a legal professional to violate an ethical duty, particularly when that duty was established by the legal profession to further its goal of protecting the public?

Certain materials relating to an attorney's preparation of a client's case for trial are protected as privileged information under what is known as the **work product** doctrine. Usually, information concerning an attorney's legal strategy for conducting a case is classified as work product and, as such, may be subject to the attorney-client privilege. Legal strategy includes the legal theories that the attorney plans to use in support of the client's claim, how the attorney interprets the evidence relating to the claim, and so on. Certain evidence gathered by the attorney to support the client's claim, however, such as financial statements relating to the client's business firm, would probably not be classified as work product. Because it is often difficult to tell what types of information (including work product) qualify as privileged, paralegals should consult closely with their supervising attorneys whenever issues arise that may require that such a distinction be made.

Work Product
An attorney's mental impressions, conclusions, and legal theories regarding a case being prepared on behalf of a client. Work product normally is regarded as privileged information.

WHEN THE ATTORNEY-CLIENT PRIVILEGE ARISES. The attorney-client privilege comes into existence the moment a client communicates with an attorney concerning a legal matter. People sometimes mistakenly assume that there is no duty to keep client information confidential unless an attorney agrees to represent a client and the client signs a retainer agreement. This is not so.

 The privilege—and thus the duty of confidentiality—arises even if the lawyer decides not to represent the client and even when the client is not charged any fee.

DURATION OF THE PRIVILEGE. The client is the holder, or "owner," of the privilege, and only the client can waive (set aside) the privilege. Unless waived by the client, the privilege lasts indefinitely. In other words, the privilege continues even though an attorney has completed the client's legal matter and is no longer working on the case. As with all confidential information relating to a client's case, privileged information is subject to the exceptions to the confidentiality rule discussed above.

Additionally, always keep in mind that privileged information is *confidential* information. If confidential information is disclosed to others, it is no longer "confidential" and can no longer be considered privileged information. This is another reason why it is so important to guard against accidental violations of the confidentiality rule: if the rule is violated, information that otherwise might have been protected by the attorney-client privilege can be used in court, which may be harmful to the the client's interests. For example, consider the e-mail example given earlier, in which the paralegal inadvertently sent a confidential document to opposing counsel instead of the client. The document, because it contained the attorney's analysis of confidential client information, might be classified as privileged information under the work product doctrine. The disclosure of the information to the opposing counsel destroyed its confidential character—and therefore any possibility that it might be protected as privileged information.

Conflict of Interest

If an attorney engages in an activity that adversely affects a client's interests (such as simultaneously representing opposing parties in a legal proceeding), the attorney faces a **conflict of interest.** Model Rules 1.7, 1.8, 1.9, and 1.10 all pertain to conflict-of-interest situations. Rule 1.7 states the general rule: "A lawyer shall not represent a client if the representation of the client will be directly adverse to another client."

A classic example of a conflict of interest exists when an attorney simultaneously represents two adverse parties in a legal proceeding. Clearly, in such a situation, the attorney's loyalties must be divided. It would be as if a football player agreed to play on both teams during a game—half of the time with one team and half with the other.

SIMULTANEOUS REPRESENTATION. If an attorney decides that representing two parties in a legal proceeding will not adversely affect either party's interest, then the attorney is permitted to do so—but only if both parties agree. Normally, attorneys avoid this kind of situation because what might start out as a simple, uncontested proceeding may evolve into a legal battle. Divorce proceedings, for example, may begin amicably but end up in heated disputes over child-custody arrangements or property division. The attorney then faces a conflict of interest: assisting one party will necessarily be adverse to the interests of the other. Note that because of the potential for a conflict of interest in divorce proceedings, some courts do not permit attorneys to represent both spouses, even if the spouses consent to such an arrangement.

Similar conflicts arise when the "family attorney" is asked to handle a family matter and the family members eventually disagree on what the outcome should be. For example, consider a situation in which two adult children request the family lawyer to handle the procedures required to settle their deceased parent's estate. The parent's will favors one of the children, and the other child decides to challenge the will's validity. The attorney cannot represent both sides in this dispute without facing a conflict of interest.

Attorneys representing corporate clients may face conflicts of interest when corporate personnel become divided on an issue. For example, assume that ABC Corporation has retained Carl Finn, an attorney, to represent the corporation. Finn typically deals with the corporation's president, Julie Johnson, when rendering legal assistance and advice. At times, however, Finn deals with other corporate personnel, including Seth Harrison, the corporation's accountant. Harrison and Johnson disagree with each other on several major issues, and eventually

---

Conflict of Interest
A situation in which two or more duties or interests come into conflict, as when an attorney attempts to represent opposing parties in a legal dispute.

Johnson arranges to have Harrison fired. Harrison wants attorney Finn to represent him in a lawsuit against the corporation for wrongful termination of his employment. Finn now faces a conflict of interest.

FORMER CLIENTS.   A conflict of interest may also involve former clients. Model Rule 1.9 states that "[a] lawyer who has formerly represented a client in a matter shall not thereafter represent another person in the same or substantially related matter in which that person's interests are materially adverse to the interests of the former client unless the former client consents after consultation." The rule regarding former clients is closely related to the rule on preserving the confidentiality of a client. The rationale behind the rule is that an attorney, in representing a client, is entrusted with certain information that may be unknown to others, and that information should not be used against the client—even after the represention has ended.

For example, assume that a year ago an attorney defended a company against a lawsuit for employment discrimination brought by one of the company's employees. During the course of the representation, the attorney learned a great deal about the company. Now, someone who was injured while using one of that same company's products consults with the attorney about the possibility of bringing a product-liability lawsuit against the company. The attorney normally must refuse to represent this person. Because the attorney has confidential information about the company that could be used to harm the company's interest, a conflict of interest exists.

Job Changes and Former Clients.   The rule concerning former clients does not prohibit an individual from working at a firm or agency that may represent interests contrary to those of a former client. If that were the situation, many of those who have worked for very large firms would be unable ever to change jobs. Generally, the rules vary, depending on the specific circumstances. In some situations, when a conflict of interest results from a job change, the new employer can avoid violating the rules governing conflict of interest through the use of screening procedures. The new employer can erect an impenetrable screen, referred to as an **ethical wall,** around the new employee so that the new employee remains ignorant about the case giving rise to the conflict of interest.

Walling-Off Procedures.   Law offices usually have special procedures for "walling off" an attorney or other legal professional from a case when a conflict of interest exists. The firm may announce in a written memo to all employees that a certain attorney or paralegal should not have access to specific files, for example, and may set out procedures to be followed to ensure that access to those files is restricted. Computer documents relating to the case may be protected by warning messages or in some other way. Commonly, any hard-copy files relating to the case are flagged with a sticker to indicate that access to the files is restricted.

Firms normally take great care to establish such procedures and observe them carefully, because if confidential information is used in a way harmful to a former client, the firm may be sued by the client and have to pay steep damages. In defending against such a suit, the firm will need to demonstrate that it took reasonable precautions to protect that client's interests.

OTHER CONFLICT-OF-INTEREST SITUATIONS.   There are several other types of situations that may give rise to conflicts of interest. Gifts from clients may create conflicts of interest, because they tend to bias the judgment of the attorney or paralegal. Some types of gifts are specifically prohibited. For example, Rule 1.8(c)

Ethical Wall
A term that refers to the procedures used to create a screen around a legal employee to shield him or her from information about a case in which there is a conflict of interest.

DEVELOPING PARALEGAL SKILLS
Building an Ethical Wall

Lana Smith, a paralegal, has been asked by her supervising attorney to set up an ethical wall because a new attorney, Sandra Piper, has been hired from the law firm of Nunn & Bush. While employed by Nunn & Bush, Piper represented the defendant, Seski Manufacturing, in the ongoing case of *Tymes v. Seski Manufacturing Co.* Lana's firm represents the plaintiff, Joseph Tymes, in that same case, so Piper's work for Nunn & Bush creates a conflict of interest. Lana makes a list of the walling-off procedures to use to ensure that the firm cannot be accused of violating the rules on conflict of interest.

CHECKLIST FOR BUILDING AN ETHICAL WALL
- Prepare a memo to the office manager regarding the conflict and the need for special arrangements.
- Prepare a memo to the team representing Tymes to inform them of the conflict of interest and the special procedures to be used.
- Prepare a memo to the firm, giving the case name, the nature of the conflict, the parties involved, and instructions to maintain a blanket of silence with respect to Sandra Piper.
- Arrange for Piper's office to be on a different floor from the team to demonstrate, if necessary, that the firm took steps to prevent Piper and the team from having access to one another or each other's files.
- Arrange with the office manager for special computer passwords to be issued to the team members so that access to computer files on the *Tymes* case is restricted to team members only.
- Place "ACCESS RESTRICTED" stickers on the files for the *Tymes* case.
- Develop a security procedure for signing out and tracking the case files in the *Tymes* case—to prevent inadvertent disclosure of the files to Piper or her staff members.

of the Model Rules of Professional Conduct prohibits an attorney from preparing documents (such as wills) for a client that gives the attorney or a member of the attorney's family a gift. (An exception to this rule exists, of course, when the attorney is a relative of the client.) Note that as a paralegal, you may be offered gifts from appreciative clients at Christmas or other times. Generally, such gifts pose no ethical problems. If a client offers you a gift that has substantial value, however, you should discuss the issue with your supervising attorney.

Attorneys also need to be careful about taking on a client whose case may create an "issue conflict" for the attorney. Generally, an attorney cannot represent a client with respect to a substantive legal issue if the client's position is directly contrary to that of another client being represented by the lawyer—or the lawyer's firm—in a case being brought within the same jurisdiction (the geographic area or subject matter over which a specific court has authority to decide legal disputes). The reason for this rule, which is set forth in Model Rule 1.7 and has been clarified by an opinion on the matter issued by the American Bar Association (ABA),[7] is that courts are obligated to follow precedents—earlier decisions on cases involving similar facts and issues (see Chapter 5). The court's ruling in one of the attorney's cases could therefore alter the outcome of the other case.

Occasionally, conflicts of interest may arise when two family members who are both attorneys or paralegals are involved in the representation of adverse parties in a legal proceeding. Model Rule 1.8(i) prohibits an attorney from representing a client if the adverse party to the dispute is being represented by a member of the attorney's family (such as a spouse, parent, child, or sibling). If you, as a

---
7. American Bar Association Formal Opinion 93–377, October 16, 1993.

paralegal, are married to or living with another paralegal or an attorney, you should inform your firm of this fact if you ever suspect that a conflict of interest might result from your relationship.

CONFLICTS CHECKS. Whenever a potential client consults with an attorney, the attorney will want to make sure that no potential conflict of interest exists before deciding whether to represent the client. Running a **conflicts check** is a standard procedure in the law office and one that is frequently undertaken by paralegals. Before you can run a conflicts check, you need to know the name of the prospective client, the other party or parties that may be involved in the client's legal matter, and the legal issue involved. Normally, every law firm has some established procedure for conflicts checks, and in larger firms there is usually a computerized database containing the names of former clients and the other information you will need in checking for conflicts of interest.

Conflicts Check
A procedure for determining whether an agreement to represent a potential client will result in a conflict of interest.

THE INDIRECT REGULATION OF PARALEGALS

Paralegals are regulated *indirectly* in several ways. Clearly, the ethical codes for attorneys just discussed indirectly regulate the conduct of paralegals. Additionally, paralegal conduct is regulated indirectly by standards and guidelines created by paralegal professional groups as well as guidelines for the utilization of paralegals developed by the American Bar Association and various states.

Paralegal Ethical Codes

In addition to indirect regulation through attorney ethical codes, paralegals are becoming increasingly self-regulated. Recall from Chapter 1 that the two major national paralegal associations in the United States—the National Federation of Paralegal Associations, or NFPA, and the National Association of Legal Assistants, or NALA—were formed to define and represent paralegal professional interests on a national level. Shortly after they were formed, both of these associations adopted codes of ethics defining the ethical responsibilities of paralegals.

NFPA's CODE OF ETHICS. In 1977, NFPA adopted its first code of ethics, called the Affirmation of Responsibility, which has since been revised several times and, in 1993, was renamed the Model Code of Ethics and Professional Responsibility. In 1997, NFPA revised the code, particularly its format, and took the bold step of appending to its code a set of enforcement guidelines setting forth recommendations on how to discipline paralegals who violate ethical standards promulgated by the code. The full title of NFPA's current code is "Model Code of Ethics and Professional Responsibility and Guidelines for Enforcement."

Exhibit 3.2 on pages 92–94 presents the preamble to the revised document as well as Section 1, which contains the ethical standards under the title, "NFPA Model Disciplinary Rules and Ethical Considerations." (For the full text of the code, including Section 2, which consists of the enforcement guidelines, see Appendix C at the end of this text.)

NALA's CODE OF ETHICS. In 1975, NALA issued its Code of Ethics and Professional Responsibility, which, like NFPA's code, has since undergone several revisions. Exhibit 3.3 on page 95 presents NALA's code in its entirety. Note that NALA's code, like the Model Code of Professional Responsibility discussed earlier in this chapter, presents ethical precepts as a series of "canons." (Prior to the 1997 revision of its code, NFPA also listed its ethical standards as "canons.")

On the Web
You can find NALA'S Code of Ethics and Professional Responsibility online at www.nala.org/stand.htm.

FEATURED GUEST: MICHAEL A. PENER
Ten Tips for Ethics and the Paralegal

BIOGRAPHICAL NOTE

Michael A. Pener developed the Paralegal Program at Johnson County Community College in 1977. It was approved by the American Bar Association (ABA) in 1980. He was the program's first director and continued in that capacity until 1987, when he became one of its full-time professors. Pener is one of the founders of the American Association for Paralegal Education (AAfPE). He served on its initial board of directors and, in 1985 and 1986, as its president. He is a long-time member of the Ethics Advisory Services Committee and Legal Assistant Committee of the Kansas Bar Association (KBA). *Starting in 1992, he served for three years as one of the AAfPE's representatives on the Approval Commission of the ABA Standing Committee on Legal Assistants.*

As a legal-assistant educator and practicing attorney, I have developed several ethics-related "truths" for my students that I think are essential for their professional survival as working legal assistants. Each of these truths is important, and the legal assistant must adhere to all of them if he or she wants to avoid, or lessen the impact of, situations involving ethical problems. While I believe the following tips will keep you out of trouble, no list of this type is ever complete without your own input—so use it to develop ethical "rules" appropriate for your work and legal practice area.

1. Obtain Copies of State and Local Ethical Rules. Keep up with current state ethical rules for attorneys and paralegals and continually review their application in cases, disciplinary proceedings, and ethical opinions of local, state, and national lawyer associations. Specifically, there are now many guidelines on major areas of concern to the legal profession, including the use of legal assistants by lawyers, confidentiality, the unauthorized practice of law, conflicts of interest, and legal competence.

2. Attend Continuing Legal Education (CLE) Programs on Legal Ethics. In many states, lawyers are required to have CLE hours on legal ethics. Attending CLE programs not only reminds you of what the rules require but also helps you remain current in ethical developments within the profession.

3. Network with Other Legal Assistants. Network with other legal assistants through local paralegal organizations and education programs and through the National Federation of Paralegal Associations and the National Association of Legal Assistants. Both of the national organizations have professional ethical codes and are involved in court cases affecting paralegals.

4. Make No Assumptions about Others. In an ideal world, all legal professionals would act ethically at all times. In such a world, there would be no need for rules to govern attorney behavior and no need for disciplinary actions. As a paralegal, you may encounter situations in which you suspect unethical behavior on the part of someone with whom you work. Ignor-

On the Web
You can find NFPA's Model Code of Ethics and Professional Responsibility and Guidelines for Enforcement on the Web at **www.paralegals.org/ Development/ modelcode.html.**

COMPLIANCE WITH PARALEGAL CODES OF ETHICS. Paralegal codes of ethics state the ethical responsibilities of paralegals generally, but they particularly apply to members of paralegal organizations that have adopted the codes. Any paralegal who is a member of an organization that has adopted one of these codes is expected to comply with the code's requirements. Note that compliance with these codes is not legally mandatory. In other words, if a paralegal does not abide by a particular ethical standard of a paralegal association's code of ethics, the association cannot initiate state-sanctioned disciplinary proceedings against the paralegal. The association can, however, expel the paralegal from the association, which may have significant implications for the paralegal's future career opportunities.

FEATURED GUEST, Continued

ing unethical behavior will not necessarily make it go away. Always keep your professional ethical requirements in mind; at times, this may mean you need to discuss the matter with someone in authority.

5. Double-Check Your Work. Expect the unexpected, especially when dealing with unfamiliar matters or with strangers. Don't assume that the documents you produce will be checked for accuracy by others. As a legal assistant, you will need to pay the utmost attention to detail and double-check everything that you do to make sure it is accurate. Also, make sure that all written communications are sent to the proper person.

6. Review All Documents That You Receive. When documents are being exchanged in the drafting stage with opposing counsel or during negotiations, always review the documents that you receive in their entirety.

7. Anticipate and Prepare for Ethical Problems. Anticipate and prepare for situations in your work and professional relationships that may give rise to ethical problems. In this chapter, you will encounter a number of "real-life" situations that will test your understanding and application of legal ethics. Study them carefully, because they most likely will happen to you. Also, note that clients want to know how their legal matters are progressing, but lawyers are sometimes too busy to attend to their clients' needs in this respect. Legal assistants may end up communicating more frequently with clients than attorneys do. If the lawyer for whom you work puts you in this role, you should feel complimented by the lawyer's confidence in you. Watch out, however, for a client who becomes overly dependent on you and your judgment. Very soon he or she may be asking you for your "legal opinion" and guidance in dealing with the lawyer. If you respond to this, you will get into trouble very quickly.

8. Use Caution When Notarizing Documents or Signing Documents as a Witness. If you are a notary public, only notarize those documents that were signed in your presence. As a notary public, you have a statutory requirement to perform the duties of your appointed office. Failure to act as required may subject you to personal liability. This means that you must refuse a lawyer's request to notarize a document that was not signed in your presence. Similarly, never sign any

> "Ignoring unethical behavior will not necessarily make it go away."

document as a witness without first reviewing it to make sure that your signature is properly requested.

9. Maintain a Balance Between Personal and Legal Ethics. Try to maintain a proper balance between your personal ethics and legal ethics. This may be the most difficult thing for you to do. You may be a party to confidential communications by clients that concern unethical, and even immoral, behavior on their part. Your law firm may have a policy or engage in an activity that is acceptable by legal ethical standards but that you personally consider to be unethical. Professionally, you must accept this. If you personally cannot, then you may have no other choice but to seek employment elsewhere.

10. Rely on Your Common Sense and Intuition. Use your common sense and intuition. Develop an awareness of what is right and wrong behavior in any given situation and then seek the answer to any legal ethical problem that you encounter.

Guidelines for the Utilization of Paralegals

As mentioned earlier in this chapter, the reason attorneys are regulated by the state is to protect the public from the harms that could result from incompetent legal advice and representation. Licensing requirements for attorneys thus serve the public interest. At the same time, they give lawyers something of a monopoly over the delivery of legal services—a monopoly that, in turn, may have detrimental effects on those who cannot afford to pay attorneys for their services. The increased use of paralegals stems, in part, from the legal profession's need to reduce the cost of legal services. The use of paralegals to do substantive legal work

EXHIBIT 3.2
NFPA's Code of Ethics and Professional Responsibility and Guidelines for Enforcement (Preamble and Section 1 Only)

Courtesy: National Federation of Paralegal Associations, Inc.

MODEL CODE OF ETHICS AND PROFESSIONAL RESPONSIBILITY AND GUIDELINES FOR ENFORCEMENT

PREAMBLE

The National Federation of Paralegal Associations, Inc. ("NFPA") is a professional organization comprised of paralegal associations and individual paralegals throughout the United States and Canada. Members of NFPA have varying backgrounds, experiences, education and job responsibilities that reflect the diversity of the paralegal profession. NFPA promotes the growth, development and recognition of the paralegal profession as an integral partner in the delivery of legal services.

In May 1993 NFPA adopted its Model Code of Ethics and Professional Responsibility ("Model Code") to delineate the principles for ethics and conduct to which every paralegal should aspire.

Many paralegal associations throughout the United States have endorsed the concept and content of NFPA's Model Code through the adoption of their own ethical codes. In doing so, paralegals have confirmed the profession's commitment to increase the quality and efficiency of legal services, as well as recognized its responsibilities to the public, the legal community, and colleagues.

Paralegals have recognized, and will continue to recognize, that the profession must continue to evolve to enhance their roles in the delivery of legal services. With increased levels of responsibility comes the need to define and enforce mandatory rules of professional conduct. Enforcement of codes of paralegal conduct is a logical and necessary step to enhance and ensure the confidence of the legal community and the public in the integrity and professional responsibility of paralegals.

In April 1997 NFPA adopted the Model Disciplinary Rules ("Model Rules") to make possible the enforcement of the Canons and Ethical Considerations contained in the NFPA Model Code. A concurrent determination was made that the Model Code of Ethics and Professional Responsibility, formerly aspirational in nature, should be recognized as setting forth the enforceable obligations of all paralegals.

The Model Code and Model Rules offer a framework for professional discipline, either voluntarily or through formal regulatory programs.

§1. NFPA MODEL DISCIPLINARY RULES AND ETHICAL CONSIDERATIONS

1.1 A PARALEGAL SHALL ACHIEVE AND MAINTAIN A HIGH LEVEL OF COMPETENCE.

Ethical Considerations

EC-1.1(a) A paralegal shall achieve competency through education, training, and work experience.

EC-1.1(b) A paralegal shall participate in continuing education in order to keep informed of current legal, technical and general developments.

EC-1.1(c) A paralegal shall perform all assignments promptly and efficiently.

1.2 A PARALEGAL SHALL MAINTAIN A HIGH LEVEL OF PERSONAL AND PROFESSIONAL INTEGRITY.

Ethical Considerations

EC-1.2(a) A paralegal shall not engage in any ex parte communications involving the courts or any other adjudicatory body in an attempt to exert undue influence or to obtain advantage or the benefit of only one party.

EC-1.2(b) A paralegal shall not communicate, or cause another to communicate, with a party the paralegal knows to be represented by a lawyer in a pending matter without the prior consent of the lawyer representing such other party.

EC-1.2(c) A paralegal shall ensure that all timekeeping and billing records prepared by the paralegal are thorough, accurate, honest, and complete.

EC-1.2(d) A paralegal shall not knowingly engage in fraudulent billing practices. Such practices may include, but are not limited to: inflation of hours billed to a client or employer; misrepresentation of the nature of tasks performed; and/or submission of fraudulent expense and disbursement documentation.

EC-1.2(e) A paralegal shall be scrupulous, thorough and honest in the identification and maintenance of all funds, securities, and other assets of a client and shall provide accurate accounting as appropriate.

> EC-1.2(f) A paralegal shall advise the proper authority of non-confidential knowledge of any dishonest or fraudulent acts by any person pertaining to the handling of the funds, securities or other assets of a client. The authority to whom the report is made shall depend on the nature and circumstances of the possible misconduct (e.g., ethics committees of law firms, corporations and/or paralegal associations, local or state bar associations, local prosecutors, administrative agencies, etc.). Failure to report such knowledge is in itself misconduct and shall be treated as such under these rules.
>
> **1.3 A PARALEGAL SHALL MAINTAIN A HIGH STANDARD OF PROFESSIONAL CONDUCT.**
>
> *Ethical Considerations*
>
> EC-1.3(a) A paralegal shall refrain from engaging in any conduct that offends the dignity and decorum of proceedings before a court or other adjudicatory body and shall be respectful of all rules and procedures.
>
> EC-1.3(b) A paralegal shall avoid impropriety and the appearance of impropriety and shall not engage in any conduct that would adversely affect his/her fitness to practice. Such conduct may include, but is not limited to: violence, dishonesty, interference with the administration of justice, and/or abuse of a professional position or public office.
>
> EC-1.3(c) Should a paralegal's fitness to practice be compromised by physical or mental illness, causing that paralegal to commit an act that is in direct violation of the Model Code/Model Rules and/or the rules and/or laws governing the jurisdiction in which the paralegal practices, that paralegal may be protected from sanction upon review of the nature and circumstances of that illness.
>
> EC-1.3(d) A paralegal shall advise the proper authority of non-confidential knowledge of any action of another legal professional that clearly demonstrates fraud, deceit, dishonesty, or misrepresentation. The authority to whom the report is made shall depend on the nature and circumstances of the possible misconduct, (e.g., ethics committees of law firms, corporations and/or paralegal associations, local or state bar associations, local prosecutors, administrative agencies, etc.). Failure to report such knowledge is in itself misconduct and shall be treated as such under these rules.
>
> EC-1.3(e) A paralegal shall not knowingly assist any individual with the commission of an act that is in direct violation of the Model Code/Model Rules and/or the rules and/or laws governing the jurisdiction in which the paralegal practices.
>
> EC-1.3(f) If a paralegal possesses knowledge of future criminal activity, that knowledge must be reported to the appropriate authority immediately.
>
> **1.4 A PARALEGAL SHALL SERVE THE PUBLIC INTEREST BY CONTRIBUTING TO THE DELIVERY OF QUALITY LEGAL SERVICES AND THE IMPROVEMENT OF THE LEGAL SYSTEM.**
>
> *Ethical Considerations*
>
> EC-1.4(a) A paralegal shall be sensitive to the legal needs of the public and shall promote the development and implementation of programs that address those needs.
>
> EC-1.4(b) A paralegal shall support bona fide efforts to meet the need for legal services by those unable to pay reasonable or customary fees; for example, participation in pro bono projects and volunteer work.
>
> EC-1.4(c) A paralegal shall support efforts to improve the legal system and access thereto and shall assist in making changes.
>
> **1.5 A PARALEGAL SHALL PRESERVE ALL CONFIDENTIAL INFORMATION PROVIDED BY THE CLIENT OR ACQUIRED FROM OTHER SOURCES BEFORE, DURING, AND AFTER THE COURSE OF THE PROFESSIONAL RELATIONSHIP.**
>
> *Ethical Considerations*
>
> EC-1.5(a) A paralegal shall be aware of and abide by all legal authority governing confidential information in the jurisdiction in which the paralegal practices.
>
> EC-1.5(b) A paralegal shall not use confidential information to the disadvantage of the client.
>
> EC-1.5(c) A paralegal shall not use confidential information to the advantage of the paralegal or of a third person.

EXHIBIT 3.2

NFPA's Code of Ethics and Professional Responsibility and Guidelines for Enforcement (Preamble and Section 1 Only)—Continued

EXHIBIT 3.2

NFPA's Code of Ethics and Professional Responsibility and Guidelines for Enforcement (Preamble and Section 1 Only)—Continued

EC-1.5(d) A paralegal may reveal confidential information only after full disclosure and with the client's written consent; or, when required by law or court order; or, when necessary to prevent the client from committing an act that could result in death or serious bodily harm.

EC-1.5(e) A paralegal shall keep those individuals responsible for the legal representation of a client fully informed of any confidential information the paralegal may have pertaining to that client.

EC-1.5(f) A paralegal shall not engage in any indiscreet communications concerning clients.

1.6 A PARALEGAL SHALL AVOID CONFLICTS OF INTEREST AND SHALL DISCLOSE ANY POSSIBLE CONFLICT TO THE EMPLOYER OR CLIENT, AS WELL AS TO THE PROSPECTIVE EMPLOYERS OR CLIENTS.

Ethical Considerations

EC-1.6(a) A paralegal shall act within the bounds of the law, solely for the benefit of the client, and shall be free of compromising influences and loyalties. Neither the paralegal's personal or business interest, nor those of other clients or third persons, should compromise the paralegal's professional judgment and loyalty to the client.

EC-1.6(b) A paralegal shall avoid conflicts of interest that may arise from previous assignments, whether for a present or past employer or client.

EC-1.6(c) A paralegal shall avoid conflicts of interest that may arise from family relationships and from personal and business interests.

EC-1.6(d) In order to be able to determine whether an actual or potential conflict of interest exists a paralegal shall create and maintain an effective recordkeeping system that identifies clients, matters, and parties with which the paralegal has worked.

EC-1.6(e) A paralegal shall reveal sufficient non-confidential information about a client or former client to reasonably ascertain if an actual or potential conflict of interest exists.

EC-1.6(f) A paralegal shall not participate in or conduct work on any matter where a conflict of interest has been identified.

EC-1.6(g) In matters where a conflict of interest has been identified and the client consents to continued representation, a paralegal shall comply fully with the implementation and maintenance of an Ethical Wall.

1.7 A PARALEGAL'S TITLE SHALL BE FULLY DISCLOSED.

Ethical Considerations

EC-1.7(a) A paralegal's title shall clearly indicate the individual's status and shall be disclosed in all business and professional communications to avoid misunderstandings and misconceptions about the paralegal's role and responsibilities.

EC-1.7(b) A paralegal's title shall be included if the paralegal's name appears on business cards, letterhead, brochures, directories, and advertisements.

EC-1.7(c) A paralegal shall not use letterhead, business cards or other promotional materials to create a fraudulent impression of his/her status or ability to practice in the jurisdiction in which the paralegal practices.

EC-1.7(d) A paralegal shall not practice under color of any record, diploma, or certificate that has been illegally or fraudulently obtained or issued or which is misrepresentative in any way.

EC-1.7(e) A paralegal shall not participate in the creation, issuance, or dissemination of fraudulent records, diplomas, or certificates.

1.8 A PARALEGAL SHALL NOT ENGAGE IN THE UNAUTHORIZED PRACTICE OF LAW.

Ethical Considerations

EC-1.8(a) A paralegal shall comply with the applicable legal authority governing the unauthorized practice of law in the jurisdiction in which the paralegal practices.

EXHIBIT 3.3

NALA's Code of Ethics and Professional Responsibility

© 1975, 1977, 1994 National Association of Legal Assistants, Inc. Reprinted with permission.

A legal assistant must adhere strictly to the accepted standards of legal ethics and to the general principles of proper conduct. The performance of the duties of the legal assistant shall be governed by specific canons as defined herein so justice will be served and goals of the profession attained. (See Model Standards and Guidelines for Utilization of Legal Assistants, Section II.)

The canons of ethics set forth hereafter are adopted by the National Association of Legal Assistants, Inc., as a general guide intended to aid legal assistants and attorneys. The enumeration of these rules does not mean there are not others of equal importance although not specifically mentioned. Court rules, agency rules and statutes must be taken into consideration when interpreting the canons.

Definition: Legal assistants, also known as paralegals, are a distinguishable group of persons who assist attorneys in the delivery of legal services. Through formal education, training and experience, legal assistants have knowledge and expertise regarding the legal system and substantive and procedural law which qualify them to do work of a legal nature under the supervision of an attorney.

Canon 1.
A legal assistant must not perform any of the duties that attorneys only may perform nor take any actions that attorneys may not take.

Canon 2.
A legal assistant may perform any task which is properly delegated and supervised by an attorney, as long as the attorney is ultimately responsible to the client, maintains a direct relationship with the client, and assumes professional responsibility for the work product.

Canon 3.
A legal assistant must not: (a) engage in, encourage, or contribute to any act which could constitute the unauthorized practice of law; and (b) establish attorney-client relationships, set fees, give legal opinions or advice or represent a client before a court or agency unless so authorized by that court or agency; and (c) engage in conduct or take any action which would assist or involve the attorney in a violation of professional ethics or give the appearance of professional impropriety.

Canon 4.
A legal assistant must use discretion and professional judgment commensurate with knowledge and experience but must not render independent legal judgment in place of an attorney. The services of an attorney are essential in the public interest whenever such legal judgment is required.

Canon 5.
A legal assistant must disclose his or her status as a legal assistant at the outset of any professional relationship with a client, attorney, a court or administrative agency or personnel thereof, or a member of the general public. A legal assistant must act prudently in determining the extent to which a client may be assisted without the presence of an attorney.

Canon 6.
A legal assistant must strive to maintain integrity and a high degree of competency through education and training with respect to professional responsibility, local rules and practice, and through continuing education in substantive areas of law to better assist the legal profession in fulfilling its duty to provide legal service.

Canon 7.
A legal assistant must protect the confidences of a client and must not violate any rule or statute now in effect or hereafter enacted controlling privileged communications.

Canon 8.
A legal assistant must do all other things incidental, necessary, or expedient for the attainment of the ethics and responsibilities as defined by statute or rule of court.

Canon 9.
A legal assistant's conduct is guided by bar associations' codes of professional responsibility and rules of professional conduct.

benefits clients because the hourly rate for paralegals is, of course, substantially lower than that for attorneys.

For this reason, bar associations (and courts, when approving fees) encourage attorneys to delegate work to paralegals whenever feasible to lower the costs of legal services for clients—and thus provide the public with greater access to legal services. In fact, some courts, when determining awards of attorneys' fees, have refused to approve fees at the attorney's hourly rate for work that could have been performed by a paralegal at a lower rate.

NALA, the ABA, and many of the states have adopted guidelines for the utilization of paralegal services. These guidelines were created in response to a variety of questions concerning the role and function of paralegals within the legal arena that had arisen during the 1970s and 1980s, including the following: What are paralegals? What kinds of tasks do they perform? What are their professional responsibilities? How can attorneys best utilize paralegal services? What responsibilities should attorneys assume with respect to their assistants' work?

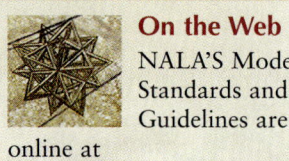

On the Web
NALA'S Model Standards and Guidelines are online at www.nala.org/stand.htm.

NALA'S MODEL STANDARDS AND GUIDELINES. In 1984, NALA adopted its Model Standards and Guidelines for the Utilization of Legal Assistants. This document addresses and provides guidance on several issues of paramount importance to legal assistants today. It begins by listing the minimum qualifications that legal assistants should have and then, in a series of guidelines, indicates what legal assistants may and may not do. We will examine these guidelines in more detail shortly. (See Appendix B for the complete text of the annotated version of NALA's Model Standards and Guidelines, as revised in 1997.)

THE ABA'S MODEL GUIDELINES. The ABA adopted its Model Guidelines for the Utilization of Legal Assistant Services in 1991. The ABA Standing Committee on Legal Assistants, which drafted the guidelines, based them on the NALA guidelines, various state codes and guidelines on the use of paralegals, and relevant state court decisions. The document consists of ten guidelines, each of which is followed by a lengthy comment on the derivation, scope, and application of the guideline. The ten guidelines are presented in Exhibit 3.4. (For reasons of space, Exhibit 3.4 presents only the guidelines; for the comments, refer to the version of the Model Guidelines in Appendix D of this text.)

STATE GUIDELINES. Over two-thirds of the states have adopted some form of guidelines concerning the use of legal assistants by attorneys, the respective responsibilities of attorneys and legal assistants in performing legal work, the types of tasks paralegals may perform, and other ethically challenging areas of legal practice. Although the guidelines of some states reflect the influence of NALA's standards and guidelines, the state guidelines focus largely on state statutory definitions of the practice of law, state codes of ethics regulating the responsibilities of attorneys, and state court decisions. As a paralegal, you should make sure that you become familiar with your state's guidelines.

The Increasing Scope of Paralegal Responsibilities

The ethical standards and guidelines just discussed, as well as court decisions concerning paralegals, all support the goal of increasing the use of paralegals in the delivery of legal services. Today, paralegals can perform virtually any legal task as long as the work is supervised by an attorney and does not constitute the unauthorized practice of law (to be discussed shortly). Guideline 2 of the ABA's Model Guidelines indicates the breadth of paralegal responsibilities:

EXHIBIT 3.4
The ABA's Model Guidelines for the Utilization of Legal Assistant Services (Comments Not Included)

© 1999. Reprinted by permission of the American Bar Association. Annotations and commentary to the Guidelines are not included in this Exhibit. A copy of the Guidelines with annotations and commentary is available through the ABA Legal Assistants Department staff office. Phone: (312) 988-5616; Fax: (312) 988-5677; E-mail: legalassts@abanet.org.

Guideline 1: A lawyer is responsible for all of the professional actions of a legal assistant performing legal assistant services at the lawyer's direction and should take reasonable measures to ensure that the legal assistant's conduct is consistent with the lawyer's obligations under the ABA Model Rules of Professional Conduct.

Guideline 2: Provided the lawyer maintains responsibility for the work product, a lawyer may delegate to a legal assistant any task normally performed by the lawyer except those tasks proscribed to one not licensed as a lawyer by statute, court rule, administrative rule or regulation, controlling authority, the ABA Model Rules of Professional Conduct, or these Guidelines.

Guideline 3: A lawyer may not delegate to a legal assistant:
(a) Responsibility for establishing an attorney-client relationship.
(b) Responsibility for establishing the amount of a fee to be charged for a legal service.
(c) Responsibility for a legal opinion rendered to a client.

Guideline 4: It is the lawyer's responsibility to take reasonable measures to ensure that clients, courts, and other lawyers are aware that a legal assistant, whose services are utilized by the lawyer in performing legal services, is not licensed to practice law.

Guideline 5: A lawyer may identify legal assistants by name and title on the lawyer's letterhead and on business cards identifying the lawyer's firm.

Guideline 6: It is the responsibility of a lawyer to take reasonable measures to ensure that all client confidences are preserved by a legal assistant.

Guideline 7: A lawyer should take reasonable measures to prevent conflicts of interest resulting from a legal assistant's other employment or interests insofar as such other employment or interests would present a conflict of interest if it were that of the lawyer.

Guideline 8: A lawyer may include a charge for the work performed by a legal assistant in setting a charge for legal services.

Guideline 9: A lawyer may not split legal fees with a legal assistant nor pay a legal assistant for the referral of legal business. A lawyer may compensate a legal assistant based on the quantity and quality of the legal assistant's work and the value of that work to a law practice, but the legal assistant's compensation may not be contingent, by advance agreement, upon the profitability of the lawyer's practice.

Guideline 10: A lawyer who employs a legal assistant should facilitate the legal assistant's participation in appropriate continuing education and *pro bono publico* activities.

Provided the lawyer maintains responsibility for the work product, a lawyer may delegate to a legal assistant any task normally performed by the lawyer except those tasks proscribed to one not licensed as a lawyer by statute, court rule, administrative rule or regulation, controlling authority, the ABA Model Rules of Professional Conduct, or these Guidelines.

Paralegals working for attorneys may interview clients and witnesses, investigate legal claims, draft legal documents for attorneys' signatures, attend will executions (in some states), appear at real-estate closings (in some states), and undertake numerous other types of legal work, as long as the work is supervised by attorneys. When state or federal law allows them to do so, paralegals can also represent clients before government agencies. Paralegals are allowed to perform freelance services for attorneys and, depending on state law and the type of service, perform limited independent services for the public.

Legal assistants are also permitted to give information to clients on many types of matters relating to a case or other legal matter. When arranging for client interviews, they let clients know what kind of information is needed and what documents to bring to the office. They inform clients about legal procedures and what the client should expect to experience during the progress of a legal proceeding. For example, in preparing for trial, legal assistants instruct clients on trial procedures, what they should wear to the trial, and so on. Clearly, as a legal assistant, you will be permitted to give clients all kinds of information. Nonetheless, you must make sure that you know where to draw the line between giving permissible types of advice and giving "legal advice"—advice that only attorneys are licensed to give under state laws.

The specific types of tasks that paralegals are legally permitted to undertake are described throughout this book; it would be impossible to list them all here. Generally, Guideline 2 of the ABA's Model Guidelines makes it clear that paralegals can engage in a wide spectrum of legal activities.

> **Apart from tasks that only attorneys can legally perform, paralegals may perform almost any type of legal work as long as the attorney authorizes the work and assumes responsibility for the paralegal's work product.**

As you can see from the ABA's guidelines, paralegals may not perform "tasks that only attorneys can legally perform." If they do so, they risk liability for the unauthorized practice of law—an important topic to which we now turn.

THE UNAUTHORIZED PRACTICE OF LAW

An awareness of what kinds of activities constitute the unauthorized practice of law (UPL) is vitally important for practicing paralegals. Paralegals judged to have engaged in the UPL may be subject to fines and possibly imprisonment. UPL actions are complicated by the fact that state statutes stipulating that only licensed attorneys can engage in the practice of law rarely indicate with any specificity what constitutes the "practice of law." For example, Ethical Consideration (EC) 3–5 to Canon 3 of the ABA's Model Code reads as follows:

> Functionally, the practice of law relates to the rendition of services for others that call for the professional judgment of a lawyer. The essence of the professional judgment of the lawyer is his educated ability to relate the general body and philosophy of law to a specific legal problem of a client.

Model Rule 5.5 is also vague on this issue. It essentially states that the practice of law varies from state to state, that restricting the practice of law to attorneys benefits the public interest, and that attorneys can delegate functions to paralegals as long as attorneys supervise the work and retain responsibility for it. Both the Model Code and the Model Rules also specifically prohibit lawyers from assisting in the "unauthorized practice of law."

Because of this lack of specificity with respect to what constitutes the practice of law, it is difficult to predict with certainty what type of action may constitute the "unauthorized" practice of law. Generally, though, state statutes regulating the practice of law, as well as court decisions concerning the authorized (and unauthorized) practice of law, indicate that certain types of activities, because they lie at the heart of the attorney-client relationship, can be performed *only* by attorneys. Otherwise stated, paralegals are prohibited from performing such activities. NALA's Model Standards and Guidelines summarize these prohibited activities in Guideline 2, which states that legal assistants should not perform any of the following actions:

- Establish attorney-client relationships.
- Set legal fees.
- Give legal opinions or advice.
- Represent a client before a court, unless authorized to do so by the court.
- Engage in, encourage, or contribute to any act which could constitute the unauthorized practice of law.

The first two activities in that list—establishing attorney-client relationships and setting legal fees—are fairly straightforward. The others, however, are less so and merit further discussion.

On the Web
A good starting point for locating your state's UPL statute and UPL court cases is FindLaw's Web site at **www.findlaw.com/casecode/state.html**.

Giving Legal Opinions and Advice

Clearly, giving legal advice goes to the essence of legal practice. After all, a person would not seek out a legal expert if he or she did not want legal advice on some matter. Although a paralegal may communicate an attorney's legal advice to a client, the paralegal may not give legal advice.

You need to be extremely careful to avoid giving legal advice even when discussing matters with friends and relatives. Although other nonlawyers often give advice affecting others' legal rights or obligations, paralegals may not do so. For example, when an individual receives a speeding ticket, a friend or relative who is a nonlawyer might suggest that the person should argue the case before a judge and explain his or her side of the story. When a paralegal gives such advice, however, he or she may be accused of engaging in the unauthorized practice of law. Legal assistants are prohibited from giving even simple, common-sense advice because of the understandably greater weight given to the advice of someone who has legal training.

Similarly, you need to be cautious in the workplace. Although you may have developed great expertise in a certain area of law, you must refrain from advising clients with respect to their legal obligations or rights. For example, suppose that you are a bankruptcy specialist and know that a client who wants to petition for bankruptcy has two realistic options to pursue under bankruptcy law. Should you tell the client about these options and their consequences? No, you should not. In effect, advising someone of his or her legal options is very close to advising a person of his or her legal rights and may therefore—in the view of many courts, at least—constitute the practice of law. Also, even though you may qualify what you say by telling the client that he or she needs to check with an attorney, this does not alter the fact that you are giving advice on which the client might rely.

What constitutes the giving of legal advice is difficult to pin down. As you read earlier, paralegals are permitted to advise clients on a number of matters, and drawing the line between permissible and impermissible advice may at times be difficult. To be on the safe side (and avoid potential liability for the unauthorized practice of law), a good rule of thumb is the following:

> **Never advise a client or other person on any matter if the advice may alter the legal position or legal rights of the one to whom the advice is given.**

Whenever you are pressured to render legal advice—as you surely will be at one time or another, by your firm's clients or others—simply say that you cannot

On the Web
For some tips on how to avoid the UPL, go to **www.paralegals.org/Development/upl.html**.

give legal advice because it is against the law to do so. Paralegals usually find that this frank and honest statement provides an easy solution to the problem.

Representing Clients in Court

The rule that only attorneys—with limited exceptions—can represent others in court has a long history. Recall from the discussion of attorney regulation earlier in this chapter that attorney licensing was initially required only for court representation. In the last few decades, the ethical reasoning underlying this rule has been called into question by two developments.

First, in 1975 the United States Supreme Court held that people have a constitutional right to represent themselves in court.[8] Some people have questioned why a person can represent himself or herself in court but cannot hire a person more educated in the law to do so unless that person is a licensed attorney. Second, the fact that paralegals are allowed to represent clients before some federal and state government agencies, such as the federal Social Security Administration and state welfare departments (as will be discussed in Chapter 9), has called into question the ethical underpinnings of this rule. Nonetheless, as a paralegal you should know that you are not allowed to appear in court on behalf of your supervising attorney—although local courts in some states are carving out exceptions to this rule for limited purposes.

Disclosure of Paralegal Status

Because of the close working relationship between an attorney and a paralegal, a client may have difficulty perceiving that the paralegal is not also an attorney. For example, a client's call to an attorney may be transferred to the attorney's paralegal if the attorney is not in the office. The paralegal may assume that the client knows that he or she is not an attorney and may speak freely with the client about a legal matter, advising the client that the attorney will be in touch with the client shortly. The client, however, may assume that the paralegal is an attorney and may make inferences based on the paralegal's comments that result in actions with harmful consequences—in which event the paralegal might be charged with the unauthorized practice of law.

To avoid such problems, you should always do the following:

 When dealing with clients or potential clients, disclose your paralegal status to ensure that they realize that you are a paralegal and not an attorney.

Similarly, in correspondence with clients or others, you should indicate your nonattorney status by adding "Paralegal" or "Legal Assistant" after your name. If you have printed business cards or if your name is included in the firm's letterhead or other literature, also make sure that your nonlawyer status is clearly indicated.

Guideline 1 of NALA's Model Standards and Guidelines emphasizes the importance of the disclosure of paralegal status by stating that all legal assistants have an ethical responsibility to "[d]isclose their status as legal assistants at the outset of any professional relationship with a client, other attorneys, a court or administrative agency or personnel thereof, or members of the general public." Disciplinary Rule 1.7 of NPFA's Model Code of Ethics and Professional Responsibility also stresses the importance of disclosing paralegal status. Guideline 4 of

---

8. *Faretta v. California*, 422 U.S. 806, 95 S.Ct. 2525, 45 L.Ed.2d 562 (1975).

> ### DEVELOPING PARALEGAL SKILLS
> ## Avoiding UPL Problems
>
>
>
> Jenna Martin, a paralegal, is attending a client's holiday party. She is the first person from her firm to arrive at the party. As she enters the room, Mr. Holbrook, the president of the company, introduces himself to Jenna. She responds, saying, "It's nice to meet you. I'm Jenna Martin, with the firm of Atkins & White." Assuming that Jenna is an attorney, Holbrook begins to ask her for legal advice about a tax problem that the company is having. Jenna now needs to take action to avoid the unauthorized practice of law.
>
> TIPS ON HOW TO AVOID UPL PROBLEMS
> - Always introduce yourself as a paralegal, or legal assistant.
> - Always include your title when signing letters or other documents.
> - Make sure that your nonattorney status is clearly indicated on business cards and company letterhead.
> - Always disclose your status to a court or other tribunal.
> - If a client does not understand your role, explain it. Make it clear that paralegals may not give legal advice.
> - Refer the client to an attorney for legal advice.

the ABA's Model Guidelines places on attorneys the responsibility for disclosing the nonattorney status of paralegals:

> It is the lawyer's responsibility to take reasonable measures to ensure that clients, courts, and other lawyers are aware that a legal assistant, whose services are utilized by the lawyer in performing legal services, is not licensed to practice law.

Paralegals Freelancing for Attorneys

Some paralegals have their own businesses and work as freelance paralegals for attorneys, as you learned in the previous chapter. In the early 1990s, there was some concern over whether freelance paralegals were, by definition, sufficiently supervised by attorneys to avoid liability for the unauthorized practice of law. In a landmark decision in 1992, the New Jersey Supreme Court stated that it could find no reason why freelance paralegals could not be just as adequately supervised by the attorneys for whom they worked as those paralegals working in attorneys' offices. Since that decision, courts in several other states and ethical opinions issued by various state bar associations have held that freelance paralegals who are adequately supervised by attorneys are not engaging in the unauthorized practice of law.

In its opinion, the New Jersey Supreme Court also called for the establishment of a Committee on Paralegal Education and Regulation to study the practice of paralegals and make recommendations to the court. The committee's report, submitted to the court in 1998, recommended that paralegals in New Jersey should be subject to state licensing requirements. This recommendation has caused widespread debate among legal professionals in New Jersey and elsewhere—as you will read shortly.

Paralegal Profile

Freelance Paralegal

DOROTHY SECOL *has worked in the legal profession for over thirty years and has been a freelance paralegal since 1982. She maintains an office in Allenhurst, New Jersey. Secol is a graduate of Monmouth University, West Long Branch, New Jersey.*

Secol is a member of the National Association of Legal Assistants (NALA) and received her CLA status in 1978. In addition, she is a former trustee of the Central Jersey Paralegal Association and a former vice president and trustee of the Legal Assistants Association of New Jersey. She is also an associate member of the New Jersey State Bar Association and serves on its Paralegal Committee and Foreclosure Committee. She is also on the Paralegal Advisory Boards of Brookdale Community College and Ocean County College. Secol is also a mediator for three courts in her area.

Secol is the author of Starting and Managing Your Own Business: A Freelancing Guide for Paralegals, *published by Aspen Publishing Company, and has written articles for the* New Jersey Law Journal *and* New Jersey Lawyer. *In addition, Secol was a petitioner in the case of* In re Opinion 24 of the Committee on the Unauthorized Practice of Law, 128 N.J. 114 (1992). *In that case, the court held that "there is no distinguishable difference between an in-house and freelance paralegal working under the direct supervision of an attorney."*

What do you like best about your work?

"The aspect I like most about my work is the creativity. Whether it's defining an issue and then researching it, writing an argument to oppose or support your position, drafting a contract or a pleading, or working up a file, I am using my intellect and judgment. I love the fact that the law changes constantly—no day is ever the same. There is never any boredom to contend with, and you constantly have to be on your toes to keep up with the changes."

"I love the excitement of running a business. The entrepreneurial aspect of being a freelance paralegal has allowed me the opportunity to grow and to learn how to be a businessperson as well as a paralegal. I have to deal with employees, vendors, clients, and suppliers, as well as provide for insurance, office equipment, advertising, marketing, technology, and much, much more. The flexibility of being in business has allowed me to spend time with my family when needed. I have had a chance to meet people from all over, to learn how different attorneys tackle problems, and to learn from different experiences. Working for many attorneys at one time gives you a different perspective than you would have if you worked for one attorney or for attorneys in one firm with a specific ideology."

What is the greatest challenge that you face in your area of work?

"The greatest challenge I have is consistently providing excellent services, maintaining professionalism at all times, and producing a product for the attorney that is as near perfect as it can get. Attorneys use the services of a freelance paralegal because they are short staffed, they do not have personnel with knowledge in a certain area of substantive law, or someone on their staff is on vacation or taking sick leave. It is up to me to ensure that the product they receive is perfect; otherwise, they don't need us. We must provide a better service than they are used to. Our services are our marketing tools."

What advice do you have for would-be paralegals in your area of work?

"Freelancing is not for the recent college graduate or someone with one or two years of experience; it is for the seasoned, experienced paralegal. To freelance, you must have a certain business acumen. Freelancing is more than just being a paralegal; it means running a business, whether it is out of your house or out of an office. You must have a certain temperament and personality. Some of the necessary characteristics are: (1) you must be a perfectionist—you are committed to be the very best you can be and you are not afraid of meeting change or of being different; (2) you must be a risk taker—you have to look for opportunities where your services are needed, and you also must learn to create a need where there was none before; (3) you must have a positive attitude and a good self-image, and you must know that you can do the job; and (4) you must have the necessary skills in order to be successful, which means being up to date on your market areas and

> **PARALEGAL PROFILE**
>
> ## Freelance Paralegal *Continued*
>
> *"Freelancing is more than just being a paralegal; it means running a business. . . . "*
>
> your areas of substantive law, as well as having the very latest knowledge on which to base your business decisions (including knowledge of new technology, equipment, and so forth)."
>
> **What are some tips for success as a paralegal in your area of work?**
> "You must have a quality program for your services. Offer services above and beyond that which are required, and make your service indispensable. You should also know your market and your competition. If you are a real-estate paralegal, be sure you are in an area where there is a need for those services. Choose your areas of substantive law based on your expertise, and then market them to those attorneys that will need your services. Additionally, you should establish goals. Be sure to have a business plan in place. Know where you want to be and how you expect to get there. You also need to plan your finances carefully. You will not have a weekly paycheck. Be sure you have enough capitalization to tide you over until your business picks up enough for you to meet all your financial obligations. Remember, you are now in business and will have certain responsibilities to meet, such as buying and maintaining equipment, supplies, rent, insurance, and subscriptions."

Independent Paralegals and the UPL

As mentioned in Chapter 2, independent paralegals (also called legal technicians) provide "self-help" legal services directly to the public. Since the 1970s, when these types of services began to spring up around the country, the courts have had to wrestle with questions such as the following: If an independent paralegal advises a customer on what forms are necessary to obtain a simple, uncontested divorce, how those forms should be filed with the court, how the court hearing should be scheduled, and so on, do those activities constitute the practice of law?

Generally, the mere dissemination of legal information does not constitute the unauthorized practice of law. There is a fine line, however, between the dissemination of legal information (by providing legal forms to a customer, for example) and giving legal advice (which may consist of merely selecting the forms that best suit the customer's needs)—and the courts do not always agree on just where this line should be drawn.

EARLY CASES. An early case on this issue was *The Florida Bar v. Brumbaugh*,[9] which was decided in 1978 by the Florida Supreme Court. The case was brought by the Florida Bar Association against Ms. Brumbaugh, who prepared legal documents for people who sought a simple, uncontested divorce. Brumbaugh prepared all the necessary court documents and told her customers how to file the documents with the court, how to schedule the court hearings, and—in a conference the day before the hearing—what would occur at the hearing.

---

9. 355 So.2d 1186 (Fla. 1978).

The Florida Bar Association claimed that Brumbaugh was engaging in the practice of law in violation of the state's UPL statute. The Florida Supreme Court held that Brumbaugh could sell legal forms and other printed information regarding divorces and other legal procedures, that she could fill in the forms as long as the customer provided the information in writing, and that she could advertise her services. She could not, however, advise customers of their legal rights; tell them which forms should be used, how they should be filled out, and where to file them; or how to present their cases in court.

A year later, the same court decided *The Florida Bar v. Furman*,[10] which involved a woman who performed legal services very similar to those performed by Brumbaugh. The court held that the woman, Ms. Furman, had engaged in the unauthorized practice of law by failing to comply with the decision in *Brumbaugh*. The *Furman* case received substantial publicity when Ms. Furman disobeyed a later *injunction* (a court order to cease engaging in the prohibited activities) and was sentenced to prison for **contempt of court** (failing to cooperate with a court order).

Contempt of Court
The intentional obstruction or frustration of the court's attempt to administer justice. A party to a lawsuit may be held in contempt of court (punishable by a fine or jail sentence) for refusing to comply with a court's order.

AN ONGOING PROBLEM.   Independent paralegals continue to face UPL allegations against them brought by bar associations and others. In 1995, an Oregon independent paralegal, Robin Smith, was taken to court by the Oregon Bar Association for engaging in the UPL. The trial court agreed with the bar association that Smith's activities constituted the practice of law and thus violated the state's UPL statute. The court stated that "the practice of law includes the drafting or selection of documents and the giving of advice in regard thereto any time an informed or trained discretion must be exercised in the selection or drafting of a document to meet the needs of the persons being served." The court ordered Smith to cease conducting her business activities, and the decision was upheld on appeal.[11]

In 1998, a UPL case was under way in California against a number of independent paralegals. The case was settled after the California legislature passed Senate Bill 1418, which provided that independent paralegals—referred to as "Legal Document Assistants" in the bill—could perform only certain types of services (generally, assist clients in filling out legal forms) and not others. The settlement incorporated the restrictions set forth in Senate Bill 1418.

Notably, even Nolo Press, the well-known publisher of self-help law books, has been under attack for the UPL. An official Texas UPL committee, acting on behalf of the Texas Supreme Court, claimed that Nolo Press, merely by publishing self-help law publications in Texas, violated the Texas UPL statute. (Texas is the only state that prohibits publishers of such books from selling them in its state.) The committee would not disclose which Nolo books were involved—or any other information Nolo asked for—because of an apparent requirement that the committee keep all information confidential. Nolo requested the Texas Supreme Court to order the committee to open up the process. As of early 1999, the Texas Supreme Court had not yet ruled on this matter. According to Nolo Press, the Texas state bar association was also planning to create a committee to review the methods used by the Texas UPL committee.

Generally, unless a state statute or rule specifically allows paralegals to directly assist the public without the supervision of an attorney, paralegals should be wary of engaging in such practices. Because the consequences of violating state UPL statutes can be so serious, we cannot emphasize enough the following advice:

On the Web
Nolo Press has placed all of the documents it has produced in response to the Texas UPL Committee's charges on its Web site. If you are interested in reading this information, go to www.nolo.com/texas.

---

10. 376 So.2d 378 (Fla. 1979).
11. *Oregon State Bar v. Smith,* 149 Or.App. 171, 942 P.2d 793 (1997).

> ## ETHICAL CONCERN
> ### Saying "If I were you . . ." and the UPL
>
> Any time that a paralegal, in responding to someone concerned about legal rights, says, "If I were you, I would . . . ," the paralegal is, in effect, giving legal advice—and engaging in the unauthorized practice of law. For example, assume that a client calls your law office, and you take the call. The client, Mrs. Rabe, is an older woman who is very upset about the fact that an insurance company did not pay on a $1,000 life insurance policy that she had purchased covering the life of her grandson, who had just died. Mrs. Rabe tells you all of the details, and even though you feel she might win a lawsuit against the insurance company, it would probably cost her a lot more than $1,000 in the process. Mrs. Rabe wants to know if your supervising attorney will see her about the case, and when you tell her the attorney is out of town, she presses you for advice. Finally, you say, "Well, if I were you, I'd take the case to small claims court. You would not have to hire an attorney, it would be less costly, and you might recover some of the money." What the paralegal did not tell Mrs. Rabe is that if she sues the insurance company, she might win not just the $1,000 payment but also substantial punitive damages for the insurance company's wrongful behavior—and possibly have benefited by other penalties imposed under the state's insurance statute.

 Any paralegal who contemplates working as an independent paralegal must thoroughly investigate the relevant state laws and court decisions on UPL before offering any services directly to the public and must rigorously abide by the letter of the law.

SHOULD PARALEGALS BE LICENSED?

One of the major issues facing legal professionals and other interested groups today is whether paralegals should be subject to direct regulation by the state through licensing requirements. Unlike certification, which was discussed in Chapter 1, licensing involves direct and mandatory regulation, by the state, of an occupational or professional group. When licensing requirements are established for a professional group, such as for attorneys, a license is required before a member of the group can practice his or her profession.

Much of the impetus toward paralegal regulation has been fueled by the activities of independent paralegals, or legal technicians—those who provide legal services directly to the public without attorney supervision. Many independents call themselves paralegals even though they have little, if any, legal training, background, or experience. Yet at the same time, those who cannot afford to hire an attorney can benefit by the self-help services provided by paralegals who do have training and experience.

General versus Limited Licensing

A number of states—most prominently, New Jersey, Utah, Wisconsin, California, New York, Texas, and Minnesota—have considered implementing a **general licensing** program. A general licensing program would require all paralegals to

General Licensing
A type of licensing in which all individuals within a specific profession or group (such as paralegals) must meet licensing requirements imposed by the state before they may legally practice their profession.

meet certain educational requirements and other specified criteria before being allowed to practice their profession.

For example, New Jersey is considering recommendations by the New Jersey Supreme Court Committee on Paralegal Education and Regulation that would require paralegals to be licensed to practice their profession. The committee's report and its recommendations, which are the most detailed ever devised by a state body on the topic, propose that paralegals be subject to state licensure based on demonstrated educational requirements and knowledge of the ethical rules governing the legal profession. If these recommendations are adopted by the New Jersey Supreme Court, they will become law in that state, and other states may look to the New Jersey scheme for guidance. In other words, what happens in New Jersey could have a significant impact on paralegal practice throughout the country.

The Utah state bar association has issued a report recommending mandatory licensure that includes passing the CLA exam. A number of other states, including Wisconsin, are also recommending licensing programs for paralegals.

As an alternative to general licensing, over half the states are considering **limited licensing**, which would limit licensing requirements to those paralegals (independent paralegals, or legal technicians) who wish to provide specified legal services directly to the public. With limited licensing, qualified paralegals would be authorized to handle routine legal services traditionally rendered only by attorneys, such as advising clients on simple divorces, will executions, bankruptcy petitions, incorporation, real-estate transactions, selected tax matters, and other specified services as designated by the state licensing body. Already, at least twenty-two states allow some form of limited nonlawyer practice, and some states would like to establish a regulatory mechanism—such as a limited licensing program—to protect the consumers of these services.

On the Web
The entire report issued by the New Jersey Supreme Court Committee on Paralegal Education and Regulation, including its recommendations for the licensure of New Jersey paralegals, can be downloaded from the following Web site: www.state.nj.us/judiciary/index.html.

Limited Licensing
A type of licensing in which a limited number of individuals within a specific profession or group (such as independent paralegals within the paralegal profession) must meet licensing requirements imposed by the state before those individuals may legally practice their profession.

Direct Regulation—The Pros and Cons

A significant part of the debate over direct regulation has to do with the issue of who should do the regulating. Certainly, state bar associations and government authorities would want to have a say in the matter. Yet paralegal organizations and educators, such as NALA, NFPA, and the American Association for Paralegal Education (AAfPE), would also want to play a leading role in developing the education requirements, ethical standards, and disciplinary procedures required by a licensing program.

The problem is, NALA, NFPA, and the AAfPE have different views on these matters. Furthermore, as you learned in Chapter 1, these organizations have not adopted a uniform definition of a paralegal—the definitions vary from one organization to another. Until legal professionals can agree on a definition of the term *paralegal*, it will be difficult to regulate the paralegal profession in a way that is acceptable to the majority of the group being regulated—paralegals.

NFPA's Position. NFPA endorses the regulation of the paralegal profession on a state-by-state basis insofar as regulation expands the utilization of paralegals to deliver cost-efficient legal services. If it can be demonstrated that there is a public need for lower-cost legal services, NFPA is in favor of the regulation of paralegals, providing the paralegals meet certain minimum criteria.

NFPA contends that the licensing of paralegals would accomplish several goals. First, attorneys and the public would benefit because only demonstrably qualified paralegals would be licensed to practice the profession. Second, attorneys' search costs in finding competent assistance would be reduced. Third, the licensing of paralegals would be a step forward in the development of the paralegal profession. Fourth, licensing would permit paralegals to legally perform specified tasks, and therefore they would not be at risk for the unauthorized practice of law to the extent they are today. And finally, the licensing of paralegals would give consumers greater access to low-cost legal assistance for routine legal matters. NFPA argues that the latter issue (access to legal services) provides a compelling reason to expand the role of paralegals.

NFPA proposes a two-tiered system of licensing: general licensing and specialty licensing. General licensing by a state board or agency would require all paralegals within the state to satisfy stipulated requirements in regard to education, experience, and continuing education; it would also subject practicing paralegals to disciplinary procedures by the licensing body. (As mentioned, NFPA has already developed a set of model enforcement guidelines, which were appended to its code of ethics in 1997—see Appendix C.) Specialty licensing would require paralegals who wish to practice in a specialized area to demonstrate, by an examination (see the discussion of the PACE examination in Chapter 1), their proficiency in that area.

As to the regulatory developments in New Jersey, NFPA has taken the position that the requirements suggested by the New Jersey Supreme Court Committee on Paralegal Education and Regulation are a positive development for the paralegal profession. The requirements will help to weed out the "bad apples" in the profession—including those who call themselves paralegals but do not have the necessary education or experience to practice competently and those who violate UPL statutes. According to Laurel Bielec, a past vice president of NFPA, the New Jersey requirements have "the potential to fulfill the hopes of those in the profession that paralegal regulation will finally allow paralegals to provide the legal services they are competent to perform."[12]

NALA's Position. While NALA supports voluntary certification, it believes that imposing licensing requirements on paralegals would be premature. Currently, paralegals perform a wide range of tasks and work in a variety of settings. In NALA's opinion, to impose mandatory, uniform requirements on a group of professionals whose function is not yet sufficiently defined would limit paralegal opportunities, closing the door to those paralegals who could not meet the requirements for licensing and prohibiting activities that paralegals are currently authorized to undertake.

NALA looks at certification and the development of paralegal education programs as being, at least at this point in time, a reasonable alternative to licensing. NALA emphasizes that most paralegals work under the supervision of attorneys and are thus already subject to regulation via attorney codes. NALA takes the position that the licensure recommendations issued by the New Jersey Supreme Court Committee on Paralegal Education and Regulation, if adopted by the New Jersey Supreme Court, would be harmful to the growth of the profession. The regulatory scheme would not allow paralegals to qualify for employment in New Jersey based on experience alone. Rather, under the proposed rules, only those who completed an ABA-approved educational program would be able to obtain a

---

12. Laurel Bielec, "A Giant Leap towards Regulation: What's Going on in New Jersey, and How Could It Affect You?" *Legal Assistant Today*, November/December 1998, pp. 12–15.

license to practice their profession in New Jersey. According to NALA, this would curb competition in paralegal education as well.[13]

NALA's objections to specific limited licensing proposals for independent paralegals (legal technicians) do not reflect opposition to the idea of limited licensing for independent paralegals so much as disagreement with specific aspects of the proposed regulatory schemes.

THE AAFPE'S POSITION. The major concern of the American Association for Paralegal Education (AAfPE) is that paralegals and paralegal educators should have some kind of a voice in determining the educational and ethical requirements that would be required for a licensing program. This prospect is dimmed by the competition between NALA and NFPA, which have conflicting views on significant issues facing the profession, ranging from the definition of a paralegal to the educational standards that paralegals should meet. According to Diane Petropulos, a former president of the AAfPE, these competing paralegal organizations need to put forth a unified front if paralegals are to have any influence over the future regulation of the profession. Otherwise, by default, the decision will not be theirs to make. In an article published in *Legal Assistant Today,* Petropulos stated, "We have our own profession to craft and significant contributions to make, but we must close the gap between NALA and NFPA to effectively set standards."[14]

On the Web
For updates on the positions taken by NFPA, NALA, and the AAfPE on regulation, as well as regulatory developments, check their Web sites: for NFPA, www.paralegals.org; for NALA, www.nala.org; for the AAfPE: www.aafpe.org.

Other Considerations

While the positions taken by NFPA, NALA, and the AAfPE outline the main contours of the debate over regulation, other groups emphasize some different considerations. For example, one of the concerns of lawyers is that if independent paralegals are licensed—through limited licensing programs—to deliver low-cost services directly to the public, this would cut into the business (and profits) of law firms. Many lawyers are also concerned that if paralegals are subject to mandatory licensing requirements, law firms will not be able to hire and train persons of their choice to become paralegals.

Some paralegals and paralegal associations are concerned that mandatory licensing would require all paralegals to be "generalists." As it is, a large number of paralegals specialize in particular areas, such as bankruptcy or family law, and do not need to have the broad knowledge of all areas of paralegal practice that licensing might require.

A FINAL NOTE

As a professional paralegal, you will have an opportunity to voice your opinion on whether paralegals should be directly regulated by state governments and, if so, what qualifications should be required before a license to practice your profession will be granted. Keep in mind, though, that all of the issues discussed in this chapter are directly relevant to your paralegal career. The most important

---

13. For further details on NALA's response to the New Jersey proposed regulatory scheme, see "Special Report: Executive Summary: NALA Statement re Report of the New Jersey Supreme Court Committee on Paralegal Education and Regulation," *NALA Newsletter,* Fall 1998, pp. 4–7.
14. "Who's in Charge?" *Legal Assistant Today,* January/February 1999, pp. 14–15.

TODAY'S PROFESSIONAL PARALEGAL
Working for the Attorney Discipline Board

Denise James is a legal assistant who works for the Attorney Discipline Board in her state. She has an interesting job that entails a variety of responsibilities. One of Denise's job responsibilities is to contact attorneys to sit on the Attorney Discipline Board's hearing panel. She consults the list of attorneys who have volunteered to sit on the panel and calls them to make arrangements for the hearing panels. She forwards to them background information and briefs on the cases that they will hear. On the day of the hearing, she meets the attorneys, escorts them to the hearing room, provides them with hearing examiners' robes, and assists them in getting the hearing started.

PREPARING "NOTICES OF DISCIPLINE"

Another of Denise's duties is to prepare the "Notices of Discipline" that are published every month in the state bar association journal, which is a monthly publication that is sent to all licensed attorneys in the state. These notices identify which attorneys have been subject to disciplinary actions and for what reasons. To prepare this month's notices, Denise pulls out all of the "final orders of discipline" that were entered this month. Then she reads through and summarizes each order.

SUMMARIZING DISCIPLINARY PROCEEDINGS

Denise reads through a final order sanctioning an attorney. The attorney, who commingled a client's funds with her own personal funds, was suspended. The funds involved consisted of a check in the settlement of a personal-injury lawsuit. The attorney deposited the check to her personal checking account and then used the money to pay her monthly bills. She did not issue a check to the client for the money until three months later. The client continually called the attorney's office and demanded the settlement check. The attorney kept stalling and then simply refused to return the client's phone calls.

Denise then summarized the disciplinary proceedings against the attorney as follows: "[attorney's name], P12345, Binghamton, by Attorney Discipline Board, Binghamton County, Hearing Panel #6, effective June 3, 2000. Respondent commingled client's funds by using the client's money, received in a settlement, to pay her personal bills, then paid the client three months later. The hearing panel found respondent's conduct to be in violation of Court Rule 1.15 and the state Rules of Professional Conduct. A suspension was issued and costs were assessed in the amount of $751.53."

There is never a dull moment working for the Attorney Discipline Board. The unfortunate part is that Denise sees many cases in which clients have lost legal rights because their cases were neglected for a variety of reasons.

point to remember as you embark on a paralegal career is that you need to think and act in a professionally responsible manner in your particular workplace. Although this takes time and practice, in the legal arena there is little room for learning ethics by "trial and error." Therefore, you need to be especially attentive to the ethical rules governing attorneys and paralegal practice discussed in this chapter.

The *Ethical Concerns* throughout this book will offer further insights into some of the ethical problems that can arise in various areas of paralegal performance. Understanding how violations can occur will help you anticipate and guard against them as you begin your paralegal career. Once on the job, you can continue your preventive tactics by asking questions whenever you are in doubt and by making sure that your work is adequately supervised.

Key Terms and Concepts

attorney-client privilege 83	ethical wall 87	suspension 75
breach 78	general licensing 105	third parties 82
conflict of interest 86	licensing 74	unauthorized practice of law (UPL) 74
conflicts check 89	limited licensing 106	work product 85
contempt of court 104	malpractice 77	
damages 77	reprimand 75	
disbarment 75	self-regulation 72	

Chapter Summary

1. The legal profession is regulated by licensing requirements and ethical rules adopted and enforced by state authorities. The purpose of attorney regulation is to protect the public against incompetent legal professionals and unethical attorney behavior. Key participants in the regulation of attorneys are state bar associations, state supreme courts, state legislatures, the United States Supreme Court (occasionally), and the American Bar Association, which establishes model rules and guidelines relating to attorney conduct to be adopted by the various states.

2. Most states have adopted a version of either the 1969 Model Code of Professional Responsibility or the 1983 revision of the Model Code, called the Model Rules of Professional Conduct, both of which were published by the American Bar Association. The majority of the states have adopted the Model Rules. The Model Code and Model Rules spell out the ethical and professional duties governing attorneys and the practice of law. Attorneys who violate the duties imposed by these rules may be subject to sanctions in the form of a reprimand, a suspension, or a disbarment. Additionally, attorneys (as well as paralegals) are subject to potential liability for malpractice or for violations of criminal statutes.

3. Some of the ethical rules governing attorney behavior pose particularly difficult problems for paralegals. One of the most frequently violated rules is the duty of competence. This duty is violated whenever a client suffers harm as a result of the attorney's incompetent action or inaction. Breaching the duty of competence may lead to a lawsuit against the attorney (and perhaps the paralegal) for negligence.

4. Another ethical pitfall for paralegals is inadvertently breaching the rule of confidentiality. The confidentiality rule requires that all information relating to a client's representation must be kept in confidence and not revealed to third parties who are not authorized to know the information. Some client information is regarded as privileged information. An attorney may reveal privileged information only if the client consents, if a court orders the attorney to reveal the information, or in special circumstances, as when revealing the information is necessary to protect another from bodily harm or death. Paralegals need to constantly guard against revealing confidential information to third parties both on and off the job.

5. Attorneys are prohibited from representing a client if the attorney's representation of that client will adversely affect the interests of another client, including former clients. An attorney may represent both sides in a legal proceeding only if the attorney feels that neither party's rights will be adversely affected and only if both clients are aware of the conflict of interest and consent to the representation. Paralegals also fall under this rule. If a firm is handling a case that one of the firm's attorneys or paralegals cannot work on, owing to a conflict of interest, that attorney or paralegal must be "walled off" from the case—that is, prevented from having any access to files or other information relating to the case. Normally, whenever a prospective client consults with an attorney, a conflicts check is done to ensure that if the attorney or firm accepts the case, no conflict of interest will exist.

6. Paralegals are regulated indirectly by attorney ethical rules, by ethical codes created by paralegal professional associations, and by guidelines on the utilization of paralegals, which define the status and function of paralegals and the scope of their

authorized activities. The American Bar Association and several states have also adopted guidelines on the utilization of paralegals. These codes and guidelines provide paralegals, attorneys, and the courts with guidance on the paralegal's role in the practice of law.

7. Court decisions, state attorney ethical rules, paralegal ethical codes and guidelines, and the guidelines on the use of legal assistants that have been adopted by the American Bar Association and several states all express a general consensus that paralegals, under attorneys' supervision, may perform virtually any legal task that attorneys can, with five exceptions. A paralegal may not (1) establish an attorney-client relationship, (2) set the fees to be charged for an attorney's services, (3) give legal advice or opinions, (4) represent a client in court (with some exceptions), or (5) engage in the unauthorized practice of law.

8. The fact that both paralegals working for attorneys and independent paralegals engage in work that traditionally only attorneys have performed raises concerns about the unauthorized practice of law. Lawsuits against independent paralegals, particularly, focused attention on the unauthorized practice of law. Determining what constitutes the unauthorized practice of law is complicated by the fact that state UPL statutes generally offer only vague or very broad definitions of what constitutes the practice of law. Generally, the paralegal must be extremely cautious when contemplating the possibility of working without attorney supervision.

9. A major concern today for both legal professionals and the public is whether paralegals should be directly regulated by the state through licensing requirements. General licensing would establish minimum standards that every paralegal would have to meet in order to practice as a paralegal in the state. Limited licensing would require paralegals wishing to offer routine legal services directly to the public in certain areas, such as family law and bankruptcy law, to demonstrate their proficiency in that area. The pros and cons of direct regulation through licensing are being debated vigorously by the leading paralegal and paralegal education associations, state bar associations, state courts, state legislatures, and public-interest groups.

QUESTIONS FOR REVIEW

1. Why is the legal profession regulated? Who are the regulators? How is regulation accomplished?

2. What are the two primary sets of ethical rules that guide the legal profession in the United States? Who created these rules?

3. How is the paralegal profession regulated by attorney ethical codes?

4. What does the duty of competence involve? How can violations of the duty of competence be avoided?

5. What is the attorney-client privilege? What is its relationship to the rule of confidentiality? What are some potential consequences of violating the confidentiality rule?

6. What is a conflict of interest? How do law firms "wall off" an attorney or a paralegal when a conflict of interest exists?

7. How is the paralegal profession regulated by paralegal codes of ethics? Why have model guidelines been established on the utilization of paralegals?

8. What types of tasks may legally be performed by paralegals? What types of tasks may normally be performed only by attorneys?

9. What is the practice of law? What is the unauthorized practice of law (UPL)? How might paralegals violate state statutes prohibiting the UPL?

10. What would the general licensing of paralegals involve? What is limited licensing? What are some of the pros and cons in the debate over paralegal licensing?

ETHICAL QUESTIONS

1. Anton Snow, a paralegal, has been asked to research the cases decided by courts in his state to see if he can find a case in which a landlord was held liable for crimes caused by a third party (someone other than the landlord or the tenant) on leased premises. Anton finds a case in which the trial court held that a landlord was liable for harms suffered by a plaintiff when she was mugged and robbed in an apartment com-

plex's parking lot. Anton does not take the time to update the case. He therefore fails to find out that the state court of appeals later reversed the trial court's decision. Thus, the trial court's decision, which Anton gives to his supervising attorney, is no longer "good law." The supervising attorney, relying on Anton's research, advises the client accordingly. Discuss the potential problems that the client, the attorney, and Anton might face as a result of Anton's failure to update the trial court's decision.

2. Norma Sollers works as a paralegal for a small law firm. She is a trusted, experienced employee who has worked for the firm for twelve years. One morning, Linda Lowenstein, one of the attorneys, calls in from her home and asks Norma to sign Linda's name to a document that must be filed with the court that day. Norma had just prepared the final draft of the document and placed it on Linda's desk for her review and signature. Linda explains to Norma that because her child is sick, she does not want to the leave home to come into the office. Norma knows that she should not sign Linda's name—only the client's attorney can sign the document. She mentions this to Linda, but Linda says, "Don't worry. No one will ever know that you signed it instead of me." How should Norma handle this situation?

3. Matthew Hinson is an independent paralegal. He provides divorce forms and typing and filing services to the public at very low rates. Samantha Eggleston uses his services. She returns with the forms filled out, but she has one question: How much in monthly child-support payments will she be entitled to receive? How may Matthew legally respond to this question?

PRACTICE QUESTIONS AND ASSIGNMENTS

1. Kathryn Borstein works as a legal assistant for the legal department of a large manufacturing corporation. In the process of interviewing a middle-management accountant with the company relating to an employment discrimination lawsuit, Kathryn discovers that a few of the top executives cheat on their income tax returns by not declaring a portion of their bonuses. Kathryn becomes disenchanted with her job with the corporation for these and other reasons and finds a new job with a law firm. Her supervising attorney in the new law firm is involved in a case against her former employer. The attorney tells Kathryn that the only way to deal with these big corporations is to get whatever dirt you can on them and then threaten to go to the press. He wants to know if she can give him any such information. Can she tell him the "dirt" about the executives who cheat on their income taxes? Why or why not? What ethical rules are involved in her decision?

2. Peter Smith, a paralegal, is using the Internet to find property tax records for a client. The client has come to the firm because he wants to buy a parcel of property, but he also wants to make sure that the property taxes have been paid. Peter finds a Web site for the county register of deeds. He locates the property and notes that, according to the information given on the Web page, the taxes have been paid. He prints the page and writes a brief memo to the attorney. The attorney then advises the client that the taxes have been paid and that it is okay to go ahead and purchase the property. The client does so, but several weeks later he receives a notice that he owes $6,500 in back taxes. The client, who is understandably upset, complains to Peter's boss. Peter is sent to the county register of deeds to look up the records relating to the property. Peter finds that the correct information was in the county's records but was not on the Web site. He makes a copy of what he finds and returns to the office. What ethical rule has been violated here? What do these "facts" reveal about the reliability of information posted on the Internet?

3. In which of the following instances may confidential client information be disclosed?

   a. During an emotional divorce trial, the client suffers a nervous breakdown and admits herself to the psychiatric ward of the local hospital. Her nervous breakdown will strengthen her case.

   b. A client's daughter calls to find out whether her mother has left her certain property in her will. The mother does not want the daughter to know that the daughter has been disinherited until the will is read after the mother's death.

   c. The client in a divorce case threatens to hire a hit man to kill her husband because she perceives that killing her husband is the only way that she can stop him from stalking her. It is clear that the client intends to do this.

d. A former client sues her attorney for legal malpractice in the handling of a breach-of-contract case involving her cosmetics home-sale business. The attorney discloses that the client is having an affair with her next-door neighbor, a fact that is unrelated to the malpractice or breach-of-contract case.

4. According to this chapter's text, which of the following tasks may a paralegal legally perform?

    a. Draft a complaint at an attorney's request.
    b. Interview a witness to a car accident.
    c. Represent a client before an administrative agency.
    d. Investigate the facts of a car-accident case.
    e. Work as a freelance paralegal for attorneys.
    f. Work as an independent paralegal providing legal services directly to the public.

5. Review the facts in Ethical Question 3 above. What do the following ethical codes say about the unauthorized practice of law, and how would these statements apply to Hinson's situation? Could Hinson be disciplined if he gives Samantha the information she requested?

    a. NFPA's Model Code of Ethics and Professional Responsibility (see Appendix C or visit NFPA's Web site at www.paralegals.org).
    b. NALA's Code of Ethics and Professional Responsibility (see Appendix A or visit NALA's Web site at www.nala.org).

Do your answers differ? If so, how?

QUESTIONS FOR CRITICAL ANALYSIS

1. Why is the legal profession regulated? What could happen if it were not? Why are ethical rules needed? What might happen if, for example, there was no rule governing competence in the profession?

2. The material in the chapter indicates that lawyers essentially regulate themselves through bar associations, state supreme courts, and state legislatures. What do you think of a system in which members of a profession regulate themselves? Is this a good system? Would it be better if the profession were regulated from the outside?

3. An experienced legal secretary opened a business, Northside Secretarial Services, for the purpose of delivering certain legal services directly to the public. Specifically, she prepared legal documents—and provided detailed instructions for filing the documents with the court and for service of process—in divorce and adoption cases. She held briefing sessions during which she gave detailed instructions about trials and hearings, including the types of questions that the court would ask and the responses that her "clients" should give to the court. The secretary advertised her services in a local newspaper, holding herself out to be an "expert in family law." She also advertised the sale of "do-it-yourself" divorce kits. She charged no more than $50 for her services, and many of her "clients" were indigent and illiterate.

   The bar association in her state charged her with the unauthorized practice of law. A former client gave testimony that she advised her to lie about the date of her second marriage, because she could not remember it, in the complaint that was filed with the court to start divorce proceedings. Another former client testified that when he found out that his wife was abusing the children, he was advised he should not try to change the petition for divorce to seek custody of the minor children but should leave it to the state agency to handle abuse and custody issues.

   What was the likely result of the state bar association's filing of unauthorized-practice-of-law charges against the legal secretary? How might the legal secretary have responded to these charges? What would result if the legal secretary was enjoined by court order from engaging in these activities and continued to do so anyway?

4. In your view, are personal and legal ethics totally distinct? How, generally, do (or should) personal and legal ethical standards interrelate?

5. If it were up to you to devise a set of ethical standards for the legal profession, would they be any different from those presented in the chapter? If so, in what ways?

6. Compare the activities that constitute the unauthorized practice of law with the activities that paralegals may lawfully engage in under the guidelines for the utilization of legal assistants. Why do you think that the activities that constitute the unauthorized practice of law are prohibited for nonlawyers? Could someone with training as a legal assistant competently handle some of these activities? If so, which ones?

7. What is the difference between a freelance paralegal and an independent paralegal, or legal technician? What are the advantages and disadvantages of each type of status? Would you prefer to work as a freelance paralegal or as an independent paralegal (legal technician)? Why?

8. Do you think that paralegals should be licensed? Why or why not? If you think that they should be licensed, what type of license should they be granted—general or limited? What impact would this have on paralegals? What impact would it have on the legal profession as a whole?

Projects

1. Go to the library and find out the requirements for becoming licensed to practice law in your state. These rules may be located in your state's court rules. Do your state's rules differ from the requirements mentioned in the text? If so, how?

2. Obtain a copy of your state's ethics rules for attorneys. These rules may be located in your state's court rules. How do the competence, confidentiality, and conflict-of-interest rules in your state compare with the ABA's Model Rules on these topics presented in this chapter? Using Microsoft's *PowerPoint* software or Corel's *Presentations* software, prepare a slide show comparing the two sets of rules.

3. Look in your local telephone book or in a directory of attorneys issued by your state bar association for an agency or commission that is responsible for disciplining attorneys. Contact the agency or commission to find out how attorneys are disciplined in your state. Learn about the various degrees of discipline that may be imposed. If disciplinary hearings are open to the public, try to attend one of the hearings. What is your impression?

4. Contact your state bar association to find out if paralegals may join. If they may, present the material, including the requirements for admission and fees, to the class.

5. Go to the library and find materials on the ethical standards of professions other than the legal profession. What ethical concerns do the rules of other professions cover? How are the rules of other professions similar to or different from the legal profession's ethical rules?

Using Internet Resources

1. Go to **www.paralegals.org**, the home page for the National Federation of Paralegal Associations (NFPA). Click on the box titled "Professional Development," which will take you to a page that lists, among other things, "NFPA Informal Ethics and Disciplinary Opinions" on various issues. Then do the following:

   a. List five issues that NFPA has addressed in these opinions.

   b. Choose one opinion and write a paragraph explaining why the issue dealt with in the opinion is important for paralegals.

   c. Choose the same or a different opinion, read completely through it, and write a paragraph summarizing NFPA's "advice" on the issue being addressed in the opinion.

2. Go online and find the case *Oregon State Bar Association v. Smith,* 149 Or.App. 171, 942 P.2d 793 (1997). It can be accessed through the FindLaw Web site at **www.findlaw.com**. Click on "State Law Resources," scroll down to "Oregon," and when the Oregon page appears, select "Primary Materials, Cases, Codes, and Regulations." When that page appears, scroll down to "Archived since 1997," and click on it. This should retrieve a query box. Enter "paralegals & UPL" (do not include quote marks). Scroll through the cases found through this search until you see *Oregon State Bar Association v. Smith*. Read through the first four paragraphs of the decision and then answer the following questions.

   a. Who is Robin Smith, and what was she accused of?

   b. What is an injunction? Why, and against whom, was an injunction issued in this case?

   c. What does "enjoined" mean? What was the People's Paralegal Service, Inc., enjoined from doing?

   d. Did these activities constitute the unauthorized practice of law?

e. How did People's Paralegal Service, Inc., argue against the injunction?

3. Go online to **www.findlaw.com** to access information on state bar associations, membership rules, ethics rules, and attorney discipline. Then answer the following questions:

   a. What are the requirements for an attorney to become licensed to practice law in your state? (Hint: The way that these requirements are listed varies from state to state. You may find these requirements under such listings as "Admissions," "Board of Law Examiners," "Supreme Court Rules," or "Court of Appeals Rules.") Do they differ from the requirements described in this chapter? If so, how?

   b. How are attorneys disciplined in your state? What are the various sanctions that may be imposed? Are disciplinary hearings open to the public? If so, try to attend one.

   c. Look up your state's ethical rules on competence, confidentiality, and conflict of interest. Are those rules the same as the rules discussed in this chapter? If not, what are the differences? Are the rules in your state stricter or more lenient?

   d. Look for rules on the admission of paralegals to the state bar association in your state. Also look for your state's guidelines on the utilization of legal assistants. What did you find?

4. Go to **www.legalethics.com**, which covers ethical issues related to the use of the Internet, and answer the following questions:

   a. Click on "Ethics Sites." Which version of the ABA's ethical rules has your state enacted? Has your state enacted a non-ABA version? Click on your state. Summarize the ethical rules or opinions that have been issued by your state regarding the use of the Internet.

   b. Click on "E-Mail." Does your state have an ethical opinion or rule regarding the use of e-mail? If so, summarize the opinion or rule.

   c. Click on "Other Issues (UPL/Referral Services)." Locate articles discussing practicing law across state boundaries by participating in listservs and discussion groups. Are such activities considered to be the unauthorized practice of law? Explain.

CHAPTER 4
The Legal Workplace

Chapter Outline

▪ Introduction ▪ The Organizational Structure of Law Firms ▪ Law-Office Management and Personnel ▪ Employment Policies ▪ Filing Procedures ▪ Financial Procedures ▪ Communicating with Clients ▪ Law-Office Culture and Politics

After completing this chapter, you will know:

- How law firms may be organized and managed.
- Some typical policies and procedures governing paralegal employment.
- The importance of an efficient filing system in legal practice and some typical filing procedures.
- How clients are billed for legal services.
- How law-office culture and politics affect the paralegal's working environment.

Introduction

The wide variety of environments in which paralegals work makes it impossible to describe in any detail how the particular firm with which you find employment will be run. Typically, though, the way in which that firm operates will relate, at least in part, to the firm's specific form of business organization. Because most paralegals are employed by private law firms, this chapter focuses on the organization, management, and procedures characteristic of these firms.

In the beginning of the chapter, we look at how the size and organizational structure of a law firm affects the paralegal's working environment. As you might imagine, the working environment in a firm owned and operated by one attorney is significantly different from that in a large law firm with two or three hundred attorneys or a large corporate enterprise—or even a government agency.

We then look at other aspects of the working environment of paralegals. Typically, the firm you work for will have specific policies and procedures relating to employment conditions, filing systems, billing and timekeeping procedures, and financial procedures. We conclude the chapter with a brief discussion of law-office culture and politics.

The Organizational Structure of Law Firms

Law firms range in size from the small, one-attorney firm to the huge megafirm that consists of hundreds of attorneys. Regardless of their size differences, though, in terms of business organization, law firms typically organize their businesses as sole proprietorships, partnerships, or professional corporations. Because the way in which a business is organized affects the law-office environment, we look briefly at each of the three major organizational forms here. These types of business organizations, and others less widely used, will be discussed in greater detail in Chapter 8.

Sole Proprietorships

Many law firms, particularly smaller firms, are **sole proprietorships**. Sole proprietorships are the simplest business form and are often used by attorneys when they first set up legal practices. In a sole proprietorship, one individual—the sole proprietor—owns the business. The sole proprietor is entitled to any profits made by the firm but is also personally liable for all of the firm's debts or obligations. **Personal liability** means that the business owner's personal assets (such as a home, automobile, savings or investment accounts, and other property) may have to be sacrificed to pay business obligations if the business fails.

An attorney who practices law as a sole proprietor is often called a *sole (solo) practitioner*. Although a sole practitioner may at times hire a staff attorney to help with the legal work, the attorney will be paid a specific sum for his or her time and will not share in the profits or losses of the firm itself.

Working for a sole practitioner is a good way for a paralegal to learn about law-office procedures because the paralegal will typically perform a wide variety of tasks. Many sole practitioners hire one person to perform the functions of secretary, paralegal, administrator, and manager. Paralegals holding this kind of position would probably handle the following kinds of tasks: receiving and date-stamping the mail, organizing and maintaining the filing system, interviewing clients and witnesses, bookkeeping (receiving payments from clients, preparing and sending bills to clients, and so on), conducting investigations and legal

Sole Proprietorship
The simplest form of business, in which the owner is the business. Anyone who does business without creating a formal business entity has a sole proprietorship.

Personal Liability
An individual's personal responsibility for debts or obligations. The owners of sole proprietorships and partnerships are personally liable for the debts and obligations incurred by their business firms. If their firms go bankrupt or cannot meet debts as they become due, the owners will be personally responsible for paying the debts.

research, drafting legal documents, assisting the attorney in trial preparation and perhaps in the courtroom, and numerous other tasks, including office administration.

Working for a sole practitioner is also a good way to find out which area of law you most enjoy because the paralegal will learn about procedures relating to many different areas of legal work. Alternatively, if you work for a sole practitioner who specializes in one area of law, you will have an opportunity to develop expertise in that area. In sum, working in a small law firm gives you a broad overview of law-office procedures and legal practice. This knowledge will help you throughout your career.

Partnerships

> **Partnership**
> An association of two or more persons to carry on, as co-owners, a business for profit.
>
> **Partner**
> A person who has undertaken to operate a business jointly with one or more other persons. Each partner is a co-owner of the business firm.
>
> **Managing Partner**
> The partner in a law firm who makes decisions relating to the firm's policies and procedures and who generally oversees the business operations of the firm.

The majority of law firms are either partnerships or professional corporations. In a **partnership**, two or more individuals undertake to do business jointly as **partners**. A partnership may consist of just a few attorneys or over a hundred attorneys. In a partnership, each partner owns a share of the business and shares jointly in the firm's profits or losses. Like sole proprietors, partners are personally liable for the debts and obligations of the business if the business fails.

In smaller partnerships, the partners may participate equally in managing the partnership. They will likely meet periodically to make decisions relating to clients, policies, procedures, and other matters of importance to the firm. In larger partnerships, managerial decisions are usually made by a committee consisting of some of the partners, one of whom may be designated as the **managing partner**.

The partnership may hire associate attorneys, but, as in a sole proprietorship, the associates will not have ownership rights in the firm. Normally, an associate hopes to become a partner, and if the associate's performance is satisfactory, the partners may invite the associate to become a partner in the firm.

Professional Corporations

> **Professional Corporation (P.C.)**
> A firm that is owned by shareholders, who purchase the corporation's stock, or shares. The liability of shareholders is often limited to the amount of their investments.
>
> **Shareholder**
> One who purchases corporate stock, or shares, and who thus becomes an owner of the corporation.

A **professional corporation (P.C.)** is owned by **shareholders,** so called because they purchase the corporation's stock, or shares, and thus own a share of the business. The shareholders share in the profits and losses of the firm in proportion to how many shares they own. Their personal liability, unlike that of partners, may or may not be limited to the amount of their investments, depending on the circumstances and on state law. As you will read in Chapter 8, limited personal liability is one of the key advantages of the corporate form of business.

In many respects, the professional corporation is run like a partnership, and the distinction between these two forms of business organization is often more a legal formality than an operational reality. Because of this, attorneys who organize their business as a professional corporation are nonetheless sometimes referred to as partners. For the sake of simplicity, in this chapter we will refer to anyone who has ownership rights in the firm as a partner.

LAW-OFFICE MANAGEMENT AND PERSONNEL

When you take a job as a paralegal, one of the first things you will want to learn is the relative status of the office personnel. Particularly, you will want to know who has authority over you and to whom you are accountable. You also want to know who will be accountable to you—whether you have an assistant or a secretary (or share an assistant or a secretary with another paralegal), for example. In

EXHIBIT 4.1

A Sample Organizational Chart for a Law Partnership

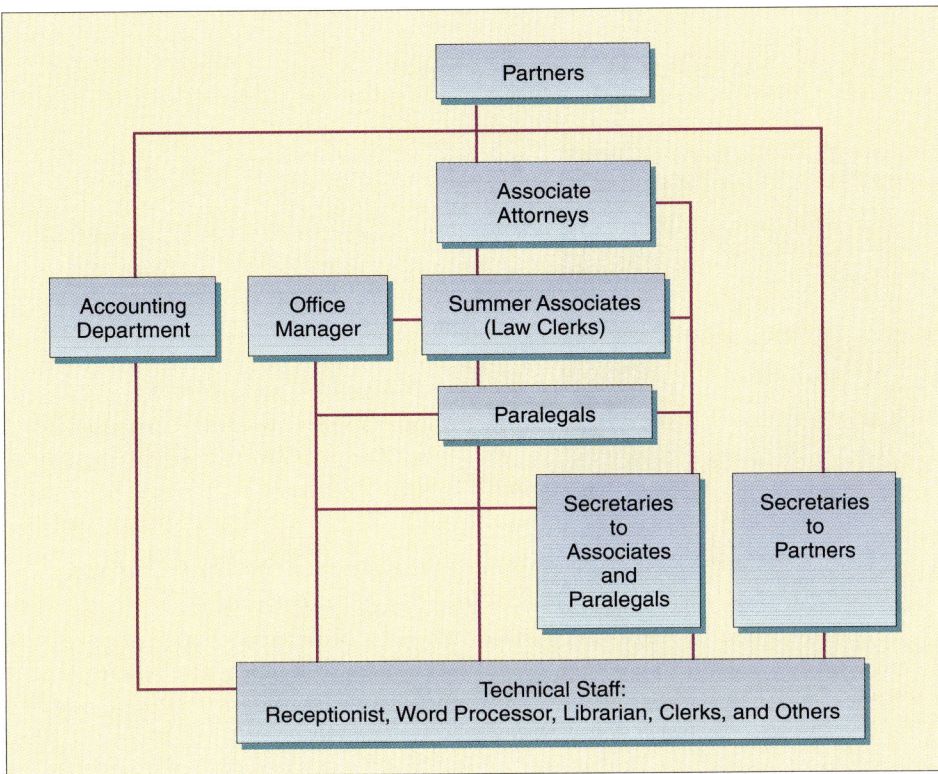

a small firm, you will have no problem learning this information. If you work for a larger law firm, however, the lines of authority may be more difficult to perceive. Your supervisor will probably instruct you, either orally or in writing, on the relative status of the firm's personnel. If you are not sure about who has authority over whom and what kinds of tasks are performed by various employees, you should ask your supervisor.

The lines of authority and accountability vary from firm to firm, depending on the firm's size and its organizational and management preferences. A sample organizational chart for a relatively small law partnership is shown in Exhibit 4.1 above. The ultimate decision makers in the hypothetical firm represented by that chart are the partners. Next in authority are the associate attorneys and summer associates (law clerks—see Chapter 1). The paralegals in this firm are supervised by both the attorneys (in regard to legal work) and the office manager (in regard to office procedural and paralegal staffing matters). In larger firms, there may be a **legal-assistant manager,** who coordinates and oversees paralegal staffing and various programs relating to paralegal educational and professional development.

In addition to attorneys and paralegals, law-firm employees include administrative personnel. In large firms, the partners may hire a **legal administrator** to run the business end of the firm. The legal administrator might delegate some of his or her authority to an office manager and other supervisory employees. In small firms, such as that represented by the chart in Exhibit 4.1, an **office manager** handles the administrative aspects of the firm. The legal administrator or office manager typically is in charge of docketing (calendaring) legal work undertaken by the attorneys; establishing and overseeing filing procedures; implementing new legal technology, such as new docketing software; ordering and monitoring supplies; and generally making sure that the office runs smoothly and that office procedures are established and followed. In a small firm, the office manager might also handle

Legal-Assistant Manager
An employee in a law firm who is responsible for overseeing the paralegal staff and paralegal professional development.

Legal Administrator
An administrative employee of a law firm who manages the day-to-day operations of the firm. In smaller law firms, legal administrators are usually called office managers.

Office Manager
An administrative employee who manages the day-to-day operations of a business firm. In larger law firms, office managers are usually called legal administrators.

Paralegal Profile

Legal Support Supervisor

ANITA HONG graduated from the paralegal program of St. Mary's College in 1984. She has worked as a paralegal since 1985. Her first paralegal job was with the Oakland city attorney's office, where she started out as one of two paralegals in a pilot program. The program was a success. Since then, Hong has gone on to supervise a paralegal staff for that office and subsequently became the legal support supervisor for the Oakland city attorney's office. Today, in addition to her supervisory duties, she also provides paralegal and administrative assistance to the city attorney's office's executive management team. Hong is currently serving as a primary representative in the National Federation of Paralegal Associations (NFPA) on behalf of the San Francisco Paralegal Association.

What do you like best about your work?

"Challenge! From day one, I've been challenged to succeed in various tasks given to me since I began my career as a paralegal in 1985. From there, I was promoted to a legal-assistant supervisor in 1989, and I went on to supervising a staff of paralegals and legal secretaries in 1994. This eventually evolved into a legal support supervisor position in 1997. What I enjoy most is the camaraderie among legal secretaries, paralegals, and attorneys."

What is the greatest challenge that you face in your area of work?

"Communication and customer service. When problems arise, I am one of the problem solvers and troubleshooters for my staff and the office as a whole. The types of problem solving range from customer service, to discovery issues, to staff issues. I have to be fast on my feet and resolve issues as quickly as possible. As a supervisor, I work very hard to stay on top of my work and deal with staff and office issues as they come up."

What advice do you have for would-be paralegals in your area of work?

"Be a mentor to paralegals new to the field. Give back what you've gained. As with any profession, it's okay to be the 'new kid on the block.' Look for mentors to guide you. I was very blessed to have a mentor to guide me as a paralegal and, eventually, as a supervisor. Also, I am fortunate to have a supervisor to help me to become a better supervisor."

What are some tips for success as a paralegal in your area of work?

"Besides having excellent analytical skills and common sense, you must have good people skills. It is important to have good relationships with your clients and your co-workers. Be a quick learner and be a team player. Show a 'can do' attitude, and be flexible about new tasks given to you. Show that you are 'in control.' Be ready to ask for guidance. If you make a mistake, be accountable for your actions without being defensive. Otherwise, people will lose confidence in your credibility and professional ability. As paralegals, we must hold ourselves to the same level of professional and ethical standards as the attorneys in the legal profession."

> "As paralegals, we must hold ourselves to the same level of professional and ethical standards as the attorneys in the legal profession."

client billing procedures. The hypothetical firm represented in Exhibit 4.1 on page 119 has an accounting department to perform this function.

The **support personnel** in a large law office may include secretaries, receptionists, bookkeepers, file clerks, messengers, and others. Depending on their functions and specific jobs, support personnel may fall under the supervision of any number of other personnel in the firm. In a very small firm, just one person—the legal secretary, for example—may perform all of the above-mentioned functions.

Support Personnel
Those employees who provide clerical, secretarial, or other support to the legal, paralegal, and administrative staff of a law firm.

EMPLOYMENT POLICIES

Employees of a law firm, which include all personnel other than the firm's owners or freelance paralegals who work for the firm on a contract basis, are subject to the firm's specific employment policies and procedures. A firm's basic rules or policies governing employment relationships may be set forth in an **employment manual** in larger firms. In smaller firms, these rules and policies are often unwritten. In either situation, when you take a job as a paralegal, or perhaps before you accept a position, you will want to become familiar with the firm's basic conditions of employment. There will be an established policy, for example, on how much vacation time you are entitled to during the first year, second year, and so on. There will also be a policy governing which holidays are observed by the firm, how much sick leave you can take, when you are expected to arrive at the workplace, and what will serve as grounds for the employer to terminate your employment.

Employment Manual
A firm's handbook or written statement that specifies the policies and procedures that govern the firm's employees and employer-employee relationships.

Employment policies and benefits packages vary from firm to firm. A foremost concern of paralegals (and employees generally) is how much they will be paid for their work, how they will be paid (that is, whether they will receive salaries or hourly wages), and what job benefits they will receive. These issues were discussed in detail in Chapter 2, so we will not examine them here. Rather, we look at some other areas of concern to paralegals in regard to employment policies, including performance evaluations and termination procedures.

Performance Evaluations

Many law firms have a policy of conducting periodic performance evaluations. Usually, performance is evaluated annually, but some firms conduct evaluations every six months.

Because paralegal responsibilities vary from firm to firm, no one evaluation checklist applies to every paralegal. Some of the factors that may be considered during a performance evaluation are indicated in Exhibit 4.2 on the next page. Note, though, that performance evaluations are much longer and more detailed than the list shown in the exhibit. For example, each major item in that list may have several subheadings and perhaps further subheadings under those subheadings. Normally, under each item listed on a performance evaluation is a series of options—ranging from "very good" to "unsatisfactory" or something similar—for the supervisor or attorney to check.

When you begin work as a paralegal, you should learn at the outset what exactly your duties will be and what performance is expected of you. This way, you will be able to prepare for your first evaluation from the moment you begin working. You will not have to wait six months or a year before you learn that you were supposed to be doing something that you failed to do.

In the busy workplace, you will probably not have much time available to discuss issues with your supervisor that do not relate to immediate needs. And even

EXHIBIT 4.2
Factors That May Be Considered in a Performance Evaluation

> 1. **RESPONSIBILITY**
> Making sure that all tasks are performed on time and following up on all pending matters.
> 2. **EFFICIENCY**
> Obtaining good results in the least amount of time.
> 3. **PRODUCTIVITY**
> Producing a sufficient quantity of work in a given time period.
> 4. **COMPETENCE**
> Knowledge level and skills.
> 5. **INITIATIVE**
> Applying intelligence and creativity to tasks and making appropriate recommendations.
> 6. **COOPERATION**
> Getting along well with others on the legal team.
> 7. **PERSONAL FACTORS**
> Appearance, grooming habits, friendliness, poise, and so forth.
> 8. **DEPENDABILITY**
> Arriving at work consistently on time and being available when needed.

if you do find a moment, you may feel awkward in broaching a discussion about your performance or about workplace problems. Performance evaluations are designed specifically to allow both the employer and the employee to exchange their views on such issues.

During performance reviews, you can learn how the firm rates your performance. You can gain valuable feedback from your supervisor, learn more about your strengths and weaknesses, and identify the areas in which you need to improve your skills or work habits. You can also give feedback to your supervisor on how you feel about the workplace. For example, if you think that your expertise is not being fully utilized, this would be a good time to discuss that issue and perhaps suggest some ways in which your knowledge and experience could be put to better use.

Some paralegals, particularly in smaller firms, have found that their busy supervising attorneys sometimes put off conducting "promised" evaluations. If you ever find yourself in this situation, consider preparing your own evaluation and presenting it to your supervising attorney for review.

Employment Termination

Virtually all policy manuals deal with the subject of employment termination. If you work for a firm that has prepared such a manual for its employees, the manual will likely specify what kind of conduct serves as a basis for firing employees. For example, the manual might specify that if an employee is absent more than twelve days a year for two consecutive years, the employer has grounds to terminate the employment relationship. The manual will also probably describe employment-termination procedures. For example, the firm might require that it be notified one month in advance if an employee decides to leave the firm; if the employee fails to give one month's notice, he or she may forfeit accumulated vacation time or other benefits on termination.

Employment Discrimination

Traditionally, employment relationships have been governed by the common law doctrine of employment at will. Under this doctrine, employers may hire and fire employees "at will"—that is, for any reason or no reason. Today, courts have created several exceptions to this doctrine, and state and federal statutes now regulate numerous aspects of the employment relationship. Under federal law (and many state statutes), employers may not refuse to hire job applicants, refuse to promote employees, or fire employees for discriminatory reasons—because of the employee's age, gender, or race, for example. These and other laws regulating employment relationships will be discussed in Chapter 9, but it should be mentioned here that virtually every large law firm today has special policies and procedures that must be followed with respect to claims of employment discrimination.

For example, an employee who experiences sexual harassment—a form of gender-based discrimination that is prohibited by federal law and most state laws—may be required by the firm's harassment policy to follow formal complaint channels to resolve the issue. If an employee fails to follow the required procedures, the firm may be able to avoid legal responsibility for the harassment. Similarly, if an employer does not have established procedures in place for dealing with harassment or other forms of discrimination, the employer may find it difficult to avoid liability for the harassment or discriminatory treatment initiated by supervisors or others against a particular employee.

> **On the Web**
> For information on federal laws governing employment discrimination, access the Equal Employment Opportunity Commission's Web site at **www.eeoc.gov**.

FILING PROCEDURES

Every law firm, regardless of its size or organizational structure, has some kind of established filing procedures. Efficient filing procedures are important in any law firm, because the paperwork generated by even a small firm can be substantial. Efficient filing procedures are particularly necessary in law offices because important and confidential documents must be safeguarded yet be readily retrievable when they are needed. If a client file is misplaced or lost, the client may suffer irreparable harm.

Additionally, documents must be filed in such a way as to protect client confidentiality. The duty of confidentiality was discussed at length in Chapter 3, but it deserves special mention here because of the extent to which it frames all legal work and procedures. This is particularly true of filing procedures. All information received from or about clients, including client files and documents, is considered confidential.

> **A breach of confidentiality by a paralegal or other employee can cause the firm to incur potentially extensive liability.**

If you work for a small firm, filing procedures may be rather informal, and you may even assume the responsibility for organizing and developing an efficient filing system. Larger firms normally have specific procedures concerning the creation, maintenance, use, and storage of office files. If you take a job with a large firm, a supervisor will probably spend some time training you in routine office procedures, including filing procedures. Although the trend today, particularly in larger firms, is toward computerized filing systems, firms routinely create "hard copies" to ensure that files are not lost if a computer system crashes.

Generally, law offices maintain several types of files. Typically, a law firm's filing system will include client files, work-product files and reference materials, and forms files (as well as personnel files, which we do not discuss here).

Client Files

To illustrate client filing procedures, we present below the phases in the "life cycle" of a hypothetical client's file. The name of the client is Katherine Baranski;

DEVELOPING PARALEGAL SKILLS

Client File Confidentiality

Robert James, a paralegal with the law firm of Jenkins & Fitzgerald, takes a client's file with him to the law library to do some legal research. While he walks several aisles away to look for a particular legal reference book, Lori Sanger, an attorney from another firm, walks by and notices the file. She can see on the file the law firm's name, the client's name (Purdy Contracting, Inc.), the court's docket number, and the firm's file number. Because she recognizes the client's name, she writes down the docket number, goes to the court clerk's office, and requests the court's file, which is public information. She reads through the file and sees that Purdy Contracting, Inc., a construction company, is being sued for a substantial amount of damages.

Lori has a client who is about to award a big construction project to Purdy Contracting. She calls her client and warns the client that this lawsuit could bankrupt Purdy. As a result, Purdy Contracting does not get the job and complains to Jenkins & Fitzgerald. The firm changes its policy so that client names no longer appear on the outside of client files.

CHECKLIST FOR CLIENT FILE CONFIDENTIALITY

- Create a confidential name for the client file, using alphabetical and/or numerical sequences.
- Do not leave files out in the open in public places, such as libraries or courts, where their contents can be observed by others.
- Do not leave files in areas within the law firm where other clients might observe the file and its contents.
- Follow the law firm's procedures for closing a file to ensure that extra copies of the documents and letters are destroyed.
- Destroy old files that no longer need to be retained by shredding them.

---

she has just retained one of your firm's attorneys to represent her in a lawsuit that she is bringing against Tony Peretto. Because Baranski is initiating the lawsuit, she is referred to as the *plaintiff*. Peretto, because he has to defend against Baranski's claims, is the *defendant*. The name of the case is *Baranski v. Peretto*. Assume that you will be working on the case and that your supervising attorney has just asked you to open a new case file. Assume also that you have already verified, through a "conflicts check" (discussed in Chapter 3), that no conflict of interest exists.

OPENING A NEW CLIENT FILE. The first step that you (or a secretary, at your request) will take in opening a new file is to assign the case a file number. For reasons of both efficiency and confidentiality, many firms identify their client files by numbers or some kind of numerical and/or alphabetical sequence instead of the clients' names, as mentioned earlier. The *Baranski v. Peretto* case file might be identified by the letters BARAPE—the first four letters of the plaintiff's name followed by the first two letters of the defendant's name. Increasingly, law firms are using computerized databases to record and track case titles and files. For example, some firms have file labels containing bar codes in which are embedded attorney codes, subject-matter codes, the client's name and file number, and so on.

Typically, law firms maintain a master client list on which clients' names are entered alphabetically and cross-referenced to the clients' case numbers. If file numbers consist of numerical sequences, there is also a master list on which the file numbers are listed in numerical order and cross-referenced to the clients' names.

ADDING SUBFILES. As the work on the *Baranski* case progresses and more documents are generated or received, the file will expand. To ensure that documents will be easy to locate, you will create subfiles. A special subfile might be created for client documents (such as a contract, will, stock certificate, or photograph) that the firm needs for reference or for evidence at trial. As correspondence relating to the *Baranski* case is generated, you will probably add a correspondence subfile. You will also want a subfile for your or the attorney's notes on the case, including research results.

As you will read in Chapters 10 and 11, litigation involves several stages. As the *Baranski* litigation progresses through these various stages, subfiles for documents relating to each stage will be added to the *Baranski* file. Many firms find it useful to color-code or add tabs to subfiles so that they can be readily identified. Often, in large files, an index of each subfile's contents is created and attached to the inside cover of the subfile.

Documents are typically filed within each subfile in reverse chronological order, with the most recently dated document on the top. Usually, to safeguard the documents, they are punched at the top with a two-hole puncher so that they can be secured within the file with a clip. Note, though, that original client documents should not be punched or altered in any way. They should always be left loose within the file. For example, if you were holding in the file a property deed belonging to a client, you would not want to alter that document in any way.

FILE USE AND STORAGE. Typically, files are stored in a central file room or area. Most firms have some kind of procedure for employees to follow when removing files from the storage area. For example, a firm might require the office staff to replace a removed file with an "out card" indicating the date, the name of the file, and the name or initials of the person who removed it.

Note that documents should never be removed from a client file or subfile. Rather, the entire file or subfile should be removed for use. This ensures that important documents will not be separated from the file and possibly mislaid or lost. Many paralegals and other users make copies of documents in the file for their use. For example, if you are working on the *Baranski* case and need to review certain documents in the file, you might remove those documents from the file temporarily, copy them, and immediately return the file to storage.

CLOSING A FILE. Assume that the *Baranski* case has been settled out of court and that no further legal work on Baranski's behalf needs to be done. For a time, her file will be retained in the inactive files, but when it is fairly certain that no one will need to refer to it very often, if ever, it will be closed. Closed files are often stored in a separate area of the building or even off-site. Traditionally, many larger law firms stored the contents of old files on microfilm. Today, firms can use scanning technology to scan file contents for storage on CD-ROMs, Zip disks, magnetic tapes, or other data-storage devices.

Specific procedures for closing files vary from firm to firm. Typically, when a case is closed, original documents provided by the client (for example, a deed to property) are returned to the client, and extraneous materials, such as extra copies of documents or cover letters, are destroyed.

DESTROYING OLD FILES. Law firms do not have to retain client files forever, and at some point, the *Baranski* case file will be destroyed. Old files are normally destroyed by shredding them so that confidentiality is preserved. Law firms exercise great care when destroying client files because a court or government agency

FEATURED GUEST: KATHLEEN MERCER REED
Ten Tips for Creating and Maintaining an Efficient File System

BIOGRAPHICAL NOTE

Kathleen Mercer Reed holds a bachelor of science degree in legal administration from the University of Toledo and has a law degree. She currently works as an associate professor and as the director of Legal Assistant Technology at the University of Toledo's Community and Technical College, the same program from which she received her associate's degree in 1985. A member of many legal-assistant advisory committees, Reed is a former president of the Toledo Association of Legal Assistants. She is active in national paralegal education issues and a frequent speaker on the paralegal profession.

File maintenance is one of the most important aspects of legal work. Without an organized case file, the attorney is unable to make sure that the case is on track and deadlines are being met. This can mean unhappy clients and a resulting loss of business. Generally, attorneys rely on their paralegals to assume responsibility for the essential task of maintaining (or supervising the maintenance of) the files. Filing systems vary. In some firms, they are highly structured and efficient; in other firms, they may be virtually nonexistent. If you are ever faced with the challenge of setting up (or reorganizing) a file system, here are some tips to consider.

1. Set Aside Time for Planning. The major problem relating to filing systems is the time factor. Law offices are extremely busy places. Time is money in the law firm. Everyone wants to get on with the important job of performing work for the client. But filing systems must be planned. You need to recognize this fact and allow time for the planning process.

2. Create a System That Is Simple, Yet Effective. Remember that you and the attorney will not be the only ones working with the file. Secretaries, receptionists, and file clerks may also need to use client files. Don't create a system that generates confusion about where certain documents are to be filed or where they can be found. Try to establish a simple, logical system that can be readily understood by everybody.

3. Make Sure That the Files Are Clearly Labeled. Each file should be clearly labeled so that it can be easily located. Files are more easily recognized when the labels are consistently placed on files and consistently typed, printed, or handwritten.

4. Don't Be Afraid to Create as Many Files as You Need. Don't hesitate to create additional files, especially subfiles, if you think that they are necessary. Generally, the more subfiles you create, the better organized your file will be—and the easier it will be to retrieve specific documents.

5. Make Sure That the Filing System Ensures Client Confidentiality. When setting up your file system, make sure that the system protects client confidentiality to the greatest possible extent. Some law firms are eliminating alphabetical systems (files in which the client's name is clearly identified on the file folder) and are using numeric filing systems instead. Numeric file systems eliminate the risk of one client seeing another client's name when the file is opened. Remember, a firm can breach a client's right to confidentiality simply

---

Statute of Limitations
A statute setting the maximum time period within which certain actions can be brought or rights enforced. After the period of time has run, no legal action can be brought.

may impose a heavy fine on a law firm that destroys a file that should have been retained for a longer period of time. How long a particular file must be retained depends on many factors, including the nature of the client's legal matters and governing statutes, such as the statute of limitations.

State **statutes of limitations** limit the time period during which specific types of legal actions may be brought. Statutes of limitations for legal-malpractice actions vary from state to state—from six months to ten years after the attorney's last contact with the client. When the statute of limitations in your state expires is thus an important factor in determining how long to retain a client file, because an attorney or law firm will need the information contained in the client's file to

FEATURED GUEST, Continued

by divulging (inadvertently or otherwise) the fact that the client consulted the firm, even as a potential client.

6. Set Up Efficient Case-Opening Procedures. A client file should be set up within twenty-four hours of the initial client interview and sent back to the attorney assigned to the file. This means that conflict-of-interest checks and initial file organization must be done quickly. A thorough conflict's check must be done to prevent the necessity of spending hours on a plaintiff's case only to find out that another attorney in the law firm is representing the defendant in that same case. At the same time, the file must be given to the attorney promptly so that he or she can begin working for the client and avoid missing any deadlines.

7. Establish an Efficient Check-Out System. No matter how well organized your file is, you can't work on the file if you can't find it! In a very small law office, this may not be a great concern. But the larger the firm, the more difficult it becomes to locate files—because more people have access to them. A file that you or an attorney needs urgently may be sitting on a partner's desk, but you do not know this. You need to establish and enforce some kind of sign-out system, such as placing "out cards" or "sign-out cards" in the file whenever a file folder is removed.

8. Establish Proper Procedures for Closing and Storing Files. Closed files must be properly stored and maintained for several reasons. First, a client may contact the firm—sometimes months after his or her case has been closed—to obtain documents or information from the client's file. Second, work that you did on past cases can be a great resource when working on current cases, and if old files are easily accessible, you will not have to "reinvent the wheel" whenever you work on a case that is similar to a case already in the firm's files. Third, and most important, there are state and national standards governing file retention. Find out how long your law firm is legally required to store and maintain closed files. For all of these reasons, closed files must be maintained with as much integrity as active files.

9. Establish Proper Procedures for Destroying Files. Client confi-

> "[B]y getting involved in file organization, your job as a paralegal is made easier."

dentiality must be maintained even when destroying very old closed files. One lawyer was shocked to find out that the paper from his closed files had been made into note pads and donated to a local school! There are a number of companies nationwide that deal exclusively with the destruction of confidential files. Use one of them or encourage your firm to invest in a paper shredder.

10. Keep in Mind the Ultimate Goal of Your Filing System. When setting up and maintaining a filing system, you should always keep in mind your primary goal—to help the firm deliver legal services more efficiently and economically. With an organized case file, the attorney can make sure that the case is on track and that deadlines are being met. Clients are happier, and malpractice actions are avoided. Additionally, by getting involved in file organization, your job as a paralegal is made easier. You not only stay well informed on file contents but also don't have to waste time searching for needed files or documents.

---

defend against a malpractice action. If the file has been destroyed, the firm will not be able to produce any documents or other evidence to refute the plaintiff's claim.

Work-Product Files and Reference Materials

Many law firms keep copies of research projects, legal memoranda, and various case-related documents prepared by the firm's attorneys and paralegals so that these documents can be referred to in future projects. In this way, legal personnel do not have to start all over again when working on a claim similar to one dealt with in the past.

Traditionally, hard copies of work-product files, or legal-information files, were filed in the firm's law library with other reference materials and publications. Today, work-product documents and research materials are often generated on computers and stored on diskettes, Zip disks, CD-ROMs, or other data-storage devices. Often, in large firms, these materials will be kept in a central data bank that is readily accessible by the firm's personnel.

Forms Files

Forms File
A reference file containing copies of the firm's commonly used legal documents and informational forms. The documents in the forms file serve as a model for drafting new documents.

Every law firm keeps on hand various forms that it commonly uses. These forms may be kept in various files or, as is often the case, stored in a **forms file**. A forms file might include forms for retainer agreements (to be discussed shortly), for filing lawsuits in specific courts, for bankruptcy petitions, for real-estate matters, and for numerous other types of legal matters. Often, to save time, copies of documents relating to specific types of cases are kept for future reference. Then, when the attorney or paralegal works on a similar case, those documents can serve as models, or guides. (These forms may be kept in a work-product file, as just mentioned.)

Increasingly, forms files are being computerized. Computerized forms have simplified legal practice by allowing legal personnel to generate customized documents within minutes. Forms for many standard legal transactions are now available from legal-software companies on disk or CD-ROM. They are also available online at an increasing number of Web sites, as you will read in Chapter 15.

On the Web
For a sampling of the types of legal forms available on the Web, check the following sites: www.lectlaw.com/form.html and www.legaldocs.com.

FINANCIAL PROCEDURES

Like any other business firm, a law firm needs to at least cover its expenses or it will fail. In the business of law, the product is legal services, which are sold to clients for a price. A foremost concern of any law firm is therefore to establish a clear policy on fee arrangements and efficient procedures to ensure that each client is billed appropriately for the time and costs associated with serving that client. Efficient billing procedures require, in turn, that attorneys and paralegals keep accurate records of the time that they spend working on a given client's case or other legal matter.

Fee Arrangements

A major ethical concern of the legal profession has to do with the reasonableness of attorneys' fees and the ways in which clients are billed for legal services. Among other things, state ethical codes governing attorneys require legal fees to be reasonable. For example, Rule 1.5 of the Model Rules of Professional Conduct states, "A lawyer's fees shall be reasonable." The rule then lists the factors that should be considered in determining the reasonableness of a fee. The factors include the time and labor required to perform the legal work, the fee customarily charged in the locality for similar legal services, and the experience and ability of the lawyer performing the services.

Retainer Agreement
A signed document stating that the attorney or the law firm has been hired by the client to provide certain legal services and that the client agrees to pay for those services in accordance with the terms set forth in the retainer agreement.

Normally, fee arrangements are discussed and agreed on at the outset of any attorney-client relationship. Most law firms require each client to agree, in a signed writing called a **retainer agreement**, to whatever fee arrangements have been made. (Some states also require, by law, that fee arrangements be stated in writing.) The agreement specifies that the client is retaining (hiring) the attorney and/or firm to represent the client in a legal matter and states that the client agrees

EXHIBIT 4.3

A Sample Retainer Agreement

RETAINER AGREEMENT

I, Katherine Baranski, agree to employ Allen P. Gilmore and his law firm, Jeffers, Gilmore & Dunn, as my attorneys to prosecute all claims for damages against Tony Peretto and all other persons or entities that may be liable on account of an automobile accident that caused me to sustain serious injuries. The accident occurred on August 4, 1999, at 7:45 A.M., when Tony Peretto ran a stop sign on Thirty-eighth Street at Mattis Avenue and, as a result, his car collided with mine.

I agree to pay my lawyers a fee that will be one-fourth (25 percent) of any sum recovered in this case, regardless of whether the sum is received through settlement, lawsuit, arbitration, or any other way. The fee will be calculated on the sum recovered, after costs and expenses have been deducted. The fee will be paid when any money is actually received in this case. I agree that Allen P. Gilmore and his law firm have an express attorney's lien on any recovery to ensure that their fee is paid.

I agree to pay all necessary costs and expenses, such as court filing fees, court reporter fees, expert witness fees and expenses, travel expenses, long-distance telephone and facsimile costs, and photocopying charges. I understand that these costs and expenses will be billed to me by my attorney on a monthly basis and that I am responsible for paying these costs and expenses, even if no recovery is received.

I agree that this agreement does not cover matters other than those described above. It does not cover an appeal from any judgment entered, any efforts necessary to collect money due because of a judgment entered by a court, or any efforts necessary to obtain other benefits, such as insurance.

I agree to pay a carrying charge amounting to the greater of two dollars ($2.00) or two percent (2%) per month on the average daily balance of bills on my account that are thirty days overdue. If my account is outstanding by more than sixty (60) days, all work by the attorney shall cease until the account is paid in full or a monthly payment plan is agreed on.

This contract is governed by the law of the state of Nita.*

I AGREE TO THE TERMS AND CONDITIONS STATED ABOVE:

Date: 2 / 4 / 2000   *Katherine Baranski*
                            Katherine Baranski

I agree to represent Katherine Baranski in the matter described above. I will receive no fee unless a recovery is obtained. If a recovery is obtained, I will receive a fee as described above.

I agree to notify Katherine Baranski of all developments in this matter promptly, and I will make no settlement of this matter without her consent.

I AGREE TO THE TERMS AND CONDITIONS STATED ABOVE:

Date: 2 / 4 / 2000   *Allen P. Gilmore*
                            Allen P. Gilmore
                            Jeffers, Gilmore & Dunn
                            553 Fifth Avenue
                            Suite 101
                            Nita City, Nita 48801

---

*A hypothetical state.

---

to the fee arrangements set forth in the agreement. Exhibit 4.3 above shows a sample retainer agreement.

Basically, there are three types of fee arrangements: fixed fees, hourly fees, and contingency fees. We examine here each of these types of fees, as well as some alternative fee arrangements that have recently come into use.

> ### ETHICAL CONCERN
> ## Handling Clients' Questions about Fees
>
> Suppose that you work as a paralegal for a sole practitioner, Marina Tesner, who is just setting up practice. You know that the attorney is soliciting new clients and that she relies on you, when she is out of the office, to make sure that potential clients are not turned away for any reason. One day, while Tesner is out of town, a man named Henry Roth calls the office. He is purchasing a home and wants to consult with an attorney before signing the final papers four days from now. You explain that Ms. Tesner is out of the office but will return in two days and could see him then. Roth says that he would wait for a couple of days if he knew what Tesner would charge for her services. Should you tell him that Ms. Tesner usually bills clients $125 an hour for her services, which is a low billable rate for your community? No, you should not. As discussed in Chapter 3, professional ethical codes prohibit anyone but an attorney from setting legal fees. If you told Roth what he wanted to know, you may be engaging in the unauthorized practice of law.

Fixed Fee
A fee paid to the attorney by his or her client for having rendered a specified legal service, such as the creation of a simple will.

FIXED FEES. The client may agree to pay a **fixed fee** for a specified legal service. Certain procedures, such as incorporation and simple divorce filings, are often handled on a fixed-fee basis because the attorney can estimate fairly closely how much time will be involved in completing the work. Charging fixed fees is increasingly becoming a preferred method of billing. This is because it helps attorneys avoid lawsuits and other problems that can result when clients allege that their legal fees were excessive.

HOURLY FEES. Traditionally, with the exception of litigation work done on a contingency-fee basis (discussed below), most law firms have charged clients hourly rates for legal services. Hourly rates vary widely from firm to firm. Some litigation firms, for example, can charge extremely high hourly rates ($500 an hour or more) for their services because of their reputation for obtaining favorable settlements or court judgments for their clients. In contrast, an attorney just starting up a practice as a sole practitioner will have to charge a lower, more competitive rate (which may be as low as $75 per hour) to attract clients.

Today, law firms also bill clients for hourly rates for paralegal services. Because the hourly rate for paralegals is lower than that for attorneys, clients benefit from attorneys' use of paralegal services. Generally, the billing rate for paralegal services depends on the size of the firm. According to the compensation survey conducted by the National Federation of Paralegal Associations (NFPA) in 1997, in firms with less than ten attorneys, the range of billing rates for paralegals was from $61 to $71 per hour; in firms with over two hundred attorneys, the range was from $81 to $90 per hour. The average billing rate, according to the 1997 survey conducted by the National Association of Legal Assistants (NALA), was $64.

Note that although your services might be billed to the client at a certain rate, say $70, that does not mean that the firm will actually pay you $70 an hour as wages. The billable rate for paralegal services, as for attorney services, has to take into account the firm's expenses for overhead (rent, utilities, employee benefits, supplies, and so on).

CONTINGENCY FEES. A common practice among litigation attorneys, especially those representing plaintiffs in certain types of cases (such as personal-injury or negligence cases) is to charge the client on a contingency-fee basis. A **contingency fee** is contingent (dependent) on the outcome of the case. If the plaintiff wins the lawsuit and recovers damages or settles out of court, the attorney will be entitled to a certain percentage of the amount recovered. If the plaintiff loses the lawsuit, the attorney gets nothing—although the client normally will reimburse the attorney for the costs and expenses involved in preparing for trial (costs and expenses are discussed below, in regard to billing procedures).

Often, the attorney's contingency fee is one-fourth or one-third of the amount recovered. The agreement may provide for modification of the amount depending on how and when the dispute is settled. For example, an agreement that provides for a contingency fee of 25 percent of the amount recovered for a plaintiff may state that the amount will be reduced to a lower percentage if the case is settled out of court. In this situation, the agreement might provide that if the case is settled before trial, the attorney's fee will be one-tenth of the amount recovered in the settlement.

While some people maintain that the use of contingency fees is ethically questionable (because it may motivate attorneys to resort to aggressive tactics just to win a case), the legal profession deems it ethical because it allows the public to have broader access to legal services. Contingency-fee arrangements allow clients who otherwise could not afford legal services to have their claims settled, in or out of court, by competent attorneys.

Note that contingency-fee agreements only apply if an attorney represents the client in a civil lawsuit. In a civil case, the plaintiff frequently seeks money damages from the defendant to compensate the plaintiff for harms suffered. If the plaintiff "wins" the case, the attorney's fee will be a percentage of the amount awarded. Criminal cases, in contrast, are brought by the state (through the district attorney, county attorney, or other attorney working for the government)—as you will read in Chapter 12. If the court finds the defendant guilty, the state imposes a penalty (a fine and/or imprisonment) on him or her. If the defendant is deemed innocent in the eyes of the court, no money is awarded to the defendant. In criminal cases, contingency fees are thus not an option.

ALTERNATIVE FEE ARRANGEMENTS. Recently, some attorneys have been creating alternative fee arrangements with their clients. One relatively new billing practice, called "task-based billing," is similar to a fixed-fee arrangement: a fixed fee is charged for specific types of tasks that are involved in a legal matter. For example, the attorney might charge a flat fee for conducting a pretrial deposition (in which a party in a lawsuit or a witness gives sworn testimony—see Chapter 10). Another alternative billing practice is sometimes referred to as "value billing." When this arrangement is used, the fees charged to the client vary, depending on the results of the representation—if a lawsuit is lost, won, or settled, for example.

Client Trust Accounts

Law firms often require new clients to pay a **retainer**—an initial advance payment to the firm to cover part of the fee and various costs that will be incurred on the client's behalf (such as mileage or other travel expenses, phone and fax charges, and so on). Funds received as retainers, as well as any funds received on behalf of the client (such as a payment to a client to settle a lawsuit), are placed in a special bank account. This account is usually referred to as a client **trust account** (or escrow account).

Contingency Fee
A legal fee that consists of a specified percentage (such as 30 percent) of the amount the plaintiff recovers in a civil lawsuit. The fee must be paid only if the plaintiff prevails in the lawsuit (recovers damages).

Retainer
An advance payment made by a client to a law firm to cover part of the legal fees and/or costs that will need to be incurred on that client's behalf.

Trust Account
A bank or escrow account in which one party (the trustee, such as an attorney) holds funds belonging to another person (such as a client); a bank account into which funds advanced to a law firm by a client are deposited.

ETHICAL CONCERN
Trust Accounts

Suppose that a legal professional who has access to funds held in trust for clients borrows money from those funds for temporary personal use. Would such borrowing be unethical? Would it be illegal? The answer to both questions is a resounding "Yes!" By law, anyone who takes for personal use any property (including money) that is legally entrusted to his or her care commits a form of theft called embezzlement. It does not matter whether the person who used the funds intended to replace them the next day, week, or month. The fact is, a crime has been committed.

 It is extremely important that the funds held in a trust account be used *only* for expenses relating to the costs of serving that client's needs.

Misuse of client funds constitutes a breach of the firm's duty to its client. An attorney's personal use of the funds, for example, can lead to disciplinary action and possible disbarment, as well as criminal penalties. *Commingling* (mixing together) a client's funds with the firm's funds also constitutes abuse and is one of the most common ways in which attorneys breach their professional obligations. If you handle a client's trust account, you should be especially careful to document fully your use of the funds to protect yourself and your firm against the serious problems that may arise if there are any discrepancies in the account.

The Prohibition against Fee Splitting

An important ethical rule with which paralegals should be familiar is Rule 5.4 of the Model Rules of Professional Conduct. That rule states, "A lawyer or law firm shall not share legal fees with a nonlawyer." For this reason, paralegals cannot become partners in a law partnership (because the partners share the firm's income), nor can they have a fee-sharing arrangement with an attorney in any way.

One of the reasons for this rule is that it protects the attorney's independent judgment concerning legal matters. For example, if an attorney became partners with two or three nonattorneys, the nonattorneys would have a significant voice in determining the firm's policies. In this situation, a conflict might arise between a policy of the firm and the attorney's duty to exercise independent professional judgment in regard to a client's case. The rule against fee splitting also protects against the possibility that nonlawyers would, indirectly through attorneys, be able to engage in the practice of law, which no one but an attorney can do.

Billing and Timekeeping Procedures

As a general rule, a law firm bills its clients monthly. Each client's bill reflects the amount of time spent on the client's matter by the attorney or other legal personnel. In the context of legal work, client billing serves an obvious financial function (collecting payment for services rendered). It also serves a communicative function, as you will learn later in this chapter.

DEVELOPING PARALEGAL SKILLS

Creating a Trust Account

Louise Larson has been hired to work for Don Jones. Don is just starting his own sole practice of law after many years of working with a medium-sized law firm in which he had nothing to do with the firm's financial management. Louise's first assignment is to establish a client trust account. Don and Louise review the ethical rules regarding client property and funds. These rules require that client funds not be commingled with the lawyer's funds. "It's too easy to 'borrow' from a client's funds when they are in the lawyer's own bank account," explains Don.

CHECKLIST FOR CREATING A CLIENT TRUST ACCOUNT

- Obtain and prepare the necessary forms from the bank in which the account will be maintained.
- Devise a bookkeeping method for tracking all fees and expenses for a particular case and/or client.
- Retain all deposit slips and canceled checks.
- Keep a record of payments made to clients.
- Decide who will have access to the account.

Generally, client bills are prepared by a legal secretary or a bookkeeper or, in larger firms, by someone in the accounting department. The bills are based on the fee arrangements made with the client and the time slips collected from the firm's attorneys and paralegals. The time slips (discussed below) indicate how many hours are to be charged to each client at what hourly rate.

The *legal fees* billed to clients will be based on the number of billable hours generated for work requiring legal expertise. **Billable hours** are the hours or fractions of hours that attorneys and paralegals spend in client-related work that requires legal expertise and that can be billed directly to clients. The *costs* billed to clients will include expenses incurred by the firm (such as court fees, travel expenses, phone and fax charges, express-delivery charges, and copying costs) on the client's behalf. If an attorney is retained on a contingency-fee basis, the client is not billed monthly for legal fees. The client is normally billed monthly for any costs incurred on the client's behalf, however.

Typically, a preliminary draft of the client's bill will be given to the attorney responsible for that client's account. After the attorney reviews and possibly modifies the bill, the final draft of the bill is generated and sent to the client. Exhibit 4.4 on the next page illustrates a sample client bill in its final form.

Most law firms today have computerized their billing procedures, using time-and-billing software designed specifically for law-office use. Because it would be impossible to describe in this section each of the hundreds of such programs that are used, we look here at traditional timekeeping and billing procedures. A knowledge of these procedures, which illustrate the basic principles involved in client billing, will help you understand whatever type of time-and-billing software your employer may use.

DOCUMENTING TIME AND EXPENSES. Accurate timekeeping by attorneys and paralegals is crucial because clients cannot be billed for time spent on their behalf unless that time is documented. Attorneys and paralegals normally keep track of the time they spend on each client's work. Traditionally, **time slips** have been used for this purpose. Each time slip documents in hours and fractions of hours (commonly in tenths or quarters of an hour) the amount of time spent on a particular day on a particular task for a particular client. Usually, an attorney or a paralegal

Billable Hours
Hours or fractions of hours that attorneys and paralegals spend in work that requires legal expertise and that can be billed directly to clients.

On the Web
You can obtain information on selected time-and-billing software at the following Web sites: www.pclaw.com/pclawjr.htm, www.timeslips.com, and www.intuit.com.

Time Slip
A record documenting, for billing purposes, the hours (or fractions of hours) that an attorney or a paralegal worked for each client, the date on which the work was done, and the type of work that was undertaken.

EXHIBIT 4.4
A Sample Client Bill

Jeffers, Gilmore & Dunn
553 Fifth Avenue
Suite 101
Nita City, NI 48801

BILLING DATE: February 28, 2000

Thomas Jones, M.D.
508 Oak Avenue
Nita City, Nita 48802

RE: Medical-Malpractice Action Brought against Dr. Jones, File No. 15789

DATE	SERVICES RENDERED	PROVIDED BY	HOURS SPENT	TOTAL
1/30/96	Initial client consultation	APG (attorney)	1.00	$150.00
1/30/96	Client interview	EML (paralegal)	1.00	74.00
1/30/96	Document preparation	EML (paralegal)	1.00	74.00
2/5/96	Interview: Susanne Mathews (nurse)	EML (paralegal)	1.50	111.00
	TOTAL FOR LEGAL SERVICES			$409.00

DATE	EXPENSES			
2/5/96	Hospital charges for a copy of the medical documents			$75.00
	TOTAL FOR EXPENSES			$75.00
	TOTAL BILL TO CLIENT			$484.00

Expense Slip
A slip of paper on which any expense, or cost, that is incurred on behalf of a client (such as the payment of court fees or long-distance telephone charges) is recorded.

includes on the time slip his or her initials, the date, the client number, and a description of the type of legal services performed. (This description will appear on the client's bill.) Exhibit 4.5 shows a sample time slip. Any costs incurred on behalf of clients are entered on **expense slips**. Exhibit 4.6 shows a sample expense slip.

BILLABLE VERSUS NONBILLABLE HOURS. The time recorded on time slips is charged either to a client (billable hours) or to the firm (nonbillable hours). As mentioned, billable time generally includes the hours or fractions of hours that attorneys and paralegals spend in client-related work that requires legal expertise. For example, the time you spend researching or investigating a client's claim is billable time. So is the time spent in conferences with or about a client, drafting documents on behalf of a client, interviewing clients or witnesses, and traveling (to and from the courthouse to file documents, for example).

Time spent on other tasks, such as administrative work, staff meetings, or performance reviews, is nonbillable time. For example, suppose that you spend thirty

> **EXHIBIT 4.5**
> A Sample Time Slip

TIME SLIP

Name of timekeeper_____ Client name/number_____

File number_____ Time allocated_____

Hourly rate_____ Billable/nonbillable_____

Date service rendered_____

Brief description of legal service:_____

_____

_____

minutes photocopying forms for the forms file, time sheets, or a procedures manual for the office. That thirty minutes would not be considered billable time.

Generally, law firms have a legitimate reason for wanting to maximize their billable hours:

> **The financial well-being of a law firm depends to a great extent on how many billable hours are generated by its employees.**

Nonbillable time ultimately cuts into the firm's profits. Of course, as mentioned earlier, nonbillable time is factored into the hourly rate charged for legal services. But to remain competitive, a law firm cannot charge too high an hourly rate. Therefore, the more billable hours generated by the firm's legal professionals, the more profitable the business will be.

Law firms normally tell their paralegals and associate attorneys how many billable hours they are expected to produce and the consequences of not being able to meet that number. Some firms expect associate attorneys to produce a minimum of 2,200 billable hours per year; other firms require fewer or more hours. Depending on the firm, a paralegal may be expected to generate between 1,250 and 2,000 billable hours per year.

Attorneys and paralegals face substantial pressure to produce billable hours for the firm. As a paralegal, you may be subject to this pressure and must learn how to handle it. For example, suppose that your employer expects you to produce 1,800 billable hours per year. Discounting vacation time and holidays (assuming a two-week vacation and ten paid holidays), this equates to 37.5 hours

> **EXHIBIT 4.6**
> A Sample Expense Slip

EXPENSE SLIP

Name_____

Client name and file number_____

Billable/nonbillable_____

Date of expense_____

Brief description of expense incurred:_____

_____

_____

Quantity and rate (if applicable)_____

> ## ETHICAL CONCERN
> ### Back Up Your Work
>
> Even a person who uses computers on a routine basis can easily forget—while the computer system is working—that a power failure or other problem can occur at any time. Should this happen, you may lose all current work that has not been saved to your hard disk. Surge protectors help to protect against "computer meltdown," but you should have, in addition, back-up copies of all of your work as well as a contingency plan—such as a second computer available to use.
>
> Backing up your work frequently on a diskette or other external storage device is particularly important and can "save the day" if the computer system crashes or fails to the extent that data on the hard drive cannot be retrieved. If you routinely back up documents, you may save yourself the hours of valuable time that could be required to recreate a document or file. You will also save yourself and the firm from the problem of deciding who will pay—the client or the law firm—for the extra time you had to spend to complete the work. Moreover, with back-up copies available, your employer will never have to be without a crucial document when it's needed. Another important precaution you can take to prevent loss of work is to have a crash-saving program, such as Norton Utilities, available to recover lost data.

weekly. Assuming that you work 40 hours a week, you will have 2.5 hours a week for such nonbillable activities as interoffice meetings, performance reviews, coffee breaks, tidying up your desk, reorganizing your work area, or chatting with others in the office. As you can imagine, unless you are willing to work more than eight hours a day, you may have difficulty meeting the billable-hours requirement.

Ethics and Client Billing Practices

Because attorneys have a duty to charge their clients "reasonable" fees, legal professionals must be careful in their billing practices. They must not "pad" their clients' bills by including more billable hours than actually worked on behalf of those clients. They also must avoid **double billing**—billing more than one client for the same time.

Double Billing
Billing more than one client for the same billable time period.

DOUBLE BILLING. Sometimes, situations arise in which it is difficult to determine which client should be billed for a particular segment of time. For example, suppose that you are asked to travel to another city to interview a witness in a case for Client A. You spend three hours traveling in an airplane, travel time that is necessary in working on behalf of Client A. You spend two hours in the airplane summarizing a document relating to a case for Client B. Who should pay for those two hours, Client A, Client B, or both? In this situation, you could argue—as many attorneys do in similar circumstances—that you generated five billable hours, three on Client A's work and two on Client B's case. This is an example of how double billing can occur.

Double billing also occurs when a firm bills a new client for work that was done for a previous client. For example, suppose that an attorney is working on a case for Client B that is very similar to a case handled by the firm a year ago for Client A. The firm charged Client A $2,000 for the legal services. Because much of the research, writing, and other work done on Client A's case can transfer over

DEVELOPING PARALEGAL SKILLS

A Client Complains about a Bill

Joni Winston takes a phone call for her supervising attorney, Mary Perkins. The caller, Joe Hendry, wants to leave a message regarding the bill for settling his father's estate. Joni tells Mr. Hendry that she worked with him on the estate matter and identifies herself as Mary's legal assistant. She asks Mr. Hendry for the details of the billing problem. He tells her that he was "double-billed" for the filing of the letters of authority with the probate court and threatens to file a grievance against Mary with the bar association if the matter is not resolved by 5:00 P.M. that day.

Joni sympathizes with Mr. Hendry and promises to look into the problem and call him back by the end of the day. Joni and Mary review the bill and determine that a temporary secretary had mislabeled the second billing

entry. The entry should have read "Preparing estate tax return" instead of "Filing letters of authority with the probate court." The amount billed remains the same. Joni returns Mr. Hendry's call, as promised, and explains to him what happened.

TIPS FOR AVOIDING BILLING ERRORS
- Select a billing system that is "user friendly."
- Carefully record your time.
- Establish procedures for regularly turning in time sheets and for recording your time.
- Assign billing tasks to one reliable staff member.
- Have attorneys review bills before they are sent to clients.

---

to Client B's case, the firm is able to complete the work for Client B in half the time. In this situation, would it be fair to bill Client B $2,000 also? After all, $1,000 of that amount represents hours spent on Client A's case (and for which Client A has already been billed). At the same time, would it be fair to Client A to bill Client B less for essentially the same services? Would it be fair to the firm if it was not allowed to profit from cost efficiencies generated by overlapping work?

Some firms today are tackling this ethical problem by splitting the benefits derived from cost efficiencies between the client and the firm. For example, the attorney in the above example might split the savings created by the overlapping research ($1,000) with Client B by billing Client B $1,500 instead of $2,000. Other firms still bill their clients for the time spent on previous work that transfers over to new clients' cases.

THE AMERICAN BAR ASSOCIATION'S RESPONSE TO DOUBLE BILLING. The American Bar Association (ABA) addressed this ethical "gray area" in the legal profession—double billing—in an ethical opinion issued in 1993. In its first formal opinion on the issue, the ABA stated that attorneys are prohibited from charging more than one client for the same hours of work. Additionally, the ABA rejected the notion that the firm, and not the client, should benefit from cost efficiencies created by the firm's work for previous clients. "The lawyer who has agreed to bill solely on the basis of time spent is obliged to pass the benefit of these economies on to the client." Although ABA opinions do not become legally binding on attorneys until they are adopted by the states as law, they do carry much weight in the legal profession.

COMMUNICATING WITH CLIENTS

Sending monthly bills to clients is one way to keep attorney-client communication channels open. Such communication is important because attorneys have a duty

TECHNOLOGY AND TODAY'S PARALEGAL
Cyberspace Communications

In the past few years, e-mail has become a standard communication tool used by business and professional firms, including law firms. The reason why e-mail is among the fastest-growing technologies is simple: it is a quick, easy-to-use, and inexpensive way to communicate. In large law firms or corporate enterprises, as well as in government agencies, e-mail messages are rapidly replacing the printed "interoffice memos" of the past. E-mail is also becoming a standard way for attorneys and paralegals to communicate with clients, opposing counsel, witnesses, and others.

Because e-mail is transmitted through an electronic medium—computer networks—it is difficult to remember that it is also a *written communication*. In other words, writing skills still apply. If you want to convey a written message to someone, you need to make sure that you use clear and effective language. Also, e-mail messages frequently are printed out and retained in client or correspondence files, so that a record exists of the communication. This means that any typos, misspellings, and incorrect usage in a message may be more permanent than you realize at the time you send the message.

One thing you can do to ensure that your e-mail messages are professional in tone and quality is to make sure that your e-mail program has a spell checker. Additionally, before you send important e-mail messages, you should print them out first and read them carefully to confirm that the grammar, spelling, and punctuation are correct—just as you would review and proofread a written letter. It often helps to print out important messages, let them sit a while, and review and proofread them later when your "eye" is fresher.

There are several other things that you can do to enhance e-mail communications and ward off potential problems. One is to request feedback for important messages. For example, if you send a message to a client informing him or her of an important court date or other matter, request the client to verify that the message was received. Similarly, you should respond immediately to incoming e-mail whenever possible so that the sender knows the message has been received and (perhaps) what actions are being taken on it. Finally, as in all other communications, such as phone calls and face-to-face encounters, you should remember to disclose your paralegal status in your e-mail communications. This is important to avoid potential liability for the unauthorized practice of law (discussed in Chapter 3).

---

to keep a client reasonably informed. Rule 1.4 of the Model Rules of Professional Conduct reads as follows:

> (a) A lawyer shall keep a client reasonably informed about the status of a matter and promptly comply with reasonable requests for information.
> (b) A lawyer shall explain a matter to the extent reasonably necessary to permit the client to make informed decisions regarding the representation.

As a paralegal, you need to be aware that keeping clients reasonably informed about the progress being made on their cases goes beyond courtesy and the cultivation of a client's goodwill—it is a legal duty of attorneys. The meaning of "reasonably informed" varies, of course, depending on the client and on the nature of the work being done by the attorney. In some cases, a phone call every week or two will suffice to keep the client informed. In other cases, the attorney may ask the paralegal to draft a letter to a client explaining the status of the client's legal matter. Some firms institute a regular monthly mailing to update clients on the status of their claims or cases. Generally, as a paralegal, you should discuss with your supervising attorney how each client should be kept informed of the status of his or her case.

Copies of all letters to a client should, of course, be placed in the client's file. Additionally, the client's file should contain a written record of each phone call

TODAY'S PROFESSIONAL PARALEGAL

Managing Conflict in the Legal Workplace

On Cheryl Hardy's first day at her new job as a legal assistant at Comp-Lease, Inc., a computer leasing corporation, Cheryl is introduced to the department staff by her boss, Dennis Hoyt. Dennis then takes her to meet the legal team. When she meets Jackie, the team secretary, Jackie gives her a frosty "Hello," without a handshake or smile, and then looks down at the desk. Cheryl does not understand why Jackie seems hostile. She has just met Jackie and has not done or said anything to offend her.

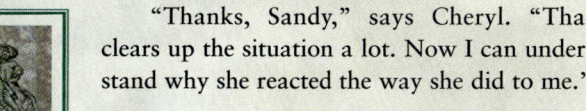

After her lunch break, Cheryl is given her first lease package to prepare. The work consists of drafting a lease (rental) agreement and giving it to the secretary to input into the computer and print out the agreement form. Cheryl prepares the draft and gives it to Jackie. Cheryl is very polite and tells Jackie not to rush because the agreement does not have to be sent out for two days. When Cheryl asks Jackie for the lease two days later, it is not done. Jackie tells Cheryl to check with her after lunch to see how it is coming. "Great," thinks Cheryl to herself, as she walks back to her desk. "My first week on the job and I'll be in trouble because of Jackie."

Analyzing the Problem

Cheryl decides to talk to a co-worker, Sandy, about the problem. At lunch, Cheryl explains the situation to Sandy. "She probably resents you," says Sandy. "You see, Jackie has always wanted to be a paralegal. The company has a policy that you have to have a degree or a certificate, even if you have experience, and so she cannot move into a paralegal position without some education. She has not been able to attend a paralegal training program because of family obligations and the expense involved. I'm sure that she knows that you were a legal secretary and that you worked your way through school. When Dennis told us that he had hired a new paralegal, he made your experience and education quite clear."

"Thanks, Sandy," says Cheryl. "That clears up the situation a lot. Now I can understand why she reacted the way she did to me."

Solving the Problem

Cheryl has an idea. She invites Jackie to lunch. Jackie talks about her interest in becoming a paralegal, her frustration with the company's policy, and her inability to get a certificate or degree because of her family obligations and the cost of going back to school. Cheryl tells Jackie that she was in a similar situation and that she got a scholarship from her school to pay for most of her education. She tells Jackie that she might be able to get one, too. She encourages Jackie by telling her, truthfully, that she is obviously bright enough to be a paralegal. Cheryl gives Jackie the name and phone number of Lois Allison, the director of the program that Cheryl attended. "Why don't you call her and tell her that I referred you? Explain that you are in the same situation that I was in when I started. She can tell you what might be available," suggested Cheryl.

When Cheryl returns to her office from lunch, she calls Lois Allison. She explains Jackie's situation and tells Lois that Jackie might be calling to get information on the program and scholarships. Lois replies that she will be happy to talk to Jackie and to help her if she can.

Later that afternoon, when Cheryl gives Jackie a lease package to prepare, Jackie prepares it right away. She even brings it into Cheryl's office, which she does not have to do. "I just want to thank you for going out of your way for me," says Jackie. "I called Lois Allison, and she wants me to come in and fill out some application forms. She thinks that I might qualify for a scholarship. So I might get to go to school after all." Cheryl smiles and replies, "I am glad that Lois could help you."

---

made to or received from a client. That way, there is a "paper trail" in the event it is ever necessary to provide evidence of communication with the client. (Actually, this is a good practice for all phone calls relating to a client's matter.) You will learn about the various forms of letters that attorneys send to clients in Chapter 16. Increasingly, attorneys and paralegals communicate with clients via e-mail, which can pose special problems—as discussed in this chapter's *Technology and Today's Paralegal: Cyberspace Communications* on the previous page.

Law-Office Culture and Politics

As a paralegal, you will find that each law firm you work for is unique. Even though two firms may be the same size and have similar organizational structures, they will have different cultures, or "personalities." The culture of a given legal workplace is ultimately determined by the attitudes of the firm's owners (the partners, for example) in regard to the fundamental goals of the firm.

Additionally, you will find that each firm has a political infrastructure that may have little to do with the lines of authority and accountability that are spelled out in the firm's employment manual or other formal policy statement. An up-and-coming younger partner in the firm, for example, may in fact exercise more authority than one of the firm's older partners who is about to retire. There may be rivalry between associate attorneys for promotion to partnership status, and you may be caught in the middle of it. If you are aware (and you may not be) of the rivalry and your position relative to it, you may find yourself tempted to take sides—which could jeopardize your own future with the firm.

Unfortunately, paralegals have little way of knowing about the culture and politics of a given firm until they have worked for the firm a while. Of course, if you know someone who works for or who has worked for a firm and value that employee's opinion, you might gain some advance knowledge about the firm's environment from that source. Otherwise, when you start to work for a firm, you will need to learn for yourself about interoffice politics. One way to do this is to listen carefully whenever a co-worker discusses the firm's staff and ask discreet questions to elicit information from co-workers about office politics and unwritten policies. This way, you can both prepare yourself to deal with these issues and protect your own interests. Ultimately, after you've worked for the firm for a time, you will be in a position to judge whether the firm you have chosen is really the "right firm" for you.

Key Terms and Concepts

- **billable hours**   133
- **contingency fee**   131
- **double billing**   136
- **employment manual**   121
- **expense slip**   134
- **fixed fee**   130
- **forms file**   128
- **legal administrator**   119
- **legal-assistant manager**   119
- **managing partner**   118
- **office manager**   119
- **partner**   118
- **partnership**   118
- **personal liability**   117
- **professional corporation (P.C.)**   118
- **retainer**   131
- **retainer agreement**   128
- **shareholder**   118
- **sole proprietorship**   117
- **statute of limitations**   126
- **support personnel**   121
- **time slip**   133
- **trust account**   131

Chapter Summary

1. In terms of business organization, a law firm may take the form of a sole proprietorship, in which one individual owns the business; a partnership, in which two or more individuals—called partners—jointly own the business; or a professional corporation, in which two or more individuals—called shareholders—own the business. The sole proprietor is entitled to all the firm's profits, bears the burden of any losses, and is personally liable for the firm's debts or other obligations. Partners share jointly the profits or losses of the firm

and are subject to personal liability for all of the firm's debts or other obligations. The owner-shareholders of a professional corporation, like partners, share the firm's profits or losses but, unlike partners, are normally not liable for the firm's debts or other obligations beyond the amount they invested in the corporation.

2. Law-firm personnel include the owners of the firm (partners, for example); associate attorneys, who are hired as employees and do not have ownership rights in the business; summer associates, or temporary law clerks; paralegals; administrative personnel, who are supervised by the legal administrator or office manager; and support personnel, including receptionists, secretaries, clerks, and others. Paralegals should learn, on first taking a job in a law firm, the relative status of law-firm personnel. Particularly, they should learn to whom they are accountable and who, in turn, is accountable to them.

3. Employment policies relate to compensation and employee benefits, performance evaluations, employment termination, and other rules of the workplace, such as office hours. Usually (particularly in larger firms), these policies are spelled out in an employment manual or other writing. Most large firms today have policies and procedures governing discrimination in the workplace.

4. Confidentiality is a major concern and a fundamental policy of every law firm. A breach of confidentiality by anyone in the law office can subject the firm to extensive legal liability. The requirement of confidentiality lends a unique character to the law-office experience and shapes, to a significant extent, law-office procedures.

5. Every law firm follows certain procedures in regard to its filing system. In larger firms, these procedures may be written up in a procedural book. In smaller firms, procedures may be more casual and based on habit or tradition. A typical law firm has client files, work-product files and reference materials, forms files, and personnel files. Proper file maintenance is crucial to a smoothly functioning firm. An efficient filing system helps to ensure that important documents will not be lost or misplaced and will be available when needed. Filing procedures in a law office must also maximize client confidentiality and the safekeeping of documents and other evidence.

6. A foremost concern of any law firm is to establish a clear policy on fee arrangements and efficient billing procedures, so that each client is billed appropriately. Types of fee arrangements include fixed fees, hourly fees, and contingency fees. Clients who pay hourly fees are billed monthly for the time spent by attorneys or other legal personnel on the clients' cases or projects, as well as all costs incurred on behalf of the clients.

7. Firms require attorneys and paralegals to document how they use their time. Because the firm's income depends on the number of billable hours produced by the firm's legal personnel, firms usually require attorneys and paralegals to generate a certain number of billable hours per year. This requirement subjects legal personnel to significant pressure. Double billing presents a major ethical problem for law firms.

8. Attorneys have a duty to keep their clients reasonably informed of the matters being handled by the attorneys for the clients. Paralegals should be aware that this is a legal duty and that they can play a significant role in keeping attorney-client communication channels open. Billing statements to clients serve as a method of communicating with clients, as do periodic phone calls, letters, or e-mail messages.

9. Each office has its own culture, or personality, which is largely shaped by the attitudes of the firm's owners and the qualities they look for when hiring personnel. Each firm also has a political infrastructure that is not apparent to outsiders. Office culture and politics make a great difference in terms of job satisfaction and comfort. Wise paralegals will learn as soon as possible after taking a job, from co-workers or others, about these aspects of the legal workplace.

QUESTIONS FOR REVIEW

1. What are the three basic organizational structures of law firms?
2. What is the difference between an associate and a partner?
3. Who handles the administrative tasks of a law firm? Who supervises the work performed by paralegals in a law firm?
4. Name some of the topics that might be included in an employment policy manual. How do firms evaluate paralegal performance?

5. Why is maintaining confidentiality so important in law offices? How does the confidentiality requirement affect law-office procedures and practices?

6. What kinds of files do law firms maintain? What general procedures are typically followed in regard to client files?

7. How does a law firm arrange its fees with its clients? What ethical obligations do attorneys have with respect to legal fees?

8. How do lawyers and legal assistants keep track of their time? What is the difference between billable and nonbillable hours? What is a client trust account?

9. Describe some of the ways that attorneys communicate with clients. Why is communicating with clients important?

10. What is meant by the phrase, "law-office culture and politics"? How might law-office culture and politics affect a paralegal?

ETHICAL QUESTIONS

1. Catherine works as a paralegal for a sole practitioner. Catherine and the legal secretary both work in a large reception area. A client is waiting in the reception area to see the attorney. The legal secretary brings a fax of a real-estate contract that she just received from a client, Mrs. Henley. Then she transfers the client to Catherine. Mrs. Henley tells her that your supervising attorney had promised to review the real-estate contract prior to the *closing* (the final step in the sale of real estate) and that the closing will take place at 4 P.M. today. Before becoming a paralegal, Catherine worked as a realtor and is very experienced in real-estate closings. Mrs. Henley knows this and insists that Catherine review and approve the contract if the attorney does not have time to review it. With what ethical problem is Catherine faced? How can these problems be resolved in a sole practitioner's office?

2. Carla Seegen is an experienced legal assistant who is also a licensed realtor. She sold real estate for eight years before becoming a paralegal. Carla works in a small law firm and has recently been assigned to work for Mike McAllister, who is a new attorney and the son of one of the firm's founding partners, John McAllister. Mike is asked to handle a real-estate closing for the firm's biggest client. Mike is unfamiliar with the client's business. Furthermore, he studied property law only briefly in law school and has no experience in real-estate transactions. Carla soon learns of Mike's lack of knowledge and experience because he does not ask her to draft the appropriate documents and undertake the kinds of tasks that are necessary for the closing. Whenever she mentions these things to Mike, however, or offers to show him what must be done, Mike becomes annoyed. Carla likes her job and knows that if she continues to annoy Mike, she may be fired. At the same time, she is concerned about the client's welfare and legal protection. Should she talk to one of the partners about the problem? Should she discuss the issue with John McAllister, Mike's father? How would you handle the situation?

3. Roberta Miller works as a paralegal, secretary, and receptionist for a sole practitioner. She is working on a bankruptcy file for a client, Gina Thomas. Because Roberta is running late for a meeting with a client, James Archer, she leaves the file—which is clearly marked, "Gina Thomas/Bankruptcy"—on her desk. Mr. Archer comes into her office for the meeting. During the meeting, Roberta turns to her computer to print a document for Mr. Archer to sign. While her back is turned, Mr. Archer notices the Gina Thomas file on Roberta's desk. Gina Thomas is his neighbor. When Roberta turns around, Mr. Archer begins to ask her questions about the file. Has an ethical violation occurred? If so, by whom and of what rule, and how could the violation have been avoided?

4. Attorney Smith represents Mrs. White in a divorce and custody action against Mr. White. At the outset of the representation, Mrs. Smith makes it clear that all that she is interested in is obtaining custody of her children. She even suggests that they propose trading the house for custody of the children in the settlement of the dispute. Attorney Smith tells Mrs. White, "Don't worry, I can get your kids. I don't suggest offering to trade the house for the children, though, because custody rights can always change, and once you give away the house, it's gone and you have nothing." The case drags on for over three years. Mrs. White pays attorney Smith $30,000. At the end of the

trial, which lasted for three months, the outstanding bill is over $100,000, and, while Mrs. White lost custody of the children, she is awarded the house. The house has enough equity to pay attorney Smith's bill, including significant fees for his legal assistant's time. The attorney demands that Mrs. White give him a lien against her house. She refuses to do so, and they are thrown into a fee dispute. Mrs. White discovers that attorney Smith's fees for his services are significantly higher than what other family-law attorneys in her area normally charge. What ethical rule comes into play here? What arguments would Mrs. White make against attorney Smith? What would be his counterarguments?

5. Sam Martin, an attorney, receives a settlement check for a client's case. It is made out jointly to Sam and his client. Sam signs it and instructs his paralegal to deposit it into his law firm's bank account, instead of the client's trust account, because he wants to take out his fee before he gives the client his portion of the money. May Sam do this? Why or why not?

6. Tom Baker, a paralegal, has been doing research for a client using Westlaw® (a computerized research service discussed in Chapter 15). Tom's supervising attorney tells him to bill the Westlaw® charges that he just incurred on behalf of one client to both that client's and another client's account. The second client to be billed is a large and prosperous corporation, and the research Tom conducted applies to the second client as well. What ethical violation has occurred? What should Tom do?

Practice Questions and Assignments

1. Using the material presented in the chapter, identify the following law practices by their organizational structure:

   a. Bill James is an attorney who practices law on his own. He owns his legal practice, the building in which he works, and most of the office furniture. He leases his office equipment. Bill has one secretary and one paralegal who work for him.

   b. Roberta Wagner owns a law firm with Joe Rosen. They own equal interests in the firm, participate equally in the firm's management, and share jointly in its profits and losses. Wagner & Rosen has three associates, six secretaries, and three paralegals who work for the firm.

   c. Randall Smith and Susan Street own a law firm together as shareholders. They employ eight associate attorneys, twelve secretaries, and five legal assistants.

2. Using the material presented in the chapter, identify the following law-office personnel:

   a. Martha Marsh works as a paralegal in a large law firm. After thirteen years with the firm, Martha is promoted. She now oversees paralegal staffing, assignments, and professional development.

   b. Mark James was hired by the partners of a large law firm, Smith & Smith, to manage the day-to-day operations of the firm.

   c. Rhonda Allen is an attorney who works as an employee for Marsh & Martin, a law firm with 250 attorneys.

   d. Tom is a file clerk for Jepp & Allen, P.C.

   e. Michael O'Dowd is a lawyer. He owns O'Dowd & O'Dowd, P.C., with his sister, Jane.

3. Henry Hampton III, a senior partner in the all-male law firm of Willette, Hampton & Kohl, hired Karla Black, the first woman attorney in the history of the firm. She was a top graduate from the number one law school in the country. After six months, the "boys" decided they did not like having a woman in their "club," and they fired Karla, claiming this was legitimate under the employment-at-will doctrine. Write one paragraph explaining the employment-at-will doctrine; then write a second paragraph analyzing this situation and explaining whether Willette, Hampton & Kohl could legally fire Karla Black under this doctrine.

4. Mary Anne is a paralegal student who has taken a job with a sole practitioner. The attorney has a general practice and handles legal matters relating to family law, real estate, estate planning and probate, and general civil litigation. He is very busy and, consequently, very disorganized. Mary Anne's first task is to help him organize his office, especially his client files. When Mary Anne arrives for her first day of work, she finds that he does not keep his files in the filing

cabinets in the office. Rather, they are on his desk, credenza, piled up on the floor, and anywhere else that he happens to leave them. Using the material in this chapter, how would you create a filing system for the attorney's office? Be sure to include a discussion of how you would store, maintain, and destroy files.

5. Identify the type of billing that is being used in each of the following examples:
   a. The client is billed $150 per hour for a partner's time, $100 per hour for an associate attorney's time, and $70 per hour for a legal assistant's time.
   b. The attorney's fee is one-third of the amount that the attorney recovers for the client, either through a pretrial settlement or through a trial.
   c. The client is charged $175 to change the name of the client's business firm.

6. Louise Lanham hires John J. Roberts, an attorney with the law firm of Sands, Roberts & Simpson, located at 1000 Plymouth Road, Phoenix, Arizona, to represent her in a divorce. She agrees to pay attorney Roberts a rate of $150 per hour and to pay a legal-assistant rate of $75 per hour. She also agrees to pay all costs and expenses, such as filing fees, expert-witness fees, court-reporter fees, and other fees incurred in the course of her representation. Using Exhibit 4.3, *A Sample Retainer Agreement*, draft a retainer agreement between Louise Lanham and John J. Roberts.

QUESTIONS FOR CRITICAL ANALYSIS

1. Explain what *personal liability* means. What do you think of this concept? Is it fair to require that the personal assets of a partner, such as his or her house, be used to pay partnership debts?

2. The limitation on personal liability for professional corporations varies by state, with some states limiting personal liability for shareholders of a professional corporation, and other states treating them more like partnerships for liability purposes. Should liability be limited for shareholders of a professional corporation? Why or why not? Is it fair to allow shareholders of business corporations to have limited liability but not to let shareholders who are members of a profession, such as law or medicine, limit their liability?

3. Legal assistants, who started out as support personnel in most law firms (because they evolved from the secretarial staff) are increasingly treated as professional staff members. What are the reasons for this change in treatment? Make a list of the reasons why legal assistants should be treated as professional staff members instead of support staff.

4. Do you think that performance evaluations are beneficial? What would happen if performance evaluations were not used? What types of information are included in them? What would you include to make them better?

5. Do you think that it is fair that employers are allowed to hire and fire employees for any reason or no reason under the employment-at-will doctrine? What might have led to the creation of the exceptions to the doctrine that now exist?

6. An employee who experiences sexual harassment may have to file a formal complaint and follow the firm's established procedures for resolving the issue. What impact might this requirement have on sexual-harassment complaints? What might happen if these procedures are not followed?

7. Why are efficient and confidential filing systems and procedures particularly necessary in law offices, more so than in other types of businesses? What might happen without them?

8. Why is it so important for members of a legal team to meticulously keep track of their hours? Why are some hours billable and others not? What happens if accurate billing records are not kept? Why are client trust funds required? Why are these accounts so important? What can happen if client funds are misused?

9. James Johnson is a sole practitioner. His office is about an hour's drive from the federal district court in which he files many of his lawsuits. He used to talk on the car phone to clients as he traveled the two hours to and from the courthouse. He would then bill the client on whose behalf he was going to the courthouse for two hours and the clients with whom he talked on the phone for increments of the same two hours. When the American Bar Association issued its rule prohibiting double billing, he was concerned that the rule would drive him out of business. Johnson feels that there should be different billing rules for lawyers in large firms and lawyers in small practices, such as his. What do you think?

10. Many law firms require their legal assistants to meet a quota of billable hours. Often, legal assistants can only generate the number of billable hours required per week by working more than the number of hours that they are paid to work. This can lead to the temptation to "pad the bill." Can you think of ways to meet the quota without breaching ethical standards?

11. Other than courtesy and building good client relations, what are the reasons for communicating with clients? Make a list of the ways in which good client communication can be accomplished.

12. Every workplace, business, or law firm has its own personality or culture. How can you find out what a particular firm's culture is? Is this something you should try to determine before accepting employment with a particular firm? Why or why not?

Projects

1. Obtain a page from the "want ads" in your local newspaper or from another source that advertises for legal professionals. Try to determine from the ads whether the firms advertising openings are organized as sole proprietorships, partnerships, or professional corporations.

2. Research legal periodicals, such as *Legal Assistant Today* or the ABA's *Journal of Law Practice Management,* for articles on document assembly and word-processing software. Write a one-page paper summarizing your findings. Be sure to describe how the software works, the advantages and disadvantages of the various programs on the market, their cost, and which program was the most highly recommended.

3. Research *Law Office Computing* magazine for articles on law-office accounting software. Can you find any that is specifically designed for trust accounts? Write a one-page paper summarizing your findings. Include a discussion of the pros and cons of each type of software, their cost, and which one was the most highly recommended.

4. Research various computer publications, such as *PC World, New Media,* and *Law Office Computing,* for articles discussing Zip disks and Zip drives. Write a one-page paper summarizing what they are, how they are used, and any pitfalls encountered in using this technology. Explain the uses for this technology in a law firm.

Using Internet Resources

1. Go online and access the following site: **www.bizfilings.com.** Select the link to "frequently asked questions" (FAQs) about incorporation. Summarize in writing the answers given to the following questions:
   a. What are the advantages of incorporation?
   b. What are the disadvantages of incorporation?
   c. How many directors must a corporation have?
   d. What factors should be considered when deciding on a corporate name?

2. Find legal forms on the Internet by going to the following Web site: **www.legaldocs.com.** Make a list of the types of forms that are available. Are they free? If not, how much do the forms cost? How can they be purchased? What methods of payment are accepted?

3. Research time-and-billing software on the Internet by going to the following Web site: **www.timeslips.com.** Click on the brochure and read about the software. Is it limited to one type of billing arrangement, or is it flexible? Can it create reports? What else can it do?

PART 2
INTRODUCTION TO LAW

CHAPTER 5
Sources of American Law

CHAPTER 6
The Court System and Alternate Dispute Resolution

CHAPTER 7
Substantive Law I

CHAPTER 8
Substantive Law II

CHAPTER 9
Administrative Law and Government Regulation

CHAPTER 5

Sources of American Law

Chapter Outline
▪ Introduction ▪ What Is Law? ▪ Constitutional Law
▪ Statutory Law ▪ Administrative Law ▪ Case Law and the Common Law Tradition ▪ National and International Law

After completing this chapter, you will know:
- The meaning and relative importance in the American legal system of constitutional law, statutory law, administrative law, and case law.
- How English law influenced the development of the American legal system.
- What the common law tradition is and how it evolved.
- The difference between remedies at law and equitable remedies.
- Some of the terms that are commonly found in case law.
- How national law and international law differ and why these bodies of law sometimes guide judicial decision making in American courts.

INTRODUCTION

Like the legal systems of many other countries, the American legal system is based on tradition. For the most part, the colonists who first came to America were governed by English law. As a result, the law of England continued to be the paramount model for American jurists and legislators after the colonists declared their independence from England in 1776. English common law from medieval times onward thus became part of the American legal tradition as well, modified as necessary to suit conditions unique to America.

This chapter opens with a discussion of the nature of law and then focuses on the sources of American law, including constitutional law, statutory law, administrative law, and case law. We then examine the common law tradition and its significance in the American legal system. You will also read how the law of other countries and international law affect judicial decision making in American courts. Another component of the American legal structure—the court system—will be examined in Chapter 6.

On the Web
The University of Michigan maintains a useful site with links to almost all U.S. governement Web sites at www.lib.umich.edu/libhome/Documents.center/govweb.html.

WHAT IS LAW?

Paralegals spend their entire careers dealing with legal matters. But even the most experienced paralegal might be hard pressed to give you a useful definition of *law*. What is law? There is no one answer to this question because how law is defined depends on the speaker's personal philosophy about such matters as morality, ethics, and truth. As a result, there have been and will continue to be different definitions of *law*. Although the various definitions differ in their particulars, they all are based on the following general observation concerning the nature of **law:**

 Law consists of a body of rules of conduct with legal force and effect, prescribed by the controlling authority (the government) of a society.

In the United States, these "rules of conduct" are embodied in numerous sources, including constitutions, statutes, administrative law, case law, and the common law tradition.

Law
A body of rules of conduct with legal force and effect, prescribed by the controlling authority (the government) of a society.

CONSTITUTIONAL LAW

Courts have numerous sources of law to consider when making their decisions, including constitutional law. The federal government and the states have separate constitutions that set forth the general organization, powers, and limits of their respective governments.

On the Web
The national Constitution Center provides extensive information on the Constitution, including its history and current debates over constitutional provisions, at members.constitutioncenter.org.

The Federal Constitution

The U.S. Constitution, as amended, is the supreme law of the land. This principle is set forth in Article VI of the Constitution, which provides that the Constitution, laws, and treaties of the United States are "the supreme Law of the Land." This provision is commonly referred to as the **supremacy clause**. A law in violation of the Constitution (including its amendments), no matter what its source, will be declared unconstitutional if it is challenged. For example, if a state legislature enacts a law that conflicts with the federal Constitution, a person or business firm that is subject to that law may challenge its validity in a court action. If the court

Supremacy Clause
The provision in Article VI of the U.S. Constitution that provides that the Constitution, laws, and treaties of the United States are "the supreme Law of the Land." Under this clause, state and local laws that directly conflict with federal law will be rendered invalid.

Bill of Rights
The first ten amendments to the Constitution.

agrees with the complaining party that the law is unconstitutional, it will declare the law invalid and refuse to enforce it.

The U.S. Constitution sets forth the powers of the three branches of the federal government and the relationship between the three branches. The need for a written declaration of the rights of individuals eventually caused the first Congress of the United States to submit twelve amendments to the Constitution to the states for approval. Ten of these amendments, commonly known as the **Bill of Rights,** were adopted in 1791 and embody a series of protections for the individual—and in some cases, business entities—against various types of interference by the federal government.[1]

CONSTITUTIONAL RIGHTS.   Summarized below are the protections guaranteed by the Bill of Rights. The full text of the Constitution, including its amendments, is presented in Appendix J at the end of this book.

1. The First Amendment guarantees the freedoms of religion, speech, and the press and the rights to assemble peaceably and to petition the government.
2. The Second Amendment guarantees the right to keep and bear arms.
3. The Third Amendment prohibits, in peacetime, the lodging of soldiers in any house without the owner's consent.
4. The Fourth Amendment prohibits unreasonable searches and seizures of persons or property.
5. The Fifth Amendment guarantees the rights to indictment by grand jury and to due process of law, and prohibits compulsory self-incrimination and double jeopardy. (These terms and concepts will be defined in Chapter 12, which deals with criminal law and procedure.) The Fifth Amendment also prohibits the taking of private property for public use without just compensation.
6. The Sixth Amendment guarantees the accused in a criminal case the right to a speedy and public trial by an impartial jury and the right to counsel. The accused has the right to cross-examine witnesses against him or her and to solicit testimony from witnesses in his or her favor.
7. The Seventh Amendment guarantees the right to a trial by jury in a civil case involving at least twenty dollars.[2]
8. The Eighth Amendment prohibits excessive bail and fines, as well as cruel and unusual punishment.
9. The Ninth Amendment establishes that the people have rights in addition to those specified in the Constitution.
10. The Tenth Amendment establishes that those powers neither delegated to the federal government nor denied to the states are reserved for the states.

THE COURTS AND CONSTITUTIONAL LAW.   You should realize that the rights secured by the Bill of Rights are not absolute. The broad principles enunciated in the Constitution are given form and substance by the courts. For example, even though the First Amendment guarantees the freedom of speech, we are not, in fact, free to say anything we want. In interpreting the meaning of the First Amendment's guarantee of free speech, the United States Supreme Court has made it clear that certain types of speech will not be protected. For example, speech that harms the

On the Web
For information on the role of the United States Supreme Court in interpreting the Constitution, go to www.usscplus.com.

---

1. One of these proposed amendments was ratified 203 years later (in 1992) and became the Twenty-seventh Amendment to the Constitution. See Appendix J.
2. Twenty dollars was forty days' pay for the average person when the Bill of Rights was written.

SUBSTANTIVE LAW CONCEPT SUMMARY
Constitutional Law

The Nature of Constitutional Law	Constitutional law is all law that is based on the provisions in the U.S. Constitution and the various state constitutions. The U.S. Constitution is the supreme law of the land. State constitutions are supreme within state borders to the extent that they do not conflict with the U.S. Constitution or a federal law.
The Bill of Rights	The Bill of Rights consists of the first ten amendments to the U.S. Constitution. The amendments embody a series of protections for the individual—and in some cases, business entities—against various types of government actions.
The Courts and Constitutional Law	The rights secured by the Constitution are not absolute. Ultimately, the United States Supreme Court interprets and defines the boundaries of the rights guaranteed by the Constitution. In doing so, the Court balances constitutional rights against other rights, such as the right to be protected from the harmful acts of others.

good reputation of another is deemed a tort, or civil wrong. If the speaker is sued, he or she may be ordered by a court to pay damages to the harmed person.

Courts often have to balance the rights and freedoms enunciated in the Bill of Rights against other rights, such as the right to be free from the harmful actions of others. Ultimately, it is the United States Supreme Court, as the final interpreter of the Constitution, that both gives meaning to our constitutional rights and determines their boundaries.

State Constitutions

Each state also has a constitution that sets forth the general organization, powers, and limits of the state government. The Tenth Amendment to the U.S. Constitution, which defines the powers and limitations of the federal government, reserves all powers not granted to the federal government to the states. Unless they conflict with the U.S. Constitution, state constitutions are supreme within the states' respective borders. State constitutions are thus important sources of law.

On the Web
If you are interested in looking at state constitutions, including the one for your state, go to www.findlaw.com/casecode/state.html.

Constitutional Law and the Paralegal

Many paralegals assist attorneys in handling cases that involve constitutional provisions or rights. For example, a corporate client might claim that a regulation issued by a state administrative agency, such as the state department of natural resources, is invalid because it conflicts with a federal law or regulation. (Administrative agencies are discussed later in this chapter.) You may be assigned the task of finding out which regulation takes priority. Many cases arise in which the plaintiff claims that his or her First Amendment rights have been violated. Suppose that a plaintiff's religious beliefs forbid working on a certain day of the week. If he or she is required to work on that day, the plaintiff may claim that the employer's requirement violates the First Amendment, which guarantees the free exercise of religion.

No matter what kind of work you do as a paralegal, you will find that a knowledge of constitutional law will be beneficial. This is because the authority

DEVELOPING PARALEGAL SKILLS

State versus Federal Regulation

Stephanie Wilson works as a paralegal in the legal department of National Pipeline, Inc., whose business is transporting natural gas to local utilities, factories, and other sites throughout the country. Last month, a pipeline running under a suburban street in Minneapolis, Minnesota, exploded, resulting in several severe injuries and one death.

The federal government has regulated pipeline safety and maintenance since 1968, under the Natural Gas Pipeline Safety Act. As a result of the explosion, the state of Minnesota wants to regulate pipeline safety as well. Stephanie's boss, the general counsel, and several other executives believe that the federal act preempts, or occupies, this field of law, preventing the state from enacting another layer of safety legislation. Stephanie is assigned the task of researching the statute and relevant case law to determine if the federal law does in fact preempt the state's regulation.

TIPS FOR DETERMINING
FEDERAL PREEMPTION

- Read through the statute to see if it expressly states that Congress intended to preempt the field.
- Look for an actual conflict between a federal and state law.
- Look for indications that Congress has impliedly occupied the field: Is the federal regulatory scheme pervasive? Is federal occupation of the field necessitated by the need for national uniformity? Is there a danger of conflict between state laws and the administration of the federal program?
- Locate and read through cases discussing the issue of federal preemption in this area.

and underlying rationale for the substantive and procedural laws governing many areas of law are ultimately based on the Constitution. For example, a knowledge of constitutional law is helpful to paralegals working in the area of criminal law, because criminal procedures are essentially designed to protect the constitutional rights of accused persons—as you will read in Chapter 12.

Statute
A written law enacted by a legislature under its constitutional lawmaking authority.

Statutory Law
Laws enacted by a legislative body.

Ordinance
An order, rule, or law enacted by a municipal or county government to govern a local matter unaddressed by state or federal legislation.

STATUTORY LAW

Laws passed by the federal Congress and the various state legislatures are called **statutes**. These statutes make up another source of law, which, as mentioned earlier, is generally referred to as **statutory law**. When a legislature passes a statute, that statute is ultimately included in the federal code of laws or the relevant state code of laws. The California Code, for example, contains the statutory law of the state of California.

Statutory law also includes local ordinances. An **ordinance** is a statute (law, rule, or order) passed by a municipal or county government unit to govern matters not covered by federal or state law. Ordinances commonly have to do with city or county land use (zoning ordinances), building and safety codes, and other matters affecting the local unit. Persons who violate ordinances may be fined or jailed, or both. No state statute or local ordinance may violate the U.S. Constitution—due to the supremacy clause, as mentioned earlier—or the state constitution.

The Expanding Scope of Statutory Law

Today, legislative bodies and administrative agencies assume an ever-increasing share of lawmaking. Much of the work of modern courts consists of interpreting what the rulemakers intended to accomplish when a particular law was drafted and enacted and deciding how the law applies to a specific set of facts.

On the Web
A good starting point to access federal statutes, as well as state statutes that are now online, is www.findlaw.com.

SUBSTANTIVE LAW CONCEPT SUMMARY	
Statutory Law	
The Nature of Statutory Law	Statutory law consists of all laws enacted by the federal Congress, a state legislature, a county, a municipality, or some other governing unit. Laws passed by Congress and state legislatures are called *statutes* and are published in federal or state statutory codes. Laws passed by local governing units (counties or cities) are called *ordinances*.

Statutory Law and the Paralegal

As a paralegal, you may often be dealing with cases that involve violations of statutory law. If you work for a small law firm, you may become familiar with the statutory law governing a wide spectrum of activities. If you specialize in one area, such as bankruptcy law, you will become very familiar with the federal statutory law governing bankruptcy and bankruptcy procedures. Here are just a few examples of the areas in which you might work that are governed extensively by statutory law:

- *Corporate law*—governed by state statutes.
- *Patent, copyright, and trademark law*—governed by federal statutes.
- *Employment law*—governed to an increasing extent by federal statutes concerning discrimination in employment, workplace safety, labor unions, pension plans, Social Security, and other aspects of employment. Each state also has statutes governing certain areas of employment, such as safety standards in the workplace and employment discrimination.
- *Antitrust law*—governed by federal statutes prohibiting specific types of anticompetitive business practices.
- *Consumer law*—governed by state and federal statutes protecting consumers against deceptive trade practices (such as misleading advertising), unsafe products, and generally any activities that threaten consumer health and welfare.
- *Wills and probate administration* (relating to the transfer of property on the property owner's death)—governed by state statutes.

You will read about some of these areas of law in later chapters. A paralegal working in an area (or on a case) governed by statutory law needs to know how to both locate and interpret the relevant state or federal statutes. You will learn how to find and analyze statutory law in Chapters 14 and 16.

ADMINISTRATIVE LAW

There is virtually no way that the federal Congress or a state legislature can oversee the actual implementation of all the laws that it enacts. To assist them in their governing responsibilities, legislatures at all levels of government often delegate such tasks to **administrative agencies**, particularly when the issues relate to highly technical areas. By creating and delegating some of its authority to an administrative agency, a legislature may indirectly monitor a particular area in which it has passed legislation without becoming bogged down in the details relating to enforcement—details that are best left to specialists.

Administrative Agency
A federal or state government agency established to perform a specific function. Administrative agencies are authorized by legislative acts to make and enforce rules relating to the purpose for which they were established.

PARALEGAL PROFILE

Legal Assistant in a General Law Practice

KAREN DUNN works as a legal assistant in a small law firm. She has worked for several law firms in the past, all of them small (the largest had thirteen lawyers). Dunn started her career in law as a legal secretary when she was nineteen years old. After working as a legal secretary for eleven years, she was promoted to the position of legal assistant and eventually passed the Certified Legal Assistant exam. Dunn's responsibilities at her current job include handling various documents associated with the litigation process. She performs these tasks with a minimum of supervision and works extensively with clients, particularly in the area of domestic relations. Dunn has been actively involved in the National Association of Legal Assistants (NALA) and served as NALA's president for two terms, the second term ending in July 1994.

What do you like best about your work?

"The thing that I like best about my job is the variety. The law is challenging and always different. I also enjoy the fact that everything done in a law firm is important and affects somebody's life. I find this exciting and challenging. Even a routine task, such as handling a contract for the sale of real estate, can be extremely important for the buyer and seller."

What is the greatest challenge that you face in your area of work?

"One of the challenges of my job is dealing with clients because something is usually wrong; that is the reason that they are in the office. If I am drawing up a will, I am dealing with people who find it stressful because they are forced to think about the end of their lives. I enjoy gaining their confidence and trust and easing their concerns about the legal process. I find that I can often help them and gain their trust through difficult situations. For example, in one situation I dealt with a very difficult divorce client. I found the client challenging but continually tried to make the process easier for that person. Even though I didn't particularly like the person, I enjoyed getting a note from the client after the case was over in which the client thanked me for my assistance.

"I also find that people tend to confide in legal assistants. They tell the legal assistant things that they would not take time to tell the lawyer. Sometimes these are things that are very important to the client's case. Perhaps this is because with a lawyer, they feel they are being charged high rates per hour, and they are also intimidated by the fact that they are speaking with a lawyer."

> "The law is challenging and always different."

What advice do you have for would-be paralegals in your area of work?

"My advice is to prepare well and learn as many skills as you can. For example, don't be afraid of keyboards. Also, I strongly recommend that you be willing to learn everything and anything."

What are some tips for success as a paralegal in your area of work?

"My tips for success as a paralegal include the following: pay attention to detail, know what you like to do, and come to grips with the fact that legal assistants don't make the final decisions. Legal assistants are not the stars. If they are comfortable with this, then they will be comfortable and happy in their career choice. Also, don't be afraid to try new things. For example, ask an attorney to give you a shot at doing an answer or a motion. Don't wait for something to be assigned to you. The more you experiment and learn, the more interesting assignments you will get in the future."

SUBSTANTIVE LAW CONCEPT SUMMARY
Administrative Law

The Nature of Administrative Law	Administrative law consists of the rules, orders, and decisions of administrative agencies at all levels of government.
Agency Creation and Function	Federal administrative agencies are created by enabling legislation enacted by the U.S. Congress, which specifies the name, purpose, composition, and powers of each agency created. State administrative agencies are created by state legislatures in a similar manner. Administrative agencies administer and enforce legislation and issue rules to implement the goals of specific legislation.

Agency Creation and Function

To create an administrative agency at the federal level, Congress passes **enabling legislation**, which specifies the name, purpose, composition, and powers of the agency being created. The Occupational Safety and Health Act of 1970, for example, provided for the creation of the Occupational Safety and Health Administration to administer and implement the provisions of the act, to issue rules as necessary to protect employees from dangerous conditions in the workplace, and to enforce the act's provisions and the agency's rules.

There are dozens of federal administrative agencies, each of which has been established to perform specific governing tasks. For example, the federal Environmental Protection Agency coordinates and enforces federal environmental laws. The Food and Drug Administration enforces federal laws relating to the safety of foods and drugs. The Federal Trade Commission issues and enforces rules relating to unfair advertising or sales practices. Each state also has a number of administrative agencies, many of which parallel agencies at the federal level. For example, state environmental laws are implemented by state environmental agencies, such as a state's department of natural resources. The rules, orders, and decisions of administrative agencies at all levels of government constitute what is known as **administrative law**.

Administrative Law and the Paralegal

Paralegals frequently deal with administrative agencies. If you work for a law firm that has many corporate clients, you may be involved extensively in researching and analyzing agency regulations and their applicability to certain business activities. If you work for a corporate legal department, you will probably assist the attorneys in the department in a vital task—determining which agency regulations apply to the corporation and whether the corporation is complying with those regulations. If you work for an administrative agency, you may be involved in drafting new rules, in analyzing survey results to see if a new rule is necessary, in mediating disputes between a private party and an agency, in investigations to gather facts about compliance with agency rules, and numerous other tasks. In any law practice, you may be asked to assist clients who are involved in disputes with administrative agencies.

Paralegals often become very familiar with administrative process when helping clients obtain needed benefits from state or federal administrative agencies. You may work with local agencies in helping the homeless obtain medical

Enabling Legislation
A statute enacted by a legislature that authorizes the creation of an administrative agency and specifies the name, purpose, composition, and powers of the agency being created.

Administrative Law
A body of law created by administrative agencies in the form of rules, regulations, orders, and decisions in order to carry out their duties and responsibilities.

On the Web
The *United States Government Manual* describes the origins, purposes, and administrators of every federal department and agency. You can access this publication online at **www.gpo.ucop.edu**.

assistance, for example. As noted in Chapter 2, some administrative agencies, including the Social Security Administration, allow paralegals to represent clients at administrative agency hearings and other procedures.

We list below a few federal government agencies and describe how paralegals may be involved with administrative law and procedures relating to those agencies. (Administrative law and agency procedures will be covered in greater detail in Chapter 9.)

On the Web
Links to federal government administrative agencies can be found at FedWorld's Web site. Go to www.fedworld.gov.

- *Equal Employment Opportunity Commission (EEOC).* If a client wants to pursue a claim against his or her employer for employment discrimination, the client must first contact the EEOC. The EEOC may investigate and try to settle the claim. If the problem cannot be resolved by the EEOC or if the EEOC decides not to take action on the matter, the client will be entitled to sue the employer directly. You may be involved in contacting the EEOC and assisting the client in complying with procedures required by the EEOC for handling complaints of employment discrimination.
- *Internal Revenue Service (IRS).* If you work for a corporate law department, you might be asked to assist corporate counsel in handling corporate taxes and related IRS requirements. If you work in a law firm, a corporate client may request legal assistance in settling a dispute with the IRS or in complying with tax laws.
- *Securities and Exchange Commission (SEC).* If you work for a corporation that sells shares of stock in its company to the public, you may be asked to assist in drafting the documents necessary to fulfill registration requirements under federal securities law. If you work for a law firm, you may perform similar tasks for corporate clients. You may also assist in the defense of a client who has been charged with "insider trading" in violation of securities law (which prohibits the purchase or sale of securities for personal gain based on knowledge available only to corporate officers or employees and not to the general public).
- *Food and Drug Administration (FDA).* Any firm that places foods or drugs on the market must make sure that those products are safe and properly labeled. If you work for a corporation or on behalf of a corporate client that markets food or drug products, you may be involved in procedures required by the FDA for product testing and labeling or for seeking FDA approval to market a firm's product.

CASE LAW AND THE COMMON LAW TRADITION

Another important source of law consists of the decisions rendered by judges in cases that come before the courts. This body of law is called **case law.** To understand the importance of case law in the United States, you need to first understand what is meant by the common law tradition, which originated in medieval England.

Case Law
Rules of law announced in court decisions.

As mentioned earlier, because of our colonial heritage much of American law is based on the English legal system. After the United States declared its independence from England, American jurists continued to be greatly influenced by English law and English legal writers. Indeed, much of American law in such areas as contracts, torts (types of civil wrongs), property law, and criminal law derives in large part from the English legal system.

Early English Courts of Law

In 1066, the Normans conquered England, and William the Conqueror and his successors began the process of unifying the country under their rule. One of the means they used to this end was the establishment of the king's courts, or *curiae regis*. Before the Norman Conquest, disputes had been settled according to the local legal customs and traditions in various regions of the country. The king's courts sought to establish a uniform set of customs for the country as a whole. What evolved in these courts was the beginning of the **common law**—a body of general rules that prescribed social conduct and applied throughout the entire English realm.

Courts developed the common law rules from the principles underlying judges' decisions in actual legal controversies. Judges attempted to be consistent. When possible, they based their decisions on the principles suggested by earlier cases. They sought to decide similar cases in a similar way and considered new cases with care because they knew that their decisions would make new law. Each interpretation became part of the law on the subject and served as a legal **precedent**. Later cases that involved similar legal principles or facts could be decided with reference to that precedent. The courts were thus guided by traditions and legal doctrines that evolved over time.

In the early years of the common law, there was no single place or publication in which legal opinions could be found. In the late thirteenth and early fourteenth centuries, however, decisions of each year were gathered together and recorded in *Year Books*. These books were informal, containing only notes of cases made by lawyers and law students, and were not organized according to different legal topics. They were not official reports, did not include every case, and sometimes did not include cases until two or three years after the cases had been decided. Nevertheless, the *Year Books* were useful to lawyers and judges. In the sixteenth century, the *Year Books* were discontinued, and other compilations of cases became available.

Common Law
A body of law developed from custom or judicial decisions in English and U.S. courts and not attributable to a legislature.

Precedent
A court decision that furnishes an example or authority for deciding subsequent cases in which identical or similar facts are presented.

The Doctrine of *Stare Decisis*

The practice of deciding new cases with reference to former decisions, or precedents, eventually became a cornerstone of the English and American judicial systems. It forms a doctrine called *stare decisis*[3] ("to stand on decided cases"). Under this doctrine, judges are obligated to follow the precedents established by their own courts or by higher courts within their jurisdictions.

The doctrine of *stare decisis* performs many useful functions. It helps the courts to be more efficient because if other courts have carefully reasoned through a similar case, their legal reasoning and opinions can serve as guides. *Stare decisis* also creates consistency. It makes the law more stable and predictable, because if the law on a given subject is well settled, someone bringing a case to court can usually rely on the court to make a decision based on what the law has been.

Stare Decisis
A flexible doctrine of the courts, recognizing the value of following prior decisions (precedents) in cases similar to the one before the court; the courts' practice of being consistent with prior decisions based on similar facts.

DEPARTURES FROM PRECEDENT.   Sometimes a court will depart from the rule of precedent if it decides that the precedent should no longer be followed. If a court decides that a ruling precedent is simply incorrect or that technological or social changes have rendered the precedent inapplicable, the court might rule contrary to the precedent. Cases that overturn precedent often receive a great deal of publicity.

In *Brown v. Board of Education of Topeka*[4] (decided in 1954), for example, the United States Supreme Court expressly overturned precedent when it concluded

On the Web
To learn how the Supreme Court justified its departure from precedent in the 1954 *Brown* decision, you can access the Court's opinion online at **www.findlaw.com**.

---

3. Pronounced *ster*-ay dih-*si*-ses.
4. 347 U.S. 483, 74 S.Ct. 686, 98 L.Ed. 873 (1954). (Legal citations are briefly explained later in this chapter and discussed in detail in Chapter 14.)

> ### ETHICAL CONCERN
> ### Legal Research and *Stare Decisis*
>
> One of the challenges faced by legal professionals is keeping up with the ever-changing law. For example, suppose that you are asked to do research on a case involving issues similar to those in a case you researched just three months ago. If you apply your previous research results to the current client's case, you need to verify that your earlier research still applies—that is, that previous case decisions are still "good law." In three months' time, an appeals court might have created a new precedent, and failure to update your research (how to do this is explained in Chapters 14 and 15) can lead to serious consequences for the client—and for you and the attorney, if the client decides to sue the attorney for negligence (specifically, for breaching the duty of competence).

that separate educational facilities for whites and African Americans, which had been upheld as constitutional in numerous previous cases,[5] were inherently unequal. The Supreme Court's departure from precedent in *Brown* received a tremendous amount of publicity as people began to realize the ramifications of this change in the law. It also spearheaded the civil rights movement, which led to further lawsuits involving claims of racial discrimination.

CASES OF FIRST IMPRESSION. Sometimes, there is no precedent on which to base a decision. For example, in 1986, a New Jersey court had to decide whether a surrogate-parenting contract should be enforced against the wishes of the surrogate parent (the natural mother).[6] This was the first such case to reach the courts, and there was no precedent in any jurisdiction to which the court could look for guidance. Developments in technology, which often outpace the law, sometimes result in cases for which there is no precedent. For example, suppose that an employee views sexually offensive images on a co-employee's computer monitor, and the employee claims that this constitutes "hostile-environment" sexual harassment. There may be no controlling state or federal law that deals with the employee's complaint.

Case of First Impression
A case presenting a legal issue that has not yet been addressed by a court in a particular jurisdiction.

Public Policy
A governmental policy based on widely held societal values.

When deciding cases such as these, called **cases of first impression,** or when there are conflicting precedents, courts may consider a number of factors, including legal principles and policies underlying previous court decisions or existing statutes, fairness, social values and customs, **public policy** (a governmental policy based on widely held societal values), and data and concepts drawn from the social sciences. Which of these sources is chosen or receives the greatest emphasis will depend on the nature of the case being considered and the particular judge hearing the case.

---

5. See, for example, *Plessy v. Ferguson,* 163 U.S. 537, 16 S.Ct. 1138, 41 L.Ed. 256 (1896). In *Plessy,* the United States Supreme Court upheld a Louisiana statute providing for separate railway cars for whites and African Americans. The Court held that the statute did not violate the U.S. Constitution, which mandates equal protection under the laws, because the statute provided for equal facilities for African Americans. Lower courts interpreted this decision to apply to other types of facilities as well, and the "separate-but-equal doctrine" prevailed until the *Brown* decision in 1954.
6. *In re Baby M,* 217 N.J.Super. 313, 525 A.2d 1128 (1987).

Judges always strive to be free of subjectivity and personal bias in deciding cases. Each judge, however, has his or her own unique personality, set of values or philosophical leanings, and intellectual attributes—all of which necessarily frame the decision-making process.

Remedies at Law versus Remedies in Equity

In the early English king's courts, the kinds of remedies that the courts could grant were severely restricted. If one person wronged another in some way, the king's court could award as compensation only land, items of value, or money. The courts that awarded these things became known as **courts of law,** and the three remedies awarded by these courts—land, items of value, and money—became known as **remedies at law.**

Even though this system helped to standardize the ways in which disputes were settled, those parties who wanted a remedy other than economic compensation could not be helped. Because the courts of law could not grant noneconomic remedies, many disappointed litigants became very frustrated with the court system. Some of the more persistent parties petitioned the king for relief. Most of these petitions were decided by an adviser to the king, called a **chancellor.** The chancellor, who was also the head of the Church of England, was said to be the "keeper of the king's conscience." When the chancellor thought that the claim was a fair one for which there was no adequate remedy at law, he would fashion new and unique remedies, called **remedies in equity,** to resolve the case. In this way, a new body of rules and remedies came into being and eventually led to the establishment of formal courts of chancery, or **courts of equity.**

Equity is that branch of law, founded on what might be described as notions of justice and fair dealing, that seeks to supply a remedy when there is no adequate remedy available at law. Once the courts of equity were established, plaintiffs could pursue their claims in either courts of law (if they sought money damages) or courts of equity (if they sought equitable remedies). Plaintiffs had to specify whether they were bringing an "action at law" or an "action in equity," and they chose their courts accordingly. Only one remedy could be granted for a particular wrong.

EQUITABLE PRINCIPLES AND MAXIMS. Courts of equity often supplemented the common law by making decisions based on considerations of justice and fairness. Today, the same court can award both legal and equitable remedies so plaintiffs may request both equitable and legal relief in the same case. (A court, however, will not grant both kinds of remedies in the same case.) Yet judges continue to be guided by so-called **equitable principles and maxims** when deciding whether to grant equitable remedies. Maxims are propositions or general statements of rules of law that courts often use in arriving at a decision. Some of the more influential maxims of equity are listed in Exhibit 5.1 on the next page.

The last maxim listed in the exhibit ("Equity aids the vigilant, not those who slumber on their rights") has become known as the equitable doctrine of **laches.** The doctrine of laches encourages people to bring lawsuits while the evidence is still fresh. What constitutes a reasonable time, of course, varies depending on the circumstances of the case. The time period for pursuing a particular claim against another party is now usually fixed by a **statute of limitations.** After the time allowed under the statute of limitations has expired, further action on that claim is barred.

For torts, or civil wrongs, the statute of limitations varies from state to state. It may be two years, three years, or even longer for certain types of wrongs. The

Court of Law
A court in which the only remedies that could be granted were things of value, such as money damages. In early England, courts of law were distinct from courts of equity.

Remedy at Law
A remedy available in a court of law. Money damages are awarded as a remedy at law.

Chancellor
An adviser to the king in medieval England. Individuals petitioned the king for relief when they could not obtain an adequate remedy in a court of law, and these petitions were decided by the chancellor.

Remedy in Equity
A remedy allowed by courts in situations where remedies at law are not appropriate. Remedies in equity are based on settled rules of fairness, justice, and honesty.

Court of Equity
A court that decides controversies and administers justice according to the rules, principles, and precedents of equity.

Equitable Principles and Maxims
Propositions or general statements of rules of law that are frequently involved in equity jurisdiction.

Laches
The equitable doctrine that bars a party's right to legal action if the party has neglected for an unreasonable length of time to act on his or her rights.

Statute of Limitations
A statute setting the maximum time period within which certain legal actions can be brought or rights enforced. After the period of time has run, normally no legal action can be brought.

EXHIBIT 5.1
Equitable Principles and Maxims

> **EQUITABLE PRINCIPLES AND MAXIMS**
>
> - Whoever seeks equity must do equity. (Anyone who wishes to be treated fairly must treat others fairly.)
> - One who seeks the aid of an equity court must come to the court with clean hands. (The plaintiffs must have acted fairly and honestly.)
> - Equity will not suffer a right to exist without a remedy. (Equitable relief will be awarded when there is a right to relief and there is no adequate legal remedy.)
> - Equity regards substance rather than form. (Equity is more concerned with fairness and justice than with legal technicalities.)
> - Equity aids the vigilant, not those who slumber on their rights. (Individuals who fail to assert their legal rights until after a reasonable period of time has passed will not be helped.)

statute of limitations for contracts involving the sale of goods is normally four years. In regard to criminal actions, the duration of the statute of limitations is often directly related to the seriousness of the offense. The statute of limitations for petty theft (the theft of an item of insignificant value), for example, may be a year while the statute of limitations for armed robbery might be twenty years. (For certain crimes, such as treason and first degree murder, there is no statute of limitations.)

EQUITABLE REMEDIES. A number of equitable remedies are available. As mentioned above, equitable remedies are normally granted only if the court concludes that the remedy at law (money damages) is inadequate. Three equitable remedies—specific performance, rescission, and injunction—are briefly discussed here.

Specific Performance. A judge's decree of **specific performance** is an order to perform what was promised. This remedy was, and still is, only available when the dispute before the court involves a contractual transaction involving something unique and money damages are inadequate. Contracts for the sale of goods that are readily available on the market rarely qualify for specific performance. Money damages ordinarily are adequate in such situations because substantially identical goods can be bought or sold in the market.

If the goods are unique, however, a court of equity may decree specific performance. For example, paintings, sculptures, and rare books and coins are so unique that money damages will not enable a buyer to obtain substantially identical substitutes in the market. The same principle applies to contracts relating to sales of land or interests in land, because each parcel of land is unique.

Rescission. In certain situations, if the legal remedy of money damages is unavailable or inadequate, the equitable remedy of rescission may be given. **Rescission**[7] is an action to undo a contract—to return the parties to the positions they occupied prior to the contract. If a customer agrees to purchase a vacuum cleaner because the seller misrepresents its quality, for example, the buyer might want merely to rescind, or cancel, the agreement if he or she discovers the fraud before any money changes hands. If the money has already changed hands, rescission would also involve *restitution*—returning to each party any money or other items of value that had been exchanged by the parties.

Specific Performance
An equitable remedy requiring exactly the performance that was specified in a contract; usually granted only when money damages would be an inadequate remedy and the subject matter of the contract is unique (for example, real property).

Rescission
A remedy whereby a contract is terminated and the parties are returned to the positions they occupied before the contract was made.

---

7. Pronounced reh-*sih*-zhen.

Developing Paralegal Skills

Analyzing a Case for Specific Performance

Louise Lassen, a wealthy heiress, buys a famous painting for $2.5 million at an auction in New York. She returns home and hires an architect and interior designer to create a room in which to display the painting. After completion of the room, Louise learns that the seller has changed his mind and is no longer interested in selling the painting. Louise contacts the firm of Murdoch & Larson to have the contract enforced. Paralegal Bob Humboldt is assigned the task of analyzing Louise's problem to determine if the remedy of specific performance may be sought.

CHECKLIST FOR ANALYZING A LEGAL PROBLEM

- Gather the facts involved in the problem.
- Determine whether unique or rare articles are involved.
- Find out what type of remedy the client wants.
- Determine whether an adequate legal remedy, such as money damages, will compensate the client.
- Apply the law to the client's facts to reach a conclusion regarding the appropriate remedy.

Injunction. An **injunction** is a court order directing the defendant to do or to refrain from doing a particular act. For example, an injunction may be obtained to stop a neighbor from burning trash in his or her yard or to prevent an estranged husband from coming near his wife. Persons who violate injunctions are typically held in *contempt of court* (discussed in Chapter 3) and punished with a jail sentence or a fine.

Injunction
A court decree ordering a person to do or refrain from doing a certain act or activity.

THE MERGING OF LAW AND EQUITY. During the nineteenth century, most states adopted rules of procedure that combined courts of law and equity—although some states, such as Arkansas, still retain the distinction. Today, a plaintiff, or a petitioner in equity (the person bringing the action), may request both legal and equitable remedies in the same action, and the trial court judge may decide whether to grant either or both forms of relief.

Despite the merging of the courts, remnants of the procedures used when law and equity courts were separate still exist. Courts still distinguish between remedies at law and equitable remedies, and differences in procedure sometimes also depend on whether the civil lawsuit involves an action in equity or an action at law. For example, in actions at law, a party has the right to demand a jury trial, but actions in equity are not decided by juries. (A judge may, however, call in a jury to serve in an advisory capacity.) The procedural differences between an action at law and an action in equity are summarized in Exhibit 5.2, which is applicable to most states.

PROCEDURE	ACTION AT LAW	ACTION IN EQUITY
Initiation of lawsuit	By filing a complaint	By filing a petition
Decision	By judge or jury	By judge (no jury)
Result	Judgment	Decree
Remedy	Monetary damages	Injunction, decree of specific performance, or rescission

EXHIBIT 5.2

Procedural Differences between an Action at Law and an Action in Equity

> ### ETHICAL CONCERN
> ## The Statute of Limitations and the Duty of Competence
>
> The duty of competence requires, among other things, that attorneys and paralegals be aware of the statute of limitations governing a client's legal matter. Assume, for example, that a client of your firm, a restaurant owner, wants to sue a restaurant-supply company for breaking a contract for the sale of dishes. If the attorney asks you to look into the matter, the first thing you should check is your state's statute of limitations covering contracts for the sale of goods. If the time period has already expired, then your attorney will need to advise the client accordingly. If the time period is about to expire, then you and your supervising attorney need to act quickly to make sure that the complaint (the document that initiates a lawsuit) is filed before the time period expires.

The Common Law Today

The common law developed in England and still used in the United States consists of the rules of law announced in court decisions, or case law. These rules of law include interpretations of constitutional provisions, of statutes enacted by legislatures, and of regulations created by administrative agencies, such as the federal Environmental Protection Agency.

To summarize and clarify common law rules and principles, the American Law Institute (ALI) drafted and published compilations of the common law called *Restatements of the Law*. The ALI, which was formed in the 1920s, consists of practicing attorneys, legal scholars, and judges. There are *Restatements of the Law* in several common law areas, including contracts and torts. The *Restatements*, which generally summarize the common law rules followed by most states, do not in themselves have the force of law but are an important secondary sources of legal analysis and opinion on which judges often rely in making their decisions. You will read more about the *Restatements of the Law* in Chapter 14, in the context of legal research.

Statutory Law and the Common Law

The common law governs all areas not covered by *statutory law*, which (as discussed previously) generally consists of those laws enacted by state legislatures and by the federal Congress. In the early years of this nation, the body of statutory law was relatively small compared to the body of common law principles and doctrines. The body of statutory law has expanded greatly since then, however, and continues to grow. To some extent, this expansion has resulted from the enactment of statutes that essentially **codify** (systematize, or arrange in a topical order) common law doctrines. For example, criminal law was at one time governed extensively by common law. Over time, common law doctrines were codified, expanded on, and enacted in statutory form. Today, criminal law is primarily statutory law.

The expansion of statutory law has also resulted from the need to regulate business and other activities for various purposes. For example, many federal and state statutes have been enacted in an attempt to protect consumers, employees, investors, and other groups from business practices that are potentially harmful to the rights or interests of these groups. Numerous statutes and regulations exist to

---

Codify
To collect and organize systematically and logically a body of concepts, principles, decisions, or doctrines.

protect the environment, and a whole body of law, antitrust law, is based on statutes passed to protect the public's interest in a freely competitive society. Another reason why the body of statutory law has expanded is to address the need for uniform laws among the states, such as the laws governing commercial transactions.

Even when legislation has been substituted for common law principles, a court's interpretation and application of a statute may become a precedent that lower courts in the jurisdiction must follow. Furthermore, courts often look to the common law when determining how to interpret a statute, on the theory that the people who drafted the statute intended to codify an existing common law rule. In a sense, then, common law and statutory law are never totally separate bodies of law, because the courts must interpret and apply statutory law.

The Terminology of Case Law

Throughout the remainder of this text, you will encounter various terms that have traditionally been used to describe parties to lawsuits, case titles, and the types of decisions that judges author. Although details on how to research case law will be given in Chapter 14, it is worthwhile at this point to explain some of the basic terminology of case law.

CASE TITLES.   The title of a case, which is sometimes referred to as the *style* of the case, indicates the names of the parties to the lawsuit. Note that a case title, such as *Baranski v. Peretto,* includes only the parties' surnames, not their first names. The *v.* in the case title stands for versus, which means "against." In the trial court (the court in which the lawsuit was first brought and tried), Baranski was the plaintiff, so Baranski's name appears first in the case title. If the case is appealed to a higher court for review, however, the appeals court sometimes places the name of the party appealing the decision first, so that the case may be called *Peretto v. Baranski.* Because some appeals courts retain the trial court order of names, it is often impossible to distinguish the plaintiff from the defendant in the title of a reported appeals court decision. You must carefully read the facts of the case to identify the parties. Otherwise, the discussion by the appeals court will be difficult to understand.

On the Web
If you are interested in learning more about the justices of the Supreme Court, go to the "Oyez" site sponsored by Cornell University at www.oyez.nwu.edu.

Usually, whenever attorneys or paralegals refer to a court decision, they give not only the title of the case but also the case citation. The **citation** indicates the reports or reporters in which the case can be found (reports and reporters are volumes in which cases are published, or "reported"). For example, a citation to 251 Kan. 728 following a case title would indicate that the case could be found in volume 251 of the Kansas reports on page 728. You will read in further detail about how to read case citations and locate case law in Chapter 14.

Citation
A citation indicates where a particular constitutional provision, statute, reported case, or article may be found.

THE PARTIES.   The **parties** to a lawsuit are the plaintiff, who initiates the lawsuit, and the defendant, against whom the lawsuit is brought. Lawsuits frequently involve multiple parties—that is, more than one plaintiff or defendant. For example, a person who is injured by a defective product might sue both the manufacturer of the product and the retailer from whom the product was purchased to obtain compensation for injuries caused by the product. In this situation, the manufacturer and the retailer would be *co-defendants*.

Party
With respect to lawsuits, the plaintiff or the defendant. Some cases involve multiple parties (more than one plaintiff or defendant).

JUDGES AND JUSTICES.   The terms *judge* and *justice* are usually synonymous and represent two designations given to judges in various courts. All members of the United States Supreme Court, for example, are referred to as justices. Justice

> ## ETHICAL CONCERN
> ### What to Do When Someone Asks You about Remedies
>
> Suppose you learn that Lewis, one of your friends, recently broke his hip when he fell off a new ladder while painting his house. He fell because one of the steps wasn't securely attached and came loose as he was climbing the ladder. He had to pay $1,000 of the medical costs out of pocket. Also, his doctor told him that he probably wouldn't be able to work at his construction job for at least two months and maybe longer. Knowing that you are trained in law, Lewis asks you whether he can obtain compensation for the out-of-pocket medical expenses and for the lost wages. Should you advise him that he could sue the ladder's manufacturer and the owner of the hardware store that sold him the ladder for money damages, a remedy at law? No, you should not. Such a statement could subject you to liability for the unauthorized practice of law. The best thing to do in this situation is simply tell Lewis that because you are a paralegal, you cannot give legal advice, but that he should check with an attorney to see what remedies he might pursue to compensate him for his injuries.

is also the formal title usually given to judges of appeals courts, although this is not always the case. Justice is commonly abbreviated to J., and justices to JJ. A Supreme Court case might refer to Justice Kennedy as Kennedy, J., or to Chief Justice Rehnquist as Rehnquist, C.J.

In a trial court, a case is heard by one judge. In an appeals court, normally a panel of three or more judges (or justices) sits on the bench. Most decisions reached by appeals courts are explained in written court opinions.

Opinion
A statement by the court setting forth the applicable law and the reasons for its decision in a case.

DECISIONS AND OPINIONS. The **opinion** contains the court's reasons for its decision, the rules of law that apply, and the judgment. There are four different types of opinions. When all judges or justices unanimously agree on an opinion, the opinion is written for the entire court and can be deemed a *unanimous opinion*. When there is not a unanimous opinion, a *majority opinion* is written, outlining the views of the majority of the judges or justices deciding the case. The name of the judge or justice immediately preceding the unanimous or majority opinion indicates the author of the opinion—that is, the judge or justice who wrote the opinion on behalf of the others.

Often, a judge or justice who feels strongly about making or emphasizing a point that was not made or emphasized in the majority opinion writes a *concurring opinion*, which appears just following the majority opinion. In a concurring opinion, the judge or justice agrees (concurs) with the decision given in the majority opinion but for different reasons. In other than unanimous opinions, a *dissenting opinion* may also be written by a judge or justice who does not agree with the majority. The dissenting opinion, which follows the concurring opinion, if any, is important because it may form the basis of the arguments used years later in overruling the precedential majority opinion. The names of the judges or justices authoring any concurring or dissenting opinions are also indicated at the beginning of those opinions.

SUBSTANTIVE LAW CONCEPT SUMMARY
Case Law and the Common Law Tradition

Case Law	The body of law that consists of the decisions rendered by judges in cases that come before the court.
The Nature of the Common Law	The common law tradition originated in medieval England with the creation of the king's courts. Portions of the decisions rendered by these courts were collected into volumes and referred to by judges in rendering subsequent decisions. The practice of deciding new cases with reference to former decisions, or precedents, forms the doctrine of *stare decisis*, which is often referred to as the cornerstone of the common law tradition. The doctrine obligates judges to follow precedents established by their own court or by higher courts within their jurisdictions.
Remedies at Law and Remedies in Equity	In medieval England, two types of courts emerged: courts of law and courts of equity. Courts of law granted remedies at law (such as money damages). Courts of equity arose in response to the need for other types of remedies. Remedies in equity, which are normally only available when the remedy at law (money damages) is inadequate, include the following: 1. *Specific performance*—A court decree ordering a party to perform a contractual promise. Specific performance may be granted when a contract involves something unique, such as a painting or parcel of land. 2. *Injunction*—A court order directing someone to do or refrain from doing a particular act. 3. *Rescission*—An action to undo a contract and return the parties to their precontractual positions; all duties under the contract are abolished.
Statutory Law and the Common Law	The common law governs all areas not covered by statutory law. As the body of statutory law grows to meet different needs, the common law governs fewer areas. Even if an area is governed by a statute, the common law plays an important role, however, because statutes are interpreted and applied by the courts, and their decisions may become precedents that must be followed by lower courts within the jurisdiction.
Case Law Terminology	1. *Case title and citation*—A case title consists of the surnames of the parties, such as *Baranski v. Peretto*. The "v." stands for versus. The citation indicates the volume and page number of the reporter in which the case can be found. 2. *Party*—The plaintiff or the defendant. Some cases involve multiple parties—that is, more than one plaintiff or defendant. 3. *Judge and justice*—These terms are often used synonymously. Usage of the terms varies. The term *justice* is traditionally used to designate judges who sit on the bench of the United States Supreme Court. 4. *Opinion*—A document containing the court's reasons for its decision, the rules of law that apply, and the judgment. If the opinion is not unanimous, a majority opinion—reflecting the view of the majority of the judges or justices—will be written. There may also be concurring and dissenting opinions.

DEVELOPING PARALEGAL SKILLS
Following Up with a Client

Maggie Sufuentes is a paralegal with the law firm of Ramirez & Sanchez in Miami, Florida. Maggie's parents immigrated to the United States from Cuba and speak only Spanish at home. Maggie is bilingual, which makes her invaluable to her firm because she can speak Spanish with the firm's Spanish-speaking clients and act as an interpreter. She also handles all of the follow-up meetings and interviews with clients. Today, Maggie and Mr. Sanchez have interviewed Bianca Martinez, a college student who wants to immigrate to the United States from Cuba and work her way through college as a nanny. Mr. Sanchez has decided that it is best for Bianca to obtain an immigrant visa under the Cuban Adjustment Act of 1980. Bianca will return tomorrow with her visa, college applications, and other documents.

TIPS FOR COLLECTING DOCUMENTS FROM A CLIENT

- Prepare a written list of documents for the client to bring in.
- Make sure that the client knows what the documents are.
- Clearly explain the significance of the documents to the clients.
- Make sure that the client understands the necessary time frame.
- Meet with the client briefly to collect and review the documents.

Common Law and the Paralegal

As a paralegal, you will find that a basic understanding of the common law tradition will serve you well whenever you need to research and analyze case law. The doctrine of *stare decisis* and the distinction between legal and equitable remedies are critical concepts when applied to real-life situations faced by clients.

For example, suppose that a client wants to sue another party for breaching a contract to perform computer consulting services. In this situation, the common law of contracts would apply to the case. (As you will read in Chapter 7, contracts for the sale of *goods* are governed by statutory law in virtually all of the states.) If you were asked to research the case, you would search for previous cases dealing with similar issues to see how those cases were decided. You would want to know of any precedents set by a higher court in your jurisdiction—and, of course, by the United States Supreme Court—on that issue. Even in an area governed by statutory law, such as sales contracts, you will want to find out how the courts have interpreted and applied the relevant state statute or statutory provision.

In addition to lawsuits involving contract law, the common law also applies to *tort law* (the law governing civil wrongs, such as negligence or assault and battery, as opposed to criminal wrongs). As a paralegal, you may be working on behalf of clients bringing or defending against the following types of actions, all of which involve tort law:

- *Personal-injury lawsuits*—actions brought by plaintiffs to obtain compensation for injuries allegedly caused by the wrongful acts of others, either intentionally or through negligence.
- *Malpractice lawsuits*—actions brought by plaintiffs against professionals, such as physicians and attorneys, to obtain compensation for injuries allegedly caused by professional negligence (breach of professional duties).
- *Product-liability lawsuits*—actions brought by plaintiffs to obtain compensation for injuries allegedly caused by defective products.

Numerous other areas, such as property law and employment law, are also still governed to some extent by the common law. Depending on the nature of your job as a paralegal, you may be dealing with many cases that are governed by the common law.

NATIONAL AND INTERNATIONAL LAW

Because business and other activities are becoming increasingly global in scope, numerous cases now brought before American courts relate to issues involving foreign parties or governments. The laws of other nations and international doctrines or agreements may affect the outcome of these cases, and thus those laws, doctrines, and agreements are also sources of law that guide judicial decisions in American courts. Many paralegals, particularly those who work for law firms that service clients operating in foreign countries, may need to become familiar with the legal systems of other nations during the course of their careers. For example, if you

On the Web
The Library of Congress offers extensive information on national and international law at **law.house.gov**.

TECHNOLOGY AND TODAY'S PARALEGAL
Finding Information on Other Nations' Laws

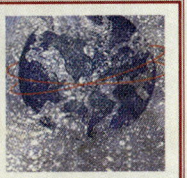

One of the things you may be asked to do, when you are working as a paralegal, is to locate information about another country's laws or customs. The Internet has made this task far less daunting for today's paralegals. You can now go online and obtain a wide variety of information about the national laws of other countries in a very short amount of time. For example, suppose that one of your firm's clients is planning a business trip to a foreign nation. You can find out what forms and what types of information are required by that country's government for businesspersons traveling into the country by going online to one of several Web sites that have links to other nations' laws.

One such site is maintained by the Northwestern University Library at: **www.library.nwu.edu/govpub/resource/internal/foreign.html**. If, in the example just mentioned, the client's business trip is to Australia, you can access the Northwestern University Library's site and find a link to the Australian Department of Immigration and Multicultural Affairs. Within minutes, you can find the relevant information (and even download the appropriate application forms) from this site for your client.

To find an extensive list of "facts" about a particular country, you can access the Central Intelligence Agency's *Factbook*, which is now published online by the agency at **www.odci.gov/cia/publications/factbook**. For example, if you want to find information on Egypt, you can go to this Web site and click on the link to Egypt. When the page opens, you will find a map of Egypt, showing the major cities and a mileage scale, as well as an abundance of data on that nation—including its population, religious and ethnic groups, languages, legal system, political parties and leaders, branches of government, economy, transportation, and so on.

Other useful online resources for national laws include FindLaw (at **www.findlaw.com**) and the Internet Law Library of the U.S. House of Representatives (at **law.house.gov**). At these (and other) Web sites, you can find extensive legal information about other nations, including constitutions, statutory laws, key administrative agencies, and court systems. You can also locate, for some countries, recent court decisions rendered by the nations' highest courts. For example, judgments delivered by Britain's highest court since 1996 are now available online at **www.parliament.the-stationery-office.co.uk/pa/ld199697/ldjudgmt/ldjudgmt.htm**.

These are just a few examples of the types of resources on national laws that are now online. You will read about a number of other Web sites that you can access for information on national (and international) topics in Chapter 15, in the context of online legal research.

FEATURED GUEST: DANIEL F. HINKEL

Pro Bono for Paralegals

BIOGRAPHICAL NOTE

Daniel F. Hinkel is a graduate of the University of Illinois College of Law and is licensed to practice law in Indiana and Georgia. He is a corporate real-estate attorney with the ING Group in Atlanta, Georgia, and an instructor of real estate for the National Center for Paralegal Training, also in Atlanta. Hinkel has written numerous articles on real-estate and construction law. He is the author of Practical Real Estate Law *and* Essentials of Practical Real Estate Law, *both published by West Legal Studies, and* Georgia Construction Mechanics' and Materialmen's Liens, *published by the Harrison Company.*

My grandfather's creed for living was "Work hard and be generous to people in need." Long before my grandfather, the Romans had a word for it, *pro bono publico,* roughly translated from the Latin to mean "for the public good." Attorneys have always considered it a professional obligation to volunteer legal services for the poor. Most state bar associations have adopted either voluntary or compulsory *pro bono* participation by their memberships. The rules of professional conduct that govern attorneys in most states include a public-service obligation as one of the ethical requirements of being an attorney. *Pro bono* participation, however, should not be limited to attorneys. A paralegal should consider voluntary *pro bono* participation a necessary part of his or her professional life as well.

LEGAL NEEDS OF THE POOR

The criminal legal needs of the poor are generally satisfied by state and federal constitutional requirements, which provide that anyone accused of a crime has a right to counsel. Through a public-defender program or court-appointed attorneys, the legal needs of poor persons accused of crimes are generally met.

One of the major problems of the American justice system is the unmet civil legal needs of the poor. The right to legal counsel in civil cases is less well defined; and it is generally provided by a number of quasi-governmental or voluntary associations that usually depend on full-time paid staff and volunteers to provide the necessary legal services.

It is estimated that a poor household is faced with from one to six legal problems a year and that most of these problems are not solved. Some of the common and serious civil legal problems faced by the poor relate to housing, securing public benefits (such as Social Security), consumer issues (such as consumer fraud and debt-collection problems), health needs, difficulties with utility companies, family disputes, and discrimination. It is within these problem areas that *pro bono* participants are most greatly needed.

PRO BONO OPPORTUNITIES

Voluntary *pro bono* activities are usually performed within the structure of a nonprofit legal aid or legal service organization. Most states have legal service organizations, which have offices in various cities within the state to provide services to the poor. In addition, city and county governments may establish neighborhood legal service centers. Private, nonprofit organizations may also provide specialized legal services to certain groups, such as elderly per-

---

work in a firm in Texas, New Mexico, Arizona, or California, you may assist in the representation of Mexican clients. In this situation, you will want to have some familiarity with Mexican law and any international agreements that regulate U.S.–Mexican relations, such as the North American Free Trade Agreement. (See the feature *Technology and Today's Paralegal* for online sources you can use to find information on other nations' laws.)

National Law

National Law
Law that pertains to a particular nation (as opposed to international law).

The law of a particular nation is referred to as **national law**. The laws of nations differ from country to country because each country's laws reflect that nation's

FEATURED GUEST, Continued

sons, migrant workers, battered women, and abused children. A list of organizations that welcome and encourage *pro bono* participation can generally be obtained from the state bar association.

PRO BONO WORK CAN MAKE A DIFFERENCE

Donating your time to provide legal services to the poor is the right thing to do, and it can make you feel good about yourself and your profession. A paralegal participating in *pro bono* activities makes a difference in his or her clients' lives. For example, assisting an indigent person in obtaining deserved and needed Social Security benefits or protecting a family from an unlawful eviction from their apartment can be a gratifying work experience. In a small way, paralegals who work with the legal needs of the poor help to resolve some of the pressing social issues of our time, and in many instances *pro bono* work may have a far greater real value than compensated work.

Pro bono participation also provides the paralegal with an opportunity to develop and improve skills in specialty areas. The *pro bono* experience may also offer a paralegal an opportunity to work in areas of the law in which he or she would not otherwise have the opportunity to work.

GETTING STARTED

Many private law firms and corporate legal departments have implemented a *pro bono* policy or program. Generally, these *pro bono* policies or programs state the firm's commitment to *pro bono* work and encourage the firm's attorneys and paralegals to participate in *pro bono* activities. A law firm or corporation with a *pro bono* program will probably have a *pro bono* coordinator who is responsible for managing the *pro bono* efforts of the firm and its employees. This coordinator can help the paralegal match his or her talents and interests with the *pro bono* opportunities available within the community. The assignment of a paralegal to a *pro bono* project should be cleared in advance with the coordinator. Most firms with such programs count time spent on authorized *pro bono* matters as part of the total productive hours required of a paralegal for purposes of performance evaluations and compensation.

> "A paralegal should consider voluntary *pro bono* participation a necessary part of his or her professional life."

Paralegals employed with firms that do not have *pro bono* programs should investigate and identify *pro bono* opportunities. Once a *pro bono* opportunity has been identified, the paralegal should discuss this opportunity with his or her supervisor and obtain permission to participate. Hopefully, the firm will consider time spent on the *pro bono* matter the same as other firm time spent in determining performance evaluations and compensation.

---

own unique cultural, historical, economic, and political background. Broadly speaking, however, there are two types of legal systems used by the various countries of the world. We have already discussed one of these systems—the common law system of England and the United States. Generally, those countries that were once colonies of Great Britain retained their English common law heritage after they achieved their independence. Today, common law systems exist in several countries, including Ireland, Canada, Australia, New Zealand, and India.

In contrast to Great Britain and the common law countries, most of the other European nations base their legal systems on Roman *civil law*, or "code law." The term *civil law*, as used here, refers not to civil as opposed to criminal law but to *codified law*—an ordered grouping of legal principles enacted into law by a

On the Web
To find information on the laws governing other nations, including constitutions around the world, go to **www.uni-wuerzburg.de/law/home.html**.

SUBSTANTIVE LAW CONCEPT SUMMARY
National and International Law

National Law	National law is the law of a particular nation. Each nation's law is different because it has evolved from varying customs and traditions. Most countries have adopted one of the following types of legal systems: 1. *The common law system*—Great Britain and the United States have a common law system. Generally, countries that were once colonies of Great Britain retained their English common law heritage after achieving independence. Under the common law, case precedents are judicially binding. 2. *The civil law system*—Many of the continental European countries and nations that were formerly their colonies have civil law systems. Based on Roman codified law, civil law (or code law) is an ordered grouping of legal principles enacted into law by a legislature or governing body. The primary source of law is a statutory code. Although important, case precedents are not judicially binding.
International Law	International law is a body of laws that governs relationships among nations. International laws allow nations to enjoy harmonious relations with each other and to benefit economically from international trade. Sources of international law include international customs and traditions developed over time, treaties among nations, and international organizations and conferences.

Civil Law System
A system of law derived from that of the Roman Empire and based on a code rather than case law; the predominant system of law in the nations of continental Europe and the nations that were once their colonies.

legislature or governing body. In a **civil law system,** the primary source of law is a statutory code, and case precedents are not judicially binding, as they normally are in a common law system. This is not to say that precedents are unimportant in a civil law system. On the contrary, judges in such systems commonly refer to previous decisions as sources of legal guidance. The difference is that judges in a civil law system are not obligated to follow precedent to the extent that judges in a common law system are; in other words, the doctrine of *stare decisis* does not apply.

Today, the civil law system is followed in most of the continental European countries, as well as in the Latin American, African, and Asian countries that were once colonies of the continental European nations. Japan and South Africa also have civil law systems. Ingredients of the civil law system are also found in the Islamic courts of predominantly Muslim countries. In the United States, the state of Louisiana, because of its historical ties to France, has in part a civil law system. The legal systems of Puerto Rico, Québec, and Scotland are similarly characterized as having elements of a civil law system.

International Law

International Law
The law that governs relations among nations. International customs and treaties are generally considered to be two of the most important sources of international law.

Relationships between countries are regulated to an extent by international law. **International law** can be defined as a body of written and unwritten laws observed by independent nations and governing the acts of individuals as well as governments. The key difference between national law and international law is the fact that national law can be enforced by government authorities, whereas international law is enforced primarily for reasons of courtesy or expediency. In essence, international law is the result of centuries-old attempts to reconcile the traditional need of each nation to be the final authority over its own affairs with the desire of nations to benefit economically from trade and harmonious relations with one another. Although no independent nation can be compelled to obey a law external to itself, nations can and do voluntarily agree to be governed in certain respects by international law for the purpose of facilitating international trade and commerce and civilized discourse.

Traditional sources of international law include the customs that have been historically observed by nations in their dealings with each other. Other sources are treaties and international organizations and conferences. A **treaty** is an agreement between two or more nations that creates rights and duties binding on the parties to the treaty, just as a private contract creates rights and duties binding on the parties to the contract. To give effect to a treaty, the supreme power of each nation that is a party to the treaty must ratify it. For example, the U.S. Constitution requires approval by two-thirds of the Senate before a treaty executed by the president will be binding on the U.S. government. *Bilateral agreements*, as their name implies, occur when two nations form an agreement that will govern their commercial exchanges or other relations with one another. *Multilateral agreements* are formed by several nations. The European Union, for example, which regulates commercial activities among its European member nations, is the result of a multilateral trade agreement. Other multilateral agreements have led to the formation of regional trade associations, such as the North American Free Trade Agreement, which was formed by Canada, Mexico, and the United States.

Treaty
An agreement, or compact, formed between two independent nations.

International organizations and conferences also play an important role in the international legal arena. International organizations and conferences adopt resolutions, declarations, and other types of standards that often require a particular behavior of nations. The General Assembly of the United Nations, for example, has adopted numerous resolutions and declarations that embody principles of international law and has sponsored conferences that have led to the formation of international agreements. The United States is a member of more than one hundred multilateral and bilateral organizations, including at least twenty through the United Nations.

International Law and the Paralegal

Communications technology, improved transportation facilities, and international organizations and treaties have all helped to form a global environment of business. What this means for attorneys and paralegals is that there is an international dimension to an increasing amount of legal work. As a paralegal, you may be asked to assist your supervising attorney in many tasks that involve an international aspect, including the following:

- Research the law of a foreign country on a particular issue, such as labor law, to determine whether a corporate client (or your corporate employer) with business operations overseas is complying with the laws of the host country.
- Assist a client who has a manufacturing plant overseas in forming employment policies that are consistent with the national law of the host country and (if U.S. employees work at the plant) with U.S. employment laws.
- Determine whether a client's patented product will be protected under the patent laws of a specific foreign country or whether an international treaty provides for such protection.
- Determine what special contractual provisions should be included in a client's contract for the international sale of goods to protect the client's interest.
- Send communications via mail, express delivery services, telephone, e-mail, or fax to the foreign offices of an American firm or a foreign firm with which an American client has business dealings.

Today's Professional Paralegal
Legal and Paralegal Practice in England

Linda Lowden, a legal assistant with the large New York firm of Stone & Stone, has just received an exciting new assignment. She is going to work in the firm's London, England, office for several months to perform "due-diligence" work for a joint venture involving an American client, USA-Tech, Inc., and a British company, BritTech, Inc. Due-diligence work is the background research that is done on a company's financial records to make sure that these records accurately reflect the true financial situation of the company.

Paralegals in England

Linda arrives at Heathrow Airport and is greeted by RuthAnne Coddens, a legal executive with whom she will be working. In England, legal assistants are called legal executives. On the drive into London, RuthAnne explains that legal executives have been used for many years in England and are very well accepted. They are required to earn a degree and to obtain work experience prior to accepting employment as legal executives. Once they are employed, they assist attorneys by preparing legal documents, interviewing clients, and representing clients in the inferior (lower) courts. Legal executives work for solicitors' firms.

Attorneys in England

"What is a solicitor's firm?" asks Linda. RuthAnne explains that in England, lawyers practice either as solicitors or as barristers. Solicitors advise clients on legal matters and prepare briefs, contracts, wills, and other legal documents for their clients. Barristers, in contrast, only represent clients in court. They are not allowed to form law partnerships, which is why most legal executives work for solicitors' firms. RuthAnne drops Linda off at the apartment where she will be living for the next several months.

Linda's Work Begins

On Monday, RuthAnne picks Linda up for work, and they drive to the London offices of Stone & Stone. Linda begins her day with a tour of the offices. She meets the people with whom she will be working. She also talks to Stephen Markham, the attorney for BritTech, on the phone and arranges to meet with him at BritTech's offices the next day. Finally, by the end of the day, she settles into her temporary office and begins to organize a plan for tackling the due-diligence work that she has come to London to perform.

She begins her due-diligence research the next day by going to BritTech and talking to Stephen Markham. She requests that she be given access to BritTech's financial records so that she can review them and, if necessary, make copies to be examined by a certified public accountant. She also needs to verify the number of years that BritTech has been in business, which she can tell from its financial data.

Title Searches and Insurance Policies

As a result of her preliminary review of the financial records, Linda finds that the company owns all of the real estate on which its manufacturing operations are located. The next step is to perform title searches on the property to be certain that there are no liens on (legal claims to) the property. Linda returns to the office to find out how to go about a title search in London. She completes the title searches, finds nothing unusual, and forwards the results to her supervising attorney in New York.

The next step is to go to BritTech and look at the insurance policies for the business. It is important to verify that they exist and to look at the type of coverage they provide. Linda returns once more to the offices of BritTech and spends many days reviewing and copying the company's insurance policies.

Linda Completes Her Task

Linda has now been in London for four months. Her research has gone well. She has one more major project. It is to review court dockets for litigation pending against BritTech. For this project, she needs the assistance of RuthAnne, who is familiar with the courts in London. She can tell Linda which courts would be handling cases in which BritTech would be a defendant and in which BritTech could lose large sums of money if the plaintiffs won. Linda and RuthAnne begin their tour of the courts in London. After two weeks, they find one case that may have significant financial consequences for BritTech, should the company lose the case. They obtain a copy of the documents relating to the case from the file, and Linda sends them to New York for further analysis of the potential liability. She is now ready to return home.

CHAPTER 5   *Sources of American Law*   **173**

▩ KEY TERMS AND CONCEPTS

administrative agency 153	enabling legislation 155	public policy 158
administrative law 155	equitable principles and maxims 159	remedies at law 159
Bill of Rights 150	injunction 161	remedies in equity 159
case law 156	international law 170	rescission 160
case of first impression 158	laches 159	specific performance 160
chancellor 159	law 149	*stare decisis* 157
citation 163	national law 168	statute 152
civil law system 170	opinion 164	statute of limitations 159
codify 162	ordinance 152	statutory law 152
common law 157	party 163	supremacy clause 149
court of equity 159	precedent 157	treaty 171
court of law 159		

▩ CHAPTER SUMMARY

1. Law has been defined variously over the ages, yet all definitions of law rest on the following assumption about the nature of law: law consists of a body of rules of conduct with legal force and effect, prescribed by the controlling authority (the government) of a society.

2. An important source of American law is constitutional law—the law established by the U.S. Constitution and the constitutions of the various states. The U.S. Constitution, as amended, is the supreme law of the land. A law in violation of the Constitution or one of its amendments, no matter what its source, will be declared unconstitutional and will not be enforced. A state constitution, so long as it does not conflict with the U.S. Constitution, is the supreme law within the state's borders.

3. Statutory law consists of statutes enacted by the U.S. Congress and state legislatures, as well as ordinances passed by local governing bodies. Statutory law takes precedence over the common law.

4. Administrative law consists of the rules and regulations issued and enforced by administrative agencies at both the state and federal levels. Administrative agencies are created by legislatures to administer and enforce legislation and to issue rules to implement the goals of specific legislation. Examples of federal administrative agencies are the Environmental Protection Agency, the Occupational Safety and Health Administration, and the Food and Drug Administration.

5. A major source of American law is case law—the decisions embodied in court cases—and the common law. The common law tradition originated in medieval England with the creation of the king's courts. The common law tradition was established in America during the colonial era and was continued in the United States after the Revolutionary War. A cornerstone of the common law tradition is the doctrine of *stare decisis*, which means "to stand on decided cases." Under this doctrine, judges are expected to abide by the law as established by previous court decisions—although occasionally a court will depart from precedent if the precedent is based on a clearly erroneous application of the law or if the political, economic, or cultural environment has changed so significantly that the precedent is no longer relevant.

6. Two parallel court systems emerged in medieval England: courts of law and courts of equity. Courts of law granted remedies at law, which consisted primarily of money damages. Courts of equity granted remedies in equity (equitable remedies), which were sought by plaintiffs for whom remedies at law could not provide adequate relief. Remedies in equity

include specific performance (an order to perform the specific terms of a contract), rescission (the cancellation of a contract so that the parties are returned to their precontractual status), and injunction (an order to engage or refrain from engaging in certain conduct).

7. Today, the common law governs all areas that are not covered by statutory law. Because the body of statutory law has expanded greatly in the last century, the scope of activities governed by common law has diminished. Nonetheless, many statutes embody common law concepts, and the courts continue to establish precedents when interpreting particular statutes or ordinances.

8. Because of the international scope of much of today's business and other dealings, the laws of other nations (national law) and the law governing relationships between nations (international law) also affect the outcome of cases brought in American courts. Many nations—generally, the continental European countries and the nations that were once colonies of those European countries—have civil law systems, in which the primary source of law is a statutory code. Many other nations—including England and the United States, as well as other countries that were formerly colonies of England—have common law systems, in which case precedents play a leading role.

QUESTIONS FOR REVIEW

1. What is law? Why are there so many different definitions of law?
2. What is constitutional law? If a state constitution conflicts with the U.S. Constitution, which constitution takes priority?
3. What is a statute? How is statutory law created?
4. What is an administrative agency? How are such agencies created?
5. Where, when, and how did the common law tradition begin?
6. What does *stare decisis* mean? Why is it said that the doctrine of *stare decisis* became the cornerstone of English and American law?
7. What is the difference between courts of law and courts of equity? Why did courts of equity evolve?
8. What kinds of remedies could be granted by a court of law? Name three remedies that could be granted by a court of equity.
9. How does the enactment of statutes affect the common law?
10. Explain the difference between national law and international law. What are some important sources of international law?

ETHICAL QUESTIONS

1. Lon Thompson is a paralegal who works for a New York law firm. One of the firm's clients wants to open a chain of restaurants (including bars) in Michigan, and Lon has been asked to research the Michigan statutes to find out the legal drinking age in that state. Lon looks in the hardbound volume of the Michigan statutes and sees that the legal drinking age is eighteen. Lon forgets to check the "pocket part," which is inserted into a "pocket" in the inside back cover of the book. The pocket part contains amendments, indicates if a statute has been repealed, and generally updates the law as described in the volume. Because of this oversight, Lon does not learn that the legal drinking age in Michigan was recently raised to twenty-one. He tells his supervising attorney that the legal drinking age in Michigan is eighteen, and the attorney passes that information on to the client. Has Lon violated any ethical rule? If so, which one? What consequences might the attorney face as a result of Lon's oversight? What consequences might Lon face?

2. John Scott, an attorney, has asked his legal assistant, Nanette Lynch, to do some research. Nanette is to research the state statutes to find out how many persons are required to witness a will. Nanette looks up the relevant state statute and finds it difficult to understand because it is so poorly written. After studying the statute for a while, Nanette decides that two witnesses are required and conveys this information to John. Actually, the statute requires that

three persons witness a will or it will not be valid. John, relying on Nanette's conclusion, has two persons witness a client's will the next day. Have John and Nanette violated any ethical rules? Explain.

3. Marilyn Clark works as a paralegal in a small general law practice. After work one day, she receives a telephone call from her Aunt May, who is in distress. Her Aunt May and Uncle Bill went to open their summer cottage and found that beavers had made a dam in the lake, which caused severe flooding on their property and in their basement. Uncle Bill is threatening to take his rifle and put an end to the beavers and their mess. Aunt May, an environmentalist, does not want Uncle Bill to shoot the beavers, so she asks Marilyn if it is illegal to shoot beavers. Marilyn knows that beavers are protected as an endangered species under federal or state environmental statutes. How should Marilyn answer this question?

4. A legal assistant in your law firm is working on a case law research project for a class that she is taking. She spends two hours doing personal case law research for her project on a computerized legal-research service that charges the firm several dollars per minute of online time. The legal assistant bills the two hours to a major client's file, assuming that no one will ever learn what she has done. You happen to be sitting at the terminal next to her, and you notice that she bills the time to one of the firm's clients. What should you do? What would you do if you learned that your supervising attorney had billed personal research time to a client's file?

Practice Questions and Assignments

1. Identify the constitutional amendment being violated in the following hypothetical situations:
   a. Jeremy's boss threatens to fire him if he does not work on Saturday nights, even though that is when he attends worship services.
   b. The city proposes an ordinance requiring that anyone caught stealing be punished by having his or her hand cut off for the first offense and the other hand cut off for the second offense.
   c. Because Robert's house is located in a poor neighborhood, the police decided that he must be a drug dealer. The police burst in and tear the place apart searching for drugs. They find nothing.
   d. The federal government bans all advertising of cigarettes.

2. In the following hypothetical situations, identify the type of case, the remedy being sought, and whether it is a remedy at law or a remedy in equity:
   a. Beth files a petition with the court. She is seeking a decree that would undo a contract into which she entered.
   b. Jim sues Bob, seeking to be reimbursed for the cost of replacing several trees that Bob's dog had destroyed.
   c. Laurie seeks to have a contract for the sale of an antique Mercedes enforced.
   d. Sam files a petition seeking to prevent the electric company from cutting down a large tree on his property.

3. Identify the type of law (common law, constitutional law, statutory law, or administrative law) that applies in each of the following scenarios:
   a. Jean Gorman strongly disagrees with the U.S. government's decision to declare war on a foreign country. She places an antiwar sign in the window of her home. The city passes an ordinance that bans all such signs.
   b. An official of the state department of natural resources learns that the Ferris Widget Company has violated the state's Hazardous Waste Management Act. The official issues a complaint against the company for not properly handling and labeling its toxic waste.
   c. Mrs. Sams was walking down a busy street when two teenagers on rollerblades crashed into her because they weren't watching where they were going. As a result of the teenagers' conduct, Mrs. Sams broke her hip, and according to her doctor, she will never walk normally again. She sues the teenagers for damages.
   d. Joseph Barnes is arrested and charged with the crime of murder.

4. Identify the following statutory law concepts:
   a. A state law enacted to require that teenagers receive expanded driving privileges at the ages of sixteen and seventeen.
   b. A rule requiring that trash be placed on the curb no sooner than 3:00 P.M. on the day before trash pickup.

c. The changing and organizing of criminal law into a statute.

5. Which of the following legal specialties are governed primarily by statutory law?
    a. Tort law.
    b. Family law.
    c. Corporate law.
    d. Property law.

6. Which of the following is an example of an administrative law case?
    a. An employment-discrimination case that is filed with the EEOC.
    b. A family-law case pending in circuit court.
    c. A dispute pending before the Internal Revenue Service.
    d. An issue of securities law.
    e. A tax matter pending before the Court of Federal Claims.

7. Identify whether each of the following is a national or international law concept:
    a. The rule that in Germany there is no speed limit on the *autobahn*.
    b. The French legal system in which the doctrine of *stare decisis* does not apply.
    c. The World Trade Organization, which governs trade among all member nations.
    d. The documents governing and establishing the European Union.

Questions for Critical Analysis

1. Rosa Jennings is an experienced paralegal. One day, while visiting with one of her neighbors, Lori Dolan, Lori asks Rosa some general questions about American law. Lori wants to know, for example, what the Bill of Rights is and what is meant by the common law tradition. Write one paragraph on each amendment in the Bill of Rights and a one-paragraph description of the common law tradition. Explain these concepts in your own words and include examples.

2. The rights guaranteed by the U.S. Constitution would be of little significance if they were not enforced by the government. In view of this fact, is a written constitution really necessary? Would the rights and privileges enjoyed by Americans be any different if we did not have a written constitution?

3. Locate *Jones v. Clinton,* 520 U.S. 681, 117 S.Ct. 1636, 137 L.Ed. 2d 945 (1997). Answer the following questions about the case:
    a. Read the first paragraph of the Court's syllabus, or summary. Who filed the lawsuit in the federal district court? For what reason(s)? What did the federal district court decide?
    b. The Eighth Circuit Court of Appeals affirmed, or upheld, the district court's decision in part, and reversed it in part. Using the syllabus, explain what the Eighth Circuit Court of Appeals did.
    c. Find the heading, "*Held.*" Paragraph 2 contains subparagraphs (a)–(d). This is a summary of the Supreme Court's reasons for affirming the decision of the Eighth Circuit Court of Appeals. For each subparagraph, summarize the Court's reasoning in one to two sentences.

4. Laws in the United States come primarily from four sources: the federal Constitution and state constitutions, statutes, administrative agencies, and the courts. Why are there so many different sources? What might happen if there were not? How could the law be changed if only courts made the law?

5. Judges, particularly the justices of the United States Supreme Court, play a paramount role in the American legal system. Why is this?

6. Why does the body of statutory law continue to expand?

7. Why do legislatures delegate authority to administrative agencies? How is the delegation of authority to agencies accomplished? Give examples of two federal administrative agencies and the type of work that paralegals might perform with respect to the areas regulated by these agencies.

8. Of what does "law" consist? How does common law fit into the definition of law given in this chapter? How did the common law develop?

9. What does the phrase *stare decisis* mean? What obligation does *stare decisis* impose on judges? How did this doctrine develop? What do courts do when declining to follow precedent? What do they do when there is no precedent?

10. Why were the courts of law and the courts of equity separate? Are they still separate? How do legal and equitable remedies differ?

Projects

1. Look at the Constitution in Appendix J of this text. Identify the amendment and quote the relevant language in the Bill of Rights that gives U.S. citizens the following rights and protections:
   a. The right to freely exercise one's religion.
   b. Protection against unreasonable searches and seizures.
   c. Protection against self-incrimination.
   d. The right to counsel in criminal prosecutions.
   e. The right to free speech.

2. Look in the white pages of your local telephone directory for your federal representative and senator. Write down their names, addresses, and telephone numbers. Consider writing or calling their offices to request information on internships.

3. Look in your local telephone directory for listings under the name of your state. Write down the names of three administrative agencies listed there and see if you can determine from their names what areas or activities they regulate. Write down your conclusions.

4. Find out if your state's courts use different procedures for cases that involve equity matters than they use for cases that do not. Are there any trial courts in your state that cannot grant equitable remedies?

5. Read through the sample court case presented as Exhibit 16.1 in Chapter 16. Identify the case name, the citation, the parties, the judge or justice who authored the opinion, the type of opinion (for example, majority, unanimous, and so on), and the first five words of the opinion.

6. Research the North American Free Trade Agreement (NAFTA) in periodicals, such as *Time* magazine or *Newsweek*. Write a one-page paper explaining what the treaty involves and who the signatories are.

Using Internet Resources

1. Go to FindLaw's home page at **www.findlaw.com.** This site offers links to many of the federal and state sources of law that you have read about in this chapter. In this exercise, you will be examining state laws, so click on "U.S. State Resources." The page you reach will list all of the states in alphabetical order. Open the site for your state, and then select "Primary Materials." Browse through the state sources of law that can be accessed online, and then answer the following questions:
   a. Were you able to access the text of your state's constitution?
   b. Did the site include your state's code (compilation of statutes) and administrative regulations?
   c. What other primary materials were included in the site?
   d. Now browse through the "Primary Materials" sites for three other states. How did your state's site compare to those of other states in terms of comprehensiveness and ease of use?

2. The Web site of the United State's Supreme Court, located at **www.usscplus.com**, contains a description of the Court's role in interpreting the Constitution. Go to this Web site and click on "The Court and Constitutional Interpretation." Explain what "judicial review" means. How did the United States Supreme Court obtain the power of judicial review?

3. The Internet Law Library Web site, located at **law.house.gov**, contains information on international laws. Go to this Web site and click on "Laws of Other Nations." Pick your favorite country and list four laws that appear in the Web site. Are any of the laws in English? Next, click on "Treaties and International Law." Click on "Treaty Collection (Compiled by Cornell Law School)." List four treatises that appear in the Web site. Click on "Agreement on the Rescue of Astronauts." When was this treaty formed? What does Article 4 of the treaty provide?

CHAPTER 6

THE COURT SYSTEM AND ALTERNATIVE DISPUTE RESOLUTION

Chapter Outline

▪ INTRODUCTION ▪ THE AMERICAN SYSTEM OF JUSTICE
▪ STATE COURT SYSTEMS ▪ THE FEDERAL COURT SYSTEM
▪ ALTERNATIVE DISPUTE RESOLUTION

After completing this chapter, you will know:

- The requirements that must be met before a lawsuit can be brought in a particular court by a particular party.
- The difference between jurisdiction and venue.
- The types of courts that make up a typical state court system and the different functions of trial courts and appellate courts.
- The organization of the federal court system and the relationship between state and federal jurisdiction.
- How cases reach the United States Supreme Court.
- The various ways in which disputes can be resolved outside the court system.

Introduction

As explained in Chapter 5, American law is based on numerous elements—the federal Constitution and state constitutions, statutes passed by federal and state legislatures, administrative law, the case decisions and legal principles that form the common law, and, to an extent, the laws of other nations and international law. But the laws would be meaningless without the courts to interpret and apply them, and for this reason the court system is a vital component of the American legal system.

Paralegals working in all areas of the law, and particularly litigation paralegals, need to have a basic understanding of the different types of courts that make up the American court system. Even though there are fifty-two court systems—one for each of the fifty states, one for the District of Columbia, and a federal system—similarities abound. Keep in mind that the federal courts are not superior to the state courts. They are simply an independent court system, which derives its authority from Article III, Section 2, of the U.S. Constitution.[1]

In the first part of this chapter, we examine the structure of the American court system. Because of the costs, both in time and money, and the potential publicity attending court trials, many individuals and firms today are turning to alternative methods of dispute resolution that allow parties to resolve their disputes outside of court. In some cases, parties are required by the courts to try to resolve their disputes by one of these methods before they can take their cases to court. In the latter part of this chapter, we provide an overview of these alternative methods of dispute resolution and the role that attorneys and paralegals play in facilitating out-of-court dispute settlements.

The American System of Justice

Before a lawsuit can be brought before a court, certain requirements must be met. We examine here these important requirements and some of the basic features of the American system of justice.

Types of Jurisdiction

In Latin, *juris* means "law," and *diction* means "to speak." Thus, "the power to speak the law" is the literal meaning of the term **jurisdiction**. Before any court can hear a case, it must have jurisdiction over the person against whom the suit is brought or over the property involved in the suit. The court must also have jurisdiction over the subject matter.

Jurisdiction
The authority of a court to hear and decide a specific action.

JURISDICTION OVER PERSONS. Generally, a court can exercise personal jurisdiction (*in personam* jurisdiction) over residents of a certain geographical area. A state trial court, for example, normally has jurisdictional authority over residents within the state or within a particular area of the state, such as a county or district. A state's highest court (often called the state supreme court[2]) has jurisdictional authority over all residents within the state.

In some cases, under the authority of a long arm statute, a court can exercise personal jurisdiction over nonresidents as well. A **long arm statute** is a state law

Long Arm Statute
A state statute that permits a state to obtain jurisdiction over nonresident individuals and corporations. Individuals or corporations, however, must have certain "minimum contacts" with that state for the statute to apply.

---

1. See Appendix J for the full text of the U.S. Constitution.
2. As will be discussed shortly, a state's highest court is often referred to as the state supreme court, but there are exceptions. For example, in New York the supreme court is a trial court.

permitting courts to exercise jurisdiction over nonresident defendants. Before a court can exercise jurisdiction over a nonresident under a long arm statute, though, it must be demonstrated that the nonresident had sufficient contacts (*minimum contacts*) with the state to justify the jurisdiction. For example, if a California citizen committed a wrong within the state of Arizona, such as causing an automobile injury or selling defective goods, an Arizona state court usually could exercise jurisdiction over the California citizen. Similarly, a state may exercise personal jurisdiction over a nonresident defendant who is sued for breaching a contract that was formed within the state.

In regard to corporations, the minimum-contacts requirement is usually met if the corporation does business within the state. A Maine corporation that has a branch office or manufacturing plant in Georgia, for example, has sufficient minimum contacts with the state of Georgia to allow a Georgia court to exercise jurisdiction over the Maine corporation. If the Maine corporation advertises and sells its products in Georgia, those activities may also suffice to meet the minimum-contacts requirements. A state court may also be able to exercise jurisdiction over a corporation in another country if it can be demonstrated that the foreign corporation has met the "minimum-contacts" test. For example, consider an Italian corporation that markets its products through an American distributor. If the corporation knew that its products would be distributed to local markets throughout the United States, it could be sued in any state by a plaintiff who was injured by the corporation's product.

JURISDICTION OVER PROPERTY. A court can also exercise jurisdiction over property that is located within its boundaries. This kind of jurisdiction is known as *in rem* jurisdiction, or "jurisdiction over the thing." For example, suppose that a dispute arises over the ownership of a boat in dry dock in Fort Lauderdale, Florida. The boat is owned by an Ohio resident, over whom a Florida court cannot normally exercise personal jurisdiction. The other party to the dispute is a resident of Nebraska. In this situation, a lawsuit concerning the boat could be brought in a Florida state court on the basis of the court's *in rem* jurisdiction.

JURISDICTION OVER SUBJECT MATTER. Jurisdiction over subject matter is a limitation on the types of cases a court can hear. In both the state and federal court systems, there are courts of *general jurisdiction* and courts of *limited jurisdiction*. The basis for the distinction lies in the subject matter of cases heard. For example, **probate courts**—state courts that handle only matters relating to the transfer of a person's assets and obligations on that person's death, including matters relating to the custody and guardianship of children—have limited subject-matter jurisdiction. A common example of a federal court of limited subject-matter jurisdiction is a bankruptcy court. **Bankruptcy courts** handle only bankruptcy proceedings, which are governed by federal bankruptcy law (bankruptcy law allows debtors to obtain relief from their debts when they cannot make ends meet). In contrast, a court of general jurisdiction can decide virtually any type of case.

The subject-matter jurisdiction of a court is usually defined in the statute or constitution creating the court. In both the state and federal court systems, a court's subject-matter jurisdiction can be limited not only by the subject of the lawsuit, but also by the amount of money in controversy, by whether a case is a felony (a more serious type of crime) or a misdemeanor (a less serious type of crime), or by whether the proceeding is a trial or an appeal.

ORIGINAL AND APPELLATE JURISDICTION. The distinction between courts of original jurisdiction and courts of appellate jurisdiction normally lies in whether

Probate Court
A court having jurisdiction over proceedings concerning the settlement of a person's estate.

Bankruptcy Court
A federal court of limited jurisdiction that hears only bankruptcy proceedings.

the case is being heard for the first time. Courts having **original jurisdiction** are courts of the first instance, or **trial courts**—that is, courts in which lawsuits begin, trials take place, and evidence is presented. In the federal court system, the *district courts* are trial courts. In the various state court systems, the trial courts are known by different names. The key point here is that normally, any court having original jurisdiction is known as a trial court. Courts having **appellate jurisdiction** act as reviewing courts, or **appellate courts**. In general, cases can be brought before them only on appeal from an order or a judgment of a trial court or other lower court. State and federal trial and appellate courts will be discussed more fully later in this chapter.

Jurisdiction of the Federal Courts

Because the federal government is a government of limited powers, the jurisdiction of the federal courts is limited. Article III of the U.S. Constitution established the boundaries of federal judicial power. Section 2 of Article III states that "[t]he judicial Power shall extend to all Cases, in Law and Equity, arising under this Constitution, the Laws of the United States, and Treaties made, or which shall be made, under their Authority."

FEDERAL QUESTIONS. Whenever a plaintiff's cause of action is based, at least in part, on the U.S. Constitution, a treaty, or a federal law, then a **federal question** arises, and the case comes under the judicial power of federal courts. Any lawsuit involving a federal question can originate in a federal court. People who claim that their constitutional rights have been violated can begin their suits in a federal court.

DIVERSITY JURISDICTION. Federal district courts can also exercise original jurisdiction over cases involving **diversity of citizenship**. Such cases may arise between (1) citizens of different states, (2) a foreign country and citizens of a state or of different states, or (3) citizens of a state and citizens or subjects of a foreign country. The amount in controversy must be more than $75,000 before a federal court can take jurisdiction in such cases. For purposes of diversity-of-citizenship jurisdiction, a corporation is a citizen of the state in which it is incorporated and of the state in which its principal place of business is located. A case involving diversity of citizenship can be filed in the appropriate federal district court.

As an example of diversity jurisdiction, assume that the following events have taken place. Maria Ramirez, a citizen of Florida, was walking near a busy street in Tallahassee, Florida, one day when a large crate flew off a passing truck and hit and seriously injured her. She incurred numerous medical expenses and could not work for six months. She now wants to sue the trucking firm for $500,000 in damages. The trucking firm's headquarters are in Georgia, although the company does business in Florida.

In this situation, Maria could bring suit in a Florida court because she is a resident of Florida, the trucking firm does business in Florida, and that is where the accident occurred. She could also bring suit in a Georgia court, because a Georgia court could exercise jurisdiction over the trucking firm, which is headquartered in that state. As a third alternative, Maria could bring suit in a federal court because the requirements of diversity jurisdiction have been met—the lawsuit involves parties from different states, Florida and Georgia, and the amount in controversy (the damages Maria is seeking) exceeds $75,000.

Note that in a case based on a federal question, a federal court will apply federal law. In a case based on diversity of citizenship, however, a federal court will normally apply the law of the state in which the court sits. This is because cases

Original Jurisdiction
The power of a court to take a case, try it, and decide it.

Trial Court
A court in which most cases usually begin and in which questions of fact are examined.

Appellate Jurisdiction
The power of a court to hear and decide an appeal; that is, the power and authority of a court to review cases that already have been tried in a lower court and the power to make decisions about them without actually holding a trial. This process is called appellate review.

Appellate Court
A court that reviews decisions made by lower courts, such as trial courts; a court of appeals.

Federal Question
A question that pertains to the U.S. Constitution, acts of Congress, or treaties. A federal question provides a basis for jurisdiction by the federal courts. This jurisdiction is authorized by Article III, Section 2, of the Constitution.

Diversity of Citizenship
Under Article III, Section 2, of the Constitution, a basis for federal court jurisdiction over certain disputes, including disputes between citizens of different states.

EXHIBIT 6.1
Exclusive and Concurrent Jurisdiction

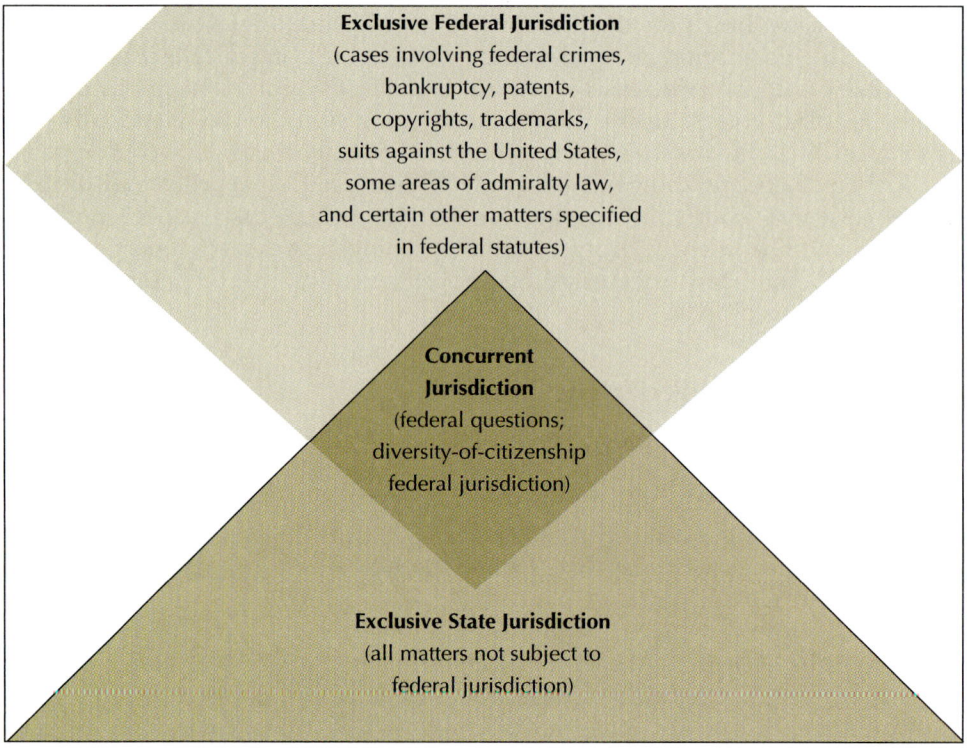

based on diversity of citizenship normally do not involve activities that are regulated by the federal government. Therefore, federal laws do not apply, and state law will govern the issue.

EXCLUSIVE VERSUS CONCURRENT JURISDICTION. When both federal and state courts have the power to hear a case, as is true in suits involving diversity of citizenship (such as Maria's case described above), **concurrent jurisdiction** exists. When cases can be tried only in federal courts or only in state courts, **exclusive jurisdiction** exists. Federal courts have exclusive jurisdiction in cases involving federal crimes, bankruptcy, patents, trademarks, and copyrights; in suits against the United States; and in some areas of admiralty law (law governing transportation on the seas and ocean waters). States also have exclusive jurisdiction in certain subject matters—for example, in divorce and adoptions. The concepts of concurrent and exclusive jurisdiction are illustrated in Exhibit 6.1.

When concurrent jurisdiction exists, a plaintiff bringing a lawsuit has a choice: he or she may bring the case in either a state court or a federal court. Normally, an attorney will look at several factors before advising a client on which court would be more advantageous. These factors include convenience (the physical location of the court), how long it would take in either type of court to get the case to trial (state courts often have heavier caseloads, and thus the wait may be longer), and the temperaments and judicial philosophies of the judges of the courts.

Concurrent Jurisdiction
Jurisdiction that exists when two different courts have the power to hear a case. For example, some cases can be heard in either a federal or a state court.

Exclusive Jurisdiction
Jurisdiction that exists when a case can be heard only in a particular court, such as a federal court.

Venue
The geographical district in which an action is tried and from which the jury is selected.

Venue

Jurisdiction has to do with whether a court has authority to hear a case involving specific persons, property, or subject matter. **Venue**[3] is concerned with the most

---
3. Pronounced *ven*-yoo.

DEVELOPING PARALEGAL SKILLS
Choice of Courts: State or Federal?

Susan Radtke, a lawyer specializing in the area of employment discrimination, and her legal assistant, Joan Dunbar, are meeting with a new client. The client wants to sue her former employer for gender discrimination. The client complained to her employer when she was passed over for a promotion. She was fired, she claims, as a result of her complaint. The client appears to have a strong case, because several of her former co-workers have agreed to testify that they heard the employer say on many occasions that he would never promote a woman to a managerial position.

Since both state and federal laws prohibit gender discrimination, the case could be brought in either state or federal court. The client tells Susan that because of Susan's experience, she wants her to decide whether the case should be filed in a state or federal court. Joan will be drafting the complaint, so Susan and Joan discuss the pros and cons of filing the case in each court. Joan reviews a list of considerations with Susan.

TIPS FOR CHOOSING A COURT
- Review the jurisdiction of each court.
- Evaluate the strengths and weaknesses of the case.
- Evaluate the remedy sought.
- Evaluate the jury pool available for each court.
- Evaluate the likelihood of winning in each court.
- Evaluate the length of time it will take each court to decide the case.

---

appropriate location for a trial. For example, two state courts may have the authority to exercise jurisdiction over a case, but it may be more appropriate or convenient to hear the case in one court than in the other.

Basically, the concept of venue reflects the policy that a court trying a suit should be in the geographic neighborhood (usually the county) in which the incident leading to the lawsuit occurred or in which the parties involved in the lawsuit reside. Pretrial publicity or other factors, though, may require a change of venue to another community, especially in criminal cases in which the defendant's right to a fair and impartial jury has been impaired. For example, a change of venue from Oklahoma City to Denver, Colorado, was ordered for the trials of Timothy McVeigh and Terry Nichols after they had been indicted in connection with the 1995 bombing of the Alfred P. Murrah Federal Building in Oklahoma City. The bombing killed more than 160 persons and injured hundreds of others. In view of these circumstances, it was thought that to hold the trial in Oklahoma City would prejudice the rights of the defendants to a fair trial.

Standing to Sue

To bring a lawsuit before a court, a party must have **standing to sue,** or a sufficient "stake" in a matter to justify seeking relief through the court system. In other words, a party must have a legally protected and tangible interest at stake in the litigation in order to have standing. The party bringing the lawsuit must have suffered a harm as a result of the action about which he or she complained. For example, assume that a friend of one of your firm's clients was injured in a car accident caused by defective brakes. The client's friend would have standing to sue the automobile manufacturer for damages. The client, however, would not have standing because the client was not injured and therefore has no legally recognizable stake in the controversy.

Standing to Sue
The requirement that an individual must have a sufficient stake in a controversy before he or she can bring a lawsuit. The plaintiff must demonstrate that he or she either has been injured or threatened with injury.

Note that in some cases, a person will have standing to sue on behalf of another person. For example, suppose that a child suffered serious injuries as a result of a defectively manufactured toy. Because the child is a minor, a lawsuit could be brought on his or her behalf by another person, such as the child's parent or legal guardian.

Standing to sue also requires that the controversy at issue be justiciable. A **justiciable**[4] **controversy** is one that is real and substantial, as opposed to hypothetical or academic. For example, in the above situation, the child's parent could not sue the toy manufacturer merely on the ground that the toy was defective. The issue would become justiciable only if the child had actually been injured due to a defect in the toy as marketed. In other words, the parent normally could not ask the court to determine what damages might be obtained *if* the child had been injured, because this would be merely a hypothetical question.

Justiciable Controversy
A controversy that is real and substantial, as opposed to hypothetical or academic.

On the Web
The Federal Rules of Civil Procedure are now available online at www.cornell.edu.

Judicial Procedures

Litigation in court, from the moment a lawsuit is initiated until the final resolution of the case, must follow specifically designated procedural rules. The procedural rules for federal court cases are set forth in the Federal Rules of Civil Procedure. State rules, which are often similar to the federal rules, vary from state to state—and even from court to court within a given state. Rules of procedure also differ in criminal and civil cases. Paralegals who work for trial lawyers need to be familiar with the procedural rules of the relevant courts. Because judicial procedures will be examined in detail in Chapters 10 through 12, we do not discuss them here.

The American System of Justice and the Paralegal

Paralegals should be familiar with the concepts of jurisdiction, venue, and standing to sue because these concepts affect pretrial litigation procedures. For example, a defendant in a lawsuit may claim that the court in which the plaintiff filed the lawsuit cannot exercise jurisdiction over the matter—or over the defendant or the defendant's property. If you are working on behalf of the defendant, you may be asked to draft a motion to dismiss the case on this ground. You may also be asked to draft a legal memorandum in support of the motion, outlining the legal reasons why the court cannot exercise jurisdiction over the case. (Motions to dismiss and supporting documents are discussed in Chapter 10.) Additionally, a party to a lawsuit may request that a case filed in a state court should be "removed" to a federal court (if there is a basis for federal jurisdiction) or vice versa. You may also be asked to draft a document requesting a change of venue (or objecting to an opponent's request for a change of venue) or to dismiss the case because the plaintiff lacks standing to sue.

If you work for a plaintiff's attorney, you might be asked to draft a complaint to initiate a lawsuit. Once the attorney reviews the facts with you, he or she may expect you to know whether concurrent jurisdiction exists. If concurrent jurisdiction exists, the attorney may expect you to ask whether the suit should be filed in a state or a federal court. If concurrent jurisdiction does not exist, the attorney may assume that you know in which court the case will be filed and that you know how to prepare the complaint for the appropriate court.

---

4. Pronounced jus-*tish*-a-bul.

PROCEDURAL LAW CONCEPT SUMMARY
The American System of Justice

Jurisdiction	1. *Jurisdiction over persons, or* in personam *jurisdiction*—The geographic boundaries within which a court has the right and power to decide cases concerning a defendant. State long arm statutes may allow state courts to exercise jurisdiction over nonresident defendants.
	
	2. *Jurisdiction over property, or* in rem *jurisdiction*—The geographic boundaries within which a court has the right and power to decide cases concerning a defendant's property.
	
	3. *Jurisdiction over subject matter*—
	   a. Limited jurisdiction—Exists when a court's jurisdiction is limited to a specific subject matter, such as probate or divorce proceedings.
	   b. General jurisdiction—Exists when a court can hear a broad array of cases.
	
	4. *Original jurisdiction*—Exists with courts that have the authority to hear a case for the first time (trial courts).
	
	5. *Appellate jurisdiction*—Exists with courts of appeal and review; generally, appellate courts do not have original jurisdiction.
	
	6. *Federal jurisdiction*—Arises in the following situations:
	   a. When a federal question is involved (when the plaintiff's cause of action is based at least in part on the U.S. Constitution, a treaty, or a federal law).
	   b. In diversity-of-citizenship cases between (1) citizens of different states, (2) a foreign country and citizens of a state or different states, or (3) citizens of a state and citizens or subjects of a foreign country. The amount in controversy must exceed $75,000.
	
	7. *Concurrent jurisdiction*—Exists when two different courts have authority to hear the same case.
	
	8. *Exclusive jurisdiction*—Exists when only state courts or only federal courts have authority to hear a case.

Venue	The most appropriate location for a trial. The concept of venue reflects the policy that a court trying a suit should be in the geographic neighborhood (usually the county) in which the incident leading to the lawsuit occurred or in which the parties involved in the lawsuit reside.
Standing to Sue	A party must have a sufficient "stake" in a controversy (a legally protected and tangible interest in the litigation) to justify seeking relief through the court system.
Judicial Procedures	Rules governing procedures relating to lawsuits and proceedings before the courts. Civil litigation in the federal courts is governed by the Federal Rules of Civil Procedure. Each state has its own procedural rules, and each court within a state has specific court rules that must be followed.

Recall from Chapter 1 that paralegal education and training emphasizes both substantive and procedural law. A paralegal can be a valuable member of a legal team if he or she has adequate knowledge of the procedural requirements relating to litigation and to different types of legal proceedings. You will read in detail about litigation procedures in Chapters 10 through 12.

ETHICAL CONCERN
Meeting Procedural Deadlines

One of the paralegal's most important responsibilities is making sure that court deadlines are met. For example, suppose that your supervising attorney asks you to file with the court a motion to dismiss (a document requesting the court to dismiss a lawsuit for a specific reason). You know that the deadline for filing the motion is three days away. You plan to deliver the motion to the court the next day, so you don't place a reminder note on your calendar. In the meantime, you place the motion in the client's file. The next morning, you arrive at work and immediately are called to help your supervising attorney with last-minute trial preparations on another case. You are busy all afternoon interviewing witnesses in still another case. You have totally forgotten about the motion to dismiss and do not think of it again until a week later—when the deadline for filing the motion has passed. Because you forgot to file the motion, your supervising attorney has breached the duty of competence. How can you make sure that you remember important deadlines? The answer is simple: *always* enter deadlines on the office calendaring system and *always* check your calendar several times a day. Also, realize that missed deadlines provide the basis for many malpractice suits against attorneys.

On the Web
State court systems vary widely from state to state. To learn about your state's court system, go to the Center for Information Law and Policy's Web site at www.cilp.org/tblhome.html.

STATE COURT SYSTEMS

Each state has its own system of courts, and no two state systems are the same. As Exhibit 6.2 indicates, there may be several levels, or tiers, of courts within a state court system: (1) state trial courts of limited jurisdiction, (2) state trial courts of general jurisdiction, (3) appellate courts, and (4) the state's highest court (often called the state supreme court). Judges in the state court system are usually elected by the voters for a specified term.

Generally, any person who is a party to a lawsuit has the opportunity to plead the case before a trial court and then, if he or she loses, before at least one level of appellate court. Finally, if a federal statute or federal constitutional issue is involved in the decision of a state supreme court, that decision may be further appealed to the United States Supreme Court.

Trial Courts

Trial courts are exactly what their name implies—courts in which trials are held and testimony taken. You will read in detail about trial procedures in Chapter 11. In that chapter, we follow a hypothetical case through the various stages of a trial. Briefly, a trial court is presided over by a judge, who issues a decision on the matter before the court. If the trial is a jury trial (many trials are held without juries), the jury will decide the outcome of factual disputes, and the judge will issue a judgment based on the jury's conclusion. During the trial, the attorney for each side introduces evidence (such as relevant documents, exhibits, and testimony of witnesses) in support of his or her client's position. Each attorney is given an opportunity to cross-examine witnesses for the opposing party and challenge evidence introduced by the opposing party.

State trial courts have either general or limited jurisdiction. Trial courts that have general jurisdiction as to subject matter may be called county, district, supe-

On the Web
The Web site of the National Center for State Courts offers links to the Web pages of all state courts. Go to www.ncsc.dni.us/court/sites/courts.htm.

EXHIBIT 6.2
State Court Systems

State court systems vary widely from state to state, and it is therefore impossible to show one "typical" state court system. This exhibit is typical of the court systems in several states, however, including Texas, California, Arizona, and Nevada.

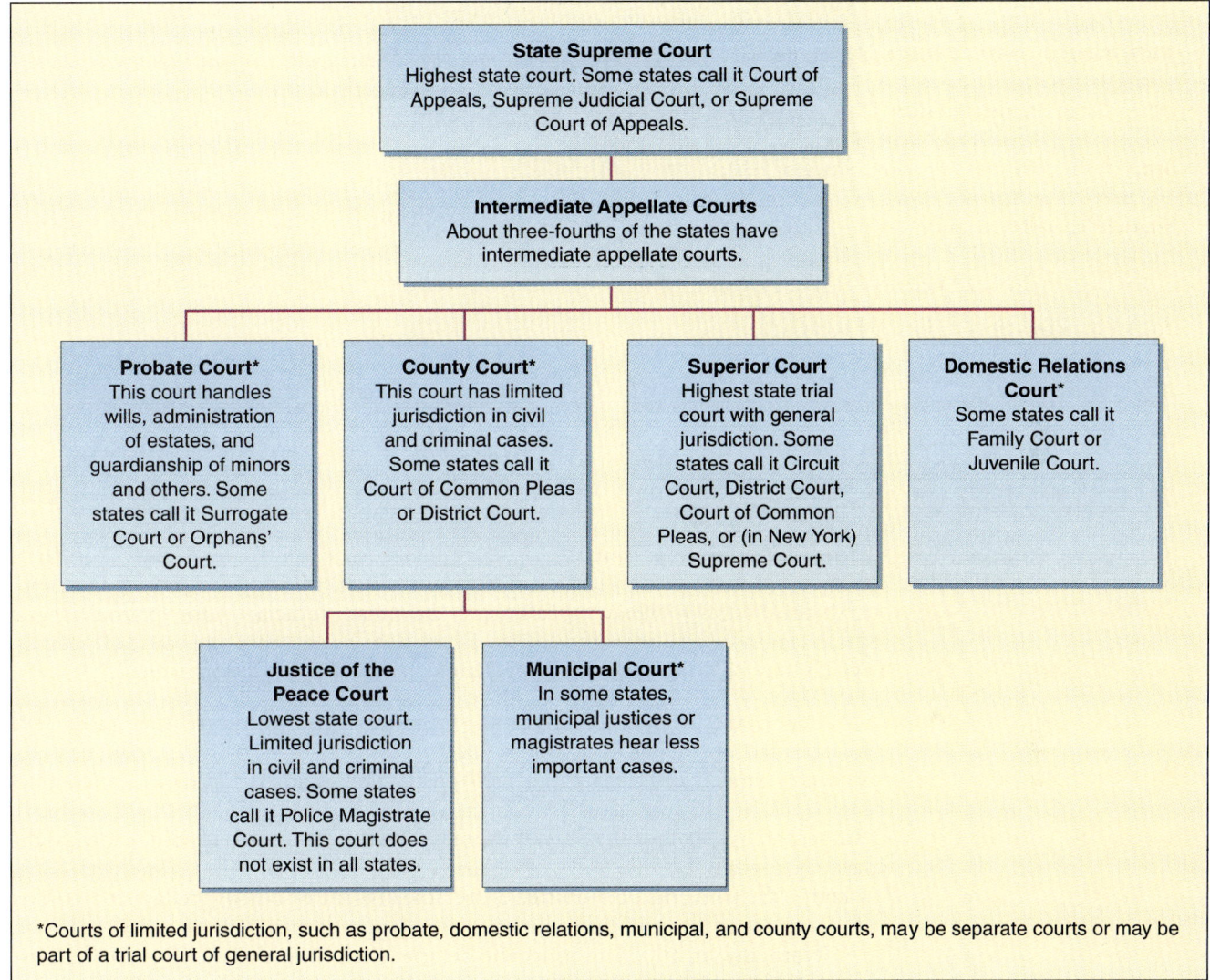

rior, or circuit courts.[5] The jurisdiction of these courts is often determined by the size of the county in which the court sits. State trial courts of general jurisdiction have jurisdiction over a wide variety of subjects, including both civil disputes (such as landlord-tenant matters or contract claims) and criminal prosecutions.

Courts with limited jurisdiction as to subject matter are often called special inferior trial courts or minor judiciary courts. Courts of limited jurisdiction include domestic relations courts, which handle only divorce actions and child-custody cases; local municipal courts, which mainly handle traffic cases; and probate courts, which, as previously mentioned, handle the administration of wills, estate-settlement problems, and related matters.

---

5. The name in Ohio is Court of Common Pleas; the name in New York is Supreme Court.

Developing Paralegal Skills

Trial Emergency

David Garner, a legal assistant, arrives at work a few minutes before 9:00 A.M. Shirley, the secretary, is overjoyed to see him. It seems that Helen Schmidt, the attorney for whom they work, is in trial, and the judge has decided to instruct the jury this morning between 9:30 and 10:00 A.M. The judge started the trial an hour earlier today because her docket was so congested. Shirley has just finished typing the jury instructions and wants David to deliver them to Helen in the court.

Tips for Handling Trial Emergencies

- Stay calm and think clearly.
- Gather all necessary/requested materials.
- Try to anticipate any additional materials that might be needed.
- Find out the judge's name and courtroom number.
- Be familiar with the court by visiting it early on.
- Anticipate security problems caused by metal detectors and other devices.

Courts of Appeals

Generally, courts of appeals (appellate courts, or reviewing courts) are not trial courts. In some states, however, trial courts of general jurisdiction may have limited jurisdiction to hear appeals from the minor judiciary—for example, from small claims courts or traffic courts. Every state has at least one court of appeals, which may be an intermediate appellate court or a state supreme court.

INTERMEDIATE APPELLATE COURTS. About three-fourths of the states have intermediate appellate courts. The subject-matter jurisdiction of these courts is substantially limited to hearing appeals. Appellate courts do not retry cases (conduct new trials, in which evidence is submitted to the court and witnesses are examined). Rather, an appellate court panel of three or more judges reviews the record of the case on appeal, which includes a transcript of the trial proceedings, and determines whether the trial court committed a prejudicial error of law. Appellate courts look at questions of law and procedure but usually not at questions of fact.

Normally, an appellate court will defer to a trial court's finding of fact because the trial court judge and jury were in a better position to evaluate testimony; they could directly observe witnesses' gestures, demeanor, and nonverbal behavior generally during the trial. At the appellate level, the judges review the written transcript of the trial, which does not include these nonverbal elements. An appellate court will challenge a trial court's finding of fact only when the finding is clearly erroneous (that is, when it is contrary to the evidence presented at trial) or when there is no evidence to support the finding. For example, if a jury concluded that a manufacturer's product harmed the plaintiff but no evidence was submitted to the court to support that conclusion, the appellate court would hold that the trial court's decision was erroneous. The options exercised by appellate courts will be further discussed in Chapter 11.

HIGHEST STATE COURTS. The highest appellate court in a state is usually called the supreme court but may be called by some other name. For example, in both New York and Maryland, the highest state court is called the Court of Appeals. The decisions of each state's highest court on all questions of state law

PROCEDURAL LAW CONCEPT SUMMARY
State Court Systems

Trial Courts	State trial courts have either general or limited jurisdiction. Those with limited jurisdiction hear cases on a particular subject matter, such as divorce or probate. Those with general jurisdiction can hear many types of cases.
Intermediate Appellate Courts	State appellate courts are generally without original jurisdiction. These courts determine whether an error was made by the trial court. Appellate courts ordinarily examine questions of law and procedure, while deferring to the trial court's findings of fact. Only if the appellate court determines that the trial court's finding of fact was clearly erroneous (contrary to the evidence presented at trial) or unsupported by evidence will it challenge the trial court's findings.
Highest State Courts	A state's highest court is its supreme court (although it may have some other title). Decisions of a state's highest court on all questions of state law are final. If a federal question is at issue, however, the case may be appealed to the United States Supreme Court.
State Court Judges and Justices	Judges and justices who sit on the benches of state courts are normally elected by the voters for specified terms.

are final. Only when issues of federal law are involved can a decision made by a state's highest court be overruled by the United States Supreme Court.

State Court Systems and the Paralegal

Because each state has its own unique system of courts, you will need to become familiar with the court system of your particular state. What is the official name of your state's highest court, or supreme court? How many intermediate state appellate courts are in your state, and to which of these courts should appeals from your local trial court or courts be appealed? What courts in your area have jurisdiction over what kinds of disputes?

In addition to knowing the names of your state's courts and their jurisdictional authority, you will also need to become familiar with the procedural requirements of specific courts. Paralegals frequently assist their attorneys in drafting legal documents to be filed in state courts, and the required procedures for filing these documents may vary from court to court. You will read more about court procedures in Chapters 10 and 11.

As indicated earlier and illustrated in Exhibit 6.1, state courts exercise exclusive jurisdiction over all matters that are not subject to federal jurisdiction. Family law (see Chapter 2) and probate law (discussed in Chapter 7), for example, are two areas in which state courts exercise exclusive jurisdiction. If you work in these or other areas of the law over which state courts exercise jurisdiction, you will need to be familiar with procedural requirements established by state (or local) courts relating to those areas.

Realize also that many paralegals work within the court system, both in state courts and county courts (which are part of the state court system). Some paralegals work as assistants to court clerks. A knowledge of state courts and procedures can thus be a valuable tool in your career as a paralegal. In addition, many paralegals work for bankruptcy courts, which are part of the federal court system—a topic to which we now turn.

On the Web
The Web site for the federal courts offers information on the federal court system and links to all federal courts at **www.uscourts.gov**.

THE FEDERAL COURT SYSTEM

The federal court system is basically a three-tiered model consisting of (1) U.S. district courts (trial courts of general jurisdiction) and various courts of limited jurisdiction, (2) U.S. courts of appeals (intermediate courts of appeals), and (3) the United States Supreme Court. Exhibit 6.3 shows the organization of the federal court system.

According to the language of Article III of the U.S. Constitution, there is only one national Supreme Court. All other courts in the federal system are considered "inferior." Congress is empowered to create other inferior courts as it deems necessary. The inferior courts that Congress has created include those on the first and second tiers in our model—the district courts and various courts of limited jurisdiction, as well as the U.S. courts of appeals.

Unlike state court judges, who are usually elected, federal court judges are appointed by the president of the United States, subject to the approval of the U.S. Senate. Federal judges receive lifetime appointments (because under Article III they "hold their Offices during good Behavior").

On the Web
Superior Information Services, a Michigan Internet consulting company, provides a single site from which you can access Web pages for trial courts. Go to www.courts.net.

U.S. District Courts

At the federal level, the equivalent of a state trial court of general jurisdiction is the district court. There is at least one federal district court in every state. The number of judicial districts can vary over time, primarily owing to population changes and corresponding caseloads. Currently, there are ninety-four judicial districts.

U.S. district courts have original jurisdiction in federal matters. Federal cases typically originate in district courts. There are other trial courts with original, but special (or limited) jurisdiction, such as the federal bankruptcy courts and others shown in Exhibit 6.3.

EXHIBIT 6.3
The Organization of the Federal Court System

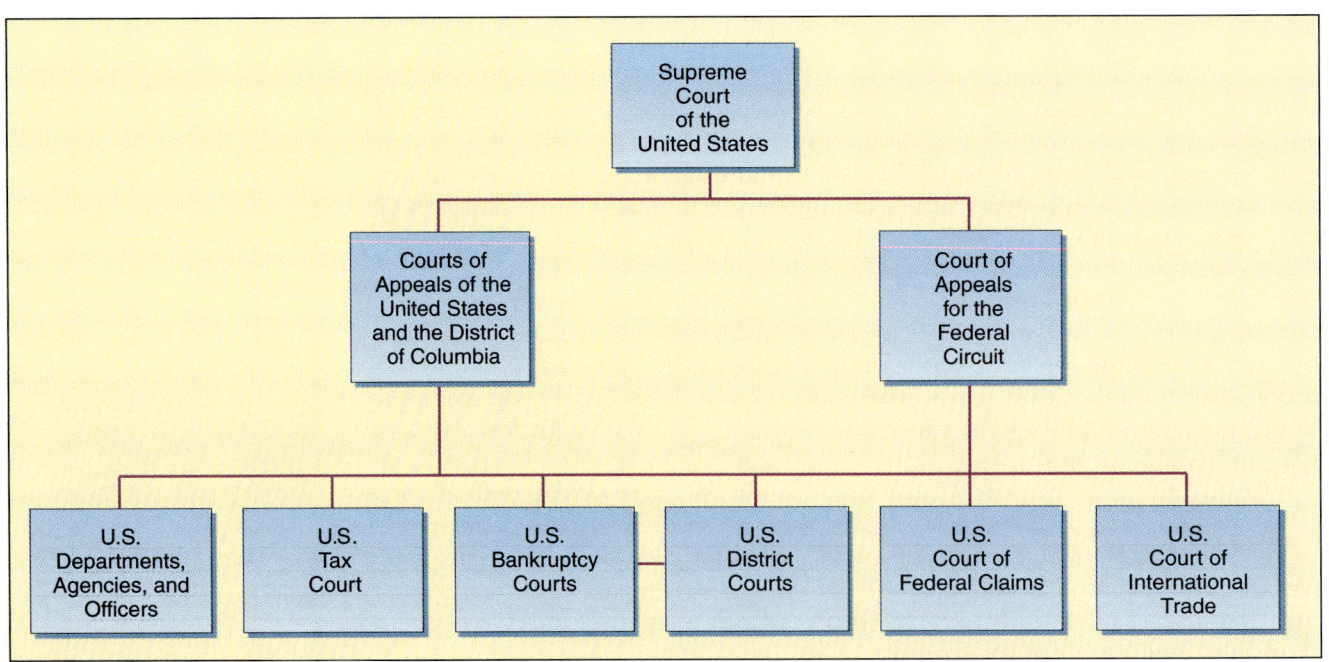

U.S. Courts of Appeals

In the federal court system, there are thirteen U.S. courts of appeals—also referred to as U.S. circuit courts of appeals. The federal courts of appeals for twelve of the circuits (including the District of Columbia Circuit) hear appeals from the federal district courts located within their respective judicial circuits. The court of appeals for the thirteenth circuit, called the Federal Circuit, has national appellate jurisdiction over certain types of cases, such as cases involving patent law and cases in which the U.S. government is a defendant.

A party who is dissatisfied with a federal district court's decision on an issue may appeal that decision to a federal circuit court of appeals. As in state courts of appeals, the decisions of the circuit courts are made by a panel of three or more judges. The judges review decisions made by trial courts to see if any errors of law were made, and the judges generally defer to a district court's findings of fact. The decisions of the circuit courts of appeals are final in most cases, but appeal to the United States Supreme Court is possible. Exhibit 6.4 shows the geographical boundaries of U.S. circuit courts of appeals and the boundaries of the U.S. district courts within each circuit.

On the Web
At the following Web site, you can use a single query form to search the opinions of U.S. circuit courts: www.law.cornell.edu/opinions.html.

EXHIBIT 6.4
U.S. Courts of Appeals and U.S. District Courts

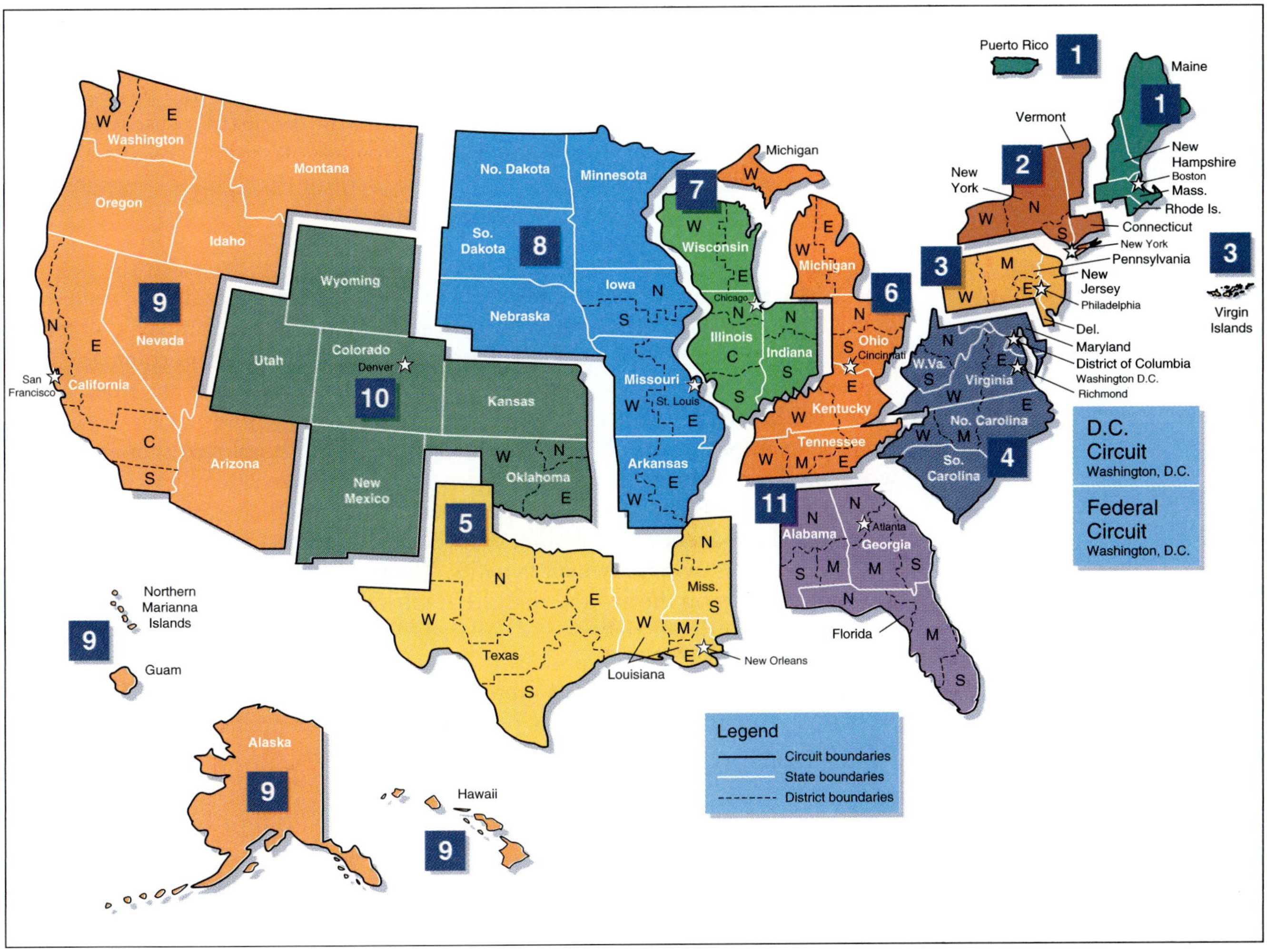

The United States Supreme Court

On the Web
An excellent site for information on the United States Supreme Court—including its basic functions and procedures, biographies and photographs of the justices, and even the history of the Supreme Court building—is the following: www.usscplus.com/info/index.htm.

The United States Supreme Court consists of nine justices. These justices, like all federal judges, are nominated by the president of the United States and confirmed by the Senate.

The Supreme Court is given original, or trial court, jurisdiction in a small number of situations. Under Article III, Section 2, of the U.S. Constitution, the Supreme Court can exercise original jurisdiction in all cases "affecting Ambassadors, other public Ministers and Consuls, and those in which a State shall be a Party." In all other cases, the Supreme Court may exercise only appellate jurisdiction "with such Exceptions, and under such Regulations as the Congress shall make." Most of the Supreme Court's work is as an appellate court. The Supreme Court can review any case decided by any of the federal courts of appeals, and it also has appellate authority over some cases decided in the state courts.

Writ of *Certiorari*
A writ from a higher court asking the lower court for the record of a case for review.

Rule of Four
A rule of the United States Supreme Court under which the Court will not issue a writ of *certiorari* unless at least four justices approve of the decision to issue the writ.

HOW CASES REACH THE SUPREME COURT. Many people are surprised to learn that there is no absolute right of appeal to the United States Supreme Court. Thousands of cases are filed with the Supreme Court each year, yet in recent years, it has heard fewer than one hundred cases each year.

To bring a case before the Supreme Court, a party requests the Court to issue a writ of *certiorari*. A **writ of *certiorari***[6] is an order issued by the Supreme Court to a lower court requiring the latter to send it the record of the case for review. Parties can petition the Supreme Court to issue a writ of *certiorari*, but whether the Court will issue one is entirely within its discretion. The Court will not issue a writ unless at least four of the nine justices approve of it. This is called the **rule of four**. The Court is not required to issue a writ of *certiorari*, and most petitions for writs are denied. A denial is not a decision on the merits of a case, nor does it indicate agreement with the lower court's opinion. It simply means that the Supreme Court declines to grant the request (petition) for appeal. Furthermore, denial of the writ has no value as a precedent.

TYPES OF CASES REVIEWED BY THE SUPREME COURT. Typically, the petitions granted by the Court involve cases that raise important constitutional questions or that conflict with other state or federal court decisions. Similarly, if federal appellate courts are rendering inconsistent opinions on an important issue, the Supreme Court may review a case involving that issue and generate a decision to define the law on the matter.

For example, suppose that an employer fires an employee who refuses to work on Saturdays, which is forbidden by the employee's religion. The fired employee applies for unemployment benefits from the state unemployment agency, and the agency, concluding that the employer had good reason to fire the employee, denies unemployment benefits. The fired employee sues the state unemployment agency on the ground that the employee's right to freely exercise her religion—a constitutional right—was violated. The case is ultimately appealed to a state supreme court, which decides the issue in a way that is contrary to several recent federal appellate courts' interpretations of freedom of religion in the employment context. If the losing party petitions the Supreme Court for a writ of *certiorari*, the Court may grant the petition and review the case.

The Federal Court System and the Paralegal

In your work as a paralegal, you will probably be dealing occasionally with the federal court system. As discussed above, certain cases involving diversity of citi-

---
6. Pronounced sur-shee-uh-*rah*-ree.

Procedural Law Concept Summary
The Federal Court System

U.S. District Courts	The federal district court is the equivalent of the state trial court. The district court exercises general jurisdiction over claims arising under federal law or based on diversity of citizenship. Federal courts of limited jurisdiction include bankruptcy courts and the other courts listed on the lowest tier of Exhibit 6.3.
U.S. Courts of Appeals	There are thirteen intermediate courts of appeals (or circuit courts of appeals) in the federal court system. Of those circuit courts, twelve hear appeals from the district courts within their circuits. The thirteenth circuit court has national appellate jurisdiction over certain types of cases, such as cases involving patent law (see Chapter 8) and cases in which the U.S. government is a defendant.
United States Supreme Court	The United States Supreme Court is the highest court in the federal court system and the final arbiter of the Constitution and federal law. Although the Supreme Court has original jurisdiction in some cases, it functions primarily as an appellate court. If the Supreme Court decides to review a case, it will issue a writ of *certiorari,* an order to a lower court requiring the latter to send it the record of the case for review.
Federal Court Judges and Justices	Judges and justices in the federal court system are appointed by the president of the United States and confirmed by the Senate. Federal court judges and justices receive lifetime appointments.

zenship may be brought in either a state or a federal court. Many litigants who could sue in a state court will opt for a federal court if diversity of citizenship exists for the reasons mentioned earlier.

You may also be working on behalf of plaintiffs whose claims concern a federal question. An increasing number of cases in federal courts are brought by plaintiffs who allege employment discrimination in violation of federal laws, such as Title VII of the Civil Rights Act of 1964, which prohibits employment discrimination based on race, color, national origin, gender, or religion. Other federal laws prohibit discrimination based on age or disability. Sexual harassment and pregnancy discrimination are considered by the courts to fall under the protective umbrella of Title VII's prohibition against gender discrimination, and such cases frequently come before federal courts.

As indicated in Exhibit 6.1, federal courts exercise exclusive jurisdiction over cases relating to bankruptcy, patents, copyrights, trademarks, federal crimes, and certain other claims. If you work on such cases, you will be dealing with the federal court system and the court procedures set forth in the Federal Rules of Civil Procedure. As with state courts, you should make sure that you know the specific requirements of the particular federal court in which a client's lawsuit is to be filed, because each federal court has some discretionary authority over its procedural rules. (Among other things, you will need to know whether you can file documents with the relevant federal court electronically. For more information on electronic filing, see this chapter's feature *Technology and Today's Paralegal: Filing Court Documents Electronically.*) You will read in detail about the procedural rules governing litigation proceedings in federal courts in Chapters 10 and 11.

On the Web
United States Supreme Court cases since 1893 can be accessed online at www.findlaw.com.

DEVELOPING PARALEGAL SKILLS

Federal Court Jurisdiction

Mona, a new client, comes to the law offices of Henry, Jacobs & Miller in Detroit, Michigan. She wants to file a lawsuit against a New York hospital where she had emergency gallbladder surgery. Mona contracted an infection as a result of the surgery and nearly died. She was so sick that she missed several months of work and lost wages of $18,000. She also has medical expenses exceeding $60,000. Jane Doyle, a paralegal, is asked to review the case to determine if it can be filed in federal court.

CHECKLIST FOR DETERMINING FEDERAL COURT JURISDICTION

- Is the case based, at least in part, on the U.S. Constitution, a treaty, or other question of federal law?
- If the case does not involve a question of federal law, does it involve more than $75,000 and one of the following:
   ✓ Citizens of different states?
   ✓ A foreign country and citizens of a state or different states?
   ✓ Citizens of a state and a foreign country?
- If it involves a combination of more than $75,000 and one of the citizenship requirements above, then diversity jurisdiction exists.

ALTERNATIVE DISPUTE RESOLUTION

Litigation in court is generally a last resort because of the high costs associated with litigating even the simplest complaint. In addition, because of the growing backlog of cases pending in the courts, it may sometimes be several years before a case is actually tried. Finally, the legal process is beset with uncertainties. One cannot know in advance how effectively the opposing side will argue its case or how the personal views and perceptions of judges and jurors may affect the outcome of the trial.

For these and other reasons, more and more individuals and business firms are turning to **alternative dispute resolution (ADR)** instead of resolving their disputes in court. Approximately 95 percent of all civil lawsuits are settled without a trial. Sometimes, a claim is settled before a lawsuit has been initiated. Most frequently, a settlement is achieved after the lawsuit is filed but before a trial takes place. In such situations, pretrial investigations give the parties and their attorneys an opportunity to assess the plaintiff's damages realistically and determine the relative strengths and weaknesses of the disputants' cases. Because so many cases are settled before they reach trial, attorneys and paralegals usually devote as much attention to these possibilities as to trial preparations.

As a paralegal, you may find that expertise in the area of ADR will serve you well in terms of career possibilities and advancement. Indeed, paralegals can play a significant role in many of the ADR options discussed in the following pages.

We now look at the various methods employed for settling disputes outside the court system. We begin by discussing the three basic (and traditional) forms of ADR—negotiation, mediation, and arbitration.

Negotiation

Negotiation is one alternative means of resolving disputes. Attorneys frequently advise their clients to try to negotiate a settlement of their disputes voluntarily

---

Alternative Dispute Resolution (ADR)
The resolution of disputes in ways other than those involved in the traditional judicial process. Mediation and arbitration are forms of ADR.

Negotiation
A method of alternative dispute resolution in which disputing parties, with or without the assistance of their attorneys, meet informally to resolve the dispute out of court.

Technology and Today's Paralegal

Filing Court Documents Electronically

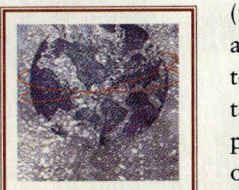

During the course of a lawsuit, many documents are filed with the court. Typically, paralegals or their support staff are the persons who make sure that the necessary paperwork reaches the relevant court in a timely fashion. The cumbersome task of physically delivering litigation documents to courthouses may be eased considerably in the future, however, depending on the success of current experiments with electronic filing, such as by e-mail or by CD-ROM.

The federal court system first experimented with an electronic filing system in January 1996 (in an asbestos case heard by the U.S. District Court for the Northern District of Ohio). Since that time, the project has been expanded, and currently at least nine federal courts allow attorneys to file documents electronically in certain types of cases. At last count, more than 130,000 documents in approximately 10,000 cases had been filed electronically in federal courts.

A number of state courts have also undertaken pilot projects to see whether electronic filing systems are feasible. For example, since late 1997 the Pima County, Arizona, court system has been accepting pleadings (documents filed at the beginning of a lawsuit) via e-mail. In early 1998, the supreme court of the state of Washington also began to accept online filings of litigation documents. (For a list of the courts experimenting with electronic filing, go to the Web site sponsored by Maryland Judge Arthur Ahalt, at www.mdlaw.net/efile.htm.)

To date, electronic filing typically has been permissible only in cases specifically approved by the court and (usually) only if all parties involved in the case agree to the procedure. The parties' agreement to electronic filing is important because if certain hardware or software is required, one party may bear more of a burden than the other. For example, in 1997 a federal court of appeals refused to accept a brief (an attorney's written argument supporting his or her client's position in a case) filed on a CD-ROM because the other party to the lawsuit did not have the equipment to "read" the brief and access the hypertext links included on the CD-ROM.

For paralegals, electronic filing—if and when it is fully implemented—will be a boon. As you might imagine, generating legal documents, filing them with the court, and making the documents available to all parties involved in the litigation are time-consuming responsibilities (see Chapter 10 for more details on pretrial litigation procedures). With electronic filing, tasks that now take hours to complete may require only minutes in the future. Because of the reduced time and paperwork involved, electronic filing will also mean substantial savings for attorneys, their clients, and the courts.

Although electronic filing creates many benefits, there are numerous hurdles to overcome on the road to this "paperless" future. Many of these hurdles are, of course, technological in nature. Some of them, though, are human. In fact, probably the most important factor in determining the success of electronic filing is the commitment of the legal community, including paralegals, to using new technology to make traditional legal procedures simpler and less costly to perform.

---

before they proceed to trial. During pretrial negotiation, the parties and/or their attorneys may meet informally one or more times to see if a mutually satisfactory agreement can be reached.

For example, assume that Katherine Baranski is suing Tony Peretto for damages. Peretto ran a stop sign, and as a result, his van crashed into Baranski's car, causing her to sustain numerous injuries and damages exceeding $100,000. After pretrial investigations into the matter, both plaintiff Baranski and defendant Peretto realize that Baranski has a good chance of winning the suit. At this point, Peretto's attorney may make a settlement offer on behalf of Peretto. Baranski may be willing to accept a settlement offer for a lower amount than the amount of damages she claimed in her complaint simply to avoid the time, trouble, and expense involved in taking the case to trial.

On the Web
You can find publications pertaining to ADR by accessing the Federal Judicial Center at **www.fjc.gov**.

Settlement Agreement
An out-of-court resolution to a legal dispute, which is agreed to by the parties in writing. A settlement agreement may be reached at any time prior to or during a trial.

Mediation
A method of settling disputes outside of court by using the services of a neutral third party, who acts as a communicating agent between the parties; a method of dispute settlement that is less formal than arbitration.

To facilitate an out-of-court settlement, Baranski's attorney may ask his paralegal to draft a letter to Baranski pointing out the strengths and weaknesses of her case against Peretto, the ADR options for settling the case before trial, and the advantages and disadvantages associated with each ADR option. Additionally, the paralegal may be asked to draft a letter to Peretto's attorney indicating the strengths of Baranski's case against him and the advantages to Peretto of settling the dispute out of court.

As a result of these pretrial negotiations, a **settlement agreement,** such as that shown in Exhibit 6.5, may be reached between Baranski and Peretto. Baranski would give up her right to continue the litigation in return for Peretto's payment to her of a designated, agreed-on sum of money.

Mediation

Another alternative method of resolving disputes is to enlist the aid of a mediator. A mediator is expected to propose solutions, but he or she does not *impose* any solution or decision on the parties. In the **mediation** process, the parties themselves must reach agreement; the role of the mediator is to help the parties view their dispute more objectively and find common grounds for agreement.

The parties may select a mediator on the basis of his or her expertise in a particular field or reputation for fairness and impartiality. The mediator does not need to be a lawyer. The mediator may be one person, such as a paralegal, an attorney, or a volunteer from the community, or a panel of mediators may be used. Usually, a mediator charges a fee, which can be split between the parties. Many state and federal courts now require that parties mediate their disputes before being allowed to resolve the disputes through trials. When mediation is required by a court before the parties can have the court hear their dispute, the mediators may be appointed by the court.

Mediation usually results in the quick settlement of disputes. Initial meetings between the parties and the mediator often occur within several weeks after a voluntary request to mediate has been made by one or both parties. Additionally, unlike litigation (and, to a certain extent, negotiation), mediation is not adversarial in nature. Rather, a mediator tries to find common grounds on which an agreement can be based. Therefore, the process tends to reduce the antagonism between the disputants and to allow them to resume their former relationship. For this reason, mediation is often the preferred form of ADR for disputes involving employers and employees, partners in a business, family members, or other parties involved in long-term relationships.

Because a mediator need not be a lawyer, this field is open to paralegals who acquire training and expertise in this area. If you are interested in becoming a mediator, you should, first of all, discuss the possibilities with your supervising attorney. He or she may be interested in having you mediate disputes involving the firm's clients. Alternatively, you might check with your local paralegal association or with one of the national paralegal associations to find out how you might pursue this career goal. You might also check with a county, state, or federal court in your area to see if you can qualify as a mediator for court-referred mediation (to be discussed shortly). Generally, any paralegal aspiring to work as a mediator must have excellent communication skills. This is because, as a mediator, it will be your job to listen carefully to each party's complaints and communicate possible solutions to a dispute in a way that is not offensive to either party. (See this chapter's featured-guest article entitled "Mediation and the Paralegal" for further details on the functions performed by mediators and the role played by paralegals in the mediation process.)

EXHIBIT 6.5
A Sample Settlement Agreement

SETTLEMENT AGREEMENT

THIS AGREEMENT is entered into this twelfth day of May, 1999, between Katherine Baranski and Tony Peretto.

WITNESSETH

WHEREAS, there is now pending in the U.S. District Court for the District of Nita* an action entitled *Baranski v. Peretto,* hereinafter referred to as "action."

WHEREAS, the parties hereto desire to record their agreement to settle all matters relating to said action without the necessity of further litigation.

NOW, THEREFORE, in consideration of the covenants and agreements contained herein, the sufficiency of which is hereby mutually acknowledged, and intending to be legally bound hereby, the parties agree as follows:

1. Katherine Baranski agrees to accept the sum of seventy-five thousand dollars ($75,000) in full satisfaction of all claims against Tony Peretto as set forth in the complaint filed in this action.

2. Tony Peretto agrees to pay Katherine Baranski the above-stated amount, in a lump-sum cash payment, on or before the first day of July, 1999.

3. Upon execution of this agreement and payment of the sum required under this agreement, the parties shall cause the action to be dismissed with prejudice.

4. When the sum required under this agreement is paid in full, Katherine Baranski will execute and deliver to Tony Peretto a release of all claims set forth in the complaint filed in the said action.

Katherine Baranski
Katherine Baranski

Tony Peretto
Tony Peretto

Sworn and subscribed before me this twelfth day of May, 1999.

Leela M. Shay
Leela M. Shay
Notary Public
State of Nita

*A hypothetical state.

FEATURED GUEST: ANDREA NAGER CHASEN

Mediation and the Paralegal

BIOGRAPHICAL NOTE

Andrea Nager Chasen received her master's degree in public administration, specializing in the theory and practice of decision-making processes, from New York University. Four years later, she earned her law degree at the American University School of Law. Following graduation from law school, through her work as a litigator, she became interested in alternative methods of dispute resolution. Her interest led her to an in-depth exploration of mediation as one method of resolving disputes out of court. As a consequence, she has developed and taught courses in mediation and has served as a mediator. Currently, she mediates and arbitrates disputes on a full-time basis in her private practice.

With all of the attention on alternative dispute resolution (ADR) methods as tools for conflict resolution, how is the traditional law firm to respond? Will the availability of ADR result in the end of the trial as we know it and the exhaustive amount of work that goes into preparing for trial? Rest assured, there is still work (and lots of it) to be done. But the type of work will differ from what the average attorney and paralegal are used to doing. This feature focuses on just one method of ADR—mediation—and the paralegal's role in this process.[a]

WHAT DOES A MEDIATOR DO?

Before considering the paralegal's role in the mediation process, it is important to know how mediators help parties in settling their conflicts. Generally, the mediator undertakes to do the following:

1. Learn what the parties' real interests are (as opposed to the positions that the parties have put forward).
2. Assess realistically the alternative ways in which the dispute might be resolved.
3. Deal with the differences between the parties' perceptions of the issues involved in the dispute.
4. Learn (in private sessions with each party) what information the parties are unwilling to disclose to each other.
5. Devise options and solutions that meet the interests of all parties involved in the dispute.

Throughout the proceedings, the mediator maintains a neutral position

---

a. *Editor's Note*: The author of this article describes some of the general features of the mediation process and the paralegal's role in mediation. Realize, however, that the mediation process may be voluntary or mandated by a court, and different states (and different courts within a state) may have different mediation procedures.

---

and focuses on the parties' feelings and statements that can be used productively. The mediator never imposes a judgment but acts as a facilitator to help the parties reach their own agreement.

THE PARALEGAL'S ROLE IN THE MEDIATION PROCESS

What tasks does the paralegal perform in relation to the mediation process? Perhaps the best way to answer this question is to divide the mediation process into various stages and examine the role of the paralegal during each stage. Generally, as with cases that go to trial, a good deal of the paralegal's efforts will be involved in overall case management.

Stage One: Premediation. The first stage of the mediation process consists of finding out the facts about a client's claim against another party and determining whether mediation might be appropriate at this point. In divorce or custody matters, if the couple has retained attorneys but negotiations appear to be failing, then an attempt to mediate the dispute may be useful. Sometimes, the client's case will already be in the initial stages of litigation, and pretrial investigations will be underway. Mediation may also be forced on the parties by a court or other authority at almost the "eleventh hour" prior to trial—after both parties are fully prepared to present their respective cases to the court.

Paralegals play an important role during the premediation stage by investigating the factual background of the dispute. Preliminary investigations should also include, where appropriate, valuations and appraisals of personal and real property, damages, and

FEATURED GUEST, Continued

compensatory payments. Finally, the paralegal should make necessary contacts with the parties and continue to generally manage the case.

Stage Two: Selecting Mediation. Certain factors should be considered in reviewing the available tools (including litigation) for conflict resolution. If the disputing parties have a continuing relationship—as business partners, for example—court-imposed decisions may alienate the parties and intensify the conflict. Also, having the conflict resolved by a court can be costly and time consuming.

Generally, mediation can be arranged to meet the scheduling demands of the parties and is far less costly than litigation. Furthermore, because the mediator does not impose the decision, the parties control how the agreement is shaped. Unlike litigation, mediation is not adversarial in nature; rather, it seeks to find common grounds on which an agreement can be based. Therefore, the process tends to reduce the antagonism between the disputants and to allow them to resume their former relationship more easily.

The paralegal's role during this preliminary stage is to develop a clear understanding of the client's needs and interests so that the attorney can better assess whether mediation would be a desirable alternative for resolving the dispute. The paralegal can also provide the attorney with a list of prescreened, qualified mediators. (Such lists can be obtained from numerous organizations, including the American Arbitration Association, the federal Mediation and Conciliation Service, local courts, bar associations, and chambers of commerce.) Once the lists are obtained, then a further screening of potential mediators may be desirable. Each mediator brings a specific style to mediation. Some mediators may act more as case evaluators, while others may use certain techniques to help the parties carefully examine their relationship issues. The kind of case for which mediation is sought may indicate the type of mediation style that is desirable. For example, if the matter is a straightforward negligence case where the relationship between the parties is secondary, the selection of a mediator who provides case evaluation may be appropriate. If the relationship issues require more attention, as with business partners, employers and employees, or a divorcing couple, this calls for the selection of a mediator who is skilled in assisting the parties in recognizing their relationship issues in addition to the other matters involved in the case.

Stage Three: Mediation Sessions. During the mediation sessions, the mediator allows both sides to present their views and spends time with the parties, either jointly or in private meetings with each party, to uncover the real interests and needs of the disputants. Sometimes, the parties may reach agreement after just one mediation session, but commonly several sessions are held so that the parties have the time and opportunity to obtain information on issues that need to be addressed. It may be necessary, for example, to obtain financial data relating to one or both of the parties. And, of course, several sessions may be required simply to reach a satisfactory agreement.

> *"The mediator never imposes a judgment but acts as a facilitator to help the parties reach their own agreement."*

The paralegal can play a crucial role during this stage of the mediation process by helping to provide additional information for the sessions as they progress. The paralegal can also help in the drafting of any preliminary responses that are required during the course of the mediation. The paralegal may also draft the final agreement—unless that duty is assumed by the mediator.

Conclusion

Mediation can be useful at many stages of a dispute between parties. Mediation may help to resolve the entire dispute or just one aspect of it. Case management within the legal office is as important for the cases that are to be mediated as it is for the cases that will be tried in court. The paralegal can play a significant role in overall case management by doing the following:

1. Maintaining good methods of tracking and organizing data during the premediation stage.

2. Assisting the parties in selecting an appropriate mediator.

3. Providing necessary data and information during mediation sessions.

Arbitration
The settling of a dispute by submitting it to a disinterested third party (other than a court), who renders a decision that may or may not be legally binding.

Arbitration

A more formal method of alternative dispute resolution is **arbitration.** The key difference between arbitration and the forms of ADR just discussed, negotiation and mediation, is that in those forms of ADR, the parties themselves settle their dispute—although a third party may assist them in doing so. In arbitration, the third party hearing the dispute normally makes the decision for the parties. In a sense, the arbitrator becomes a private judge, even though the arbitrator does not have to be a lawyer. Frequently, a panel of experts arbitrates the dispute.

Depending on the parties' circumstances and preferences, the arbitrator's decision may be legally binding or nonbinding on the parties. In nonbinding arbitration, the parties submit their dispute to a third party but remain free to reject the third party's decision. Nonbinding arbitration is more similar to mediation than to binding arbitration. As will be discussed later in this chapter, arbitration that is mandated by the courts is often not binding on the parties. If, after mandatory arbitration, the parties are not satisfied with the results of arbitration, they may then ignore the arbitrator's decision and have the dispute litigated in court. Even if the arbitrator's decision is legally binding, a party can appeal the decision to a court for judicial review—as will be discussed below.

Arbitration Clause
A clause in a contract that provides that, in case of a dispute, the parties will determine their rights by arbitration rather than through the judicial system.

ARBITRATION CLAUSES AND STATUTES.   Virtually any commercial matter can be submitted to arbitration. When a dispute arises, parties can agree to settle their differences through arbitration rather than through the court system. Frequently, however, disputes are arbitrated because of an arbitration clause in a contract entered into before the dispute arose. An **arbitration clause** provides that any disputes arising under the contract will be resolved by arbitration. For example, an arbitration clause in a contract for the sale of goods might provide that "any controversy or claim arising under this contract will be referred to arbitration before the American Arbitration Association."[7]

If parties enter into a contract containing an arbitration clause, it is likely that either a state or a federal statute will compel them to arbitrate any dispute arising under the contract. Most states have statutes under which arbitration clauses are enforced, and some state statutes compel arbitration of certain types of disputes, such as those involving public employees. At the federal level, the Federal Arbitration Act (FAA) of 1925 enforces arbitration clauses in contracts relating to certain types of activities, such as those involving interstate commerce (commerce between two or more states). Even business activities that have only remote or minimal effects on commerce between two or more states may be regarded as interstate commerce. Thus, arbitration agreements involving transactions only slightly connected to the flow of interstate commerce may fall under the FAA.

On the Web
The Virtual Magistrate Project, which is sponsored by several ADR organizations (including the American Arbitration Association), offers a forum for online dispute resolution at vmag.vcilp.org.

The FAA does not establish a set arbitration procedure. The parties themselves must agree on the manner of resolving their disputes. The FAA only provides that if the parties have agreed to arbitrate disputes arising in relation to their contract, through an arbitration clause, the arbitration clause will be enforced. In other words, arbitration must take place before a party can take a dispute to the courts.

Submission Agreement
A written agreement to submit a legal dispute to an arbitrator or arbitrating panel for resolution.

THE ARBITRATION PROCESS.   The first step in the arbitration process is the **submission agreement,** which occurs when the parties agree to submit their dispute for arbitration. (If an arbitration clause is included in a contract, the clause itself is the submission to arbitrate.) Most states require that an agreement to sub-

---

7. As will be discussed shortly, the American Arbitration Association is a leading provider of arbitration services in the United States.

> ### ETHICAL CONCERN
> ## Potential Arbitration Problems
>
> Many individuals and business firms prefer to arbitrate disputes rather than take them to court. For that reason, they often include arbitration clauses in their contracts. These clauses normally specify who or what organization will arbitrate the dispute and where the arbitration will take place. To safeguard a client's interests, when drafting and reviewing arbitration clauses in contracts, the careful paralegal will be alert to the possibility that those who arbitrate the dispute might not be totally neutral or that the designated place of arbitration is so geographically distant from the client's location that it may pose a great inconvenience and expense for the client should an arbitrable dispute arise. The paralegal should call any such problems to his or her supervising attorney's attention. The attorney can then discuss the problem with the client and help the client negotiate an arbitration clause that is more favorable to the client's position.

mit a dispute to arbitration must be in writing. The submission agreement typically identifies the parties, the nature of the dispute to be resolved, the monetary amounts involved in the dispute, the place of arbitration, and the powers that the arbitrator will exercise. Frequently, the agreement includes a signed statement that the parties intend to be bound by the arbitrator's decision.

The next step in the process is the *hearing*. Normally, the parties agree prior to arbitration—in an arbitration clause or in a submission-to-arbitrate agreement, for example—on what procedural rules will govern the proceedings. In a typical hearing, the parties begin as they would at a trial by presenting opening arguments to the arbitrator and stating what remedies should or should not be granted. After the opening statements have been made, evidence is presented. Witnesses may be called and examined by both sides. After all evidence has been presented, the parties give their closing arguments. Although arbitration is in some ways similar to a trial, the rules (such as those regarding what kinds of evidence may be introduced) are usually much less restrictive than those involved in formal litigation.

After each side has had an opportunity to present evidence and to argue its case, the arbitrator reaches a decision. The final decision of the arbitrator is called an **award**, even if no money is conferred on a party as a result of the proceedings. Under most arbitration statutes, the arbitrator must render an award within thirty days of the close of the hearing.

Award
In the context of ADR, the decision rendered by an arbitrator.

A paralegal may become extensively involved in preparations for arbitration, just as he or she would in preparing for a trial. The paralegal will assist in obtaining and organizing all evidence relating to the dispute, may interview witnesses and prepare them for the hearing, and generally will assist in other tasks commonly undertaken prior to a trial (see Chapter 10).

THE ROLE OF THE COURTS IN THE ARBITRATION PROCESS. The role of the courts in the arbitration process is limited. One important role is played at the prearbitration stage. When a dispute arises as to whether the parties have agreed in an arbitration clause to submit a particular matter to arbitration, one party may file suit to compel arbitration. The court before which the suit is brought will not decide the basic controversy but must decide whether the dispute is *arbitrable—*

that is, whether the matter is one that can be resolved through arbitration. For example, if the dispute involves a claim of employment discrimination on the basis of age, the court will have to decide whether the Age Discrimination in Employment Act of 1967 (which protects persons forty years of age and older against employment discrimination on the basis of age) permits claims brought under this act to be arbitrated. As for any other court trial, the attorney's legal team will gather all the evidence and facts relating to the dispute, research the relevant arbitration statute and previous case law, and so on, as necessary to support the client's position.

Courts also may play an important role at the postarbitration stage. If the arbitration has produced an award, one of the parties may appeal the award or may seek a court order compelling the other party to comply with the award. In determining whether an award should be enforced, a court conducts a review that is much more restricted in scope than an appellate court's review of a trial court decision. The general view is that because the parties were free to frame the issues and set the powers of the arbitrator at the outset, they cannot complain about the result. An arbitration award may be set aside, however, if the award resulted from the arbitrator's misconduct or "bad faith," or if the arbitrator exceeded his or her powers in arbitrating the dispute. An arbitrator is permitted to resolve only those issues that are covered by the agreement to submit to arbitration.

Other ADR Forms

The three forms of ADR just discussed are the oldest and traditionally the most commonly used forms. In recent years, a variety of new types of ADR have emerged. Some of them combine elements of mediation and arbitration. For example, in **binding mediation,** a neutral mediator tries to facilitate agreement between the parties, but if no agreement is reached the mediator issues a legally binding decision on the matter. In **mediation arbitration (med-arb),** an arbitrator attempts first to help the parties reach an agreement, just as a mediator would. If no agreement is reached, then formal arbitration is undertaken, and the arbitrator issues a legally binding decision.

Other ADR forms are sometimes referred to as "assisted negotiation" because they involve a third party in what is essentially a negotiation process. For example, in **early neutral case evaluation,** the parties select a neutral third party (generally an expert in the subject matter of the dispute) to evaluate their respective positions. The parties explain their positions to the case evaluator however they wish. The case evaluator then assesses the strengths and weaknesses of the parties' positions, and this evaluation forms the basis of negotiating a settlement.

The mini-trial is a form of assisted negotiation that is often used by business parties. In a **mini-trial,** each party's attorney briefly argues the party's case before representatives of each firm who have the authority to settle the dispute. Typically, a neutral third party (usually an expert in the area being disputed) acts as an adviser. If the parties fail to reach an agreement, the adviser renders an opinion as to how a court would likely decide the issue. The proceeding assists the parties in determining whether they should negotiate a settlement of the dispute or take it to court.

Court-Referred ADR

Today, the majority of states either require or encourage parties to undergo mediation or arbitration prior to trial. Generally, when a trial court refers a case for arbitration, the arbitrator's decision is not binding on the parties. If the parties do not agree with the arbitrator's decision, they can go forward with the lawsuit.

Binding Mediation
A form of ADR in which a mediator attempts to facilitate agreement between the parties, but if no agreement is reached the mediator issues a legally binding decision.

Mediation Arbitration (Med-Arb)
A form of ADR in which an arbitrator attempts first to help the parties reach an agreement, just as a mediator would. If no agreement is reached, then formal arbitration is undertaken, and the arbitrator issues a legally binding decision.

Early Neutral Case Evaluation
A form of ADR in which a neutral third party evaluates the strengths and weaknesses of the disputing parties' positions; the evaluator's opinion forms the basis for negotiating a settlement.

Mini-Trial
A private proceeding that assists disputing parties in determining whether to take their case to court. During the proceeding, each party's attorney briefly argues the party's case before the other party and (usually) a neutral third party, who acts as an adviser. If the parties fail to reach an agreement, the adviser renders an opinion as to how a court would likely decide the issue.

The types of court-related ADR programs in use vary widely. In some states, such as Missouri, ADR is voluntary. In other states, such as Minnesota, parties are required to undertake ADR before they can have their cases heard in court. Some states, such as Minnesota, offer a menu of options. Other states, including Florida (which has a statewide, comprehensive mediation program), offer only one alternative.

Several federal courts have also instituted ADR programs. Courts in several federal districts require arbitration prior to trial in cases involving less than $100,000, and a number of other federal courts provide for voluntary arbitration. Additionally, numerous federal courts hold summary jury trials. In a **summary jury trial (SJT)**, the parties present their arguments and supporting evidence (other than witness testimony—witnesses are not called in an SJT), and the jury then renders a verdict. Unlike in an actual trial, the jury's verdict is not binding. The verdict does, however, act as a guide to both sides in reaching an agreement during the mandatory negotiations that immediately follow the SJT. The SJT is much speedier than a regular trial, and frequently the parties are able to settle their dispute without resorting to an actual trial. If no settlement is reached, both sides have the right to a full trial later.

Today's courts are experimenting with a variety of other alternatives to speed up (and reduce the cost of) justice. These alternatives include summary procedures for commercial litigation, the appointment of special masters to assist judges in deciding complex issues, and permitting an expanded use of paralegals in the handling of routine legal matters.

Summary Jury Trial (SJT)
A method of settling disputes (used in some federal courts) in which a trial is held but the jury's verdict is not binding. The verdict only acts as a guide to both sides in reaching an agreement during the mandatory negotiations that immediately follow the trial. If a settlement is not reached, both sides have the right to a full trial later.

Providers of ADR Services

ADR services are provided by both government agencies and private organizations. A major provider of ADR services is the **American Arbitration Association (AAA)**. Most of the nation's largest law firms are members of this nonprofit association. Founded in 1926, the AAA now settles about seventy thousand disputes a year in its numerous offices around the country. Cases brought before the AAA are heard by an expert or a panel of experts in the area relating to the dispute and are usually settled quickly. Generally, about half of the panel members are lawyers. To cover its costs, the AAA charges a fee, paid by the party filing the claim. In addition, each party to the dispute pays a specified amount for each hearing day, as well as a special additional fee for cases involving personal injuries or property loss.

American Arbitration Association (AAA)
The major organization offering arbitration services in the United States.

ETHICAL CONCERN
Private Justice

The use of for-profit arbitration providers has been controversial. Critics raise the ethical question as to whether it is fair to put a "price tag" on justice by making dispute-settlement forums more available to those who can afford them than to those who cannot. Supporters of private ADR services maintain that any alternative that can help reduce the heavy caseload of the courts ultimately helps everybody. As a concerned citizen, you may have strong views on the matter. In your capacity as a paralegal, however, you should not let your personal ethical standards prevent you from implementing whatever (legal) course of action the client, in consultation with your supervising attorney, chooses to undertake.

Procedural Law Concept Summary
Alternative Dispute Resolution

Negotiation	A method of ADR in which the parties come together, with or without attorneys to represent them, and try to reach a settlement without the involvement of a third party.
Mediation	A method of ADR in which the parties themselves try to reach an agreement but with the help of a third party, called a mediator, who proposes solutions.
Arbitration	A more formal method of ADR in which the parties submit their dispute to a neutral third party, the arbitrator (or panel of arbitrators), who renders a decision. The decision may or may not be legally binding, depending on the circumstances. Court-mandated arbitration, for example, is normally nonbinding. In arbitration proceedings voluntarily entered into by parties, such as through a voluntarily agreed-on arbitration clause in a contract, the arbitrator's decision is usually binding. Arbitrators' decisions, even in binding arbitration, may be appealed to the courts for review if a party claims that the award should be set aside because the arbitrator exceeded his or her authority or for some other reason.
Binding Mediation	A proceeding in which a mediator attempts to facilitate agreement between the parties, but if no agreement is reached the mediator issues a legally binding decision.
Mediation Arbitration (Med-Arb)	A proceeding in which an arbitrator attempts first to help the parties reach an agreement, but if no agreement is reached formal arbitration is undertaken and the arbitrator issues a legally binding decision.
Early Neutral Case Evaluation	A proceeding in which a neutral third party evaluates the strengths and weaknesses of disputing parties' positions and renders an opinion, which becomes the basis for negotiating a settlement.
Mini-Trial	A private proceeding in which each party's attorney argues the party's case before a panel of representatives from both sides. A neutral third party often acts as an adviser and renders an opinion on how a court would likely decide the issue.
Court-Referred ADR	Many federal and state courts today encourage or require parties to lawsuits to undergo some form of ADR (mediation or arbitration, for example) before bringing their lawsuits before the courts. Some federal courts use summary jury trials with nonbinding jury verdicts to facilitate pretrial settlements.
Providers of ADR Services	ADR services are provided by both government agencies and private organizations. The American Arbitration Association (AAA) is the leading provider of such services. Numerous for-profit firms in the country also provide ADR services, often hiring retired judges to conduct arbitration or other ADR proceedings.

Hundreds of for-profit firms around the country also provide ADR services. Typically, these firms hire retired judges to conduct arbitration hearings or otherwise assist parties in settling their disputes. The leading firm in this relatively new private system of justice is JAMS/Endispute, which is based in Santa Ana, California. Private ADR firms normally allow the parties to decide on the date of the hearing, the presiding judge, whether the judge's decision will be legally binding, and the site

Today's Professional Paralegal

Arbitrating Commercial Contracts

Julia Lorenz has worked as a legal assistant for International Airlines (IA) for ten years. She works in the legal department on the staff of the general counsel. Her job has been to work with Jim Manning, senior attorney. This attorney is responsible for all of the corporation's contracts, including the following: major contracts with jet manufacturers for the purchase of aircraft, contracts with catering companies to supply food during flights, fuel contracts, employment and labor contracts, and many small contracts for the purchase and lease of equipment and supplies for the numerous airline offices and ticket counters.

Reviewing Proposed Contracts

Julia's job is to review the provisions of proposed major contracts, such as the contracts to purchase jet aircraft, and to provide Jim with an article-by-article summary of the contracts' provisions. Jim then negotiates these contracts to obtain the most favorable terms possible for the airline. Once he has negotiated a contract, Julia makes the final changes and forwards it to the appropriate IA corporate official to review and sign.

Attending Arbitration Proceedings

All of the airline's major contracts contain arbitration clauses that require all contract disputes to be resolved through binding arbitration services provided by the American Arbitration Association (AAA). On numerous occasions, Julia has attended arbitration proceedings with Jim. In preparing for arbitration, Julia obtains affidavits, prepares subpoenas, and arranges for witnesses to be present to testify. During the arbitration proceedings, she assists in presenting material into evidence. She and Jim have developed a good rapport with several arbitrators at the local AAA office, and they usually request these arbitrators when they have a case that must be arbitrated.

Becoming an Arbitrator

Julia's knowledge of arbitration procedures and her outstanding work in preparing for arbitration, as well as during the proceedings, won her significant recognition from this group of arbitrators. One of the arbitrators eventually approached Julia and suggested that she apply for approval as an arbitrator. She said that she would consider it.

Julia later mentioned the arbitrator's suggestion to Jim. He thought that Julia had been paid quite a compliment. He encouraged her to contact the AAA to inquire about the possibility of being approved as an arbitrator. When Julia called the AAA, she learned that arbitrators in the area of commercial arbitration are not required to be attorneys. She would need eight years of experience in her field and would have to meet certain educational requirements. When Julia realized that she had the necessary qualifications, she submitted an application. About two months later, she was approved as an arbitrator.

---

of the hearing—which may be a conference room, a law-school office, or a leased courtroom. The judges follow procedures similar to those of the federal courts and use similar rules. Usually, each party to the dispute pays a filing fee and a designated fee for a hearing session or conference.

As mentioned, courts also have ADR programs in which disputes are resolved by court-appointed attorneys or paralegals who are qualified to act as arbitrators or mediators in certain types of disputes. Many paralegals have found that becoming a mediator or an arbitrator is an especially rewarding career option.

ADR and the Paralegal

The time and money costs associated with litigating disputes in court continue to rise, and, as a result, disputing parties are increasingly turning to ADR as a means of settling their disagreements. As a way to reduce their caseloads, state and federal courts are also increasingly requiring litigants to undergo arbitration prior to

Paralegal Profile

LEE A. PAIGE graduated from the University of West Los Angeles School of Paralegal Studies with an ABA-approved paralegal certificate. He holds paralegal specialist certificates in litigation, real estate, environmental law, and intellectual-property law. His experience includes state and federal litigation, copyrights, patent and trademark prosecution, assignments, and licensing. He is currently employed as a senior paralegal in the Los Angeles office of the Seattle-based law firm of Preston, Gates & Ellis, where he assists attorneys with railroad litigation and environmental-law research.

In 1998 Paige served as president of the Los Angeles Paralegal Association, the largest association of paralegals in the nation. For the past ten years he has been extremely active in the promotion and development of the paralegal profession both in California and nationally. He is frequently called on to serve as a motivational speaker and paralegal expert by high schools, colleges, paralegal schools, and paralegal and legal associations. As a representative of the California Alliance of Paralegal Associations, he has lobbied the state bar association and the state legislature in an effort to codify a legal definition of the term *paralegal* and specific educational standards for traditional paralegals. He has authored several articles on the paralegal profession and is a contributing writer to *Legal Assistant Today* magazine.

Litigation Paralegal

What do you like best about your work?

"I very much enjoy research! To some paralegals, such a statement might sound a little crazy, but I really do enjoy researching more than any other part of my job. As a former news writer, my natural penchant for 'digging' for a story comes in quite handy. It is very gratifying to me for an attorney to give me a problem and rely on me to find the answer. I get quite an adrenaline rush from 'fact-finding' missions and a wealth of satisfaction from 'delivering the goods' that are the result of my computerized or manual research."

What is the greatest challenge that you face in your area of work?

"The greatest challenge I currently face is keeping ahead of our ever-mounting litigation schedule. I primarily assist a partner in my firm who represents a major railway company and juggles a huge caseload. My boss is an excellent attorney, but, as is the case with many litigators, he is frequently overloaded. His secretary and I must be constantly vigilant with his weekly calendar and daily schedule to prevent time conflicts and make sure that he does not miss any crucial dates or court appearances."

> "One success tip that I always give to students and working paralegals is to never stop learning."

What advice do you have for would-be paralegals in your area of work?

"I frequently lecture at local paralegal schools, and the advice I normally give paralegal students is to focus their studies on areas of law that are of interest to them. This will give them an idea of where their real strengths are. I work in litigation, but it is not for everyone. Litigation is very complex and demanding, and if students go into it blindly they may be disappointed. Many people enter into the paralegal profession as a second career, perhaps as a result of a layoff, forced relocation, or downsizing. Other people see becoming a paralegal as a way of getting a "foot in the door" of the legal profession, and still others use it as a proving ground in anticipation of going on to law school and becoming an attorney. Whatever their reasons for becoming paralegals, I always advise would-be paralegals to investigate the profession before they jump in, and to only attend an ABA-approved school."

What are some tips for success as a paralegal in your area of work?

"One success tip that I always give to students and working paralegals is to never stop learning. Paralegals should voluntarily take additional classes and seminars beyond their paralegal certificates. Such classes will keep them abreast of new developments in law and procedure that can affect their ability to assist their attorneys in the representation of their clients and increase their value to their employers."

bringing their suits before the courts. Although paralegals have always assisted attorneys in work relating to the negotiation of out-of-court settlements for clients, they may play an even greater role in the future. Some paralegals are qualified mediators and directly assist parties in reaching a mutually satisfactory agreement. Some paralegals serve as arbitrators. As more and more parties utilize ADR, paralegals will have increasing opportunities in this area of legal work.

If you are interested in becoming a mediator, you need to be thoroughly familiar with ADR law in the state in which you work. Some states do not require mediators to meet any special training requirements. For example, Florida law requires that a family mediator "shall be a person with the appropriate attributes who can demonstrate sensitivity toward the parties involved and facilitate solutions to the problem." Other states require mediators to have up to sixty hours of training in certain fields, such as family law, child development, or family dynamics.

KEY TERMS AND CONCEPTS

alternative dispute resolution (ADR) 194	diversity of citizenship 181	negotiation 194
American Arbitration Association (AAA) 203	early neutral case evaluation 202	original jurisdiction 181
appellate court 181	exclusive jurisdiction 182	probate court 180
appellate jurisdiction 181	federal question 181	rule of four 192
arbitration 200	jurisdiction 179	settlement agreement 196
arbitration clause 200	justiciable controversy 184	standing to sue 183
award 201	long arm statute 179	submission agreement 200
bankruptcy court 180	mediation 196	summary jury trial (SJT) 203
binding mediation 202	mediation arbitration (med-arb) 202	trial court 181
concurrent jurisdiction 182	mini-trial 202	venue 182
		writ of *certiorari* 192

CHAPTER SUMMARY

1. Before a court can hear a case, the court must have jurisdiction over the person against whom the suit is brought or over the property involved in the suit. It must also have jurisdiction over the subject matter of the dispute. Courts of general jurisdiction can hear most types of disputes. Courts of limited jurisdiction are restricted in the types of actions they can decide. Courts having original jurisdiction are courts in which the trial of a case begins. Courts having appellate jurisdiction are reviewing courts. They do not try cases anew but review the decisions of trial courts.

2. Federal courts can exercise jurisdiction over claims involving (1) a federal question, which arises when the plaintiff's claim is based at least in part on the U.S. Constitution, a treaty, or a federal law; or (2) diversity of citizenship, which arises when the case involves citizens of different states, a foreign country and citizens of a state or different states, or citizens of a state and citizens or subjects of a foreign country. The amount in controversy must exceed $75,000 for jurisdiction based on diversity of citizenship to arise.

3. Venue has to do with the appropriate geographical area in which a case should be brought. The concept of venue reflects the policy that a court trying a suit should be in the geographic neighborhood (usually the county) in which the incident leading to

the suit occurred or in which the parties involved in the suit reside.

4. Before a plaintiff can bring a lawsuit, he or she must have standing to sue. To have standing, a plaintiff must have a sufficient stake in a controversy to justify taking the issue before a court. Additionally, the controversy must be justiciable—that is, it must be actual and real, not hypothetical or academic.

5. Paralegals should become familiar with the procedural rules of the specific court in which a case is filed. Federal court procedures are set forth in the Federal Rules of Civil Procedure. States rules vary from state to state—and even from court to court within a given state. Also, court procedural rules are different for civil cases than for criminal cases.

6. The structure of state court systems varies from state to state. A typical state court system may consist of several tiers. On the bottom tier are courts of limited jurisdiction. On the next tier are usually the trial courts of general jurisdiction. Trial courts are courts of original jurisdiction—in other words, courts in which lawsuits are initiated, trials are held, and evidence is presented. The upper tier consists of appellate courts, to which trial court decisions can be appealed. Appellate courts are reviewing courts; their function is to review the trial court's decision in cases that are appealed. The highest state appellate court is typically called the state supreme court, although there are exceptions. Cases can be appealed from a state's highest court to the United States Supreme Court only if a federal question is involved.

7. The federal court system consists of U.S. district courts (trial courts), U.S. courts of appeals (intermediate appellate courts), and the United States Supreme Court. Decisions from a district court can be appealed to the court of appeals of the circuit (geographical area) in which the district court is located. There are thirteen circuit courts of appeals. Decisions rendered by these circuit courts may be appealed to the United States Supreme Court.

8. The United States Supreme Court is the highest court in the land. There is no absolute right of appeal to the Supreme Court, and the Court hears only a fraction of the cases that are filed with it each year. If the Court decides to review a case, it will issue a writ of *certiorari*, which is an order by the Supreme Court to a lower court requiring the latter to send it the record of the case for review. As a rule, only those petitions that raise the possibility of important constitutional questions are granted.

9. The costs and time-consuming character of litigation, as well as the public nature of court proceedings, have caused many to turn to various forms of alternative dispute resolution (ADR) for settling their disagreements. Out-of-court settlements are reached in the majority of lawsuits, usually before the trial begins.

10. Negotiation, the simplest method of ADR, may or may not involve a third party; the parties to the dispute simply try to work out their problems to avoid going to court. Mediation is a form of ADR in which the parties attempt to reach agreement with the help of a neutral third party, called a mediator (or a panel of mediators), who helps the disputants explore alternative possibilities for settling their differences as amicably as possible. The mediator proposes various solutions for the parties to consider.

11. Arbitration is the most formal method of ADR. In arbitration, a neutral third party (a lawyer, expert, panel of specialists, or other party) renders a decision after the parties present their cases and evidence in a hearing. Normally, in voluntary arbitration (as opposed to court-mandated ADR), the parties agree at the outset to be legally bound by the arbitrator's decision, which is called an award. Increasingly, parties are including in their contracts arbitration clauses—provisions by which the parties agree to arbitrate any disputes that may arise under the contract. Arbitration clauses will likely be enforced under a federal or state arbitration statute.

12. Other forms of ADR include binding mediation, mediation arbitration (med-arb), early neutral case evaluation, and mini-trials.

13. To ease their heavy caseloads, numerous state and federal courts today encourage or require parties to disputes to mediate or arbitrate their disputes before they can be heard in court. If a party is not satisfied with the results of mediation or arbitration, however, that party normally can take the issue to court.

14. Both government agencies and private organizations provide ADR services. The leading provider of such services is the American Arbitration Association (AAA). Numerous for-profit firms in the nation also provide ADR services. For-profit firms usually hire retired judges to conduct ADR procedures.

Questions for Review

1. Define *jurisdiction* and explain why jurisdiction is important.
2. What is the difference between personal jurisdiction and subject-matter jurisdiction? What is a long arm statute?
3. Define *original jurisdiction* and *appellate jurisdiction*. What is the difference between the two?
4. Over what types of cases may federal courts exercise jurisdiction?
5. What is the relationship between state and federal jurisdiction?
6. What is venue? What is the difference between venue and jurisdiction?
7. Describe the functions of a trial court. How do they differ from the functions of an appellate court?
8. What are the typical courts in a state court system? What are the three basic tiers, or levels, of courts in the federal court system?
9. How do cases reach the United States Supreme Court?
10. List and explain the various methods of alternative dispute resolution.

Ethical Questions

1. Larry Simpson is working on a lawsuit that was recently filed in a federal district court on the basis of diversity-of-citizenship jurisdiction. Larry, a legal assistant, just received the plaintiff's answers to interrogatories (attorneys' written questions to the parties in a lawsuit), which he has been assigned by his supervising attorney to summarize. Larry discovers that the plaintiff's damages are nowhere near the $75,000 required for diversity jurisdiction. What should Larry do?

2. Diane Post, a paralegal, is working on the defense team in a civil lawsuit that has just been filed in the county court, which has limited jurisdiction over civil lawsuits. The plaintiff is seeking an injunction and $3,000 in damages. (Recall from Chapter 5 that an injunction is an equitable remedy in which a court orders a person to do or refrain from doing a particular act.) The superior court is the only court with jurisdiction over equitable remedies. No one but Diane has noticed that the plaintiff is seeking a remedy that the county court does not have the jurisdictional authority to grant. What should Diane do?

3. Suzanne Andersen's supervising attorney, Amy Lynch, works occasionally as a mediator for family-law cases in the local courts. Amy has mediated a divorce case today involving the property settlement of a wealthy businessperson, who happens also to be a defendant in another lawsuit in which Amy represents the plaintiff. As a result of her mediation today, Amy has learned some confidential financial information about this man. She now has come to Suzanne, her paralegal, and asked her to use this information to his disadvantage in the lawsuit. How should Suzanne handle this situation?

4. Mr. James, a divorce client, is concerned because Ms. James, his former wife, refused to deliver their two children, aged nine and eleven, for their parenting time with him on Thanksgiving and on his two weekends in December. She claimed that it was up to the children to decide their parenting time and that they did not want to see him. In their state, children aged nine and eleven are not considered old enough to decide when they will visit their parents. Mr. James now wants to file a motion to ensure that he will see his children for the New Year's holiday.

    Marla, a paralegal, is assigned the task of drafting a motion and filing it with the family court for a hearing before the holidays. Marla timely completes the assignment and takes the motion to the court to file it, only to find out that the court had changed its Christmas holiday schedule and is closed until January 2, which is after New Year's Day. Fliers announcing the change had been posted around the courthouse for two weeks, but Marla had not been at the courthouse during this time. What is the result? What remedy might be available to Mr. James if he misses his New Year's holiday parenting time with his children?

5. Steve is a paralegal with a New Jersey corporation. He reviewed a contract for the purchase of engine

parts for which his company would spend $500,000. Steve told his supervising attorney that the contract met the corporation's checklist of requirements. The contract contained a provision stating that the parties agreed to submit any dispute arising from the contract to binding arbitration in the state of California. When the parts were defective and his company wanted to sue, it could not. What is the result? What should Steve have done differently?

▣ Practice Questions and Assignments

1. A plaintiff and defendant are involved in an auto accident. Both are residents of the county and state in which the accident took place. The plaintiff files an auto negligence lawsuit in the county circuit court where the trial will occur. What types of jurisdiction does the court have? Compare it to the other types of jurisdiction discussed in the chapter.

2. The Brown family from Chicago, Illinois, owns a vacation home in Harbor Springs, Michigan. A dispute arises over the ownership of the property, and an action to partition, or divide, the ownership of the property is filed in the Michigan courts. What type of jurisdiction does the Michigan court have?

3. Renee Clark is a victim of gender discrimination in the workplace. She can file a lawsuit against her employer under either Title VII, a federal statute, in a federal district court, or under her state's civil rights act in a state court. What types of jurisdiction do the courts in this example have?

4. Family courts hear cases involving divorce, custody, and other family matters. What types of jurisdiction do family courts have?

5. The court system in the state of Utopia has two levels of trial courts. The lower-level trial court has jurisdiction over civil cases under $25,000, misdemeanors, local ordinance violations, and small claims. The upper-level trial court has jurisdiction over civil cases exceeding $25,000, felonies and serious misdemeanors, divorce, injunctions, and review of the lower-level trial court's decisions. What are the various types of jurisdiction that each trial court in the state of Utopia has?

6. Marcia, who is from Toledo, Ohio, drives to Troy, Michigan, and shops at a popular mall. When leaving the parking lot, Marcia causes a car accident to occur when she runs a stop sign. On what basis could a Michigan court obtain jurisdiction over Marcia?

7. Louise sues the manufacturer of her automobile, which is defective, under the Magnuson-Moss Warranty Act, a federal consumer-protection statute. In which court may Louise bring her action and on what jurisdictional basis?

8. Identify each of the following courts:

   a. This state court takes testimony from witnesses and receives evidence. It may have either general or limited subject-matter jurisdiction.

   b. This court has appellate jurisdiction and is part of a court system that is divided into geographical units called *circuits*.

   c. This state court usually has a panel of three or more judges who review the record of a case for errors of law and procedure. It does not have original jurisdiction.

   d. This court can exercise diversity-of-citizenship jurisdiction and receives testimony and other evidence.

   e. The decisions of this court are usually final. It is the highest appellate court in its geographical area.

   f. This federal court has nine justices. It has original jurisdiction over a few types of cases but functions primarily as an appellate court. There is no automatic right to appeal cases to this court.

9. Look at Exhibit 6.4. In which federal circuit is your state located? How many federal judicial districts are located in your state? In which federal district is your community located?

10. Based on the information provided in this chapter, including the exhibits, determine which federal court (or courts) could hear the following cases and on what jurisdictional grounds:

    a. A case in which the Internal Revenue Service sues a taxpayer for back taxes.

    b. A case involving an automobile accident between a citizen of Chicago, Illinois, and a citizen of St. Louis, Missouri, in which the plaintiff is seeking damages of $100,000.

    c. A bankruptcy case.

d. A lawsuit claiming sexual harassment in violation of Title VII of the federal Civil Rights Act of 1964.

e. A lawsuit claiming that the defendant violated the federal statute prohibiting racketeering crimes.

11. Suppose that you are a plaintiff in a case brought against the defendant for damages in the amount of $250,000. The case arose as a result of injuries and property damage that you incurred in a car accident caused by the defendant's reckless driving. You know that you have a good chance of winning that amount of damages if the case goes to trial. The defendant offers to settle the case for $175,000. Assume that it would take three years before the court could hear the case. What factors would you consider in deciding this question? What would your decision be?

12. Using Exhibit 6.5 as a model, draft a settlement agreement for a lawsuit involving the following facts:

    Harry Jones is suing Burt Gaston in the U.S. District Court for the Western District of Kentucky, docket number 99-123456. On June 12, 1999, Harry agrees to accept $100,000 in settlement of the lawsuit. Harry's attorney will prepare a settlement agreement for their signatures on June 30. Harry will be paid in one lump-sum cash payment on the execution of the settlement agreement, and he will give up his right to all claims against Burt and release Burt from all future liability for all claims arising out of this occurrence.

13. Using the materials presented in the chapter, identify the following methods of alternative dispute resolution:

    a. The parties to a divorce meet with a neutral third party who proposes solutions to resolve their dispute. After several hours, the parties come to a solution.

    b. The parties to a contract dispute submit it to a neutral third party for a legally binding resolution. The neutral third party is not a court.

    c. The plaintiff and defense attorneys in a personal-injury case propose settlement figures to one another and their clients, in an effort to voluntarily resolve the lawsuit.

    d. The attorneys from the personal-injury example above are able to reach an acceptable figure of $100,000. They draft an agreement whereby the plaintiff gives up her right to sue in exchange for the defendant paying her $100,000.

    e. A commercial dispute involving $95,000 in damages was filed in a federal court. The judge requires the parties' attorneys to present their arguments and supporting evidence, excluding witnesses, to the jury. The jury then renders a nonbinding verdict. Once the nonbinding verdict is rendered, the parties reach a settlement.

QUESTIONS FOR CRITICAL ANALYSIS

1. Before a case can be heard by a court, the court must have jurisdiction to hear and decide the case. What types of jurisdiction exist? What would happen if a case were filed in a court that did not have jurisdiction over it?

2. The federal courts have jurisdiction primarily over diversity cases and over questions of federal law. State courts have jurisdiction over matters such as wills, divorces, and property concerns. Why? What would happen if federal courts decided divorce cases, for example? What would happen if state courts decided cases between a citizen of the state and a foreign citizen?

3. The decision changing the venue of the trial of McVeigh and Nichols from Oklahoma City, Oklahoma, to Denver, Colorado, is *United States v. McVeigh*, 918 F.Supp. 1467 (1996). Review this case. What constitutional issues were involved in the court's decision allowing a change of venue? Do death-penalty cases require a different standard? If so, what is the standard? What evidence did the court review in reaching its decision? Why did the court conclude that the federal district court in Denver, Colorado, met the requirements for an alternative venue? Given the outcome of the case, was the change of venue effective? Given the pretrial publicity, would the defendants have been convicted if venue had been changed to Maine?

4. What is the difference in the roles that the trial and appellate courts play in a lawsuit? Why is it that

appellate courts only rarely decide questions of fact? When does an appellate court review facts?

5. Most state court judges are elected, while federal court judges are appointed. Which system, in your opinion, is fairer? Does either system affect the quality of the judiciary?

6. Do you think that it is fair that in most cases there is no right to appeal to the United States Supreme Court? Should citizens have to petition for *certiorari* to be heard by the Supreme Court? What does the requirement of a grant of *certiorari,* coupled with the limited number of cases that the Supreme Court hears, tell you about the role and purpose of the Supreme Court?

7. Why are Americans increasingly turning to ADR as a way of settling their disputes? What are the implications of ADR, including the increased use of "private justice," for the American system of justice generally?

8. Some individuals have claimed that mandatory ADR infringes on a person's constitutional right to a jury trial. Do you agree with this view? Why or why not?

Projects

1. Contact a local trial court and request a copy of a chart, pamphlet, or other publication that lists the courts in your state and describes the jurisdiction of each. Check with your instructor prior to undertaking this assignment for any special instructions.

2. Contact the local federal district court clerk's office and ask if electronic filings are accepted. If accepted, ask whether filings are accepted via e-mail or CD-ROM. Ask if any other form of filings, such as tax filings, are accepted. Find out if electronic filing is limited to certain types of documents or cases. Check with your instructor prior to undertaking this assignment for any special instructions.

3. Review a local legal newspaper or bar association journal. Locate advertisements for firms offering ADR services. Call one of these firms and find out what services are offered and what rates are charged.

4. Contact the American Arbitration Association and ask what kind of disputes (contract disputes, employment disputes, and so on) they arbitrate. Request a copy of its procedural rules for the arbitration of disputes in one of the areas it handles. Review the rules and summarize the procedures involved.

5. Review the table of contents of the court rules of your state courts or the federal courts. What subjects are covered? How do these subjects relate to the topics discussed in this chapter? You should be able to locate these rules in your school's library or in a law-school library.

Using Internet Resources

1. Paralegals frequently assist in ADR proceedings or even, in some cases, serve as mediators or arbitrators. To learn more about ADR procedures, go to **www.adr.org,** the home page for the American Arbitration Association (AAA). Browse through the site's offerings and find the answers to the following questions:

    a. Where on the AAA's site is the "Demand for Arbitration" form located? How long is the form? In what circumstances would it be used? What procedure is involved in filing the document (for example, who should receive copies of the form, how many copies must be sent, and so on)? Under AAA rules, within how many days must an answering statement be filed?

    b. Where on the site is the "Submission to Dispute Resolution" form located? What kind of information is required to fill out the form? How does this form differ from the "Demand for Arbitration" form? What ADR options are listed on the form? How many copies of the form must be filed with the AAA?

2. The United States Supreme Court Web site contains useful information on the United States Supreme Court. Go to its Web site at **www.usscplus.com.**

a. Click on "Current Term." What are the names of the cases and subjects included in this term?

b. Click on "The Court," and then select "Justices." How many justices are on the Supreme Court? What are their names? What law schools did they attend? Who appointed each justice?

3. Go to the Web site, **www.courts.net**. This useful Web site provides a directory to courts throughout the country. This information is helpful for learning about the court system in a particular state, as well as locating the court. Click on your state. What information is available about the courts in your state? Make a list of the courts that are included. Click on the various courts, and make a list of the type of information that is available, such as judges' names, telephone numbers, court addresses, and so on.

CHAPTER 7

SUBSTANTIVE LAW I

Chapter Outline
▣ INTRODUCTION ▣ TORTS ▣ CONTRACTS
▣ REAL PROPERTY ▣ WILLS, TRUSTS, AND ESTATES

After completing this chapter, you will know:

- The purpose of tort law, two basic categories of torts, how torts differ from crimes, and when the doctrine of strict liability is applied.

- The elements of a valid contract, defenses that can be raised in actions for breach of contract, and the law governing contracts for the sale of goods.

- The difference between real property and personal property.

- How one acquires, holds, and transfers ownership rights in property and the procedures that are involved in the sale of real estate.

- Devices used in estate planning and the laws and procedures that come into play when property is transferred on a person's death.

Introduction

The law governs virtually every transaction or activity that individuals engage in across the nation. Simple, everyday transactions—such as purchasing a carton of milk from your corner grocer or loaning a friend your paralegal textbook—are subject to specific laws that define the rights and duties of the parties involved in the transaction.

As a paralegal, you will be directly involved in the process of applying legal concepts and principles to specific situations that arise in the everyday world around you. Some of your work may involve drafting, or filing with the appropriate court or agency, documents relating to concepts discussed in this chapter. Your work may also involve legal research and analysis. You may be asked, for example, to find cases on point (cases in which the facts and legal issues are similar to those in a case that your supervising attorney is litigating). A basic understanding of the legal principles involved in the case will help direct your research efforts.

In the pages that follow, you will read about some of the fundamental concepts of American law. Some of these principles and concepts originated centuries ago, in the common law of medieval England. Others are of more recent origin; they have been formed by the courts or enacted by legislatures to solve problems unique to life in the modern United States.

Torts

The common law of torts is an area of particular importance for paralegals. Tort lawsuits are frequent occurrences in the American legal arena, and many attorneys and paralegals devote a substantial amount of their time to serving clients who either want to bring or need to defend against tort lawsuits.

The word **tort** is French for "wrong." Of course, crimes also involve wrongs. A crime, however, is an act so reprehensible that it is considered to be a wrong against the state (and normally defined as such by statute), as well as against the individual victim. Therefore, a public official representing the state (such as a district attorney, or D.A.) prosecutes a person who has been accused of committing a criminal act (see Chapter 12). The object of a criminal action is to punish the wrongdoer. The object of a tort action, in contrast, is to recover compensation (damages) for the harm suffered because of another's wrongful act. (Occasionally, however, an injured person is given extra compensation in the form of what are called **punitive damages,** in an attempt to punish the wrongdoer and deter other members of society from engaging in similar actions.)

In this section, we will discuss the two basic categories of torts: intentional torts and torts resulting from negligence. We will also examine the concept of *strict liability,* a tort doctrine under which a defendant may be liable for harm or injury to another regardless of intention or fault.

Tort
A civil (as opposed to a criminal) wrong not arising from a breach of contract. A breach of a legal duty, owed by the defendant to the plaintiff, that caused the plaintiff to suffer harm.

Punitive Damages
Damages that are awarded in a civil lawsuit to punish the wrongdoer. Punitive damages are usually awarded only in cases involving willful or malicious misconduct.

Intentional Torts

An **intentional tort,** as the term implies, is a wrongful action that involves an element of *intent.* In tort law, intent means that the actor intended the consequences of his or her act or knew with substantial certainty that certain consequences would result from the act. Note that the intent requirement does not necessarily mean that the actor intended to harm someone; only that he or she intended to commit the act and, implicitly, intended the act's consequences.

Intentional Tort
A wrongful act knowingly committed that interferes with the interests of another in a way not permitted by law.

 The law generally assumes that individuals intend the normal consequences of their actions.

Assault
Any word or action intended to make another person fearful of immediate physical harm; a reasonably believable threat.

Battery
The unprivileged, intentional touching of another.

Thus, forcefully pushing another—even if done in jest and without any wish to harm the person—is an intentional tort (if injury results) because someone who is forcefully pushed can ordinarily be expected to fall down and possibly be injured.

Some intentional torts are similar to acts prohibited by state criminal laws. For example, both state criminal codes and tort law provide for a legal action in cases of assault and battery. An **assault** is an intentional, unexcused act that causes another to reasonably fear immediate harmful or offensive contact. A **battery** is the completion of the fear-inducing act or any actual contact with another that is offensive to the other person (a person does not have to be afraid, or fear immediate harm, for an act to constitute a battery). For example, if Chris threatens to hit Cynthia with his fist, Chris's action constitutes assault. If Chris actually hits Cynthia with his fist, Chris's action constitutes a battery.

In addition to assault and battery, intentional torts include the following:

- *Defamation*—The making of a false statement that harms another's good reputation. The law imposes a general duty on all persons to refrain from making false statements about others. Breaching this duty orally constitutes the tort of *slander;* breaching it in writing or in any permanent form (such as in a videotape) constitutes the tort of *libel.* For defamation to occur, the false statement must be communicated to a third party.

- *Fraudulent misrepresentation*—An intentional misrepresentation of facts that causes another person who justifiably relied on the misrepresentation to suffer harm.

- *Intentional infliction of emotional distress*—An intentional act that amounts to extreme and outrageous conduct resulting in severe emotional distress to another. Because it is difficult to prove the existence of emotional distress, a few states require that the mental or emotional disturbance be evidenced by some physical symptom or illness.

- *False imprisonment*—The act of intentionally confining or restraining another person's activities without justification, such as when a merchant delays a sus-pected shoplifter without sufficient reason and for an unreasonable period of time.

- *Invasion of privacy*—The act of intruding on the privacy or seclusion of another. Taking unwanted photographs of another may constitute an invasion of privacy, as might using another's name or picture for commercial purposes without permission.

- *Trespass to land*—The act of entering onto another's land without permission, thus interfering with that person's right to the exclusive possession of his or her property. If it can be shown that the trespass was warranted, however, as when a trespasser enters onto another's property to help someone in danger, a complete defense exists. (A **defense** is a legally acceptable reason, raised by a defendant in a lawsuit, why the court should not grant what the plaintiff is seeking.)

Defense
A legally acceptable reason, raised by a defendant, as to why the plaintiff should not be granted whatever it is the plaintiff is seeking.

Negligence
The failure to exercise the standard of care that a reasonable person would exercise in similar circumstances.

Negligence

In tort law, **negligence** occurs when someone suffers an injury because of another's failure to live up to a required *duty of care*—a concept that will be explored shortly. In contrast to intentional torts, torts involving negligence do not involve the element of intent. In fact, many of the actions discussed in the section on intentional torts would constitute negligence if the element of intent were missing. For example, if Sarah intentionally shoves Tony, who falls and breaks an arm as a result, Sarah has committed an intentional tort—battery. In contrast, if Sarah carelessly bumps into Tony, and Tony falls and breaks an arm as a result, Sarah's action constitutes negligence. In either situation, Sarah has committed a tort.

THE ELEMENTS OF NEGLIGENCE. The tort of negligence occurs when someone *breaches* a *duty of care* and that breach *causes* another person to suffer *injury or harm*. For negligence to occur, all of the elements italicized in this definition must be present.

The Duty of Care and Its Breach. When evaluating a negligence claim, then, the first question you need to ask is whether the defendant had a duty of care with respect to the plaintiff and, if so, whether that duty was breached. The concept of a duty of care arises from the notion that if we are to live in society with other people, some actions can be tolerated and some cannot, some actions are right and some are wrong, and some actions are reasonable and some are not.

Generally, the duty of care is measured under a **reasonable person standard**, which reflects society's judgment as to how a reasonably prudent person would act in a specific set of circumstances. (This hypothetical "reasonable person" appears again and again in the law.) When determining whether a duty of care has been breached, a court will compare the defendant's actions against those that would have been taken (or not taken) by a reasonably prudent person *in the defendant's position*. A reasonably prudent person would not drive carelessly and create the risk of harming others. A reasonably prudent attorney would not miss a filing deadline and thus harm his or her client's interests. A reasonably prudent seller would not market a product that had not been sufficiently tested for safety. And a reasonably prudent retail business owner would ensure that his or her customers were safe while on the owner's business premises.

Reasonable Person Standard
The standard of behavior expected of a hypothetical "reasonable person." The standard against which negligence is measured and that must be observed to avoid liability for negligence.

The Injury Requirement. Even if it can be established that the defendant breached a duty of care, to recover in a negligence action the plaintiff must also show that the breach caused the plaintiff to suffer some legally recognizable injury or harm. Remember that the purpose of tort law is to obtain compensation for harms suffered because of another's wrongdoing. If no harm or injury results from a given negligent action, there is nothing to compensate—and thus no tort.

Causation. Additionally, in a negligence action, to be compensated for the injury the plaintiff must show that the injury was *caused* by the defendant's breach of the duty of care. In deciding whether the requirement of causation is met, two questions must be addressed:

- *Is there causation in fact?*
- *Was the act the proximate cause of the injury?*

Causation in fact exists if the plaintiff can show that the injury would not have occurred "but for" the defendant's act. Theoretically, causation in fact is limitless. For example, one could say that "but for" the creation of the world, a particular injury would not have occurred. Thus, as a practical matter, the law has to establish limits, and it does so through the concept of **proximate cause** (sometimes called *legal cause*).

Proximate Cause
Legal cause. Proximate cause exists when the connection between an act and an injury is strong enough to justify imposing liability.

For example, suppose that the defendant carelessly left a campfire burning. The fire not only burned down the forest but also set off an explosion in a nearby chemical plant that spilled chemicals into a river, killing all the fish for one hundred miles downstream and ruining the economy of a tourist resort. Should the defendant be liable to the resort owners? To the tourists whose vacations were ruined? These are questions of proximate cause. Generally, the courts use foreseeability as the test for proximate cause: A plaintiff can only recover damages if the defendant could reasonably have foreseen that the consequences of his or her actions would create a risk of injury to the plaintiff.

> ## ETHICAL CONCERN
> ### Malpractice Suits
>
> Paralegals are not perfect and occasionally fail to perform a required duty. But the law will not "look the other way" if a client is harmed as the result of that negligence and then brings a malpractice suit against the attorney. It will not matter that the attorney specifically requested his or her paralegal to send a settlement letter to a defendant's attorney by a certain date. Nor will it matter that the attorney was under the impression that the letter had actually been sent by that date. The attorney, as the person responsible for the paralegal's work, will bear the legal consequences of the paralegal's negligent action if the client is harmed as a result and brings suit. The paralegal might also be held liable. As a paralegal, you should always make sure that you carry out instructions to the letter and perform your tasks accurately and in a timely manner, so that you do not expose your supervising attorney or yourself to liability for malpractice.

DEFENSES TO NEGLIGENCE. Certain defenses are available to defendants in negligence cases, depending on the circumstances. The defense of *assumption of risk* may be raised if the defendant can show that the plaintiff voluntarily entered into a risky situation and was fully aware of the risk involved. The risk can be assumed by express agreement or can be implied by the plaintiff's knowledge of the risk and subsequent conduct. For example, a driver entering a race knows that there is a risk of being injured or killed if another vehicle in the race crashes into his. The driver thus assumes the risk of injury.

In a few states, if a defendant can show that the plaintiff's own negligence contributed to his or her injury, the plaintiff is completely barred from recovery under the doctrine of *contributory negligence*. In a majority of states, however, courts have now adopted a *comparative negligence* standard. Under this standard, the court determines the degree to which each party was negligent, and the liability for damages is distributed accordingly. For example, if a court concludes that the plaintiff and defendant were equally negligent, the court may allow the plaintiff to recover only 50 percent of the damages incurred. Thus, if the jury finds that the plaintiff incurred damages of $30,000, this amount would be reduced to $15,000.

Another defense to negligence is known as the *last clear chance doctrine*. This doctrine operates when the plaintiff or the plaintiff's property, through the plaintiff's own negligence, is endangered by a defendant who missed an opportunity to avoid causing damage. For example, if Callahan walks across the street against the light and Riggs, a motorist, sees her in time to avoid hitting her but hits her anyway, Riggs normally is not permitted to use Callahan's prior negligence as a defense. (The adoption of the comparative negligence rule has effectively abolished the last clear chance doctrine in most jurisdictions.)

Strict Liability

Strict Liability
Liability regardless of fault. In tort law, strict liability may be imposed on those who engage in abnormally dangerous activities that cause harm to others, on merchants who introduce into commerce goods that are unreasonably dangerous, and in certain other situations.

Intentional torts and torts of negligence are based on fault. They involve acts that depart from a reasonable standard of care and cause injuries. Under the doctrine of **strict liability,** liability for injury is imposed without considering fault. Strict liability for damages proximately caused by abnormally dangerous activities, such as blasting with dynamite, is one application of this doctrine. Strict liability is applied in such cases because of the extreme risk of the activities. For example, even if

> # DEVELOPING PARALEGAL SKILLS
> ## Product-Liability Paralegals
>
>
>
> Sylvia is a paralegal working in the legal department of an automobile company. The company is frequently the defendant in product-liability lawsuits. In these lawsuits, during the discovery phase of the litigation (see Chapter 10), attorneys for the plaintiffs normally request information about the design and manufacturing process used by the company in producing its vehicles.
>
> Sylvia's job is to work with the corporate attorneys to gather this information and provide it to the plaintiffs' attorneys, as allowed or required by court rules. Frequently, Sylvia meets with the company's engineers to discuss these information requests and to obtain the necessary information. Sylvia then reviews with her supervising attorney the material to be sent out.
>
> ### TIPS FOR OBTAINING INFORMATION
> - Good communication skills help when making requests for information.
> - Good interpersonal skills help you develop good relationships with those from whom you need information.
> - Analytical skills help determine what information is needed.
> - Good writing skills assist you in preparing the responses to requests for information.
> - Send out the responses in a timely fashion.

blasting with dynamite is performed with all reasonable care, there is still a risk of injury. Because of the potential for harm, the courts have deemed it fair to ask the person who engaged in the activity to pay for any injuries caused by that activity. Although there may be no fault, there is still responsibility because of the dangerous nature of the undertaking.

There are other applications of the strict liability principle. Persons who keep dangerous animals, for example, are strictly liable for any harm inflicted by the animals. A significant application of strict liability is in the area of product liability. **Product liability** is the term given to the legal liability of manufacturers and sellers to buyers, users, and bystanders for injuries or damages suffered because of defects in goods. Liability arises when a product has a defective condition that makes it unreasonably dangerous and the product causes damage or injury to a person using the product. Product liability may be based on strict liability, as well as on negligence and misrepresentation. Strict product liability may also be imposed on the basis of warranty theory, a topic you will read about shortly.

Strict product liability is a matter of social policy and is based on two considerations: (1) the manufacturing company is making a profit from its activities and therefore should bear the cost of injury as an operating expense, and (2) the manufacturing company can better bear the cost of injury because it can spread the cost throughout society by increasing the prices of its goods or services.

Product Liability
The legal liability of manufacturers and sellers to buyers, users, and bystanders for injuries or damages suffered because of defects in goods purchased. Liability arises when a product has a defective condition that makes it unreasonably dangerous to the user or consumer.

Tort Law and the Paralegal

Many paralegals become involved in tasks relating to tort lawsuits. If you work for a litigation firm, chances are that you will handle numerous assignments involving tort claims. Many law firms specialize in personal-injury litigation and represent plaintiffs who have been injured in car accidents or other incidents resulting from the defendants' alleged negligence. Many law firms or departments of law firms also specialize in other areas of tort litigation, such as medical malpractice and product liability.

SUBSTANTIVE LAW CONCEPT SUMMARY
Torts

Intentional Torts	An intentional tort is an intended act whose consequences cause another to suffer a harm or an injury. The actor must intend the act and know with substantial certainty that certain consequences will result from the act. (The law assumes that persons intend the normal consequences of their actions.) Intentional torts include the following: **1.** *Assault and battery*—An *assault* is an unexcused and intentional act that causes another person reasonably to fear immediate harmful or offensive contact. A *battery* is the completion of the fear-inducing act or any actual contact with another that is offensive to the other person. **2.** *Defamation*—A false statement of fact that is communicated to a third person and that causes damage to a person's reputation. Defamation is called *slander* when defamatory statements are made orally and *libel* when defamatory statements are made in writing or in any permanent form. **3.** *Fraudulent misrepresentation*—A false representation made by one party through misstatement of facts or through conduct, with the intention of deceiving another and on which the other reasonably relies to his or her detriment. **4.** *Intentional infliction of emotional distress*—An intentional act that amounts to extreme and outrageous conduct resulting in severe emotional distress to another. **5.** *False imprisonment*—Intentional confinement or restraint of another person's movement without justification. **6.** *Invasion of privacy*—An action that intrudes on the privacy or seclusion of another person without that person's permission or approval. **7.** *Trespass to land*—Invasion of another's real property without consent or privilege.
Negligence	**1.** *Definition of negligence*—The careless performance of a legally required duty or the failure to perform a legally required act. More generally, the failure to exercise a reasonable standard of care.

If you work for a corporation, your responsibilities might include assisting attorneys in work relating to tort lawsuits brought by or against the corporation. A consumer who was injured by one of the corporation's products, for example, might initiate a product-liability suit against the firm. A person who was injured in an accident caused by one of the company's truck drivers might sue the corporation for damages under negligence theory.

Specific types of tasks that paralegals perform in personal-injury cases are listed in Chapter 2, in the section describing personal-injury law. When working on medical-malpractice or product-liability cases, as well as on personal-injury cases, you might be asked to undertake any of the tasks typically performed by litigation paralegals, including those listed in Chapter 2 in the section on the litigation paralegal (and described at length in Chapters 10 and 11). You will find that in any tort litigation, you will profit from a knowledge of the fundamental concepts of tort law discussed in this section. Another broad area of the common law with which paralegals should be familiar is contract law, which we discuss next.

SUBSTANTIVE LAW CONCEPT SUMMARY
Torts—Continued

Negligence—continued	2. *Elements required for negligence*—To succeed in a negligence action, the plaintiff must prove the following:
	   a. That the defendant owed a duty of care to the plaintiff.
	   b. That the defendant breached the duty of care.
	   c. That the plaintiff sustained a legally recognizable injury.
	   d. That the plaintiff's injury was caused by the defendant's breach of the duty of care.
	3. *Defenses to negligence*—
	   a. Assumption of risk—The plaintiff was fully aware of the risk of injury attending a certain action or event and voluntarily assumed that risk.
	   b. Contributory negligence—The plaintiff's own negligence contributed to his or her injury. In a few states, contributory negligence on the part of the plaintiff is a complete defense against liability for the plaintiff's injury.
	   c. Comparative negligence—If the plaintiff was also negligent, the degree of negligence on the part of both the plaintiff and defendant is computed, and the liability for damages is distributed accordingly.
	   d. Last clear chance—If the defendant missed the last opportunity to avoid causing harm to the plaintiff or the plaintiff's property, the defendant may not raise the plaintiff's contributory negligence as a defense. The last clear chance doctrine has been effectively abolished in those states that have adopted a comparative negligence standard.

Strict Liability	Liability for injury imposed for reasons other than fault because of the inherent danger of an activity (such as blasting with dynamite) or situation (such as the possession of dangerous animals). Strict liability may also be imposed for reasons of public policy, as when strict product liability is imposed on manufacturers and sellers of products that are unreasonably dangerous when used as intended and that harm consumers as a result.

CONTRACTS

Contract law deals with, among other things, the keeping of promises. A promise is a declaration that something either will or will not happen in the future. A **contract** is an exchange of promises that can be enforced in court. It is an agreement (made orally or in writing) formed by two or more parties who promise to perform or refrain from performing some act now or in the future. If the contractual promise is not fulfilled, the party who made it is subject to the sanctions of a court for **breach of contract** (failure to perform what was promised in the contract). The breaching party may be required to pay money damages to compensate the other party for losses caused by the breach or, in some situations, may be ordered to perform the contract as promised.

In your work as a paralegal, you may deal extensively with contract formation or claims for breach of contract. A basic understanding of contract law will help guide your understanding and serve as a point of departure for all work that you do involving contracts. This section will explain what elements must be

Contract
An agreement or bargain struck between parties, in which each party assumes a legal duty to the other party. The requirements for a valid contract are agreement, consideration, contractual capacity, and legality.

Breach of Contract
The failure of a contractual party to perform the obligations assumed in a contract.

FEATURED GUEST: JOHN DeLEO, J.D.
The Paralegal's Relationship to the Law

BIOGRAPHICAL NOTE

John D. DeLeo received his bachelor of arts degree in political science from Pennsylvania State University. He received his paralegal certificate from Long Island University and was a practicing paralegal for two years before starting law school. He earned a J.D. degree from Loyola University School of Law, New Orleans, in 1984 and has been licensed to practice law in Louisiana and Pennsylvania. After practicing law for a time, DeLeo joined the faculty of Central Pennsylvania Business School in Summerdale, Pennsylvania, in 1984. Mr. DeLeo teaches a variety of courses in the legal assistant program at that school, including torts, constitutional law, evidence, and civil procedure. Mr. DeLeo was named faculty member of the year in 1990 and 1993.

Working in the legal field can be a daunting and sometimes mystifying experience. "The law" is so vast that no matter how long you study, you can never completely master it. Here are some suggestions on how you, as a paralegal, can start to get a handle on this potential quagmire.

WHAT IS THE PURPOSE OF YOUR TASK?

Whenever you receive an assignment, you should ask yourself why you are being asked to do it. What is the legal purpose of the task? The answer to this question will aid you in your work and bring things into focus.

DOES THE ISSUE RELATE TO PROCEDURAL OR SUBSTANTIVE LAW?

Also ask yourself whether the issue relates to procedural or substantive law. Procedural law concerns the method of enforcing legal rights. Substantive law defines what those rights are. Examples of substantive law are contract law, tort law, and property law (topics covered in this chapter). You will learn more about these areas of law in your paralegal program. Procedural law involves knowing the appropriate court in which to file a case, the appropriate time for filing

---

present for a contract to be enforceable and what remedies are available when a contract is breached. These principles apply to all contracts unless statutory law has modified the common law—as it has in the area of contracts for the sale of goods, for example, as you will read shortly.

Contract Requirements

If a client alleges that a party has breached a contract, the first issue to be decided is whether a valid contract was ever formed. To be considered valid, the elements of agreement, consideration, contractual capacity, and legality must all be present. We look here at each of these requirements.

Agreement
A meeting of the minds, and a requirement for a valid contract. Agreement involves two distinct events: an offer to form a contract and the acceptance of that offer by the offeree.

Offer
A promise to do something in return for something of value.

AGREEMENT. A contract is, in essence, an **agreement** between two or more parties. Therefore, if the parties failed to reach an agreement, no contract exists. To determine whether the parties agreed to form a contract, the courts separate contractual agreement into two events—one party's offer to form a contract and the other party's acceptance of that offer.

A contractual **offer** is a promise to do something (such as sell your car) in return for something of value (such as money). To be legally effective, an offer must reflect a serious and objective intention on the part of the *offeror* (the person making the offer) to enter into a contract with the *offeree* (the person to whom the offer is made). Offers made in jest, in undue excitement, or in obvious anger

Featured Guest, Continued

various documents relating to litigation, and other rules. With the procedural and substantive distinction in mind, you can better separate and analyze the issues of the case. It is also important to know that when you do legal research, you will use different references for procedural issues than for substantive issues.

Be Aware of the Larger Picture

A key factor in paralegal work is the ability to be aware of the overarching situation in any case on which you are assigned to work. Different rules and procedures apply depending on the facts of the case before you. When working on a file, you should know, for example, whether this is a civil or criminal case, whether it has been filed in a federal court or a state court, and what general area of law governs the claims being made. The answers to these questions will direct your actions and work on the case.

For example, assume that your supervising attorney is defending a client who has been sued for negligence. The plaintiff claims that the defendant ran a red light, that the defendant's car crashed into hers as a result, and that the defendant therefore should be liable for the plaintiff's injuries from the accident.

The plaintiff has filed suit in a federal court, alleging diversity-of-citizenship jurisdiction. You have been asked to gather medical records, physicians' reports, medical bills, and other information relating to the plaintiff's claim.

If you are aware that in order for federal courts to take jurisdiction based on diversity of citizenship, the amount in controversy must be more than $75,000, you will have a better understanding of what you should be looking for during your investiga-

> "A key factor in paralegal work is the ability to be aware of the overarching situation."

tion. For example, if it appears that the plaintiff's damages are less than $75,000, you should advise your supervising attorney of your findings. Your attorney could then file with the federal court a *motion to dismiss* the case for lack of subject-matter jurisdiction.

Generally, a paralegal who can keep in mind the larger framework of an issue while still doing a particular assignment will be a valuable asset to a law firm. When you receive an assignment and you know why this task is important as well as the legal basis of the lawsuit, you will be able to do your job in a more effective way.

---

do not meet the intent requirement, and an offeree's acceptance of such an offer does not create a contractual agreement. The terms of an offer must also be sufficiently definite so that if the offer is accepted, the specific terms of the resulting contract will be clear to a court if a dispute arises. For example, if James says to Kim, "I'll buy the encyclopedias and pay you some money for them next week," no valid contract has been formed—because "some" money is not a definite term.

Once an offer is made, the offeree can accept or reject it. **Acceptance** occurs when the offeree indicates, by words or actions, that he or she agrees to the terms of the offer. On acceptance, a contract is formed. If the offeree wants to modify the terms of the offer, he or she can make a *counteroffer,* thus assuming the role of an offeror. For example, assume that Kirk offers to sell Christina his van for $6,000. Christina responds that she will not pay that much for the car, but she is willing to buy it for $5,500. Christina has both rejected Kirk's offer and created another offer—a counteroffer. Now Christina is the offeror, and if Kirk (the offeree in this situation) accepts Christina's offer, a contract normally will result.

Note that only the offeree can accept an offer. A third party who heard about the offer cannot accept it and form a valid contract. Note also that an acceptance must be timely. If the offeror states that the offer will be open for ten days, acceptance must normally occur within that period of time for a contract to result. If the offeror does not indicate how long the offer will remain open, then acceptance must occur within a reasonable period of time. (What constitutes a reasonable

Acceptance
In contract law, the offeree's indication to the offeror that the offeree agrees to be bound by the terms of the offeror's offer, or proposal to form a contract.

period of time in the eyes of a court varies, depending on the circumstances.) Normally, an offeror can *revoke* (take back) an offer at any time before it is accepted, although there are some exceptions to this rule.

CONSIDERATION.   Another requirement of a valid contract is that consideration be exchanged. **Consideration** in contract law is normally defined as "something of value"—which may be money or the performance of certain actions that are not otherwise required. For example, suppose that you give your friend $1,000 in exchange for her promise to take care of your house and garden for six months. This promise normally will be enforceable, because consideration has been given. Your consideration is the one thousand dollars; your friend's consideration is the assumption of an obligation that she otherwise would not assume.

The requirement of consideration distinguishes contracts from gifts. For example, if you promise to give your friend $1,000 as a gift and she promises to accept your gift, no contract results, because your friend has given no consideration for the contract.

> **Consideration**
> Something of value, such as money or the performance of an action not otherwise required, that motivates the formation of a contract. Each party must give consideration for the contract to be binding.

CONTRACTUAL CAPACITY.   The third element required for the formation of a valid contract is **contractual capacity**, which exists when a person has the mental competence to enter into a contract. A person adjudged by a court to be mentally incompetent, for example, cannot form a legally binding contract with another party. A contract entered into by an intoxicated person who did not comprehend the legal consequences of his or her actions normally is not binding on that person.

Laws governing contracts made by minors (in most states, persons under the age of eighteen) vary from state to state. Although minors may enter into contracts, normally they can also legally avoid contractual obligations by *disaffirming* (in effect, canceling) the contracts. A common exception to this rule is made in contracts for *necessaries*—essential items, such as food.

> **Contractual Capacity**
> The threshold mental capacity required by law for a party who enters into a contract to be bound by that contract.

LEGALITY.   The fourth requirement for a valid contract is legality. A contract to do something that is prohibited by federal or state legislation is illegal and, as such, void at the outset (that is, no contract exists). For example, a contract to purchase cocaine from a drug dealer is void because it is illegal. No court would enforce the contract if a lawsuit was brought for breach of the contract.

Defenses to Contract Enforceability

In an action for breach of contract, if a defendant can show that one of the four elements for a valid contract is missing, the contract will not be enforced—because no valid contract ever came into existence. The defendant can thus raise the lack of contract formation as a defense. Even a valid contract, however, may not be enforceable in certain circumstances.

For example, each state has a **Statute of Frauds**[1] specifying that certain types of contracts must be in writing to be enforceable, including the following: (1) contracts for the sale of land; (2) contracts for the sale of goods priced at $500 or more; (3) contracts made in consideration of marriage, such as prenuptial agreements; (4) contracts that are impossible to perform within one year; and (5) contracts in which one party assumes responsibility for another's debts or obligations. If one of these types

> **Statute of Frauds.**
> A state statute that requires certain types of contracts to be in writing to be enforceable.

---

1. These laws are the American counterparts of a seventeenth-century English statute, the purpose of which was to prevent fraud by requiring contracts relating to important transactions to be in writing. In those days, "hiring" witnesses to testify to the existence of an oral contract was not uncommon.

of contracts is formed orally, a defendant in an action for breach of contract can raise the Statute of Frauds as a defense against the contract's enforceability.

A party may also claim that a contract should not be enforced because he or she did not genuinely assent to its terms—due to fraud, for example, or because of a mistake. Additionally, some contracts will not be enforced by the courts because they are contrary to public policy, or contrary to what are considered by the courts to be the interests of society as a whole. For example, suppose that a salesperson persuades an uneducated and economically disadvantaged customer to buy a refrigerator on the installment plan. The customer signs an agreement promising to pay $50 a month for five years, without realizing that she has obligated herself to pay $3,000 for a refrigerator worth $900. A court may consider such a contract to be an **unconscionable contract**—a contract so oppressive, one sided, or unfair that it "shocks the conscience" of the court—and refuse to enforce it.

Unconscionable Contract
A contract so unfair, oppressive, or one sided that it "shocks the conscience" of the court. If a court deems a contract to be unconscionable, the court will not enforce it.

Still another defense against a claim for breach of contract is the assertion that the contract cannot be performed because it is objectively impossible to perform it. If the subject matter of the contract (such as a computer) is destroyed, for example, the contract cannot be performed because the computer no longer exists. Similarly, if one of the parties to the contract dies or becomes incapacitated, or if a law enacted after the contract was made makes the contract illegal, performance will normally be deemed impossible.

Sales Contracts and Warranties

Sales contracts, or contracts for the sale of goods, are governed by state statutes that are based on Article 2 of the **Uniform Commercial Code (UCC).** The UCC is one of the many—and one of the most significant—uniform laws created by the American Law Institute and the National Conference of Commissioners on Uniform State Laws. The UCC was first issued in 1952 and has since been revised to reflect the changing customs and needs of business and society. The UCC has been adopted, in whole or in part, by all of the states. State statutory codes are not necessarily called the Uniform Commercial Code, however. In Ohio, for example, UCC provisions are incorporated into the Ohio Commercial Code.

Sales Contract
A contract for the sale of goods, as opposed to a contract for the sale of services, real property, or intangible property. Sales contracts are governed by Article 2 of the Uniform Commercial Code.

Uniform Commercial Code (UCC)
A uniform code of laws governing commercial transactions that has been adopted in part or in its entirety by all of the states. Article 2 of the UCC governs contracts for the sale of goods.

THE SCOPE OF ARTICLE 2. In regard to Article 2 of the UCC, two things should be kept in mind. First, Article 2 deals with the sale of *goods*, not real property (real estate), services, or intangible property. Second, the rules may vary quite a bit, depending on whether the buyer or seller is a merchant. You should always note the subject matter of a dispute and the kind of people (merchants or consumers) involved when you are dealing with cases involving contractual disputes. If the subject is goods, then the UCC will govern. If it is real estate or services, then the common law principles discussed earlier will apply.

As under the common law of contracts, the parties to sales contracts are free to fashion the terms of their contracts as they wish. The UCC normally comes into play only when a dispute arises over ambiguous or missing terms. Note also that the UCC does not replace the common law of contracts—the body of contract law discussed in the previous section. A contract for the sale of goods is also subject to the common law requirements of agreement, consideration, contractual capacity, and legality. Similarly, the common law defenses against contract formation or enforceability also apply to sales contracts. If the UCC has not modified a common law principle, then the common law governs. The general rule is thus as follows:

> **When the UCC speaks, its principles apply; when the UCC is silent on a particular matter, then the common law of contracts applies.**

Warranty
An express or implied promise by a seller that specific goods to be sold meet certain criteria, or standards of performance, on which the buyer may rely.

WARRANTIES UNDER THE UCC. The UCC provides that a **warranty** of title arises in any sale of goods—that is, a seller automatically warrants (promises) to a buyer that the seller has good title to (legitimate ownership rights in) the goods being sold and can transfer that good title to the buyer. If the goods turn out to be stolen, for example, and the buyer has to return the goods to the real owner, the seller will be liable to the buyer for the value of the goods.

The UCC also contains provisions on express and implied warranties as to the quality or nature of the goods being sold. An *express warranty* is an oral or written promise made by a seller concerning the nature of the goods being sold. For example, the statement, "This is a new Black & Decker lawn mower" is an express warranty, or promise, that the lawn mower is indeed a Black & Decker lawn mower and that it is new. If you purchase the lawn mower and learn that it is not new but used, the seller has breached an express warranty.

Under the UCC, implied warranties arise in all sales transactions. Every merchant makes an *implied warranty of merchantability* when goods are sold. The goods must be merchantable—that is, they must be "reasonably fit for the ordinary purposes for which such goods are used." Some examples of unmerchantable goods are a light bulb that explodes when switched on, hamburger meat that contains fragments of glass, and a new boat that leaks. Goods sold by merchants must also be fit for the particular purpose for which they are sold. For this *implied warranty of fitness for a particular purpose* to arise, the buyer must rely on the seller's skill or judgment in selecting suitable goods.

On the Web
The UCC is available online at www.law.cornell.edu/uniform/ucc.html.

The UCC permits express and implied warranties to be disclaimed, provided that the buyer is made aware of the disclaimers at the time the sales contract is formed. To disclaim an implied warranty of fitness for a particular purpose, the disclaimer must be in writing and be conspicuous (printed in larger or contrasting type or in a different color, for example). A merchantability disclaimer must mention the word *merchantability*, but it need not be in writing. If it is made in writing, the writing must be conspicuous. Generally speaking, unless circumstances indicate otherwise, the implied warranties are disclaimed by the expression "as is," "with all faults," or similar language that is commonly understood by both parties as meaning that there are no implied warranties.

Remedies for Breach of Contract

Recall from Chapter 5 that there are two basic types of remedies: remedies at law (money damages) and remedies in equity (remedies that are granted when money damages are inadequate). In cases involving breached contracts, plaintiffs often seek money damages to compensate them for the expenses they incurred as a result of the breach of contract.

In certain situations, such as contracts for the sale of unique goods or items, money damages may be an inadequate remedy. In such a situation, a plaintiff might ask the court to grant an equitable remedy, such as *specific performance* (the performance of what was promised in the contract) or *rescission* (cancellation) of the contract. (These equitable remedies were both described in Chapter 5.) Note, though, that when rescission is granted as a remedy and the contract is rescinded (or canceled), each party must make **restitution** to the other by returning goods, property, or money previously conveyed. An equitable remedy that was not mentioned in Chapter 5 is **reformation**. In cases involving breaches of contracts, this remedy occurs when the court revises a contract to reflect the true intention of the parties—if a mutual mistake occurred, for example.

Remedies for breach of a contract for the sale of goods are designed to put the aggrieved party in as good a position as if the other party had fully performed.

Restitution
An equitable remedy under which a person is restored to his or her original position prior to loss or injury, or placed in the position that he or she would have been in had the breach not occurred.

Reformation
An equitable remedy granted by a court to correct, or "reform," a written contract so that it reflects the true intentions of the parties.

Developing Paralegal Skills

Contract Review

Samantha Thompson works as a paralegal for a corporation. One of her jobs is to review contracts between the corporation and outside vendors. She is reviewing a contract for the corporation's purchase of fifty new personal computers from an outside vendor. The contract, which is a preprinted form contract, was submitted by the vendor and consists of thirty paragraphs of "fine print." The blanks in the form, for such terms as price and quantity, have been filled in by the vendor. As Samantha reads through the contract, she comes across a warranty disclaimer provision. Samantha realizes that this contract provision means that there will be no warranty of merchantability or fitness for a particular purpose for the new computers that the company is purchasing. She makes a note to inform her supervising attorney of this important provision. The attorney will want to inform management of this limitation on warranties.

TIPS FOR REVIEWING A CONTRACT
- Find out which contract provisions are acceptable to the client.
- Obtain the original copy of the contract.
- Read through each provision carefully.
- Be certain you understand the meaning of each provision. If you are uncertain, find out what a provision means; do not rely on "boilerplate" language.
- Prepare a memo to the client explaining the client's rights and liabilities under the contract.
- In the memo, mention the contract terms and provisions that the client might find objectionable.

The seller's remedies for breach include the right to stop or withhold delivery of the goods and the right to recover damages or the purchase price of the goods from the buyer. The buyer's remedies include (1) the right to reject nonconforming goods (goods that do not conform to those specifically agreed on in the contract) or improperly delivered goods; (2) the right to cover (to buy the goods elsewhere and recover from the seller the extra cost of obtaining the substitute goods); (3) the right to recover damages; and (4) in certain circumstances, the right to obtain specific performance of the sales contract.

Contract Law and the Paralegal

As a legal professional, it is vital that you have some knowledge of contract law. Regardless of where you work (for a large or small law firm, for a corporation, or for the government) and regardless of your area of specialty as a paralegal, you may be asked to handle matters that require an understanding of the basic principles of contract law. This is because contracts are so pervasive in our society. Business firms and government agencies routinely form contracts. Individuals in all walks of life commonly make contracts with others for goods or services. (Today, forms for numerous types of contracts are available online—see this chapter's *Technology and Today's Paralegal: Contract Forms* for information on how to access Web sites offering contract forms.)

Here are just a few of the tasks you might perform, in any workplace and in any capacity, that involve contracts:

- Interview a client or other person to obtain information about a contract to be drafted or a claim for breach of contract.
- Review a contract to make sure that its terms are sufficiently definite and that it has met all of the requirements for a valid contract.
- Research previous cases decided by courts in your jurisdiction to determine whether a defense raised against a claim for breach of contract will likely

Substantive Law Concept Summary
Contract Law

Requirements of a Valid Contract	A contract is an exchange of promises that can be enforced in court. For a contract to be valid, the following four requirements must be met: 1. *Agreement*—The making of an offer (a promise to do something in return for something else) and the acceptance of that offer by the one to whom the offer was made. 2. *Consideration*—Something of value (such as money or an action one would not otherwise be required to undertake) given in exchange for performance or a promise of performance. 3. *Contractual capacity*—The required level of mental competence to enter into a legally binding contract. 4. *Legality*—The contract must be for a legal purpose.

Defenses to Contract Enforceability	1. *Failure to comply with the Statute of Frauds*—The following types of contracts fall under the Statute of Frauds and must be in writing to be enforceable:
	   a. Contracts involving interests in land.
	   b. Contracts for the sale of goods priced at $500 or more.
	   c. Contracts made in consideration of marriage.
	   d. Contracts whose terms cannot be performed within one year.
	   e. Contracts in which one party agrees to be responsible for the debts or obligations of another.
	
	2. *Lack of genuineness of assent*—If a defendant can prove that he or she did not genuinely assent to the terms of the contract (because of mistake or fraud, for example), the contract normally will not be enforceable.
	
	3. *Unconscionable contract*—A contract that is so oppressive, one sided, or unfair to the defendant that it "shocks the conscience" of the court is not enforceable.
	
	4. *Impossibility of performance*—A court will not enforce a contractual obligation that is objectively impossible to perform, as when the subject matter of the contract has been destroyed.

Sales Contracts and Warranties	1. *Sales contracts*—Contracts for the sale of goods (tangible, movable property) are governed by Article 2 of the Uniform Commercial Code (UCC). Buyers and sellers are free to fashion their own contracts. The UCC normally comes into play if a dispute arises over ambiguous or absent contractual terms. The UCC does not displace the common law of contracts but modifies common law doctrines as necessary to facilitate commercial transactions. If the UCC *has* modified a common law principle, then the UCC will govern. If the UCC *has not* modified a common law principle, then the common law will govern.

Substantive Law Concept Summary
Contract Law—Continued

Sales Contracts and Warranties—continued	2. *Types of warranties*—
	  a. Warranty of title—Arises in any sale of goods. The seller automatically warrants (promises) to the buyer that the seller has good title to the goods being sold.
	  b. Express warranty—The seller's oral or written promise concerning the nature of the goods being sold.
	  c. Implied warranty of merchantability—An implied warranty that the goods sold are reasonably fit for the ordinary purposes for which such goods are used.
	  d. Implied warranty of fitness for a particular purpose—An implied warranty that the goods sold are fit for the particular purpose for which they are sold. The buyer must have relied on the seller's skill or judgment in selecting suitable goods.
	
	3. *Warranty disclaimers*—Express and implied warranties may be disclaimed, but the buyer must be made aware of any warranty disclaimers or modifications *at the time the sales contract is formed.*

Remedies for Breach of Contract	When a contract is breached, the remedies available to the nonbreaching party include remedies at law (money damages) and remedies in equity (normally not granted unless the remedy at law is inadequate):
	
	1. *Money damages*—Compensation for the losses incurred because of the breach.
	2. *Equitable remedies*—
	  a. Specific performance—The breaching party is ordered by the court to perform the promised contractual obligation.
	  b. Rescission—Cancellation of the contract.
	  c. Restitution—When a contract is rescinded, or canceled, both parties must make restitution to each other by returning the goods, property, or money previously exchanged under the contract.
	  d. Reformation—The court revises the contract to reflect the true intention of the parties.
	3. *Sales contracts: Seller's remedies*—
	  a. The right to stop or withhold delivery of the goods.
	  b. The right to recover damages or the purchase price of the goods from the buyer.
	4. *Sales contracts: Buyer's remedies*—
	  a. The right to reject nonconforming goods or improperly delivered goods.
	  b. The right to buy the goods elsewhere and recover from the seller the extra cost of obtaining the substitute goods.
	  c. The right to recover damages.
	  d. In some circumstances, the court will order the seller to undertake the specific performance promised in the contract.

TECHNOLOGY AND TODAY'S PARALEGAL

Contract Forms

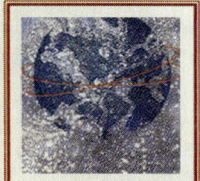

Before the printing press was invented, every contract form had to be handwritten. Since the advent of printing, in contrast, most standard contract forms have been readily available at low cost. The introduction of computers into legal practice obviated the need to use preprinted forms and further allowed attorneys and paralegals to customize contract forms for each given situation. This procedure has been both simplified and expanded by the inclusion of contract forms on simple-to-use CD-ROMs, such as Quicken's *Business Law Partner*.

Now the Internet has made available an even larger variety of contract forms, as well as other legal and business forms. For example, over five thousand forms are available at www.legal-businessforms.com. Sources for the forms include publishing houses, law firms, and law journals, as well as various government entities and bar associations. At that site, you can preview the forms you need. If you want to download an entire form, you have to pay a fee ranging from $10 to $45.

Another source for contract forms is the 'Lectric Law Library's collection of forms at www.lectlaw.com/form.html. In addition to actual forms, there are comments on how the forms should be used and filled out. The site includes forms for the assignment of a contract, a contract for the sale of a motor vehicle, and many others.

At www.legaldocs.com you will find an electronic forms book that offers hundreds of standardized legal forms, some of which are free.

Finally, at www.findlaw.com/16forms/index.html you will find hyperlinks to other online collections of con-

---

succeed or to determine how the courts have interpreted a certain type of contract provision.
- Gather evidence to determine the amount of damages sustained as a result of a breach of contract.
- Assist in litigating a breach of contract.
- Draft a settlement letter to settle a contract dispute.
- Assist in arbitration or other proceedings held for the purpose of settling a contract dispute.
- Contact representatives of business firms (perhaps in foreign countries) for the purpose of contract negotiations or the settlement of contract disputes.

In addition to these tasks, you may be involved in legal work that arises only in relation to sales contracts. You may need to determine, for example, whether one of the parties to a contract qualifies as a "merchant" as defined by Article 2 of the UCC. If so, different rules may apply to the contract. You may be asked to investigate a claim for breach of warranty to determine whether a warranty was made and whether the seller's actions (or failure to act) constituted a breach of warranty.

Many paralegals assist in work relating to product-liability lawsuits. Product liability may be based on warranty theory or, as mentioned earlier, on the tort theories of negligence, fraudulent misrepresentation, or strict liability.

REAL PROPERTY

Real Property
Immovable property consisting of land and the buildings and plant life thereon.

From an early period, the law has divided property into two classifications: real property and personal property. **Real property,** or *real estate,* is land and all things attached to the land (such as trees and buildings), as well as the minerals below the surface of the land and the air above the land. **Personal property** is all other property. Personal property can be either tangible or intangible. *Tangible* personal property, such as a television set or a car, has physical substance. *Intangible* personal property represents a set of rights and interests but has no real physical existence. Stocks and bonds are examples of intangible personal property.

Personal Property
Any property that is not real property. Generally, any property that is movable or intangible is classified as personal property.

Ownership Rights in Property

Property ownership is often viewed as a "bundle of rights." One who owns the entire bundle of rights—ownership rights to the greatest degree possible—is said to own the property in **fee simple**.

 An owner in fee simple is entitled to use, possess, or dispose of the real or personal property (by sale, gift, or other means) however he or she chooses during his or her lifetime. On the owner's death, the interests in the property descend to the owner's heirs.

Fee Simple
Ownership rights entitling the holder to use, possess, or dispose of the property however he or she chooses during his or her lifetime.

Of course, those who own real property even in fee simple may be subject to certain restrictions on their right to use the property absolutely as they choose. For example, zoning laws may prohibit an owner of property in a given area from conducting certain types of activities (such as running a business) on the property. Also, under its power of **eminent domain,** the government has a right to take private property for public use (for a highway, for example), as long as the government compensates the owner for the value of the land taken.

Eminent Domain
The power of a government to take land for public use from private citizens for just compensation.

Property owned in fee simple may also be subject to an *easement,* which is the right of another to use the owner's land for a limited purpose—a neighbor's right to use the land to reach a roadway, for example, or a utility company's right to erect and maintain power lines and poles or gas lines on the land.

In contrast to ownership in fee simple, other forms of ownership, including those discussed below, involve limited ownership rights.

CONCURRENT OWNERSHIP. Persons who share the bundle of ownership rights to either real or personal property are said to be concurrent owners. There are two principal types of concurrent ownership: tenancy in common and joint tenancy.

A **tenancy in common** is a form of co-ownership in which two or more persons own undivided interests in certain property. If a tenant in common dies, the tenant's ownership rights pass to his or her heirs.

Tenancy in Common
A form of co-ownership of property in which each party owns an undivided interest that passes to his or her heirs at death.

A **joint tenancy** is also a form of co-ownership in which two or more persons own undivided interests in property. The key feature of a joint tenancy is the "right of survivorship." When a joint tenant dies, that tenant's interest passes to the surviving joint tenant or tenants and not to the deceased tenant's heirs, as it would with a tenancy in common. If a joint tenant transfers his or her interest in the property while he or she is living, the joint tenancy terminates. The new co-owner (the one to whom the rights were transferred) and the other tenant or tenants become tenants in common.

Joint Tenancy
The joint ownership of property by two or more co-owners in which each co-owner owns an undivided portion of the property. On the death of one of the joint tenants, his or her interest automatically passes to the surviving joint tenant or tenants.

Two other types of concurrent ownership take the form of a tenancy by the entirety and community property. A *tenancy by the entirety* is a form of co-ownership by husbands and wives that is similar to a joint tenancy, except that the spouses cannot separately transfer their interests in the property during their lifetimes. In a few states, husbands and wives can hold property as community property. In those states, *community property* is all property acquired during the marriage; each spouse technically owns an undivided one-half interest in the property.

LIFE ESTATES. A *life estate* is an interest in real property that is transferred to another for the life of that individual. A conveyance "to Allison for her life" creates a life estate. In a life estate, the life tenant cannot injure the land in a manner that would adversely affect its value for the owner of the future interest in it.

FUTURE INTERESTS. When someone who owns real property in fee simple conveys the property conditionally to another or for a limited period of time (such as with a life estate), the original owner still retains an interest in the land. This interest is called a *future interest* because it will only arise in the future. The holder of a future interest may transfer it to another during his or her lifetime; if the interest is not transferred, it will pass to the owner's heirs on his or her death.

The Transfer and Sale of Real Property

Property can be transferred in numerous ways. Property can be given to another as a gift or transferred to another by inheritance, leased to another, or sold. Most commonly, though, property is transferred by sale. The sale of tangible personal property (goods) is covered by the common law of contracts, as modified by Article 2 of the Uniform Commercial Code, which we have already discussed. Rights in certain types of intangible property (such as checks, money orders, and other documents) are covered by other articles of the UCC. The sale of real property is governed by both the common law of contracts as well as state (and, to a limited extent, federal) statutory law.

Here we look at some of the basic steps and procedures involved in the sale of real estate. These steps and procedures are summarized in Exhibit 7.1.

EXHIBIT 7.1
Steps Involved in the Sale of Real Estate

BUYER'S PURCHASE OFFER

Buyer offers to purchase Seller's property. The offer may be conditioned on Buyer's ability to obtain financing, on satisfactory inspections of the premises, and so on. Included with the offer is earnest money.

SELLER'S RESPONSE

If Seller accepts Buyer's offer, then a contract is formed. Seller could also reject the offer or make a counteroffer that modifies Buyer's terms. Buyer may accept or reject Seller's counteroffer or make a counteroffer that modifies Seller's terms.

PURCHASE AND SALE AGREEMENT

Once an offer or a counteroffer is accepted, a purchase and sale agreement is formed.

TITLE EXAMINATION AND INSURANCE

Title examiner investigates and verifies Seller's rights in the property and discloses any claims or interests held by others. Buyer (and/or Seller) may purchase title insurance to protect against a defect in title.

CLOSING

After financing is obtained and all inspections have been completed, the closing takes place. The escrow agent (such as a title company or a bank) transfers the deed to Buyer and the proceeds of the sale to Seller. The proceeds are the purchase price less any amount already paid by Buyer and any closing costs to be paid by Seller. Included in the closing costs are fees charged for services performed by the lender, escrow agent, and title examiner. The purchase and sale of the property is complete.

> ## ETHICAL CONCERN
> ### Real-Estate Sales and the Duties of Competence and Diligence
>
> Remember from Chapter 3 that Rule 1.1 of the Model Rules of Professional Responsibility imposes on attorneys the duty of competence. Attorneys also are obligated to be diligent in their representation. Model Rule 1.3 states that "[a] lawyer shall act with reasonable diligence" when representing a client. As a paralegal, you need to make sure that you also act with competence and diligence when assisting in transfers of real property. For most individuals, the purchase of real property is the most expensive purchase they will ever make. You need to take great care to make sure that the client's legal interests are protected in every respect. This means, among other things, that you should become familiar with your state's requirements relating to real-estate transactions.

CONTRACT FORMATION—OFFER AND ACCEPTANCE. The common law contractual requirements of agreement (offer and acceptance), consideration, contractual capacity, and legality all apply to real-estate contracts. When a buyer wishes to purchase real estate, he or she submits an offer to the seller. The offer specifies all of the terms of the proposed contract—a description of the property, the price, and any other conditions that the buyer wishes to include. Often, a buyer conditions the offer on the buyer's ability to obtain financing. The offer might also specify which party will bear the cost of any repairs that need to be made. The purchase and sale agreement presented in Exhibit 7.2 beginning on page 234 illustrates the terms and conditions that might be included in an offer to purchase real estate. When signed by the buyer and the seller, the offer constitutes a contract for the sale of land that is binding on the parties.

The buyer normally tenders a sum of money, called *earnest money,* along with the offer. By paying earnest money, the buyer indicates that he or she is making a serious offer. Normally, the offer will provide that if the seller accepts the offer (and forms a contract with the buyer), the buyer will forfeit this money if he or she breaches the contract. Other damages for breach might also be specified in the agreement. If the deal goes through, the earnest money is usually applied to the purchase price of the real estate.

Once the offer is submitted to the seller, the seller has three options: he or she can accept the offer, reject it, or modify its terms—thus creating a counteroffer. The buyer, in turn, can then accept, reject, or modify the terms of the counteroffer—thus creating yet another counteroffer for the seller to consider. In real-estate transactions, bargaining over price and other conditions of the sale frequently involves the exchange of one or more counteroffers. Once one of the parties accepts an offer or counteroffer, a contract is formed by which both parties normally must abide.

THE ROLE OF THE ESCROW AGENT. The sale of real property normally involves three parties: the seller, the buyer, and the escrow agent. Frequently, both the buyer and the seller are assisted by real-estate agents, attorneys, and paralegals. The escrow agent, which may be a title company, bank, or special escrow company, acts as a neutral party in the transaction and facilitates the sale by

EXHIBIT 7.2
A Sample Purchase and Sale Agreement

BUY AND SELL AGREEMENT

THIS IS A LEGALLY BINDING CONTRACT, READ ALL PARTS CAREFULLY BEFORE SIGNING.
Buyers & Sellers are advised to seek legal counsel. Buyer and Seller acknowledge that agency relationship has been disclosed.

DATE: _____, 20___, _____ A.M./P.M.

SELLING OFFICE _____, REALTOR _____, AGENT FOR: Seller/Buyer
LISTING OFFICE _____, REALTOR _____, AGENT FOR: Seller/Buyer

1. BUYER'S OFFER
The undersigned _____, hereinafter called the Buyer hereby, offers to buy the following property commonly known as (Address) _____ located in the City/Twp. of _____, County of _____ Michigan, Legally described as: _____
_____
_____ and/or tax ID # _____ subject to any existing building and use restrictions, zoning ordinances and easements, for the sum of _____ Dollars ($ _____)

2. TERMS OF PURCHASE as indicated by "X" below: (other unmarked terms of purchase do not apply). Payment of such money shall be made in cash, certified check, or bank money order.

CASH ☐ The full purchase price upon execution and delivery of Warranty Deed.

NEW MORTGAGE ☐ The full purchase price upon the execution and delivery of Warranty Deed, contingent upon Buyer's ability to obtain a _____ Mortgage for no less than _____ years, for no less than _____ % of purchase price at no more than _____ % interest per annum which Buyer agrees to apply for within _____ calendar days after acceptance and secure and accept commitment on or before _____ (date).

CONTRACT ☐ $ _____ upon execution and delivery of Land Contract, wherein the balance of $ _____ shall be payable in monthly installments of $ _____ or more including interest at _____ % per annum, interest to start on date of closing and the first such payment to become due one month after closing date. This contract shall be payable in full _____ months/years from date of closing.

EQUITY ☐ Upon execution and delivery of: ( ) Assignment of vendee interest in land contract ( ) Warranty Deed subject to existing mortgage. Buyer to pay the difference (Approximately $ _____) between the purchase price and balance of said Mortgage or Land Contract which Buyer ☐ formally ☐ informally assumes and/or agrees to pay. Buyer agrees to reimburse Seller for any funds held in escrow for payment of future taxes and insurance premiums.

3. CREDIT REPORT ☐ Buyer hereby agrees to provide a credit report satisfactory to seller and/or lender and release necessary information. _____
4. OTHER PROVISIONS: _____
_____
_____
_____
_____

5. PROPERTY TAXES: For purposes of this agreement, taxes are to be prorated in arrears, on a calendar year basis, the amount to be based on the latest assessment and millage figures. The seller is responsible for taxes through _____ and the buyer is responsible for taxes thereafter. Exceptions: _____.

6. ASSESSMENTS: Perpetual assessments shall be assumed and paid by the buyer. All other assessments which become a lien on the property at time of closing shall be:
☐ Assumed by the buyer. Any current year's installments shall be prorated on a calendar year basis with the seller paying the prorated amount through closing.
☐ Paid in full by seller. ☐ _____

7. TITLE: Seller shall: ☐ Furnish an owner's policy of title insurance covering the foregoing described property in the amount of the purchase price.
☐ Pay $ _____ toward owner's title insurance costs for the buyer. ☐ _____
IT IS RECOMMENDED THAT ANY EVIDENCE OF TITLE AND SUPPORTING DOCUMENTS BE EXAMINED BY AN ATTORNEY.

8. SALE IS TO BE CLOSED by _____, subject to paragraph 4 above. An additional period of up to thirty (30) days shall be allowed for closing to accommodate delays in title work or the correction of title defects which can be readily corrected, delays in obtaining any required inspections, surveys, or repairs, or if the terms of purchase require participation of a lender and the lender has issued a commitment consistent with the requirement but is unable to participate in a closing on the agreed date. Any further extension shall be by written mutual agreement.

9. THE SELLER SHALL DELIVER and the purchaser shall accept possession of said property subject to the rights of the following tenants _____.
If the Seller occupies the property, it shall be vacated _____ closing. From the date after closing until the date of vacating the property as agreed, Seller shall pay the sum of $ _____ per day.

allowing the buyer and the seller to complete the transaction without having to exchange documents and funds directly with each other.

To understand the vital role played by the escrow agent, consider the problems that might otherwise arise. Essentially, in the sale of property, the buyer gives the seller money, and the seller conveys (transfers) to the buyer a deed, representing ownership rights in the property (deeds will be discussed shortly). Neither the buyer nor the seller wishes to part with the money or the deed until all conditions of the sale and purchase have been met.

The solution is the use of an escrow agent. The escrow agent holds the deed until the buyer pays the seller for the property at the closing (the final step in the

EXHIBIT 7.2—Continued
A Sample Purchase and Sale Agreement

---

10. For valuable consideration Buyer gives seller _____ calendar day(s) for written acceptance of this offer. This offer, when signed, will constitute a binding agreement between Buyer and Seller. Buyer herewith deposits $ _____ evidencing Buyer's good faith, said deposit to be held by said REALTOR®/Broker, and to apply as part of the purchase price. If this sale is not consummated, the deposit made herein shall be subject to the provisions of Paragraph 106 on the reverse side of this Agreement.

11. INSPECTIONS: This agreement is contingent upon buyer's satisfaction of the following (check box) indicated inspections:

   a) Buyer to pay for ☐ water; ☐ well; ☐ septic; ☐ mechanical; ☐ structural; ☐ plumbing; ☐ heating; ☐ electrical; ☐ pest; ☐ environmental; ☐ Lender Req.; ☐ other

   b) Seller to pay for ☐ water; ☐ well; ☐ septic; ☐ mechanical; ☐ structural; ☐ plumbing; ☐ heating; ☐ electrical; ☐ pest; ☐ environmental; ☐ Lender Req.; ☐ other

   c) ☐ Inspections shall be deemed acceptable to buyer unless written notice of objection is delivered to seller, or seller's agent by _____. Failure to submit written notice of said objection shall be deemed a waiver of buyer's inspection and repair rights and buyer agrees to accept the property in its present condition. In the event of any claim or demand to remedy or repair any item, The Seller shall have the option of: 1) making said items operational provided the Seller agrees to the expense in writing, 2) Giving the Buyers a credit for the items, providing the expense has been approved by the Seller, or 3) Cancelling the contract of sale and refunding the Buyer any earnest money deposit held by Broker less any expenses incurred on Buyers behalf.

   d) ☐ Buyer(s) waive all inspections without benefit of an opinion by a licensed contractor.

12. Buyer hereby acknowledges receipt of a copy of this agreement.

13. NOTE: GENERAL CONDITIONS OF SALE PRINTED ON REVERSE SIDE NUMBERED 101 THROUGH 119 HAVE BEEN REVIEWED AND ARE INCORPORATED HEREIN AND MADE A PART OF THIS AGREEMENT.

_____ _____
Initial   Initial

14. Witness _____ X _____ Buyer
Buyer's Address _____ X _____ Buyer
_____ Zip _____ Buyer's Phone: (Res.) _____ (Bus.) _____
Received from above named buyer deposit monies in the form of _____ by _____
                                                                    Realtor/Broker

15. SELLER'S ACCEPTANCE   Date: _____, 20_____, _____ AM/PM
The above agreement is hereby accepted _____

NOTE: GENERAL CONDITIONS OF SALE PRINTED ON REVERSE SIDE NUMBERED 101 THROUGH 119 HAVE BEEN REVIEWED AND ARE INCORPORATED HEREIN AND MADE A PART OF THIS AGREEMENT.

Seller Has Read This Agreement And Acknowledges Receipt Of A Copy.
_____ _____
Initial   Initial

Witness _____ X _____ Seller
Buyer's Address _____ X _____ Seller
_____ Zip _____ Seller's Phone: (Res.) _____ (Bus.) _____

BUYER'S RECEIPT OF SELLER'S ACCEPTANCE   Date: _____, 20_____, _____ AM/PM

16. Receipt is Hereby Acknowledged by Buyer of Seller's acceptance of Buyer's offer. In the event the acceptance was subject to certain changes from Buyer's offer, Buyer agrees to accept said changes, ALL OTHER TERMS AND CONDITIONS REMAINING UNCHANGED, EXCEPT: _____

Witness _____ X _____ Buyer
                                 X _____ Buyer

SELLER'S RECEIPT OF ACCEPTANCE   Date: _____, 20_____, _____ AM/PM

17. Seller's Receipt of Acceptance: Seller hereby Acknowledges receipt of a copy of Buyer's acceptance of his counter offer (in the event Seller has made a counter offer).

Witness _____ X _____ Seller
Revised and approved 4/94   Gratiot-Isabella Board of Realtors®   X _____ Seller

---

sale of real estate). The escrow agent also holds any money paid by the buyer, including the earnest money mentioned above, until the sale is completed. At the closing, the escrow agent receives money from the buyer, the buyer is given the deed, and the seller is given the money. The triangular relationship that exists among the buyer, the seller, and the escrow agent is depicted in Exhibit 7.3 on page 238.

FINANCING. Because few buyers can or want to pay cash for real property, buyers generally need to secure financing. Commonly, a buyer of real property finances the purchase by obtaining a loan—called a **mortgage**—from a bank, a mortgage company, or some other party. When a buyer obtains a mortgage, the bank or mortgage company takes a security interest in the property. That is, the

Mortgage
A written instrument giving a creditor an interest in the debtor's property as security for a debt.

EXHIBIT 7.2—Continued
A Sample Purchase and Sale Agreement

---

101. THE PROPERTY INCLUDES ANY OF THE FOLLOWING PRESENTLY ON THE PREMISES: All buildings; TV antenna and controls; satellite dish and controls; garage door opener and transmitter(s); carpet; light fixtures and shades; drapery and curtain hardware; window shades and blinds; screens; storm windows and doors; stationary laundry tubs; water softener (unless rented); water heater; incinerator; sump pump; heating and air conditioning equipment, (window units excluded); water pump and pressure tank; built-in kitchen appliances including garbage disposal; awnings; mail box; all plantings; fence(s); attached fireplace screens, doors, and equipment; attached supplemental heating units; all attached mirrors and all bathroom mirrors; smoke, heat, and fire detectors; burglar alarms; and any gas, oil, and mineral rights owned by the seller. ADDITIONS OR EXCEPTIONS SHOULD BE NOTED IN # 4.

102. Seller shall be responsible for fire and extended coverage insurance until sale is closed, and buyer is responsible thereafter.

103. Prorations: Rent; casualty insurance, if assigned; fuel; interest on any existing land contract, mortgage, or other lien assumed and/or to be paid by the Buyer shall be adjusted to the date of closing of the sale. Security deposits and lease agreements shall be assigned to Buyer at closing.

104. It is agreed by the REALTOR®/Broker and Seller or Lessor, parties to this agreement, that as required by law, discrimination because of race, creed, color, national origin, sex, marital status, height, weight, age or handicap by said parties with respect to the sale or lease of the subject property is prohibited.

105. The convenants herein shall bind and insure to the benefit of the executors, administrators, successors, personal representatives and assigns of the parties hereto. SELLER ALSO AGREES to pay Listing REALTOR®/Broker named on the face hereof a commission as stated in the Listing Agreement corresponding to the property described herein for negotiating this sale. All deposits are to be held by Selling REALTOR®/Broker in accordance with the terms hereof and in accordance with the Occupational Code and the rules of the Bureau of Occupational and Professional Regulation of the Michigan Department of Commerce.

106. DEFAULT: If Seller refuses to complete the sale, the full commission shall be due and payable upon such refusal. If a Buyer refuses to complete the sale, the Buyer's earnest money deposit shall be forfeited. The deposit shall be first applied to reimburse the Broker for all expenses incurred by the Listing Broker on Seller's behalf including, but not limited to, abstracting charges, counsel, and fees of public officers. One-half of the remainder of such deposit (but not in excess of the amount of the full commission) shall be retained by the Listing Broker in full payment for services rendered and the balance of the deposit shall be paid over to the Seller. If this transaction is subject to any contingencies which cannot be met, Buyer's earnest money deposit shall be first applied to reimburse the Broker for all expenses incurred by the Broker on Buyer's behalf. The balance of the deposit shall be paid over to the Buyer.

107. SELLER understands that consummation of the sale or transfer of the property described in this agreement shall not relieve the Seller of any liability that Seller may have under the mortgage(s) to which the property is subject unless otherwise agreed to by the lender or required by law or regulation.

108. INFORMATION DISCLOSURE: The purchase price and terms of this sale shall be disclosed to the Gratiot-Isabella Board of REALTORS® in the ordinary conduct of business.

109. MERGER: This agreement supersedes any and all representations and agreements and constitutes the entire agreement between the parties, and no prior representations or agreements, oral or written, shall be considered a part hereof.

110. TIME shall be deemed as of the very essence of this agreement.

111. TO SELLERS BEST KNOWLEDGE:

   A. No other person or persons have any right, title, or interest in said real estate (except as Seller discloses herein or shown by title insurance commitment); that said owners have made no deeds of conveyance or deeds to change title, that they have not entered into any contracts to convey said real estate or any agreements for the sale of said real estate, or any mineral, oil, gravel, rental or other leases affecting said real estate except under this Purchase Agreement.

   B. The title to the premises has never been disputed, questioned, or rejected to the sellers knowledge: that there is no suit or proceeding pending affecting the premises; that all bills and charges for work, labor and services rendered and materials furnished in the improvement of the premises or nay part thereof have been paid, and that no person or corporation has filed or has a right to file a mechanic's lien thereon; that no financing statement has been filed against any fixtures or chattels attached to or used in the operation of the premises; that the premises upon closing will be free and clear of all encumbrances, liens or charges of every nature or description, save and except: (TO BE SET FORTH UNDER PARAGRAPH 4 REVERSE SIDE)

   C. There are no judgements or tax liens against them unsatisfied of records in the courts of the State or the United States, and that no proceedings in bankruptcy have been instituted by or against them.

112. THE BUYER ACKNOWLEDGES that the REALTOR® cannot warrant the condition of any fixtures, equipment, or personal property being purchased by Buyer from Seller.

113. THE SELLER ACKNOWLEDGES THE FOLLOWING:

   A. That a credit report on the Buyer has been recommended by REALTOR®; and that if a credit report is not obtained, the Seller is accepting Buyer on Buyer's own merit trust.

---

bank or mortgage company secures the right to claim ownership of the property if the buyer fails to make the scheduled payments.

INSPECTION OF THE PREMISES. In addition to obtaining financing, buyers may have the premises inspected to see if there are any major electrical or plumbing problems, structural defects, termite or insect infestations, or other problems. Often, the contract of sale is conditioned on the outcome of these inspections. If problems surface during the inspections, the buyer and seller may negotiate (or

EXHIBIT 7.2—Continued
A Sample Purchase and Sale Agreement

B. That REALTOR® cannot warrant that the Buyer will be able to obtain financing at the time of any balloon payment specified in this agreement.

114. **TYPICAL SELLERS COST:**
Transfer tax on deed;
All costs required and necessary to clear title;
Accumulated interest on any existing indebtedness;
Updated abstract or Owner's Title, Insurance Policy;
Preparation of Deed, Land Contract, Bill of Sale and/or other documents necessary to convey clear title, if required.

TYPICAL BUYERS COST:
Preparation of Mortgage, Note, or any other security instruments except Land Contract
Mortgage Title Insurance Policy;
Mortgage Inspection Survey Report, if required;
Recording of Deed and/or Security Instruments;
Attorney's Opinion and/or services on behalf of the Buyer;
Mortgage closing cost as required by mortgagee including appraisal and closing fees (except V.A.)
Transfer fee on Mortgage Assumption;
Closing Fee

115. **EXAMINATION OF TITLE:** In addition to any encumbrances referred to herein, Purchaser shall take title to the property subject to: 1) Real Estate Taxes not yet due, and 2) Covenants, Conditions, Restrictions, Rights of Way, and Easements of record, if any, which do not materially affect the value or intended use of the property.

116. **CONTINGENCIES SATISFIED IN WRITING:** Each contingency contained herein shall be satisfied according to its terms or waived in writing by the party responsible within the time specified for any extension thereof agreed to by the parties in writing. This paragraph contemplates that each party shall diligently pursue the completion of this transaction.

117. **NO TAX ADVICE:** Purchaser and Seller acknowledge that they have not received or relied upon any statements or representations by the REALTOR®, regarding the effect of this transaction upon their tax liability.

118. **FAX TRANSMISSION:** The facsimile transmission of a signed copy hereof or any counter offer to the other party or his/her agent, followed by faxed acknowledgment of receipt, shall constitute delivery of said signed document. The parties agree to confirm such delivery by mailing or personally delivering a signed copy to the other party or agent.

119. **CONDITION OF PREMISES:** Buyer has personally inspected the property and agrees to accept it in "as is" condition except as otherwise provided in this agreement. Buyer acknowledges that it has been recommended the buyer seek and secure inspections of the property not limited to matters of survey, use permits, easements, rights of way, water, well, septic systems, municipal systems, structural, plumbing, heating, electrical, pest, environmental concerns, subdivision restrictions, zoning, soil borings, franchising, use permits, ADA requirements, etc.

Purchaser acknowledges that he/she has not relied upon any representations either expressed or implied, by brokers and/or agents as to the condition of the premises or contents thereof and that they are not relying on any such warranty or representation as a condition to purchase except as specifically set forth in writing, fully executed by all parties and attached hereto.

ALL BUYERS AND SELLERS OF REAL ESTATE ARE ADVISED TO SEEK LEGAL COUNSEL.

DISCLAIMER: This form is provided as a service of the Gratiot-Isabella Board of REALTORS®. Please review both the form and details of the particular transaction to ensure that each section is appropriate for the transaction. The Gratiot-Isabella Board of REALTORS® is not responsible for use or misuse of the form, for misrepresentation, or for warranties made in connection with the form.

---

may have included in the contract) arrangements specifying which party will pay what portion of the costs of any necessary repairs.

TITLE EXAMINATION AND INSURANCE. Whenever title to property is transferred from one party to another, that transfer is recorded by the county recording office. A *title examination* involves checking these records carefully to make sure that the seller is actually the owner of the property described in the purchase offer and to determine whether claims (such as a tax lien for overdue taxes) on the

EXHIBIT 7.3

The Concept of Escrow

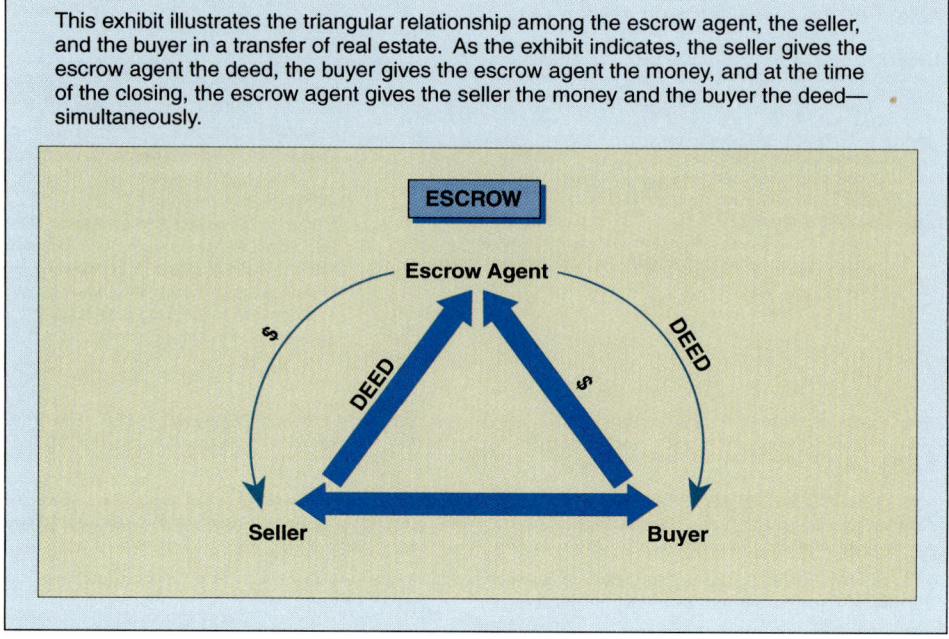

property exist that were not disclosed by the seller. The title examination is an important task to be accomplished prior to the purchase of real estate. The title examination may be undertaken by the buyer or the buyer's attorney (paralegals frequently assume this responsibility), or by the lending institution, a title insurance company, or another party.

Normally, the history of past ownership and transfers of the property is already summarized in a document called an *abstract*, which may be in the possession of the seller (or the holder of the seller's mortgage or other company or institution). After examining the abstract, the title examiner gives an opinion as to the validity of the title. Title examinations are not foolproof, though, and buyers of real property generally purchase title insurance to protect their interests in the event that some defect in the title was not discovered during the examination.

THE CLOSING. One of the terms specified in the contract is when the closing will take place. The closing—also called the settlement or the closing of escrow— is coordinated by the escrow agent. At the closing, several events happen nearly simultaneously: the buyer signs the mortgage note (if the purchase was financed by a mortgage), title insurance is obtained, the seller receives the proceeds of the sale (the purchase price less the amount previously paid by the buyer and less closing costs), and the deed to the property is delivered to the buyer.

A **deed** is the instrument of conveyance (transfer) of real property. As indicated on the sample deed in Exhibit 7.4 on page 240, a deed gives the names of the seller (grantor) and buyer (grantee), describes the property being transferred, evidences the seller's intent to convey (for example, "I hereby bargain, sell, grant, or give") the property, and contains the seller's signature.

Closing costs comprise fees for services, including those performed by the lender, escrow agent, and title company. These costs can range from several hundred to several thousand dollars, depending on the amount of the mortgage loan and other conditions of the sale, and must be paid, in cash, at the closing. Usually,

Deed
A document by which title to property is transferred from one party to another.

> ## ETHICAL CONCERN
> ### Accurate Paperwork and the Sale of Real-Estate
>
> Art Guthrie, a paralegal, was drafting a real-estate offer for one of the firm's corporate clients. Instead of keying in $90,000 as the amount being offered for the property, Art accidentally entered $900,000. No one detected the error. The seller accepted the offer, and only when Art was reviewing the closing package did he notice the mistake and tell his supervising attorney about it. The seller agreed to cancel the contract (because in the meantime she had received an offer of $110,000 for the property). Eventually the client paid $115,000—$25,000 more than he otherwise would have had to pay—for the desired property. The client sued the attorney for negligence, alleging that the attorney had breached the duty of competence and seeking the extra $25,000 in damages. The picture emerging from this hypothetical scenario is clear: when handling paperwork relating to real-estate transactions, as with other legal documents, the paralegal must make absolutely sure that the documents are accurate.

the buyer and seller can learn in advance, by checking (or having their attorneys or real-estate agents check) with the escrow agent handling the closing, what the closing costs will be. Also, under the federal Real Estate Settlement Procedures Act of 1976, lending institutions must notify—within a specified time period—each applicant for a mortgage loan of the precise costs that must be paid at the closing.

Leases

An owner of either personal or real property can lease, or rent, the property to another person or a business firm. A **lease** is a contractual agreement under which a property owner (the lessor) agrees to rent his or her property to another (the lessee) for a specified period of time. Leases of personal property (cars or equipment) are covered by the Uniform Commercial Code, which spells out the rights and duties of lessors and lessees.

Leases of real property are governed in part by the common law of contracts and in part (and to an increasing extent) by state statutory law. Although under the common law, an oral lease is valid, a party who seeks to enforce an oral lease may have difficulty proving its existence. In most states, statutes mandate that leases exceeding one year's duration must be in writing. When real property is leased, the lessor (landlord) retains ownership rights to the property, but the lessee (tenant) obtains the right to the exclusive possession of the property. Most leases, however, give the landlord the right to come onto the property for certain purposes—to make repairs, for example.

Paralegals frequently draft or review lease agreements for clients (or for corporate employers), and you should be familiar with the types of terms that are typically included in a lease agreement, or contract. Normally, a lease contract will specify the names of the lessor and lessee, the location of the premises being leased, the amount of rent to be paid by the lessee, the duration of the lease, and the respective rights and duties of the parties in regard to the use and maintenance of the leased premises. Exhibit 7.5 on page 242 illustrates the kinds of provisions that are commonly included in lease agreements.

Lease
In real-property law, a contract by which the owner of real property (the landlord) grants to a person (the tenant) an exclusive right to use and possess the property, usually for a specified period of time, in return for rent or some other form of payment.

On the Web
If you are interested in learning why the Real Estate Settlement Procedures Act of 1976 was passed and what it requires of lending institutions, you can find the act online at www.law.cornell.edu/uscode/12/2601.shtml.

EXHIBIT 7.4
A Sample Deed

Date: May 31, 1999

Grantor: RAYMOND A. GRANT AND WIFE, JOANN H. GRANT

Grantor's Mailing Address (including county):
4106 North Loop Drive
Austin, Travis County, Texas

Grantee: DAVID F. FRIEND AND WIFE, JOAN E. FRIEND, AS JOINT TENANTS WITH RIGHT OF SURVIVORSHIP

Grantee's Mailing Address (including county):
5929 Fuller Drive
Austin, Travis County, Texas

Consideration:
For and in consideration of the sum of Ten and No/100 Dollars ($10.00) and other valuable consideration to the undersigned paid by the grantees herein named, the receipt of which is hereby acknowledged, and for which no lien is retained, either express or implied.

Property (including any improvements):
Lot 23, Block "A", Northwest Hills, Green Acres Addition, Phase 4, Travis County, Texas, according to the map or plat of record in volume 22, pages 331-336, of the Plat Records of Travis County, Texas.

Reservations from and Exceptions to Conveyance and Warranty:

This conveyance with its warranty is expressly made subject to the following: Easements and restrictions of record in volume 7863, page 53, volume 8430, page 35, volume 8133, page 152, of the Real Property Records of Travis County, Texas; and to any other restrictions and easements affecting said property which are of record in Travis County, Texas.

Grantor, for the consideration and subject to the reservations from and exceptions to conveyance and warranty, grants, sells, and conveys to Grantee the property, together with all and singular the rights and appurtenances thereto in any wise belonging, to have and hold it to Grantee, Grantee's heirs, executors, administrators, successors, or assigns forever. Grantor binds Grantor and Grantor's heirs, executors, administrators, and successors to warrant and forever defend all and singular the property to Grantee and Grantee's heirs, executors, administrators, successors, and assigns against every person whomsoever lawfully claiming or to claim the same or any part thereof, except as to the reservations from and exceptions to conveyance and warranty.

When the context requires, singular nouns and pronouns include the plural.

BY: *Raymond A. Grant*
Raymond A. Grant

BY: *JoAnn H. Grant*
JoAnn H. Grant

STATE OF TEXAS
COUNTY OF TRAVIS
This instrument was acknowledged before me on the 31st day of May 1999 by Raymond A. and JoAnn H. Grant

Rosemary Potter
Notary Public, State of Texas
Notary's name (printed): ROSEMARY POTTER

Notary Seal

Notary's commission expires: 1/31/2002

Property Law and the Paralegal

Paralegals frequently undertake tasks that require an understanding of the law governing real property. If you work for a small legal practice, some of your work may involve assisting your supervising attorney in handling real-estate transactions. If you work for a law firm (or a department within a law firm) that spe-

PARALEGAL PROFILE

Real-Estate Paralegal

CAROL D. HOLLER, a Certified Legal Assistant Specialist (CLAS), has worked in the largest law firm in Fort Lauderdale, Florida, for fifteen years and practices in the area of commercial real estate. She is also the supervisor in the real-estate department in her firm and oversees fourteen real-estate paralegals. Holler started her career in law with a small law firm in Towson, Maryland. The firm performed all of the closings for a Maryland savings and loan association. Holler's career took her to various law firms and corporations throughout the country, but her work always dealt primarily with real estate. This extensive experience, coupled with a real-estate sales and appraisal background, has proved invaluable in her paralegal career.

Holler has been actively involved in Florida Legal Assistants, Inc., as its president for the past two years and in numerous other board positions. She has also served on the Continuing Education Council of the National Association of Legal Assistants, Inc., for many years.

What do you like best about your work?
"The everyday challenges of different real-property issues keep my work varied and interesting. The variety of problems with each commercial real-property transaction makes every closing exciting and new; I never get bored with the work. I feel this is one of the best parts about my work because I am constantly learning something new. Additionally, there is a great deal of client contact as well as contact with opposing counsel."

What is the greatest challenge that you face in your area of work?
"Millions of real-property issues and people problems are associated with real property. Every day, we learn of another problem on a parcel of property, caused by either humans or the environment. Our job is to find a resolution to the problem and to create a smooth and pleasant closing for our client. Many of our clients feel that we are miracle workers, and keeping them thinking that way is the greatest challenge of my job."

What advice do you have for would-be paralegals in your area of work?
"When I have the opportunity to discuss becoming a paralegal with would-be paralegals (and it seems these opportunities are frequent), I tell them to take any job they can get in a law firm or title company and become a sponge—absorb everything they can from the people that work there and volunteer for everything they can to learn more. Prior knowledge is one of the best things you can have when you are finding a better job. Use your prior work experiences to build into the position you ultimately want."

What are some tips for success as a paralegal in your area of work?
"Knowledge, knowledge, knowledge are the best tips for success in my area of work. Much of this comes from years of experience and from handling a variety of transactions. Do not get stuck in a job where you are not continuously learning something new. Take the knowledge you have gained from one job and move on to something better and more challenging; keep the learning curve always moving upward."

> "Do not get stuck in a job where you are not continuously learning something new."

---

cializes in real-estate transactions, you will have extensive contact with buyers and sellers of real property, as well as with real-estate agents, title companies, banking institutions that finance real-estate purchases, and the attorneys and paralegals who work on behalf of the other parties in real-estate sales.

If a real-estate agent is involved, the agent will assist the seller or the buyer in drawing up a purchase contract, in arranging for inspections, in having the title

EXHIBIT 7.5
Typical Lease Terms

Term of lease: Indicates the duration of the lease, including the beginning and ending dates.
Rental: Indicates the amount of the rent payments and the intervals (monthly, yearly, etc.) at which rent will be paid.
Maintenence and use of leased premises: Describes which areas will be repaired and maintained by the landlord and which by the tenant.
Utilities: Stipulates which utilities (electricity, water, etc.) will be paid by the landlord and by the tenant.
Alterations: Normally states that no structural alterations to the property will be made by the tenant without the landlord's consent.
Assignment: States whether the tenant's rights in the lease can be assigned (transferred) by the tenant to a third party.
Insurance: Indicates whether the landlord or the tenant will insure the premises against damage. (Normally, the landlord secures insurance coverage for the building, and the tenant obtains a "renter's policy" for his or her own personal property—furniture and other possessions—that will be housed in the building.)
Taxes: Designates which party will be liable for taxes or special assessments on the property. (Normally, the landlord assumes this responsibility, but in some commercial leases, the tenant agrees to take on this responsibility.)
Destruction: States what will happen in the event that the premises are totally destroyed by fire or other casualty.
Quiet enjoyment: A covenant (promise) by the landlord that the tenant shall possess and enjoy the premises without interference by any third party.
Termination: Usually specifies that the tenant's right to possession of the premises ends when the lease expires.
Renewal: Indicates that the tenant has an option to renew the lease if the landlord is notified of the intent to renew within a certain period of time (such as one month or three months) before the lease expires.

examined and title insurance procured, and in preparing the closing papers. In this situation, your job will be to assist the attorney in verifying, on behalf of your client, that all of the documents needed have been prepared and that the documents contain the correct purchase price, mortgage amount, property description, and other terms. Generally, you will be responsible for making sure that the documents are in order and that the client's interests are fully protected.

Here are just some of the types of tasks that you might perform as a real-estate paralegal working for a law firm, many of which were also mentioned in Chapter 2 as tasks of the paralegal who specializes in real-estate law:

- Interview a client who wants to buy or sell property.
- Assist the client with the preliminary negotiations (offers and counteroffers) leading up to the purchase contract.

DEVELOPING PARALEGAL SKILLS
Reviewing the Closing Package

Andy Casmis, a paralegal, is reviewing a closing package for his supervising attorney, a sole practitioner. Andy's job is to request the closing package from the lender and review it before the closing takes place. The closing package consists of the purchaser's requirements, closing statement, settlement statement, deed, bill of sale, mortgage documents, and title insurance policy. Andy needs to make sure that there are no mistakes in the closing documents.

CHECKLIST FOR REVIEWING A CLOSING PACKAGE

- Order the closing package as far in advance as possible.
- Set aside uninterrupted time for reviewing the closing package.
- Review the address and legal description of the property in the mortgage note and the deed for accuracy.
- Using a calculator, review the purchaser's requirements sheet, the closing statement, the bill of sale, and the mortgage documents to make sure that there are no numerical errors.
- Review each document to make sure that the parties' names are listed and spelled correctly.
- Review the deed to ensure that the ownership rights are correctly listed and that the names are correct.
- Contact the client and remind him or her of the items that need to be brought to the closing.

- Draft the offers and counteroffers, as well as other documents necessary to the sale.
- Conduct a title examination by going to the county courthouse and examining previous property transfers.
- Obtain or create a title abstract.
- Contact the title company to arrange for the closing.
- Handle the escrow account.
- Attend the closing. (In some states, paralegals are allowed to represent clients at closings.)

Corporations also purchase and sell property, and some larger corporations have real-estate groups within their legal departments. If you work for a corporation that buys and sells a significant amount of property, your employer will be the "client," and you will perform similar tasks on the corporation's behalf.

The law governing real property also comes into play in other contexts than real-estate purchases or sales. If you work in the area of probate administration, for example, you will need to have an understanding of how ownership rights in property may be acquired and transferred.

WILLS, TRUSTS, AND ESTATES

All of the real and personal property that a person owns will be transferred to others on that person's death. For that reason, the laws governing the succession of property are a necessary corollary to the concept of private ownership of property. As discussed in Chapter 2, people usually undertake *estate planning* to control how the transfer of their property ("estate") will occur when they die. *Wills* and *trusts* are two basic devices used in the estate-planning process. We look at these devices, as well as others, in this section. We also discuss the process of *estate administration,* which involves collecting and transferring a decedent's (deceased person's) property.

SUBSTANTIVE LAW CONCEPT SUMMARY
Property Law

Property Classifications	1. *Real property*—Immovable property, including the land and all things attached to it, the minerals below the surface of the land, and the air above the surface of the land. 2. *Personal property*—All property that is not real property (movable property, intangible property).

Ownership Rights in Property	1. *Fee simple*—The most complete form of ownership.
	
	2. *Concurrent ownership*—An interest in property held jointly with others. Types of concurrent ownership include the following:
	  a. Tenancy in common—A form of co-ownership of property in which two or more persons own an undivided interest in the property. On one tenant's death, the property passes to his or her heirs.
	  b. Joint tenancy—A form of co-ownership in which two or more persons own an undivided interest in property. On the death of a joint tenant, the property interest passes to the remaining tenant(s), not to the heirs of the deceased tenant.
	  c. Tenancy by the entirety—A form of co-ownership between a husband and wife that is similar to a joint tenancy, except that a spouse cannot transfer separately his or her interest during his or her lifetime.
	  d. Community property—A form of co-ownership between a husband and wife in which each spouse owns an undivided one-half interest in the property acquired during the marriage (exists in only a few states).
	
	3. *Life estate*—An ownership interest in property that lasts for the life of a specified individual.
	
	4. *Future interest*—A residuary interest (such as the interest of an owner who transfers property to another as a life estate) in existing property that arises only in the future (such as when the holder of the life estate dies).

The Transfer and Sale of Real Property	Property may be transferred by gift, by will or inheritance, by lease, or by sale. Commonly, property is transferred by sale. The sale of real property is governed by the common law of contracts as well as by state (and, to a limited extent, federal) statutory law. For a summary of the basic steps and procedures involved in the sale of real estate, see Exhibit 7.1.
Leases	A lease is a contractual agreement under which a property owner (the lessor) agrees to rent his or her property to another (the lessee) for a specified period of time. Both personal and real property can be leased. 1. *Personal property*—Leases of personal property (cars or equipment) are covered by the Uniform Commercial Code, which spells out the rights and duties of lessors and lessees. 2. *Real property*—Leases of real property are governed in part by the common law of contracts and in part (and to an increasing extent) by state statutory law.

Wills

Testator
One who makes a valid will.

As you learned in Chapter 2, a *will* is the final declaration of how a person desires to have his or her property disposed of after death. The maker of a will is also called a **testator** (from the Latin *testari,* "to make a will"). A will is referred to as a *testamentary disposition* of property, and one who dies after having made a valid will is said to have died **testate**. If no valid will has been executed, a decedent is said to have died **intestate**. When a person dies intestate, state **intestacy laws** govern the distribution of the property among heirs or next of kin.

A will can serve other purposes besides the distribution of property. It can appoint a guardian for minor children or incapacitated adults. It can also appoint a *personal representative* to settle the affairs of the deceased. An **executor** is a personal representative named in a will. An **administrator** is a personal representative appointed by the court for a decedent who dies without a will or who fails to name an executor in the will.

Laws Governing Wills. The laws governing wills come into play when a will is probated. To **probate** (prove) a will means to establish its validity and carry the administration of the estate through a process supervised by a *probate court*. When drafting wills for clients, attorneys and paralegals must make sure that the wills meet the specific requirements imposed by state statute.

Probate laws vary from state to state. In 1969, however, the American Bar Association and the National Conference of Commissioners on Uniform State Laws approved the Uniform Probate Code (UPC). The UPC, which has since been significantly revised, codifies general principles and procedures for the resolution of conflicts in settling estates and relaxes some of the requirements for a valid will contained in earlier state laws. Like other "uniform" laws, the UPC is a model act that does not become law in a state until adopted by that state's legislature. Many states have enacted some part of the UPC and incorporated it into their own probate codes. Nonetheless, succession and inheritance laws vary widely among states, and paralegals should always check the particular laws of the state involved.

Requirements for a Valid Will. A will must comply with state statutory requirements and formalities. If it does not, it will be declared void and the decedent's property will be distributed according to state intestacy laws. Generally, most states uphold the following basic requirements for executing a will:

- *The testator must have testamentary capacity.* In other words, the testator must be of legal age and sound mind *at the time the will is made.*
- *Generally, a will must be in writing.* Exceptions include wills that are completely in the handwriting of the testator and, in a few states, oral "deathbed" wills, made before witnesses, that dispose of personal property.
- *A will must be signed by the testator, generally at the end of the document.*
- *A will must be witnessed.* The number of witnesses (often two, sometimes three), their qualifications, and the manner in which the witnessing must be done are generally determined by state law.
- *In some states, a will must be published.* A will is "published" by an oral declaration by the maker to the witnesses that the document they are about to sign is his or her "last will and testament."

The Probate Process. Typically, probate procedures vary, depending on the size of the decedent's estate. For smaller estates, most state statutes provide for the distribution of assets without formal probate proceedings. Faster and less expensive methods are then used. For example, property can be transferred by *affidavit* (a written statement taken in the presence of a person who has authority to affirm it), and problems or questions can be handled during an administrative hearing. In addition, some state statutes provide that title to cars, savings and checking accounts, and certain other property can be passed merely by filling out forms.

Testate
The condition of having died with a valid will.

Intestate
The state of having died without a valid will.

Intestacy Laws
State statutes that specify how property will be distributed when a person dies intestate (without a valid will).

Executor
A person appointed by a testator to serve as a personal representative on the testator's death.

Administrator
A person appointed by a court to serve as a personal representative for a person who died intestate (without a valid will) or if the executor named in the will cannot serve.

Probate
To prove and validate a will. The process of proving and validating a will and the settling of matters pertaining to the administration of a decedent's estate, guardianship of a decedent's children, and similar matters.

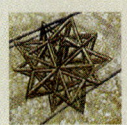

On the Web
To learn more about wills and probate procedures, you can access the UPC online at www.law.cornell.edu/uniform/probate.html.

On the Web
To find the wills of over one hundred famous people from 1493 to the present, go to www.ca-probate.com/wills.

DEVELOPING PARALEGAL SKILLS
Drafting a Client's Will

Mr. Perkins has come to the law firm of Smith & Hardy to have his will prepared. He had previously met with attorney Jennifer Hardy, who has been assisting him in estate planning. Today, Mr. Perkins meets with Jennifer Hardy's paralegal, James Reese, who will review with Mr. Perkins the information that is needed to prepare the will. After the meeting, James returns to his office, inserts a disk into his computer, and begins drafting Mr. Perkins's will. Later in the week, after going over the will with Jennifer Hardy, James will meet with Mr. Perkins so that he can review and sign the will.

CHECKLIST FOR DRAFTING A WILL
- Start with a standard will form.
- Review each provision, or clause, in the standard form.
- Input the client's name, address, and other information.
- Modify the clauses as necessary to fit the client's needs.
- Specifically describe all of the client's assets in the will.
- Number each page and clause of the will.

A majority of states also provide for *family settlement agreements,* which are private agreements among the beneficiaries. Once a will is admitted to probate, the family members can agree to settle among themselves the distribution of the decedent's assets. Although a family settlement agreement speeds the settlement process, a court order is still needed to protect the estate from future creditors and to clear title to the assets involved. The use of these and other types of summary procedures in estate administration can save time and money.

For larger estates, formal probate proceedings are normally undertaken, and the probate court supervises every aspect of the settlement of the decedent's estate. Additionally, in some situations—such as when a guardian for minor children or for an incompetent person must be appointed and a trust has been created to protect the minor or the incompetent person—more formal probate procedures cannot be avoided. Formal probate proceedings may take several months to complete. As a result, a sizable portion of the decedent's assets (up to perhaps 10 percent) may have to go toward payment of fees charged by attorneys and personal representatives, as well as court costs.

Trusts

Trust
An arrangement in which property is transferred by one person (the grantor, or settlor) to another (the trustee) for the benefit of a third party (the beneficiary).

Like wills, trusts are important estate-planning devices. A **trust** involves any arrangement by which legal title to property is transferred from one person to be administered by a trustee for another's benefit. If Mendel conveys his farm to Western Bank to be held for the benefit of his daughters, Mendel has created a trust. Mendel is the *settlor,* or *grantor* (the one creating the trust), Western Bank is the *trustee,* and Mendel's daughters are the *beneficiaries.* A trust can be created for any purpose that is not illegal or against public policy.

There are numerous kinds of trusts, each with its own special characteristics. We look here at some of the most common types of trusts.

Inter Vivos Trust
A trust created by the grantor (settlor) and effective during the grantor's lifetime—that is, a trust not established by a will.

LIVING TRUSTS. A living trust—or **inter vivos** trust (*inter vivos* is Latin for "between or among the living")—is a trust executed by a grantor during his or her lifetime. A living trust may be an attractive estate-planning option because living trusts are not included in the property of a decedent's estate that is probated.

Living trusts can be irrevocable or revocable. The distinction between these two types of living trusts is an important one for estate planners. In an *irrevocable* living trust, the grantor permanently gives up control over the property. In a *revocable* living trust, in contrast, the grantor retains control over the trust property during his or her lifetime.

To establish an irrevocable living trust, the grantor executes a trust deed, and legal title to the trust property passes to the named trustee. The trustee has a duty to administer the property as directed by the grantor for the benefit and in the interest of the beneficiaries. The trustee must preserve the trust property; make it productive; and, if required by the terms of the trust agreement, pay income to the beneficiaries, all in accordance with the terms of the trust. Once an irrevocable *inter vivos* trust has been created, the grantor has, in effect, given over the property for the benefit of the beneficiaries.

To establish a revocable living trust, the grantor deeds the property to the trust but retains the power to amend, alter, or revoke the trust during his or her lifetime. The grantor may also arrange to receive income earned by the trust assets during his or her lifetime. Unless the trust is revoked, the principal of the trust is transferred to the trust beneficiary on the grantor's death.

TESTAMENTARY TRUSTS. A trust created by will to come into existence on the settlor's death is called a **testamentary trust.** Although a testamentary trust has a trustee who maintains legal title to the trust property, actions of the trustee are subject to judicial approval. This trustee can be named in the will or appointed by the court. Thus, a testamentary trust does not fail because a trustee has not been named in the will. The legal responsibilities of the trustee are the same as in an *inter vivos* trust.

Testamentary Trust
A trust that is created by will and that does not take effect until the death of the testator.

If a will that establishes a testamentary trust is invalid, then the trust will also be invalid. The property that was supposed to be in the trust will then pass according to intestacy laws, not according to the terms of the trust.

SPECIAL TYPES OF TRUSTS. A trust designed for the benefit of a segment of the public or the public in general is a *charitable trust*. It differs from other types of trusts in that the identities of the beneficiaries are uncertain. Usually, to be deemed a charitable trust, a trust must be created for charitable, educational, religious, or scientific purposes.

In a *spendthrift trust*, the beneficiary is permitted to draw only a certain portion of the total amount to which he or she is entitled at any one time. The majority of states allow spendthrift trust provisions to prohibit creditors from attaching such trusts. A divorced spouse or a minor child of the beneficiary may be permitted to obtain alimony or child-support payments, however.

A special type of trust created when one person deposits money in his or her own name as a trustee for another is a *Totten trust*,[2] or *tentative trust*. This trust is tentative in that it is revocable at will until the depositor dies or completes the gift in his or her lifetime by some unequivocal act or declaration (for example, delivery of the funds to the intended beneficiary). If the depositor dies before the beneficiary dies and if the depositor has not revoked the trust, normally the beneficiary obtains property rights to the balance on hand.

---

2. This type of trust derives its unusual name from *In the Matter of Totten*, 179 N.Y. 112, 71 N.E. 748 (1904).

On the Web
You can find links to a number of Web sites relating to estate planning at www.ca-probate.com/links.htm.

Other Estate-Planning Devices

Commonly, beneficiaries under a will must wait until the probate process is complete—which can take several months if formal probate proceedings are undertaken—to have access to money or other assets received under the will. For this and other reasons, some persons arrange to have property transferred in ways other than by will and outside the probate process.

One method of accomplishing this is by establishing a living trust, as has already been discussed. A person can also arrange to hold title to certain real or personal property as a joint tenant with a spouse or other person. Remember from earlier in this chapter that in a joint tenancy, when one joint tenant dies, the other joint tenant or tenants automatically inherit the deceased tenant's share of the property. (This is true even if the deceased tenant has provided otherwise in his or her will.) Yet another way of transferring property outside the probate process is by making gifts to children or others while one is still living. Finally, to make sure that a spouse, children, or some other dependent is provided for, many people take out life insurance policies. On the death of the policyholder, the proceeds of the policy go directly to the beneficiary and are not involved in the probate process.

Estate Administration

Estate Administration
The process in which a decedent's personal representative settles the affairs of the decedent's estate (collects assets, pays debts and taxes, and distributes the remaining assets to heirs); the process is usually overseen by a probate court.

Estate administration is the process of collecting a decedent's assets, settling his or her debts, and distributing all remaining assets. These tasks are undertaken by the decedent's personal representative. In every state, however, a special court, usually called a probate court, oversees the administration of decedents' estates. The rights of both creditors and beneficiaries must be protected during the estate-administration proceedings.

If a will exists, it probably names a personal representative (executor) to administer the estate. If there is no will, or if the will fails to name a personal representative, then the court must appoint one (an administrator). The personal representative must inventory and collect the assets of the decedent and, if necessary, have them appraised to determine their value. In addition, the personal representative is responsible for managing the assets of the estate during the administration period and for preventing them from being wasted or unnecessarily depleted.

The personal representative pays debts owed by the decedent and also arranges for the estate to pay taxes. A federal tax is levied on the total value of the estate after debts and expenses for administration have been deducted and after various exemptions have been allowed. The tax is on the estate itself rather than on the beneficiaries. In most states, a state inheritance tax is imposed on the recipient of a decedent's property rather than on the estate. Some states also have a state estate tax similar to the federal estate tax. In general, inheritance tax rates are graduated according to the type of relationship between the beneficiary and the decedent. The lowest rates and largest exemptions are applied to a surviving spouse and the children of the decedent.

When the ultimate distribution of assets to the beneficiaries is determined, the personal representative is responsible for distributing the estate pursuant to the court order. Once the assets have been distributed, an accounting is rendered to the court, the estate is closed, and the personal representative is relieved of any further responsibility or liability for the estate.

Wills, Trusts, and Estates and the Paralegal

Paralegals are often involved in legal work relating to wills, trusts, other estate-planning devices, and estate administration. If you work for a general law prac-

SUBSTANTIVE LAW CONCEPT SUMMARY
Wills, Trusts, and Estates

Wills	1. *Definition*—A will is the final declaration of how a person desires to have his or her property disposed of after death. 2. *Terminology*—A person who dies without a valid will is said to have died *intestate*, and the decedent's property is distributed under state *intestacy laws*. The maker of a will is called a *testator*. A personal representative appointed in a will to settle the affairs of a decedent is called an *executor*. A personal representative appointed by the court for an intestate decedent is an *administrator*. 3. *Requirements of a valid will*—A testator must have testamentary capacity (be of legal age and sound mind at the time the will is made); and the will must be in writing (with some exceptions), must be signed by the testator, must be witnessed, and (in a few states) must be published—the testator must announce to witnesses that the will is his or her "last will and testament." 4. *Probate procedures*—To *probate* a will means to establish its validity and to carry the administration of the estate through a court process. Probate laws vary from state to state. Probate procedures may be informal or formal, depending on the size of the estate and other factors, such as whether a guardian for minor children must be appointed.
Trusts	1. *Definition*—A trust is any arrangement by which property is transferred from one person (the grantor, or settlor) to be administered by another (the trustee) for the benefit of a third party (the beneficiary). 2. *Living* (inter vivos) *trust*—A trust executed by a grantor during his or her lifetime. A living trust may be revocable or irrevocable. 3. *Testamentary trust*—A trust created by will and coming into existence on the death of the grantor. 4. *Special types of trusts*—Include charitable trusts, spendthrift trusts, and Totten trusts.
Other Estate-Planning Devices	1. *Joint ownership of property.* 2. *Gifts to children or others while one is still living.* 3. *Life insurance policies.*
Estate Administration	Estate administration is the process in which a decedent's personal representative (named in the will or appointed by a court) collects the assets, settles the debts, and distributes the remaining assets of the decedent's estate. The rules and procedures for managing the estate of a deceased are controlled by state laws and thus vary from state to state. Estate administration is overseen by a special court, usually called a probate court.

tice, you may be required to assist in handling tasks relating to all of these areas at one time or another. If you specialize in estate planning and administration, you may work for a law firm or a probate court and work extensively with probate proceedings. Among other things, you might be responsible for coordinating the efforts of the personal representative with those of the probate court. An increasing number of paralegals today are specializing in trust law and finding career opportunities in trust departments of banking institutions.

Today's Professional Paralegal

Relocation Assistance

Paralegal Marla Mann works in the real-estate group in the legal department of a large corporation that has offices throughout the United States. Marla works for the attorney who handles employee relocations. Whenever an employee is transferred, the company takes care of all of the arrangements for selling the house that the employee is vacating. Marla works extensively with real-estate agents, attorneys for the purchasers, title companies, and banks and other institutions that provide mortgage financing.

Meeting with a Real-Estate Agent

Marla's telephone rings. It is Lou Holt, a real-estate agent. He has an offer on a transferred employee's house. He will drop it off in about an hour. Marla continues to review the closing documents for the sale of another transferred employee's home. An hour later, the receptionist announces that Lou Holt is in the lobby. Marla walks to the lobby, meets Lou, and takes the offer. Lou tells Marla that he will be out of the office tomorrow and to call his partner, John Stoff, if Marla or her supervising attorney has any questions or if they want to negotiate any of the terms of the offer.

Dealing with Appraisals

Marla's telephone rings again. This time it is June Sember, a loan officer at the National Bank. She has some questions about an appraisal on another house. Marla answers June's questions. June's call reminds Marla that she was going to call Bob Redding, a real-estate appraiser, to set up an appraisal for another house. She calls Bob, and he tells Marla that this afternoon would be the best time for him to appraise the property. They agree to meet at the property at 2 P.M. Marla notes it on her calendar. Marla continues to review the closing package until lunch time.

After lunch, Marla leaves to meet Bob Redding for the appraisal. They walk through the house. Bob looks at every room, takes measurements, and makes notes. He walks around the outside of the house, inspects it, and takes some more measurements. He looks at a book containing the prices for which comparable houses have been sold in the neighborhood. He agrees that this house is worth the price that was offered for it, based on the prices at which other, similar homes have been sold. Bob tells Marla that he will prepare a written appraisal and forward it to the bank, with a copy to her. She thanks him and returns to her office to continue her other work.

Here is just a sampling of the tasks paralegals perform in the areas of wills, trusts, and estates:

- Interview clients to obtain information about their assets and liabilities for estate-planning purposes.
- Draft a will for a client.
- Create the necessary documents to establish a trust for a client.
- Monitor a trust fund's investments to ensure that the funds are not unnecessarily depleted.
- Locate beneficiaries named in a will or the next of kin of a person who died intestate.
- File a will with the probate court to initiate probate procedures.
- Research laws governing estate and inheritance taxes to determine how they apply to a decedent's estate.
- Research state laws governing wills and probate procedures.

KEY TERMS AND CONCEPTS

acceptance 263
administrator 245
agreement 222
assault 216
battery 216
breach of contract 221
consideration 224
contract 221
contractual capacity 224
deed 238
defense 216
eminent domain 231
estate administration 248
executor 245
fee simple 231
intentional tort 215

inter vivos trust 246
intestacy laws 245
intestate 245
joint tenancy 231
lease 239
mortgage 235
negligence 216
offer 222
personal property 231
probate 245
product liability 219
proximate cause 217
punitive damages 215
real property 230
reasonable person standard 217
reformation 226

restitution 226
sales contract 225
Statute of Frauds 224
strict liability 218
tenancy in common 231
testamentary trust 247
testate 245
testator 244
tort 215
trust 246
unconscionable contract 225
Uniform Commercial Code (UCC) 225
warranty 226

CHAPTER SUMMARY

1. A tort is a wrongful act that harms another or another's property. The purpose of tort law is to compensate victims who are harmed by the actions of others, not to punish the wrongdoers; but punitive damages may be awarded to deter certain types of acts.

2. Intentional torts require intention—that is, the wrongdoer must intend to undertake an act and intend the normal consequences of the act, although the intent to harm another is not required. Intentional torts include defamation of character, fraudulent misrepresentation, intentional infliction of emotional distress, false imprisonment, invasion of privacy, and trespass to land.

3. The tort of negligence occurs when an individual's breach of a duty of care causes another to suffer a legally recognized injury. To prove negligence, a plaintiff must show that the defendant had a duty of care, the defendant breached that duty of care, the plaintiff suffered a legally recognizable injury, and the defendant's breach of the duty of care caused that injury.

4. Under the tort doctrine of strict liability, a party may be held liable for a tort even though he or she exercised reasonable care and was not at fault for the harm caused. Examples of the application of strict liability include liability for dangerous animals and product liability.

5. A contract is an exchange of promises, either oral or in writing, that can be enforced in court. Four elements must exist for a valid contract to be formed: agreement (offer and acceptance), consideration, contractual capacity, and a legal purpose. Defenses against contract formation or enforceability include the Statute of Frauds, which requires certain types of contracts to be in writing to be enforceable, as well as the claim that the defendant did not genuinely assent to the terms of the contract. Additionally, contracts that are deemed unconscionable or that are objectively impossible to perform will not be enforced.

6. Contracts for the sale of goods are covered by the Uniform Commercial Code (UCC), which applies when certain terms in a sales contract are absent or unclear. The UCC also has provisions on the types of warranties that can arise when a sales contract is formed.

7. Remedies for breach of contract include money damages to compensate the nonbreaching party for

losses caused by the breach and, when money damages are inadequate, the equitable remedies of specific performance, rescission and restitution, and reformation. The UCC spells out the remedies that are available to the buyer and seller when a sales contract is breached.

8. Real property is land and all things permanently affixed to the land. Personal property includes all other property, as well as intangible property (property—such as ownership rights in stock—that has no physical existence). The most complete form of property ownership is the fee simple. One can also own property concurrently with others (as in a joint tenancy and a tenancy in common) or conditionally, as when property is held as a life estate (for the duration of the life of the holder). Ownership rights in real property can be transferred by gift, will, inheritance, lease, or sale. Most commonly, property is transferred by sale.

9. When real property is sold, the parties form a contract specifying the terms and conditions of the sale. Frequently, the contract is conditioned on the buyer's ability to obtain financing. Buyers normally have the premises inspected to learn of any defects, have the title examined, and (often) obtain title insurance. At the closing, which is the final step in the sales transaction, the deed is transferred to the buyer, the seller receives the proceeds of the sale, and all other accounts are settled, including the payment of closing costs by the buyer and the seller.

10. Estate-planning devices include wills, trusts, life insurance policies, joint ownership, and gifts to heirs made before death. A will, to be valid, must meet specific state statutory requirements. On the death of the testator, the will is probated. The property of a person who dies without a valid will is distributed according to state intestacy laws. A trust is an arrangement in which a property owner transfers property to another for the benefit of a third party. When a person dies, a personal representative collects the assets of the decedent's estate, pays all bills and taxes owed by the decedent, and distributes the remaining assets to the decedent's heirs. Normally, the estate-administration process is overseen by a probate court.

QUESTIONS FOR REVIEW

1. How are torts different from crimes? List and define four intentional torts.

2. How do intentional torts differ from torts arising from negligence? How does the tort doctrine of strict liability differ from the law governing intentional torts and torts arising from negligence?

3. What requirements must be met for a valid contract to be formed? What defenses can be raised against a claim for breach of contract? What remedies are available to the nonbreaching party when a contract is breached?

4. What law governs contracts for the sale of goods (sales contracts)? What is a warranty, and what types of warranties are made in the sale of goods?

5. What is the difference between real property and personal property? What is a fee simple? What are some other ways in which ownership rights in property can be held?

6. What is the most common way of transferring ownership rights in property?

7. What law governs the sale of real property? Describe the basic steps involved in the sale of real estate.

8. What is a lease? Describe some of the provisions that are typically included in lease contracts when real property is involved.

9. What is estate planning? What are the requirements of a valid will? What happens to a person's property if that person dies without a valid will? What is a trust? Name and describe two basic types of trusts.

10. Why and how are wills probated? What are the duties of a personal representative?

ETHICAL QUESTIONS

1. Douglas Coleman works as a paralegal for an oil company. The attorney he works for is responsible for negotiating franchise contracts with people who want to purchase gas-station franchises. Most of those applying for franchises have lawyers who negotiate for them. Bob Little is applying for a franchise with-

out a lawyer to represent him. It is apparent from talking to Little that he does not have much education, and he has indicated that he has never owned a gas station before. He has, however, recently inherited some money, and he wants to achieve his lifelong dream of owning his own gas station.

He has been sent a copy of the standard-form franchise agreement. The standard-form contract is very one sided and unfair to the franchisee (the person purchasing the franchise). Little calls and says that he is ready to negotiate his franchise agreement with the oil company and asks Douglas to set up a telephone conference for that purpose. Douglas would like to tell Little that he really should have a lawyer represent his interests during the negotiations. Can he recommend to Little that he retain a lawyer? Should he give Little any tips about how to negotiate a franchising arrangement with the oil company? What might happen if Douglas does either of these things? What might happen if he does nothing?

2. Jeffrey Singleman is an experienced legal assistant in a tort-law practice. He is given a great deal of responsibility and has minimal supervision. One day, Georgia Wellington, an associate with the firm, has two court appearances scheduled at the same time. One appearance is in federal court, which is on one side of town, and the other is in the county circuit court, which is on the other side of town. Georgia asks Jeffrey to handle the hearing in the county circuit court for her. What should Jeffrey do?

3. Melinda Park has been asked to review an offer to purchase real estate. The offer was made by a client who is a first-time buyer and who has no experience in real-estate transactions. The client wants to understand what the legal obligations of the buyer and the seller are before he signs the offer. Melinda is a new paralegal with the law firm for which she is working, and her supervising attorney, Chad Abraham, gives her the offer to review because he thinks it would be good experience for her. She is to go through the offer, summarize each provision, and note the legal effect of each provision on both the buyer and the seller.

Melinda begins to read the offer, and she sees a paragraph that states that the premises are being sold "as is." Melinda thinks that she understands what this provision means, so she doesn't check on its actual meaning. Instead, she writes, "The house is sold as it appears, and there is no legal effect on the buyer." (The "as is" clause in fact means that there is no warranty on the house; and if there is anything wrong with it, such as a leaking roof, the seller is not obligated to cover repair costs. The buyer must pay for the repairs himself or herself.) What has Melinda done? How could she have better handled the situation?

4. Using the facts from the situation in Ethical Question 3 above, assume that Melinda's supervising attorney did not have time to review her work before giving it to the client. Has the attorney violated any ethical or legal obligation? What effect might Melinda's explanation of the legal effect of the "as is" clause have on the client? On Melinda? On the attorney?

5. Cynthia Warner works as a legal assistant for a sole practitioner, Samuel Weingarten. Mr. Weingarten's practice consists mainly of estate planning and probate. Today, Mr. Weingarten has received a check for $100,000 from the sale of real property that was in an estate that he is probating. Mr. Weingarten instructs Cynthia to deposit the check into the firm's bank account, not the client trust account, because he has some bills to pay. What should Cynthia do? How might she handle this situation with Mr. Weingarten?

Practice Questions and Assignments

1. Using the information on intentional torts and negligence presented in this chapter, identify the following torts:
   a. Mary receives a telephone call at 5:25 P.M. while she is making dinner for her husband, who will be home shortly. The caller says, "I've got your husband and his money, and I'm taking him to Brazil. You'll never see him again." In a panic, Mary, knowing that her husband has just received a large bonus from his employer, suffers a heart attack. The call was actually made by her husband's friend, Joe. Joe frequently plays practical jokes on Mary and her husband, and the call was another one of his pranks.
   b. Susan Stetson has difficulty paying a large bill for a business dinner in a restaurant due to an error by her credit-card company. The restaurant owner takes Susan's purse, which contains her car keys, and prevents Susan from leaving for over two hours while the matter is being resolved.
   c. The *Local Inquirer* publishes an article that claims that the sister of a famous movie star, whose name

it mentions, is dying from AIDS. The article is false and is published without having been investigated by the reporter.

    d. Jennifer is driving her children home from school. The two oldest children are fighting in the back seat. She turns to scold them, taking her eyes off the road temporarily. When she turns back, there is a child on a bike crossing the street in front of her. Jennifer tries but is unable to swerve to avoid hitting the boy.

2. Using the material on ownership rights in property presented in this chapter, identify the types of ownership rights described in the following statements.

    a. John and Linda, a brother and a sister, jointly own a cottage that they inherited from their mother. They have rights of survivorship.

    b. Jeannette conveys her beach-front property to her mother for as long as her mother lives. On her mother's death, the property is to go to Jeanette's daughter.

    c. Louise Winter owns her home, and she may use, possess, or dispose of it as she pleases. On Louise's death, the property will descend to her heirs.

    d. John Tully and Sam Marsh jointly own a large farm in Iowa. If either of them dies, the heirs of the deceased owner will inherit that owner's share of the farm.

3. Using the material on contract law presented in this chapter, identify which defenses the defendants in the following hypothetical cases might use to defend against an action for breach of contract:

    a. Mrs. Martinez, a Spanish-speaking immigrant, buys a washing machine and signs a financing agreement that allows her to pay for it in monthly installments. The agreement contains a clause that allows the store to repossess the appliance if she misses a payment. Mrs. Martinez misses the next-to-the-last payment. The store notifies Mrs. Martinez that she has breached their contract and that it intends to repossess the washing machine. How might Mrs. Martinez defend against the store's action?

    b. Sally orally agrees to purchase a farm from her lifelong friend, Fred. She promises to pay Fred $120,000 for the farm. She trusts Fred, so she does not put the deal in writing. A few days later, Fred sells the same property to Nell for $140,000. Fred and Nell put their agreement in writing. When Sally learns of Fred's contract with Nell, she sues Fred for breach of contract. What is Fred's defense?

    c. Rob enters into a contract with Tom to sell Tom fifty sweaters in Christmas colors and featuring Christmas designs. The first shipment of sweaters is due on October 1, 1999. When the sweaters are not delivered, Tom calls Rob and learns that the factory where the sweaters are produced has burned down. Tom, who is upset because he needed the sweaters for his Christmas catalogue sales, sues Rob for breach of contract. What is Rob's defense?

4. Using the material presented in this chapter on remedies for breach of contract, identify the remedies available to the innocent parties in the following situations:

    a. Mike sells two hundred computers to Heartland University for $100,000. Mike's secretary makes a typographical error when she types the contract, keying in $1,000,000 instead of $100,000. Heartland signs the contract without noticing the error, but later refuses to pay more than $100,000. Mike, taking advantage of the error and Heartland's unwitting agreement to a price of $1,000,000 for the computers, sues Heartland for the full $1,000,000. What remedy will the court likely grant in this situation?

    b. Mrs. Wilcox sells her house to a young couple, the Warners. Among other things, Mrs. Wilcox guarantees that the basement does not leak. Two weeks after the Warners move into the house, the basement floods severely during a rainstorm. The Warners are upset and investigate the problem. They learn that the foundation is cracked and that the basement has always leaked. They contact their lawyer, demanding to get their money back in exchange for returning the house to Mrs. Wilcox. What remedy will the Warners' lawyer seek?

    c. Martha discovers an old painting in the attic of her grandmother's house. Martha has an antiques dealer come to the house and appraise the painting. The dealer offers her $1,000 for it. Martha accepts the dealer's offer and signs a contract of sale. The dealer is to pick up the painting, along with other items that Martha is selling to him, on the following Tuesday. Before the dealer returns, Martha's sister says that she would like to have the painting. Martha then calls the dealer and tells him that she will not be selling him the painting after all. The dealer sues Martha for breach of contract. What remedy might he seek?

5. Using the material presented in this chapter on the sale of real estate, identify the following steps in a real-estate sales transaction:
   a. An offer or counteroffer is accepted.
   b. Title to the property is reviewed to determine the seller's ownership interest and to determine if any liens against the property exist.
   c. The escrow agent transfers the deed to the buyer and the proceeds of the sale to the seller to complete the sale.
   d. The buyer tenders a sum of money, along with the offer.

6. Using the material presented in this chapter, identify which of the following terms belong in a lease agreement:
   a. Buyer's purchase offer.
   b. Quiet enjoyment.
   c. Taxes.
   d. Closing.
   e. Termination.
   f. Title examination.

7. Using the terminology relating to wills, trusts, and estates described in this chapter, identify the term that is normally used to describe each of the following persons (indicated by italics):
   a. *Helen* died without a valid will.
   b. *Anne* is appointed by the court to settle the affairs of her sister, Helen, who died without having made a will.
   c. *Mark* died after having created a valid will.
   d. *Bill*, Mark's brother, was appointed by Mark to settle Mark's affairs on Mark's death.

8. Using the material presented in this chapter on trusts, identify each of the following types of trusts:
   a. Barbara inserts a trust provision in her will requiring that all of her property be held in trust for her children until they reach the age of thirty.
   b. Steve, who is seventy years old, transfers his home into a trust for the benefit of his children and their spouses.
   c. Kathy creates a trust in her will for cancer research.

9. Using the material presented in this chapter on other estate-planning devices, identify which of the following types of estate-planning devices allow property to be transferred outside of the probate process:
   a. Living trusts.
   b. Life insurance.
   c. Testamentary trusts.
   d. Holding property as joint tenants with rights of survivorship.
   e. Gifts to children.

QUESTIONS FOR CRITICAL ANALYSIS

1. Tort law distinguishes between intentional actions that harm others and unintentional acts that harm others. How are they different? Are the consequences any different? Should they be?

2. The tort of intentional infliction of emotional distress imposes liability on a person who engages in extreme and outrageous conduct that causes another to suffer severe emotional distress. How can these types of "injuries" be measured? How can they be compensated? Should this tort be allowed?

3. Negligence law imposes a duty on every member of society to act like a "reasonable person." How did the concept of a duty of care arise? What societal judgment does the reasonable person standard reflect?

4. Proximate cause, also known as legal cause, must be proved to succeed in a negligence case. Foreseeability is one commonly used test of proximate cause. What impact does foreseeability have on the issue of causation? What might happen without such a test?

5. Mrs. Palsgraf was standing on a platform at a train station waiting for a train. Another train pulled up, and two men ran to catch it. The first man boarded the train without incident. The second man, however, ran into difficulty because the train had already begun to move. As he attempted to board the train, a guard on the train pulled him forward, and another guard on the platform pushed him from the platform onto the train. Unbeknownst to the guards, the

package carried by the man, which was covered in newspaper, contained fireworks. When the package fell, it exploded. The explosion caused baggage scales some distance away to tip over and injure Palsgraf, who was standing near the scales. Palsgraf sued the Long Island Railroad. Do you think a court would find that the railroad owed a duty of care to Palsgraf? How would a court view the issue of proximate cause in this case? Write two paragraphs, one analyzing the issue of duty of care and the other the issue of proximate cause.

6. Even if the elements of duty, breach of duty, and causation are met, there can be no recovery in a negligence action if the injury requirement is not met. Why not? Is this principle of tort law fair?

7. In a few states, if a plaintiff in a negligence case can be shown to have contributed at all to the injury, then the plaintiff is completely barred from recovering any damages by the defense of contributory negligence. Is this a fair outcome? With what doctrine have the majority of the states replaced the contributory negligence doctrine?

8. Strict liability imposes liability for injuries suffered by defendants without considering fault. Is this fair in any situation? If so, in which situations? What is the underlying rationale behind imposing strict product liability on defendants?

9. Consideration, a requirement for a valid contract, is defined as *something of value*. What items, other than money, meet this definition? Why does consideration distinguish a contract from a gift?

10. Why are minors allowed to avoid contractual obligations by canceling or disaffirming contracts? Are there any types of contracts that minors may *not* disaffirm? If so, what types of contracts, and why?

11. Legality, a requirement for a valid contract, makes contracts in violation of federal or state laws illegal and void from the outset. Give examples of three different types of contracts that would violate federal or state laws.

12. Our day-to-day transactions, such as buying a can of cola from a vending machine or purchasing groceries with a debit card, involve contracts. Explain how these contracts meet the requirements of a valid contract. Do they meet the requirements of the Statute of Frauds? Would a court enforce these contracts?

13. What does the Statute of Frauds require? How is it used in a contract dispute? Why, during the seventeenth century, might the need have arisen for the Statue of Frauds? Can you think of any reasons, in addition to those given in the chapter, that might have created the need for the Statute of Frauds?

14. A woman agrees that in exchange for $10,000, she will be artificially inseminated, conceive a child, carry the child to term, and after delivery of the baby surrender it to the father and his wife. The mother will terminate her parental rights, and the father's wife will adopt the child. Is this a valid contract? What are the arguments in favor of it being upheld as valid? What are the arguments favoring its invalidation?

15. Why is property ownership described as a "bundle of rights"? What is one called who owns the entire bundle? Is it ever possible to own less than the entire bundle? How? Give an example. Is it possible to share the bundle of rights? How? Give examples.

16. Why is the relationship that exists among an escrow agent, a seller, and a buyer of real estate described as triangular?

17. In a real-estate sales transaction, the buyer is usually the offeror. Is there any situation in which the seller might become the offeror? Explain.

18. Why do people make wills? What happens if they do not? Is it more advantageous for those inheriting property to inherit it by will or through state laws governing intestate succession? Explain.

19. What is the difference between an *inter vivos* trust and a testamentary trust? When would each type of trust be used? Give an example of each.

20. Many attorneys have probate practices in which they administer estates, with paralegals assisting in the collection of a decedent's assets, settling the debts of the estate, or working with the personal representative to accomplish these tasks on behalf of the decedent. How do you feel about performing these types of tasks? Would you be interested in the area of probate administration? Why or why not?

Projects

1. Find out what defenses against negligence are used in your state. Do the courts in your state allow the defense of contributory negligence, or have they adopted the comparative negligence doctrine?

2. Find out what the law is in your state regarding surrogate-parenting contracts. Are they regulated at all? If so, are they legal or illegal? Write a one-page paper summarizing your state's law on this topic.

3. Visit the register of deeds office for your county. Ask to see how and where deeds are recorded. Find out what the term *liber* means. Write a one-page paper summarizing your visit and explaining the meaning of the term *liber*. Check with your instructor prior to undertaking this project for any special instructions or considerations for your county.

4. Easy Soft, Inc., sells software for legal professionals to use. One of its software packages contains real-estate documents. Write to Easy Soft, Inc., at 475 Watchung Ave., Watchung, NJ 07060, or call 1-800-905-SOFT to request information on its real-estate software. Write a three-paragraph summary of the types of real-estate documents available. Explain how these documents would be used in a law office.

5. One task performed by paralegals in a probate-law practice is locating the heirs of a person who died without a will, or intestate. Occasionally, these heirs are unknown or difficult to find. In these instances, a law firm may hire a search business to locate missing heirs. One such firm is International Genealogical Search, Inc. Contact the firm via e-mail at igs@heirsearch.com or by telephone at 1-800-663-2255 to find out what services the company provides and what its rates are. Write a three-paragraph summary of your findings.

Using Internet Resources

1. To learn more about intestacy laws, access the Uniform Probate Code (UPC) at the Web site given below, offered by Cornell University, and then answer the following questions:

    www.law.cornell.edu/uniform/probate.html

    a. How many states have adopted the UPC in its entirety?

    b. How many states have adopted it in part or with modifications?

2. The wills of famous people can be viewed by accessing the wills section of the Court TV Web site at www.ca-probate.com/wills. Go to this Web site and click on the will of Jacqueline Kennedy Onassis. Then answer the following questions:

    a. What did she leave to her children?

    b. What did she leave to Maurice Templesman?

    c. Were any trusts established in her will? If so, for whom? What are the terms of the first trust that was created in her will?

    d. What is a residuary clause? Was one included in this will?

CHAPTER 8

SUBSTANTIVE LAW II

Chapter Outline
■ INTRODUCTION   ■ AGENCY LAW
■ FORMS OF BUSINESS ORGANIZATION   ■ INTELLECTUAL PROPERTY

After completing this chapter, you will know:
- What agency relationships are and why they are established.
- The significance of agency law for business relationships.
- The most common forms of business organizations and how each type of business organizational form is created and operated.
- How profits, losses, risks, and liabilities are distributed in each business organizational form.
- What constitutes intellectual property and the basic forms it takes.

INTRODUCTION

A basic knowledge of the substantive law discussed in the preceding chapter is fundamental for practicing paralegals. Even if you specialize in just one area of the law, you will find that legal concepts overlap considerably. This is certainly true with *agency law,* which we discuss in the beginning of this chapter. Tort law and contract law both overlap with the law of agency, as do many other areas of law, such as employment (discussed in Chapter 9).

Agency is a pervasive common law concept that permeates the business world. Because of this, a discussion of agency relationships provides an excellent background for an examination of business organizations, a topic with which much of this chapter is concerned. Following a description of the various types of business organizations available to entrepreneurs today, we look at intellectual property—a form of property that is increasingly important for business firms.

AGENCY LAW

The common law of agency involves concepts and principles with which all paralegals should be familiar. Agency is a pervasive concept in our society because little work could get done without agents. An **agency** relationship exists when one party, called the **agent,** agrees to represent or act for another party, called the **principal.** If you are working as a paralegal employee, in essence you are an agent of your employer. Attorneys, because they represent and act for their clients, are agents of those clients. All forms of business organizations involve agents. Indeed, a business world without agents is hard to imagine. Picture Henry Ford trying to sell all of the cars that Ford Motor Company manufactured. Obviously, other people must be appointed to fill in—act as agents—for the owner of a large company—the principal.

Normally, all employees who deal with third parties are deemed to be agents. Agency relationships can also arise between employers and independent contractors (such as real-estate agents) who are hired to perform special tasks or services (such as the sale of property).

Fiduciary Duties

An important concept in agency law is that an agency is a **fiduciary relationship**—one involving a high degree of trust and confidence. Because of this, certain legal (fiduciary) duties arise whenever an agency relationship comes into existence.

The principal is obligated to cooperate with the agent, provide safe working conditions for the agent, and reimburse the agent for work performed and for any expenses incurred while working on the principal's behalf. The agent, in turn, must perform his or her tasks competently, obey and be loyal to the principal, notify the principal of knowledge or events significant to the agency, and render an accounting to the principal of how and for what purpose the principal's funds were used. Duties also imply rights. In general, the principal has a right corresponding to every duty owed by the agent, and vice versa. If you read through your state's ethical rules governing attorneys, you will find that many of the rules governing attorney-client relationships are rooted in these agency concepts.

Agency Relationships and Third Parties

Agency law also comes into play when disputes arise over who should be liable—the principal, agent, or both—when an agent forms a contract with a third party or

Agency
A relationship between two persons in which one person (the agent) represents or acts in the place of another (the principal).

Agent
A person who is authorized to act for or in the place of another person (the principal).

Principal
In agency law, a person who, by agreement or otherwise, authorizes another person (the agent) to act on the principal's behalf in such a way that the acts of the agent become binding on the principal.

Fiduciary Relationship
A relationship involving a high degree of trust and confidence.

> # ETHICAL CONCERN
> ## The Paralegal as Agent and Subagent
>
> Whenever an attorney agrees to represent a client, the attorney becomes an agent of the client. But what is the status of the paralegal who works for the attorney-agent on the client's behalf? In this situation, the paralegal becomes both an agent (of the attorney) and a subagent (of the client). Subagents also owe fiduciary duties to the principal. A paralegal who works for a law firm thus has fiduciary duties (as an agent) to the firm and (as a subagent) to the client. As a general rule, you should treat both your attorney and the client as principals and serve their interests with the utmost loyalty and care.

an agent's action causes a third party to suffer harm. Generally, a principal is liable only for the authorized actions of his or her agent. If an agent is not authorized to enter into a contract on behalf of the principal, then normally the principal will not be bound by the contract unless he or she voluntarily accepts (ratifies) it.

An agent may be expressly authorized, either orally or in writing, to form certain contracts; or the agent's authority may be implied by custom—that is, an agent normally has the authority to do whatever is customary or necessary to fulfill the purpose of the agency. A paralegal office manager, for example, has the implied authority to enter into a contract to purchase office supplies on behalf of the firm because the office manager needs to have the authority to purchase supplies to fulfill his or her duties.

A third party injured as a result of an employee's negligence or intentional tort can sue either the employee or the employer. Under the doctrine of *respondeat superior*,[1] the principal-employer is liable for any harm caused to a third party by an agent-employee within the scope of employment. The doctrine imposes **vicarious liability** on the employer—that is, liability without regard to the personal fault of the employer—for torts committed by an employee in the course or scope of employment. The theory of *respondeat superior* is similar in this respect to the theory of strict liability covered in Chapter 7.

Respondeat Superior
A doctrine in agency law under which a principal-employer may be held liable for the wrongful acts committed by agents or employees while acting within the scope of their agency or employment.

Vicarious Liability
Legal responsibility placed on one person for the acts of another.

Agency Law and the Paralegal

A knowledge of agency law is important for the paralegal for several reasons. As a paralegal employee, you will be directly involved in an agency relationship, and it is to your advantage to know what kinds of rights and duties are involved in that relationship. A knowledge of agency law also helps you understand the ethical rules of the legal profession, many of which, as already mentioned, are derived from the common law of agency.

Furthermore, in your work as a paralegal, you will often be dealing with agents. As you will read shortly, each partner in a partnership, for example, is considered an agent of every other partner in the firm and thus has fiduciary duties to the other partners. Corporate officers (such as corporate presidents and vice presidents) are agents of the corporation and, as such, assume the fiduciary duties that arise in agency relationships. Paralegals who work on behalf of corporate clients

---

1. Pronounced ree-*spahn*-dee-uht soo-*peer*-ee-your. The doctrine of *respondeat superior* applies not only to employer-employee relationships but also to principal-agent relationships as long as the principal has the right of control over the agent.

SUBSTANTIVE LAW CONCEPT SUMMARY
The Law of Agency

Agency Law	An agency relationship arises when one person (called the *agent*) agrees to act for or in the place of another person (called the *principal*). Employees who deal with third parties are normally considered to be agents of their employers. Independent contractors may or may not be agents.
Fiduciary Duties	1. *Duties of the principal*—The principal must cooperate with the agent, provide safe working conditions for the agent, and reimburse the agent for work performed and for any expenses incurred while working on the principal's behalf. 2. *Duties of the agent*—The agent must perform his or her tasks competently, obey and be loyal to the principal, notify the principal of knowledge or events significant to the agency, and render an accounting to the principal of how and for what purpose the principal's funds were used.
Agency Relationships and Third Parties	1. *Liability for an agent's contracts*—In an agency relationship, the principal normally is bound by all contracts formed by the agent on behalf of the principal, as long as the action was authorized. If the action was not authorized, the principal will not be liable unless he or she voluntarily agrees to be bound by (ratifies) the contract. 2. *Liability for an agent's torts*—Agents are personally liable for the torts that they commit. If an agent commits a tort within the scope of his or her employment as an agent, the principal may also be held liable under the doctrine of *respondeat superior*.

or who specialize in the area of corporate law will find that agency law permeates the corporate environment.

For paralegals working in the employment context, the doctrine of *respondeat superior* is particularly important because the outcome of many employment cases is influenced by this legal concept. For example, when an employee sues an employer for a supervisor's harassment, the employer may have to pay damages to the employee even though the employer was unaware of the supervisor's actions.

FORMS OF BUSINESS ORGANIZATION

Traditionally, there were three basic forms of business organization: the sole proprietorship, the partnership, and the corporation. These forms continue to be used. In addition, today's business owners and professionals are turning to newer, alternative business organizational forms known as limited liability partnerships or corporations.

Each business form involves different relationships, rights, obligations, and regulatory schemes. In your work as a paralegal, you will want to have some idea of what these rights and duties are when you work on behalf of clients.

Sole Proprietorships

Remember from Chapter 4 that the simplest form of business is the *sole proprietorship*, in which one person—the sole proprietor—owns the business. The sole

On the Web
To learn more about how agency doctrines apply to sexual harassment in today's workplace, access the Supreme Court opinions at www.findlaw.com, and browse through the following two cases decided by the Court in 1998: *Burlington Industries, Inc. v. Ellerth* and *Faragher v. City of Boca Raton*.

Developing Paralegal Skills

A Case of *Respondeat Superior*

Tom Mintin works as a paralegal in a plaintiff's personal-injury litigation firm. A new client, Ms. Bolls, has come into the office seeking representation. Ms. Bolls met with Tom's supervising attorney, Jared Mills. Ms. Bolls, a single parent, and her son Steven were driving home from the grocery store one winter evening in their late-model Volkswagen. They were slowly making their way down an icy street. As they approached an intersection with a stop sign for oncoming traffic, their car was hit by an oncoming Jaguar, which failed to stop at the stop sign. The car was speeding, and the driver went through the stop sign at forty-five miles per hour. In the accident, Steven sustained a severe head injury that resulted in irreparable brain damage.

The wealthy drivers of the Jaguar, a married couple, had gone out for dinner, had several drinks, and then stopped to purchase Christmas cards for clients of the husband's employer, a multimillion-dollar business. The driver's license was suspended for driving under the influence of alcohol. Jared Mills asks Tom to research the issue of whether the multimillion-dollar business can be held liable for the car accident under a theory of *respondeat superior*, given that the wealthy couple had stopped to purchase Christmas cards on their way home from dinner. Tom researches the issue and learns that an employer is liable under *respondeat superior* for the negligent acts of an employee if the acts were committed in the scope of his or her employment. The employer may also be liable for an employee's acts if the acts occur while the employee is on a brief "detour" from the employer's work—such as when a paralegal employee stops by the dry cleaners for personal reasons while on the way to the courthouse for his employer. The employer is not liable, however, if the employee is on a "frolic" of his or her own and is not pursuing work that he or she was hired to perform.

Checklist for Determining Liability under the Doctrine of *Respondeat Superior*

- Did the employee commit a tort?
- If so, was the tort one of negligence, as opposed to an intentional tort such as an assault or battery?
- Was the negligence committed by the employee within the scope or course of his or her employment?
- If the answer to the question above is no, then was the act committed during a brief detour from the employee's course of employment, or was the employee on a "frolic" of his or her own when the act was committed?

---

proprietor is entitled to all of the business's profits and bears personal responsibility for all of the business's debts and other obligations. Sole proprietors can own and manage any type of business, from an informal, home-office undertaking to a large restaurant or construction firm. Sole proprietorships are very common. In fact, they constitute over two-thirds of all American businesses. They are also usually small enterprises—fewer than 1 percent of the sole proprietorships in the United States earn over $1 million per year.

FORMATION OF A SOLE PROPRIETORSHIP. The sole proprietorship is usually easier and less costly to start than any other kind of business, as few legal forms are involved. No partnership agreement need be devised, because there are no partners. No papers need be filed with the state (as when a corporation is formed) to establish the business. At most, there will be only minor paperwork involved, depending on the law of the city in which the business is located. Generally, anyone who does business without creating a separate business entity, such as a partnership or a corporation, has a sole proprietorship.

Because it is the simplest business form to create, persons first starting up a business often choose to operate as sole proprietors. An attorney or a freelance paralegal might begin doing business as a sole proprietor. (Recall from Chapter 4 that an attorney who practices law as a sole proprietor is often called a *sole practitioner,* or *solo practitioner.*)

ADVANTAGES OF SOLE PROPRIETORSHIPS. A major advantage of the sole proprietorship is that the sole proprietor is entitled to all the profits made by the firm (because he or she takes all the risk). The sole proprietor is also free to make any decision he or she wishes concerning the business—whom to hire, when to take a vacation, what kind of business to pursue, and so on. Additionally, sole proprietors are allowed to establish tax-exempt retirement accounts, such as Keogh plans. (A Keogh plan is a retirement program designed for self-employed persons by which such persons can shelter a certain percentage of their income from taxation. The principal and interest earnings are not taxed until funds are withdrawn from the plan.)

DISADVANTAGES OF SOLE PROPRIETORSHIPS. A major disadvantage of the sole proprietorship is that the proprietor alone, as the firm's sole owner, is personally liable for any losses, debts, and obligations incurred by the business enterprise. As discussed in Chapter 4, *personal liability* means that the personal assets of the business owner (such as a home, car, savings account, or other tangible or intangible property) may be subject to creditors' claims if the business fails.

As a paralegal, if you are asked to do a preliminary investigation of a client's claim against a business entity, one of the first things you should check is the form of the business. For example, suppose that your firm's client wants to sue a business firm for damages. If you learn that the firm is a sole proprietorship, then you will know that if the firm itself has insufficient assets to pay damages to the client (should the client win in court), the firm's owner will personally be liable for the damages. Depending on what you learn about the firm's financial condition, you may want to investigate the owner's personal financial position as well.

Another disadvantage of the sole proprietorship is that if its owner wishes to expand the business, it is difficult to obtain capital. The sole proprietor is dependent on loans made by lending institutions and others. For this reason, sole proprietors sometimes decide to take on partners, who will contribute capital to the business, or to incorporate and sell shares in the business to raise funds.

TAXATION AND SOLE PROPRIETORSHIPS. A sole proprietor must pay income taxes on business profits, but he or she does not have to file a separate tax return for the business. Rather, the profits are reported on the sole proprietor's personal tax return and taxed as personal income.

TERMINATION OF THE SOLE PROPRIETORSHIP. In a sole proprietorship, the owner is the business. For that reason, when the owner dies, so does the business—it is automatically dissolved. If the business is to be transferred to family members or other heirs, a new proprietorship is created. Similarly, if the proprietor sells the business, whoever purchases it must establish either a new sole proprietorship or some other business form, such as a partnership or a corporation.

Partnerships

As discussed in Chapter 4, many law firms organize their business in the form of a *partnership,* which arises when two or more individuals undertake to do business together as *partners.* Each partner owns a portion of the business and shares jointly in the firm's profits or losses. Partners are personally liable for the debts and obligations of the business if the business fails, just as sole proprietors are.

On the Web
You can find links to most uniform laws online at www.lawsource.com.

The Uniform Partnership Act (UPA) governs the operation of partnerships. (The UPA is one of a number of "uniform" laws drafted by legal experts and submitted to the states for adoption. Uniform laws, like the American Bar Association's codes and rules, are model laws. They become actual law only when adopted by the states.) Except for Louisiana, the UPA has been adopted in all of the states, as well as in the District of Columbia. A revised version of the UPA, known as the Revised Uniform Partnership Act (RUPA), has been adopted by several states, and other states are considering its adoption. Always keep in mind, however, the following rule:

 The provisions of the UPA (or the RUPA) govern a partnership only if the partners have not expressly agreed otherwise.

PARTNERSHIP FORMATION.   Under the UPA, a partnership is defined as "an association of two or more persons to carry on as co-owners a business for profit." To create a partnership, two or more persons interested in establishing a profit-making business simply agree to do so, as partners. The partnership agreement can be expressed orally or in writing, or it can be implied by conduct. If the partnership is to continue for over a year, then the agreement must be in writing to satisfy the Statute of Frauds, a state statute that specifies what types of contracts must be in writing to be enforceable (discussed in Chapter 7).

RIGHTS AND DUTIES OF PARTNERS.   When two or more persons agree to do business as partners, they enter into a special relationship with one another. To an extent, their relationship is similar to an agency relationship because each partner is deemed the agent of the other partners and of the partnership.

Partnership law is distinct from agency law in one significant way, however. A partnership is based on a voluntary contract between two or more competent persons who agree to place some or all of their money or other assets, labor, and skill in a business, with the understanding that profits and losses will be proportionately shared. In a nonpartnership agency relationship, the agent usually does not have an ownership interest in the business, nor is he or she obligated to bear a portion of the ordinary business losses.

The rights of partners are often written into the partnership agreement. If the agreement does not specify these rights, then the UPA comes into play (the state's version of the UPA or RUPA, as adopted). Some of the important rights of partners are listed in Exhibit 8.1.

LIABILITY OF PARTNERS.   Historically, a partnership could not be sued or initiate a lawsuit in its own name. This traditional rule treated all partnerships as aggregates of individuals. Under this rule, which is still followed in some states,

EXHIBIT 8.1
Rights of Partners

PARTNERS HAVE THE RIGHT:

- To hold an ownership interest in the firm and to receive a share of the profits.
- To inspect partnership books and records.
- To an accounting of partnership assets and profits (for example, to determine the value of each partner's share in the partnership). An accounting can be performed voluntarily or can be compelled by a court order. Formal accounting occurs by right in connection with partnership dissolution proceedings.
- To participate in the management of the business operation unless the partnership agreement specifies otherwise.

> ## ETHICAL CONCERN
> ### The Paralegal as an Apparent Partner
>
> If you work as a paralegal for a law partnership, you need to be especially careful to ensure that clients do not mistakenly conclude that you are an attorney-partner of the firm. For example, assume that you and your supervising attorney are waiting for a client to arrive for an intake interview. You are sitting in the attorney's office talking about another matter when the client arrives. During the course of the interview, the attorney asks you about an ordinance just passed by the city that might affect the client's planned renovations of an office building. Your answer indicates that you are knowledgeable in the law. The client leaves the office assuming that you are an attorney, even though you were introduced as the attorney's legal assistant. Should the client ever sue the firm and/or the partners, you may be subject to liability as an "apparent partner" if the client convinces the court that you "held yourself out as an attorney."

only the individual partners—not the partnership—can be sued. Because this approach is so cumbersome, most states today recognize the partnership as an entity that may sue or be sued and collect judgments in the partnership's name.

A distinguishing feature of the partnership, and one that is often regarded as a disadvantage of this form of business, is the potentially extensive personal liability faced by partners for partnership obligations and for the actions of the other partners. Partners have **joint liability,** or shared liability. In other words, partners may be held personally liable not only for their own actions and those of the partnership as an entity but also for the actions of other partners.

Partners may also be subject to **joint and several liability**—*several* liability means *individual* liability.[2] Joint and several liability allows a plaintiff to sue and seek judgment against any one—or all—of the jointly liable defendants. Fault is not an issue. In a partnership, joint and several liability gives a third party the option of suing any one or more of the partners without suing all of them or the partnership itself. The third party may even sue a partner who had no knowledge of the circumstances that gave rise to the cause of action.

For example, suppose that a plaintiff wants to recover for damages allegedly caused by a physician's negligence (medical malpractice). The physician is one of four partners who own a partnership. The plaintiff could sue the physician who allegedly caused the harm, the partnership, one of the other physicians (even if that physician had nothing to do with the plaintiff's treatment), or all of the physicians to recover damages. The liability faced by partners is a major reason for the rapid growth of a new form of partnership, the limited liability partnership, which will be discussed later.

TAXATION OF PARTNERSHIPS. The partnership itself, as an entity, does not pay federal income taxes. The partnership as an entity files an information return with the Internal Revenue Service on which the income received by the partnership is reported. The partners declare their shares of the partnership's profits on their personal income tax returns and pay taxes accordingly.

Joint Liability
Shared liability. In partnership law, partners incur joint liability for partnership obligations and debts.

Joint and Several Liability
In partnership law, joint and several liability means that a third party may sue one or more of the partners separately or all of them together. This is true even if one of the partners sued did not participate or know about whatever gave rise to the cause of action.

---

2. The term *several* stems from the medieval English term *severall,* which meant "separately," or "severed from" one another. As used here, *several* liability means *separate* (individual) liability.

PARTNERSHIP TERMINATION. The partnership agreement may specify the duration of the partnership by indicating that the partnership will end on a certain date or on the occurrence of a certain event. It would be a breach of the partnership agreement for one partner to withdraw from the partnership before the specified date arrived or the specified event occurred. The withdrawing partner would be liable to the remaining partners for any related losses.

When an agreement does not specify the duration of the partnership, the partners are free to withdraw at any time without incurring liability to the remaining partners. Under the UPA, withdrawal by a partner results in the **dissolution** (the formal disbanding) of the partnership (although a new partnership may arise among those who stay with the enterprise). Under the revised UPA (RUPA), however, the withdrawal of a partner causes a partnership to be dissolved only if the withdrawal results in the breakup of the partnership itself and the business cannot continue. The occurrence of certain events also results in partnership termination. The death or bankruptcy of a partner, for example, terminates the partnership.

Partnership termination is a two-step process. Dissolution is the first step in the process. The second step is the **winding up** of partnership affairs. Once the firm is dissolved, it continues to exist legally until the process of winding up all business affairs (collecting and distributing the firm's assets) is complete.

LIMITED PARTNERSHIPS. Ordinary partnerships, such as those just discussed, are often referred to as *general partnerships*. The **limited partnership,** in contrast, is a special form of partnership involving two different types of partners—general partners and limited partners. The *general partners* manage the business and have the rights and liabilities of partners in a general partnership. The *limited partners* are, for the most part, simply investors in the business. A limited partnership may be formed, for example, to purchase and develop real estate. The limited partners play a passive role. Their funds help to finance the venture, and they receive a share of the profits in return.

The limited partner does not participate in the management of the partnership and, in return, enjoys limited liability status. Unlike general partners, who are personally liable for partnership obligations, limited partners are liable only up to the amount that they have invested. In other words, if the partnership goes bankrupt they will lose their investments but cannot be held liable for partnership debts beyond that amount.

In contrast to the informal, private, and voluntary agreement that usually suffices to create a general partnership, the formation of a limited partnership is a public and formal proceeding that must follow state statutory requirements. The partners must sign a *certificate of limited partnership*, which requires information similar to that found in a corporate charter. The certificate must be filed with the designated state official (usually, the secretary of state). In this respect, the limited partnership resembles the corporation—another creature of statute.

Corporations

Paralegals frequently work on behalf of corporate clients or on legal matters involving corporations. An increasing number of paralegals are also now working for corporate employers. As a paralegal, you should thus have a basic knowledge of how corporations are formed and operated. You should also be familiar with the basic rights and responsibilities of corporate personnel. As discussed in Chapter 4, corporate personnel include the *shareholders* (the owners of the business, called shareholders because they purchase corporate **shares,** or stock), the **directors** (persons

---

Dissolution
The formal disbanding of a partnership or a corporation.

Winding Up
The process of winding up all business affairs (collecting and distributing the firm's assets) after a partnership or corporation has been dissolved.

Limited Partnership
A partnership consisting of one or more general partners (who manage the business and are liable to the full extent of their personal assets for debts of the partnership) and of one or more limited partners (who contribute only assets and are liable only up to the amount of their contributions).

Share
A unit of stock; a measure of ownership interest in a corporation.

Director
A person elected by the shareholders to direct corporate affairs.

elected by the shareholders to direct corporate affairs), and the **officers** (persons hired by the directors to manage the day-to-day operations of the corporation).

Although it is owned by individuals, the corporation is a separate legal entity, which is created and recognized by state law. In the eyes of the law, a corporation is a legal "person" that enjoys many of the rights and privileges that U.S. citizens enjoy, such as the right of access to the courts as an entity that can sue or be sued. It also has, among other rights, the right to due process of law and the right to freedom from unreasonable searches and seizures.

The Model Business Corporation Act (MBCA) is a codification of modern corporation law that has been influential in the codification of corporation statutes. Today, the majority of state statutes are guided by a revision of the MBCA known as the Revised Model Business Corporation Act (RMBCA). There is, however, considerable variation among the statutes of the states that have based their statutes on the MBCA or the RMBCA, and several states do not follow either act.

> **Because of this, as a paralegal you will need to rely on individual state corporation laws rather than the MBCA or RMBCA.**

We look now at corporate formation; various classifications of corporations; the rights and responsibilities of corporate personnel; and corporate mergers, consolidations, and termination.

CORPORATE FORMATION. Generally, forming a corporation involves two steps. The first step consists of preliminary organizational and promotional undertakings—particularly, obtaining capital for the future corporation. Before a corporation becomes a reality, people invest in the proposed corporation as *subscribers*. The subscribers become the shareholder-owners of the corporation when the corporation becomes a legal entity.

Contracts to purchase corporate shares (stock) are frequently made by *promoters* on behalf of the future corporation. Promoters are those who, for themselves or others, take the preliminary steps in organizing a corporation. One of the tasks of the promoter is to issue a prospectus. A **prospectus** is a document that describes the corporation and its operations so that those who wish to purchase stock (invest) in the corporation have the basis for making an informed decision.

The second step in forming a corporation is the process of incorporation. Exact procedures for incorporation differ among states, but the basic requirements are similar. The primary document needed to begin the incorporation process is called the **articles of incorporation** (see Exhibit 8.2 on page 268 for sample articles of incorporation for a small corporation). The articles include basic information about the corporation and serve as a primary source of authority for its future organization and business functions. Once they have been filed in the appropriate state office, the articles of incorporation will become a public record.

Paralegals frequently assist their supervising attorneys in preparing incorporation papers and filing them with the appropriate state office. Also, as a paralegal, you may need to obtain information about a corporation—for example, when you are conducting an investigation. For both of these reasons, you should know what information is generally included in the articles of incorporation. Exhibit 8.3 on page 269 lists and describes this kind of information.

After the articles of incorporation have been prepared, signed, and authenticated by the incorporators, they are sent to the appropriate state official, usually the secretary of state, along with the appropriate filing fee. In many states, the secretary of state then issues a **certificate of incorporation** representing the state's authorization for the corporation to conduct business. (This may be called the **corporate charter**.) The certificate and a copy of the articles are returned to the

Officer
A person hired by corporate directors to assist in the management of the day-to-day operations of the corporation. Corporate officers include the corporate president, vice president, secretary, treasurer, and possibly others, such as a chief financial officer and chief executive officer. Corporate officers are employees of the corporation and subject to employment contracts.

On the Web
Corporate statutes for all but a few states are now online at fatty.law.cornell.edu/topics/state_statutes.html.

Prospectus
A document that discloses relevant facts about a company and its operations so that those who wish to purchase stock (invest) in the corporation have the basis for making an informed decision.

Articles of Incorporation
The document filed with the appropriate governmental agency, usually the secretary of state's office, when a business is incorporated. State statutes usually prescribe what kind of information must be contained in the articles of incorporation.

Certificate of Incorporation (Corporate Charter)
The document issued by a state official (usually the secretary of state) granting a corporation legal existence and the right to function.

EXHIBIT 8.2
Articles of Incorporation

Filed with Secretary of State
_____, 20_____

SHORT FORM
ARTICLES OF INCORPORATION
OF
Hiram, Inc.

ARTICLE I

The name of this corporation ___Hiram, Inc.___

ARTICLE II

The purpose of this corporation is to engage in any lawful act or activity for which a corporation may be organized under the General Corporation Law of New Pacum other than the banking business, the trust company business, or the practice of a profession permitted to be incorporated by the New Pacum Corporation Code.

ARTICLE III

The name and address in the State of New Pacum of this corporation's initial agent for service of process is: ___Hiram Galliard, 8934 Rathburn Avenue, North Bend, New Pacum 98754___

ARTICLE IV

The corporation is authorized to issue only one class of shares of stock; and the total number of shares that this corporation is authorized to issue is ___10,000.___

ARTICLE V

The corporation is a close corporation. All the corporation's issued shares of stock shall be held of record by not more than ten (10) persons.

DATED: ___June 3, 2000___

___Hiram Galliard___ ___Martha Bonnell___
[Signature(s) of Incorporator/ Directors(s)]

I (we) hereby declare that I (we) am (are) the person(s) who executed the foregoing Articles of Incorporation, which execution is my (our) act and deed.

___Hiram Galliard___ ___Martha Bonnell___

---

incorporators, who then hold the initial organizational meeting that completes the details of incorporation.

CLASSIFICATIONS OF CORPORATIONS. Corporations are classified in several ways. How a corporation is classified depends on its purpose, ownership characteristics, and location. A *private corporation* is, as the term indicates, a corporation that is privately owned. A *public corporation* is formed by the government for a political or governmental purpose, as when a town incorporates. Note that a public corporation is not the same as a publicly held corporation. A *publicly held corporation* is any corporation whose shares are publicly traded in securities markets, such as the New York Stock Exchange.

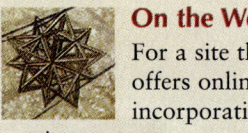

On the Web
For a site that offers online incorporation services, go to www.bizfilings.com.

EXHIBIT 8.3

Information Generally Included in the Articles of Incorporation

---

THE NAME OF THE CORPORATION

- The choice of a corporate name is subject to state approval to ensure against duplication or deception. State statutes usually require that the secretary of state run a check on the proposed name in the state of incorporation. Once cleared, a name can be reserved for a short time, for a fee, pending the completion of the articles of incorporation.

THE NATURE AND PURPOSE OF THE CORPORATION

- The intended business activities of the corporation must be specified in the articles, and, naturally, they must be lawful. Stating a general corporate purpose (for example, "to engage in the production and sale of agricultural products") is usually sufficient to give rise to all of the the powers necessary or convenient to the purpose of the organization.

THE DURATION OF THE CORPORATION

- A corporation can have perpetual existence under most state corporate statues. A few states, however, prescribe a maximum duration after which the corporation must formally renew its existence.

THE CAPITAL STRUCTURE OF THE CORPORATION

- The captial structure of the corporation is generally set forth in the articles. A few state statutes require relatively small capital investment (for example, $1,000) for ordinary business corporations but a greater capital investment for those engaged in insurance or banking. The number of shares of stock authorized for issuance, their valuation, the various types or classes of stock authorized for issuance, and other relevant information concerning equity, capital, and credit must be outlined in the articles.

THE INTERNAL ORGANIZATION OF THE CORPORATION

- Whatever the internal management structure of the corporation, it should be described in the articles, although it can be included in bylaws adopted after the corporation is formed.

THE REGISTERED OFFICE AND AGENT OF THE CORPORATION

- The corporation must be indicate the location and address of its registered office within the state. Usually, the registered office is also the principal office of the corporation. The corporation must give the name and address of a specific person who has been designated as an agent and who can receive legal documents (including service of process) on behalf of the corporation.

THE NAMES AND ADDRESSES OF THE INCORPORATORS

- Each incorporator must be listed by name and must indicate an address. An incorporator is a person—often, the corporate promoter—who applies to the state on behalf of the corporation to obtain its corporate charter. The incorporator need not be a shareholder and need not have any interest at all in the corporation. Many states do not impose residency or age requirements for incorporators. States vary on the required number of incorporators; it can be as few as one or as many as three. Incorporators are required to sign the articles of incorporation when they are submitted to the state; often this is their only duty. In some states, they participate at the first organizational meeting of the corporation.

Corporations may also be classified as either *for-profit corporations* or *not-for-profit* (or *nonprofit*) *corporations*. Not-for-profit corporations may be formed by a group—such as a charitable association, a hospital, or a religious organization—to conduct its business without exposing the individual owners to personal liability.

DEVELOPING PARALEGAL SKILLS
Reserving a Corporate Name

Jon Thomas is a paralegal in a law firm that specializes in corporate law. Jon and his supervising attorney have just concluded a meeting with new clients who want to incorporate their existing partnership. They want to use their current name, L&J Building Construction. Jon's assignment is to find out if the name is available and then, if it is, to reserve it. He calls the 900 number for the state's department of commerce and learns that the name is available. Next, Jon goes online, accesses the department of commerce's Web site, and downloads and prints out the corporate name reservation form. He prepares the form and immediately faxes it to the department.

TIPS FOR RESERVING A CORPORATE NAME

- Have the preferred name and several alternatives available.
- Make sure the client understands that the name selected may not be available.
- Determine whether the name is available before reserving it.
- Once you learn that the name is available, file the corporate name reservation form immediately.

Corporations owned by a small group of shareholders, such as family members, are called *close,* or *closely held, corporations.* Unlike large corporations, close corporations cannot sell their shares on public securities markets and usually place restrictions on the transfer of corporate shares—to keep the business in the family, for example, or for some other reason. State laws may provide more flexibility for close corporations, in terms of statutory formalities that must be observed, than for other corporations. Also, certain close corporations are permitted to elect a special corporate tax status under Subchapter S of the Internal Revenue Code. These corporations are called *S corporations.*

Lawyers, physicians, accountants, architects, engineers, and other professionals frequently incorporate as *professional corporations.* As discussed in Chapter 4, law firms often prefer to incorporate as professional corporations (P.C.s) rather than operate as partnerships. A professional corporation may also be designated as a service corporation (S.C.) or a professional association (P.A.).

DIRECTORS AND OFFICERS. The articles of incorporation name the initial board of directors, which is appointed by the incorporators. Thereafter, the board of directors is elected by a majority vote of the shareholders. The board holds formal meetings and records the minutes. Each director has one vote, and generally the majority rules. The directors' rights include the right to participate in board meetings and the right to inspect corporate books and records. The director's responsibilities to the corporation and its shareholders include declaring and paying **dividends** (payments to shareholders representing their share of corporate profits), appointing and removing officers, and making significant policy decisions.

The board of directors appoints the corporate officers, who manage the day-to-day operations of the firm. They include the president, vice president, secretary, treasurer, chief financial officer, and chief executive officer. The officers are employees of the corporation and are subject to employment contracts. As employees, they are also agents of the corporation.

Directors and officers have fiduciary duties to the corporation and its shareholder-owners, including the duty of loyalty and the duty to exercise reasonable care when conducting corporate business. The duty of loyalty is breached when an officer or director uses corporate funds or confidences for personal gain,

Dividend
A distribution of profits to corporate shareholders, disbursed in proportion to the number of shares held.

as when an officer discloses company secrets (such as a proposed merger) to an outsider. The duty of care is breached when a director's or officer's negligence—failure to exercise reasonable care in corporate operations or decision making—results in harmful consequences for the corporate entity.

SHAREHOLDERS. Any person who purchases a share in a corporation becomes an owner of the corporation. Through shareholders' meetings, the shareholders play an important role in the corporate entity—they elect the directors who control the corporation, and they have a right to vote (one vote per share) on decisions that significantly affect the corporation. They also have a right to a share in corporate profits proportionate to the number of shares they hold. Shareholders do not manage the daily affairs of the corporation, nor are they liable for corporate debts or other obligations beyond the amount of their investments. Corporate owners, or shareholders, thus have *limited liability*—a key advantage of the corporate form of business.

CORPORATE TAXATION. The corporation as an entity pays income taxes on corporate profits. Then, when the profits are distributed to the shareholders in the form of dividends, the shareholders pay personal income taxes on the income they receive. This double-taxation feature of the corporate form of business is one of its major disadvantages.

Some small (close) corporations are permitted to avoid the double taxation of corporate profits by electing S corporation status under Subchapter S of the Internal Revenue Code. An S corporation, like a partnership, is a "pass-through" entity for tax purposes. This means that the corporation itself does not pay income taxes. Instead, it files an information return only, as a partnership does, indicating the corporation's net profits. The S corporation shareholders declare their proportionate shares of the corporation's net income on their personal tax returns and pay taxes on that income accordingly.

CORPORATE MERGER AND CONSOLIDATION. As a paralegal, you may be asked to help a corporate client in procedures relating to major corporate changes, such as a merger or a consolidation. A **merger** is a process through which one corporation (the surviving corporation) acquires all of the assets and liabilities of another corporation (the merged corporation). The shareholders of the merged corporation receive payment for their shares, either in cash or in shares in the surviving corporation. A **consolidation** is a similar process. The difference is that in a consolidation, both existing corporate entities disappear and a completely new corporation is formed. The differences between a merger and a consolidation are illustrated graphically in Exhibit 8.4 on the next page.

State laws vary somewhat as to the procedures that must be undertaken to accomplish a merger or a consolidation. As a paralegal, you will need to find out what the specific requirements are in your state. Generally, the following requirements must be met:

- The boards of directors and the shareholders of each corporation involved must approve the merger or consolidation.
- Once the merger or consolidation is approved by these groups, articles of merger or articles of consolidation must be filed with the state, usually with the secretary of state's office.
- When state formalities have been satisfied, the state issues a certificate of merger to the surviving corporation or a certificate of consolidation to the newly consolidated corporation.

Merger
A process in which one corporation (the surviving corporation) acquires all of the assets and liabilities of another corporation (the merged corporation).

Consolidation
A process in which two or more corporations join to become a completely new corporation. The original corporations cease to exist.

EXHIBIT 8.4
Merger and Consolidation

A merger involves the legal combination of two or more corporations in such a way that only one of the corporations continues to exist. For example, Corporation A and Corporation B decide to merge. It is agreed that A will absorb B, so after the merger, B ceases to exist as a separate entity and A continues as the surviving corporation. Consolidation occurs when two or more corporations combine in such a way that both corporations cease to exist and a new one emerges. For example, Corporation A and Corporation B consolidate to form an entirely new organization, Corporation C. In the process, A and B both are terminated as legal entities, and C comes into existence as an entirely new entity.

```
        Merger                    Consolidation

      A     B                       A     B
        ↓                             ↓
        A                             C
```

On the Web
Hoover's Online has an extensive collection of data on U.S. corporations at www.hoovers.com.

As a paralegal, you should realize the difference in legal effect between a merger or a consolidation and an *acquisition,* which occurs when one corporation acquires or purchases all or almost all of the assets of another company. In a merger or a consolidation, the surviving corporation or the newly consolidated corporation assumes not only the assets but also the liabilities of the previously existing entities. If a person has a valid claim against one of those entities, this claim is a liability that will be assumed by the surviving or newly consolidated corporation. A person injured by a defective product manufactured by one of the previously existing corporations, for example, could sue the surviving or new corporation and recover damages. In contrast, if an acquisition has occurred, the acquiring corporation has acquired the assets of the other corporation but normally has not assumed responsibility for the liabilities of that corporation.

CORPORATE TERMINATION. As with partnership termination, the process of corporate termination involves two steps. The first step, dissolution, extinguishes the legal existence of the corporation. The second step, **liquidation,** involves the winding up of the corporation's business affairs. After creditors have been paid, all remaining assets are distributed to the shareholders.

Corporations can be terminated at a time specified in the articles of incorporation or by the agreement of the shareholders and the board of directors. In certain circumstances, a court may dissolve a corporation. For example, if the directors are deadlocked and cannot agree on the management of the corporation, a court may grant a shareholder's petition to dissolve the corporation. A corporation may also be terminated by law if it fails to meet certain statutory requirements, such as the payment of taxes or annual fees.

Liquidation
In regard to corporations, the process by which corporate assets are converted into cash and distributed among creditors and shareholders according to specific rules of preference.

Limited Liability Companies and Partnerships

In recent years, two new forms of limited liability business organizations have emerged, the limited liability company and the limited liability partnership. The use of these new forms is spreading quickly because of the advantages they offer to businesspersons in regard to business taxation and liability—advantages not available through the partnership and corporate forms of business.

For example, one of the major tax advantages of a partnership is that the partnership's income passes through to the partners as personal income. Consequently, partners avoid the double-taxation feature of the corporate form of business. But there is a price to pay for this tax advantage: partners face unlimited personal liability. The partners can avoid unlimited personal liability by incorporating their business, because corporate owners (shareholders) have limited liability. But again, there is a price to pay for this limited liability: the double taxation of profits characteristic of the corporate form of business.

As mentioned, one way to achieve both goals—limited liability and single taxation of profits—is to elect S corporation status. Certain requirements must be met, however, before a corporation can qualify for S corporation status. One requirement is that the corporation have seventy-five or fewer shareholders, thus excluding large firms. Another requirement is that an S corporation may only have one class of stock (meaning that there is little flexibility in how corporate profits are distributed). Additionally, certain entities (such as partnerships and, with some exceptions, corporations) cannot be shareholders in an S corporation.

LIMITED LIABILITY COMPANIES. The **limited liability company (LLC)** is a hybrid form of business enterprise that combines the pass-through tax benefits of S corporations and partnerships with the limited liability of limited partners and corporate shareholders. Like the limited partnership and the corporation, an LLC must be formed and operated in compliance with state law. To form an LLC, *articles of organization* must be filed with a central state agency, such as the secretary of state's office. The business's name must include the word "Limited Liability Company" or the initials "L.L.C."

A major advantage of the LLC is that, as indicated, it does not pay taxes as an entity. Rather, profits are "passed through" the LLC and paid personally by the owners of the company, who are called *members* instead of shareholders. Another key advantage is that the liability of members is limited to the amount of their investments. In an LLC, members are also allowed to participate fully in management activities, and under some state statutes, the firm's managers need not even be members of the LLC. Yet another advantage is that corporations and partnerships, as well as foreign investors, can be LLC members. Additionally, in contrast to S corporations, there is no limit on the number of members of the LLC. Finally, part of the LLC's attractiveness to businesspersons is the flexibility it offers. The members can themselves decide how to operate the various aspects of the business through a simple operating agreement.

The disadvantages of the LLC are relatively few. Generally, the major disadvantage has been the lack of uniformity among state statutes with respect to LLCs. The differences among the states are rapidly disappearing, however.

LIMITED LIABILITY PARTNERSHIPS. The **limited liability partnership (LLP)** is similar to the LLC. The difference between an LLP and an LLC is that the LLP is designed more for professionals, such as attorneys, who normally do business as partners in a partnership. Like LLCs, LLPs must be formed and operated in compliance with state statutes. The appropriate form must be filed with a central state

Limited Liability Company (LLC)
A hybrid form of business organization authorized by a state in which the owners of the business have limited liability and taxes on profits are passed through the business entity to the owners.

Limited Liability Partnership (LLP)
A hybrid form of business organization authorized by a state that allows professionals to enjoy the tax benefits of a partnership while limiting in some way the normal joint and several liability of partners.

Featured Guest: Lloyd G. Pearcy
The Paralegal and Projects Involving Business Organizations

Biographical Note

Lloyd G. Pearcy, an attorney for over thirty years, has taught business organizations at Denver Paralegal Institute for two decades and business law classes in both undergraduate and MBA programs at the University of Phoenix. He has presented Continuing Legal Education (CLE) seminars on business organizations to trade associations throughout the United States. He has contributed to a book on employment law and has written numerous columns on business law in various trade journals.

The paralegal who is assigned projects involving business organizations will experience many opportunities to excel and achieve personal satisfaction. An understanding of the practical and frequently overlooked issues discussed here may help you attain recognition and professional fulfillment.

Practical Considerations in Analyzing Jurisdictional Choices

Today, states compete to attract new businesses by making their statutes regulating business organizations more user friendly. Yet the statutes tend to level out. As soon as one state modifies its statute or regulations, other states quickly copy the modifications. The tendency of state legislatures to enact model acts more or less intact adds to this process.

In most cases, I advise clients to charter their businesses in their home states. The business owners and their legal counsel will be more familiar with all of the home state's statutes, not just those directly pertaining to business entities. They will also be more likely to keep abreast of periodic legislative revisions.

There are some situations, however, in which it is strategically, if not legally, advantageous to incorporate in another state. If the company's business plan is to make a public stock offering several years down the line, some underwriters will counsel the business owners to incorporate in the state of Delaware, because prospective investors often regard Delaware corporations as more sophisticated. If the company that is going public is in the medical field, the preferred state of incorporation may be Tennessee. If it is a credit-card issuing company, the

> "Limited liability companies (LLCs) are the 'new kid on the block' in the world of business entities."

jurisdiction of choice may be South Dakota, not because that state's corporation statute is preferred but because its law governing lenders is considered desirable.

An Unexpected Advantage of Par-Value Stock

Par-value stock has always been misunderstood. The term is a misnomer. It has nothing to do with the book value or market value of stock. It is a minimum issuance price in that the corporation cannot sell par stock for less than the designated par value. Another rule is that the funds the corporation receives from the issuance of par stock cannot be used for the payment of dividends.

Many legal scholars believe that the usefulness of the distinction between par-value and no-par-value stock has ended. With the development of sophisticated accounting procedures, the information that the designation conveys has become outdated. Some states have abolished the distinction or made it optional.

Designating stock as par value may nonetheless be advantageous to your firm's client. This is because some states base their franchise taxes or registration fees on a formula computed by multiplying the number of authorized shares by their par value. If the stock is no-par stock, these states impute a value to those shares, often $1 per share. A corporation operating in numerous states and thus needing to qualify as a foreign corporation in

FEATURED GUEST, Continued

multiple jurisdictions can incur significant qualification fees. This is especially true if its articles of incorporation authorize a large number of shares. By designating a par value below one dollar—for example, one cent per share—the corporation is assured that it will qualify for the lowest tax or fee available.

DO NOT OVERLOOK SHARES IN SERIES

An underutilized feature of corporation law is the opportunity to designate a corporation's stock as "shares in series." When a class of stock is so designated in the articles of incorporation, it enables the company to vary the attributes of different blocks of *the same class of stock* at different issuance dates. Such shares are known informally as "blank stock."

Suppose that your law firm has a business client who is incorporating. The client wants maximum flexibility in conforming the sale of its shares of stock to market conditions, which change from time to time. The client does not want to bother with several classes of stock, nor with having to amend the articles of incorporation in the future. The "shares in series" alternative is designed for this scenario. There is a single class of stock, but certain characteristics can be varied each time the corporation sells a different block of shares. Attributes that can be varied in this way include such matters as voting rights, dividend rates, liquidation priorities, conversion rights, and redemption terms. The allowable variations are defined in each state's statute. To reserve this flexibility, the class must be designated as "series shares" in the articles of incorporation. Thereafter, each time the corporation issues a block of shares the board of directors defines the specific attributes of the stock.

CONSIDER THE ADVANTAGES OF A LIMITED LIABILITY COMPANY

Limited liability companies (LLCs) are the "new kid on the block" in the world of business entities. Most states have adopted enabling legislation that not only authorizes the formation of domestic LLCs but also allows foreign LLCs to qualify to do business within the state.

LLCs are a blend of other business forms. Like limited and general partnerships and S corporations, the LLC is a "pass-through" entity. The LLC does not pay income taxes as an entity and files only an "informational tax return" with the Internal Revenue Service (IRS). Available tax credits or deductions pass through the entity to the owners personally. None of the owners of an LLC (called "members") is personally liable for business debts. Furthermore, none of the limitations placed on S corporations applies to LLCs. There is no limit on the number of owners, there can be more than one class of securities, nonresident aliens are allowed to be owners, affiliated ownership with other entities is not disqualifying, and so on.

MAKE THE LIMITED LIABILITY ELECTION FOR GENERAL OR LIMITED PARTNERSHIPS

In recent years, virtually all states have enacted laws allowing general partnerships to register as limited liability partnerships (LLPs). Generally, limited partnerships are allowed to register as limited liability limited partnerships (LLLPs). Registration as an LLP or LLLP affords significant protection against personal liability for all partners in a general partnership and for the general partners of limited partnerships. Without the election to operate as an LLP, general partners are personally liable for all of the business debts. If the assets of the business are insufficient to pay its creditors, the personal assets of the partners can be reached. If a partner cannot pay his or her proportionate share, the entire obligation falls on the partner or partners who can.

If the LLP election is made, partners remain liable for their own misconduct but not for that of their partners. This protection is acquired by filing the appropriate document with the secretary of state. The name of the general partnership is required to include the words "Limited Liability Partnership," or the abbreviation "L.L.P." Similarly, the name of a limited partnership that makes the election must include the words "Limited Liability Limited Partnership," or the abbreviation "L.L.L.P." Thereafter, businesses that extend credit to, or enter into other business relationships with, the partnership are deemed to have notice that the partners will not be personally liable for payment of business debts. Consistent with the law governing other entity forms that limit personal liability, such as corporations and limited liability companies, it is not sufficient for the partnership to merely *acquire* the limited liability designation through registration. It must consistently display the designation in its business documents so there is a continuing notice as to the limitation on personal liability of the partners.

agency, usually the secretary of state's office, and the business's name must include either "Limited Liability Partnership" or the initials "L.L.P."

The major advantage of the LLP is that it allows a partnership to function as a pass-through entity for tax purposes but limits the personal liability of the partners for partnership tort liability. Consider an example. A group of lawyers operates as a partnership. A client sues one of the attorneys for malpractice and wins a large judgment, and the firm's malpractice insurance is insufficient to cover the obligation. Under traditional partnership law, the partners are jointly and severally (individually) liable. This means, in this example, that when the attorney's personal assets are exhausted, the personal assets of the other, innocent partners can be used to satisfy the judgment.

Although LLP statutes vary from state to state, generally each state statute limits in some way the liability of partners. For example, Delaware law protects each innocent partner from the "debts and obligations of the partnership arising from negligence, wrongful acts, or misconduct." In North Carolina, Texas, and Washington, D.C., the statutes protect innocent partners from obligations arising from "errors, omissions, negligence, incompetence, or malfeasance."

In most states, it is relatively easy to convert a traditional partnership into an LLP because the firm's basic organizational structure remains the same. Additionally, all of the laws governing partnerships still apply (apart from those modified by the LLP statute). Normally, an LLP statute is simply an amendment to a state's already existing partnership law.

Family Limited Liability Partnership (FLLP)
A limited liability partnership (LLP) in which the majority of the partners are persons related to each other or persons acting in a fiduciary capacity for persons so related. All partners must be natural persons.

FAMILY LIMITED LIABILITY PARTNERSHIPS. A **family limited liability partnership (FLLP)** is an LLP in which the majority of the partners are persons related to each other, such as spouses, siblings, parents, grandparents, or other relatives. Persons acting in a fiduciary capacity for persons so related can also be partners. All of the partners must be natural persons or persons acting in a fiduciary capacity for the benefit of natural persons.

Probably the most significant use of the FLLP form of business is in agriculture. Family-owned farms sometimes find this form beneficial. The FLLP has the same advantages as other LLPs as well as some additional advantages. In Iowa, for example, partners doing business as an FLLP can avoid certain real-estate taxes when transferring real estate from one partner to another.

Limited Liability Limited Partnership (LLLP)
A type of limited partnership in which the general partner has the same liability as the limited partner. In other words, the liability of all partners is limited to the amount of their investments in the firm.

LIMITED LIABILITY LIMITED PARTNERSHIPS. A **limited liability limited partnership (LLLP)** is a type of limited partnership. The difference between a limited partnership and an LLLP is that the liability of a general partner in an LLLP is the same as the liability of a limited partner. In other words, the liability of all partners is limited to the amount of their investments in the firm.

A few states (including Colorado, Delaware, Florida, Missouri, Pennsylvania, Texas, and Virginia) provide expressly for LLLPs. In states that do not provide for LLLPs but that allow for limited partnerships and limited liability partnerships, a limited partnership will probably still be able to register with the state as an LLLP.

Business Organizations and the Paralegal

We have already mentioned many of the ways in which paralegals benefit from a knowledge of business organizations. Because so much legal work has to do with business clients, it is impossible to summarize the many tasks involving business organizations that paralegals carry out. The following list, however, will give you an idea of some of the types of work that paralegals frequently perform in this area:

Substantive Law Concept Summary
Forms of Business Organization

Sole Proprietorships	1. *Creation*—The simplest form of business; used by anyone who does business without creating an organization. 2. *Operation*—The owner is the business. The owner can conduct all business operations himself or herself (such as in a small home office) or hire employees to run the business. 3. *Taxation*—The owner pays personal income taxes on all profits. 4. *Liability*—The owner is personally liable for all business debts and obligations. 5. *Termination*—A sole proprietorship terminates on the owner's death or whenever the owner ceases doing business.
Partnerships	1. *Creation*—Created by the written or oral agreement of the parties to do business jointly as partners. (The creation of a limited partnership is a formal proceeding that must comply with state statutory requirements.) 2. *Operation*—Each partner has an equal voice in management, unless otherwise provided for in the partnership agreement. The partners may hire employees to assist them in running the business. (In a limited partnership, only the general partners may participate in management.) 3. *Taxation*—The partnership as an entity does not pay income taxes but files an informational tax return with the Internal Revenue Service each year. Each partner pays personal income taxes on his or her share of the profits of the partnership. 4. *Liability*—Partners are personally liable for partnership debts and obligations. (In a limited partnership, only the general partners have unlimited personal liability; the liability of limited partners is limited to the amount of their investments in the enterprise.) 5. *Termination*—A partnership may be terminated by the agreement of the partners or by the occurrence of certain events, such as the death or bankruptcy of a partner.
Corporations	1. *Creation*—A corporation is created by a state-issued charter. 2. *Operation*—The shareholders elect directors, who set policy and appoint officers to manage the day-to-day corporate affairs. 3. *Taxation*—The corporation pays income tax on net profits; shareholders again pay income tax on profits distributed as dividends. 4. *Liability*—Shareholders have limited liability and are not personally liable for the debts of the corporation (beyond the amount of their investments). 5. *Termination*—A corporation may be terminated at a time specified in the articles of incorporation, by the agreement of the shareholders and the board of directors, or by court decree.
Limited Liability Organizations	Two relatively new forms of business organization are the limited liability partnership (LLP) and the limited liability company (LLC). Generally, these organizations and special forms of these organizations (such as the family limited liability partnership, or FLLP) allow business owners to combine the tax advantages of the partnership with the limited liability of limited partners or corporate shareholders.

> ## ETHICAL CONCERN
> ### Meeting Federal Court Deadlines
>
> As yet another example of the consequences of missing a court procedural deadline, suppose that a client of your firm has been sued in tort for the conversion of intellectual property. *Conversion* is the wrongful taking of another's property—the civil counterpart of theft. The plaintiff, an author, filed suit against the client in a state court, alleging that the defendant had used portions of a textbook written by the plaintiff without permission. You are asked to prepare a "notice of removal" so that the case can be removed (transferred) from the state court to a federal court, because the claim is essentially a copyright claim, over which federal courts exercise jurisdiction. If the notice is not filed with the federal court within thirty days of the defendant's receipt of the complaint and summons (and nothing is filed with the state court), the defendant may lose the right to defend against the suit and may end up having to pay whatever damages the plaintiff is seeking. If this happened, the client, in turn, could then sue the attorney, and possibly the paralegal, to recover the damages that the defendant had to pay the plaintiff due to the attorney's breach of the duty of competence.

- Research state laws governing partnerships, corporations, and limited liability organizations.
- Assist in litigation relating to a corporate employer or a corporate client.
- Prepare applications for licenses, certificates, and permits on behalf of a corporation.
- Draft a partnership agreement.
- Draft documents necessary to form a limited partnership, corporation, or limited liability company or partnership and file the required papers with the appropriate state office.
- Maintain corporate stock-transfer records on the sale or purchase of stocks.
- Reserve a corporate name for an incorporator.
- Draft a corporate prospectus.
- Draft stock-option agreements for use by corporate clients. (A stock option is an option to purchase the corporation's stock at a specified price, ordinarily below the market value.)
- Schedule directors' and shareholders' meetings.
- Maintain corporate records, including minutes of directors' and shareholders' meetings.
- Draft articles of merger or consolidation.
- Assist in the dissolution of a partnership or corporation.

Intellectual Property
Property resulting from intellectual, creative processes—the products of an individual's mind. Examples of intellectual property are patents, trademarks, copyrights, and trade secrets.

INTELLECTUAL PROPERTY

Today, one of the most valuable forms of property owned by business organizations is **intellectual property**—intangible personal property that consists of the products resulting from intellectual creative processes. Although it is an abstract

PARALEGAL PROFILE

Debtor/Creditor and Real-Estate Paralegal

SONIA LEVINE *works as a paralegal at Pierce Atwood, Maine's largest law firm. She began her career at Pierce Atwood as a legal secretary in 1992. The attorneys immediately recognized her abilities and soon gave her more challenging responsibilities. In May 1998, the firm promoted her to paralegal. She works mostly in the areas of debtor/creditor law and real-estate law, assisting in multimillion-dollar commercial real-estate and loan transactions. She also handles various litigation and bankruptcy matters. Sonia received an associate's degree in paralegal studies and office management from Andover College and has completed numerous liberal arts and business classes at the University of Southern Maine.*

> **"[I]t is important that paralegals take a leadership role in the area of technology."**

What do you like best about your work?

"What I like best about my job is the ever-increasing responsibility. I work without direct, day-to-day supervision and exercise my own judgment when responding to client needs. I initiate, prioritize, and complete tasks with minimal input from the attorneys. This independence creates a challenging and rewarding working environment. My position also enables me to take the initiative and to take on additional responsibilities without being asked. Increased responsibility leads to increased professional recognition and respect within the legal and business community."

What is the greatest challenge that you face in your area of work?

"The greatest challenge I face in my job is working with so many different attorneys. Each attorney has his or her preferred way of handling things. It is often a challenge to keep track of which attorneys prefer which work styles and to alter my own work styles based on the preferences of the attorney with whom I will be working. Following instructions effectively from a diverse group of attorneys (as well as clients and staff) often requires diplomacy and tact. Though challenging, this diversity creates a work environment that enables me to learn from many intelligent and talented professionals."

What advice do you have for would-be paralegals in your area of work?

"The best advice I can give to a 'would-be' paralegal in my work area or any other is to become efficient with new computer technology and to keep up to date with recent developments and changes in online information resources. With constant advancement in electronic information, such as Internet access, it is important that paralegals take a leadership role in the area of technology. There will be an increasing demand for paralegals with ability to locate, analyze, and sort information into organized, manageable formats (and to teach attorneys to do the same)."

What are some tips for success as a paralegal in your area of work?

"One of the most important tips for success as a paralegal is keeping up with your work at all times. Falling behind in your work can lead to missed court or client deadlines. Last-minute 'crunches' before real-estate or loan closings leave too much room for error and sloppiness. Also, don't be afraid to ask the attorneys questions if you are confused or need additional information in order to timely complete your tasks. Just make sure you express your questions and concerns clearly. Finally, don't 'reinvent the wheel.' It is not necessary to draft a lengthy or complex legal document from scratch every time that particular type of document is needed. Check with attorneys and other paralegals in your firm to see if a form exists within your firm's files. And when you do have to prepare a new document, save it in a forms file for future use."

> ## SUBSTANTIVE LAW CONCEPT SUMMARY
> ### Intellectual Property
>
> | | |
> |---|---|
> | **Patents** | A patent is a grant from the federal government that gives an inventor the exclusive right to make, use, and sell his or her invention for a period of twenty years after the patent application has been filed. The inventor must demonstrate that the invention is genuine, useful, and not obvious in light of current technology. |
> | **Trademarks** | A trademark is a distinctive mark or motto that a manufacturer stamps, prints, or affixes to goods so that its products are distinguishable from those of others. The owner of a trademark has the exclusive right to use that mark. |
> | **Copyrights** | The right of an author or creator of a literary work, artistic creation, or other production (such as a computer program) to have the exclusive use of that work for a statutory period of time. |
> | **Trade Secrets** | A trade secret is a valuable business secret that makes a particular company or product unique and that would be of value to a competitor. Trade secrets include customer lists, plans, research and development, and pricing information. Trade secrets are protected under the law. |

term for an abstract concept, intellectual property is familiar to virtually everyone. Patents, trademarks, and copyrights are all forms of intellectual property. The book you are reading is copyrighted. Undoubtedly, the computer you use in your workplace or at home is trademarked.

For paralegals, a basic knowledge of intellectual-property law is important because intellectual property is an expanding area of legal practice. Paralegals who specialize in this area are finding a growing market for their services (see the feature *Technology and Today's Paralegal: The Expanding World of Intellectual Property*).

Forms of Intellectual Property

Patent
A government grant that gives an inventor the exclusive right or privilege to make, use, or sell his or her invention for a limited time period.

A **patent** is a grant from the federal government that allows an inventor to have the exclusive right to make, use, and sell his or her invention for a period of up to twenty years following the date of filing the application for a patent. To secure a patent, an inventor must demonstrate to the satisfaction of the U.S. Patent and Trademark Office that the invention is genuine, useful, and not obvious in light of the technology of the time. Anyone who makes, uses, or sells another's patented product or process without the patent holder's permission commits the tort of patent infringement.

Trademark
A distinctive mark or motto that a manufacturer affixes to the goods it produces to distinguish the goods from goods produced by other manufacturers.

A **trademark** is a distinctive mark or motto that a manufacturer stamps, prints, or otherwise affixes to the goods it produces so that those goods can be distinguished from those of other manufacturers and merchants. Generally, to be protected under trademark law, a mark must be distinctive. A distinctive mark might consist of uncommon words (such as *Kodak* or *Xerox*) or words that are used in an uncommon or fanciful way (such as *English Leather* for an after-shave lotion instead of for leather processed in England). Someone who uses another's trademark without permission commits the tort of trademark infringement.

Technology and Today's Paralegal

The Expanding World of Intellectual Property

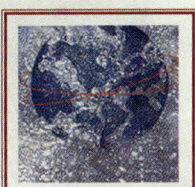

Intellectual property—the products of creative processes—is taking on added significance in today's world. Our increasingly high-tech society requires high-tech products, and these products would not exist without laws protecting ownership rights in such intellectual property. For example, lifesaving medical equipment and drugs would not be developed and sold if their creators could not profit from their efforts. Neither would the computer hardware and software that are essential to virtually all major business and government operations today. Indeed, today ownership rights in intangible intellectual property are more important to the prosperity of many U.S. companies than are their tangible assets.

What does all this mean for paralegals? For one thing, the expanding realm of intellectual property means more work for paralegals. There is a seemingly constant supply of new high-tech products, such as software, for which patents or copyrights must be obtained. There are more licensing agreements (allowing others, for a price, to use one's intellectual property) to be drafted. There is a greater need to do research on how international treaties and national laws do (or do not) protect the intellectual-property rights of U.S. businesses.

There is also more litigation over claims of intellectual-property infringement, and this litigation is often quite complicated. Paralegals who work for a law firm or department that specializes in patent cases, for example, often must manage voluminous materials and paperwork for just one case. A lawsuit for the alleged infringement of patent rights in a sophisticated product, such as a genetically engineered drug for treating leukemia, can result in thousands of exhibits and other documents that must be organized, safeguarded, and retrieved at the right moment. Because of the complexity of the work involved, paralegals who specialize in intellectual property are the highest-paid paralegals in today's job market (see Chapter 2).

Although technology has made certain tasks relating to intellectual property more complex, it has simplified others. To learn about copyright procedures and obtain copyright application forms, today's paralegal need only go online to the site of the U.S. Copyright Office (at **lcweb.loc.gov/copyright**). To conduct a trademark search, a paralegal can access the trademark database offered on the Web (at **www.uspto.gov**). To find experts in patent law to testify in patent-infringement cases or other cases involving intellectual property, paralegals can search online databases (for example, that of Hieros Gamos at **www.hg.org/expert-serv.html**). Paralegals can also learn about current developments in intellectual-property law and some of the legal issues it raises by accessing one of a number of legal Web sites (see Chapter 15).

A **copyright** gives the creator of a literary or artistic production, including computer software, the right to the exclusive use of that work for a specified period of time—for sole authors, the life of the author plus seventy years. A literary or artistic work is protected under copyright law regardless of whether its creator applied to the U.S. Copyright Office for a copyright on the work. If another person uses a significant portion of the work without the author's permission, the author can sue that person for copyright infringement. All the author has to do is demonstrate that he or she produced the work prior to the publication of the copied version. (Note, though, that the "fair use" provision of the federal Copyright Act allows certain persons or organizations, such as nonprofit educational institutions, to reproduce copyrighted material for certain purposes without the copyright holder's permission.)

Some business processes and information that are not (or cannot be) patented, copyrighted, or trademarked are nevertheless protected under the law as **trade secrets.** Customer lists, plans, research and development, pricing information,

Copyright
The exclusive right of an author to publish, print, or sell an intellectual production for a statutory period of time.

Trade Secret
Information or a process that gives a business an advantage over competitors who do not know the information or process.

Today's Professional Paralegal
Preparing Articles of Incorporation

Hiram Galliard and Martha Bonnell have decided to incorporate their business, Hiram's Pub and Brewery. They have met with John Roberts, an attorney in the corporate law firm of Roberts, Bassette & Wolfe, who has advised them on what type of corporation to set up and various stock and tax matters. John has requested that Mr. Galliard and Ms. Bonnell meet with his legal assistant, Marge Finch, to give Marge the information needed to prepare the articles of incorporation for filing.

Preparing for the Meeting

Several days prior to the meeting, Marge reserves the law firm's conference room. On the day of the meeting, she makes certain that it is free of any confidential client files left from previous projects. She also organizes her articles of incorporation file and makes extra copies of the forms and the checklist of information that she will need. She gathers needed supplies, such as legal pads and pens, and brings them to the conference room. Marge asks the receptionist to make sure that there is a fresh pot of coffee ready for her meeting.

The Meeting

Marge's phone rings at 11:00 A.M. The receptionist announces that Mr. Galliard and Ms. Bonnell are in the lobby for their 11:00 A.M. appointment. Marge walks to the lobby and introduces herself, saying, "Hello, Mr. Galliard, Ms. Bonnell, I'm Marge Finch, John Roberts's legal assistant." Mr. Galliard and Ms. Bonnell each respond with, "Hello, it's nice to meet you." They both ask Marge to call them by their first names, Hiram and Martha. Marge escorts the clients around the corner to the conference room.

Martha, Hiram, and Marge sit down at the conference table and begin to review the information that is required to prepare the articles of incorporation. Marge begins, "I know that the name of the corporation that you have decided on is Hiram, Inc. I have contacted the secretary of state's office to see if the name is available, but it has not yet responded. We need a couple of alternative names in case Hiram, Inc., is unavailable." "We haven't thought about it," responds Hiram. "But if we couldn't call it Hiram, Inc., I would want to call it either Galliard, Inc., or Bonnell, Inc." Marge makes a note of the names on her checklist.

"John also informed me that 10,000 shares of stock would be issued, that the two of you would be the incorporators, and that it will be a closely held corporation. Is that correct?" asks Marge. "Yes," responds Martha. "The next item is the nature and purpose of the corporation. I know that you are incorporating the brewery and pub business that you started several years ago as a sole proprietorship. What we normally do is insert a general statement indicating that the purpose of the business is to engage in any lawful business act or activity allowed under the corporation laws of the state," explains Marge.

Marge continues down her checklist. "We no longer have to insert the duration of the corporation into the articles, now that the state corporation statute has been amended," says Marge. "But I do need the management structure of the corporation." Hiram responds, "I am going to be the chief financial officer, and Martha will be the chief executive officer. Then we will have an executive vice president, a treasurer, a secretary, and other executives to be appointed as needed from time to time." Marge notes this information on her checklist as well. "I also need the names of the members of the board of directors," says Marge. "I brought the list with me," responds Martha as she hands the list to Marge.

"Now I need the name and address of the registered agent," says Marge. "I will be the registered agent, and my address for service of process is 8934 Rathburn Avenue, North Bend, New Pacum 98754," responds Hiram. "Will that be the address that you will use when you sign as an incorporator?" asks Marge. "Yes," responds Hiram. "What is your address, Martha?" asks Marge. "I'll be using the Rathburn Street address as well," answers Martha.

"That takes care of the information that I needed. If you wouldn't mind waiting for a few minutes, I have the incorporation forms on a computer disk and I can quickly input this information. That way you can sign the forms before you leave, and we can file them as soon as we find out if the name, Hiram, Inc., is available," explains Marge. "Would you like a cup of coffee while you wait?" she asks. Marge pours coffee for both Hiram and Martha. Then she excuses herself and returns to her office to prepare the forms.

Signing the Articles of Incorporation

Marge returns shortly with the prepared forms. Hiram and Martha both sign the articles of incorporation as the incorporators. Then they must attest to the act and to who they are by signing the attestation clause at the bottom of the form. The clause reads: "I (we) hereby declare that I (we) am (are) the person(s) who executed the foregoing Articles of Incorporation, which execution is my (our) act and deed." "Now that you have signed the articles of incorporation, John wanted me to call him. He wants us to go out to lunch to celebrate!" Marge calls John and then puts the forms on her desk so that she can follow up on the name and file the articles of incorporation after lunch.

marketing techniques, and generally anything that makes a particular company unique and that would have value to a competitor constitute trade secrets.

Intellectual Property and the Paralegal

An increasing number of lawsuits involve alleged infringements of intellectual-property rights. If you work for a law practice, one of the firm's clients may seek legal assistance when the client discovers that someone has used, without permission, something that he or she created—such as a software program, the words or music to a song, a novel, a patented invention, or a trademark. If you work for a corporation, you might be responsible for much of the document preparation and control necessary to protect rights in intellectual property or to litigate cases involving the infringement of intellectual-property rights. The U.S. Patent and Trademark Office and the U.S. Copyright Office also employ paralegals. If you work for either of these offices, you would be handling exclusively applications and other records relating to patents and trademarks or copyrights.

On the Web
You can find answers to frequently asked questions (FAQs) about patent and trademark law, as well as a host of other information, at the Web site of the U.S. Patent and Trademark Office. Go to **www.uspto.gov**. For information on copyrights, go to the U.S. Copyright Office at **lcweb.loc.gov/copyright**.

Here are some specific types of tasks you might undertake in the area of intellectual-property law (many of which were also mentioned in Chapter 2):

- Interview a client (or a manager of a corporation for which you work) to obtain information regarding intellectual property to be registered.
- Call the U.S. Patent and Trademark Office to find out if someone has applied for patent or trademark protection for a certain type of product that your firm's client (or your corporate employer) wants to develop and register.
- Draft the documents necessary to apply for patent, trademark, or copyright protection.
- Draft contracts that provide for another's authorized use of a copyrighted, patented, or trademarked product in return for royalties (a percentage of the proceeds received as a result of the authorized use of the intellectual property).
- Review marketing data and sales statements to verify royalties due for another's authorized use of your employer's trademarked, patented, or copyrighted product.
- Assist in litigation resulting from the infringement of rights in intellectual property.

KEY TERMS AND CONCEPTS

agency 259
agent 259
articles of incorporation 267
certificate of incorporation (corporate charter) 267
consolidation 271
copyright 281
director 266
dissolution 266
dividend 270
family limited liability partnership (FLLP) 276

fiduciary relationship 259
intellectual property 278
joint and several liability 265
joint liability 265
limited liability company (LLC) 273
limited liability limited partnership (LLLP) 276
limited liability partnership (LLP) 273
limited partnership 266
liquidation 272

merger 271
officer 267
patent 280
principal 259
prospectus 267
respondeat superior 260
share 266
trade secret 281
trademark 280
vicarious liability 260
winding up 266

Chapter Summary

1. In an agency relationship, one party (the agent) agrees to represent or act for another party (the principal). Employees who deal with third parties are normally considered to be agents of their employers. Independent contractors may or may not be agents.

2. Certain legal duties arise when an agency is formed. The principal has a duty to cooperate with, provide safe working conditions for, reimburse, and compensate the agent. The agent has a duty to perform work competently, obey and be loyal to the principal, notify the principal of knowledge or events significant to the agency, and render an accounting to the principal of how the principal's funds were used. A principal is bound by an agent's authorized actions and may be held liable for an agent's torts committed within the scope of employment.

3. The three major traditional forms of business organization are the sole proprietorship, the partnership, and the corporation. The simplest form of business is the sole proprietorship. Anyone who does business without creating an organization is a sole proprietor. The owner is entitled to enjoy the firm's profits, assumes full responsibility for the firm's operations and obligations, and pays personal income taxes on all profits. If the owner dies or ceases doing business, the sole proprietorship terminates.

4. A partnership is created when two or more persons, orally or in writing, agree to undertake business jointly for a profit. Each partner is deemed the agent of the other partners and, as a result, assumes certain rights and fiduciary duties. The partnership as an entity does not pay income taxes; rather, each partner pays personal income taxes on his or her share of the profits. Partners assume personal liability for business obligations, and, depending on state law, their liability may be joint and several. A partnership may be terminated by the agreement of the partners, when the goal of the partnership has been achieved, when a certain time period lapses, or by certain events, such as the death or bankruptcy of a partner.

5. The formation of a limited partnership is a formal undertaking involving compliance with specific state-imposed requirements. In a limited partnership, the general partners manage the business operations and assume personal responsibility for the firm's obligations. The limited partners are investors only; they do not participate in management, and their liability for business obligations is limited to the amount of their investments in the enterprise.

6. A corporation is formed with the state's permission (by a state-issued charter) and governed by state corporation laws. Corporate personnel include the shareholders (who purchase shares in the corporation's stock and thus become the owners of the business), the directors (who are elected by the shareholders to establish corporate policy and oversee the firm's operations), and the officers (who are appointed by the directors to manage the day-to-day affairs of the corporation).

7. Corporate income is subject to "double taxation"—the corporation as an entity pays income taxes on its profits, and the shareholders again pay personal taxes on the profits when they are distributed in the form of dividends. Unlike sole proprietors and partners, corporate shareholders have limited liability and are not personally liable (beyond the amount of their investments in the business) for corporate obligations. A corporation may be terminated at a time specified in the articles of incorporation, by the agreement of the directors and shareholders, and, in some circumstances, by a court.

8. Two relatively new forms of business organization are the limited liability company (LLC) and the limited liability partnership (LLP). These organizations combine the tax benefits of the partnership form of business (the business entity does not pay income taxes) with the limited personal liability of the corporate form of business. Special forms of LLPs include family limited liability partnerships and limited liability limited partnerships.

9. Intellectual property consists of the products of one's mind—creative works such as inventions, artistic creations, and literary works. Federal statutory law (patent, copyright, and trademark law) grants to individuals the exclusive right (for a limited period of time) to use or sell their intellectual property. Trade secrets, another form of intellectual property, are also protected under the law. Intellectual property is increasingly important in today's world and an expanding area of law.

CHAPTER 8 *Substantive Law II*

QUESTIONS FOR REVIEW

1. What is an agency relationship? How is an agency formed? What fiduciary duties arise in an agency relationship?
2. Why are agency relationships important in the business world?
3. When is a principal liable for the contracts formed by an agent? Under what common law doctrine may a principal be held liable for the torts of the agent?
4. What are the three most common traditional forms of business organization? How is each form created and terminated?
5. How are the profits distributed in each of the three major traditional forms of business organization?
6. How do the three forms compare in terms of the liability of the owners and taxation?
7. What is a limited liability company? What advantages does this business organizational form offer to businesspersons?
8. What are limited liability partnerships? Name and describe two types of limited liability partnerships.
9. What is intellectual property? Why is this form of property important for businesses today?
10. List and describe four categories of intellectual property.

ETHICAL QUESTIONS

1. Peter works as a legal assistant for a law firm. The firm's client is suing her former employer for wrongful termination of the employment relationship. The employee-plaintiff has financial records that prove that her supervisor authorized the nondisclosure of income to the Internal Revenue Service. Disclosing these records would seriously affect her supervisor's credibility and would strengthen the employee-plaintiff's case. Peter contacts the client to obtain the records. She refuses, fearing the repercussions it might have on her ability to find a future job. Peter's supervising attorney was adamant about the need to obtain these records. The attorney was concerned that it would be malpractice for the firm not to introduce this evidence. To whom is Peter obligated, the client or the firm? Why? How should Peter resolve this conflict?
2. Marcia Moore, a paralegal, and her supervising attorney, Brenda Thomas, meet with a new client for an intake interview concerning a probate matter. Brenda never introduces Marcia as a paralegal, and the client assumes that she is an attorney because she is so knowledgeable about probate procedures. Marcia does not inform the client that she is a paralegal, either. Marcia has continued contact with the client throughout the case. The case becomes contested and requires a costly trial. When the client is dissatisfied with the outcome, she sues Marcia's firm and names Marcia as a defendant, because she believes Marcia to be an attorney. How should Marcia have handled the situation from the beginning? How should Marcia's supervising attorney have handled it?
3. Amy Mehall is a paralegal in the legal department of a large corporation. One day, her good friend Sarah, who works in the company's purchasing department, asks Amy for help. Sarah is being sexually harassed by her boss. Amy tells Sarah that she cannot give her any legal advice. Sarah asks Amy to make an appointment for her with Amy's supervising attorney, so that she can get the legal advice that she needs. May employees of a corporate legal department represent other employees of a corporation? Why or why not?
4. Paralegal Mike Fassen works in a law firm that specializes in intellectual-property law. His supervising attorney, Margaret Gorman, is attending an out-of-town hearing today, and the receptionist has transferred a call from a client to Mike. The client states that he heard a song that he composed and copyrighted being performed on the radio by a famous rock band. The client is very upset because the band recorded the song without his permission. The client demands to speak to Margaret Gorman, Mike's supervising attorney. When Mike tells the client that Margaret is not available, the client insists that Mike answer his legal questions. How should Mike handle this situation?

Practice Questions and Assignments

1. Using the material on agency presented in this chapter, identify the parties involved in the relationships described below as either principals or agents:
   a. Bob drives a delivery van for a retail florist chain, Forget-Me-Not Flowers, Inc. Forget-Me-Not Flowers, Inc., owns the delivery truck and provides Bob with a delivery schedule.
   b. Tim owns Forget-Me-Not Flowers, Inc. He hired Bob to drive the delivery van.
   c. Attorney Mary Hacker represents Tom Smith in a drunk-driving case.
   d. Attorney Hacker's paralegal, Amy Wilson, files a motion with the court in Tom Smith's case.

2. Using the material presented in the chapter on agency relationships and third parties, explain why the principal is (or is not) liable for the actions of the agent in each of the following situations:
   a. Attorney Tom Moran tells his paralegal Jane Davis to purchase litigation software.
   b. Attorney Jane Smith leaves a written memo to her paralegal David Hayes instructing David to solicit bids for a computer network for the law firm from three computer consulting firms. David not only obtains three bids, but he hires one of the firms to set up the network at a cost of $10,000.
   c. Paralegal Megan Meldrum has office management duties in addition to her paralegal responsibilities at the sole practitioner's for whom she works. When the photocopier no longer functions, she enters into a lease for a new machine at the same cost of the old one without discussing it with her supervising attorney. Would it make any difference if the cost of the new machine were significantly greater than the old one?

3. Using the material presented in this chapter on business organizational forms, identify whether each of the business firms described below is a sole proprietorship, a partnership, or a corporation, and why:
   a. Terrence and Lars have owned a business together for three months. Terrence contributed 60 percent of the capital needed to start the business, and Lars contributed the other 40 percent. Each owner is responsible for a proportionate share of the profits and losses of the business, and each owner participates in managing the business.
   b. Four wealthy individuals create a business for the purpose of funding the construction of a new commerce center to revitalize the downtown business district in their city. Each individual contributes 25 percent of the funds necessary for the project, and each individual is liable for only 25 percent of the firm's losses. They all sign an agreement.
   c. Anne Hall, Joe Richie, and Mike Werner are all certified public accountants. They decide to do business together. By the end of its first year, the firm has become very profitable. As a result, the firm has to pay a substantial amount in income taxes on its profits.
   d. Dr. Menendez practices medicine on his own; he has not incorporated his business.
   e. The Pear Company is a for-profit business that has a charter issued by the state and that provides for the limited liability of its owners.

4. Identify the type of business entity being used in each of the following examples:
   a. Jones & Smith is a firm that consists of accountants. The firm itself does not pay taxes, and the partners have limited liability.
   b. The General Company is a business entity that consists of members. The firm itself does not pay taxes, and its members have limited liability.
   c. Family Farms is a partnership that does not pay taxes, whose partners are mostly family members, and whose members have limited liability.
   d. Neighborhood Drugs is a retail drugstore owned by Sara Katz. She is entitled to all of the business's profits and is personally liable for all of the business's debts and obligations.
   e. The Enging Company is owned by shareholders who are only liable for the company's debts to the extent of their investments; the firm pays taxes.
   f. West & West is a partnership. The firm does not pay taxes, and its partners are personally liable for the firm's debts and obligations.

5. Using Exhibit 8.2, *Articles of Incorporation*, draft a set of short-form articles of incorporation using the following facts:

   Richard Hart, Steve Grable, and Lucy White decide to incorporate the restaurant that they have been operating for the past six months. All three will be the incorporators. The name of the corporation, which is available, is Lucy's Tavern. Steve Grable will be the registered agent, and the address for service of process will be the restaurant's address, 1000 Audubon Road, Anytown, Anystate 10010. The purpose of the corporation will be any lawful act or activity for which a corporation may be organized under the general corporation law of Anystate. The corporation shall be for profit, and 15,000 shares of stock shall be issued.

6. Using the material on intellectual property presented in this chapter, identify the type of legal protection that applies to each form of intellectual property described below:

   a. Karen Wilson designs book bags for students. Her logo is a small schoolhouse stamped on the book bag. Karen's logo distinguishes her book bags from those of other manufacturers.

   b. Mike Pierson has developed a highly successful strategy for marketing his pizza and for locating his pizza shops. This strategy has made his company, Pizza Express, unique and prosperous.

   c. Carol Garcia writes a textbook, which is published. The publisher's payments to Carol are in the form of royalties.

   d. Dr. Alston invents a unique type of windshield wipers. He wants the right to sell his invention.

QUESTIONS FOR CRITICAL ANALYSIS

1. What is a fiduciary relationship? Why does the law impose such a relationship on parties involved in agency relationships?

2. Attorneys are agents of their clients and thus are governed by the principles of agency law discussed in this chapter. Do you see any similarities between the duties of agents to their principals and the ethical rules governing attorneys (discussed in Chapter 3)? If so, what are the similarities? In other words, which duties of agents, if any, correspond to the specific ethical rules discussed in Chapter 3?

3. Review the *Developing Paralegal Skills* feature entitled "A Case of *Respondeat Superior.*" Apply the various requirements for determining liability found in the checklist to the case discussed in the feature. Make a list of arguments for and against finding liability under the theory of *respondeat superior*. Which arguments should prevail? Why?

4. What protection does the corporation provide that sole proprietorships and partnerships do not? Why might this protection have come into existence? Whom does it favor? Is is detrimental to anyone?

5. What are the advantages of running a business as a sole proprietorship? How do these advantages compare to the costs and risks involved?

6. How do the rights among partners under partnership law differ from the rights of agents under agency law? What is the reason for these differences?

7. How do sole proprietorships, partnerships, and corporations pay income taxes? When would it be advantageous for tax purposes to be incorporated? When would it be more advantageous not to be incorporated?

8. What types of duties do directors and officers owe to a corporation? How do these duties compare to those of an agent? Is it possible for an individual to serve as both an officer and director of a corporation at the same time?

9. What are limited liability companies and partnerships? What are the advantages of these forms of business organization? Give an example of a situation in which each type of entity would be used.

10. Why are patents, trademarks, and copyrights known as intellectual property? What type of property is protected by a patent, a trademark, and a copyright, respectively? How is a trade secret protected?

PROJECTS

1. Find out if your state's corporation statute is based on the Model Business Corporation Act or the Revised Model Business Corporation Act.

2. Look in your telephone directory or in a state administrative agency manual in your library for the name and telephone number of the state department or agency that regulates businesses and accepts corporate filings, such as articles of incorporation. Call this department for information about a company located in your area. See how much information you can acquire about that company from the government office.

3. Call the agency located in question 2 above. Find out if forms are required to be filed to form a partnership. If they are required, request a copy of the forms.

4. Call or write the U.S. Copyright Office, which is located in the Library of Congress in Washington, D.C. Ask for information on copyright law and for copyright registration forms.

USING INTERNET RESOURCES

1. Go online and access the following site: **www.bizfilings.com**. Here you will find a series of "frequently asked questions" (FAQs) about incorporation. Summarize in writing the answers given on the Web page to the following questions:

   a. What are the advantages of incorporation?

   b. What are the disadvantages of incorporation?

   c. How many directors must a corporation have?

   d. What factors should be considered when deciding on a corporate name?

2. Research the Cornell Law Library Web site at **www.law.cornell.edu**, and try to find your state's corporation statute. If your state's corporation statute is located on the Web site (most are), see if you can locate the requirements for corporate formation. What are they? If your state's statute is not on the Web site, use New York's corporation statute for this exercise.

CHAPTER 9

Administrative Law and Government Regulation

Chapter Outline
❈ Introduction ❈ Administrative Law ❈ Consumer Law
❈ Environmental Law ❈ Employment Relationships

After completing this chapter, you will know:
- The purpose, types, powers, and essential functions of administrative agencies.
- How administrative agencies establish and enforce rules.
- Some of the ways in which the government protects consumers against unfair business practices and harmful products.
- The major laws regulating environmental pollution.
- How the government regulates employer-employee relationships.

INTRODUCTION

In the early years of American history, legal professionals were not very concerned about administrative law and government regulation. This is because in those years the United States had a relatively simple, nonindustrial economy that required little regulation—and hence few administrative agencies were needed to create and enforce rules. Today, in contrast, there are rules concerning virtually every aspect of a business's operations. Keeping up with the seemingly ever-changing rules and regulations issued by administrative agencies has become not only a major challenge for business owners but also for the lawyers and paralegals who assist them. Indeed, much of the work undertaken by attorneys and paralegals today touches, either directly or indirectly, on agency regulations.

Whenever the government decides to regulate a certain area, such as the hiring and firing practices of employers, it passes legislation setting forth the reasons why the area should be regulated and the general way in which the regulations will be carried out. Typically, the law will authorize the creation of a new administrative agency—or authorize an existing agency—to fill in the gaps of the broadly defined legislation by issuing and enforcing specific rules and regulations.

In this chapter, we first examine administrative agencies and their procedures. We then look at three areas of the law that involve extensive government regulation: consumer law, environmental law, and employment law.

ADMINISTRATIVE LAW

As you read in Chapter 5, legislation that creates an administrative agency is called *enabling legislation*, and the rules and regulations created by administrative agencies are known as *administrative law*.[1] Paralegals often deal with administrative agencies in their work. A client may need assistance in obtaining benefits under the Medicare program, which is administered by the federal Social Security Administration. A corporate client or employer may need legal advice on how to comply properly with the workplace safety regulations created and enforced by the federal Occupational Safety and Health Administration (or a parallel state agency). In these and numerous other similar situations, you would need to contact and work with agency representatives and know how to find existing and proposed agency rules.

In this section, you will learn about the powers delegated to administrative agencies in their enabling acts, the different types of administrative agencies that exist, how agencies establish rules, and how they investigate and enforce those rules. You will also read about how an agency's decision can be challenged both formally and informally through a pathway of administrative proceedings (and ultimately through the court system). Although our discussion focuses on federal administrative agencies, we will also examine the relationship between state and federal agencies.

Types of Administrative Agencies

There are two basic types of administrative agencies, executive agencies and independent regulatory agencies. Federal **executive agencies** include the cabinet departments of the executive branch, which were formed to assist the president in carrying out executive functions, and the subagencies within the cabinet departments. The Occupational Safety and Health Administration, for example, is a subagency within the Department of Labor. Exhibit 9.1 on the next page lists the

Executive Agency
A type of administrative agency that is either a cabinet department or a subagency within a cabinet department. Executive agencies fall under the authority of the president, who has the power to appoint and remove federal officers.

---

1. Administrative law is variously defined. Some scholars define administrative law as the law that governs the authority, powers, and functions of administrative agencies.

EXHIBIT 9.1
The Government of the United States

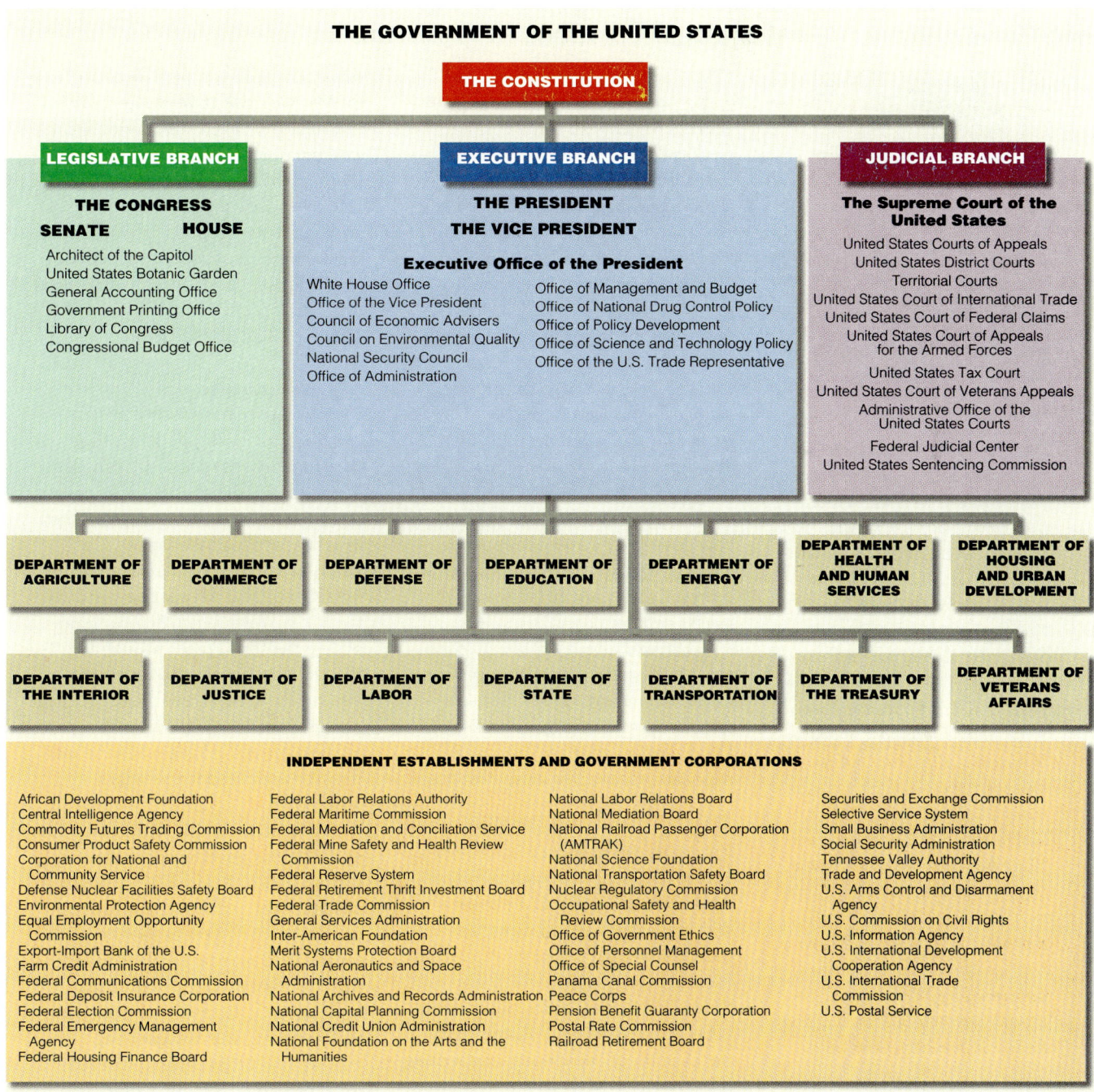

SOURCE: *United States Government Manual, 1997/98* (Washington, D.C.: U.S. Government Printing Office, 1997), p. 22.

cabinet departments and illustrates how administrative agencies fit into the organizational structure of the U.S. government.

Although all administrative agencies are part of the executive branch of government, **independent regulatory agencies** are outside the major executive departments, as you can see in Exhibit 9.1. The Federal Trade Commission and the Securities and Exchange Commission are examples of independent regulatory agencies.

Independent Regulatory Agency
A type of administrative agency that is more independent of presidential control than an executive agency. Officials of independent regulatory agencies cannot be removed without cause.

FEATURED GUEST: JUDY A. LONG
Paralegal Positions in Government

BIOGRAPHICAL NOTE

Judy A. Long received her bachelor's degree and master's degree in business administration from California State University at Long Beach. She received her J.D. with honors from Western State University College of Law and is a member of the California State Bar Association. She developed the ABA-approved paralegal program at Rio Hondo College in Whittier, California, and is presently the paralegal coordinator at Rio Hondo College, where she also teaches classes. Long has been involved in the legal profession for many years as a paralegal, an attorney, and a professor. She has authored a text on law-office procedures, published by West Legal Studies, and co-authored a textbook on basic business law.

The federal government and state, county, and local governments all offer positions for paralegals. Duties and responsibilities are as varied as the different government departments and agencies.

Unlike paralegals in private law firms, who often work long hours, paralegals employed by the government usually work a standard thirty-five or forty hours a week. There are many other advantages to working for the government. These advantages include good salaries, excellent benefits (such as medical and dental insurance), and time off for vacations, government holidays, and sick leave. Paralegals receive regularly scheduled performance reviews and are usually given annual salary increases. In some cases, however, they must pass tests to receive promotions.

The working environment is generally more structured in government offices than in private law firms, corporations, or other organizations. Depending on your preferences, this may also be perceived as an advantage.

THE FEDERAL GOVERNMENT

Paralegals are employed by the federal government in several different departments. To obtain a position with the federal government, you must contact the Office of Personnel Management (OPM), which has thirty-nine branch offices in various areas of the country. You can learn the location of these offices by writing the OPM at 1900 E Street N.W., Washington, DC 20415-0001, or contacting the OPM by phone at (202) 606-1800. You can also check the OPM's Web site at **www.opm.gov** for information. The OPM administers examinations to all entry-level paralegal applicants. After the results have been obtained, the applicants' names are placed on a register from which federal agencies select job candidates.

When applying for a federal position, you need to complete Form 171. This form, which can be obtained from the OPM, is similar to an employment application. You must complete a separate form for each position for which you apply. It is therefore a good idea to fill out the form, leaving the specific position blank, and make several copies. Then, as you apply for different jobs, all you have to do is type in the position. You should also keep a copy of each form that you submit. Before completing the form, read through the booklet titled *Hiring Standards for Paralegals,* which can also be obtained from the OPM, so that your application will be geared to the qualifications required for the open position.

The largest employer of paralegals in the federal government is the Department of Justice (DOJ), which has branches in many cities throughout the country. Paralegals who work for the DOJ may be involved in investigating criminal cases, conducting legal research, interviewing witnesses, and gathering and documenting exhibits and other evidence needed for prosecuting criminal violations. Subagencies within the DOJ include the Drug Enforcement Administration

The significant difference between the two types of agencies lies in the accountability of the regulators. Agencies that are considered part of the executive branch are subject to the authority of the president, who has the power to appoint and remove federal officers. In contrast, those who run independent agencies serve for fixed terms and cannot be removed without just cause.

FEATURED GUEST, Continued

(DEA), the Office of the Solicitor General, and the Immigration and Naturalization Service. Other government departments and agencies that employ paralegals include the military, the Civil Rights Commission, the Equal Employment Opportunity Commission (EEOC), the Department of Transportation, the United States Postal Service, and the Federal Deposit Insurance Corporation. The kinds of cases paralegals might work on vary depending on the agency and range from prosecuting drug dealers (DEA) to employment discrimination (EEOC) to securities fraud (the Securities and Exchange Commission, or SEC), along with numerous other possibilities.

STATE AND COUNTY GOVERNMENTS

Many state and county departments employ paralegals in the criminal justice field. Paralegals in these areas assist in preparing cases for trial, undertaking legal research, finding and preparing witnesses for trial, and investigating cases. If they work for the public defender's office, they may spend time interviewing accused persons and investigating their backgrounds. The state attorney general's office employs paralegals for investigation, legal research, document preparation, and assistance with litigation.

County governments also employ paralegals in various capacities. For instance, some of my former paralegal students are employed as consumer counselors and investigators for the Los Angeles County Department of Consumer Affairs. Their duties and responsibilities include handling and investigating consumer complaints against businesses.

"GETTING YOUR FOOT IN THE DOOR"

Spending time as a student intern in a government office prepares you for a government position after graduation. Volunteer assistance from student interns is often welcomed. When these interns graduate, they have an inside track to a permanent position with a government office.

Our paralegal program also includes an internship class in which students work for unit credits but are not paid. Some of the students work in government offices.

If there is a particular government office in which you are interested, invite a guest speaker from that office to speak to your class (with your instructor's permission, of course). Not only will this enable you to learn more about what paralegals do in that office, but you will have made a contact that may prove valuable when you graduate and are looking for a job.

Visiting government offices is an excellent way to learn about different areas of government. If you would like to know more about the state attorney general's office, for instance, call that office and set up an appointment to interview an attorney or paralegal there to see

> "Spending time as a student intern in a government office prepares you for a government position after graduation."

what this person does. Again, you will establish a contact that you may be able to use after graduation.

In our paralegal program, a fieldwork class has been established in conjunction with the Los Angeles County Department of Consumer Affairs. Students learn consumer law in the classroom and then work as volunteers doing consumer counseling in the Department of Consumer Affairs. They also assist litigants in Small Claims Court. Several of the students have obtained positions as a direct result of this experience.

If you are interested in a position that has regular hours, good benefits, and a competitive salary, you should consider working for the government. Start your investigation today by contacting the departments in which you are interested, or call the nearest branch of the federal Office of Personnel Management to obtain more information about positions in the federal government. You may find that the steady, secure government position suits you better than the stress and long hours associated with working for a private law firm. It is never too early to start your job search! Every contact you make while you are a student is a potential employer when you graduate.

Agency Powers

Federal administrative agencies are created by Congress. Because Congress cannot possibly oversee the actual implementation of all the laws it enacts, it must delegate such tasks to others, particularly when the issues relate to highly technical

>  **On the Web**
> The home pages for all of the federal administrative agencies discussed in this chapter, as well as more than 750 other federal agencies, can be located easily using the Federal Web Locator. Go to www.law.vill.edu/Fed-Agency/fedwebloc.html.

areas, such as air and water pollution. By delegating some of its authority to make and implement laws, Congress is able to monitor indirectly a particular area in which it has passed legislation without becoming bogged down in the many details relating to enforcement—details that are often best left to specialists.

ENABLING LEGISLATION. As you learned in Chapter 5, when Congress wants to create an administrative agency, it passes enabling legislation, which specifies the name, purpose, function, and powers of the agency being created. The agency may exercise only those powers delegated to it by Congress in the enabling act. State agencies are created by state legislatures through similar enabling acts.

Enabling acts are important sources of information for paralegals who are researching legal matters involving administrative agencies. Suppose, for example, that you are employed by a law firm and that a client is being investigated by the Federal Trade Commission (FTC) for deceptive advertising practices. In your research, you would learn that the FTC was created by the Federal Trade Commission Act of 1914, which prohibits unfair and deceptive trade practices. You would learn what procedures the agency must follow to charge persons or organizations with a violation and whether the act provides for judicial review of agency orders. You would also discover that the act grants to the FTC the power to do the following:

- Create "rules and regulations for the purpose of carrying out the Act."
- Conduct investigations of business practices.
- Obtain reports from interstate corporations concerning their business practices.
- Investigate possible violations of federal antitrust statutes (laws prohibiting certain kinds of anticompetitive business behavior).
- Publish the findings of its investigations.
- Recommend new legislation.
- Hold trial-like hearings to resolve certain kinds of trade disputes that involve FTC regulations or federal antitrust laws.

AGENCY POWERS AND THE CONSTITUTION. Administrative agencies occupy an unusual niche in the American legal system because they exercise powers that are normally divided among the three branches of government. Notice that in the FTC's enabling legislation discussed above, the FTC's grant of power incorporates functions associated with the legislature (rulemaking), the executive branch (enforcement of the laws), and the courts (**adjudication,** or the formal resolution of disputes).

The constitutional principle of *checks and balances* allows each branch of government to act as a check on the actions of the other two branches. Furthermore, under the Constitution, only the legislative branch is authorized to create laws. Yet administrative agencies, which are not specifically referred to in the Constitution, make **legislative rules** that are as legally binding as laws passed by Congress.

The constitutional authority for delegating such powers to administrative agencies—and the basis of all administrative law—is generally held to be implied by Article I of the U.S. Constitution. Section 1 of that article grants all legislative powers to Congress and requires Congress to oversee the implementation of all laws. Article I, Section 8, gives Congress the power to make all laws necessary for executing its specified powers. These passages have been interpreted by the courts, under what is known as the **delegation doctrine,** as granting to Congress the power to establish administrative agencies that can create rules for implementing those laws.

Adjudication
The act of resolving a controversy and rendering an order or decision based on a review of the evidence presented.

Legislative Rule
A rule created by an administrative agency that is as legally binding as a law enacted by a legislature.

Delegation Doctrine
A doctrine that authorizes Congress to delegate some of its lawmaking authority to administrative agencies. The doctrine is implied by Article I of the U.S. Constitution, which grants specific powers to Congress to enact and oversee the implementation of laws.

> ### ETHICAL CONCERN
> #### Putting the Client's Interests First
>
> Many paralegals dealing with administrative agencies know how frustrating this can sometimes be. You are told what the requirements are, comply with those requirements exactly, and then learn that yet another requirement must be met. Or the person you need to contact is unavailable or doesn't return your calls. If you, as a paralegal, are working with a particular agency for the first time, your patience may be tested by these or other obstacles to communication efficiency. In the interests of the client you are assisting, you should always try to avoid letting your frustration interfere with your goal, which is to enlist the agency staff members' cooperation in settling the client's claim as quickly as possible. A good way to learn about agency requirements and personnel is to talk to co-workers who have dealt with the agency. Once you become familiar with agency procedures and personnel, either through your co-workers' assistance or through your own experience, you can develop strategies for dealing efficiently with the agency.

Although administrative agencies have significant powers, these powers are also limited. Remember from Chapter 6 that the courts have the authority to invalidate legislative acts that violate the Constitution. Thus, if a court concludes that Congress has enabled, through legislation, an agency to exercise lawmaking powers that rightfully should be exercised only by Congress, the court can invalidate the law. Additionally, Congress itself exercises controls over administrative agencies. Just as Congress can delegate powers to an agency, so can it take away those powers, or even abolish the agency. Congress can also revise funding limits to restrict an agency's scope of operations.

Administrative Process

Rulemaking, enforcement, and adjudication constitute the three main functions of an administrative agency. How these functions are carried out make up what has been termed **administrative process.** The Administrative Procedure Act (APA) of 1946 imposes detailed procedural requirements that all federal agencies must follow when engaging in formal rulemaking and adjudication. The act does not apply to certain agency proceedings, however, such as some informal rulemaking procedures or hearings.

RULEMAKING. A major function of an administrative agency is **rulemaking**—the formulation of new regulations. As mentioned, an agency's power to make rules is conferred on it by Congress in its enabling legislation. For example, the Occupational Safety and Health Administration (OSHA) was authorized by the Occupational Safety and Health Act of 1970 to develop and issue rules governing safety in the workplace. In formulating its rules, OSHA has to follow specific rulemaking procedures required under the APA. The most common rulemaking procedure involves three basic steps.

First, when a federal agency decides to create a new rule, it publishes a notice of the proposed rulemaking proceedings in the *Federal Register*, a daily publication of the executive branch that prints government orders, rules, and regulations. The notice states where and when the proceedings will be held, the agency's legal

Administrative Process
The procedure used by administrative agencies in the administration of law.

Rulemaking
The actions undertaken by administrative agencies when formally adopting new regulations or amending old ones.

On the Web
You can access the text of the APA online at www.law.cornell.edu/uscode/5/ch5.html.

Paralegal Profile

Immigration Paralegal

DIANE S. GALLO has been a practicing paralegal for twelve years, concentrating in the regulatory-law areas of immigration and naturalization, telecommunications, and environment. She coordinates the firm's immigration practice, which meets the ongoing needs of corporations that employ foreign nationals as professionals and managers. She is generally well versed in the requirements of immigration law.

Gallo graduated from Georgia State University with a bachelor of arts degree in sociology. In 1985, she earned a paralegal certificate with honors from the National Center for Paralegal Training. She is actively involved with the National Federation of Paralegal Associations and has held several offices, including the presidency.

What do you like best about your work?
"What I like most about my job is the client contact. I work primarily with immigration and naturalization. A typical day for me involves planning strategies and assisting clients. I enjoy working with people and building relationships to achieve goals. The failure or success of our efforts in areas such as immigration can dramatically affect clients' lives."

What is the greatest challenge that you face in your area of work?
"The greatest challenge for me is the cross-cultural dimension of my job. I deal with many international clients, and cultural differences can be challenging. I have to be sensitive to other perspectives, viewpoints, and customs."

What advice do you have for would-be paralegals in your area of work?
"I recommend a focus on both communication and writing skills. Organizational skills are also critical for all paralegal work and especially in the area of immigration law."

What are some tips for success as a paralegal in your area of work?
"Tips for success as an immigration paralegal include having excellent writing, communication, and computer skills. People skills are also an important asset. Don't be afraid to carve out a niche for yourself and aggressively seek what you want to do."

> "The greatest challenge for me is the cross-cultural dimension of my job."

 **On the Web** The *Code of Federal Regulations* and the *Federal Register* can be found online at the following government Web site: www.access.gpo.gov/nara/cfr/index.html.

authority for making the rule (usually, its enabling legislation), and the terms or subject matter of the proposed rule.

A "comment period" follows during which interested parties have the opportunity to express their views on the proposed rule in an effort to influence agency policy. Finally, after the comments have been received and reviewed, the agency drafts the final rule and publishes it in the *Federal Register.* Later, the rule is compiled in the *Code of Federal Regulations,* an important source for paralegals researching administrative law, as you will learn in Chapter 14.

ENFORCEMENT—INVESTIGATION. Administrative agencies conduct investigations of regulated entities to monitor compliance with agency rules. A typical agency investigation might begin when a paralegal on the agency's staff takes a statement from someone who wants to report a violation of an agency rule. Alternatively, an investigation may begin when an agency determines that it needs to gather information about a certain individual, firm, or industry. An agency may also gather information by requesting that a firm or individual submit certain documents and records to the agency for examination.

> ## DEVELOPING PARALEGAL SKILLS
> ### Preparing for an Administrative Hearing
>
> Brent Moore is a nurse and a paralegal. He represents clients before the Social Security Administration (SSA). His nursing background helps him to evaluate medical claims and to argue on behalf of his client when a dispute arises between a client and the SSA. One of his clients, Margarete Sufuentes, has just been denied disability benefits by the SSA. Brent is preparing to argue Margarete's case at an agency hearing.
>
>
>
> TIPS FOR PREPARING FOR AN ADMINISTRATIVE HEARING
> - Be certain to file the "Hearing Request" form within the required time limits.
> - Obtain copies of all reports and other documents well in advance of the hearing.
> - Explain the hearing procedure to the client.
> - Prepare exhibits to display critical evidence, such as reports, medical records, and so on.
> - Compile all documents and other evidence in the order in which it will be presented at the hearing.
> - Include documents and other evidence that you will attempt to discredit at the hearing.
> - Prepare and submit a written argument, or brief, if necessary.
> - Rehearse your oral argument.

Normally, business firms comply with agency requests to inspect facilities or business records because it is in any firm's interest to maintain good relationships with regulatory bodies. In some instances, though, such as when a firm thinks an agency request is unreasonable and may be detrimental to the firm's interest, the firm may refuse to comply with the request. In such situations, an agency may need to resort to the use of a subpoena (see Chapter 11) or a search warrant (see Chapter 12).

ENFORCEMENT—ADJUDICATION. Once its investigation is concluded, an agency may begin an administrative action against an individual or organization. The majority of such actions are resolved through negotiated settlements at their initial stages, without the need for formal adjudication. Depending on the agency, negotiations may take the form of a casual conversation or a series of special conferences. Whatever form the negotiations take, their purpose is to rectify the problem to the agency's satisfaction and eliminate the need for additional proceedings.

If a settlement cannot be reached, the agency may issue a formal complaint against the offending party and adjudicate the dispute. The case will then be heard by an **administrative law judge (ALJ)**. The ALJ presides over the hearing and has the power to administer oaths, take testimony, rule on questions of evidence, and make determinations of fact. Although the ALJ works for the agency prosecuting the case, he or she is required by law to be an unbiased adjudicator (judge). Hearing procedures vary widely from agency to agency. They may be informal meetings conducted at a table in a conference room, or they may be formal adjudicatory hearings resembling trials. In some agencies, paralegals are allowed to represent clients at these hearings (paralegal practice before administrative agencies will be discussed shortly).

Following the hearing, the ALJ renders a decision on the matter. Either party may appeal the ALJ's decision to the commission or board that governs the agency. If a party is dissatisfied with the commission's decision, it may normally appeal the decision to a federal court of appeals. The APA provides for judicial review of most agency decisions. Appellate courts normally defer to agency decisions on questions of fact, just as they do when reviewing trial court decisions (see Chapter 6). Usually,

Administrative Law Judge (ALJ)
One who presides over an administrative agency hearing and who has the power to administer oaths, take testimony, rule on questions of evidence, and make determinations of fact.

> ### ETHICAL CONCERN
> ## Decorum before Agency Hearings
>
> What do you do when an administrative law judge (ALJ) is obviously biased against you or your client? Suppose that you are authorized to represent a client before a certain state agency, and your client, who is suffering from alcoholism and related medical problems, is trying to obtain disability benefits from the agency. The ALJ makes it clear that he does not believe that those who voluntarily abuse alcohol should be entitled to state disability or medical assistance for alcohol-related problems. Throughout the hearing, your patience and poise are put to the test by the judge's perceptibly hostile attitude and intimidating words. In situations such as these, you need to remember that you are not at the hearing to serve your own interests but those of the client. Angry responses to the ALJ will only worsen your client's chances for a favorable decision, and if the decision is appealed your heated responses will be on the record for review. As Rule 3.5 of the Model Rules of Professional Conduct points out, no matter what judges may do, the advocate must "protect the record for subsequent review and preserve professional integrity by patient firmness."

when a court reviews an administrative agency decision, the court considers whether the agency exceeded its authority under its enabling legislation, interpreted applicable laws properly, based its decision on substantial evidence, acted in an "arbitrary and capricious" manner in drawing its conclusions, and similar factors.

State Administrative Agencies

So far, you have been reading about federal administrative agencies. State agencies, however, also play a significant regulatory role. As a paralegal, you may find yourself working with a state agency, a federal agency, or perhaps both simultaneously. Not all states publish agency regulations in a compiled form, as the federal government does, which makes it difficult to research state regulations in those states, at least until you become familiar with the workings of a particular agency. Many states, however, do have administrative codes, which make it easier to locate the rules and regulations of specific agencies.

On the Web
To find information on state administrative agencies, use the State Web Locator at www.law.vill.edu/ State-Agency/ statewebloc.html.

Commonly, a state agency is created as a parallel to a federal agency to provide similar services on a more localized basis. Such parallel agencies include the federal Social Security Administration and the state welfare agency, the Internal Revenue Service and the state revenue agency, and the Environmental Protection Agency and the state pollution-control agency. Not all federal agencies have parallel state agencies, however. The U.S. Postal Service, the Federal Bureau of Investigation, and the Nuclear Regulatory Commission have no parallel state agencies.

In the event that the actions of parallel state and federal agencies come into conflict, the actions of the federal agency will prevail. For example, if the Federal Aviation Administration specifies the hours during which airplanes may land at and depart from airports, a state or local government is prohibited from issuing inconsistent laws or regulations governing the same activity. The priority of federal law over conflicting state laws is based on the supremacy clause of the U.S. Constitution. This clause, which is found in Article VI of the Constitution, states that the U.S. Constitution and "the Laws of the United States which shall be made in Pursuance thereof . . . shall be the supreme Law of the Land."

DEVELOPING PARALEGAL SKILLS
Approval to Practice before the IRS

Damian Forsythe has an associate's degree in accounting and is also interested in law. He has just completed Law 100, "Introduction to Law," and learned that some administrative agencies allow nonlawyers to practice before them. One of those agencies is the Internal Revenue Service (IRS). Damian would be allowed to represent clients before the IRS and to advise clients on tax matters without engaging in the unauthorized practice of law.

Damian contacts the Office of the Director of Practice in Washington, D.C. The administrative assistant who answers the telephone explains that the IRS allows nonlawyers and noncertified public accountants to practice before the agency, but they first must pass the "Enrolled Agents" exam and be admitted to practice. Form 23 must be submitted to apply for admission to practice, and applicants must meet certain requirements, such as being current with personal income tax payments. There are no educational requirements to become an enrolled agent. The exam is very difficult, though, and requires a knowledge of accounting, tax laws, and regulations. It is only given once a year, usually in September.

Damian is told that Form 2587, which he can use to register for the exam, is available online at the IRS's Web site at www.irs.ustreas.gov. He can also obtain a copy of Form 23 from the Web site. Damian uses his computer to explore the possibility of representing clients before the IRS.

TIPS FOR CONTACTING
AN ADMINISTRATIVE AGENCY

- Try to identify a person at the agency who can help you obtain whatever information you seek.
- Consider checking online sources to see if there is an agency directory that lists employee names and departments.
- If you place a blind call, think about your question ahead of time and about which department might be able to answer it.
- Obtain the name and telephone number of the person you are trying to reach before being transferred.
- Be patient and polite.

Paralegal Practice before Administrative Agencies

Paralegals, as well as other qualified nonlawyers, are permitted to practice administrative law in some situations under Section 555 of the APA, which reads, in part, as follows:

> A person compelled to appear in person before an agency or representative thereof is entitled to be accompanied, represented, and advised by counsel or, if permitted by the agency, by other qualified representative[s].

By allowing "other qualified representative[s]" to practice administrative law, an agency increases efficiency while reducing the costs involved—the client is not required to hire an attorney to pursue an administrative claim (unless, of course, court action is required). Federal agencies that allow representation by nonlawyers include the Social Security Administration and the Wage and Appeals Board within the Department of Labor.

One agency, the Federal Maritime Commission, requires nonlawyer representatives to register, pay a small fee, and satisfy certain educational requirements. To represent someone before the Social Security Administration, in contrast, one need only obtain from the agency an "Appointment of Representative" form and have the client sign it. Other agencies that allow nonlawyers to represent clients may require the nonlawyer to pass an examination or to meet specific educational requirements.

Although only federal agencies must follow the APA, state agency procedures are usually similar to those required by the APA, and both federal and state agencies may allow paralegals to represent clients. If you, as a paralegal, want to practice in a certain area of administrative law, you should do the following:

 Contact the relevant agency and ask about its specific representation requirements and procedures.

Administrative Law and the Paralegal

The functions of administrative agencies permeate almost every area of legal practice. No matter where you work, you should anticipate that sooner or later you will be interacting with a government agency. Suppose that you work for a

SUBSTANTIVE LAW CONCEPT SUMMARY
Administrative Law

Types of Administrative Agencies	1. *Executive agencies*—These agencies include the cabinet departments of the executive branch and the subagencies within those departments; the president has the power to appoint and remove officials who run the agencies. 2. *Independent regulatory agencies*—These are agencies outside the major executive departments; officials who run the agencies serve for fixed terms and cannot be fired without just cause.
Agency Powers	1. *Agency creation*—An agency is created by enabling legislation passed by Congress, which specifies the name, purpose, function, and powers of the agency being created. An agency cannot legitimately exercise powers that exceed those delegated to it by Congress in the enabling legislation. 2. *Agencies and the Constitution*—The courts have traditionally held, under what is known as the delegation doctrine, that Congress has the authority to delegate some of its lawmaking powers to administrative agencies based on Sections 1 and 8 of Article I of the Constitution.
Administrative Process	Administrative agencies exercise three basic functions: 1. *Rulemaking*—Agencies form rules governing activities within the area of their authority. 2. *Investigation*—Agencies conduct investigations of regulated entities to monitor compliance with agency rules or to gather information. 3. *Adjudication*—When a regulated entity fails to comply with an agency rule, the agency can issue a complaint against the entity. In adjudication proceedings, which may be formal or informal, an administrative law judge presides over the hearing and renders a decision on the matter. Most agency decisions may be appealed to a court.
State Administrative Agencies	State administrative agencies regulate state affairs. Often, a state agency is created as a parallel to a federal agency. If the actions of parallel state and federal agencies come into conflict, the actions of the federal agency will prevail, based on the supremacy clause of the U.S. Constitution, which states that the Constitution and the laws of the federal government are the "supreme Law of the Land."
Paralegal Practice before Administrative Agencies	Paralegals and other qualified nonlawyers are permitted to represent clients before certain federal and state agencies.

> ### ETHICAL CONCERN
> ## Confidentiality and Administrative Practice
>
> One of the challenges facing paralegals who deal with administrative agencies is remembering at all times the duty to keep client information confidential. Suppose, for example, that you are working on behalf of a client who is trying to obtain disability benefits. In pursuing the client's claim, you deal with a number of employees of the relevant state agency. One day, you receive a phone call from a person who states that he is working for the agency. He asks you to send him information on your client's financial position (income, property holdings, and other assets) and gives you his fax number. Without thinking twice, you fax him this confidential information and then continue with your work on another case. What if the person who requested the information is not an employee of the agency after all but someone who, for any number of reasons, wants to learn of the client's financial condition? This can and does happen. To avoid breaching the duty of confidentiality, you should always verify that anyone requesting information has a right to obtain it. Generally, you should not transmit confidential information by fax.

small law firm (or sole practitioner) that specializes in personal-injury claims. You may communicate directly with an investigator for the Occupational Safety and Health Administration when the firm handles a personal-injury claim involving an employer's violation of workplace safety standards.

If you work for a large law firm, you may be required to deal with several agencies simultaneously. The firm's department that handles legal issues involving the elderly may ask you to request blank forms from the federal Social Security Administration to keep on file. The firm's antitrust department (which deals with anticompetitive business practices) may require that you send exhibits to the Federal Trade Commission. The firm's employment-law department may request that you contact the Equal Employment Opportunity Commission to reschedule a hearing date.

Of course, you may work as an employee of an administrative agency. If you do, you will become especially knowledgeable about that agency's procedures and requirements. Generally, the paralegal specializing in administrative law will find that opportunities for paralegals in this area continue to expand.

CONSUMER LAW

During the 1960s, an era that saw increased focus on individual rights, many Americans became concerned over the health and safety of consumers. This concern grew into what has often been called the consumer movement. A **consumer** is a person who purchases, for private use, goods or services from business firms. By the early 1960s, the American public had felt the impact of the technology explosion as it affected production, transportation, and information systems. Consumers found themselves having to cope with ever-increasing amounts of information and complex products that they could no longer understand.

To a significant extent, the consumer movement was sparked by the activities of Ralph Nader, whose 1965 book *Unsafe at Any Speed* focused public attention on the issue of automobile safety. Since that time, Nader and the consumer organizations he founded have continued to advocate laws protecting consumers, as

Consumer
An individual who purchases products and services for personal or household use.

have other consumer activists. The consumer movement was particularly effective during the 1960s and 1970s. Indeed, some people refer to those decades as "the age of the consumer" because so much legislation was passed in an attempt to protect consumers against unfair practices and unsafe products.

Since the 1980s, the impetus driving the consumer movement has lessened, to a great extent because so many of its goals have been achieved. Both state and federal legislation now regulates how businesses may advertise, engage in mail-order and electronic transactions, package and label their products, and so on. In addition, numerous local, state, and federal agencies now exist to help consumers settle their grievances with sellers and producers. **Consumer law** consists of all of the statutes, agency rules, and common law judicial rulings that protect the interests of consumers.

Attorneys and paralegals frequently handle claims brought by consumers against sellers of goods and services. As a paralegal, you may be asked to investigate or do research relating to such a claim. Your task will be simpler if you understand some of the ways in which the government protects consumers. In this section, you will read about how the government regulates advertising practices, the labeling and packaging of products, certain types of sales transactions, consumer health and safety, and credit transactions.

Consumer Law
Statutes, agency rules, and judicial decisions protecting consumers of goods and services from dangerous manufacturing techniques, mislabeling, unfair credit practices, deceptive advertising, and so on. Consumer laws provide remedies and protections that are not ordinarily available to merchants or to businesses.

Deceptive Advertising

Over the past three decades, consumers have received increased protection against **deceptive advertising.** This protection has come more from statutes and government agency rules than from the common law. Under the common law, if a seller misrepresented the quality, price, or availability of a certain product, the consumer's only recourse was to sue the seller for fraud. Fraud requires proof of *intent* to misrepresent the product's usefulness to the buyer. Frequently, the burden of having to prove intent was too great, and consumers were left with little or no legal recourse against such deceptive practices.

Deceptive Advertising
Advertising that misleads consumers, either by unjustified claims concerning a product's performance or by the failure to disclose relevant information concerning the product's composition or performance.

Today, numerous government agencies, both federal and state, are empowered to protect consumers from deceptive advertising. At the federal level, the most important agency regulating advertising is the Federal Trade Commission (FTC). The Federal Trade Commission Act of 1914 authorizes the FTC to determine what constitutes a deceptive practice within the meaning of the act.

Deceptive advertising comes in many forms. Deception may arise from a false statement or claim about a company's own products or a competitor's products. Some advertisements contain "half-truths," meaning that the presented information is true but incomplete, leading consumers to a false conclusion. For example, the makers of Campbell's soups advertised that most Campbell's soups were low in fat and cholesterol and thus were helpful in fighting heart disease. What the ad did not say was that Campbell's soups are high in sodium and that high-sodium diets may increase the risk of heart disease. The FTC ruled that Campbell's claims were thus deceptive. Generally, the test for whether an ad is deceptive is *whether a reasonable consumer would be deceived by the ad.*

On the Web
A good source for information on the FTC, its regulations protecting consumers, and other government sites dealing with consumer issues is the FTC itself. You can access its home page at **www.ftc.gov**.

If a sufficient number of consumers complain to the FTC about the deceptive practices of a given retailer, the FTC has the power to investigate the problem and take action. If, after its investigation, the FTC believes that a given advertisement is unfair or deceptive, it drafts a formal complaint and sends it to the alleged offender. The company may agree to settle the complaint without further proceedings. If the company does not agree to a settlement, the FTC can conduct a hearing, at which the company can present its defense. If the FTC succeeds in proving that an advertisement is deceptive, it usually issues a *cease-and-desist* *orde*r requiring that the challenged advertising be stopped. It might also impose a sanction known as *counteradvertising* by requiring the company to supply new advertising—in print, on radio, and on television—to inform the public about the earlier misinformation.

Labeling and Packaging Laws

A number of federal and state laws now require manufacturers and sellers to provide labels that give consumers accurate information or warnings about products or their possible misuse. In general, labels must be accurate, which means they must use words as they are ordinarily understood by consumers. For example, a regular-size box of cereal cannot be labeled "giant" if that word would exaggerate the amount of cereal contained in the box. Labels often must specify the raw materials used in the product, such as the percentage of cotton, nylon, or other fibers in a shirt.

An important federal law in this area is the Fair Packaging and Labeling Act of 1966. This act requires that consumer goods have labels that identify the product, the manufacturer, the packer or distributor and its place of business, the net quantity of the contents, and the quantity of each serving if the number of servings is stated. This statute also governs product descriptions and savings claims, disclosure of ingredients of nonfood products, and the partial filling of packages.

The federal Food and Drug Administration (FDA) implements food labeling acts. The FDA has guidelines to standardize nutritional information on packaged foods. These guidelines require, among other things, that producers of similar products use the same portion size to designate the products' nutritional content, such as the amount of saturated fat, sodium, and calories they contain. The guidelines specify that, for example, businesses that manufacture and market food products cannot label a salad dressing as "low-calorie" or "light" when in fact its caloric value is the same as that of regular salad dressing but the recommended serving size is smaller. The FDA also defines some popular terms used to promote products, such as *healthy, light,* and *low-fat*. These laws and guidelines are designed to reduce consumer confusion over the contents of packaged foods.

Sales Transactions

As discussed in Chapter 7, Article 2 of the Uniform Commercial Code (UCC), which has been adopted by virtually all of the states, is the law that governs the purchase and sale of goods in the marketplace. Numerous UCC provisions protect consumers from unfair or deceptive sales practices. Particularly important are the provisions relating to unconscionable contracts (contracts that are so one sided and unfair to the buyer that they "shock the conscience" of the court) and warranties. Product-liability laws—which are based on the tort theories of negligence and strict liability as well as warranty law—also afford consumers a degree of protection by allowing them to sue manufacturers and sellers for compensation when they are harmed or injured by faulty products.

Federal and state statutes and regulations also protect consumers who purchase specific types of goods or services. For example, the Federal Trade Commission has issued rules requiring sellers of certain types of goods or services (such as used cars and funeral services) to disclose pertinent information to consumers.

Of growing concern today is how the government can regulate sales transactions over the Internet to protect consumers from deceptive practices. This topic is explored in this chapter's *Technology and Today's Paralegal*.

TECHNOLOGY AND TODAY'S PARALEGAL
Consumer Protection against Internet Fraud

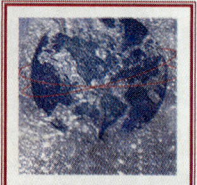

A significant number of sales transactions now take place over the Internet. In many ways, consumers benefit greatly from the ease with which goods can be ordered online. At the same time, Internet transactions can result in problems that are difficult to resolve when the sellers engage in deceptive practices. As a paralegal, you should be aware of some of the steps that are being taken to curb deceptive sales practices and online fraud in the interest of protecting consumers.

You can find out about current fraudulent schemes being perpetrated against consumers online by going to the "Consumer Alerts" page of the U.S. Consumer Gateway Web site at www.consumer.gov. You can also obtain information on online consumer fraud, including the ten most common Internet scams, from the Web site of the National Consumers League at www.fraud.org/ifw.htm. This organization has devoted time and effort to develop Web pages to help consumers, as well as lawyers who deal in Internet consumer fraud.

The Federal Trade Commission (FTC) can, of course, bring actions against entities that make false or unsubstantiated claims in their Internet ads, and it has already done so on several occasions. It also has provided "hot links" on Web sites that have engaged in deceptive advertising. A hot link takes the user to the FTC's own Web site, on which the complaint, restraining order, and other documents in the case can be read and downloaded. The FTC has also joined the Coupon Information Center in order to identify Internet advertisements that might be potentially fraudulent coupon-related schemes.

At the state level, some states are setting up information sites to help consumers protect themselves. One of the most well designed is New Hampshire's consumer's source book at www.state.nh.us/oag/ctb.html. Numerous states have also expanded their consumer-protection statutes to cover Internet transactions. For example, the California legislature revised Section 17538 of its Business and Professional Code to protect consumers against deceptive trade practices involved in transactions conducted over the Internet or by "any other electronic means of communication." Previously, that section only covered telephone, mail-order catalogue, radio, and television sales. Now anybody selling over the Internet in California must explicitly create an on-screen notice indicating its refund and return policy, the physical location of its business, its legal name, and a number of other details.

Through these and other efforts, consumers are gaining some protection against online deceptive sales practices. Yet given the immense number of Web sites advertising products, it is virtually impossible to prevent online fraud against consumers without extensive government regulation of the Internet—something that, at least to date, neither buyers nor sellers would like to see happen.

Consumer Health and Safety

In 1906, Congress passed the Pure Food and Drug Act, which was the first step toward protecting consumers against adulterated and misbranded food and drug products. In 1938, the Federal Food, Drug and Cosmetic Act was passed to strengthen the 1906 legislation. These acts and subsequent amendments established standards for foods, specified safe levels of potentially dangerous food additives, and created classifications of foods and food advertising. They also required that drugs must be proved effective as well as safe before they are marketed. Also in 1906, Congress passed the Meat Inspection Act, the first of a series of laws that established inspection requirements for all meat and poultry sold for human consumption. Most of the statutes involving food and drugs are monitored and enforced by the Food and Drug Administration.

Congress has enacted a number of statutes in an attempt to protect individuals from harmful products as well. In response to public concern over the dangers of cigarette smoking, for example, Congress required that warnings be placed on cigarette and little-cigar packages, as well as on containers of smokeless tobacco. Statutes categorized as product-safety acts protect consumers by carefully regulating the distribution of hazardous or defective products. One example is the Flammable Fabrics Act of 1953, which prohibits the sale of highly flammable fabrics and clothing. Another is the Consumer Product Safety Act of 1972, which was enacted to protect consumers from unreasonably dangerous products. The Consumer Product Safety Commission, which was created by the act to implement its provisions, sets standards of product safety, is empowered to ban the production of unreasonably hazardous products, and keeps the public informed about unsafe products.

Consumer Credit Protection

Because of the extensive use of credit by American consumers, credit protection has become an important area regulated by consumer protection legislation. One of the most significant statutes regulating the credit and credit-card industry is the Truth-in-Lending Act (TILA), the name commonly given to Title 1 of the Consumer Credit Protection Act, which was passed by Congress in 1974.

THE TRUTH-IN-LENDING ACT. The TILA requires sellers and lenders to disclose credit terms or loan terms so that individuals can more effectively shop around for the best financing arrangements. TILA requirements apply to any transaction involving an installment sales contract by which payment is to be made in more than four installments. These transactions typically include installment loans, retail and installment sales, car loans, home-improvement loans, and certain real-estate loans if the amount of financing is less than $25,000. Under the provisions of the TILA, all of the terms of a credit instrument must be fully disclosed. The TILA provides that a consumer can cancel the contract if a creditor fails to follow exactly the procedures required by the act.

In 1974, Congress enacted the Equal Credit Opportunity Act (ECOA) as an amendment to the TILA. The ECOA prohibits the denial of credit solely on the basis of race, religion, national origin, color, gender, marital status, or age. The act also prohibits credit discrimination on the basis of whether an individual receives certain forms of income, such as public-assistance benefits. Creditors are prohibited from requesting any information from a credit applicant that could be used for the type of discrimination covered by the act and its amendments. Under the ECOA, a creditor may not require the signature of an applicant's spouse, other than as a joint applicant, on a credit instrument if the applicant qualifies under the creditor's standards of creditworthiness for the amount and terms of the credit requested.

The TILA also contains provisions regarding credit cards. One provision limits the liability of a cardholder to $50 per card for unauthorized charges made before the creditor is notified that the card has been lost. Another provision prohibits a credit-card company from billing a consumer for any unauthorized charges on a credit card that was improperly issued by the company. For example, if a consumer receives an unsolicited credit card in the mail and the card is later stolen and used by the thief to make purchases, the consumer to whom the card was sent is not liable for the unauthorized charges. Further provisions of the act concern billing disputes related to credit-card purchases. A debtor may think that an error has occurred in billing or may wish to withhold payment for a faulty product purchased by credit card. The act outlines specific procedures for both the consumer and the credit-card company to follow in settling such a dispute.

FAIR CREDIT REPORTING. To ensure that consumers can find and alter any inaccurate information about their credit records, Congress passed the Fair Credit Reporting Act (FCRA) in 1970. The FCRA covers all credit bureaus, investigative reporting companies, detective and collection agencies, and computerized information-reporting companies. Under the act, the consumer has the right to be notified of reporting activities, to have access to information contained in reports, and to demand the correction of any erroneous information on which a denial of credit, employment, or insurance might have been based.

On request and proper identification, any consumer is entitled to know what information about him or her is contained in the agency's file, as well as the sources of the information and the identity of those who have received a consumer credit report, such as businesses that may wish to extend credit to the consumer. Under the act, no investigative report can be prepared on an individual consumer unless that person is notified and given the right to request information on the nature and scope of the pending investigation.

FAIR DEBT-COLLECTION PRACTICES. In 1977, Congress passed the Fair Debt Collection Practices Act in an attempt to curb what were perceived to be abuses by collection agencies. The act applies only to debt-collection agencies that, usually for a percentage of the amount owed, regularly attempt to collect debts on behalf of someone else. Creditors who attempt to collect debts are not covered by the act unless, by misrepresenting themselves to the debtor, they cause the debtor to believe they are collection agencies.

The act prohibits such debt-collection practices as contacting the consumer at his or her place of employment if the employer objects, contacting the consumer at inconvenient or unusual times, and contacting the consumer if he or she is represented by an attorney. The act also prohibits debt-collection agencies from contacting third parties (other than parents, spouses, or financial advisers) about the payment of a debt unless authorized to do so by a court, using harassment and intimidation (such as abusive language), using false or misleading information (such as posing as a police officer), and communicating with the consumer after receipt of a notice that the consumer is refusing to pay the debt (except to advise the consumer of further action to be taken by the collection agency).

GARNISHMENT PROCEEDINGS. Creditors have numerous remedies available to them when consumers fail to pay their debts. Among these remedies is garnishment. **Garnishment** occurs when a creditor, after complying with procedures mandated by state law, legally seizes a portion of a debtor's property (such as wages) in the possession of a third party (such as an employer). The creditor must first obtain an *order of garnishment* from the court, which allows the creditor to have access to the debtor's wages while they are still in the control of the employer. State laws governing garnishment vary from state to state, and some states (for example, Texas) do not permit garnishment of wages by private parties except under a child-support order.

Garnishment can create a hardship for the consumer-debtor if he or she is relying on wages for support. To protect consumers, both federal and state laws limit the amount of income that can be taken from a debtor's weekly take-home pay. The federal Consumer Credit Protection Act of 1968 provides that a debtor can keep either 75 percent of the net earnings per week or a sum equivalent to the pay for thirty hours of work at federal minimum wage rates, whichever is greater. State laws also provide dollar exemptions, and these amounts are often larger than those provided by federal law. State and federal statutes can be applied together to create a pool of funds to enable a debtor to continue to provide for family needs while reducing the amount of the debt in a reasonable way.

Garnishment
A proceeding in which a creditor legally seizes a portion of a debtor's property (such as wages) that is in the possession of a third party (such as an employer).

DEVELOPING PARALEGAL SKILLS

Discharged for Garnishment

Eva White works as a paralegal for a firm that specializes in labor law. A business client has called Eva's supervising attorney to ask for advice concerning garnishment. Basically, the client wants to know if he can fire an employee so that he can avoid having to comply with garnishment proceedings that have been initiated against the employee. The attorney, Melinda Jenks, has asked Eva to research recent case law on the question of whether an employer may fire an employee for such a reason.

Eva walks down the hall to the firm's library. She researches the topic of garnishment and locates a case in which an employee was fired two days after his employer received notice of the garnishment. The case turned on whether the employer had notice that the garnishment proceedings had already been initiated against the employee. She reads through the case and finds a citation, or reference, to the statute. Eva's next step is to check the statute itself to ensure that she has up-to-date knowledge of how the statute is being applied.

CHECKLIST FOR LEGAL RESEARCH
- Locate case law.
- Locate statutes.
- Update your case law findings by checking in a *Shepard's* citator (see Chapter 14) to make sure that the holding in the case is still good law.
- Update the statute by checking the paper insert in the back of the book called the "pocket part" and a *Shepard's* citator to see if the statute has been amended or repealed.

Understandably, employers dislike garnishment proceedings. After all, such proceedings impose time costs on employers (appearance at court hearings, record-keeping costs, and so on). To protect the job security of employees whose wages are subject to garnishment, federal law provides that garnishment of an employee's wages for any one indebtedness cannot be grounds for that employee's dismissal.

Consumer Law and the Paralegal

Because consumer laws protect all individuals, as a paralegal you will undoubtedly encounter a client with a claim that falls under a federal or state consumer-protection law. You might even find yourself working for a consumer group. In the area of consumer law, paralegals may be asked to perform the following types of tasks:

- Investigate a client's complaint alleging deceptive advertising.
- Assist in work relating to a business client who has been charged with violating Federal Trade Commission rules governing deceptive trade practices.
- Develop acceptable standards for a food producer to ensure compliance with the labeling laws implemented by the Food and Drug Administration.
- Investigate a client's use of hazardous products to ensure compliance with Consumer Product Safety Commission standards.
- Draft a letter to a credit-reporting agency to rectify an error on a client's credit report.
- Assist a client in collecting a debt through garnishment proceedings.
- Maintain and keep current the law firm's consumer law library.

Substantive Law Concept Summary
Consumer Law

Deceptive Advertising	Advertising that misleads consumers or that is based on false claims is prohibited by the Federal Trade Commission (FTC). Generally, the test for whether an ad is deceptive is whether a reasonable consumer would be deceived by the ad.
Labeling and Packaging Laws	Manufacturers must comply with labeling or packaging requirements for their specific products. In general, all labels must be accurate and not misleading.
Sales Transactions	Consumers are protected in sales transactions by numerous provisions of the Uniform Commercial Code (discussed in Chapter 7), including the provisions on unconscionability and warranties. Consumers are also protected by laws allowing product-liability lawsuits to be brought against sellers. Additionally, state and federal statutes protect consumers who purchase certain types of goods, and federal regulations impose requirements on sellers of certain types of products or services.
Consumer Health and Safety	Laws protecting the health and safety of consumers include laws governing the processing and distribution of meat and poultry, poisonous substances, and drugs and cosmetics; laws requiring warnings of health hazards associated with certain products, such as cigarettes; and the Consumer Product Safety Act of 1972, which created the Consumer Product Safety Commission to inspect consumer products, ban the manufacture of hazardous products, and remove from the market products that are deemed to be imminently hazardous.

Consumer Credit Protection	1. *Truth-in-Lending Act (TILA) (1974)*—A disclosure law requiring sellers and lenders to disclose credit terms or loan terms. Transactions covered by the act typically include retail and installment sales and loans, car loans, home-improvement loans, and certain real-estate loans. The TILA also provides for the following:
	   a. Equal credit opportunity—Prohibits creditors from discriminating on the basis of race, religion, marital status, gender, national origin, color, or age.
	   b. Credit-card protection—Limits the liability of cardholders for unauthorized charges and protects consumers from liability for unauthorized charges made on unsolicited credit cards.
	   c. Credit-card rules—Allows credit-card users to withhold payment for faulty products purchased by credit cards and to withhold payment for charges billed in error until disputes are resolved.
	
	2. *Fair Credit Reporting Act (1970)*—Entitles consumers to be informed when credit-reporting agencies send credit reports to third parties, to request verification of the accuracy of the reports, and to have unverified information removed from their files.
	
	3. *Fair Debt Collection Practices Act (1977)*—Prohibits debt-collecting agencies from using unfair collection practices (such as calling at unreasonable times, contacting certain third parties about the debt, harassment, and intimidation).

Garnishment Proceedings	Garnishment occurs when a creditor legally seizes a portion of a debtor's property (such as wages) in the possession of a third party (such as an employer). Both state and federal laws regulate garnishment proceedings to protect individuals from unfair procedures or from being deprived of too much of their income. Federal law also prohibits an employer from firing an employee because of a single garnishment proceeding.

Environmental Law

We now turn to a discussion of the various ways in which businesses are regulated by the government in the interest of protecting the environment. Remember from Chapter 2 that *environmental law* is defined as all law pertaining to environmental protection.

Environmental law is not new. Indeed, the federal government began to regulate some activities, such as those involving the pollution of navigable waterways, in the late 1800s. In the last few decades, however, the body of environmental law has expanded substantially as government has attempted to control industrial waste and to protect dwindling natural resources and endangered species. Today, businesses face the task of complying with numerous environmental regulations. Because of the complexity of many of these regulations, businesses often need legal assistance to make sure that they meet environmental requirements imposed by law. For this reason, many attorneys and paralegals now specialize in environmental law.

In this section, we first discuss the common law actions that can be brought against business firms and individuals for damages caused by polluting activities. We then look at some of the most significant statutes and regulations that have been created to protect the environment.

Common Law Actions

Common law remedies against environmental pollution originated centuries ago in England. Today, injured individuals continue to rely on the common law to obtain damages and injunctions against business polluters. For example, an injured party may sue a business polluter in tort under the negligence and strict liability theories discussed in Chapter 7. A developing area of tort law, and legal practice, involves **toxic torts**—actions against toxic polluters.

Businesses that engage in ultrahazardous activities—such as the transportation of radioactive materials—are strictly liable for whatever injuries the activities cause. In a strict liability action, the injured party does not need to prove that the business failed to exercise reasonable care.

Toxic Tort
A wrongful act (tort) that occurs when a person or business fails to properly use or clean up toxic chemicals that cause harm to a person or to society.

Federal Regulation of the Environment

Congress has passed a number of statutes to control the impact of human activities on the environment. Some of these statutes were passed in an attempt to improve the quality of air and water. Some of them specifically regulate toxic chemicals, including pesticides, herbicides, and hazardous wastes.

ENVIRONMENTAL REGULATORY AGENCIES. Much of the body of federal law governing business activities consists of the regulations issued and enforced by administrative agencies. The most well known of the agencies regulating environmental law is, of course, the Environmental Protection Agency (EPA), which was created in 1970 to coordinate federal environmental responsibilities. Other federal agencies with authority for regulating specific environmental matters include the Department of the Interior, the Department of Defense, the Department of Labor, the Food and Drug Administration, and the Nuclear Regulatory Commission. These regulatory agencies—and all other agencies of the federal government—must take environmental factors into consideration when making significant decisions.

On the Web
For information on the standards, guidelines, and regulations of the Environmental Protection Agency, go to www.epa.gov.

ENVIRONMENTAL IMPACT STATEMENTS. The National Environmental Policy Act (NEPA) of 1969 requires that for every major federal action that significantly

Environmental Impact Statement (EIS)
A statement required by the National Environmental Policy Act for any major federal action that will significantly affect the quality of the environment. The statement must analyze the action's impact on the environment and explore alternative actions that might be taken.

affects the quality of the environment, an **environmental impact statement (EIS)** must be prepared. Construction by a private developer of a ski resort on federal land, for example, may require an EIS. Building or operating a nuclear power plant, which requires a federal permit, or constructing a dam as part of a federal project would require an EIS. An EIS must analyze (1) the impact on the environment that the action will have, (2) any adverse effects on the environment and alternative actions that might be taken, and (3) irreversible effects the action might generate.

Air Pollution

Federal involvement with air pollution goes back to the 1950s, when Congress authorized funds for air-pollution research. In 1963, the federal government passed the Clean Air Act, which focused on multistate air pollution and provided assistance to states. Various subsequent amendments to the act strengthened the government's authority to regulate air quality. These laws provide the basis for issuing regulations to control pollution coming primarily from mobile and stationary sources.

Mobile sources include automobiles and other moving sources of pollution. The Clean Air Act of 1970 and its amendments require automobile manufacturers to cut new automobiles' exhaust emissions by a certain percentage by a given date. For example, the 1990 amendments to the Clean Air Act required manufacturers to reduce new automobiles' emissions of nitrogen oxide by 35 percent. By 1998, all new cars had to meet these standards. Another set of emission controls may be ordered after 2000.

On the Web
The Virtual Law Library of the Indiana University School of Law provides numerous links to online environmental law resources. Go to www.law.indiana.edu.

Stationary sources include manufacturing plants, electric utilities, and other nonmoving sources of pollution. The Clean Air Act authorizes the EPA to establish air-quality standards for these sources. The EPA sets the maximum levels of certain pollutants that may be emitted by stationary sources, and the states formulate plans to achieve those standards. Different standards apply to sources of pollution in clean areas and sources in polluted areas. Different standards also apply to existing sources of pollution and major new sources. Performance standards for major sources require the use of "maximum achievable control technology" to reduce emissions from the combustion of fossil fuels (coal and oil). The EPA issues guidelines as to what equipment meets this requirement.

The EPA can assess civil penalties of up to $25,000 per day for violations of emission limits under the Clean Air Act. Additional fines of up to $5,000 per day can be assessed for other violations, such as failing to maintain required records. To penalize those for whom it is more cost effective to violate the act than to comply with it, the EPA is authorized to obtain a penalty equal to the violator's economic benefits from noncompliance. Persons who provide information about violators may be paid up to $10,000. Private citizens can also sue violators. Those who knowingly violate the act may be subject to criminal penalties, including fines of up to $1 million and imprisonment for up to two years (for false statements or failures to report violations). Corporate officers are among those who may be subject to these penalties.

Water Pollution

Federal regulations governing water pollution can be traced back to the Rivers and Harbors Appropriations Act of 1899. These regulations prohibited ships and manufacturers from discharging or depositing refuse in navigable waterways.

NAVIGABLE WATERS.   Navigable waters include coastal waters, freshwater wetlands, and lakes and streams used by interstate travelers and industry. In 1948, Congress passed the Federal Water Pollution Control Act (FWPCA), but its regulatory system and enforcement proved inadequate. In 1972, amendments to the FWPCA—known as the Clean Water Act—were enacted to (1) make waters safe for swimming, (2) protect fish and wildlife, and (3) eliminate the discharge of pollutants into the water. The amendments required that municipal and industrial polluters apply for permits before discharging wastes into navigable waters.

They also set forth specific time schedules, which were extended by amendment in 1977 and by the Water Quality Act of 1987. Under these schedules, the EPA establishes limits for discharges of different types of pollutants based on the technology available for controlling them. Regulations, for the most part, specify that the "best available control technology" be installed. The EPA issues guidelines as to what equipment meets this standard, which essentially requires the most effective pollution-control equipment available.

Under the Clean Water Act, violators are subject to a variety of civil and criminal penalties. Civil penalties for each violation range from a maximum of $10,000 per day, and not more than $25,000 per violation, to as much as $25,000 per day. Criminal penalties range from a fine of $2,500 per day and imprisonment for up to one year to a fine of $1 million and fifteen years' imprisonment. Injunctive relief and damages can also be imposed. The polluting party can be required to clean up the pollution or pay for the cost of doing so. Criminal penalties apply only if a violation was intentional.

DRINKING WATER.   Another statute governing water pollution is the Safe Drinking Water Act of 1974, which requires the EPA to set maximum levels for pollutants in public water systems. Operators of public water supply systems must come as close as possible to meeting the EPA's standards by using the best available technology that is economically feasible. The EPA is particularly concerned with contamination from underground sources. Pesticides and wastes leaked from landfills or disposed of in underground injection wells are among the more than two hundred pollutants known to exist in groundwater used for drinking in at least thirty-four states. The act was amended in 1996 to give the EPA more flexibility in setting regulatory standards governing drinking water.

OCEAN DUMPING.   The Marine Protection, Research, and Sanctuaries Act of 1972 (known popularly as the Ocean Dumping Act), as amended in 1983, prohibits entirely the ocean dumping of certain materials, including chemical and high-level radioactive waste. The act establishes a permit program for transporting and dumping other materials. There are specific exemptions, including pollutants subject to the permit provisions of other environmental legislation.

Each violation of any provision or permit may result in a civil penalty of not more than $50,000 or revocation or suspension of the permit. A knowing violation is a criminal offense that may result in a $50,000 fine, imprisonment for not more than a year, or both. An injunction may also be imposed.

OIL POLLUTION.   In 1989, the supertanker *Exxon Valdez* caused the worst oil spill in North American history in the waters of Alaska's Prince William Sound. A quarter of a million barrels of crude oil—more than ten million gallons—leaked out of the ship's broken hull. In response to the *Exxon Valdez* oil spill disaster, Congress passed the Oil Pollution Act of 1990. Any onshore or offshore oil facility, oil shipper, vessel owner, or vessel operator that discharges oil into navigable waters or onto an adjoining shore may be liable for clean-up costs, as well as damages. The act created a $1 billion oil clean-up and economic compensation fund and decreed that by the year 2011, oil tankers using U.S. ports must be double hulled to limit the severity of accidental spills.

Under the act, damage to natural resources, private property, and the local economy, including the increased cost of providing public services, is compensable. The act provides for civil penalties of $1,000 per barrel spilled or $25,000 for each day of the violation. The party held responsible for the clean-up costs can bring a civil suit for contribution from other potentially liable parties.

Toxic Chemicals

Originally, most environmental clean-up efforts were directed toward reducing smog and making water safe for fishing and swimming. Over time, however, control of toxic chemicals became an important part of environmental law.

PESTICIDES AND HERBICIDES. The first toxic chemical problem to receive widespread public attention was that posed by pesticides and herbicides. Using these chemicals to kill insects and weeds has increased agricultural productivity, but their residue remains in the environment. In some instances, accumulations of this residue have killed animals, and scientists have identified potential long-term effects that are detrimental to humans. Under the Federal Insecticide, Fungicide, and Rodenticide Act of 1947, pesticides and herbicides must be registered before they can be sold, used only for approved applications, and used in limited quantities when applied to food crops. If a substance is identified as harmful, the EPA can cancel its registration.

Under 1996 amendments to the act, for a pesticide to remain on the market, there must be a "reasonable certainty of no harm" to people from exposure to the pesticide. This means that there must be no more than a one-in-a-million risk to people of developing cancer from exposure in any way, including eating food that contains residues from the pesticide.

Penalties for registrants and producers for violating the act include imprisonment for up to one year and a fine of no more than $50,000. Penalties for commercial dealers include imprisonment for up to one year and a fine of no more than $25,000. Farmers and other private users of pesticides or herbicides who violate the act are subject to a $1,000 fine and imprisonment for up to thirty days.

TOXIC SUBSTANCES. The Toxic Substances Control Act of 1976 regulates chemicals and chemical compounds that are known to be toxic (such as asbestos and polychlorinated biphenyls, popularly known as PCBs) and authorizes investigation of any possible harmful effects from new chemical compounds. The regulations permit the EPA to require that manufacturers, processors, and other organizations planning to use chemicals first determine their effects on human health and the environment. The EPA may require special labeling, limit the use of a substance, set production quotas, or prohibit the use of a substance altogether.

HAZARDOUS WASTES. Some industrial, agricultural, and household wastes pose more serious threats than others. If not properly disposed of, these toxic chemicals may present a substantial danger to human health and the environment. If released into the environment, they may contaminate public drinking water resources.

Resource Conservation and Recovery Act. In 1976, Congress passed the Resource Conservation and Recovery Act (RCRA) in reaction to an ever-increasing concern about the effects of hazardous waste materials on the environment. The RCRA required the EPA to establish regulations to monitor and control hazardous waste disposal and to determine which forms of solid waste should be considered hazardous and thus subject to regulation. The act authorized the EPA to promulgate various technical requirements for some types of facilities for storage and treatment of hazardous waste. The act also requires all producers of hazardous waste materials to label and package properly any hazardous waste that is to be transported.

The RCRA was amended in 1984 and 1986 to decrease the use of land containment in the disposal of hazardous waste and to require compliance with the act by some generators of hazardous waste—such as those generating less than 1,000 kilograms (2,200 pounds) a month—that had previously been excluded from regulation under the RCRA.

Under the RCRA, a company may be assessed a civil penalty based on the seriousness of the violation, the probability of harm, and the extent to which the violation deviates from RCRA requirements. The assessment may be up to $25,000 for each violation. Criminal penalties include fines up to $50,000 for each day of violation, imprisonment for up to two years (in most instances), or both. Criminal fines and the time of imprisonment can be doubled for certain repeat offenders.

Superfund. In 1980, Congress passed the Comprehensive Environmental Response, Compensation, and Liability Act (CERCLA), commonly known as Superfund. The basic purpose of Superfund, which was amended in 1986, is to regulate the clean-up of disposal sites in which hazardous waste is leaking into the environment. A special federal fund was created for this purpose.

Superfund provides that when a release or a threatened release of hazardous chemicals from a site occurs, the following persons are responsible for cleaning up the site: (1) the person who generated the wastes disposed of at the site, (2) the person who transported the wastes to the site, (3) the person who owned or operated the site at the time of the disposal, or (4) the current owner or operator. A person falling within one of these categories is referred to as a **potentially responsible party** (PRP). If the PRPs do not clean up the site, Superfund authorizes the EPA to clean up the site and recover clean-up costs from the PRPs.

Superfund imposes strict liability on PRPs. Also, liability under Superfund is usually joint and several—that is, a PRP who generated only a fraction of the hazardous waste disposed of at the site may nevertheless be liable for all of the clean-up costs. CERCLA authorizes a party who has incurred clean-up costs to bring a "contribution action" against any other person who is liable or potentially liable for a percentage of the costs.

State and Local Regulation

Many states regulate the degree to which the environment may be polluted. Thus, for example, even when state zoning laws permit a business's proposed development, the proposal may have to be altered to change the development's impact on the environment. State laws may restrict a business's discharge of chemicals into the air or water or regulate its disposal of toxic wastes. States may also regulate the disposal or recycling of other wastes, including glass, metal, and plastic containers and paper. Additionally, states may restrict emissions from motor vehicles.

City, county, and other local governments control some aspects of the environment. For instance, local zoning laws control some land use. These laws may be designed to inhibit or direct the growth of cities and suburbs or to protect the

Potentially Responsible Party (PRP) A party who may be liable under the Comprehensive Environmental Response, Compensation, and Liability Act, or Superfund. Any person who generated hazardous waste, imported hazardous waste, owned or operated a waste site at the time of disposal, or currently owns or operates a site may be responsible for some or all of the clean-up costs involved in removing the hazardous chemicals.

DEVELOPING PARALEGAL SKILLS
Monitoring the *Federal Register*

Robin Hayes is a legal assistant for CARCO, Inc., a large company that manufactures automobile parts. She works in the environmental-law practice group, within the corporation's legal department. One of her responsibilities is to monitor the *Federal Register* on a daily basis for newly proposed environmental regulations and for changes to existing rules. Today, Robin notices a change to the hazardous waste manifest, a form that CARCO is required to use when shipping hazardous waste to a disposal facility. The change requires the company to certify its efforts in reducing the amount of hazardous waste that it generates. Robin prepares a memo to the attorneys in the group, because they will need to inform management of the change.

CHECKLIST FOR MONITORING THE *FEDERAL REGISTER*

- Have your name put at the top of the routing slip that circulates the *Federal Register* to personnel in your firm or department.
- Review the *Federal Register* every day without fail.
- Begin by perusing the table of contents to locate relevant topics affecting your client.
- Next, review the subtopics to determine if notices, rules, or proposed rules have been issued on topics affecting your client.
- Skim through any notices, rules, and proposed rules that may apply to your client.
- Read in detail the relevant notices, rules, and proposed rules that may apply to your client.
- Photocopy relevant notices, rules, and proposed rules for circulation to the attorneys and others who should be advised of this information.
- Notify the attorneys and others of upcoming deadlines for comments on proposed rules and changes.

---

natural environment. Numerous other environmental concerns, including methods of waste and garbage removal, are typically subject to local regulation.

Environmental Law and the Paralegal

Paralegals who specialize in environmental law find employment in a number of settings. A paralegal specialist in this area may work for a federal or state environmental agency, a local government agency concerned with natural resources, a law firm's environmental department, a corporate legal department, and in many other situations.

If you work for a government environmental agency, you may be involved in the research and writing necessary to create new rules or revise existing ones. You may be asked to assist in monitoring compliance with a particular regulation. You might draft documents relating to legal actions brought against violators. In a corporate environment, you may be asked to help draft the firm's environmental policies and procedures or to obtain and fill out forms required to be submitted by the firm to an environmental agency.

Some paralegals working in the area of environmental law may be involved in extensive litigation concerning environmental claims. For example, a government agency may bring an action against a business that has failed to comply with a particular law or regulation. A company may sue another company who refuses to contribute to the cost of cleaning up a hazardous site to which the other company furnished materials. An individual or group of individuals may sue a company for health injuries suffered because of the company's polluting activities.

SUBSTANTIVE LAW CONCEPT SUMMARY
Environmental Law

Common Law Actions	Parties may recover damages for injuries sustained as a result of pollution-causing activities of a firm under the theories of negligence and strict liability (see Chapter 7). Businesses engaging in ultrahazardous activities are liable for whatever injuries the activities cause, regardless of whether the firms exercise reasonable care.
Federal Regulation	The Environmental Protection Agency was created in 1970 to coordinate federal environmental programs; it administers most federal environmental policies and statutes. The National Environmental Policy Act of 1969 imposes environmental responsibilities on all federal agencies and requires for every major federal action the preparation of an environmental impact statement (EIS). An EIS must analyze the action's impact on the environment, its adverse effects and possible alternatives, and its irreversible effects on environmental quality. Areas regulated by the federal government include the following: 1. *Air pollution*—Regulated under the authority of the Clean Air Act of 1963 and its amendments. 2. *Water pollution*—Regulated under the authority of the Rivers and Harbors Appropriations Act of 1899, as amended, and the Federal Water Pollution Control Act of 1948, as amended by the Clean Water Act of 1972. 3. *Toxic chemicals*—Pesticides and herbicides, toxic substances, and hazardous waste are regulated under the authority of the Federal Insecticide, Fungicide, and Rodenticide Act of 1947, the Toxic Substances Control Act of 1976, and the Resource Conservation and Recovery Act of 1976, respectively. The Comprehensive Environmental Response, Compensation, and Liability Act (CERCLA) of 1980, as amended, regulates the clean-up of hazardous waste disposal sites.
State and Local Regulation	Activities affecting the environment are controlled at the local and state levels through regulations relating to land use, the disposal and recycling of garbage and waste, and pollution-causing activities in general.

Often, such litigation involves massive amounts of paperwork and exhibits—and case management becomes a challenge. A paralegal who can meet this challenge will be a valuable asset to his or her employer.

Here are some of the many types of tasks that you might perform as a paralegal working in the area of environmental law (many of these were also mentioned in Chapter 2):

- Obtain permits from federal, state, or local environmental agencies to use property in certain ways (such as clearing trees or filling wetlands).
- Draft and file the documents necessary to include another polluting company as a defendant in an action brought by a government agency.
- Monitor the *Federal Register* on a routine basis to determine if new environmental regulations have been proposed by the EPA.
- Research the scope and applicability of a particular regulation to find out whether a client's planned action may violate that rule, whether a permit is required, and so on.
- Prepare for and perhaps attend hearings before environmental agencies.

- Assist in negotiations between an environmental agency and a business firm or group of firms to settle a dispute over a claimed violation of an environmental law or regulation.
- Coordinate a corporate employer's environmental programs and policies and monitor corporate activities to ensure proper compliance with environmental laws.

EMPLOYMENT RELATIONSHIPS

Whenever a business organization hires an employee, an employment relationship is established. Both the employer and the employee acquire legal rights and duties as a result of the relationship. These rights and duties have evolved over time to meet changing economic and social conditions that affect the workplace. A century ago, employers had numerous rights but few duties. Conversely, employees had numerous duties but few rights. Today, federal and state statutes have dramatically altered the character of the traditional workplace and employment relationships.

Because attorneys and paralegals are frequently involved in legal work relating to employment relationships, you should have a basic understanding of employment law. In this section, after a brief discussion of the common law doctrine governing employment relationships, we look at some of the ways in which the government regulates today's workplace.

Employment at Will

Prior to the 1930s, employment relationships between employers and employees were governed largely by the common law, including the common law of agency (see Chapter 8). A pervasive common law concept in those days was the doctrine of **employment at will.** According to this doctrine, an employment relationship could be terminated at any time by either the employee or the employer—for any reason or for no reason at all. Since the 1930s, however, numerous federal and state statutes have been enacted to regulate employment relationships. Therefore, even though at-will employment is still the law in several states, statutes governing the workplace have significantly curbed the right of employers to hire and fire employees at will.

Employment at Will
A common law doctrine under which employment is considered to be "at will"—that is, either party may terminate the employment relationship at any time and for any reason, unless a contract specifies otherwise.

Labor Laws

In the early decades of the twentieth century, employees began to organize to protect their interests. They formed associations called *labor unions* and elected union representatives to bargain with employers for improved wages and working conditions. The ultimate weapon of the labor union was, of course, the *strike*. By their organized refusal to work, employees could bring their employer's operations to a halt—to the financial detriment of the employer.

In 1932, Congress established the legal right of employees to organize labor unions with the passage of the Norris-LaGuardia Act. The act protected peaceful strikes, picketing, and boycotts and restricted the power of the federal courts to enjoin (stop or prohibit) labor unions from engaging in peaceful strikes. Other acts, including those discussed below, granted further protections to workers.

NATIONAL LABOR RELATIONS ACT. The Norris-LaGuardia Act was strengthened by the enactment of the National Labor Relations Act (NLRA) of 1935. The twin goals of the NLRA were to protect workers' efforts to organize into unions and to promote *collective bargaining* (bargaining between union representatives and employers) as a peaceful method of dispute resolution. The NLRA sought to curb activities that would discourage or prevent collective bargaining efforts conducted on behalf of the workers. The NLRA also created the National Labor Relations Board (NLRB) to oversee the enforcement of the statute. Congress gave the NLRB the power to investigate alleged NLRA violations and to prevent continued violations by particular employers.

FAIR LABOR STANDARDS ACT. The Fair Labor Standards Act (FLSA) of 1938, among other things, prohibited the oppression or exploitation of children by regulating the employment of minors. For example, under the act, children below the age of sixteen cannot be employed on a full-time basis except in very limited circumstances. The FLSA also established guidelines regulating overtime pay and minimum hourly wages. The act provided that if in any week an employee works more than forty hours, the hours in excess of the first forty must be compensated at one and a half times the employee's regular hourly rate. As for the minimum hourly wage, it represents the absolute minimum amount that an employer can pay an employee per hour. The minimum wage rate, which is set by Congress, is changed periodically to reflect inflation.

On the Web
Several law firms that specialize in labor law publish on the Web newsletters that discuss current issues relating to labor and employment law. For examples of the kind of information that you can find in such newsletters, go to the following Web sites:
www.arentfox.com/
   newslett/employ/
   employ.htm
and
www.haledorr.com.

The FLSA exempts certain employees (including administrative and professional employees) from its provisions. You will remember from Chapter 2 that one of the issues facing paralegals today is whether they should be classified as professional employees who are exempt from the act's requirements regarding overtime pay.

Family and Medical Leave

In 1993, Congress passed the Family and Medical Leave Act (FMLA) to protect employees who need time off work for family or medical reasons. A majority of the states also have legislation allowing for employment leave for family or medical reasons, and many employers maintain private family-leave plans for their workers.

The FMLA requires employers who have fifty or more employees to provide employees with up to twelve weeks of family or medical leave during any twelve-month period. During the employee's leave, the employer must continue the worker's health-care coverage and guarantee employment in the same position or a comparable position when the employee returns to work. An important exception to the FMLA, however, allows the employer to avoid reinstatement of a *key employee*—defined as an employee whose pay falls within the top 10 percent of the firm's work force. Additionally, the act does not apply to employees who have worked less than one year or less than twenty-five hours a week during the previous twelve months.

Generally, an employee may take family leave when he or she wishes to care for a newborn baby, a newly adopted child, or a foster child just placed in the employee's care. An employee may take medical leave when the employee or the employee's spouse, child, or parent has a "serious health condition" requiring care. For most absences, the employee must demonstrate that the health condition requires continued treatment by a health-care provider and includes a period of incapacity of more than three days.

Remedies for violations of the FMLA include (1) damages for unpaid wages (or salary), lost benefits, denied compensation, and actual monetary losses (such as the cost of providing for care) up to an amount equivalent to the employee's wages for twelve weeks; (2) job reinstatement; and (3) promotion. The successful plaintiff is entitled to court costs, attorneys' fees, and—in cases involving bad faith on the part of the employer—double damages.

State Workers' Compensation Laws

State **workers' compensation laws** establish an administrative procedure for compensating workers injured on the job. Instead of suing, an injured worker files a claim with the administrative agency or board that administers the local workers' compensation claims. State workers' compensation statutes normally allow employers to purchase insurance from a private insurer or a state fund to pay workers' compensation benefits in the event of a claim. Most states also allow employers to be *self-insured*—that is, employers who show an ability to pay claims do not need to buy insurance.

In general, the right to recover benefits is based wholly on the existence of an employment relationship and the fact that the injury was *accidental* and *occurred on the job or in the course of employment*, regardless of fault. Intentionally inflicted self-injury, for example, would not be considered accidental and hence would not be covered. If an injury occurred while an employee was commuting to or from work, it would not usually be considered to have occurred on the job or in the course of employment and hence would not be covered.

An employee must notify his or her employer of an injury promptly (usually within thirty days of the injury's occurrence). Generally, an employee also must file a workers' compensation claim with the appropriate state agency or board within a certain period (sixty days to two years) from the time the injury is first noticed, rather than from the time of the accident.

An employee's acceptance of workers' compensation benefits bars the employee from suing for injuries caused by the employer's negligence. By barring lawsuits for negligence, workers' compensation laws also bar employers from raising common law defenses to negligence, such as contributory negligence. For example, an employer can no longer raise such defenses as contributory negligence or assumption of risk (see Chapter 7) to avoid liability for negligence. A worker may sue an employer who *intentionally* injures the worker, however.

> **Workers' Compensation Laws**
> State statutes that establish an administrative procedure for compensating workers for injuries that arise out of or in the course of their employment, regardless of fault.

Employment Discrimination

The early 1960s marked a period in our history in which we, as a nation, focused on the civil rights of all Americans, regardless of race, color, national origin, gender, or religion. It was during this period that consumer protection also became an issue, as mentioned earlier. Out of the movement to end racial and other forms of discrimination grew a body of law protecting workers against discrimination in employment. Although our discussion focuses on the federal laws prohibiting discrimination in the workplace, state laws also prohibit employment discrimination, sometimes to an even greater degree than do federal laws.

TITLE VII OF THE CIVIL RIGHTS ACT OF 1964. The most significant federal law prohibiting discrimination is the Civil Rights Act of 1964. The law was enacted to protect certain groups from the discriminatory practices of business owners, educational institutions, employers, and other groups. One section of the act, known as Title VII, pertains to employment practices. Title VII prohibits employers from discriminating against employees or potential employees on the basis of race, color, national origin, religion, or gender. The Pregnancy Discrimination Act of 1978 amended Title VII to expand the definition of gender-based discrimination to include discrimination based on pregnancy.

The Application of Title VII. Title VII of the 1964 Civil Rights Act has been interpreted by the courts to prohibit both intentional and unintentional discrimination. The latter occurs when certain employer practices or procedures have a discriminatory effect, even though they were not intended to be discriminatory. For example, suppose that a city requires all of its firefighters to be at least six feet tall. In effect, that job requirement discriminates against women, because few women are that tall. The effect of the rule is discriminatory, even though the intent in adopting the rule might have been merely to ensure an able-bodied firefighting crew.

The courts have also extended Title VII protection to those who are subject to **sexual harassment** in the workplace. There are two types of sexual harassment. *Quid pro quo harassment* occurs when a superior doles out awards (promotions, raises, benefits, or other advantages) to a subordinate in exchange for sexual favors. (*Quid pro quo* in Latin means "this for that" or "something for something.") In contrast, *hostile-environment harassment* occurs when an employee is subjected to offensive sexual comments, jokes, or physical contact in the workplace that makes it difficult or impossible for the employee to perform a job satisfactorily.

Sexual Harassment
In the employment context, the hiring or granting of job promotions or other benefits in return for sexual favors (*quid pro quo* harassment) or language or conduct that is so sexually offensive that it creates a hostile working environment (hostile-environment harassment).

The Equal Employment Opportunity Commission. The Equal Employment Opportunity Commission (EEOC) is a federal agency that administers and enforces Title VII and the laws prohibiting employment discrimination based on disability or age (to be discussed shortly), as well as some other federal antidiscrimination laws. Claims of Title VII violations must first be filed with the EEOC. The EEOC will either investigate and take action on the claim, on behalf of the employee, or allow the employee to file a civil suit against the employer.

Employers' Liability under Title VII. An employer's liability under Title VII can be extensive. In general, the court can order injunctive relief against the employer (a judicial order to prevent future discrimination), retroactive promotions that were wrongfully withheld from the employee, and past wages to compensate the employee for the time he or she was wrongfully unemployed. Damages are also available in cases involving *intentional* discrimination.

DISCRIMINATION BASED ON AGE. The Age Discrimination in Employment Act of 1967 prevents employers from discriminating against workers between the ages of forty and seventy on the basis of their age. The act was passed, in part, in response to an increasing tendency on the part of employers to reduce costs by excluding older workers from their work forces and hiring younger workers (at lower salaries) instead.

On the Web
You can find the complete text of Title VII, the ADEA, and the ADA (and other federal antidiscrimination laws), as well as information about the activities of the EEOC, at the EEOC's Web site. Go to www.eeoc.gov.

DISCRIMINATION BASED ON DISABILITY. Congress enacted the Americans with Disabilities Act (ADA) in 1990 to strengthen existing laws prohibiting discrimination in the workplace against individuals with disabilities. Employers with fifteen or more employees are obligated to satisfy the requirements of the ADA.

As defined by the 1990 statute, disabilities include heart disease, cancer, blindness, paralysis, acquired immune deficiency syndrome (AIDS), emotional illnesses, and learning disabilities. Under the ADA, an employer is not permitted to discriminate against a person with a disability if *reasonable accommodations* can be provided to assist the worker in satisfactorily performing the job. An employer is not required to accommodate a worker with a disability if the accommodation would constitute an undue hardship for the employer, however. For example, if the cost of accommodating the employee is extremely high, that high cost might constitute an undue hardship for the employer. Although enforcement of the ADA falls within the jurisdiction of the EEOC, the paralegal should note that the

> ## SUBSTANTIVE LAW CONCEPT SUMMARY
> ### Employment Relationships
>
> | | |
> |---|---|
> | **Employment at Will** | Traditionally, the employment relationship has been "at will"—that is, the relationship can be terminated at any time for any reason by either the employer or the employee. Statutes have limited the application of the at-will doctrine. |
> | **Labor Laws** | 1. *Norris-LaGuardia Act (1932)*—Permitted employees to organize into unions and to engage in peaceful strikes.

2. *National Labor Relations Act (1935)*—Established the right of employees to engage in collective bargaining and to strike. The act also created the National Labor Relations Board (NLRB) to oversee elections and to prevent employers from engaging in unfair and illegal labor practices.

3. *Fair Labor Standards Act (1938)*—Established guidelines regulating overtime pay and minimum hourly wages. Prohibited the exploitation of children by regulating their employment. |
> | **Employment Discrimination** | 1. *Title VII of the Civil Rights Act (1964)*—Prohibits employment discrimination against job applicants and employees on the basis of race, color, national origin, gender, or religion. Title VII has been interpreted by the courts to prohibit both intentional and unintentional discrimination as well as pregnancy discrimination and sexual harassment.

2. *Age Discrimination in Employment Act (1967)*—Prohibits employment discrimination on the basis of age (against employees or job applicants aged forty or older).

3. *Americans with Disabilities Act (1990)*—Prohibits discrimination on the basis of disability against individuals qualified for a given job. Employers must reasonably accommodate the needs of persons with disabilities. |

worker alleging discrimination in violation of the ADA may also file a civil lawsuit against the employer for violation of the act.

Employment Relationships and the Paralegal

Employment relationships necessarily affect the paralegal. As an employee, you will be subject to the laws governing employment relationships. As a legal professional, depending on the firm or organization for which you are employed, you may be extensively involved in work relating to labor and employment laws. If you work in the corporate counsel's office of a large corporate enterprise, for example, the corporation's employees may belong to a labor union. The corporate counsel's office will then need to handle matters governed by labor laws, such as collective bargaining agreements and labor-management disputes. As a paralegal in a law firm or a government agency, you might assist in work relating to claims of employment discrimination, which may require you to interact with the EEOC or a relevant state agency. Here are just a few tasks that paralegals commonly undertake in the area of labor and employment law:

- Draft employment contracts for an employer.
- Assist with contract negotiations between labor and management.
- Prepare for arbitration proceedings before the NLRB.

Today's Professional Paralegal

Developing a Policy on Sexual Harassment

Erika Delong, a legal assistant, works in the office of the general counsel at ABC Manufacturing Corporation. She works closely with the personnel department. Today, she is attending a meeting with her supervisor, Gene Tompkins, who is the general counsel, to discuss the company's policy on sexual harassment with the vice president of human resources, the president of the corporation, and the vice presidents of several of the corporation's divisions. Erika has been asked to attend the meeting because her supervisor will ultimately be responsible for preparing the policy and he wants her to draft it. Erika has already obtained copies of other companies' policies to use as samples in the meeting.

The meeting is held in a large conference room. The president opens the meeting by explaining its purpose—to develop a policy on sexual harassment. "We want to discourage it and to have a written policy that includes reporting and investigation procedures. Erika and Gene have several samples that we can review," says the president.

Setting Policy Goals and Defining Sexual Harassment

Erika passes out the sample policies. The group then reviews the various policies, with Gene explaining the legal ramifications of each one. The president remarks that he thinks the policy should begin with a statement that the corporation wants to promote an atmosphere in which authority and power are not abused and in which sexual harassment is not condoned. He points out some language that he likes in one of the samples. Erika highlights it so she will have an idea of how to draft the introduction.

Gene then states, "After an introduction and general statement of the corporation's policy, we should give the legal definition of what constitutes sexual harassment. The definition in sample three is very good from both a legal and a practical point of view because it also gives examples." Erika highlights the definition paragraph in sample three and puts a number 2 next to it, so she knows that it should come second. She flips back to the sample the president referred to and she puts a number 1 next to it.

Developing Procedures

As the discussion continues, the vice president of human resources comments on the procedure for filing a complaint, the investigation that will take place, and the disciplinary measures that will be imposed for sexual harassment. The vice president does not like any of the samples, and the group spends quite a bit of time working through specific language to pin down what he wants. When the meeting is over, the group goes to lunch in the executive dining room. After lunch, Gene informs the others that Erika will prepare a draft of the policy and will circulate it among them for review and comment. Once all of their comments have been collected, the group will meet again to decide on the final provisions. Erika will then prepare and circulate a final draft of the policy. Erika returns to her office to begin working on the initial draft.

- Respond to inquiries from the NLRB regarding a client's alleged unfair labor practices.
- Prepare for and attend administrative hearings before the EEOC.
- Gather factual information to counter or support a claim of employment discrimination.
- Prepare reports and furnish documentation in response to an EEOC investigation into an employee's claim of employment discrimination.
- Draft a policy manual for a business client concerning what actions constitute discriminatory employment practices.
- Research the EEOC's guidelines on sexual harassment and relevant case law to determine what type of policies and procedures will help a client avoid liability for sexual harassment.
- Prepare notices regarding a firm's employment policies, important changes in employment laws, and so on.

Key Terms and Concepts

adjudication 294
administrative law judge (ALJ) 297
administrative process 295
consumer 301
consumer law 302
deceptive advertising 302
delegation doctrine 294
employment at will 316
environmental impact statement (EIS) 310
executive agency 290
garnishment 306
independent regulatory agency 291
legislative rule 294
potentially responsible party (PRP) 313
rulemaking 295
sexual harassment 319
toxic tort 309
workers' compensation laws 318

Chapter Summary

1. Congress and state legislatures create administrative agencies by passing enabling legislation, which specifies the name, purpose, function, and powers of the agency being created. Federal agencies include executive agencies (cabinet departments and subagencies) and independent regulatory agencies (agencies outside of the executive branch).

2. Administrative agencies combine functions normally associated with the three branches of government—the executive, legislative, and judicial branches. The constitutional authority for delegating such powers to administrative agencies is generally held to be implied by various sections in Article I of the Constitution, which deals with congressional powers.

3. The administrative process includes rulemaking, enforcement, and judicial functions. Agency rulemaking typically involves a three-step process: notifying the public of a proposed rule, receiving and reviewing comments from interested parties on the proposed rule, and publishing the final rule in the *Federal Register,* a daily government publication. The agency's enforcement function involves investigation (including on-site inspections, if necessary to obtain information) and adjudication in a hearing conducted by an agency's administrative law judge. A party may appeal the ALJ's decision to the commission or board that heads the agency and, ultimately, to a federal court.

4. Administrative agencies exist at all levels of American government—federal, state, and local. Many federal agencies have parallel state agencies. If a conflict of law arises between a federal and a state agency, the supremacy clause of the U.S. Constitution requires that the federal agency's decisions or rules take priority over those of the state agency. Some agencies permit qualified paralegals to represent and advise clients during administrative proceedings.

5. Numerous federal and state statutes have been enacted to protect consumers from harmful products or unfair practices on the part of sellers. The Federal Trade Commission prohibits deceptive advertising, which is usually defined as any advertising that would deceive a reasonable consumer. Packaging and labeling laws protect consumers by requiring producers to label their products accurately and truthfully and to disclose certain information on product labels. In addition to the Uniform Commercial Code's provisions that protect consumers (the provisions on warranties and unconscionability, for example), federal and state statutes and regulations also regulate certain types of sales transactions in the interest of protecting consumers.

6. Consumers are also protected by federal laws and regulations governing the sale of foods and drugs, which establish standards relating to health and safety that must be met by producers of foods and drugs before their products can be marketed. Federal laws also provide protection for consumers in credit transactions by imposing specific requirements on institutions that extend credit to consumers, credit-card companies, credit-reporting agencies, and credit-collection agencies. Federal and state laws also regulate garnishment proceedings against debtors.

7. Both state and federal statutes and agency regulations protect the environment from pollution caused by business activities. Additionally, businesses whose pollution causes others to be injured may be sued in tort on the basis of negligence or strict liability. The federal Environmental Protection Agency was established in 1970 to coordinate and administer federal

environmental protection laws. The major federal law regulating air pollution is the Clean Air Act of 1963, as amended. The major federal law governing water pollution is the Clean Water Act of 1972, as amended. A number of federal laws have also been enacted to protect the environment from toxic chemicals, including pesticides and herbicides, other toxic substances, and hazardous waste.

8. Under the common law, employment in the United States has traditionally been "at will"—both the employer and employee could terminate the employment relationship at any time for any reason. State and federal statutes regulating employment now govern employment relationships to a significant extent. Since the 1930s, a number of federal laws have been enacted to allow employees to form labor unions, strike peacefully, and bargain collectively with management for improved working conditions and benefits. Labor laws generally regulate union-management relations and prohibit both employers and unions from engaging in certain types of activities. Federal law also requires most employers to give their employees time off for family and medical purposes. Workers are also protected under state workers' compensation statutes, which allow workers to obtain compensation for injuries incurred while on the job, without regard to fault.

9. Title VII of the Civil Rights Act of 1964 prohibits employment discrimination against job applicants and employees on the basis of race, color, national origin, gender, and religion. The courts have interpreted Title VII to prohibit not only intentional discrimination but also unintentional discrimination, as well as sexual harassment. The Age Discrimination in Employment Act of 1967 prohibits employment discrimination based on age, and other statutes, including the Americans with Disabilities Act of 1990, prohibit employment discrimination against persons with disabilities. Employees with disabilities must be reasonably accommodated by employers. Laws prohibiting employment discrimination are administered by the Equal Employment Opportunity Commission.

QUESTIONS FOR REVIEW

1. How are administrative agencies created? What are two types of federal agencies?

2. What powers can an administrative agency exercise? Why is it said that administrative agencies exercise powers—executive, legislative, and judicial—that are usually divided among the three branches of government? Does the Constitution authorize Congress to delegate some of its law-making powers to administrative agencies?

3. Describe the most commonly used procedure for agency rulemaking. Where can a paralegal find an agency rule?

4. How do agencies enforce laws and regulations?

5. What are some of the ways in which the law attempts to protect consumers? Name some of the most important consumer-protection statutes.

6. What are the major federal statutes that protect the environment? What federal agency is charged with administering federal environmental laws? Do states also pass laws and issue regulations protecting the environment?

7. What is Superfund? What parties are responsible for the clean-up of hazardous waste sites?

8. What is meant by employment at will? When did the government begin to regulate employment relationships? What was the purpose of the National Labor Relations Act, and what agency administers and enforces the act's provisions?

9. What are state workers' compensation statutes? How do they protect workers?

10. What federal statutes prohibit employment discrimination? What kinds of discrimination are prohibited under these statutes? What federal agency handles claims of employment discrimination?

ETHICAL QUESTIONS

1. Trevor Holland is an independent paralegal who is interested in the area of workers' compensation. He contacts the state workers' compensation board to request information on whether a nonlawyer may represent clients who have workers' compensation claims. He is told that nonlawyers are not allowed to

practice before the agency. What would happen if he began practicing in this area anyway?

2. Janet Koons is a paralegal working for the state unemployment office. A young woman comes into the office to file a claim for unemployment compensation. The woman states that she was fired from her job while on maternity leave, although the duration of the leave did not exceed the leave time allotted by the company. The woman asks Janet if her job termination constitutes gender-based discrimination. Should Janet answer her question? What should Janet say?

3. Mark Anderson has been the operations manager of Division B of the Wicks Company for fifteen years. The Wicks Company is now undergoing a reorganization and is combining the management of Division B with that of Division A. The operations manager of Division A, a younger man who has been with the firm for only three years, has been asked to take over Mark's responsibilities. The net result for Mark is that he has been given the choice of retiring earlier than planned (with a special retirement bonus) or taking another job with the company with less pay and little job security. Mark has always received favorable performance evaluations and does not want to retire. He concludes that he is being discriminated against on the basis of age and calls to make an appointment with an attorney to seek legal advice. His main question is whether the company would have a legitimate reason to fire him if he discusses the matter with the Equal Employment Opportunity Commission. The attorney is out of town, and the attorney's paralegal, June Carter, takes the call. How should June respond to Mark's question?

4. The state Department of Environmental Quality is holding a hearing. CARCO, an automobile manufacturing company, has been accused of violating the air-emissions standards in the state. An administrative law judge (ALJ) is presiding over the hearing. The ALJ makes several comments about lawless corporate polluters and refers to the state's environmental laws as "polluter pay acts." Julie Marks, a paralegal, is attending the hearing with Jeffrey Nelson, a CARCO attorney. How should they respond to the ALJ's remarks?

PRACTICE QUESTIONS AND ASSIGNMENTS

1. Using the material on administrative agencies presented in Exhibit 9.1, *The Government of the United States,* identify the agencies described below by name and type:

   a. This department oversees education and reports to the secretary of education.

   b. This agency oversees transportation issues and gets involved in major disasters, such as plane crashes.

   c. This department oversees the military and reports to the secretary of defense.

   d. This agency oversees issues related to consumer products.

2. Using the material in the chapter discussing the functions performed by administrative agencies, identify which function is being carried out in each of the following scenarios:

   a. The Environmental Protection Agency publishes a notice of proposed rulemaking in the *Federal Register.* The proposed rule creates three categories of generators of hazardous waste and imposes various regulations on the different types of generators.

   b. Robert is denied disability benefits by the Social Security Administration (SSA). Robert's attorney challenges the denial, and a hearing on the matter is held by the SSA's administrative law judge.

   c. Louise calls the state department of health to report unsanitary conditions that she has observed at a local restaurant. The health department visits the restaurant to determine whether the conditions there are unsanitary.

3. Using the material on the agency rulemaking process discussed in this chapter, discuss the steps that an agency would follow if it wanted to create the following rule:

   Every paralegal shall be entitled to have the day off on his or her birthday. If the birthday falls on a weekend or a holiday, the paralegal shall be given a day off during the week to celebrate his or her birthday.

4. Rhonda Raines works as a paralegal for a busy attorney. While the attorney is taking a deposition in the firm's conference room, a client calls. The client owns a restaurant and has just returned from out of town to find an inspector from the state's health department at the restaurant's door. The client has not inspected the kitchen yet, and he wants to look it over himself before the inspector sees it. If the restaurant receives another citation for violating the health code, the agency could put the restaurant out of business permanently.

The client wants to know if there is any way he can prevent the inspector from coming in and inspecting the restaurant. Rhonda tells him the attorney is tied up but she can slip into the conference room and hand him a note asking him what the client can do to put off the inspection. On the basis of what you have learned in this chapter, write a note from the attorney to Rhonda instructing the client on how to keep the inspector out of his kitchen.

5. Using the material on labor laws presented in this chapter, identify each of the following statutes or employment doctrines:

   a. A federal statute regulating minimum hourly wages and overtime pay.

   b. A federal statute prohibiting age discrimination.

   c. A federal statute allowing employees to organize into unions and to strike.

   d. A federal statute prohibiting employment discrimination on the basis of race, color, national origin, gender, or religion.

   e. A federal statute authorizing collective bargaining and strikes, and establishing an agency to oversee union elections and other union activities.

   f. A doctrine allowing employment relationships to be terminated at any time for any reason by either party.

   g. A federal statute prohibiting employment discrimination on the basis of disability.

   h. State statutes that allow workers to be compensated for on-the-job injuries.

6. Using the material on consumer law presented in this chapter, identify the law that would apply to each of the following situations and explain how it would resolve the problem:

   a. Mary purchases a new computer system for $2,500 and pays for it with a credit card. The first week that Mary has her new computer, she has serious difficulty operating many of the programs, the computer constantly freezes up, and she loses work that she has prepared on the word processor. Mary complains to the company from which she purchased the computer. When the problem is not resolved, she withholds payment to her credit-card company and notifies them of the reason.

   b. Dick has a credit card with an $8,000 balance. He loses his job and stops paying the credit-card company. The company begins to harass him at all hours of the day and even calls his former employer to verify that Dick had been fired.

7. Using the materials on environmental law presented in the chapter, identify the law that applies to each of the following situations and explain how it would resolve the problem:

   a. The foreman at a manufacturing plant disposes of a fifty-five-gallon drum of spent solvents, a toxic waste, every week by pouring it on the ground "out back."

   b. An investigation reveals that the local gas utility company has PCBs in its pipeline in excess of those allowed.

   c. An oil company releases hundreds of gallons of oil into a local river, contaminating the river, which is a major source of drinking water for the area.

   d. A manufacturing plant that produces metallic paint for use on motor vehicles releases more pollutants into the air than the allowable emissions limits for its vicinity.

   e. In the 1950s, five large manufacturing companies disposed of hazardous waste by burying the waste on the property of a farmer forty miles away from the city and its inhabitants, where it could do no harm. The rural farm is now part of a suburb. The suburb's ground water and drinking water are found to be contaminated by the waste buried on the site of the former farm. The citizens demand that the waste disposal site be cleaned up.

8. Identify what type of employment discrimination, if any, is being practiced in each of the following hypothetical situations:

   a. Lana Ronsky, a legal assistant in an all-male law firm, is the subject of constant sexual jokes, comments, and occasional uninvited touching—all of which are offensive to her and make it difficult for her to do her job.

   b. Monica Pierson, a partner in a large law firm, interviews seven potential legal assistants, including an Asian American. Although the Asian American is the best qualified for the job, Monica does not hire him because he speaks English with an accent, which might offend some of the firm's clients.

   c. Diana Bekins, the manager of an insurance agency, makes it clear to Jack McBride, a new sales representative, that she will promote him only if he provides sexual favors in return.

   d. A post office has a rule that all mail carriers must be able to bench-press two hundred pounds, because the mailbags are so heavy. As a result, only 3 out of 150 mail carriers are women.

QUESTIONS FOR CRITICAL ANALYSIS

1. Why are so many administrative agencies needed? What do they regulate? Do government agencies assist those groups that they were created to help, or are agencies unnecessarily burdensome?

2. The heads of independent regulatory agencies serve fixed terms and cannot be removed without cause. What are the benefits of this arrangement? What problems might it cause? Is this a good system?

3. The U.S. Constitution provides for a separation of powers among the executive, legislative, and judicial branches of government. Why, then, are administrative agencies allowed to exercise executive, legislative, and judicial powers? What would be the result if agencies could not exercise this combination of powers?

4. Federal administrative agencies typically have parallel agencies at the state level. Why? What happens if there is a conflict between a state and a federal regulation? If a citizen wants to challenge an agency rule or decision, must he or she go through two layers of government bureaucracy to do so? If so, is this a good system?

5. Some administrative agencies allow nonlawyers, including paralegals, to represent clients before the agencies, yet paralegals are not allowed to represent clients in courts. What is the difference between paralegals' representation of clients before agencies and representing clients in courts?

6. What debt-collection practices does the Fair Debt Collection Practices Act prohibit? How would these practices assist a debt-collection agency in collecting debts? What can debt-collection agencies legally do to collect debts?

7. Why do employers dislike garnishment proceedings? What action might an employer take to avoid a garnishment situation with a specific employee? How can the employee be protected? Is garnishment fair to the employer? Is it fair to the employee? Why or why not?

8. Make a list of the consumer laws presented in this chapter. What rights do these laws protect? Why are they needed? What does the necessity for consumer-protection laws say about our society?

9. What tort actions exist for environmental pollution? How do tort actions fit into the environmental regulatory scheme? What would happen if tort actions were the only remedy for environmental pollution?

10. The Clean Air Act, the Clean Water Act, and the Toxic Substances and Control Act, among others, regulate the amount of pollution allowed into the air, water, and other aspects of the environment. Should any pollution be allowed into the environment? Who should determine how "clean" air or water should be? What might happen if no pollution at all were allowed?

11. In addition to imposing joint liability, Superfund also imposes strict liability—that is, liability without regard to fault—on generators and transporters of hazardous waste, and owners and operators of the site at the time of the disposal and at the time of the clean-up. Is it fair to hold companies liable who did not know that the waste they were disposing of was harmful? Is it fair to hold a subsequent purchaser of contaminated property liable who did not know that the property was polluted when he or she purchased it? Who ultimately pays for the clean-up costs?

12. Employers typically want their employees to be bright, young people who are dedicated to their work. Some employers do not want to hire people who need to take family or maternity leaves, who are old, or whose racial or ethnic background is dissimilar to theirs. Should employers be allowed to hire only the people they want to hire? Should they be able to limit their employees to certain age groups or ethnic backgrounds? Should they be able to refuse to hire job candidates with disabilities? Why or why not? What laws protect people in these groups from employment discrimination?

13. What laws were the result of the efforts of labor unions? What other benefits have workers realized as a result of labor unions' efforts? What might happen if labor unions did not exist?

PROJECTS

1. Visit a local law library to determine if your state has an administrative code similar to the federal government's *Code of Federal Regulations*. If your state has such a code, what is it called? Does your state also have a publication similar to the *Federal Register*? If so, what is it called? How often is it published?

2. Using a telephone book or a state directory (or an online directory of state agencies), make a list of five

state administrative agencies for which you would be interested in working, along with the phone number of each agency. Call each agency and ask if non-lawyers are allowed to practice before it. Record your results and report them to the class. Discuss with others in the class for which agency each would prefer to work, and why.

3. Contact one of the agencies listed in your answer to Project 2. Arrange to visit the agency to observe what kind of work paralegals perform at that agency. Discuss this project with your instructor before you undertake it to learn if any limitations apply.

4. Locate your state employment agency in the telephone directory. Contact the agency and find out whether your state adheres to the employment-at-will doctrine. Also find out if, and in what circumstances, exceptions to this doctrine are made.

5. Call the Equal Employment Opportunity Commission at 1-800-669-4000 and find out where the nearest regional office of the agency is located. Also, find out what the time frames and procedures are for filing claims of gender-based discrimination, age discrimination, and disability-based discrimination, respectively.

6. Contact the Federal Trade Commission by telephone at 1-202-382-4357, or in writing at the following address: Federal Trade Commission, CRC-240, Washington, DC 20580. Find out how to file a complaint for deceptive advertising. Does the agency resolve complaints submitted by individuals?

7. Contact a credit-reporting agency and obtain a credit report on yourself, if one exists. Does the report contain accurate information about your credit transactions? If not, and if a denial of credit, employment, or insurance might have been based on the report, you can and should have it corrected, as permitted under the Fair Credit Reporting Act.

Using Internet Resources

1. Many paralegals, at one time or another, are asked to assist in cases dealing with employment discrimination. For that reason, it is a good idea to become familiar with the agency that administers federal laws prohibiting various forms of employment discrimination, the Equal Employment Opportunity Commission (EEOC). This exercise will help you learn more about this agency and its activities. First, access the EEOC's Web site at **www.eeoc.gov**. Browse through the site, and then find answers to the following questions:

    a. What federal law (enabling legislation) established the EEOC? What federal acts does it enforce?

    b. Within how many days after a discriminatory action must an employee file a charge (claim) with the EEOC? Can employees first file a charge with a state or local agency that implements state and local laws?

    c. How many charges of discrimination were filed with the EEOC in the most recent year listed? What percentage of the total annual claims dealt with each of the following types of discrimination: sex discrimination, disability-based discrimination, and race-based discrimination?

    d. Give the titles of two recent "Enforcement Guidelines" issued by the EEOC.

2. The Federal Trade Commission (FTC) provides information on consumer law issues through its Web site, located at **www.ftc.gov**. Go to this Web site, follow the directions given below, and then answer these questions:

    a. Select "Who We Are & How We Serve You." What are the vision, mission, and goals of the FTC?

    b. Click on "How the FTC Brings an Action." Summarize in two paragraphs how the FTC brings an action.

    c. Click on "Privacy Policy." What is the FTC's privacy policy regarding those who visit its Web site?

    d. Click on "Where to Go for More Information." Make a list of the offices, including their names and addresses, to contact for additional information, along with any other sources included.

    e. Go back to the home page and select "Consumer Protection." What areas of consumer protection does the FTC regulate?

    f. From the home page, access "Current News Releases." Do any of these news releases deal with false advertising? Prepare a one-paragraph summary of one of the news releases.

PART 3
LEGAL PROCEDURES AND PARALEGAL SKILLS

CHAPTER 10
Civil Litigation—Before the Trial

CHAPTER 11
Trial Procedures

CHAPTER 12
Criminal Law and Procedures

CHAPTER 13
Conducting Interviews and Investigations

CHAPTER 14
Legal Research

CHAPTER 15
Computer-Assisted Legal Research

CHAPTER 16
Legal Analysis and Writing

CHAPTER 10

Civil Litigation— Before the Trial

Chapter Outline

- Introduction
- Civil Litigation—A Bird's Eye View
- The Preliminaries
- The Pleadings
- Pretrial Motions
- Traditional Discovery Tools
- Revised Discovery Procedures under FRCP 26

After completing this chapter, you will know:

- The basic steps involved in the civil litigation process and the types of tasks that may be required of paralegals during each step of the pretrial phase.

- What a litigation file is, what it contains, and how it is organized, maintained, and reviewed.

- How a lawsuit is initiated and what documents are filed during the pleadings stage of the civil litigation process.

- What a motion is and how certain pretrial motions, if granted by the court, will end the litigation before the trial begins.

- What discovery is and the kind of information that attorneys and their paralegals obtain from parties to the lawsuit and from witnesses when preparing for trial.

INTRODUCTION

The paralegal plays a particularly important role in helping the trial attorney prepare for and conduct a civil trial. Popular television shows and movies tend to glamorize courtroom trials as semantic battles between quick-witted litigators, but the success of any trial depends primarily on how well the attorney and the paralegal have prepared for it.

Preparation for trial involves a variety of tasks. The law relating to the client's case must be carefully researched. Evidence must be gathered and documented. The litigation file must be created and carefully organized. Procedural requirements and deadlines for filing certain documents with the court must be met. **Witnesses**—persons asked to testify at trial—must be prepared in advance and be available to testify at the appropriate time during the trial. Any exhibits, such as charts, photographs, or videotapes, to be used at the trial must be properly prepared, mounted, scanned into the computer, or filmed. Arrangements must be made to have any necessary equipment, such as a VCR, videodisc, or CD-ROM player and projector, available for use at the trial. The paralegal's efforts are critically important in preparing for trial, and attorneys usually rely on paralegals to ensure that nothing has been overlooked during trial preparation.

Attorneys may request that their paralegals assist them during the trial as well. In the courtroom, the paralegal can perform numerous tasks. For example, the paralegal can locate documents or exhibits as they are needed. The paralegal can also observe jurors' reactions to statements made by attorneys or witnesses, check to see if a witness's testimony is consistent with sworn statements made by the witness before the trial, and perhaps give witnesses some last-minute instructions outside the courtroom before they are called to testify.

The complexity of even the simplest civil trial requires that the paralegal have some familiarity with the litigation process and the applicable courtroom procedures. Much of this expertise, of course, can only be acquired through hands-on experience. Yet every paralegal should be acquainted with the basic phases of civil litigation and the forms and terminology commonly used in the process. In this chapter, you will learn about the pretrial stages of a civil lawsuit, from the initial attorney-client meeting to the time of trial. In the next chapter, you will read about trial and posttrial procedures.

Witness
A person who is asked to testify under oath at a trial.

On the Web
For a summary of the step-by-step procedures followed during a civil law case in one state court (Arizona), go to www.supreme.state.az.us/courts/guide.htm#How.

CIVIL LITIGATION—A BIRD'S EYE VIEW

Although civil trials vary greatly in terms of complexity, cost, and detail, they all share similar structural characteristics. They begin with an event that gives rise to the legal action, and (provided the case is not settled by the parties at some point during the litigation process—as most cases are) they end with the issuance of a **judgment**, the court's decision on the matter. In the interim, the litigation itself may involve all sorts of twists and turns. Even though each case has its own "story line," most civil lawsuits follow some version of the course charted in Exhibit 10.1.

Judgment
The court's final decision regarding the rights and claims of the parties to a lawsuit.

Pretrial Settlements

As just mentioned, in most cases, the parties reach a *settlement*—an out-of-court resolution of the dispute—before the case goes to trial. Lawsuits are costly in both time and money, and it is usually in the interest of both parties to settle the case out of court. Throughout the pretrial stage of litigation, the attorney will therefore attempt to help the parties reach a settlement. At the same time, though, the attorney and the paralegal will operate under the assumption that the case will go to trial because if it does, all pretrial preparation must be completed prior to the trial date.

EXHIBIT 10.1
A Typical Case Flow Chart

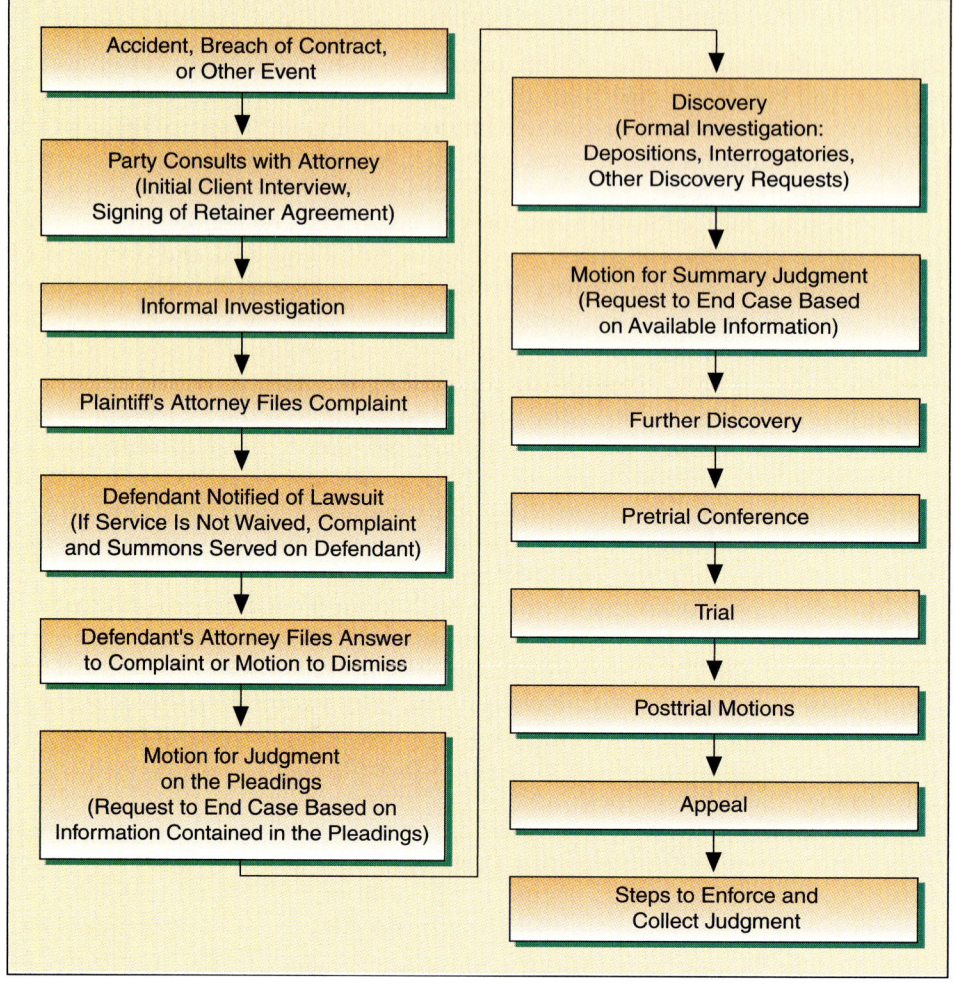

Procedural Requirements

Understanding and meeting procedural requirements is essential in the litigation process. These requirements are spelled out in the procedural rules of the court in which a lawsuit is brought. All civil trials held in federal district courts are governed by the **Federal Rules of Civil Procedure (FRCP)**.[1] These rules specify what must be done during the various stages of the federal civil litigation process. For example, FRCP 4 (Rule 4 of the FRCP) describes the procedures that must be followed in notifying the defendant of the lawsuit. Each state also has its own rules of civil procedure (which in many states are similar to the FRCP). In addition, many courts have their own local rules of procedures that supplement the federal or state rules. The attorney and the paralegal must comply with the rules of procedure that apply to the specific court in which the trial will take place.

A Hypothetical Lawsuit

To illustrate the procedures involved in litigation, we present a hypothetical civil lawsuit. The case involves an automobile accident in which a car driven by Tony Peretto collided with a car driven by Katherine Baranski. Baranski suffered numer-

Federal Rules of Civil Procedure (FRCP)
The rules controlling all procedural matters in civil trials brought before the federal district courts.

---

1. Some practitioners use the abbreviation FRCivP to distinguish the Federal Rules of Civil Procedure from the Federal Rules of Criminal Procedure.

ous injuries and incurred substantial medical and hospital costs. She also lost wages for the five months that she was unable to work. Baranski has decided to sue Peretto for damages. Because Baranski is the person initiating the lawsuit, she is the plaintiff. Peretto, because he must defend against Baranski's claims, is the defendant. The plaintiff and the defendant are referred to as the *parties* to the lawsuit, as discussed in Chapter 5. (Some cases involve several plaintiffs and/or defendants.)

The attorney for the plaintiff (Baranski) is Allen P. Gilmore. Gilmore is assisted by paralegal Elena Lopez. The attorney for the defendant (Peretto) is Elizabeth A. Cameron. Cameron is assisted by paralegal Gordon McVay. Throughout this chapter and the following chapter, *Case at a Glance* features in the page margins will remind you of the names of the players in this lawsuit.

> **Case at a Glance**
>
> **The Plaintiff—**
> Plaintiff: Katherine Baranski
> Attorney: Allen P. Gilmore
> Paralegal: Elena Lopez
>
> **The Defendant—**
> Defendant: Tony Peretto
> Attorney: Elizabeth A. Cameron
> Paralegal: Gordon McVay

THE PRELIMINARIES

Katherine Baranski arranges to meet with Allen P. Gilmore, an attorney with the law firm of Jeffers, Gilmore & Dunn, to see if Gilmore will represent her in the lawsuit. Gilmore asks paralegal Elena Lopez to prepare the usual forms and information sheets, including a retainer agreement and a statement of the firm's billing procedures, and to bring them with her to the initial interview with Baranski.

The Initial Client Interview

Most often, an initial client interview is conducted by the attorney—for several reasons. First, if attorney Gilmore is interested in taking on a new client, he will want to explain to the client the value of his services and those of his firm. Second, only an attorney can agree to represent a client. Third, only an attorney can set fees, and if Gilmore decides to take Baranski on as a client, fee arrangements will be discussed, and possibly agreed on, during the initial client interview. Finally, only an attorney can give legal advice, and the initial client interview may involve advising Baranski of her legal rights and options. In short, what transpires during the initial client interview normally falls under the umbrella of "the practice of law," and, as you read in Chapter 3, only attorneys are permitted to practice law.

Because attorney Gilmore and paralegal Lopez will be working together on the case, however, Gilmore will ask Lopez to sit in on the interview. Gilmore will want Lopez to meet Baranski, become familiar with Baranski's claim, and perhaps make arrangements for follow-up interviews with Baranski should Gilmore decide to take the case.

During the initial client interview, Katherine Baranski explains to attorney Gilmore and paralegal Lopez the facts of her case as she perceives them. Baranski tells them that Tony Peretto, who was driving a Dodge van, ran a stop sign and crashed into the driver's side of her Ford Escort as she was driving through the intersection of Mattis Avenue and Thirty-eighth Street in Nita City, Nita. The accident occurred at 7:45 A.M. on August 4, 1998. Baranski has misplaced Peretto's address, but she knows that he lives in another state, the state of Zero.[2] Baranski claims that as a result of the accident, she has been unable to work for five months and has lost approximately $15,000 in wages. Her medical and hospital expenses total $85,000, and the property damage to her car is estimated to be $10,000.

Gilmore agrees to represent Baranski in the lawsuit against Peretto. He explains the fee structure to Baranski, and she signs the retainer agreement.[3] He also has Baranski sign forms authorizing Gilmore to obtain relevant medical,

---

2. Nita and Zero are fictitious states invented for the purpose of this hypothetical.
3. See Chapter 4 for a discussion of legal fees and the form and function of the retainer agreement.

> ## ETHICAL CONCERN
> ### The Unauthorized Practice of Law
>
> When a paralegal conducts an initial client interview, the paralegal must be constantly aware of the ethical pitfalls inherent in these situations. Suppose that attorney Gilmore is out of town but wants to obtain information about Baranski's legal matter as soon as possible. In this situation, he might ask Lopez to conduct an initial interview solely for the purposes of gaining information from Baranski about her claim. To avoid potential liability for the unauthorized practice of law, Lopez must be careful not to advise Baranski in regard to fees or her legal rights and obligations.

employment, and other records relating to the claim. (These forms, which are called *release forms,* will be discussed in Chapter 13.) At the end of the interview, Gilmore also asks Lopez to schedule a follow-up interview with Baranski. Lopez will conduct the follow-up interview and obtain more details from Baranski about the accident and its consequences.

Preliminary Investigation

After Baranski leaves the office, attorney Gilmore asks paralegal Lopez to undertake a preliminary investigation to glean as much information as possible concerning the factual circumstances of Baranski's accident. Sources of this information will include the police report of the accident, medical records, employment data, and eyewitness accounts of the accident.

You will read in Chapter 13 about the steps that a paralegal can take when investigating the facts of a client's case, and therefore we will not discuss investigation here. Bear in mind, though, that at this point in the pretrial process, the paralegal may engage in extensive investigation. Legal investigation is an important part of pretrial work, and facts discovered (or not discovered) by the legal investigator may play an important role in determining the outcome of the lawsuit.

Creating the Litigation File

Attorney Gilmore also asks paralegal Lopez to create a litigation file for the case. As the litigation progresses, Lopez will carefully maintain the file to make sure that such items as correspondence, bills, research and investigation results, and all documents and exhibits relating to the litigation are in the file and segregated in an organized manner.

Each law firm or legal department has its own specific organizational scheme to follow when creating and maintaining client files. Recall from Chapter 4 that there are three goals of any law-office filing system: to preserve confidentiality, to safeguard legal documents, and to ensure that the contents of files can be easily and quickly retrieved when needed. Usually, it is the paralegal's responsibility to make sure that the litigation file is properly created and maintained.

As a case progresses through the litigation process, subfiles may be created for documents relating to the various stages. For example, at this point in the Baranski case, the litigation file will contain notes taken during the initial client interview, the signed retainer agreement, and information and documents gathered

DEVELOPING PARALEGAL SKILLS

File Work-Up

Once a litigation file has been created, the paralegal typically "works up" the file. In the Baranski case, after paralegal Lopez has completed her initial investigation into Baranski's claim, she will review and summarize the information that she has amassed so far, including the information that she has gathered through the initial client interview, subsequent client interviews, and any investigation that she has conducted.

Lopez will also identify areas that might require the testimony of an expert witness. For example, if Baranski claimed that as a result of the accident she had broken her hip and would always walk with a limp, Gilmore would want a medical specialist to give expert testimony to support Baranski's claim. (How to locate expert witnesses will be discussed in later chapters.)

Lopez would prepare a list of potential experts for Gilmore to review. Once Lopez has worked up the file, she will prepare a memo to Gilmore summarizing the file. This memo will provide Gilmore with factual information for deciding which legal remedy or strategy to pursue, what legal issues need to be researched, and generally how to proceed with the case.

TIPS FOR PREPARING A FILE WORK-UP MEMO

- Summarize the information that has been obtained about the case.
- Suggest a plan for further investigation in the case (you will read about investigation plans in Chapter 13).
- Suggest additional information that might be obtained during discovery (discussed later in this chapter).
- Include a list of expert witnesses to contact, explaining which witnesses might be preferable and why.

---

by paralegal Lopez during her preliminary investigation of the claim. As the lawsuit progresses, Lopez will make sure that special subfiles are created for documents relating to the pleadings and discovery stages (to be discussed shortly). Depending on the office filing system, the file folders for these subfiles may be color coded or numbered so that each subfile can be readily recognized and retrieved. Lopez will also prepare an index for each subfile to indicate what documents are included in it. The index will be placed at the front of the folder for easy reference.

A properly created and maintained litigation file will provide a comprehensive record of the case so that others in the firm who become involved with it can quickly acquaint themselves with the progress of the proceedings. Because well-organized files are critical to the success of any case, Lopez should take special care to properly maintain the file.

THE PLEADINGS

The next step will be for plaintiff Baranski's attorney (Gilmore) to file a complaint in the appropriate court. The **complaint**[4] is a document that states the claims the plaintiff is making against the defendant. The complaint also contains a statement regarding the court's jurisdiction over the dispute and a demand for a remedy (such as money damages).

The filing of the complaint is the initial step that begins the legal action against the defendant, Peretto. The plaintiff's complaint and the defendant's answer—both of which are discussed below—are **pleadings**. The pleadings inform

Complaint
The pleading made by a plaintiff or a charge made by the state alleging wrongdoing on the part of the defendant.

Pleadings
Statements by the plaintiff and the defendant that detail the facts, charges, and defenses involved in the litigation.

---
4. In state courts, this document may be called a *petition*.

EXHIBIT 10.2
Types of Pleadings

Initial Pleadings

Complaint Filed by the plaintiff to initiate the lawsuit.
Answer Filed by the defendant in response to the plaintiff's complaint.

Counterclaim and Reply

Counterclaim Filed by the defendant against the plaintiff, asserting a claim for an injury arising from the same incident that forms the basis for the plaintiff's claim. There are two types of counterclaims:

1. A *compulsory* counterclaim must be asserted if it arises out of the same transaction or event that gave rise to the plaintiff's complaint or the right to assert the claim will be waived (forgone). Example: Defendant Peretto claims that plaintiff Baranski's negligence caused him to suffer injuries for which he should be compensated.

2. A *permissive* counterclaim arises from a separate transaction than the one forming the basis for the original lawsuit. Example: Defendant Peretto claims that plaintiff Baranski, prior to the accident had purchased a used Rolls-Royce from him, and Baranski's check bounced. Peretto has the option of either bringing a separate lawsuit against Baranski to collect the amount of the bounced check or filing a permissive counterclaim for that amount in this lawsuit.

Reply Filed by the plaintiff in response to the defendant's counterclaim.

Cross-Claim and Answer

Cross-claim Filed by a defendant against another defendant or a plaintiff against another plaintiff. When cross-claims are made, the defendants are suing one another (or the plaintiffs are suing one another). Example: Assume that plaintiff Baranski had been struck by two vehicles, one belonging to defendant Peretto and one belonging to Leon Balfour. If Peretto and Balfour had been named as co-defendants in Baranski's complaint, then Peretto's attorney could also file a cross-claim on behalf of Peretto against Balfour.

Answer Filed by the party against whom a cross-claim is brought.

Third Party Complaint and Answer

Third Party Complaint Filed by the defendant (in response to the plaintiff's complaint) or by the plaintiff (in response to the defendant's counterclaim) to bring into the litigation a third party who could be liable. Example: Defendant Peretto files a third party complaint against the manufacturer of the van that he was driving. Peretto asserts that the manufacturer should be liable for Baranski's injuries because the van's brakes were defective and therefore Peretto was unable to stop at the stop sign.

Answer Filed by the third party in response to the third party complaint.

---

each party of the claims of the other and specify the issues (disputed questions) involved in the case. We examine here the complaint and answer, two basic pleadings. Exhibit 10.2 above includes other types of pleadings that, under the FRCP, may also be filed with the court during this stage of the litigation.

The complaint must be filed within the period of time allowed by law for bringing legal actions. The allowable period is fixed by state statutes of limitations (discussed in Chapter 5), and this period varies for different types of lawsuits. For example, state statutes of limitations governing breaches of sales contracts are usually four years. For negligence lawsuits, statutes of limitations vary from state to state. After the time allowed under a statute of limitations has expired, normally no action can be brought, no matter how strong the case was originally. For example, if the statute of limitations covering the auto-negligence lawsuit that plaintiff Baranski is bringing against defendant Peretto is two years, Baranski normally has to initiate the lawsuit within that two-year period or forgo (give up) forever the possibility of suing Peretto for damages caused by the car accident.

Drafting the Complaint

The complaint itself may be no more than a few paragraphs long, or it may be many pages in length, depending on the complexity of the case. In the Baranski case, the complaint will probably be only a few pages long unless special circumstances justify additional details. The complaint will include the following sections, each of which we discuss below:

- Caption.
- Jurisdictional allegations.
- General allegations (the body of the complaint).
- Prayer for relief.
- Signature.
- Demand for a jury trial.

Exhibit 10.3 on pages 338 and 339 shows a sample complaint. The sections of the complaint are indicated in the marginal annotations.

Baranski's case is being filed in a federal court, so the Federal Rules of Civil Procedure (FRCP) apply. If Baranski's case were filed in a state court, paralegal Lopez might need to review the appropriate state rules of civil procedure. The rules for drafting pleadings in state courts differ from the FRCP. The rules also differ from state to state and even from court to court within the same state. Lopez could obtain pleading forms, either from "form books" available in the law firm's files or library (or on computer disk or online) or from pleadings drafted previously in similar cases litigated by the firm in the court in which the Baranski case will be filed.

THE CAPTION. All documents submitted to the court or other parties during the litigation process begin with a caption. The caption of the complaint identifies the court in which the action is being filed, the names of the parties, and the designation of the document as a "Complaint." The caption leaves a space for the court to insert the name of the judge who will be hearing the case. The caption also leaves a space for the court to insert the file number, or case number, that it assigns to the case. (The court's file number may also be referred to as the *docket number.* A **docket** is the list of cases entered on a court's calendar and thus scheduled to be heard.) Exhibit 10.3 shows how the caption will read in the case of *Baranski v. Peretto.*

Docket
The list of cases entered on a court's calendar and thus scheduled to be heard by the court.

JURISDICTIONAL ALLEGATIONS. Because attorney Gilmore is filing the lawsuit in a federal district court, he will have to include in the complaint an allegation that the federal court has jurisdiction to hear the dispute. (An **allegation** is an assertion, claim, or statement made by one party in a pleading that sets out what the party expects to prove to the court.) Recall from Chapter 6 that federal courts can exercise jurisdiction over disputes involving either a *federal question* or *diversity of citizenship.* A federal question arises whenever a claim in a civil lawsuit relates to a federal law, the U.S. Constitution, or a treaty executed by the U.S. government. Diversity of citizenship exists when the parties involved in the lawsuit are citizens of different states and the amount in controversy exceeds $75,000. Because Baranski and Peretto are citizens of different states (Nita and Zero, respectively)

Allegation
A party's statement, claim, or assertion made in a pleading to the court. The allegation sets forth the issue that the party expects to prove.

EXHIBIT 10.3
The Complaint

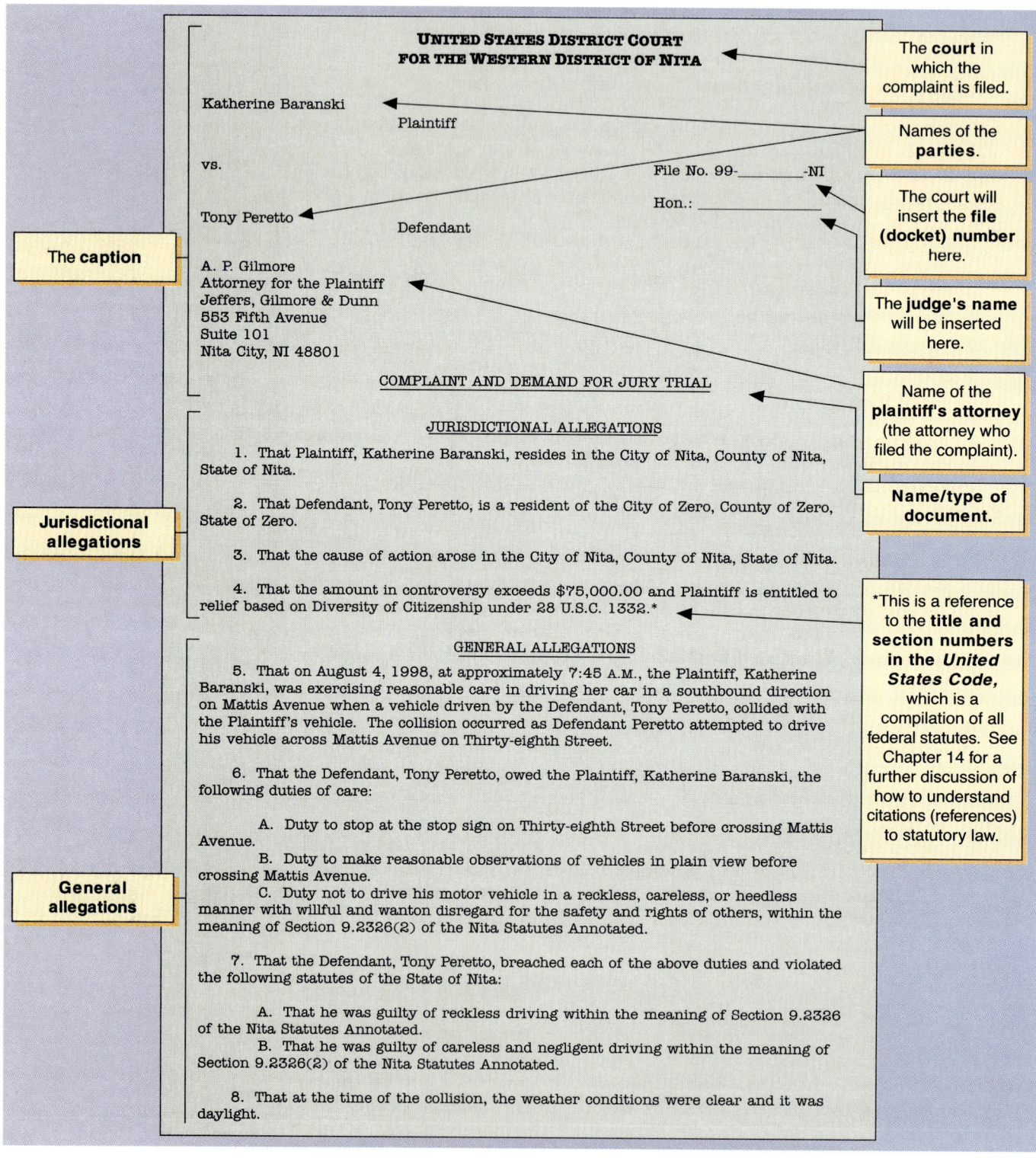

EXHIBIT 10.3
The Complaint—Continued

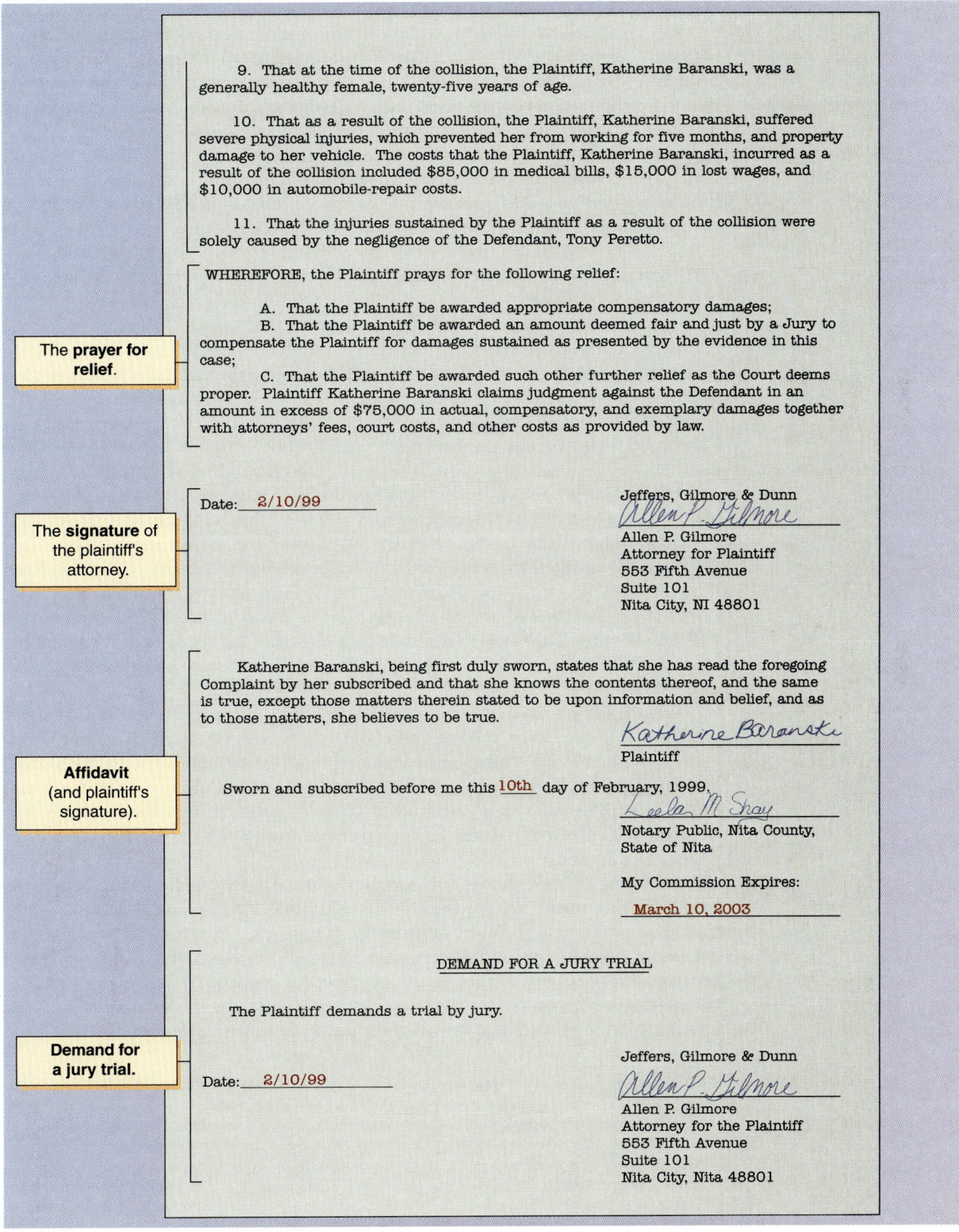

9. That at the time of the collision, the Plaintiff, Katherine Baranski, was a generally healthy female, twenty-five years of age.

10. That as a result of the collision, the Plaintiff, Katherine Baranski, suffered severe physical injuries, which prevented her from working for five months, and property damage to her vehicle. The costs that the Plaintiff, Katherine Baranski, incurred as a result of the collision included $85,000 in medical bills, $15,000 in lost wages, and $10,000 in automobile-repair costs.

11. That the injuries sustained by the Plaintiff as a result of the collision were solely caused by the negligence of the Defendant, Tony Peretto.

WHEREFORE, the Plaintiff prays for the following relief:

The prayer for relief.

A. That the Plaintiff be awarded appropriate compensatory damages;
B. That the Plaintiff be awarded an amount deemed fair and just by a Jury to compensate the Plaintiff for damages sustained as presented by the evidence in this case;
C. That the Plaintiff be awarded such other further relief as the Court deems proper. Plaintiff Katherine Baranski claims judgment against the Defendant in an amount in excess of $75,000 in actual, compensatory, and exemplary damages together with attorneys' fees, court costs, and other costs as provided by law.

Date: 2/10/99

The signature of the plaintiff's attorney.

Jeffers, Gilmore & Dunn

Allen P. Gilmore
Allen P. Gilmore
Attorney for Plaintiff
553 Fifth Avenue
Suite 101
Nita City, NI 48801

Affidavit (and plaintiff's signature).

Katherine Baranski, being first duly sworn, states that she has read the foregoing Complaint by her subscribed and that she knows the contents thereof, and the same is true, except those matters therein stated to be upon information and belief, and as to those matters, she believes to be true.

Katherine Baranski
Plaintiff

Sworn and subscribed before me this 10th day of February, 1999.

Leela M Shay
Notary Public, Nita County,
State of Nita

My Commission Expires:

March 10, 2003

DEMAND FOR A JURY TRIAL

The Plaintiff demands a trial by jury.

Demand for a jury trial.

Jeffers, Gilmore & Dunn

Date: 2/10/99

Allen P. Gilmore
Allen P. Gilmore
Attorney for the Plaintiff
553 Fifth Avenue
Suite 101
Nita City, Nita 48801

and because the amount in controversy exceeds $75,000, the case meets the requirements for diversity-of-citizenship jurisdiction. Gilmore thus asserts that the federal court has jurisdiction on this basis, as illustrated in Exhibit 10.3.

As explained in Chapter 6, certain matters—such as those involving patent or copyright disputes, the Internal Revenue Service, or bankruptcy—can *only* be brought in federal courts. Certain other cases, however, including those involving diversity of citizenship, may be brought in either a state court or a federal court. Thus, an attorney in Gilmore's position can advise the client that he or she has a choice. Gilmore probably considered several factors when advising Baranski on which court would be preferable for her lawsuit. An important consideration is how long it would take to get the case to trial. Many courts are overburdened by their caseloads, and sometimes it can take years before a court will be able to hear a case. If Gilmore knows that the case could be heard two years earlier in the federal court than in the state court, that will be an important factor to consider.

GENERAL ALLEGATIONS (THE BODY OF THE COMPLAINT). The body of the complaint contains a series of allegations, stated in numbered paragraphs. In plaintiff Baranski's complaint, the allegations outline the factual events that gave rise to Baranski's claims.[5] The events are described in a series of chronologically arranged, numbered allegations so that the reader can understand them easily. As Exhibit 10.3 shows, the numbers of the paragraphs in the body of the complaint continue the sequence begun in the section on jurisdictional allegations.

When drafting the complaint, paralegal Lopez will play the role of advocate. She must present the facts forcefully and in a way that supports and strengthens the client's claim. The recitation of the facts should demonstrate that defendant Peretto had engaged in conduct that entitles plaintiff Baranski to relief. Even though she will want to present the facts in a light most favorable to Baranski, Lopez must be careful not to exaggerate the facts or make false statements. Rather, she must present the facts in such a way that the reader could reasonably infer that defendant Peretto was negligent and that Peretto's negligence caused Baranski's injuries and losses.

What if her research into the case had given Lopez reason to believe that a fact was probably true even though she could not be certain as to its validity? She could still include the statement in the complaint by prefacing it with the phrase, "On information and belief . . . ." This language would indicate to the court that the plaintiff, Baranski, had good reason to believe the truth of the statement but that the evidence for it either had not yet been obtained or might not hold up under close scrutiny.

The most effective complaints are those that are clear and concise. Moreover, brevity and simplicity are required under FRCP 8(a). As in all legal writing, Lopez should strive for clarity. When drafting the complaint, Lopez should use clear language and favor simple and direct statements over more complex wording. This is because the court may, at the request of opposing counsel, strike (delete) from the complaint ambiguous phrases—phrases whose meaning is unclear or that may be interpreted in more than one way. Lopez should also resist the temptation to include

---

5. The body of the complaint described in this section is a *fact pleading,* in which sufficient factual circumstances must be alleged to convince the court that the plaintiff has a cause of action. State courts often require fact pleadings, whereas federal courts only require *notice pleading.* FRCP 8(a) requires only that the complaint have "a short and plain statement of the claim showing that the pleader is entitled to relief." Fact pleading and notice pleading are not totally different—that is, the same allegation of facts could be in the body of a complaint submitted to either a federal or a state court. Federal courts simply have fewer requirements in this respect, and therefore they are often more attractive to litigants.

facts that are not absolutely necessary for the complaint. By reducing the body of the complaint to the simplest possible terms, Lopez will not only achieve greater clarity but also minimize the possibility of divulging attorney Gilmore's trial strategies or hinting at a possible defense that the opponent might use to defeat the claim.

After telling plaintiff Baranski's story, paralegal Lopez will add one or more paragraphs outlining the harms suffered by the plaintiff and the remedy (in money damages) that the plaintiff seeks. In general, it is preferable that all allegations of damages—such as hospital costs, lost wages, and auto-repair expenses—be included in a single paragraph, as in Exhibit 10.3. Lopez should check the relevant court rules, however, to see whether the court requires that certain types of damages (Baranski's lost wages, for example) be alleged in a separate paragraph.

PRAYER FOR RELIEF. Paralegal Lopez will include at the end of the complaint a paragraph, similar to that shown in Exhibit 10.3, asking that judgment be entered for the plaintiff and appropriate relief be granted. This **prayer for relief** will indicate that plaintiff Baranski is seeking money damages to compensate her for the harms that she suffered.

Prayer for Relief
A statement at the end of the complaint requesting that the court grant relief to the plaintiff.

SIGNATURE. In federal practice, the signature following the prayer for relief certifies that the plaintiff's attorney (or the plaintiff, if he or she is not represented by an attorney) has read the complaint and that the facts alleged are true to the best of his or her knowledge. In addition to the attorney's signature, some courts require an affidavit signed by the plaintiff verifying that the complaint is true to the best of the plaintiff's knowledge. **Affidavits** are sworn statements attesting to the existence of certain facts. They are acknowledged by a notary public or another official authorized to administer such oaths or affirmations. Exhibit 10.3 illustrates an affidavit for the Baranski complaint.

Affidavit
A written statement of facts, confirmed by the oath or affirmation of the party making it and made before a person having the authority to administer the oath or affirmation.

DEMAND FOR A JURY TRIAL. A trial can be held with or without a jury. If there is no jury, the judge determines the truth of the facts alleged in the case. The Seventh Amendment to the U.S. Constitution guarantees the right to a jury trial in federal courts in all "suits at common law" when the amount in controversy exceeds $20. Most states have similar guarantees in their own constitutions, although many states put a higher minimum dollar restriction on the guarantee (for example, in Iowa the minimum amount is $1,000). If this threshold requirement is met, either party may request a jury trial.

The right to a trial by jury does not have to be exercised, and many cases are tried without one. In most states and in federal courts, one of the parties must request a jury or the right is presumed to be waived (that is, the court will presume that neither party wanted a jury trial). The decision to exercise the right to a jury trial usually depends on what legal theory the party is using and which judge is assigned to the trial. In the Baranski case, plaintiff Baranski's attorney, Gilmore, may advise Baranski to demand a jury trial if he believes that a jury would be sympathetic to Baranski's position. If plaintiff Baranski wants a jury trial, Gilmore will ask paralegal Lopez to include a demand for jury trial (similar to the one illustrated in Exhibit 10.3) with the complaint.

Filing the Complaint

Once the complaint has been prepared, carefully checked for accuracy, and signed by attorney Gilmore, paralegal Lopez will file the complaint with the court in which the action is being brought. To file the complaint, Lopez will deliver it to the clerk of the court, together with a check payable to the court in the amount of

Developing Paralegal Skills
Federal Court Rules—Creating a Complaint Checklist

Ann Marston is a paralegal who works in a firm with a federal court practice. A new paralegal, Brian Blake, is joining the firm, and Ann has been asked to train Brian. Her supervising attorney suggested that she create a checklist for drafting federal court complaints. The checklist could be used to train not only Brian but also new associates in the firm.

Before she begins drafting a complaint, Ann meets with Brian and explains what she does. Ann tells Brian that she starts by getting the file and reviewing her notes, memos from the client interview, and any reports, such as police reports, that are in the file. She explains that these sources will assist her in describing how, for example, a personal injury occurred in an accident case. She also checks to see if she made any notes, during her meeting with the attorney who will handle the case, regarding the court in which the case will be filed, because in some cases the state and federal courts have concurrent jurisdiction. Next, she finds out the plaintiff's and the defendant's correct legal names. If necessary, she contacts the secretary of state to obtain the legal name of a corporation. Lastly, she takes out her copy of the Federal Rules of Civil Procedure and reviews Rule 8, 10, and 11, which specify the kind of information that should be included in complaints filed in a federal court.

CHECKLIST FOR DRAFTING A COMPLAINT

- Determine when the statute of limitations expires by checking the file for the relevant dates.
- Locate a previously drafted complaint form for the types of cases involved.
- Determine the court's basis for jurisdiction in the case, and draft an allegation explaining it.
- Determine the facts that create the cause of action, or the legal basis for the lawsuit.
- Draft the "general allegations," or the body of the complaint. If the plaintiff has more than one legal basis for the relief sought, draft as many "counts" as the plaintiff has.
- Determine the specific type of relief, such as money damages, that the plaintiff is seeking, and draft a prayer for relief.
- Insert a signature block for an attorney's signature after a reasonable inquiry into the facts that support the claim.
- Determine if a jury trial is desired, and draft a demand for a jury trial if needed.

On the Web
To find out whether a particular court permits documents to be filed electronically and, for some courts, to obtain the appropriate forms, visit that court's Web page (or the home page for the state court system). You can find links to federal and state courts at www.findlaw.com.

the required filing fee. (If Lopez is not aware of the court's specific procedures for filing the complaint, she should call the court clerk to verify the amount of the filing fee and how many copies of the complaint need to be filed.) The court clerk files the complaint by stamping the date on the document; assigning the case a file number, or docket number; and assigning the case to a particular judge. (In state courts, the file number may not be assigned until later.)

Although traditionally a complaint or other litigation-related document has been delivered personally to the court clerk, the 1993 revision of Rule 5(a) of the FRCP provides that federal courts may permit filing by fax or "other electronic means." As you read in Chapter 6, several jurisdictions now permit electronic filing. In the future, filing court documents electronically will likely become a common method of filing.

After the complaint has been filed, the court will consult with the attorneys for both sides, often through a scheduling conference. Following this meeting, the judge will enter a *scheduling order* that sets out the time limits within which pretrial events (such as the pleadings, discovery, and the final pretrial conference) must be completed and the date of the trial. Under FRCP 16(b), the scheduling order should be entered "as soon as practicable and in no event more than 120 days after the complaint is filed."

EXHIBIT 10.4

A Summons in a Civil Action

United States District Court

__WESTERN__ DISTRICT OF __NITA__

Katherine Baranski

v.

Tony Peretto

SUMMONS IN A CIVIL ACTION

CASE NUMBER:

TO:

Tony Peretto
1708 Johnston Drive
Zero City, ZE 59806

YOU ARE HEREBY SUMMONED and required to file with the Clerk of this Court and serve upon

PLAINTIFF'S ATTORNEY

Allen P. Gilmore
Jeffers, Gilmore & Dunn
553 Fifth Avenue
Suite 101
Nita City, NI 48801

an answer to the complaint which is herewith served upon you, within __20__ days after service of this summons upon you, exclusive of the day of service. If you fail to do so, judgment by default will be taken against you for the relief demanded in the complaint.

C. H. Hynek
CLERK

February 10, 1999
DATE

John Dolan
BY DEPUTY CLERK

Service of Process

Before the court can exercise jurisdiction over the defendant—in effect, before the lawsuit can begin—the court must have proof that the defendant was notified of the lawsuit. If defendant Peretto did not agree to *waive* service of process (waiver of service will be discussed later) or if the case against Peretto had been filed in a state court, Peretto would be served with a summons. Serving the summons and complaint—that is, the delivery of these documents to the defendant in a lawsuit—is referred to as **service of process**.

THE SUMMONS. The **summons** identifies the parties to the lawsuit, as well as the court in which the case will be heard, and directs the defendant to respond to the complaint within a specified period of time. In the Baranski case, paralegal Lopez will prepare a summons by filling out a form similar to that shown in Exhibit 10.4. Lopez will also prepare a cover sheet for the case, which is required in the federal courts and in most state courts. A sample cover sheet is shown in Exhibit 10.5 on page 344.

Service of Process
The delivery of the summons and the complaint to a defendant.

Summons
A document served on a defendant in a lawsuit informing the defendant that a legal action has been commenced against him or her and that the defendant must appear in court on a certain date to answer the plaintiff's complaint.

EXHIBIT 10.5
A Federal Civil Cover Sheet

CIVIL COVER SHEET

JS 44 (Rev. 07/86)

The JS 44 civil cover sheet and the information contained herein neither replace nor supplement the filing and service of pleadings or other papers as required by law, except as provided by local rules of court. This form, approved by the Judicial Conference of the United States in September 1974, is required for the use of the Clerk of Court for the purpose of initiating the civil docket sheet. (SEE INSTRUCTIONS ON THE REVERSE OF THE FORM.)

I. (a) PLAINTIFFS
Katherine Baranski

DEFENDANTS
Tony Peretto

(b) COUNTY OF RESIDENCE OF FIRST LISTED PLAINTIFF Nita
(EXCEPT IN U.S. PLAINTIFF CASES)

COUNTY OF RESIDENCE OF FIRST LISTED DEFENDANT Zero
(IN U.S. PLAINTIFF CASES ONLY)
NOTE: IN LAND CONDEMNATION CASES, USE THE LOCATION OF THE TRACT OF LAND INVOLVED

(c) ATTORNEYS (FIRM NAME, ADDRESS, AND TELEPHONE NUMBER)
Allen P. Gilmore
Jeffers, Gilmore & Dunn
553 Fifth Avenue, Suite 101
Nita City, NI 48801

ATTORNEYS (IF KNOWN)

II. BASIS OF JURISDICTION (PLACE AN X IN ONE BOX ONLY)
- [ ] 1 U.S. Government Plaintiff
- [ ] 2 U.S. Government Defendant
- [ ] 3 Federal Question (U.S. Government Not a Party)
- [X] 4 Diversity (Includes Citizenship of Parties in Item III)

III. CITIZENSHIP OF PRINCIPAL PARTIES (For Diversity Cases Only)
(PLACE AN X IN ONE BOX FOR PLAINTIFF AND ONE BOX FOR DEFENDANT)

	PTF	DEF		PTF	DEF
Citizen of This State	[X] 1	[ ] 1	Incorporated or Principal Place of Business in This State	[ ] 4	[ ] 4
Citizen of Another State	[ ] 2	[X] 2	Incorporated and Principal Place of Business in Another State	[ ] 5	[ ] 5
Citizen or Subject of a Foreign Country	[ ] 3	[ ] 3	Foreign Nation	[ ] 6	[ ] 6

IV. CAUSE OF ACTION (CITE THE U.S. CIVIL STATUTE UNDER WHICH YOU ARE FILING AND WRITE A BRIEF STATEMENT OF CAUSE. DO NOT CITE JURISDICTIONAL STATUTES UNLESS DIVERSITY.)

28 U.S.C. 1332. Action for damages caused by negligent operation of motor vehicle.

V. NATURE OF SUIT (PLACE AN X IN ONE BOX ONLY)

CONTRACT	TORTS		FORFEITURE/PENALTY	BANKRUPTCY	OTHER STATUTES
❏ 110 Insurance	**PERSONAL INJURY**	**PERSONAL INJURY**	❏ 610 Agriculture	❏ 422 Appeal 28 USC 158	❏ 400 State Reapportionment
❏ 120 Marine	❏ 310 Insurance	❏ 362 Personal Injury—Med Malpractice	❏ 620 Food & Drug	❏ 423 Withdrawal 28 USC 157	❏ 410 Antitrust
❏ 130 Miller Act	❏ 315 Airplane Product Liability	❏ 365 Personal Injury—Product Liability	❏ 630 Liquor Laws		❏ 430 Banks and Banking
❏ 140 Negotiable Instrument	❏ 320 Assault, Libel & Slander	❏ 368 Asbestos Personal Injury Product Liability	❏ 640 R.R. & Truck	**PROPERTY RIGHTS**	❏ 450 Commerce/ICC Rates/etc.
❏ 150 Recovery of Overpayment & Enforcement of Judgment	❏ 330 Federal Employers' Liability		❏ 650 Airline Regs	❏ 820 Copyrights	❏ 460 Deportation
❏ 151 Medicare Act	❏ 340 Marine	**PERSONAL PROPERTY**	❏ 660 Occupational Safety/Health	❏ 830 Patent	❏ 470 Racketeer Influenced and Corrupt Organizations
❏ 152 Recovery of Defaulted Student Loans	❏ 345 Marine Product Liability	❏ 370 Other Fraud	❏ 690 Other	❏ 840 Trademark	❏ 810 Selective Service
❏ 153 Recovery of Overpayment of Veteran's Benefits	[X] 350 Motor Vehicle	❏ 371 Truth in Lending	**LABOR**	**SOCIAL SECURITY**	❏ 850 Securities/Commodities/Exchange
❏ 160 Stockholders' Suits	❏ 355 Motor Vehicle Product Liability	❏ 380 Other Personal Property Damage	❏ 710 Fair Labor Standards Act	❏ 861 HIA (1395ff)	❏ 875 Customer Challenge 12 USC 3410
❏ 190 Other Contract	❏ 360 Other Personal Injury	❏ 385 Property Damage Product Liability	❏ 720 Labor/Mgmt. Relations	❏ 862 Black Lung (923)	❏ 891 Agricultural Acts
❏ 195 Contract Product Liability			❏ 730 Labor/Mgmt. Reporting & Disclosure Act	❏ 863 DIWC (405(g))	❏ 892 Economic Stabilization
REAL PROPERTY	**CIVIL RIGHTS**	**PRISONER PETITIONS**	❏ 740 Railway Labor Act	❏ 863 DIWW (405(g))	❏ 893 Environmental Matters
❏ 210 Land Condemnation	❏ 441 Voting	❏ 510 Motions to Vacate Sentence	❏ 790 Other Labor Litigation	❏ 864 SSID Title XVI	❏ 894 Energy Allocation Act
❏ 220 Foreclosure	❏ 442 Employment	❏ 530 Habeas Corpus	❏ 791 Empl. Ret. Inc. Security Act	❏ 865 RSI (405(g))	❏ 895 Freedom of Information Act
❏ 230 Rent Lease & Ejectment	❏ 443 Housing/Accommodations	❏ 540 Mandamus & Other		**FEDERAL TAX SUITS**	❏ 900 Appeal of Fee Determination Under Equal Access to Justice
❏ 240 Torts to Land	❏ 444 Welfare	❏ 550 Civil Rights		❏ 870 Taxes (U.S. Plaintiff or Defendant)	❏ 950 Constitutionality of State Statutes
❏ 245 Tort Product Liability	❏ 440 Other Civil Rights			❏ 871 IRS—Third party 26 USC 7609	❏ 890 Other Statutory Actions
❏ 290 All Other Real Property					

VI. ORIGIN (PLACE AN X IN ONE BOX ONLY)
- [X] 1 Original Proceeding
- [ ] 2 Removed from State Court
- [ ] 3 Remanded from Appellate Court
- [ ] 4 Reinstated or Reopened
- [ ] 5 Transferred from Another District (specify)
- [ ] 6 Multidistrict Litigation
- [ ] 7 Appeal to District Judge from Magistrate Judgment

VII. REQUESTED IN COMPLAINT:
CHECK IF THIS IS A **CLASS ACTION** [ ] UNDER F.R.C.P. 23
DEMAND $ Excess of $75,000
Check YES only if demanded in complaint:
JURY DEMAND: [X] YES [ ] NO

VII. RELATED CASE(S) IF ANY (See Instructions)
JUDGE _____ DOCKET NUMBER _____

DATE: 2/10/99
SIGNATURE OF ATTORNEY OF RECORD: *Allen P. Gilmore*

UNITED STATES DISTRICT COURT

If the case were being brought in a state court, paralegal Lopez would deliver the summons to the court clerk at the same time she delivered the complaint. (In federal court cases, as will be discussed below, the complaint may already have been filed under the new FRCP provisions relating to waiver of notice.) After the clerk files the complaint and signs, seals, and issues the summons, attorney Gilmore will be responsible for making sure that the documents are served on defendant Peretto. The service of the complaint and summons must be effected within a specified time—120 days under FRCP 4(m)—after the complaint has been filed.

SERVING THE COMPLAINT AND SUMMONS. How service of process occurs depends on the rules of the court or jurisdiction in which the lawsuit is brought. Under FRCP 4(c)(2), service of process in federal court cases may be effected "by any person who is not a party and who is at least 18 years of age." Paralegal Lopez, for example, could serve the summons by personally delivering it to defendant Peretto or to someone living in his home. Alternatively, she could make arrangements for someone else to do so, subject to the approval of attorney Gilmore. In some types of cases, Gilmore might request that the court have a U.S. marshal or other federal official serve the summons.

Under FRCP 4(e)(1), service of process in federal court cases may also be effected "pursuant to the law of the state in which the district court is located." Many state courts require that the complaint and summons be served by a public officer, such as a sheriff.

Regardless of how the summons is served, attorney Gilmore will need some kind of proof that defendant Peretto actually received the summons. In federal court cases, unless service is made by a U.S. marshal or other official, proof of service can be established by having the process server fill out and sign a form similar to the **return-of-service form** shown in Exhibit 10.6 on page 346. This form can then be submitted to the court as evidence that service has been effected.

Return-of-Service Form
A document signed by a process server and submitted to the court to prove that a defendant received a summons.

Paralegal Lopez must be very careful to comply with the service requirements of the court in which plaintiff Baranski's suit has been filed. If service is not properly made, defendant Peretto will have a legal ground (basis) for asking the court to dismiss the case against him, thus delaying the litigation. As mentioned earlier, the court will not be able to exercise jurisdiction over Peretto until he has been properly notified of the lawsuit being brought against him.

SERVING CORPORATE DEFENDANTS. In cases involving corporate defendants, the summons and complaint may be served on an officer or a *registered agent* (representative) of the corporation. The name of a corporation's registered agent is usually obtainable from the secretary of state's office in the state in which the company incorporated its business (and, usually, the secretary of state's office in any state in which the corporation does business).

FINDING THE DEFENDANT. Because some defendants may be difficult to locate, paralegals sometimes have to investigate and attempt to locate a defendant so that process may be served. Information sources that may be consulted to help locate a defendant include telephone directories, banks, former business partners or fellow workers, credit bureaus, Social Security offices, insurance companies, landlords, state and county tax rolls, utility companies, automobile-registration bureaus, bureaus of vital statistics, and the post office. (Chapter 13 discusses these and other possible sources, including various online sources, that the paralegal might consult when trying to locate parties or witnesses involved in lawsuits.)

EXHIBIT 10.6
A Return-of-Service Form

RETURN OF SERVICE

Service of the Summons and Complaint was made by me[1]   DATE **2/11/99**

NAME OF SERVER **Elena Lopez**   TITLE **Paralegal**

Check one box below to indicate appropriate method of service

[X] Served personally upon the defendant. Place where served: **Defendant Peretto's Home: 1708 Johnston Drive, Zero City, Zero 59806**

[ ] Left copies thereof at the defendant's dwelling house or usual place of abode with a person of suitable age and discretion then residing therein. Name of person with whom the summons and complaint were left.

[ ] Returned unexecuted:

[ ] Other (specify):

STATEMENT OF SERVICE FEES

TRAVEL	SERVICES	TOTAL
40 miles @ 33¢/mile	1 hour @ $56/hour	$69.20

DECLARATION OF SERVER

I declare under penalty of perjury under the laws of the United States of America that the foregoing information contained in the Return of Service and Statement of Service Fees is true and correct.

Executed on **2/11/99**   *Signature of Server:* Elena Lopez

308 University Avenue, Nita City, Nita 48804
Address of Server

Notice and Waiver of Service—FRCP 4(d)

The 1993 revision of the FRCP added Rule 4(d), which allows for a simpler and less costly alternative to service of process. Under this rule, a plaintiff's attorney is permitted to notify the defendant directly, through the mails or "other reliable means," of the lawsuit. After the complaint has been filed, attorney Gilmore will thus probably ask paralegal Lopez to follow the procedures outlined in FRCP 4(d).

EXHIBIT 10.7

Form 1A—Notice of Lawsuit and Request for Waiver of Service of Summons

TO: _____(A)_____
[as _____(B)_____ of _____(C)_____]

    A lawsuit has been commenced against you (or the entity on whose behalf you are addressed). A copy of the complaint is attached to this notice. It has been filed in the United States District Court for the _____(D)_____ and has been assigned docket number _____(E)_____.

    This is not a formal summons or notification from the court, but rather my request that you sign and return the enclosed waiver of service in order to save the cost of serving you with a judicial summons and an additional copy of the complaint. The cost of service will be avoided if I receive a signed copy of the waiver within _____(F)_____ days after the date designated below as the date on which this Notice and Request is sent. I enclose a stamped and addressed envelope [or other means of cost-free return] for your use. An extra copy of the waiver is also attached for your records.

    If you comply with this request and return the signed waiver, it will be filed with the court and no summons will be served on you. The action will then proceed as if you had been served on the date the waiver is filed, except that you will not be obligated to answer the complaint before 60 days from the date designated below as the date on which this notice is sent (or before 90 days from that date if your address is not in any judicial district of the United States).

    If you do not return the signed waiver within the time indicated, I will take appropriate steps to effect formal service in a manner authorized by the Federal Rules of Civil Procedure and will then, to the extent authorized by those Rules, ask the court to require you (or the party on whose behalf you are addressed) to pay the full costs of such service. In that connection please read the statement concerning the duty of parties to waive the service of the summons, which is set forth on the reverse side [or at the foot] of the waiver form.

    I affirm that this request is being sent to you on behalf of the plaintiff, this _____ day of _____, _____.

                                      _____
                                      Signature of Plaintiff's Attorney or
                                      Unrepresented Plaintiff

Notes:
    A—Name of individual (or name of officer or agent of corporate defendant)
    B—Title, or other relationship of individual to corporate defendant
    C—Name of corporate defendant, if any
    D—District
    E—Docket number of action
    F—Addressee must be given at least 30 days (60 days if located in foreign country) in which to return waiver

    To comply with FRCP 4(d), Lopez will need to fill out two forms. Form 1A, which is shown in Exhibit 10.7, is entitled "Notice of Lawsuit and Request for Waiver of Service of Summons." This form, which must be signed by attorney Gilmore, requests defendant Peretto to waive the requirement that he be notified of the lawsuit by having a summons served on him. Next, Lopez will fill out Form 1B, entitled "Waiver of Service of Summons." Exhibit 10.8 on page 348 indicates the information that must be included in this form. Once these forms are filled out and attorney Gilmore has reviewed and signed them, paralegal Lopez will send to defendant Peretto a packet containing the following contents:

- Two copies each of Form 1A and Form 1B.
- A copy of the complaint.
- An addressed, stamped envelope for defendant Peretto to use when returning Form 1B.

EXHIBIT 10.8
Form 1B—Waiver of Service of Summons

TO: _____(name of plaintiff's attorney or unrepresented plaintiff)_____

    I acknowledge receipt of your request that I waive service of a summons in the action of __(caption of action)__, which is case number __(docket number)__ in the United States District Court for the _____(district)_____. I have also received a copy of the complaint in the action, two copies of this instrument, and a means by which I can return the signed waiver to you without cost to me.

    I agree to save the cost of service of a summons and an additional copy of the complaint in this lawsuit by not requiring that I (or the entity on whose behalf I am acting) be served with judicial process in the manner provided by Rule 4.

    I (or the entity on whose behalf I am acting) will retain all defenses or objections to the lawsuit or to the jurisdiction or venue of the court except for objections based on a defect in the summons or in the service of the summons.

    I understand that a judgment may be entered against me (or the party on whose behalf I am acting) if an answer or motion under Rule 12 is not served upon you within 60 days after __(date request was sent)__, or within 90 days after that date if the request was sent outside the United States.

_____
Date

Signature _____
Printed/typed name: _____
[as_____]
[of_____]

[To be printed on foot of or on reverse side of form:]

DUTY TO AVOID UNNECESSARY COSTS OF SERVICE OF SUMMONS

Rule 4 of the Federal Rules of Civil Procedure requires parties to cooperate in saving unnecessary costs of service of the summons and complaint. A defendant located in the United States, who, after being notified of an action and asked by a plaintiff located in the United States to waive service of a summons, fails to do so will be required to bear the cost of such service unless good cause be shown for its failure to sign and return the waiver.

    It is not good cause for a failure to waive service that a party believes that the complaint is unfounded, or that the action has been brought in an improper place or in a court that lacks jurisdiction over the subject matter of the action or over its person or property. A party who waives service of the summons retains all defenses and objections (except any relating to the summons or to the service of the summons), and may later object to the jurisdiction of the court or to the place where the action has been brought.

    A defendant who waives service must within the time specified on the waiver form serve on the plaintiff's attorney (or unrepresented plaintiff) a response to the complaint and must also file a signed copy of the response with the court. If the answer or motion is not served within this time, a default judgment may be taken against that defendant. By waiving service, a defendant is allowed more time to answer than if the summons had been actually served when the request for waiver of service was received.

    If defendant Peretto agrees to waive service of process, he will need to sign and return the waiver to attorney Gilmore within thirty days after the waiver form was sent by Gilmore. (For defendants located in a foreign country, the time period is extended to sixty days.)

    The aim of FRCP 4(d) is to eliminate the costs associated with service of process and to foster cooperation among adversaries. To encourage defendants to agree to the waiver of service, FRCP 4(d)(3) provides that defendants who return the required waiver are not required to respond to the complaint for sixty days (ninety days for defendants outside the United States) after the date on which the request for waiver of service was sent. In contrast, if a defendant does not agree to waive service and a complaint and summons must be served, then (under FRCP 12) the defendant must respond to the complaint within twenty days after process is served.

The Defendant's Response

Once a defendant receives the plaintiff's complaint, either via mail or through service of process, the defendant must respond to the complaint within a specified time period (in federal cases, within the time periods specified above). If the defendant fails to respond within that time period, the court, on the plaintiff's motion, will enter a **default judgment** against the defendant. The defendant will then be liable for the entire amount of damages that the plaintiff is claiming and will lose the opportunity to either defend against the claim in court or settle the issue with the plaintiff out of court.

In the Baranski case, assume that defendant Peretto consults with an attorney, Elizabeth A. Cameron, to decide on a course of action. Before Cameron advises Peretto on the matter, she will want to investigate plaintiff Baranski's claim and obtain evidence of what happened at the time of the accident. She may ask her paralegal, Gordon McVay, to call anyone who may have witnessed the accident and any police officers who were at the scene. Attorney Cameron will also ask McVay to gather relevant documents, including the traffic ticket that Peretto received at the time of the accident and any reports that might have been filed by the police. If all goes well, attorney Cameron and paralegal McVay will complete their investigation in a few days and then meet to assess the results.

As mentioned earlier, most cases are settled out of court before they go to trial. But even if Peretto's attorney suspects that an out-of-court settlement might be financially preferable to a trial, she will still draft a response to plaintiff Baranski's claim. She knows that if defendant Peretto does not respond to the plaintiff's complaint within the proper time period, the court will enter a default judgment against Peretto. In deciding how best to respond to the complaint, Peretto's attorney, Cameron, must consider whether to file an answer or a motion to dismiss the case.

THE ANSWER. A defendant's **answer** must respond to each allegation in the plaintiff's complaint. FRCP 8(b) permits the defendant to admit or deny the truth of each allegation. Defendant Peretto's attorney may advise Peretto to admit to some of the allegations in plaintiff Baranski's complaint, because doing so narrows the number of issues in dispute.

> Any allegations that are not denied by the defendant will be deemed to have been admitted.

If defendant Peretto has no knowledge as to whether a particular allegation is true or false, then his attorney, Cameron, may indicate that in the answer. This puts the burden of proving the allegation on plaintiff Baranski, just as if it were an outright denial. It is not necessary for Peretto's attorney to include in the answer any of the reasons for the denial of particular allegations in Baranski's complaint. These reasons may be revealed during the discovery phase of the litigation process (discussed later in this chapter).

Exhibit 10.9 on pages 350 and 351 illustrates the types of responses that defendant Peretto might make in his answer. Like the complaint, the answer begins with a caption and ends with the attorney's signature. It may also include, following the attorney's signature, an affidavit signed by the defendant, as well as a demand for a jury trial, as in Exhibit 10.9.

Answer and Affirmative Defenses. A defendant may assert, in the answer, a reason why he or she should not be held liable for the plaintiff's injuries even if the facts, as alleged by the plaintiff, are true. This is called raising an **affirmative defense.**

Default Judgment
A judgment entered by a clerk or court against a party who has failed to appear in court to answer or defend against a claim that has been brought against him or her by another party.

Answer
A defendant's response to a plaintiff's complaint.

Case at a Glance

The Plaintiff—
　Plaintiff: Katherine Baranski
　Attorney: Allen P. Gilmore
　Paralegal: Elena Lopez

The Defendant—
　Defendant: Tony Peretto
　Attorney: Elizabeth A. Cameron
　Paralegal: Gordon McVay

Affirmative Defense
A response to a plaintiff's claim that does not deny the plaintiff's facts but attacks the plaintiff's legal right to bring an action.

EXHIBIT 10.9
The Answer

UNITED STATES DISTRICT COURT
FOR THE WESTERN DISTRICT OF NITA

Katherine Baranski
        Plaintiff

vs.

Tony Peretto
        Defendant

File No. 99-14335-NI

Hon. Harley M. LaRue

Elizabeth A. Cameron
Attorney for the Defendant
Cameron & Strauss, P.C.
310 Lake Drive
Zero City, ZE 59802

<u>ANSWER AND DEMAND FOR JURY TRIAL</u>

<u>JURISDICTIONAL ALLEGATIONS</u>

1. Defendant lacks sufficient information to form a belief as to the truth of the allegations contained in paragraph 1 of Plaintiff's Complaint.

2. Defendant admits the allegations contained in paragraph 2 of Plaintiff's Complaint.

3. Defendant admits the allegations contained in paragraph 3 of Plaintiff's Complaint.

4. Defendant lacks sufficient information to form a belief as to the truth of the allegations contained in paragraph 4 of Plaintiff's Complaint.

<u>GENERAL ALLEGATIONS</u>

5. Defendant admits the allegations contained in paragraph 5 of Plaintiff's Complaint.

6. Defendant admits the allegations contained in paragraph 6 of Plaintiff's Complaint.

7. Defendant contends that he was operating his vehicle properly and denies the allegations contained in paragraph 7 of Plaintiff's Complaint for the reason that the allegations are untrue.

8. Defendant admits the allegation contained in paragraph 8 of Plaintiff's Complaint.

9. Defendant lacks sufficient information to form a belief as to the truth of the allegation contained in paragraph 9 of Plaintiff's Complaint.

10. Defendant lacks sufficient information on the proximate cause of Plaintiff's injuries to form a belief as to the truth of the averments contained in paragraph 10 of Plaintiff's Complaint.

11. Defendant denies the allegation of negligence contained in paragraph 11 of Plaintiff's Complaint.

EXHIBIT 10.9
The Answer—Continued

NEW MATTER AND AFFIRMATIVE DEFENSES

Although denying that the Plaintiff is entitled to the relief prayed for in the Plaintiff's Complaint, Defendant further states that the Plaintiff is barred from recovery hereunder by reason of the following:

1. That the Plaintiff's injuries were proximately caused by her own contributory negligence and want of due care under the circumstances prevailing at the time of the accident.

2. That the Plaintiff was exceeding the posted speed limit at the time and place of the accident and therefore was guilty of careless and negligent driving within the meaning of Section 9.2325(1) of the Nita Statutes Annotated.

3. That the Plaintiff failed to exercise that standard of care that a reasonably prudent person would have exercised under the same or similar conditions for her own safety and that her own negligence, contributory negligence, and/or comparative negligence caused or was a contributing factor to the incident out of which the Plaintiff's cause of action arises.

4. The Defendant reserves the right, by an appropriate Motion, to move the Court to amend the Defendant's Answer to the Plaintiff's Complaint, to allege other New Matters and Affirmative Defenses as may be revealed by discovery yet to be had and completed in this case.

WHEREFORE, the Defendant prays for a judgment of no cause of action with costs and attorneys' fees to be paid by the Plaintiff.

Cameron & Strauss, P.C.

Elizabeth A. Cameron

Date: 2/25/99

Elizabeth A. Cameron
Attorney for the Defendant

310 Lake Drive
Zero City, ZE 59802

Tony Peretto, being first duly sworn, states that he has read the foregoing Answer by him subscribed and that he knows the contents thereof, and the same is true, except those matters therein stated to be upon information and belief, and as to those matters, he believes to be true.

Tony Peretto
Defendant

Sworn and subscribed before me this 25th day of February, 1999.

Laura Curtis
Notary Public, Zero County,
State of Zero

My Commission Expires:
December 8, 2001

DEMAND FOR A JURY TRIAL

The Defendant demands a trial by jury.

Date: 2/25/99

Cameron & Strauss, P.C.

Elizabeth A. Cameron

Elizabeth A. Cameron
Attorney for the Defendant
310 Lake Drive
Zero City, Zero 59802

> **Case at a Glance**
>
> **The Plaintiff—**
> Plaintiff: Katherine Baranski
> Attorney: Allen P. Gilmore
> Paralegal: Elena Lopez
>
> **The Defendant—**
> Defendant: Tony Peretto
> Attorney: Elizabeth A. Cameron
> Paralegal: Gordon McVay

For example, Peretto might claim that someone else was driving his Dodge van when it crashed into Baranski's car. Peretto's attorney might also raise the defense of *contributory negligence*. That is, she could argue that even though defendant Peretto's car collided with Baranski's, plaintiff Baranski was also negligent because she was exceeding the speed limit when the accident occurred and was thus unable to avoid being hit by Peretto's car. As discussed in Chapter 7, in a few states, if it can be shown that the plaintiff was contributorily negligent, the plaintiff will be completely barred from recovery, and the judge would likely grant a defendant's motion to dismiss the case on this basis. Most states, however, have abandoned the doctrine of contributory negligence in favor of a *comparative negligence* standard. In these states, a plaintiff whose own negligence contributed to an injury can still recover damages, but the damages are reduced by a percentage that represents the degree of the plaintiff's negligence. Although affirmative defenses are directed toward the plaintiff, the plaintiff is not required to file additional pleadings in response to these defenses.

Answer and Counterclaim. Peretto's attorney may follow the answers to the plaintiff's allegations with one or more counterclaims. A **counterclaim** is like a reverse lawsuit in which the defendant asserts a claim against the plaintiff for injuries that the defendant suffered from the same incident. For example, defendant Peretto might contend that plaintiff Baranski lost control of her car and skidded into Peretto's car, causing Peretto to be injured. This allegation would be a counterclaim. The plaintiff is required to reply to any counterclaims made by the defendant.

Counterclaim
A claim made by a defendant in a civil lawsuit against the plaintiff; in effect, a counterclaiming defendant is suing the plaintiff.

MOTION TO DISMISS. A **motion** is a procedural request submitted to the court by an attorney on behalf of his or her client. When one party files a motion with the court, they must also send to, or serve on, the opposing party a *notice of motion*. The notice of motion informs the opposing party that the motion has been filed and indicates when the court will hear the motion. The notice of motion gives the opposing party an opportunity to prepare for the hearing and argue before the court why the motion should not be granted.

The **motion to dismiss**, as the phrase implies, requests the court to dismiss the case for reasons provided in the motion. Defendant Peretto's attorney, for example, could file a motion to dismiss if she believed that Peretto had not been properly served, that the complaint had been filed in the wrong court, that the statute of limitations for that type of lawsuit had expired, or that the complaint did not state a claim for which relief (a remedy) could be granted. See Exhibit 10.10 for an example of a motion to dismiss.

If defendant Peretto's attorney decides to file a motion to dismiss plaintiff Baranski's claim, she may want to attach one or more **supporting affidavits**—sworn statements as to certain facts that may contradict the allegations made in the complaint. Peretto's attorney may also have her paralegal draft a **memorandum of law** (which is called a *brief* in some states) to be submitted along with the motion to dismiss and the accompanying affidavits. The memorandum of law will present the legal basis for the motion, citing any statutes and cases that support it. A supporting affidavit gives factual support to the motion to dismiss, while the memorandum of law provides the court with the legal grounds for the dismissal of the claim.[6]

Motion
A procedural request or application presented by an attorney to the court on behalf of a client.

Motion to Dismiss
A pleading in which a defendant admits the facts as alleged by the plaintiff but asserts that the plaintiff's claim fails to state a cause of action (that is, has no basis in law) or that there are other grounds on which a suit should be dismissed.

Supporting Affidavit
An affidavit accompanying a motion that is filed by an attorney on behalf of his or her client. The sworn statements in the affidavit provide a factual basis for the motion.

Memorandum of Law
A document (known as a brief in some states) that delineates the legal theories, statutes, and cases on which a motion is based.

---

6. The memorandum of law described here should not be confused with the legal memorandum discussed in Chapter 16. The latter is an internal memorandum (that is, a memo submitted—usually by the paralegal—to an attorney).

> **EXHIBIT 10.10**
> A Motion to Dismiss
>
> ---
>
> **UNITED STATES DISTRICT COURT**
> **FOR THE WESTERN DISTRICT OF NITA**
>
> Katherine Baranski
>   Plaintiff   File No. 99-14335-NI
>
> vs.   Hon. Harley M. LaRue
>
> Tony Peretto
>   Defendant
>
> Elizabeth A. Cameron
> Attorney for the Defendant
> Cameron & Strauss, P.C.
> 310 Lake Drive
> Zero City, ZE 59802
>
> **MOTION TO DISMISS**
>
> The Defendant, Tony Peretto, by his attorney, moves the court to dismiss the above-named action because the statute of limitations governing the Plaintiff's claim has expired, as demonstrated in the memorandum of law that is being submitted with this motion. The Plaintiff therefore has no cause of action against the Defendant.
>
>   Cameron & Strauss, P.C.
>
>   *Elizabeth A. Cameron*
> Date: 2/20/99   Elizabeth A. Cameron
>   Attorney for the Defendant
>   310 Lake Drive
>   Zero City, ZE 59802

Amending the Pleadings

An attorney may be called on by a client to file a complaint or an answer without having much time to become familiar with the facts of the case. Because no attorney can anticipate how a case will evolve, the complaint or answer may have to be amended to account for newly discovered facts or evidence. Amendments may also be desirable when circumstances dictate that a different legal theory or defense be put forward.

PRETRIAL MOTIONS

Many motions may be made during the pretrial litigation process, including those listed and described in Exhibit 10.11 on page 355. Some pretrial motions, if granted by the court, will end a case before trial. These motions include the motion to dismiss (which has already been discussed), the motion for judgment on the pleadings, and the motion for summary judgment. Here we examine the latter two motions.

Motion for Judgment on the Pleadings

Once the two attorneys in the Baranski case, Gilmore and Cameron, have finished filing their respective pleadings and amendments, either one of them may file a

> ## ETHICAL CONCERN
> ### Deadlines and the Duty of Competence
>
> Experienced paralegals often stress how easy it is to miss deadlines. A very important deadline that the paralegal should always check is when the statute of limitations expires for the type of claim being made. For example, suppose that the state of Nita's statute of limitations requires Baranski to file her complaint against Peretto within two years or forever forgo the right to sue him. Also suppose that Baranski did not realize that she would always have a limp until a year or so after the accident. Baranski consults with attorney Gilmore about the matter a month before the two-year statute of limitations expires. Gilmore and his paralegal, Lopez, should immediately check the statute of limitations to make sure that they do not miss any deadlines. Otherwise, by the time Lopez completes her initial investigation into the matter, has further consultations with Baranski, and completes other preliminaries—including the drafting of the complaint—the statute might expire before the complaint is filed. All attorneys (and their paralegals) are charged with a duty of competence, and a breach of this duty (such as failing to notice and advise a client of the date on which a statute of limitations expires) may subject the attorney to a lawsuit for professional negligence (malpractice).

Motion for Judgment on the Pleadings
A motion, which can be brought by either party to a lawsuit after the pleadings are closed, for the court to decide the issue without proceeding to trial. The motion will be granted only if no facts are in dispute and the only issue concerns how the law applies to a set of undisputed facts.

Motion for Summary Judgment
A motion requesting the court to enter a judgment without proceeding to trial. The motion can be based on evidence outside the pleadings and will be granted only if no facts are in dispute and the only issue concerns how the law applies to a set of undisputed facts.

motion for judgment on the pleadings. Motions for judgment on the pleadings are often filed when it appears from the pleadings that the plaintiff has failed to state a cause of action for which relief may be granted. They may also be filed when the pleadings indicate that no facts are in dispute and the only question is how the law applies to a set of undisputed facts. For example, assume for a moment that in the Baranski case, defendant Peretto admitted to all of plaintiff Baranski's allegations in his answer and raised no affirmative defenses. In this situation, Baranski's attorney, Gilmore, would file a motion for judgment on the pleadings in Baranski's favor.

Motion for Summary Judgment

A **motion for summary judgment** is similar to a motion for judgment on the pleadings in that the party filing the motion is asking the court to grant a judgment in its favor without a trial. As with a motion for judgment on the pleadings, a court will only grant a motion for summary judgment if it determines that no facts are in dispute and the only question is how the law applies to a set of facts agreed on by both parties.

When the court considers a motion for summary judgment, it can take into account *evidence outside the pleadings*. This distinguishes the motion for summary judgment from the motion to dismiss and the motion for judgment on the pleadings. To support a motion for summary judgment, one party can submit evidence obtained at any point prior to trial (including during the discovery stage of litigation—to be discussed shortly) that refutes the other party's factual claim. In the Baranski case, for example, suppose that Peretto was in another state at the time of the accident. Defendant Peretto's attorney could make a motion for summary judgment in Peretto's favor and attach to the motion a witness's sworn statement that Peretto was in the other state at the time of the accident. Unless plaintiff Baranski's attorney could bring in sworn statements by other witnesses to show

EXHIBIT 10.11
Pretrial Motions

MOTION TO DISMISS

A motion filed by the defendant in which the defendant asks the court to dismiss the case for a specified reason, such as improper service, lack of personal jurisdiction, or the plaintiff's failure to state a claim for which relief can be granted.

MOTION TO STRIKE

A motion filed by the defendant in which the defendant asks the court to strike (delete from) the complaint certain of the paragraphs contained in the complaint. Motions to strike help to clarify the underlying issues that form the basis for the complaint by removing paragraphs that are redundant or irrelevant to the action.

MOTION TO MAKE MORE DEFINITE AND CERTAIN

A motion filed by the defendant to compel the plaintiff to clarify the basis of the plaintiff's cause of action. The motion is filed when the defendant believes that the complaint is too vague or ambiguous for the defendant to respond to it in a meaningful way.

MOTION FOR JUDGMENT ON THE PLEADINGS

A motion that may be filed by either party in which the party asks the court to enter a judgment in its favor based on information contained in the pleadings. A judgment on the pleadings will only be made if there are no facts in dispute and the only question is how the law applies to a set of undisputed facts.

MOTION TO COMPEL DISCOVERY

A motion that may be filed by either party in which the party asks the court to compel the other party to comply with a discovery request. If a party refuses to allow the opponent to inspect and copy certain documents, for example, the party requesting the documents may make a motion to compel production of documents.

MOTION FOR SUMMARY JUDGMENT

A motion that may be filed by either party in which the party asks the court to enter judgment in its favor without a trial. Unlike a motion for judgment on the pleadings, a motion for summary judgment can be supported by evidence outside the pleadings, such as witnesses' affidavits, answers to interrogatories, or other evidence obtained prior to or during discovery.

---

that Peretto was at the scene of the accident, Peretto would normally be granted his motion for summary judgment.

A motion for summary judgment would be particularly appropriate if plaintiff Baranski had previously signed a release waiving her right to sue defendant Peretto on the claim. In that situation, Peretto's attorney, Cameron, would attach a copy of the release to the motion before filing the motion with the court. Cameron would also prepare and attach a memorandum of law in support of the motion. When the motion is heard by the court, Cameron would argue that the execution of the waiver barred plaintiff Baranski from pursuing her claim against defendant Peretto.

The burden would then shift to plaintiff Baranski's attorney, Gilmore, to demonstrate that the release was invalid or otherwise not binding on Baranski. If the judge believes that the release had been voluntarily signed by plaintiff Baranski, then the judge might grant the motion for summary judgment in Peretto's favor. If

> **Case at a Glance**
>
> **The Plaintiff—**
> Plaintiff: Katherine Baranski
> Attorney: Allen P. Gilmore
> Paralegal: Elena Lopez
>
> **The Defendant—**
> Defendant: Tony Peretto
> Attorney: Elizabeth A. Cameron
> Paralegal: Gordon McVay

Paralegal Profile

Litigation Paralegal

Charisse A. Charles-Hampton *received her bachelor of arts degree,* cum laude, *in legal administration in December 1993 from the University of West Florida. Her first paralegal job was as an intern for a judge. After graduation, she was hired by a small law firm as a workers' compensation litigation paralegal and is currently working as a litigation paralegal, primarily in the area of personal injury.*

She is an active member of the Pensacola Legal Assistants Association and serves as chairperson for the Scholarship Awards Committee.

What do you like best about your work?

"What I like best about my work is being able to communicate with people in various offices to assist our clients in defending their claims. I have met a lot of people via the telephone and in so doing, have established great working relationships with many doctors' offices, judges' offices, clerks at the courthouse, and adjusters at various insurance companies, to just list a few. My working relationships with these people make my job much easier when I need to call on their assistance for our clients."

What is the greatest challenge that you face in your area of work?

"The greatest challenge for me is playing the role of both a plaintiff's paralegal and a defense paralegal. Some days it is very hard to empathize with clients who I know in my heart are not seriously injured and are only looking for a handout. On the flip side, it is sometimes very difficult to not allow my emotions to come into play when defending a matter for an insurance company regarding an individual who has been seriously injured."

> "Communication can help you or destroy you."

What advice do you have for would-be paralegals in your area of work?

"I suggest that they focus heavily on their communication skills. Communication can help you or destroy you. I encourage them to attend workshops that focus on communicating with clients who are both difficult and not so difficult. I also encourage would-be paralegals to be detail oriented. Lastly, I suggest that they welcome challenges, big or small."

What are some tips for success as a paralegal in your area of work?

"Tips for success as a personal-injury paralegal include good communication skills, organizational skills, computer skills, timeliness, a willingness to accept changes, and a willingness to make changes that will benefit all parties involved."

---

attorney Gilmore is able to convince the judge that the release signed by Baranski had been procured by coercive or fraudulent practices, however, then the judge would deny the motion for summary judgment and permit the case to go to trial.

TRADITIONAL DISCOVERY TOOLS

Before a trial begins, the parties can use a number of procedural devices to obtain information and gather evidence about the case. Plaintiff Baranski's attorney, for example, will want to know how fast defendant Peretto was driving, whether he had been drinking, whether he saw the stop sign, and so on. The process of

Discovery
Formal investigation prior to trial. During discovery, opposing parties use various methods, such as interrogatories and depositions, to obtain information from each other and from witnesses to prepare for trial.

> ### ETHICAL CONCERN
> ## Keeping Client Information Confidential
>
> As it happens, attorney Gilmore's legal assistant, Lopez, is a good friend of plaintiff Baranski's daughter. Lopez learns from the results of Baranski's medical examination that Baranski has a terminal illness. Lopez is sure that the daughter, who quarreled with her mother two months ago and hasn't spoken to her since, is unaware of the illness and would probably be very hurt if she learned that Lopez knew of it and didn't tell her. Should Lopez tell her friend about the illness? No. This is confidential information at this point, which Lopez only became aware of by virtue of her job. Should the information be revealed publicly during the course of the trial, then Lopez would be free to disclose it to her friend if the friend still remained unaware of it. In the meantime, Lopez is ethically (and legally) obligated not to disclose the information to anyone who is not working on the case, including her friend.

obtaining information from the opposing party or from other witnesses is known as **discovery**.

Discovery serves several purposes. It preserves evidence from witnesses who might not be available at the time of the trial or whose memories will fade as time passes. It can pave the way for summary judgment if both parties agree on all of the facts. It can lead to an out-of-court settlement if one party decides that the opponent's case is too strong to challenge. Even if the case does go to trial, discovery prevents surprises by giving parties access to evidence that might otherwise be hidden. This allows both parties to learn as much as they can about what to expect at a trial before they reach the courtroom. It also serves to narrow the issues so that trial time is spent on the main questions in the case.

The FRCP and similar rules in the states set forth the guidelines for discovery activity. Discovery includes gaining access to witnesses, documents, records, and other types of evidence. The rules governing discovery are designed to make sure that a witness or a party is not unduly harassed, that **privileged information** (communications that may not be disclosed in court) is safeguarded, and that only matters relevant to the case at hand are discoverable. Currently, the trend is toward allowing more discovery and thus fewer surprises. The 1993 revision of the FRCP significantly changed the rules governing discovery in federal court cases. To the extent that state courts decide to follow the new federal rules, discovery in such cases will also be affected. You will learn how the revised rules affect the traditional discovery process in the next section.

Privileged Information
Confidential communications between certain individuals, such as an attorney and his or her client, that are protected from disclosure except under court order.

Traditional discovery devices include interrogatories, depositions, requests for documents, requests for admissions, and requests for examinations. Each of these discovery tools is examined below.

Interrogatories

Interrogatories are written questions that must be answered, in writing, by the parties to the lawsuit and then signed by the parties under oath. Typically, the paralegal drafts the interrogatories for the attorney's review and approval. In the Baranski case, for example, attorney Gilmore will probably ask paralegal Lopez to draft interrogatories to be sent to defendant Peretto.

Interrogatories
A series of written questions for which written answers are prepared and then signed under oath by a party to a lawsuit (the plaintiff or the defendant).

Featured Guest: James W. H. McCord
Ten Tips for Drafting Interrogatories

Biographical Note

Since 1978, James McCord has been active in paralegal education as the director of paralegal programs at Eastern Kentucky University. He has served as president of the American Association for Paralegal Education, as a member of the American Bar Association Legal Assistant Program Approval Commission, and as chair of the Kentucky Bar Association Committee on Paralegals. He received his law degree from the University of Wisconsin and practiced law before taking the position at Eastern Kentucky University. McCord is the author of The Litigation Paralegal: A Systems Approach, which is now in its third edition; ABA Approval: An Educator's Guide; and (as co-author) Criminal Law and Procedure for the Paralegal.

Interrogatories that are well thought out and carefully phrased can help to clarify the factual circumstances of the case, the types of evidence that can be obtained, and the issues in dispute. Because they help to define and shape a lawsuit, your ability to draft good interrogatories will make you a valued member of the litigation team. Here are some tips that you might find useful when you are asked to draft interrogatories.

1. Know the Limits of Interrogatories. Interrogatories have limits. The questions must seek information that is relevant to the issues or that will lead to relevant facts. The number of questions may be limited by the relevant rules or by the judge. Ethical standards explicitly forbid using interrogatories to harass a party or for the primary purpose of swamping the opponent with paperwork. Objections to interrogatories cause unwanted delay and possible loss of valuable information. Opponents usually object to questions that are irrelevant, vague or ambiguous, unduly burdensome, too numerous, or too broad in scope (covering too great a time span, for example). An attorney will also object to questions that seek protected information (such as the privileged communication between spouses or between an attorney and his or her client) or the ideas and strategies that make up the attorney's work product.

2. Develop Objectives for the Interrogatories. Review the case file to familiarize yourself with its contents. Meet with your supervising attorney to discuss the attorney's approach to the case. Identification of the key issues in the case, as well as the strategies and directions the attorney intends to pursue at trial, will help you streamline your work. With your attention focused on only the pertinent matters, reread the complaint, answer, and any other pleadings. Identify the elements to be proved and the defenses to be asserted, then list possible evidence that would support or disprove those elements or defenses. Divide the list into three parts: the information you already possess, information you have that needs to be clarified, and information that you need but do not yet possess. For items in the last two groups, indicate likely persons, files, documents, or other sources that will provide the information or give you leads to the information.

3. Refer to Form Books or Previous Interrogatories. Collections of commonly used interrogatories can be found in the firm's library, a law library, or practice manuals. These are frequently categorized by the type of case—personal injury, contract, antitrust, and so on. Check interrogatories from similar cases in the firm's files to locate pertinent questions. Local examples keyed to local practice are especially helpful. Use the gathered examples as a guide only, then shape your questions to the unique needs of your case. Input useful examples into your computer and edit them to your satisfaction. Add your own questions to fully address the elements of the case at hand.

4. Use Preliminary Sections to Define and Instruct. Following the desired case caption, draft an introductory paragraph stating the name of the person to whom the questions are directed, that answers to the questions are requested, the date answers are due, and the applicable rule or rules of procedure. A subsequent section should define any terms or identify any acronyms that will be

FEATURED GUEST, Continued

repeated in the questions. This promotes clarity and avoids repetitious language. It reduces evasiveness by giving you the power to define the terms as broadly or as narrowly as needed. Interrogatories from previous cases define commonly repeated terms, such as *document, identify, you,* and *corporate officer,* and thus are good sources for the definitions section. Review your proposed definitions in light of your case to make sure that they do not exclude a particularly valuable area of information. The definition and instruction sections should not be so long that they are difficult to read.

5. **Cover the "Who, What, Why, When, Where, and How."** When planning your interrogatories, try to cover the "who, what, why, when, where, and how." Focus on the pleadings. Include in the interrogatories questions that will elicit the basis for each allegation and each denial made in the pleadings. Also include questions that will help you locate evidence that goes beyond the allegations and denials in the pleadings. You might draft questions that ask, for example, for the address and custodian of certain documents, physical evidence, exhibits and witnesses to be relied on, and other items. (Under the revised FRCP, much of the information will already have been disclosed by the parties.)

6. **Phrase Your Questions Simply, Concisely, and Accurately.** The questions should be written simply and concisely. Try to eliminate all unnecessary adjectives and adverbs. Break complex questions into shorter and simpler components.

Avoid giving the defendant options that allow the defendant to select the easiest and least informative answer. Be reasonable in the scope of your requests. For example, you should limit the time span for which records or other kinds of information are sought.

Also, make sure that no words are misspelled. Misspellings create an impression of incompetence and may allow respondents to answer legitimately that they have no knowledge of the whereabouts of "Mr. Fones" when you need information about "Mr. Jones."

7. **Avoid Questions Calling for a "Yes" or "No" Answer.** Questions that permit a "yes" or "no" response are of little value unless you include follow-up questions. Questions should determine if the person's statement is based on personal observation or secondhand knowledge. "Why" questions are easily circumvented with such responses as "That is what he wanted to do," or "He believed he should."

8. **Make Effective Use of Opinion and Contention Questions.** Opinion and contention questions are permitted by federal and most state rules. They identify where the opponent stands on key factual questions. For example, "Do you contend that the intersection light was red before the defendant entered the intersection? If so, on what do you base your contention? What persons have knowledge of these facts?" and so forth. The answers to these types of questions identify the facts in contention and the evidence on which the contention is based. This is extremely useful because other discovery devices do not get at the reasons or evidence that forms the basis for a contention or opinion. It is best to reserve this kind of question for a time later in the discovery process when previous discovery has revealed the contentions and most of the investigation in the case is completed. Otherwise, "I do not know yet" is a likely response.

> "Your ability to draft good interrogatories will make you a valued member of the litigation team."

9. **Add Concluding or Summary Interrogatories.** Include one or more questions to provide some protection for anything you forgot to address. This may prevent the opponent from using evidence at trial that you should have learned about earlier. A concluding request might be, "Identify any additional information pertinent to this lawsuit but not set out in your previous answers."

10. **Employ the Evasiveness Test and Submit the Document to Your Supervising Attorney.** Proofread the drafted interrogatories. Test your questions by placing yourself in the position of the other party and seeing if you can weasel your way around and out of providing such information. Redraft questions if necessary. Once this is done, give the document to your supervising attorney for any final review and signature. Have the interrogatories served on defendant.

On the Web

The first set of interrogatories submitted by Paula Jones to President Bill Clinton in Jones's lawsuit against Clinton for sexual harassment are included in Court TV's online library at **www.courttv.com/library/government/jones/questions.html**.

DRAFTING INTERROGATORIES. All discovery documents, including interrogatories, normally begin with a caption similar to the complaint caption illustrated earlier in this chapter. Following the caption, Lopez will add the name of the party who must answer the interrogatories, instructions to be followed by the party, and definitions of certain terms that are used in the interrogatories. The body of the document consists of the interrogatories themselves—that is, the questions that the opposing party must answer. The interrogatories should end with a signature line for the attorney below which appears the attorney's name and address.

Before drafting the questions, Lopez will want to review carefully the contents of the case file (including the pleadings and the evidence and other information that she obtained during her preliminary investigation into plaintiff Baranski's claim) and consult with attorney Gilmore on what litigation strategy should be pursued. For further guidance, she might consult form books containing sample interrogatories as well as interrogatories used in similar cases previously handled by the firm. (For tips on how to draft effective interrogatories, see this chapter's featured-guest article on that topic.)

Depending on the complexity of the case, interrogatories may be few in number, or they may run into the hundreds. Exhibit 10.12, which begins on the following page, illustrates the types of interrogatories that have traditionally been used in cases similar to the Baranski-Peretto case. Depending on the rules of the court in which the Baranski case is being filed, paralegal Lopez might draft similar interrogatories for defendant Peretto to answer. Realize that some state courts now limit the number of interrogatories that can be used, and the 1993 revision of FRCP 33 limits the number of interrogatories in federal court cases to twenty-five (unless a greater number is allowed by stipulation of the parties or by court order). Therefore:

 Before drafting interrogatories, the paralegal should always check the rules of the court in which an action is being filed to find out if that court limits the number of interrogatories that can be used.

ANSWERING INTERROGATORIES. After receiving the interrogatories, defendant Peretto must answer them within a specified time period (thirty days under FRCP 33) in writing and under oath, as mentioned above. Very likely, he will have substantial guidance from his attorney and his attorney's paralegal in forming his answers. Peretto must answer each question truthfully, of course, because he is under oath. His attorney and her paralegal would counsel him, though, on how to phrase his answers so that they are both truthful and strategically sound. For example, they would advise Peretto on how to limit his answers to prevent disclosing more information than is necessary.

Depositions

Deposition
A pretrial question-and-answer proceeding, usually conducted orally, in which an a party or witness answers an attorney's questions. The answers are given under oath, and the session is recorded.

Like interrogatories, **depositions** are given under oath. Unlike interrogatories, however, depositions are usually conducted orally (except in certain circumstances, such as when the party being deposed is at a great distance and cannot be deposed via telephone). Furthermore, they may be taken from nonparty witnesses. As indicated earlier, interrogatories can only be taken from the parties to the lawsuit.

The attorney wishing to depose a party must give that party's attorney reasonable notice in writing by serving the attorney with a notice similar to that shown in Exhibit 10.13 on page 365. Typically, the notice will be accompanied by a cover letter to the attorney.

EXHIBIT 10.12
Sample Interrogatories

UNITED STATES DISTRICT COURT
FOR THE WESTERN DISTRICT OF NITA

Katherine Baranski
                Plaintiff

vs.

Tony Peretto   Defendant

File No. 99-14335-NI

Hon. Harley M. LaRue

A. P. Gilmore
Attorney for the Plaintiff
Jeffers, Gilmore & Dunn
553 Fifth Avenue
Suite 101
Nita City, NI 48801

<u>PLAINTIFF'S FIRST INTERROGATORIES TO DEFENDANT</u>

    PLEASE TAKE NOTICE that the following Interrogatories are directed to you under the provisions of Rule 26(a)(5) and Rule 33 of the Federal Rules of Civil Procedure. You are requested to answer these Interrogatories and to furnish such information in answer to the Interrogatories as is available to you.
    You are required to serve integrated Interrogatories and Answers to these Interrogatories under oath, within thirty (30) days after service of them upon you. The original answers are to be retained in your attorney's possession and a copy of the answers are to be served upon Plaintiff's counsel.
    The answers should be signed and sworn to by the person making answer to the Interrogatories.
    When used in these Interrogatories the term "Defendant," or any synonym thereof, is intended to and shall embrace and include, in addition to said Defendant, all agents, servants and employees, representatives, attorneys, private investigators, or others who are in possession or who may have obtained information for or on behalf of the Defendant.
    These Interrogatories shall be deemed continuing and supplemental answers shall be required immediately upon receipt thereof if Defendant, directly or indirectly, obtains further or different information from the time answers are served until the time of trial.

1. Were you the driver of an automobile involved in an accident with plaintiff on the _____ day of _____, 19 ___, at about _____ o'clock _____ A.M. at the intersection of _____ and _____, in the city of _____ in the county of _____, state of _____? If so, please state the following:

    (a) Whether your name is correctly spelled in the complaint in this cause of action;
    (b) Any other names by which you have been known, including the dates during which you have used those names;
    (c) Your Social Security number and place and date of birth;
    (d) Your height, weight, and eye and hair color;
    (e) Your address at the time of the accident;
    (f) The names, addresses, and phone numbers of your present and former spouses (if any) and all of your children, whether natural or adopted, who were residing with you at the time of the accident (if any).

2. Please list your places of residence for the last five years prior to your current residence, including complete addresses and dates of residence as well as the names of owners or managers.

EXHIBIT 10.12

Sample Interrogatories—Continued

3. Please indicate where you have worked during the five years prior to and including your present employment. When so doing, please indicate the following:

    (a) The names, addresses, and telephone numbers of each employer or place of business, including the dates during which you worked there;
    (b) How many hours you worked, on average, per week;
    (c) The names, addresses, and telephone numbers of your supervisors (or owners of the business);
    (d) The nature of the work that you performed.

4. Please give all relevant information with respect to your driver's license that you had on the date of the accident, including the following:

    (a) The state of issuance and the number of your license;
    (b) The type and date of issuance as well as its expiration date;
    (c) Any violations, offenses, or restrictions that were recorded against your license.

5. Indicate whether you have ever had your driver's license suspended, revoked, or canceled, and whether you have ever been denied the issuance of a driver's license for mental or physical reasons. If you have, please indicate the date and state of such an occurrence as well as the reasons for it.

6. Do you have normal vision without the use of glasses or contact lenses? If your answer is in the negative, please indicate the following:

    (a) The date on which glasses or contact lenses were prescribed and the name and address of the prescriber;
    (b) The date and complete address of the business from which they were purchased;
    (c) The present location of the glasses or contact lenses;
    (d) Whether or not you were wearing the glasses or contact lenses at the time of the accident.

7. Do you have normal hearing without the use of a hearing aid? If your answer is in the negative, please indicate the following:

    (a) The date on which the hearing aid was prescribed and the name and address of the prescriber;
    (b) The date and complete address of the business from which it was purchased;
    (c) The present location of the hearing aid;
    (d) Whether or not you were wearing the hearing aid at the time of the accident.

8. When is the last time you had your vision checked within the last five years?

9. If you have had your vision checked, please indicate the following:

    (a) The date and reason for the vision examination;
    (b) The name, address, and telephone number of the examiner;
    (c) The results and/or actions taken.

10. When is the last time you had your hearing checked within the last five years?

11. If you have had your hearing checked, please indicate the following:

    (a) The date and reason for the hearing examination;
    (b) The name, address, and telephone number of the examiner;
    (c) The results and/or actions taken.

EXHIBIT 10.12
Sample Interrogatories—Continued

12. Have you ever suffered from any form of fits or convulsions, fainting spells, epilepsy, mental illness, nervous breakdowns, alcoholism, or drug addiction? If your answer is yes, for each such occurrence or reoccurrence within one year prior to this accident, please indicate the following:

    (a) The date of onset;
    (b) The actual condition;
    (c) Your address at the time of onset;
    (d) The names and addresses of those qualified persons who treated you for the condition, including the dates of such treatment;
    (e) The names and addresses of hospitals or other institutions in which you were treated for such condition, including the dates of treatment;
    (f) The date of termination or present status of the condition.

* * * *

[Now would come various interrogatories about whether the defendant in the automobile accident owned the automobile, and, if not, who the owner was and the relationship between the owner and the defendant. There might also be questions relating to the defendant's military service record.]

* * * *

30. When the accident occurred, did you have full use of all of your limbs and extremities? If you answer is in the negative, please state the following:

    (a) The limbs or extremities affected;
    (b) The dates and causes of any impairments;
    (c) The details of any impairments.

31. Within the twenty-four hours preceding the accident, did you ingest any narcotic, tranquilizer, drug, sedative, or other form of medication? If so, please state the following:

    (a) The identity of the drug or medication and the reason for taking it;
    (b) The dosage and the number of times taken;
    (c) The date and address where the medication was purchased;
    (d) The name, address, and phone number of the person who prescribed the medication;
    (e) The prescription number.

32. Within twenty-four hours prior to the accident, were you in a residence or an establishment in which liquor was served? If so, for each occasion, please state the following:

    (a) The name and address of the residence or establishment;
    (b) The time during which you were at such residence or establishment;
    (c) The names and addresses of the persons accompanying you;
    (d) The name, type, and quantity of each alcoholic beverage consumed;
    (e) The time of consumption of each drink.

33. After the accident, did any authority request that you undergo a sobriety test? If so, please indicate the following:

    (a) The type of test;
    (b) How long after the accident the test was given;
    (c) The name and address of the person and place where the test was given;
    (d) The results of the test;

EXHIBIT 10.12
Sample Interrogatories—Continued

     (e) The name and address of the person currently having custody of the records indicating the test results;
     (f) If you were requested to take such a test and refused, the name, address, and telephone number of each person whom you refused.

34. For the twenty-four hours preceding the accident, please describe in hourly detail your general activities, including your hours of employment and what you did during each of those hours.

35. Please answer the following questions with respect to the trip you were taking by automobile at the time of the accident:

     (a) From what point did you start and where were you going?
     (b) What time was it when you started and what time were you scheduled to arrive at your destination?
     (c) What was the purpose of your trip?
     (d) What was the address of each place where you stopped during the trip?
     (e) What were the exact routes that you took, by street and by compass direction?
     (f) What is the name, address, phone number, and present whereabouts of each passenger who accompanied you at any time during the trip?

36. At the time of the accident, please state the following to the best of your recollection:

     (a) The time, day of the week, and date;
     (b) The direction in which you were traveling prior to impact;
     (c) The visibility and light conditions;
     (d) The weather, including the temperature, wind, rain, fog, etc.;
     (e) The speed at which you were traveling just prior to the point of impact;
     (f) The speed at which you were traveling 50 feet before the impact;
     (g) The speed at which you were traveling 250 feet before the impact;
     (h) The speed at which you were traveling one-quarter mile before the impact;
     (i) The speed at which you were traveling one-half mile before the impact;
     (j) The speed at which you were traveling one mile before the impact.

37. The general character of the neighborhood.

* * * *

[Additional interrogatories would probably be asked. Some interrogatories would relate to the scene of the accident, including road surface, coloring, posted speed limits, shoulders and curbs on the side of the road, whether the surface was wet, etc. There would be further interrogatories about whether the defendant's attention was diverted from traffic just prior to the accident and whether there were traffic controls at or near the accident scene. The defendant would be asked to indicate when he or she noticed the plaintiff's vehicle and where it was located. There would be further questions about the plaintiff's speed, whether the plaintiff braked, whether the plaintiff remained in the defendant's line of vision, whether there were other vehicles between the defendant's and plaintiff's vehicles, etc. Other interrogatories would include information about the defendant's car, lighting, etc. and whether the defendant applied his or her brakes prior to impact, whether he or she blew the horn, and so on. Information about the extent of damages to the parties involved and to the vehicles would then be asked.]

Dated: March 15, 1999

                                                                           Jeffers, Gilmore & Dunn

                                                                           Allen P. Gilmore
                                                                           Allen P. Gilmore
                                                                           Attorney for Plaintiff
                                                                           553 Fifth Avenue
                                                                           Suite 101
                                                                           Nita City, NI 48801
                                                                           (618) 555-1212

EXHIBIT 10.13
Notice of Taking Deposition

**UNITED STATES DISTRICT COURT
FOR THE WESTERN DISTRICT OF NITA**

Katherine Baranski
        Plaintiff

vs.
                                        File No. 99-14335-NI

Tony Peretto   Hon. Harley M. LaRue
        Defendant

Allen P. Gilmore
Attorney for the Plaintiff
Jeffers, Gilmore & Dunn
553 Fifth Avenue
Suite 101
Nita City, NI 48801

Elizabeth A. Cameron
Attorney for the Defendant
Cameron & Strauss, P.C.
310 Lake Drive
Zero City, ZE 59802

TO: Elizabeth A. Cameron
        Cameron & Strauss, P.C.
        310 Lake Drive
        Zero City, ZE 59802

<u>NOTICE OF TAKING DEPOSITION</u>

PLEASE TAKE NOTICE that Katherine Baranski, by and through her attorneys, Jeffers, Gilmore & Dunn, will take the deposition of Tony Peretto on Wednesday, April 15, 1999, at 1:30 P.M., at the law offices of Cameron & Strauss, P.C., 310 Lake Drive, Zero City, ZE 59802, pursuant to the Federal Rules of Civil Procedure, before a duly authorized and qualified notary and stenographer.

Dated: March 20, 1999   Jeffers, Gilmore & Dunn

                                                                     Allen P. Gilmore
                                                                     Allen P. Gilmore
                                                                     Attorney for Katherine Baranski
                                                                     553 Fifth Avenue, Suite 101
                                                                     Nita City, NI 48801

Normally, the defendant's attorney deposes the plaintiff first, and then the plaintiff's attorney deposes the defendant. Following these depositions, the attorneys may depose witnesses and other parties to obtain information about the event leading to the lawsuit. When both the defendant and the plaintiff are located in the same jurisdiction, the site of the deposition will usually be the offices of the attorney requesting the deposition. When the parties are located in different jurisdictions, other arrangements may be made. In the Baranski case, attorney Gilmore will travel to defendant Peretto's city, which is located in another state, and depose Peretto in the office of Peretto's attorney, Cameron.

Deponent
A party or witness who testifies under oath during a deposition.

When an attorney takes the deposition of a party or witness, the attorney is able to question the person being deposed (the **deponent**) in person and then follow up with any other questions that come to mind. Even though the deposition is usually taken at the offices of one of the party's attorneys, the fact that the deponent has sworn to tell the truth necessitates that both the attorney and the deponent treat the deposition proceedings as seriously as they would if the deponent were on the witness stand in court.

FRCP 30, as revised in 1993, prohibits the taking of any depositions in federal court cases before the parties have made the disclosures required under revised Rule 26 and discussed in the next section. Revised Rule 30 also states that the court's approval is required if, without written agreement by the parties, either attorney wants to take more than one deposition from the same party or witness, or more than a total of ten depositions.

DRAFTING DEPOSITION QUESTIONS. Depositions are conducted by attorneys. Although paralegals may attend depositions, they do not ask questions during the deposition. Deposition questions are often drafted by paralegals, however. In the Baranski case, for example, attorney Gilmore might ask paralegal Lopez to draft questions for a deposition of defendant Peretto or someone else, such as an eyewitness to the accident. For Peretto's deposition, Lopez might draft questions similar to those presented in Exhibit 10.14. Attorney Gilmore can then use Lopez's questions as a kind of checklist during the deposition. Note, though, that Gilmore's questions will not be limited to the questions included in the list. Other, unforeseen questions may arise as Gilmore learns new information during the deposition. Also, the deponent's answer to one question may reveal the answer to another, so that not all questions will need to be asked.

PREPARING THE CLIENT FOR A DEPOSITION. No attorney can predict a deponent's answers beforehand. Spontaneous and perhaps even contradictory statements can seriously damage the deponent's case. For this reason, the deposed party and his or her lawyer will want to prepare for the deposition by formulating mock answers to anticipated questions. For example, if defendant Peretto's attorney plans to depose plaintiff Baranski, attorney Gilmore and paralegal Lopez might have Baranski come into their office for a run-through of possible questions that Peretto's attorney might ask her during the deposition. This kind of preparation does not mean that the lawyer tells the deponent what to say. Instead, the lawyer offers suggestions as to how the answers to certain questions should be phrased. The answers must be truthful, but the truth can be presented in many ways.

THE ROLE OF THE DEPONENT'S ATTORNEY. The deponent's attorney will attend the deposition, but the attorney's role will be limited. The attorney may make occasional objections to the opposing attorney's questions if the questions appear to be irrelevant to the case or ask for privileged information. If plaintiff Baranski were to be deposed by defendant Peretto's attorney, Cameron, then Baranski's attorney, Gilmore, would object to any of Cameron's questions that were misleading or ambiguous or that wandered too far from the issues relating to the claim.

Gilmore would also caution Baranski to limit her responses to the questions and not to engage in speculative answers that might prejudice her claim. If plaintiff Baranski was asked whether she had ever been involved in an automobile accident before, for example, Gilmore would probably caution her to use a simple (but truthful) "yes" or "no" answer. Attorney Gilmore normally would permit Baranski to volunteer additional information only in response to precisely phrased questions.

Case at a Glance

The Plaintiff—
 Plaintiff: Katherine Baranski
 Attorney: Allen P. Gilmore
 Paralegal: Elena Lopez

The Defendant—
 Defendant: Tony Peretto
 Attorney: Elizabeth A. Cameron
 Paralegal: Gordon McVay

EXHIBIT 10.14
Deposition Questions

DEPOSITION QUESTIONS

1. Please state your full name and address for the record.
2. What is your age, birth date, and Social Security number?
3. What is your educational level and what employment position do you hold?
4. Do you have a criminal record and if so, for what?
5. Have you ever been involved in previous automobile accidents? What driving violations have you had? Has your driver's license ever been suspended?
6. What is your medical history? Have you ever had health problems? Are you in perfect health? Were you in perfect health at the time of the accident?
7. Do you wear glasses or contact lenses? If so, for what condition? Were you wearing your glasses or contacts at the time the accident occurred?
8. Do you take medication of any kind?
9. Do you have any similar lawsuits or any claims pending against you?
10. Who is your automobile insurer? What are your policy limits?
11. Were there any passengers in your vehicle at the time of the accident?
12. Describe your vehicle. What was the mechanical condition of your vehicle at the time of the accident? Do you do your own mechanical work? What training do you have in maintaining and repairing automobiles? Had you taken your vehicle to a professional mechanic's shop prior to the accident?
13. State the date the accident occurred.
14. Where were you prior to the accident, at least for the six hours preceding the accident?
15. Where were you going when the accident occurred, and for what purpose?
16. What were you doing during the last few moments before the accident? Were you smoking, eating, drinking, or chewing gum?
17. What were you thinking about just before the accident occurred?
18. What route did you take to reach your destination, and why did you take this particular route?
19. Describe the weather conditions at the time of the accident.
20. Please recite the facts of how the accident occurred.
21. Please describe the area in which the accident occurred. Were there many cars and pedestrians on the streets? Were there traffic controls, obstructions, or the like?
22. What was your location and in what direction were you going?
23. When did you see the Plaintiff's automobile approaching?
24. How far away were you when you first saw the auto? What was your rate of speed?
25. Did your vehicle move forward or was it pushed backward by the impact?
26. When did you first apply your brakes? Were your brakes functioning properly?
27. Did you attempt to avoid the accident? If so, how?
28. Did you receive a traffic ticket as a result of the accident?
29. Do you own the vehicle that you were driving at the time of the accident?
30. Were you acting within the scope of your employment when the accident occurred?
31. What were the conditions of the parties affected by the accident just after the accident occurred?
32. Did you attempt to provide first aid to any party?
33. How did the Plaintiff leave the scene and what was her physical condition?
34. What was the damage to your vehicle, and has it been repaired?

As will be discussed below, deposition proceedings are recorded. If both attorneys agree to do so, however, they can go "off the record" to clarify a point or discuss a disputed issue. Depositions are stressful events, and tempers often flare. In the event that the deposition can no longer be pursued in an orderly fashion, the attorney conducting the deposition may have to terminate it.

The above description of the role of the deponent's attorney at a deposition is typical for cases filed in state courts and, until the 1993 revision of the FRCP, in federal courts as well. The revised FRCP, however, imposes strict limitations on an attorney's right to object to questions asked of his or her client during a

DEVELOPING PARALEGAL SKILLS

Deposition Summaries

After a deposition is taken, each attorney orders a copy of the deposition transcript. Copies may be obtained in printed form or on a computer disk. When the transcript is received, the legal assistant's job is to prepare a summary of the testimony that was given. The summary is typically only a few pages in length.

The legal assistant must be very familiar with the lawsuit and the legal theories that are being pursued so that he or she can point out inconsistencies in the testimony and how the testimony varies from the pleadings. The paralegal might also give special emphasis to any testimony given by deponents that will help to prove the client's case in court.

After the deposition summary has been created, the paralegal places the summary in the litigation file, usually in a special discovery folder or binder within the larger file. The deposition summary will be used to prepare for future depositions, to prepare pretrial motions, and to impeach witnesses at the trial, should they give contradictory testimony.

TIPS FOR SUMMARIZING A DEPOSITION

- Find out how the deposition is to be summarized—by chronology, by legal issue, by factual issues, or otherwise.
- Read through the deposition transcript and mark important pages.
- Using a dictaphone or dictation software, dictate a summary of the information on the marked pages.
- Be sure to include a reference to the page and line that is being summarized.
- Take advantage of software that will assist in summarizing the deposition transcript.

---

deposition. Rule 30(d)(1) now requires that an attorney may instruct a deponent not to answer only "when necessary to preserve a privilege, to enforce a limitation on evidence directed by the court, or to present a motion [to terminate the deposition]." The revised rule also states that all objections during a deposition must be stated concisely and in a nonargumentative, nonsuggestive manner. This rule is consistent with the revised FRCP 26, which imposes an ongoing duty on each party to disclose relevant information to the other party in the lawsuit.

THE DEPOSITION TRANSCRIPT. Every utterance made during a deposition is recorded. A court reporter will usually record the deposition proceedings and create an official **deposition transcript**. Methods of recording a deposition include stenographic recording (a traditional method that involves the use of a shorthand machine), tape recording, videotape recording, or some combination of these methods. Revised Rule 30(b)(2) of the FRCP states that unless the court orders otherwise, a deposition "may be recorded by sound, sound-and-visual, or stenographic means."

Deposition Transcript
The official transcription of the recording taken during a deposition.

Impeach
To call into question the credibility of a witness by challenging the truth or accuracy of his or her trial statement.

The deposition transcript may be used by either party during the trial to prove a particular point or to **impeach** (call into question) the credibility of a witness who says something during the trial that is different from what he or she stated during the deposition. For example, a witness in the Baranski case might state during the deposition that defendant Peretto *did not* stop at the stop sign before proceeding to cross Mattis Avenue. If at trial, the witness states that Peretto *did* stop at the stop sign before crossing Mattis Avenue, plaintiff Baranski's attorney (Gilmore) could challenge the witness's credibility on the basis of the deposition transcript. Exhibit 10.15 shows a page from a transcript of a deposition conducted by attorney Gilmore in the Baranski case. The deponent was Julia Williams, an eyewitness to

EXHIBIT 10.15
A Deposition Transcript (Excerpt)

67	Q: Where were you at the time of the accident?
68	A: I was on the southwest corner of the intersection.
69	Q: Are you referring to the intersection where Thirty-eighth Street crosses Mattis Avenue?
70	A: Yes.
71	Q: Why were you there at the time of the accident?
72	A: Well, I was on my way to work. I usually walk down Mattis Avenue to the hospital.
73	Q: So you were walking to work down Mattis Avenue and you saw the accident?
74	A: Yes.
75	Q: What did you see?
76	A: Well, as I was about to cross the street, a dark green van passed within three feet of me and ran the
77	stop sign and crashed into another car.
78	Q: Can you remember if the driver of the van was a male or a female?
79	A: Yes. It was a man.
80	Q: I am showing you a picture. Can you identify the man in the picture?
81	A: Yes. That is the man who was driving the van.
82	Q: Do you wear glasses?
83	A: I need glasses only for reading. I have excellent distance vision.
84	Q: How long has it been since your last eye exam with a doctor?
85	A: Oh, just a month ago, with Dr. Sullivan.

page 4

the accident. On the transcript, the letter "Q" precedes each question asked by Gilmore, and the letter "A" precedes each of Williams's answers.

SUMMARIZING AND INDEXING THE DEPOSITION TRANSCRIPT. Typically, the paralegal will summarize the deposition transcript. The summary, which along with the transcript will become part of the litigation file, allows the members of the litigation team to review quickly the information obtained from the deponent during the deposition.

In the Baranski case, assume that paralegal Lopez is asked to summarize the deposition transcript of Julia Williams. A commonly used format for deposition summaries is to summarize the information sequentially—that is, in the order that it was given during the deposition—as shown in Exhibit 10.16 on the next page. Notice that the summary includes the page and line numbers in the deposition transcript where the full text of the information can be found.

Often, in addition to summarizing the transcript, the paralegal provides an index to the document. The index consists of a list of topics (such as education, employment status, injuries, medical costs, and so on) followed by the relevant page and line numbers of the deposition transcript. Together, the summary and the index

On the Web
If you are interested in the history of court reporting, visit the Web site of the National Court Reporters Association at www.vervbatimreports.com.

EXHIBIT 10.16
A Deposition Summary (Excerpt)

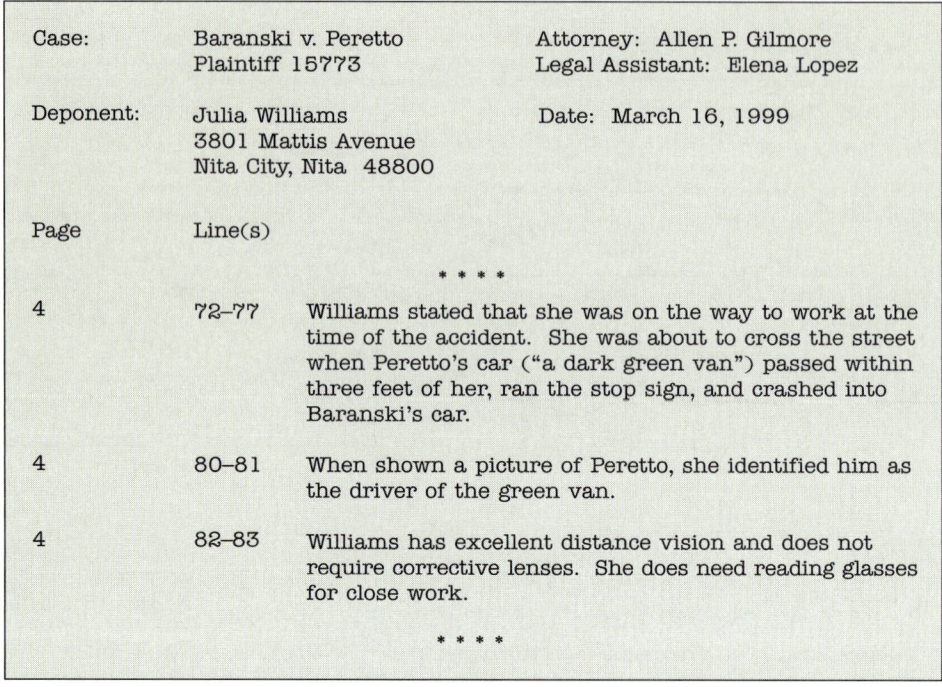

allow anyone involved in the case to locate information quickly. Today, key-word indexes allow attorneys and paralegals to locate within seconds deposition testimony on a particular topic. Often, court reporters will provide key-word indexes on request. (For a discussion of the services offered by today's court reporters, see the feature *Technology and Today's Paralegal: Indexing the Deposition Transcript*.)

Other Discovery Requests

During the discovery phase of litigation, attorneys often request documents so that they may familiarize themselves with specific facts or events that were earlier disclosed by the parties or learned on investigation. In federal court cases, the revised FRCP 34 authorizes each party to request documents and other forms of evidence held by other parties and witnesses, but such requests cannot be made until after the initial prediscovery meeting of the parties (discussed below) has taken place. In most state courts, and depending on the nature of the case, the inspection of documents may be the first step in the discovery process if document inspection will facilitate the widest possible scope of discovery.

During discovery, a party can also request that the opposing party admit the truth of matters relating to the case. For example, plaintiff Baranski's attorney can request that defendant Peretto admit that he did not stop at the stop sign before crossing Mattis Avenue at Thirty-eighth Street. Such admissions save time at trial because the parties will not have to spend time proving facts on which they already agree. Any matter admitted under such a request is conclusively established as true for the trial. FRCP 36 permits requests for admission, but the 1993 revision of this rule stipulates that a request for admission cannot be made, without the court's permission, prior to the prediscovery meeting of the attorneys. In view of the limitations on the number of interrogatories under the revised FRCP (and under some state procedural rules that impose similar limitations), requests for admissions are a particularly useful discovery tool.

Case at a Glance

The Plaintiff—
Plaintiff: Katherine Baranski
Attorney: Allen P. Gilmore
Paralegal: Elena Lopez

The Defendant—
Defendant: Tony Peretto
Attorney: Elizabeth A. Cameron
Paralegal: Gordon McVay

Technology and Today's Paralegal

Indexing the Deposition Transcript

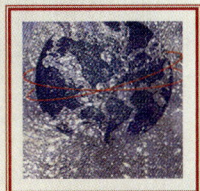

Depositions have always played a key role in the litigation process. In the pretrial phase, they enable the parties' attorneys to gain information about the case. In the trial phase, they are often used as a weapon in the legal battle. An attorney can impeach (call into question) a witness's credibility during cross-examination by pointing to discrepancies between what a witness said during a deposition and what that witness has just said on the stand at trial.

As you might imagine, using deposition testimony in this way requires that the attorney and his legal assistant be able to access quickly the relevant portion of the deposition transcript. This is why carefully prepared deposition indexes are so important to the litigation process and its outcome. Typically, it is the paralegal's responsibility to index the deposition, and this can be a time-consuming task.

What many attorneys and paralegals do not realize is that technological advances have allowed court-reporting firms to offer a variety of services for just a nominal fee—and sometimes for free. For example, a court reporter can generate a concordant index of each word in the deposition transcript by both page and line number, as well as a key-word index of referenced terms. Searches for a key word can be designed so that they call up not only the key word but also a specified number of transcript lines above and below the word. Key-word indexes make it easy for the paralegal, during trial, to instantly retrieve deposition testimony on a particular topic. For example, in the Baranski case, if a witness is testifying that Peretto stopped at a stop sign, the paralegal could search that witness's deposition testimony for the word "stop sign" to verify whether the witness's testimony on the stand was consistent with that given during the deposition.

When depositions are videotaped, as they often are, the court reporter can synchronize his or her computer clock with the videographer's time stamps. When concordant indexing is combined with video time stamps, every word in the videotape is also indexed. This means that, using a splitscreen monitor, a particular portion of the transcript can be viewed simultaneously with the corresponding portion of the videotape. Many attorneys are finding that presenting at trial such synchronized text-video presentations of deposition testimony is far more effective than simply reading the witness's words.

As a paralegal, you will benefit by being aware of the variety of services that today's court reporters offer. To learn more about court-reporting technology and services, visit the Web site of the National Court Reporters Association at www.verbatimreporters.com. You can also locate court reporters in your area and learn what services they offer by doing a "Geo search" at that site.

During discovery, the defendant's attorney may also want to verify the nature and extent of any injuries alleged by the plaintiff. If a defendant has genuine doubts as to the nature of the plaintiff's injuries the defendant may petition the court to order that the plaintiff submit to a medical examination. Although a medical examination may appear to be overly intrusive, FRCP 35(a) permits such an examination when the existence of the plaintiff's claimed injuries is in dispute. The examination, however, must be preceded by a court order. Because plaintiff Baranski is suing defendant Peretto for injuries arising from the accident, the existence, nature, and extent of her injuries is vitally important in calculating the damages that she might be able to recover from Peretto. Consequently, Baranski will probably be ordered by the court to undergo a physical examination if Peretto's attorney submits such a request.

Revised Discovery Procedures under FRCP 26

The 1993 amendments to the FRCP significantly changed discovery procedures in the federal courts. Under the revised rules, each party to a lawsuit has a duty to disclose to the other party specified types of information prior to the discovery stage of litigation. Under revised Rule 26(f), once a lawsuit is brought, the parties (the plaintiff and defendant and/or their attorneys, if the parties are represented by counsel) must schedule a prediscovery meeting to discuss the nature of the lawsuit, any defenses that may be raised against the claims being brought, and possibilities for promptly settling or otherwise resolving the dispute. The meeting should take place as soon as practicable but at least fourteen days before a scheduling conference is held or a scheduling order issued. Either at this meeting or within ten days after it, the parties must also make the initial disclosures described below and submit to the court a plan for discovery. As the trial date approaches, the attorneys must make subsequent disclosures relating to witnesses, documents, and other information that is relevant to the case.

The new discovery rules do not replace the traditional methods of discovery discussed in the preceding section. Rather, the revised rules impose a duty on attorneys to disclose specified information automatically to opposing counsel early in the litigation process so that the time and costs of traditional discovery methods can be reduced. Under the revised rules, attorneys may still use the traditional discovery tools (depositions, interrogatories, and so on) to obtain information, but they cannot use these methods until the prediscovery meeting has been held and initial disclosures have been made. Also, to save the court's time, the revised rules give attorneys a freer hand in crafting a discovery plan that is appropriate to the nature of the claim, the parties' needs, and so on.[7]

Initial Disclosures

FRCP 26(a)(1) requires each party to disclose the following information to the other party either at an initial meeting of the parties or within ten days following the meeting:

- The name, address, and telephone number of any person who is likely to have "discoverable information" and the nature of that information.
- A copy or "description by category and location" of all documents, data, and other "things in the possession, custody, or control of the party" that are relevant to the dispute.
- A computation of the damages being claimed by the disclosing party. The party must make available to the other party, for inspection and copying, documents or other materials on which the computation of damages is based, "including materials bearing on the nature and extent of injuries suffered."
- Copies of any insurance policies that cover the injuries or harms alleged in the lawsuit and that may pay part or all of a judgment (damages, for example) resulting from the dispute.

In the Baranski case, following the new requirements under revised Rule 26 would mean that attorney Gilmore and paralegal Lopez would have to work quickly to assemble all relevant information, documents, and other evidence that Lopez had gathered during client interviews and during her preliminary investigation into the case. Lopez would have to prepare copies of the documents or other information—or a description of them—for attorney Gilmore's review and signa-

---

7. The 1993 revision of the FRCP, including the revision of Rule 26 governing discovery requirements, allows federal district courts to modify, or opt not to follow, these rules requiring early disclosures. About one-fourth of the existing ninety-four U.S. federal districts have opted not to follow these rules.

ture. The copies or descriptions would then have to be filed with the court and delivered to defendant Peretto's attorney.

Note that in the information disclosed to defendant Peretto's attorney, paralegal Lopez would have to include even information that might be damaging to Baranski's position. Lopez would not need to disclose *privileged information*, however. If defendant Peretto's attorney seeks information that attorney Gilmore claims is privileged, Peretto's attorney will be able to obtain that information only through a court order.

A party will not be excused from disclosing relevant information simply because the party has not yet completed an investigation into the case or because the other party has not yet disclosed the required information. Revised FRCP 37(c) makes it clear that the failure to make these initial disclosures can result in serious sanctions. That rule states that if a party fails to disclose certain relevant information, that party will not be able to use the information as evidence at trial. In addition, the court may impose other sanctions, such as ordering the party to pay reasonable expenses, including attorneys' fees, created by the failure to disclose. In sum, attorney Gilmore and paralegal Lopez would need to make sure that all relevant information (that is not privileged) was disclosed, or Gilmore would not be able to use it in court (and may face other sanctions as well).

Discovery Plan

As mentioned above, at the initial meeting of the parties, the attorneys must also work out a **discovery plan** and submit a report describing the plan to the court within ten days of the meeting. The type of information to be included in the discovery plan is illustrated in Exhibit 10.17 on the following page, which shows Form 35, which was generated for this purpose. As indicated by that form, the revised Rule 26(f) allows the attorneys substantial room to negotiate the details of discovery, including the time schedules to be followed.

In the Baranski case, paralegal Lopez will make sure that attorney Gilmore takes a copy of Form 35 with him to the initial prediscovery meeting of the parties to use as a checklist. After the attorneys decide on the details of the plan to be proposed to the court, attorney Gilmore will probably have paralegal Lopez draft a final version of the plan for his review and signature.

Discovery Plan
A plan formed by the attorneys litigating a lawsuit, on behalf of their clients, that indicates the types of information that will be disclosed by each party to the other prior to trial, the testimony and evidence that each party will or may introduce at trial, and the general schedule for pretrial disclosures and events.

Subsequent Disclosures

In addition to the initial disclosures just discussed, each party must make other disclosures prior to trial. All subsequent disclosures must also be made in writing, signed by the attorneys, and filed with the court. Subsequent disclosures include information relating to expert witnesses and other witnesses and exhibits that will or may be used at trial.

EXPERT WITNESSES. Under FRCP 26(a)(2), each party must disclose to the other party the names of any expert witnesses who may be called to testify during the trial. Additionally, the following information about each expert witness must be disclosed in a report signed by the expert witness:

- A statement by the expert witness indicating the opinions that will be expressed, the basis for the opinions, and the data or information considered by the witness when forming the opinions.
- Any exhibits that will be used to summarize or support the opinions.

EXHIBIT 10.17
Form 35—Report of Parties' Planning Meeting

[Caption and Names of Parties]

1. Pursuant to Fed. R. Civ. P. 26(f), a meeting was held on __(date)__ at __(place)__ and was attended by:

   __(name)__ for plaintiff(s) __(party name)__
   __(name)__ for defendant(s) __(party name)__
   __(name)__ for defendant(s) __(party name)__

2. Pre-Discovery Disclosures. The parties [have exchanged] [will exchange by __(date)__] the information required by [Fed. R. Civ. P. 26(a)(1)] [(local rule _____)].

3. Discovery Plan. The parties jointly propose to the court the following discovery plan: [Use separate paragraphs or subparagraphs as necessary if parties disagree.]

   Discovery will be needed on the following subjects:
   __(brief description of subjects on which discovery will be needed)__
   All discovery commenced in time to be completed by __(date)__. [Discovery on __(issue for early discovery)__ to be completed by __(date)__.]
   Maximum of ____ interrogatories by each party to any other party. [Responses due ____ days after service.]
   Maximum of ____ requests for admission by each party to any other party. [Responses due ____ days after service.]
   Maximum of ____ depositions by plaintiff(s) and ____ by defendant(s).
   Each deposition [other than of _____] limited to maximum of ____ hours unless extended by agreement of parties.
   Reports from retained experts under Rule 26(a) (2) due:
      from plaintiff(s) by __(date)__
      from defendant(s) by __(date)__
   Supplementations under Rule 26(e) due __[time(s) or intervals(s)]__.

4. Other Items. [Use separate paragraphs or subparagraphs as necessary if parties disagree.]

   The parties [request] [do not request] a conference with the court before entry of the scheduling order.
   The parties request a pretrial conference in __(month and year)__.
   Plaintiff(s) should be allowed until __(date)__ to join additional parties and until __(date)__ to amend the pleadings.
   Defendant(s) should be allowed until __(date)__ to join additional parties and until __(date)__ to amend the pleadings.
   All potentially dispositive motions should be filed by __(date)__.
   Settlement [is likely] [is unlikely] [cannot be evaluated prior to __(date)__] [may be enhanced by use of the following alternative dispute resolution procedure: _____].
   Final lists of witnesses and exhibits under Rule 26(a) (3) should be due
      from plaintiff(s) by __(date)__.
      from defendant(s) by __(date)__.
   Parties should have _____ days after service of final lists of witnesses and exhibits to list objections under Rule 26(a)(3).
   The case should be ready for trial by __(date)__ [and at the time is expected to take approximately __(length of time)__].
   [Other matters.]

   Date: _____

- The qualifications of the expert witness, including a list of all publications authored by the witness within the preceding ten years.
- The compensation to be paid to the expert witness.
- A list of any other cases in which the witness has testified as an expert at trial or by deposition within the preceding four years.

These disclosures must be made either at times set by the court or, if the court does not indicate any times, at least ninety days prior to the trial date.

Today's Professional Paralegal
Witness Coordination

Barbara Lyons works as a paralegal for a busy litigation firm. Today she is assisting with a medical-malpractice trial. Susan Weiss, the attorney for whom Barbara works, has asked Barbara to coordinate Susan's witnesses. It is 8:30 A.M., and Barbara and Susan are waiting in the courtroom for Dr. Max Brennan, the first witness that Susan will call today.

Planning a Witness's Arrival Time

While they are waiting, Susan fills Barbara in on how the trial went yesterday and what she expects to happen today. Susan tells Barbara that she expects Dr. Brennan to be on the stand testifying from 9 A.M. until at least the lunch break. Then she expects that he will be cross-examined for an hour or two after lunch. Susan wants Barbara to have the next witness, Laura Lang, at the courthouse and ready to testify by 11 A.M., though, in the event that Dr. Brennan is excused earlier than expected.

Barbara had previously arranged with the witness to arrive at the courthouse by 11 A.M. but is concerned that Lang will not be on time. Even though Barbara met with Lang two times to review her testimony and prepare her for the trial experience, she was always late. Barbara tells this to Susan. Susan tells Barbara to go out into the hallway at 9 A.M. and call Lang. "Tell her that things are moving along more quickly than planned and to be here at ten o'clock. That should help to make sure that she will be here by eleven."

A Witness Is Delayed

It is 8:35 A.M., and Dr. Brennan has not yet arrived. Susan asks Barbara to go out to the hallway and call him, first in his car and then his office, to find out where he is. Barbara opens her trial notebook to the witness section. Dr. Brennan's page is first because he is the first witness scheduled to appear. She locates the number for his car phone, jots it down on a scrap of paper, and leaves the courtroom. As she starts dialing Dr. Brennan's number, she sees him walk out of the elevator. Barbara puts the phone back and greets Dr. Brennan. "Sorry I'm running late, but I had an emergency this morning and I had to stop by the hospital before I came here," explains Dr. Brennan.

"I'm just glad to see you!" exclaims Barbara. "Let's go into the courtroom. You are the first witness, and Susan wants to see you," instructs Barbara. Barbara and Dr. Brennan enter the courtroom. Susan and Dr. Brennan talk briefly before the judge enters the courtroom. The court is called to order, and the trial resumes. Barbara sits at the counsel table while Susan questions Dr. Brennan on the stand. At 9:00 A.M., Barbara leaves the courtroom and calls Laura Lang.

Taking Precautions—Arranging for a Witness to Arrive Early

Lang answers the phone. "Hello Ms. Lang. It's Barbara Lyons from Smith, White & White. Susan Weiss asked me to call you and tell you that the trial is moving faster than we anticipated. Susan would like you to be here at ten o'clock instead of eleven, if that's possible," advises Barbara. "Oh. Well, I suppose I can be there by then," responds Lang. "Do you remember how to get here?" asks Barbara. "Yes, I have the directions," answers Lang. "Good. I'll see you soon then, at ten o'clock," says Barbara. She returns to the courtroom.

At 9:55 A.M., Barbara leaves the courtroom again to wait in the hallway for Laura Lang. By 10:15 A.M., Lang has still not arrived. Barbara opens the courtroom door to listen. The testimony is going faster than Susan had anticipated, and Barbara can tell that Susan will probably be ready to put Lang on the stand in another thirty minutes or so. Barbara closes the courtroom door. She goes to the pay phone and dials Lang's telephone number. There is no answer. I hope that she is on her way, thinks Barbara.

A Timely Arrival

Now it is 10:45 A.M., and Lang is still not there. Barbara opens the courtroom door again and can tell that there is only about five minutes left in Dr. Brennan's testimony. She dials Lang's number again. No answer. Barbara continues to wait in the hallway, and a few minutes later Lang appears. Barbara breathes a sigh of relief. She opens the courtroom door, catches Susan's eye, and nods her head.

OTHER PRETRIAL DISCLOSURES. Under revised FRCP 26(a)(3), each party must also disclose to the other party the following information about other witnesses that will testify at trial or any exhibits that will or may be used:

- A list containing the names, addresses, and telephone numbers of other witnesses that may or will be called during the trial to give testimony. The witness list must indicate whether the witness "will be called" or "may be called."
- A list of any witnesses whose deposition testimony may be offered during the trial and, if not taken stenographically, a transcript of the relevant sections of the deposition testimony.
- A list of exhibits that indicates which exhibits will be offered and which exhibits may be offered if the need arises.

These disclosures must be made at least thirty days before trial, unless the court orders otherwise. Once the disclosures have been made, the opposing party has fourteen days within which to file with the court any objections to the use of any deposition or exhibit. If objections are not made, they are deemed to be waived (unless a party can show good cause why he or she failed to object to the disclosures within the fourteen-day time period).

An attorney's duty to disclose relevant information is ongoing throughout the pretrial stage. Any time an attorney learns about relevant supplemental information concerning statements or responses made earlier, that information must be disclosed to the other party.

Key Terms and Concepts

affidavit 341
affirmative defense 349
allegation 337
answer 349
complaint 335
counterclaim 352
default judgment 349
deponent 366
deposition 360
deposition transcript 366
discovery 356

discovery plan 373
docket 337
Federal Rules of Civil Procedure (FRCP) 332
impeach 366
interrogatories 357
judgment 331
memorandum of law 352
motion 352
motion for judgment on the pleadings 354

motion for summary judgment 354
motion to dismiss 352
pleadings 335
prayer for relief 341
privileged information 357
return-of-service form 345
service of process 343
summons 343
supporting affidavit 352
witness 331

Chapter Summary

1. The paralegal assists the attorney in a variety of tasks in the pretrial civil litigation process. The paralegal's efforts are of critical importance because attorneys rely on paralegals to make sure that nothing has been overlooked in preparing for the trial.

2. Although civil lawsuits vary from case to case in terms of their complexity, cost, and detail, all civil litigation involves similar procedural steps, as described in Exhibit 10.1.

3. The first step in the civil litigation process occurs when the attorney initially meets with a client who wishes to bring a lawsuit against another party or parties. The attorney normally conducts this initial client interview, although the paralegal often attends the interview, meets the client, and may make arrangements with the client for subsequent interviews.

4. Once the attorney agrees to represent the client in the lawsuit and the client has signed the retainer agreement, the attorney and the paralegal undertake a preliminary investigation into the matter to ascertain the facts alleged by the client and gain other factual information relating to the case.

5. A litigation file is also created for the case. All documents and records pertaining to the lawsuit will be kept in the litigation file. Each law firm or department usually has specific procedures for organizing and maintaining litigation files. Generally, the litigation file will expand, as the case progresses, to include subfiles for the pleadings, discovery, and other documents and information relating to the litigation.

6. The pleadings—which consist of the plaintiff's complaint, the defendant's answer, and any counterclaim or other pleadings listed in Exhibit 10.2—inform each party of the claims of the other and delineate the details of the dispute.

7. A lawsuit in a federal or state court normally is initiated by the filing of a complaint with the clerk of the appropriate court. The complaint includes a caption, jurisdictional allegations, general allegations (the body of the complaint) detailing the cause of action, a prayer for relief, a signature, and, if appropriate, a demand for a jury trial.

8. Typically, the defendant is notified of a lawsuit by the delivery of the complaint and a summons (service of process). The summons identifies the parties to the lawsuit, identifies the court in which the case will be heard, and directs the defendant to respond to the complaint within a specified time period. In federal court cases, revised FRCP 4 permits the plaintiff's attorney to notify the defendant, by first-class mail or other reliable means, of the lawsuit and enclose with the notice a form that the defendant can sign to waive the requirement of service of process. If the defendant does not sign and return the form, then the plaintiff's attorney will arrange to have the defendant served with the complaint and summons.

9. On receiving the complaint (and summons, if process is served), the defendant has several options. The defendant may submit an answer. The answer may deny any wrongdoing, or it might assert an affirmative defense against the plaintiff's claim, such as the plaintiff's contributory negligence. The answer may be followed by a counterclaim, in which the defendant asserts a claim against the plaintiff arising from the event giving rise to the lawsuit. Both the complaint and the answer may be amended as the case evolves and more evidence is discovered, subject to procedural rules. Alternatively or simultaneously, the defendant might make a motion to dismiss the case, perhaps on the ground that the relevant statute of limitations has expired.

10. A motion for judgment on the pleadings is a pretrial motion that may be filed by either party after all pleadings and amendments have been filed. The motion may be granted if it can be shown that no factual dispute exists. A motion for summary judgment may be filed by either party during or after the discovery stage of litigation. The latter motion is distinguished from a motion for judgment on the pleadings by the fact that the judge, in determining whether to grant the motion, can consider evidence apart from the pleadings—such as evidence contained in affidavits, depositions, and interrogatories. The motion for summary judgment will not be granted if any facts are in dispute.

11. In preparing for trial, the attorney for each party undertakes a formal investigative process called discovery to obtain evidence helpful to his or her client's case. Traditional discovery tools include interrogatories and depositions. Interrogatories are written questions that the parties to the lawsuit must answer, in writing and under oath. Depositions, like interrogatories, are given under oath, but unlike interrogatories, depositions may also be taken from witnesses. Furthermore, the attorney is able to question the deponent (the person being deposed) in person. Usually, a court reporter records the official transcript of the deposition. During discovery, the attorney for either side may also submit various requests, including a request for documents in the possession of the other party or opposing counsel (or a third party), a request for admission (of the truth of certain statements) by the opposing party,

and a request for examination (to establish the truth of claimed injuries or health status).

12. In federal court cases, revised FRCP 26 requires that the attorneys cooperate in forming a discovery plan early in the litigation process. The rule also requires attorneys to automatically disclose relevant information. Under FRCP 26, only after initial disclosures have been made can attorneys resort to the use of traditional discovery tools.

❋ QUESTIONS FOR REVIEW

1. What happens during the initial client interview? Who normally conducts this interview, the attorney or the paralegal? Why?
2. What are the basic steps in the litigation process prior to the trial? How does the paralegal assist the attorney in each of these steps?
3. What kinds of documents are contained in a litigation file? How might these documents be classified, or organized, within the file?
4. What documents constitute the pleadings in a civil lawsuit? What is the effect of each type of document on the litigation?
5. How are defendants notified of lawsuits that have been brought against them? What new procedures are required under revised FRCP 4 for notifying the defendant in a lawsuit?
6. What is service of process? Why is it important?
7. Name three pretrial motions and state the purpose of each.
8. What is a counterclaim? What is an affirmative defense? What is the effect of each of these on the litigation?
9. What is discovery? When does it take place? List three discovery devices that can be used to obtain information prior to trial.
10. How have the 1993 amendments to the FRCP affected the discovery process in federal court cases?

❋ ETHICAL QUESTIONS

1. Pamela Hodges has just started working as a paralegal for Lawyers, Inc., a high-volume, low-overhead law firm that handles mostly simple and routine litigation. Her supervising attorney, Carol Levine, has two initial client meetings scheduled at the same time. Carol tells Pam to handle one, and she (Carol) will come in to sign the retainer agreement. After one and a half hours, Carol is still tied up, and the client is demanding that Pam sign the retainer agreement or he will find another attorney. Should Pam let the client leave and risk losing his business, or should Pam sign the retainer agreement? Does she have other options?
2. Your next-door neighbor's son was beaten up while at school. The boy's mother is facing over $1,000 in medical and dental expenses as a result of his injuries, which she cannot afford to pay. She knows that you work as a paralegal in a law firm that specializes in personal-injury litigation, so she asks you if you will help her. She wants you to write a letter threatening legal action, which she will then sign, and she also wants to know whether she can sue the parents of the boys who beat up her son. Should you write the letter? Should you advise her on what action she might take against the other boys' parents? What are your ethical obligations in this situation? How could you help her without violating professional ethical standards?
3. Bruce Miller, a paralegal, is meeting with a client, Callie Nelson, to prepare answers to interrogatories. In the course of preparing the answers, Callie asks Bruce if he thinks that she has a good case, if there are better legal theories that she should pursue to win her case, and what her options are if she loses. How should Bruce answer these questions?
4. Scott Emerson takes a job as a paralegal with a large law firm that specializes in defending clients against product-liability claims. The firm's clients are some of the largest manufacturing companies in the country. Mark Jones, an associate attorney, assigns Scott the job of drafting and sending out interrogatories to the plaintiff in a case brought against one of the firm's clients. Specifically, Scott is told to send out a standard set of one hundred interrogatories, each with five parts. Scott eventually learns that one of the favorite discovery tactics of the firm is to inundate

plaintiffs with discovery requests, interrogatories, and depositions to cause continuous delays and to outspend the plaintiffs. Scott knows that the relevant state court rules do not limit the number of interrogatories that can be used, but he suspects that the firm's tactics are ethically questionable. Are they? What should Scott do?

Practice Questions and Assignments

1. Assume that you work for attorney Tara Jolans of Adams & Tate, 1000 Town Center, Suite 500, White Tower, Michigan. Jolans has decided to represent Sandra Nelson in her lawsuit against David Namisch. Based on the following information, draft a complaint to be filed in the U.S. District Court for the Eastern District of Michigan.

   Sandra Nelson is a plaintiff in a lawsuit resulting from an automobile accident. Sandra was turning left at a traffic light at the intersection of Jefferson and Mack Streets, while the left-turn arrow was green, when she was hit from the side by a car driven by David Namisch, who failed to stop at the light. The accident occurred on Friday, June 3, 1999, at 11:30 P.M. David lives in New York, was visiting his family in Michigan, and just prior to the accident had been out drinking with his brothers. Several witnesses saw the accident. One of the witnesses called the police.

   Sandra was not wearing her seat belt at the time of the accident, and she was thrown against the windshield, sustaining massive head injuries. When the police and ambulance arrived, they did not think that she would make it to the hospital alive, but she survived. She wants to claim damages of $500,000 for medical expenses, $65,000 for lost wages, and $35,000 for property damage to her Rolls Royce. The accident was reported in the local newspaper, complete with photographs.

2. Using Exhibit 10.4, *A Summons in a Civil Action*, draft a summons to accompany the complaint against David Namisch. David's address is 1000 Main Street, Apartment 63, New York, NY 10009. The court clerk's name is David T. Brown.

3. Using Exhibit 10.5, *A Federal Civil Cover Sheet*, go through the exhibit and prepare a list of information to be inserted into a cover sheet to accompany the complaint against David Namisch.

4. Draft the first ten questions for a set of interrogatories to be directed to the plaintiff, Sandra Nelson, based on the facts given in Question 1 above.

5. Using Exhibit 10.13, *Notice of Taking Deposition*, draft a notice that Sandra Nelson's attorneys will be taking the deposition of David Namisch on September 10, 1999, at 9:00 A.M., at the law offices of Adams & Tate. Mr. Namisch's attorney is Mark Simmons of Simmons & Smith, 444 Park Avenue, New York, NY 10007.

6. Using the material presented in the chapter on pretrial motions, identify each of the following motions:

   a. Tom Smith is a defendant in an auto-negligence case. His attorney files a motion requesting that a judgment be granted in Tom's favor without a trial. He attaches to the motion an affidavit of an eyewitness, who saw the plaintiff run a stop sign.

   b. Dr. Higgins is sued for medical malpractice. The plaintiff recovered completely and has no damages. Dr. Higgins's attorney files a motion asking that the case against his client be dismissed for failure to state a claim on which relief can be granted.

   c. After the answer is filed in a case brought by a plaintiff who slipped and fell on a broken egg on a grocery store floor, her attorney files a motion requesting that the court enter a judgment in the plaintiff's favor based on the undisputed facts contained in both the answer and the complaint.

   d. Dr. Higgins's attorney loses the motion discussed above. When the plaintiff's attorney requests medical records, Dr. Higgins instructs his attorney to refuse to provide the records. The plaintiff's attorney files a motion to obtain the records.

Questions for Critical Analysis

1. Most cases are settled before trial. Why is this? What does it say about our system of justice? Does it place certain parties at a disadvantage?

2. What is the difference between preliminary investigation and discovery? What impact does this difference have on a case? Which would you

prefer to undertake to determine the facts of a case?

3. A complaint is required to be served on the defendant in a lawsuit. What happens if the plaintiff is not properly served? Is this a fair result? Why or why not?

4. Why are defendants in federal courts that have adopted the 1993 revisions to the FRCP allowed to waive service of process? What is it that these defendants actually waive?

5. Why does a complaint contain jurisdictional allegations and general allegations? What is the difference between these types of allegations? Why is each type necessary? What might happen if jurisdictional allegations were not included in a complaint?

6. How can a legal professional include a fact in a complaint if he or she has reason to believe that the fact is true but is uncertain as to its truth? Does including such a fact have any impact on the attorney's signing of the complaint or an affidavit?

7. What is the difference between a cross-claim and a counterclaim? How is each pleading used? Why are these claims allowed? Should they be?

8. If a defendant fails to respond to the plaintiff's complaint within a specified time period, what can happen? Is this a fair rule? Why?

9. In answering a complaint, what happens if a defendant fails to deny an allegation? Is this fair to the defendant? What happens if a defendant is uncertain as to the truth of a matter being alleged by a plaintiff in a complaint?

10. What is the difference between a motion for summary judgment and a motion for judgment on the pleadings? Is one motion preferable to the other? Give an example of how each motion is used.

11. What is the difference between interrogatories and depositions? Which is more efficient? Which is more cost effective? Which would you prefer to use?

12. Most state court rules require the use of traditional discovery tools. The FRCP, on the other hand, has authorized the use of "auto discovery" in the courts adopting these rules. Which system of discovery is better? Which is faster? Which is more realistic?

Projects

1. Litigation is paper and document intensive, and computers can help tame the "paper dragon." Software has been developed and is constantly being updated that can organize and coordinate various pieces of evidence and testimony by using a combination of imaging software, database software, and full-text searching. This allows evidence, including documents and deposition transcripts, to be scanned into the computer, indexed, and easily located or retrieved. Two of the companies that sell the software are Summation Legal Technologies, Inc., and INMAGIC. Call one of these companies for a free demonstration kit or CD. Summation can be reached at 1-800-735-7866. INMAGIC can be reached at 1-800-229-8398. Ask for the livenote software. When you receive the software, try the demonstration. Write a one-page paper describing how the software works.

2. Visit the county court clerk's office (or the clerk's office of a local court) and obtain the following: local court rules, summons and return-of-service forms, and a filing-fee schedule.

3. Review your state's court rules to find out if counterclaims and the other types of pleadings listed in Exhibit 10.2 are permissible. If so, when are they permitted?

4. Review your state's court rules to determine which, if any, of the pretrial motions covered in this chapter are used in the courts in your state. Are the rules the same for all courts in your state? If not, how are they different?

5. Find out when a local court's "motion day" is and attend court for two to three hours on that day. Observe as many motions for summary judgment as possible. Write a one-page summary of what you observed. Be sure to include the name of the court you visited, the date, and the judge's name.

Using Internet Resources

1. Access the Web site of the National Court Reporters Association at **www.verbatimreporters.com**.

   a. Click on "Site Map" and then go to the "About Court Reporting" page. Read about the history of court reporting, and then answer the following questions:
   - When was the stenotype first invented? How does this machine work?
   - What is computer-aided transcription (CAT)? What is "realtime" translation?

   b. Now go to the "Geo search" page, and do a search for your city (if you live in a smaller community, enter the name of a large city in your area or state) and answer these questions:
   - How many court reporters or court-reporting firms offer services in that area?
   - List five types of services that one (or more) of these court reporters or firms offer.

2. The O. J. Simpson deposition can be found at **www.courttv.com/old/casefiles/simpson**. Access this Web site and select "Documents and Depositions." Then click on "Pre-Trial Depositions."

   a. Choose "O. J. Simpson Deposition—View the Deposition—Day 1." Answer the following questions:
   - What type of deposition was taken?
   - When was the deposition taken?
   - Where was it taken?
   - Pursuant to what was it taken?
   - What opening statement did the videographer make?
   - What were some of the opening questions that attorney Petrocelli asked?

   b. Choose "Denise Brown Deposition—View the Deposition." Answer the following questions:
   - What type of deposition was taken?
   - When and where was it taken?
   - Before whom was it taken?
   - Who was the attorney taking the deposition?
   - What were the opening questions?
   - What was the subject of the deposition?

CHAPTER 11
TRIAL PROCEDURES

Chapter Outline
- Introduction
- Preparing for Trial
- Pretrial Conference
- Jury Selection
- The Trial
- Posttrial Motions and Procedures
- Enforcing the Judgment

After completing this chapter, you will know:

- How attorneys prepare for trial and the ways in which paralegals assist in this task.
- How jurors are selected and the role of attorneys and their legal assistants in the selection process.
- The various phases of a trial and the kinds of trial-related tasks that paralegals often perform.
- The options available to the losing party after the verdict is in.
- How a case is appealed to a higher court for review.

CHAPTER 11 *Trial Procedures* 383

INTRODUCTION

Trials are costly in terms of both time and money. For this reason, parties to lawsuits often try to avoid going to trial. Pretrial negotiations between the parties and their respective attorneys may lead to an out-of-court settlement. Using the pretrial motions discussed in Chapter 10, the parties may attempt to end the litigation after the pleadings are filed or while discovery takes place. In many cases, parties opt for alternative methods of dispute resolution, such as mediation or arbitration, to avoid the time, expense, and publicity of courtroom trials. Recall from Chapter 6 that alternative dispute resolution is not always an option—many state and federal courts *mandate* that a dispute be mediated or arbitrated by the parties before they are permitted to bring the dispute before a court. If the parties fail to settle their dispute through any of these means, the case will go to trial.

To illustrate how attorneys and paralegals prepare for trial, we will continue using the hypothetical scenario developed in Chapter 10, in which Katherine Baranski (the plaintiff) was suing Tony Peretto (the defendant) for negligence. In the Baranski-Peretto case, Allen P. Gilmore is the attorney for plaintiff Baranski, and Gilmore's legal assistant is Elena Lopez. Defendant Peretto's attorney is Elizabeth A. Cameron, and Cameron's legal assistant is Gordon McVay.

> **Case at a Glance**
>
> **The Plaintiff—**
> Plaintiff: Katherine Baranski
> Attorney: Allen P. Gilmore
> Paralegal: Elena Lopez
>
> **The Defendant—**
> Defendant: Tony Peretto
> Attorney: Elizabeth A. Cameron
> Paralegal: Gordon McVay

PREPARING FOR TRIAL

As the trial date approaches, the attorneys for the plaintiff and the defendant and their respective paralegals complete their preparations for the trial. The paralegals collect and organize all of the documents and other evidence relating to the dispute. They may find it useful to create a trial-preparation checklist similar to the one in Exhibit 11.1 on the next page. Even though settlement negotiations may continue throughout the trial, both sides assume, for planning purposes, that the trial court will have to decide the issue.

At this point in the litigation process, plaintiff Baranski's attorney, Gilmore, will focus on legal strategy and how he can best use the information learned during the pleadings and discovery stages when presenting Baranski's case to the court. He will meet with his client and with his key witnesses to make last-minute preparations for trial. He might also meet with defendant Peretto's attorney to try once more to settle the dispute. Gilmore's legal assistant, Elena Lopez, will be notifying witnesses of the trial date and helping Gilmore prepare for trial. For example, she will make sure that all exhibits to be used during the trial are ready and verify that the trial notebook (to be discussed shortly) is in order.

Contacting and Preparing Witnesses

Typically, the paralegal is responsible for ensuring that witnesses are available and in court on the day of the trial. As mentioned in Chapter 10, a witness is any person asked to testify at trial. The person may be an eyewitness (that is, someone who saw the accident or event leading to a lawsuit), a person who has knowledge that is relevant to the lawsuit (such as an ambulance driver who assisted the accident victims or anyone who can testify to the truth of a claim being made by one of the parties), an official witness (such as a police officer), or an expert witness.

Several types of negligence lawsuits require expert witnesses. As discussed in Chapter 10, an expert witness is one who has specialized knowledge in a particular field. Such witnesses are often called to testify in negligence cases, because one element to be proved in a negligence case is the reasonableness of the defendant's actions. In medical-malpractice cases, for example, it takes someone with

EXHIBIT 11.1

Trial-Preparation Checklist

TWO MONTHS BEFORE THE TRIAL

- Review the status of the case and inform the attorney of any depositions, interrogatories, or other discovery procedures that need to be undertaken prior to trial.
- Interview witnesses and prepare witness statements.
- Review deposition transcripts/summaries, answers to interrogatories, witness statements, and other information obtained about the case. Inform the attorney of any further discovery procedures that should be undertaken prior to trial.
- Begin preparing the trial notebook.

ONE MONTH BEFORE THE TRIAL

- Make a list of the witnesses who will testify at the trial for the trial notebook.
- Prepare a subpoena for each witness, and arrange to have the subpoenas served.
- Prepare any exhibits that will be used at trial, and reserve any special equipment (such as a VCR) that will be needed at the trial.
- Draft *voir dire* questions and perhaps prepare a jury profile.
- Prepare motions and memoranda.
- Continue assembling the trial notebook.

ONE WEEK BEFORE THE TRIAL

- Check the calendar and call the court clerk to confirm the trial date.
- Complete the trial notebook.
- Make sure that all subpoenas have been served.
- Prepare the client and witnesses for trial.
- Make the final arrangements (housing, transportation, and so on) for the client or witnesses, as necessary.
- Check with the attorney to verify how witnesses should be paid (for lost wages, travel expenses, and so on).
- Make final arrangements to have all equipment, documents, and other items in the courtroom on the trial date.

ONE DAY BEFORE THE TRIAL

- Meet with others on the trial team to coordinate last-minute efforts.
- Have a final pretrial meeting with the client.

---

specialized knowledge in the defendant physician's area of practice to establish the reasonableness of the defendant's actions. A layperson does not know what is reasonably required in diagnosing or treating a specific illness or injury.

CONTACTING WITNESSES AND ISSUING SUBPOENAS. In the Baranski case, attorney Gilmore and paralegal Lopez will have lined up witnesses to testify on behalf of their client, plaintiff Baranski. In preparing for the trial, Lopez will inform each of the witnesses that the trial date has been set and that they will be expected to appear at the trial to testify. A **subpoena**—an order issued by the court clerk directing a person to appear in court—will be served on each of the witnesses to ensure their presence in court. A subpoena to appear in a federal court is shown in Exhibit 11.2. (Although not shown in the exhibit, a return-of-service form, similar to the one illustrated in Chapter 10, will be attached to the subpoena to verify that the witness received it.)

Unless she is already familiar with the court's requirements, paralegal Lopez will want to check with the court clerk to find out about what fees and documents she needs to take to the court to obtain the subpoena. The subpoena will then be served on the witness. Most subpoenas to appear in federal court can be served by

Subpoena
A document commanding a person to appear at a certain time and place to give testimony concerning a certain matter.

EXHIBIT 11.2
A Subpoena

United States District Court	DISTRICT	Nita
Katherine Baranski	DOCKET NO.	99-14335-NI
v.	TYPE OF CASE	[X] CIVIL [ ] CRIMINAL
Tony Peretto	SUBPOENA FOR	[X] PERSON [ ] DOCUMENT(S) or OBJECT(S)

TO: Julia Williams
3765 Mattis Avenue
Nita City, NI 48803

YOU ARE HEREBY COMMANDED to appear in the United States District Court at the place, date, and time specified below to testify in the above-entitled case.

PLACE	COURTROOM
4th and Main Nita City, NI	B
	DATE AND TIME
	8/4/99 10:00 A.M.

YOU ARE ALSO COMMANDED to bring with you the following document(s) or Object(s): (1)

[ ] See additional information on reverse

This subpoena shall remain in effect until you are granted leave to depart by the court or by an officer acting on behalf of the court.

U.S. MAGISTRATE (2) OR CLERK OF COURT	DATE
C. H. Hynek	July 13, 1999
(BY) DEPUTY CLERK *John Dolan*	

This subpoena is issued upon application of the:	ATTORNEY'S NAME AND ADDRESS
[X] Plaintiff [ ] Defendant [ ] U.S. Attorney	Allen P. Gilmore Jeffers, Gilmore & Dunn 553 Fifth Avenue, Suite 101 Nita City, NI 48801

(1) If not applicable, enter "none"
(2) A subpoena shall be issued by a magistrate in a proceeding before him, but need note be under the seal of the court. (Rule 17(a). Federal Rules of Criminal Procedure.)

---

anyone who is eighteen years of age or older, including paralegals, who often serve subpoenas. Subpoenas to appear in state court are often served by the sheriff or other process server.

When contacting *friendly witnesses* (those favorable to Baranski's position), Lopez should take care to explain that all witnesses are served with subpoenas, as a precaution, and to tell each witness when he or she can expect to receive the subpoena. Otherwise, a friendly witness might assume that Gilmore and Lopez did not trust the witness to keep his or her promise to appear in court.

PREPARING WITNESSES FOR TRIAL.   No prudent attorney ever puts a party or a witness on the stand unless the attorney has discussed the testimony beforehand with the party or witness. Prior to the trial, attorney Gilmore and paralegal Lopez will meet with each witness and prepare him or her for trial. Gilmore will prepare the witness for the types of questions to expect from himself and from opposing counsel during the trial. He might do some role-playing with the witness to help the witness understand how the questioning will proceed during the trial and to

DEVELOPING PARALEGAL SKILLS

Locating Expert Witnesses

Patricia Wolf is a paralegal in a law firm that specializes in defending physicians in medical-malpractice cases. Patricia's role is to locate expert witnesses. These experts testify in defense of the physicians' actions. When expert witnesses may be needed, Patricia lines the witnesses up early. This ensures that they will be available on the date that they are needed in court. It also allows the attorney to interview the experts in advance to determine more precisely what legal theories or defenses should be used in court.

CHECKLIST FOR LOCATING EXPERT WITNESSES

- Start with resources within the law firm. These resources may include the firm's expert-witness file and the firm's expert-witness resource person (in law firms that specialize in medical malpractice).
- If necessary, go outside the firm to these resources: professional associations, such as the American Medical Association; expert-witness directories; and online databases of experts.
- Prepare a letter to each expert describing the case and asking the expert to contact the firm.
- If the expert responds to the letter, arrange for a meeting.

---

prepare him or her for the opposing attorney's questions. Gilmore will also review with the witness any sworn statements made during discovery (during a deposition, for example). Additionally, Gilmore will review the substantive legal issues involved in the case and how the witness's testimony will affect the outcome of those issues.

Lopez will handle other aspects of witness preparation. She will advise the witness on trial procedures, when and where the witness will testify, and so on. Lopez might take the witness to the courtroom in which the trial will take place (if the courtroom is not in use) and familiarize the witness with the courtroom environment. She will show the witness where he or she will sit while giving testimony, where the judge and jurors will be, and where the attorneys will be seated.

ETHICAL CONCERN

Why Subpoena Friendly Witnesses?

The beginning paralegal might logically ask why it is necessary to subpoena friendly witnesses. The answer to this question is twofold. First, subpoenas make it easier for witnesses to be excused from their jobs and any other obligations on the date that they are to appear in court. Second, attorneys must take reasonable steps (and serving witnesses with subpoenas is a reasonable measure) to ensure that the clients' interests are best served. If a witness had not been subpoenaed and for some reason failed to appear at trial, the lack of his or her crucial testimony could jeopardize the client's chances of winning the case. By serving the witness with a subpoena, the attorney has proof that he or she has not breached the duty of competence to the client.

If necessary, Lopez might also do some role-playing, acting out the parts of the attorneys and asking the kinds of questions they might ask the witness during the trial.

Additionally, Lopez will advise witnesses on other details involved in trial preparation. For example, she might recommend appropriate clothing and grooming or tell them where to look when giving testimony and how to remain calm and poised when speaking to the court. After going over the trial procedures and the witness's role during the trial, Lopez may follow up on the discussion with a letter to the witness. Familiarity with the trial setting and what will be expected of him or her at trial will help to reduce a witness's discomfort in facing a new situation and allow the witness to control better his or her responses when called to testify.

Exhibits and Displays

Paralegals are frequently asked to prepare exhibits or displays that will be presented at trial. Attorney Gilmore may wish to present to the court a photograph of plaintiff Baranski's car taken after the accident occurred, a diagram of the intersection, an enlarged document (such as a police report), or other relevant evidence. Paralegal Lopez will be responsible for making sure that all exhibits are properly prepared and ready to introduce at trial. If any exhibits require special equipment, such as an easel or a VCR, Lopez must also make sure that these will be available in the courtroom and properly set up when they are needed. Increasingly, attorneys are using high-tech equipment to prepare their trial presentations. For a discussion of how high-tech presentations are altering the paralegal's trial-preparation tasks, see the feature *Technology and Today's Paralegal: Presentation Technology*.

The Trial Notebook

To present plaintiff Baranski's case effectively, attorney Gilmore will need to have in the courtroom all of the relevant documents; he will also need to be able to locate them quickly. To accomplish both of these goals, Lopez will prepare a **trial notebook**. The notebook will contain copies of the pleadings, interrogatories, deposition transcripts and summaries, pretrial motions, a list of exhibits and when they will be used, a witness list and the order in which the witnesses will testify, relevant cases or statutes that Gilmore plans to cite, and generally any document or information that will be important to have close at hand during the trial.

Trial Notebook
A binder that contains copies of all of the documents and information that an attorney will need to have at hand during the trial.

 Unless the paralegal knows from prior experience what his or her supervising attorney wants to include in the trial notebook and how it should be organized, the paralegal should discuss these matters with the attorney.

Typically, the trial notebook is a three-ring binder (or several binders, depending on the complexity of the case). The contents of the notebook are separated by divider sheets with tabs on them. Paralegal Lopez will create a general index to the notebook's contents and place this index at the front of the notebook. She may also create an index for each section of the binder and place those indexes at the beginnings of the sections. Some paralegals use a computer notebook and a software retrieval system to help them quickly locate documents, especially in complicated cases involving thousands of documents.

When preparing the trial notebook, always remember the following:

 The documents in the trial notebook should not be the original documents but rather copies of them.

> **Case at a Glance**
>
> **The Plaintiff—**
> Plaintiff: Katherine Baranski
> Attorney: Allen P. Gilmore
> Paralegal: Elena Lopez
>
> **The Defendant—**
> Defendant: Tony Peretto
> Attorney: Elizabeth A. Cameron
> Paralegal: Gordon McVay

TECHNOLOGY AND TODAY'S PARALEGAL

Presentation Technology

Attorneys and paralegals involved in complex litigation no longer have to lug piles of paper into the courtroom and then, during trial, search through them for key documents and exhibits. Today, advances in technology have made it possible for documents and exhibits to be presented to the court on computer monitors. With the click of a mouse or the wave of a wand over a computer bar code, the attorney can call up a particular document or other exhibit to support the client's case. The attorney might highlight a particular portion of a document or exhibit by using an electronic yellow "highlighter," a red electronic circle, or arrows. Certain text or areas of an exhibit might be emphasized by enlarging them while they are being displayed.

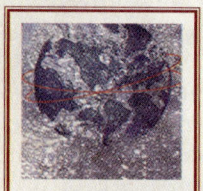

Video clips and slides can also be incorporated into the presentation. For example, a witness's pretrial deposition can be integrated into the presentation so that the attorney can impeach a witness on the spot if the witness gives inconsistent or contradictory evidence at trial. During closing arguments, attorneys can display photos of the witnesses who testified, along with key quotes from each witness, to remind the jury about the person who testified while emphasizing that witness's remarks.

As you might imagine, presentation technology has significantly changed the ways in which paralegals prepare for trial. Instead of making sure that an easel is in the courtroom for displaying an enlargement of a particular document, the paralegal may be asked to rent and use a digital camera to photograph key exhibits so that they can be incorporated into the computerized presentation. Instead of preparing copies of photos to hand out to the judge and jury, paralegals may be asked to scan the photos into a computerized presentation system. When witnesses are testifying at trial, instead of looking at a hard copy of the witness's pretrial deposition, the paralegal may be requested to compare the witness's trial testimony with what he or she said during the deposition, using key-word searches (see the *Technology and Today's Paralegal* feature in Chapter 10).

Of course, an important consideration in preparing for trial is the preferences of the court. Not every court welcomes high-tech presentations, and not every court is equipped to handle them. Therefore, when preparing for trial, the paralegal would be wise to check with the court in which the trial is to be held to find out, in advance, what equipment can be used in the courtroom, as well as what presentation practices are generally approved by the court.

The original documents (unless they are needed as evidence at trial) should always remain in the firm's files, both for reasons of security (should the trial notebook be misplaced) and to ensure that Lopez or others in the office will have access to the documents while the notebook is in court with the attorney.

Paralegal Lopez will not wait until the last minute to prepare the trial notebook. Rather, at the outset of the lawsuit, she will make copies of the pleadings and other documents as they are generated to include in the notebook. That way, she will not have to spend valuable time just before the trial, when there are other pressing needs, to do work that could have been done earlier. For further suggestions on how to prepare a trial notebook, see this chapter's featured-guest article on that topic.

PRETRIAL CONFERENCE

Pretrial Conference
A conference prior to trial in which the judge and the attorneys litigating the suit discuss settlement possibilities, clarify the issues in dispute, and schedule forthcoming trial-related events.

Before the trial begins, the attorneys usually meet with the trial judge in a **pretrial conference** to explore the possibility of resolving the case and, if a settlement is not possible, at least agree on the manner in which the trial will be conducted. In particular, the parties may attempt to clarify the issues in dispute and establish ground

DEVELOPING PARALEGAL SKILLS

Trial Support

Scott Greer, a paralegal with the firm of Dewey & Stone, is helping an attorney prepare for a trial in a personal-injury lawsuit. The client was injured in an automobile accident and is now a paraplegic. Scott has received a memo from his supervising attorney requesting that he prepare a diagram of the accident and arrange to have a "day in the life" videotape created for presentation to the jury. The video will show what a typical day in the life of the plaintiff is like as a result of the injuries sustained in the accident. Scott contacts Trial Support Services, Inc., a firm that specializes in litigation support, to make the video. Scott also obtains permission to have Trial Support Services, Inc., create the diagram as well.

TIPS FOR CREATING TRIAL VIDEOS

- Use a reliable trial-support services provider or vendor.
- Arrange to meet the vendor at the location where the videotape will be made.
- Make sure that the videotape is realistic, so that the court will allow its use.
- Preview the video before giving it to the attorney.
- Make sure that the vendor is timely paid.

---

rules to restrict such matters as the admissibility of certain types of evidence. For example, attorney Gilmore might have paralegal Lopez draft a **motion *in limine***[1] (a motion to limit evidence) to submit to the judge at this time. The motion will request the judge to order that certain types of evidence not be brought out at trial.

To illustrate: Suppose that plaintiff Baranski had been arrested in the past for illegal drug possession. Gilmore knows that evidence of the arrest, if introduced by the defense at trial, might prejudice the jury against Baranski. In this situation, Gilmore might submit a motion *in limine* to keep the defense from presenting the evidence. Exhibit 11.3 on page 392 presents a sample motion *in limine*. Note that Gilmore would include with the motion affidavits and/or a memorandum of law (brief)—these documents were discussed in Chapter 10—to convince the judge that the motion should be granted.

Once the pretrial conference has concluded, both parties turn their attention to the trial itself. Assuming that the trial will be heard by a jury, however, one more step is necessary before the trial begins: selecting the jurors who will hear the trial and render a verdict on the dispute.

Motion *in Limine*
A motion requesting that certain evidence not be brought out at the trial, such as prejudicial, irrelevant, or legally inadmissible evidence.

JURY SELECTION

Before the trial gets under way, a panel of jurors must be assembled. The clerk of the court usually notifies local residents by mail that they have been selected for jury duty. The process of selecting the names of these prospective jurors varies, depending on the court, but often they are randomly selected by the court clerk from lists of registered voters or those within a state to whom driver's licenses have been issued. The persons selected then report to the courthouse on the date specified in the notice. At the courthouse, they are gathered into a single pool of jurors, and the process of selecting those jurors who will actually hear the case begins.

On the Web
Numerous firms offer trial consulting services, including assistance in jury selection. You can access the Web site of one such firm, Jury Research Institute, at **www.jri-inc.com**.

---

1. Pronounced in *leem*-in-ay.

FEATURED GUEST: VITONIO F. SAN JUAN

Ten Tips for Preparing a Trial Notebook

BIOGRAPHICAL NOTE

Vitonio F. San Juan is a graduate of the University of the Philippines College of Law. He has a Master of Law degree (an advanced law degree) from the University of California School of Law in Los Angeles. He is also a J.S.D. (Doctor of the Science of Law) candidate at the University of California School of Law in Berkeley (Boalt Hall). He practiced corporate and securities law before devoting his time to legal education and to the law governing international trade and investments. At present, he is the director of paralegal studies at the University of La Verne in La Verne, California. The program offers a paralegal certificate, an associate's degree, and a bachelor of science degree in paralegal studies.

The trial notebook compiles all of the essential case information for the ready reference of the trial attorney. Prepared by the paralegal, the notebook reorganizes the central office file in such a way that the trial attorney has quick access to the information he or she needs during the trial. In preparing the notebook, the paralegal might find it helpful to follow the tips given below.

1. **Check with the Attorney before Creating the Notebook.** The one hard-and-fast rule for organizing the trial notebook is that it must be organized so that it assists the attorney during the trial. To learn the attorney's preferences, the legal assistant should check with the attorney. The trial attorney will be the one presenting the evidence during trial, anticipating the opposition's moves, and ultimately summarizing the client's case in the closing argument. As a member of the trial team, you must communicate closely with the attorney during the pretrial stages to make sure that the trial notebook is organized efficiently for the attorney's use during the trial.

2. **Prepare the Notebook Early.** The paralegal must keep track of many things while helping prepare for a trial. With the increasing number of jobs to be done and the accompanying details, it is very easy to forget something. To avoid this possibility, start preparing the notebook once you learn what the trial attorney wants included in it. Having the notebook not only makes you feel more confident and in control, but it could also help the attorney in the settlement stage. During that stage, the notebook will send a message to opposing counsel that your side is prepared and that you have a strong case. In any event, even if the case goes to trial, the notebook will show the client just how well your firm works.

3. **Think "Easy Access."** In preparing the notebook you should try to make every document easily retrievable. The attorney who can easily locate the document that he or she needs, at the moment that it is needed, projects a positive image to the jury. If it takes more than a few seconds to get the document or to access prior testimony, the jury can easily lose confidence in the attorney and brand him or her as a fumbler. Normally, a three-ring binder is used. This will make the notebook flexible; it can be expanded and updated as needed. If there will be a large number of pages, a large-size binder might be used. The color of the binder should be coordinated with the colors of any other binders. A unique color will assist you in finding a specific item in a hurry and can again create the impression in court that the case has been carefully thought out and organized.

4. **Create a Notebook That Works.** Once you've talked to the trial attorney and determined his or her preferences, you can start creating the notebook. Most notebooks have a table of contents and are divided into sections.

Although some types of trials require twelve-person juries, most civil matters can be heard by a jury of six persons.

Voir Dire

Both the plaintiff's attorney and the defendant's attorney have some input into the ultimate make-up of the jury. Each attorney will question prospective jurors in a

FEATURED GUEST, Continued

There could be sections for the pleadings and pretrial motions; the opening statement and the discovery plan; jury research notes, proposed *voir dire* questions, and notes on the accepted jurors; witnesses (subdivided into friendly, hostile, and expert); and notes regarding closing arguments. Various indexes may also be included (such as a deposition index, a key-document index, an exhibit index, and a demonstrative-evidence index).

Each section should be tabbed. Consider using colored tabs that match a predetermined color code (for example, red for exhibits, yellow for witnesses, blue for documents, and so on).

Use notebook dividers and be sure to have extra ones handy. You can put extra tabs and dividers in a prepunched pocket envelope. The pocket envelope can also contain extra yellow pads of paper. Attorneys often need to make notes during a trial, and the yellow paper can be easily distinguished from the rest of the white paper in the notebook.

Finally, cases vary in complexity and length. If you can't fit all the information into one notebook, use more notebooks.

5. **Have a Section for Contact Information.** This section of the trial notebook should include the names, addresses (including e-mail addresses), and phone and fax numbers of all of the parties and attorneys involved in the case. It is also a good idea to include a section for your vendors (suppliers), including your graphics vendors, photocopying vendors, and couriers.

6. **Create a Back-Up Trial Notebook.** Keep a duplicate copy of the main trial notebook so that a copy will be available if the original is lost or, more likely, a portion of its contents is misplaced.

If the technology is available, consider scanning your trial notebook's contents into a computer file.

7. **Create Your Own Paralegal Notebook.** This notebook should contain key information for your use. While the trial notebook is assembled to meet the trial needs of the attorney, this notebook will enable you to have key information at your fingertips. It should contain some of the information found in the trial notebook and checklists to help you remember all the various deadlines and details. You may also include a section for adding notes during the trial. For example, you could jot down jury responses to the behavior of certain witnesses—information that may be helpful to you when you are preparing witnesses for trial in the future.

8. **Consult with Other Paralegals.** If you have questions, consult with other, more experienced paralegals when preparing your trial notebook. Some of their ideas and experiences may help you avoid mistakes.

> "The attorney who can easily locate the document that he or she needs, at the moment that it is needed, projects a positive image to the jury."

9. **Review the Contents Periodically.** Check and recheck the contents of the trial notebook periodically. Make sure that the sections are complete and that all information is current. If the attorney removes a section from the notebook, make sure before the trial begins that the section is in its proper place.

10. **Check with the Attorney Again.** Once you've put together the trial notebook, make sure that it contains everything that is needed. Schedule some convenient time with the trial attorney to go over the notebook. He or she may want to include other sections or indexes. Try to anticipate any problems and take care of them before they occur. Remember that you must be flexible and take every new problem in stride. The trial notebook is an essential tool for the attorney trying a case. A very personalized tool, it contains information that must be readily accessible. Remember: when in doubt, check with the attorney.

---

proceeding known as *voir dire*.[2] Legal assistants often work with their attorneys to write up the questions that will be asked of jurors during *voir dire*. Because all

Voir Dire
A proceeding in which attorneys for the plaintiff and the defendant ask prospective jurors questions to determine whether potential jury members are biased or have any connection with a party to the action or with a prospective witness.

---

2. Pronounced vwahr *deehr*. Literally, these French verbs mean "to see, to speak." During the *voir dire* phase of litigation, attorneys do in fact see the jurors speak. In legal language, however, the phrase refers to the process of interrogating jurors to learn about their backgrounds, attitudes, and so on.

EXHIBIT 11.3
Motion *in Limine*

**UNITED STATES DISTRICT COURT
FOR THE WESTERN DISTRICT OF NITA**

Katherine Baranski
                    Plaintiff

vs.
                                        File No. 99-14335-NI

Tony Peretto
                    Defendant   Hon. Harley M. LaRue

A. P. Gilmore
Attorney for the Plaintiff
Jeffers, Gilmore & Dunn
553 Fifth Avenue
Suite 101
Nita City, NI 48801

<u>MOTION *IN LIMINE*</u>

    The Plaintiff respectfully moves the Court to prohibit counsel for the Defendant from directly or indirectly introducing or making any reference during the trial to the Plaintiff's arrest in 1984 for the possession of illegal drugs.
    The grounds on which this motion is based are stated in the accompanying affidavits and memorandum.

Date: <u>6/18/99</u>
                                                    Allen P. Gilmore
                                                    Allen P. Gilmore
                                                    Attorney for the Plaintiff
                                                    Jeffers, GIlmore & Dunn
                                                    553 Fifth Avenue
                                                    Suite 101
                                                    Nita City, NI 48801

On the Web
If you want to try your hand at being a juror, go to www.cyberjury.com. This interactive Web site allows visitors to act as jurors in deciding cases.

of the jurors will have previously filled out forms giving basic information about themselves, the attorneys and their paralegals can tailor their questions accordingly. They fashion the questions in such a way as to uncover any biases on the part of prospective jurors and to find persons who might identify with the plights of their respective clients. When large numbers of jurors are involved, during the *voir dire* process the attorneys may direct their questions to groups of jurors, as opposed to individual jurors, to minimize the amount of time needed to choose the jurors who will sit on the jury. Note that in some courts, judges may question the jurors, using questions prepared by the attorneys.

Challenges during *Voir Dire*

During *voir dire*, the attorney for each side may exercise a certain number of **challenges** to prevent particular persons from being allowed to serve on the jury. As plaintiff Baranski's attorney, Gilmore will want to exclude jurors who may already have formed an unfavorable impression about the validity of Baranski's claim. To uncover any underlying hostility toward Baranski, Gilmore might ask a

Challenge
An attorney's objection, during *voir dire*, to the inclusion of a particular person on the jury.

> ### ETHICAL CONCERN
> #### Should You Tell Your Supervising Attorney What You Know about a Prospective Juror?
>
> During *voir dire*, paralegal Lopez notices one of her neighbors among the prospective jurors. Lopez knows that her neighbor is strongly biased against foreigners and will probably not be an impartial juror in the case against Tony Peretto, who has a slight foreign accent. Lopez also knows that she and attorney Gilmore want their client, plaintiff Baranski, to win the case, and a juror biased against Peretto would definitely help them achieve this goal. Should Lopez tell Gilmore what she knows about this prospective juror? Yes. It is to Gilmore's—and his client's—advantage to know all he can about the prospective jurors, and it is up to Gilmore to decide how to use whatever information he obtains. Furthermore, Lopez has no duty to keep confidential any information that she has learned about her neighbor.

juror whether he or she has ever been sued. Defendant Peretto's attorney, in contrast, will want to ferret out jurors who might be inclined to render a verdict against Tony Peretto, perhaps because they have been injured in a car accident caused by another person's negligent driving. Experienced litigators try to conserve their challenges so that they may eliminate the prospective jurors who are the most hostile.

During the jury-selection process, attorney Gilmore may have paralegal Lopez observe the prospective jurors carefully as they respond to the attorneys' questions. Lopez, because she is not participating in the questioning process, is free to observe the jurors more closely than Gilmore. As a result, she may uncover a verbal or nonverbal response that Gilmore might not notice.

TYPES OF CHALLENGES. Both attorneys can exercise two types of challenges: challenges "for cause" and peremptory challenges. If attorney Gilmore concludes that a particular prospective juror is biased against Baranski for some reason, he may exercise a **challenge for cause** and request that the prospective juror not be included in the jury. Each attorney may also exercise a limited number of peremptory challenges. Attorneys may exercise **peremptory challenges** without giving any reason for their desire to exclude a particular juror. Peremptory challenges based on racial criteria or gender, however, are illegal.[3]

After both sides have completed their challenges, those jurors who have been excused are permitted to leave. The remaining jurors, those found to be acceptable by both attorneys, will be seated in the jury box.

ALTERNATE JURORS. Because unforeseeable circumstances or illness may necessitate that one or more of the sitting jurors be dismissed, the court also seats several *alternate jurors* who will also hear the entire trial. Depending on the rules of

> **Case at a Glance**
>
> **The Plaintiff—**
> Plaintiff: Katherine Baranski
> Attorney: Allen P. Gilmore
> Paralegal: Elena Lopez
>
> **The Defendant—**
> Defendant: Tony Peretto
> Attorney: Elizabeth A. Cameron
> Paralegal: Gordon McVay

Challenge for Cause
A *voir dire* challenge for which an attorney states the reason why a prospective juror should not be included in the jury.

Peremptory Challenge
A *voir dire* challenge to exclude a potential juror from serving on the jury without any supporting reason or cause. Peremptory challenges based on racial or gender criteria are illegal.

---

3. Discriminating against prospective jurors on the basis of race was prohibited by the United States Supreme Court in *Batson v. Kentucky,* 476 U.S. 79, 106 S.Ct. 1712, 90 L.Ed.2d 69 (1986). Discriminating against prospective jurors on the basis of gender was prohibited by the Supreme Court in *J.E.B. v. Alabama ex rel. T.B.,* 511 U.S 127, 114 S. Ct. 1419, 128 L.Ed.2d 89 (1994). See Chapter 14 for an explanation of how to read court citations.

Paralegal Profile

Litigation Paralegal

VICTORIALEI "NOHEA" NAKAAHIKI *is a paralegal in the litigation and maritime/admiralty sections of the Carlsmith Ball Law Firm in Honolulu, Hawaii, and has been a paralegal for ten years. Nohea received her A.S. degree in Paralegal Studies from Kapiolani Community College. She is a former president of the Hawaii Paralegal Association and the current secondary representative to the National Federation of Paralegal Associations (NFPA). Nohea is also an affiliate member of the Native Hawaiian Bar Association, American Bar Association, Federal Bar Association, Monterey County Women Lawyers' Association, and Hawaii State Bar Association. Nohea is also a member of the paralegal editor's board for* Legal Assistant Today *magazine.*

What do you like best about your work?

"As a member of both litigation and maritime/admiralty sections at my firm, I work on an assortment of cases, including construction, product liability, and toxic torts on the litigation side and maritime personal injury, wrongful death, vessel stranding, collision, sinking, and shipping-related cases on the maritime/admiralty side. Although I enjoy the variety of work, I especially enjoy working on the maritime cases. Living and working in Hawaii, the 'Gateway to the Pacific Rim,' I am afforded the opportunity to work with many shipping agents, ship owners, marine underwriters, and marine consultants/experts throughout the world."

What is the greatest challenge that you face in your area of work?

"The greatest challenge I face in my area of work is the ability to balance my typically smaller maritime cases with my larger and more complex litigation cases. Approximately 90 percent of my maritime cases are in federal court, and therefore they follow a pretty set time line as directed by scheduling and pretrial orders, while my nonmaritime cases (such as an action filed by the Hawaii state attorney general against the tobacco industry) are filed in state court with no set pretrial dates provided until a week before trial. Just recently, I was faced with preparing a maritime case for a jury trial in a federal court while simultaneously preparing a product-liability case in a state court—that was a challenge! But I faced it head-on. What helped me get through preparing the two cases for trial was knowing the rules and procedures of both courts and properly managing both of my cases."

the particular jurisdiction, a court might have two or three alternate jurors present throughout the trial. If a juror has to be excused in the middle of the trial, then an alternate may take his or her place without disrupting the proceedings. Unless they replace jurors, alternate jurors do not participate in jury deliberations at the end of the trial. Once the jury members are seated, the judge swears in the jury and the trial itself can begin.

THE TRIAL

During the trial, the attorneys, Allen Gilmore and Elizabeth Cameron, will present their cases to the jury. Because the attorneys will be concentrating on the trial, it will fall to their paralegals to coordinate the logistical aspects of the trial and observe as closely as possible the trial proceedings. Because paralegal Lopez is thoroughly familiar with the case and Gilmore's legal strategy, she will be a valuable ally during the trial. She will be able to anticipate Gilmore's needs and provide appropriate reminders or documents as Gilmore needs them.

PARALEGAL PROFILE

Litigation Paralegal *Continued*

"Learn all you can about the area of the law with which you are dealing."

What advice do you have for would-be paralegals in your area of work?

"Learn all you can about the area of the law with which you are dealing, whether it is maritime law, construction law, or personal-injury law; attend continuing legal education seminars and read legal reference materials, hornbooks, and treaties; know your court rules (this includes state, federal, and local rules); always be one step ahead of your attorney—if you know a discovery response is due, take the initiative to draft it without being asked; continuously offer your assistance with anything that needs to be done. Attorneys appreciate the interest you show in a case, as well as the initiative you take."

What are some tips for success as a paralegal in your area of work?

"Here is my "Top Ten List of Tips" for success as a paralegal: (1) take the initiative; (2) be confident in your role as the paralegal (this can be done by knowing and/or learning court procedures, applicable court rules, and elements of the law with which you are dealing); (3) be organized; (4) develop document-management skills (document management and organization are crucial to your success as a paralegal); (5) take an interest in the issues of a case and focus on how you can efficiently and effectively assist the attorney to prove or disprove those issues; (6) learn to use a database program and apply it to a case (using a database will help you with document management, especially with larger, more complex litigation cases); (7) develop your online factual research skills (Internet, public-information computer databases such as InfoTech, DBT Autotrek, and LexisNexis, and other methods); (8) expand your communication skills to include familiarity with and/or knowledge of other languages and cultures; (9) develop and follow a tickler and calendaring system that will assist in your efforts to ensure that your attorney meets pretrial deadlines; and last but surely not least, (10) be a team player—do not exhibit an attitude because you are the paralegal. Remember, you are a member of a team with a common goal: to achieve the best results for your client. You should never be above photocopying, date stamping, or filing documents with a court."

Prior to each trial day, for example, Lopez will assemble the documents and materials that will be needed in court. During the court proceedings, Lopez will make sure that attorney Gilmore has within reach any documents or exhibits that he will need to have at hand for questioning parties or witnesses. When attorney Gilmore no longer needs the documents or exhibits, Lopez will put them aside in an appropriate place. At the end of the day, she will again organize the documents and materials, decide what will be needed for the next day, and file the documents that can remain in the office.

Paralegal Lopez must also monitor each witness's testimony to ensure that it is consistent with previous statements made by the witness. Lopez will have the relevant deposition transcript (and summary) at hand when a witness takes the stand. She will follow the deposition transcript (or summary) of each witness as that witness testifies. This way, she can pass a note to Gilmore if he misses any inconsistencies in the witness's testimony.

Lopez will also act as a second pair of eyes and ears during the trial. She will observe how the jury is responding to various witnesses and their testimony or to the attorneys' demeanor and questions. She will take notes during the trial on

Case at a Glance

The Plaintiff—
Plaintiff: Katherine Baranski
Attorney: Allen P. Gilmore
Paralegal: Elena Lopez

The Defendant—
Defendant: Tony Peretto
Attorney: Elizabeth A. Cameron
Paralegal: Gordon McVay

these observations as well as on the points being stressed and the types of evidence introduced by the opposing counsel, Cameron. At the end of the day, Lopez and Gilmore may review the day's events, and Lopez's "trial journal" will provide a ready reference to the major events that transpired in the courtroom.

Opening Statements

The trial both opens and closes with attorneys' statements to the jury. In their **opening statements,** the attorneys will give a brief version of the facts and the supporting evidence that they will use during the trial. Because some trials can drag on for weeks or even months, it is extremely helpful for jurors to hear a summary of the story that will unfold during the trial. Otherwise, they may be left wondering how a particular piece of evidence fits into the dispute.

In short, the opening statement is a kind of "road map" that describes the destination that each attorney hopes to reach and outlines how he or she plans to reach it. Plaintiff Baranski's attorney, Gilmore, will focus on such things as his client's lack of fault and the injuries that she sustained when she was hit by defendant Peretto's car. Peretto's attorney, Cameron, will highlight the points that weaken plaintiff Baranski's claim (for example, Cameron might point out that Baranski was speeding) or otherwise suggest that defendant Peretto had not committed any wrongful act.

The Plaintiff's Case

Once the opening statements have been made, Gilmore will present the plaintiff's case first. Because he is the plaintiff's attorney, he has the burden of proving that defendant Peretto was negligent.

DIRECT EXAMINATION. Attorney Gilmore will call several eyewitnesses to the stand and ask them to tell the court about the sequence of events that led to the accident. This form of questioning is known as **direct examination.** For example, Gilmore will call Julia Williams, an eyewitness who saw the accident occur, and ask her questions such as those presented in Exhibit 11.4 on page 397. He will also call other witnesses, including the police officer who was summoned to the accident scene and the ambulance driver. Gilmore will try to elicit responses from these witnesses that strengthen plaintiff Baranski's case—or at least that do not visibly weaken the claim.

During direct examination, attorney Gilmore will not usually be permitted to ask **leading questions,** which are questions that lead the witness to a particular desired response. A leading question might be something like the following: "So, Mrs. Williams, you noticed that the defendant ran the stop sign, right?" If Mrs. Williams says "yes" to this question, she has, in effect, been "led" to this conclusion by Gilmore's leading question. The fundamental purpose behind a trial is to establish what actually happened, not to tell witnesses what to say.

> Leading questions may distort the testimony by discouraging witnesses from telling their stories in their own words.

When Gilmore is dealing with *hostile witnesses* (uncooperative witnesses or those who are testifying on behalf of the other party), however, he is normally permitted to ask leading questions. This is because hostile witnesses may be uncommunicative and unwilling to describe the events they witnessed. If Gilmore asked a hostile witness what he or she observed on the morning of August 4 at 7:45 A.M., for example, the witness might respond, "I saw two trucks driving down Mattis

---

Opening Statement
An attorney's statement to the jury at the beginning of the trial. The attorney briefly outlines the evidence that will be offered during the trial and the legal theory that will be pursued.

Direct Examination
The examination of a witness by the attorney who calls the witness to the stand to testify on behalf of the attorney's client.

Leading Question
A question that suggests, or "leads to," a desired answer. Generally, leading questions may be asked only of hostile witnesses.

Avenue." That answer is true, but it has nothing to do with the Baranski-Peretto accident. Therefore, to elicit information from this witness, Gilmore would be permitted to use leading questions, which would force the witness to respond to the question at issue.

CROSS-EXAMINATION. After attorney Gilmore has finished questioning a witness on direct examination, defendant Peretto's attorney, Cameron, will begin her **cross-examination** of that witness. During her cross-examination, Cameron will be primarily concerned with reducing the witness's credibility in the eyes of the jury and the judge. Cameron's questions for Gilmore's witnesses will be based on their answers to interrogatories and depositions submitted during discovery. Consequently, Cameron will have a fairly good idea as to what areas of questioning may prove fruitful. Moreover, she can attack the credibility of these witnesses if their answers on the witness stand vary considerably from answers they gave in response to the same questions during discovery or if other evidence obtained during discovery contradicts their testimony.

The defendant's attorney, Cameron, must confine her cross-examination to matters that were—or could have been—brought up during direct examination and those that relate to a witness's credibility. She normally may not introduce evidence that a witness for the plaintiff is a smoker or dislikes children, for example, unless she can demonstrate that such facts are relevant to the case. In general, Cameron will try to uncover relevant physical infirmities of the plaintiff's witnesses (such as poor eyesight or hearing) as well as any evidence of bias (such as a witness's habit

Cross-Examination
The questioning of an opposing witness during the trial.

Case at a Glance

The Plaintiff—
  Plaintiff: Katherine Baranski
  Attorney: Allen P. Gilmore
  Paralegal: Elena Lopez

The Defendant—
  Defendant: Tony Peretto
  Attorney: Elizabeth A. Cameron
  Paralegal: Gordon McVay

EXHIBIT 11.4
Direct Examination—Sample Questions

ATTORNEY:	Mrs. Williams, please explain how you came to be at the scene of the accident.
WITNESS:	Well, I was walking north on Mattis Avenue toward Nita City Hospital, where I work as a nurse.
ATTORNEY:	Please describe for the court, in your own words, exactly what you observed when you reached the intersection of Mattis Avenue and Thirty-eighth Street.
WITNESS:	I was approaching the intersection when I saw the defendant run the stop sign on Thirty-eighth Street and crash into the plaintiff's car.
ATTORNEY:	Did you notice any change in the speed at which the defendant was driving as he approached the stop sign?
WITNESS:	No. He didn't slow down at all.
ATTORNEY:	Mrs. Williams, are you generally in good health?
WITNESS:	Yes.
ATTORNEY:	Have you ever had any problems with your vision?
WITNESS:	No. I wear reading glasses for close work, but I see well in the distance.
ATTORNEY:	And how long has it been since your last eye examination?
WITNESS:	About a month or so ago, I went to Dr. Sullivan for an examination. He told me that I needed reading glasses but that my distance vision was excellent.

of playing a friendly round of golf with plaintiff Baranski every Saturday). When cross-examining Gilmore's witnesses for the plaintiff, Cameron is permitted to ask leading questions because Gilmore's witnesses will be hostile witnesses with respect to Peretto's defense. Some questions that Cameron might ask Julia Williams, Gilmore's eyewitness, are presented in Exhibit 11.5.

REDIRECT AND RECROSS. After defendant Peretto's attorney, Cameron, has finished cross-examining each witness, plaintiff Baranski's attorney, Gilmore, will need to repair any damage done to the credibility of the witness's testimony—or, indeed, to the case itself. Gilmore will do this by again questioning the witness and allowing the witness to explain his or her answer. This process is known as **redirect examination**.

If Cameron's cross-examination revealed that one of Gilmore's eyewitnesses to the accident had vision problems, for example, Gilmore could ask the witness whether he or she was wearing corrective lenses at the time of the accident. Gilmore might also have the witness demonstrate to the court that he or she has good vision by having the witness identify a letter or object at the far end of the courtroom. Because redirect examination is primarily used to improve the credibility of cross-examined witnesses, it is limited to matters raised during cross-examination. (If attorney Cameron chooses not to cross-examine a particular witness, then, of course, there can be no redirect examination by Gilmore.)

Following Gilmore's redirect examination, defendant Peretto's attorney, Cameron, will be given an opportunity for **recross-examination**. When both attorneys have finished with the first witness, Gilmore will call the succeeding witnesses in plaintiff Baranski's case, each of whom will be subject to cross-examination (and redirect and recross, if necessary).

Redirect Examination
The questioning of a witness following the adverse party's cross-examination.

Recross-Examination
The questioning of an opposing witness following the adverse party's redirect examination.

EXHIBIT 11.5
Cross-Examination— Sample Questions

ATTORNEY:	You have just testified that you were approaching the intersection when the accident occurred. Isn t it true that you stated earlier, under oath, that you were at the intersection at the time of the accident?
WITNESS:	Well, I might have, but I think I said that I was close to the intersection.
ATTORNEY:	In fact, you said that you were at the intersection. Now, you say that you were approaching it. Which is it?
WITNESS:	I was approaching it, I suppose.
ATTORNEY:	Okay. Exactly where were you when the accident occurred?
WITNESS:	I think that I was just in front of the Dairy Queen when the accident happened.
ATTORNEY:	Mrs. Williams, the Dairy Queen on Mattis Avenue is at least seventy-five yards from the intersection of Mattis Avenue and Thirty-eighth Street. Were you watching the defendant s car as it proceeded north on Mattis Avenue toward the intersection?
WITNESS:	Well, not at first, I guess.
ATTORNEY:	When did you start observing the defendant s car?
WITNESS:	I believe it was when the defendant ran the stop sign.
ATTORNEY:	Mrs. Williams, I suggest that you did not really look at the defendant s car until after the collision focused your attention on it. Isn t that true?

Motion for a Directed Verdict (Motion for Judgment as a Matter of Law)

After attorney Gilmore has presented his case for plaintiff Baranski, then Cameron, as counsel for defendant Peretto, may decide to make a **motion for a directed verdict** (now also known as a **motion for judgment as a matter of law** in federal courts). Through this motion, attorney Cameron will be saying to the court that the plaintiff's attorney, Gilmore, has not offered enough evidence to support a claim against defendant Peretto. If the judge agrees to grant the motion, then a judgment will be entered for defendant Peretto, plaintiff Baranski's case against him will be dismissed, and the trial will be over. A sample motion for judgment as a matter of law is shown in Exhibit 11.6 on the following page.

The motion for a directed verdict (judgment as a matter of law) is seldom granted because only those cases that involve genuine factual disputes are permitted to proceed to trial in the first place. If the judge had believed that Baranski's case was that weak before the trial started, then the judge would probably have granted a pretrial motion to dismiss the case, thereby avoiding the expense of a trial. Occasionally, however, the occurrence of certain events—such as the death of a key witness—might mean the plaintiff has no evidence at all to support his or her allegations. In that event, the court may grant the defendant's motion for a directed verdict, or judgment as a matter of law.

The Defendant's Case

Assuming that the motion for directed verdict (motion for judgment as a matter of law) is denied by the court, the two attorneys, Gilmore and Cameron, will now reverse their roles. Attorney Cameron will now begin to present evidence demonstrating the weaknesses of plaintiff Baranski's claims against defendant Peretto. She will essentially follow the same procedure used by Gilmore when he presented plaintiff Baranski's side of the story. Cameron will call witnesses to the stand and question them. After Cameron's direct examination of each witness, that witness will be subject to possible cross-examination by Gilmore, redirect examination by Cameron, and recross-examination by Gilmore.

In her presentation of the defendant's case, attorney Cameron will attempt to counter the points made by attorney Gilmore during his presentation of plaintiff Baranski's side of the story. To that end, Cameron and her paralegal, Gordon McVay, may have to prepare exhibits and assorted memoranda of law in addition to those originally prepared. The need to prepare additional exhibits and memoranda sometimes arises when the plaintiff's attorney pursues a different strategy from the one anticipated by the defense team. Depending on Cameron's preference or strategy, she may choose to begin by exposing the weaknesses in the plaintiff's case (by asserting that the plaintiff was speeding, for example) or by presenting defendant Peretto's version of the accident. Regardless of the procedure taken, however, paralegal McVay, like paralegal Lopez, will have to keep track of the materials brought to court each day to faciliate Cameron's presentation.

Once Cameron has finished presenting her case on behalf of defendant Peretto, Gilmore will be permitted to offer evidence to *rebut* (refute) evidence introduced by Cameron in Peretto's behalf. After Gilmore's rebuttal, if any, both attorneys will make their closing arguments to the jury.

Closing Arguments

In their **closing arguments**, the attorneys summarize their presentations and argue in their clients' favor. A closing argument should include all of the major points that

---

Motion for a Directed Verdict (Motion for Judgment as a Matter of Law)
A motion requesting that the court grant a judgment in favor of the party making the motion on the ground that the other party has not produced sufficient evidence to support his or her claim.

On the Web
For an example of how witnesses are examined at trial, you can read through one or more of the trial transcripts from O. J. Simpson's trial, which are online at **www.courttv.com/old/casefiles/simpson/transcripts**.

Closing Argument
An argument made by each side's attorney after the cases for the plaintiff and defendant have been presented. Closing arguments are made prior to the jury charge.

EXHIBIT 11.6

Motion for Judgment as a Matter of Law

**UNITED STATES DISTRICT COURT
FOR THE WESTERN DISTRICT OF NITA**

Katherine Baranski

          Plaintiff

vs.

Tony Peretto

          Defendant

File No. 99-14335-NI

Hon. Harley M. LaRue

Elizabeth A. Cameron
Attorney for the Defendant
Cameron & Strauss, P.C.
310 Lake Drive
Zero City, ZE 59802

MOTION FOR JUDGMENT AS A MATTER OF LAW

The Defendant, Tony Peretto, at the close of the Plaintiff's case, moves the court to withdraw the evidence from the consideration of the jury and to find the Defendant not liable.

As grounds for this motion, Defendant Peretto states that:

(1) No evidence has been offered or received during the trial of the above-entitled cause of action to sustain the allegations of negligence contained in Plaintiff Baranski's complaint.

(2) No evidence has been offered or received during the trial proving or tending to prove that Defendant Peretto was guilty of any negligence.

(3) The proximate cause of Plaintiff Baranski's injuries was not due to any negligence on the part of Defendant Peretto.

(4) By the uncontroverted evidence, Plaintiff Baranski was guilty of contributory negligence, which was the sole cause of the Plaintiff's injuries.

Date: 7/21/99

Elizabeth A. Cameron
Elizabeth A. Cameron
Attorney for the Defendant
Cameron & Strauss, P.C.
310 Lake Drive
Zero City, ZE 59802

---

support the client's case. It should also emphasize the shortcomings of the opposing party's case. Jurors will view a closing argument with some skepticism if it merely recites the central points of a party's claim or defense without also responding to the unfavorable facts or issues raised by the other side. Of course, neither attorney wants to focus too much on the other side's position, but the elements of the opposing position do need to be acknowledged and their flaws highlighted.

Both attorneys will want to organize their presentations so they can explain to the jury their respective arguments and show how their arguments are supported

ETHICAL CONCERN
Communicating with Jurors

Suppose that you are the paralegal working on the Baranski case with attorney Allen Gilmore, and one of your neighbors is a juror in the case. One evening, while you are gardening in your back yard, your neighbor approaches you and says, "You know, I didn't really understand what that witness, Williams, was saying. Did she really see the accident? Also, is it true that Mrs. Baranski will never be able to walk normally again?" You know the answers to these questions, and you would like the juror to know the truth. You also know that it would enhance Baranski's chances of winning the case if this juror were as familiar with the factual background as you are. What should you do? First, you should inform your neighbor that as a paralegal, you have an ethical duty to abide by the professional rules of conduct governing the legal profession. One of these rules prohibits *ex parte* (private) communications with jurors about a case being tried. Second, you should remind your neighbor that jurors are not permitted to discuss a case they are hearing with anyone.

by the evidence. Once both attorneys have completed their remarks, the case will be submitted to the jury and the attorneys' role in the trial will be finished.

Jury Instructions

Before the jurors begin their deliberations, the judge gives the jury a **charge**, in which the judge sums up the case and instructs the jurors on the rules of law that apply to the issues involved in the case. Because the jury's role is to serve as the fact finder, the factual account contained in the charge is not binding on them. Indeed, the jurors may disregard the facts as noted in the charge. They are *not* free to ignore the statements of law, however. The charge contains a request for findings of fact, which is typically phrased in an "if, then" format. For example, in the charge presented in Exhibit 11.7 on page 403, the jury is first asked to decide if the defendant was negligent. The next question states that *if* the jury decides that the defendant was negligent, *then* the jury must decide whether the defendant's negligence caused the plaintiff's injuries. This format helps to channel the jurors' deliberations.

Charges, which are also called jury instructions, are usually drafted by the attorneys before the trial begins, and an attorney's trial strategy will likely be linked to the charges. Often, the paralegal drafts the charge for the attorney's review. The judge, however, has the final decision as to what charge will be submitted to the jury.

Charge
The judge's instruction to the jury, following the attorneys' closing arguments, setting forth the rules of law that the jury must apply in reaching its decision, or verdict.

On the Web
To find information on jury verdicts in assorted trials throughout the country, including the amount of damages awarded in each case, go to www.morelaw.com.

The Verdict

Following its receipt of the charge, the jury begins its deliberations. Once it has reached a decision, the jury issues a **verdict** in favor of one of the parties. If the verdict is in favor of the plaintiff, the jury will specify the amount of damages to be paid by the defendant. Following the announcement of the verdict, the jurors are discharged. Usually, immediately after the verdict has been announced and the jurors discharged, the party in whose favor the verdict was issued makes a motion asking the judge to issue a *judgment*—which is the court's final word on the

Verdict
A formal decision made by a jury.

> **Case at a Glance**
>
> **The Plaintiff—**
>   Plaintiff: Katherine Baranski
>   Attorney: Allen P. Gilmore
>   Paralegal: Elena Lopez
>
> **The Defendant—**
>   Defendant: Tony Peretto
>   Attorney: Elizabeth A. Cameron
>   Paralegal: Gordon McVay

matter—consistent with the jury's verdict. For example, if the jury in the Baranski case finds that defendant Peretto was negligent and awards plaintiff Baranski damages in the amount of $75,000, the judge will order defendant Peretto to pay the plaintiff that amount.

POSTTRIAL MOTIONS AND PROCEDURES

Every trial must have a winner and a loser. Although civil litigation is an expensive and cumbersome process, the losing party may wish to pursue the matter further after the verdict has been rendered. Assume that plaintiff Baranski wins at trial and is awarded $75,000 in damages. Cameron, as defendant Peretto's attorney, may wish to file a posttrial motion or appeal the decision to a higher court. Note that plaintiff Baranski, even though she won the case, could also appeal the judgment. For example, she might appeal the case on the ground that she should have received $110,000 in damages instead of $75,000, arguing that the latter amount inadequately compensates her for the harms that she suffered as a result of defendant Peretto's negligence.

Posttrial Motions

Assume that defendant Peretto's attorney, Cameron, believes that the verdict for plaintiff Baranski is not supported by the evidence. In this situation, she may file a **motion for judgment notwithstanding the verdict** (also known as a *motion for judgment as a matter of law* in the federal courts).[4] By filing this motion, attorney Cameron asks the judge to enter a judgment in favor of defendant Peretto on the ground (basis) that the jury verdict in favor of plaintiff Baranski was unreasonable and erroneous. Cameron may file this motion only if she previously filed a motion for a directed verdict (or judgment as a matter of law) during the trial and the motion was denied at that time. If she decides to file this motion, she must file it within ten days of the date that the judgment is entered against defendant Peretto following the conclusion of the trial.

Like virtually all motions in federal court, this motion must be accompanied by a supporting affidavit or a memorandum of law, or brief (these documents were discussed in Chapter 10). Assuming that attorney Cameron files the motion, it will fall on the judge to determine whether the jury's verdict was reasonable in view of the evidence presented at trial. If the judge concludes that the verdict was reasonable, then he will deny Cameron's motion. If he agrees with Cameron, however, then he will set the jury's verdict aside and enter a judgment in favor of defendant Peretto.

Rule 50 of the Federal Rules of Civil Procedure permits either party to file a **motion for a new trial**. Such a motion may be submitted along with a motion for a judgment notwithstanding the verdict. A motion for a new trial is a far more drastic tactic because it asserts that the trial was so pervaded by error or otherwise fundamentally flawed that a new trial should be held. Because such a motion reflects adversely on the way in which the judge conducted the trial, it should only be filed if the attorney truly believes that a miscarriage of justice will otherwise result.

Motion for Judgment Notwithstanding the Verdict
A motion (also referred to as a motion for judgment as a matter of law in federal courts) requesting that the court grant judgment in favor of the party making the motion on the ground that the jury verdict against him or her was unreasonable or erroneous.

Motion for a New Trial
A motion asserting that the trial was so fundamentally flawed (because of error, newly discovered evidence, prejudice, or other reason) that a new trial is needed to prevent a miscarriage of justice.

---

4. Amendments to the FRCP in 1991 designated both the motion for a directed verdict and the motion for judgment notwithstanding the verdict as motions for judgment as a matter of law. One of the reasons for the change was to allow both the preverdict and postverdict motions to be referred to with a terminology that does not conceal their common identity (both motions claim, at different times during the proceedings, that there is insufficient evidence against the defendant to justify a claim—or a verdict—against the defendant). Many judges and attorneys continue to use the former names of these motions, however, so we include them in our discussion.

> The jury is requested to answer the following questions:
>
> (1) Was the defendant negligent?
>
>   Answer: (yes or no) _____
>
> (2) If your answer to question (1) is "yes," then you must answer this question: Was the defendant's negligence a proximate (direct) cause of the plaintiff's injuries?
>
>   Answer: (yes or no) _____
>
> (3) Was the plaintiff negligent?
>
>   Answer: (yes or no) _____
>
> (4) If your answer to question (3) is "yes," then you must answer this question: Was the plaintiff's negligence a proximate (direct) cause of the accident and injuries that she suffered?
>
>   Answer: (yes or no) _____
>
> (5) If your answer to either question (1) or question (3) is "yes," then answer the following:
>
>   Taking 100% as the total fault causing the accident and injuries, what percentage of the total fault causing the accident and injuries do you attribute to:
>
>   _____ the defendant
>
>   _____ the plaintiff
>
>   (If you find that a party has no fault in causing the accident, then attribute 0 percentage of the fault to that party.)
>
> (6) Regardless of how you answered the previous questions, answer this question:
>
>   Disregarding any negligence or fault on the part of the plaintiff, what sum of money would reasonably compensate the plaintiff for her claimed injury and damage?
>
>   Answer: $ _____

EXHIBIT 11.7
Jury Charge—Request for Findings of Fact

For a motion for a new trial to have a reasonable chance of being granted, the motion must allege such serious problems as jury misconduct, prejudicial jury instructions, excessive or inadequate damages, or the existence of newly discovered evidence (but not if the evidence could have been discovered earlier through the use of reasonable care). As with other posttrial motions in federal courts, the motion for a new trial must be filed within ten days following the entry of the judgment. Exhibit 11.8 on page 405 illustrates a motion for judgment as a matter of law or, in the alternative, for a new trial.

Appealing the Verdict

If attorney Cameron's posttrial motions are unsuccessful or if she decides not to file them, she may still file an **appeal**. The purpose of an appeal is to have the trial

On the Web
The Federal Rules of Appellate Procedure are online at **www.law.cornell.edu/ topics/archive/ appellate_procedure.html**.

Appeal
The process of seeking a higher court's review of a lower court's decision for the purpose of correcting or changing the lower court's judgment or decision.

court's decision either reversed or modified by an appellate court. As discussed in Chapter 6, appellate courts, or courts of appeals, are *reviewing* courts, not trial courts. In other words, no new evidence will be presented to the appellate court, and there is no jury. The appellate court will review the trial court's proceedings to decide whether the trial court erred in applying the law to the facts of the case, in instructing the jury, or in administering the trial generally. Appellate courts rarely tamper with a trial court's findings of fact because the judge and jury were in a better position than the appellate court to evaluate the credibility of witnesses, the nature of the evidence, and so on.

As grounds for the appeal, defendant Peretto's attorney, Cameron, might argue that the trial court erred in one of the ways mentioned in the preceding paragraph. Unless she believes that a reversal of the judgment is likely, however, she will probably advise Peretto not to appeal the case, as an appeal will simply add to the costs and expenses already incurred by Peretto in defending against plaintiff Baranski's claim.

NOTICE OF APPEAL. When the appeal involves a federal district court decision, as in the Baranski case, the **appellant** (the party appealing the decision) must file a notice of appeal with the district court that rendered the judgment. The clerk of the court then notifies the **appellee** (the party against whom the appeal is taken) as well as the court of appeals. The clerk then forwards a transcript of the trial court proceedings along with any related pleadings and exhibits; these materials together constitute the **record on appeal.**

THE APPELLATE BRIEF AND ORAL ARGUMENTS. When a case is appealed, the attorneys for both parties submit written *briefs* that present their positions regarding the issues to be reviewed by the appellate court. The briefs outline each party's view of the proper application of the law to the facts. (Appellate briefs will be discussed further in Chapter 16.)

After the appellate court has had an opportunity to review the briefs, the court sets aside a time for both attorneys to argue their positions before the panel of judges. The attorneys will then present their arguments and answer any questions that the judges might have. Generally, the attorneys' arguments before an appellate court are limited in terms of both the time allowed for argument and the scope of the argument. Following the oral arguments, the judges will decide the matter and then issue a formal written opinion, which normally will be published in the relevant reporter (see Chapter 14 for a detailed discussion of how court opinions are published).

THE APPELLATE COURT'S OPTIONS. Once they have reviewed the record and heard oral arguments, the judges have several options. For example, in the Baranski case, if the appellate court decided to uphold the trial court's decision, then the judgment for plaintiff Baranski would be **affirmed**. If the judges decided to **reverse** the trial court's decision, however, then Peretto would no longer be obligated to pay the damages awarded to Baranski by the trial court. The court might also affirm or reverse a decision *in part*. For example, the judges might affirm the jury's finding that Peretto was negligent but **remand** the case—that is, send it back to the trial court—for further proceedings on another issue (such as the extent of Baranski's damages). An appellate court can also *modify* a lower court's decision. If, for example, the appellate court decided that the jury awarded an excessive amount in damages, the appellate court might reduce the award to a more appropriate, or fairer, amount.

Appellant
The party who takes an appeal from one court to another; sometimes referred to as the petitioner.

Appellee
The party against whom an appeal is taken—that is, the party who opposes setting aside or reversing the judgment; sometimes referred to as the respondent.

Record on Appeal
The items submitted during the trial (pleadings, motions, briefs, and exhibits) and the transcript of the trial proceedings that are forwarded to the appellate court for review when a case is appealed.

Affirm
An appellate court's decision to uphold the trial court's judgment in a case.

Reverse
An appellate court's decision that is contrary to the judgment of the trial court.

Remand
An appellate court's decision to send a case back to the trial court for further proceedings.

EXHIBIT 11.8

Motion for Judgment as a Matter of Law or for a New Trial

UNITED STATES DISTRICT COURT
FOR THE WESTERN DISTRICT OF NITA

Katherine Baranski

        Plaintiff

vs.

Tony Peretto

        Defendant

File No. 99-14335-NI

Hon. Harley M. LaRue

Elizabeth A. Cameron
Attorney for the Defendant
Cameron & Strauss, P.C.
310 Lake Drive
Zero City, ZE 59802

<u>MOTION FOR JUDGMENT AS A MATTER OF
LAW OR, IN THE ALTERNATIVE,
MOTION FOR A NEW TRIAL</u>

    The Defendant, Tony Peretto, moves this Court, pursuant to Rule 50(b) of the Federal Rules of Civil Procedure, to set aside the verdict and judgment entered on August 15, 1999, and to enter instead a judgment for the Defendant as a matter of law. In the alternative, and in the event the Defendant's motion for judgment as a matter of law is denied, the Defendant moves the Court to order a new trial.

    The grounds for this motion are set forth in the attached memorandum.

Date: 8/16/99

Elizabeth A. Cameron
Elizabeth A. Cameron
Attorney for the Defendant
Cameron & Strauss, P.C.
310 Lake Drive
Zero City, ZE 59802

The decision of the appellate court may sometimes be appealed further. A state appellate court's decision, for example, may be appealed to the state supreme court. A federal appellate court's decision may be appealed to the United States Supreme Court. It will be up to these higher courts to decide whether they will review the case. In other words, these courts are not normally *required* to review cases. Recall from Chapter 6 that although thousands of cases are submitted to the United States Supreme Court each year, it hears less than one hundred. (An action decided in a state court, however, has a somewhat greater chance of being reviewed by the state supreme court.)

ENFORCING THE JUDGMENT

The uncertainties of the litigation process are compounded by the lack of guarantees that any judgment will be enforceable. It is one thing to have a court enter a

Developing Paralegal Skills

Locating Assets

Paralegal Myra Cullen works for a law firm that represented Jennifer Roth in a lawsuit brought against Best Eatery, a local restaurant. Roth won $100,000 in a lawsuit for damages resulting from falling and breaking her leg in the restaurant's lobby on a rainy morning. Best Eatery's only insurance coverage is a small liability policy that will only pay a portion of Roth's damage award. Myra has been assigned the task of investigating Best Eatery's assets to determine how the judgment can be collected. Myra learned through pretrial discovery that John Dobman owns Best Eatery as a sole proprietor, which means that he is personally liable for the debts of the business. Myra goes to the register of deeds for the county and researches the property. She determines that Dobman's equity in the property is $110,000, which will cover any shortfall in the damages.

Tips for Locating Assets

- Ask what property the defendant owns during discovery, such as in interrogatories.
- Ask for the address of the property.
- Go to the register of deeds to learn about any liens filed against the property and the amount of any mortgage loan.
- Check with a realtor or an appraiser as to the market value of the property.
- Deduct the liens and the mortgage debt from the market value to determine the defendant's equity.

Writ of Execution
A writ that puts in force a court's decree or judgment.

Judgment Creditor
A creditor who is legally entitled, by a court's judgment, to collect the amount of the judgment from a debtor.

judgment in your favor; it is quite another to collect the money to which you are entitled from the opposing party. Even if the jury awarded Baranski the full amount of damages requested ($110,000), for example, she might not, in fact, "win" anything at all. Peretto's auto insurance coverage might have lapsed, in which event the company would not cover any of the damages. Alternatively, Peretto's insurance coverage may be limited to $20,000, meaning that Peretto would have to pay personally the remaining $90,000. If Peretto personally did not have that amount of money available, then Baranski would need to go back to court and request that the court issue a **writ of execution**—an order, usually issued by the clerk of the court, directing the sheriff to seize (take temporary ownership of) and sell Peretto's assets. The proceeds of the sale would then be used to pay the damages owed to Baranski. Any excess proceeds of the sale would be returned to Peretto.

Even as a **judgment creditor** (one who has obtained a court judgment against his or her debtor), Baranski may not be able to obtain the full amount of the judgment from Peretto. Laws protecting debtors provide that certain property (such as a debtor's home up to a certain value, tools used by the debtor in his or her trade, and so on) is *exempt*. Exempt property cannot be seized and sold to pay debts owed to judgment creditors. Similar exemptions would apply if Peretto declared bankruptcy. Thus, even though Baranski won at trial, she, like many others who are awarded damages, might not be able to collect them. Realize, though, that judgments constitute liens (legal claims) for significant time periods. If the financial circumstances of the debtor—such as Peretto—change in the future, recovery may be possible.

The difficulty of enforcing court judgments, coupled with the high costs accompanying any litigation (including attorneys' fees, court costs, and the litigants' time costs), is a major reason why most disputes are settled out of court, either before or during the trial.

Today's Professional Paralegal

Drafting *Voir Dire* Questions Like a Pro

Andrea Leed, a legal assistant, is preparing for trial. Her boss is a famous trial attorney, Mary Marshall. Mary rarely loses a case. One of her many secrets to success is that she always draws up a jury profile and prepares carefully for *voir dire*.

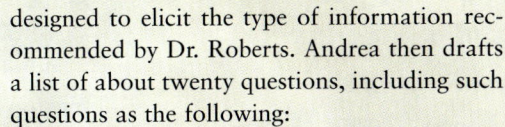

Mary is defending a corporation in an environmental liability case. The case involves many complex engineering and scientific issues that the jury will need to understand in order to reach its verdict. It is a common practice in these types of cases to select a "blue ribbon" jury—a jury consisting of persons who are very well educated. Mary has suggested that Andrea locate and hire a psychologist to prepare a jury profile.

Consulting with an Expert Witness

Andrea contacts TrialPsych, Inc., a consulting firm headed by Dr. Linda Robertson, who specializes in jury selection. Dr. Robertson would be delighted to work on the case, but her services are very expensive, and Andrea must find out whether the client is willing to pay Dr. Robertson's fee. The client agrees to pay the fee, so Andrea meets with Dr. Robertson to discuss the case. Andrea explains that the client is a corporation and that the case involves complex scientific and engineering issues. Dr. Robertson consults her files for statistical information on these types of cases. She finds that the ideal jury would be made up of white-collar professionals holding advanced degrees in engineering or another applied science. Also, the prospective jurors would ideally be against extensive government regulation of the corporate world.

Drafting *Voir Dire* Questions

Andrea returns to the office and discusses with Mary the results of her consultation with Dr. Roberts. Mary and Andrea decide to draft questions for *voir dire* that are designed to elicit the type of information recommended by Dr. Roberts. Andrea then drafts a list of about twenty questions, including such questions as the following:

1. Please state your name and address.
2. Where are you employed, and how long have you been employed there?
3. What is the highest level of education that you have attained: high school diploma, some college but no degree, college degree, advanced degree (please specify)?
4. If you have attended college or received a college degree, what was your field of study?
5. Have you ever been fired by a corporate employer in a way that you believed was unfair?
6. Have you ever worked for a government regulatory agency, and, if so, what were your responsibilities in that position?
7. Have you, or persons or business firms with whom you are or have been associated, ever been sued for violating environmental statutes or regulations? If so, what were the violations?
8. In your opinion, what should be the government's role in regulating a company's operations?

Reviewing the *Voir Dire* Questions

Andrea faxes the list of questions to Dr. Robertson, who reviews them and faxes back some suggested changes, which Andrea incorporates. When the final list of questions is drawn up, Andrea presents it to Mary and places a copy of the list in the trial notebook. Mary asks Andrea to call Dr. Robertson and ask her if she is available to sit in on the actual *voir dire* process to ensure that jury selection goes smoothly.

Key Terms and Concepts

affirm 404	leading question 396	record on appeal 404
appeal 403	motion for a directed verdict (motion for judgment as a matter of law) 399	recross-examination 398
appellant 404		redirect examination 398
appellee 404		remand 404
challenge 392	motion for a new trial 402	reverse 404
challenge for cause 393	motion for judgment notwithstanding the verdict 402	subpoena 384
charge 401		trial notebook 387
closing argument 399	motion *in limine* 389	verdict 401
cross-examination 397	opening statement 396	*voir dire* 391
direct examination 396	peremptory challenge 393	writ of execution 406
judgment creditor 406	pretrial conference 388	

Chapter Summary

1. Before the trial begins, attorneys for both sides and their paralegals gather and organize all evidence, documents, and other materials relating to the case. It is helpful to create a trial-preparation checklist to ensure that nothing is overlooked during this stage. Paralegals often assist in contacting and issuing subpoenas to witnesses, as well as in preparing witnesses for trial. Paralegals also assume responsibility for making sure that all exhibits and displays are ready by the trial date and that the trial notebook is prepared.

2. Prior to the trial, the attorneys for both sides meet with the trial judge in a pretrial conference to decide whether a settlement is possible or, if not, to decide how the trial will be conducted and what types of evidence will be admissible. A motion *in limine* (to limit evidence) may be made by one or both of the attorneys at this time.

3. The jury-selection process is called *voir dire*. During this process, attorneys for both sides may question individual jurors or groups of jurors to determine if bias exists or if for other reasons certain jurors should not be included in the jury. The attorneys can exclude certain persons in the jury pool from sitting on the jury through the exercise of challenges for cause and a limited number of peremptory challenges.

4. Once the jury has been selected and seated, the trial begins. The paralegal, if he or she attends the trial, coordinates witnesses' appearances, tracks the testimony of witnesses and compares it with sworn statements that the witnesses made prior to the trial, and provides the attorney with appropriate reminders or documents when necessary. The paralegal generally acts as a second set of eyes and ears for the attorney during the trial.

5. The trial begins with opening statements in which both attorneys briefly give their versions of the facts of the case and the evidence supporting their views.

6. Following the attorneys' opening statements, the plaintiff's attorney presents evidence supporting the plaintiff's claim, including the testimony of witnesses. The attorney's questioning of the witnesses whom he or she calls is referred to as direct examination. The defendant's attorney may then cross-examine the witness, after which the plaintiff's attorney may question the witness on redirect examination, followed by possible recross-examination by the defendant's attorney.

7. After the plaintiff's attorney has presented his or her client's case, the defendant's attorney may make a motion for a directed verdict, also called a motion for judgment as a matter of law. This motion asserts that the plaintiff has not offered enough evidence to support the validity of the plaintiff's claim against the defendant. If the judge grants the motion, the case will be dismissed.

8. The attorneys then reverse their roles, and the defendant's attorney presents evidence and testimony to refute the plaintiff's claims. Any witnesses called to the stand by the defendant's attorney will be subject to direct examination by that attorney, cross-

examination by the plaintiff's attorney, and possibly redirect examination and recross-examination.

9. After the defendant's attorney has finished his or her presentation, both attorneys give their closing arguments. Each attorney summarizes the major points that he or she made during the trial and attempts to show how the evidence presented favors a verdict in his or her client's favor.

10. Following the attorneys' closing arguments, the judge instructs the jury in a charge—a document that includes statements of the applicable law and a review of the facts as they were presented during the trial. The jury must not disregard the judge's instructions as to what the applicable law is and how it should be applied to the facts of the case as interpreted by the jury. The jury then begins its deliberations. When the jury has reached a decision, it issues a verdict in favor of one party or the other.

11. After the verdict has been pronounced and the trial concluded, the losing party's attorney may do any of the following: He or she may file a motion for judgment notwithstanding the verdict (motion for judgment as a matter of law), alleging that the judge should enter a judgment in favor of the losing party in spite of the verdict because the verdict was not supported by the evidence or was otherwise erroneous. In conjunction with the motion, or in the alternative, the attorney may also file a motion for a new trial, asserting that the trial was so flawed—by judge or juror misconduct or by other pervasive errors—that a new trial should be held. Finally, the attorney may, depending on the client's wishes, appeal the decision to an appellate court for further review and decision.

12. Even though a plaintiff wins a lawsuit for damages, it may be difficult to enforce the judgment against the defendant, particularly if the defendant has few assets.

Questions for Review

1. What role does the paralegal play in preparing witnesses, exhibits, and displays for trial? How can the paralegal assist the attorney in preparing the trial notebook?

2. What is a pretrial conference? What issues are likely to be raised and decided at a pretrial conference?

3. How are jurors selected? What role does the attorney play in the selection process? Does the paralegal play a role in the process?

4. What is the difference between a peremptory challenge and a challenge for cause?

5. What role might the paralegal play during the trial? What types of trial-related tasks may the paralegal perform?

6. How are witnesses examined during trial? What is the difference between direct examination and cross-examination?

7. What is a jury charge? Can the jury decide matters of law?

8. Name the posttrial motions that are available. In what situation is each of them used?

9. Describe the procedure for filing an appeal. What factors are considered by an attorney when deciding whether a case should be appealed?

10. Why do appellate courts defer to trial courts' findings of fact? What options might an appellate court pursue after it has completed its review of a case?

Ethical Questions

1. Anthony Paletti, a paralegal, is attending a trial with his supervising attorney. Anthony leaves the courtroom to meet a witness. On his way down the hall, he runs into the defendant in the case. The defendant says to Anthony, "You work for the plaintiff's attorney, don't you? I have a question for you about that contract that your attorney offered into evidence." Should Anthony answer the defendant's question? Why or why not?

2. A client claiming to have severely injured his back at work comes into the office of a law firm. The client, in a wheelchair, seeks legal advice about filing a lawsuit, and the attorney decides to take the case. Two days later, Alvin Kerrigan, the attorney's paralegal, sees the new client on the roof of a building installing shingles. What should Alvin do?

3. During a lunch break in the course of a trial, Louise Lanham, a paralegal, was washing her hands in the rest room. One of the members of the trial jury came up to her and said, "I don't understand what negligence is. Can you explain it to me?" How should Louise answer this question?

Practice Questions and Assignments

1. Paralegal Patricia Smith is assisting her supervising attorney, who has received a trial date for an auto-accident case. The trial is set to begin in ten weeks. Discovery has been completed in the case. The depositions of the plaintiff and defendant were taken, along with those of two eyewitnesses, a police officer and Dr. Black, the plaintiff's physician. Patricia's firm represents the plaintiff, and they plan to call not only their client to testify, but also the defendant, Mr. Sams (one of the eyewitnesses), and the police officer. All of the witnesses are local. Additionally, the plaintiff and the defendant answered interrogatories. The file also contains police reports, newspaper articles about the accident, and medical records. Using the material presented in Exhibit 11.1, *Trial-Preparation Checklist*, prepare a checklist for Patricia to complete.

2. A product-liability trial is about to begin. It involves the death of Tom Bert, resulting from a defective industrial press. The plaintiff's wife is suing as Tom's personal representative. One of her claims is for *loss of consortium*, which is a claim for the loss of her relationship with her husband. Tom's wife remarried three weeks after the plaintiff's funeral, however, and there exists evidence that she was having an affair with her second husband prior to Tom's death. The defense attorney wants to be able to address the plaintiff as Mrs. Ross, her new name resulting from her recent marriage, throughout the trial. By calling the wife by her new name in front of the jury, it will emphasize to the jury that she did not have much of a relationship with Tom Bert. The defense attorney hopes that this will significantly decrease any damages that might be awarded to Mrs. Ross on the loss-of-consortium claim. The defense attorney assigns you the task of drafting a motion *in limine* to present to the judge at the pretrial conference. Prepare an outline of the argument that would be included in the motion.

3. Using Exhibit 11.2, *A Subpoena*, draft a subpoena for a friendly witness using the following facts:

   > Simon Kolstad, whose address is 100 Schoolcraft Road, Del Mar, California, is a witness to be subpoenaed in *Sumner v. Hayes*, a civil lawsuit filed in the U.S. District Court for the Eastern District of Michigan, docket number 99-123492. He is being subpoenaed by the plaintiff's attorney, Marvin W. Green, whose office is located at 300 Penobscot Building, Detroit, Michigan. Kolstad is to appear in room number 6 of the courthouse, which is located at 231 Lafayette Boulevard, Detroit, Michigan, at 2:30 P.M. on January 10, 1999. Kolstad is to bring with him a letter from the defendant to Kolstad dated February 9, 1996.

4. Draft a series of questions for the plaintiff's attorney and for the two defendants' attorneys (the attorneys representing the doctor and the pharmaceutical company, respectively) to use during *voir dire* in a case involving the following facts:

   > The plaintiff's daughter died five days after starting on a regimen of taking weight-control pills. The daughter died because the pills were incompatible with her blood type. Prior to taking the pills, she was a perfectly healthy, twenty-five-year-old law student. The mother is bringing a medical-malpractice suit against the doctor for prescribing the wrong type of pill. The mother is also suing the pharmaceutical company that manufactured the pill on the ground that it failed to warn of the dangers of its pill for those persons, including her daughter, whose blood types were incompatible with the pill.

5. Using the scenario from question 4 above, involving the law student who died after taking weight-control pills that were incompatible with her blood type, select a jury of your classmates for a trial of the case. Plaintiff and defense teams, each consisting of at least one attorney and paralegal, will need to be selected. The rest of the class will serve as the jury pool to be questioned during *voir dire*. You will need to use the questions that you drafted for question 4 above. Your assignment is to select the jurors most favorable to their respective clients' positions. Additional factual information relating to the two defendants includes the following:

   a. The physician has prescribed this pill on numerous occasions and has never had a patient die as a result of taking it. The doctor did not take a thorough medical history of the plaintiff, nor did he note her blood type.

   b. The pharmaceutical company did include a package insert warning physicians of the dangers involved in taking the drug and instructing them as to the types of tests that should be undertaken before the pill is prescribed.

6. Your client, a surgeon, is suing a lawyer for slander (a tort arising when someone makes a verbal statement that harms another's good name or reputation—see

Chapter 7). The lawyer was representing the surgeon in a malpractice case. In the presence of several other physicians, the lawyer told the surgeon that he "ought to have his head examined" and that he was so "incompetent at his job" that the lawyer had decided not to defend him against the malpractice claim. The surgeon is suing the lawyer for slander because, as a result of the lawyer's comments, the physician's staff privileges at a major hospital have been suspended and he can no longer perform surgery there.

Using the material presented in the chapter, draft questions for your supervising attorney to ask your client, the surgeon, during trial.

7. Using the material presented in the chapter, identify the motion that would be filed in each of the following situations:

   a. A plaintiff's attorney loses a case, and she believes that her loss is due to prejudicial jury instructions given by the judge.

   b. The defendant's key witness was hospitalized during a trial and was unable to testify. As a result, key evidence is not presented, and the defendant is unable to prove his case.

   c. In the example above, the plaintiff's attorney made the appropriate motion, which was not granted, and ultimately lost the lawsuit. Thus, according to the plaintiff's attorney, the judgment was not supported by the evidence.

   d. The defense attorney has seen grotesque photographs of an accident that the plaintiff's attorney has in her file. The defense attorney is concerned that these photographs would unfairly prejudice a jury against the defendant during the trial.

8. Using the material presented in the chapter, indicate whether the appellate court will affirm, modify, or reverse the trial court's decision or remand the case for further proceedings:

   a. A trial court finds for the plaintiff in the amount of $150,000 in a case in which the plaintiff slipped and fell in a grocery store. The court of appeals found that while the plaintiff was entitled to damages, the damages awarded by the jury were excessive. The appellate court sent the case back to the trial court to reevaluate the amount of damages awarded.

   b. A trial court finds that the plaintiff was slandered by the defendant. On appeal, the court of appeals finds that the trial court admitted evidence that it should not have allowed and holds that without this evidence, there was no slander.

   c. A trial court finds that the defendant breached a contract and owes the plaintiff $1,000,000 in damages. The defendant appeals, claiming that the damages are not supported by the evidence. The court of appeals agrees with the trial court's decision.

QUESTIONS FOR CRITICAL ANALYSIS

1. Typically, all witnesses to appear at a trial to testify are served with a subpoena, even friendly witnesses. Why is this? What might happen if they were not subpoenaed? How can the service of subpoenas be handled with friendly witnesses so that they are not offended?

2. Most prudent attorneys do not put a witness on the stand without discussing the witness's testimony beforehand or at least learning what the witness will say. What might happen if a witness whose testimony has not been discussed ahead of time, or whose testimony is unknown, takes the stand? What effect might this have on the outcome of the case?

3. Much preparation and organization goes into trial work, from preparing witnesses and trial notebooks, to drafting questions, to creating exhibits and displays. Why is this done? What impact do these preparations have on the jury? What impact would (or does) it have when an attorney is unprepared and disorganized?

4. The mother of a minor child filed a complaint for paternity and child support against the alleged father. The case went to trial, and a jury was selected. Thirty-six potential jurors were assembled, twelve males and twenty-four females. Three jurors were excused for cause, and ten of the remaining prospective jurors were males. The mother's attorney then used nine of her ten peremptory strikes to remove male jurors, and the attorney for the alleged father used all but one of his challenges to remove female jurors. As a result, the jury was all female. The jury found the alleged father to be the child's father and ordered him to pay child support. The father appealed, claiming that the plaintiff's use of peremptory challenges to exclude men from the jury was unconstitutional. What arguments might

the alleged father's attorney make to support this claim? How might the mother's attorney respond? [HINT: See *J.E.B. v. Alabama ex rel. T.B.*, 511 U.S. 127, 114 S. Ct. 1419, 128 L.Ed.2d 89 (1994).]

5. Certain types of cases, such as product-liability cases, require complex evidence. Should certain types of jurors be required in these complex cases? Why or why not?

6. What is the difference between redirect examination and recross-examination? When is each type of examination used? What is allowed during each type of examination?

7. Why are leading questions not allowed during direct examination? Why are leading questions allowed during cross-examination? Is the use of leading questions fair to the witness being cross-examined?

8. What is the basis for a motion for a directed verdict? Why would a trial start if the grounds for a motion for a directed verdict existed? Are these motions frequently granted?

9. Why do you think that attorneys and paralegals, instead of judges, draft jury instructions? Does this surprise you? Why or why not?

10. Is there a difference between a verdict and a judgment? If so, what is the difference? Who do you think drafts the judgment? Why?

11. After a trial, the losing party may file a motion for a judgment notwithstanding the verdict and/or a motion for a new trial. What is the likelihood that a judge will grant such a motion? Why would a losing party file these types of motions as opposed to appealing the case?

12. How is a judgment paid when there is no insurance or other cash assets available to pay the judgment? Is all of a defendant's property subject to the judgment? If not, what property is exempt? Why might these exemptions have been created?

Projects

1. Call a local court clerk or administrator (not a judge) to obtain a list of the cases on the court's trial docket. Arrange to attend a trial that is not expected to last longer than a few days. Attend the trial for as many days as you can and observe carefully the following proceedings: *voir dire*, opening statements, the presentation of evidence, and closing arguments. Also note how paralegals are used. Prepare a three-page summary of your observations, making sure to include the name and docket number of the case, the name of the court, and the name of the judge.

2. Look up your state's court rules and find out how many challenges for cause are allowed during *voir dire*. How many peremptory challenges are permitted during *voir dire*?

3. Look for advertisements for vendors of trial-support services, such as video or exhibit preparers, in a legal newspaper or legal-assistant journal. Call at least two of the vendors and request a brochure on their services. Write a one-page summary of your research.

4. Call your local sheriff's office and find out what happens when a writ of execution is carried out. Ask if there is any printed information available on this procedure. If so, request a copy. Share the results of your research with the class. (Discuss this assignment with your instructor prior to undertaking it.)

5. Research a computer magazine, such as *Law Office Computing* or *Law Technology Product News*, for articles on the use of technology, such as digital cameras or scanners, to prepare or present evidence during a trial. If possible, obtain demo disks or videos of the technology. Present your findings to the class.

Using Internet Resources

1. If you are assisting an attorney in litigating a case, you may be asked to do some research on jury verdicts in similar cases. To date, there are not very many fully searchable databases on the Web that contain this information, but their number is expanding. One site is that offered by MoreLaw at www.morelaw.com. Access this site, and spend some time browsing through its offerings. Then select a large state, such as California or New York, and answer the following questions:

   a. How many cases/verdicts were listed for the state you selected?

b. Choose five cases and, for each case, describe briefly what it was about, who "won" the case (the plaintiff or the defendant), and, if the plaintiff won, what amount of damages were awarded.

c. Choose one of these cases and describe it in further detail. Who initiated the lawsuit? Who was the defendant? Why? What general area of law was involved (torts, product liability, contracts, and so on)? How did the jury decide the issue? Did the jury award damages? If so, what amount? Were punitive damages also awarded?

d. Generally, what are the advantages of this site for paralegals doing research on jury verdicts? What are the disadvantages?

2. The Court TV Web site contains the transcripts of O. J. Simpson and others involved in his trial. Access the Web site at: **www.courttv.com/old/casefiles/simpson**. Click on "transcripts." Click on "Read excerpts from the three-day direct examination of O. J. Simpson." Read the transcripts and then answer the following questions:

a. What is the date of the first transcript?

b. What subject is addressed in the first transcript?

c. What type of question is the first question asked of O. J. Simpson?

d. What types of questions are included in the third and fifth questions?

e. Why were these types of questions being asked during direct examination?

f. Compare the first, third, and fifth questions to the second, fourth, and sixth questions. How do they differ?

CHAPTER 12

Criminal Law and Procedures

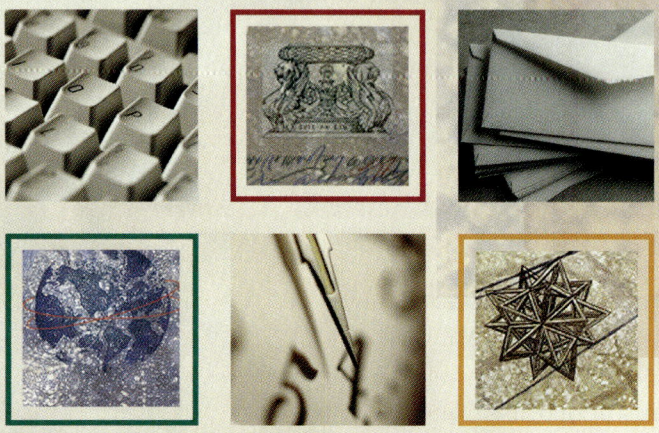

Chapter Outline

Introduction ▪ What Is a Crime? ▪ Elements of Criminal Liability
▪ Constitutional Safeguards ▪ Criminal Procedures Prior to Prosecution
▪ The Prosecution Begins ▪ The Trial

After completing this chapter, you will know:

- The difference between crimes and other wrongful acts.
- The elements that are required for criminal liability and some of the more common defenses that are raised when defending against criminal charges.
- The constitutional rights of persons accused of crimes.
- The basic steps involved in criminal procedure from the time a crime is reported to the resolution of the case.
- Why a criminal suspect may be released and the case dismissed prior to trial.
- How and why criminal litigation procedures differ from civil litigation procedures.

CHAPTER 12 *Criminal Law and Procedures*

INTRODUCTION

More than one million people are arrested for crimes and enter the criminal justice system each year. As the crime rate continues to increase, so does the work of attorneys and legal assistants involved in criminal law cases. Criminal cases are prosecuted by **public prosecutors,** who are employed by the government. The public prosecutor in federal criminal cases is called a U.S. attorney. In cases tried in state or local courts, the public prosecutor may be referred to as a *prosecuting attorney, state prosecutor, district attorney, county attorney, or city attorney.*

Defendants in criminal cases may hire private attorneys to defend them. If a defendant cannot afford to hire an attorney, the court will appoint one for him or her. Everyone accused of a crime that may result in a jail sentence has a right to counsel, and this right is ensured by court-appointed attorneys, called **public defenders,** who are paid by the state.

There are many opportunities for paralegals in the area of criminal law. Some paralegals work for state prosecutors. Others work for public defenders or private attorneys who specialize in criminal defense. Still others may work for victims' rights organizations. All states now operate victims' rights programs that provide compensation and counseling services to victims of crimes. The police departments of larger cities often provide counseling and other services to crime victims also. Additionally, numerous private groups work for increased recognition of crime victims' rights.

Paralegals may also come into contact with criminal defendants in the course of their work in a general law practice or in a corporate legal department. A client may be arrested for driving while intoxicated or for the possession of illegal drugs, for example, or a corporation might need legal assistance in defending against alleged criminal violations of federal environmental laws.

This chapter begins by explaining the legal nature of crime, the elements of criminal liability, and the constitutional protections that come into play when a person is accused of a crime. The rest of the chapter focuses on criminal procedures. Because many of the procedures involved in criminal litigation are similar to those discussed in Chapters 10 and 11, details of these procedures will not be repeated here. Rather, in this chapter, we offer an overview of criminal law and procedure and the ways in which criminal litigation differs from civil litigation.

Public Prosecutor
An individual, acting as a trial lawyer, who initiates and conducts criminal cases in the government's name and on behalf of the people.

Public Defender
A court-appointed attorney who is paid by the state to represent a criminal defendant who is unable to hire private counsel.

WHAT IS A CRIME?

A **crime** can be distinguished from other wrongful acts, such as torts, in that a crime is an *offense against society as a whole*. Criminal defendants are prosecuted by public officials on behalf of the state, as mentioned above, not by their victims or other private parties. In addition, those who have committed crimes are subject to penalties, including fines, imprisonment, and in some cases, death. As discussed in Chapter 7, tort remedies—remedies for civil wrongs—are generally intended to compensate the injured party (by awarding money damages, for example). Criminal law, however, is concerned with punishing the wrongdoer in an attempt to deter others from similar actions.

Another factor distinguishing criminal law from tort law is that criminal law is primarily statutory law. Essentially, a crime is whatever a legislature has declared to be a crime. Although federal crimes are defined by the U.S. Congress, most crimes are defined by state legislatures. As mentioned in Chapter 5, at one time criminal law was governed primarily by the common law. Over time, common law doctrines and principles were codified, expanded on, and enacted in statutory form. Although many crimes were originally defined by the common

Crime
A broad term for violations of law that are punishable by the state and are codified by legislatures. The objective of criminal law is to protect the public.

law, the statutory definitions of those crimes may differ significantly from these common law definitions.

For example, under the common law, the crime of *burglary* was defined as the breaking and entering of another's dwelling at night with the intent to commit a felony. Originally, the definition was aimed at protecting an individual's home and its occupants. Most state statutes have eliminated some of the requirements found in the common law definition. Thus, the time at which the breaking and entering occurs is usually immaterial, and many state statutes do not require that the building that is entered need be a person's dwelling or home.

Still another factor distinguishes criminal law from tort law: a criminal act does not necessarily involve a victim, in the sense that the act directly and physically harms another. If Jeffers grows marijuana in her backyard for her personal use, she may not be physically or directly harming another's interests, but she is nonetheless committing a crime. Why? Because she is violating a rule of society that has been enacted into law by duly elected representatives of the people. She has committed an offense against society's values, safety, and welfare.

Note that it is possible for the same act to constitute both a crime and a tort. For example, if Jackson intentionally shot and killed Avery, the state could prosecute Jackson for the crime of murder. Avery's wife could also bring a civil lawsuit in tort law against Jackson to obtain compensation (in the form of money damages) for the losses she suffered as a result of Avery's death.

On the Web
Many state criminal codes are now online. To find your state's code, go to **www.findlaw.com** and select "State Codes."

Classifications of Crimes

Crimes are generally divided into the following two broad classifications: felonies and misdemeanors.

Felony
A crime—such as arson, murder, rape, or robbery—that carries the most severe sanctions. Sanctions range from one year in a state or federal prison to life imprisonment or (in some states) the death penalty.

FELONIES.   A **felony** is a serious crime that may be punished by imprisonment for more than one year or (in some states) death. Examples of felonies include *murder, rape, robbery* (theft involving the use of force or fear), *arson* (the intentional burning of another's building or structure), and *grand larceny*. Larceny is the nonviolent theft of another's money or property. Larceny is referred to as grand larceny when the theft involves more than a threshold amount defined by state law. Threshold amounts range from $50 to $2,000.

Felonies are commonly classified by degree. The Model Penal Code,[1] for example, provides for four degrees of felony: capital offenses for which the maximum penalty is death, first degree felonies punishable by a maximum penalty of life imprisonment, second degree felonies punishable by a maximum of ten years' imprisonment, and third degree felonies punishable by up to five years' imprisonment.

Misdemeanor
A less serious crime than a felony, punishable by a fine or incarceration for up to one year in jail (not a state or federal penitentiary).

MISDEMEANORS.   A **misdemeanor** is a crime that may be punished by incarceration for not more than one year. A misdemeanor, by definition, is a less serious crime. Under federal law and in most states, a misdemeanor is any crime that is not defined by law as a felony. State legislatures specify what crimes are classified as felonies or misdemeanors and what the potential punishment for each type of criminal act may be. Examples of misdemeanors include *petty larceny* (the non-

---

1. The American Law Institute (discussed in Chapter 5) issued the Official Draft of the Model Penal Code in 1962. The Model Penal Code is a rational and integrated body of material drafted for the purpose of assisting state legislatures in reexamining and recodifying state criminal laws. Uniformity among the states is not as important in criminal law as in other areas of the law. Crime varies with local circumstances, and it is appropriate that punishments vary accordingly.

violent theft of another's property worth less than the threshold amount required for grand larceny), *prostitution, disturbing the peace,* and *public intoxication.*

PETTY OFFENSES.   Certain types of criminal or quasi-criminal actions, such as violations of building codes, are termed **petty offenses,** or *infractions.* In most jurisdictions, such actions are considered a subset of misdemeanors. Some states, however, classify them separately.

Petty Offense
In criminal law, the least serious kind of wrong, such as a traffic or building-code violation.

The Variety of Criminal Acts

The number of actions classified as criminal is nearly endless. Besides variations on the crimes mentioned above, criminal acts also include writing bad checks, credit-card violations, resisting arrest, disorderly conduct, obstruction of highways and public places, vagrancy, loitering, and numerous other actions.

Federal jurisdiction is limited to certain types of crimes. If a federal law or a federal government agency (such as the U.S. Department of Justice or the federal Environmental Protection Agency) defines a certain type of action as a crime, federal jurisdiction exists. Generally, federal criminal jurisdiction is limited to crimes occurring outside the jurisdiction of any state, crimes involving interstate commerce or communications, crimes that interfere with the operation of the federal government or its agents, and crimes directed at citizens or property located outside the United States. A challenging legal issue today concerns how a state or the federal government can exercise jurisdiction over criminal acts that are committed via the Internet, which knows no geographical borders. (See the feature entitled *Technology and Today's Paralegal: Keeping Up with Cyber Crimes.*)

On the Web
A good source for statistical data and other information on crime is the Bureau of Justice Statistics, an agency within the U.S. Department of Justice. Go to **www.ojp.usdoj.gov/bjs**. Another good source is the Federal Bureau of Investigation, which is online at **www.fbi.gov**.

ELEMENTS OF CRIMINAL LIABILITY

For a person to be convicted of a crime, two elements must exist simultaneously: (1) the performance of a criminal act and (2) a specified state of mind, or intent. This section describes these two elements of criminal liability and some of the defenses that can be used to avoid liability for crimes.

The Criminal Act

A criminal act is known as the ***actus reus,***[2] or guilty act. Most crimes require an act of *commission*; that is, a person must *do* something in order to be accused of a crime. In some cases, an act of *omission* can be a crime, but only when a person has a legal duty to perform the omitted act. Failure to file a tax return is an example of an omission (failure to act) that is a crime.

The guilty-act requirement is based on one of the premises of criminal law—that a person is punished for *harm done* to society. As in tort law, which deals with civil wrongs, a criminal wrong will not exist unless the act or failure to act caused another (or society generally) to suffer an injury, or harm. Thinking about killing someone or about stealing a car may be wrong, but the thoughts do no harm unless they are translated into action. Of course, a person can be punished for *attempting* murder or robbery, but normally only if substantial steps toward the criminal objective have been taken.

Actus Reus
A guilty (prohibited) act. The commission of a prohibited act is one of the two essential elements required for criminal liability; the other element is the intent to commit a crime.

---
2. Pronounced *ak*-tuhs *ray*-uhs.

TECHNOLOGY AND TODAY'S PARALEGAL
Keeping Up with Cyber Crimes

Advances in technology, and particularly the communications revolution brought about by the Internet, continue to transform the legal landscape. Certainly, this is true with respect to crimes. While technology has many benefits, it also has brought about new types of crimes—or new ways of committing old crimes.

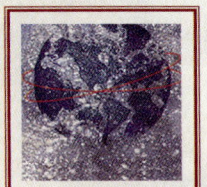

Consider just one example. Gambling is usually illegal, except when specific forms of gambling (including lotteries) are permitted by state law. A state law, however, can govern only activities within the state's borders. What happens if a citizen of Nebraska plays blackjack on the Internet, and the gambling entity resides in some offshore location, such as Finland? Even if Nebraska's criminal code defines such gambling as a crime, what can that state's government do about the illegal activity? Its courts cannot exercise jurisdiction over a company located in Finland (see Chapter 6 for a discussion of jurisdictional requirements).

How can paralegals working in the area of criminal law keep abreast of new developments, including new laws (or amendments to old laws) that are being enacted to govern crimes perpetrated online? One way to keep current on cyberspace crimes is to search through online law journals. A good starting point is FindLaw's database of law review articles at **www.findlaw.com/lawreviews/index.html**. At that site, you can look through the journals listed in the "criminal law" category or search the entire database using key words. For example, if you enter "electronic crimes," you will obtain a long list of articles dealing with that general topic. You can find information on various issues relating to computer crime and security at a Web site maintained by the U.S. Department of Justice at **www.usdojgov/criminal/cybercrime/crimes.html**.

To learn about proposed federal and state legislation governing cyberspace crimes, a good site to access is **www.house.gov**. There you will find the full text of all pending bills before Congress, as well as links to state legislatures and pending state legislation. Another good site for information on state legislation is that sponsored by the Center for Information Law and Policy, the URL for which is **www.cilp.org/tblhome.html**.

State of Mind

Mens Rea
A wrongful mental state, or intent. A wrongful mental state is a requirement for criminal liability. What constitutes a wrongful mental state varies according to the nature of the crime. For the crime of murder to exist, for example, the required *mens rea* is the intent to take another person's life.

Even a completed act that harms society is not legally a crime unless the court finds that the second element—the required state of mind—was present. A wrongful mental state, or ***mens rea***,[3] normally is as necessary as a wrongful act in establishing criminal liability. What constitutes such a mental state varies according to the wrongful action. For murder, the criminal act is the taking of a life, and the mental state is the intent to take life. For theft, the guilty act is the taking of another person's property, and the mental state involves both the knowledge that the property belongs to another and the intent to steal that property. Without the mental state required by law for a particular crime, there is no crime.

The same criminal act can result from varying mental states, and how a crime is defined and punished depends on the degree of "wrongfulness" of the defendant's state of mind. For example, taking another's life is *homicide*, a criminal act. The act can be committed coldly, after premeditation, as in *murder in the first degree*, which carries the most severe criminal penalty. The act can be committed in the heat of passion, as in *voluntary manslaughter*, which carries a less severe penalty than murder. Or the act can be committed as a result of criminal negligence (reckless driving or driving while intoxicated, for example), as in *involuntary manslaughter*. In each of these situations, the law recognizes a different degree of wrongfulness, and the harshness of the punishment depends on the degree to which the act of killing another was an *intentional* act.

---
3. Pronounced mehns *ray*-uh.

Defenses to Criminal Liability

Asserting that a defendant lacks the required degree of criminal intent for a specific crime is, of course, one way of defending against criminal liability. This defense and other defenses against criminal liability are discussed below.

THE REQUIRED MENTAL STATE IS LACKING. Proving that a defendant did or did not possess the required mental state for a given crime is difficult because a person's state of mind is, by nature, a subjective attribute. For example, assume that Jackson shot and killed Avery. Jackson is arrested and charged with the crime of murder. Jackson contends that he did not commit murder because he was too drunk to know what he was doing and thus lacked the required mental state for murder—intent to kill. Jackson may have committed a criminal act (homicide). In view of his mental state, however, he committed not the crime of murder but (probably) the crime of involuntary manslaughter. Of course, there will most certainly have to be some facts in evidence tending to show that Jackson was indeed so drunk that he could not have intended to kill Avery.

Criminal defendants may assert they lacked the required degree of criminal intent for other reasons, including *insanity* (the inability to distinguish between right and wrong due to diminished mental capacity), *duress* (which exists when one is forced to commit a specific act), or *mistake* (for example, taking someone else's property, such as a briefcase, thinking that it is one's own).

PROTECTION OF PERSONS OR PROPERTY. We all have the right to protect ourselves from physical attacks by others; this is the right of **self-defense**. The force we use to protect ourselves must be reasonable under the circumstances, though. The force used must be justified by the degree of threat posed in a given situation. If someone is about to take your life, the use of *deadly force* (shooting that person with a gun, for example) might be deemed reasonable, depending on the circumstances. If, however, someone in a shopping mall tries to pick your pocket to steal your wallet, you normally do not have a right to shoot him or her, because there was no physical threat to your person.

Similarly, we have the right to use force in **defense of others** if they are threatened with imminent harm. If you and a friend are walking down a city street one night and someone attacks and threatens to kill your friend, you are justified in using whatever force is reasonable under the circumstances to protect your friend. As with self-defense, it must be shown that the force used was reasonable in view of the nature of the threat.

We also have the right to use reasonable force in the **defense of property**. In particular, if someone is illegally trespassing on our property or is stealing our property, we have the right to use force to stop the trespassing or prevent the theft; again, the amount of force used must be reasonable. Because human life has a higher value than property, deadly force is normally not allowed in the protection of property unless the thief or trespasser poses a threat to human life.

STATUTES OF LIMITATIONS. With some exceptions, such as for the crime of murder, statutes of limitations apply to crimes just as they do to civil wrongs. In other words, criminal cases must be prosecuted within a certain number of years. If a criminal action is brought after the statutory time period has expired, the accused person can raise the statute of limitations as a defense.

OTHER DEFENSES. Further defenses include *mistaken identity* and other reasons why the criminal charges might not be valid. For example, a defendant may

Self-Defense
The legally recognized privilege to protect oneself or one's property against injury by another. The privilege of self-defense only protects acts that are reasonably necessary to protect oneself or one's property.

Defense of Others
The use of reasonable force to protect others from harm.

Defense of Property
The use of reasonable force to protect one's property from the harm threatened by another. The use of deadly force in defending one's property is seldom justified.

Paralegal Profile

Criminal Law Paralegal

MICHELE D. DOYLE *works as a legal assistant in a small law firm. She has been employed by several law firms during the past fifteen years, working for the prosecution as well as for the defense in criminal matters and working in the area of civil litigation. Doyle started her career as an employee of the police department, then changed vocations when the career option of legal assistant first arose. She subsequently passed the Certified Legal Assistant exam. Doyle's responsibilities encompass document handling and control, investigations, case management, client relations, witness interviews, courtroom case management, and computer technologies in and out of the courtroom. Doyle has been actively involved in both her local paralegal association and in the National Association of Legal Assistants (NALA). She presently serves on NALA's professional development committee.*

What do you like best about your work?

"I thoroughly enjoy meeting and helping the people I encounter, learning from individuals no matter what their age, occupation, or talent. Everyone has needs; with respect to the law, some have greater needs than others. Taking up the challenge a case offers, strategizing and fighting to the end, gives me great joy and satisfaction. I gain the confidence, respect, and friendship of many individuals along the way. I also enjoy learning about so many facets of the law from the past and look forward to the future. I am very proud of my chosen profession. There is always a new challenge around every corner, and instead of giving up when the challenge gets tough, I look for ways to counter the challenge. I have yet to throw in the towel, and I suspect that I will never give up—I will only find new ways to shape what is important to me."

What is the greatest challenge that you face in your area of work?

"Keeping myself educated is my greatest challenge. I'm fearful that I will not have the proper resources, tools, and training to do the job. No one wants to fail, especially me. And I'm not just talking about losing a case. I'm speaking about failing to do an important task—one that was thought to be unimportant at the time but that turned out to be crucial later on. I'm also speaking about failing to keep oneself educated, even if it is reading the daily newspaper or case law. The law is constantly changing, and education in this area is the key element. Lawyers are busy people, and they rely on legal assistants who have the desire, drive, and fortitude to come up with the fact-saving element to the case. I seek out seminars to attend, and I read case law and opinions wherever I can find them. Online reading has become a daily habit for me."

offer an *alibi* (proof that the defendant was somewhere else at the time of the crime, for example) as a defense. Still other defenses to criminal liability have to do with violations of procedural law. For example, the police officer or officers who arrested the defendant must have had the proper authority to do so, and the court in which the action is brought must have jurisdiction over the subject matter of the case and over the person brought before the court.

Because criminal law brings the force of the state, with all its resources, to bear against the individual, law enforcement authorities must be sure they abide by the letter of procedural law when arresting and prosecuting a person accused of a crime. If they do not, the defendant may be able to use the prosecution's violations of procedural laws as a defense against criminal liability, depending on the nature of the defendant's right that was violated and the degree of violation.

PARALEGAL PROFILE

Criminal Law Paralegal *Continued*

"The law is constantly changing, and education in this area is the key element."

What advice do you have for would-be paralegals in your area of work?
"Start with the task at hand, ask questions, leave no stone unturned, be creative, go the extra mile, plan every move strategically, honestly, and with fortitude and integrity. Above all, enjoy what you do. No matter which side you may happen to be on, perform your duties honestly and hold your adversary in great esteem. Be honest with your work and with yourself. Do not be afraid to say no if the task calls for a dishonest measure to get the job done. Even if no one discovers the dishonesty, you know the truth. Keep yourself educated and up to date. Become involved in your local and national paralegal associations. Share your ideas—don't keep them to yourself. Smile and be respectful and polite. Our main objective is not to argue in court, but to provide the fuel for the argument."

What are some tips for success as a paralegal in your area of work?
"Listen, communicate, and perform the detail work that no one else wants to do. Never badmouth your adversary, your employer, your client, the court, or anyone you might encounter. Do not let yourself become stagnant, thereby being nonproductive. Really believe in what you are doing. Search for new ways to perform tasks and prove yourself valuable. I keep a daily notebook. At the start of every day, I date and highlight the top of the page. For every task I receive, there is some kind of note. Every phone call is logged, and every 'to-do' and thought is written down. It doesn't need to be a book, just a memory jog-log, a place to store the events of your day. Don't be afraid to try new and different things. Ask your employer if you might try a new task or challenge. Be open to new ideas and change. By taking on new challenges and ideas, you will save yourself from burnout and boredom."

CONSTITUTIONAL SAFEGUARDS

From the very moment a crime is reported until the trial concludes, law enforcement officers and prosecutors must be careful to abide by the specific criminal procedures that have been established to protect an accused person's constitutional rights. Before allowing a case to go to trial, the prosecutor and legal assistants assigned to the case review all pretrial events very closely to make sure that all requirements were properly observed. Defense attorneys and their legal assistants also investigate and review closely the actions of arresting and investigating police officers in an attempt to obtain grounds for a dismissal of the charges against their clients.

The U.S. Constitution provides specific procedural safeguards to protect persons accused of crimes against the potentially arbitrary or unjust use of government power. These safeguards are stated in the first ten amendments to the Constitution, which constitute the Bill of Rights. As you will see in the following pages, criminal procedure is rooted in the constitutional rights and protections

On the Web
The American Civil Liberties Union (ACLU) has long acted as a guardian of Americans' civil liberties. You can learn about some of the constitutional questions raised by various criminal laws and procedures by going to the ACLU's Web site at **www.aclu.org**.

Developing Paralegal Skills

Year-and-a-Day Defense

Jennifer Wall and Ed Roper are paralegals in a criminal defense firm. The firm is defending Robert Baines, who has been charged with murder. Baines got into a fight in a bar with Gerald Litton on January 1, 1998. Baines beat Litton so severely that he went into a coma, and, without ever regaining consciousness, died, on January 4, 1999. The senior attorney remembers the year-and-a-day defense from law school.

The rule requires that the victim must die within a year and a day from defendant's conduct, or the defendant cannot be prosecuted for murder. This is an old rule, originating when the quality of medical care was not as advanced as it is today and when people had much shorter life expectancies. If a victim lived for more than a year and a day, it could not be said with reasonable certainty that intervening causes, such as illness or infirmities, were not the cause of the victim's death, thus providing a defense for the accused. Because this is an old rule, the attorney assigns Jennifer and Ed to research their state's law to see if the defense still applies. They find that their state's law

requires that the victim must live for three years from the date of attack for the defendant to use this defense to evade prosecution. Thus, the defense is not available for their client, Baines.

Checklist for Locating and Applying Criminal Defenses

- Obtain a list of defenses from a general legal source, such as a legal encyclopedia.
- Look in your state's statutes to determine whether these defenses are authorized in your state.
- If the defenses are not authorized by state statute, review your state's case law to determine if the courts have authorized the use of these defenses. Reviewing state case law will also allow you to determine the situations in which particular defenses are used.
- Determine whether the available defenses apply to your client's case.

Due Process of Law
The Fifth Amendment to the U.S. Constitution prohibits the deprivation of "life, liberty, or property without due process of law," meaning that fair, reasonable, and standard procedures must be used by the government in any legal action against a citizen.

Double Jeopardy
To place at risk (jeopardize) a person's life or liberty twice. The Fifth Amendment to the Constitution prohibits a second prosecution for the same criminal offense in all but a few circumstances.

spelled out in the Fourth, Fifth, Sixth, and Eighth Amendments. These rights and protections are summarized below. The full text of the U.S. Constitution, including the Bill of Rights, is presented in Appendix J.

1. The Fourth Amendment requires that no warrants for a search or an arrest may be issued without probable cause (to be discussed shortly).
2. The Fifth Amendment requires that no one shall be deprived of "life, liberty, or property without due process of law." **Due process of law** means that the government must follow a set of reasonable, fair, and standard procedures (that is, criminal procedural law) in any action against a citizen.
3. The Fifth Amendment prohibits **double jeopardy** (trying someone twice for the same criminal offense).
4. The Fifth Amendment guarantees that no person shall be "compelled in any criminal case to be a witness against himself."
5. The Sixth Amendment guarantees a speedy and public trial, a trial by jury, the right to confront witnesses, and the right to a lawyer at various stages in some proceedings.
6. The Eighth Amendment prohibits excessive bail and fines, and cruel and unusual punishment.

The *Miranda* Rule

In regard to criminal procedure, one of the questions that had been facing many courts in the 1950s and 1960s was not whether suspects had constitutional rights—that was not in doubt—but how and when those rights could be exercised. For example, the Fifth Amendment to the Constitution guarantees the privilege against compulsory **self-incrimination**. As indicated in the list presented above, that amendment states, among other things, that no person "shall be compelled in any criminal case to be a witness against himself." But could this right be exercised during pretrial interrogation proceedings or only during the trial? Were confessions obtained from suspects admissible in court if the suspects had not been advised of their right to remain silent and other constitutional rights?

To clarify these issues, in 1966 the United States Supreme Court issued a landmark decision, *Miranda v. Arizona*.[4] The *Miranda* decision established the rule that individuals who are arrested and taken into custody must be informed of certain constitutional rights, which have come to be called the ***Miranda* rights**, before any statements they make can be admissible in court. These rights, which include the right to remain silent and the right to counsel, are listed in Exhibit 12.1.

Under what is known as the **exclusionary rule**, all evidence obtained in violation of a defendant's constitutional rights must normally be excluded, as well as all evidence derived from the illegally obtained evidence. For example, if a police officer or a private investigator breaks into a suspect's home (that is, enters the home illegally with neither the suspect's permission nor a search warrant) and obtains evidence that the suspect committed a crime, that evidence normally will not be admissible in court.

The Erosion of the *Miranda* Rule

Although the Supreme Court and lower courts have enforced the rules discussed above hundreds of times since the *Miranda* decision, the *Miranda* rights of defendants have been gradually eroded. Congress, in 1968, passed the Omnibus Crime Control and Safe Streets Act, which provided—among other things—that in cases involving federal crimes a voluntary confession could be used as evidence even if the accused was not informed of his or her rights.

Several subsequent decisions by the United States Supreme Court also eroded the rule. In 1984, for example, the Court recognized a "public safety"

---

4. 384 U.S. 436, 86 S.Ct. 1602, 16 L.Ed.2d 694 (1966). How to read case citations is discussed in Chapter 14.

Self-Incrimination
The act of giving testimony that implicates one's own guilt or participation in criminal wrongdoing. The Fifth Amendment to the Constitution states that no person "shall be compelled in any criminal case to be a witness against himself."

***Miranda* Rights**
The constitutional rights of accused persons taken into custody by law enforcement officials. Following the United States Supreme Court's decision in *Miranda v. Arizona*, on taking an accused person into custody, the arresting officer must inform the person of certain constitutional rights, such as the suspect's right to remain silent or right to counsel.

Exclusionary Rule
In criminal procedure, a rule under which any evidence that is obtained in violation of the accused's constitutional rights guaranteed by the Fourth, Fifth, and Sixth Amendments, as well as any evidence derived from illegally obtained evidence, will not be admissible in court.

EXHIBIT 12.1
The *Miranda* Rights

Upon taking a criminal suspect into custody and before any interrogation takes place, law enforcement officers are required to communicate the following rights and facts to the suspect:

1. The right to remain silent.
2. That any statements made may be used against the person in a court of law.
3. The right to talk to a lawyer and have a lawyer present while being questioned.
4. If the person cannot afford to hire a lawyer, the right to have a lawyer provided at no cost.

In addition to being advised of these rights, the suspect must be asked if he or she understands the rights and whether he or she wishes to exercise the rights or waive (not exercise) the rights.

FEATURED GUEST: PAMELA POOLE WEBER
Paralegals and Criminal Litigation

BIOGRAPHICAL NOTE

Pamela Poole Weber graduated from Stetson University College of Law and is licensed to practice law in Florida. In 1989, after working in both the corporate and public sectors as a litigator, she joined Seminole Community College in Central Florida. There she developed and was the director of a two-year legal-assistant program. She is now the executive director of the Seminole Community College Foundation. Weber remains active in various legal areas, teaching police recruits in the area of juvenile law and lecturing to seniors on issues relating to the rights of elderly persons.

The gavel strikes, the trial is over, and the jury is escorted to the jury room to deliberate. Your pulse begins to pound, and the gravity of the situation overwhelms you. This is the first time that you, as a paralegal, have assisted your supervising attorney in a criminal case. Now comes the most difficult time—waiting for the decision. But you take satisfaction in knowing that you have done the best job you can.

* * * * *

Criminal litigation is a very fast-paced area of law that is continually changing. Many people do not understand what is involved in defending or prosecuting someone accused of a crime. First and foremost, both sides must be familiar with current laws and especially with changes or new interpretations of those laws. Attorneys do not always have the time required to keep up with these changes. A paralegal can be a valuable asset to a law office by keeping informed on current developments—by reading current court decisions, by reviewing summaries of new laws or modifications to existing laws, by being alert for emerging trends reported in the media, and by generally keeping their eyes and ears open. This behind-the-scenes work is in many ways just as interesting as the spectacular trial scenes on television, and a paralegal's input with respect to current law may well determine the outcome of a case.

Both the defense and the prosecution must review every aspect of the case. This requires combining legal research with critical analysis. Attorneys and paralegals work together in planning a course of action for each case, regardless of whether the case is simple or highly complex. This team approach is becoming more widely accepted because of the results it generates. As the old saying goes, "Two minds are better than one."

OPPORTUNITIES FOR PARALEGALS

Criminal litigation may present paralegals with a variety of opportunities, although paralegals are not utilized as extensively in criminal litigation as they are in civil litigation. Some attorneys do not use paralegals to their fullest capabilities because they do not know how to maximize paralegal services. Often, paralegals must suggest tasks that they can perform or, if appropriate, must simply go ahead and perform the tasks on their own. Remember, though, that paralegals cannot engage in any actions that only attorneys are licensed to perform.

What are some of the services that paralegals can provide? Obviously, legal research is critical to successful criminal litigation, and paralegals can perform this research for attorneys. Such research may involve a review and analysis of the law or laws that allegedly have been violated by the defendant, various defense strategies, procedural problems, and evidentiary problems—just to name a few. Sometimes, research is very detailed, requiring days and even weeks to complete. At other times, research may have to be done at the last minute within only an hour or two.

Paralegals who want more contact with people can involve themselves in the evidentiary side of the case. Both the defense attorney and the prosecuting attorney in a criminal case have some sort of evidence—physical evidence, witnesses' testimony, or confessions, for example—with which to work. The paralegal may interview witnesses, prepare deposition

FEATURED GUEST, Continued

questions, review police and laboratory reports, or identify photographs that may be useful at trial.

Many paralegals enjoy the challenge of critical analysis and strategic thinking. The criminal litigation paralegal is continually provided with challenges in this respect. In this area, the paralegal can assist in actually preparing the case for trial. The paralegal may be asked to draft pretrial motions, review the available research and documents, draft responses to the opposing side's motions, prepare questions for jury selection, and prepare jury instructions for the conclusion of the case.

How Can I Assist in the Defense of a Criminal?

This question, long asked by attorneys, is now being asked by paralegals. Many people look at this area of law and say that they could never represent such defendants as Ted Bundy or Jeffrey Dahmer (convicted serial killers). Perhaps these people believe that by representing such defendants, the attorneys are somehow condoning their criminal actions. Or perhaps they detest those defendants so much that they want them convicted and punished without the benefit of due process. But attorneys and their legal assistants must remind themselves that until the verdict is in, the defendants are only *accused* of committing the criminal acts. They are guilty of no crime until the jury decides they are guilty *beyond a reasonable doubt*. Our country's criminal justice system is founded on the principle that a person is "innocent until proven guilty." The paralegal must remember that his or her job is not to decide the guilt or innocence of an accused person. Rather, it is to ensure that *justice* is being served.

A paralegal working for the prosecutor will strive to ensure that the people of a particular city, county, or state, or even the United States, are having their interests protected. The prosecution does not represent the victim of a criminal act but rather the citizens of a community.

The defense paralegal will work to ensure the protection of the rights of the accused. The U.S. Constitution guarantees that all persons have certain rights, including the right to a trial in which they may confront their accusers and the right to be represented by legal counsel during that trial. These rights apply to everyone—including those who actually commit the crimes with which they are charged. It is up to the defense team to make sure that the defendant has not been deprived of any of his or her constitutional rights.

The defense attorney and his or her legal assistants will examine closely all the circumstances, procedures, and evidence involving the defendant to make sure that the defendant has been allowed to exercise these rights. It may be the task of the paralegal to determine if evidence, including a confession, was properly obtained. If it was not, the paralegal may assist in drafting motions to bring this to the attention of the court. The defense team will also explore various defenses that may be available to the accused.

> "The defense paralegal will work to ensure the protection of the rights of the accused."

Paralegals who wish to work in the area of criminal justice must be prepared to be highly objective about criminal proceedings. They must be able to separate their personal and emotional responses to a particular defendant's alleged criminal acts from their professional goal of serving that defendant's best interests by doing all they can to ensure that his or her rights have been observed.

Conclusion

Criminal litigation offers numerous opportunities for legal assistants, but it is important to remember that in some cases it may be difficult to achieve the necessary personal and emotional distance from a case to deal with it objectively and professionally.

* * * * *

The bailiff returns and announces that the jury has reached a verdict. Your heart leaps into your throat. You take a deep breath and wait. The jury returns a verdict for your side, and you realize that you have just experienced a first victory as a paralegal. After all, you say to yourself, your efforts were crucial to the success of your attorney's case. You know that not all future cases will be "won," but you experience the rewarding feeling of being an integral part of the system seeking justice for all Americans.

On the Web

If you are interested in reading the Supreme Court's opinion in *Miranda v. Arizona*, go to www.law.cornell.edu/supct.

On the Web

An excellent site for information on the criminal justice system is tqd.advanced.org/2760/homep.htm. Here, you can follow a fictional criminal case through the courts, find a glossary of terms used in criminal law, view actual forms that are filled out during the course of an arrest, and learn about some controversial issues in criminal law.

Arrest
To take into custody a person suspected of criminal activity.

Citation
In criminal procedure, an order for a defendant to appear in court or indicating that a person has violated a legal rule.

Probable Cause
Reasonable grounds to believe the existence of facts warranting certain actions, such as the search or arrest of a person.

exception to the *Miranda* rule.[5] The need to protect the public warranted the admissibility of statements made by the defendant (in this case indicating where he placed the gun) as evidence in a trial, even when the defendant was not informed of his *Miranda* rights. In 1990, the Court recognized a "routine booking questions" exception to *Miranda*.[6] The statements made by the defendant to the police in response to questions regarding "biographical data necessary to complete booking or pretrial services" were exempted from *Miranda*. Today, juries are permitted to accept confessions without being convinced of their voluntariness. Even in cases that are not tried in federal court, confessions made by criminal suspects who have not been completely informed of their legal rights may be taken into consideration. In *Minnick v. Mississippi*,[7] however, a 1990 case heard by the Supreme Court, the Court held that once a defendant has requested counsel, the defendant cannot be questioned by police unless the defendant's attorney is present.

CRIMINAL PROCEDURES PRIOR TO PROSECUTION

In most matters, the police (or other persons or agencies authorized by the state to do so) control the criminal justice process up to the time a case is turned over for prosecution. Although lawyers and legal assistants are usually not extensively involved in this initial stage of the criminal process, events that take place at this stage may affect the final outcome of the case. Therefore, paralegals—and especially those working with criminal defense attorneys—need to be familiar with the basic steps that occur in this phase of the criminal process.

We offer in this section (and illustrate graphically in Exhibit 12.2) a general version of the procedural steps involved in the criminal process. Bear in mind, however, that procedural details vary significantly, depending on the locality and jurisdiction in which an accused person is arrested and prosecuted and depending on the nature of the crime. Realistically, there is no way that an introductory paralegal text such as this one can describe the many procedural variations involved in the criminal process. As a paralegal, if you work in the area of criminal law or on a case involving criminal law, you therefore must do the following:

 Check with your supervising attorney or the court hearing the case to learn the specific procedural requirements that apply to the case.

Arrest

In a lawful **arrest**, the suspect is taken into custody by the police, may be searched for weapons or evidence, and is taken to the police station to be formally charged with the crime. Most arrests are for misdemeanors, and in such situations the arresting officers often release the suspects with citations rather than taking them to the police station. The **citation** instructs the defendant to appear in court at some later date to respond to the charges.

PROBABLE CAUSE. Before an individual can be arrested, the requirement of probable cause must be met. **Probable cause** exists if there is a substantial likelihood that (1) a crime was committed and (2) the individual committed the crime.

---

5. *New York v. Quarles*, 467 U.S. 649, 104 S.Ct. 2626, 81 L.Ed.2d 550 (1984).
6. *Pennsylvania v. Muniz*, 496 U.S. 582, 110 S.Ct. 2638, 110 L.Ed.2d 528 (1990).
7. 498 U.S. 146, 111 S.Ct. 486, 112 L.Ed.2d 489 (1990).

EXHIBIT 12.2

Major Procedural Steps in a Criminal Case

ARREST

Police officer takes suspect into custody. Most arrests are made without a warrant. After the arrest, the officer searches the suspect, who is then taken to the police station.

↓

BOOKING

At the police station, the suspect is searched again, photographed, fingerprinted, and allowed at least one telephone call. After the booking, charges are reviewed, and if they are not dropped a complaint is filed and a magistrate reviews the case for probable cause.

↓

INITIAL APPEARANCE

The suspect appears before the magistrate, who informs the suspect of the charges and of his or her rights. If the suspect requires a lawyer, one is appointed. The magistrate sets bail (conditions under which a suspect can obtain release pending disposition of the case).

↓

PRELIMINARY HEARING

In a proceeding in which both sides are represented by counsel, the magistrate determines whether there is probable cause to believe that the suspect committed the crime, based on the evidence.

↓

GRAND JURY REVIEW ↔ **PROSECUTOR REVIEW**

The federal government and about half of the states require grand jury indictments for at least some felonies. In those states, a grand jury determines whether the evidence justifies a trial on the charge sought by the prosecutor.

In jurisdictions that do not require grand jury indictments, a prosecutor issues an information. An information is similar to an indictment: both are charging instruments that replace the complaint.

↓

ARRAIGNMENT

The suspect is brought before the trial court, informed of the charges, and asked to enter a plea.

↓

PLEA BARGAIN

A plea bargain is a prosecutor's promise to make concessions (or promise to seek concessions) in return for a suspect's guilty plea. Concessions may include a reduced charge or a lesser sentence.

↓

GUILTY PLEA ↔ **TRIAL**

In most jurisdictions, most cases that reach the arraignment stage do not go to trial but are resolved by a guilty plea, often as a result of a plea bargain. The judge sets the case for sentencing.

Generally, most felony trials are jury trials, and most misdemeanor trials are bench trials (trials before judges). If the verdict is "guilty," the judge sets the case for sentencing. Everyone convicted of a crime has the right to an appeal.

EXHIBIT 12.3
An Arrest Warrant

```
                    United States District Court
                    _____ DISTRICT OF _____

    UNITED STATES OF AMERICA
              v.                              WARRANT FOR ARREST

                                    CASE NUMBER:

    To: The United States Marshal
        and any Authorized United States Officer

        YOU ARE HEREBY COMMANDED to arrest _____
                                                    Name

    and bring him or her forthwith to the nearest magistrate to answer a(n)

    ☐ Indictment  ☐ Information  ☐ Complaint  ☐ Order of Court  ☐ Violation Notice  ☐ Probation Violation Petition

    charging him or her with (brief description of offense)




    in violation of Title _____ United States Code, Section(s) _____

    _____        _____
    Name of Issuing Officer                Title of Issuing Officer

    _____        _____
    Signature of Issuing Officer           Date and Location


    Bail fixed at $ _____ by _____
                                          Name of Judicial Officer

                                RETURN
    This warrant was received and executed with the arrest of the above-named defendant at _____

    ─────────────────────────────────────────────────────────────
    DATE RECEIVED    | NAME AND TITLE OF ARRESTING OFFICER | SIGNATURE OF ARRESTING OFFICER
    DATE OF ARREST   |                                     |
                                                                  [G13861]
```

Note that probable cause involves a *likelihood*—not just a possibility—that the suspect committed the crime. For example, if Castle observed Jackson running from the scene of a homicide, gun in hand, Castle's observation would probably constitute probable cause to arrest Jackson. If Castle observed Jackson walking unhurriedly away from the vicinity of the homicide, with no gun in hand, Castle's observation would not constitute probable cause. In the latter situation, although Jackson might have been the perpetrator, more evidence would be required to demonstrate that it was *likely* that Jackson committed the crime.

The requirement of probable cause is based on the Fourth Amendment, which prohibits unreasonable searches and seizures (and an arrest is a "seizure" of a person). The Fourth Amendment reads as follows:

> **EXHIBIT 12.3**
> An Arrest Warrant—Continued

```
THE FOLLOWING IS FURNISHED FOR INFORMATION ONLY:

DEFENDANT'S NAME: _____
ALIAS: _____
LAST KNOWN RESIDENCE: _____
LAST KNOWN EMPLOYMENT: _____
PLACE OF BIRTH: _____
DATE OF BIRTH: _____
SOCIAL SECURITY NUMBER: _____
HEIGHT: _____      WEIGHT: _____
SEX: _____      RACE: _____
HAIR: _____      EYES: _____
SCARS, TATTOOS, OTHER DISTINGUISHING MARKS: _____
_____
_____
FBI NUMBER: _____
COMPLETE DESCRIPTION OF AUTO: _____
_____
INVESTIGATIVE AGENCY AND ADDRESS: _____
_____
_____
                                                          [G13862]
```

The right of the people to be secure in their persons, houses, papers, and effects, against unreasonable searches and seizures, shall not be violated, and no Warrants shall issue, but upon probable cause, supported by Oath or affirmation, and particularly describing the place to be searched, and the persons or things to be seized.

If a police officer observes a crime being committed, the officer can arrest the wrongdoer on the spot without a warrant, because the probable-cause requirement is satisfied (the officer knows that a crime was committed and that the person being arrested did, in fact, commit the crime). If a crime is reported to the police by a victim or some other person, however, the police must decide if a crime has really been committed and, if so, whether there is enough information about the alleged wrongdoer's guilt to justify an arrest.

ARREST WARRANTS. Often, the police try to gather more information to help them determine whether a suspect should be arrested. If, after investigating the matter, the police decide to arrest the suspect, they must obtain an **arrest warrant,** such as that shown in Exhibit 12.3, from a judge or other public official. To obtain this warrant, the police will have to convince the official, usually through supporting affidavits, that probable cause exists. Probable cause is also required to obtain a **search warrant,** which authorizes police officers or other criminal investigators to search specifically named persons or property to obtain evidence (see Exhibit 12.4 on page 430).

Arrest Warrant
A written order, based on probable cause and issued by a judge or public official (magistrate), commanding that the person named on the warrant be arrested by the police.

Search Warrant
A written order, based on probable cause and issued by a judge or public official (magistrate), commanding that police officers or criminal investigators search a specific person, place, or property to obtain evidence.

EXHIBIT 12.4
A Search Warrant

Ch. 89　　　　　SEARCH AND SEIZURE　　　　　§ 7942
　　　　　　　　　　　　　　　　　　　　　　　Rule 41

§ 7942.　Search Warrant

AO 93 (Rev. 5/85) Search Warrant

United States District Court

_____ DISTRICT OF _____

In the Matter of the Search of
(Name, address or brief description of person or property to be searched)

SEARCH WARRANT

CASE NUMBER:

TO: _____ and any Authorized Officer of the United States

Affidavit(s) having been made before me by _____ who has reason to
　　　　　　　　　　　　　　　　　　　　　　　Affiant
believe that ☐ on the person of or ☐ on the premises known as (name, description and/or location)

in the _____ District of _____ there is now
concealed a certain person or property, namely (describe the person or property)

I am satisfied that the affidavit(s) and any recorded testimony establish probable cause to believe that the person or property so described is now concealed on the person or premises above-described and establish grounds for the issuance of this warrant.

YOU ARE HEREBY COMMANDED to search on or before _____
　　　　　　　　　　　　　　　　　　　　　　　　　　　　　　　Date
(not to exceed 10 days) the person or place named above for the person or property specified, serving this warrant and making the search (in the daytime—6:00 A.M. to 10:00 P.M.) (at any time in the day or night as I find reasonable cause has been established) and if the person or property be found there to seize same, leaving a copy of this warrant and receipt for the person or property taken, and prepare a written inventory of the person or property seized and promptly return this warrant to _____
as required by law.　　　　　　　　　　　　　　　　U.S Judge or Magistrate

_____ at _____
Date and Time Issued　　　　　　　　　　City and State

_____　　　　　　_____
Name and Title of Judicial Officer　　　　　Signature of Judicial Officer　　[G13950]

Booking

Booking
The process of entering a suspect's name, offense, and arrival time into the police log (blotter) following his or her arrest.

Magistrate
A public civil officer or official with limited judicial authority, such as the authority to issue an arrest warrant.

After the arrest, the police take the suspect to the police station, a jail, or some other *holding facility* where the booking occurs. **Booking** takes place when an officer enters the suspect's name, offense, and time of arrival on the police log, or *blotter*. Then the suspect is fingerprinted and photographed, told the reason for the arrest, and allowed to make a phone call.

For most lesser offenses, after booking the suspect may be released on his or her promise to appear at some later date before a **magistrate** (a civil official or officer who has limited judicial authority, such as a justice of the peace). Sometimes, the suspect is required to deposit a small amount of cash, or bail (dis-

EXHIBIT 12.4

A Search Warrant—Continued

§ 7942	SPECIAL PROCEEDINGS	Ch. 89
Rule 41		

AO 93 (Rev. 5/85) Search Warrant

RETURN

DATE WARRANT RECEIVED	DATE AND TIME WARRANT EXECUTED	COPY OF WARRANT AND RECEIPT FOR ITEMS LEFT WITH

INVENTORY MADE IN THE PRESENCE OF

INVENTORY OF PERSON OR PROPERTY TAKEN PURSUANT TO THE WARRANT

CERTIFICATION

I swear that this inventory is a true and detailed account of the person or property taken by me on the warrant.

Subscribed, sworn to, and returned before me this date.

_____ _____
U.S. Judge or Magistrate   Date

[G13951]

---

cussed below), as security for his or her later appearance before the magistrate. For more serious offenses (and for some minor offenses), the suspect will be incarcerated (locked up in a jail cell) until the date of his or her appearance before a magistrate. Before being incarcerated, the suspect is thoroughly searched to make sure that no weapons get into the jail. Personal effects are listed and stored.

Investigation after the Arrest

As already mentioned, when a suspect is "caught red-handed," the police may arrest the suspect without an arrest warrant and may not have to undertake much of an investigation of the alleged offense after the arrest. In other cases, however, the police must find and interview witnesses and conduct searches (of the suspect's home or car, for example) to collect evidence. Witnesses may view the suspect individually in a *line-up,* in which the suspect appears with a group of several others. In more serious cases, detectives may take charge of the investigation.

As the police review the evidence at hand, they may conclude there is insufficient evidence to justify recommending the case for prosecution. If they reach this conclusion, the suspect may be released and the case may be closed. Alternatively, the police may decide to change the charge that was initially brought against the suspect, usually reducing the charge to a lesser offense. The police may also decide to release the suspect with a warning or a referral to a social service agency. Unless the suspect is released, at this point in the criminal process, control over the case moves from the police to the public prosecutor.

THE PROSECUTION BEGINS

On the Web
You can find summaries of famous criminal cases, and sometimes related pleadings and other documents, at the Web site of Court TV. Go to www.courttv.com/trials.

The prosecution of a criminal case begins when the police inform the public prosecutor of the alleged crime, provide the reports written by the arresting and investigating officers, and turn over evidence relating to the matter. The prosecutor has the discretion to investigate the case further by personally interviewing the suspect, the arresting and investigating officers, and witnesses and gathering other evidence. The prosecutor's legal assistants often participate in these tasks. Based on a review of the police file or an investigation, the prosecutor decides whether to take the case to trial or drop the case and allow the suspect to be released. Major reasons for releasing the suspect include insufficient evidence and unreliable witnesses.

Because prosecutions are expensive and resources are limited, most prosecutors do not go forward with cases unless they think that they have a strong chance of proving the charges against the suspects in court. In many jurisdictions, at least half of all felony suspects are released or offered the alternative of participating in a diversion program to avoid being prosecuted and to clear their records. **Diversion programs** attempt to deter the suspect from further wrongdoing by, for example, requiring the suspect to stay employed, to attend special classes (perhaps on drug education), or to perform special community services. In some cases, the suspects may be required to make restitution (by returning or paying for stolen property, for example) to the victims of their crimes to avoid prosecution.

Diversion Program
In some jurisdictions, an alternative to prosecution that is offered to certain felony suspects to deter them from future unlawful acts.

If the decision is to prosecute the case, then a complaint is filed and other procedures undertaken. The procedures discussed below (and summarized earlier in Exhibit 12.2) assure that the accused person's Fifth Amendment right to due process of law is not jeopardized.

Filing the Complaint

The criminal litigation process may begin with the filing of a *complaint* (see Exhibit 12.5). Once the decision to prosecute the case is made, then the prosecutor files a complaint against the suspect, usually with the magistrate's court. (In some cases, however, a grand jury is called at this point to determine probable cause, as will be discussed below.) The complaint includes a statement of the charges that are being brought against the suspect. The suspect now becomes a criminal defendant. Because the defendant is in the court system, prosecutors must show that they have legal grounds to proceed. They must show probable cause that a crime was committed and that the defendant committed the crime. Note

EXHIBIT 12.5
A Complaint

```
United States District Court
                    DISTRICT OF

UNITED STATES OF AMERICA
        V.
                                CRIMINAL COMPLAINT

                            CASE NUMBER:

(Name and Address of Defendant)

I, the undersigned complainant being duly sworn state the following is true and correct to the best of my knowledge and belief. On or about _____ in _____ county, in the _____ District of _____ defendant(s) did, (Track Statutory Language of Offense)




in violation of Title ____ United States Code, Section(s) _____.
I further state that I am a(n) _____ and that this complaint is based on the following
                                  Official Title
facts:




Continued on the attached sheet and made a part hereof:  ☐ Yes  ☐ No

                                                    _____
                                                    Signature of Complainant
Sworn to before me and subscribed in my presence,

_____ at _____
Date                                City and State
```

that the Fourth Amendment requirement of probable cause comes under scrutiny several times during the prosecution of a criminal offense.

Initial Appearance

In most jurisdictions, defendants are taken before a magistrate very soon after arrest, usually within twenty-four hours. During this *initial appearance*, a brief proceeding takes place. The magistrate makes sure that the person presented is the person named in the complaint, informs the defendant of the charge or charges made in the complaint, and explains to the defendant his or her constitutional rights—particularly the right to remain silent (under the Fifth Amendment) and the right to be represented by counsel (under the Sixth Amendment). If the defendant cannot afford to hire a private attorney, a public defender may be appointed, or private counsel may be hired by the state to represent the defendant.

Bail
The amount of money or conditions set by the court to assure that an individual accused of a crime will appear for further criminal proceedings. If the accused person provides bail, whether in cash or by means of a bail bond, then the person is released from jail.

The magistrate may release the defendant from jail pending further legal proceedings on certain conditions. Defendants who have been arrested for misdemeanors, for example, may be released on their own recognizance (on their promise to return at a later date for further proceedings). For more serious crimes, the defendant will be released only if he or she posts **bail**—an amount of money paid by the defendant to the court and retained by the court until the defendant returns for further proceedings. For some serious crimes, bail may be denied.

Often, defendants are unable to pay the amount of bail set by the court. In such a situation, the defendant may make arrangements with a *bail bondsperson* to post a bail bond on behalf of the defendant. The bondsperson, in effect, promises the court that he or she will turn over to the court the full amount of the bail if the defendant fails to return for the further proceedings. The defendant usually must give the bondsperson a certain percentage of the bail (often 10 percent) in cash. This amount, which is often not returned to the defendant later, is considered as payment for the bondsperson's assistance and assumption of risk. Depending on the amount of the bail bond, the defendant may also be required to sign over to the bondsperson rights to certain property (such as a car, a valuable watch, or other asset) as security for the bond.

Motion to Reduce the Amount of Bail
A motion requesting that the bail needed to release the defendant be lowered because it is unreasonably high under the circumstances and may violate the Eighth Amendment's prohibition against excessive bail.

Normally, the defendant's attorney (or the attorney's paralegal) makes arrangements for bail with the court or a bail bondsperson. A paralegal working on a criminal case may also be asked to draft a **motion to reduce the amount of bail** if the defendant's attorney deems that the amount of bail set by the judge is unreasonably high. Under the Eighth Amendment to the Constitution, "excessive bail shall not be required." In a motion to reduce the amount of bail, the attorney may argue that the bail set by the court is "excessive" in view of the nature of the crime or the circumstances in which the crime was committed.

Preliminary Hearing

Preliminary Hearing
An initial hearing in which a magistrate decides if there is probable cause to believe that the defendant committed the crime for which he or she is charged.

The defendant again appears before a magistrate or judge at a **preliminary hearing**. During this hearing, the magistrate or judge determines whether the evidence presented is sufficient to establish probable cause to believe the defendant committed the crime for which he or she is charged. This may be the first adversarial proceeding in which both sides are represented by counsel. Paralegals may become extensively involved in the process at this point by assisting in preparation for the hearing. The prosecutor may present witnesses, who may be cross-examined by defense counsel (the defense rarely presents its witnesses prior to trial). If the defendant intends to plead guilty, he or she usually waives the right to a preliminary hearing to help move things along more quickly. In many jurisdictions, however, the preliminary hearing is required in certain felony cases.

If the magistrate finds the evidence insufficient to establish probable cause, either the charge is reduced to a lesser one, or charges are dropped altogether and the defendant is released. If the magistrate believes there is sufficient evidence to establish probable cause, the prosecutor issues an information. The **information** replaces the complaint as the formal charge against the defendant and binds over the defendant for further proceedings, which usually means that the case proceeds to trial.

Information
A formal accusation or complaint, usually issued by a prosecuting attorney, against a criminal suspect. The information initiates the criminal litigation process.

Grand Jury Review

The federal government and about half of the states require a grand jury, and not the prosecutor, to make the decision as to whether a case should go to trial. In other words, a grand jury's indictment is an alternative to a prosecutor's

> **EXHIBIT 12.6**
> An Indictment
>
> [*Title of Court and Cause*]
>
> The Grand Jury charges that:
>
> On or about _____, 20__, at _____, _____, in the _____ District of _____, _____ having been convicted of knowingly acquiring and possessing food stamp coupons in a manner not authorized by the provisions of Chapter 51, Title 7, United States Code, and the regulations issued pursuant to said chapter, a felony conviction, in the federal district court for the _____ District of _____, and sentenced on _____, 20__, did knowingly possess a firearm that had been transported in and affecting commerce, to wit: an OMC Pistol, Back Up 380 Caliber, serial number _____; all in violation of Section 1202(a)(1) of Title 18, United States Code, Appendix.
>
> A True Bill
>
> _____,
> Foreperson.
>
> _____,
> United States Attorney.

information as the formal complaint that initiates the criminal litigation process.

A **grand jury** is a group of citizens called to decide whether probable cause exists—that is, whether it is likely that the defendant committed the crime for which he or she is charged and therefore whether the case should go to trial. Even in those courts in which grand jury review is not required, the prosecutor may call a grand jury to evaluate the evidence against a suspect, which will indicate to the prosecutor the relative strength or weakness of the case.

The grand jury sits in closed session and only hears evidence presented by the prosecutor—the defendant cannot present evidence at this hearing. Normally, the defendant and his or her attorney are not even allowed to attend a grand jury hearing—although in some cases the defendant may be required to testify. The prosecutor presents to the grand jury whatever evidence the state has against the defendant, including photographs, documents, tangible objects, test results, the testimony of witnesses, and other items. If the grand jury finds that probable cause exists, it issues an **indictment** against the defendant called a *true bill*. The indictment is filed with the trial court and becomes the formal charge against the defendant. An example of an indictment is shown in Exhibit 12.6 above.

Arraignment

Based on the information or the indictment filed, the prosecutor submits a motion to the court, similar to that shown in Exhibit 12.7 on the next page, to order the defendant to appear before the trial court for an **arraignment**. Due process of law, which is guaranteed by the Fifth Amendment, requires that a criminal defendant be informed of the charges brought against him or her and be offered an opportunity to respond to those charges. The arraignment is one of the ways in which due process requirements are satisfied by criminal procedural law.

Grand Jury
The group of citizens called to decide whether probable cause exists to believe that a suspect committed the crime with which he or she has been charged.

Indictment
A charge or written accusation, issued by a grand jury, that probable cause exists to believe that a named person has committed a crime.

Arraignment
A court proceeding in which the suspect is formally charged with the criminal offense stated in the indictment. The suspect then enters a plea (guilty, not guilty, or *nolo contendere*) in response.

EXHIBIT 12.7
Motion for Order Directing Defendant to Appear for Arraignment

> The United States of America by _____, United States Attorney for the _____ District of _____, by direction of the Attorney General, requests the Court to issue an order directing the defendant herein, _____, to be and appear before the United States District Court for the _____ District of _____ at _____, in person, on _____, 20__, at 10:00 A.M. for arraignment. This request is made in compliance with the order for warrant of removal issued on the _____ day of _____, 20__, by United States District Judge _____ in the United States District Court for the District of _____.
>
> _____
> United States Attorney.

Nolo Contendere
Latin for "I will not contest it." A criminal defendant's plea in which he or she chooses not to challenge, or contest, the charges brought by the government. Although the defendant may still be sentenced or fined, the plea neither admits nor denies guilt.

Plea Bargaining
The process by which the accused and the prosecutor in a criminal case work out a mutually satisfactory disposition of the case, subject to court approval. Usually, plea bargaining involves the defendant's pleading guilty to a lesser offense in return for a lighter sentence.

Motion to Suppress Evidence
A motion requesting that certain evidence be excluded from consideration during the trial.

Motion Challenging the Sufficiency of the Indictment
A motion claiming that the evidence submitted by the prosecutor was insufficient to establish probable cause that the defendant committed the crime with which he or she has been charged.

Motion for a Change of Venue
A motion requesting that a trial be moved to a different location to ensure a fair and impartial proceeding, for the convenience of the parties, or for some other acceptable reason.

At the arraignment, the defendant is informed of the charges against him or her, and the defendant must respond to the charges by pleading not guilty or guilty. The defendant may also enter a plea of *nolo contendere*, which is Latin for "I will not contest it." The plea of *nolo contendere* is neither an admission of guilt nor a denial of guilt. It merely admits to the truth of the facts as presented by the prosecution. *Nolo* pleas are rarely used in felony cases.

At the arraignment, the defendant can move to have the charges dismissed, which happens in a fair number of cases for a variety of reasons. The defendant may claim, for example, that the case should be dismissed because the statute of limitations for the crime in question has lapsed. Most frequently, however, the defendant pleads guilty to the charge or to a lesser charge that has been agreed on through **plea bargaining** between the prosecutor and defendant. If the defendant pleads guilty, no trial is necessary, and the defendant is sentenced based on the plea. If the defendant pleads not guilty, the case will go to trial.

Pretrial Motions

Defense attorneys and their paralegals will search for and be alert to any violation of the defendant's constitutional rights. Many pretrial motions are based on possible violations of the defendant's rights as provided by the Constitution and criminal procedural law. The motion to reduce the amount of bail, for example, which has already been discussed, is rooted in the Eighth Amendment's prohibition against excessive bail. A motion to dismiss the case (see Chapter 10) is usually based on an assertion that a constitutional right—or a criminal procedure stemming from that right—has been violated. For example, a motion to dismiss might assert that the evidence against the defendant was obtained illegally (without a search warrant, for instance, if in the circumstances a search warrant should have been obtained). Alternatively, the attorney may ask the paralegal to draft a **motion to suppress evidence**. Exhibit 12.8 on page 438 illustrates a motion to suppress evidence seized illegally (without a search warrant).

Other pretrial motions include a **motion challenging the sufficiency of the indictment** (claiming that there was insufficient evidence to establish probable cause), a motion *in limine* (to limit evidence that may be submitted—see Chapter 11), and a **motion for a change of venue** (to a more convenient venue, for example, or to ensure the defendant's right to a fair and impartial trial).

> ## ETHICAL CONCERN
> ### The Ethics of Plea Bargaining
>
> Paralegals who work on criminal cases may be ethically troubled by plea bargaining. In such situations, it may be helpful to view the issues in the larger context of the American justice system and American society. American courts are overburdened with cases, and it is in the public interest to reduce their caseloads. American jails are overcrowded, and reducing prison sentences is one way to deal with this issue. In the larger context, then, the ethical issue is whether you believe that it is fair to balance society's interest in obtaining strict justice against society's interest in lowering the social costs (more prisons, more courts, more judges, and so on) of that justice. Also, and more directly to the point, your job as a paralegal is to serve the client's best interests—and it may be in the client's best interests to plea bargain. In such a situation, you will need to set your personal feelings aside.

Various other motions—including motions to reduce the charges against the defendant, to obtain evidence (during discovery), or to extend the trial date—may also be made prior to the trial. As with motions made during the civil litigation process, each motion must be accompanied by supporting affidavits and/or legal memoranda.

Discovery

In preparing for trial, public prosecutors, defense attorneys, and paralegals engage in discovery proceedings (including depositions and interrogatories), interview and subpoena witnesses, prepare exhibits and a trial notebook, examine relevant documents and evidence, and do other tasks necessary to most effectively prosecute or defend the defendant. Although similar to civil litigation in these respects, criminal discovery is generally more limited, and the time constraints relating to discovery also are different in criminal cases.

During discovery, defendants are generally entitled to obtain any evidence in the possession of the prosecutor relating to the case, including statements previously made by the defendant, objects, documents, and reports of tests and examinations. Defendants are given this right to offset the fact that the prosecution (the state) has more resources at its disposal than the defendant (an individual citizen).

To obtain evidence from the prosecutor's office, the defense attorney asks his or her legal assistant to draft a **motion for discovery and inspection** similar to that shown in Exhibit 12.9 on page 440. The motion must be submitted to the court within a specified period of time (for a case being tried in a federal court, the motion must be submitted within ten days following the arraignment). The legal assistant will also draft an affidavit in support of the motion. The affidavit contains the sworn testimony of the defendant as to the defendant's knowledge of papers, documents, and other evidence in the possession of the prosecutor.

Motion for Discovery and Inspection
A motion requesting permission from the court to obtain evidence in the adversary's possession.

THE TRIAL

You have already seen that after arrest, in most cases, either (1) the suspect is released or the charges are dropped for lack of probable cause or some other

EXHIBIT 12.8
Motion to Suppress Evidence

> [*Title of Court and Cause*]
> MOTION TO SUPPRESS
>
> The Defendant, _____, by and through his/her attorney of record, moves this Court for an order pursuant to the Federal Rules of Criminal Procedure suppressing the use or any reference at any stage of the legal proceedings, to evidence taken from the person, property, or the premises of the Defendant, _____, under the following grounds.
>
> 1. The search and seizure were made without lawful authority or jurisdiction.
>
> 2. The arrest and detention was illegal, unconstitutional, and unreasonable, in that at the time the arrest was made, no offense was being committed in the officer's presence, the arrest was made without probable cause, the detention was without legal justification, and the arrest came after the search and seizure.
>
> 3. There were no circumstances justifying or authorizing the search and seizure.
>
> 4. The search and seizure were the fruits of a previous illegal, unconstitutional, and unreasonable search, arrest, detention, intrusion, and/or statement.
>
> 5. The search and seizure violated the defendant's rights granted him by the Fourth, Fifth, and Fourteenth Amendments of the United States Constitution.
>
> 6. Any statements given were given without legal counsel and without the defendant's waiver of his/her rights to counsel.
>
> 7. All such statements, whether oral or written, were obtained from defendant in violation of his/her rights under the Fifth, Sixth, and Fourteenth Amendments to the United States Constitution, and Article I, Sections 19, 18(a), and 10 of the Constitution.

reason, or (2) the suspect pleads guilty to the crime (or to a lesser crime as a result of plea bargaining) prior to trial, usually at the arraignment, in which case sentencing occurs and no trial takes place. As a result, only a small fraction of all criminal cases actually go to trial.

Very few misdemeanor cases go to trial, and when they do, the trials are usually quite short. Most criminal trials involve felonies. Although some criminal trials are spectacular trials that go on for weeks and become newsworthy, most are over very quickly, usually within two days.

There are many procedural similarities between a civil trial and a criminal trial. As in a civil trial, the prosecutor and the defendant's attorney make their opening statements to the court, examine and cross-examine witnesses, and summarize their positions in closing arguments. The jury is charged (instructed), and when the jury renders its verdict, the trial comes to an end. Despite these similarities, there are some significant procedural differences between civil and criminal litigation, including those discussed below.

EXHIBIT 12.8

Motion to Suppress Evidence—Continued

> 8. All such statements, whether oral or written, were made before the defendant was offered an opportunity to consult with counsel, without counsel present, and without warning to the defendant of his constitutional rights.
>
> 9. All such statements, whether oral or written, were involuntary in that defendant was induced and coerced to make such statements by threats, promises, and actions of the investigative officers.
>
> 10. All such statements, whether oral or written, were obtained in violation of defendant's rights under *Miranda v. Arizona,* 384 U.S. 436 (1966), in that defendant did not make a knowing, voluntary, and intelligent waiver of his/her *Miranda* rights because interrogating officers misrepresented the nature, character, and sufficiency of the evidence against him/her. See *Woods v. Clusen,* 794 F.2d 293, 296 (7th Cir. 1986).
>
> The items sought to be suppressed are as follows:
>
> a. Any and all clothes, baggage, papers, books, documents, records notes, correspondence, currency, financial statements, photographs, furnishings, narcotics, narcotics paraphernalia, or weapons seized during or in relation to a search and arrest that occurred on or about _____ , 20 ___ , at approximately _____ and _____ .
>
> b. Any and all pre- and postarrest statements made by the defendant in relation to the above-named incident.
>
> c. Any and all clothes, baggage, papers, books, documents, records, notes, correspondence, currency, financial statements, photographs, furnishings, narcotics, narcotics paraphernalia, or weapons seized during or in relation to a search and arrest that occurred on or about _____ 20 ___ , at or near _____ .
>
> d. Any and all pre- and postarrest statements made by the defendant in relation to the above-named incident.
>
> WHEREFORE, Defendant, _____ , moves this Court for an Order consistent with the relief requested herein.
>
> Respectfully submitted,
>
> _____

Special Features of Criminal Trials

As mentioned earlier, criminal procedures are designed to protect the individual from the state. Criminal trial procedures reflect this greater need for protection of the criminal defendant. Many of the significant rights of the criminal defendant, including his or her right to a "speedy and public trial" and the right to a jury trial, are spelled out in the Sixth Amendment. That amendment reads, in part, as follows:

> In all criminal prosecutions, the accused shall enjoy the right to a speedy and public trial, by an impartial jury of the State and district wherein the crime shall have

EXHIBIT 12.9
Motion for Discovery and Inspection

> [*Title of Court and Cause*]
>
> MOTION OF DEFENDANT FOR DISCOVERY AND INSPECTION
>
> The above-named defendant moves this Honorable Court, pursuant to the provisions of Rule 16(a), Title 18, United States Code, to permit the defendant to inspect and copy or photograph the following items:
>
> 1. All written or recorded statements made by the defendant, or copies thereof, within the possession, custody, or control of the government, the existence of which is known, or by the exercise of due diligence may become known, to the attorney for the government;
>
> 2. The substance of any oral statement which the government intends to offer in evidence at the trial made by the defendant whether before or after arrest in response to interrogation by any person then known to the defendant to be a government agent;
>
> 3. The recorded testimony of the defendant, if any, before a grand jury which relates to the offense charged herein;
>
> 4. The defendant's prior criminal record, if any, which is within the possession, custody, or control of the government, the existence of which is known, or by the exercise of due diligence may become known, to the attorney for the government;
>
> 5. All books, papers, documents, photographs, tangible objects, buildings or places, or copies or portions thereof, which are within the possession, custody, or control of the government, and which are material to the preparation of the defendant's defense, or are intended for use by the government as evidence in chief at the trial, or were obtained from or belong to the defendant;
>
> 6. The results or reports of physical or mental examinations, and of scientific tests or experiments, if any, or copies thereof, which are within the possession, custody, or control of the government, the existence of which are known, or by the exercise of due diligence may become known, to the attorney for the government, and which are material to the preparation of the defense or are intended for use by the government as evidence in chief at trial.
>
> Respectfully submitted,
>
> _____

been committed, . . . and to be informed of the nature and cause of the accusation; to be confronted with the witnesses against him; to have compulsory process for obtaining witnesses in his favor; and to have the Assistance of Counsel for his defence.

A "SPEEDY AND PUBLIC TRIAL." The right to a jury trial in civil cases is stated in the Seventh Amendment, but that amendment does not say anything about a

Developing Paralegal Skills

The Prosecutor's Office—Warrant Division

Kathy Perello works as a legal assistant in the warrant division of the county prosecutor's office. Officer Ryan McCarthy is at her door with a burglary report. The police have a suspect they want to arrest. Officer McCarthy presents the paperwork from the prosecutor that authorizes the arrest and requests that Kathy prepare an arrest warrant. Officer McCarthy will then take the warrant over to the court, swear to the truth of its contents, and ask the judge to sign the warrant so that McCarthy can make the arrest.

Checklist for Preparing a Warrant

- Obtain written authorization from a prosecutor before initiating the warrant procedure.
- Obtain a copy of the suspect's criminal history.
- Use the above to prepare the warrant.
- Verify that the criminal history matches the suspect.
- Make sure that the crime and the suspect are both specifically described.
- Review the typed warrant to ensure that any other required terms are contained in it.
- Call the officer to pick up the warrant and take it to a judge for a probable-cause determination.

"speedy and public" trial. In contrast, the Sixth Amendment requires a speedy and public trial for criminal prosecutions. The reason for this requirement is obvious—depending on the seriousness of the crime with which a defendant is charged, the defendant may lose his or her right to move freely (and may remain incarcerated prior to trial). Also, the accusation that a person has committed a crime jeopardizes that person's reputation in the community. If the defendant is innocent, the sooner the trial is held, the sooner the defendant can establish his or her innocence in the eyes of the court (and of the public).

The Sixth Amendment does not specify what is meant by the term *speedy*. Generally, in determining whether a defendant's right to a speedy trial has been violated, courts will examine several factors, including the reason for the delay and how the delay affects the defendant's position.

The criminal defendant's right to a *public* trial is an important constitutional protection. It helps to ensure that the prosecution of the defendant will be undertaken fairly and honestly.

THE ROLE OF THE JURY. In all felony cases, the defendant is entitled to a jury trial. In some states, juries may also be requested for misdemeanor cases. If the defendant waives his or her right to trial by jury, the waiver must be documented by a form such as that shown in Exhibit 12.10 on the next page or otherwise be made on the record in court. Of the criminal cases that go to trial, a majority are tried by a jury. If the right to a jury trial is waived, the case will be decided by the judge.

While the jury is traditionally composed of twelve persons, many states have reduced the size of juries to six persons for lesser offenses. In most jurisdictions, jury verdicts in criminal cases must be *unanimous* for **acquittal** or conviction. If the jury cannot obtain unanimous agreement on whether to acquit or convict the defendant, the result is a **hung jury**, and the judge may order a new trial.

THE PRESUMPTION OF A DEFENDANT'S INNOCENCE. A presumption in criminal law is that a defendant is innocent until proved guilty. The burden of proving

Acquittal
A certification or declaration following a trial that the individual accused of a crime is innocent, or free from guilt, in the eyes of the law and is thus absolved of the charges.

Hung Jury
A jury whose members are so irreconcilably divided in their opinions that they cannot reach a verdict. The judge in this situation may order a new trial.

EXHIBIT 12.10
Waiver of Trial by Jury

[*Title of Court and Cause*]

WAIVER OF JURY TRIAL

_____, this defendant herein having been furnished a copy of the _____ [*insert indictment and/or information*] and informed of his rights waives trial by jury and requests that he be tried by the court.

_____
Defendant.

The government consents.
_____,
United States Attorney.

Approved by the Court.

---

guilt falls on the state (the public prosecutor). Even if a defendant in fact committed the crime, he or she will be "innocent" in the eyes of the law unless the prosecutor can substantiate the charge with sufficient evidence to convince a jury (or judge in a nonjury trial) of the defendant's guilt.

A STRICT STANDARD OF PROOF. In a criminal trial, the defendant has no burden of proof. As mentioned, the burden of proving the defendant's guilt lies entirely with the state. In other words, it is up to the state to prove that the defendant committed the crime with which the defendant is charged. Furthermore, the state must prove the defendant's guilt **beyond a reasonable doubt**. The prosecution must show that, based on all the evidence, the defendant's guilt is clear and unquestionable. This strict standard of proof is higher than in civil proceedings, in which the case is usually decided on a preponderance of the evidence. A "preponderance of the evidence" means that the evidence offered in support of a certain claim outweighs the evidence offered to negate the claim.

Beyond a Reasonable Doubt
The standard used to determine the guilt or innocence of a person charged with a crime. To be guilty of a crime, a suspect must be proved guilty "beyond and to the exclusion of every reasonable doubt."

ETHICAL CONCERN
Preparing Exhibits for Trial

In preparing exhibits for trial, especially when creating an exhibit from raw data, it is important that the paralegal ensure that the exhibit is accurate and not misleading. An attorney has a duty not to falsify evidence, and if erroneous evidence is introduced in court and challenged by opposing counsel, your supervising attorney may face serious consequences. By preparing an inaccurate exhibit (for example, by miscalculating a column of figures), the paralegal may jeopardize the attorney's professional reputation by causing the attorney to breach a professional duty.

DEVELOPING PARALEGAL SKILLS
Discovery in the Criminal Case

The law firm of McCoy & Warner is defending Taylor Rogers in a case of attempted murder. Rogers allegedly shot a person in a drive-by shooting on the expressway. Lee Soloman, a paralegal, is working on the case. Today, as the result of a discovery motion that his supervising attorney won in court, Lee has received copies of all of the evidence that the prosecuting attorney has in his file. Lee's job is to create the discovery file and then to work with the material in the file to prepare the case.

Tips for Criminal Discovery

- Create a discovery file containing sections for the defendant's statements, witnesses' statements, police reports, tests, and other evidence.
- Review the evidence and prepare a memo summarizing it.
- Review the memo and/or evidence with your supervising attorney.
- If the supervising attorney agrees, contact witnesses and obtain statements.
- Interview the police officers who were involved in the arrest or who were at the crime scene.

The higher standard of proof in criminal cases reflects a fundamental social value—a belief that it is worse to convict an innocent individual than to let a guilty person go free. The consequences to the life, liberty, and reputation of an accused person from an erroneous conviction for a crime are usually more serious than the effects of an erroneous judgment in a civil case. Placing a high burden of proof on the prosecution reduces the margin of error in criminal cases.

THE PRIVILEGE AGAINST SELF-INCRIMINATION. The Fifth Amendment to the U.S. Constitution states that no person can be forced to give testimony that might be self-incriminating. Therefore, a defendant does not have to testify at trial. Witnesses may also refuse to testify on this ground. For example, if a witness, while testifying, is asked a question and answering the question would reveal his or her own criminal wrongdoing, the witness may "take the Fifth" and refuse to testify on the ground that the testimony may incriminate him or her.

RULES OF EVIDENCE. Courts have complex rules about what types of evidence may be presented and how the evidence may be brought out in criminal cases, especially in jury trials. These rules are designed to ensure that evidence presented to the judge and jury is relevant, reliable, and not unfairly prejudicial to the defendant. Often, one of the tasks of the defense attorney is to challenge evidence presented by the prosecution and the prosecution's witnesses to establish that the evidence is not reliable. Of course, the prosecutor also tries to demonstrate the irrelevance or unreliability of exhibits or testimony brought forward by the defense.

Rules of evidence will be discussed further in Chapter 13, which deals with legal investigation. Paralegals who undertake legal investigations must be especially careful to collect and preserve evidence properly. Otherwise, it may not be admissible in court.

On the Web
You can access the Federal Rules of Evidence online at www.law.cornell.edu/rules/fre/overview.html.

> ## ETHICAL CONCERN
> ### The Benefits of Good Record Keeping
>
> One of your jobs as a paralegal is to make sure that witnesses are in court at the proper time. This job relates to the attorney's duty of competence, which, if breached, could expose the attorney to potential liability for malpractice. For all your efforts, however, a key witness fails to appear in court. Your supervising attorney is understandably upset about this and asks you how this could have happened. You show the attorney the memorandum of your interview with the client, in which you noted that the witness was willing to testify; the receipt from the certified letter that you sent to the witness, which contained the subpoena, indicating that the witness had received it; and a telephone memo of a call that you made to the witness a week prior to the trial in which the witness agreed to be in court on the date of the trial. Although your documentation is not a cure for the problem presented by the missing witness, it does provide evidence—should it be necessary—that neither you nor the attorney was negligent.

Sentencing

Sentence
The punishment, or penalty, ordered by the court to be inflicted on a person convicted of a crime.

When a defendant is found guilty by a trial court (or pleads guilty to a crime and no trial takes place), the judge will pronounce a **sentence**, which is the penalty imposed on anyone convicted of a crime. Often, the sentence is pronounced in a separate proceeding at a later time.

According to the punishment prescribed by law for the crime involved, which frequently involves minimum and maximum penalties, the judge may sentence the defendant to one or more of the following:

- Incarceration in a jail (for less serious crimes involving short sentences) or imprisonment in a state or federal penitentiary (for serious crimes involving long sentences).
- Death (in some states).
- Probation, house arrest, or other form of supervised release.
- Financial penalties—including fines, restitution to victims, and payment of litigation costs.

On the Web
The U.S. Sentencing Guidelines can be found online at www.ussc.gov.

Although juries decide whether a criminal defendant is guilty or innocent and often make recommendations concerning sentencing, the judge has the final authority in regard to sentencing. In federal criminal cases, judges must follow mandatory sentencing guidelines that have been established by the U.S. government. The guidelines specify a range of penalties to be imposed for different types of crimes. The judge is free to select an appropriate penalty within the range, however, as long as it is at least the minimum mandatory sentence. In deciding which penalty should be imposed, a judge may be guided by his or her personal evaluation of the defendant's actions, by recommendations from the prosecuting attorney and other court aides, by recommendations from social service administrators, and by state laws.

TODAY'S PROFESSIONAL PARALEGAL

Working for the District Court

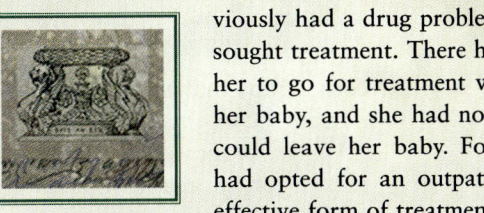

Amanda Bowin is a legal assistant who is assigned to work for six of the twelve judges who serve the district court. Today is "criminal call," and she is in the courtroom observing an arraignment. She has in front of her a docket sheet for the defendant. She listens while the judge explains the criminal charges. The defendant pleads not guilty, and the date for the pretrial hearing is set. (If the defendant had pled guilty, then a sentencing date and probation interview would have been scheduled.) Amanda notes the plea and the pretrial hearing date on the docket sheet. She then observes five more arraignments and notes the defendants' pleas on their respective docket sheets.

"Show Cause" Motions

Several attorneys enter the courtroom. They are present for "show cause" motions. A "show cause" motion is made when a defendant has violated the terms of his or her probation or sentence. The first motion is made by an assistant prosecutor against a defendant who was stopped on the highway for speeding and was found to be carrying a handgun. The judge evaluates the evidence and gives the defendant the option of either pleading guilty to the violation of probation or going to trial on the issue. The defendant chooses to plead guilty and is sentenced by the judge. Amanda notes all of the information on her docket sheet for this case. She listens to the remaining "show cause" motions and makes notes on the pleas and sentences.

Sentencing Hearings

Next, the sentencing hearings begin. Amanda listens and notes the sentences on the relevant docket sheets. The last item up this morning is the sentencing of a woman who has been convicted for criminal neglect—she had abandoned her two-year-old child at a gas station. The child has been placed in a foster home. The defense attorney is allowed to call a witness to testify as to the defendant's character and how well she cared for her daughter. This is an attempt to convince the judge to impose the lightest possible sentence allowable for this crime.

The attorney calls a social worker to the stand. The social worker testifies that the defendant-mother had previously had a drug problem for which she had sought treatment. There had been no place for her to go for treatment where she could take her baby, and she had no one with whom she could leave her baby. For those reasons, she had opted for an outpatient program, a less effective form of treatment. She had tried hard to fight her addiction to "crack" cocaine and had been doing well, but sometimes it takes more than one attempt at treatment to succeed. The social worker continues by telling the court that unfortunately, the defendant mother had strayed from her treatment and was under the influence of cocaine at the time that her friend talked her into abandoning her child.

The mother is very remorseful and regrets her actions. She truly loves her daughter and does not want to lose custody of her permanently. If the judge gives her a long jail sentence, she is afraid that she will ultimately lose custody of her child. After this testimony, the social worker steps down from the stand.

The judge considers the testimony. He knows that if he puts the defendant-mother in jail, she will not receive the treatment that she needs. This will not help either the defendant or her daughter. He sentences her to one year of drug rehabilitation in a live-in facility. This means that her child will remain in foster care for that time. The decision regarding her daughter's custody after that time will be left up to the agency that placed the daughter in the foster home. If the mother's treatment is successful, the agency might consider returning the child to the mother's custody. The defendant is to appear before the court every three months and give a progress report.

Criminal Call Ends

Amanda notes this sentence on her docket sheet. She leaves the courtroom now that the criminal call is over. She takes the files containing the docket sheets and her notes for the cases to the Records Department. There the information will be entered into the county's computer system to update the status of these cases.

On the Web

For an example of an appeal petition in an actual criminal case, go to www.courttv.com/trials/woodward/appeal.html.

Appeal

Persons convicted of crimes have a right of appeal. (The prosecution may appeal certain types of decisions, but it may not appeal a *not-guilty* verdict.) Most felony convictions are appealed to an intermediate court of appeal, although in some states there is no intermediate court of appeal, so the appeal goes directly to the state's highest appellate court, usually called the supreme court of the state. Most convictions that result in supervised release or fines are not appealed, but a high percentage of the convictions that result in prison sentences are appealed. About 10 to 20 percent of such convictions are reversed on appeal. The most common reason for reversal is that the trial court admitted improper evidence, such as evidence obtained by a search that did not meet constitutional requirements.

If a conviction is overturned on appeal, the defendant may or may not be tried again, depending on the reason for the reversal and on whether or not the case was reversed with or without prejudice. A decision reversed "with prejudice"

KEY TERMS AND CONCEPTS

acquittal 441
actus reus 417
arraignment 435
arrest 426
arrest warrant 429
bail 434
beyond a reasonable doubt 442
booking 430
citation 426
crime 415
defense of others 419
defense of property 419
diversion program 432
double jeopardy 422
due process of law 422

exclusionary rule 423
felony 416
grand jury 435
hung jury 441
indictment 435
information 434
magistrate 430
mens rea 418
Miranda rights 423
misdemeanor 416
motion challenging the sufficiency of the indictment 436
motion for a change of venue 436
motion for discovery and inspection 437

motion to reduce the amount of bail 434
motion to suppress evidence 436
nolo contendere 436
petty offense 417
plea bargaining 436
preliminary hearing 434
probable cause 426
public defender 415
public prosecutor 415
search warrant 429
self-defense 419
self-incrimination 423
sentence 444

CHAPTER SUMMARY

1. Crimes are defined as such by state legislatures or the federal government. A crime is distinguished from other types of wrongs, such as torts, by the fact that crimes are deemed to be offenses against society as a whole. Whereas tort litigation involves private parties suing each other, criminal litigation involves the state prosecuting a wrongdoer.

2. Crimes fall into two basic classifications—felonies and misdemeanors. Felonies are more serious crimes (such as murder, rape, and robbery) for which the penalty may include imprisonment for a year or longer or (in some states) death. Misdemeanors are less serious crimes (such as prostitution, disturbing the peace, and public intoxication) for which the penalty may include imprisonment for up to a year. A seemingly endless variety of acts have been defined as crimes by either state or federal statutes.

3. Two elements are required for criminal liability to exist: a wrongful act (*actus reus*) and a specified state of mind (*mens rea*). Criminal liability may be avoided if the state of mind required for the crime was lacking or some other defense against liability can be raised. Defenses against criminal liability include self-defense, defense of others, defense of property, the running of a statute of limitations, and others (procedural violations, alibi, and so on).

4. Because criminal law involves bringing the substantial resources of the state against an individual, specific procedures must be followed in arresting and prosecuting a criminal suspect to safeguard the suspect's constitutional rights. The U.S. Constitution guarantees that every person accused of a crime has specific rights, including the right to due process of law, the right to an attorney, the privilege against self-incrimination (the right to remain silent), and the right to a speedy trial. At the time of the arrest and taking into custody of a criminal suspect, the arresting officers must inform the suspect of his or her rights by reading the *Miranda* warnings. Any evidence or confession obtained in violation of the suspect's rights will normally not be admissible in court.

5. The initial procedures undertaken by the police after a crime is reported include arrest, booking, and investigation after arrest. Criminal litigation against a suspect begins when the prosecutor decides to prosecute the case and files a complaint. See Exhibit 12.2 for a graphical illustration and summary description of the major steps in the criminal justice process.

6. Prior to the trial, the defendant's attorney may file pretrial motions requesting the court to dismiss the case for various reasons. A pretrial motion may challenge the sufficiency of the evidence, may assert that certain key evidence was obtained illegally, or may argue that for some other reason the case should be dismissed.

7. Prior to the trial of a criminal case, discovery takes place. The defendant in a criminal case is entitled to obtain any evidence relating to the case possessed by the prosecution, including documents, statements previously made by the defendant, objects, reports of tests or examinations, and other evidence.

8. Most trials involving felonies are tried by a jury; most trials involving misdemeanors are decided in a bench trial (by the judge). Criminal trials differ from civil trials in a number of ways. Special features of criminal trials include the right to a speedy and public trial, unanimous agreement by the jury on the verdict, a presumption of the defendant's innocence, a higher standard of proof (the defendant must be found guilty "beyond a reasonable doubt"), the privilege against self-incrimination, and complex rules covering what types of evidence can be introduced at trial and how the evidence is introduced.

9. A defendant who has been found guilty is sentenced by the judge. The sentence may involve fines, imprisonment, or (in some states) death. Alternatively, the defendant may be sentenced to a diversion program, probation, or some other type of supervised release.

10. If the defendant loses at trial, he or she may appeal the case to a higher court. Only a minority of decisions are reversed on appeal, however.

QUESTIONS FOR REVIEW

1. How does a crime differ from a tort? What are the major classifications of crimes?

2. What elements are required for criminal liability? What defenses can be raised against criminal liability?

3. What are the constitutional rights of a person accused of a crime? Which constitutional amendments provide these rights?

4. What are the basic steps involved in criminal procedure from the time a crime is reported to the resolution of the case?

5. How is probable cause defined? Who determines whether probable cause exists?

6. What is the difference between an indictment and an information? When is each used?

7. What different pleas may a defendant enter during an arraignment? What is plea bargaining, and when does it typically occur?

8. When may a criminal suspect be released and the case dismissed prior to trial?

9. What pretrial motions may be filed in a criminal case?

10. What are the major procedural differences between civil litigation and criminal litigation? What are the reasons for these differences?

ETHICAL QUESTIONS

1. Linda Lore is an experienced paralegal who works for a criminal defense firm. The lawyers trust her implicitly and feel that she is as knowledgeable as they are. One Monday morning, John Dodds, an attorney with the firm, is scheduled to be in court for a motion and, at the same time, at a deposition. John calls Linda into his office and asks her to take the deposition. Should Linda take it? Why or why not?

2. Janice Henley is a legal assistant to a criminal defense attorney. They are defending a notorious drug dealer who was arrested in a huge drug bust. The drug bust was videotaped by the agents of the Drug Enforcement Administration who carried it out. The videotape is their best evidence against the client.

    In the hall outside the courtroom, Janice observes the girlfriend of the defendant approach the federal prosecutor and talk to him. He happens to be holding the videotape, along with some papers, in his hand. The girlfriend pulls what appears to be a large magnet from her oversized purse and leans toward the videotape. If the magnet makes contact with the tape, it will erase it. What should Janice do?

3. Larry Dow works as a paralegal for the criminal defense firm of Rice & Rowen. He and his boss have just met with Joe Dollan, an attorney from another well-known law firm. Joe has been arrested for embezzling (stealing) funds from an estate he was managing for a client and needs a criminal defense attorney to handle the case. Embezzlement is a felony, and if convicted, Joe will lose his license to practice law. Larry knows that a good friend of his recently retained Joe to handle the estate of her uncle. Should Larry tell his friend that Joe has been charged with embezzlement? Is there anything that Larry can do to help his friend?

4. Melinda Johns works as a legal assistant for the county prosecutor. She is working with Ms. Roberts, the victim of a robbery. They are preparing for trial. The prosecutor gives Ms. Roberts several options for proving the case and tells her to think about it overnight. The next morning, Ms. Roberts, still undecided, asks Melinda which strategy she should pursue. How should Melinda answer Ms. Roberts's question?

PRACTICE QUESTIONS AND ASSIGNMENTS

1. Using the material presented in the chapter, identify each of the following crimes by its classification:

    a. Jerry refuses to mow his lawn, and it grows to a height of seven inches. The local police department receives complaints from his neighbors and gives Jerry a citation for violating the local lawn-height ordinance.

    b. Nancy is arrested for being drunk in public. She faces a possible jail sentence of six months in prison.

    c. Susan is arrested for arson. The penalty includes a confinement for over one year in prison on conviction.

2. Review the material presented in this chapter on the *Miranda* rights. Summarize these rights. Now review Appendix J containing the Constitution and the Bill of Rights. From which amendment(s) are the *Miranda* rights derived?

3. Review the material presented in the chapter on the major procedural steps in a criminal case. Prepare a one-page summary of these steps. Identify which steps involve constitutional rights and the amendments on which these rights are based.

4. Using Exhibit 12.3, *An Arrest Warrant,* and the following information, draft an arrest warrant.

    Raymond Samuels, also known as Raymond Sams, of 1032 Whittier, Detroit, Michigan, employed by Bob's Supermarkets, is suspected of illegally acquiring and possessing food stamps in violation of Chapter 51, Title 7, of the United States Code. His Social Security number is 100-23-9876, and his birth date is June 17, 1948. Raymond is a white male, who is approximately 5'10" tall and who weighs two hundred pounds. He has brown hair, blue eyes, and a scar on his chin. He was investigated by the Detroit office of the Federal Bureau of Investigation (FBI), located at 1000 McNamara Building, 300 Second Street, Detroit MI 48226, file number 99-77863. Raymond Samuels owns a red 1989 Ford pickup truck.

5. Using Exhibit 12.4, *A Search Warrant*, the facts given in question 3 above, and the following information, draft a search warrant to search the home and person of Raymond Samuels for illegal food stamps.

   Raymond Samuels resides at 1032 Whittier, Detroit, MI 48228. The warrant in case number 99-123456 (FBI File number 99-77863) will be issued to the FBI, based on an affidavit provided by Officer James McCullough. The search warrant will be presented to the Federal District Court for the Eastern District of Michigan, located in Detroit, Michigan, before Magistrate Virginia M. Hacket. It is to be carried out within ten days from today's date, and the search may be made at any time, day or night.

6. A suspect is arrested, taken into custody, and interrogated at the police station. The police are determined to get him to confess to a murder. They confront him with an accomplice who accuses him of having committed the murder. The accused denies the allegation and says, "I didn't do it, you did." When the accused denies the murder, the police take him, handcuffed, into an interrogation room and question him for hours until he confesses. He is never told that he has the right to remain silent or to consult an attorney. Additionally, they refused him the right to talk to his attorney when he requested to do so during the interrogation, and they refused to allow his retained attorney to speak with him when his attorney arrived at the police station.

   Using the material presented in the chapter, analyze the facts of this situation and explain what rights the accused should have been accorded and why.

7. Using the material presented in the chapter on state of mind, identify the type of homicide committed in each of the following situations:

   a. David, while driving in an intoxicated state, crashes into another car and kills its occupants.

   b. David, after pulling up next to his wife at a stoplight and observing her passionately kissing another man, smashes into her car and kills his wife.

   c. David, who is angry with his boss for firing him, plans to kill his boss by smashing his car into his boss's car, killing his boss, and making it look like a car accident. David carries out his plan, kills his boss, and survives the accident.

8. Using the material presented in the chapter, discuss the following defenses:

   a. Mary is waiting for her bus to work at a dimly lit bus stop at 6:30 A.M. A man approaches her from behind and pulls out a gun, puts it to her head, and starts laughing, telling her there is one bullet in the barrel and that he is going to pull the trigger until it goes off. Mary pulls a gun out of her pocket, puts her hand behind her back, and shoots her assailant in the stomach, killing her assailant.

   b. Jennifer and Kathy are walking on a crowded downtown street. Suddenly, from behind, someone grabs Jennifer's purse. Kathy pulls a gun out of her pocket and shoots and kills the purse-snatcher.

   c. Joan is lying in bed at night, drifting off to sleep, when her bedroom window breaks. A man dressed in black with a stocking over his head jumps through it and attacks her. Joan, aware that a serial rapist has attacked several of her neighbors, pulls out a gun from under her mattress and shoots and kills her assailant.

   d. Jan arrives home from grocery shopping on a Tuesday morning at 10:00 A.M. and enters her house through the kitchen door. She hears a noise upstairs and goes to investigate. She finds a burglar loading her jewelry into a small felt bag. Jan pulls out a handgun and shoots and kills the burglar.

9. Using the material presented in the chapter, identify the following criminal procedures:

   a. Terrible Tom is charged with the crime of arson. He pleads not guilty and is bound over for trial in the district court.

   b. Naughty Ned is taken to the police station, searched, photographed, fingerprinted, and allowed to make one telephone call.

   c. A jury of Bad Barbara's peers reviews the evidence against her and determines whether probable cause exists and whether the prosecutor should proceed to trial for manslaughter.

   d. The police stop Larcenous Larry on the street when his description matches that of reported gas-station robber. He is three blocks from the gas station when they stop him. They question him, search him, and find that he has a pocketful of $20 and $50 dollar bills—the same denominations that were reported by the gas-station attendant as having been stolen. The police read Larcenous Larry his rights and take him into the station.

- e. Larcenous Larry is taken before a magistrate where the charges against him are read and counsel is appointed. His request to be set free on bail is denied.
- f. In exchange for a guilty plea to manslaughter, the prosecutor agrees to drop the more serious murder charges against Malicious Mary.

10. Using Exhibit 12.7 and the following information, draft a motion for an order directing the defendant to appear in your local district court for an arraignment.

Paul M. James, the U.S. attorney for your district, requests the defendant, Patrick C. Duffy, to appear for his arraignment on June 3, 1999, at 10:00 A.M., pursuant to a warrant issued on March 12, 1999, by Judge William T. Richardson of the federal district court in your district.

QUESTIONS FOR CRITICAL ANALYSIS

1. Crimes are classified into three categories: felonies, misdemeanors, and petty offenses. What is the difference between these classifications? What does the difference indicate about the reasons for such classifications?

2. When is a crime a federal crime? Why is there a difference between state and federal crimes? Should there be?

3. A guilty act is typically required in order for a crime to be committed. Is it ever possible for a crime to be committed without a guilty act? If so, how? Give an example of such a crime.

4. What role does the mental state of an accused play in the definition of a crime? How does the degree of wrongfulness affect the crime? What would be the result if intent were not considered? Would this be a fair outcome for the accused? For society?

5. Do cyber crimes need to include the elements of traditional crimes? Why or why not? Do the traditional elements of a crime assist or hamper the definition of cyber crimes? Why or why not?

6. Should people who are insane be convicted of crimes? If so, should they be convicted of all crimes or only certain types of crimes? What should the test be for determining if someone is insane? Should insane persons who are convicted of crimes be placed in a mental institution instead of a prison?

7. The statute of limitations is a defense to some crimes. Should it be allowed as a defense to crimes? What about the crime of murder?

8. Why do you think so many procedural safeguards were included in the Constitution for the protection of criminal defendants?

9. Look at the U.S. Constitution in Appendix J. Is there anything in the Bill of Rights that requires the police to give criminal suspects the *Miranda* warnings upon arrest?

10. The United States Supreme Court has eroded the *Miranda* rule in subsequent decisions that have recognized public-safety and routine booking exceptions to it. Additionally, juries are permitted to accept confessions without being convinced that they were voluntarily made. What does this say about the way in which the rule has been applied? What does this say about the way in which criminals' rights are enforced by the courts in general?

11. How is "probable cause" defined? What might be the historical reasons for this requirement?

12. Make a list of the differences between the requirements for a civiwl trial and for a criminal trial. What is the reason for these differences?

13. On conviction of a crime in federal court, the defendant is sentenced by a judge who applies the federal sentencing guidelines. These guidelines provide a range of penalties from which the judge may choose. Should the judge be able to choose a sentence, or should sentences be mandatory? Should the defendant be given the opportunity to present evidence to minimize his or her sentence?

14. In a recent case, Timothy McVeigh was sentenced to death for the bombing of a federal building in Oklahoma City, Oklahoma. Do you think that this was a fair penalty for the crime committed? Why or why not? He appealed his conviction and sentence to the United States Supreme Court, which ruled against him. What arguments might he have made in an attempt to persuade the Supreme Court to rule against the death penalty?

Projects

1. Call the state court in your city that handles pretrial criminal procedures, such as initial hearings, arraignments, and other procedures. Arrange to be in court when these matters are being heard.

2. Call the state court in your city that handles more serious crimes (for example, felonies and/or serious misdemeanors) and obtain a list of the criminal trials that are on the docket. Arrange to attend one of the trials for as long as possible. Observe how legal assistants are used by the trial attorneys.

3. Call the county prosecutor's office in your area and ask if it gives tours to students. If so, arrange to go on a tour of the prosecutor's office and try to learn how warrants are issued and how the prosecutor prepares for trial. Also observe how paralegals are utilized in the office.

4. Contact your local police department and ask if it gives tours to students. If so, arrange to take a tour of the department and learn, to the extent possible, what procedures are followed in regard to booking and investigation.

5. Call your local criminal court. Ask if they have copies of the state court's standard-form criminal arrest warrant and search warrant. Request a copy of each. Compare the state court forms to the standard federal court arrest-warrant and search-warrant forms contained in the chapter as Exhibits 12.3 and 12.4, respectively. Write a one-page paper summarizing the differences and similarities.

6. Review your state's court rules to see how the rules for criminal cases differ from those for civil cases. List and describe the major differences.

Using Internet Resources

1. Go to **tqd.advanced.org/2760/homep.htm.** This site, which has become well known primarily for its "Anatomy of a Murder," also provides a list of "Landmark Supreme Court Cases" in criminal law. Select "Rockin' Supreme Court Cases" to view a list of these cases. Select one of the cases, scan through it, and then answer the following questions:

   a. Who was the defendant, and with what crime or crimes was he or she charged?

   b. What defenses were raised by the defendant?

   c. What constitutional issue was involved?

   d. What was the Supreme Court's decision on the issue?

2. Go to the Web site of the Federal Bureau of Investigation (FBI) at **www.fbi.gov.**

   a. Click on "Your FBI." Next, click on "General Information" and then on "A Brief History of the FBI." Answer the following questions:

   - When was the FBI founded and by whom?
   - What was the agency's original name? When and how was it changed to the FBI?
   - Prior to 1920, what types of crimes did the FBI investigate? Were there many crimes to be investigated? Why or why not?
   - When did the FBI become a large agency? Why?

   b. Return to the FBI home page. Click on "Freedom of Information and Privacy Act." Answer the following questions:

   - When did the Freedom of Information Act (FOIA) first apply to FBI records? Why?
   - What is the FBI's procedure on receiving a FOIA request?
   - How many FOIA requests has the FBI handled since 1975? How many employees work in the FOIA section?

   c. Click the "Back" button to return to the "Freedom of Information Act Reading Room." Click on the "Electronic Reading Room." Answer the following questions:

   - What is required to view the cases contained in the Electronic Reading Room? Do you have this software available on your computer? How can you obtain it? If you are not using your own computer, check with a supervisor to make sure that you can load this software.
   - Scroll down to "Categories." Click on the "Alphabetical Listing of All Cases Presented on This Site." List the names of four famous celebrities (actors, singers, and so on) for whom the FBI has files. Why might the FBI have investigated these people?

CHAPTER 13

Conducting Interviews and Investigations

Chapter Outline
▣ Introduction ▣ Planning the Interview ▣ Interviewing Skills
▣ Interviewing Clients ▣ Interviewing Witnesses
▣ Planning and Conducting Investigations

After completing this chapter, you will know:

- How to prepare for an interview and the kinds of skills employed during the interviewing process.

- The common types of client interviews paralegals may conduct and the different types of witnesses paralegals may need to interview during a preliminary investigation.

- How to create an investigation plan.

- The variety of sources that you can use when trying to locate information or witnesses.

- Rules governing the types of evidence that are admissible in court.

- How to summarize your investigation results.

Introduction

Paralegals frequently interview clients. After the initial client interview (which is usually conducted by the supervising attorney), the paralegal may conduct one or more subsequent interviews to obtain detailed information from the client. How the paralegal relates to the client has an important effect on the client's attitude toward the firm and the attorney or legal team handling the case.

Additionally, paralegals often conduct pretrial investigations to learn as much as possible about the case. As part of a preliminary investigation into a client's claim, the paralegal may interview one or more witnesses to gain as much information as possible. The more factual evidence that can be gathered in support of a client's claim, the better the client's chances in court—or in any other dispute-settlement proceeding.

Learning how to conduct interviews and investigations is thus an important part of preparing for your career as a paralegal. In this chapter, you will read about the basic skills and concepts that you can apply when interviewing clients or witnesses, and when conducting investigations.

Planning the Interview

Planning an interview involves organizing many details. As a paralegal, you may be responsible for locating a witness, scheduling the interview, determining where the interview should take place, arranging for the use of one of the firm's conference rooms or other office space for the interview, and additional related details. Crucial to the success of any interview is how well you prepare for it.

Know What Information You Want to Obtain

Prior to any interview, you should have clearly in mind the kind of information you want to obtain from the client or witness being interviewed—the **interviewee**. You should know what questions you want to ask and have them prepared in advance. Advance preparation for an interview depends, of course, on the type of interview being conducted. In many situations, the paralegal (or the firm) will already have created specific preprinted or computerized forms indicating what kind of information should be gathered during client interviews relating to particular types of claims. Using preprinted forms ensures that all essential information will be obtained.

Interviewee
The person who is being interviewed.

If you are interviewing a client who is petitioning for bankruptcy, for example, you will need to obtain from the client the types of information that must be included on the bankruptcy forms to be submitted to the court. The bankruptcy forms will serve as a checklist for you to follow during the client interview. Similarly, if your firm frequently handles personal-injury cases, you will probably have available a preprinted or computerized personal-injury intake sheet, such as that shown in Exhibit 13.1 on the following two pages, to use as a guide when obtaining client information during the initial client interview.

Recording the Interview

Some interviewers tape-record their interviews. Before you tape-record an interview, you should always do the following:

 Obtain permission to tape-record the interview from both your supervising attorney and the person being interviewed.

EXHIBIT 13.1
Personal-Injury Intake Sheet

PERSONAL-INJURY INTAKE SHEET

Prepared for Clients of
Jeffers, Gilmore & Dunn

1. **Client Information:**

   Name: Katherine Baranski
   Address: 335 Natural Blvd.
   Nita City, NI   48802
   Social Security No.: 206-15-9858
   Marital Status: Married   Years Married: 3
   Spouse's Name: Peter Baranski
   Children: None

   Phone Numbers: Home (473) 555-2211   Work (473) 555-4849
   Employer: Nita State University
   Mathematics Department
   Position: Associate Professor of Mathematics
   Responsibilities: Teaching
   Salary: $ 46,000

2. **Related Information:**

   Client at Scene: Yes
   Lost Work Time: 5 months
   Client's Habits: Normally drives south on Mattis Avenue on way to university each morning at about the same time.

When you are using a tape recorder, you should state or include at the beginning of the tape the following identifying information:

- The name of the person being interviewed and any other relevant information about the interviewee.
- The name of the person conducting the interview.
- The names of other persons present at the interview, if any.
- The date, time, and place of the interview.
- On the record, the interviewee's consent to having the interview tape-recorded.

If more than one tape is used, you should indicate at the end of each tape that the interview will be continued on the next tape in the series, and each subsequent tape should contain identifying information.

EXHIBIT 13.1

Personal-Injury Intake Sheet—Continued

3. **Incident/Accident:**
   Date: August 4, 1998   Time: 7:45 A.M.
   Place: Mattis Avenue and 38th Street, Nita City, Nita

   Description: Mrs. Baranski was driving south on Mattis Avenue when a car driven by Tony Peretto, who was attempting to cross Mattis at 38th Street, collided with Mrs. Baranski's vehicle.

   Witnesses: None known by Mrs. Baranski
   Defendant: Tony Peretto
   Police: Nita City
   Action Taken: Mrs. Baranski was taken to City Hospital by ambulance (Nita City Ambulance Co.).

4. **Injuries Sustained:**
   Nature: Multiple fractures to left hip and leg; lacerations to left eye and left side of face; multiple contusions and abrasions

   Medical History: No significant medical problems prior to the accident

   Treating Hospital: Nita City Hospital
   Treating Physician: Dr. Swanson
   Hospital Stay: August 4, 1998   to November 20, 1998
   Insurance: Southwestern Insurance Co. of America
   Policy No: 00631150962-B

   Interview Conducted by:
   Allen P. Gilmore   January 30, 1999
   Attorney   Date
   Elena Lopez   January 30, 1999
   Paralegal/Witness   Date

There are several advantages to tape-recording an interview. For one thing, having a record of the interview on tape reduces the need to take extensive notes during the interview. You can either have the tape transcribed for future reference, or you can listen to the tape later (when creating an interview summary, for example—discussed later) to refresh your memory of how the interviewee responded to certain questions. You may also want to have other members of the legal team read the transcript or listen to the tape. Sometimes, what might not have seemed significant to you may seem significant to someone else working on the case. Also, as a case progresses, a remark made by the interviewee that did not seem important at the time of the interview may take on added importance in view of evidence gathered after the interview was held.

Developing Paralegal Skills

The Tape-Recorded Interview

Justin Hooper is preparing for an interview that will be tape-recorded. He takes the tape recorder to the conference room where the interview will take place and sets up the tape recorder. The witness arrives and is shown into the conference room by the receptionist. Justin takes a prepared statement from a file folder containing the introductory remarks used in a tape-recorded interview. He reads it into the tape recorder:

"My name is Justin Hooper. I am a paralegal at the law firm of Smith & Howard. The firm is representing Mr. Barry Buckner, the defendant in *Jones v. Buckner*. This tape-recorded interview is taking place in the law offices of Smith & Howard on January 6, 1999. The time is two o'clock P.M."

Justin then turns to the witness and asks the witness to state and spell her name into the tape recorder. Justin also asks the witness for her consent to have the interview tape-recorded, so that the witness's consent will be on record. Then the interview begins.

Tips for Conducting a Tape-Recorded Interview

- Test the tape-recorder before the interview to ensure that it is working properly.
- Create a prepared introductory statement that gives the name of the interviewer; the date, time, and location of the interview; the case name; and other relevant information.
- Ask the witness to state and spell his or her name into the tape recorder.
- Ask the witness for permission to tape-record the interview—be certain the witness's answer is tape-recorded.
- Ask all others present during the interview to state and spell their names.
- Have additional tapes available, and immediately label additional tapes as they are used.
- If more than one tape is used, be certain to state on each tape which number the tape is and state how many tapes were used.

There are also some disadvantages to tape-recording interviews. A major disadvantage is that some clients and witnesses may be uncomfortable and less willing to disclose information freely if they know everything they are saying is being recorded. Such reluctance is understandable in view of the fact that the interviewee cannot know in advance what exactly will transpire during the course of the interview or how the tape may later be used. When asking an interviewee for his or her permission to tape-record an interview, you should therefore evaluate carefully how the interviewee responds to this question. Depending on the interviewee's response, you might consider taking notes instead of tape-recording the session.

Interviewing Skills

Interviewing skills are essentially any skills—particularly interpersonal and communication skills—that help you to conduct a successful interview. In this section, you will learn how the use of interpersonal and communication skills can help you establish a comfortable relationship with the interviewee. Then, you will read about specific questioning and listening techniques that can help you control the interview and elicit various types of information.

Interpersonal Skills

At the outset of any interview, remember that your primary goal is to obtain information from the client or witness being interviewed. Although some people communicate information and ideas readily and effectively, others may need considerable coaching and encouragement. If they feel comfortable in your presence and in the interviewing environment, they will generally be more willing to disclose information.

As you begin an interview, you should remember that the interviewee may be very nervous or at least uncomfortable. Because the time you have to talk with a client or witness will be limited, you should put that individual at ease as quickly as possible. A minute or two spent chatting casually with the client or witness is time well spent. Also, saying or doing something that shows your concern for the interviewee's physical comfort helps to make the interviewee feel more relaxed. For example, you might offer the individual a cup of coffee or other beverage.

Using language that the interviewee will understand is essential in establishing a good working relationship with that person. If you are interviewing a client with only a grade school education, for example, do not use the phrase "facial lacerations" when talking about "cuts on the face." If you are interviewing a witness who does not speak English very well, arrange to have an interpreter present unless you are fluent in the witness's native language. Because most clients and witnesses are not familiar with legal terminology, you should always abide by the following rule of thumb when conducting interviews:

 Avoid using legal terms that will not be clearly understood by the interviewee.

If you must use a specific legal term to express an idea, be sure that you define the term and that it is clearly understood.

Questioning Skills

When questioning witnesses or clients, you should remember to remain objective at all times and gather as much relevant factual information as possible. Sometimes, you may have difficulty remaining objective when questioning witnesses because you sympathize with the client and may not want to hear about facts that are contrary to the client's position. But relevant factual information includes those details that adversely affect the client's case as well as those that support his or her position. Indeed, your supervising attorney must know *all* of the facts, especially any that might damage the client's case in court.

The experienced legal interviewer uses certain questioning techniques to prompt interviewees to communicate the information needed. There are several types of questions, including open-ended, closed-ended, hypothetical, pressure, and leading questions.

OPEN-ENDED QUESTIONS. The **open-ended question** is a broad, exploratory question that invites any number of possible responses. The open-ended question can be used when you want to give the interviewee an opportunity to talk at some length about a given subject. "What happened on the night of October 28—the night of the murder?" is an open-ended question. Other examples of open-ended questions are "And what happened next?" and "What did you see as you approached the intersection?" When you ask a question of this kind, be prepared

Open-Ended Question
A question that is phrased in such a way that it elicits a relatively detailed discussion of an experience or event.

for a lengthy response. If a witness has difficulty narrating the events he or she observed or if a lull develops during the explanation, you will need to encourage the witness to continue through the use of various prompting responses (which will be discussed shortly in the context of listening skills).

Open-ended questions are useful in interviewing clients or friendly witnesses (witnesses who favor the client's position). This is because these kinds of interviewees are usually forthcoming, and you will be able to gain information from them by indicating in broad terms what you want them to describe.

Closed-Ended Question
A question that is phrased in such a way that it elicits a simple "yes" or "no" answer.

CLOSED-ENDED QUESTIONS. The **closed-ended question,** in contrast, is intended to elicit a "yes" or "no" response from the interviewee. "Did you see the murder weapon?" is an example of a closed-ended question. Although closed-ended questions tend to curb communication, they are useful in some situations. For example, if an interviewee tends to digress frequently from the topic being discussed, using closed-ended questions can help keep him or her on track. Closed-ended questions, because they invite specific answers, also may be useful in relaxing the interviewee in preparation for more difficult questions that may follow later in the interview. In addition, closed-ended questions may help to elicit information from adverse witnesses (those who are not favorable to the client's position) who may be reluctant to volunteer information.

Hypothetical Question
A question based on hypothesis, conjecture, or fiction.

HYPOTHETICAL QUESTIONS. As a paralegal, you may be asked to interview an expert witness either to gather information about a case or to evaluate whether that person would be an effective expert witness at trial (expert witnesses will be discussed later in this chapter). The **hypothetical question** is frequently used with expert witnesses. Hypothetical questions allow you to obtain an answer to an important question without giving away the facts (and confidences) of a client's case. For example, you might invent a hypothetical situation involving a certain type of knee injury (the same kind of injury as that sustained by a client) and then ask an orthopedic surgeon what kind of follow-up care would ordinarily be undertaken for that type of injury.

Pressure Question
A question intended to make the interviewee feel uncomfortable and respond emotionally. Pressure questions are sometimes used by interviewers to elicit answers from interviewees who may otherwise be unresponsive.

PRESSURE QUESTIONS. Sometimes interviewers use a type of question known as a pressure question. **Pressure questions** are intended to make the interviewee feel uncomfortable and to induce him or her to respond emotionally. The pressure question may be useful in eliciting a response from an interviewee who is reluctant to discuss a matter with you. If an eyewitness, for example, refuses to state whether he or she saw the murderer, an interviewer might pressure him or her into responding by asking a question such as the following: "The murder weapon—a heavy board—was found a mile from the victim's body. Did you know that the board was traced to the construction site right next door to your store?"

Note that pressure questions should be used only as a last resort, and then used very carefully. As an interviewer, you want to enlist the interviewee's cooperation, not alienate him or her.

Leading Question
A question that suggests, or "leads to," a desired answer. Interviewers may use leading questions to elicit responses from witnesses who otherwise would not be forthcoming.

LEADING QUESTIONS. The **leading question** is one that suggests to the listener the answer to the question. "Isn't it true that you were only ten feet away from where the murder took place?" is a leading question. This question, of course, invites a "yes" answer. Leading questions are very effective for drawing information out of eyewitnesses or clients, particularly when they are reluctant to disclose information. They are also useful when interviewing adverse witnesses who are hesitant to communicate information that may be helpful to the client's

Q. You were drinking beer in the parking lot during lunch and then got behind the wheel to drive anyway, didn't you?	**EXHIBIT 13.2** Leading Questions
A. Yes.	
Q. You saw the driver of the green van run the stop sign, right?	
A. Yes.	
Q. Isn't it true that you were so intoxicated at the time of the accident that you can't remember what happened?	
A. Yes.	

position. When used with clients and friendly witnesses, however, leading questions have a major drawback:

 Leading questions may lead to distorted answers because the client or witness may tailor the answer to fit his or her perception of what the interviewer wants to know.

For this reason, in the interviewing context, leading questions should be used cautiously and only when the interviewer is fully aware of the possible distortions that might result. For other examples of leading questions, see Exhibit 13.2 above.

Listening Skills

The interviewer's ability to listen is perhaps the most important communication skill used during the interviewing process. Whenever you conduct an interview, you will want to absorb fully the interviewee's verbal answers, as well as his or her nonverbal messages. Prior to the interview, you should make sure that the room in which it is to be held will be free of noises, phone calls, visitors, and other interruptions or distractions. During the interview itself, you can use several listening techniques to maximize communication and guide the interviewee toward the fullest disclosure of needed information.

For communication to be truly an interactive process, the listener must engage in active listening. **Active listening** requires the listener to pay close attention to what the speaker is saying. Active listening is critical to a productive interview. A paralegal's lack of attention during the interview may mean important details could be missed, and ultimately, the client could suffer.

Active Listening
The act of listening attentively to the speaker's verbal or nonverbal messages and responding to those messages by giving appropriate feedback.

 If you ever find your attention wandering during an interview, have the interviewee repeat what he or she just said to make sure that you have not missed anything.

You do not have to admit that your attention was wandering, of course. Simply say that you want to make sure that your impression of what the interviewee said is accurate.

Active listening also involves feedback. As a listener, you can give feedback, in the form of both verbal and nonverbal cues, to encourage the speaker to continue discussing a topic. An example of a verbal cue is "I'm listening, please go on" or "And then what happened?" Verbal feedback can also be given by simply murmuring an "uh huh" or a "hmm" here and there to let the speaker know you are attentive. A nonverbal cue can be any facial expression or body language that shows you are interested in what is being said. Nodding positively, for example, is an effective way to convey, nonverbally, your interest. Maintaining eye contact is another nonverbal cue to indicate your interest in what is being said.

Finally, active listening involves the ability to analyze on the spot the interviewee's comments in the context of the larger picture. Often, something that the interviewee says opens a door to another area that should be explored. When this happens, you need to decide whether to explore that area now or later (perhaps at a subsequent interview).

 In general, you need to be constantly analyzing your interviewee's responses and deciding how those responses should direct your further questioning.

INTERVIEWING CLIENTS

Typically, the paralegal interviews either clients or witnesses. Here we look at client interviews. (We will discuss witness interviews shortly.) The various types of client interviews include the initial client interview, subsequent client interviews to obtain further information, and informational interviews, or meetings, to inform the client of the status of his or her case and to prepare the client for trial or other legal proceedings. We look next at each of these types of interviews.

The Initial Client Interview

As discussed in Chapter 4, when a client seeks legal advice from an attorney, the attorney normally holds an initial interview with the client. During this interview, the client explains his or her legal problem so that the attorney can advise the client on possible legal options and the legal fees that may be involved. Either then or at a later time, the client and the attorney will agree on the terms of the representation, if the attorney decides to take the case.

Paralegals often attend initial client interviews. Although the attorney normally conducts this first interview, the paralegal plays an important role. Usually, you will observe the client, take notes on what the client is saying, and provide the client with forms, statements explaining the firm's fees, and other prepared information normally given to new clients. Following the interview, you and the attorney may compare your impressions of the client and of what the client said during the interview.

All of the people present at the interview should be introduced to the client, their titles given, and the reason for their presence at the interview made known to the client. In introducing you, the paralegal, to the potential client, the attorney will probably stress that you are not a lawyer.

 If your supervising attorney does not indicate your nonattorney status to the client, you must do so.

If a firm decides to take a client's case, the client should be introduced to every member of the legal team who will be working on the case.

A follow-up letter, such as the one shown in Exhibit 13.3, will be sent to the client after the interview. The letter will state whether or not the attorney has decided to accept the case or, if the attorney orally agreed during the initial client interview to represent the client, will confirm the oral agreement in writing.

Subsequent Client Interviews

Paralegals are often asked to conduct additional interviews with clients whose cases have been accepted. For example, assume that a client wants to obtain a

EXHIBIT 13.3
A Sample Follow-Up Letter to a Client

Jeffers, Gilmore & Dunn
553 Fifth Avenue
Suite 101
Nita City, NI 48801

Telephone: (616) 555-9690
Fax: (616) 555-9679
e-mail: jgd@nitanet.net

February 2, 1999

Ms. Katherine Baranski
335 Natural Boulevard
Nita City, Nita 48802

Dear Ms. Baranski:

It was a pleasure to meet and talk with you on January 30. Jeffers, Gilmore & Dunn will be pleased to act as your representative in your action against Tony Peretto to obtain compensation for your injuries.

I am enclosing a fee agreement for your review. If you wish this firm to act as your legal counsel, please sign and date the agreement and return it to me as soon as possible. A self-addressed, stamped enveloped is enclosed for your convenience. As soon as I receive the completed agreement, we will begin investigating your case.

As I advised during our meeting, to protect your rights, please refrain from speaking with the driver of the vehicle, his lawyer, or his insurance company. If they attempt to contact you, simply tell them that you have retained counsel and refer them directly to me. I will handle any questions that they may have.

If you have any questions, please do not hesitate to call me or my paralegal, Ms. Elena Lopez.

Sincerely,

Allen P. Gilmore
Allen P. Gilmore
Attorney at Law

APG/db

Encs.

---

divorce. After the initial interview, your supervising attorney may ask you to arrange for a subsequent interview with the client to obtain all the information necessary to prepare the divorce pleadings. When scheduling the interview, you should tell the client what kinds of documents or other data he or she should bring to the interview. During the interview, you will fill out the form that the firm uses to record client information in divorce cases. Paralegals often assume responsibility for gathering most of the information needed to file for a divorce or to begin child-custody proceedings.

When conducting a client interview, the paralegal should always disclose his or her nonlawyer status if this fact was not made clear at an earlier session. Remember, even if you had been introduced to the client as a "legal assistant," the client may not realize that a legal assistant is not an attorney. To protect yourself against potential claims that you have engaged in the unauthorized practice of law, you should clearly state to the client that you are "not an attorney."

FEATURED GUEST: ANNA DURHAM BOLING
Ten Tips for More Effective Interviewing

BIOGRAPHICAL NOTE

Anna Durham Boling graduated from the University of Georgia School of Law in 1984 and is licensed to practice law in the state of Georgia. Following graduation from law school, Boling practiced real-estate law for four years. She then accepted a position as an instructor in the paralegal studies program at Athens Area Technical Institute in Athens, Georgia. She was named director of the program in July 1989. Under her direction, the program was approved by the American Bar Association in February 1992. Boling currently works for the Institute of Government at the University of Georgia.

Interviewing clients and witnesses is a learned skill. Interviewers, whether they are lawyers, legal assistants, or others, become more effective over time as they acquire more interviewing experience. There are many interviewing "tips" that can enhance the abilities of even the novice interviewer, however. The following suggestions are ones I have found to be particularly helpful. As you develop your interviewing skills, you may find that the tips that serve you best are the ones you develop yourself. In the meantime, you can learn from the experiences of others.

1. **Verify Information.** When interviewing clients and witnesses, realize that every bit of information obtained must be verified. I do not mean to suggest that all clients or all witnesses lie (although, unfortunately, some do). On the contrary, each individual client or witness will describe his or her perception of what happened, and you will find that no two people ever perceive the same factual occurrence in exactly the same way. A good method to verify information is therefore to interview several people about the event or issue under investigation. Another way to verify information is to use additional sources, such as documentary evidence.

2. **Let the Interviewee Vent His or Her Emotions.** Sometimes, clients or witnesses come to interviews with heightened emotions regarding the matters about which they are to be questioned. In such situations, they may need an opportunity to vent their feelings before they can relax enough to discuss a subject that is painful or bothersome to them. When this happens, it is often helpful to put the time clock aside and interact with the interviewee on a personal level. Showing compassion for the interviewee's emotional needs will help you establish a rapport with that person, which will enhance the possibility of effective communication.

3. **Keep an Open Mind.** Be careful not to categorize a client's problem. Both the interviewer and the person being interviewed can fall prey to this trap, particularly during the initial interview. For example, a client in financial distress might say that he wants to declare bankruptcy. All he knows is that his financial situation is worsening and that he wants to obtain some relief. He thinks that bankruptcy is the only answer, but there may be other answers to the client's dilemma, and other legal issues may be involved. Explore the client's entire situation. In this example, find out what caused the financial distress so that you can better understand the client's specific circumstances. In this way, the legal team will be better able to offer the best and most complete service possible.

4. **Listen Carefully.** Listen carefully to the person being interviewed. Do not make assumptions about the inter-

The Informational Interview

The informational interview, or meeting, is an interview in which the client is brought in to discuss upcoming legal proceedings. Most clients know very little about the procedures involved in litigation, and firms often have their paralegals

FEATURED GUEST, Continued

viewee or anticipate a particular answer before asking the question. An interviewer taking this approach may miss important or even critical information. Learn to listen to the interviewee's answers and "digest" the information objectively—without letting any assumptions interfere with the listening process. In this way, you may discern valuable pieces of information that could significantly affect the outcome of the case.

5. **Record Information.** Write down everything that is learned in the course of an interview. Recording the information on paper, on a computer, or with a tape recorder is especially important for the beginner because of the level of detail that must be reported. You may think, "I could never forget that piece of information." But in a busy practice full of distractions, you may have forgotten that information by the end of the interview.

6. **Engage in Interactive Communication.** Interviewing should be interactive. It should involve a meaningful exchange between the interviewer and the interviewee. When listening to the answers to your questions, ask yourself, "In light of this response, what else would I like to know?" By posing this question to yourself, you will be able to carry each line of questioning to its logical extreme and, in doing so, arrive at the most complete picture possible.

7. **Be Prepared for the Interview.** Be thoroughly prepared for your interview. Preparation is particularly important for the inexperienced interviewer. Reviewing closed files in your law firm that are similar to the case at hand is often very helpful. Determine what information in those files is significant. Notice which questions recur from file to file. This will enable you to construct a line of questioning that will elicit the desired information. Interview preparation is time consuming, but the benefits can be enormous. As your interviewing skills develop, the preparation time for subsequent interviews will decrease significantly.

8. **Learn the Chronology of the Factual Circumstances.** If possible, have the person being interviewed relate what he or she knows about the subject matter of your investigation in the order in which the events occurred. If the interviewee can relay his or her story in this manner, then the risk of omitting important facts is lessened substantially. Encourage your interviewee to supply as complete a description as possible and to avoid omitting any details. Although this request may elicit some useless information, it is better to have too much, rather than too little, information. You will be able to weed out unimportant or irrelevant information after the interview.

"Interviewing clients and witnesses is a learned skill."

9. **Remain Objective.** It is important to have an objective understanding of the client's problem. When assisting in the representation of a client, it is quite natural to feel sympathy for that person, particularly if he or she has suffered a substantial hardship. But too much sympathy may prevent you from objectively evaluating the factual circumstances of the client's case. Remember that your supervising attorney will be in a better position to defend the client's interests if the attorney is aware of all information relating to the case, including information that appears to be unfavorable to the client.

10. **Evaluate the Results.** Just as it is important to prepare for interviews, it is important to review your work once the case has been resolved. In retrospect, you can determine whether any information that turned out to be important to the case was missed and if so, how or why it was missed. You can also learn how important information was successfully obtained. This evaluation exercise will enhance your effectiveness as an interviewer and help you prepare for interviews in future cases.

explain these procedures to clients and prepare clients for the trial experience. For example, the paralegal can describe to clients what will take place during the trial, how to groom themselves appropriately for trial, where to look when they testify, and so on. The informational interview helps the client understand why certain proceedings are taking place and his or her role in those proceedings.

ETHICAL CONCERN
Handling Client Documents

Clients frequently give paralegals important documents relating to their cases during interviews. State codes of ethics impose strict requirements on attorneys in regard to the safekeeping of clients' funds and other property, including documents. Suppose, for example, that a client gives you the only copy she has of her divorce agreement. You should never rely on memory when it comes to client documents. Instead, immediately after the conclusion of the interview, you should record the receipt of any documents or other items received from the client. The information may be recorded in an evidence log (discussed later in this chapter) or in some other way, depending on the procedures established by your firm to govern the receipt and storage of such property. An evidence log or other method of recording documents and items received from clients provides you with evidence—should it be necessary—of what you did (or did not) receive from a client.

Summarizing the Interview

The interviewing process does not end with the close of the interview. A final and crucial step in the process involves summarizing the results of the interview for the legal team working on the case. As a paralegal, you will create an intake memorandum following each initial client interview. If the firm has a prepared intake form for particular types of cases, such as the personal-injury intake sheet referred to earlier and illustrated in Exhibit 13.1, the completed form might constitute the interview summary. Information obtained during any subsequent interviews with a client should be analyzed and summarized in a memo for your supervising attorney or other team members to review and for later inclusion in the client's file.

Your interview summary should be created immediately after the interview, while the session is still fresh in your mind. When summarizing the results of a client interview, you should carefully review your notes and, if the session was tape-recorded, review the tape. You should never rely totally on your memory of the statements made during the interview. It is very easy to forget the client's specific words, and it may be very important later to know exactly how the client phrased a certain comment or response. Relying on memory is also risky because, as mentioned earlier, sometimes a statement that seemed irrelevant at the time of the interview may turn out to be very important to the case. You should thus make sure that the facts are accurately recorded and are as reliable as possible.

On the Web
You can find databases containing numerous expert witnesses at various Web sites, including www.experts.com, www.hg.org/expert-serv.html, and www.claims.com.

INTERVIEWING WITNESSES

Witnesses play a key role in establishing the facts of an event. As a legal investigator, your goal is to elicit as much relevant and reliable information as possible from each witness about the event that you are investigating. Interviewing witnesses is in many ways similar to interviewing clients, and many of the interviewing skills, such as listening skills, that we have already discussed apply to interviews of witnesses. A major difference between clients and witnesses, however, is that the latter may not always be friendly to the client's position. Here we

ETHICAL CONCERN
The Unauthorized Practice of Law

Paralegals must be especially careful not to give legal advice when interviewing clients. Suppose that you are conducting a follow-up interview of a client, Sue Collins. Collins was injured in a car accident and is suing the driver of the other car involved for negligence. During the initial client interview, Collins told you and your supervising attorney that the accident was totally the result of the other driver's negligence. During the course of your follow-up interview, however, Collins presents you with an interesting hypothetical. She says to you, "What would happen, in a lawsuit such as mine, if the plaintiff was not watching the road when the accident occurred? What if the plaintiff was looking in the back seat to see why her baby was crying? Could the plaintiff still expect to win in court?" You know that under the laws of your state, contributory negligence on the part of the plaintiff (discussed in Chapter 7) is an absolute bar to the recovery of damages. Should you explain this to Collins? No. Even though the question is phrased as a hypothetical, it is possible that your answer could affect Collins's future actions. Your best option is to tell Collins that you are not permitted to give legal advice but that you will relay the "hypothetical" question to your supervising attorney.

---

describe the various types of witnesses as well as some basic skills and principles that are particularly relevant to investigative interviews.

Types of Witnesses

Witnesses include expert witnesses, lay witnesses, and eyewitnesses. Witnesses are also sometimes classified as friendly witnesses or hostile (or adverse) witnesses.

EXPERT WITNESSES. An **expert witness** is an individual who has professional training, advanced knowledge, or substantial experience in a specialized area, such as medicine, computer technology, ballistics, or construction techniques. Paralegals often arrange to hire expert witnesses either to testify in court or to render an opinion on some matter relating to the client's case. Expert witnesses are often used in cases involving medical malpractice and product liability to establish the duty, or standard of care, that the defendant owed to the plaintiff. For example, if a client of your firm is suing a physician for malpractice, your supervising attorney might arrange to have another physician testify as to the standard of care owed by a physician to a patient in similar circumstances.

> **Expert Witness**
> A witness with professional training or substantial experience qualifying him or her to testify on a particular subject.

LAY WITNESSES. Most witnesses in court are lay witnesses. In contrast to expert witnesses, **lay witnesses** do not possess any particular skill or expertise relating to the matter before the court. They are people who happened to observe or otherwise have factual knowledge about an event. A professional or expert in one field may be a lay witness in regard to another field about which he or she does not have expert knowledge. A physician involved in a fraud claim, for example, might give testimony about the fraud as a lay witness but not as an expert witness.

> **Lay Witness**
> A witness who can truthfully and accurately testify on a fact in question without having specialized training or knowledge; an ordinary witness.

EYEWITNESSES. In attempting to gain more information about an event relating to a client's legal claim, paralegals may be required to interview eyewitnesses.

> # ETHICAL CONCERN
> ## Keeping the Client Informed
>
> Attorneys have a duty to keep their clients reasonably informed about their cases or claims. As a paralegal, you should assume the responsibility for making sure that the attorney does not breach this duty. Periodic notes or phone calls to the client not only keep the client informed about progress on the case but also keep you in touch with the case status—and you and your supervising attorney will be less likely to miss important deadlines relating to the litigation. Frequent communications with clients also cultivate goodwill. Clients generally welcome any news from their attorneys' offices. Even a letter saying "nothing is happening" is usually appreciated. To make sure that the client is kept informed, you will want to have some kind of a tickler system to remind you to contact the client at periodic intervals.

Eyewitness
A witness who testifies about an event that he or she observed or has experienced firsthand.

Eyewitnesses are lay witnesses who have witnessed an event and who may testify in court as to what they observed. The term *eyewitness* is deceiving, and perhaps a better term might be "sense" witness. This is because an eyewitness may have firsthand knowledge of an event, but this knowledge need not have been derived from the sense of sight—that is, from actually seeing the event. An eyewitness may be someone who listened in on a telephone conversation between an accused murderer and his or her accomplice. A blind man may have been an eyewitness to a car crash, because he heard it.

In interviews, eyewitnesses are ordinarily asked to describe an event, in their own words and as they recall it, that relates to the client's case. Eyewitness accounts may be lengthy, and the paralegal may want to tape-record the interview session to ensure accuracy. The experienced paralegal may also find that different eyewitnesses to the same event have contradictory views on what actually took place. People's perceptions of reality differ, as paralegals often find when comparing eyewitness reports.

Friendly Witness
A witness who gives voluntary testimony at an attorney's request on behalf of the attorney's client; a witness who is prejudiced against the client's adversary.

FRIENDLY WITNESSES. Some witnesses to an event may be the client's family, friends, co-workers, neighbors, or other persons who know the client and who want to be helpful in volunteering information. These witnesses are regarded as **friendly witnesses.** You may think that friendly witnesses are the best kind to interview, and they often are. They may also be biased in the client's favor, however, so the paralegal should look closely for the actual facts (and not the witness's interpretation of the facts) when interviewing friendly witnesses.

Hostile Witness
A witness for the opposing side in a lawsuit or other legal proceeding; an adverse witness.

HOSTILE WITNESSES. Witnesses who may be prejudiced against your client or friendly to your client's adversary are regarded as **hostile witnesses** (or *adverse witnesses*). Interviewing hostile witnesses can be challenging. Sometimes the witness has an interest in the outcome of the case and would be in a better position if your client lost in court. For example, if the client is a tenant who refuses to pay rent until the landlord makes a structural repair to the roof, then the paralegal interviewing the landlord's manager should be prepared to deal with that person as a potentially hostile witness.

Sometimes, hostile witnesses refuse to be interviewed. On learning that the alternative might be a subpoena, however, a hostile witness may consent to at least a limited interview. If you plan to interview hostile witnesses, keep in mind the following rule of thumb:

 Contact and interview hostile witnesses in the early stages of your investigation. The longer you wait, the greater the chance that they may be influenced by the opposing party's attorney or the opinions of persons sympathetic to the opposing party.

When interviewing hostile witnesses, you need to be especially careful to be objective, fair, and unbiased in your approach. This does not mean that you have to ignore your client's interests. On the contrary, you will best serve those interests by doing all you can to keep from further alienating a witness whose information might ultimately help your client's case.

Questioning Witnesses

When you are asking questions as a legal investigator, you should follow this rule of thumb:

 Phrase your questions so that they lead to the most complete answer possible.

Investigative questions should be open ended. Compare, for example, the following two questions:

1. "Did you see the driver of the green van run the stop sign?"
2. "What did you see at the time of the accident?"

The first question calls for a "yes" or "no" answer. The second question, in contrast, invites the witness to explain fully what he or she actually saw. Something else that the witness saw could be important to the case—but unless you allow room for the witness's full description, you will not learn about this information.

Notice that the first question also assumes a fact—that the driver of the green van ran the stop sign. The second question, however, makes no assumptions and conveys no information to the witness that may influence his or her answer. Generally, the less the witness knows about other witnesses' descriptions, the better, because those other descriptions could influence the witness's perception of the event. You want to find out exactly what the witness observed, in his or her own words.

Checking the Witness's Qualifications

When you are interviewing a witness during the course of an investigation, you often will not know whether the testimony of that witness will be needed in court or even whether the claim you are investigating will be litigated. Nonetheless, you should operate under the assumption that each witness is a potential court witness. Thus, you should make sure that the witness is competent to testify and reliable. Is there any indication that the witness has a physical or mental disability that might interfere with the accuracy of his or her perception of the witnessed event? Has the witness ever been convicted of a crime? Does he or she abuse drugs or have a reputation in the community as a troublemaker? If it can be shown that a witness is unreliable or incompetent to testify, the witness's testimony normally will not be admitted in court.

Also investigate the witness's possible biases. Does the witness have an interest in the claim being investigated that would tend to make his or her testimony prejudicial? Is the witness a relative or close friend of one of the parties involved

EXHIBIT 13.4
Information Contained in a Witness Statement

---

1. **Information about the Witness**
   —Name, address, and phone number
   —Name, address, and phone number of the witness's employer or place of business
   —Interest, if any, in the outcome of the claim being investigated

2. **Information about the Interview**
   —Name of the interviewer
   —Name of the attorney or law firm for which the claim is being investigated
   —Date, time, and place of the interview

3. **Identification of the Event Witnessed**
   —Nature of the action or event observed by the witness
   —Date of the action or event

4. **Witness's Description of the Event**

5. **Attestation Clause**
   —Provision or clause at the end of the statement affirming the truth of the witness's description as written in the statement.

[Witness's Signature]

---

in the claim? Does the witness hold a grudge against one of the parties? If the answer to any of these questions is yes, the witness's testimony may be discredited in court. In any event, it will probably not be as convincing as testimony given by a neutral, unbiased witness.

Witness Statements

Whenever you interview a witness, you should take notes and prepare a memorandum of the interview. Depending on the procedures followed by your firm, you may want to have the witness—particularly if he or she is a hostile witness—sign a statement. A **witness statement** is a written statement setting forth what the witness said during the interview. Exhibit 13.4 shows the type of information normally contained in a witness statement, and Exhibit 13.5 presents an excerpt from a sample witness statement.

Statutes and court rules vary as to the value of witness statements as evidence. Usually, statements made by witnesses during interviews cannot be introduced as evidence in court, but they can be used for other purposes. For example, if a hostile witness's testimony in court contradicts something he or she said during your interview, the witness statement may be used to impeach the witness—that is, to call into question the witness's testimony or demonstrate that the witness is unreliable. Witness statements also can be used to refresh a witness's memory.

Witness Statement
The written transcription of a statement made by the witness during an interview and signed by the witness.

PLANNING AND CONDUCTING INVESTIGATIONS

Because factual evidence is crucial to the outcome of a legal problem, investigation is necessarily an important part of legal work. Attorneys often rely on paralegals to conduct investigations, and you should be prepared to accept the

> **EXHIBIT 13.5**
> A Sample Witness Statement (Excerpt)

> **STATEMENT OF JULIA WILLIAMS**
>
> I, Julia Williams, am a thirty-five-year-old female. I reside at 3801 Mattis Avenue, Nita City, Nita 48800, and my home telephone number is (408) 555-8989. I work as a nurse at the Nita City Hospital & Clinic, 412 Hospital Way, Nita City, Nita 48802. My work telephone number is (408) 555-9898. I am making this statement in my home on the afternoon of February 8, 1999. The statement is being made to Elena Lopez, a paralegal with the law firm of Jeffers, Gilmore & Dunn.
>
> In regard to the accident on the corner of Mattis Avenue and Thirty-eighth Street on August 4, 1999, at approximately 7:45 A.M. on that date, I was standing at the southwest corner of that intersection, waiting to cross the street, when I observed . . .
>
> * * * *
>
> I affirm that the information given in this statement is accurate and true to the best of my knowledge.
>
> *Julia Williams*
> Julia Williams

responsibility for making sure that an investigation is conducted thoroughly and professionally. In the following pages, you will read about the basics of legal investigation—how to plan and undertake an investigation, how the rules of evidence shape the investigative process, and the importance of carefully documenting the results of your investigation.

Of course, you have already read about one aspect of investigations—interviewing witnesses. A preliminary investigation, however, can involve much more. For one thing, before witnesses can be interviewed, they must be located. Information relating to the case may also have to be obtained from a police department, weather bureau, or other source.

Where Do You Start?

Assume that you work for Allen Gilmore, the attorney who represented the plaintiff in the hypothetical case discussed in Chapters 10 and 11. Recall that the plaintiff in that case, Katherine Baranski, sued Tony Peretto for negligence. Peretto had run a stop sign at an intersection and as a result, his car collided with Baranski's. Further assume that the case is still in its initial stages. Attorney Gilmore has just met with Katherine Baranski for the initial client interview. You sat in on the interview, listened carefully to Baranski's description of the accident and of the damages she sustained as a result (medical expenses, lost wages, and so on), and took thorough notes.

After the interview, Gilmore asks you to do a preliminary investigation into Baranski's claim. It is now your responsibility to find the answers to a number of questions. Did the accident really occur in the way perceived by the client, Katherine Baranski? Exactly where and when did it happen? How does the police report describe the accident? Were there any witnesses? Was Tony Peretto insured and, if so, by what insurance company? What other circumstances (such as weather) are relevant? Your supervising attorney will want to know the answers to these and other questions before advising Baranski as to what legal action should be pursued.

In undertaking any legal investigation, your logical point of departure is the information you have already acquired about the legal claim or problem. In the

EXHIBIT 13.6
An Investigation Plan

```
                    INVESTIGATION PLAN
                       File No. 15773

                                              Date        Date
                                           Requested   Received

1. Contact Police Department
    —To obtain police report
    —To ask for photographs of accident scene
    —To talk with investigating officer      _____    _____

    —SOURCE:  Nita City Police Dept.
    —METHOD:  Request in person or by mail

2. Contact Known Witnesses
    —Tony Peretto, van driver
    —Michael Young, police officer at accident scene
    —Julia Williams, witness at accident scene
    —Dwight Kelly, witness at accident scene   _____    _____

    —SOURCE:  Police report
    —METHOD:  Contact witnesses by initial phone
              call and personal interview when possible

3. Obtain Employment Records
    —To learn employment status and income of
      Mrs. Baranski                             _____    _____

    —SOURCE:  Nita State University
    —METHOD:  Written request by mail with
              Mrs. Baranski's release enclosed

4. Obtain Hospital Records
    —To learn necessary information about
      Mrs. Baranski's medical treatment and costs  _____    _____

    —SOURCE:  Nita City Hospital
    —METHOD:  Written request by mail with
              Mrs. Baranski's release enclosed
```

Baranski case, this information consists of the statements made by Baranski during the initial client interview and summarized in your notes. Baranski had described what she remembered about the accident, including the date and time it occurred. She said she thought that the police investigator had the names of some persons who had witnessed the accident. She also stated that she was employed as an assistant professor in the math department at Nita State University, earning approximately $46,000 a year. By using common sense and a little imagination, you can map out a fairly thorough investigation plan based on this information.

Creating an Investigation Plan

Investigation Plan
A plan that lists each step involved in obtaining and verifying the facts and information that are relevant to the legal problem being investigated.

An **investigation plan** is simply a step-by-step list of the tasks that you plan to undertake to verify or obtain factual information relating to a legal problem. In the Baranski case, the steps in your investigation plan would include those summarized in Exhibit 13.6 above and discussed in the following pages. The paralegal should make sure that his or her supervising attorney approves the investigation plan. Generally, throughout the investigation, it is important to keep in close touch with your supervising attorney about progress being made.

EXHIBIT 13.6

An Investigation Plan—Continued

	Date Requested	Date Received

5. Contact National Weather Service
—To learn what the weather conditions were on the day of the accident _____ _____

—SOURCE: National Weather Service or newspaper
—METHOD: Phone call or written request

6. Obtain Title and Registration Records
—To verify Tony Peretto's ownership of the vehicle _____ _____

—SOURCE: Department of Motor Vehicles
—METHOD: Order by mail

7. Contact Tony Peretto's Insurance Company
—To find out about insurance coverage _____ _____
—To check liability limits _____ _____

—SOURCE: Insurance company
—METHOD: Written request by mail

8. Use a Professional Investigator
—To contact such witnesses as _____ _____
  – ambulance attendants
  – doctors
  – residents in neighborhood of accident scene
—To inspect vehicle
—To take photos of accident site _____ _____
—To investigate accident scene, etc. _____ _____

—SOURCE: Regular law-firm investigator
—METHOD: In person

CONTACTING THE POLICE DEPARTMENT. The initial step in your plan should be to contact the police department. You will want to look at a copy of the police report of the accident, view any photographs that were taken at the scene, obtain the names of persons who may have witnessed the accident, and, if possible, talk to the investigating officer.

CONTACTING AND INTERVIEWING WITNESSES. Next, you will want to contact and interview any known witnesses and document their descriptions of what took place at the time of the accident. Known witnesses include the driver (Tony Peretto) of the vehicle that hit Katherine Baranski, the police officer at the scene, and the other witnesses noted in the police investigation report. Keep in mind that if Tony Peretto is aware of Baranski's intention to sue him, he will probably have retained an attorney. If he has, then you are not permitted to contact him directly—all communications with him will have to be through his attorney.

OBTAINING MEDICAL AND EMPLOYMENT RECORDS. To justify a claim for damages, you will need to ascertain the nature of the injuries sustained by Baranski as a result of the accident, the medical expenses that she incurred, and her annual or monthly income (to determine the amount of wages she lost as a

DEVELOPING PARALEGAL SKILLS

Keeping an Evidence Log

Steve Fessler works as a paralegal for Marty Melman, a sole practitioner. Marty is representing June Linden, the plaintiff in a personal-injury case. Marty asked Steve to obtain X-rays of the plaintiff's fractured ankle. The fracture occurred as a result of an auto accident.

Steve receives a phone call from the hospital indicating that the X-rays are ready to be picked up. Steve drives to the hospital, picks up the X-rays, and brings them back to the office. He places them in a special folder and applies an exhibit label to the folder, which contains a thorough description of the X-rays for purposes of identification. The special folder will preserve the X-rays. Next, he places the folder in the evidence cabinet, which is kept locked so that access to the cabinet is controlled. He takes out a notebook entitled "Evidence Log" and places a clean log sheet in it.

TIPS FOR CREATING AN EVIDENCE LOG

- The form should contain blanks for the file name, a description of the evidence, and information about its acquisition, such as the date and by whom and how it was acquired.
- Additionally, the form should contain information blanks for identifying marks on the evidence, where the evidence is kept within the firm, and the name of the evidence custodian.
- The form should include columns that show the chain of custody of the evidence, such as columns for the name, date, and purpose of each release of the evidence.
- There should be a prominent statement on the form that the evidence must be safeguarded and returned in the same condition. Anyone removing the evidence should be required to sign this statement.
- Consider taking a Polaroid snapshot before and after each transfer of the evidence.

This way, if the evidence needs to be removed and reviewed by someone, such as an expert witness, there will be a record of the evidence and who has or had custody of it. Maintaining an evidence log also helps to protect against claims that the evidence is not authentic or has been altered while in the law firm's possession.

---

result of the accident). To obtain this information, you will need copies of her medical and employment records.

Note that the institutions holding these records will not release them to you unless Katherine Baranski authorizes them to do so. Therefore, you will also need to arrange with Baranski to sign release forms to include with your requests for copies. A sample authorization form to release medical records is shown in Exhibit 13.7. You should make sure that Baranski signs these forms before she leaves the office after the initial interview. Otherwise, waiting for her to return the signed forms may delay your investigation.

In addition to obtaining medical records, you may be asked to do some research on the type of injury sustained by Baranski and related statistical or other information. Some helpful online sources for medical information are discussed in the feature *Technology and Today's Paralegal: Online Medical Research* on page 474.

CONTACTING THE NATIONAL WEATHER SERVICE. Weather conditions at the time of the accident may have an important bearing on the case. If it was snowing heavily at the time of the Baranski-Peretto accident, for example, Peretto's attorney may argue that Peretto did not see the stop sign or that ice on the road prevented him from stopping. You will therefore want to ascertain what the weather conditions were at the time of the accident by contacting the National Weather Service. Also, when you interview eyewitnesses, you should ask them about weather conditions at the place and time of the accident.

On the Web
The National Weather Service is online at www.nws.noaa.gov.

EXHIBIT 13.7
Authorization to Release Medical Records

TO: Nita City Hospital & Clinic
Nita City, NI 48803

PATIENT: Katherine Baranski
335 Natural Boulevard
Nita City, NI 48802

You are hereby authorized to furnish and release to my attorney, Allen P. Gilmore of Jeffers, Gilmore & Dunn, all information and records relating to my treatment for injuries incurred on August 4, 1998. Please do not disclose information to insurance adjusters or to other persons without written authority from me. The forgoing authority shall continue in force until revoked by me in writing, but for no longer than one year following the date given below.

Date: January 30, 1999.   *Katherine Baranski*
Katherine Baranski

Please attach your invoice for any fee or photostatic costs and send it with the information requested above to my office.

Thank you,

Allen P. Gilmore
Allen P. Gilmore
Jeffers, Gilmore & Dunn
Attorneys at Law
553 Fifth Avenue
Suite 101
Nita City, NI 48801

Helena Moritz
Helena Moritz
Notary Public State of Nita
Nita County
My Commission Expires November 12, 2002

OBTAINING VEHICLE TITLE AND REGISTRATION RECORDS. To verify that Tony Peretto owns the vehicle that he was driving at the time of the accident, you will need to obtain title and registration records. Usually, these can be acquired from the state department of motor vehicles, although in some states the secretary of state's office handles such records. The requirements for obtaining such information vary from state to state and may include the submission of special forms and fees. Therefore, you should call the relevant state department or office in advance to find out what procedures should be followed.

CONTACTING THE INSURANCE COMPANY. If you learned the name of Peretto's insurance company from Baranski or from the police report, you will want to contact that company to find out what kind of insurance coverage Peretto has and the limits of his liability under the insurance policy. Insurance companies usually are reluctant give this information to anyone other than the policyholder. They sometimes cooperate with such requests, however, because

On the Web
Relevant driving and vehicle-registration records may be on the Web. See, for example, the list of licensed drivers in the state of Texas at **www.publicdata.com**. To find the home pages of your state's government agencies, go to **www.findlaw.com**.

Technology and Today's Paralegal

Online Medical Research

Attorneys and paralegals frequently deal with cases involving personal injuries, medical malpractice, product liability, or other health-related problems. In such cases, paralegals may be asked to do some research on a particular medical topic, procedure, or device. (A paralegal may also be asked to locate an expert witness in the medical field; you will read about online databases of expert witnesses in Chapter 15.)

You might want to begin your research by familiarizing yourself with the relevant medical terminology. To do this, you can access medical dictionaries and glossaries online. For example, you can find the "Online Medical Dictionary" maintained by CancerWEB at www.graylab.ac.uk/omd/index.html. To find online medical glossaries, you can go to www.va-business.com/electro/hmos/gloss.html or www.hmri.com/onthehealthcareteam/index.html.

Some medical journals are also available online if what you need is an article on a particular medical subject. For example, the *Journal of the American Medical Association* can be found at www.ama-assn.org/public/journals/jama/jamahome.htm. Reuters Health Information Services provides current news on medical topics for both health professionals and the general public (see www.reutershealth.com). There are also many medical texts on the Web. Good, comprehensive sources include Martindale's Health Science Guide at www.sci.lib.uci.edu/~martindaleHSGuide.html and the Multimedia Medical Reference Library at www.med-library.com/medlibrary.

Information about medical devices, drugs, and medical procedures can be found at the Food and Drug Administration's site (at www.fda.gov) or at Yahoo's medical site (at www.yahoo.com/Health/Medicine). Links to other medical sites are available on the American Medical Association's Web pages at www.ama-assn.org/med_link/med_link.html.

Other useful medical-research sites include Health-Gate's site at www.healthgate.com/index.shtml, which gives you free access to MEDLINE and other medical databases, and the Web site of the National Institutes of Health at www.nih.gov. The latter site has a wealth of information and offers links to a number of other sites, including the National Library of Medicine and MEDLINE.

---

they know that if they do not, the information can be obtained during discovery, should a lawsuit be initiated.

USING A PROFESSIONAL INVESTIGATOR'S SERVICES. Some law firms routinely use the services of professional investigators. Depending on the circumstances, your supervising attorney may decide to use a professional investigator for certain tasks, including those described above. You might be responsible for working with the investigator. For example, you might arrange for the investigator to inspect and take photographs of the accident scene.

Locating certain witnesses (witnesses who have moved, for example) may be difficult and time consuming. This is another task that your supervising attorney may prefer the professional investigator to handle, particularly if the attorney needs your assistance in the office. The investigator might also be asked to locate other witnesses, such as the ambulance driver or attendants, physicians who treated Baranski, or residents in the area who might have observed the accident.

Locating Witnesses

Perhaps one of the most challenging tasks for the legal investigator is locating a witness whose address is unknown or who has moved from a previous, known address. Suppose, for example, that in the Baranski case the police investigation report lists the name, address, and telephone number of Edna Ball, a witness to the accident. When you call her number, a recording informs you that the phone has been disconnected. You go to her address, and the house appears to be vacant. What is your next step?

At this point, many paralegals suggest to their supervising attorneys that a professional investigator take over the search. But if you alone must locate the witness, there are several sources to which you can turn. A good starting point is to visit other homes in the neighborhood. Perhaps someone living nearby knows Edna Ball and can give you some leads as to where she is or what happened to her. Other sources are discussed below.

TELEPHONE AND CITY DIRECTORIES. The telephone directory can sometimes be a valuable source of information for the investigator. In trying to locate Edna Ball, for example, you might check to see if her name is still listed in the current directory and, if so, whether it is listed jointly with someone, such as her husband. Your local telephone information service might have a new number listed for her. If the information-service operator indicates that the number is unlisted, you can explain the nature of your concern and request that the operator phone Edna Ball at that number to see if she is willing to call you.

City directories are also good potential sources of information. Such directories may be available in the local library or the law firm's library. A city directory generally contains more information than a phone book. For example, some city directories list places of employment and spouses' names in addition to addresses and telephone numbers. Typically, city directories provide a listing of names and phone numbers by street address. In the Baranski case, if you wanted to obtain the telephone numbers of persons who live in the area of the Baranski-Peretto accident, you could consult a city directory for addresses near the intersection where the accident occurred.

On the Web
To find telephone book Web sites, you can do a broad search using a search engine, such as that of Infoseek at www.infoseek.com.

OTHER INFORMATION SOURCES. Other sources of information are media reports (newspaper and magazine articles and television videos covering the event being investigated); court records (probate proceedings, lawsuits, and so on); deeds to property (usually located in the county courthouse); birth, marriage, and death certificates; voter registration lists; the post office (to see if the witness left a forwarding address); credit bureaus; the tax assessor's office; and city utilities, such as the local electric or water company.

Professional organizations may be useful sources as well. For example, if you have learned from one of Edna Ball's neighbors that she is a paralegal, you can check with state and local paralegal associations to see if they have current information on her. You might also check with federal, state, or local governmental agencies or bureaus (discussed in the following section) to see if the information contained in public records will be helpful in locating Edna Ball.

Accessing Government Information

Records and files acquired and stored by government offices and agencies can be a tremendous resource for the legal investigator. Public records available at local government buildings or offices (such as the county courthouse or post office) were mentioned above. Additionally, it is possible to obtain information from federal agencies, such as the Social Security Administration, and from state departments or agencies, such as the state revenue department or the secretary of state's office. If you wish to obtain information from any government files or records, you should check with the specific agency or department to see what rules apply.

On the Web
You can access the home pages of federal agencies by going to www.findlaw.com.

Paralegal Profile

Insurance Paralegal

KIRTRENA S. DEEN received her bachelor of arts degree in legal administration from the University of West Florida in Pensacola, Florida, in 1996. On graduation, she worked at a large law firm as a legal assistant for approximately a year and a half in the area of personal-injury and employment law. Currently, she is employed as a claims representative for a national automobile insurance company. In September 1998, she received her Florida Department of Insurance Adjusters License. Additionally, she serves on the University of West Florida Legal Administration Program Advisory Board as a paralegal representative in the corporate/public sector.

What do you like best about your work?

"I enjoy the responsibility and exposure of investigating, evaluating, and negotiating a variety of automobile claims as opposed to adjusting only specific types of automobile claims. Some examples of the claims I am assigned to adjust include property, bodily-injury, arson, theft, vandalism, and weather-related claims. I also enjoy the investigative process of meeting the parties involved, securing recorded statements, conducting scene investigations, and canvassing for witnesses."

What is the greatest challenge that you face in your area of work?

"Once a claim has been reported, the claims representative must investigate to establish coverage, finalize legal liability, and inspect the reported damage. Once the claim has been thoroughly investigated, it must be evaluated to determine a fair settlement and negotiated accordingly. Therefore, the greatest challenge of adjusting claims is completing the investigation, evaluation, and negotiation process promptly and fairly while complying with the terms of the insurance policy and governing statutory laws."

What advice do you have for would-be paralegals in your area of work?

"My advice is to possess strong interpersonal skills, as well as superior writing and oral communication skills. Due to the variety of claims assigned, claims representatives in my area daily communicate and negotiate with insureds, claimants, and other claims representatives, as well as attorneys, regarding the settlement of claims. Additionally, regular meetings and communication with paint and body shop managers is needed regarding the assessment of automobile damage. Thus, the ability to communicate effectively with all kinds of people is a great asset to possess in my area of work."

What are some tips for success as a paralegal in your area of work?

"Know the terms and conditions of the insurance policy and regularly refer to the policy to substantiate them. The insurance policy is the contract between the insurance company and the insured to which they must adhere. Know the statutory laws governing claims handling in your area and keep abreast of changes. Be detail oriented and analytical in the investigation process. Feel passionate about your work. Passion for your work will enable you to go that extra mile to handle claims promptly and fairly."

> "[T]he ability to communicate effectively with all kinds of people is a great asset to possess in my area of work."

EXHIBIT 13.8

Freedom of Information Act Request Form

Agency Head or FOIA Officer
Title
Name of Agency
Address of Agency
City, State, Zip

Re: Freedom of Information Act Request.

Dear _____:

    Under the provisions of the Freedom of Information Act, 5 U.S.C. 552, I am requesting access to [identify the records as clearly and specifically as possible].

    If there are any fees for searching for, or copying, the records I have requested, please inform me before you fill the request. [Or: . . . please supply the records without informing me if the fees do not exceed $_____.]

    [Optional] I am requesting this information [state the reason for your request if you think it will assist you in obtaining the information].

    [Optional] As you know, the act permits you to reduce or waive fees when the release of the information is considered as "primarily benefiting the public." I believe that this request fits that category and I therefore ask that you waive any fees.

    If all or any part of this request is denied, please cite the specific exemption(s) that you think justifies your refusal to release the information, and inform me of the appeal procedures available to me under the law.

    I would appreciate your handling this request as quickly as possible, and I look forward to hearing from you within ten days, as the law stipulates.

Sincerely,

Signature
Name
Address
City, State, Zip

The Freedom of Information Act (FOIA), which was enacted by Congress in 1966, requires the federal government to disclose certain records to any person on request. A request that complies with the FOIA procedures need only contain a reasonable description of the information sought. Exhibit 13.8 above illustrates the proper format for a letter requesting information under the FOIA. Note that the FOIA exempts some types of information from the disclosure requirement, including classified information (information concerning national security), confidential material dealing with trade secrets, government personnel rules, and personal medical files.

Investigation and the Rules of Evidence

Because an investigation is conducted to obtain information and verify facts that may eventually be introduced as evidence at trial, you should know what kind of evidence will be admissible in court before undertaking your investigation.

Evidence is anything that is used to prove the existence or nonexistence of a fact. Whether evidence will be admitted in court is determined by the **rules of evidence**—rules that have been created by the courts to ensure that any evidence presented in court is fair and reliable. The Federal Rules of Evidence govern the admissibility of evidence in federal courts. For cases brought in state courts, state rules of evidence apply. (Many states have adopted evidence rules patterned on the

Evidence
Anything that is used to prove the existence or nonexistence of a fact.

Rules of Evidence
Rules governing the admissibility of evidence in trial courts.

DEVELOPING PARALEGAL SKILLS
Accessing Government Information

Ellen Simmons has started a new job as a paralegal for Smith & Case, a law firm that handles Superfund cases. Ellen is about to request copies of documents from the EPA. Ellen calls and speaks to Christopher Peter, a paralegal with the EPA. She identifies herself as a paralegal from Smith & Chase, which is representing a client involved at the Suburban Landfill Superfund site. Ellen is greeted with an icy silence and wonders what she might have said to offend Christopher. She asks if the EPA has the waste-in/waste-out report that gives the total volume of hazardous waste at the site and lists the potentially responsible parties.

Christopher responds, in a surprised voice, that the EPA does have the documents. "Are you new?" asks Christopher. "Is it that obvious?" jokes Ellen. Christopher responds that it's not really that obvious and explains that her predecessor always just sent in a FOIA request for everything that the EPA had in its files and that it took weeks to respond to requests from her firm. "Believe me, your firm has quite a reputation around here," says Christopher.

Ellen knows that she is off to a good start in her new job and with an important legal assistant at the EPA. She smiles to herself as she promises to submit the FOIA request for only the waste-in/waste-out report.

TIPS FOR WORKING WITH GOVERNMENT AGENCIES

- Review the file to familiarize yourself with the case before calling the agency.
- Review the agency's regulations to ascertain which documents the agency prepares in specific types of cases, such as Superfund cases.
- Make a list of the various documents.
- Determine in advance (from the list) which documents you will be requesting.
- Develop a list of alternatives to use in the event that the documents that you request have not been prepared or are not available.
- Make reasonable requests from the agency.
- Cultivate good working relationships with agency staff members.

Direct Evidence
Evidence establishing the existence of a fact that is in question without relying on inferences.

Circumstantial Evidence
Indirect evidence that is offered to establish, by inference, the likelihood of a fact that is in question.

federal rules.) Of course, you will not need to become an expert in evidentiary rules, but a basic knowledge of how evidence is classified and what types of evidence are admissible in court will greatly assist your investigative efforts.

DIRECT VERSUS CIRCUMSTANTIAL EVIDENCE. Two types of evidence may be brought into court—direct evidence and circumstantial evidence. **Direct evidence** is any evidence that, if believed, establishes the truth of the fact in question. For example, bullets found in the body of a shooting victim provide direct evidence of the type of gun that fired them. **Circumstantial evidence** is indirect evidence that, even if believed, does not establish the fact in question but only the degree of likelihood of the fact. In other words, circumstantial evidence can create an inference that a fact exists.

For example, suppose that your firm's client owns the type of gun that shot the bullets found in the victim's body. This circumstantial evidence does not establish that the client committed the crime. Combined with other circumstantial evidence, however, it is possible that a jury could be convinced that the client committed the crime. For instance, if other circumstantial evidence indicates that your firm's client had a motive for harming the victim and that the client was at the scene of the crime at the time the crime was committed, a jury might conclude that the client committed the crime.

RELEVANCE.   Evidence will not be admitted in court unless it is relevant to the matter in question. **Relevant evidence** is evidence that tends to prove or disprove the fact in question. For example, evidence that the gun belonging to your firm's client was in the home of another person when the victim was shot would be relevant, because it would tend to prove that the client did not shoot the victim.

Even relevant evidence may not be admitted in court if its probative (proving) value is substantially outweighed by other important considerations. For example, even though evidence is relevant, it may not be necessary—the fact at issue may already have been sufficiently proved or disproved by previous evidence. In that situation, the introduction of further evidence would be a waste of time and would cause undue delay in the trial proceedings. Relevant evidence may also be excluded if it would tend to distract the jury from the main issues of the case, mislead the jury, or cause the jury to decide the issue on an emotional basis.

Relevant Evidence
Evidence tending to make a fact in question more or less probable than it would be without the evidence. Only relevant evidence is admissible in court.

AUTHENTICATION OF EVIDENCE.   At trial, an attorney must lay the proper foundation for the introduction of certain evidence, such as documents, exhibits, and other objects, and must demonstrate to the court that the evidence is what the attorney claims. The process by which this is accomplished is referred to as **authentication**. The authentication requirement relates to relevance, because something offered in evidence becomes relevant to the case only if it is authentic, or genuine.

Authentication
Establishing the genuineness of an item that is to be introduced as evidence in a trial.

 As a legal investigator, you therefore need to make sure that the evidence you obtain is not only relevant but also capable of being authenticated if introduced at trial.

Commonly, evidence is authenticated by the testimony of witnesses. For example, if an attorney wants to introduce an autopsy report as evidence in a case, he or she can have the report authenticated by the testimony of the medical examiner who signed it. Generally, an attorney must offer enough proof of authenticity to convince the court that the evidence is, in fact, what it is purported to be.

The rules of evidence require authentication because certain types of evidence, such as exhibits and objects, cannot be cross-examined by opposing counsel, as witnesses can, yet such evidence may have a significant effect on the jury. The authentication requirement provides a safeguard against the introduction of non-verified evidence that may strongly influence the outcome of the case.

The Federal Rules of Evidence provide for the self-authentication of specific types of evidence. In other words, certain documents or records need not be authenticated by testimony. Certified copies of public records, for example, are automatically deemed authentic. Other self-authenticating evidentiary documents include official publications (such as a report issued by the federal Environmental Protection Agency), documents containing a notary public's seal or the seal of a public official, newspaper or magazine articles, and manufacturers' trademarks or labels.

HEARSAY.   When interviewing witnesses, you need to make sure that a witness's statements are based on the witness's own knowledge and not hearsay. **Hearsay** is defined as any testimony given in court about a statement made by someone else. Literally, it is what someone heard someone else say. For example, if a witness in the Baranski case testified in court as to what he or she heard another observer say about the accident, that testimony would be hearsay. Generally, hearsay is not admissible as evidence. To a great extent, this is because the listener may have misunderstood what another person said, and without the opportunity of cross-examining the originator of the statement, the misperception cannot be challenged.

Exceptions to the hearsay rule are made in certain circumstances. Generally, these exceptions allow hearsay to be considered as evidence when the hearsay

Hearsay
An oral or written statement made by an out-of-court declarant that is later offered in court by a witness (not the declarant) concerning a matter before the court. Hearsay is generally not admissible as evidence.

Today's Professional Paralegal
Interviewing a Client

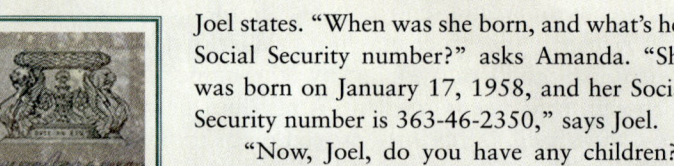

Amanda Blake, a paralegal, works for John Kerrigan, a sole practitioner. A new client, Joel Sontag, calls for an appointment to make his will. The attorney has to go out of town for a court hearing. Because Sontag seems to be anxious to get the will done, the attorney asks Amanda to meet with Sontag and interview him to obtain some basic information. The attorney will review the information when he returns from his trip and then call Sontag to advise him on the will and other estate-planning possibilities.

Preparing for the Interview

Amanda reserves the conference room. On the day of Sontag's visit, she has it set up for the interview. She has already made a copy of the will and estate-planning checklist that she will use to ensure that she gets all of the essential information from Sontag. The secretary shows Sontag into the conference room when he arrives.

Meeting the Client

Amanda introduces herself, saying, "Hello, Mr. Sontag, I'm Amanda Blake, John Kerrigan's legal assistant. I'll be meeting with you today to obtain the estate-planning information that Mr. Kerrigan needs if he is to advise you. Sontag responds, "Mr. Kerrigan told me that we would be meeting today. He also told me how capable you are." Amanda smiles and says, "Thanks. And did Mr. Kerrigan explain to you that I'm not an attorney?" Sontag responds, "Yes, he did." Amanda then removes her checklist and note pad from her file.

Obtaining Information about the Client

"I'll be reviewing this checklist to make sure that we obtain all of the information that we need for your will," Amanda informs Joel. "First, I need you to fill out the client information form," instructs Amanda. "As you can see, it requires you to give us personal information, such as your name, legal residence, date of birth, and other data." Joel takes the form and fills it out. When he is finished, he hands it to Amanda.

"Now I need some other information. First, I need to know if you're married," states Amanda. "Yes, I am," responds Joel. "Your wife's name is?" asks Amanda. "Nicole Lynn Sontag," answers Joel. "And your wife resides with you at the address that you've given on the client information form?" asks Amanda. "Yes, she does," Joel states. "When was she born, and what's her Social Security number?" asks Amanda. "She was born on January 17, 1958, and her Social Security number is 363-46-2350," says Joel.

"Now, Joel, do you have any children?" asks Amanda. "Yes, we have one son, Joel, Jr., age four," answers Joel. "Do you want to provide for both of them in your will?" asks Amanda. "Yes," responds Joel. "Do you have any other relatives for whom you want to provide?" asks Amanda. "Yes, I have a brother, Alfred Sontag, who lives in a home for autistic people," answers Joel. "I'll need the address for the home," responds Amanda. Joel takes an address book out of his briefcase and gives her the address. "Is there anyone else whom you want to provide for in your will?" asks Amanda. "No," responds Joel.

Obtaining Information about the Client's Property

"Now we need to discuss property," Amanda informs Joel. "Do you own a home?" she asks. "Yes," he answers. Amanda says, "I need to know if the home is located at the address you gave on the form, when you bought it, what it cost, what its present approximate market value is, whether you own it jointly with your wife, and the balance on your mortgage." Joel gives her all of the requested information. Amanda continues questioning Joel about his property holdings until she has covered all the items on her checklist.

Concluding the Interview

"Well," says Amanda, "we've covered everything on the checklist. Now we need to set up a time for you to meet with Mr. Kerrigan to discuss estate-planning procedures and your will. Because you jointly own property with your wife, Mr. Kerrigan may want both of you to meet with him. Would two o'clock next Tuesday afternoon be a good time for you both to come in to meet with Mr. Kerrigan?" Joel tells Amanda that he thinks that both he and his wife could arrange to meet with the attorney at that time. They tentatively schedule an appointment for that date. Joel will call Amanda if the appointment must be changed. Joel gets up to leave the office, saying that he'll probably see her again next Tuesday. "I'll look forward to that," says Amanda. Amanda then begins to prepare a detailed summary of the interview to give to her supervising attorney on his return.

consists of statements that are highly reliable or believable, such as a dying person's statement on the cause or circumstances of his or her impending death. Statements made by persons in a moment of excitement caused by a startling event or condition may be admissible.

Summarizing Your Results

The final step in any investigation is summarizing the results. Generally, your investigation report should provide an overall summary of your findings, a summary of the facts and information gathered from each source that you investigated, and your general conclusions and recommendations based on the information obtained during the investigation.

OVERALL SUMMARY. The overall summary of the investigation should thoroughly describe for the reader all of the facts you have gathered about the case. This section should be written in such a way that someone not familiar with the case could read it and become adequately informed of the case's factual background.

SOURCE-BY-SOURCE SUMMARIES. You should also create a list of your information sources, including witnesses, and summarize the facts gleaned from each of these sources. Each "source section" should contain all of the information gathered from that source, including direct quotes from witnesses. Each source section should also contain a subsection giving your personal comments on that particular source. You might comment on a witness's demeanor, for example, or on whether the witness's version of the facts was consistent or inconsistent with that of other witnesses. Your impressions of the witness's competence or reliability could be noted. If the witness provided you with further leads to be explored, this information could also be included.

GENERAL CONCLUSIONS AND RECOMMENDATIONS. In the final section, you will present your overall conclusions about the investigation, as well as any suggestions that you have on the development of the case. Attorneys rely heavily on their investigators' impressions of witnesses and evaluations of investigative results because the investigators have firsthand knowledge of the sources. Your impression of a potentially important witness, for example, may help the attorney decide whether to arrange for a follow-up interview with the witness. Usually, the attorney will want to interview only the most promising witnesses, and your impressions and comments will serve as a screening device. Based on your findings during the investigation, you might also suggest to the attorney what further information can be obtained during discovery, if necessary, and what additional research needs to be done.

KEY TERMS AND CONCEPTS

active listening 459	**eyewitness** 466	**lay witness** 465
authentication 479	**friendly witness** 466	**leading question** 458
circumstantial evidence 478	**hearsay** 479	**open-ended question** 457
closed-ended question 458	**hostile witness** 466	**pressure question** 458
direct evidence 478	**hypothetical question** 458	**relevant evidence** 479
evidence 477	**interviewee** 453	**rules of evidence** 477
expert witness 465	**investigation plan** 470	**witness statement** 468

CHAPTER SUMMARY

1. Paralegals often interview clients and witnesses. Interviewing skills include interpersonal skills, questioning skills, and communication skills, particularly listening skills.

2. Paralegals can use several types of questions during the interviewing process, including open-ended, closed-ended, hypothetical, pressure, and leading questions.

3. Prior to the interview, the paralegal should prepare the interview environment to ensure that interruptions, noises, and delays will be minimized, that the client will be comfortable, and that any necessary supplies, forms, and equipment are at hand. If an interview is to be tape-recorded, the paralegal must obtain permission from both his or her supervising attorney and the interviewee to tape the session.

4. There are basically three types of client interviews: the initial interview (usually conducted by the attorney but often attended by the paralegal), the subsequent interview (often conducted by the paralegal), and the informational interview (or meeting, also typically handled by the paralegal). As soon as possible after an interview is concluded, the paralegal should summarize in a written memorandum the information gathered in the interview.

5. Witnesses interviewed by paralegals include expert witnesses (who have specialized training in a given area), lay witnesses (ordinary witnesses who have factual information about the matter being investigated), eyewitnesses (who have firsthand knowledge of an event—because they saw it happen, for example), friendly witnesses (who are favorable to the client's position), and hostile witnesses (who are prejudiced against the client or resent being interviewed for other reasons). Following an interview of a witness, the paralegal should create a witness statement that identifies the witness, discloses what was discovered during the interview, and is signed by the witness.

6. Factual evidence is crucial to the outcome of a legal problem, and paralegals are often asked to conduct investigations to discover any factual evidence that supports (or contradicts) a client's claims. Before starting an investigation, the paralegal should create an investigation plan—a step-by-step list of what sources will be investigated to obtain specific types of information. The paralegal should discuss the plan with his or her supervising attorney before embarking on the investigation.

7. There are several information sources available to paralegals who wish to locate factual information regarding witnesses or other persons involved in a lawsuit. These sources include telephone and city directories, media reports, court records, utility companies, professional organizations, and information recorded, compiled, or prepared by federal, state, and local government entities. The Freedom of Information Act of 1966 requires that federal agencies disclose certain of their records to any person on request, providing that the form of the request complies with the procedures mandated by the act.

8. Evidence is anything that is used to prove the existence or nonexistence of a fact. Direct evidence is any evidence that, if believed, establishes the truth of the fact in question. Circumstantial evidence is evidence that does not directly establish the fact in question but that indicates the degree of likelihood of the fact's existence. Because an investigation is undertaken to verify or uncover factual information that may eventually be used at trial, the paralegal should be familiar with what kind of evidence is admissible in court. Rules of evidence established by the federal and state courts spell out what types of evidence may or may not be admitted in court.

9. To be admissible in court, evidence must be relevant. Evidence must also be authenticated by a demonstration (usually by the testimony of a witness) that the evidence is what the attorney claims it to be. Some forms of evidence, such as certified copies of public records, are automatically deemed to be authentic and need not be authenticated by testimony. Hearsay (secondhand knowledge) is generally not admissible, although there are certain exceptions to this rule.

10. When the investigation is complete, the paralegal should summarize the results. The summary should include an overall summary, a source-by-source summary, and a final section giving the paralegal's conclusions and recommendations.

Questions for Review

1. What kinds of skills do interviewers employ during interviews?

2. What are the different types of questions that can be used in an interview? When would you use each type?

3. What takes place during the initial client interview? What is the paralegal's role at this interview? What other types of client interviews are commonly conducted by paralegals? What is the purpose of each type?

4. List and describe the various types of witnesses. In what kinds of situations might each of these types of witnesses be used?

5. What is a witness statement? How is it used?

6. Why and how do you create an investigation plan? What types of actions might be included in an investigation plan?

7. List five sources that you would consult in attempting to locate a witness. Which would be the most useful? Which would be the least useful? Why?

8. What is evidence? How are the rules of evidence used?

9. Define and give examples of the following types of evidence: direct evidence, circumstantial evidence, relevant evidence, authenticated evidence, and hearsay.

10. What is included in an investigation summary? Why should one be prepared?

Ethical Questions

1. Leah Fox, a legal assistant, has been asked by the attorney for whom she works to contact several potential witnesses to see what they know about an event. The first witness that Leah calls says, "I don't know if I should get involved. I don't want to get in trouble. You see, I was supposed to be at work, but I called in sick. If I get involved and my employer finds about where I really was, I might get fired. You're a lawyer, what do you think?" How should Leah respond?

2. Leah Fox, a legal assistant, is conducting a follow-up interview with a new client, who is seeking a divorce. Leah is asking the client about the couple's marital property. According to the client, the couple wants to divide the property evenly on their divorce. When Leah asks the client about checking or savings accounts, the client says to Leah, "You know, Leah, I have this 'secret' savings account, but I don't want anybody to know about it. Please don't tell Mr. Harcourt [Leah's supervising attorney] what I've just told you." What should Leah do in this situation?

3. Jeffrey Jones starts a new job as a paralegal. He reviews a file and notices that the client has not been contacted and updated on the status of the case in three months. He also notices that there is a settlement conference scheduled for tomorrow and that the client needs to be in court. What should Jeffrey do?

4. Jeffrey is asked to review the *Clemmons v. Auto Manufacturer of America* file and to continue the investigation in the case. His boss represents the auto manufacturer in this product-liability case and believes, based on the evidence uncovered so far, that he has an open-and-shut case against the plaintiff, who claims that her husband was killed when the car exploded on impact during an auto accident. Jeffrey begins interviewing witnesses, including an engineer who works for the company. The engineer states that he knew the car was defective and would explode on impact. Jeffrey is worried that his boss will be upset about this fact, because it damages his "open-and-shut" case. What should Jeffrey do?

5. Thomas Lent is a new legal assistant with a law firm that specializes in personal-injury cases. He is reviewing a "Request to Produce Documents" that was recently received in a case that his supervising attorney is handling for the plaintiff. The document requests the plaintiff's medical records, but it does not state specifically which records or for what injuries. Thomas's supervising attorney instructs Thomas to obtain copies of all of the plaintiff's medical records. The plaintiff's medical-records file is several inches thick because the plaintiff is an elderly person and has various medical problems. Thomas is instructed to bury the relevant medical records in the stack and not to make them obvious to the defendant's attorney. If she wants these records, she will have to sort through the file, says the attorney. What should Thomas do? Can the attorney be disciplined for this kind of behavior?

6. In response to a discovery request, Lynnette Banks, a paralegal in a corporate law firm, receives a package of documents in the mail. She opens the package and begins to read through the documents. As she does so, she discovers some that have the words "Privileged and Confidential" stamped on them. She scans a document and realizes that it is a letter from the opposing counsel to his client. The letter reveals the opposing attorney's legal strategy for the case on which Lynette is now working. What should Lynnette do?

Practice Questions and Assignments

1. Review the Baranski-Peretto hypothetical case discussed earlier in this text (see Chapter 10). Then write sample questions that you would ask the interviewee when interviewing eyewitnesses to the accident. Phrase at least one question in each of the question formats discussed in this chapter.

2. Using the information in this chapter on questioning skills, identify the following types of questions:
   a. "From January 10 through January 17, 1999, you were on a cruise in the Bahamas, Mr. Johnson. Your credit-card records, which were subpoenaed, indicate that you purchased two tickets. If your wife did not accompany you on that cruise, who did?"
   b. "Did you go on a cruise in the Bahamas with another woman, Mr. Johnson?"
   c. "Isn't it true, Mr. Johnson, that someone other than your wife accompanied you on a cruise in the Bahamas?"
   d. "Mr. Johnson, will you please describe your whereabouts between January 10 and January 17, 1999?"

3. Lena Phillips, a fifty-two-year-old, self-employed seamstress, fell down the three steps in front of her house and fractured her right wrist. She was treated in the emergency room at the Neighborhood Hospital by Dr. Ralph Dean on the day that she fell, January 10, 1999, and released. On January 17, January 25, and February 11, 1999, she visited Dr. Dean's office for follow-up care to make sure that the wrist was healing properly. It appeared that the wrist was healing properly during the month in which she was treated by Dr. Dean. She noticed, however, that even though she had a full range of motion in her wrist, the wrist angled inward somewhat. When she queried Dr. Dean about this, he told her that some angling of the wrist was inevitable.

   Over the course of the following year her wrist became increasingly crooked and bent inward. She went to an orthopedist, Dr. Alicia Byerly, on March 30, 2000. Dr. Byerly tried a splint, but without success. She eventually performed surgery on the wrist at the Neighborhood Hospital on May 3, 2000, but was unable to correct the problem. Dr. Byerly told Ms. Phillips that she should have had surgery on the wrist during the first three weeks after it was broken to correct the angling problem.

   Lena Phillips has come to the firm for which you work, the law firm of Samson & Gore, 5000 West Avenue, Northville, NH 12345, because she wants to sue Dr. Dean for medical malpractice. On May 15, 2000, you are asked to investigate her case. Draft an investigation plan.

4. Using Exhibit 13.3, *A Sample Follow-Up Letter to a Client,* as an example, draft a follow-up letter to Lena Phillips based on the facts from question 3 above. The attorney that gave you the assignment is Alan Samson. You will need to include a retainer agreement and instruct the client not to talk to Dr. Dean.

5. Using the factual background presented in question 3, draft an "Authorization to Release Medical Information" letter for Lena Phillips to sign. Her name and address are Lena A. Phillips, 150 North Street, Northville, NH, 12345.

6. Using the information in Exhibit 13.4, *Information Contained in a Witness Statement,* and Exhibit 13.5, *A Sample Witness Statement (Excerpt),* draft a witness statement based on the following facts.

   You work for the law firm of Thomas & Snyder and on April 1, 2000, you are interviewing a witness to a car-train accident that happened a few hours earlier. The interview takes place at the police station. The witness's name is Henry Black. Henry is retired and lives at 2002 Stephens Road, Clinton Township, Pennsylvania. His telephone number is (123) 456–7890.

   Henry was in his Cadillac, stopped in front of the railroad tracks on Jefferson Avenue in Clinton Township, Pennsylvania, at approximately 10:00 A.M., when a red 1999 Mercury Villager sped past him and across the tracks. He was very surprised that a car would not stop at the tracks because the train was only about thirty feet away and was blowing its whistle. There were no gates or guard rails in front of the tracks. Henry looked over at the driver of the Villager and saw that she was talking on a cellular phone as she was driving. She did not appear to hear the train. As her Villager crossed the tracks, the train struck the passenger side of her vehicle. Fortunately, there appeared to be no one else in the vehicle.

7. Assume that a witness is being questioned about statements that she heard a third party make. Determine which of the following statements would qualify as exceptions to the hearsay rule:

    a. The third party exclaimed, "Watch out, he's not stopping at the red light!"

    b. The third party apologized, "Are you all right? I am so sorry. I didn't mean to hurt you."

    c. The third party uttered just before he died, "Make sure you find Joe. He is the one who shot me. Tom didn't have anything to do with this."

    d. The third party exclaimed, "I smell gas fumes!"

    e. The third party, who was the defendant's mistress, said, "He couldn't have killed Bob. He was with me last night."

8. During the course of a murder trial, a prosecuting attorney paraded through the courtroom carrying a hand that had been unearthed the day before and that had been widely publicized as belonging to the murder victim. The defense attorney strenuously objected on the ground that the hand was not relevant. Should the judge sustain the objection?

9. Determine whether each of the following statements is a statement of fact or a statement of opinion, and explain why:

    a. I am sure that the suspect took the money because when I saw him near the cash register, he looked around suspiciously and then tried to sneak away without being seen.

    b. The man who took the money from the cash register was wearing a green trench coat, brown pants, and black boots and was carrying a large tan briefcase.

10. Working in groups of three, role-play the initial client interview described in Chapter 10 between Katherine Baranski and the legal team—attorney Allen Gilmore and paralegal Elena Lopez. Attorney Gilmore will need to prepare a list of questions and will ask most of the questions during the interview. Paralegal Lopez will take notes during the interview, provide the retainer-agreement and release forms, and schedule the follow-up interview. Change roles if time allows.

QUESTIONS FOR CRITICAL ANALYSIS

1. Some attorneys ask their legal assistants to conduct initial client interviews alone, without the attorney being present. During these types of interviews, clients often ask legal assistants for legal advice. Is it fair to put the legal assistant in this position? How would you handle an attorney who asks you to handle initial client interviews? How would you handle a client who asks for legal advice?

2. Why do you think you need to obtain the client's or witness's permission to tape-record an interview? What might happen if you did not obtain permission?

3. Leading questions tend to lead to distorted answers and may typically be used only on cross-examination. Why would an attorney want to use this type of question on cross-examination? Is this misleading to the court? Is the use of leading questions ethical?

4. There are several different types of client interviews. Make a list of the different types of client interviews and the kinds of questions that would be most effective to use during each one.

5. Expert witnesses give testimony relating to incidents they have not observed or people they may never have met. What, then, is the value of expert testimony? Why do courts allow expert witnesses to testify?

6. Several different types of witnesses were described in this chapter. Do any of these types, or categories, of witnesses overlap—that is, could one witness fall into more than one of the categories? Explain.

7. Hostile witnesses are often interviewed, but usually they are not called to testify at trial by the party to whom they are hostile. Why is this? How would an attorney handle a witness who is hostile to his or her client's case?

8. Witnesses' qualifications are checked out during the course of investigation. Why is this? What might happen if a witness's qualifications were not checked?

9. Why should you use an investigation plan? What might happen without one? What if you find information that requires you to drastically modify your plan? How should you proceed?

10. Clients are often required to sign releases authorizing an entity (such as a hospital) to turn over information to a particular party (such as an attorney). Why is this? What might happen if releases were not required?

Projects

1. Watch an interview on television. Write a two-page, double-spaced paper describing the interview. Include in your description the following information:
   a. The names of the interviewer and the interviewee.
   b. The subject of the interview.
   c. The date and time of the interview and the television channel over which it was broadcast.
   d. The different types of questions (open ended, closed ended, and so on) used by the interviewer and the types of responses elicited by the different kinds of questions.
   e. The ways in which the interviewer and interviewee communicated nonverbally.
   f. Your overall evaluation of the interviewer's skill at interviewing this particular interviewee.
2. Using public records only, find out the name of the spouse of the person sitting next to you in class (if he or she is married). If he or she is not married, find out the name of at least one of his or her siblings or another relative. Start by making a list of the public sources that you could search.
3. Locate law libraries in your city or county that are open to the public. What resources does each library have that would help you locate expert witnesses?
4. Call the county offices for your county and ask if they give tours. If they do, arrange to go on a tour of the offices. Find out what information is kept there, such as data on births, deaths, marriages, and property. Also find out what information is available to the public and what procedures must be followed to obtain this information.
5. Go to a library and do some research on listening skills. Write a one-page, double-spaced paper giving additional information on the listening techniques discussed in this chapter.

Using Internet Resources

1. Access the following Web site to find the Federal Rules of Evidence:

   www.law.cornell.edu/rules/fre/overview.html#1007.

   Browse through these rules and then answer the following questions:
   a. How do the Federal Rules of Evidence define "relevant evidence"?
   b. Summarize the "General Rule of Competency" set forth in the these rules.
   c. Look at Rule 803, which lists several exceptions to the "Hearsay Rule." List and describe five of these exceptions.
2. KnowX.com is a public records Web site. Much of the information that can be located at this site is information that a private investigator (or a paralegal) might want to find when investigating a case. Access the site at **www.KnowX.com**. From the information contained on the home page, what can you find using KnowX.com?
   a. Click on "Locate People." What databases does KnowX.com search to find people? Is there any cost involved? If so, how much does KnowX.com charge? Click on "Start the Demo" to run the "Quick Demo." What is the result of the search?
   b. Return to the home page and select "Research Businesses." Next, click on "The Ultimate Business Finder." What databases does KnowX.com search for business information?
   c. Return to the home page and choose "Run a Background Check." What types of background checks does KnowX.com perform? What databases does it search? Is there any cost involved? If so, how much does KnowX.com charge?
   d. Return to the home page. Click on "Other Searches." Make a list of five other searches that KnowX.com can perform.

CHAPTER 14

LEGAL RESEARCH

Chapter Outline

- Introduction
- Primary and Secondary Sources
- Researching Case Law—The Preliminary Steps
- Secondary Sources of Case Law
- The Case Reporting System
- Researching Statutory Law
- Researching Administrative Law
- Finding Constitutional Law
- Updating the Law—Learning to Use Citators

After completing this chapter, you will know:

- How primary and secondary sources of law differ and how to use each of these types of sources in the research process.
- How to use legal encyclopedias and other secondary sources to find case law relevant to your research topic.
- How court decisions are published and how to read case citations.
- How federal statutes and regulations are published and the major sources of statutory and administrative law.
- What kinds of resources are available for researching the legislative history of a statute.
- Why finding current law is important and how to verify that your research results are up to date.

INTRODUCTION

For many paralegals, legal research is a fascinating part of their jobs. They find it intrinsically interesting to read the actual words of a court's opinion on a legal question or the text of a statute. Additionally, they acquire a firsthand knowledge of the law and how it applies to actual people and events. Research is also a crucial part of the paralegal's job, and the ability to conduct research thoroughly yet efficiently enhances a paralegal's value to the legal team.

As a paralegal, you may be asked to perform a variety of research tasks. Some research tasks will be simple. You may be asked to locate and copy a court case, for example. Other research tasks may take days or even weeks to complete. In almost all but the simplest of research tasks, legal research overlaps extensively with legal analysis, which is covered in the following chapter. To find relevant case law, for example, you need to be able to analyze the cases you find to ensure that they are indeed relevant. Although we discuss research and analysis separately, keep in mind that the two processes are closely related.

Many paralegals now conduct research without even entering a law library. Computerized legal services such as Westlaw® and Lexis® allow legal professionals to find the text of cases, statutes, and other legal documents without leaving their desks. As you will read in Chapter 15, these and an abundance of other sources are now available online. An increasing number of law firms today are also purchasing reference materials on CD-ROMs. To a great extent, how you do your research—that is, whether you conduct research online or in a law library—will depend on your employer and the computer facilities available to you. In some workplaces, paralegals are expected to conduct much of their research using computerized legal services or other online sources. In other workplaces, paralegals may be asked to do the bulk of their legal research using printed legal sources in law libraries.

Regardless of whether legal research is conducted online or in a law library, it is essential to know what sources to consult for different types of information. You will learn about these sources in this chapter. You will also learn how to make sure that the law you find is up to date and still "good law."

PRIMARY AND SECONDARY SOURCES

Primary Source
In legal research, a document that establishes the law on a particular issue, such as a case decision, legislative act, administrative rule, or presidential order.

Secondary Source
In legal research, any publication that indexes, summarizes, or interprets the law, such as a legal encyclopedia, a treatise, or an article in a law review.

Generally, research sources fall into two broad categories—primary sources and secondary sources. Printed decisions of the various courts in the United States, statutes enacted by legislative bodies, rules and regulations created by administrative agencies, presidential orders, and generally any documents that *establish* the law are **primary sources** of law. **Secondary sources** of law consist of books and articles that summarize, systematize, compile, or otherwise interpret the law. Legal encyclopedias, which summarize the law, are secondary sources of law.

Normally, researchers in any field or profession begin their research with secondary sources. Secondary sources are often referred to as *finding tools*, because they help the researcher to find primary sources on the topics they are researching and to learn how those sources have been interpreted by others. If you are asked to research case law on a certain issue, you should do likewise. You should first refer to secondary sources to learn about the issue and find relevant primary sources concerning it. Then you can go to the primary sources themselves (such as statutes or court cases) to research the established law on the issue.

In the following sections, you will read about the primary and secondary sources that are most frequently used in researching case law, statutory law and legislative history, administrative law, and constitutional law.

> ## ETHICAL CONCERN
> ### Efficiency in Research
>
> Attorneys have a duty to charge their clients reasonable fees. As a paralegal, you help your attorney fulfill this duty by working efficiently—to minimize the number of hours you spend on work relating to the client's matter. Legal research can be extremely time consuming, as every paralegal knows. To reduce the time spent in researching a particular legal issue, start out on your quest with a clear idea of your research task. After all, your time is expensive not only for the client (who pays for it) but also for your supervising attorney (who may need your assistance on other cases as well). By knowing as precisely as possible what the goal of your research is, you can reach that goal more quickly and thus better serve the interests of both the client and your supervising attorney.

RESEARCHING CASE LAW—THE PRELIMINARY STEPS

Any research project normally involves the following five steps:

- Defining the issue(s) to be researched.
- Determining the goal of the research project.
- Consulting relevant secondary sources.
- Researching relevant primary sources.
- Synthesizing and summarizing research results.[1]

To illustrate how you would follow the first two steps when researching case law, we present a hypothetical case. The case involves one of your firm's clients, Trent Hoffman, who is suing Better Homes Store for negligence. During the initial client interview, Hoffman explained to you and your supervising attorney that he had gone to the store to purchase a large mirror. As he was leaving the store through the store's side entrance, carrying the bulky mirror, he ran into a large pole just outside the door. He did not see the pole because the mirror blocked his view. On hitting the pole, the mirror broke, and a piece of glass entered Hoffman's left eye, causing permanent loss of eyesight in that eye. Hoffman claims that the store was negligent in placing a pole so close to the exit and is suing the store for $3 million in damages.

You have already undertaken a preliminary investigation into the matter and obtained evidence supporting Hoffman's account of the facts. Your supervising attorney now asks you to do some research. Your job is to research case law to find other cases with similar fact patterns and see how the courts decided the issue in those cases.

Defining the Issue

Before you consult any source, primary or secondary, you must know the legal issue that needs to be researched. Your first task will be to examine closely the facts of Hoffman's case to determine the nature of the legal issue involved. Based on Hoffman's description of the factual circumstances (verified through your preliminary investigation) and on his allegation that Better Homes Store should

---

1. This final step—because it involves legal analysis and writing—is covered in Chapter 16.

not have placed a pole just outside one of the store's entrances, you know that the legal issue relates to the tort of negligence. As a starting point, you should therefore review what you know about negligence theory.

Recall from Chapter 7 that the tort of negligence is defined as the failure to exercise reasonable care, and to succeed in a negligence action, a plaintiff must establish that (1) the defendant had a duty of care to the plaintiff, (2) the defendant breached that duty, (3) the plaintiff suffered a legally recognizable injury, and (4) the injury was caused by the defendant's breach of the duty of care. A knowledge of these elements will help you determine the issue that needs to be researched in Hoffman's case. There is little doubt that the third requirement has been met—Hoffman's loss of sight in his left eye is a legally recognizable injury for which he can be compensated—*if* he succeeds in proving the other three elements of negligence. The fourth element, causation, is largely dependent on proving the first two elements. In your research, you will therefore want to focus on the first two elements. Specifically, you need to find answers to the following questions:

- Did Better Homes Store owe a duty of care to its customer, Hoffman? You might phrase this question in more general terms: Do business owners owe a duty of care to **business invitees**, customers and others whom they invite onto their premises?
- If so, what is the extent of that duty, and how is it measured? In other words, are business owners always liable, in all circumstances, when customers are injured on their premises? Or must some condition be met before store owners will be liable? For example, must a customer's injury be a *foreseeable* consequence of a condition on the premises, such as the pole outside the store's door, for the store owner to be liable for the injury?
- If the injury must be a foreseeable consequence of a condition, would a court find that Hoffman's injury in this case was a foreseeable consequence of the pole's placement just outside the store's door?

These, then, are the issues you need to research. Notice how the term *issue* has become plural. You will find that this is a common occurrence in legal research—only rarely will you be researching a single legal issue.

Determining Your Research Goals

Once you have defined the issue or issues to be researched, you will be in a better position to determine your research goals. Remember that you are working on behalf of a client, who is paying for your services. Your overall goal is thus to find legal support for Hoffman's claim. To achieve this goal, you will want to do two things: find cases on point and cases that are mandatory authorities. Depending on what you find, you may also need to look for persuasive authorities.

CASES ON POINT. One of your research goals is to find a case (or cases) on point in which the court held for the plaintiff. A **case on point** is a previous case involving fact patterns and legal issues that are similar to those in a case that has not yet been decided by a court. In regard to Hoffman's negligence claim, a case on point would be one in which the plaintiff alleged that he or she was injured while on a store's premises because of a dangerous condition on those premises.

The ideal case on point, of course, would be a case in which all four elements of a case (the parties, the circumstances, the legal issues involved, and the remedies sought by the plaintiff) are very similar. Such a case is called a **case on "all fours."**[2]

Business Invitee
A person, such as a customer or client, who is invited onto business premises by the owner of those premises for business purposes.

Case on Point
A case involving factual circumstances and issues that are similar to a case before the court.

Case on "All Fours"
A case in which all four elements of a case (the parties, the circumstances, the legal issues involved, and the remedies sought by the plaintiff) are very similar.

---

2. Some scholars maintain that this phrase originated from the Latin adage that "nothing similar is identical unless it runs on all four feet."

DEVELOPING PARALEGAL SKILLS
Defining the Issues to Be Researched

Federal government agents observed Bernie Berriman in his parked car talking on his cellular phone. Later, other cars were seen driving up to Bernie's car and stopping. The drivers received brown paper bags in exchange for money. Bernie was questioned, and his car was searched. Cocaine was found in the car. He was arrested for transporting and distributing cocaine, and the police took his car and cellular phone. Bernie's lawyer is arguing that the government agents did not have the authority to require Bernie to forfeit his car and cellular phone. Natalie Martin, a legal assistant with the U.S. attorney's office, has been assigned the task of researching the federal statutes and cases on this issue.

Before Natalie can begin her research project, she must thoroughly review the case to determine what specific issues need to be researched. Using a checklist method that she learned in school, she breaks the facts of

the case down into five categories and inserts the relevant facts from her assignment:

- Parties: Who are the people involved in the action or lawsuit?
- Places and Things: Where did the events take place, and what items are involved in the action or lawsuit?
- Basis of Action or Issue: What is the legal claim or issue involved in the action or lawsuit?
- Defenses: What is the legal reason why the accused should not be held responsible?
- Relief Sought: What is the legal remedy or penalty sought in the case?

Now Natalie is ready to go the library and begin her research.

In regard to Hoffman's claim, a case on "all fours" would be a case on point, such as just described, in which the plaintiff-customer did not expect a condition (such as an obstacle in his or her path) to exist and was prevented from seeing the obstacle by some action that a customer would reasonably undertake (such as carrying a large box out of a store). The parties and the circumstances of the case would thus be very similar to those in Hoffman's case. If the plaintiff also sustained a permanent injury, as Hoffman did, and sought damages for negligence, then the case would be, relative to Hoffman's case, a case on "all fours."

MANDATORY AUTHORITIES. In researching Hoffman's case, another goal is to find cases (on point or on "all fours") that are also mandatory authorities. A **mandatory authority** is any authority that the court must rely on in its determination of the issue. A mandatory authority may be a statute, regulation, or constitution that governs the issue, or it may be a previously decided court case that is controlling in your jurisdiction.

For a case to serve as a mandatory authority, it must be on point and decided by a superior court. A superior court, in the sense that it is used here, is any court that is on a higher tier in the court system. Recall from Chapter 6 that both the federal and state court systems consist of several levels, or tiers, of courts. *Trial courts*, in which evidence is presented and testimony given, are on the bottom tier (which also includes lower courts handling specialized issues). Decisions from a trial court can be appealed to a higher court, which commonly is an intermediate *court of appeals*, or *appellate court*. Decisions from these intermediate courts of appeals may be appealed to an even higher court, such as a state supreme court or, if a federal question is involved, the United States Supreme Court.

A lower court is bound to follow the decisions set forth by a higher court in the same jurisdiction. An appellate court's decision in a case involving facts and

Mandatory Authority
Any source of law that a court must follow when deciding a case. Mandatory authorities include constitutions, statutes, and regulations that govern the issue before the court, and court decisions made by a superior court in the jurisdiction.

issues similar to a case brought in a trial court in the same jurisdiction would thus be a mandatory authority—the trial court would be bound to follow the appellate court's decision on the issue. A higher court is never required to follow an opinion written by a lower court in the same jurisdiction, however. For example, if a California intermediate appellate court is deciding a case, it does not have to abide by decisions previously made by California trial courts on the issue, although it might take these decisions into consideration. But the court is obligated to abide by a decision on the issue rendered by the California Supreme Court.

State courts have the final say on state law, and federal courts have the final say on federal law. Thus, except in deciding an issue that involves federal law, state courts do not have to follow the decisions of federal courts. In deciding issues that involve federal law, however, state courts must abide by the decisions of the United States Supreme Court.

 When you are performing research, look for cases on point decided by the highest court in your jurisdiction, because those cases carry the most weight.

Persuasive Authority
Any legal authority, or source of law, that a court may look to for guidance but on which it need not rely in making its decision. Persuasive authorities include cases from other jurisdictions and secondary sources of law, such as scholarly treatises.

PERSUASIVE AUTHORITIES.   A **persuasive authority** is not binding on a court. In other words, the court is not required to follow that authority in making its decision. Examples of persuasive authorities are (1) prior court opinions of other jurisdictions, which, although they are not binding, may be suggestive as to how a particular case should be decided; (2) legal periodicals, such as law reviews, in which the issue at hand is discussed by legal scholars; (3) encyclopedias summarizing legal principles or concepts relating to a particular issue; and (4) legal dictionaries that describe how the law has been applied in the past.

Often, a court refers to persuasive authorities when deciding a *case of first impression*, which is a case involving an issue that has never been addressed by that court before. For example, if in your research of Hoffman's claim you find that no similar cases have ever reached a higher court in your jurisdiction, you would look for similar cases decided by courts in other jurisdictions. If courts in other jurisdictions have faced a similar issue, the court may be guided by those other courts' decisions when deciding Hoffman's case. Your supervising attorney will want to know about these persuasive authorities so that he can present them to the court for consideration.

SECONDARY SOURCES OF CASE LAW

Finding cases that are both on point and mandatory legal authorities is not always easy. The body of American case law consists of about five million decisions. Each year, more than forty thousand new cases are added to this collection. Because the decisions of the courts are published in chronological order, finding relevant precedents would be a Herculean task if it were not for secondary sources of law that classify decisions according to subject. A logical place to begin your research is thus with secondary sources of case law. In researching Hoffman's claim, you might look first at a legal encyclopedia to learn more about the topic of negligence and the duty of care of business owners to business invitees. Generally, to help you find topics that shed light on your subject, you should make a list of all relevant legal terms and phrases, as well as their synonyms, before beginning the research process.

Legal Encyclopedias

Legal encyclopedias provide detailed summaries of legal rules and concepts. Legal encyclopedias also arrange topics alphabetically and refer readers to leading cases in that area of law.

Encyclopedias are helpful resources for the student who is new to legal research or for an experienced legal professional who is researching an unfamiliar area of law. By referring to an encyclopedia, you can obtain background information on the topic that will help you direct your research more effectively. Two popular legal encyclopedias are *American Jurisprudence*, Second Edition, and *Corpus Juris Secundum*. Another popular legal resource is *Words and Phrases*. We discuss each of these works here. (Note that there are also state-specific encyclopedias—that is, encyclopedias that refer readers to state cases or statutes relating to a specific topic. You can check with the reference librarian in your local law library to find a state-specific encyclopedia, if your state has one.)

AMERICAN JURISPRUDENCE, SECOND EDITION. *American Jurisprudence*, Second Edition, is commonly referred to as *American Jurisprudence 2d* or, more briefly, as *Am. Jur. 2d*. (A photograph of one of the volumes of this encyclopedia is shown in Exhibit 14.1.) This encyclopedia is published by the Lawyers Cooperative Publishing Company. (Because this company is now part of West Group, in the remainder of this chapter we refer to its publications as West Group publications.) *American Jurisprudence 2d*. offers a detailed discussion of virtually every area of American law. The encyclopedia covers more than 440 topics in 58 volumes. Each topic is further divided into various subtopics containing narrative descriptions of the general rules of law that have emerged from generations of court decisions. If there are conflicting decisions on an issue or topic, the encyclopedia indicates this and offers explanations for the differing opinions. The encyclopedia also provides various cross-references to specific court cases, annotations in *American Law Reports* (to be discussed shortly), law reviews, and other relevant sections of *American Jurisprudence*. The volumes are kept current through supplements called **pocket parts** (because they slip into a pocket in the front or back of the volume), which contain additions to the various topics and subtopics.

As with any encyclopedia, topics in *American Jurisprudence 2d* are presented alphabetically. Each general topic is organized to allow a researcher to find quickly the specific area of interest. Each volume of the encyclopedia also contains an index, located at the back of the volume. A separate index is also provided for the entire encyclopedia once a series, or edition, is completed. The indexes can be very helpful to the researcher. For example, in researching the issue in Hoffman's lawsuit against Better Homes Store for negligence, you could look in the index for such terms as *premises liability, business invitees, duty of care, landowners,* or some other term or phrase. Exhibit 14.2 on the next page shows the first page of the discussion of premises liability. Although not shown in the exhibit, an outline of the major topics of the section follows, complete with descriptive subsections. The outline allows the researcher to locate easily any relevant areas within the general subject matter.

CORPUS JURIS SECUNDUM Another enclopedia helpful to the legal researcher is *Corpus Juris Secundum*, or *C.J.S.*, which is published by West Group. This encyclopedia, like *American Jurisprudence 2d*, provides detailed information on almost every area of the law. *C.J.S.* consists of 101 volumes and covers 433 topics, each of which is further divided into subtopics. One of the volumes of this set is depicted in Exhibit 14.3 on page 495.

The approaches of *C.J.S.* and *American Jurisprudence 2d* are very similar. *C.J.S.* offers an explanation of contradictory court decisions on an issue, if there are any, and provides the names of these cases and of the published sources in which they can be found. *C.J.S.* also contains alphabetical entries as well as indexes for locating relevant legal information. The indexes are located at the end of each volume and in a multivolume index at the end of a set. To keep its information up

EXHIBIT 14.1
American Jurisprudence 2d

Reproduced with permission of West Group.

Pocket Part
A separate pamphlet containing recent cases or changes in the law that is used to update hornbooks, legal encyclopedias, and other legal authorities. It is called a "pocket part" because it slips into a sleeve, or pocket, in the front or back binder of the volume.

EXHIBIT 14.2
Excerpt from *American Jurisprudence 2d*

Reproduced with permission of West Group.

PREMISES LIABILITY
by
Irwin J. Schiffres, J.D. and Sheila A. Skojec, J.D.

Scope of topic: This article discusses the principles and rules of law applicable to and governing the liability of owners or occupants of real property for negligence causing injury to persons or property by reason of defects therein or hazards created by the activities of such owners or occupants or their agents and employees. Treated in detail are the classification of persons injured as invitees, licensees, or trespassers, and the duty owed them, as well as the rules applicable in those jurisdictions where such status distinctions are no longer determinative of the duty owed the entrant; the effect of "recreational use" statutes on the duty owed persons using the property for such purposes; the greater measure of duty owed by the owner to children as compared to adult licensees and trespassers, including the attractive nuisance doctrine; and the specific duties and liabilities of owners and occupants of premises used for business or residential purposes. Also considered is the effect of the injured person's negligence on the plaintiff's right to recover under principles of contributory or comparative negligence.

Federal aspects: One injured on premises owned or operated by the United States may seek to recover under general principles of premises liability discussed in this article. Insofar as recovery is sought under the Federal Torts Claims Act, see 35 Am Jur 2d, FEDERAL TORTS CLAIMS ACT § 73.

Treated elsewhere:
   Mutual obligations and liabilities of adjoining landowners with respect to injuries arising from their acts or omissions, see 1 Am Jur 2d, ADJOINING LANDOWNERS AND PROPERTIES §§ 10, 11, 28 et seq., 37 et seq.
   Liability for the acts or omissions of the owners or occupants of premises abutting on a street or highway which cause injury to those using the way, see 39 Am Jur 2d, HIGHWAYS, STREETS, AND BRIDGES §§ 517 et seq.
   Liability for violation of building regulations, see 13 Am Jur 2d, BUILDINGS §§ 32 et seq.
   Liability of employer for injuries caused employees on the employer's premises, see 53 Am Jur 2d, MASTER AND SERVANT §§ 139 et seq.
   Liability for injuries caused by defective products on the premises, see 63 Am Jur 2d, PRODUCTS LIABILITY
   Respective rights and liabilities of a landlord and tenant where one is responsible for an injury suffered by the other, or by a third person, on leased premises or on premises provided for the common use of tenants, see 49 Am Jur 2d, LANDLORD AND TENANT §§ 761 et seq.
   Liability of a receiver placed in charge of property for an injury sustained thereby or thereon by someone other than the persons directly interested in the estate, see 66 Am Jur 2d, RECEIVERS § 364
   Duties and liabilities of occupiers of premises used for various particular types of businesses or activities, see 4 Am Jur 2d, AMUSEMENTS AND EXHIBITIONS §§ 51 et seq.; 14 Am Jur 2d, CARRIERS §§ 964 et seq.; 38 Am Jur 2d, GARAGES, AND FILLING AND PARKING STATIONS §§ 81 et seq.; 40 Am Jur 2d, HOSPITALS AND ASYLUMS § 31; 40 Am Jur 2d, HOTELS, MOTELS, AND RESTAURANTS §§ 81 et seq.; 50 Am Jur 2d, LAUNDRIES, DYERS, AND DRY CLEANERS §§ 21, 22; 54 Am Jur 2d, MOBILE HOMES, TRAILER PARKS, AND TOURIST CAMPS § 17; 57 Am Jur 2d, MUNICIPAL, COUNTY, SCHOOL, AND STATE TORT LIABILITY; and 59 AM JUR 2D, PARKS, SQUARES, AND PLAYGROUNDS §§ 43 et seq.
   Duties and liabilities with respect to injuries caused by particular agencies, such as

317

---

to date, *C.J.S.* also provides supplements (pocket parts) containing current materials. In regard to Hoffman's claim, if you looked up the word *business* in the *C.J.S.*, you would find a discussion of that topic, including a reference to business invitees (as shown on the page from the *C.J.S.* presented in Exhibit 14.4 on page 496).

WORDS AND PHRASES. *Words and Phrases* is a forty-six-volume encyclopedia of definitions and interpretations of legal terms and phrases published by West Group. It is a useful tool for learning how the courts have interpreted a particular term or phrase. The words and phrases covered are arranged in alphabetical order. Each is followed by abstracts (brief summary statements) from federal or state court decisions in which the word or phrase has been interpreted or defined. The abstract also indicates the names of the cases and the reporters in which they can be located. **Reporters** are publications containing the actual texts of court cases, as will be discussed later in this section. When researching Hoffman's claim, you could find out how various courts have defined *negligence* by looking up that term in *Words and Phrases*. Part of the entry for this term is shown in Exhibit 14.5 on page 497. *Words and Phrases* is updated by annual supplementary pocket parts.

Case Digests

In researching the issue in Hoffman's case against Better Homes Store, you might want to check a case digest as well as a legal encyclopedia for references to relevant case law. **Digests**, which are produced by various publishers, are helpful research tools because they provide indexes to case law—from the earliest recorded cases through the most current opinions. Case digests arrange topics alphabetically and provide information to help you locate referenced cases, but they do not offer the detail found in legal encyclopedias. Collected under each topic heading in a case digest are annotations. **Annotations** are comments, explanatory notes, or case summaries. In case digests, annotations consist of very short statements of relevant points of law in reported cases.

The digests published by West Group offer the most comprehensive system for locating cases by subject matter. West publishes digests of both federal court opinions and state court opinions, as well as regional digests, and digests that correspond with its reporters covering specialized areas, such as bankruptcy.

THE WEST KEY-NUMBER SYSTEM. West's key-number system has simplified the task of researching case law. The system divides all areas of American law into specific categories, or topics, arranged in alphabetical order. The topics are further divided into many specific subtopics, each designated by a **key number,** which is accompanied by the West key symbol: ⚷. Exhibit 14.6 on page 498 shows some of the key numbers used for subtopics under the topic of negligence.

West editors provide abstracts, or **headnotes,** for every area of the law discussed within each decision appearing in the West reporters. Every headnote is described by its topic name, which is followed by a key number indicating the specific subject discussed. This system of arranging legal and factual issues by subject matter allows West to gather all headnotes under the same topic and key number into one published work—the digest. If you consulted a West digest when researching Hoffman's case, the digest would indicate the names of cases relating to the topic as well as the reporters in which the texts of those cases can be found.

WEST'S FEDERAL DIGESTS. West's federal digests cover cases from the United States Supreme Court, the U.S. courts of appeals, the U.S. district courts, and various specialized federal courts, such as bankruptcy courts. Cases from all of these courts are organized according to the West key-number system. Headnotes from the United States Supreme Court are listed first, followed by appellate court and district court cases.

There are five separate federal digests, providing coverage from 1754 to the present. The *Federal Digest* covers the years 1754 through 1939. The *Modern Federal Digest* begins coverage in 1939 and ends with the year 1961. The *Federal Practice Digest 2d* covers the time period from 1961 to 1975, and the *Federal Practice Digest 3d* covers 1975 through 1991. The *Federal Practice Digest 4th*, the current edition, begins with 1991. Exhibit 14.7 on page 499 shows excerpts from

EXHIBIT 14.3
Corpus Juris Secundum

Reproduced with permission of West Group.

Reporter
A publication in which court cases are published, or reported.

Digest
A compilation in which brief summaries of court cases are arranged by subject and subdivided by jurisdiction and court.

Annotation
A brief comment, an explanation of a legal point, or a case summary found in a case digest or other legal source.

Key Number
A number (accompanied by the symbol of a key) corresponding to a specific topic within West's key-number system to facilitate legal research of case law.

Headnote
A note near the beginning of a reported case summarizing the court's ruling on an issue.

EXHIBIT 14.4
Excerpt from *Corpus Juris Secundum*

Reproduced with permission of West Group.

BUSINESS

12A C.J.S.

Business time. The term "business time" has been held to mean the ability to engage in a sustained effort of a character sufficiently substantial to negative the idea that there was not a total loss of power reasonably to continue a business or profession.[18]

Business use. The phrase "business use" may have different meanings in different statutes, ordinances, and other writings.[19] The generally accepted meaning of the term necessarily implies employment of one or more persons for the purpose of earning a livelihood, activities of persons to improve their economic conditions and desires, and generally relates to commercial and industrial engagements.[20]

Business visitor. "Business visitors" are deemed to fall into two classes, first, those who enter upon the premises of another for a purpose connected with the business which the possessor conducts thereon, and, second, those who come upon the premises for a purpose connected with their own business which is connected with any purpose, business or otherwise, for which the possessor uses the premises.[21]

The phrase "business visitor" has been held equivalent to "invitee,"[22] and has been compared or contrasted with "licensee"[23] and "gratuitous licensee."[24]

Other phrases employing the word "business," as an adjective, are set out in the note.[25]

Iowa.—Crane Co. v. City Council of Des Moines, 225 N.W. 344, 345, 208 Iowa 164.
N.J.—Duke Power Co. v. Hillsborough Tp., Somerset County, 26 A.2d 713, 729, 20 N.J.Misc. 240.
N.C.—Mecklenburg County v. Sterchi Bros. Stores, 185 S.E. 454, 457, 459, 210 N.C. 79.
Okl.—State v. Atlantic Oil Producing Co., 49 P.2d 534, 538, 174 Okl. 61—Grieves v. State ex rel. County Attorney, 35 P.2d 454, 456, 168 Okl. 642.
Or.—Endicott, Johnson & Co. v. Multnomah County, 190 P. 1109, 1111, 96 Or. 679.
18. Ark.—Pacific Mut. Life Ins. Co. v. Riffel, 149 S.W.2d 57, 59, 202 Ark. 94.
19. Ga.—Snow v. Johnston, 28 S.E.2d 270, 277, 197 Ga. 146.

Test
Definite test of business use would usually be whether or not profit was being made, directly or indirectly, by owner, on particular occasion.
N.Y.—Juskiewicz v. New Jersey Fidelity & Plate Glass Ins. Co., 206 N.Y.S. 566, 568, 210 App.Div. 675.
20. Ga.—Snow v. Johnston, 28 S.E.2d 270, 277, 197 Ga. 146.
21. Kan.—Bessette v. Ernsting, 127 P.2d 438, 440, 155 Kan. 540—Kurre v. Graham Ship by Truck Co., 15 P.2d 463, 465, 136 Kan. 356.
See generally C.J.S. Negligence §§ 63(41)–63(56).

What constitutes
Cal.—Crane v. Smith, 144 P.2d 356, 361, 362, 23 Cal.2d 288.

Held "business visitors"
Cal.—Turnipseed v. Hoffman, 144 P.2d 797, 798, 23 Cal.2d 532—Hill v. Eaton & Smith, 149 P.2d 762, 763, 65 Cal.App.2d 11.
Mass.—Fortier v. Hibernian Bldg. Ass'n of Boston Highlands, 53 N.E.2d 110, 113, 315 Mass. 446.
N.Y.—Haefeli v. Woodrich Engineering Co., 175 N.E. 123, 125, 255 N.Y. 442.
Vt.—Rheaume v. Goodro, 34 A.2d 315, 316, 113 Vt. 370.
22. U.S.—Robey v. Keller, C.C.A.Va., 114 F.2d 790, 794—McCann v. Anchor Line, C.C.A.N.Y., 79 F.2d 338, 339.
Conn.—Knapp v. Connecticut Theatrical Corporation, 190 A. 291, 292, 122 Conn. 413.
Kan.—Kurre v. Graham Ship by Truck Co., 15 P.2d 463, 465, 136 Kan. 356.
Mo.—Stevenson v. Kansas City Southern Ry. Co., 159 S.W.2d 260, 263, 348 Mo. 1216.

Pa.—Hartman v. Miller, Super., 17 A.2d 652, 653, 143 Pa.Super. 143.
R.I.—Royer v. Najarian, 198 A. 562, 564, 60 R.I. 368.
23. U.S.—McCann v. Anchor Line, C.C.A.N.Y., 79 F.2d 338, 339.
Cal.—Oettinger v. Stewart, 148 P.2d 19, 20, 21, 24 Cal.2d 133, 156 A.L.R. 1221.
24. Cal.—Oettinger v. Stewart, 148 P.2d 19, 20, 21, 24 Cal.2d 133, 156 A.L.R. 1221.
N.H.—Sandwell v. Elliott Hospital, 24 A.2d 273, 274, 92 N.H. 41.
N.Y.—Haefeli v. Woodrich Engineering Co., 175 N.E. 123, 125, 255 N.Y. 442.
Petluck v. McGolrick Realty Co., 268 N.Y.S. 782, 786, 240 App.Div. 61.
25. **Particular terms**
(1) "Business compulsion" as analogous to "duress."
Cal.—Sistrom v. Anderson, 124 P.2d 372, 376, 51 C.A.2d 213.
(2) "Business assets" distinguished from "personal asset."
Cal.—In re Friedrichs' Estate, 290 P. 54, 55, 107 Cal.App. 142.
(3) "Business compulsion" contrasted with "duress."
Wash.—Ramp Buildings Corporation v. Northwest Bldg. Co., 4 P.2d 507, 509, 164 Wash. 603, 79 A.L.R. 651.
(4) "Business district" defined in statute and contrasted with "residential district."
N.C.—Mitchell v. Melts, 18 S.E.2d 406, 410, 220 N.C. 793.
(5) "Business enterprise" requires investment of capital, labor, and management.
U.S.—Helvering v. Jewel Mining Co., C.C.A.8, 126 F.2d 1011, 1015.
(6) One's home is not a "business enterprise."
Minn.—State v. Cooper, 285 N.W. 903, 905, 205 Minn. 333, 122 A.L.R. 727.
(7) Renting rooms in dwelling house is not engaging in a "business enterprise."
Tex.—Austin v. Richardson, Com.App., 288 S.W. 180, 181.
(8) "Business establishment" held to be a statutory phrase restricted to one resembling a mill, workshop, or other manufacturing establishment.
N.Y.—O'Connor v. Webber, 147 N.Y.S. 1053, 163 App.Div. 175, 178.
(9) "Business loss (or losses)" contrasted with "damage to property."

West's *Federal Practice Digest 4th* on the topic of negligence. As shown in the exhibit, the section begins with a general topical outline (shown in the lower right-hand portion of the exhibit). You can scan through the outline to find the specific subtopic covering the issue you are researching. Then, you can turn to the pages covering that subtopic (the beginning page of one of the subtopics is shown in the upper left-hand side of the exhibit) to find references to relevant case law.

Each of these federal digests provides headnotes for cases appearing in the *Supreme Court Reporter* (which reports cases decided by the United States Supreme Court), the *Federal Reporter* (which reports cases from the federal courts of appeals), the *Federal Supplement* (which reports cases from the federal district courts), and the *Federal Rules Decisions* (which covers federal rules of procedure). As mentioned, West also publishes specialized digests corresponding to its special

EXHIBIT 14.5
Excerpt from *Words and Phrases*

Reproduced with permission of West Group.

NEGLIGENCE

Estoppel by Negligence
Fault
General Negligence
Gross Negligence
Hazardous Negligence
Heedlessness
High Degree of Negligence
Homicide by Negligence
Imputed Contributory Negligence
Imputed Negligence
Incurred Without Fault or Negligence
Independent Act of Negligence
Independent Negligence
Injury Resulting from Negligence
Insulated Negligence
Intentional Negligence
Joint Negligence
Legal Negligence
Liability Created by Law
Marine Cause
Mistake, Error or Negligence
Mutual Contributory Negligence
Negligent
Notice of Negligence
Nuisance
Nuisance Dependent Upon Negligence
Ordinary Care
Ordinary Negligence
Otherwise
Persistent Negligence
Preponderance
Presumption of Negligence
Prima Facie Case of Negligence
Prima Facie Negligence
Prior Negligence
Proof of Negligence
Proximate Contributory Negligence
Reckless; Recklessly; Recklessness
Separate Negligence
Simple Negligence
Situation Created by Actor's Negligence
Slight Negligence
Specific Negligence
Subsequent Negligence
Supervening Negligence
Trespass
Wanton Negligence
Wantonness
Willful and Intentional Negligence
Willful Negligence
Willfulness
Without Negligence

In general

"Negligence", in absence of statute, is defined as the doing of that thing which a reasonably prudent person would not have done, or the failure to do that thing which a reasonably prudent person would have done, in like or similar circumstances. Biddle v. Mazzocco, Or., 284 P.2d 364, 368.

"Negligence" is a departure from the normal or what should be the normal, and is a failure to conform to standard of what a reasonably prudent man would ordinarily have done under the circumstances, or is doing what such man would not have done under the circumstances. Moran v. Pittsburgh-Des Moines Steel Co., D.C.Pa., 86 F. Supp. 255, 266.

"Negligence" being failure to do that which ordinarily prudent man would do or doing of that which such a man would not do under same circumstances, an ordinary custom, while relevant and admissible in evidence of negligence, is not conclusive thereof, especially where it is clearly a careless or dangerous custom. Tite v. Omaha Coliseum Corp., 12 N.W.2d 90, 94, 144 Neb. 22, 149 A.L.R. 1164.

Whether or not an act or omission is "negligence" seems to be determined by what under like circumstances would men of ordinary prudence have done. Cleveland, C., C. & St. L. R. Co. v. Ivins, Ohio, 12 O.C.D. 570.

"Negligence" means simply the want of ordinary care under the circumstances surrounding that particular case and the transaction in question, and "negligently" simply means doing an act in such a manner that it lacks the care which men of ordinary prudence and foresight use in their everyday affairs of life under the same or similar circumstances. Smillie v. Cleveland Ry., Ohio, 31 O.C.D. 323, 325, 20 Cir.Ct.R.,N.S., 302.

"Negligence" is the failure to do what a reasonable and prudent man would ordinarily have done under circumstances of situation or doing what such a person, under existing circumstances, would not have done. Judt v. Reinhardt Transfer Co., 17 Ohio Supp. 105, 107, 32 O.O. 161.

By "negligence" is meant negligence of such character that in the discretion of the court, the defendant should have inflicted upon him the punative penalties of having his license suspended and that the public required such protection. Com. v. Galley, 17 Som. 54.

"Negligence" is a failure to use ordinary care, that is, such care as persons of ordinary prudence are accustomed to exercise

524

federal reporters. Examples of these digests are *West's Bankruptcy Digest, Military Justice Digest, Education Law Digest, Reporting Services Digest,* and *United States Claims Digest.* West also provides exclusive digest coverage of the decisions of the United States Supreme Court in the *United States Supreme Court Digest.*

EXHIBIT 14.6
Subtopics and Key Numbers in a West Digest

Reproduced with permission of West Group.

NEGLIGENCE.

Scope-Note.

INCLUDES failure to use due care, either in respect of acts or of omissions, in performance or observance of a duty not founded on contract, which failure is the proximate cause of unintended injury to the person to whom such duty is owing; nature and extent of liability for such injuries in general; nature and effect of negligence or other fault on the part of the person injured contributing to his injury; comparison of negligence of the parties; imputation to the person injured of others' negligence; civil remedies for such injuries; and criminal responsibility for such negligence in general, and prosecution and punishment thereof as a public offense.

Matters not in this topic, treated elsewhere, see Descriptive-Word Index.

Analysis.

I. ACTS OR OMISSIONS CONSTITUTING NEGLIGENCE, ⬅1–55.
    A. Personal Conduct in General, ⬅1–15.
    B. Dangerous Substances, Machinery, and Other Instrumentalities, ⬅16–27.
    C. Condition and Use of Land, Buildings, and Other Structures, ⬅28–55.

II. PROXIMATE CAUSE OF INJURY, ⬅56–64.

III. CONTRIBUTORY NEGLIGENCE, ⬅65–101.
    A. Persons Injured in General, ⬅65–83.
    B. Children and Others under Disability, ⬅84–88.
    C. Imputed Negligence, ⬅89–96.
    D. Comparative Negligence, ⬅97–101.

IV. ACTIONS, ⬅102–143.
    A. Right of Action, Parties, Preliminary Proceedings, and Pleading, ⬅102–119.
    B. Evidence, ⬅120–135.
    C. Trial, Judgment, and Review, ⬅136–143.

V. CRIMINAL RESPONSIBILITY, ⬅144.

I. ACTS OR OMISSIONS CONSTITUTING NEGLIGENCE.
  A. Personal Conduct in General.
    ⬅1. Nature and elements of negligence in general.
       2. Duty to use care.
       3. Degrees of care in general.
       4. Ordinary or reasonable care.
       5. Customary methods and acts.
       6. Requirements of statutes or ordinances.
       7. Care as to children.
       8. Care as to infirm or helpless persons.

48 F.D.—1

WEST'S STATE AND REGIONAL DIGESTS. West's digest system also provides state digests for the cases of all states except Utah, Nevada, and Delaware. State digests include references to decisions issued by federal courts located within the state. Some state court decisions are also represented in West's regional digests. West currently publishes four regional digests, corresponding to four of its seven regional reporters (the names and coverage of West's regional reporters will be discussed later in this chapter).

EXHIBIT 14.7
West's *Federal Practice Digest 4th* on Negligence

Reproduced with permission of West Group.

⚷26 NEGLIGENCE   77 F P D 4th—530

For later cases see same Topic and Key Number in Pocket Part

imposition of strict liability under Louisiana law; contractor had no scheduling authority and performed repairs only in accordance with specific directions from premises owner. LSA-C.C. art. 2317.

In re Shell Oil Refinery, 765 F.Supp. 324.

⚷27.
See PRODUCTS LIABILITY.

(C) CONDITION AND USE OF LAND, BUILDINGS, AND OTHER STRUCTURES.

⚷28. Care required in general.
Library references
C.J.S. Negligence §§ 63(1), 63(57) et seq., 74.

C.A.7 (Ind.) 1990. Person may not use his land in such way as unreasonably to injure interests of persons not on his land—including owners of adjacent lands, as well as other landowners and users of public ways.

Justice v. CSX Transp., Inc., 908 F.2d 119, rehearing denied.

C.A.1 (Mass.) 1990. Under traditional Massachusetts landowner liability principles, there must be a defect, apart from natural accumulation of water, ice, or snow, in order to hold landowner liable in slip-and-fall action for negligence.

Athas v. U.S., 904 F.2d 79.

C.A.9 (Mont.) 1986. Under Montana law, duty of care owed by a landowner does not depend on whether the injured party was a trespasser, licensee or invitee.

Berge v. Boyne USA, Inc., 779 F.2d 1445.

D.D.C. 1990. In slip and fall case, burden was on plaintiff to prove that defendant was negligent either in creating a dangerous condition or in allowing one to continue without correction and that such negligence was proximate cause of the injuries, and to make out prima facie case of liability predicated on existence of dangerous condition, it was necessary to show that defendant had actual notice of dangerous condition or that condition existed for such length of time that, in the exercise of reasonable care, its existence should have become known and corrected.

Thomas v. Grand Hyatt Hotel, 749 F.Supp. 313.

N.D.Ill. 1990. Liability of owners and occupiers of land is evaluated under principles of ordinary negligence, under Illinois law. Ill. S.H.A. ch. 80, ¶ 302.

O'Clair v. Dumelle, 735 F.Supp. 1344, affirmed 919 F.2d 143.

D.Kan. 1991. Under Kansas law, person is entitled to use their own premises for any lawful purpose; however, landowner's freedom to use his premises is not absolute, but is subject to important qualification that such use be ordinary and usual, conforming to standard of care expected of reasonably prudent person, and failure to conform to this standard may constitute negligence.

Reese Exploration, Inc. v. Williams Natural Gas Co., 768 F.Supp. 1416.

D.Mass. 1990. Under Massachusetts law, landowner is not under legal duty to remove natural accumulations of ice or snow.

Swann v. Flatley, 749 F.Supp. 338.

For cited U.S.C.A. sections and legislative

NEGLIGENCE

SUBJECTS INCLUDED

Failure to use due care, either in respect of acts or of omissions, in performance or observance of a duty not founded on contract, which failure is the proximate cause of unintended injury to the person to whom such duty is owing

Nature and extent of liability for such injuries in general

Nature and effect of negligence or other fault on the part of the person injured contributing to his injury

Comparison of negligence of the parties

Imputation to the person injured of others' negligence

Civil remedies for such injuries

Criminal responsibility for such negligence in general, and prosecution and punishment thereof as a public offense

SUBJECTS EXCLUDED AND COVERED BY OTHER TOPICS

Death, actions for damages for, see DEATH

Manslaughter by negligence, see AUTOMOBILES, HOMICIDE

Particular kinds of property, negligence in care and use of, see MINES AND MINERALS, WATERS AND WATER COURSES, ANIMALS, SHIPPING, COLLISION, and other specific topics

Particular kinds of works, public improvements, etc., negligence in construction and use of, see RAILROADS, BRIDGES, HIGHWAYS, MUNICIPAL CORPORATIONS, and other specific topics

Particular personal relations, occupations, employments, contracts, etc., negligence in respect of duties incident to, see ATTORNEY AND CLIENT, EMPLOYERS' LIABILITY, PHYSICIANS AND SURGEONS, CARRIERS, LANDLORD AND TENANT, BAILMENT and other specific topics

For detailed references to other topics, see Descriptive-Word Index

---

Analysis

I. ACTS OR OMISSIONS CONSTITUTING NEGLIGENCE, ⚷1–55.
(A) PERSONAL CONDUCT IN GENERAL, ⚷1–15.
(B) DANGEROUS SUBSTANCES, MACHINERY, AND OTHER INSTRUMENTALITIES, ⚷16–27.
(C) CONDITION AND USE OF LAND, BUILDINGS, AND OTHER STRUCTURES, ⚷28–55.

PARALEGAL PROFILE

Litigation Paralegal

PAMELA JO RAYBOURN serves as a legal assistant in the areas of product liability, business and employment litigation, and antitrust. Her work includes undertaking factual investigations, drafting and responding to discovery requests (including motion practice), and organizing large documents. She has extensive experience in preparing for and assisting at trial, arbitration, and mediation. She is also involved in supervising and training support staff.

Raybourn has served as chair of NFPA's Ethics Committee since 1998, has written numerous articles for newsletters published by the Oregon State Bar Association and the Oregon Legal Assistants Association, and was a PACE exam preparer for NFPA from 1996–1997.

What do you like best about your work?

"I like the responsibility of searching for the factual information that makes or breaks the case. I like digging and asking questions to gather all the information necessary to prepare the case. I also enjoy working with the employees of our corporate clients. It is easy to zealously represent a client when you know the client has integrity and strong business ethics."

What is the greatest challenge that you face in your area of work?

"It doesn't help the client if you complete the assignment and it sits on the attorney's desk for weeks. I find myself in the role of a prodder, checking to see that the work gets off the attorney's desk and out the door."

What advice do you have for would-be paralegals in your area of work?

"Get a well-rounded education in all areas of law. Because litigation can involve any legal theory, I have found it necessary to understand the legal principles involved in probate and estates, real estate, contracts, patents, bankruptcy, business organizations, and product liability in addition to understanding tort and negligence theory. The better you understand a legal theory, the more able you are to review documents and locate facts to support that theory."

> "There is no such thing as a dumb question."

What are some tips for success as a paralegal in your area of work?

"Ask questions. There is no such thing as a dumb question. You will exert less wasted energy and effort if you ask a question to be sure you understand the assignment. Sometimes I go back to the attorney more than once to ensure that I am on the right track. Sometimes a review of documents will lead to other questions. If you ask questions, you can direct your efforts to efficiently completing the assignment. This will benefit you as well as the client."

WEST'S COMPREHENSIVE *AMERICAN DIGEST SYSTEM.* West's *American Digest System* is a comprehensive set of volumes incorporating case abstracts from West's state, federal, and regional digests. Most of the cases catalogued are from appellate courts, although some trial court decisions are included. The *American Digest System* is particularly helpful when you are looking for persuasive authorities. To find persuasive authorities, you will want to consider cases from all jurisdictions. The *American Digest System* will help you locate them efficiently.

Sequential Sets. The *American Digest System* is divided into three different sets, each covering a specific period of time. The *American Digest Century Edition* provides coverage of all cases from 1658 through 1896. The *Decennial Digest* includes all cases issued from 1896 to the present. Each volume in the set covers a ten-year period; for example, the *Eighth Decennial Digest* covers cases reported between 1966 and 1976. West has slightly changed the decennial digest publication schedule because of the increased number of reported cases. Today, "decennial" digests are issued every five years, rather than every ten years. The most recently published cases can be found in West's *General Digest*, which is an annual publication. Three volumes of these digests are shown in Exhibit 14.8.

Advantages of the **American Digest System.** The advantage of the *American Digest System* is its vast coverage of cases from different courts. The digests cover almost every topic, and most key numbers are represented, even though they may relate to only a few cases. Some of the more common areas of the law contain hundreds of different case abstracts, offering the researcher a wide variety of resources to consider. Under each key number, cases are listed by type of court. Federal court cases appear first, starting with a listing of decisions issued by the United States Supreme Court. This listing is followed by listings of appellate court decisions and, finally, district court cases. State court cases follow the federal court listings and are arranged in alphabetical order by state.

Each of West's decennial digests also offers the researcher many helpful finding tools. The **table of cases** lists all of the cases included in the digest, in alphabetical order. This listing usually appears in the last volume of the set. The decennial digests also have topical outlines that list various subtopics. If you know the specific topic on which you want to focus, all you need to do is locate the digest containing that topic and review the outline for specific subtopics. Exhibit 14.9 on the next page shows outlines for the topic and subtopics relating to negligence, as well as key-numbered annotations. Each volume of the digest system lists the various topics that it contains.

OTHER DIGESTS. There are other digests for specific jurisdictions and specialized interest areas. The *Lawyers' Edition of the Digest of the Supreme Court Reports* corresponds to decisions listed in the *Lawyers' Edition of the Supreme Court Reports*. Both are published by West Group and are similar in organizational style to the West digests. Each topic begins with an outline of contents and headnotes are arranged according to section number. The classification system is limited to United States Supreme Court cases and is not applicable to similar cases found in lower federal courts or state courts. The digest provides cross-references to the *American Law Reports* and other legal publications. Other publishers also publish state-specific digests, such as Callahan's *Michigan Digest*.

Annotations: *American Law Reports*

The *American Law Reports (A.L.R.)* and *American Law Reports Federal (A.L.R. Federal)*, published by West Group, are also useful resources for the legal researcher. An *A.L.R.* volume is shown in Exhibit 14.10 on page 503. These reports are multivolume sets that present the full text of selected cases in numerous areas of the law. They are helpful in finding cases from jurisdictions throughout the country with similar factual and legal issues.

There are five different series of *American Law Reports,* covering case law since 1919. The fifth series *(A.L.R.5th)* is the current edition. *A.L.R. Federal* is the current edition for coverage of federal decisions. The *A.L.R.1st* and *A.L.R.2d*

EXHIBIT 14.8
West's *Digests*

Reproduced with permission of West Group.

Table of Cases
An alphabetical list of the cases that have been cited or reproduced in a legal text, case digest, or other legal source.

EXHIBIT 14.9
Outlines for Topics and Subtopics in a West *Decennial Digest*

Reproduced with permission of West Group.

---

29 10th D Pt 1—1117

NEGLIGENCE

SUBJECTS INCLUDED

Failure to use due care, either in respect of acts or of omissions, in performance or observance of a duty not founded on contract, which failure is the proximate cause of unintended injury to the person to whom such duty is owing

Nature and extent of liability for such injuries in general

Nature and effect of negligence or other fault on the part of the person injured contributing to his injury

Comparison of negligence of the parties

Imputation to the person injured of others' negligence

Civil remedies for such injuries

Criminal responsibility for such negligence in general, and prosecution and punishment thereof as a public offense

SUBJECTS EXCLUDED AND COVERED BY OTHER TOPICS

Death, actions for damages for, see DEATH

Manslaughter by negligence, see AUTOMOBILES, HOMICIDE

Particular kinds of property, negligence in care and use of, see MINES AND MINERALS, WATERS AND WATER COURSES, ANIMALS, SHIPPING, COLLISION, and other specific topics

Particular kinds of works, public improvements, etc., negligence in construction and use of, see RAILROADS, BRIDGES, HIGHWAYS, MUNICIPAL CORPORATIONS, and other specific topics

Particular personal relations, occupations, employments, contracts, etc., negligence in respect of duties incident to, see ATTORNEY AND CLIENT, EMPLOYERS' LIABILITY, PHYSICIANS AND SURGEONS, CARRIERS, LANDLORD AND TENANT, BAILMENT and other specific topics

For detailed references to other topics, see Descriptive-Word Index

Analysis

I. ACTS OR OMISSIONS CONSTITUTING NEGLIGENCE, ⚖1–55.
  (A) PERSONAL CONDUCT IN GENERAL, ⚖1–15.
  (B) DANGEROUS SUBSTANCES, MACHINERY, AND OTHER INSTRUMENTALITIES, ⚖16–27.
  (C) CONDITION AND USE OF LAND, BUILDINGS, AND OTHER STRUCTURES, ⚖28–55.

II. PROXIMATE CAUSE OF INJURY, ⚖56–64.

III. CONTRIBUTORY NEGLIGENCE, ⚖65–101.
  (A) PERSONS INJURED IN GENERAL, ⚖65–83.11.
  (B) CHILDREN AND OTHERS UNDER DISABILITY, ⚖84–88.
  (C) IMPUTED NEGLIGENCE, ⚖89–96.
  (D) COMPARATIVE NEGLIGENCE, ⚖97–101.

IV. ACTIONS, ⚖102–143.
  (A) RIGHT OF ACTION, PARTIES, PRELIMINARY PROCEEDINGS, AND PLEADING, ⚖102–119.
  (B) EVIDENCE, ⚖120–135.

NEGLIGENCE

29 10th D Pt 1—1118

IV. ACTIONS, ⚖102–143—Cont'd
  (B) EVIDENCE, ⚖120–135.—Cont'd
    1. PRESUMPTIONS AND BURDEN OF PROOF, 121–123.
    2. ADMISSIBILITY, 124–133.
    3. WEIGHT AND SUFFICIENCY, ⚖134–135.
  (C) TRIAL, JUDGMENT, AND REVIEW, ⚖136–143.

V. CRIMINAL RESPONSIBILITY, ⚖144.

I. ACTS OR OMISSIONS CONSTITUTING NEGLIGENCE.

(A) PERSONAL CONDUCT IN GENERAL.

⚖1. Nature and elements of negligence in general.
2. Duty to use care.
3. Degrees of care in general.
4. Ordinary or reasonable care.
5. Customary methods and acts.
6. Requirements of statutes or ordinances.
7. Care as to children.
8. Care as to infirm or helpless persons.
9. Inadvertent acts or omissions.
10. Unintended consequences.
11. Willful, wanton, or reckless acts or conduct.
12. Acts in emergencies.
13. Degrees of negligence.
14. Persons liable.
15. Joint and several liability.

(B) DANGEROUS SUBSTANCES, MACHINERY, AND OTHER INSTRUMENTALITIES.

⚖16. Care required in general.
17. Customary methods and acts.
18. Requirements of statutes or ordinances.
19. Injurious substances and articles.
20. Defective and dangerous machinery, tools, and appliances.
21. Fires.
22. Dangerous instrumentalities and operations.
22½. Private vehicles.
23. Machinery and other things as attractions to children.
  (1). In general.
  (2). Railroad turntables and cars.
24. Knowledge of defect or danger.
25. Precautions against injury.
26. Persons liable in general.

(C) CONDITION AND USE OF LAND, BUILDINGS, AND OTHER STRUCTURES.

⚖28. Care required in general.
29. Duty to use care.
30. Customary methods and acts.
31. Requirements of statutes or ordinances.
32. Care as to licensees or persons invited.
  (1). In general.
  (2). Who are licensees, and status of person going on land of another in general.
  (2.1). Classes of licensees, and distinction between them in general.
  (2.2). Bare licensees.
  (2.3). Invitees in general.
  (2.4). Implied invitation in general.
  (2.5). Automobile service stations and parking service.
  (2.6). Bill collectors.
  (2.7). Buildings in process of construction, alteration, or demolition.
  (2.8). Business visitors, and store and restaurant patrons.
  (2.9). Deliverymen and haulers.
  (2.10). Employees and contractors.
  (2.11). Frequenters.
  (2.12). Gratuitous licensees.
  (2.13). Guests in private homes.
  (2.14). Meter readers.
  (2.15). Persons accompanying invitees.
  (2.16). Postmen.
  (2.17). Public officials in general.
  (2.18). Firemen and policemen.
  (3). Exceeding or abusing license or invitation.
  (4). Children and others under disability.
33. Care as to trespassers.
  (1). In general.
  (2). Who are trespassers.
  (3). Children.
34. Care as to persons on adjacent premises.
35. Care as to persons on adjacent highway.
36. Private grounds in general.
37. Places open to public; recreational use.
38. Places abutting on or near highways.
39. Places attractive to children.
40. Streams, ponds, and wells.
41. Excavations.
42. Embankments and piling of materials.
43. Buildings and other structures.
44. Elevators, hoistways, and shafts.
45. Use of property.
46. Traps, pitfalls, and harmful devices.
47. Knowledge of defect or danger.
48. Precautions against injury.
49. — In general.
50. — Barriers, or covering or guarding dangerous places.
51. — Notices and warnings.
52. Persons liable.
53. — In general.
54. — Acts or omissions of independent contractors.

---

series contain separate digests that provide references to cases and also have word indexes to assist the researcher in locating specific areas.

QUICK INDEXES. *A.L.R.3d, A.L.R.4th, A.L.R.5th,* and *A.L.R. Federal* use a new method of accessing information through the *Quick Index* approach (see Exhibit 14.11 on page 504), which is a combination of the topical approach and the factual-word approach in an alphabetical listing. This approach is now the standard means used to access annotations throughout all of the series. The *A.L.R. Federal's Quick Index* covers the annotations in *A.L.R. Federal,* as well as the annotations in the *Lawyers' Edition of the Supreme Court Reports* (mentioned previously) and other federal law research tools.

ANNOTATIONS. The cases presented in these reporters are followed by annotations. In the *A.L.R.,* annotations consist of articles that focus on specific issues; these reports can therefore be an excellent source to turn to in researching case law. The annotations also present an overview of the specific area of law addressed by the case, indicate current trends in that area, and refer to other case law relating to the specific issue or issues.

As shown in Exhibit 14.12 on page 505, an annotation begins with an outline of the subject matter or topic discussed and is followed by a detailed index of subtopics. This is followed by a table of the jurisdictions represented in the discussions of the topic. The annotations contain cross-references to other publications, such as *American Jurisprudence 2d*.

UPDATING SUPPLEMENTS.   *A.L.R.* annotations are periodically updated by the addition of relevant recent cases. The annotations in *A.L.R.1st* are supplemented by a six-volume set called *A.L.R.1st Blue Book of Supplemental Decisions* (see Exhibit 14.13 on page 506). *A.L.R.2d* is updated by the *A.L.R. Later Case Service* (see Exhibit 14.14 on page 507). *A.L.R.3d, A.L.R.4th, A.L.R.5th,* and *A.L.R. Federal* are made current by pocket-part supplements located in the front of each volume. An additional updating tool for *A.L.R.2d, A.L.R.3d, A.L.R.4th, A.L.R.5th,* and *A.L.R. Federal* is the Annotation History Tables located at the end of the Quick Indexes for *A.L.R.3d* and *A.L.R.4th* and at the end of each pocket-part supplement. *A.L.R.1st* contains annotations of supplementing and superseding (overruling or modifying) cases in the last volume of the *A.L.R.1st Blue Book*. The history tables allow the researcher to see if any new annotations supplement or supersede an earlier annotation.

Treatises

A **treatise** is a formal scholarly work that treats a given subject systematically and in detail. Treatises are written by individuals such as law professors, legal scholars, and practicing attorneys. Law treatises are commentaries that summarize, interpret, or evaluate different areas of substantive and procedural law. Some treatises are published in multivolume sets, and others are contained in a single book. The organization of the text of a treatise is easy to follow. Each text contains a table of contents and an index or indexes for efficient reference, and most contain a table of cases referred to within the text. Although treatises are secondary materials and have no binding effect on courts, they may merit particular judicial respect and recognition when written by leading scholars in the field. Many of these scholarly works are classics and serve as valuable sources of information many years after publication.

Hornbooks are single-volume treatises that synthesize the basic principles of an area of the law. Paralegals who seek to familiarize themselves with a particular area of the law, such as torts or contracts, should review one of the many available hornbooks. For example, in researching the issue in Trent Hoffman's negligence case, you might want to locate the learned treatise *Prosser and Keeton on the Law of Torts*, Fifth Edition, which is included in West's Hornbook Series, and read the sections on negligence in that volume. (Exhibit 14.15 on page 508 shows the page of this book that opens the chapter on defenses to negligence.) This text was written by distinguished lawyers from leading law schools. In addition to providing a clear and organized discussion of the subject matter, hornbooks present many examples of case law and references to cases that may be helpful in searching for cases with similar facts and issues.

Treatises are usually organized by section numbers rather than by page numbers. And, as is characteristic of other legal sources, they are divided into topics and subtopics. Most treatises are updated by supplementary loose-leaf pages or pocket-part additions.

Restatements of the Law

Other sources of general background information are the *Restatements of the Law*, produced by the American Law Institute (ALI), an organization established in 1923

EXHIBIT 14.10
American Law Reports

Reproduced with permission of West Group.

Treatise
In legal research, a text that provides a systematic, detailed, and scholarly review of a particular legal subject.

Hornbook
A secondary source presented as a single-volume scholarly discussion, or treatise, on a particular legal subject (such as property law).

On the Web
You can learn more about the American Law Institute (ALI) and its publications, including information on which *Restatements of the Law* are in the process of being revised, by accessing the ALI's Web site at www.ali.org.

EXHIBIT 14.11

Excerpt from the *A.L.R. Federal's Quick Index*

Reproduced with permission of West Group.

ALR 3d
QUICK INDEX

ABANDONMENT

Contracts (this index)

Criminal enterprise: withdrawal from or abandonment of criminal enterprise, 8 Am Jur POF 2d, pp 231–266

Disclosure of trade secret in court proceedings as abandonment of secrecy, 58 ALR3d 1318

Easement: abandonment of easement, 3 Am Jur POF 2d, pp 647–674

Eminent domain: what constitutes abandonment of eminent domain proceeding so as to charge condemnor with liability for condemnee's expenses or the like, 68 ALR3d 610

Felony-murder: what constitutes termination of felony for purpose of felony-murder rule, 58 ALR3d 851

Fire insurance: obtaining new property insurance as cancellation of existing insurance, 3 ALR3d 1072

Harassment or other mistreatment by employer or supervisor as "good cause" justifying abandonment of employment, 76 ALR3d 1089, 9 Am Jur POF2d, pp 697–728

Home, abandonment of: what voluntary acts of child, other than marriage or entry into military service, terminate parent's obligation to support, 32 ALR3d 1055

Infestation of leased dwelling or apartment with vermin as entitling tenant to abandon premises or as constructive eviction by landlord in absence of express covenant of habitability, 27 ALR3d 924

Mechanics' lien: abandonment of construction or of contract as affecting time for filing mechanics' liens or time for giving notice to owner, 52 ALR3d 797

Mines and Minerals (this index)

Mitigation: landlord's duty, on tenant's failure to occupy, or abandonment of, premises, to mitigate damages by accepting or procuring another tenant, 21 ALR3d 534

Nonconforming use: zoning-abandonment of lawful nonconforming use, 18 Am Jur POF 2d, pp 731–777

Oil or gas: duty and liability as to plugging oil or gas well abandoned or taken out of production, 50 ALR3d 240

Physician's abandonment of patient, 3 Am Jur POF 2d, pp 117–165

Principal and agent: insurance agent's statement or conduct indicating that insurer's cancellation of policy shall not take effect as binding on insurer, 3 ALR3d 1135

Proofs: abandonment, 1 Am Jur POF, pp 1–10

Real estate contract: purchaser's abandonment of land sales contract, 5 Am Jur POF 2d, pp 165–188

Trade Secrets (this index)

Unemployment Compensation (this index)

Withdrawal, after provocation of conflict, as reviving right of self-defense, 55 ALR3d 1000

Zoning (this index)

ABANDONMENT OF CASE

Condemnation of rural property for highway purposes, abandonment of action involving, 8 Am Jur Trials, pp 57–102

ABANDONMENT-OF-SHIP DRILL

Liability for injury to or death of passenger in connection with a fire drill or abandonment-of-ship drill aboard a vessel, 8 ALR3d 650

ABANDONMENT OF SPOUSE OR CHILD

Desertion (this index)

ABATEMENT

Action.

Consult POCKET PART for later annotations   1

---

by a group of prominent judges, law professors, and practicing attorneys. The *Restatements* present an overview of the basic principles of the common law in ten specific fields: agency law, conflict of laws, contracts, foreign relations law, judgments, property, restitution, security, torts, and trusts. Most of the *Restatements* have been updated by the issuance of second or third editions. The *Restatements* are often abbreviated when referred to by legal professionals. The *Restatement of the Law of Torts*, Second Edition, is often referred to as the *Restatement (Second) of the Law of Torts*, or, more simply, as the *Restatement (Second) of Torts*. The ALI is cur-

EXHIBIT 14.12
Annotation from *American Law Reports*

Reproduced with permission of West Group.

ANNOTATION

VALIDITY AND CONSTRUCTION, AS TO CLAIM ALLEGING DESIGN DEFECTS, OF STATUTE IMPOSING TIME LIMITATIONS UPON ACTION AGAINST ARCHITECT OR ENGINEER FOR INJURY OR DEATH ARISING OUT OF DEFECTIVE OR UNSAFE CONDITION OF IMPROVEMENT TO REAL PROPERTY

by

Jane Massey Draper, B.C.L.

I. PRELIMINARY MATTERS

§ 1. Introduction:
    [a] Scope
    [b] Related matters

TOTAL CLIENT-SERVICE LIBRARY® REFERENCES

5 Am Jur 2d, Architects § 25; 51 Am Jur 2d, Limitation of Actions §§ 27–30, 136

2 Am Jur Pl & Pr Forms (Rev), Architects, Form 33; 17 Am Jur Pl & Pr Forms (Rev), Limitation of Action, Forms 121–151

2 Am Jur Legal Forms 2d, Architects, Engineers, and Surveyors §§ 24:62, 24:65, 24:111; 12 Am Jur Legal Forms 2d, Limitation of Actions §§ 167:14, 167:20, 167:53

24 Am Jur Proof of Facts 285, Architect's Negligence

USCS Constitution, Amendment 14

US L Ed Digest, Constitutional Law §§ 496, 780, 784; Limitation of Actions §§ 5, 6, 121, 179

ALR Digests, Architect § 2; Limitation of Actions §§ 2, 133, 134, 141, 195, 196, 200

L Ed Index to Annos, Architects; Limitation of Actions

ALR Quick Index, Architects; Death; Defects and Irregularities; Engineers; Improvement; Limitation of Actions; Plans and Specifications; Property Damage

Federal Quick Index, Architects; Death; Engineers; Limitation of Actions; Property Damage

Consult POCKET PART in this volume for later cases

1242

---

93 ALR3d   TIME LIMITATION—ACTION AGAINST ARCHITECT
                                     93 ALR3d 1242

§ 2. Background, summary, and comment:
    [a] Generally
    [b] Practice pointers

II. VALIDITY

§ 3. Generally:
    [a] Statute held valid
    [b] Statute held invalid

III. CONSTRUCTION

§ 4. Effect of statute, generally:
    [a] Commencement of limitation period
    [b] Duration of limitation period
§ 5. Effect on other statutes of limitation
§ 6. Applicability to particular types of actions:
    [a] Breach of contract or warranty; negligence
    [b] Indemnity
§ 7. Infancy as tolling statute
§ 8. Construction of particular terms:
    [a] "Improvement to real property"
    [b] "Owners, tenants, or otherwise"
    [c] "Limitation shall not apply"

INDEX

Air conditioning machinery, negligent design of rooms housing, § 3
Alumni building, design and construction of, §§ 4[b], 6[b]
Apartment house, unsafe condition of, § 4[b, c]
Asphyxiation of city employees by sewer gas, § 8[c]
Automobile manufacturer, action against, § 8[a]
Background, summary, and comment, § 2
Bank complex, design and construction of, § 5
Breach of contract or warranty, § 6[a]
Bridge, negligent design, construction, maintenance and control of, § 8[a]
Ceiling, sagging of suspended ceiling resulting in building becoming untenantable, § 4[a]
Commencement of limitation period, § 4[a]
Construction of statute, generally, §§ 4-8
Contract, breach of, § 6[a]
Conveyor system, negligence in design of alterations of, § 3
Courthouse building, negligent construction of, § 6[a]
Drainage system for townhouse complex, faulty design of, § 3
Duration of limitation period, § 4[b]
Effect of statute, § 4
Heater, building burning as result of installation of, § 3
Hospital building, negligent design in construction of, § 6[a]
"Improvement to real property", construction of, § 8[a]
Indemnity, § 6[b]
Infancy as tolling statute, § 7
Introduction, § 1
"Limitation shall not apply", construction of, § 8[c]
Minor injured as result of running through glass side light, action by, §§ 5, 7
Municipal building, action involving preparation of plans and specifications for, § 4[b]
Negligence, § 6[a]
Other statutes of limitation, effect on, § 5

1243

---

rently in the process of creating a new edition of the *Restatement of the Law of Torts*. To date, one volume has been completed, covering product liability. Exhibit 14.16 on page 511 shows a photograph of this volume. (For some suggestions on how you can keep up to date on new developments with respect to legal publications and laws, see the feature *Technology and Today's Paralegal: Looking Ahead*.)

Restatements are helpful resources when researching issues involving common law doctrines, such as negligence. Each section in the *Restatements* contains a statement of the principles of law that are generally accepted by the courts and/or embodied in statutes on the topic, followed by a discussion of these principles. The *Restatements* are useful research tools because they present particular cases as examples and also discuss variations on the general propositions of the law. The overall organization of the texts is easy to follow. There is a general index for the *Restatements* in the first series, in addition to the separate indexes available for the individual *Restatements*. Later editions contain appendices, including notes of decisions citing the first series, Reporter's Notes, and cross-references to *A.L.R.* annotations.

EXHIBIT 14.13

A Page from the *A.L.R. 1st Blue Book* of *Supplemental Decisions*

Reproduced with permission of West Group.

Seventh Permanent Volume
OF
SUPPLEMENTAL DECISIONS
FOR
ANNOTATIONS IN THE
AMERICAN LAW REPORTS
Vols. 1–175

1 ALR 39-136
U.S.—Davis v F. (ND Ill) 717 F Supp 614
Mass.—Ogden Suffolk Downs, Inc. v B., 18 Mass App 101, 463 NE2d 575
Tex.—Stafford v J. (App Houston (14th Dist)) 687 SW2d 784

1 ALR 143-145
Supplemented 38 ALR 229 and 89 ALR 966♦

1 ALR 148-149
Superseded 74 ALR2d 828♦

1 ALR 156-162
Supplemented 99 ALR 938♦

1 ALR 203-218
Supplemented 2 ALR 767 and 41 ALR 405♦

1 ALR 222-264
Supplemented 102 ALR 174 and 116 ALR 1064♦
Subdiv VIII superseded 71 ALR2d 1140♦

1 ALR 272-274
Supplemented 18 ALR 87♦

1 ALR 276-297
R.I.—Celona v R. I. E. C., 544 A2d 582

1 ALR 329-331
Superseded 36 ALR2d 861♦

1 ALR 336-338
Supplemented 20 ALR 1535 and 73 ALR 1494♦

1 ALR 343-349
Superseded 51 ALR2d 1404♦

1 ALR 362-365
La.—Ursin v N. O. A. B. (App 5th Cir) 506 So 2d 947

1 ALR 374-380
Supplemented 101 ALR 1282 and 104 ALR 1352♦

1 ALR 383-392
Superseded 13 ALR4th 1153♦

1 ALR 394-400
U.S.—Dunavant Enterprises, Inc. v S. S. Co. (CA11 Ala) 730 F2d 665
F.—Re Tinnell Traffic Services, Inc. (BC MD Tenn) 43 BR 277
Re STN Enterprises, Inc. (BC DC Vt) 45 BR 955
Re Windsor Communications Group, Inc. (BC ED Pa) 80 BR 712
Re Hawkins Co. (BC DC Idaho) 104 BR 317, 10 UCCRS2d 468
Ill.—Mueller v S. (5th Dist) 160 Ill App 3d 699, 112 Ill Dec 589, 513 NE2d 1198
Mont.—Interstate Brands Corp. v C., 708 P2d 573
Ohio.—Konicki v S., Inc., 16 Ohio App 3d 40, 16 Ohio BR 43, 474 NE2d 347, 41 UCCRS 103
Va.—Noland Co. v N.-R. Corp., 234 Va 266, 360 SE2d 852

1 ALR 403-405
Mo.—Stegman v S. E. Co. (App) 678 SW2d 416

1 ALR 436-439
Supplemented 46 ALR 1192 at p 1194♦

1 ALR 449-450
Superseded 28 ALR2d 662♦

1 ALR 459-470
Supplemented 160 ALR 295♦

1 ALR 483-488
Supplemented 46 ALR 814♦

1 ALR 498-502
Supplemented 72 ALR 278♦

1 ALR 528-532
N.Y.—Blackmore v W. L. Corp. (3d Dept) 97 App Div 2d 889, 470 NYS2d 713
Agency, Broad & Cornelia Street, Inc. v L. (3d Dept) 97 App Div 2d 934, 470 NYS2d 729
Trenga Realty v W. H., Inc. (3d Dept) 138 App Div 2d 875, 526 NYS2d 251
O'Connor Realty Services, Inc. v H. (2d Dept) 149 App Div 2d 492, 539 NYS2d 975

1 ALR 546-547
Superseded 50 ALR2d 1324♦

1 ALR 564-568
Supplemented 8 ALR 493♦

1 ALR 598-593
Ga.—Georgia Insurers Insolvency Pool v M., 175 Ga App 430, 333 SE2d 383

♦When Supplemented see later Note and Blue Book under caption of later Note

3

The *Restatements* are *not* primary sources of law and therefore are not binding on the courts. But they are highly respected secondary sources of law and are often referred to by the courts as the basis for their decisions.

Legal Periodicals

Legal periodicals are another source of secondary authority and, as such, are not binding. Legal periodicals, such as law reviews, contain thoroughly researched information on specific areas of the law. The authors are usually law professors,

EXHIBIT 14.14

A Page from the *A.L.R. Later Case Service*

Reproduced with permission of West Group.

LATER CASE SERVICE — 81 ALR2d 750–787

salary before and after accident was sufficient to establish comparative salary range and, accordingly, award for lost earning capacity was not speculative or contrary to weight of evidence. Turner v Chicago Transit Authority (1984, 1st Dist) 122 Ill App 3d 419, 77 Ill Dec 928, 461 NE2d 551.

It was not error to admit testimony regarding plaintiff's wages from last period of employment, even though plaintiff was unemployed at time of accident, where wages were probative of earning capacity at time of injury since plaintiff had held same job for ten years and wages were earned only seven months prior to accident. Cantara v Massachusetts Bay Transp. Authority, 3 **Mass** App 81, 323 NE2d 759 (citing annotation).

Evidence of wages earned by plaintiff during regular employment for five-year period ending two months before she was injured in automobile accident was not too remote on issue of impairment of earning capacity. Matthews v Porter, 239 **SC** 620, 124 SE2d 321 (quoting annotation).

[b] Change in employment; temporary or permanent nature of work.

Evidence as to deceased's past earnings as self-employed trucker-broker was admissible notwithstanding deceased was not employed in such business at time of death where other evidence indicated that deceased intended to return to such business in very short time. Blackburn v Aetna Freight Lines, Inc. (CA3 Pa) 368 **F**2d 345.

81 ALR2d 750–787

Liability of proprietor of business premises for injury from fall on exterior walk, ramp, or passageway connected with the building in which the business is conducted.

New sections and subsections added:

§ 9.1. Comparative negligence.

---

§ 1. Scope and related matters, p. 753.

Status of one who enters a store or other place of public resort solely for purpose of using facilities accessible to public, such as telephone, mailbox, lavatory, or the like. 93 ALR2d 784.

Duty of proprietor toward visitor upon premises on private business with or errand or work for employee. 94 ALR2d 6.

Liability of owner or operator of shopping center to patrons for injuries from defects or conditions in sidewalks, walks, or pedestrian passageways. 95 ALR2d 1341.

Liability of owner or operator of garage or gasoline filling station for bodily injury to nonemployees on premises. 8 ALR3d 6.

Liability for injury to patron, of owner or operator of retail store failing to provide carry-out service. 21 ALR3d 931.

Liability of owner or occupant of premises for injuries sustained by mail carrier. 21 ALR3d 1099.

Premises liability: proceeding in the dark along outside path or walkway as contributory negligence. 22 ALR3d 599.

Liability of owner or operator of self-service laundry for personal injury or damages to patron or frequenter of premises from defect in premises or appliances. 23 ALR3d 1246.

Liability of owner or occupant of premises to building or construction inspector coming upon premises in discharge of duty. 28 ALR3d 891.

Liability of owner or operator of premises for injury to meter reader or similar employee of public service corporation coming to premises in course of duties. 28 ALR3d 1344.

Liability of owner or operator of premises for injury to person coming to premises in course of delivery or pickup of merchandise or similar products. 32 ALR3d 9.

Liability of owner or operator of parking lot for personal injuries allegedly resulting from condition of premises. 38 ALR3d 10.

Liability of owner or operator of parking lot for personal injuries caused by movement of vehicles. 38 ALR3d 138.

Liability of lessee of particular premises in shopping center for injury to patron from condition on portion of premises not included in his leasehold. 48 ALR3d 1163.

Liability of landlord for personal injury or death due to inadequacy or lack of lighting on portion of premises used in common by tenants. 66 ALR3d 202.

Store or business premises slip-and-fall: Modern status of rules requiring showing of notice of proprietor of transitory interior condition allegedly causing plaintiff's fall. 85 ALR3d 1000.

Liability for injuries in connection with allegedly dangerous or defective doormat on nonresidential premises. 94 ALR3d 389.

Liability of operator of grocery store to invitee slipping on spilled liquid or semiliquid substance. 24 ALR4th 696.

Liability of operator of store, office, or similar place of business to invitee slipping on spilled liquid or semiliquid substance. 26 ALR4th 481.

81

---

attorneys prominent in their fields, judges, legal scholars, or law students. The periodicals discuss and evaluate specific laws and their implications. Additionally, they may advocate changes in the law.

Articles in legal periodicals can be extremely helpful to paralegals. For example, many law-review articles present well-written and informative overviews of areas of the law with which paralegals may be unfamiliar. Legal periodicals may be

EXHIBIT 14.15

A Page from the *Hornbook on the Law of Torts*

Reproduced with permission of West Group.

Chapter 11

NEGLIGENCE: DEFENSES

Table of Sections

Sec.
65. Contributory Negligence.
66. Last Clear Chance.
67. Comparative Negligence.
68. Assumption of Risk.

§ 65. Contributory Negligence

The two most common defenses in a negligence action are contributory negligence and assumption of risk. Since both developed at a comparatively late date in the development of the common law,[1] and since both clearly operate to the advantage of the defendant, they are commonly regarded as defenses to a tort which would otherwise be established. All courts now hold that the burden of pleading and proof of the contributory negligence of the plaintiff is on the defendant.[2]

Contributory negligence is conduct on the part of the plaintiff, contributing as a legal cause to the harm he has suffered, which falls below the standard to which he is required to conform for his own protection.[3] Unlike assumption of risk, the defense does not rest upon the idea that the defendant is relieved of any duty toward the plaintiff. Rather, although the defendant has violated his duty, has been negligent, and would oth-

---

§ 65

1. The earliest contributory negligence case is Butterfield v. Forrester, 1809, 11 East 60, 103 Eng.Rep. 926. The first American case appears to have been Smith v. Smith, 1824, 19 Mass. (2 Pick.) 621. Assumption of risk first appears in a negligence case in 1799. See infra, § 68 n. 1.

2. E.g., Wilkinson v. Hartford Accident & Indemnity Co., La.1982, 411 So.2d 22; Moodie v. Santoni, 1982, 292 Md. 582, 441 A.2d 323; Addair v. Bryant, 1981, ___ W.Va. ___, 284 S.E.2d 374; Pickett v. Parks, 1981, 208 Neb. 310, 303 N.W.2d 296; Hatton v. Chem-Haulers, Inc., Ala.1980, 393 So.2d 950; Sampson v. W. F. Enterprises, Inc., Mo.App.1980, 611 S.W.2d 333; Howard v. Howard, Ky.App.1980, 607 S.W.2d 119; cf. Reuter v. United States, W.D.Pa.1982, 534 F.Supp. 731 (presumption that person killed or suffering loss of memory was acting with due care).

Illinois and certain other jurisdictions held to the contrary for some time. See West Chicago Street Railroad Co. v. Liderman, 1900, 187 Ill. 463, 58 N.E. 367; Kotler v. Lalley, 1930, 112 Conn. 86, 151 A. 433; Dreier v. McDermott, 1913, 157 Iowa 726, 141 N.W. 315. See Green, Illinois Negligence Law II, 1944, 39 Ill.L.Rev. 116, 125–130.

3. Second Restatement of Torts, § 463. See generally, Malone, The Formative Era of Contributory Negligence, 1946, 41 Ill.L.Rev. 151; James, Contributory Negligence, 1953, 62 Yale L.J. 691; Bohlen, Contributory Negligence, 1908, 21 Harv.L.Rev. 233; Lowndes, Contributory Negligence, 1934, 22 Geo.L.J. 674; Malone, Some Ruminations on Contributory Negligence, 1981, 65 Utah L.Rev. 91; Schwartz, Contributory and Comparative Negligence: A Reappraisal, 1978, 87 Yale L.J. 697; Note, 1979, 39 La.L.Rev. 637.

451

---

a helpful case-finding aid as well. Many articles contain numerous footnotes citing relevant cases and statutes or offering factual background. Legal periodicals often contain references to other secondary sources of authority, such as treatises, other law-review articles, and legal texts as well. Additionally, articles in legal periodicals can be a good source of information on recent developments and trends in the law. As with all legal sources, articles in legal periodicals can become outdated, and it is important to remember to find up-to-date articles that discuss current law.

Paralegals can locate articles relevant to a particular issue by looking at various periodical guides in the law library. The two most popular guides are the *Index to Legal Periodicals*, covering publications beginning in 1908, and the *Current Legal Index*, which began coverage in 1980. Most law libraries contain at least one of these publications. The *Index to Legal Periodicals* (see Exhibit 14.17 on page 511) indexes articles appearing in approximately five hundred periodicals, and the *Current Legal Index* covers over seven hundred legal periodicals. Both indexes are published twelve times a year. Cumulative issues are published quarterly, and a cumulative bound volume is published at the end of the year.

FEATURED GUEST: E. J. YERA
Ten Tips for Effective Legal Research

BIOGRAPHICAL NOTE

In 1987, E. J. Yera graduated from the University of Miami School of Law, where he subsequently served as a research instructor until 1989. After clerking for the U.S. District Court for the Southern District of Florida, he served as corporate counsel for Holmes Regional Medical Center in Melbourne, Florida, and its affiliates until 1995. He then became a member of the Health Care Task Force in the Antitrust Division of the U.S. Department of Justice in Washington, D.C. Since 1997, he has been a member of the U.S. Attorney's Office in the Southern District of Florida. He has taught and lectured in various paralegal programs and has published several articles.

If you perform legal research frequently, you will develop a routine. The purpose of this article is not to give you ironclad rules but to set out ten guidelines that will help you find the routine that is most comfortable for you. You may come back to this article and reread it over time. Now, however, as you read it for the first time, think about how you can use the tips in your future research tasks.

1. Before You Start, Make Sure You Know the Exact Legal Issue You Will Be Researching. You would be surprised at how many students, paralegals, and lawyers research a question for hours only to discover they were not researching the correct legal question. Before you start your research, you should determine the legal question or issue that needs to be researched. You might learn this from reviewing information you already have available, such as a summary of a client interview. If you have an opportunity to ask questions of the attorney giving you a research assignment, do so. What counts, in the end, is coming back with the correct answers, not impressing the attorney by appearing to understand the research task completely when you first hear about it. It will take you twice as long to finish the assignment if you research the wrong issue or if you are unsure what the issue is.

2. Understand the Language of the Issue. Often, the researcher finds that he or she cannot find the answer because the legal terms used in defining the problem are unfamiliar to him or her. Legal terms, or "terms of art," as they are often called, are as unfamiliar to many people as a foreign language. If you are uncertain about the meaning of any term or phrase, look it up in a law dictionary or encyclopedia to get a general idea of its meaning. Depending on how broad the term is, you may want to read a hornbook on the topic to give you a basic understanding of it. For example, assume you are researching an issue relating to securities law. If you do not have a clear understanding of what securities are, there is no way in the world that you can conduct effective research on the issue. You will need to acquire some background knowledge before you focus on the particular research topic.

3. Be Aware of the Circular Nature of Legal Research and Use It to Your Advantage. Students often ask whether primary or secondary sources should be researched first. The answer is that it does not matter, as long as you always research both types of sources. By researching both primary and secondary sources on a topic, you can be assured that you are almost always double-checking your own work. For example, in a case (primary source of law) on a particular issue, the judge writing the opinion will discuss any pertinent statutes on the issue. Similarly, most annotated versions of a statute (annotations are secondary sources of law) give a listing, following the text of the statute, of cases applying the statute and the context in which the statute was applied. The reason you check both sources is to make sure you have found all of the relevant materials.

4. Until You Submit the Assignment, Always Assume There Are Additional Relevant Materials to Find. You need to keep on your toes until you complete your research task. Always assuming that further relevant materials must be located will help

Continued

FEATURED GUEST, Continued

you do this. Of course, there comes a point when you have to assume that you *have* covered the research territory, and knowing when to stop doing research is perhaps one of the hardest things to learn. Certain legal issues can be researched for months and even years. The intent of this tip, though, is to encourage you not to cut corners when conducting research.

5. Keep a List of What Sources You Have Found and Where They Have Led You. You do not want to spend valuable time wondering if you have already checked certain sources. Therefore, it is important to construct a "road map" of where you have been and where you are going.

6. Take the Time to Become Familiar with the Sources You Are Using. It probably seems obvious that you need to become familiar with your sources, yet this requirement is sometimes overlooked. For example, a case digest (a volume summarizing cases) may indicate on its spine that the digest covers the years "1961 to Date." "To Date," however, does not mean that it is the most current digest; it only means that the digest covers cases up to the date of publication of the new digest replacing it. You should take the time to read the first few pages of the digest to verify its contents. This is true generally for any source you are using—look it over carefully before assuming it contains the sources you need.

7. Always Be Aware of the Jurisdiction and the Time Frame You Are Researching. If you are researching an issue that will be resolved by a Florida state court, then your emphasis should be on Florida cases. Of course, there are times when no case law is available, and you must then find cases on point from other states to use as persuasive authorities. You must also be aware of the time frame covered by the source you are using (as mentioned in Tip 6). Be aware when researching any area of the law that very often there is either a loose-leaf service or a pamphlet or pocket part (a small booklet that slips into a pocket of the bound volume) containing newer information. Always ask yourself the following question: Where can the most up-to-date material be found? If you don't know, ask a law librarian who does.

8. Always Use *Shepard's* to Make Sure the Cases You Are Using Are Up to Date. *Shepard's Citations* is a set of volumes that helps the researcher of case law in two ways. First, it lists other cases that have cited the cases you have found. This information is helpful because if another case has cited a case you have found, that other case may also be relevant to your issue, and thus you may be able to use it. Also, cases that cite your case are more recent, and using one or more of those cases may thus be advantageous. Second, *Shepard's* tells you, among other things, whether the cases that you have found are still "good law"—that is, whether the cases have been overruled, reversed, or the like. Knowing this information is crucial—because presenting a case to your attorney that no longer represents good law could well be a short cut to the unemployment line.

9. Use Computerized Legal-Research Services to Update Your Research Results. Computerized legal databases such as Westlaw® and Lexis® allow you to update your research results by using online citators. Also, these services allow you to search the available case law for words or phrases. By doing so, you can actually create your own indexing system. Additionally, the Internet is a great source for legal materials. Several state and federal courts, government agencies, law schools, and bar associations have developed Web sites containing different types of primary and secondary legal materials.

10. Twice a Year, Take Three or Four Hours and Browse through Your Local Law Library. You cannot use sources effectively if you do not know that they exist. You should periodically—say, twice a year—spend an afternoon in the law library browsing through the shelves. Read the first few pages of each new source; then make a note of what the source contains. Ask the librarian for new sources in your area. The time you save later will more than compensate for an afternoon's time spent in the library. You will be surprised at how quickly the new sources you discovered or were told about at the law library come to mind when you receive a research assignment, and they may figure significantly in your research.

> "What counts, in the end, is coming back with the correct answers."

> ## ETHICAL CONCERN
> ### Avoiding Plagiarism
>
> Plagiarism—copying the exact, or nearly exact, words of another without acknowledging the author of those words—may constitute a violation of federal copyright law (discussed in Chapter 8). You should realize, though, that it is possible to plagiarize another's words *unintentionally*. Suppose, for example, that you are taking notes from a legal treatise, such as a hornbook on the law of torts, and you copy several paragraphs word for word for your future reference. You don't enclose the paragraphs in quotation marks because you know you will remember that those are not your words but the words of the hornbook's authors. A week or so later, you are preparing a brief and, referring to your notes, you include those paragraphs, assuming that they are your own version of what the authors said in the hornbook. In short, you have plagiarized a substantial portion of another's copyrighted work without even being aware of it. To ensure that your employer will not face a lawsuit for copyright infringement, always remember to include quotation marks (and the exact source of the quoted material) when copying another's words.

EXHIBIT 14.16
Restatement (Third) of Torts: Products Liability

Reproduced with permission of West Group.

These publications have both a subject index and an index of authors and titles. Exhibit 14.18 on page 513 illustrates how entries are listed in the *Index to Legal Periodicals*.

THE CASE REPORTING SYSTEM

The primary sources of case law are, of course, the cases themselves. Once you have learned what cases are relevant to the issue you are researching, you need to find the cases and examine the exact words of the court opinions. Assume, for example, that in researching the issue in Hoffman's case, you learn that your state's supreme court, a few years ago, issued a decision on a case with a very similar fact pattern. In that case, the state supreme court upheld a lower court's judgment that a retail business owner had to pay extensive damages to a customer who was injured on the store's premises. You know that the state supreme court's decision is a mandatory authority, and to your knowledge, the decision has not been overruled or modified. Therefore, the case will likely provide weighty support to your attorney's arguments in support of Hoffman's claim.

At this point, however, you have only read *about* the case in secondary sources. To locate the case itself and make sure it is applicable, you need to understand the case reporting system and the legal "shorthand" employed in referencing court cases.

State Court Decisions

New York and a few other states publish selected opinions of their trial courts, but most state trial court decisions are not published. Decisions from the state trial courts are usually just filed in the office of the clerk of the court, where they are available for public inspection.

STATE REPORTERS.   Written decisions of the appellate courts, however, are usually published and distributed. The reported appellate decisions are published—in

EXHIBIT 14.17
Index to Legal Periodicals

Reproduced with permission of H. W. Wilson Company.

TECHNOLOGY AND TODAY'S PARALEGAL

Looking Ahead

Every day, it seems, legislatures propose or pass new laws; administrative agencies propose or issue new regulations; and new cases begin to work their way through the court system. A few of these may reach the nation's highest court. As a paralegal, you can perform a valuable service for your supervising attorney by keeping up with new developments in the legal arena or in your specialty area. Online sources can help you in this task.

Suppose, for example, that you want to discover whether a new edition of one of the *Restatements* is being planned or developed. To find out, you can go to the Web site of the American Law Institute at www.ali.org. There you can find information on all of the *Restatements,* including new editions. If you are working in the area of product liability, you will pay special attention to information given about the *Restatement (Third) of Torts: Products Liability.* This volume, which was released in 1998, is the first publication in what eventually will become a series of volumes in the Third Edition of the *Restatement of Torts.* As you know, the *Restatements* are secondary sources of law, but the courts are often guided by the principles set forth in these compilations. Thus, the judgment of the scholars who created the new volume on products liability will likely influence the courts when deciding product-liability cases.

To find out about new uniform laws being developed by the National Conference of Commissioners (NCC) on Uniform State Laws, you can visit its Web site at www.nccusl.org. There you will find the text of all in-process drafts of proposed uniform acts, including drafts of revisions to the Uniform Commercial Code (UCC). Recall from Chapter 7 that Article 2 of the UCC governs sales contracts. Currently, the NCC is revising Article 2 and creating Article 2B, an addition to Article 2 that will, if and when adopted by the states, govern the licensing of intellectual property. You will also find a draft of the Uniform Electronic Transactions Act and the Limited Liability Partnership Act, plus more than a dozen other proposed uniform laws. While these drafts are just that—they are not yet laws—they may become law in the future once their final versions are approved by the NCC and submitted to the states for adoption. In the meantime, provisions in these drafts may serve as persuasive authorities.

You can find out what cases are pending before the Supreme Court from a number of online sources. A helpful site is that of Law Journal EXTRA!, which you can find at www.ljx.com. If you access the "LJX Files," you will see a brief description of each case pending before the Supreme Court, as well as articles from the *National Law Journal* and the *New York Law Journal* on recent cases decided by the Court.

Finally, if you specialize in a particular area, you should become familiar with Internet sites that offer articles or other information on current issues in that domain. If you work in the area of intellectual property, for example, you might add as a "Bookmark" the Trade Secrets Home Page™, which includes the texts of important new laws governing intellectual property as well as a regularly updated list of recent cases in that field.

On the Web
You can find information on state courts, including whether they publish any of their decisions online, at the Center for Information Law and Policy's State Court Locator. Go to www.cilp.org/tblhome.html.

chronological order by date of decision—in volumes called *reports*, which are numbered consecutively. State appellate court decisions are found in the reports of that particular state. State court decisions are usually published in both official and unofficial reporters. The official reports are designated as such by the state legislature, are issued by the individual courts, and serve as the authoritative text of the decision. Any cases on point appearing in an official report must be cited in briefs or research memoranda.

A few of the states, including New York and California, publish more than one official state reporter. These states usually have a large volume of litigation and require greater reporter coverage. For example, New York publishes three official reporters: the *New York Reports* (providing coverage of the Court of Appeals, that state's highest court), the *Appellate Division Reports* (covering decisions of the *Appellate Division of the Supreme Court*—the latter is the name of a trial court in New York), and *Miscellaneous Decisions,* offering coverage of

EXHIBIT 14.18

Entries in the *Index to Legal Periodicals*

Reproduced with permission of H.W. Wilson Company.

PERIODICALS INDEXED

All data as of latest issue received

A

ABA Journal. See American Bar Association Journal

Adelaide Law Review. $40. semi-ann (ISSN 0065-1915) University of Adelaide Law School, GPO Box 498, Adelaide, S.A. 5001, Australia
  North American distribution rights: William S. Hein & Co. Inc., 1285 Main St., Buffalo, NY 14209

The Adelphia Law Journal. $10. ann (ISSN 8756-3630) Sigma Nu Phi National Headquarters, Suite 1500, 625 Fourth Ave. South, Minneapolis, MN 55415

Administrative Law Journal. $20. q (ISSN 1052-2913) Washington College of Law, American University, 4400 Massachusetts Ave., NW, Washington, DC 20016
  Name changed to Administrative Law Journal of the American University with Vol. 6, 1992

Administrative Law Journal of the American University. $20. q (ISSN 1052-2913) Washington College of Law, American University, 4400 Massachusetts Ave., NW, Washington, DC 20016
  Formerly Administrative Law Journal; name changed with Vol. 6, 1992

Administrative Law Review. $35. q (ISSN 0001-8368) American Bar Association, Section of Administrative Law, 750 N. Lake Shore Dr., Chicago, IL 60611

The Advocates' Quarterly. $65. q (ISSN 0704-0288) Canada Law Book Inc., 240 Edward St., Aurora, Ont. L4G 3S9, Canada

AIPLA Quarterly Journal. $45. q (ISSN 0883-6078) AIPLA Headquarters, Suite 203, 2001 Jefferson Davis Highway, Arlington, VA 22202

The Air Force Law Review. $12. semi-ann (ISSN 0094-8381) Superintendent of Documents, U.S. Government Printing Office, Washington, DC 20402

Akron Law Review. $20. q (ISSN 0002-371X) University of Akron School of Law, Akron, OH 44325

Akron Tax Journal. ann (ISSN 1044-4130) University of Akron School of Law, Akron, OH 44325

Alabama Law Review. $24. tri-ann (ISSN 0002-4279) University of Alabama School of Law, Box 870382, Tuscaloosa, AL 35487-0382

The Alabama Lawyer. $20. 7 times a yr (ISSN 0002-4287) Alabama State Bar, 415 Dexter Ave., Montgomery, AL 36104

Alaska Law Review. $20. semi-ann (ISSN 0883-0568) Duke University School of Law, Room 006, Durham, NC 27706

Albany Law Review. $25. q (ISSN 0002-4678) Albany Law School of Union University, 80 New Scotland Ave., Albany, NY 12208

Alberta Law Review. $30. tri-ann (ISSN 0002-4821) Faculty of Law, University of Alberta, Edmonton, Alta. T6G 2H5, Canada

The American Bankruptcy Law Journal. $50. q (ISSN 0027-9048) The American Bankruptcy Law Journal, P.O. Box 983, Lexington, KY 40588

American Bar Association Journal. $66. m (ISSN 0747-0088) American Bar Association Journal, 750 N. Lake Shore Dr., Chicago, IL 60611

American Bar Association Section of Administrative Law. See Administrative Law Review

American Bar Association Section of Antitrust Law. See Antitrust Law Journal

American Bar Association Section of Business Law. See The Business Lawyer

American Bar Association Section of Criminal Justice. See American Criminal Law Review

American Bar Association Section of Family Law. See Family Law Quarterly

American Bar Association Section of International & Comparative Law. See The International Lawyer

American Bar Association Section of Labor and Employment Law. See The Labor Lawyer

American Bar Association Section of Natural Resources Law. See Natural Resources & Environment

American Bar Association Section of Public Contract Law. See Public Contract Law Journal

American Bar Association Section of Real Property, Probate & Trust Law. See Real Property, Probate and Trust Journal

American Bar Association Section of Taxation. See The Tax Lawyer

American Bar Association Section of Tort and Insurance Practice. See Tort & Insurance Law Journal

American Bar Association Section of Urban, State and Local Government Law. See The Urban Lawyer

American Business Law Journal. $23. q (ISSN 0002-7766) Abilene Christian University, c/o Prof. Brad Reid, Subscription Mgr., Box 8335, Abilene, TX 79699

American Criminal Law Review. $33. q (ISSN 0164-0364) American Criminal Law Review, Georgetown University Law Center, 600 New Jersey Ave., N.W., Washington, DC 20001

American Indian Law Review. $10. semi-ann (ISSN 0094-002X) College of Law, University of Oklahoma, 300 Timberdell Rd., Norman, OK 73019

American Intellectual Property Law Association Quarterly Journal. See AIPLA Quarterly Journal

The American Journal of Comparative Law. $20. q (ISSN 0002-919X) Boalt Hall, University of California, Berkeley, CA 94720

American Journal of Criminal Law. $20. tri-ann (ISSN 0092-2315) University of Texas School of Law, 727 E. 26th St., Austin, TX 78705

American Journal of Family Law. $120. q (ISSN 0891-6330) Professional Education Systems, 200 Spring St., P.O. Box 1428, Eau Claire, WI 54702

American Journal of International Law. $100. q (ISSN 0002-9300) American Journal of International Law, 2223 Massachusetts Ave., N.W., Washington, DC 20008-2864

The American Journal of Jurisprudence. $19. ann (ISSN 0065-8995) American Journal of Jurisprudence, Law Bldg., Notre Dame, IN 46556

American Journal of Law & Medicine. $70. q (ISSN 0098-8588) American Society of Law & Medicine, 765 Commonwealth Ave., Boston, MA 02215

The American Journal of Legal History. $20. q (ISSN 0002-9319) Temple University School of Law, 1719 N. Broad St., Philadelphia, PA 19122

The American Journal of Tax Policy. $22. semi-ann (ISSN 0739-7569) The American Journal of Tax Policy, P.O. Box 870382, Tuscaloosa, AL 35487

The American Journal of Trial Advocacy. $24. tri-ann (ISSN 0160-0281) Cumberland School of Law, Samford University, Box 2263, Birmingham, AL 35229

American Society of International Law Proceedings. $15. ann (ISSN 0272-5037) American Society of International Law Proceedings, 2223 Massachusetts Ave., N.W., Washington, DC 20008

The American University Journal of International Law and Policy. $22. q (ISSN 0888-630X) Washington College of Law, The American University, 4400 Massachusetts Ave., NW, Washington, DC 20016

The American University Law Review. $30. q (ISSN 0003-1453) Washington College of Law, American University, 4400 Massachusetts Ave., NW, Washington, DC 20016

The Anglo-American Law Review. £70. q (ISSN 0308-6569) Barry Rose Law Periodicals Ltd., Little London, Chichester, West Sussex, PO19 1PG England

Annals of Air and Space Law. $31.50. ann (ISSN 0701-158X) Institute and Centre of Air and Space Law, McGill University, 3690 Peel St., Montreal, Que. H3A 1W9, Canada

Annuaire canadien de droit international. See The Canadian Yearbook of International Law

Annual Conference on Intellectual Property. ann Albany Law School of Union University, 80 New Scotland Ave., Albany, NY 12208

Annual Review of Banking Law. $64. ann (ISSN 0739-2451) Warren, Gorham & Lamont, Inc., 210 South St., Boston, MA 02111

---

selected lower court decisions. In addition to this extensive state coverage, West Group publishes the *New York Supplement* series, which combines the cases from all three official publications.

WEST'S NATIONAL REPORTER SYSTEM. Additionally, state court opinions appear in regional units of the National Reporter System, published by West Group. Most libraries have the West reporters because they report cases more quickly and are distributed more widely than the state-published reports. In fact, many states have eliminated their own reporters in favor of West's National Reporter System.

The National Reporter System divides the states into the following geographical areas: *Atlantic* (A. or A.2d), *South Eastern* (S.E. or S.E.2d), *South Western* (S.W. or S.W.2d), *North Western* (N.W. or N.W.2d), *North Eastern* (N.E. or N.E.2d), *Southern* (So. or So.2d), and *Pacific* (P. or P.2d). Note that the *2d* in the preceding abbreviations refers to *Second Series.* In the near future, the designation *3d,* for *Third Series,* will be used for some of the reporters. The states included in each of these regional divisions are indicated in Exhibit 14.19 on the next page. Note that the names of the areas may not match the commonly used geographical terms. For example, the *North Western* reporter includes North Dakota, Minnesota, and other states located in the "old" Northwest—the Northwest in the United States in an earlier era.

CITATION FORMAT.   After an appellate decision has been published, it is normally referred to *(cited)* by the name of the case (often called the *style* of the case) and the volume number, abbreviated name, and page number of each reporter in which the case has been published. This information is included in what is called the **citation.** When more than one reporter contains the text of the same case, a reference to the other reporter or reporters in which the case can be found—called a **parallel citation**—is also included. The first citation will be to the state's official reporter (if different from West's National Reporter System). Note that in every citation to a reporter, the number preceding the abbreviated name of the reporter will be the volume number, and the first number following it will be the page number of the first page of the case.

To illustrate how to find case law from citations, suppose you want to find the following case: *Cirrincione v. Johnson,*184 Ill. 2d 109, 703 N.E. 2d 67 (1998). You can see that the opinion in this case may be found in volume 184 of the official *Illinois Reports, Second Series,* on page 109. The parallel citation is to volume 703 of West's *North Eastern Reporter, Second Series*, page 67. Exhibit 14.20 further illustrates how to read citations to state court decisions.

When conducting legal research, you need to include in your research notes the citations to the cases or other legal sources that you have consulted, quoted, or want to refer to in a written summary of your research results. Several guides have been published on how to cite legal sources. The most widely used guide is a book entitled *The Bluebook: A Uniform System of Citation*, which is published by the Harvard Law Review Association. This book explains the proper format for citing cases, statutes, constitutions, regulations, and other legal sources. It is a good idea to memorize the basic format for citations to cases and statutory law because these legal sources are frequently cited in legal writing. Another popular guide is a small booklet entitled *The University of Chicago Manual of Legal Citation.*

Federal Court Decisions

As mentioned earlier, court decisions from the U.S. district courts (federal trial courts) are published in West's *Federal Supplement* (F.Supp.), and opinions from the circuit courts of appeals are reported in West's *Federal Reporter* (F., F.2d, or F.3d). These are both unofficial reporters (there are no official reporters for these courts). Both the *Federal Reporter* and the *Federal Supplement* incorporate decisions from specialized federal courts. West also publishes separate reporters, such as its *Bankruptcy Reporter*, that contain decisions in certain specialized fields under federal law.

United States Supreme Court Decisions

Opinions from the United States Supreme Court are published in several reporters, including the *United States Reports,* West's *Supreme Court Reporter*, and the

---

Citation
In case law, a reference to the volume number, name, and page number of the reporter in which a case can be found. In statutory and administrative law, a reference to the title number, name, and section of the code in which a statute or regulation can be found.

Parallel Citation
A second (or third) citation to another case reporter in which a case has been published. When a case is published in more than one reporter, each citation is a parallel citation to the other(s).

On the Web
To find Supreme Court opinions and opinions issued by the federal appellate courts, a good starting point is FindLaw's site at www.findlaw.com.

EXHIBIT 14.19
National Reporter System—Regional and Federal

Regional Reporters	Coverage Beginning	Coverage
Atlantic Reporter (A. or A.2d)	1885	Connecticut, Delaware, Maine, Maryland, New Hampshire, New Jersey, Pennsylvania, Rhode Island, Vermont, and District of Columbia.
North Eastern Reporter (N.E. or N.E.2d)	1885	Illinois, Indiana, Massachusetts, New York, and Ohio.
North Western Reporter (N.W. or N.W.2d)	1879	Iowa, Michigan, Minnesota, Nebraska, North Dakota, South Dakota, and Wisconsin.
Pacific Reporter (P. or P.2d)	1883	Alaska, Arizona, California, Colorado, Hawaii, Idaho, Kansas, Montana, Nevada, New Mexico, Oklahoma, Oregon, Utah, Washington, and Wyoming.
South Eastern Reporter (S.E. or S.E.2d)	1887	Georgia, North Carolina, South Carolina, Virginia, and West Virginia.
South Western Reporter (S.W. or S.W.2d)	1886	Arkansas, Kentucky, Missouri, Tennessee, and Texas.
Southern Reporter (So. or So.2d)	1887	Alabama, Florida, Louisiana, and Mississippi.

Federal Reporters		
Federal Reporter (F., F.2d, or F. 3d)	1880	U.S. Circuit Court from 1880 to 1912; U.S. Commerce Court from 1911 to 1913; U.S. District Courts from 1880 to 1932; U.S. Court of Claims (now called U.S. Court of Federal Claims) from 1929 to 1932 and since 1960; U.S. Court of Appeals since 1891; U.S. Court of Customs and Patent Appeals since 1929; and U.S. Emergency Court of Appeals since 1943.
Federal Supplement (F.Supp.)	1932	U.S. Court of Claims from 1932 to 1960; U.S. District Courts since 1932; and U.S. Customs Court since 1956.
Federal Rules Decisions (F.R.D.)	1939	U.S. District Courts involving the Federal Rules of Civil Procedure since 1939 and Federal Rules of Criminal Procedure since 1946.
Supreme Court Reporter (S.Ct.)	1882	U.S. Supreme Court since the October term of 1882.
Bankruptcy Reporter (Bankr.)	1980	Bankruptcy decisions of U.S. Bankruptcy Courts, U.S. District Courts, U.S. Courts of Appeals, and U.S. Supreme Court.
Military Justice Reporter (M.J.)	1978	U.S. Court of Military Appeals and Courts of Military Review for the Army, Navy, Air Force, and Coast Guard.

NATIONAL REPORTER SYSTEM MAP

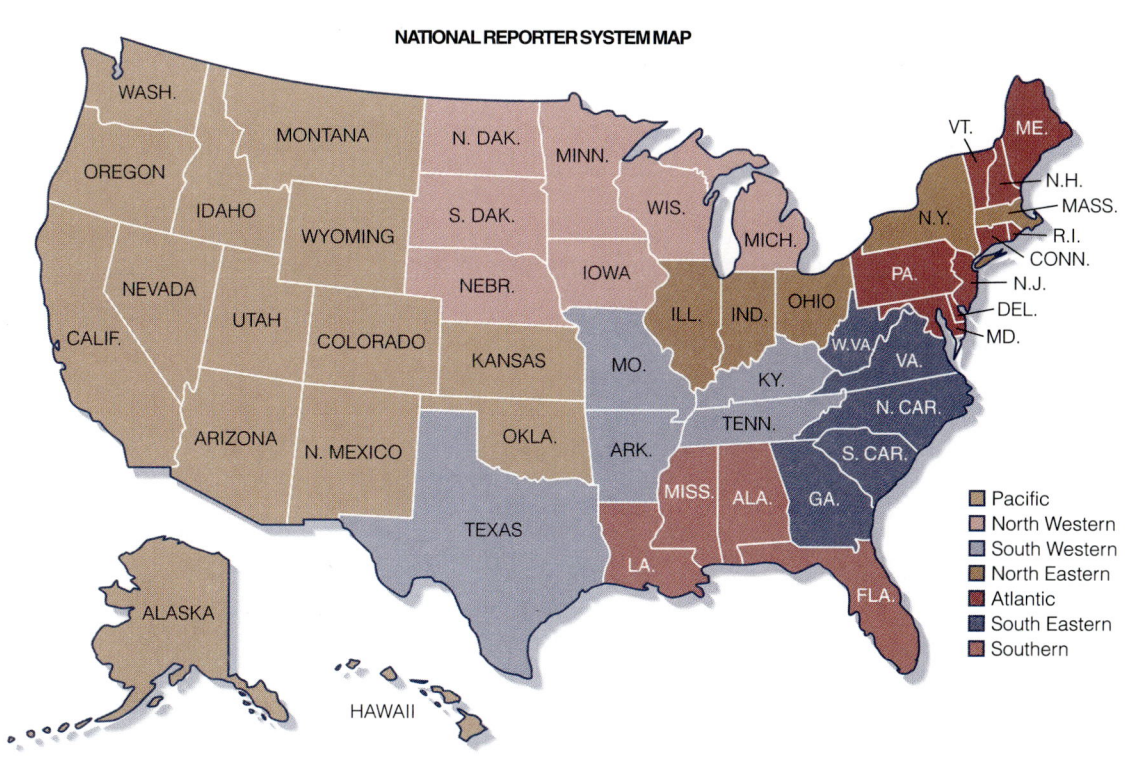

EXHIBIT 14.20
How to Read Case Citations

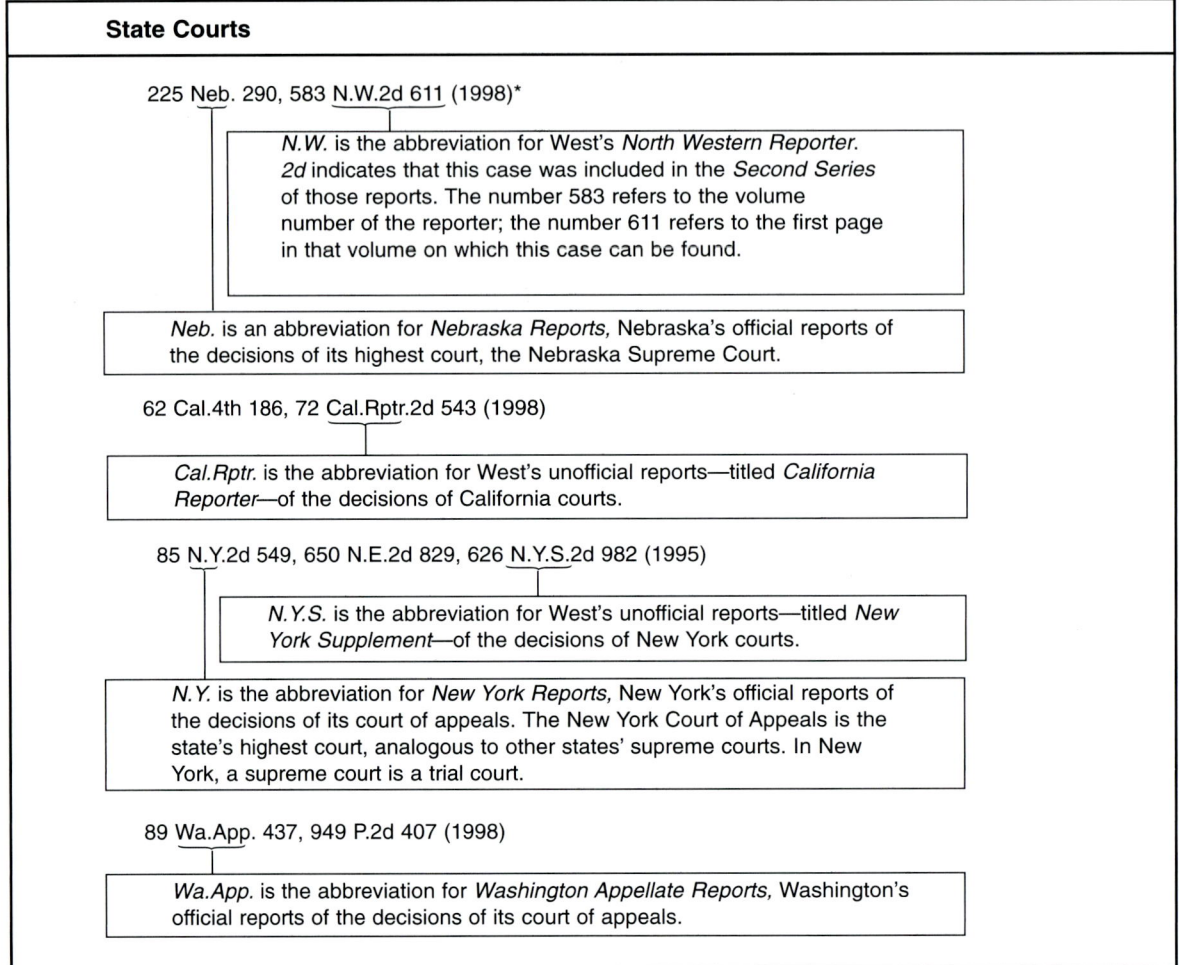

*The case names have been deleted from these citations to emphasize the publications. It should be kept in mind, however, that the name of a case is as important as the specific page numbers in the volumes in which it is found. If a citation is incorrect, the correct citation may be found in a publication's index of case names. The date of a case is also important because, in addition to providing a check on error in citations, the value of a recent case as an authority is likely to be greater than that of earlier cases.

Lawyers' Edition of the Supreme Court Reports, each of which we discuss below. A sample citation to a Supreme Court case is also included in Exhibit 14.20.

THE *UNITED STATES REPORTS*. The *United States Reports* (U.S.) is the official edition of all decisions of the United States Supreme Court for which there are written opinions. Published by the federal government, the series includes reports of Supreme Court cases dating from the August term of 1791. Approximately two to four weeks after the Supreme Court issues a decision, the official slip opinion is published by the U.S. Government Printing Office. The **slip opinion** is the first authoritative text of the opinion and is printed as an individual pamphlet. After a number of slip opinions have been issued, the advance sheets of the official *United States Reports* appear. These are issued in pamphlet form to provide a temporary resource until the official bound volume is finally published.

Slip Opinion
A judicial opinion published shortly after the decision is made and not yet included in a case reporter or advance sheets.

EXHIBIT 14.20
How to Read Case Citations—Continued

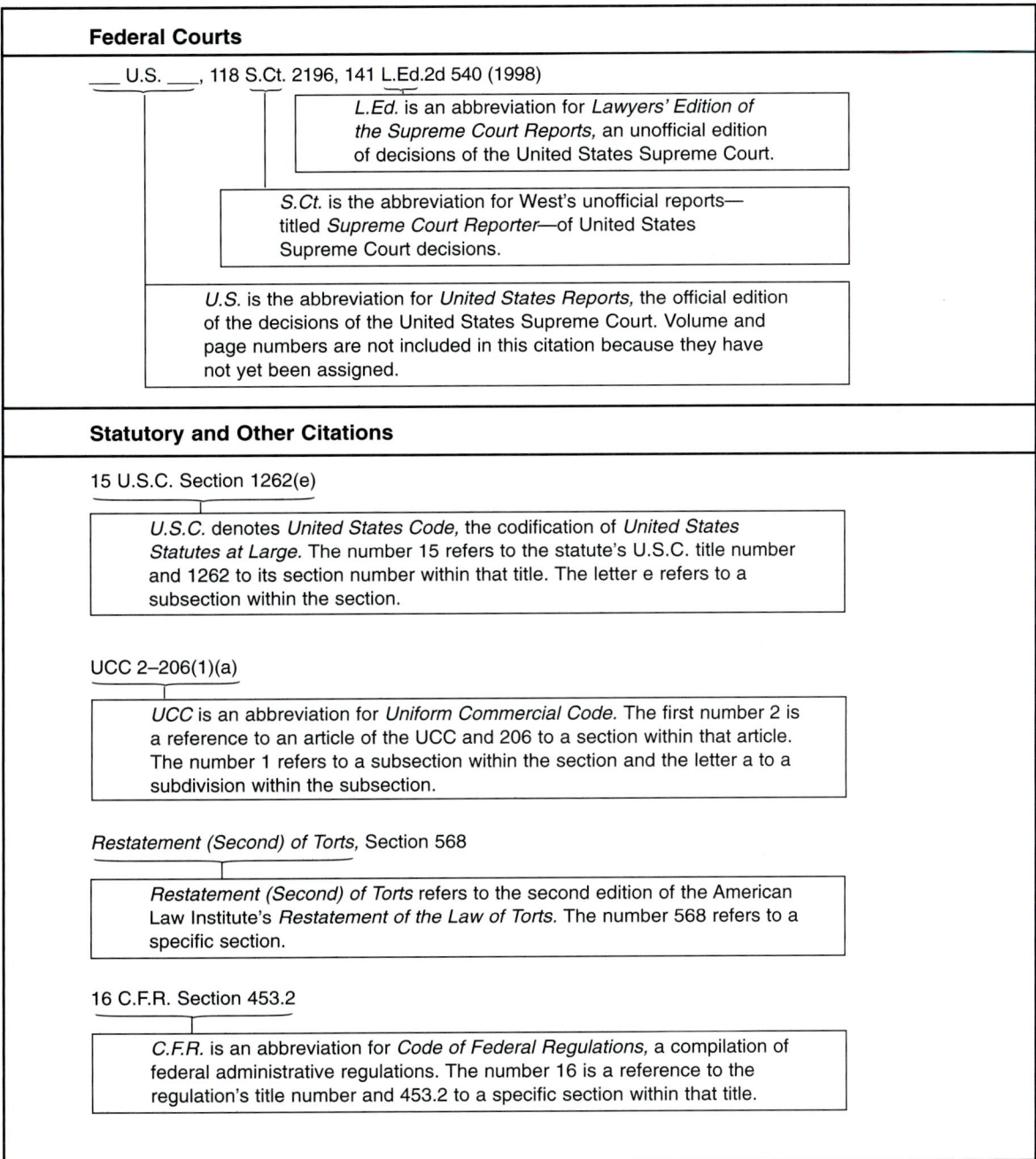

Virtually all Supreme Court decisions, as well as the text of many treaties and statutes, are now available in electronic format on the Internet. Supreme Court opinions are available on the Internet within minutes after their release. Thus, if you have access to the Internet and want to read the text of a Supreme Court decision made yesterday or even just hours ago, you may be able to view it on your computer screen.

Developing Paralegal Skills
Understanding Case Citations

Wendy Morgan is a legal secretary who is studying to become a paralegal. She has just read a chapter in her textbook on legal research and is studying the section on case citations. She shows a citation to Janet Honner, a legal assistant at the office, and asks Janet to go over the citation with her.

The name of the case is *O'Driscoll v. Hercules, Inc.*, and its citation is 55 F.3d 176 (10th Cir. 1999). Janet tells Wendy that the names in the case are the names of the parties to the lawsuit. Next is the volume number, which is 55. It is imprinted on the outside binding of the book or reporter in which the case is printed. The name, or abbreviation, of the reporter is F.3d, which stands for *West's Federal Reporter, Third Series*. The next number, 176, is the page number of volume 55 on which the case begins. The information in parentheses shows that the U.S. Court of Appeals for the Tenth Circuit decided the case in 1999. Wendy checks her understanding by reviewing the parts of another case citation.

Janet then explains to Wendy that citations for some cases (although not the *O'Driscoll* case) include a second citation as well. The second citation, which is referred to as a parallel citation, indicates where the case can be found in a different reporter.

Tips for Understanding a Case Citation
- The case name usually appears first and includes the names of parties to the lawsuit.
- The case name is either italicized or underlined.
- The first number is the volume number of the reporter in which the case appears.
- The reporter abbreviation is usually some combination of letters and/or numbers.
- The reporter abbreviation is followed by the page number on which the case begins.
- The material in parentheses contains at least the year that the court decided the case and, in some instances, the abbreviation of the name of the court that made the decision.

Syllabus
A brief summary of the holding and legal principles involved in a reported case, which is followed by the court's official opinion.

THE *SUPREME COURT REPORTER*. Supreme Court cases are also published in West's *Supreme Court Reporter* (S.Ct.), which is an unofficial edition of Supreme Court opinions dating from the Court's term in October 1882. In this reporter, the case report—the formal court opinion—is preceded by a brief **syllabus** (summary of the case) and headnotes with key numbers (used throughout the West reporters and digests) prepared by West editors.

THE *LAWYERS' EDITION OF THE SUPREME COURT REPORTS*. The *Lawyers' Edition of the Supreme Court Reports*, also published by West Group, is an unofficial edition of the entire series of the Supreme Court reports containing many decisions not reported in early official volumes. The advantage offered to the legal researcher by the *Lawyers' Edition* is its research tools. In its second series, it precedes each case report with a full summary of the case and discusses in detail selected cases of special interest to the legal profession. Also, the *Lawyers' Edition* is the only reporter of Supreme Court opinions that provides summaries of the briefs presented by counsel.

UNOFFICIAL LOOSE-LEAF SERVICES. Unofficial loose-leaf services publish Supreme Court decisions the day after a decision is announced. Two loose-leaf services cover Supreme Court opinions: *United States Law Week*, which is published by the Bureau of National Affairs, and the *Supreme Court Bulletin*, which is published by CCH, Inc.

> ## ETHICAL CONCERN
> ### Citing Sources
>
> Before returning a legal source to the library shelf (or signing off a computerized legal-research service), you should make sure that you have included in your research notes the proper reference or citation for that authority. If you forget to cite your source, you will have to spend additional time relocating the source once again to obtain the citation. As has been stressed elsewhere, your time is a valuable resource for your attorney and a costly one for your client. If you have to spend another hour's time going to and from a library to obtain a citation that you should have included in your notes in the first place, the client may not consider charges for that hour to be "reasonable"—and attorneys have a duty to charge their clients reasonable fees.

RESEARCHING STATUTORY LAW

The case law that we have been discussing up to this point is often referred to as *judge-made law* because it is made by the judges and justices of the American court system. Other primary sources of American law are the statutes and ordinances passed by legislative bodies, such as the U.S. Congress, state legislatures, and town governments. Collectively, the law created by these bodies is referred to as *statutory law*.

Statutes enacted by legislative bodies are generally intended to govern the conduct of a broad group of persons and activities. Some statutes serve to supplement the common law, and other statutes replace it. The legislature has broad power to establish laws, and if a common law principle conflicts with a statutory provision, the statute will normally take precedence. Additionally, the legislature may create statutes that deal with areas not covered by the common law, such as age discrimination in employment, workers' compensation benefits, and other employment-related issues.

The process of enacting a statute is similar at the state and federal levels. The process begins when legislation is proposed and presented to the legislature for debate. The proposed legislation is usually called a *bill*. If the bill is passed, it is sent to the president or governor, who has the authority to sign it into law. Once legislation is signed into law, it is published.

To find the relevant statutory law governing a particular legal issue or area, you will need to know, first of all, the names of the various publications in which statutory law can be found. In this section, we look first at how federal statutes are published and how you can find, within these publications, statutes governing the issue you are researching. A more difficult task in researching statutory law is deciding whether a statute you have found is really applicable to the issue being researched. This determination requires a careful reading of the statute and may require further inquiry. You may need to analyze what the legislature intended when it passed the bill and how the courts have interpreted the statute.

The Publication of Federal Statutes

Federal statutes in the United States are published in three forms. The first official publication of a statute's text is the slip law. **Slip laws** present the text of statutes

Slip Law
The first official publication of a statute that comes out shortly after the legislation is passed (presented as a single sheet or pamphlet).

Public Law Number
An identification number that has been assigned to a specific statute, or public law, following the legislative process.

Session Laws
Statutes passed by legislators that are officially published chronologically, by order of legislative session, in a multivolume set.

Code
A systematic and logical presentation of laws, rules, or regulations.

in the form of pamphlets or single sheets. These pamphlets or sheets are not indexed, but they can be identified by their **public law number**, or P.L. number—a number assigned to each statute on completion of the legislative process. Slip laws are available through the *United States Code Service (U.S.C.S.)* advance service and the *United States Code Congressional and Administrative News (U.S.C.C.A.N.)* advance service. They are published in pamphlet form by the U.S. Government Depository Library. (The *U.S.C.S.* and the *U.S.C.C.A.N.* will be discussed in greater detail shortly.)

The second form in which statutes are officially published is the session law. **Session laws** are collections of statutes contained in volumes and arranged by the year or legislative session during which they were enacted. Each volume contains an index. The session laws of the U.S. Congress appear in the *United States Statutes at Large*, which is published by the U.S. government. *Statutes at Large* volumes contain the language of the legislation as it appeared at the time of passage. They also include references to the House or Senate bill number, which can be helpful in directing the researcher to legislative sources, such as committee hearings and reports. These sources are valuable when you are trying to determine the intended meaning of a particular statute. Each state issues its own official session laws. Some states have both an official and an unofficial version. The titles of the volumes vary by state.

Finally, statutory material is published in compilations referred to as **codes**. Unlike the sources just discussed, codes arrange statutory provisions by topic, thus facilitating legal research. Most statutory codes are updated through the issuance of supplemental pocket parts or by loose-leaf services. Paralegals conducting research on statutory law should begin by reviewing the index provided for the relevant statutory code.

The *United States Code*

The *United States Code*, or *U.S.C.*, is published by the U.S. government every six years and is updated annually. The *U.S.C.* is divided into fifty topic classifications. As shown in Exhibit 14.21, each of these topics, called *titles* of the code, carries a descriptive title and a number. For example, laws relating to commerce and trade are collected in Title 15. Laws concerning the courts or judicial procedures are collected in Title 28. Titles are subdivided into chapters (sections) and subchapters. A citation to the *U.S.C.* includes title and section numbers. Thus, a reference to "28 U.S.C. Section 1346" means that the statute can be found in Section 1346 of Title 28. "Section" may also be designated by the symbol §, and "Sections" by §§.

One approach to finding statutory law in the *U.S.C.* is simply to refer to the title descriptions listed in the front of each volume. This approach is most beneficial for researchers who can quickly find the applicable title for the statute they are researching. Alternatively, the researcher can consult the index to the *U.S.C.* The index provides an alphabetical listing of all federal statutes by subject matter and by the name of the act. The researcher should consider the various ways the statute could be listed and then review the index for the appropriate description. The more descriptive words the researcher can think of, the more likely it is that he or she will be able to locate a particular statute. The index provides the exact location of the statute, by title and section.

Sometimes a researcher may know the popular name of a legislative act but not its official name. In this situation, the researcher can consult the *U.S.C.* volume entitled *Popular Name Table*, which lists statutes by their popular names. Many legislative bills enacted into law are commonly known by a popular name. Some have descriptive titles reflecting their purpose; others are named after their

On the Web
You can access and search (by title and section number) the U.S. Code online at www.law.cornell.edu/uscode.

EXHIBIT 14.21

Titles in the *United States Code*

```
                    TITLES OF UNITED STATES CODE

    *1. General Provisions.                27. Intoxicating Liquors.
     2. The Congress.                     *28. Judiciary and Judicial Procedure; and
    *3. The President.                         Appendix.
    *4. Flag and Seal, Seat of Government, 29. Labor.
        and the States.                    30. Mineral Lands and Mining.
    *5. Government Organization and       *31. Money and Finance.
        Employees; and Appendix.          *32. National Guard.
    †6. [Surety Bonds.]                    33. Navigation and Navigable Waters.
     7. Agriculture.                      ‡34. [Navy.]
     8. Aliens and Nationality.           *35. Patents.
    *9. Arbitration.                       36. Patriotic Societies and Observances.
   *10. Armed Forces; and Appendix.       *37. Pay and Allowances of the Uniformed
   *11. Bankruptcy; and Appendix.              Services.
    12. Banks and Banking.                *38. Veterans' Benefits.
   *13. Census.                           *39. Postal Service.
   *14. Coast Guard.                       40. Public Buildings, Property, and Works.
    15. Commerce and Trade.                41. Public Contracts.
    16. Conservation.                      42. The Public Health and Welfare.
   *17. Copyrights.                        43. Public Lands.
   *18. Crimes and Criminal Procedure;    *44. Public Printing and Documents.
        and Appendix.                      45. Railroads.
    19. Customs Duties.                   *46. Shipping; and Appendix.
    20. Education.                         47. Telegraphs, Telephones, and
    21. Food and Drugs.                        Radiotelegraphs.
    22. Foreign Relations and Intercourse. 48. Territories and Insular Possessions.
   *23. Highways.                         *49. Transportation; and Appendix.
    24. Hospitals and Asylums.             50. War and National Defense; and Appendix.
    25. Indians.
    26. Internal Revenue Code.

    *This title has been enacted as law. However, any Appendix to this title has not been enacted as law.
    †This title was enacted as law and has been repealed by the enactment of Title 31.
    ‡This title has been eliminated by the enactment of Title 10.

                                    Page III
```

sponsors. The Labor-Management Reporting and Disclosure Act of 1959, for example, is also known as the Landrum-Griffin Act. Searching by popular name will allow the researcher to find the title and section of the statute and therefore locate the statute in the *U.S.C.*

The *U.S.C.* also lists, after the text of the statute, citations to the *United States Statutes at Large*. These citations are helpful for paralegals who wish to examine previous versions of the statute in the *Statutes at Large*.

Unofficial Versions of the Federal Code

There are two unofficial versions of the federal code that are similar to the *U.S.C.*, but they contain some important differences. They provide annotations describing cases and other sources that have applied or interpreted a given statute. Additionally, they contain more cross-references to related sections of the code than does the *U.S.C.* These two unofficial federal codes are discussed next.

EXHIBIT 14.22
Excerpt from the *United States Code Annotated*

Reproduced with permission of West Group.

Ch. 11 PEACETIME DISABILITY   38 § 1131

CROSS REFERENCES
Rates of peacetime death compensation same as specified under this section, see 38 USCA § 1142.

LIBRARY REFERENCES
American Digest System
 Veterans' benefits; rights and disabilities in general, see Armed Services ⇔101.
Encyclopedias
 Veterans' benefits; compensation for dependents and survivors, see C.J.S. Armed Services § 254.
 Veterans' benefits; general considerations, see C.J.S. Armed Services § 251.
 Veterans' benefits; payment of benefits, see C.J.S. Armed Services § 265.
Law Reviews
 Making intramilitary tort law more civil: A proposed reform of the Feres Doctrine. David Schwartz, 95 Yale L.J. 992 (1986).

WESTLAW ELECTRONIC RESEARCH
Armed services cases: 34k[add key number].
See, also, WESTLAW guide following the Explanation pages of this volume.

NOTES OF DECISIONS
Death of claimant 1
Withdrawal of claim 2

1. Death of claimant
 Where the widow filed a claim but died before decision was made in her favor, awards were made as if there had been no surviving widow. 1943, A.D.V.A. 524.

2. Withdrawal of claim
 Where the stepfather's claim for death compensation had not yet been favorably considered, a withdrawal of his claim had the effect of entitling the mother to be considered as the only person who had established a right to the benefit under former § 472b of this title, and she was accordingly entitled to the $45 rate therein provided for one parent. 1940, A.D.V.A. 458.

SUBCHAPTER IV—PEACETIME DISABILITY COMPENSATION

CROSS REFERENCES
Amounts payable under this subchapter exempt from tax levy, see 26 USCA § 6334.

§ 1131. Basic entitlement
For disability resulting from personal injury suffered or disease contracted in line of duty, or for aggravation of a preexisting injury suffered or disease contracted in line of duty, in the active military, naval, or air service, during other than a period of war, the United States will pay to any veteran thus disabled and who was discharged or released under conditions other than dishonorable from the period of service in which said injury or disease was incurred, or preexisting injury or disease was aggravated, compensation as provided in this subchapter, but no compensation shall be paid if

237

---

38 § 1131   DISABILITY, ETC., COMPENSATION   Ch. 11

the disability is a result of the veteran's own willful misconduct or abuse of alcohol or drugs.

(Pub.L. 85–857, Sept. 2, 1958, 72 Stat. 1122, § 331; Pub.L. 101–508, Title VIII, § 8052(a)(3), Nov. 5, 1990, 104 Stat. 1388-351; renumbered Pub.L. 102–83, § 5(a), Aug. 6, 1991, 105 Stat. 406.)

HISTORICAL AND STATUTORY NOTES
Revision Notes and Legislative Reports
 1958 Act. Senate Report No. 2259 and House Report No. 1298, see 1958 U.S. Code Cong. and Adm.News, p. 4352.
 1990 Act. House Report No. 101–881 and House Conference Report No. 101–964, see 1990 U.S.Code Cong. and Adm.News, p. 2017.
Amendments
 1990 Amendment. Pub.L. 101–508 substituted "a result of the veteran's own willful misconduct or abuse of alcohol or drugs" for "the result of the veteran's own willful misconduct".
Effective Dates
 1990 Act. Amendment by Pub.L. 101–508 effective with respect to claims filed after Oct. 31, 1990, see section 8052(b) of Pub.L. 101–508, set out as a note under section 105 of this title.

LIBRARY REFERENCES
American Digest System
 Veterans' benefits; compensation for disability, see Armed Services ⇔104.
 Veterans' benefits; rights and benefits in general, see Armed Services ⇔101.
Encyclopedias
 Veterans' benefits; disability compensation, see C.J.S. Armed Services § 255.
 Veterans' benefits; general considerations, see C.J.S. Armed Services § 251.
Law Reviews
 Federal Tort Claims Act—Feres Doctrine. (1985) 24 Duquesne L.Rev. 309.

WESTLAW ELECTRONIC RESEARCH
Armed services cases: 34k[add key number].
See, also, WESTLAW guide following the Explanation pages of this volume.

NOTES OF DECISIONS
Action against government contractor 4
Civilian 2
Indemnity 3
Law governing 1

1. Law governing
 The Veterans' Benefits Act did not preempt Navy enlisted man's action under state law against private corporation which operated government-owned nuclear reactor facility, to recover for injuries sustained while enlisted man was on duty and a deck on which he was standing collapsed, despite provision in contract between corporation and the Government that Government would reimburse corporation for all judgments incurred in connection with the contract; such clause apparently was added by the parties without specific statutory or regulatory direction and, even if indemnification would frustrate the Act, preemption would operate against corporation's indemnity claim and not against the enlisted man's claim against the corporation. Chapman v. Westinghouse Elec. Corp., C.A.9 (Idaho) 1990, 911 F.2d 267.

2. Civilian
 A civilian is ineligible under this section for any injuries resulting from improper activation into military service. Valn v. U.S., C.A.Del.1983, 708 F.2d 116.

3. Indemnity
 Where this chapter is present, it is sole or exclusive remedy for claims which involve service-related injuries, irrespective of who sues United States; thus, in a case growing out of service-connected injury, there cannot be a recovery of indemnity for payments to serviceman

238

THE *UNITED STATES CODE ANNOTATED.* One of the unofficial versions of the *U.S.C.* is West's *United States Code Annotated (U.S.C.A.).* The *U.S.C.A.* contains the full text of the *U.S.C.*, the U.S. Constitution, the Federal Rules of Evidence, and various other rules, including the Rules of Civil Procedure and the Rules of Criminal Procedure. This useful set of approximately two hundred volumes offers historical notes relating to the text of each statute and any amendments to the act. As shown in Exhibit 14.22, cross-references to other titles and sections within the *U.S.C.A.* are also given. Annotations, referred to as "Notes of Decisions," offer additional research assistance by listing cases that have analyzed, discussed, or interpreted the particular statute.

The *U.S.C.A.* is more current than the *U.S.C.* The supplements updating the *U.S.C.* often lag behind current statutory law by more than a year (or sometimes, two years), whereas the *U.S.C.A.* provides updated statutory information through supplemental pocket parts and pamphlets many times a year.

Locating statutory law in the *U.S.C.A.* is similar to locating statutes in the *U.S.C.* Researchers can use the topical or index approach and, if necessary, look through the *Popular Name Table.*

THE *UNITED STATES CODE SERVICE.* The second unofficial version of the federal code is the *United States Code Service (U.S.C.S.),* published by West Group. The *U.S.C.S.* offers some of the same features offered by the *U.S.C.A.,* such as annotations. The *U.S.C.S.* and the *U.S.C.A.* are distinguishable by the research tools they provide. The research section of the *U.S.C.S.* provides references and citations to some sources that are not contained in the *U.S.C.A.,* including such publications as *American Law Reports,* legal periodicals, and *American Jurisprudence.*

Like the *U.S.C.A.,* the *U.S.C.S.* offers an effective updating service in the form of replacement volumes and pocket parts. The *U.S.C.S.* issues softbound updated volumes called *Cumulative Later Case and Statutory Service,* which compile cases—including annotations—that have been published since the last printed pocket-part supplement. Another *U.S.C.S.* updating service is the advance service, a monthly compilation of slip laws and other legislative decrees.

Paralegals can begin statutory research in the *U.S.C.S.* by reviewing the *Subject Index* or the *Popular Name Table.* Both annotated codes also have conversion charts listing all public acts by public law number, *Statutes at Large* references, and *U.S.C.* title and section numbers.

Interpreting Statutory Law

Paralegals should understand that often the key to successful statutory research is determining whether a statute is applicable to the legal issue being researched. This can prove to be a difficult task. In your analysis of a statute's applicability to a research problem, it is crucial that you read the language of the statute carefully. As will be discussed in the next chapter, there are several approaches to interpreting statutory law. One approach involves researching case law on the subject and determining how other courts—in particular, higher courts within your jurisdiction, whose decisions create binding precedents—have interpreted a given statute. Another technique, which we discuss below, involves determining what the legislature intended when it enacted the statute.

Researching Legislative History

Prior to the enactment of any statute, the U.S. Congress or a state legislature analyzes carefully the wording and the implications of the statute. Federal statutes pass through committees in both the House of Representatives and the Senate before being voted on by the legislature and signed by the president. The statutes may be debated extensively on the floor of each chamber of Congress, and a congressional hearing may be held to clarify certain issues relating to the proposed law. Committee reports and transcripts of congressional debates and hearings can shed much light on why the statute was passed, why it was worded in a certain way, what the goals of the act were, and so on. These sources are described in more complete detail below.

Before you can study these sources, however, you need to know how to find them. The easiest way to locate them is to refer to the unofficial, annotated

Developing Paralegal Skills
Researching the *U.S.C.A.*

Natalie Martin has completed her factual analysis of the case involving Bernie Berriman (see the *Developing Paralegal Skills* feature entitled "Defining the Issues to Be Researched") and begins her research. The issue she is researching is whether the government, which arrested Bernie for the transportation and distribution of cocaine, had the authority to confiscate Bernie's car and car phone. Natalie's supervising attorney has told her to start her research by going to the *United States Code Annotated* (U.S.C.A.) to find the relevant federal statutes.

Checklist for Researching the *U.S.C.A.*

- Start with general index volumes unless the *U.S.C.A.* title (topic) number or a popular name is known.
- If the specific title number is known, begin in the title index. If the popular name of a statute is known, begin in the *Popular Names Table*.
- Look up topics, either by factual categories or legal categories in the index. Here, the topic could be "drugs."
- Look up subtopics within topics. Here, "forfeiture" or "property" could be subtopics under "drugs."
- Write down the citations to the *U.S.C.A.* volumes containing the topics.
- Look up the citations in the volumes containing the various titles or topics.
- Read the relevant sections of the statute to determine if they apply to the research.
- Update the relevant sections of the statute to determine if they apply to the research.
- Check the annotations following the statute sections for case law in which the statute has been applied and interpreted.
- Review any cases that appear relevant.
- "Shepardize" both statutes and cases to make sure they are still "good law."

---

versions of the federal code, such as the *U.S.C.A.* and the *U.S.C.S.* These codes often contain information regarding the legislative history of a statute. For example, the statute's public law number and date of passage are included in these annotated codes, as are cross-references to sources that will provide you with more detailed information on a statute's legislative history. Each source that you discover will likely lead you to other useful sources.

COMMITTEE REPORTS. Committee reports provide the most important source of legislative history. Congressional committees produce reports for each bill, and these reports often contain the full text of the bill, a description of its purpose, and the committee's recommendations. Several tables are also included to set out dates for certain actions. The dates can help the researcher locate floor debates and committee testimony in the *Congressional Record* (described below) and various other publications. Committee reports are published according to a numerical series and are available through the U.S. Government Printing Office.

THE *CONGRESSIONAL RECORD*. The *Congressional Record*, which is published daily while Congress is in session, contains *verbatim* (word-for-word) transcripts of congressional debates and proceedings. The transcripts include remarks made by various members of Congress, proposed amendments, votes, and occasionally the text of the bill under discussion.

Legislative hearings, another important source of legislative research, can be found in the transcripts of testimony before the House and Senate committees considering the proposed legislation. The purpose of conducting hearings is to determine if such legislation is needed. As a result, many types of testimony are presented. The researcher may find some helpful testimony in these sources, yet it is important to remember that much of it may be biased, because of the interested positions of the parties presenting the information. Hearings may be informative but are not as authoritative as committee reports in determining legislative intent.

OTHER SOURCES OF LEGISLATIVE HISTORY. The two tools most frequently used in conducting research on legislative history are the *United States Code Congressional and Administrative News (U.S.C.C.A.N.)* and the *Congressional Information Service (C.I.S.)*. The *U.S.C.C.A.N.*, a West publication shown in Exhibit 14.23, contains reprints of statutes as published in the *Statutes at Large* and sections describing the statutes' legislative history, including committee reports. Statutes in the *U.S.C.A.* are followed by notations directing the researcher to the corresponding legislative history in the *U.S.C.C.A.N.* The *C.I.S.*, a U.S. government publication, contains information from committee reports, hearing reports, documents from both houses, and special publications. Both the *C.I.S.* and the *U.S.C.C.A.N.* provide a system of indexing and abstracting that allows quick access to information.

State Codes

State codes follow the *U.S.C.* pattern of arranging statutes by subject. They may be called codes, revisions, compilations, consolidations, general statutes, or statutes, depending on the preference of the states. In some codes, subjects are designated by number. In others, they are designated by name. For example, "13 Pennsylvania Consolidated Statutes Section 1101" means that the statute can be found in Section 1101 of Title 13 of the Pennsylvania code. "California Commercial Code Section 1101" means that the statute can be found in Section 1101 under the heading "Commercial" in the California Code. Abbreviations may be used. For example, "13 Pennsylvania Consolidated Statutes Section 1101" may be abbreviated to "13 Pa.C.S. § 1101," and "California Commercial Code Section 1101" may be abbreviated to "Cal. Com. Code § 1101."

In many states, official codes are supplemented by annotated codes published by private publishers. Annotated codes follow the numbering scheme set forth in the official state code but provide outlines and indexes to assist in locating information. These codes also provide references to case law, legislative history sources, and other documents in which the statute has been considered or discussed. Like their federal counterparts, the annotated codes at the state level are kept current with pocket parts and other supplementary materials.

RESEARCHING ADMINISTRATIVE LAW

Administrative rules and regulations constitute a growing source of American law. As discussed in Chapter 9, Congress frequently delegates authority to administrative agencies through enabling legislation. For example, in 1914 Congress passed the Federal Trade Commission Act, which established the Federal Trade Commission, or FTC. The act gave the FTC the authority to issue and enforce rules and regulations relating to unfair trade practices in the United States. Other federal administrative agencies include the Occupational Safety and Health Administration, the Consumer Product Safety Commission, and the Securities and Exchange Commission. The orders, regulations, and decisions of such agencies are legally binding and, as such, are primary sources of law.

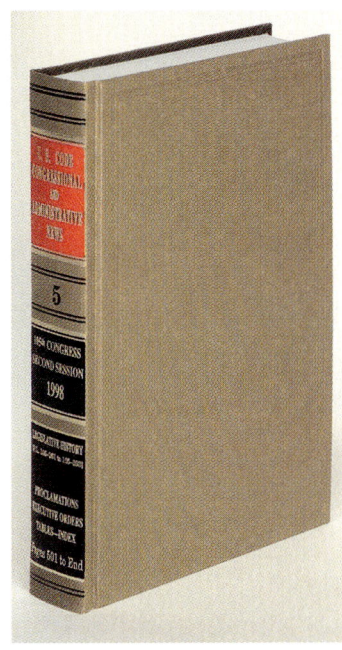

EXHIBIT 14.23
United States Code Congressional and Administrative News

Reproduced with permission of West Group.

EXHIBIT 14.24
Code of Federal Regulations

Reproduced with permission of West Group.

The *Code of Federal Regulations*

The *Code of Federal Regulations (C.F.R.)* is a government publication containing all federal administrative agency regulations (see Exhibit 14.24). The regulations are compiled from the *Federal Register*, a daily government publication consisting of executive orders and administrative regulations and in which administrative regulations are first published. (See Chapter 9 for a discussion of administrative rulemaking procedure.)

The *C.F.R.* uses the same titles as the *United States Code* (shown previously in Exhibit 14.21). This subject-matter organization allows the researcher to determine the section in the *C.F.R.* in which a regulation will appear. Each title of the *C.F.R.* is divided into chapters, subchapters, parts, and sections. Exhibit 14.25 shows some pages from *C.F.R.* Title 20 (Chapter III, Part 416) that relate to the Social Security Administration.

Publication of the *C.F.R.*

The *C.F.R.* is revised and republished four times a year. Recent regulations appear in the *Federal Register* until they are later incorporated into the *C.F.R.* If, as a paralegal, you are searching for administrative regulations in the *C.F.R.*, you should begin with the index section of the *Index and Finding Aids* volume. This index will allow you to locate the relevant title and the section of the *C.F.R.* that pertains to the problem. The next step is locating the regulation in the most recent volume of that title in the *C.F.R.* You should also review the *List of C.F.R. Sections Affected*, issued in monthly pamphlets, to determine if any changes have been made to the section since the last revision. A page from this publication is shown in Exhibit 14.26 on page 528. You can find updates to these monthly pamphlets by looking at the *Federal Register's* cumulative publication, *List of C.F.R. Parts Affected*, which reflects changes made during the current month.

Finding Tools for Administrative Law

The *Congressional Information Service (C.I.S.)* also provides an index to the *C.F.R.* The *C.I.S.* index is helpful in locating *C.F.R.* regulations by subject matter and also in determining the geographical areas affected by the regulation. The *American Digest System* can be of additional help to the paralegal, because it provides coverage of court cases dealing with administrative questions. The digests, however, do not contain any agency rulings. Additionally, certain loose-leaf services provide administrative decisions for particular specialty fields, such as taxation. If available, they are a useful research tool.

Whenever you need to research administrative law, remember that the most efficient way to find what you are looking for may be simply to call the agency and ask agency personnel how to access information relevant to your research topic.

FINDING CONSTITUTIONAL LAW

The federal government and all fifty states have their own constitutions describing the powers, responsibilities, and limitations of the various branches of government. Constitutions can be replaced or amended, and it is important that researchers have access to both current versions and older ones.

The text of the U.S. Constitution can be found in a number of publications. A useful source of federal constitutional law is *The Constitution of the United*

EXHIBIT 14.25
Subdivisions of Titles and Provisions in the *Code of Federal Regulations*

CHAPTER III—SOCIAL SECURITY ADMINISTRATION, DEPARTMENT OF HEALTH AND HUMAN SERVICES

Part		Page
400	[Reserved]	
401	Disclosure of official records and information	4
404	Federal old-age, survivors and disability insurance (1950–)	15
410	Federal Coal Mine Health and Safety Act of 1969, Title IV—Black Lung benefits (1969–)	485
416	Supplemental security income for the aged, blind, and disabled	571
422	Organization and procedures	867
423–499	[Reserved]	

Social Security Administration, HHS

filed with the Secretary of Labor. If the claimant, upon notification by the Social Security Administration of his her right to review (see 410.704(a)) requests that the claim originally filed with the Social Security Administration be forwarded to the Office of Workers' Compensation Programs for review, or if more than one claim has been filed with the Secretary of Labor by the same claimant, such claims shall be merged and processed with the first claim filed with the Office of Workers' Compensation Programs.

410.706 Effect of the Social Security Administration determination of entitlement.

Under section 435 of the BLBRA of 1977 a determination of entitlement made by the Social Security Administration under this subpart G is binding on the Office of Workers' Compensation Programs as an initial determination of eligibility.

7 Hearings and appeals.

review of any determination by the Social Security Administration of a claim under this subpart made by the Office of Workers' Compensation Programs. If the Social Security Administration does not approve the claim following its review of this subpart, the claim will be returned to the Office of Worker's Compensation Programs, and the Office of Workers' Compensation Programs will automatically review the claim. The Office of Workers' Compensation Programs will provide an opportunity for the claimant to submit additional evidence if it is needed to approve the claim. See 410.704(e)(2) of this subpart. If the Social Security Administration approves the claim but the claimant disagrees with any part of the Social Security Administration's determination, he/she may request the Office of Workers' Compensation Programs to review the Social Security Administration determination. See § 410.704 of this subpart.

Pt. 416

PART 416—SUPPLEMENTAL SECURITY INCOME FOR THE AGED, BLIND, AND DISABLED

Subpart A—Introduction, General Provisions and Definitions

Sec.
416.101 Introduction.
416.105 Administration.
416.110 Purpose of program.
416.120 General definitions and use of terms.
416.121 Receipt of aid or assistance for December 1973 under an approved State plan under title I, X, XIV, or XVI of the Social Security Act.

Subpart B—Eligibility

GENERAL

416.200 Introduction.
416.201 General definitions and terms used in this subpart.
416.202 Who may get SSI benefits.
416.203 Initial determinations of SSI eligibility.
416.204 Redeterminations of SSI eligibility.

REASONS WHY YOU MAY NOT GET SSI BENEFITS FOR WHICH YOU ARE OTHERWISE ELIGIBLE

416.210 You do not apply for other benefits.
416.211 You are a resident of a public institution.
416.212 You do not accept vocational rehabilitation services.
416.213 You are a disabled and medically determined drug addict or alcoholic and you do not accept or follow treatment.
416.214 You leave the United States.
416.215 You are a child of armed forces personnel living overseas.

ELIGIBILITY FOR INCREASED BENEFITS BECAUSE OF ESSENTIAL PERSONS

416.220 General.
416.221 Who is a qualified individual.
416.222 Who is an essential person.
416.223 What happens if you are a qualified individual.
416.250 Experimental, pilot, and demonstration projects in the SSI program.

BENEFITS FOR PERSONS WITH DISABLING IMPAIRMENTS WHO PERFORM SGA

416.260 General.

Social Security Administration, HHS § 416.204

Public institution means an institution that is operated by or controlled by the Federal government, a State, or a political subdivision of a State such as a city or county. The term *public institution* does not include a publicly operated community residence which serves 16 or fewer residents.
Resident of a public institution means a person who can receive substantially all of his or her food and shelter while living in a public institution. The person need not be receiving treatment and services available in the institution and is a resident regardless of whether the resident or anyone else pays for all food, shelter, and other services in the institution. A person is not a resident of a public institution if he or she is living in a public educational institution for the primary purpose of receiving educational or vocational training as defined in this section. A *resident of a public institution* means the same thing as an *inmate* of a public institution as used in section 1611(e)(1)(A) of the Social Security Act. (See § 416.211(b), (c), and (d) of this subpart for exceptions to the general limitation on the eligibility for Supplemental Security Income benefits of individuals who are residents of a public institution.)
SSI means supplemental security income.
State assistance means payments made by a State to an aged, blind, or disabled person under a State plan approved under title I, X, XIV, or XVI (AABD) of the Social Security Act which was in effect before the SSI Program.
We or *Us* means the Social Security Administration.
You or *Your* means the person who applies for or receives SSI benefits or the person for whom an application is filed.

[47 FR 3103, Jan. 22, 1982, as amended at 49 FR 19639, May 19, 1984; 50 FR 48570, Nov. 26, 1985; 50 FR 51517, Dec. 18, 1985; 54 FR 19164, May 4, 1989]

§ 416.202 Who may get SSI benefits.

You are eligible for SSI benefits if you meet all of the following requirements:
(a) You are—
(1) Aged 65 or older (subpart H);

(2) Blind (subpart I); or
(3) Disabled (subpart I).
(b) You are a resident of the United States (§ 416.1603), and—
(1) A citizen or a national of the United States (§ 416.1610);
(2) An alien lawfully admitted for permanent residence in the United States (§ 416.1615);
(3) An alien permanently residing in the United States under color of law (§ 416.1618); or
(4) A child of armed forces personnel living overseas as described in § 416.215.
(c) You do not have more income than is permitted (subparts K and D).
(d) You do not have more resources than are permitted (subpart L).
(e) You file an application for SSI benefits (subpart C).

[47 FR 3103, Jan. 22, 1982, as amended at 58 FR 4897, Jan. 19, 1993]

§ 416.203 Initial determinations of SSI eligibility.

(a) *What happens when you apply for SSI benefits.* When you apply for SSI benefits we will ask you for documents and any other information we need to make sure you meet all the requirements. We will ask for information about your income and resources and about other eligibility requirements and you must answer completely. We will help you get any documents you need but do not have.
(b) *How we determine your eligibility for SSI benefits.* We determine that you are eligible for SSI benefits for a given month if you meet the requirements in § 416.202 in that month. However, we usually determine the amount of your SSI benefits for that month based on your income in an earlier month (see § 416.420). Thus, it is possible for you to meet the eligibility requirements in the given month but receive no benefit payment for that month.

[47 FR 3103, Jan. 22, 1982, as amended at 50 FR 48570, Nov. 26, 1985]

§ 416.204 Redeterminations of SSI eligibility.

(a) *Redeterminations defined.* A redetermination is a review of your eligibility to make sure that you are still

EXHIBIT 14.26
A Page from the *List of C.F.R. Sections Affected*

List of CFR Sections Affected

All changes in this volume of the Code of Federal Regulations which were made by documents published in the FEDERAL REGISTER since January 1, 1986, are enumerated in the following list. Entries indicate the nature of the changes effected. Page numbers refer to FEDERAL REGISTER pages. The user should consult the entries for chapters and parts as well as sections for revisions.

For the period before January 1, 1986, see the "List of CFR Sections Affected, 1949-1963, 1964-1972, and 1973-1985" published in seven separate volumes.

1986

20 CFR   51 FR Page

Chapter III
404 Technical correction... 5989, 15883
SSA representation project........21156
404.1—404.3 (Subpart A) Heading and authority citation revised..11718
404.1 Introductory text, (c), (j), (l), (p), and (q) revised; (r) through (v) added.....................11718
404.2 (a) introductory text, (a)(1), (b) introductory text, and (b)(1) revised; (a) (2) through (13) and (b)(3) removed; (a) (14) through (19) and (b) (4) and (5) redesignated as (a) (2) through (7) and (b) (3) and (4); new (b) (3) and (4) revised................................11718
404.3 (c) amended.........................11718
404.201—404.290 (Subpart C) Authority citation revised...4482, 12603
404.211 (d)(1) revised; (d)(4) added...4482
404.212 (b)(1) amended; authority citation removed....................4482
404.270 Amended...........................12603
404.271 (a) and (c) amended.........12603
404.272 Revised.............................12603
404.273 Revised.............................12603
404.274 Revised.............................12603
404.275 Revised; authority citation removed...........................12604
404.277 (b) nomenclature change..12604
404.278 Added................................12604

20 CFR—Continued   51 FR Page

Chapter III—Continued
404.301—404.395 (Subpart D) Authority citation revised...4482, 10615, 12603, 17617
404.310 (b) amended.....................10616
404.312 (b) amended.....................12604
404.313 Added................................12605
404.315 (c) amended.......... 10616, 16166
404.316 (c)(1)(iv) and (v) removed; (c)(1)(vi) redesignated as (c)(1)(iv); (c)(1)(iii) amended; new (c)(1)(iv) *Example* revised; interim.........................17617
404.320 (b)(1) amended................10616
404.331 Introductory text revised; (f) added; authority citation removed..........................11911
404.332 (a) and (b)(3) revised; (b)(8) added; authority citation removed...........................11911
404.333 Revised.............................11912
404.335 (e) revised; authority citation removed...........................4482
(a)(2)(ii) and (c) amended...........10616
404.336 (e) revised; authority citation removed...........................4482
404.337 (b)(1) removed; (b)(2), (3), (4), and (5) redesignated as (b)(1), (2), (3), and (4)............ 4482
(c)(1)(iv) and (v) removed; (c)(1)(vi) redesignated as (c)(1)(iv); (c)(1)(iii) amended; interim..............................17617
404.338 Amended..........................4482
404.352 (c)(1)(iv) and (v) removed; (c)(1)(vi) redesignated as (c)(1)(iv); (c)(1)(iii) amended; interim..................... 17617

925

States of America, published under the authority of the U.S. Senate and available through the Library of Congress. It includes the full text of the U.S. Constitution, corresponding United States Supreme Court annotations, and a discussion of each provision, including background information on its history and interpretation. Additional constitutional sources are found in the *U.S.C.A.* and the *U.S.C.S.*, both of which contain the entire text of the Constitution and its amendments as well as citations to cases discussing particular constitutional provisions. Annotated state codes provide a similar service for their state constitutions. Constitutional annotations are updated through supplementary pocket parts. State constitutions are usually included in the publications containing state statutes.

Updating the Law—Learning to Use Citators

Almost every day, new court decisions are made, new regulations are issued, and new statutes are enacted or existing statutes amended. Because the law is ever changing, a critical factor to consider when researching a topic or point of law is whether a given court opinion, statute, or regulation is still valid. A case decided six months ago may prove to be "bad law" today (if it has been reversed or significantly modified on appeal, for example). Similarly, statutes are frequently amended and new statutes enacted. This means that statutory law, too, is constantly changing. The careful researcher will avoid assuming that the case law or statutory law on a specific issue is the same today as it was last month or last year. This section will show you how to make sure that a law or court interpretation of the law is up to date and still "good law"—that is, currently valid law.

Case Law

Shepard's Citations, which is published by Shepard's is a research tool with which all paralegals should become familiar. *Shepard's* contains the most comprehensive system of case citators in the United States. A **citator** provides a list of legal references that have cited or interpreted the case or law. A *case citator* provides, in addition, a history of the particular case. *Shepard's* lists every case published in an official or unofficial reporter by its citation.

Shepard's citators are available for many different jurisdictions. *Shepard's United States Citations* covers the decisions of the United States Supreme Court as reported in *United States Reports, Supreme Court Reporter,* and *Lawyers' Edition of the Supreme Court Reports. Shepard's Federal Reporter Citations* provides coverage of the various federal courts of appeal and district courts. *Shepard's* citators also exist for the reports of every state, the District of Columbia, and Puerto Rico. Every region of the National Reporter System is covered by *Shepard's.* Exhibit 14.27 shows a *Shepard's* case citator.

One of the most valuable functions of *Shepard's* is that it provides the researcher with a means to verify the history of a case. For example, if a paralegal wants to know whether a certain court decision has been reversed by a higher court, *Shepard's* provides that information. Note, though, that it takes some time before the printed versions of *Shepard's* citators are updated. As will be discussed later in this section, to make absolutely sure that your research is truly up to date, you will want to use one of the online citators provided by computerized legal-research services.

The Organization of *Shepard's Citations*. At first glance, the unique organizational structure and language of *Shepard's* can appear confusing. The researcher begins by finding the appropriate citator, the one that corresponds with the researched case's citation. For example, if the citation for the main case indicates that it is from the *Atlantic Reporter,* the citator to locate is *Shepard's Atlantic Citations.* Then, to locate the case in this publication, the researcher finds the pages covering the relevant volume of the *Atlantic Reporter.* The volume numbers are printed in the upper left-hand corner of each page for easy reference. Once the correct pages are found, the researcher reviews the listings to locate the page on which the case begins. Parallel citations to other reporters are listed in parentheses with the case. Following this is a listing of citations identifying any higher courts that have reviewed the case. Then comes a listing of cases that have cited the main case.

Citator
A book or online service that provides the subsequent history and interpretation of a statute, regulation, or court decision and a list of the cases, statutes, and regulations that have interpreted, applied, or modified a statute or regulation.

EXHIBIT 14.27
Shepard's Citations

Reproduced by permission of Shepard's. Further reproduction of any kind is strictly prohibited.

TYPES OF INFORMATION PROVIDED BY *SHEPARD'S CITATIONS.* Paralegals can use *Shepard's* citators to accomplish several research objectives. First, *Shepard's* provides parallel citations for the cited case, allowing the paralegal to locate the case in other official or unofficial reporters.

Second, *Shepard's* lists other cases ("citing cases") that have cited the main case (the "cited case"). For example, suppose that in researching Hoffman's claim you have found a case on point. You can check *Shepard's Citations* to find out what other cases have dealt with one or more issues in your case (the cited case). Also, *Shepard's* listing of citing cases may include other cases on point that you will want to check. *Shepard's* has an elaborate abbreviation system to provide information on how the cited case has been used in the citing case. For example, if the ruling in the cited case has been followed by a citing case, the symbol *F* (for "followed") will appear after the name of the citing case. Exhibit 14.28 explains other symbols used in *Shepard's*.

Third, if you are researching a case on point, Shepard's provides further research tips by referring to helpful periodical articles and annotations in the *American Law Reports*.

Finally, as mentioned earlier, *Shepard's* provides a history of the cited case. If the decision in your case on point has been overturned on appeal, *Shepard's* will indicate this—or any other further history of the cited case.

Statutory and Constitutional Law

Shepard's citators for constitutions and statutes are similar to the case citators. The cited constitutional or statutory sources are listed by section number on each page and appear in boldfaced print for quick reference. *Shepard's* can serve as a valuable tool in constitutional and statutory research by identifying other sources that have discussed the researched provision and by providing information on the status of the provision.

On the federal level, the *Statutes Edition of Shepard's United States Citations* contains listings of the following publications:

- The U.S. Constitution.
- The *U.S.C., U.S.C.A.,* and *U.S.C.S.*
- The *United States Statutes at Large* provisions that have not yet been incorporated into the *U.S.C.*
- *Federal Reporter* citations.
- Annotations from the *American Law Reports* and the *Lawyers' Edition of the Supreme Court Reports*.

Shepard's also cites publications for all state constitutions and statutes, including a listing of federal statutory and constitutional provisions that have been cited in state sources.

Administrative Regulations

Shepard's Code of Federal Regulations Citations provides citations to decisions of federal and state courts relating to administrative law, articles in legal periodicals discussing sections of the *C.F.R.*, and other reference sources. The citation lists in *Shepard's C.F.R.* are organized by title and *C.F.R.* section. To acknowledge the frequent republication of the *C.F.R.*, each citation is followed by either the date of the publication of the *C.F.R.* edition cited or the date of the citing reference.

EXHIBIT 14.28
Abbreviations Used in *Shepard's*

Reproduced with permission of Shepard's. Further reproduction of any kind is strictly prohibited.

ABBREVIATIONS—ANALYSIS

History of Case

a	(affirmed)	Same case affirmed on rehearing.
cc	(connected case)	Different case from case cited but arising out of same subject matter or intimately connected therewith.
m	(modified)	Same case modified on rehearing.
r	(reversed)	Same case reversed on rehearing.
s	(same case)	Same case as case cited.
S	(superseded)	Substitution for former opinion.
v	(vacated)	Same case vacated.
US	cert den	*Certiorari* denied by U.S. Supreme Court.
US	cert dis	*Certiorari* dismissed by U.S. Supreme Court.
US	reh den	Rehearing denied by U.S. Supreme Court.
US	reh dis	Rehearing dismissed by U.S. Supreme Court.

Treatment of Case

c	(criticized)	Soundness of decision or reasoning in cited case criticized for reasons given.
d	(distinguished)	Case at bar different either in law or fact from case cited for reasons given.
e	(explained)	Statement of import of decision in cited case. Not merely a restatement of the facts.
f	(followed)	Cited as controlling.
h	(harmonized)	Apparent inconsistency explained and shown not to exist.
j	(dissenting opinion)	Citation in dissenting option.
L	(limited)	Refusal to extend decision of cited case beyond precise issues involved.
o	(overruled)	Ruling in cited case expressly overruled.
p	(parallel)	Citing case substantially alike or on all fours with cited case in its law or facts.
q	(questioned)	Soundness of decision or reasoning in cited case questioned.

ABBREVIATIONS—COURTS

Cir. Fed.—U.S. Court of appeals, Federal Circuit
Cir (number)—U.S. Court of Appeals Circuit (number)
CIT—United States Court of International Trade
CCPA—Court of Customs and Patent Appeals
Cl Ct—Claims Court (U.S.)
Ct Cl—Court of Claims Reports (U.S.)
Cu Ct—Customs Court Decisions
DC—District of Columbia
EC or ECA—Temporary Emergency Court of Appeals
ML—Judicial Panel on Multidistrict Litigation
RRR—Special Court Regional Rail Reorganization Act of 1973

Shepard's uses a system of abbreviations, including those listed below, to indicate the impact that a court decision has had on the cited regulation.

- C (constitutional).
- U (unconstitutional).

> ## ETHICAL CONCERN
> ### The Importance of Finding Current Law
>
> It is easy to forget that the law is continually changing and, in certain areas, changing very quickly. Even though you might have researched a certain legal issue as recently as three months ago—and for a case very similar to the one your supervising attorney is now litigating—it is a mistake to assume that the earlier research results are still valid. Between then and now, a leading case on the issue might have been overruled or a statute amended or a regulatory guideline changed. Even though you may have checked the relevant printed volume of *Shepard's Citations*, you need to realize that the most recent changes in the law will not be included in printed legal reference materials. To make absolutely certain that your research results are still valid, you should use an online citator to see if recent cases or modifications to statutes or regulations affect your research. Failure to update your research results may seriously harm your attorney's chances at success in arguing a client's case. In sum, if your attorney trusts you to do legal research, never rely on yesterday's law.

- **Up** (unconstitutional in part).
- **V** (void).
- **Va** (valid).

Shepard's also publishes a variety of topical citators covering the regulations of federal agencies in specific areas. Examples include *Occupational Safety and Health Citations*, *Federal Energy Law Citations*, and *Bankruptcy Citations*.

Legal Periodicals

Shepard's Law Review Citations includes citations to approximately two hundred legal periodicals and law reviews. Researchers can use it to locate references to law-review articles mentioned in court decisions and other legal services. The researcher finds the cited source by looking for the name of the legal periodical and then locating the volume and page number. Once the specific article has been found, the researcher reviews the list of citing sources that have referred to the article. *Shepard's* provides coverage of local law reviews and twenty national law reviews in each of its state citators. At the federal level, *Shepard's* publishes *Federal Law Citations in Selected Law Reviews*, which provides indexes of law-review citations to federal court cases and other statutory information.

Online Citators

Several computerized legal-research services provide online citators. Online citators are extremely useful to legal researchers because they are more up to date than the printed citators just discussed. You can access Westlaw® or Lexis® online to update the law within seconds. You can also learn the previous and subsequent history of a particular case, find out what other cases have cited it, and so on. You will read about online citators in further detail in Chapter 15.

TODAY'S PROFESSIONAL PARALEGAL

Mapping Out a Research Strategy

Bill Cather is a paralegal in a criminal defense firm located in a major metropolitan area. Bill has been assigned a research project on a case involving one of the firm's clients, who was arrested for drug dealing. The police had seen the client making phone calls from a public telephone booth and suspected that he was engaged in drug trafficking. The police placed an electronic device into the phone booth—without a warrant—and learned that what they suspected was true. Bill is now going to map out his research strategy before he undertakes the project.

STEP ONE: IDENTIFYING THE ISSUE

Bill's first step is to analyze the facts and identify the issue involved. He knows that the police may search certain areas without a warrant. The courts determine which areas are entitled to the protection of a warrant by considering whether a person has a reasonable expectation of privacy in the area. Bill wonders whether a person has a reasonable expectation of privacy in a public phone booth. Do people customarily expect others to hear what they are saying on the phone when they are in a phone booth with the door closed? Bill will have to research the issue. If a person using a phone booth is entitled to a reasonable expectation of privacy, then probably the police would have to obtain a search warrant before using an electronic device to listen to—and record—any telephone conversation taking place in a public phone booth.

STEP TWO: IDENTIFYING SECONDARY SOURCES

Because he is not familiar with the topic that he is going to research, Bill will begin by doing some background research. He can choose from a variety of secondary sources, such as legal encyclopedias and treatises. He prefers legal encyclopedias because they are easy to read and understand. He particularly prefers the *Corpus Juris Secundum (C.J.S.)* because it provides numerous citations to cases. He writes *"C.J.S."* on his list as the first source to consult.

STEP THREE: IDENTIFYING PRIMARY SOURCES

Next he will want to consult the various primary sources of law. He will want to look at the Fourth Amendment to the U.S. Constitution to find the exact wording of the amendment in regard to freedom from unreasonable searches and seizures and the warrant requirement. He can find the Constitution in the *U.S.C.A.* He writes "Constitution" on his list as a primary source to consult. He will also want to consult state and federal statutory codes to find out whether the police's action violated a wiretapping statute, if one exists, so he writes "federal and state statutory codes" on his list. To find cases on point—in addition to those cited in the *C.J.S.*—relating to the topic, Bill can consult case digests.

STEP FOUR: UPDATING AND VERIFYING RESEARCH RESULTS

After Bill finds and reads through relevant cases, he will have to verify in *Shepard's* that they are still good law. *Shepard's* will also provide an additional source of case law because it includes every subsequent case that cited the case being "Shepardized." He writes *"Shepard's"* on his list.

Bill will also want to either run a computer search or return to the secondary sources, such as encyclopedias, to make certain that he has not overlooked any case law. As a final measure, he will want to use an online citator to verify that his research results are as up to date as possible. Bill writes *"C.J.S.* and online citators" as the final item on his list. Once Bill is comfortable with the results of his research, he will return to his office and prepare a memorandum of law to inform his supervisor of his findings.

Key Terms and Concepts

annotation 495
business invitee 490
case on "all fours" 490
case on point 490
citation 514
citator 529
code 520
digest 495
headnote 495
hornbook 503
key number 495
mandatory authority 491
parallel citation 514
persuasive authority 492
pocket part 493
primary source 488
public law number 520
reporter 495
secondary source 488
session law 520
slip law 519
slip opinion 516
syllabus 518
table of cases 501
treatise 503

Chapter Summary

1. Primary sources of law consist of all documents that establish the law, including court decisions, statutes, regulations, constitutions, and presidential orders. Secondary sources of law are sources written about the law, such as legal encyclopedias, digests, treatises, and periodicals.

2. The first step in the legal-research process is to identify the legal question, or issue, to be researched (often, more than one issue will be involved). The next step is to determine the goal of the research project. In researching case law, the researcher's goal is to find cases that are on point (ideally, cases on "all fours") and that are mandatory authorities. Mandatory authorities are all legal authorities (statutes, regulations, constitutions, or cases) that courts must follow in making their decisions. In contrast, courts are not bound to follow persuasive authorities (such as cases decided in other jurisdictions).

3. Legal encyclopedias and case digests are helpful secondary sources of case law for researchers who want to find background information on the issue being researched. These sources present legal topics alphabetically and contain citations to cases and statutes relating to the topic. Two popular legal encyclopedias are *American Jurisprudence,* Second Edition, and *Corpus Juris Secundum.* Both encyclopedias contain a wealth of information on the topics presented. A third encyclopedia, *Words and Phrases,* covers legal terms and phrases and cites cases in which the terms or phrases appear. West's case digests are major secondary sources of law. These digests, which use the West system of topic classification and key numbers, provide cross-references to topics contained in other West publications.

4. Other important secondary resources of case law include the *American Law Reports,* which contain leading cases, each of which is followed by an annotation that discusses the key issues in the case and that refers the researcher to other sources on the issues; law treatises, which are scholarly publications discussing specific legal topics or areas; the *Restatements of the Law,* which are highly respected scholarly compilations of the common law; and legal periodicals, such as law reviews.

5. Primary sources of case law are the cases themselves. Most state trial court decisions are not published in printed volumes. State appellate court opinions, including those of state supreme courts, are normally published in state reporters, although many states have eliminated their own reporters in favor of West's National Reporter System. Federal trial court opinions are published unofficially in West's *Federal Supplement,* and opinions from the federal circuit courts of appeals are published unofficially in West's *Federal Reporter.* United States Supreme Court opinions are published officially in the *United States Reports,* published by the federal government, and unofficially in West's *Supreme Court Reporter* and the *Lawyers' Edition of the Supreme Court Reports.*

6. Federal statutes are published officially in the *United States Code (U.S.C.).* The *U.S.C.* organizes statutes into fifty subjects, or titles, and further subdivides each title into chapters (sections) and subchapters. The researcher can find a statute in the

U.S.C. by searching through the topical outlines, by looking in the index, or by looking under the act's popular name in the volume entitled *Popular Name Table*. The *United States Code Annotated* and the *United States Code Service* are unofficial publications of federal statutes. Both of these sources are useful to researchers because they provide annotations and citations to other resources.

7. In researching statutory law, it is important to make sure that a given statute is really relevant to the issue being researched. In determining the intent of the statute, the researcher may want to investigate its legislative history. Important sources for researching legislative history include transcripts of committee reports and hearings, transcripts of congressional proceedings, and the wording of statutes as first published in the *United States Statutes at Large*. Helpful resources in this area include the *Congressional Record*, the *United States Code Congressional and Administrative News*, and the *Congressional Information Service*.

8. Regulations issued by federal administrative agencies are primary sources of law. Agency regulations are published in the *Code of Federal Regulations (C.F.R.)*. The *C.F.R.* follows a format similar to that of the *United States Code (U.S.C.)*, and the subject classifications (titles) of the *C.F.R.* correspond to the titles in the *U.S.C.* To locate recently published regulations, the researcher should refer to the *Federal Register's* cumulative *List of C.F.R. Sections Affected*, which reflects changes made during the current month. Constitutions are also primary sources of law. The U.S. Constitution can be found in a number of publications. Annotated versions of state constitutions are also available.

9. Crucial in legal research is making sure that the research results are still valid. The various volumes of *Shepard's Citations* allow the researcher to verify whether a case has been overruled or reversed, a statute repealed or amended, an agency regulation voided or superseded, and the like.

10. Online citators, including those provided by Lexis® and Westlaw®, enable the researcher to access recent cases, statutes, or regulations (or amendments or modifications to existing statutes or regulations) and thus ensure that research results are as up to date as possible. (See Chapter 15.)

Questions for Review

1. What are the differences between primary and secondary sources of law? How are each of these types of sources used in legal research?

2. What is a case on point? What is a case on "all fours"? Why is finding such a case important when researching case law?

3. What is the difference between a mandatory authority and a persuasive authority? Which type of authority should you strive to find when conducting legal research?

4. How are legal encyclopedias and other secondary sources used to find case law relevant to a research topic?

5. What is a case digest? How do case digests help legal researchers find case law? What is the West key-number system, and how does it simplify the legal-research process?

6. Describe the forms in which court decisions are published, from their initial publication to their final published form.

7. Identify the various parts of a case citation. How do they help you locate a case?

8. Describe the forms in which statutes are published, from their original issuance to their final published form. Do the same for regulations. What are the major sources for statutes and regulations?

9. What is meant by the term *legislative history*? What resources are available for researching the legislative history of a statute?

10. Why is it important to find the most current law? How can you verify that your research results are up to date?

Ethical Questions

1. Kristine Connolly, a paralegal in a litigation firm, has finished reading a brief that the opposing side submitted to the court in support of a motion for summary judgment. In the brief, she notices a citation to

a state supreme court case of which she is unaware. She is experienced in the field and keeps current with new cases as they are decided. She wants to look at the case because it gives the other side a winning edge. She checks in the advance sheets, digests, and state encyclopedias, as well as on Westlaw®. She finally calls the state supreme court clerk's office and asks about the case. The office has no record of such a case. She asks the legal assistant for the opposing counsel to give her a copy of the case. When she does not receive it, she decides that the case is probably fictional. What should Kristine do?

2. Barbara Coltiers is a legal assistant in a very busy litigation practice. She gets a call from a nervous attorney in her firm thirty minutes before the attorney is to appear in court. He wants her to do some research before he goes to court. He has just heard about a case that might help him win and gives her the citation. Because he is in a hurry, he gives her the wrong volume number. She has a hard time finding the case, but after about fifteen minutes of searching she locates the citation. She quickly copies the case and runs to his office with it so that he can hurry across the street to the court for his appearance. She is in such a hurry that she forgets to check the subsequent history of the case.

It turns out that the case had been overruled by the state supreme court and was therefore no longer controlling in the jurisdiction. The attorney is chastised by the judge for citing it. In fact, the judge is so annoyed with the attorney for making an argument that was not based on existing law that he denies the attorney's motion and makes the attorney pay the other side's court costs. When the client finds out why the motion was denied, she is irate. Does the client have any remedy against the attorney? Against Barbara?

3. John Hernandez is studying at a local college to be a legal assistant. The college has Westlaw® for its students to use. The software license specifically prohibits the faculty or students of the college from using the program for personal work. John knows that Kathy has a part-time job with a law firm, and he becomes aware that Kathy is using Westlaw® regularly to do research for her supervising attorney in that firm. What should John do?

Practice Questions and Assignments

1. Using the material presented in the chapter, identify the case name, volume number, reporter abbreviation, page number, and year of decision for each of the following case citations and their parallel cites:

    a. *Smith v. James,* 400 Mich.19, 630 N.W. 2d 98 (1999).

    b. *Johnson v. Fassler Wrecking, Inc.,* 10 Cal.4th 539, 27 Cal.Rptr.2d 201 (1999).

    c. *Barnes v. Barnes,* 95 N.Y.2d 101, 637 N.E. 2d 23, 654 N.Y.S. 13 (1999).

    d. *Miranda v. Arizona,* 384 U.S. 436, 86 S.Ct. 1602, 16 L.Ed.2d 694 (1966).

2. Using the material presented in the chapter, identify the title number, code abbreviation, and section number for the following statutory citations:

    a. 42 U.S.C. Section 1161(a).

    b. M.C.L. Section 600.1111(b).

3. Using the material presented in the chapter, indicate whether the following sources are primary or secondary sources:

    a. Digest.

    b. Case reporters.

    c. Legal encyclopedias.

    d. Statutes.

    e. The *Code of Federal Regulations.*

4. Sleeping Beauty is awakened by a kiss from Prince Charming. She can think of nothing more repulsive than to be kissed by him. Sleeping Beauty suffers from nightmares and depression as a result of this incident and contacts your law firm regarding filing a lawsuit against the prince for the damages, which include medical expenses, that she has suffered as a result of the kiss. The paralegal is assigned the task of researching Sleeping Beauty's case to determine whether or not she can sue. What are the issue(s) to be researched? What would the paralegal's research goals be?

5. Mr. John D. Consumer bought a new car eight months ago. The car frequently stalls. The problem began the first week after he purchased the vehicle. It stalled late at night on an expressway while he was returning home from a business trip. It has stalled at least monthly since then, often in potentially dangerous areas. Not only has he taken the car to the dealer, who has repeatedly attempted to repair the problem without success, but he has also notified the manu-

facturer in writing of the problem. Most states have a lemon law that requires manufacturers to replace vehicles that cannot be repaired, even if the warranty has expired. Does your state have a lemon law? If so, would the lemon law help Mr. Consumer?

Research this question and try to find the answer to Mr. Consumer's problem. Begin by analyzing the facts. Then make a list of relevant legal terms to look up in an index.

Select a legal encyclopedia—either *American Jurisprudence* or *Corpus Juris Secundum*—to use in your research. Write down the name of the encyclopedia. Consult the general index volumes.

a. Write down the index topics under which you found relevant information. (If you have difficulty locating relevant information, try checking the topic indexes in the individual volumes.)

b. Write down the citations to encyclopedia sections containing relevant information.

c. Look up these citations in the appropriate volumes of the encyclopedia to find an answer to Mr. Consumer's problem. Be sure to check the pocket part for more current citations. According to the encyclopedia, what is the answer to John D. Consumer's problem?

6. After analyzing the facts of Mr. Consumer's problem and making a list of legally and factually relevant terms, as described in Practice Question 5, do the following:

a. Locate the index to the annotated version of your state statutes. Using your list of terms, look in the index for citations to relevant statute sections. Write down the citations.

b. If you did Practice Question 5 above, compare how you found the citations in the index to your state statutes with how you found them in the legal encyclopedia. Under what topics did you look in each situation?

c. Now that you have found relevant citations, go to the volume of the statute containing the cited sections and read those sections. (Be sure to check the pocket part of the volume.) What answer does the statute in your state give to Mr. Consumer's problem? If you answered Practice Question 5 above, is the answer given in the encyclopedia? If not, how do the answers differ?

7. Using the annotated version of your state statutes, look for relevant case law on Mr. Consumer's problem. If no annotated version of your state statute exists or if no cases appear in the annotated version—or if you want to learn to use another source—locate a state digest. Find the relevant section(s) and locate case law that interprets the statute and that is as similar to Mr. Consumer's problem as possible.

a. Write down the citations to no more than three relevant cases. Now look up those cases in the case reporters.

b. Read through the summary and headnotes of each case. Do the cases still appear to be relevant? If not, go back to the annotated statute or digest and look for more relevant cases.

c. What did you find? Did the courts' application of the statute change in any way your answer to the problem facing Mr. Consumer?

8. Using the material presented in Exhibit 14.28, *Abbreviations Used in Shepard's,* answer the following questions:

a. Under the section entitled "History of Case," what does the abbreviation, "a" stand for? The abbreviation "r"? Why are these abbreviations significant?

b. Under the section entitled "Treatment of Case," what does the abbreviation "d" stand for? The abbreviation "o"? Why are these significant?

Questions for Critical Analysis

1. Sources of law are divided into two broad categories, primary and secondary sources. What is the difference between these two types? Why are only primary sources allowed to be cited in most briefs and other documents filed with the courts?

2. What is the difference between a mandatory and a persuasive authority? Why is this distinction important for the courts? Which source is preferable to find when doing legal research? Why?

3. What is the difference between a case on point and a case on "all fours"? Which is it preferable to locate? How do these cases fit into the research goals? How likely is it that you might find a case on point or on "all fours"?

4. Legal encyclopedias, legal digests, and *American Law Reports* are secondary sources. For what is each source used? How are these sources different? How are they similar? Which source is preferable to use and why?

5. What is an annotation? How is it used in a digest? In the *American Law Reports*?

6. Explain the West key-number system. What is its purpose? Is its use limited to digests? How can the key-number system be of assistance to a researcher?

7. What is a parallel citation? Why are parallel citations used?

8. The written opinions of judges sitting on state and federal appellate courts are usually published in reporters. Why is it that trial court decisions are not routinely published in reporters?

9. What is West's National Reporter System? What geographical units are included in it? Is it widely used? Why or why not? How might the West's key-number system tie into it?

10. *The Bluebook* provides rules for citation. Why are these rules needed? What would happen without these rules? Can you think of a better system?

11. What is the difference between case law and statutory law? Why is the difference significant? In what forms are statutes published? What are the parallel codes for the statutes of the U.S. government?

12. How is statutory law interpreted? What role do case law and legislative history play in its interpretation? How reliable are the sources?

13. What is the purpose of *Shepard's Citations*? What might result if *Shepard's* citators were not used? Are there other methods of accomplishing the same objective?

Projects

1. Using a state bar directory or other type of legal directory, find out which law libraries in your area are open to the public. Make arrangements to visit a law library. If tours of the library are offered, try to be present for a tour.

2. Make arrangements through your professor, a local bar association, or your personal contacts to visit the law library of a law firm or the legal department of a corporation or government office. If you also participated in Project 1 above, compare the materials available in the libraries of firms or government agencies with those available in law libraries. Why is it necessary for legal professionals to use law libraries other than those located in their offices?

3. Find out if your state has an official reporter for its appellate courts. If it does, find out where the reporter is printed and how often the advance sheets are compiled into a hardbound volume and distributed.

4. Obtain a copy of *The Bluebook: A Uniform System of Citation* and look up the citation formats for your state court reporters and statutes.

5. Using information from Chapter 6, make a diagram of the federal court system. List the reporters for each court in the system, using the information given in this chapter.

Using Internet Resources

1. Go to the home page of the American Law Institute (ALI) at www.ali.org. Browse through this site and its offerings, and then answer the following questions:
   a. Select "ALI Press Releases" and look over the list of new press releases. Have any new *Restatements* been published by the ALI? If so, on what topics?
   b. Now access the ALI's "Catalogue of Publications." How many *Restatements of the Law* have been published by the ALI? Make a list of the topics covered in the *Restatements*.

2. The *United States Code,* which contains the statutes passed by Congress, can be accessed through Cornell Law School's Legal Information Institute at www.law.cornell.edu/uscode. Access this Web site and answer the following questions:
   a. How many ways are there to access the *United States Code* within the Web site? What are they?
   b. Scroll down to the title listing. How many titles are there? For what is "title" a synonym? Click on Title 42. What does it cover? How many chapters

are in Title 42? In the "Search Title 42" box, enter "Superfund Act." What results do you obtain?

c. Go back to the *United States Code* home page. Using the section entitled "Find U.S. Code Materials by Title and Section," enter "42" in the title box and "9601" in the section box; then click on "Go to title and section." Describe what you find. In what chapter is this act located? In addition to the statutory section, what else is available?

CHAPTER 15

Computer-Assisted Legal Research

Chapter Outline
▣ INTRODUCTION ▣ CD-ROMs AND LEGAL RESEARCH
▣ WESTLAW® AND LEXIS® ▣ GOING ONLINE—INTERNET BASICS ▣ CONDUCTING ONLINE RESEARCH ▣ LOCATING PEOPLE AND INVESTIGATING COMPANIES ▣ SOME OF THE BEST LEGAL-RESOURCE SITES ON THE INTERNET

After completing this chapter, you will know:

- How CD-ROMs and legal-research services provided by Westlaw® and Lexis® help legal professionals in computer-assisted legal research (CALR).
- What the Internet is, and how it can be accessed and navigated.
- Some strategies for planning and conducting research on the Internet.
- How you can find people and investigate companies using Internet search tools and databases.
- How to find some of the best legal resources available on the Internet.

INTRODUCTION

Computers and online databases have greatly simplified the tasks of paralegals in all areas of legal work. This is particularly true in the area of legal research. One of the great benefits of computer technology for legal practitioners is **computer-assisted legal research (CALR)**. As you learned in Chapter 14, thorough and up-to-date legal research requires access to voluminous source materials, including state and federal court decisions and statutory law. Today, attorneys and paralegals can access many of these materials online—either through the use of proprietary software and a modem connection or via the Internet. Additionally, a number of primary and secondary legal sources are available on CD-ROMs.

An obvious advantage of CALR is that you can locate and print out court cases, statutory provisions, and other legal documents within a matter of minutes without leaving your work station. Another key advantage of CALR is that new case decisions and changes in statutory law are entered almost immediately into certain online legal databases, including those of Westlaw® and Lexis®. This means that you can find out easily and quickly whether a case decided three months ago is still "good law" today. The case may have been overturned by a higher court since then, and the only way you would know this would be through CALR (because the case would not yet be included in printed sources).

In this chapter, after a discussion of CD-ROMs and legal research, we look at the legal-research services available through Westlaw® and Lexis®. We then look at the Internet—what it is and how it can be used to conduct online research efficiently. You will learn about service providers, browsers, and search engines. You will discover how to evaluate whether the Internet is the best tool for particular research projects. You will also read about some of the best resources currently available on the Internet.

By the time you read this chapter, some of what we say will have changed, particularly with respect to Internet resources. Some of these resources may have improved, others may have been removed, and still others may have been added. The general approach to conducting research online will not have altered, however. If you master the basic principles of online research discussed in this chapter, you will be able to conduct research on the Internet no matter how much it changes.

Computer-Assisted Legal Research (CALR)
Any legal research conducted with the assistance of computers. CALR includes the use of CD-ROMs, fee-based legal-services providers such as Westlaw® and Lexis®, and the Internet.

CD-ROMs AND LEGAL RESEARCH

Increasingly, today's law firms are using research materials available in CD-ROM ("compact disk, read-only memory") format. CD-ROM technology allows the legal researcher to access data on a small, compact laser disk, much like the compact disks that are sold in music stores.

CD-ROMs are accessed through a CD-ROM reader, which reads and displays the contents of a CD-ROM when it is inserted into the reader. Depending on the computer system, the reader may be contained within the computer or attached to the computer with a cable. The software program accompanying a CD-ROM allows the computer operating system to communicate with the CD-ROM. A paralegal using CD-ROMs for legal research would find the CD-ROM containing the relevant reference materials—a legal encyclopedia, for example—and use the CD-ROM's index or search tool to quickly locate a given topic or subtopic.

Advantages of Using CD-ROMs

Most law firms have law libraries containing legal encyclopedias, case digests, statutory compilations, and other research materials frequently used by the firms'

EXHIBIT 15.1
West CD-ROM Libraries

Reproduced with permission of West Group.

attorneys and paralegals. Law libraries and the physical space required to house them are expensive, particularly for small law firms. An obvious advantage of using legal reference materials on CD-ROMs is that they are far less costly to purchase and require much less space than their printed counterparts.

A CD-ROM holds the equivalent of over 600 megabytes of data. This means that one CD-ROM can store approximately 300,000 pages, or over one hundred volumes of legal reference materials. For example, the entire 215-volume *United States Code Annotated* (discussed in Chapter 14) is contained on only two CD-ROMs. Many federal government publications, legal encyclopedias, West reporters, and other research sources are also available in CD-ROM format. Exhibit 15.1 shows a photograph of CD-ROM legal libraries.

CD-ROMs can also be easily transported. They can be used (on laptop or notebook computers) while traveling or even in the courtroom. A further advantage of using CD-ROMs is that searches of materials contained on them can be conducted more easily and quickly than when using printed reference sources. For example, if you are researching a state statute, you can search through the statute for certain words or section numbers using the search command, which saves valuable research time. West's CD-ROM libraries offer the advantage of the key-number system. As discussed in Chapter 14, this system simplifies legal research by allowing you to search key numbers to find relevant case law or other legal sources. You can also copy segments of the statute directly to your computer, which reduces the amount of time you spend in document preparation as well as lessening the risk of error.

Disadvantages of Using CD-ROMs

The major disadvantage of using CD-ROMs in legal research is that, like their printed equivalents, they can become outdated. Suppose that you want to locate recent court cases interpreting a particular provision of the *United States Code*. If your CD-ROM containing the *United States Code Annotated* was purchased five years ago, clearly you will be unable to find the latest annotations on that CD-ROM. In other words, just as when conducting research using printed legal reference materials, you need to keep in mind the date of the materials included on the CD-ROM.

Note that even the most recently issued CD-ROM version of a legal encyclopedia or other reference work may be somewhat outdated, just as a printed text is, because of the time it takes to create and distribute the CD-ROM. The best way to ensure that your research is really up to date is to check an online legal database.

WESTLAW® AND LEXIS®

CALR has made it possible to access legal databases containing many of the most important legal resources. By accessing databases provided through commercial legal-research services, legal professionals can obtain case law or statutory law relating to a particular issue within seconds. Although not all printed legal sources are contained on these databases, many of them are. Two premier legal-research services often used by attorneys and paralegals are Westlaw® and Lexis®. To use these legal-research services, a law firm or other user signs a contract with the provider of the services. Charges for the service are typically based on either online time (Westlaw®) or the number of database searches performed (Lexis®).

The Westlaw® and Lexis® databases contain extensive legal and business information. Westlaw®, for example, is organized into more than ten thousand databases covering all areas of the law. It is possible to access such primary sources as federal and state statutes, court cases, and administrative regulations. Some of the materials are also accessible through specialized databases, such as bankruptcy, insurance, and taxation. Secondary sources include legal texts and periodicals, public records, and other sources of business and financial information.

Accessing Westlaw® or Lexis®

To access Westlaw® or Lexis®, a subscriber can use the service's proprietary software, which allows the subscriber's computer to access the database through a modem connection over a telephone line. Traditionally, this was the only way that legal professionals could access these services. Today, both Westlaw® and Lexis® can be accessed online via the Internet as well—at www.westlaw.com and www.lexis.com, respectively. Special software is not needed to access either of these services via the Internet.

An advantage of accessing these databases on the Web is that research can be done easily with a standard browser (browsers are discussed later in this chapter) and without the extensive training needed to use the proprietary software. A disadvantage is that users who do not have the software also do not have the accompanying manuals that instruct them on how to use the services. "Help" links at both Web sites, however, give users instructions on how to perform various tasks. Another disadvantage for Lexis® users is that only a portion of the Lexis® databases are included on the Web site. In contrast, Westlaw® offers the full panoply of its services on the Web.

When you access Westlaw® or Lexis® (using proprietary software or via the Internet), you will be asked to sign onto the service with your password. After you sign on, a welcome page is displayed. (The welcome page of Westlaw® is shown in Exhibit 15.2.) From this page, you can begin your research. You can retrieve documents by citation, check citations, or search databases for cases, statutes, or other documents on a given topic or issue.

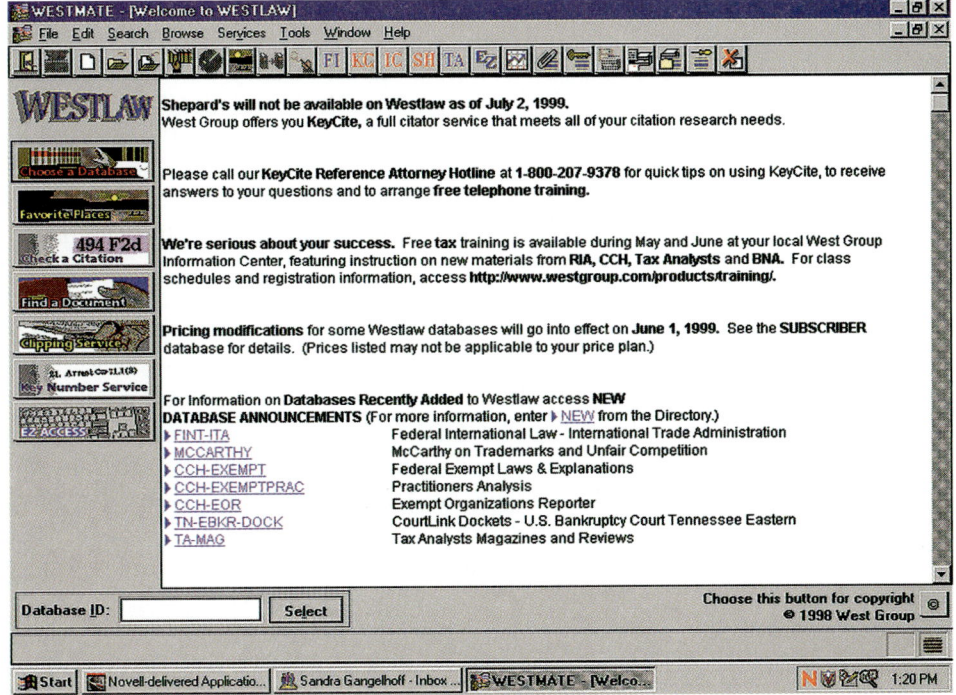

EXHIBIT 15.2

The Opening ("Welcome") Page of Westlaw®

Reproduced with permission of West Group.

Retrieving a Document by Citation

If you have the citation for a document, such as a court case or statute, you can enter the citation and call up the document. For example, on Westlaw® you would click on the "Find a Document" box on the left side of the screen. This will open a query box into which you key the citation for a case, statute, regulation, or other document. Within seconds, the cited document will appear on the screen.

Checking a Citation

Westlaw® and Lexis® both provide online citators. Recall from Chapter 14 that a citator, such as one of *Shepard's* citators, shows the history of a case and provides a list of legal references that have cited or interpreted a particular case. Online citators are extremely useful to legal researchers because they are more up to date than printed citators. For example, suppose that you want to find out whether the holding in a particular case decided by a California appellate court is still "good law." If you are using Lexis®, you can use the **Auto-Cite** citator to find out if the decision was appealed to the California Supreme Court (or to the United States Supreme Court) and, if so, whether the holding was affirmed, overturned, or modified on appeal. You can also "Shepardize" the case to find out how courts in other jurisdictions have dealt with the same issue.

If you are using Westlaw®, you can use the **KeyCite** citator service. An important editorial enhancement to documents accessible through Westlaw® are the KeyCite case status flags, which indicate when there is case history that should be investigated. Depending on the color of the flag, you are warned that a case is not good law for at least one of its points, that the case has some negative history but its holding has not been reversed, or that the case has been overruled. KeyCite provides other features to make your research more efficient. When checking the citation of your case in the KeyCite database, stars added to the citation of a citing case show the extent to which your case is discussed in the citing case. For example, four stars indicate that the citing case contains an extended discussion of your case, usually more than a printed page of text. One star indicates the reference is brief, usually no more than as part of a list of case citations.

If your search results include a statute or an agency rule, when using Westlaw® you can check for any recent changes with the "Update" service. The service displays any documents on Westlaw® that amend or repeal the statute or rule you are viewing. The "General Materials" service retrieves references, notes, or annotations that apply to the title, chapter, or subchapter of a statute or rule you are viewing. This service also displays tables that track statute numbers through amendments and other changes.

These and other tools allow you to access updated law within seconds. As stressed in Chapter 14, a crucial part of legal research is making sure your findings are accurate and up to date. If your supervising attorney is preparing for trial, for example, the attorney will want to base his or her legal argument on current authorities. A precedential case that may have been good law yesterday may not remain so today.

> **Making sure that your research results reflect current law is a crucial step in legal research.**

Selecting a Database

Much of the legal research that paralegals perform involves searching legal databases for cases or statutes relating to certain topics or legal issues. To do this, you

---

Auto-Cite
An aid to legal research developed by the editors of Lexis®. On Lexis®, Auto-Cite can be used to find the history of a case, to verify whether the case is still good law, and to perform other functions.

KeyCite
An aid to legal research developed by the editors of Westlaw®. On Westlaw®, KeyCite can trace case history, retrieve secondary sources, categorize legal citations by legal issue, and perform other functions.

DEVELOPING PARALEGAL SKILLS

Cite Checking on Westlaw®

Katie, a paralegal, needs to quickly check a citation for a case from the court of appeals to see if it is still good law. Her supervising attorney wants to use the case in a brief that must be filed within a few hours. Katie accesses Westlaw®. She enters her password and client-identifying information. Once she has gained access, she clicks on the "Check This Citation" box and enters the case cite. Then she clicks on KeyCite. The search turns up a red flag, which means that the case has been reversed or overruled and is no longer good law. Katie clicks on the red flag, which takes her to the decision in which the case was reversed or overruled. It turns out that the case was reversed on different grounds. So the rule of law for which her supervising attorney wants to cite the case is still good law. Katie and her supervisor can use the case in their brief after all.

TIPS FOR USING KEYCITE

- A red flag means that a case has been reversed or overruled and must be reviewed.
- A yellow flag means that the case has been questioned and should be checked.
- Never cite a case without verifying that it is still good law.
- Always read a citing case to find why your case has a red or yellow flag and to determine what issue in your case has been questioned, reversed, or overruled.

---

first select a database that you want to search. If you are using Westlaw®, for example, you would click on the box labeled "Choose a Database," which would open a page containing the main directory. From that page, you could select "Federal Materials," "State Materials," or another topic and then click on "Expand" in the lower right-hand corner of the screen. Eventually, you will find the particular database you want.

For example, suppose that your supervising attorney has asked you to research case law on the liability of tobacco products manufacturers for cancer caused by the use of those products. To do a thorough investigation, you will need to search the databases containing decisions from all state courts as well as from all federal courts. To find these databases on Westlaw®, you would access the main directory, select "State Materials," and click on "expand." Then you would select "Case Law" to expand this database. Eventually, you will find the database containing decisions from all state courts ("allstates"). For federal court decisions, you would select "Federal Materials" from the main directory and continue the "expand" function until you reach the database containing decisions from all federal courts ("allfeds").

After you become familiar with the database identifiers on whatever service you are using, you can access that database more directly. For example, on the opening page of Westlaw® you can enter "allfeds" or "allstates" into the database box at the bottom of the screen.

Searching a Database

Once you have chosen a specific database, such as "allfeds," a search box will open on the screen into which you can enter your *search query*. Traditionally, searches of Westlaw® and Lexis® databases had to use the "terms and connectors" (Boolean) method of searching. Today, both services also allow users to draft search queries using natural language (or "plain English"). Before beginning your search, you should indicate in the search box which method you will use.

> # ETHICAL CONCERN
> ## Cutting the Cost of Legal Research
>
> As a paralegal, you have an ethical duty to the client to minimize costs, including the cost of computerized research—which, after all, is paid for by the client. One way you can reduce research costs is to plan your search queries carefully before accessing a service such as Lexis® or Westlaw.® This way, you do not have to spend online time making such decisions.

THE TERMS AND CONNECTORS METHOD. In a search employing terms and connectors, you use numerical and grammatical connectors to specify the relationship between the terms. For example, to find cases on the liability of tobacco products manufacturers for cancer caused by the use of those products, you could type the following terms and connectors in the query box:

> liability /p cancer /s tobacco

This would retrieve all cases in which the term *liability* is in the same paragraph ("/p") as the term *cancer*, with the term *cancer* in the same sentence ("/s") as the term *tobacco*. To restrict the scope of your search, you can add a field restriction. For example, you might want to retrieve only court opinions rendered after 1995. If you are using Westlaw®, you could add the following to your query to restrict the search results to cases decided after 1995:

> & added date (after 1/1/1996)

Numerous other grammatical and numerical connectors can be used to efficiently search a database. These are listed in the instruction manuals provided to Lexis® and Westlaw® subscribers. Some of the most commonly used terms and connectors are indicated online when you are connected to one of these services. For example, on Westlaw® you will find a description of some options in the search box into which you enter your query.

Generally, when drafting queries, you want to make sure your query is not too broad (as it would be if you entered just the term *liability*). Your search will be futile because so many thousands of documents contain that term. At the same time, you do not want your search to be so narrow that no cases will be retrieved.

THE NATURAL LANGUAGE METHOD. The natural language method (called "Freestyle" on Lexis® and WIN on Westlaw®—WIN is an acronym for "Westlaw® is Natural") allows you to type a description of an issue in plain English to retrieve the most relevant documents. In searching for cases relating to the topic in the previous example, your query might read as follows:

> Is a tobacco manufacturer liable for cancer caused by the use of its products?

This query would retrieve the documents most closely matching your description. Exhibit 15.3 illustrates the results of running a search with these words on Westlaw®.

To include synonyms that might be necessary to produce more comprehensive results, there is a "Thesaurus" feature on Westlaw® that can suggest terms for your search. After entering your "natural language" query, click "Thesaurus." Select a term from the list for which you want suggestions. Then click "View

EXHIBIT 15.3
Search Results on Westlaw®

Reproduced with permission of West Group.

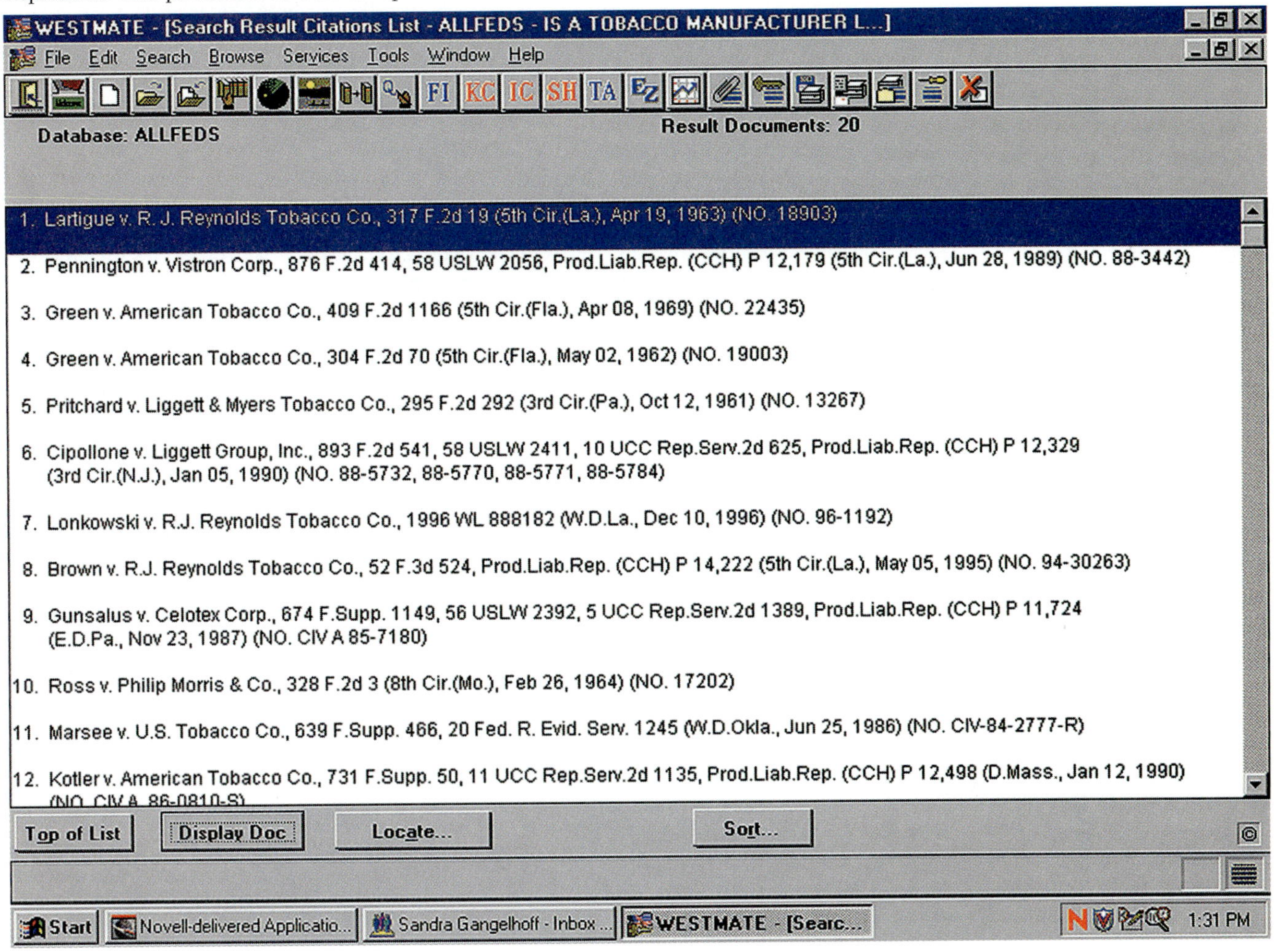

Related Terms." If you want to add one of the terms to your description, select the term and click "Add Term to Description."

Browser Enhancements

Suppose that your search resulted in a list of twenty cases relevant to your topic. At this point, there are internal browsing tools that can help you pinpoint your search more precisely. For example, Westlaw® browsing tools include "Term" browsing, "Best Section" browsing, and "Locate." Browsing by "Term" or "Best Section" allows you to find exact references to your search term.

The "Locate" tool allows you to scan the documents in your search result for terms that were not included in your query. For example, assume that your original request was, in natural language, "Is a tobacco manufacturer liable for cancer caused by the use of its products?" If you want to know whether "death" is discussed in any of your search-result documents, you can use the "Locate" tool (select "Locate" from the pull-down menu) and type "death" in the "Locate

Query" box; then click "Locate." Click the "Term" box at the bottom of the screen to continue the "Locate" function. To cancel "Locate," select "Cancel Locate" from the pull-down menu.

When browsing through your search results, remember that the time you spend using the service is costly. If you have found a case or cases that appear to be on point, you can print them out (or download them to your computer) for further study and analysis.

GOING ONLINE—INTERNET BASICS

Until the advent of the Internet, CALR generally meant research using CD-ROMs and databases provided by commercial computerized legal-research services, such as Westlaw® and Lexis®. Today, paralegals and other legal professionals can take advantage of the vast resources on the Internet to better serve their firms' clients.

As already mentioned, Westlaw® and Lexis® are both now "online"[1] (accessible through the Internet), as are numerous other legal-research services. Additionally, today's paralegals have access to a vast array of nonlegal online databases to quickly find other types of information they may be asked to locate.

In the remaining pages of this chapter, you will learn how the Internet can be used to conduct legal or fact-based research. You will also read about some of the best Web sites to access for particular types of information. We begin by looking at some Internet "basics"—what the Internet is and how it can be accessed and navigated to locate information.

What Is the Internet?

The Internet is a global communication network of interconnected computers. Business computers, university and college computers, government computers, your personal computer—all of these and more can be part of the "network of networks" that constitutes cyberspace, or the "information superhighway."

The Internet is growing so fast that estimates of its size are outdated before they make it into print. The technology that makes the Internet possible also changes quickly. The important point for a paralegal is how to use this technology to find information.

Internet Tools

User-friendly software, color monitors and printers, and faster processors have combined with other technological advances to open the Internet to anyone with a little computer knowledge. With a few points and clicks, a paralegal can get onto, and maneuver around, the Internet. Once online, the tools that a paralegal will find most useful include uniform resource locators, e-mail, file transfer protocol, and the World Wide Web.

UNIFORM RESOURCE LOCATORS. A uniform resource locator (URL) is an Internet "address." A paralegal might think of a URL as an electronic citation. Nearly every resource on the Internet is identified by a URL.

---

1. Note that Westlaw® and Lexis® have been "online" for years, in the sense that their databases can be accessed electronically. In the remaining pages of this chapter, we use the term *online* to refer specifically to the Internet.

The basic format of a URL is "service://directorypath/filename." For example, http://www.westlegalstudies.com is the URL for the West Legal Studies Web site, a resource center for paralegal instructors, students, and professionals. This URL indicates that you use the "http" service to reach the directory path (or here, host computer) www.westlegalstudies.com. This site provides access to instructor resources, new textbook and learning material releases, and an online catalogue and bookstore.

The letters **"http"** stand for **hypertext transfer protocol**. When something on the Internet is a site on the World Wide Web (to be discussed shortly), the first part of its address is "http." *Hypertext* is a database system by which disparate objects (text, graphics, and so on) can be linked to each other. With hypertext, you can move from one object to another even though their forms are different (for example, text and graphics have different forms). *Protocol* is the system of formats and rules that enable two computers to communicate. (Because "http://" is part of the URL of every site on the Web, we have omitted it from the rest of the URLs included in this chapter.)

The letters "www" stand for World Wide Web. The **World Wide Web**, or simply the Web, is a hypertext-based service through which data is made available on the Internet.

To enter a URL into a browser, usually it is not necessary to type in "http" and "www." The browser will enter these terms automatically. This saves time.

Hypertext Transfer Protocol (http)
An interface program that enables computers to communicate. Hypertext is a database system by which distinct objects, such as text and graphics, can be linked. Protocol is a system of formats and rules, such as the speed of a transmission.

World Wide Web
A hypertext-based system through which specially formatted documents are accessible on the Internet.

E-MAIL. One of the most common uses of the Internet today is for e-mail, and legal professionals and others often include e-mail addresses on their letterhead stationery and business cards. E-mail can at times be a research tool, as well. E-mail is the basis for services associated with listservs and newsgroups (discussed later in this chapter), for example.

An Internet service provider (to be discussed shortly) can supply an e-mail address and the software that allows a user to compose, send, and receive e-mail. The software is also available from other sources.

FILE TRANSFER PROTOCOL. **File transfer protocol (ftp)** is a very basic interface that connects one computer to another to copy files. The files may contain text, graphics, or software. Ftp is the tool with which a computer (called a client) copies the files onto itself or from itself onto the host computer. A host computer set up to receive ftp requests is called a server.

To find files that are available from ftp servers, researchers use an online index called Archie. This index can be found at several Web sites, including ArchiePlex (www.lerc.nasa.gov/archieplex).

File Transfer Protocol (FTP)
An interface program that connects one computer to another over the Internet to copy files.

WORLD WIDE WEB. The World Wide Web (the Web) is a data service on the Internet. The Web is accessed through a browser (browsers will be discussed shortly). The browser's basic user interface is hypertext, which means that communications between computers on the Web are primarily through links and menus (lists of commands).

When most people think of the Internet, they think of the Web. The Web consists primarily of documents, which are referred to as Web pages (sometimes **home pages**) or Web sites. These pages or sites usually contain links in boldfaced, underlined, or colored text. By selecting or clicking on a link, a user can be transported to other pages or sites, or run other software.

For example, if you access the home page of the Legal Information Institute at Cornell Law School at www.law.cornell.edu (see Exhibit 15.4 on the next page), which has one of the best law-related sites on the Internet, you will find

Home Page
The main page of a Web site. Often, the home page serves as a table of contents to other pages at the site.

EXHIBIT 15.4
The Home Page of the Legal Information Institute

Reproduced with permission.

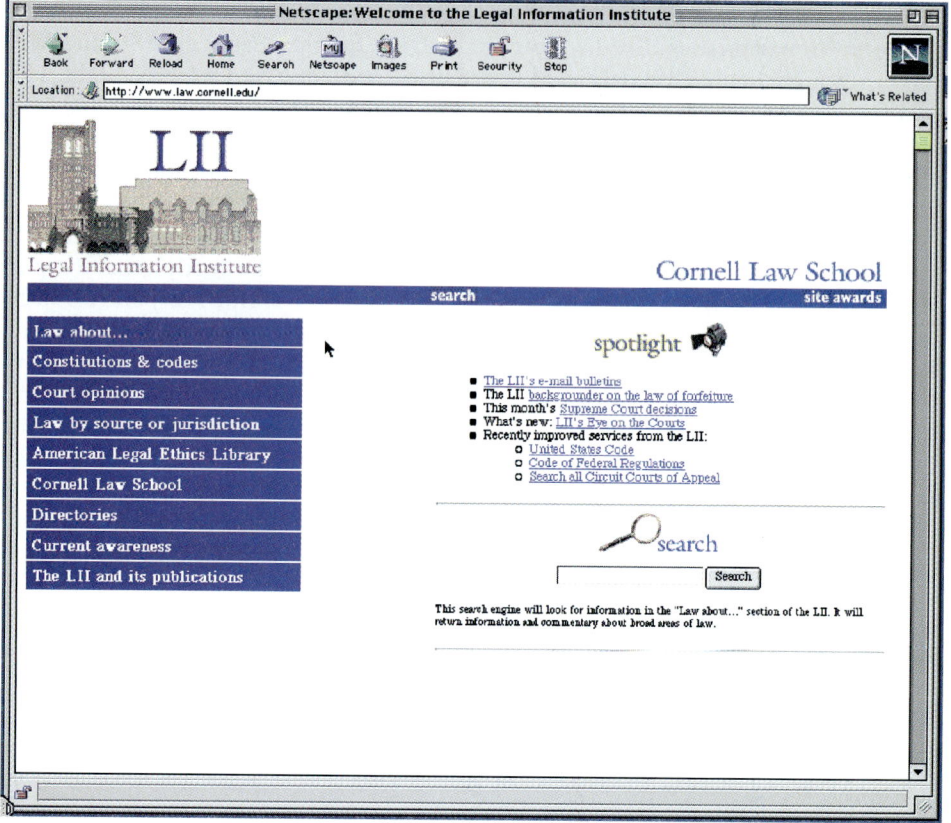

numerous links. Among other things, you will find links to the U.S. Constitution, the *United States Code,* and selected court cases—including the most recent United States Supreme Court decisions as well as some of the Court's historic decisions. You can download text, graphics, and software from Web sites (or "cut and paste" selected portions into a word-processing document).

Accessing the Internet

The Internet can be compared to an enormous library. Knowing how to get into the library—how to gain access to the information you need—is one of the most important parts of any research, and this is true of using the Internet. To get into a library, you need to know where it is and you need to go through the door. To get onto the Internet, you also need to find it and to go there—with a computer and an online service or an Internet service provider.

There are three basic types of *gateways* (methods of access) to the Internet. These methods differ in their cost and their ease of use. The most expensive method is to set up your own gateway, which a large law firm or business organization might do. This requires registering a domain name with the Internet Network Information Center (InterNIC) (see www.internic.com), paying a registration fee, and operating a computer work station with software connected to a special high-speed phone line. Other techniques to gain access are through commercial online services and Internet service providers.

Commercial Online Services
Internet service providers that, for a fee, allow their subscribers access to resources that are otherwise restricted.

COMMERCIAL ONLINE SERVICES.   Some small businesses and many individuals access the Internet through **commercial online services,** such as America Online (**www.aol.com**). There are also online services, such as Counsel Connect (**www.americanlawyer.com**), designed for legal professionals. Each of these services has advantages and disadvantages.

The chief advantages of commercial online services are that they are generally designed to be easy to use and direct you to resources that are likely to meet your needs. The chief disadvantage is that the volume of users often surpasses the ability of a service's equipment to deliver data quickly (or sometimes to deliver it at all) and to provide other support that the service may advertise. Some services may also inhibit or prevent your viewing particular sites otherwise available on the Web.

INTERNET SERVICE PROVIDERS (ISPS). An **Internet service provider (ISP)** is a service that provides dedicated access to the Internet. There are thousands of ISPs, which are usually the least expensive options for gaining access to the Internet. Most ISPs serve local regions, but there are national ISPs, including AT&T WorldNet (**www.att.com/worldnet**), Netcom (**www.netcom.com**), and Sprint Communications Company, L.P. (EarthLink Sprint TotalAccess can be accessed through **www.sprint.com**).

Internet Service Provider (ISP)
A company that provides dedicated access to the Internet, generally through a local phone number.

An ISP is often less consumer oriented than a commercial online service, while offering the same features, including basic Internet access, e-mail addresses, software, and other services. An advantage of an ISP is that it normally does not have the same volume of users as a commercial service and thus can deliver data faster. For the same reason, an ISP may respond more quickly with technical support, although it may not offer the same range of support as a commercial service advertises. A list of thousands of ISPs, organized by area code and country, is available at **thelist.internet.com**.

Navigating the Internet

Once you have access to the Internet, the next important step is to navigate through the vast number of Internet resources until you find the information you are seeking. As stated earlier, the Internet is similar to an enormous library, but there is a key difference—the Internet has no centralized, comprehensive card catalogue. In place of a card catalogue, a researcher uses browsers, guides, directories, and search engines.

BROWSERS. A browser is software that allows a computer to roam the Web. Some commercial online services build browsers into their service. The most popular browsers, however, are Microsoft Explorer (**www.microsoft.com/ie**) and Netscape Navigator (**www.netscape.com/computering/download/index.html**). These browsers can be used with any Internet service.

Improvements and other changes in browser interfaces and capabilities are so rapid and ongoing that almost any discussion of specific features would be outdated before it was published. Although each browser (and each version of each browser) has its own features, all browsers perform the same basic functions. These functions include the ability to set up automatic links (referred to as "Favorites" in Explorer and "Bookmarks" in Netscape) to Internet sites, in order to access those links easily, and to travel back and forth from resource to resource on the Web. Browsers also make it possible to copy text from Web sites and paste it into a word-processing document. With a browser, you can download images, software, and documents to your computer. Finally, with a browser you can search a single document that appears in your window. This last feature is most helpful when the document is long and your time is short.

EXHIBIT 15.5
The Home Page for FindLaw

Reproduced with permission.

GUIDES AND DIRECTORIES. The lack of a single, comprehensive catalogue of what's available on the Internet has led to hundreds of attempts to survey and map the Web. Lists of Web sites categorized by subject are organized into guides and directories, which can be accessed at Web sites online. These sites provide menus of topics that are usually subdivided into narrower subtopics, which themselves may be subdivided, until a list of URLs is reached. If you're uncertain of which menu to use, directories allow you to run a search of the directory site. Popular examples of online directories include Yahoo (**www.yahoo.com**) and, for legal professionals, FindLaw (**www.findlaw.com**). Exhibit 15.5 presents FindLaw's home page.

SEARCH ENGINES. Next to browsers, the most important tools for conducting research on the Web are search engines. Search engines include the following:

- AltaVista (**altavista.digital.com**).
- Excite (**www.excite.com**).
- HotBot (**www.hotbot.com**).
- Infoseek (**www.infoseek.com**).
- Lycos (**www.lycos.com**).

A search engine scans the Web and indexes the contents of pages into a database. There are search engines that will search only specific categories of resources. For example, FindLaw, Inc., provides a tool at **www.findlaw.com** that searches only legal resources on the Web (see Exhibit 15.5). The FindLaw tool can be further limited to search specified databases, such as federal government sites.

Search engines vary in the size and scope of searches, in the flexibility of possible queries, and in the presentation of results. When contemplating whether the Internet is the best tool for a research project, however, you should always keep the following in mind:

 For legal research, even the best search engine cannot match the results of a search conducted with the internal search engine of a commercial fee-based database such as Lexis® or Westlaw®.

For example, all search engines have the capability to use connectors, such as "and," "or," and "not." For most search engines, this is the limit of their sophistication. More precise queries can be formulated with Westlaw® or Lexis®, especially for a researcher proficient in using the service. As discussed earlier in this chapter, search tools on Lexis® or Westlaw® allow a researcher to pinpoint anything in the service's database. As of this writing, universal Web search engines cannot match this capability.

Another difficulty with Web search engines is the quality of the results. In response to a search query, a search engine often lists irrelevant sources. Some of the best search engines will categorize results by, for example, the type of Web site (commercial, educational, personal, and so on—see, for instance, Northern Light at **www.nlsearch.com**). This can be helpful, but it does not eliminate irrelevant sites. Sometimes, irrelevant sites can be eliminated only when a researcher goes to the sites and scrolls through them. Ordinarily, however, the first few hits are likely to be the most useful, and a researcher with experience can often avoid others that are inappropriate.

 To obtain the best results, a researcher must know the features of each search engine and how to focus queries to take advantage of those features most effectively.

A capable researcher will also keep abreast of changes to the search engines. Each engine includes tips at its site for searching with it. Also, of course, with practice comes proficiency.

There are two basic kinds of searches: by key word and by concept. A keyword search generates Web sources that use the exact terms that the researcher types in. A concept search adds sources that use related words. In general, the best results are obtained in a search for Web pages that contain very specific terms. Exhibit 15.6 on page 554 provides a look at the results of running a search in a search engine.

META SEARCH ENGINES. Meta search engines run searches on more than one search engine simultaneously. They are the best tools for searching the most Web space possible. It should be noted that nothing searches the entire Web, however. The most capable search engine searches less than 10 percent of all of the Web pages on the Internet. These selected pages include those that receive the most hits. (This is in sharp contrast to searches in commercial databases such as Lexis® or Westlaw®.) Meta search engines include Metacrawler (**www.metacrawler.com**) and All In One Search (**www.AllOneSearch.com**).

Using search engines, including meta search engines, is often the starting point when conducting online research—a topic to which we now turn.

CONDUCTING ONLINE RESEARCH

Your goal when conducting online research is to find accurate, up-to-date information on the topic you are researching in a minimum amount of time. As anyone

EXHIBIT 15.6
Results of a Search Using a Search Engine

Excite is a trademark of Excite, Inc. and may be registered in various jurisdictions. Excite screen display © 1995–1999 Excite, Inc.

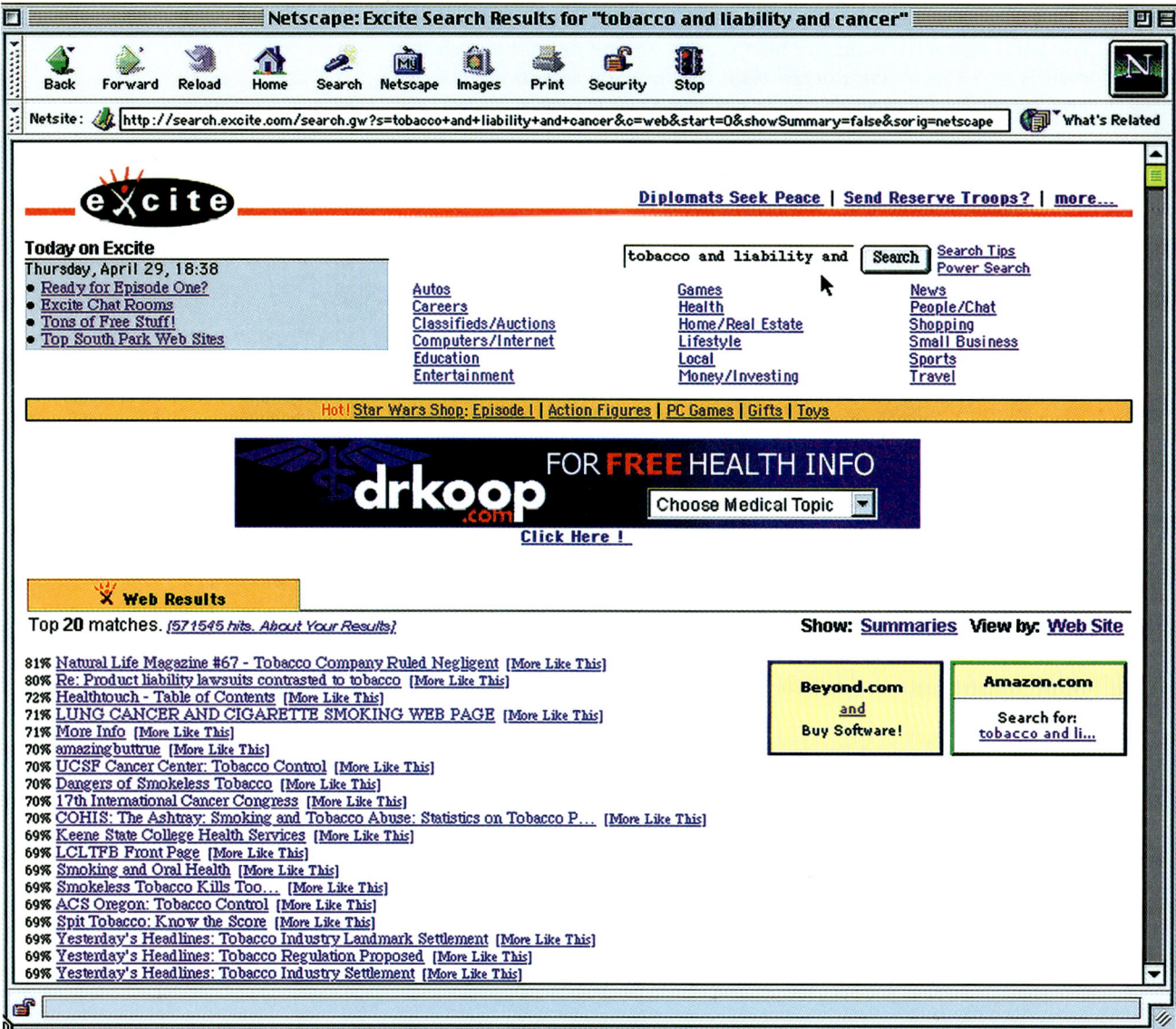

who has used the Internet knows, it is possible to spend hours navigating through cyberspace to find specific data or information. Planning your research in advance and using various research strategies, such as those discussed in this section, can help you achieve your goal of conducting online research efficiently. First, though, as a preliminary matter, you need to decide whether the Internet is the right research tool for your project.

A Threshold Question: Is the Internet the Right Research Tool for Your Project?

The Internet is only one tool for doing research. Knowing which tool to use and when to use it is the key to obtaining quick, accurate results. Ask yourself the fol-

DEVELOPING PARALEGAL SKILLS
Conducting Legal Research on the Internet

Robin Marks works as a paralegal for an attorney who practices constitutional law. Today is the first Monday in October 1999, and Robin has been assigned the task of obtaining a list of cases for which the United States Supreme Court granted *certiorari* for the Court's 1999–2000 term. Robin contemplates the fastest and most efficient method for obtaining this list of cases. She has used a United States Supreme Court Web site, www.usscplus.com, in the past for accurate information on pending Supreme Court decisions. Robin also knows from experience that the Internet is helpful for obtaining current legal information, such as recently issued court opinions. Robin turns to her computer and enters the URL into her browser to obtain the list of cases to be heard during the upcoming term.

TIPS FOR DOING LEGAL RESEARCH ON THE INTERNET
- Determine your research goals.
- Determine whether the legal material to be located is current or was published prior to 1990.
- Determine whether your legal issue is broad or narrow—narrow issues are easier to locate.
- Compile a list of legally related Web sites.
- Bookmark the Web sites that are most useful.

lowing questions: What sources are needed? Are they on the Internet? Are they available elsewhere? Either way, what is the cost? How much time do you have to produce results? The availability (accessibility) of a source, what it costs, and the time it would take to use it are the basic considerations. The Internet is most useful when the most recent information is needed.

Knowing what source to use is a skill that improves with time and experience. Being aware of a particular source is only the first step, however. A good researcher must be able to determine whether the source is available online and, if so, how to find the desired information within that source. Important points to keep in mind include the following:

- Discussion groups on the Internet cover nearly every conceivable topic.
- Most business firms, colleges, universities, and trade organizations have Web sites.
- Anything that can be subscribed to for a fee is available online, or will be available soon.
- Complete books are not online to the extent that fee-based periodicals are.

In terms of availability and cost, it should be remembered that many sources on the Internet are free, but some are not. It may be more cost effective to pull a book off a shelf than to pay for the same material online. It may also be faster to flip through the pages of a book, such as a dictionary, than to take the time to go online and click through a few links to find the same information. Additionally, if you are conducting serious legal research, the Internet may not be the research tool of choice. For other types of research, it may be the most efficient tool.

CONDUCTING LEGAL RESEARCH ON THE INTERNET. Many primary sources of law—including federal and state statutes, federal and state regulations, and the decisions of numerous courts—are now accessible via the Internet. Later in this chapter, you will learn some of the best sites to access when you are looking for online legal resources. Among the primary sources of law that you can access online are the following documents:

- The United States Constitution, U.S. treaties, the Declaration of Independence, and other selected important historical documents.
- United States Supreme Court decisions.
- Decisions issued by the U.S. Courts of Appeals over at least the last two or three years.
- The entire *United States Code* (all federal statutes) and the entire *Code of Federal Regulations* (all federal administrative agency rules). See, for example, the U.S. House of Representatives Internet Law Library at **law.house.gov** (the home page of this site is illustrated in Exhibit 15.7).
- Materials focused on specific areas of the law, such as intellectual property.
- Sources related to each state's laws—these vary in the depth of their coverage. There is a list of URLs for state resources included in "The Legal List" and indexed at **www.lcp.com/The-Legal-List/index5.html**.
- Foreign law, which can be hard to find in many law libraries, can be found at such sites as the European Union Internet Resources site at **www.lib.berkeley.edu/GSSI/eu.html**.

What is available online in terms of secondary sources of law (comments or explanations by experts on particular topics) varies. Traditional secondary sources, such as the legal encyclopedias and legal treatises familiar to paralegals and lawyers in their printed versions, are generally not available. Other types of secondary sources are online, however, and these can help a researcher focus his or her efforts (see, for example, the resources provided by Nolo Press at **www.nolo.com**). Many law firms provide background material at their sites (see, for example, the list of publications offered by Hale and Dorr, L.L.P., a Boston law firm, at **www.haledorr.com/publications.html**).

THE LIMITED SCOPE OF ONLINE LEGAL SOURCES. Although numerous legal materials are available online, their scope is limited.

 For serious, in-depth legal research, as of the time this edition is being written, the free Web sites on the Internet are not excellent resources.

For example, research into court cases to determine whether a law is constitutional must still be conducted in a law library or through a commercial, fee-based service. Although more legal resources are constantly being added to the Web, material that predates the 1990s is generally not available.

One reason for the limits to what is available online has to do with the expense of data compilation and storage. Most information providers selectively convert their data into an electronic resource. It also takes time to compile a large historical database. The limited facility of browsers and search engines also detracts from the usefulness of the free resources on the Internet for researching the law.

CONDUCTING FACT-BASED RESEARCH ON THE INTERNET. While the Internet has drawbacks as far as serious legal research is concerned, it can be very useful when you need to find peripheral materials and information. Lawyers often need to know more than the law. For example, for a case involving a personal injury, medical research may be necessary. For other cases, scientific, technical, technological, or other types of research may be needed.

EXHIBIT 15.7
The Home Page of the U.S. House of Representatives Internet Law Library

Reproduced with permission.

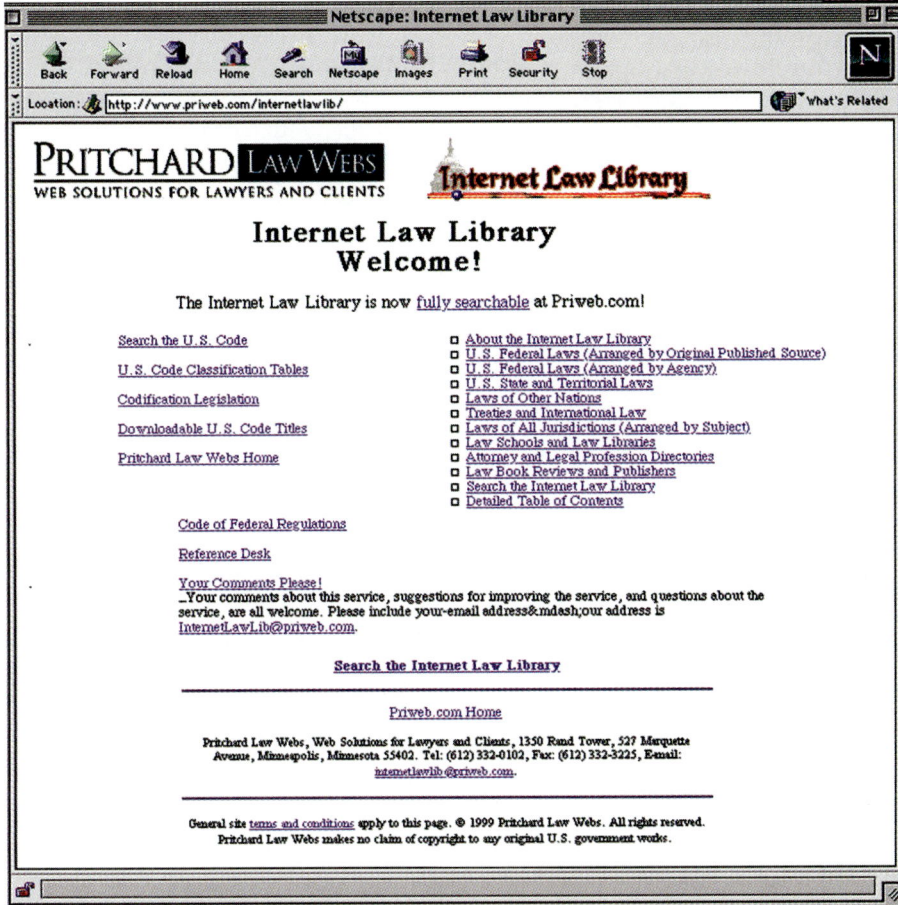

Online databases that focus on the law do not entirely fill this requirement. Other resources available on the Internet can be very useful to legal professionals, however.

 In fact, currently the great value of the Internet for legal professionals is the speed with which it allows them to locate people, investigate companies, and conduct other practical, fact-based research.

The numerous databases available on the Web make it possible to perform such research with great ease and speed. Of course, as with all research, the key to efficiency and obtaining successful results is careful planning.

Plan Ahead—Analyze the Facts and Identify the Issues

If you have decided that the Internet is the right tool for a particular research project, you should plan your research steps before going online. The first step is to know what it is you are seeking. To avoid wasting time and money, state your objectives clearly and be sure that you understand your goals. To narrow the scope

DEVELOPING PARALEGAL SKILLS
Medical Research on the Internet

Tom Shannon needs to locate information on bipolar disorder. Tom's supervising attorney is trying to prove that the defendant in a case has this mental disorder. Tom, who has worked as a paralegal for ten years, knows the Internet is an excellent source for medical information. Tom accesses the American Medical Association's Web site at www.ama-assn.org. He searches for articles describing this disorder. Tom finds several citations to articles, along with summaries of the articles, but the full text of the articles is not online. He prints out the information he found and goes to the library at the local medical school to obtain the full text of the articles.

TIPS FOR PERFORMING MEDICAL RESEARCH ONLINE

- Become familiar with medical terminology.
- Search the appropriate medical categories on the Web site.
- Locate appropriate articles and summaries.
- If the full text of the articles is not available online, go to the nearest medical school's library to obtain them.

---

of your research, you may need to know the reason for the research or how the results will be used.

The second step is to determine which sources are most likely to lead you to the desired results. One way to gain a sense of where you want to look is to use a guidebook (see, for example, the most recent edition of *The Internet for Dummies*, written by John R. Levine, Carol Baroudi, and Margaret Levine Young, and published by IDG Books Worldwide, Inc.). A good guide can point you in the direction of the right Web sites to visit to begin your research, to narrow its focus, or to find exactly what you need. Once these steps are taken, your research can begin.

Starting Points

Sometimes, a research session begins with one of the online directories or guides discussed earlier in this chapter. For example, if the object of your search is to find information on a particular case, you could start with Yahoo's "Government" menu (www.yahoo.com/Government). This is broken into submenus, including one titled "Law," which is further broken down into submenus that include "Cases." See Exhibit 15.8 beginning on page 559.

A search engine or a meta search engine may be used to compile your own list of Web sites containing certain key words. A search engine tailored to zero in on specific topical sites may be more useful than either a general search engine or a meta search engine, depending on your research goals. Keep in mind the limitations of search engines, however. Your search may locate many irrelevant sources and may not spot every site that you would find helpful. Also, different search engines will yield different results. For this reason, it is best to use more than one search engine when conducting research.

From the preliminary results of a general search, you can click on the links to visit the sites and determine which are useful. Many sites include their own links to other sources you may find helpful. Some Web sites attempt to collect links to all online resources about particular topics. These include directories, which were discussed earlier, as well as other sites such as the Federal Web Locator (www.law.vill.edu/fed-agency/fedwebloc.html), which provides links to federal

CHAPTER 15   *Computer-Assisted Legal Research*   **559**

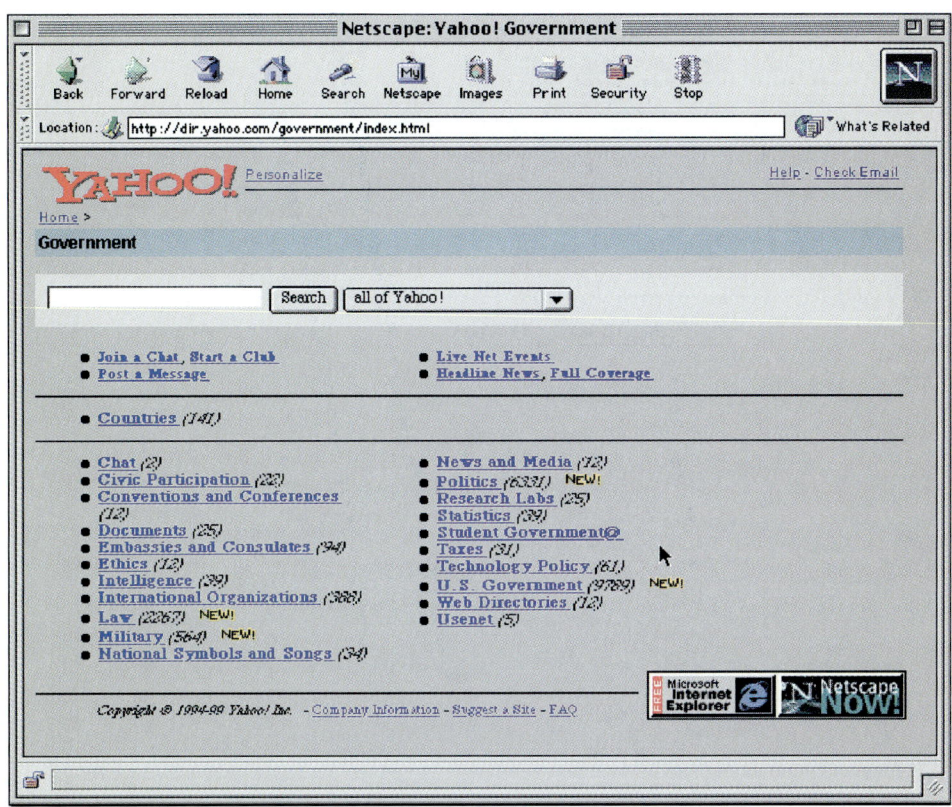

EXHIBIT 15.8a
www.yahoo.com/ Government/

Reproduced with permission.

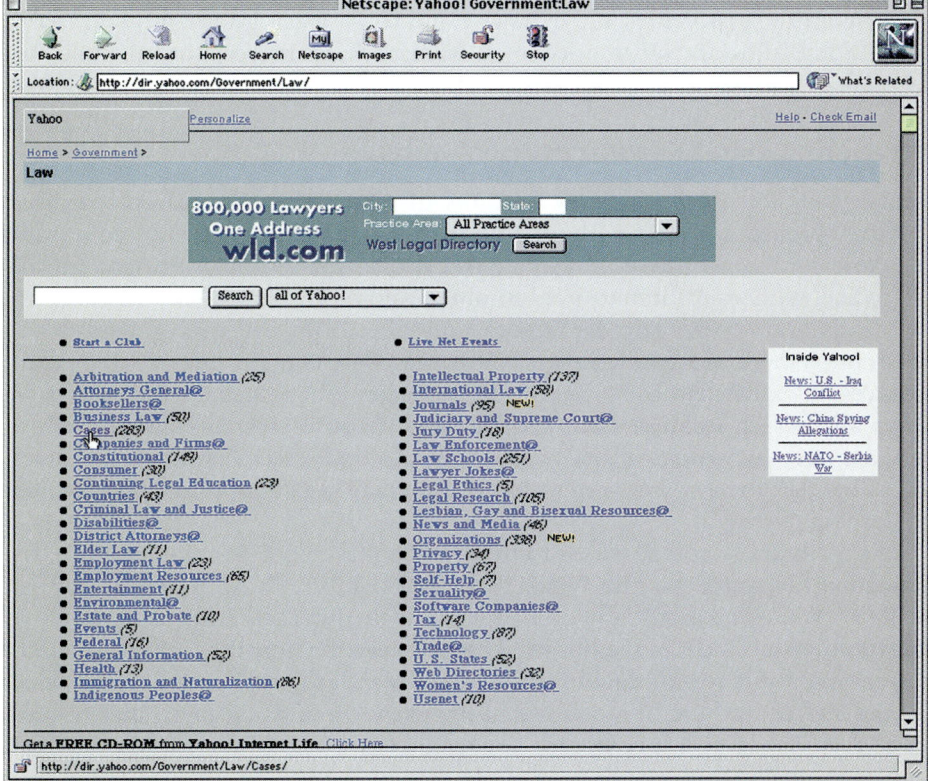

EXHIBIT 15.8b
www.yahoo.com/ Government/Law/

EXHIBIT 15.8c

www.yahoo.com/
Government/Law/Case

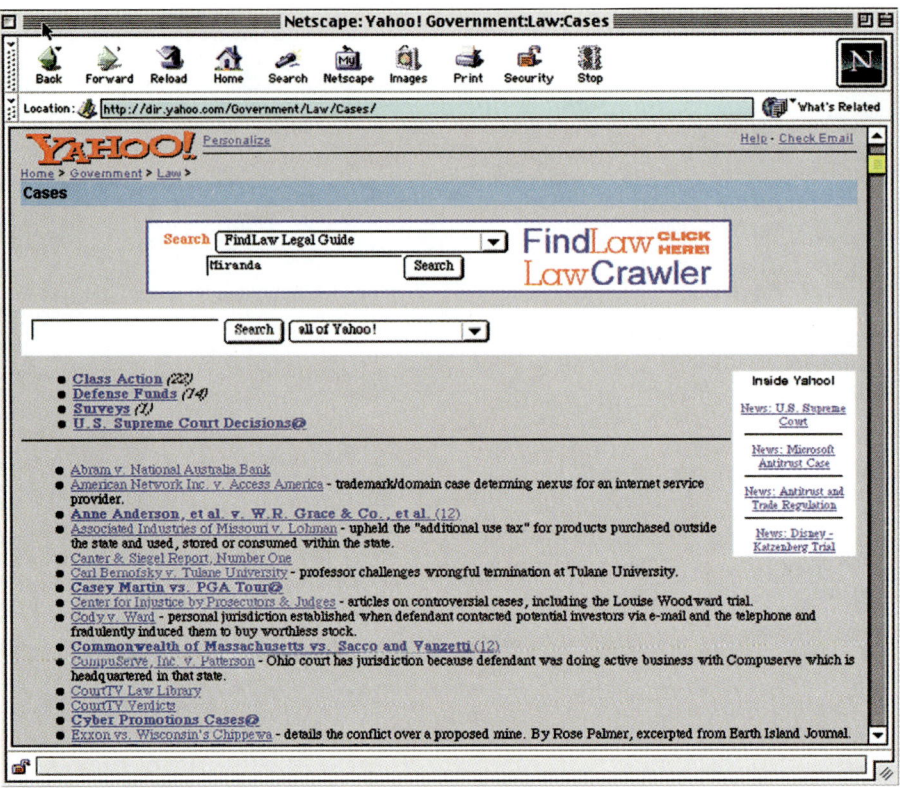

offices and agencies. For more experienced researchers, there is Hieros Gamos (www.hg.org/hg), which is an extensive guide to legal information available online. Some sites are more eclectic in what they offer (see, for example, the 'Lectric Law Library at www.lectlaw.com).

Discovering What Resources Are Available

Despite your best intentions and attempts to pinpoint your research, you may have to approach a project without a clear objective regarding what you need to find. Your initial research goal may be to discover the extent of resources available online, with your ultimate goal to obtain more precise results.

In addition to the popular guides and directories, such as Excite (www.excite.com), there are less familiar Web pages that contain links to important resources in particular topic areas. These pages often include directory-style menus and search utilities. For example, legal-resource search engines, such as CataLaw (see www.catalaw.com), are directed to find sites related to legal topics. Remember that these sources often change, and may even disappear, and new ones can develop overnight.

Many libraries provide access to their catalogues online (see, for example, the cataloguing available on the New York Public Library's Web site at catnyp.nypl.org). You can search these catalogues over the Internet in the same way that you would search them in the library. This can save the time that otherwise might be spent in a futile trip to the library. You can search the catalogues of your local libraries as well as those of more distant libraries. Often, you can arrange to have source material in a distant library delivered to a closer library, where you can more conveniently review it.

Technology and Today's Paralegal
Creative Online Searching

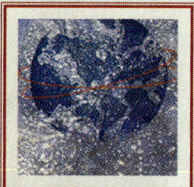

Information can be collected easily via the Internet. The only limit to what is collected and how it is analyzed is the ability of the researcher. What distinguishes a good researcher from an average researcher is the ability to obtain hard-to-find or obscure data from hard-to-reach sources that are especially reliable. Backing up a secondary source with hard-to-find primary data is qualitative, comprehensive research.

For example, the Web can be a good source for obtaining background information on people. Imagine that a lawyer for whom you work is scheduled to question a certain witness. Background information could be useful during the questioning. The witness's past can be investigated on the Web in several ways. A general search can be made to uncover any data concerning the witness. Newsgroups (discussed elsewhere in this chapter) can be searched to discover whether the person has said anything in these groups that relates to his or her testimony. Other ways to find people and information about them are discussed later in this chapter.

Interpreting the data in clever ways is another attribute that distinguishes good researchers. For example, one of your client's competitors advertises employment opportunities for engineers with certain skills. To an intelligent researcher, this may indicate a new direction for the competitor's research and development, or a new product line. A competitor's Web links could give your client insight into the competitor's operations or indicate a new market for your client's products. To discover sites that link to your competitor's home page, you could use a feature such as the Advanced Search tool at the Altavista search engine site (**www.altavista.com**). In that tool, as a search term, use **link: your competitor's home page address.**

Another way to find out what resources are available is to begin with a listserv list or a newsgroup. These can also be used to update your research.

A **listserv list** (or mailing list) is basically a list of e-mail addresses of persons interested in a particular topic. By placing their names on the list, they agree to receive e-mail from others about the topic. A message sent to the list's address is automatically sent to everyone on the list. Anyone on the list can respond to whoever sent the message. As a researcher, you might post a message that asks for suggestions about online resources for your research. You can also add your name to the list to receive the mass e-mailings. In some cases, you may be able to browse an archive of messages to see if another researcher has previously called attention to a resource that matches your search.

Listserv lists (see **tile.net/listserv**) provide more anonymity than newsgroups. There is a listserv list for paralegals and legal assistants. To subscribe to this list, send the message "subscribe paralegals <your e-mail address>" to **majordomo@ljx.com**. The address to post messages to the subscribers on this list is **PARALEGALS@ljx.com**. To add your e-mail address to other listserv lists, see **www.lawguru.com/subscribe/listtool.html**.

A **newsgroup** (also known as a **usenet group**) is a forum that resembles a community bulletin board. A newsgroup can be selected by topic. A researcher can post a question or problem (for example, "Does anyone know a good source for what I want to know?") and check back hours or days later for others' responses. A researcher might also browse the newsgroup's archive, although messages are typically stored only for limited periods of time. There are thousands of newsgroups (a few hundred of which focus on law-related topics). Newsgroup directories can be skimmed at such sites as Liszt (**www.liszt.com/news**). Newsgroups can be searched with specialized search engines, such as Dejanews (**www.dejanews.com**).

Listserv List
A list of e-mail addresses of persons who have agreed to receive e-mail about a particular topic.

Newsgroup (Usenet Group)
An online bulletin board service (BBS). A newsgroup, or BBS, is a forum, or discussion group, that usually focuses on a particular topic.

ETHICAL CONCERN
Surfing the Web

A problem faced by paralegals who are novices in conducting online research is how to avoid spending hours surfing the Web for a site that contains the information being sought. You know the information is "out there" somewhere on the Web, but how can you locate it? What key terms can you use in your search that will find the information but that will also narrow the search sufficiently—so that you do not end up retrieving hundreds of thousands of documents? Over time, of course, you will become familiar with the best sites for information in your area of practice. In the meantime, how can you avoid giving the impression to your employer that you are "wasting" time surfing the Web? One thing you can do is explain to your employer at the outset that surfing the Web is part of the learning process and that this "learning time" is essential if you are to become efficient in online research.

Browsing the Links

Traveling around on the Internet to see what data are available is known as "surfing the Web" or "browsing the links." As you browse through the links that could be potentially useful for your research, two problems will become apparent. First, you need to keep track of the Web sites you visit. Second, the speed at which your computer browses can sometimes be slow.

A browser "Favorite" (Explorer) or "Bookmark" (Netscape) is an electronic substitute for keeping a book on your desk. With one of these tools, you can create an automatic link to any point on the Web and return to it at any time. For example, you might want to create a Favorite or Bookmark to the site at which you begin your research: a directory, a search engine, or one of the sites that have many links that relate to what you need.

Slow speed can be more of a problem. It may be the result of something, such as an outmoded browser, that you can correct. It is not always so easily overcome, however. It can result from bad phone lines, your service provider's problems, the limits of equipment (yours or someone else's), quirks in the weather, and so on.

Before going online, you may want to take steps to avoid some of the causes of slow speed. For example, to avoid the difficulty of accessing a popular site during its busiest times, you might go online early in the morning or late in the day. You should be aware that if traffic is heavy at a particular site, there could be a mirror site with the same data. A site will note on its home page if a **mirror site** is available. You might also avoid downloading or uploading large files at a site's busy times. It may be possible to increase your speed by selecting the text-only option when you browse. This may be particularly helpful when you use a low-performance computer or modem to access a site that has rich graphics. With some sites, this may not be an option, however, because the graphics may be necessary to navigate the sites.

Narrowing Your Focus

Once you find a Web site that could be useful, you may need to zero in more precisely within that site on specific data. Many sites contain links to text and graph-

---

Mirror Site
A Web site that duplicates an already existing site. A mirror site is used to improve the availability of access to a site that receives a lot of traffic or is distant from some users.

ics within their pages. These links can be browsed to peruse documents within the site. Some sites include internal search utilities with which you can look for specific information within those sites. These utilities compare to an index in a book, except, of course, you choose the words in the index. Each site's internal utility can be different, but in general, it will work like a search engine. (See, for example, Harvard University's internal search tool at **search.harvard.edu:8765**.)

As pointed out earlier in this chapter, your browser also has the ability to search an individual Web page that you are viewing. This can be particularly helpful when scrolling through a document for a bit of information would be tedious and time consuming. Using your browser's "find" tool, you can search, for example, the text of a specific bill before Congress at the Library of Congress's THOMAS site (**thomas.loc.gov**), which contains legislative information. You might also use your find tool to search a company's document in the Electronic Data Gathering, Analysis, and Retrieval (EDGAR) database of the Securities and Exchange Commission (SEC) (**www.sec.gov/edgarhp.htm**). EDGAR is an indexed collection of documents and forms that public companies and others are required to file with the SEC. Exhibit 15.9 on the next page presents the first page of the EDGAR online collection.

Evaluating What You Find

After you have found what appears to be exactly what you are looking for, you need to consider its reliability. In evaluating data revealed through a search on the Internet, a researcher applies the same evaluative skills he or she would use to evaluate data found in other, more traditional ways. Because anyone with access to a computer can put anything on the Internet, however, you should abide by the following rule of thumb:

> **Every source of data obtained via the Internet needs to be evaluated carefully for its credibility.**

In evaluating a source's credibility, you need to ask yourself whether the source of the information is a primary, a secondary, or a tertiary source. Primary sources include experts and persons with firsthand knowledge. For example, the inventor of a product would be a primary source for information about his or her invention. Publicly filed documents are also good primary sources. For example, the legal forms that some companies are required to file with the Securities and Exchange Commission are good primary sources for the information that they contain (see the discussion of company investigations later in this chapter).

Secondary sources include books and periodicals (such as newspapers and magazines) and their online equivalents that contain "secondhand" information. Tertiary sources are any other sources that might be used in research.

A researcher needs to be aware, first of all, of whether online information is outdated. Often, it is difficult to ascertain when certain online articles, data, and other information were created. Also, a researcher needs to determine whether the source is reputable. A reputable source might be an organization that has established itself as an excellent resource in a particular field. A less reputable source might be an individual's own self-serving home page. Finally, the researcher should determine whether information was placed on the Web by a source that may be biased in a certain way.

In short, a researcher needs to keep in mind that anyone can provide information on the Web regardless of whether the person knows what he or she is talking about. People may not even be who they represent themselves to be. Because of this, whenever possible, you should do the following:

EXHIBIT 15.9
The Securities and Exchange Commission's EDGAR Database

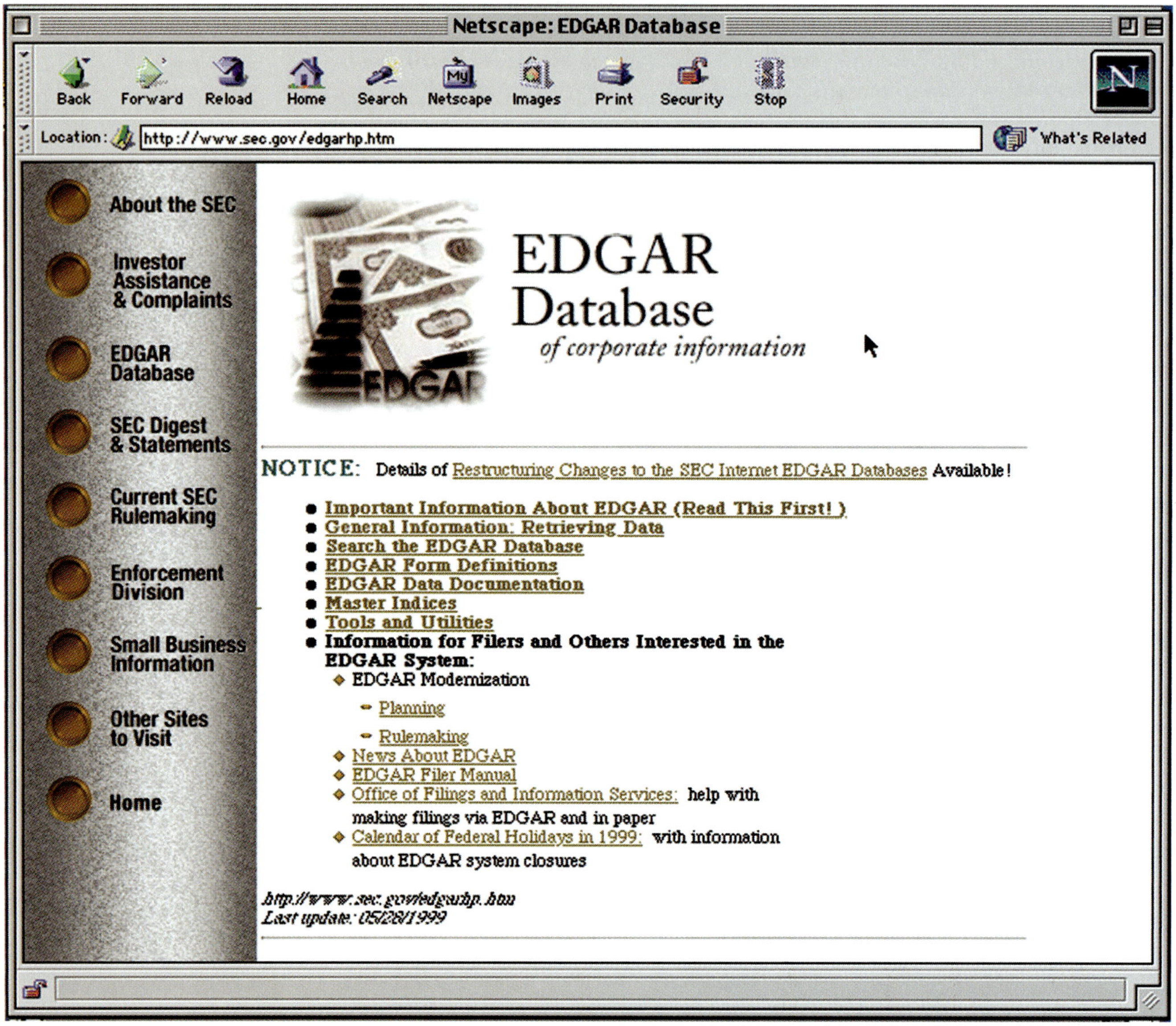

Find and interpret primary sources yourself before you form any conclusions about information retrieved from the Web.

Updating Your Results

Staying current with events in the law, and in other areas that relate to your research, is important. The speed with which information is distributed via the Internet is a boon for paralegals and other researchers, because data are often online before they are available in other media. You can confirm whether your research results represent the most recent data available by going to relevant Web sites.

For certain types of research, you may want to check one of the news sites that abound on the Internet, such as CNN (see www.cnn.com). There are sites directed at those who may be interested only in updates in specific subjects. For updates on the legal news, you might check the site of FindLaw Legal News at www.findlaw.com. Corporate press releases—current and archival—can be reviewed at PRNewswire's site (www.prnewswire.com).

You can also arrange to have selected types of news articles sent immediately to your computer (see, for example, the Yahoo news ticker at www.my.yahoo.com/ticker.html or the Pointcast site at www.pointcast.com). Other sources for updating research results include newsgroups (or usenet groups) and listserv lists, both of which have already been discussed.

LOCATING PEOPLE AND INVESTIGATING COMPANIES

Paralegals often need to locate people or find out information about specific companies. As mentioned earlier, the Internet can be an especially useful research tool when searching for this type of information.

Finding People

A paralegal may need to find particular persons to assist a lawyer in collecting debts, administering an estate, preparing a case for court, and so on. Public records are helpful in looking for people, but some records (including most historic records) are not on the Internet. Despite this limitation, Web searches can be cheaper and faster than going to a government office or a library. Sometimes, using a commercial locator service or database can also be less costly than a trip out of the office.

BROAD SEARCHES. On the Web, a researcher can run a broad search with a general search engine such as Infoseek (www.infoseek.go.com). A researcher might also narrow the focus of a search to, for example, all of the U.S. telephone books. There are several Web sites that provide telephone directories. Each of the sites has unique features. Some provide e-mail addresses (for example, Four11 Corporation at www.four11.com). Some include business listings (for example, www.companylink.com). Some can conduct a search with a telephone number or an e-mail address to reveal a name and a street address (for example, Database America at www.databaseamerica.com/html/index.htm or the Internet Address Finder at www.iaf.net). On some sites, such as WhoWhere (www.whowhere.com), a search can be based on personal characteristics, such as occupation, school, or affiliation with a certain organization. Some international telephone books can also be searched (see, for example, World Pages at www.worldpages.com).

NARROW SEARCHES. If something is known about a person, the Web can be a good source for locating him or her. For example, if you are looking for an attorney, you can link to *West's Legal Directory,* which is a comprehensive compilation of lawyers in the United States, by going to www.westbuslaw.com. From the West Legal Studies Resource Center, click on the "Student Center" link in the "Support and Services" box in the left column. When the "Student Center" page appears, scroll down to "West's Legal Directory."

LOCATING EXPERT WITNESSES. To find a person to serve as an expert witness, you can search the National Directory of Expert Witnesses at www.claims.com or choose a different Web source from the Expert Witness Info on the Internet list of the

Paralegal Profile

V. Sheri Towne has a bachelor's degree in education from the University of Arkansas. She began her career in law while serving as an officer in the United States Navy. After graduating with honors from the U.S. Naval Justice School, she served as the non-lawyer legal officer for a naval air station and later as a member of a procurement fraud task force set up by the Navy and the Federal Bureau of Investigation. She has been with the firm of Pratt-Thomas, Pearce, Epting & Walker, P.A., since 1986, became a Certified Legal Assistant (CLA) in 1988, added the civil litigation specialist credential in 1994, and has served as her firm's lead paralegal since 1990. In addition to performing general paralegal responsibilities for Andrew K. Epting, Jr., Towne provides Internet research and litigation technology support for the fourteen-member firm and is responsible for designing and maintaining its Internet Web site at www.wiselaw.com. Ms. Towne has been actively involved with the National Association of Legal Assistants (NALA) and the South Carolina Alliance for Legal Assistant Associations (SCALAA). She is a founding member and past president of the Tri-County Paralegal Association.

Litigation Paralegal and Web Site Designer

What do you like best about your work?

"I like the intellectual challenge and the opportunity for creative problem solving, the satisfaction of knowing that your efforts contribute to making a difference in people's lives and (at times) when they feel helpless, vulnerable, or overcome by events."

What is the greatest challenge that you face in your area of work?

"My greatest challenge is keeping up with the ever-growing information and technology resources available to accomplish a given task and keeping those items in perspective such that in any given situation I can provide what is needed, when it is needed, in a cost-effective and efficient manner for both the firm and the client."

What advice do you have for would-be paralegals in your area of work?

"One of the most important skills to develop is that of a good listener. Pay close attention to what you are being told, not only by the attorneys who supervise your work but also by clients and others around you. Make sure you understand the ideas and concepts being imparted to you by the *other* person. Learn the resources that are available for finding information, including print material, online information, public and private libraries, and people. For any given situation, find the method to obtain the information needed that is both effective *and* efficient. Develop the habit of being methodical and paying attention to detail."

What are some tips for success as a paralegal in your area of work?

"Be flexible. Develop more than one method or option for accomplishing a task so that when conditions change, such as a deadline being shortened, you are still able to effectively and efficiently get the job done. Learn your supervising attorney's habits and patterns, and learn to think and plan ahead several steps. When you can anticipate what will be needed and have it ready almost as quickly as it is asked for, you will have made yourself a highly valued asset. Always keep your supervisors informed of problems, not just when they occur but also when they are anticipated—and have at least two suggestions for solving them available for discussion. Never be afraid to ask questions. No matter how busy you are, always take a moment to respond to requests for information or assistance from others. Never stop learning—the moment you think you know all there is to know is the exact moment you confirm that you don't."

> "One of the most important skills to develop is that of a good listener."

Northern California Association of Law Libraries (**www.nocall.org/experts.htm**). To look for a professor at a particular university or an employee at a certain company, the staff directory of the school or business firm may be available, and searchable, online. (See, for example, the directory for the faculty of Yale Law School at **elsinore.cis.yale.edu/lawweb/lawschool/facfp.htm**.)

SEARCHES BASED ON SPECIFIC CHARACTERISTICS. A search for a person can be based on such characteristics as his or her professional status or where he or she went to school. With the right database (some sites charge a fee), a person's business license can be verified, a veteran may be located, information about a federal prison inmate can be accessed, and a federal employee can be found. (See, for example, the Federal Government Directory at **www.fed.gov**.)

Information can be obtained on persons who contribute to federal election campaigns (see the Federal Candidate Campaign Money Page at **www.tray.com/fecinfo**).

Adoptees and their birth parents may be located through certain databases on the Web such as the Webgator site at **www.inil.com/users/dguss/gator9.htm**. For genealogy searches, there are databases that include all persons who have died since 1962, American marriages before 1800, graves, and so on (see, for example, the Social Security Death Index at **www.ancestry.com**).

States' driving and vehicle registration records and motor vehicle accident data may be available on the Web (see, for example, the state of Texas list of licensed drivers at **www.publicdata.com**). Forwarding addresses and name changes for individuals and companies can be found at such databases as Semaphore Corporation's "Where Did They Go?" at **www.semaphorecorp.com/default.html**.

FEE-BASED SEARCHES. Some commercial services provide access to their compilations of information only for a price. Some of the information mentioned above can be found in fee-based databases. There are pay services through which military personnel can be found (for example, MilitaryCity Online at **www.militarycity.com**). Through a service with access to states' incorporation data and other sources' information, people can be pinpointed based on their ownership interest in business organizations. Real-property records, bankruptcy filings, and documents relating to court dockets, lawsuits, and judgments can be searched through such sites as KnowX at **www.knowx.com**. Social Security numbers can also be verified (see **www.informus.com/ssnlkup.html**).

Investigating Companies

Lawyers often need to know about their clients' companies and the companies of their clients' competitors. For example, if a client suffered an injury caused by a defectively designed product, a lawyer will need to identify the defendant manufacturer, find out whether the manufacturer is the subsidiary of a larger company, and learn the defendant's address. If a client wants to acquire or invest in a particular business firm, research into the firm's background may be vital. There are many ways to find this type of information on the Web.

It is important to remember that sites on the Web can be searched online anonymously (without the awareness of the firm about which information is sought). Because of this anonymity, your clients may learn of competitive threats and opportunities without alerting their competitors.

FINDING COMPANY NAMES AND ADDRESSES. A researcher can run a search with a telephone number to find a company's name and address (for example, see the GTE Superpages at yp.gte.net). Without a telephone number, a company's name and address can be found with the help of a directory that searches by industry and state (see the CompanyLink page at www.companylink.com, for example). A search with such a directory can also help determine whether a specific firm name is in use anywhere in the United States. The Internet Network Information Center maintains a database of registered domain names (see, for example, the Netpartners Company Site Locator at www.netpartners.com/locator.htm).

UNCOVERING DETAILED INFORMATION ABOUT PUBLIC COMPANIES. To discover more information than a company name and address, an in-depth search is necessary. A guide to uncovering company information on the Web is located at www.virtualchase.com/coinfo/index.htm. Fuld & Company provides links to a variety of business research resources from its Competitive Intelligence Guide at www.fuld.com. Most companies maintain their own Web sites, which may contain the firm's annual reports, press releases, and price lists. Some companies put their staff directories online.

Information may be available through the sites of government agencies. For example, the Occupational Safety and Health Administration (OSHA) site (www.osha.gov) identifies manufacturers whose products have caused injuries or deaths at any time in the last twelve years, and the Consumer Product Safety Commission (CPSC) site (www.cpsc.gov) lists products that have been recalled. The Securities and Exchange Commission (SEC) regulates public companies and requires them to file documents and forms revealing certain information. The documents include annual reports and proxies, which contain information on directors and stock issues. This material can be accessed through the SEC's EDGAR database (at www.sec.gov/edgarhp.htm), as already mentioned.

Some states make their corporate records available online. For links to many states' records offices, see w3.uwyo.edu/~prospect/secstate.html.

Other information about public companies can be found at other free sites and pay sites. In general, the best free sites provide data on the companies and links to the companies' home pages, EDGAR, and other resources, such as news articles. See, for example, the Wall Street Research Network at www.wsrn.com or Yahoo Company Information at biz.yahoo.com/news. Pay sites sometimes include larger databases with archives of information that may span decades and may cover companies in other countries.

LEARNING ABOUT PRIVATE COMPANIES. Data on private companies is more difficult to find because these firms are not subject to the SEC's disclosure requirements. Much of the information that is available is only what the companies want to reveal. With this limitation in mind, there are a few sites that compile some of the data on private companies, associations, and nonprofit organizations. For example, Hoover's Online at www.hoovers.com provides brief profiles of many companies, with links to other sites, including search engines. For a fee, Hoover's will provide expanded profiles. Dun & Bradstreet provides, at its site (www.companiesonline.com), links to approximately one hundred thousand public and private companies.

SOME OF THE BEST
LEGAL-RESOURCE SITES ON THE INTERNET

As we have said elsewhere in this chapter, what is available on the Web changes rapidly. New sites come online. Old favorites disappear. Familiar sites move. URLs

FEATURED GUEST: JAN RICHMOND
Keeping Current on Computer Technology

BIOGRAPHICAL NOTE

Jan Richmond completed her master of arts degree in legal studies at Webster University in St. Louis, Missouri. As an undergraduate, she specialized in systems and data processing. She received her undergraduate degree from Washington University. Richmond has been an adjunct faculty member in the legal-assisting program at St. Louis Community College since 1989. Her teaching schedule includes courses in computers and the law, advanced computer utilization, and legal administration, in additon to classes in WordPerfect 5.1 and 6.0, and Windows, Excel, Lotus, and numerous other software applications. Richmond has been a consultant in law-office training for nine years. For the past four summers, she offered computer classes for the Missouri Bar Association.

Computer technology is developing at such a rapid pace that you can almost rest assured that what's here today will be changed or gone tomorrow. That means that paralegals must learn to tackle the tremendous problem of keeping their computer systems up to date.

Here's an example: today, it is common to see a paralegal seated next to an attorney to assist with the marking of testimony that is being electronically captured by a court reporter and transmitted to the attorney's table. As testimony is being given, with the aid of online Westlaw® or Lexis®, research can begin in the electronic courtrooms of today. Courtroom presentations are no longer limited to paper-based media. PowerPoint or other software has made the changing visual image, manipulated by paralegals, instantly available as evidence in almost any jurisdiction.

There are several ways that you can learn about current developments in the area of computer technology and software. One way is to read computer magazines, such as those listed and described below. Other ways include attending computer workshops and seminars, participating in user groups, accessing online information, and attending software demonstrations or obtaining demonstration software diskettes, or "demos."

COMPUTER MAGAZINES

There are a number of monthly or bimonthly publications to which you or your firm can subscribe. By routinely scanning through some or all of these publications, you can keep abreast of what's happening in the computer world in regard to technology or software relating to law offices and legal research.

The Lawyer's PC (published by Shepard's/McGraw-Hill, P.O. Box 35300, Colorado Springs, CO 80935-3530) is a monthly publication for lawyers who use personal computers. Each month, a different topic is addressed. One issue, for example, featured an article entitled "Changing the Way We Work: Where Are Computers Taking Us?" The topic was right on target for attorneys and paralegals who wish to assess the impact of computer technology on their work habits. Each November, the entire issue is devoted to a list of application software for the law office. *The Perfect Lawyer,* a similar type of monthly publication also published by Shepard's/McGraw-Hill, deals with WordPerfect word-processing software and legal applications specific to that software.

Law Office Technology is a bimonthly publication that covers a wide variety of topics and deals with all aspects of law and computing. Topics covered range from the most commonly used WordPerfect macros to automating the job of estate management. To obtain information on this magazine, write to *Law Office Technology,* 3520 Cadillac Avenue, Suite E, Costa Mesa, CA 92626.

Legal Assistant Today (3520 Cadillac Avenue, Suite E, Costa Mesa, CA 92626) and *Legal Professional* (6060 North Central Expressway, Suite 670, Dallas, TX 75206-9947) are less oriented toward computer technology but do contain computing articles of interest and offer differing points of view on particular topics.

Last, but not least, is *AMLaw Tech* (345 Park Avenue South, New York, NY 10010), one of the newer publications that is heavily directed toward the use of technology in legal practice.

WORKSHOPS AND SEMINARS

Every professional organization offers workshops and seminars dealing with

Continued

FEATURED GUEST, Continued

computers. If you are a member of an association for paralegals, you will have an opportunity to meet and exchange ideas with others doing similar work. Check with your state, city, or county organization—or with the American Bar Association—to find out when seminars or workshops will be offered and on what specific topics. Computer workshops and seminars are not just for the technologically astute; even the novice can benefit from this type of meeting.

User Groups

User groups come in two varieties: specific and generic. Specific groups deal with one particular product, such as WordPerfect. I have attended meetings of WordPerfect users in several cities and have found that those attending these meetings have the same common goal: to get the most out of the product. You can gain invaluable information from both knowledgeable members attending these meetings and WordPerfect personnel. You will pick up tips from both groups that can help make your tasks easier.

Generic groups include groups formed by IBM computer users, Macintosh users, and others. Such groups often meet on a monthly basis and discuss different software application packages that operate on personal computers. Usually, vendors attend these meetings and give away software to the groups for their use. Although the group's interests may not be the same as yours, you will not know until you attend a meeting or two.

Bar associations are beginning to sponsor special interest groups that exchange information. In addition, a number of state bar association meetings now address special topics at the end of each meeting. These topics may include vendor displays of new computer products and programs relating to law-office management, litigation, and so on.

Using the Internet

With the explosion of the Internet, we could hardly overlook this wonderful and powerful communication tool. The amount of information that is now available to us worldwide is unbelievable and overwhelming. This tool can be used to research products and software, and even to gain access to online legal-research services such as Westlaw® and Lexis® via the Web. Often, attorneys access listservs for the purpose of exchanging information on a legal issue or a new technology tool available in the marketplace.

Be aware of the hazards as well as the benefits of using the Internet, however. One such potentially hazardous area might be using the Internet for transferring documents. Paralegals must keep their skills current on encryption software so they will be able to take advantage of sending information and documents to clients, other attorneys, medical facilities, and so on without the danger of a "surfer" picking up the firm's confidential material. There are paralegal listservs that allow paralegals and legal assistants across the world to share information.

Software Demonstrations

When a new software product piques your interest, you will not want to purchase it without having first had an opportunity to explore its capabilities and how it can be applied to your firm's needs. One way of evaluating new software is by contacting the vendor and requesting a demonstration by a local dealer. You might also request from the vendor the names of some other firms in your area using the product. Then make some telephone calls to those firms to see if they might be willing to discuss with you the advantages and disadvantages of the product. Usually, people are anxious to tell you about the problems they have experienced—which would be most helpful for you.

You can also ask the vendor for a demonstration diskette with supporting literature. Demonstration diskettes are usually very simple to use and very informative. Others in your firm can also view them and help in the evaluating process. Literature is always helpful because it will give you the hardware requirements of the program, such as how much space will be needed on the hard drive and how much internal memory is required for the program to run smoothly. The down side of demonstration diskettes is that you may receive an abbreviated version of the software and thus may not be able to see its full capabilities.

Conclusion

Computer technology is an ever-changing field. New kinds of hardware and software seem to appear every day. Keeping current in regard to computer technology can be frustrating, but it is also exciting. Generally, the best way to keep current is by reading computer literature and by communicating with others who share your needs and concerns.

> "Paralegals must learn to tackle the tremendous problems of keeping their computer systems up to date."

change. This section lists selected sites that a legal professional might find helpful. Many of these sites are not otherwise noted in this chapter. Included are references to valuable sites that have been on the Web for some time and have been kept up to date.

Basic Resources

Important Web resources for a legal professional include more than law-related sites. As indicated earlier in this chapter, other important sites can include those of your clients' competitors. Sometimes, however, all that is needed is some basic information: the meaning of a word, the area code for a telephone number, or a local map, for example. Sites with such basic information include those mentioned here.

ALMANACS AND NONLEGAL ENCYCLOPEDIAS. These may be found at a site maintained by Information Please at www.infoplease.com.

AREA CODES. See Search.com at www.555-1212.com/aclookup.html.

CASE CITATION GUIDE. *The Bluebook: A Uniform System of Citation* (discussed in Chapter 14) is accessible online at www.law.cornell.edu/citation/citation/table.html.

DICTIONARIES. "WWWebster Dictionary" (Merriam-Webster, Inc.) provides an online dictionary at www.m-w.com/netdict.htm. (Sites for legal dictionaries, multiple dictionaries, and specialized dictionaries will be mentioned shortly.)

E-MAIL ADDRESSES. E-mail addresses may be located through the Internet @ddress.finder at www.iaf.net.

INTERNET DIRECTORIES. A number of Internet directories, including Yahoo (www.yahoo.com) and Infoseek (www.infoseek.com), which were mentioned earlier in this chapter, are well known. Other Internet directories include "E-Map: The Electronic Map to the Internet" at www.e-map.com. A site titled "Librarians' Index to the Internet" is at sunsite.berkeley.edu/internetindex. The Magellan Internet Guide is online at www.mckinley.com. Another useful directory is Webcrawler at Webcrawler.com.

INTERNET SEARCH TOOLS. Inference Find will organize your results by type of Web site—for example, commercial site, nonprofit site, and so on—at www.inference.com/infind. Northern Light at www.nlsearch.com will also categorize your search results by type of Web site. SavvySearch is a meta search engine at www.savysearch.com.

INTERNET SERVICE PROVIDERS. To locate an Internet service provider, see the site ISP Finder at www.ispfinder.com. Another source for the names of providers is the "Internet Access Providers Meta-List" at www.herbison.com/herbison/iap_meta_list.html. The commercial service America Online can be accessed at www.aol.com.

LEGAL DICTIONARIES. Black's Corporation Law Dictionary is online at www.alaska.net/~winter/black_law_dictionary.html. There is a European law dictionary at www2.echo.lu/edic/. The 'Lectric Law Library provides a dictionary of legal terms at www.lectlaw.com/da.htm. There is a "plain language" legal dictionary titled "WWLIA Legal Dictionary" at www.wwlia.org/diction.htm.

> ## ETHICAL CONCERN
> ### Finding Ethical Opinions on the Web
>
> Paralegals can provide a valuable service to their employers by knowing how to access online the ethical opinions issued by the American Bar Association (ABA) or state bar associations. For example, suppose that your supervising attorney is defending a client in court, and the attorney learns that the client has given testimony that the attorney knows is false. What is the attorney's ethical responsibility in this situation? Should the attorney disclose the client's perjury to the court? Would this be a violation of the attorney-client privilege? Or suppose that the attorney learns that the client intends to testify falsely in court. Must the attorney inform the court of the client's intention? In these situations, the attorney may ask you to find out if the state bar association or the ABA has issued an ethical opinion on this issue. You can find this information quickly by going online and accessing www.abanet.org/cpr/ethicopinions.html, which is the page at the ABA's Web site where it posts summaries of its ethical opinions. To find ethical opinions issued by state bar associations, go to www.legalethics/map.htm and select "states" under the "EthicSites" heading in the index. When the link opens, click on your state.

LEGAL ETHICS. One of the best sites on the Internet to find information on legal ethics, including articles dealing with ethical issues and ethical opinions issued by the American Bar Association (ABA) and state bar associations, is www.legalethics.com, a site maintained by Internet Legal Services. (You can also access the ABA or a state bar association through the Web sites given in the margins of Chapters 1 and 3. For Web sites concerning paralegal ethics, see Chapter 3.)

LIBRARY CATALOGUES. For lists of links to the catalogues of libraries that may be accessed online, consult Yahoo's Library Collection at www.yahoo.com/Reference/Libraries. The Library of Congress offers a collection of links to other libraries' catalogues at lcWeb.loc.gov/z3950/gateway.html. For a list of the catalogues of law libraries that may be available, see "Law Library Links" at law.house.gov/114.htm.

MAPS. U.S. Street Maps is a site that provides what its name implies at www.mapblast.com. Another useful site is MapQuest at www.mapquest.com. See also World Maps at www.lib.utexas.edu/Libs/PCL/Map_collection/Map_collection.html.

MULTIPLE DICTIONARIES. On-Line Dictionaries includes links to more than 500 dictionaries in more than 140 languages at www.facstaff.bucknell.edu/rbeard/diction.html.

SPECIALIZED DICTIONARIES. One Look at www.onelook.com offers an engine that searches hundreds of dictionaries focused on such special topics as business, medicine, science, technology, and the Internet.

TELEPHONE DIRECTORIES. All U.S. telephone books are online at Switchboard at www.switchboard.com. These books are also available at www.555-1212.com. A directory of toll-free numbers can be found at "AT&T Toll-Free Internet Directory" at www.tollfree.att.net/dir800.

THESAURI. The WWWebster Dictionary site, produced by Merriam-Webster, Inc., includes a thesaurus at www.m-w.com/dictionary.htm. Roget's Thesaurus is accessible at online sites, including Web.cs.city.ac.uk/text/roget/thesaurus.html.

ZIP CODES. For zip codes, see the U.S. Postal Service site at www.usps.gov/ncsc/lookups/lookup_zip+4.html.

University Sites

Many universities, colleges, law schools, and other academic institutions are dedicated to making the Internet and its related technology an essential part of professional research. Their Web sites are often good points from which to start because in general they provide updated material and links to other resources. These sites include those discussed in the following subsections.

LAW-RELATED STARTING POINTS. The Legal Information Institute at Cornell Law School is a good starting place for online legal research. The URL is www.law.cornell.edu. This site includes many United States Supreme Court decisions (often within hours of their release) and links to many other law-related sites and services.

Another good site is the World Wide Web Virtual Law Library maintained by the Indiana University School of Law at www.law.indiana.edu/law/v-lib/lawindex.html. This is a comprehensive, up-to-date, subject index of law-related topics.

LawLists, a site produced at the University of Chicago, is online at www.lib.uchicago.edu/~llou/lawlists/info.html. This site contains an extensive listing of law-related discussion groups, including legal listservs.

Meta-Index for Legal Research at Georgia State University College of Law (gsulaw.gsu.edu/metaindex) enables a researcher to run a search in several Web sites' internal search tools simultaneously.

WashLaw WEB at www.washlaw.edu is produced by Washburn University. This site includes a comprehensive collection of links to legal resources on the Web.

Northwestern University, at Oyez Oyez Oyez: A Supreme Court Database (court.it-services.nwu.edu/oyez), provides digital audio (RealAudio) of the oral arguments in many important United States Supreme Court cases, as well as recordings of some of the announcements of the Court's opinions.

GOVERNMENT RESOURCES LISTINGS. The site of the Documents Center of the University of Michigan Library is a reference point for local, state, federal, foreign, and international law resources on the Web. The URL is www.lib.umich.edu/libhome/Documents.center/index.html. This site is one of the most comprehensive lists of links to government documents on the Web, with descriptions of what is included at each link.

LAW-RELATED DISCUSSION GROUPS. To receive information about new and updated resources related to the law, subscribe to LAWSRC-L by sending an e-mail note to mailto:listserve@listserve.law.cornell.edu. In the note, state, "subscribe LAWSRC-L <your name>."

NET-LAWYERS is a discussion group that involves primarily practicing attorneys in how to use the Internet. To subscribe, send an e-mail message to mailto:net-lawyers-request@Webcom.com. In the message, state, "subscribe NET-LAWYERS <your name>."

WEB SITE EVALUATIONS. Questions to use when considering the reliability and accuracy of a particular Web site are listed at a site titled "Ten Cs for Evaluating Internet Resources." The URL is **www.uwec.edu/Admin/Library/10cs.html**.

Questions are also listed at "Thinking Critically about World Wide Web Resources." The URL for this site is **www.library.ucla.edu/libraries/college/instruct/web/critical.htm**.

Government Sites

The government—the federal government, in particular—provides many excellent resources online. Nearly every federal agency has its own Web site. The following are some of the most useful sites for a paralegal.

LAW-RELATED STARTING POINTS. The House of Representatives Library at **www.house.gov** is one of the best government-supported sources of material on the Web. This site contains the full text of pending legislation and congressional testimony. The "Law Library" section contains a wealth of legal resources. The Library of Congress's THOMAS site (**thomas.loc.gov**) duplicates some of the House site's materials, but it does not include the "Law Library."

BUSINESS AND ECONOMIC INFORMATION. The federal Department of Commerce, at **www.doc.gov**, provides a wealth of business and economic statistical data and other information. Some of it is available only for a fee. There are links to other government agencies' sites, including the home page of the U.S. Patent and Trademark Office.

INFORMATION ABOUT PUBLIC COMPANIES. As mentioned earlier, the EDGAR database of the Securities and Exchange Commission (at **www.sec.gov/edgarhp.htm**) contains public companies' electronic filings of documents and forms that the commission requires. This is one of the best resources on the Web for information about public companies.

GOVERNMENT PUBLICATIONS. GPO Access is the title of the Government Printing Office's database. This database contains the full text of the *Code of Federal Regulations,* the *Congressional Record,* the *Federal Register,* all versions of all bills introduced in Congress, the current edition of the *United States Government Manual,* the *United States Code,* and other government publications. The URL for this site is **www.access.gpo.gov/su_docs/index.html**.

DISCUSSION GROUP. To learn about new government sources that appear on the Web, subscribe to GOVDOC-L. Send a message to *mailto:listserv@psuvm.psu.edu* or *mailto:listserv@psuvm.bitnet*. The message should read "subscribe GOVDOC-L <your name>."

Sites for Associations and Organizations

The following are some online databases that catalogue associations, professional organizations, and nonprofit organizations.

ASSOCIATIONS. Associations Online includes Web links to more than five hundred associations divided into categories. The address is **www.ipl.org/ref/AON**.

Yahoo's directory includes a list of professional associations at **www.yahoo.com/Business_and_Economy/Organizations/Professional**.

PROFESSIONAL ORGANIZATIONS.   Professional organizations indexed according to business category (accounting, banking, law, and so on) can be found at www.nvst.com/rsrc/proforg.htm. (For Web sites for bar associations and paralegal organizations, see Chapters 1 and 3.)

NONPROFIT ORGANIZATIONS.   More than one million nonprofit organizations are included in a database maintained by the Internet Nonprofit Center at www.nonprofits.org. This site includes links to the Web pages of many nonprofit organizations.

Free Commercial Sites

Commercial sites are Web pages that are maintained or supported by for-profit organizations (as opposed to academic institutions, the government, and nonprofit organizations). Some commercial sites, such as Westlaw® and Lexis®, are fee-based, or pay, commercial sites. Other sites pay for themselves with on-site advertising. These are free commercial sites. Free commercial sites that may be of value to a legal professional include those discussed next.

ALL-PURPOSE STARTING POINTS.   Yahoo organizes, categorizes, and subdivides the most comprehensive list of URLs on the Web. New Web addresses are added at the rate of hundreds per day. Yahoo's address is www.yahoo.com.

Internet orientation, Internet tools, and Internet guides are the subjects of the Internet Web Text Index at www.december.com/Web/text/index.html.

A collection of references to various subject guides can be found at the Argus Clearinghouse site at www.clearinghouse.net/searching/index.html.

LAW-RELATED STARTING POINTS.   The West Legal Studies site (www.westlegalstudies.com) is a paralegal resource center. The site provides access to resources for professionals, students, and instructors, including links to nearly one thousand legal and paralegal information Web sites.

Another West site with a similar name—West Legal Studies Resource Center—is at www.westbuslaw.com. This site includes daily law highlights, an overview of the U.S. court system, study aids for students, links to a law dictionary and a lawyers' directory, and more.

The "Internet Legal Resource Guide," at www.ilrg.com, is an index of approximately four thousand law-related Web sites, categorized by topic. The site also includes the "LawRunner: A Legal Research Tool," which is preprogrammed to run your search terms in templates across as many as thirty million Web pages.

"The Legal List" at www.lcp.com/The-Legal-List/TLL-home is both a guide to research on the Web and a good starting point with links to other online resources.

The producers of the periodical *legal.online* offer links at their site at www.legalonline.com to legal resources on the Web that the producers find to be particularly useful. These resources include government sites, as well as sites maintained by libraries, law schools, law firms, private companies, and others.

Law-related search engines are linked at "Virtual Legal Search Engines," a site produced by Virtual Search Engines, at www.dreamscape.com/frankvad/search.legal.html. This site also includes a number of basic references (dictionaries, for example) and links to search engines for other topics.

Thousands of law-related materials and products are available through the 'Lectric Law Library at www.lectlaw.com. Most of the information files are not links to other sites but are actually at this site, with plain text and simple graphics

EXHIBIT 15.10
The Home Page of the 'Lectric Law Library

Reprinted with permission. Contact http://www.LectLaw.com or staff@LectLaw.com.

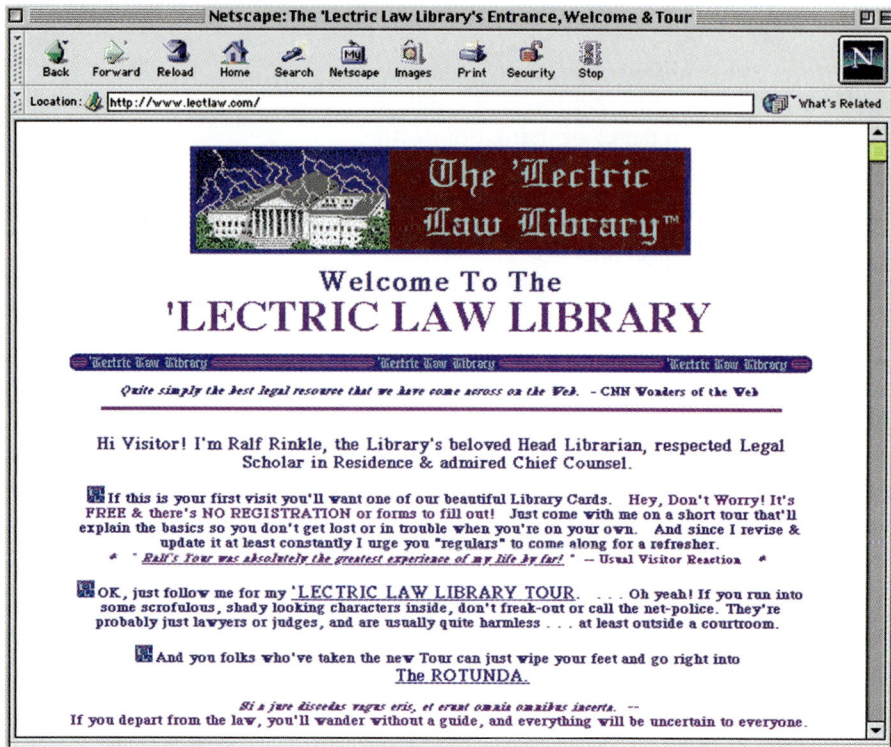

a) Home page

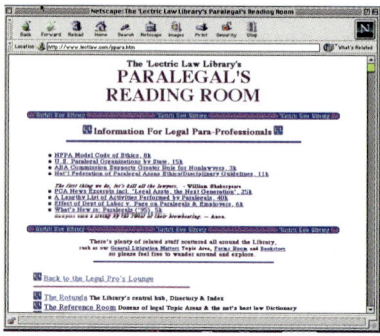

b) "Paralegal's Reading Room" in "The Rotunda"

and without frames. Most of the larger items are compressed for downloading. Also included are legal forms and a law dictionary. An illustration of the home page of the 'Lectric Law Library is in Exhibit 15.10.

"Law Library Resource Xchange" (LLRX), at www.llrx.com, provides links to a number of resource sites on the net, ranging from legal research to library products and services. This site, which is maintained by Law Library Resource Xchange, L.L.C., includes timely and updated articles relating to research and library topics.

MEDIA DIRECTORY. The American Journalism Review site contains more than eight thousand links to the online pages of newspapers, magazines, and other media, at www.newslink.org/menu.html.

Today's Professional Paralegal

Locating Guardians and Wards

Patrick Mitchell works as a legal assistant for a sole practitioner, Anne Urso. Anne takes probate court assignments in which the court appoints her *guardian ad litem*. (A *guardian ad litem* is a special guardian appointed by a court to protect the interests of minors or incapacitated persons in legal proceedings.) This requires Anne to determine whether someone who had previously been appointed as a legal guardian for an incapacitated person needs to continue on as guardian. In order to make this determination, Anne must visit the ward and meet with the guardian.

Today, Anne has received an envelope in the mail appointing her *guardian ad litem* in five cases. The paperwork that comes from the court contains the names and addresses of both the guardian and the ward. Anne knows from experience that the court's records are often out of date and that this information needs to be updated.

Anne assigns the task of locating the guardians and wards to Patrick. He will call them first to see if the information from the court is accurate and to set up a meeting between them and either Anne or himself. The forms have to be submitted to the court within two weeks of their receipt by Anne, which is a quick turnaround time, especially in light of Anne's case load. Patrick calls the ward and the guardian on the first sheet and finds that their telephone numbers have been disconnected. He sets this sheet aside and calls the people listed on the next sheet. He succeeds in contacting the guardian and learns that the ward, an eighty-five-year-old man, Mr. Ahern, died almost a year ago. Patrick continues calling the guardians and wards listed on the sheets. He is able to contact the next three and sets up appointments with them.

Now Patrick must locate the guardian and the ward from the first sheet. He decides that the fastest way to do this is to use a people locator on the Internet. From past experience, Patrick is familiar with a number of reliable Web sites. These sites include KnowX, Bigfoot, and MapQuest. He accesses www.bigfoot.com. He enters the name of the ward, Thomas Ford, and the address, 1111 Three Mile Drive, Detroit, Michigan, and clicks on "Search." Within a few seconds, the computer retrieves a telephone number and an address for Mr. Ford. The telephone number is different from the one that was on the court's forms. Patrick runs another search for the guardian and turns up a new telephone number and address for him as well. Patrick then calls the guardian and the ward and schedules an appointment to meet with them.

Patrick then goes online to the Web site www.knowx.com to verify the death records of the second ward, Mr. Ahern. Using Mr. Ahern's Social Security number, he is able to access these records and print out a copy to include with his report. Patrick places a copy in the file.

Next, Patrick needs to use a mapping Web site to create maps for, and driving directions to, the five different locations to which he and Anne will need to go. Patrick accesses www.mapquest.com. He enters the address of the office and then the address of the first ward. He clicks on "Search," and a map with driving directions soon appears on the screen. Patrick prints out the maps with driving directions and places them in the file. Having finished this project, he then turns to his next task.

Key Terms and Concepts

Auto-Cite 544
commercial online services 550
computer-assisted legal research (CALR) 541
file transfer protocol (ftp) 549
home page 549
hypertext transfer protocol (http) 549
Internet service provider (ISP) 551
KeyCite 544
listserv list 561
mirror site 562
newsgroup (usenet group) 561
World Wide Web 549

Chapter Summary

1. Computer-assisted legal research often involves using CD-ROMs. An advantage of using legal resources in CD-ROM format is that they are less costly to purchase and require less physical space than printed resources do. CD-ROMs can also be easily transported, which means they can be used while traveling, in the courtroom, or anywhere outside the office. The major disadvantage of using CD-ROMs in legal research is that they, like their printed equivalents, eventually become outdated.

2. For serious legal research, legal professionals often use online commercial legal-research services, particularly Lexis® and Westlaw®. Subscribers to these fee-based services can access the services' databases through the use of proprietary software and a modem connection via a telephone line, or via the Internet. Both Lexis® and Westlaw® provide their users with access to an extensive collection of legal, business, and other resources. Using these fee-paid legal services, paralegals can access specific documents, check citations, update the law, and search hundreds of databases. Both Lexis® and Westlaw® allow users to search databases with queries using "natural language" or "terms and connectors."

3. Today's legal professionals, including paralegals, can access a vast amount of information using the Internet, which is a global communication network of interconnected computers. Many online resources are available free, while others charge a fee for accessing their databases. The Internet tools most commonly used by paralegals include uniform resource locators (URLs), which are Internet "addresses"; e-mail, which transmits messages via the Internet to special e-mail addresses; file transfer protocol (ftp), which is a basic interface that connects computers and allows files to be transferred from one computer to another; and the World Wide Web, which is a data service on the Internet that is accessed through a browser.

4. The Internet is accessed through gateways, such as America Online or one of numerous Internet service providers. To navigate the Internet, which has no "card catalogue" as a library does, one must use browsers (software such as Microsoft Explorer or Netscape Navigator that allows a computer to roam the Web); guides and directories (menus of topics at various Web sites); and search engines (such as Alta Vista or Excite) that scan the Web for certain key words or concepts. Meta search engines run searches on more than one search engine simultaneously and thus are the best tools for searching the most Web space possible.

5. Before beginning an online research session, you should first decide whether the Internet is the right tool for your research project. At this time, there are insufficient primary and secondary legal sources on the Web to conduct in-depth legal research. For peripheral research, however, such as locating people or public records, the Internet offers an abundance of information. To avoid wasting time, you should also define what you are seeking and determine which sources are most likely to lead you to the desired results.

6. Once online, you can use various search tools and other resources (such as listservs and newsgroups) to locate data and information relevant to your topic. Often, researchers need to browse the Web (browse through the links provided at a site, which often provide links to other sites, and so on) for a time before finding a site that is particularly relevant and useful. In evaluating your research results, it is especially important to consider the reliability of any information obtained online. To update results, you can

access news sites online to see if there have been articles or press releases concerning a recent development in the area you are researching.

7. Paralegals often engage in online research to locate information about persons and to investigate companies. Sometimes, a person can be located through a broad search of the Web using a search engine such as Infoseek. Narrow searches can be conducted by accessing—for free or for a fee—specialized databases, such as compilations of physicians, lawyers, or expert witnesses. Searches for persons may also be conducted based on specific characteristics, such as professional status or campaign contributions. There are numerous online sites that contain information about both private and public companies.

8. Basic resources that you can find on the Web include almanacs, nonlegal encyclopedias, area codes, a case citation guide, dictionaries, e-mail addresses, information about the Internet, Internet directories, Internet search tools, Internet service providers, legal dictionaries, library catalogues, maps, multiple dictionaries, specialized dictionaries, telephone directories, thesauri, and zip codes. Various university and government sites offer links to a number of primary and secondary legal sources. There are also online databases that catalogue associations, professional organizations, and nonprofit organizations, as well as several free commercial sites that serve as all-purpose starting points for online research.

QUESTIONS FOR REVIEW

1. What are some of the advantages and disadvantages of using legal resources in CD-ROM format when conducting legal research?

2. What is Westlaw®? What is Lexis®? How do legal professionals access these services? What kind of legal sources do these services make available to users?

3. How can these services be used to update the law? Describe two ways in which you can search databases on Lexis® and Westlaw®.

4. What is the difference between the Internet and the World Wide Web? Name and define four useful Internet tools.

5. Define and give two examples of an Internet gateway. What is a browser? What are Internet guides and directories?

6. What should you do before going online to conduct a research session? Is the Internet a good research tool for serious legal research? Why or why not?

7. What are some starting points when doing online research? How can one discover what resources are available on the Web? Why is it important to evaluate the reliability of information found online and to update the results of an Internet research session?

8. What online search techniques could you use when trying to find information on a specific person? How would you go about finding company names and addresses in an Internet search?

9. List five basic, nonlegal resources that can be accessed via the Internet. Name five universities whose law schools or legal institutes provide extensive Internet legal libraries or links to Internet legal resources.

10. What kinds of legal resources can be obtained at various government sites? What resources or search tools can be found at sites for associations and organizations and at free commercial sites?

ETHICAL QUESTIONS

1. Janice, a paralegal in a labor law-firm, joins a listserv. It is called AWD@counterpoint.com. It is a discussion group about the Americans with Disabilities Act (ADA) of 1990 and related laws. Another member of the group posts a question about what companies the ADA applies to and whether his company is subject to the law. Janice knows the answer and could answer it. Should Janice answer the question? Why or why not?

2. The partners in the law firm of Dewey & Howe learn about a plane crash in the morning newspaper. They instruct their legal assistant to contact all of the families of the victims via e-mail to see if they are interested in filing a class-action lawsuit against the airline. Is this type of activity allowed under the ethical rules?

3. The law firm of Smith & Varney decides that it needs a Web page to advertise the law firm's services over

the Internet. They assign the task to paralegal Mark Hampton. Mark develops a Web site for the firm. The site contains a biography of each attorney, e-mail addresses for all attorneys, and Web links to helpful and related practice areas. Is this type of Web site allowable advertising under the ethical rules?

4. Samantha, a paralegal, runs a credit check on a client over the Internet without using an encryption program. The client's Visa number is intercepted, and unauthorized charges of $4,320.00 are charged on the client's account. What kind of ethical problems result?

Practice Questions and Assignments

1. Using the material presented in the chapter on Westlaw®, answer the following questions:
   a. How would you gain access to Westlaw®?
   b. How would you find the case *Del Monte Dunes at Monterey, Ltd. v. City of Monterey*, 95 F.3d 1422 (9th Cir. 1996)? How would you find out whether the holding in that case is still good law?
   c. What specific steps would you take to find the database of decisions made by courts in your state?

2. Suppose that one of your clients is suing a restaurant that served her tainted oysters. The oysters contained a bacteria that caused the client to suffer serious health injuries, including permanent nerve damage. What databases would you search on Westlaw® to find out whether there are any other cases involving this issue or a similar issue? How would you draft a query in natural language to retrieve these cases from the selected database(s)? To draft a query using terms and connectors, what key terms would you use?

3. Explain the parts of the following URL:

   http://www.urisko.edu

4. Create your own URL, using your name to create a Web site for commercial purposes.

5. Using the material presented in the chapter, make a list of the Web sites that you would search to find the name, address, and telephone number of a particular company. Would you search the same sites for more detailed information? If not, where would you search? Does it make a difference whether the company is public or private? If so, where would you search for information on public companies? Where would you search for information on private companies?

6. Assume that the legal researchers in the situations described below all have access to an excellent law library, to Westlaw® or Lexis®, and to the Internet. Which of these three research sources or tools would you advise the legal professional to use for his or her particular research need? Why?
   a. Matthew, a paralegal, needs to find out if a case cited in a legal motion he is drafting is still good law.
   b. Cindy, an attorney, needs to locate a psychiatric expert witness.
   c. Robert, a paralegal, has been asked to locate a statutory provision; he needs to make sure that the result is up to date.
   d. Tom, a paralegal, needs to locate a witness to a car accident.
   e. Megan, a paralegal, needs to find an heir who is to inherit $500,000 under her uncle's will.

Questions for Critical Analysis

1. Why would an attorney invest in a legal encyclopedia contained on a CD-ROM instead of a printed set of encyclopedias? In conducting legal research, would you prefer to use legal sources in CD-ROM format rather than printed legal sources? Why or why not?

2. Legal professionals must pay a significant fee to access legal databases provided by commercial services such as Westlaw® and Lexis®. Why would it ever be preferable to use these fee-based services for research instead of the Internet, which offers "free" access to numerous online legal and other resources?

3. What are some advantages of using Westlaw® or Lexis® when doing legal research rather than using the printed resources in a law library? Are there any disadvantages?

4. What is the Internet? What is the World Wide Web? Are they different entities, or are these terms synonyms for the same entity?
5. The Internet offers vast resources and provides these resources instantly. What are the advantages of the Internet? Are there any disadvantages? If so, what are they?
6. What impact does the Internet have on how legal professionals perform their work? What impact does it have on society as a whole? Is the impact positive or negative, or both?
7. Chat rooms provide Internet users with the ability to communicate in "real time." How does "real time" communication compare to talking on the telephone? How does it compare to writing letters or sending e-mail messages? Which method of communication do you prefer? Why?
8. What are the three basic types of gateways to the Internet? Which one is the most useful? Which one is the most cost effective? Which one is best suited for a law firm? Why?
9. What is the difference between a gateway to the Internet and a browser? How do directories and search engines differ?
10. Do you believe that the Internet will be the sole tool used by legal researchers in the future? Why or why not?

PROJECTS

1. Most colleges and universities provide Internet access to students. Find out if the school you attend provides such access. If it does, find out which gateway to the Internet is used and which Web browser. Also, find out if it is possible for students to have an e-mail account at the school.
2. Do a research project on how and why the Internet was created. Write a two-page paper summarizing the results of your research.
3. Using Corel WordPerfect 8.1, create a Web page for yourself, your employer, or your paralegal program. What information needs to be included?
4. Contact the West Group sales representative for your area. Request information on West's CD-ROM research products. Write a one-page paper describing what is available, how much the CD-ROM products cost, and how they are updated.

USING INTERNET RESOURCES

1. In this chapter, you have learned many tips about how to use the Internet to do legal research and to find useful information relating to legal work. For an online article also dealing with legal research using the Internet, go to

   www.ali-aba.org/aliaba/intro.htm.

   Read through this guide to Internet research, and then answer the following questions:
   a. What does the article say about the reliability of information available on the Web?
   b. In the author's opinion, which search engine was the "hands-down winner" in his sample search? Why?
   c. Briefly summarize the author's recommendations on how to proceed with a search on a particular topic (see "A Search Example" at the end of the article).

2. The American Bar Association's Web site contains helpful information on legal-research sources on the Internet. Access the Web site at

   www.abanet.org/lpm/writing/research.html

   Answer the following questions about the research sources available online:
   a. What categories of research materials are available?
   b. Go to the "Legal Resources" category. Click on the "Johns Hopkins University Law Collection." How is the collection organized?
   c. Click on the "Back" button. Select the "Legal Information Institute at Cornell Law School." How does it compare to the Johns Hopkins University collection? How is it organized? Which legal-research Web site would you prefer to use? Why?

CHAPTER 16

LEGAL ANALYSIS AND WRITING

Chapter Outline

▣ INTRODUCTION ▣ ANALYZING CASE LAW ▣ ANALYZING STATUTORY LAW
▣ LEGAL WRITING—THE PRELIMINARIES ▣ THE IMPORTANCE OF GOOD WRITING SKILLS ▣ PLEADINGS AND DISCOVERY ▣ GENERAL LEGAL CORRESPONDENCE
▣ THE INTERNAL MEMORANDUM ▣ THE APPELLATE BRIEF

After completing this chapter, you will know:

- How to read and analyze case law.
- Some techniques for reading statutory law and guidelines traditionally used for interpreting statutory law.
- What factors you should consider before undertaking a legal-writing assignment.
- What factors you should consider when drafting a legal document.
- The purpose and format of the most common types of legal letters.
- How to prepare a legal memorandum.
- How to prepare an appellate brief.

CHAPTER 16 Legal Analysis and Writing

INTRODUCTION

To a certain extent, legal research, analysis, and writing are all part of the same process. In Chapters 14 and 15, we looked primarily at the various types of resources available to the legal researcher and how to locate them. This chapter focuses on how to analyze those resources and communicate the research results in writing. Much legal writing, however, is not directly related to the research process. As a paralegal, your typical day will involve other types of writing responsibilities as well. You will be expected to know how to draft letters to clients or opposing counsel, internal memos, documents to be submitted to court clerks or judges in regard to pending lawsuits, and a variety of other documents.

This chapter opens with some guidelines on how to analyze legal sources, including case law, statutory law, and administrative law. The remainder of the chapter, which deals with legal writing, includes suggestions on how you can learn to write effectively and a description of the types and formats of legal documents commonly prepared by paralegals. When a case is appealed to a higher court, attorneys for both parties submit appellate briefs to the court. An *appellate brief* is an attorney's written argument setting forth the legal reasons why the court should rule in favor of the attorney's client. For those paralegals interested in learning how to draft appellate briefs, we conclude the chapter with a special section on this topic.

ANALYZING CASE LAW

As mentioned, *case law* is that body of law created by the decisions of court judges. Attorneys may rely heavily on case law to support a given position or argument. If you can find a *case on point* or a *case on "all fours,"*[1] that case may serve as a mandatory authority to support your supervising attorney's argument in a case presently being litigated.

One of the difficulties all legal professionals face in analyzing case law is the sheer length and complexity of some court opinions. While certain court opinions may be only two or three pages long, others can occupy hundreds of pages. Understanding the components of a case—that is, the basic format in which cases are presented—can simplify your task of reading and analyzing case law. You will find that over time, as you acquire experience, case analysis becomes easier.

The Components of a Case

Reported cases contain much more than just the court's decision. Cases have many different parts, and you should understand why each part is there and what information it communicates. The annotations on the sample court case shown in foldout Exhibit 16.1 indicate the various components of a case.

The case presented in Exhibit 16.1 is an actual case that was decided by the United States Supreme Court in 1998. The lawsuit was initiated by Sidney Abbott, who was infected with the human immunodeficiency virus (HIV), against a dentist who refused to treat Abbott—fill a cavity—in the dental office. (The dentist offered to fill the cavity at the hospital, but Abbott refused.) In her suit, Abbott claimed that the dentist had violated the Americans with Disabilities Act (ADA) of 1990, which mandates the accommodation of persons with disabilities.

---

1. Recall from Chapter 14 that a case on point is a previous case having fact patterns and issues similar to the case being litigated. A case on "all fours" has nearly identical fact patterns and issues.

Important sections, terms, and phrases in the case are defined or discussed in the margins. You will note also that triple asterisks (* * *) and quadruple asterisks (* * * *) frequently appear in the exhibit. The triple asterisks indicate that we have deleted a few words or sentences from the opinion for the sake of readability or brevity. Quadruple asterisks mean that an entire paragraph (or more) has been omitted. Also, when the opinion cites another case or legal source, the citation to the referenced case or source has been omitted to save space and to improve readability.

We discuss below the various components of a case. As you read through the descriptions of these components, refer to Exhibit 16.1, which illustrates most of the components discussed below.

CITATION AND CASE TITLE. Typically, the case citation is found just above or below the case title (or *style*). As discussed in Chapter 14, the *citation* indicates the name, volume number, and page number of the reporter series in which the case appears. The case presented in Exhibit 16.1 is a printout of the Westlaw® version of the case, and the parallel citations are to West's *Supreme Court Reporter* and the *Lawyers' Edition of the Supreme Court Reports*. When the parallel citation to the *United States Reports* becomes available, it will be added by Westlaw® as well. (Recall from Chapter 14 that West's *Supreme Court Reporter* and the *Lawyers' Edition of the Supreme Court Reports* are unofficial reporters; the official reporter for cases decided by the United States Supreme Court is the *United States Reports*.) In Exhibit 16.1, the case title immediately follows the citation.

On the Web
If you are interested in reading the entire opinion rendered by the United States Supreme Court in the sample case presented in Exhibit 16.1, you can access the case online at www.findlaw.com. Find the link to Supreme Court decisions, and then, when the link opens, click on "1998 cases." When that link opens, scroll down to *Bragdon v. Abbott* to access the case.

DOCKET NUMBER. The docket number immediately follows the case title. Recall from Chapter 10 that a docket number is assigned by the court clerk when a case is initially filed. The number serves as an identifier for all papers submitted in connection with the case. A case published in a reporter should not be cited by its docket number, but the docket number may serve as a valuable tool in obtaining background information on the case. Cases appearing in slip-opinion form (cases that have been decided but that are not yet published in a reporter—see Chapter 14) are usually identified, filed, and cited by docket number. After publication of the decision, the docket number may continue to serve as an identifier for appellate records and briefs (appellate briefs will be discussed in a later section of this chapter).

DATES ARGUED AND DECIDED. An important component of a case is the date on which it was decided by the court. Usually, the date of the decision immediately follows the docket number. In addition to the date of the court's decision on the matter, the date on which the case was argued before the court (in appellate court cases) may also be included here, as in Exhibit 16.1.

SYLLABUS. Following the docket number is the *syllabus*. As you will recall from Chapter 14, a syllabus is a brief synopsis of the facts of the case, the issues analyzed by the court, and the court's conclusion. In official reporters, the courts usually prepare the syllabi; in unofficial reporters, the publishers of the reporters usually prepare them. The syllabus is often a helpful research tool. It provides a clear overview of the case and points out various legal issues discussed by the court. But always keep in mind the following caution:

> **Reading the syllabus is not a substitute for reading the case.**

HEADNOTES. Often, unofficial reporters, such as those published by West Group, make extensive use of case *headnotes*. As discussed in Chapter 14,

EXHIBIT 16.1
A Sample Court Case

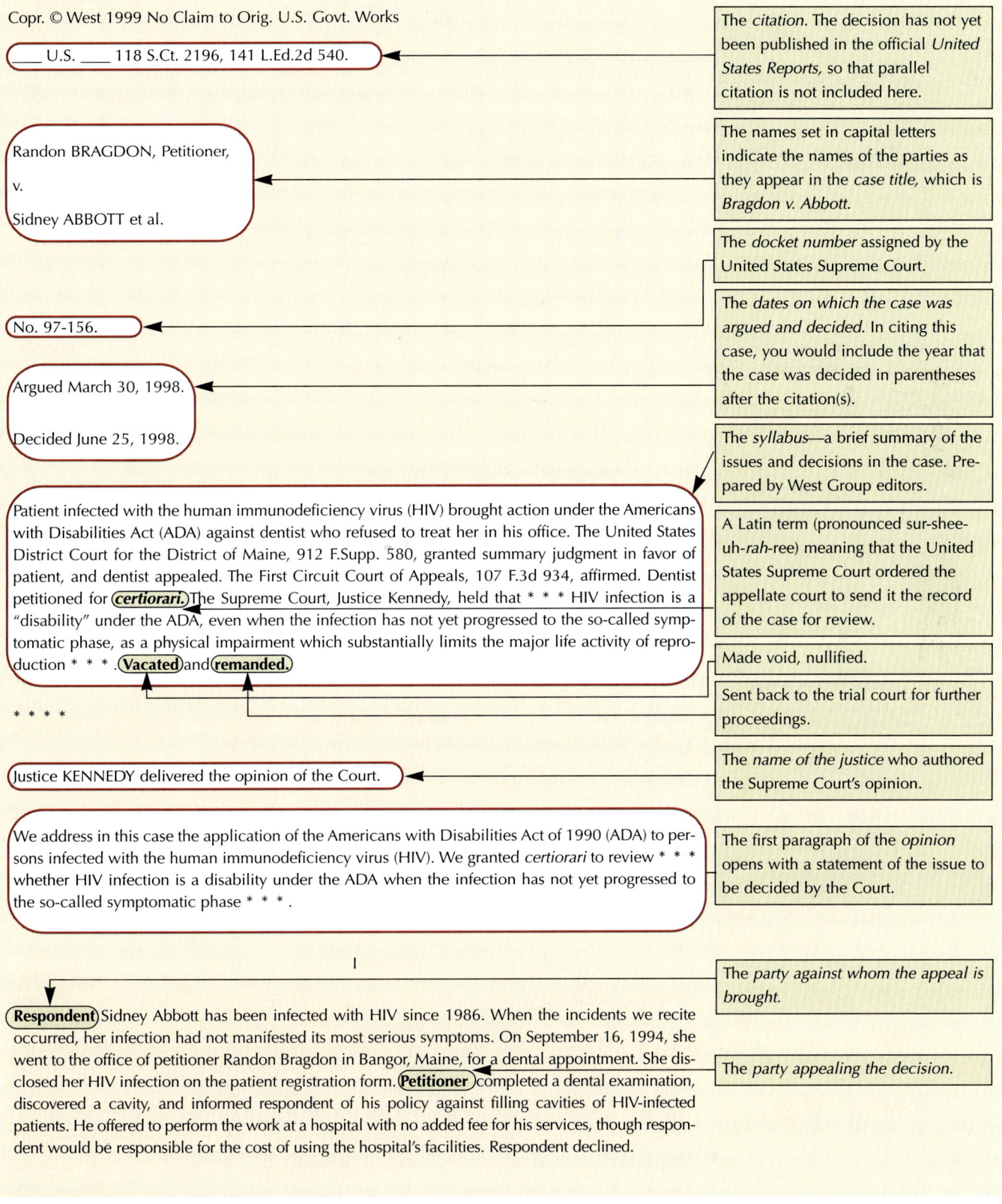

EXHIBIT 16.1
A Sample Court Case

Respondent sued petitioner under * * * the ADA. * * *

* * * *

The Court summarizes the rulings of the lower federal courts on the issue before the court.

* * * The District Court ruled in favor of [Abbott], holding that respondent's HIV infection satisfied the ADA's definition of disability. * * *

The Court of Appeals **affirmed.** It held respondent's HIV infection was a disability under the ADA, even though her infection had not yet progressed to the symptomatic stage. * * *

Confirmed, or ratified.

II

The Court cites the provision of the ADA that directly applies to the issue before the Court.

We * * * review the ruling that respondent's HIV infection constituted a disability under the ADA. The statute defines disability as:

(A) a physical or mental impairment that substantially limits one or more of the major life activities of such individual;

(B) a record of such an impairment; or

(C) being regarded as having such impairment.

We hold respondent's HIV infection was a disability under subsection (A) of the definitional section of the statute. In light of this conclusion, we need not consider the applicability of subsections (B) or (C).

The Court summarizes how it will proceed to analyze the issue.

Our consideration of subsection (A) of the definition proceeds in three steps. First, we consider whether respondent's HIV infection was a physical impairment. Second, we identify the life activity upon which respondent relies (reproduction and child bearing) and determine whether it constitutes a major life activity under the ADA. Third, tying the two statutory phrases together, we ask whether the impairment substantially limited the major life activity. * * *

* * * *

1

The Court begins the first step in its inquiry.

The first step in the inquiry under subsection (A) requires us to determine whether respondent's condition constituted a physical impairment. * * *

* * * *

The Court's conclusion on the first step.

In light of the immediacy with which the virus begins to damage the infected person's white blood cells and the severity of the disease, we hold it is an impairment from the moment of infection. * * * [I]nfection with HIV causes immediate abnormalities in a person's blood, and the infected person's white cell count continues to drop throughout the course of the disease, even when the attack is concentrated in the lymph nodes. In light of these facts, HIV infection must be regarded as a physiological disorder with a constant and detrimental effect on the infected person's hemic and lymphatic systems from the moment of infection. HIV infection satisfies the statutory and regulatory definition of a physical impairment during every stage of the disease.

EXHIBIT 16.1
A Sample Court Case

2

The statute is not operative, and the definition not satisfied, unless the impairment affects a major life activity. Respondent's claim throughout this case has been that the HIV infection placed a substantial limitation on her ability to reproduce and to bear children. Given the pervasive, and invariably fatal, course of the disease, its effect on major life activities of many sorts might have been relevant to our inquiry. * * *

— The Court begins the second step in its inquiry.

From the outset, however, the case has been treated as one in which reproduction was the major life activity limited by the impairment. * * * We ask, then, whether reproduction is a major life activity.

— This is the essential question before the court in the second step of its inquiry.

We have little difficulty concluding that it is. As the Court of Appeals held, "[t]he plain meaning of the word 'major' denotes comparative importance" and "suggest[s] that the touchstone for determining an activity's inclusion under the statutory rubric is its significance." Reproduction falls well within the phrase "major life activity." Reproduction and the sexual dynamics surrounding it are central to the life process itself.

While petitioner concedes the importance of reproduction, he claims that Congress intended the ADA only to cover those aspects of a person's life which have a public, economic, or daily character. The argument founders on the statutory language. Nothing in the definition suggests that activities without a public, economic, or daily dimension may somehow be regarded as so unimportant or insignificant as to fall outside the meaning of the word "major." The breadth of the term confounds the attempt to limit its construction in this manner.

— The Court takes issue with the petitioner's argument.

* * * *

* * * Petitioner advances no credible basis for confining major life activities to those with a public, economic, or daily aspect. In the absence of any reason to reach a contrary conclusion, we agree with the Court of Appeals' determination that reproduction is a major life activity for the purposes of the ADA.

— The Court's conclusion on the second step.

3

The final element of the disability definition in subsection (A) is whether respondent's physical impairment was a substantial limit on the major life activity she asserts. * * *

— The Court begins the third and final step in its inquiry.

Our evaluation of the medical evidence leads us to conclude that respondent's infection substantially limited her ability to reproduce in two independent ways. First, a woman infected with HIV who tries to conceive a child imposes on the man a significant risk of becoming infected. * * * Second, an infected woman risks infecting her child during gestation and childbirth * * *

— The Court's conclusion on the third step.

* * * *

The determination of the Court of Appeals that respondent's HIV infection was a disability under the ADA is affirmed. The judgment is vacated, and the case is remanded for further proceedings consistent with this opinion.

— The Court *summarizes its conclusion and gives its order* in the final portion of the opinion.

It is so ordered.

headnotes are short paragraphs following the general syllabus. They serve to highlight and summarize specific rules of law mentioned in the case. In reporters published by West Group, they are correlated to the comprehensive West key-number system. In Exhibit 16.1, the headnotes were deleted for reasons of space, as were the names of counsel.

NAMES OF COUNSEL. The published report of the case usually contains the names of the lawyers (counsel) representing the parties. The attorneys' names are typically found just following the syllabus (and headnotes, if any).

NAME OF JUDGE OR JUSTICE AUTHORING THE OPINION. The name of the judge or justice who authored the opinion in the case will also be included in the published report of the case, just before the court's opinion (discussed below). In the case presented in Exhibit 16.1, Justice Kennedy of the United States Supreme Court authored the opinion.

In some cases, instead of the name of a judge or justice, the decision will be authored *per curiam* (Latin for "by the court"), which means that the opinion is that of the whole court and not the opinion of any one judge or justice. Sometimes the phrase is used to indicate that the chief justice or presiding judge wrote the opinion. The phrase also may be used for an announcement of a court's disposition of a case that is not accompanied by a written opinion.

OPINION. As you may have noted in previous chapters, the term *opinion* is often used loosely to refer to a court case or decision. In fact, the term has a precise meaning. The formal opinion of the court contains the analysis and decision of the judge or judges that heard and decided the case. Most opinions contain a brief statement of the facts of the case, a summary of the legal issues raised by the facts, and the remedies sought by the parties. In appellate court cases, the court summarizes the errors of the lower court, if any, and the impact of these errors on the case's outcome. The main body of the court's opinion is the application of the law to the particular facts. The court often mentions case precedents, relevant statutes, and administrative rules and regulations to support its reasoning. Additionally, court opinions often contain discussions of policy and other factors that clarify the underlying reason for the court's decision.

When all of the judges unanimously agree in their legal reasoning and their decision, the opinion is deemed a *unanimous* opinion. When the opinion is not unanimous, a *majority* opinion is written, outlining the views of the majority of the judges deciding the case. There may also be a *concurring* opinion or a *dissenting* opinion. (See Chapter 5 for an explanation of these different types of opinions.)

THE COURT'S CONCLUSION. In the opinion, the judges will indicate their conclusion, or decision, on the issue or issues before the court. If several issues are involved, as often happens, there may be a conclusion at the end of the discussion of each issue. Often, at the end of the opinion, the conclusions presented within the opinion will be briefly reiterated and summarized, or, if no conclusions were yet presented, they will be presented in the concluding section of the opinion.

An appellate court also specifies what the *disposition* of a case should be. As discussed in Chapter 11, if the appellate court agrees with a lower court's decision, it will *affirm* that decision, which means that the decision of the lower court remains unchanged. If the appellate court concludes that the lower court erred in its interpretation of the law, the court may *reverse* the lower court's ruling. Sometimes, if an appellate court concludes that further factual findings are necessary or that a case should be retried and a decision made that is consistent with the appellate court's conclusions of law, the appellate court will *remand* the case to the lower court for further proceedings consistent with its opinion. In the sample case presented in Exhibit 16.1, the United States Supreme Court *vacated* (nullified) the lower court's decision and remanded the case.

Analyzing Cases

When you are researching case law, you should identify the components of the case. The syllabus and headnotes are often helpful in giving you an overview of the issues involved. Your main focus, though, should be on the opinion—the words of the court itself.

You will inevitably find that some opinions are easier to understand than others. Some judges write more clearly and logically than others do. You may need to reread a case (or a portion of a case) to understand what is being said, why it is being said at that point in the case, and what the judge's underlying legal reasoning is. Some cases contain several pages describing facts and issues of previous cases and how those cases relate to the one being decided by the court. You might want to reread these discussions several times to distinguish between comments made in the previous case and comments that are being made about the case at bar (before the court).

Often, the judge writing the opinion provides some guideposts, perhaps by indicating sections and subsections within the opinion by numbers, letters, or subtitles. Note that in Exhibit 16.1, Roman numerals are used to divide the opinion into basic sections. Arabic numerals are used to further divide portions of the opinion. Scanning through the opinion for these types of indicators can help orient you to the opinion's format.

In cases that involve dissenting or concurring opinions, you need to make sure that you identify these opinions so that you do not mistake one of them for the majority opinion. Generally, you should scan through the case a time or two to identify its various components and sections and then read the case (or sections of the case) until you understand the facts and procedural history of the case, the issues involved, the applicable law, the legal reasoning of the court, and how the reasoning leads to the court's conclusion on the issue or issues.

In reading and analyzing cases, you should also be able to determine which statements of the court are legally binding and which are not. Only the **holding** (the legal principle to be drawn from the court's decision) is binding. Other views expressed in the opinion are referred to as *dicta* and are not binding in subsequent cases. *Dicta* is the plural of *dictum*. As used here, *dictum* is an abbreviated form of the Latin term *obitur dictum*, which means "a remark by the way." *Dicta* are any statements made by a judge that go beyond the facts of the case or that do not directly relate to the facts of the case or to the resolution of the issue being addressed. *Dicta* include comments used by the court to illustrate an example and statements concerning a rule of law that is not essential to the case at hand. You can probably assume that statements are *dicta* if they begin with "If the facts were different" or "If the plaintiff had . . ." or some other "if/then" phrase.

Holding
The binding legal principle, or precedent, that is drawn from the court's decision in a case.

Dicta
A Latin term referring to nonbinding (nonprecedential) judicial statements that are not directly related to the facts or issues presented in the case and thus not essential to the holding.

Summarizing and Briefing Cases

After you have read and analyzed a case, you may decide that it is on point and that you want to include a reference to it in your legal writing. If so, you will want to summarize in your notes the important facts and issues in the case, as well as

EXHIBIT 16.2
Format for Briefing a Case

> 1. **NAME (TITLE, OR STYLE) OF CASE.** Give the full name of the case.
>
> 2. **CASE CITATION.** Give the full citation for the case, including all parallel citations, the date the case was decided, and the name of the court deciding the case.
>
> 3. **FACTS.** Briefly indicate (a) the reasons for the lawsuit; (b) the identity and arguments of the plaintiff(s) and defendant(s); and (c) if the case was decided by an appellate court, the lower court's opinion on the issues.
>
> 4. **PROCEDURE.** Summarize the judicial history of the case—that is, each court that has heard the case and each court's decision on the matter.
>
> 5. **ISSUE.** Concisely phrase the essential legal issue(s) before the court.
>
> 6. **DECISION.** Indicate here the court's decision on the issue(s).
>
> 7. **RATIONALE.** Summarize as briefly as possible the legal reasoning on which the court based its decision.
>
> 8. **HOLDING.** State the rule (or rules) of law for which the case stands.

Briefing a Case
Summarizing a case. A typical case brief will indicate the case title and citation and then briefly state the factual background and procedural history of the case, the issue or issues raised in the case, the court's decision, the applicable rule of law and the legal reasoning on which the decision is based, and conclusions or notes concerning the case made by the one briefing it.

the court's decision, or holding, and the reasoning used by the court. This is called **briefing a case**.[2]

There is a fairly standard format you can use when you brief any court case. Although the format may vary, typically it presents the essentials of the case under headings such as those illustrated and described in Exhibit 16.2. As you can see in the exhibit, in a case brief, the name and citation for the case are given first. Then, the background and facts leading up to the lawsuit are included. Also, when more than one issue is involved in a case, the issues are combined in the *Issue* section, the decisions regarding each issue may be combined under the *Decision* section, and so on. Following the *Decision* section, the court's legal reasoning is set forth under the heading *Rationale*. Finally, the *Holding* section sets forth the rule of law for which the case stands. See Exhibit 16.3 on the next page for a briefed version of the sample court case presented in Exhibit 16.1. Depending on the issue you were researching, you would add a conclusion to the brief indicating how the Supreme Court's ruling affected that issue.

Synthesizing Your Research Results

Once you have analyzed and briefed the cases you want to use in support of a legal argument, you need to synthesize your research results. In synthesizing your results, you extract the most important rules of law, issues, and defenses from the cases you have read and analyzed and combine them in such a way that they can be effectively incorporated into whatever legal document you need to draft. You can synthesize your results in three different ways:

- By grouping cases according to their *rules of law*.
- By grouping cases according to their *issues*.
- By grouping cases according to the *defenses* that were raised by the defendants.

For example, assume that you have found several cases in which the court enunciated the following rule of law: an owner of business premises is liable to a

---
2. Note that a *case brief* is not the same is a *legal brief* an attorney submits to a court.

EXHIBIT 16.3
Briefed Version of Sample Court Case

NAME OF CASE Bragdon v. Abbott.

CITATION ___ U.S. ___, 118 S.Ct. 2196, 141 L.Ed.2d 540 (1998).

FACTS Sidney Abbott, who was infected with HIV, went to the office of Randon Bragdon for a dental appointment. Abbott disclosed her HIV infection on the patient registration form. During the examination, Bragdon discovered a cavity. He told Abbott of his policy against filling the cavities of HIV-infected patients in his office. He offered to do it at a hospital with no added fee if Abbott would pay the cost of using the hospital's facilities.

PROCEDURE Abbott declined and filed a suit in a federal district court against Bragdon, alleging in part discrimination under the Americans with Disabilities Act (ADA) on the basis of a disability—her HIV infection. The federal district court granted summary judgment in favor of Abbott, and Bragdon appealed. The U.S. Court of Appeals for the First Circuit affirmed the district court's ruling, and Bragdon appealed to the United States Supreme Court.

ISSUE Is an HIV infection that has not yet progressed to the symptomatic phase a disability under the ADA?

DECISION Yes. The United States Supreme Court agreed with the court of appeals that Abbott's infection met the ADA's definition of a disability. The Court vacated the decision of the court of appeals and remanded the case to the trial court to determine whether Bragdon's actions constituted a reasonable accommodation of Abbott's disability.

RATIONALE The Supreme Court noted that the ADA defines a disability as "a physical impairment * * * that substantially limits one or more of [an individual's] major life activities." The Court then made a three-step inquiry to determine if HIV qualified as a disability under the ADA's definition of that term. First, the Court found that HIV is a physical impairment from the very outset because of its capability of rapidly advancing and affecting the hemic and lymphatic systems. Second, with respect to the "major life activity" requirement of the ADA definition, the Court reasoned that "[t]he plain meaning of the word 'major' denotes comparative importance and suggests that the touchstone is an activity's significance. Reproduction and the sexual dynamics surrounding it are central to the life process itself." As for the "substantially limits" elements, the Court found that an HIV-infected woman's ability to reproduce is substantially limited in two ways: "If she tries to conceive a child, (1) she imposes on her male partner a statistically significant risk of becoming infected; and (2) she risks infecting her child during gestation and childbirth."

HOLDING An HIV infection that has not yet progressed to the symptomatic phase

---

customer who sustained an injury as a result of the store's failure to warn the customer of a dangerous condition on the premises, if the store owner knew or should have known of the condition. You might group the cases you have found under the heading "Liability of Retail Business Owners to Customers."

Similarly, you could group cases under a heading relating more specifically to the issue with which you are directly concerned. You might have a heading such as "slip-and-fall cases" and include the cases that involve such issues under this heading.

Finally, you might arrange the cases under the various defenses that store owners can raise against liability claims. One defense that business owners sometimes raise, for example, is that a dangerous condition was so open and obvious that there was no need to warn customers of it. Another defense might be that the customer knew of a particular risk and deliberately assumed that risk. If you work for the firm representing the defendant store in a slip-and-fall case brought by one of the store's customers, grouping cases in terms of the defenses raised might be a logical organizational strategy to use when synthesizing your research results.

ANALYZING STATUTORY LAW

Because of the tremendous growth in statutory and regulatory law in the last century, the legal issues dealt with by attorneys are frequently governed by statutes and administrative agency regulations. Legal assistants must understand how to interpret and analyze this body of law. Although we use the terms *statute* and *statutory law* in this section, the following discussion applies equally well to the regulations issued by administrative agencies.

If a statute applies to the legal issues in your case, you must understand the statute thoroughly before evaluating how it does or does not apply to the issue that you are researching. The first step in statutory analysis is therefore to read the language of the statute very carefully. The next step is to interpret the meaning of the statute.

Reading Statutory Law

As with court cases, some statutes are more difficult to read than others. Some are extremely wordy or lengthy or difficult to understand for some other reason. By carefully reading and rereading a statute, however, you can usually determine the reasons for the statute's enactment, the class of people to which the statute applies, the kind of conduct being regulated by the statute, and the circumstances in which that conduct is prohibited, required, or permitted. You can also learn whether the statute allows for any exceptions and, if so, in what circumstances. When reading a statute, you can do several things to simplify your task, including those discussed below.

COVERAGE AND EFFECTIVE DATE. When researching statutory law on behalf of a client, one of the first things you should find out is whether the statute is applicable to the client's case. Suppose your firm's client is a small corporation with ten employees. Your firm is defending the client against a lawsuit for employment discrimination based on disability in violation of the Americans with Disabilities Act (ADA) of 1990. In researching this statute, the first thing you will want to check is what firms are subject to the statute. (You will find that the ADA applies only to employers who have fifteen or more employees, and thus the client is not subject to the act's provisions.)

Each statute also indicates the date on which it will become legally effective. This is something you will want to verify at the outset of your inquiry. Note that the effective date may be a year or two later than the date on which the statute was enacted into law. For example, the provisions relating to employment in the Americans with Disabilities Act of 1990 did not become legally effective until July 26, 1992. Questions also arise in regard to whether the provisions of the act will apply *retroactively*—that is, to lawsuits filed before the effective date of the statute. If the statute is unclear on its applicability in this respect, you will want to research relevant case law to find out how the courts have decided this issue.

On the Web
You can access the full text of the Americans with Disabilities Act of 1990 at the following Web site: www.usdoj.gov/crt/ada/statute.html.

DEFINITIONS. Usually, near the beginning of a statute or the beginning of each major section within the statute, you can find a list of terms followed by their

EXHIBIT 16.4
Excerpt from the Americans with Disabilities Act of 1990

> § 12112. Discrimination
>
> **(a) General rule**
> No covered entity shall discriminate against a qualified individual with a disability because of the disability of such individual in regard to job application procedures, the hiring, advancement, or discharge of employees, employee compensation, job training, and other terms, conditions, and privileges of employment.
>
> **(b) Construction**
> As used in subsection (a) of this section, the term "discriminate" includes—
>
> (1) limiting, segregating, or classifying a job applicant or employee in a way that adversely affects the opportunities or status of such applicant or employee because of the disability of such applicant or employee;
>
> (2) participating in a contractual or other arrangement or relationship that has the effect of subjecting a covered entity's qualified applicant or employee with a disability to the discrimination prohibited by this subchapter (such relationship includes a relationship with an employment or referral agency, labor union, an organization providing fringe benefits to an employee of the covered entity, or an organization providing training and apprenticeship programs);
>
> (3) utilizing standards, criteria, or methods of administration—
>   (A) that have the effect of discrimination on the basis of disability; or
>   (B) that perpetuate the discrimination of others who are subject to common administrative control;
>
> (4) excluding or otherwise denying equal jobs or benefits to a qualified individual because of the known disability of an individual with whom the qualified individual is known to have a relationship or association;
>
> (5)(A) not making reasonable accommodations to the known physical or mental limitations of an otherwise qualified individual with a disability who is an applicant or employee, unless such covered entity can demonstrate that the accommodation would impose an undue hardship on the operation of the business of such covered entity; or
>   (B) denying employment opportunities to a job applicant or employee who is an otherwise qualified individual with a disability, if such denial is based on the need of such covered entity to make reasonable accommodation to the physical or mental impairments of the employee or applicant;
>
> (6) using qualification standards, employment tests, or other selection criteria that screen out or tend to screen out an individual with a disability or a class of individuals with disabilities unless the standard, test, or other selection criteria, as used by the covered entity, is shown to be job-related for the position in question and is consistent with business necessity; and
>
> (7) failing to select and administer tests concerning employment in the most effective manner * * *.

definitions. In the hypothetical case mentioned above, which involves a lawsuit based on discrimination against a person with a disability, you will want to read carefully the statutory definition of *disability*. You will also want to learn how the ADA defines other terms or phrases that may be important in determining the defendant firm's liability. For example, the ADA requires employers reasonably to accommodate persons with disabilities. You will want to find out how the act defines *reasonable accommodation*.

SUBDIVISIONS. Another helpful tactic in reading statutory law is to identify the various sections and subsections in the statute. Often, statutes indicate subsections by letters or numbers, but it is easy to lose sight of the relationship between one subsection and another. Consider the excerpt from the ADA shown in Exhibit 16.4. You will find there are several levels of subsections within this section of the statute and that each subsection is preceded by a number or letter. You may also find that you have to scan through the section more than once to identify the relationship between the subsections. Statutes frequently contain even more levels of subsections, and at times, you may want to diagram the structure of the text to discern the interrelationship of various subsections.

AND VERSUS *OR.* When reading a statute, you should also pay careful attention to the words *and* and *or* in the text. For example, suppose that a section of a statute begins with the words "A contract which does not satisfy the requirements of subsection (1) but which is valid in other respects is enforceable if . . ." Following these words, two conditions are listed. A crucial factor in interpreting the section is whether the conditions are connected by *and* or *or*. If *and* is used, then both conditions must be met before the contract is enforceable. If *or* is used, then only one of the conditions must be met. Consciously looking for these *connectors* in positions such as the one just described can help to clarify the meaning of a statutory provision.

Interpreting Statutory Law

Generally, when trying to understand the meaning of statutes, you should do as the courts do. We therefore now look at some of the typical techniques used by courts when they are faced with the task of interpreting the meaning of a given statute or statutory provision.

Rules of Construction
The rules that control the judicial interpretation of statutes.

RULES OF CONSTRUCTION. Certain statutory rules of interpretation, called **rules of construction,** may prove helpful in your analysis of the statute's language and intent. Examples of statutory rules of interpretation used in many jurisdictions are the following:

- Specific provisions are given greater weight than general provisions when there is a conflict between the two.
- Recent provisions are given greater weight than earlier provisions when there is a conflict between the two.
- Masculine pronouns refer to both males and females.
- Singular nouns also include the plural forms of the nouns.

Plain-Meaning Rule
A rule of statutory interpretation. If the meaning of a statute is clear on its face, then that is the interpretation the court will give to it; inquiry into the legislative history of the statute will not be undertaken.

THE PLAIN-MEANING RULE. In interpreting statutory language, courts also apply the **plain-meaning rule.** Under this rule, the words chosen by the legislature must be understood according to their common meanings. If the statute is clear and unambiguous *on its face* (in its apparent and obvious meaning), and therefore capable of only one interpretation, that interpretation must be given to it. No additional inquiries, such as inquiries into legislative intent or history, are permitted when the meaning of the statute is clear on its face.

The plain-meaning rule, although seemingly simple, is usually not so simple to apply. For one thing, the plain meaning of a statute is rarely totally clear, because legal language, especially in statutes, is difficult to understand and often inherently ambiguous. Also, each word or phrase in a statute takes on meaning only in context—as it relates to the surrounding text. Thus, the interpretation of the meaning of a statutory word, phrase, or provision remains ultimately subjective.

Furthermore, laws, by their very nature, cannot be too specific. When enacting a statute, the legislators often state a broad principle of law and then leave it up to the courts to apply this principle to specific circumstances—which vary from case to case. For example, consider the final two lines of the excerpt from the ADA presented in Exhibit 16.4 on page 590. What exactly does the clause "failing to select and administer tests concerning employment in the most effective manner" mean? In interpreting this provision, you would need to research case law to see how the courts have interpreted the provision or study the legislative history of the act to understand the legislators' intent in wording the clause in that particular way.

PREVIOUS JUDICIAL INTERPRETATION.   Paralegals often find that researching statutory law also involves researching case law—to see how the courts have interpreted and applied statutory provisions. As discussed in Chapter 14, courts are obligated to follow the precedents set by higher courts in their jurisdictions. A statutory interpretation made by a higher court therefore must be accepted as binding by lower courts in the same jurisdiction. You can find citations to court cases relating to specific statutes by referring to annotated versions of state or federal statutory codes, as discussed in Chapter 14.

LEGISLATIVE INTENT.   Another common technique employed in statutory interpretation is learning the intent of the legislature. A court relying on this method determines the meaning of the statute by attempting to find out why the legislators chose to phrase the statute in the particular language they used or, more generally, what the legislators sought to accomplish by enacting the statute. To discern the intent of the legislators who drafted a particular law, it is often necessary to investigate the legislative history of the statute. This can be done by researching committee reports, records of congressional hearings or other proceedings, and other relevant documents. (Refer to Chapter 14 for a discussion of how to research the legislative history of a statute.)

LEGAL WRITING—THE PRELIMINARIES

Part of legal research involves summarizing your results in writing. As a paralegal, you will find that in addition to drafting research summaries, you will be expected to draft numerous other types of materials. In fact, much of your work as a paralegal will involve writing assignments. We will look at writing skills and the kinds of legal materials that paralegals create in subsequent sections. Here, you will read about some of the more general requirements involved in legal writing.

Whenever you receive a writing assignment, you need to understand at the outset (1) the nature of your writing assignment, (2) when it must be completed, and (3) what type of writing approach is appropriate to the assignment. We examine each of these basic requirements here.

Understanding the Assignment

The practice of law is often hectic, and frequently paralegals are asked to research, analyze, and report their results on particular issues within a short time period. When you receive a writing assignment, you should always make sure that you understand the exact nature of the request so that you can execute your task as efficiently as possible. The writing style, format, and methodological approach used in legal writing vary, depending on the specific objectives of the document you are supposed to create. If you need to ask questions, do so. You should never equate asking questions with incompetence. As the adage states, the only "dumb question" is the one that is not asked.

Developing Paralegal Skills

Interpreting Statutes

Ralph Winter, a paralegal, works for an attorney who is representing the plaintiff in a negligence case. The plaintiff stepped on a broken stair step in her apartment building, fell, and broke her hip. She is suing the owner of the building for negligence. The attorney has successfully opposed the owner-defendant's motion for summary judgment in the case, but the defense is now trying a new tactic. The defense wants to get the venue of the case changed to a county in which the landlord owns and operates a restaurant and owns a significant amount of other commercial property—on the assumption that a jury in that area might be more inclined to favor the defendant. The defense has filed a motion for change of venue, and Ralph is once again researching the law.

He has located a statute entitled "Venue in County Designated." It reads:

> Notwithstanding any provision of this article, the place of trial of an action shall be in the county designated by the plaintiff, unless the place of trial is changed to another county by order, upon motion, or by consent as provided in subdivision (b) of Rule 511. N.Y. Civil Practice Sec. 509 (McKinney 1976).

"This statute is pretty clear," thinks Ralph. Ralph turns to the annotations following section 509 to make sure the courts have applied it as he interprets it. Under note 5, he finds the title, "Motion for Change of Venue." Ralph finds a case involving an injured tenant. It holds that venue was proper in the county in which the plaintiff resided, the accident occurred, the plaintiff was treated for the resulting injuries, and the building's superintendent resided, rather than the county in which the building owner's residence and principal place of business were located. Ralph decides to pull this helpful case and read it to be certain it says what the annotation indicates.

Tips for Applying Statutes

- Read the language of the statute and summarize each provision in your mind, or on paper if it is lengthy.
- Make sure that the statute has taken effect and has not been repealed, amended, or held unconstitutional—check the pocket part or a citator.
- Apply each requirement of the statute to the facts of the problem being researched.
- Review the case annotations following each section to determine how the courts have applied the law.

Time Constraints and Flexibility

The time factor is an important consideration in legal writing. When you receive a writing assignment, you need to understand clearly when the assignment must be completed. In some situations, you will be required to submit writings to a court by a certain date, which is inflexible. Additionally, clients usually demand quick responses to questions. And frequently, during the course of litigation or other legal activities, crucial new issues arise that must be addressed immediately, often overnight or within two or three days. As a paralegal, you will need to assess such situations realistically. If little time is given for the completion of a project, you have to make informed judgment calls, deciding what information is crucial to the writing and what can be omitted.

In addition to time constraints, other circumstances may influence the way a paralegal handles an assignment. For example, external circumstances, such as newly enacted laws, may affect the legal treatment of an issue. Additionally, a client may unexpectedly demand a change in the course of action. These situations require flexibility. Whenever you undertake a writing task, you should be prepared for the possibility that you may have to make quick changes and go in new directions before your assignment is completed.

Writing Approaches

Another thing you should determine when you receive a writing assignment is what type of writing is required. Many of your writing assignments will require *objective analysis,* which either focuses on facts or discusses fairly both sides of a legal matter. Other types of assignments will require advocacy, which involves presenting the facts and issues in a light most favorable to your client.

For example, assume that your supervising attorney hands you two lease agreements and asks you to compare them and note whether the differences in the wording of the agreements lead to different obligations. Your concern will not be to point out which agreement is better but to analyze and compare the documents objectively and point out which clauses lead to what kinds of obligations. Objective analysis may also be required when an attorney seeks assistance in providing clients with information regarding a particular legal matter. Clients often seek the advice of an attorney to determine whether they have a claim that merits the filing of a lawsuit. In this situation, an attorney may request the paralegal to investigate the issues thoroughly and provide a memorandum containing an accurate and unbiased analysis of the issue.

If the writing assignment is intended to advocate a position, the style of writing will be somewhat different from that in an objective discussion of the law. In advocating a position, you are primarily concerned with convincing the reader that the argument proposed is stronger than the opposing party's position. You will need to develop supportive legal arguments and present the matter in the light most favorable to the client. (Realize, though, that attorneys have a duty of candor toward the tribunal, or court. This duty requires an attorney to disclose mandatory authorities to the court even if those authorities are adverse to the client's position.)

THE IMPORTANCE OF GOOD WRITING SKILLS

The legal profession is primarily a communications profession. Effective written communications are particularly crucial in the legal arena. For paralegals, good writing skills therefore go hand in hand with successful job performance. The more competent a writer you are, the more likely it is that your finished products will be satisfactory to the attorney with whom you are working. You should also keep in mind that some of your written projects, such as correspondence, represent the firm for which you work. A well-written document is a positive reflection on the firm and upholds the firm's reputation for good performance.

Each writing assignment you receive will give you an opportunity to improve and perfect your writing skills. In the following sections, we offer some guidelines you can follow as you strive to improve your writing. Paralegals seriously interested in improving their writing skills also will have close at hand a good dictionary, a thesaurus, a style manual (such as Strunk and White's *Elements of Style* or the *Chicago Manual of Style*), and perhaps a book or two on basic English grammar.

Organize and Outline Your Presentation

Once you know what it is you want to demonstrate, discuss, or prove to your reader, you need to decide how best to organize your ideas to achieve this end. Because organization is essential to effective legal writing, you should have your organizational framework in mind before you begin writing. Most people find that an outline—whether it is a simple sketch in pencil on a scrap of paper or a detailed outline created by a specialized computer program—makes writing easier. It not only saves time but also produces a more organized result.

When creating an outline, you decide the sequence in which topics should be discussed. Some issues will need to be addressed before others, either for logical reasons or for purposes of clarity and readability. Similar issues should be grouped together, either in the same section or under the same topic heading. Other factors you will want to consider when organizing your presentation are format and structural devices.

CHOICE OF FORMAT. An important requirement in legal writing is selecting the appropriate format. The format of a document concerns such things as how wide or narrow the margins should be, how many spaces paragraphs should be indented, how many line spaces should be between paragraphs or other sections, and so on. Documents to be filed with a court must conform to the procedural rules of the particular jurisdiction. Most law firms also adopt special formats for other types of documents, such as correspondence sent to clients and opposing counsel and internal legal memoranda. When writing these types of documents, you need to know what format your firm prefers to use.

STRUCTURAL DEVICES. If you are writing about a complex legal research project involving numerous issues, you may want to divide your presentation into several sections, with each section dealing with one issue. You can make it easier for the reader to follow the discussion by including a "road map" to the document. For example, you might preface the writing with an introduction that highlights the points that will be discussed and the conclusion that will be reached, thus orienting the reader to the document's contents. Also, try to "walk" your reader through the analysis and discussion by including descriptive headings and subheadings in the body of the document so that the reader never gets lost.

Arranging events **chronologically**—that is, in a time sequence—can also serve as a structural device. A chronologically structured discussion is sometimes easier for the reader to follow. This is particularly true when you are describing the factual background leading to a lawsuit. Presenting the facts and events in chronological order helps to orient the reader. Even if you are discussing legal issues instead of facts, you might want to use a chronological structure for at least part of your discussion. For example, if you are writing about the historical development of a particular rule of law, you will want to structure that part of the discussion chronologically.

Write to Your Audience

Paralegals prepare legal documents and correspondence for a wide range of people. Whenever you draft legal correspondence or legal documents of any kind, you should keep in mind that legal documents are not ends in themselves. They are created for someone (a judge, an attorney, a client, a witness, or some other person) to read. The ultimate goal of legal writing is to *communicate* information or ideas to your reader. It is therefore important to tailor the writing to the intended audience. For example, a letter directed to an attorney may include legal terms and concepts that would be inappropriate in a letter to a layperson, who probably would not understand them. You must therefore consider to whom the legal writing is directed and what legal understanding the reader possesses.

In addition to the reader's legal knowledge, paralegals should consider how well the reader understands the subject matter. You cannot presume, especially in cases dealing with technical and scientific matters, that your reader knows as

Chronologically
In a time sequence; naming or listing events in the time order in which they occurred.

much as the attorney or yourself. Indeed, you should normally assume the contrary—that the reader has had neither the time nor the background to gain a comprehensive understanding of every legal or factual matter presented. Both in consideration of your reader's needs and in the interests of effective communication, you should present your information or analysis clearly, carefully leading the reader from point A to point B, from point B to point C, and so on.

Avoid Legalese

As a paralegal, writing to your audience often requires you to minimize or eliminate legal jargon, or legalese. Legalese consists of terms that are used by legal professionals but that are unknown to most people outside the legal profession. Therefore, if you are writing a letter to a client, either avoid using legal terms the client may not understand or define such terms for your reader. For example, if you are advising a client of the date on which *voir dire* will take place, consider saying "jury selection"—or perhaps "*voir dire* (jury selection)"—instead. Although a certain amount of legal terminology in legal writing is unavoidable, you should minimize the use of language that may confuse the reader.

Lawyers have traditionally used certain terms in legal documents—words such as *hereof, therein,* and *thereto,* for example—that you should avoid whenever possible in your writing. These and similar words sound strange and excessively formal to the ordinary person. Legal documents are also often filled with redundancies. Consider, for example, the following sentence from an agreement to finance a business:

> If Borrower shall have made any representation or warranty herein . . . which shall be in any material respect false and/or erroneous and/or incorrect . . .

What is the difference between *false, erroneous,* and *incorrect?* Often, these terms are used synonymously, and it is hard to imagine that something could be erroneous and still be correct—so why should it be necessary to add *incorrect* to the clause?

Other commonly used legal phrases containing obvious redundancies include *all the rest, residue, and remainder; null and void; full and complete;* and *cease and desist.* In the first phrase, the words *rest, residue,* and *remainder* mean essentially the same thing. In the second phrase, the words *null* and *void* are synonymous, as are the coupled terms in the other phrases. Yet these types of phrases are commonplace in legal documents, largely because they have been traditionally used in the legal profession and because of the natural inclination of lawyers to want to make sure that all aspects of a given subject are covered.

As a paralegal, you should strive to minimize the use of legalese, including redundancies, in your own writing—but be cautious:

 When translating legalese into plain English, you need to make sure that you correctly understand the intent of the legal phrase. If you have any doubts, always ask your supervising attorney.

(See this chapter's *Technology and Today's Paralegal: Online "Plain English" Guidelines* for a discussion of online sources offering instructions on and some examples of "plain English" writing.)

Be Brief and to the Point

Just as the use of legalese can hinder communication, so, too, can the use of too many words. Writing effectively requires efficiency in word usage. Unnecessary words can

TECHNOLOGY AND TODAY'S PARALEGAL

Online "Plain English" Guidelines

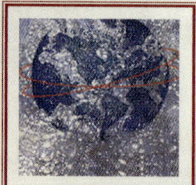

The ability to write clearly and effectively is a valuable asset to any paralegal, because virtually every paralegal is required to do a certain amount of writing as a part of his or her job. As mentioned elsewhere, clear and effective writing means keeping "legalese"—legal terminology typically understood only by legal professionals—to a minimum, or even eliminating it entirely. The problem is, how can you do this without "dummying down" a legal concept or risking inaccuracy when describing that concept?

Today's paralegal need not go far to find helpful instructions in the art of writing in "plain English." Indeed, there are a number of sites on the Web you can turn to for guidance. You can find many helpful sites simply by doing a key-word search for "plain language" or "plain English" using a search engine such as Yahoo. Some sites, such as **www.deet.gov.au/pubs/plain_en/writing.htm**, offer helpful writing tips in addition to specific examples of how you can replace cumbersome phrases (such as "at such time as" or "prior to and following") with a simpler term or phrase (such as "when" or "before and after"). Other sites, such as **www.web.net/~plain/PlainTrain** offer online training in the use of plain language in writing.

An excellent source for writing tips and using plain language is the "Plain English Handbook" that the Securities and Exchange Commission (SEC) recently published online at **www.sec.gov/consumer/plaine.htm#A3**. The Purpose of the booklet is indicated by its subtitle: "How to Create Clear SEC Disclosure Documents." Paralegals working in the area of securities law will certainly find this handbook helpful. Yet the guidelines given in the booklet can apply to any written communication.

Paralegals can also turn to other online sources for ideas on how to use language that communicates well. For example, if you want to better understand a legal term (so that you can paraphrase it in language more understandable to your audience), you can check various online dictionaries, such as Black's Corporation Law Dictionary (at **www.alaska.net/~winter/black_law_dictionary.html**) or the 'Lectric Law Library's dictionary of legal terms (at **www.lectlaw.com/d-a.htm**). A particularly helpful online source is the "plain language" legal dictionary found at **www.wwlia.org/dicion.htm**. This dictionary defines and describes legal concepts in language most people can understand.

---

become stumbling blocks for your reader and prevent a clear understanding of the point you wish to make. When proofreading your document, take time to make sure that your statements are brief and to the point. Exhibit 16.5 on the next page offers some examples of how efficient word usage can enhance clarity.

Generally, you should only use words essential to the point you are making; unnecessary words will only distract or confuse your reader. Similarly, you should include in your writing only concepts or factual information directly relevant to your topic.

Writing Basics: Sentences

A good writer uses a large proportion of short, concrete sentences because they are easier to understand. Additionally, forceful sentences include active, dynamic verbs rather than nominalizations (verbs transformed into nouns). For example, it is simpler and more effective to say "the plaintiff decided to settle the case" than "the plaintiff made a decision to settle the case." In the first example, the verb *decide* is direct and forceful. In the second example, the conversion of *decided* into *made a decision* detracts from the forcefulness of the verb.

Writing in the active voice also makes sentences easier to understand. The active voice sets up a subject-verb-object sentence structure, whereas the passive

EXHIBIT 16.5
Using Words Efficiently

Do not write:
Ms. Carpenter never drives at night due to the fact that she has poor night vision.

Write instead:
Ms. Carpenter does not drive at night because she has poor night vision.

Do not write:
The new client who brought his business to our attention yesterday has a number of issues pertaining to his legal problems that he needs to discuss with us as soon as possible.

Write instead:
The client who hired us yesterday needs to discuss his legal problems immediately.

Do not write:
The defendant worked for one of the members of an organized crime ring for a period of seven years. During that seven-year period of time, the defendant witnessed crimes numbering in the hundreds.

Write instead:
During the seven years that the defendant worked for a member of an organized crime ring, he witnessed hundreds of crimes.

---

voice uses an object-verb-subject format. For example, "The defendant stole the diamond" uses the active voice. Contrast the simplicity and strength of this statement with its passive equivalent: "The diamond was stolen by the defendant." The use of the active voice puts people, actors, movers, and doers into your writing and thus makes your writing more reflective of reality. Sometimes, however, you may want to maintain the facelessness of the actor or doer. For example, if your firm is defending a plaintiff who has been accused of stealing a diamond, consider writing "the diamond that was stolen" instead of "the diamond that the plaintiff allegedly stole." In this situation, the passive voice effectively removes the plaintiff from the action.

You should also make sure you use correct grammar when writing legal documents. Grammatical and punctuation errors, such as those in the following sentences, distract your reader and may reflect poorly on your (and your firm's) professional reputation and status.

- *Incorrect*: The plaintiff should *of* consulted with the defendant.
  Correct: The plaintiff should *have* consulted with the defendant.
- *Incorrect*: The defendant could not possibly have *did* what the plaintiff alleged.
  Correct: The defendant could not possibly have *done* what the plaintiff alleged.
- *Incorrect*: The *plaintiffs* allegations were vague and ambiguous.
  Correct: The *plaintiff's* allegations were vague and ambiguous.

When proofreading your documents, you should make sure they are free of any errors involving subject-verb agreement, punctuation, spelling, the use of apostrophes, and other elements.

Writing Basics: Paragraphs and Transitions

A paragraph is a group of sentences that develops a particular idea. A paragraph should have unity and coherence. Each paragraph should begin with a *topic sentence* that indicates what the paragraph is about. Each subsequent sentence in the paragraph should contribute to the development of the topic; if it does not, consider placing the sentence elsewhere or simply deleting it. When you write, be

EXHIBIT 16.6

Transitional Terms and Phrases

---

1. Words that indicate a conceptual or causal sequence or relationship. Examples:

The *third* element required for a cause of action under negligence theory is that the plaintiff must have suffered a legally recognizable injury.

As a result of the fall, the plaintiff was injured.

2. Words that indicate a chronological sequence of events. Examples:

After the fall, the plaintiff was taken to Nita City Hospital & Clinic.

Before the plaintiff's accident, she was in excellent health.

3. Words that refer back to the subject discussed in the previous paragraph. Examples:

Courts make exceptions to *this rule* in certain situations, however.

The act does not apply to employers who have fewer than fifteen employees, however.

If the *above-mentioned conditions* are not met, the injured party cannot recover damages.

In contrast to negligence actions, actions in strict liability do not require the plaintiff to prove that the defendant breached a duty of care.

If the *plaintiff* had not been *injured in the fall*, then she would have no cause of action against the store owner.

4. Words that introduce summaries. Examples:

In short, the plaintiff has a valid claim against the defendant.

In summary, the plaintiff met all four conditions for a negligence action against the defendant.

To conclude, the plaintiff established the element of causation by demonstrating that she would not have been injured if it had not been for the defendant's actions.

---

conscious of why you begin a new paragraph—or why you do not. When you proofread, watch carefully for how you are using paragraphs. You should create a new paragraph whenever you start discussing another idea. Paragraphs that are not logically constructed are often confusing and pointless for the reader.

Take your reader with you as you move from one paragraph to another. Although the connection between paragraphs may be clear to you, the writer, it may not be clear to your reader. You need to show, by including transitional sentences or phrases, how a topic discussed in one paragraph relates to the subsequent paragraph. Exhibit 16.6 lists some terms and phrases writers commonly use to effect smooth transitions.

Be Alert for Sexist Language

The language of the law has traditionally used masculine pronouns inclusively—that is, to refer to both males and females. Jurists, legal scholars, and others in the legal profession are consciously moving away from this tradition. As a paralegal, you should take special care to become aware of and avoid sexist language in your own writing. For example, if you see a word with "man" or "men" in it (such as

> ## ETHICAL CONCERN
> ### Ethics and Time Management
>
> Many paralegals learn the hard way—through trial and error—that the ability to manage their time effectively is an essential part of doing a good job. One of the easiest things to overlook when engaging in research and writing is that good writing takes time—you may need to revise a document more than once before you are satisfied with its quality. Whenever you are given a writing assignment, you should make sure you allow yourself enough time to revise and polish your final document. As a paralegal, you have an ethical duty to your supervising attorney, the firm, and the client to serve their best interests. In regard to legal writing, their interests are served by the production of clear and convincing legal documents—and by your ability to manage your time so that this goal can be achieved.

policeman, fireman, or *workmen's compensation*) use a gender-neutral substitute for it (such as *police officer, firefighter,* or *workers' compensation*). In the past decade or so, writers have devised various ways to avoid using masculine pronouns when the referent's gender is unknown. Some of the ways are these:

- Use *he or she* rather than *he.*
- Alternate between the use of masculine and feminine pronouns.
- Make the noun plural so that a gender-neutral plural pronoun (*they, their,* or *them*) can be used.
- Repeat the noun rather than using a pronoun.

Proofread and Revise Your Document

A crucial part of legal writing involves proofreading and revising your document. When you receive a writing assignment, you should always allow time to proofread and revise whatever you are writing. Virtually no writer can turn out an error-free document on the first try, and as a paralegal, you will be especially concerned with accuracy. Proofreading your document allows you to discover and correct typographical errors, to see whether your document reflects a logical progression of thought from one topic to another, and to verify whether you have covered all of the relevant facts or issues. You should use the spell checker in your computer, and perhaps the grammar checker as well, to assist you in proofreading. Don't, however, count on these tools to catch all your errors.

When you write your first draft, you have much to think about, and you may overlook many details. When proofreading your document, you can pay more attention to organizational coherence, transitions, paragraph construction, sentence formation, word choice, sexist language, and the like. You might find it helpful to develop a "writing checklist" to remind you of certain things you want to avoid or achieve in your writing—particularly if there is a required format for the particular type of document on which you are working. When you are writing legal documents, always keep the following advice in mind:

 Creating a polished document takes time, and a good portion of that time should be spent in proofreading and revising your written work product.

PLEADINGS AND DISCOVERY

Many writing tasks undertaken by paralegals involve forms that must be submitted to the court or to opposing counsel before a trial begins or after the trial has commenced. These documents were covered in detail earlier in this text, in Chapters 10 and 11. You can review those chapters for explanations and illustrations of the forms required for pretrial procedures (pleadings, discovery procedures, and pretrial motions) and for motions made during the trial.

It is especially important that such documents contain the required information and be presented in the appropriate format. Form books and computerized forms offer guidelines, but you should always become familiar with the rules of the court in which the documents are being filed to ensure that you use the proper format.

GENERAL LEGAL CORRESPONDENCE

Paralegals are often asked to draft letters to clients, witnesses, opposing counsel, and others. Even when a message may already have been conveyed orally (in person or by phone) to one of these parties, the paralegal may be asked to write a letter confirming in writing what was discussed. Lawyers are extremely conscious of the need to document communications to avoid future problems. The existence of the written document clarifies any ambiguities that might arise in connection with the oral conversation and confirms that the conversation took place.

Law firms normally have an official letterhead and stationery. The letterhead contains certain information about the firm. Most letterheads include the firm's name, address, and phone and fax numbers, and, more and more commonly, an e-mail address. Some firms have more descriptive letterheads that include the names of partners in the firm or the various geographical locations in which the firm has offices. You should always use your firm's letterhead when writing a letter on behalf of one of the firm's attorneys or when writing as a representative of the firm. The first page of any correspondence from the firm should be composed on letterhead paper. Any additional pages can be printed on numbered continuing sheets (plain, matching stationery).

In this section, you will read about some typical requirements relating to legal correspondence. Keep in mind, though, that the particular law firm, corporate legal department, or government agency for which you work will probably have its own specific procedures and requirements you will need to follow.

General Format for Legal Correspondence

Although there are many types of legal correspondence, the general format of a legal letter includes the components discussed below and illustrated in Exhibit 16.7 on page 604.

DATE.   Legal correspondence must be *dated*. The date appears below the official letterhead of the firm. You should make sure that the date is correctly keyed in. Be especially careful after the turn of a year. Many people continue to use the preceding year on correspondence, checks, and other documents simply out of habit. In a legal document, however, entering the wrong year could have important legal consequences.

As explained earlier, dates serve an important function in legal matters. The date of a letter may be critical in matters involving legal notice of a particular event.

Featured Guest: Richard M. Terry

Ten Tips for Effective Legal Writing

Biographical Note

Richard M. Terry received his bachelor's degree and master's degree from the University of Baltimore. He worked as a legal assistant for ten years. During that time, he was a supervisor in the Office of the Public Defender for Baltimore City. Currently, he is an assistant professor and the coordinator of the legal-assistant program at Baltimore City Community College.

Writing is a major form of communication. As a paralegal, you will be asked to write constantly throughout your career. Writing in this profession can take many forms, depending on your specialty and employer. You may be asked to prepare letters to clients and reports on client interviews and investigations, as well as responses to legal questions you have researched. Make no mistake—every document you prepare will be important. The tips for effective legal writing given below are not cast in stone. They are general guidelines that will make you a better legal writer, not only while you are in school but also when you enter the profession.

1. Plan before You Write. In this age of computerized word processing, there is a tremendous temptation just to sit down at the keyboard and begin to type, creating as you go along. Avoid this temptation at all costs. Instead, prepare a plan of action before you put the first word on paper. Your plan of action will consist of a few simple steps. First, if your supervising attorney has asked you to write the document, make sure that he or she has spelled out clearly what is needed. Second, if you are drafting a particular type of document (such as a pleading or memorandum) for the first time, ask for or find a sample to use, perhaps in your firm's files. Third, outline the document before you begin writing. Making an outline is the key to producing a well-organized document. Fourth, just before printing out the final copy of the document, check with the attorney again, to make sure you have not missed any key points.

2. Write with a Purpose. Writing with a purpose means writing with an identifiable goal in mind. The document you produce must reflect that purpose. Generally, the purpose for any legal document is either objective or adversarial. A document with an objective purpose simply passes on information, without any appearance of bias. A document with an adversarial purpose emphasizes the strong points of one position versus the weak points of another. Adversarial writing will reflect a definite bias.

3. Write Clearly. Remember that simple is usually better. Try to say exactly what you mean, and use standard vocabulary and clear and concrete terms. It is not necessary to show that you have a mastery of legal language. Identify your audience, and write to the people who will ultimately read your document. The style and tone of your writing should change with the document's intended audience, as well as with the purpose of the document. When you write to a client, for example, try to avoid the use of technical or legal terms. Your tone should be explanatory, and you should define legal terms and describe the consequences of legal actions. In contrast, when you are writing to the court or to attorneys, you will not need to explain legal concepts or terms. Remember, too, that readers normally do not have time to figure out what you are trying to say. Structure what you write, get to the point, and stick to it.

4. Use Proper Grammar and Sentence Structure. Legal documents once were routinely written in highly formal, complex language, but over the past few years, writing in plain English has become the rule. As a result, legal documents are no longer as long and complicated as they once

FEATURED GUEST, Continued

were. No matter which style you use, however, you must observe the rules of basic grammar and punctuation you learned in junior and senior high school. Make sure, for example, that you write in complete sentences and punctuate long sentences correctly.

5. **Use an Appropriate Writing Style.** Style is a broad term. In a general sense, it refers to how you express what you have to say, as opposed to the content of your writing. For example, a piece of writing can have a formal or an informal style. More narrowly, style can refer to specific forms, such as the form of a legal citation or of the names of particular courts. A good style manual can assist in determining what is an appropriate style. Style manuals give many basic rules and explain how the rules apply in different contexts. Well-known style manuals include *The Elements of Style* by William Strunk, Jr., and E. B. White, and the *Chicago Manual of Style*, currently in its fourteenth edition. For the proper format for legal citations, the source to consult is *The Blue Book: A Uniform System of Citation.*

6. **Edit Your Work.** The first draft of a document is not necessarily correct in every detail. Always go back and review objectively what you have written. If possible, have someone else read it for you. If that is not possible, try reading the document backwards—that is, from the last line to the first line. More often than not, you will catch at least some spelling and punctuation errors this way.

7. **Use Computers Effectively.** The computer has come of age in the law office of the 1990s. Using computers saves time and reduces the potential for errors in legal writing. There is no excuse for sending out any document containing spelling and grammatical mistakes if the document was produced on a computer. Use the spell-checker and grammar-checker functions to ensure that the document has no spelling or grammatical errors before you print it. Because today's law office relies heavily on computers for both research and writing, legal assistants who wish to succeed on the job should become knowledgeable in the use of computers and legal software.

8. **Keep Copies.** Whenever you create a document, keep a copy for your files. For one thing, this will help you to create a "forms file." Legal writing is somewhat repetitive.

> "Identify your audience, and write to the people who will ultimately read your document."

The form stays the same, and only the names and facts are changed. Creating a forms file will, in the long run, save you time and effort.

9. **Consider New Writing Methods and Styles.** Keeping abreast of what others in the field are doing and how they write may affect the format and style of your writing. Read as many trade publications as possible. Papers such as the *National Law Journal* are great sources of information, and magazines such as *Legal Assistant Today* often give interesting writing tips. Another way of keeping up with current information is to network with others in the profession. Maybe another legal assistant has a method or style of writing that is suited to your situation. Don't close your mind to it.

10. **Practice, Practice, Practice.** Good, effective writing is an art that requires a great deal of practice. The more you write, the better you become.

Additionally, legal correspondence normally is filed chronologically. Without any indication of when the letter was written, accurate filing of the letter would be difficult, if not impossible. As a general rule, you should always place a date on every written item that you create, including telephone messages, memos to file, and personal reminders to yourself.

Address Block
That part of a letter that indicates to whom the letter is addressed. The address block is placed in the upper left-hand portion of the letter, above the salutation (or reference line, if one is included).

METHOD OF DELIVERY AND ADDRESS BLOCK. Below the date is a line indicating the method of delivery, or how the letter was sent (if other than by U.S. mail), which is followed by the **address block,** which indicates to whom the letter is addressed. If the letter was sent by Federal Express, the line before the recipient's name and address will read VIA FEDERAL EXPRESS. If the letter is hand

EXHIBIT 16.7
Components of a Legal Letter

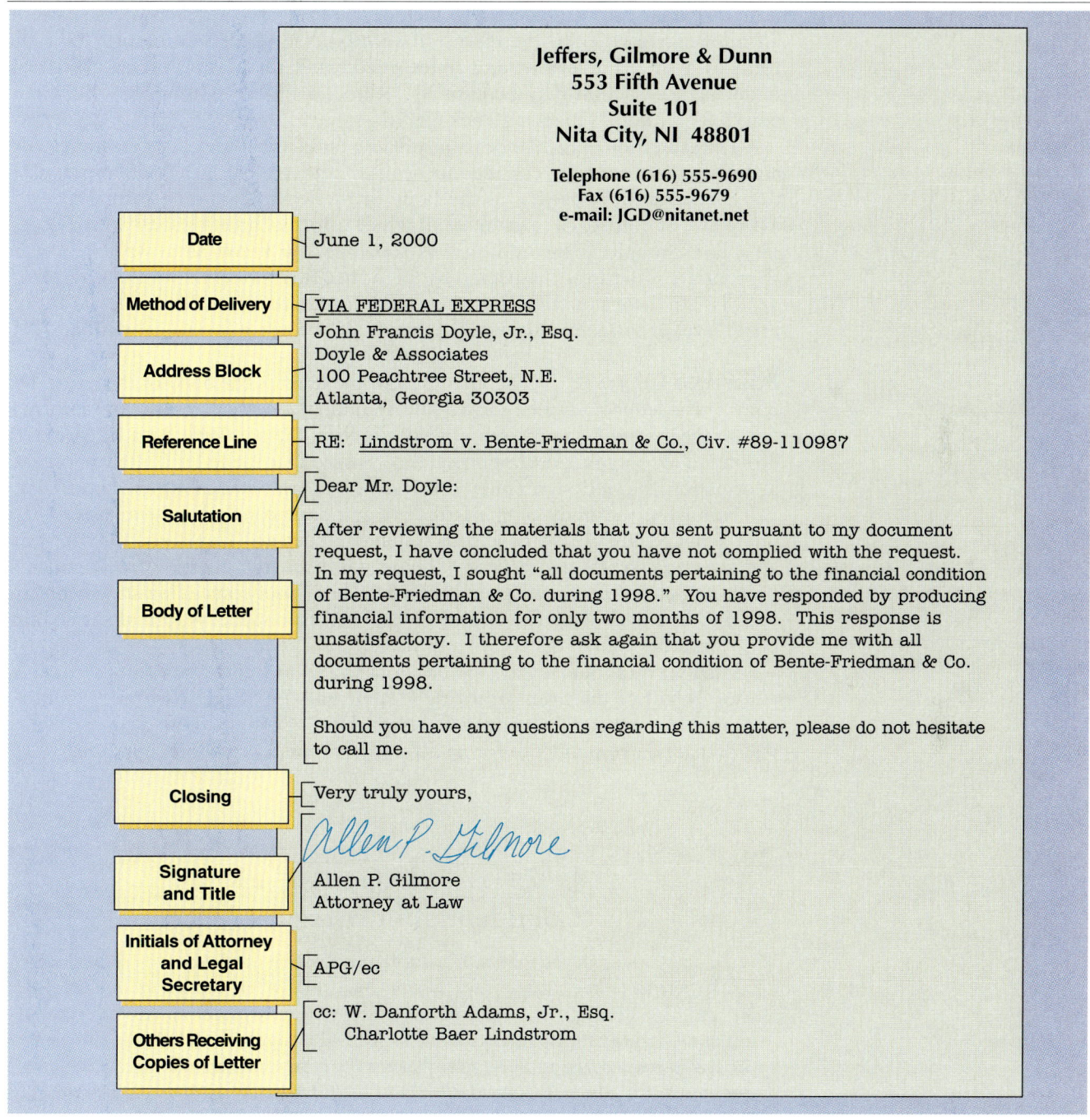

delivered, the line will read BY HAND DELIVERY. Communication by facsimile can be described by the words BY FAX or BY FACSIMILE. The address block should contain the name of the person to whom the letter is written, the person's title, and the name and address of the person's firm or place of business.

REFERENCE LINE AND SALUTATION. Following the address block, the writer may include a **reference line** identifying the matter discussed in the letter. In a

Reference Line
The portion of the letter that indicates the matter to be discussed in the letter, such as "RE: Summary of Cases Applying the Family and Medical Leave Act of 1993." The reference line is placed just below the address block and above the salutation.

letter regarding a pending lawsuit, the reference line may contain the name of the case, its case file (or docket) number, and a brief notation of the nature of the legal dispute. Many attorneys also include the firm's file number for the case. In an informative letter (to be discussed shortly), the reference line may take the form of a title. For example, a letter concerning the closing procedures for a financing transaction may be entitled "RE: Closing Procedures for ABC Company's $4,000,000 Financing Package."

> **Salutation**
> The formal greeting to the addressee of the letter. The salutation is placed just below the reference line.

The **salutation,** which appears just below the reference line, is a greeting to the addressee. Because legal correspondence is a professional means of communication, the salutation, as well as the body of the letter, should be formal in tone. There are, of course, circumstances in which a formal greeting may not be necessary. For example, if the addressee is someone you know quite well, it may be appropriate to address the person by his or her first name, rather than by "Mr." or "Ms." In these situations, you must use your discretion to determine the appropriate level of formality. Generally, when in doubt, use a formal salutation.

BODY AND CLOSING. The main part of the letter is the body of the letter. The body of the letter should be formal and should effectively communicate information to the reader. As a representative of the firm, the paralegal must be careful to proofread all outgoing correspondence to ensure that the letter contains accurate information, is clearly written, and is free of any grammatical or spelling errors.

Following the body of the letter are standard concluding sentences. These final sentences are usually courteous statements such as "Thank you for your time and attention to this matter," or "Should you have any questions or comments, please call me at the above-listed number." These brief concluding statements are followed by the **closing.** The closing in legal correspondence is formal—for example, "Sincerely yours" or "Very truly yours."

> **Closing**
> A final comment to a letter that is placed above the signature, such as "Very truly yours."

Finally, you should always include your title in any correspondence written by you on behalf of the firm. Your title ("Paralegal" or "Legal Assistant" or other title) should immediately follow your name. This, of course, is not a concern when you prepare correspondence for an attorney who will provide a signature.

ETHICAL CONCERN
"Confidential" Correspondence

As a paralegal, you may be faced with the question of whether you should open letters to the attorney for whom you work when the letters are marked "Confidential." For example, suppose that you work for an attorney who is out of the country for two weeks. Because she will be hard to reach during this time, she has instructed you to open all of her mail for her and respond appropriately to certain matters. She has explicitly told you to call her only if an emergency arises. While she is gone, you receive a letter to the attorney that is marked "Confidential." You recognize the sender's name (an attorney who is defending against a lawsuit brought by one of your supervising attorney's clients) and suspect that the letter pertains to the lawsuit. Should you open the letter? Should you hold it until your attorney returns? Or should you try to contact your attorney for advice? To avoid this kind of situation, ask your employer in advance how you should handle confidential mail. Some attorneys routinely have their paralegals open this type of mail; others do not.

> **Jeffers, Gilmore & Dunn**
> 553 Fifth Avenue
> Suite 101
> Nita City, NI 48801
>
> Telephone (616) 555-9690
> Fax (616) 555-9679
> e-mail: JGD@nitanet.net
>
> June 24, 2000
>
> Bernadette P. Williams
> 149 Snowflake Drive
> Irving, TX 75062
>
> RE: Kempf/Joseph Arbitration Proceedings
>
> Dear Ms. Williams:
>
> The arbitration will resume on Monday, August 1, 2000. Please arrive at the offices of the American Arbitration Association (the AAA) before 8:30 A.M. The offices of the AAA are located at 400 West Ferry Boulevard in Dallas. You will be called as a witness sometime before 12:00 noon.
>
> Should you have any questions or concerns regarding your responsibilities as a witness, please do not hesitate to contact me.
>
> Sincerely,
>
> *Elena Lopez*
> Elena Lopez
> Legal Assistant

EXHIBIT 16.8
A Sample Informative Letter

Types of Legal Letters

There are several types of legal correspondence, and each type serves a different purpose. Types of legal letters with which you should become familiar include the following:

- Informative letters.
- Confirmation letters.
- Opinion (advisory) letters.
- Demand letters.

INFORMATIVE LETTERS. A letter that conveys information to another party is an **informative letter**. As a paralegal, you will write many such letters—to clients, for example. Informative letters might be written to advise a client about current developments in a case, an upcoming meeting or procedure, the general background on a legal issue, or simply a breakdown of the firm's bill. The letters you write should be tailored to the client's level of legal understanding.

Informative letters are also sent to opposing counsel and other individuals. For example, law firms often send litigation-scheduling information to opposing counsel, witnesses, and other persons who may be involved in a trial. Informative letters may also be used as transmittal (cover) letters when documents or other materials are sent to a client, a court, opposing counsel, or some other person.

Informative Letter
A letter that conveys certain information to a client, a witness, an adversary's counsel, or other person regarding some legal matter (such as the date, time, place, and purpose of a meeting).

Exhibit 16.8 shows a sample letter written to an individual who will testify during an arbitration procedure.

CONFIRMATION LETTERS. Another type of letter frequently written by paralegals is the confirmation letter. **Confirmation letters** are similar to informative letters in that they communicate certain information to the reader. Confirmation letters put into written form the contents of an oral discussion. In addition to providing attorneys with a permanent record of earlier conversations, confirmation letters also safeguard against any misinterpretation or misunderstanding of what was communicated orally. See Exhibit 16.9 for an example of a confirmation letter.

OPINION LETTERS. The function of an **opinion letter**, or **advisory letter**, is to provide not only information but also advice. In contrast to informative letters, opinion letters actually give a legal opinion about the matter discussed. Attorneys providing opinion letters are required to provide a detailed analysis of the law and

---

Confirmation Letter
A letter that states the substance of a previously conducted verbal discussion to provide a permanent record of the oral conversation.

Opinion (Advisory) Letter
A letter from an attorney to a client containing a legal opinion on an issue raised by the client's question or legal claim. The opinion is based on a detailed analysis of the law.

EXHIBIT 16.9
A Sample Confirmation Letter

Jeffers, Gilmore & Dunn
553 Fifth Avenue
Suite 101
Nita City, NI 48801

Telephone (616) 555-9690
Fax (616) 555-9679
e-mail: JGD@nitanet.net

August 3, 2000

Pauline C. Dunbar
President
Minute-Magic Corporation
7689 Industrial Boulevard
San Francisco, CA 80021

RE: Purchase of real estate from C. C. Barnes, Inc.

Dear Ms. Dunbar:

The following information describes the current status of the negotiations between C. C. Barnes, Inc., and Minute-Magic Corporation:

   Selling Price: $400,000
   Financing Agreement: Citywide Bank
   Interest Rate: 8.5%

This information confirms what I told you on the phone today, August 3, 2000. I look forward to seeing you next week. Should you have any questions or comments in the meantime, please give me a call.

Very truly yours,

Allen P. Gilmore
Allen P. Gilmore
Attorney at Law

APG/ec

DEVELOPING PARALEGAL SKILLS
Writing to Clients

Leslie Linden works as a paralegal for Sandra O'Connell, a sole practitioner who owns a small family-law practice. Sandra asks Leslie to draft a letter to a client, Karen Young, explaining that her divorce hearing is scheduled for June 3, 1999, and informing Karen that she needs to be present in court on that date. Leslie sits down at the computer and drafts the following letter to the client:

The hearing for your divorce is scheduled to take place on Monday, June 3, 1999, at 10 A.M. The hearing will be conducted in Room 2B of the Jefferson County Courthouse in Jefferson City. Please arrive at the courthouse by 9:30 A.M.

Because this is a no-fault divorce state, your divorce is not contested, and we have worked out your property settlement in advance, the hearing will be brief. We expect you to be on the stand for only fifteen minutes at the most. You will be asked to make a statement concerning your reasons for wanting a divorce, and the judge will ask you a few questions.

Ms. O'Connell would like you to call the office and schedule an appointment, at your convenience, to prepare you for the hearing. She will discuss with you at that time what you will say on the stand and the kinds of questions that the judge will probably ask you. Please contact the office at your earliest convenience.

TIPS FOR DRAFTING LETTERS
- Write to your audience.
- Minimize the use of legalese, especially when writing to clients.
- Use plain English, good grammar, and correct spelling.
- Organize the letter so that it flows logically.
- Always obtain a writing sample from the attorney for whom you work.

---

to bring the analysis to a definite conclusion, setting forth the firm's opinion on the matter.

In addition to rendering the law firm's legal opinion, opinion letters may also be used to inform a client of the legal validity of a specific action. For example, a company seeking to establish operations in a foreign country may seek a lawyer's opinion on whether a certain action it plans to undertake is legally permissible. The attorney (or a paralegal) will research the issue and then draft an advisory letter to the client. Opinion letters are commonly quite long and include detailed explanations of how the law applies to the client's factual situation. Sometimes, the attorney just summarizes his or her conclusion in the opinion letter (as in the opinion letter shown in Exhibit 16.10) and attaches a legal memorandum to the letter explaining the legal sources and reasoning used in forming that conclusion.

Opinion letters issued by a firm reflect legal expertise and advice on which a client can rely. Note the following rule:

> **Opinion letters must be signed by attorneys.**

Should doubts about the legal validity of an opinion letter surface at a later date, the client may bring a malpractice suit against the firm. The signature of an attorney represents the attorney's acceptance of responsibility for what is stated in the document and can serve as the basis for liability.

DEMAND LETTERS. Another basic type of letter is the demand letter. **Demand letters** are adversarial in nature and seek to advance the interests of a client. Usually, a demand letter attempts to persuade the reader to accept the position most

Demand Letter
An adversarial letter that attempts to persuade the reader that he or she should accept a position that is favorable to the writer's client—that is, demanding that the reader do or not do a certain thing.

EXHIBIT 16.10
A Sample Opinion Letter

Jeffers, Gilmore & Dunn
553 Fifth Avenue
Suite 101
Nita City, NI 48801

Telephone (616) 555-9690
Fax (616) 555-9679
e-mail:JGD@nitanet.com

December 9, 2000

J. D. Joslyn
President and Chief Executive Officer
Joslyn Footwear, Inc.
700 Kings Avenue, Suite 4000
New City, NI 48023

Dear Ms. Joslyn:

After careful consideration of your plans to expand Joslyn Footwear, Inc., into Latin American markets, I have concluded that to implement the current plans would subject you to potentially significant liability.

The most serious flaw in the current plans concerns your construction of massive shoe-producing industrial plants. Unfortunately, the plans fail to conform to the minimum legal and industrial regulations in Mexico, Uruguay, and Argentina.

The enclosed legal memorandum explains in detail how the law applies to your situation and the reasons for my conclusion. Please call me if you have any questions.

Very truly yours,

Allen P. Gilmore

Allen P. Gilmore
Attorney at Law

APG/ec

Enclosure

---

favorable to the client. For example, your supervising attorney may ask you to draft a letter to a client's debtor, demanding payment for an amount owed. Whatever the content of a demand letter, its purpose is to demand something of the recipient on behalf of the client.

The demand letter should adopt a serious and persuasive tone, and the client's demand must not be frivolous. Although the letter should be insistent and adversarial, it should not come across as unreasonable or harassing. After all, demand letters seek to accomplish something rather than foreclose opportunities. A common form of demand letter in litigation firms is a letter in which an attorney requests a response from an adversarial party in a lawsuit to an offer to settle the case. Exhibit 16.11 on page 611 illustrates this type of demand letter.

> ### ETHICAL CONCERN
> ### Letters and the Unauthorized Practice of Law
>
> As has been stressed in other areas of this text, engaging in the unauthorized practice of law is one of the most serious potential ethical and legal problems facing paralegals. To avoid liability for the unauthorized practice of law, you should never sign opinion (advisory) letters with your own name, and when you sign other types of letters, you should always indicate your status as a paralegal. Even if the person to whom you are sending the letter knows you quite well and knows you are a paralegal, you should indicate your status on the letter itself. By doing so, you will prevent potential confusion as well as potential legal liability. Even if your name and status is included in the letterhead (as is permitted under some state laws), as a precaution, you should type your title below your name at the end of the letter as well.

The Internal Memorandum

The internal legal memorandum, as the term implies, is prepared for internal use within a law firm, legal department, or other organization or agency. As a paralegal, you may be asked to draft a legal memorandum for your supervising attorney. Generally, the legal memo presents a thorough summary and analysis of a particular legal problem.

The attorney for whom the document is prepared may be relying on the memo for a number of reasons. For example, the attorney may be preparing a brief on behalf of a client or an opinion letter regarding a client's claim. Thus, if you are asked to draft the memo, you will want it to be extremely thorough and clearly written. Because the legal memo is directed to attorneys who are knowledgeable in the law, there is no need to avoid sophisticated legal terminology or to define basic legal theories or procedures.

The purpose of the memo is to provide an attorney with all relevant information regarding the case, so the document is written objectively. It is an explanatory memo informing the attorney of all sides of the issues presented, including both the strengths and weaknesses of the client's claim or defense. You should keep the following in mind:

 Your goal in drafting a legal memorandum is to inform, explain, and evaluate the client's claim or defense.

A legal memorandum is organized in a logical manner. Although there is no one way to structure the legal memo, most are divided into sections that perform distinct functions. Of course, if the law firm or the attorney for whom you are working prefers a particular format, that format should be followed. Generally, legal memos contain the following sections:

- Heading.
- Statement of the facts.
- Questions presented.
- Brief conclusion in response to the questions presented.
- Discussion and analysis of the facts and the applicable law.
- Conclusion.

EXHIBIT 16.11
A Sample Demand Letter

> **Jeffers, Gilmore & Dunn**
> **553 Fifth Avenue**
> **Suite 101**
> **Nita City, NI 48801**
>
> Telephone (616) 555-9690
> Fax (616) 555-9679
> e-mail:JGD@nitanet.com
>
> June 15, 2000
>
> Christopher P. Nelson, Esq.
> Nelson, Johnson, Callan & Sietz
> 200 Way Bridge
> Philadelphia, PA 40022
>
> RE: Furman v. Thompson
>
> Dear Mr. Nelson:
>
> This morning, I met with my clients, Mark and Andrea Furman, the plaintiffs in the lawsuit against your client, Laura Thompson. Both Mark and Andrea expressed a desire to withdraw their complaint and settle with Ms. Thompson. The Furmans' settlement demand is $20,000, payable by certified check no later than July 7, 2000. Considering the strength of the plaintiffs' claims against Ms. Thompson and the possibility of a jury award exceeding $100,000, the Furmans and I think that you and your client will find this demand quite reasonable.
>
> Please contact me by Friday, June 25, 2000, if you plan to take advantage of the Furmans' demand. If we do not hear from you by that date, we will interpret your inaction as a rejection of the Furmans' settlement offer.
>
> Very truly yours,
>
> *Allen P. Gilmore*
>
> Allen P. Gilmore
> Attorney at Law
>
> APG/ec

Heading

The *heading* of a legal memorandum contains four pieces of information:

- The date on which the memo is submitted.
- The name of the person submitting the memo.
- The name of the person for whom the memo was prepared.
- A brief description of the matter, usually in the form of a reference line.

Exhibit 16.12 on page 613 illustrates a sample heading for a legal memorandum.

Statement of the Facts

The *statement of the facts* introduces the legal issues by describing the factual elements of the dispute. Only the relevant facts are included in this section. Thus, a

PARALEGAL PROFILE

Litigation Paralegal

MICHAEL GAIGE is a legal assistant with the Portland, Maine, law firm of Harvey & Frank, where he specializes in civil litigation. Gaige received his B.A. degree from Lock Haven University in Pennsylvania in 1974, and his paralegal certificate from Bentley College in Waltham, Massachusetts, in 1979. He began working as a legal assistant in February 1980 and received his certified legal assistant (CLA) designation from the National Association of Legal Assistants, Inc., in March 1985. He has lectured at seminars on various litigation topics and was an adjunct instructor for the National Academy for Paralegal Studies in Bangor, Maine. Gaige is a member of the board of directors of the Maine State Association of Legal Assistants and a member of the board of directors of the National Association of Legal Assistants, Inc., as its Region I Director.

What do you like best about your work?
"The thing I like best is the constant learning process. Whether it is keeping up with advances in technology or gathering and organizing facts and documents about a particular case, litigation involves a constant learning process that is challenging and stimulating. Many cases require that you develop some degree of familiarity with an industry or about a product or something of which you had little or no previous knowledge. You can never acquire too much knowledge, and a law firm is a great place to do so—just 'bring your own container.'"

What is the greatest challenge that you face in your area of work?
"The greatest challenge in litigation is keeping everything organized. Whether it involves maintaining a database or keeping track of physical documents and other evidence, it is important that at least one person attempts to maintain control over the various components of a file at all times. Seldom does a day pass that I am not asked, 'Where can I find this?' or 'Can you bring me that?' When several people are working on delegated tasks related to the same file, it can be very challenging to keep track of and help coordinate everything related to one case, let alone the ten or twenty or thirty cases on which you are working."

What advice do you have for would-be paralegals in your area of work?
"Be as organized and proactive as possible. Learn to use the technology and software programs that can make your job easier. With experience comes the ability to anticipate what needs to be done. Don't wait to receive instructions to perform a task or a project if there are things you know need to be accomplished. Although preparing for and assisting at trial can be glamorous and exciting, it also requires long hours and generous helpings of stress. If you are looking for a nine-to-five job and are not particularly adept at coping with stress, you may be better suited to areas of the law other than litigation."

What are some tips for success as a paralegal in your area of work?
"Always reduce assignments to writing. Make certain you understand precisely what your assignment is and the time constraints associated with each one. Few things are more frustrating to an attorney and more wasteful of time and energy than spending time on an assignment that does not result in what the attorney wanted accomplished. Make certain you have an understanding of all the factual and legal issues and the desired result. Otherwise, important information may be overlooked when performing isolated tasks with a limited understanding of the case. You never know when that seemingly unimportant point will become remarkably significant as the case develops."

> "Make certain you understand precisely what your assignment is and the time constraints associated with each one."

EXHIBIT 16.12
Legal Memorandum—Heading

MEMORANDUM

DATE: August 6, 2000

TO: Allen P. Gilmore, Partner

FROM: Elena Lopez, Paralegal

RE: Neely, Rachel: Emotional Distress—File No. 00-2146
Neely, Rachel, and Melanie: Emotional Distress—File No. 00-2147

key requirement of paralegals is that they learn which facts are legally significant. In other words, as a paralegal, you will need to determine which facts have a bearing on the legal issues in the case and which facts are irrelevant.

Facts presented in a legal memo must not be slanted in favor of the client. The legal memo is not an adversarial argument on the client's behalf. Rather, it is an objective presentation of both the facts and the legal issues. Therefore, you should never omit facts that are unfavorable to the client's claim or defense. The attorney for whom you work needs to know all of the facts that will influence the outcome of the case.

The statement of the facts should contain a logical and concise description of the events surrounding the conflict. Presenting events chronologically often helps to clarify the factual pattern in a case. Alternatively, facts relating to the same issue can be grouped together. The latter organizational technique is especially useful when the facts are complicated and numerous legal issues are presented.

Exhibit 16.13 on the next page indicates what kinds of information are typically included in a statement of the facts. It also shows what writing style is generally used.

Questions Presented

The *questions presented* address the legal issues presented by the factual circumstances described in the statement of the facts. The questions should be specific and straightforward. They should refer to the parties by name, succinctly set out the legal problem, and specifically indicate the important and relevant events. The questions-presented section may involve just one simple issue or a number of complex issues. Regardless of the complexity of the matter, this section helps bring the main points of the conflict into focus. See Exhibit 16.14 on page 615 for an example of how the questions presented might be phrased.

Brief Conclusion

The *brief conclusion* (or *short answer* or *brief answer*) sets forth succinct responses to the questions presented in the previous section. The responses may vary in length. For example, as indicated in Exhibit 16.15 on page 615, certain questions can be answered simply by "yes," "no," "probably so," or "probably not," followed by a brief sentence summarizing the reason for that answer. For complicated legal questions, a more detailed statement might be appropriate. Even so, each conclusion should be limited to a maximum of one paragraph. The discussion of the legal analysis, which is the main part of the memo, provides ample opportunity for supporting details.

CHAPTER 16 *Legal Analysis and Writing* 617

EXHIBIT 16.13
Legal Memorandum—
Statement of the Facts

STATEMENT OF THE FACTS

Ms. Rachel Neely ("Neely") and Ms. Melanie Neely ("Melanie"), our clients, seek advice in connection with possible emotional distress claims against Mr. Miles Thompson ("Thompson"). The claims arose as a result of (1) Neely's distress at hearing a car crash, caused by Thompson and involving her eleven-year-old daughter, Melanie, and subsequently viewing Melanie's injuries; and (2) Melanie's distress related to statements made by Thompson.

In February 1998, Neely and Melanie moved to Union City from San Francisco. Neely immediately began working for an investment firm in downtown Union City. At that firm, she became acquainted with the defendant, Thompson. Thompson was Neely's boss. At first, the two had a friendly, professional relationship. During this time, Thompson and Neely spent much time together socially and learned much about each other. Thompson, for example, knew that Neely had left San Francisco after her marriage ended. Neely had confided in Thompson that the divorce and the events preceding it were extremely traumatic for herself and for Melanie. Melanie knew Thompson and was comfortable with him. Thompson had spent time with Melanie and knew that Melanie had suffered emotionally because of her parents' bitter divorce.

The relationship between Thompson and Neely became strained approximately six months after Neely began working with Thompson. Tension between the parties arose as a result of Thompson's expression of romantic interest in Neely. Neely, who was dating someone else, had no romantic interest in Thompson and communicated to him her lack of interest in pursuing that type of relationship with him.

On April 2, 2000, Thompson visited the Neely home. Melanie was not fully aware of the problem her mother was having with Thompson. Thompson came to the door, and Melanie, who was alone in the house, let him in. Thompson invited Melanie for a ride in his Corvette. Melanie willingly went with him. Meanwhile, Neely, who had gone to the grocery store to buy some milk, returned to the house to find Melanie missing. She panicked, called the neighbors, and then called the police.

Thompson, who claims that he took Melanie for a ride so that she could be informed about her mother's "bad behavior," drove around Union City with Melanie for approximately thirty minutes. During this ride, Thompson told Melanie that her mother was a "wicked, selfish, woman, who could care less about Melanie." Thompson also told Melanie that her mother was a "no good, sex-crazed woman who would leave Melanie once the right man came along." Upon returning to the Neely home, Thompson made a left turn from Oak Street onto Maple Road, and his car was hit by an oncoming vehicle. According to the police report of the accident, Thompson's blood-alcohol level indicated that he was intoxicated.

The Neely home is located on the corner of the intersection of Maple Road and Oak Street. Neely heard the crash and ran outside. Seeing the accident and recognizing Thompson's car, she approached the site of the accident. There she saw Melanie bleeding profusely from head injuries. As a result of the accident, Melanie spent two days at Union City Memorial Hospital, where she was kept under observation for possible internal injuries. Melanie continues to be severely depressed and emotionally unstable as a result of Thompson's comments. Additionally, she has frequent nightmares and finds it difficult to speak without stuttering. Since the time of the accident, she has been under psychiatric therapy for these problems. Neely, who fainted after viewing her daughter's injuries, spent one day in Union City Memorial Hospital for extreme anxiety and trauma.

Discussion and Analysis

The *discussion and analysis* section of the legal memorandum, as the phrase implies, contains a discussion and legal analysis of each issue to be resolved. If the facts of the dispute concern only one legal issue, the entire discussion will revolve around that issue. Legal memoranda usually address multiple issues, however. When multiple issues are involved, the paralegal should organize the discussion into separate parts so that each legal issue can be analyzed separately. For example, if the dispute involves two potential legal claims, the discussion should be divided into two sections with a descriptive heading for each section. The headings of the two sections might read as follows:

I. Negligent Infliction of Emotional Distress.
II. Intentional Infliction of Emotional Distress.

EXHIBIT 16.14
Legal Memorandum—
Questions Presented

> **QUESTIONS PRESENTED**
>
> 1. Does Neely have a claim for the negligent infliction of emotional distress as a result of viewing the injuries sustained by her daughter in a car accident caused by Thompson's negligence?
>
> 2. Does Melanie have a claim for the intentional infliction of emotional distress arising out of Thompson's statements to her on April 2, 2000?

The legal analysis presented in the memo should answer the following questions:

- What options are available to the client?
- Which of the options are favorable?
- Will these options offer a reasonable resolution of the issues?
- What law supports the strongest position?
- Is it case law or statutory law?
- What law goes against the client's claim or defense?
- Are there any constitutional issues involved?
- On what law would the other side rely to support its position?
- How can the attorney respond to the other side's strongest arguments?

The discussion is the core of the legal memo. This section provides an opportunity for paralegals to demonstrate good research and writing skills. After the research is completed, you must relate the legal findings to the facts of the matter. The reader expects to find a thorough analysis of the law. One method of legal reasoning and analysis commonly used by paralegals and other legal professionals is called the *IRAC method*. IRAC is an acronym consisting of the first letters of the following words: Issue, Rule, Application, and Conclusion. To use the IRAC method, you first state the issue you are researching. Then you state the rule of law that applies to the issue. The rule of law may be a rule stated by the courts in previous decisions, a state or federal statute, or a state or federal administrative agency regulation. Next, you apply the rule of law to the set of facts involved in the client's case. Finally, you set forth your conclusion on the matter. If there are two or more issues involved in the client's case, you can analyze each issue using the IRAC method.

Points of law should be identified and supported with proper citations. Occasionally, legal sources will directly address a point that applies to the case at hand.

EXHIBIT 16.15
Legal Memorandum—
Brief Conclusion

> **BRIEF CONCLUSION**
>
> 1. Probably not. Neely cannot recover under the rule that is currently applied in this jurisdiction. This rule requires that the plaintiff be present at the scene when the accident occurs.
>
> 2. Most likely, yes. Thompson's conduct toward Melanie appears to have been (1) reckless, (2) outrageous and extreme, and (3) the direct cause of Melanie's severe emotional distress.

> ## ETHICAL CONCERN
> ### Objectivity and the Legal Memorandum
>
> Assume that you are conducting research on behalf of a client who is bringing a lawsuit against a restaurant for negligence. The client's wife choked to death on a piece of meat, and none of the restaurant's employees offered to help. As a member of the legal team representing the client's interests, your goal is to maximize the client's chances of winning in court. During your research, you discover that although no precedential cases involving a similar fact pattern have been decided in your jurisdiction, another state's supreme court has recently held for the defendant restaurant in a very similar case. Because the courts in your state are not obligated to follow this ruling, you might be tempted to downplay the case's significance in your legal memorandum. Do not do this. In deciding whether the client should sue, the attorney needs to make an informed judgment—and he or she will be relying on you to supply objective information. It is in the best interests of the client to point out to your attorney the potential arguments of opposing counsel.

In these situations, it is effective to quote directly from the text or the case, statute, or other legal source. You should not rely too heavily on quoted material, however. Although quotations from a case or other legal authority can lend extremely helpful support, you should always keep the following fact in mind:

 The attorney for whom the memo is prepared wants to see your analysis, not a reiteration of a court's opinion.

Exhibit 16.16 presents a portion of a discussion section in a legal memorandum. We have annotated the exhibit to illustrate the basic IRAC elements.

When discussing how other cases have addressed certain issues, you need to include citations to the cases. As mentioned in Chapter 14, there are various guides to citation formats, including the book entitled *The Bluebook: A Uniform System of Citation*, which is published by the Harvard Law Review Association.

Conclusion

The *conclusion* is the culmination of the legal memo. Many issues have been analyzed, and both the strengths and weaknesses of the client's matter have been evaluated. Now you should conclude the analysis by taking a position. The conclusion is your opinion of how the issues discussed may be resolved. Exhibit 16.17 shows an example of a conclusion to a legal memorandum.

The concluding section may acknowledge the fact that research into a particular area bore little fruit. For example, there may be no cases on point to support one of the issues. The conclusion also may instruct the attorney that more information is needed or may demonstrate that a certain issue needs to be evaluated further. Finally, this section presents you with an opportunity to make strategic suggestions. Paralegals should feel comfortable—especially after a careful legal analysis—in recommending a course of action. Not only do your recommendations reflect thorough analysis, but they also indicate that you are willing to exercise initiative and make a mature judgment, which will be helpful to your supervising attorney.

EXHIBIT 16.16
Legal Memorandum—
Discussion (Excerpt)

DISCUSSION (excerpt)

I. Negligent Infliction of Emotional Distress

Recovery Restriction

Issue — *Are there any restrictions on recovering for the negligent infliction of emotional distress?*

Rule — An individual's right to emotional tranquility is recognized by the law protecting persons against the negligent infliction of emotional distress. The method for determining whether protection should be afforded for emotional distress caused by the knowledge of a third person's injury as a result of a defendant's negligent actions is clear in this jurisdiction. *The rule adopted in this jurisdiction is the "impact rule," which requires that a plaintiff alleging emotional distress must also suffer a direct, physical impact from the same force that injured the victim.* Saechao v. Matsskoun, 717 P.2d 165, 168 (Or.App. 1986). This "bright line" rule provides the courts with a test from which they can easily determine the relationship between compensability and the defendant's breach of duty owed to the victim. *Id.* At 169.

Application — Neely was in her house when the accident occurred. She heard the crash and ran outside. Recognizing Thompson's car, Neely approached it and found Melanie bleeding profusely from head injuries. Neely did not suffer any direct physical impact from the car accident which injured Melanie. Thus, Neely could not recover under the impact rule because she did not suffer any direct physical impact and Thompson owed her no duty.

The impact rule, which evolved as a result of the law's early reluctance to acknowledge the authenticity of emotional distress claims, avoids the problems of floodgate litigation. *Id.* at 169. It strictly limits a victim's recovery. Some strong arguments can be made against the application of the impact rule. Although the rule limits a defendant's liability and offers an easy decision-making criterion for the courts, it also lends itself to arbitrary and often unjust results. The impact rule makes an after-the-fact determination of duty, protecting those suffering from emotional distress only if they also suffered harm directly and physically as a result of the defendant's negligence. *Id.* at 171.

THE APPELLATE BRIEF

Appellate Brief
A document submitted to an appellate court setting forth legal arguments and supporting law in favor of the appellant or the appellee.

The purpose of the **appellate brief** is to persuade a court of appeals to decide the issue in favor of your client. The brief is filed with the appellate court before the court reviews the case being appealed. The court reviews the briefs submitted by the attorneys for both sides to gain a better understanding of the issues presented in the dispute. Your goal in writing an appellate brief is to convince your

EXHIBIT 16.17
Legal Memorandum—
Conclusion

CONCLUSION

It is unlikely that Neely has a cause of action against Thompson for the emotional distress that she allegedly suffered due to Thompson's negligence.

It is likely that Melanie has a cause of action for the intentional infliction of emotional distress based on Thompson's outrageous comments to her about her mother.

Note that Neely might pursue, on her own behalf, a claim for the intentional infliction of emotional distress against Thompson for Thompson's reckless behavior in taking Melanie from her home and telling Melanie outrageous things. I recommend that we speak with Neely about the effect on her of Thompson's statements to Melanie. This, in my opinion, is a strong claim. I believe that we could argue successfully that Thompson intended to injure Neely through this egregious act.

readers that the matter must be decided in favor of the client on whose behalf the brief was written.

Although the arguments in an appellate brief should be forceful and convincing, you must not misrepresent or exaggerate the facts and issues. Always keep in mind that the goal is to persuade the court in favor of the client. If a brief is not credible, or believable, the court will lack confidence in the argument. Arguments must be presented reasonably and be based on the facts of the case and valid law.

Types of Appellate Briefs

Four types of appellate briefs may be filed with the appellate court: the appellant's brief, the appellee's brief, the reply brief, and the *amicus curiae*[3] brief. These briefs are all adversarial—that is, they present arguments on behalf of one of the parties—but they contain distinguishing characteristics.

APPELLANT'S BRIEF. The **appellant** is the party who appealed the case and who seeks to convince the appellate court to reverse the decision of the trial court. The **appellant's brief** is the first brief filed with the court and, as such, establishes the issues to be addressed. The purpose of the brief is to convince the court that the lower court's decision was erroneous.

APPELLEE'S BRIEF. The **appellee** is the party who prevailed in the lower court and against whom the appeal is brought. The **appellee's brief** will address the issues raised by the appellant's brief. It is filed as a direct response to the claims set forth by the appellant. The purpose of the appellee's brief is to rebut (counter) any arguments in the appellant's brief and to emphasize the accuracy of the earlier judgment rendered in the appellee's favor.

The appellant's brief, because it is the first brief filed with the court, will often contain more background information about the dispute than the appellee's brief. If the attorney for the appellee is satisfied with the appellant's presentation of the procedural history, facts, and issues, he or she may choose to state that the appellee adopts that portion of the appellant's brief.

REPLY BRIEF. The **reply brief** is filed by the appellant in response to the appellee's brief. The appellant, as the first party to file a brief, needs an opportunity to respond to arguments submitted in subsequent briefs. Although advocating the appellant's cause, the reply brief is narrow in scope and focuses on rebutting whatever arguments were presented in briefs submitted on behalf of the appellee.

AMICUS CURIAE BRIEF. The Latin phrase *amicus curiae* means "friend of the court." The phrase refers to individuals or organizations that submit briefs to the appellate court despite the fact that they are not parties to the lawsuit. An individual or organization seeking to file an *amicus curiae* **brief** with the court must petition the court for the right to do so. *Amicus* briefs are usually filed in cases that involve broad public issues, such as civil rights or environmental concerns. The purpose of the *amicus* brief is to convince the court to rule in favor of one of the parties because not to do so would affect a broad interest of society. For example, the American Civil Liberties Union frequently files *amicus* briefs on behalf of parties whose civil rights or liberties have allegedly been violated.

Writing an Effective Appellate Brief

An appellate brief is an important document and should be submitted to the court as a formal piece of legal writing. The court expects a document that presents clear and

On the Web
You can now find appellate briefs online at some courts' sites. For example, the Supreme Court of Florida posts briefs on its Web site at www.flcourts.org/courts/supct/oacal.html.

Appellant
The party appealing a case.

Appellant's Brief
An appellate brief that argues in favor of the appellant's position. This brief will try to convince the court that the lower court's decision was erroneous.

Appellee
The party against whom an appeal is brought.

Appellee's Brief
An appellate brief that argues in favor of the appellee's position. This brief will attempt to rebut (counter) any arguments in the appellant's brief and will emphasize the accuracy of the earlier judgment rendered in its favor.

Reply Brief
An appellate brief filed by the appellant to rebut (counter) arguments made by the appellee in the appellee's brief.

Amicus Curiae Brief
A brief filed with the court by a third party (that is, a party not directly involved in the lawsuit) that is concerned about the outcome of the litigation. The purpose of such a brief is to convince the court to rule in favor of one of the parties because not to do so would affect a broad interest of society. (*Amicus curiae* is Latin for "friend of the court.")

---

3. Pronounced ah-*mee*-cuhs *kur*-ee-ay.

concise arguments. In addition, each court has procedural rules dictating the general format required of an appellate brief. Because the prescribed format differs from one jurisdiction to another, paralegals should become familiar with the rules of the relevant court. The following sections describe the format required by most courts.

TITLE PAGE. The *title page* is the front cover of the appellate brief. The title page provides certain information about the case on appeal. Most title pages identify the court to which the case is being appealed and the lower court from which the case is being appealed. The index or docket number is also listed for easy identification. The names of both the appellant and appellee appear on the title page, but the brief clearly states for which party the document is submitted. Finally, the title page contains the name and address of the attorney or law firm filing the brief and the date of the filing. Exhibit 16.18 on the next page shows a sample title page of an appellate brief submitted by the appellee (respondent) to the United States Supreme Court.

Courts often have rules specifying the colors to be used for the covers of various types of briefs. For example, a court may require the appellant to submit a blue title page and the appellee to submit a red title page; two other colors may be assigned for reply briefs and *amicus curiae* briefs. The colors assigned may vary from one jurisdiction to another.

TABLE OF CONTENTS. The *table of contents* lists the sections of the appellate brief and gives the page number on which each section begins. The table of contents not only functions as an index to the contents of the brief but also provides the reader with a glimpse of the argument, because it outlines the points being made in the argument. This comprehensive outline allows the reader to locate a particular part of the argument without having to search through the entire document. A sample table of contents is shown in Exhibit 16.19 on page 621.

TABLE OF AUTHORITIES. The *table of authorities* provides the reader with page references for all authorities cited in the argument. The court and the parties to the dispute will want to refer to the sources of law behind certain arguments, and the table of authorities provides an efficient guide for locating them in the brief. The sources are arranged in a particular order, as shown in Exhibit 16.20 on page 622. Cases cited in the brief are listed first. The entries are presented alphabetically and contain the full name of the case followed by the proper citations. Following the list of cases are listings of statutory and constitutional provisions referred to in the brief. Additional sources, such as treatises or articles in legal periodicals, may be listed under specific categories or under "miscellaneous."

The table of authorities, which is a crucial part of the brief, is one of the last sections to be completed. When the argument is in final form, the attorney usually asks the paralegal to prepare the table of authorities. Because the court and opposing counsel will rely on the table, accuracy is extremely important. If you prepare a table of authorities, make sure that you are working from the final copy of the brief. If the attorney continues to edit and make changes to the brief, sources may be deleted or moved, making it very difficult to achieve an accurate listing.

STATEMENT OF JURISDICTION. The *statement of jurisdiction* indicates the source of authority for the appellate court's jurisdiction over the dispute. This section of the brief usually refers to the statute granting jurisdiction to the court, as in Exhibit 16.21 on page 622.

QUESTIONS PRESENTED. The *questions presented* set out the legal issues that will be argued by the parties in the dispute. This section provides the court with a

EXHIBIT 16.18
Appellate Brief—Title Page

```
IN THE SUPREME
COURT
OF THE UNITED STATES
SPRING TERM 1999
NO. 00-198
```

John Jeffries Connelly   Petitioner

—AGAINST—

United States of America   Respondent

**ON WRIT OF CERTIORARI
TO THE
UNITED STATES COURT OF APPEALS
FOR THE SECOND CIRCUIT**

BRIEF FOR RESPONDENT

Joseph P. McCaffrey
U.S. Attorney for the
District of Nita
309 Garden Boulevard,
Suite 321
Capital City, NI 49250
(417) 555-9708

---

capsule summary of why the decision of the trial court should be reversed or upheld. The number of questions presented to the court reflects the number of legal issues on which the party seeks the court's opinion. When there is more than one issue, each issue raised is numbered separately. In Exhibit 16.22 on page 623, which illustrates this section of the appellate brief, there is only one question on appeal.

The questions should be framed in such a way that they lead to a response in the client's favor. The goal is to have the reader nodding his or her head in agreement as the questions are read. The questions should also be clear and concise; they should convince—not confuse—the reader.

STATEMENT OF THE CLAIM. The *statement of the claim* usually contains two components: a preliminary statement dealing with the procedural background of

EXHIBIT 16.19
Appellate Brief—Table of Contents

TABLE OF CONTENTS

Table of Authorities ii
Statement of Jurisdiction 1
Questions Presented 1
Opinions Below 2
Statement of the Claim 2
Summary of the Argument 4

Argument:

    I. The circuits have split three ways in establishing the level of inquiry necessary for a waiver of counsel to be knowing and intelligent 8
        A. This court has never set out a specific line of inquiry for a trial judge to conduct in order to determine whether a defendant has knowingly and intelligently waived counsel 9
        B. Four circuits have adopted a minimum-inquiry approach, four circuits have adopted a middle-inquiry approach, and three circuits have adopted a searching-inquiry approach 10
    II. The Second Circuit correctly found that the district court's record, which would satisfy all inquiry approaches, supported a knowing and intelligent waiver 13
        A. The district court's inquiry and the facts and circumstances indicated in the record clearly establish that there was a knowing and intelligent waiver of counsel 15
        B. The district court's inquiry would satisfy any of the circuit's approaches 16
    III. This court should require no more than a middle-inquiry approach in the determination of a knowing and intelligent waiver of counsel 17
        A. Deference should be given to the district court judge 17
        B. A brief comment on the record both respects the discretion of the trial judge and promotes judicial economy 19

the case and a statement of the relevant facts of the case. The preliminary statement is essentially a procedural history of the dispute as viewed from the client's perspective. The procedural information in this section will explain how and from what court the case has been appealed. Additionally, this section includes information regarding the nature of the cause of action, the parties to the suit, the injuries sustained, and the relief sought.

    The statement of the facts sets forth the important factual background of the case. The facts are not presented objectively. Rather, they are presented persuasively so that the court is inclined to accept the client's perspective. At the same time, the description of the facts should not be exaggerated or misleading.

> **TABLE OF AUTHORITIES**
>
> CASES:
>   Adams v. Carroll, 875 F.2d 1441 (9th Cir. 1992)..................... 15
>   Chapman v. United States, 953 F.3d 886, 890
>   (5th Cir. 1994)... 8
>   Faretta v. California, 422 U.S. 806 (1975)............................... 5
>   Fitzpatrick v. Wainwright, 800 F.2d 1057
>   (11th Cir. 1986)... 17
>
> CONSTITUTIONAL PROVISIONS:
>   Art. 7, U.S. Constitution... 14
>
> STATUTES:
>   Mass. Code Ann., Sec. 24 (1989).. 12
>
> LAW REVIEW ARTICLES:
>   Callan, Waiver of Consent and Pro Se
>   Representation, 78 U. Co. L. Rev, 455 (1990).................... 11

EXHIBIT 16.20
Appellate Brief—
Table of Authorities

The facts that are communicated to the appellate court are limited to the facts that appear in the record of the case.[4] In presenting the facts, the writer must cite the part of the record from which that information was obtained. An excerpt from a statement of the claim is shown in Exhibit 16.23.

SUMMARY OF THE ARGUMENT. The *summary of the argument* is a condensed version of the developed argument made in the main text of the brief. This section should not attempt to match the main body of the argument in detail and depth, but should present the reader with an overview that mentions each major section of the argument. This section of the brief is relied on heavily by those who have not had an opportunity to review the argument section thoroughly.

The summary is usually one or two pages in length, although the length varies, depending on the size and complexity of the argument. It is not necessary to include citations or quotations in the summary, as they will appear in the main part of the argument. See Exhibit 16.24 on page 624 for an excerpt from a sample summary of the argument.

ARGUMENT. In the *argument* section, which is the core of the appellate brief, the legal arguments are developed and analyzed in detail. This is the section in

---

4. The record of the case, or record on appeal, consists of the following: (1) the pleadings, (2) a transcript of the trial testimony and copies of the exhibits, (3) the judge's rulings on motions made by the parties, (4) the arguments of counsel, (5) the instructions to the jury, (6) the verdict, (7) the posttrial motions, and (8) the judgment order from which the appeal is taken.

> **STATEMENT OF JURISDICTION**
>
> This Court has jurisdiction under 28 U.S.C. Sec. 1298 (1977).

EXHIBIT 16.21
Appellate Brief—
Statement of Jurisdiction

EXHIBIT 16.22
Appellate Brief—
Question Presented

> **QUESTION PRESENTED**
>
> Whether a waiver of a defendant's constitutional right to counsel is knowing and intelligent when a district court judge does not conduct a sweeping inquiry before allowing that defendant to proceed *pro se* [on his or her own behalf].

which the writer seeks to convince the court that a decision should be rendered in favor of the client. The section sets forth the reasons why the court should decide the case in the client's favor and supports these reasons by referring to case law, statutes, and other legal sources. The argument should be persuasive and convincingly advocate the client's position. The decision of the appellate court is influenced by both the logic and forcefulness of the argument.

Each section of the argument has two main components: the *point heading* and the *body of the argument*. These components are discussed below and illustrated in Exhibit 16.25 on the next page.

Point Headings and Subheadings. Each section that discusses one of the legal arguments begins with a point heading, which usually begins with a roman numeral. **Point headings** are brief recapitulations of the argument. Effective point headings enhance the argument's presentation. These headings serve as a road map for the reader, setting out the points to be made and separating the text into logical sections. Point headings, if written clearly and concisely, make the argument much easier to follow.

A section of the argument may warrant more than a point heading. If the discussion is particularly complex, the addition of subheadings may help to clarify the structure of the presentation. There should not be too many subheadings under a point heading, however. Excessive divisions in the argument make the argument choppy and confusing. Point headings and subheadings should be distinguishable from one another. It is helpful to review forms for point headings and subheadings, which are on file at most law firms, to gain insight into both organizational and stylistic presentation.

Point Heading
A brief recapitulation of the point being made in a section of an appellate brief. Point headings separate the text into logical sections and make the argument easier to follow.

EXHIBIT 16.23
Appellate Brief—Statement of the Claim (Excerpt)

> **STATEMENT OF THE CLAIM (Excerpt)**
>
> Three weeks before his trial for charges of violating the National Firearms Act, petitioner, John J. Connelly, filed a motion to proceed *pro se* with the district court. A week after his motion was filed, the district court held a hearing specifically to consider petitioner's request to represent himself at trial. The trial judge's discussion of the matter with petitioner was thorough, covering the crimes with which he was charged, the statutes he had violated, and the maximum penalties that applied. The judge reiterated petitioner's right to counsel and stressed that the court would appoint counsel should petitioner lack sufficient funds.
>
> During the hearing, petitioner unequivocally stated his intention to proceed *pro se* and conceded full awareness of the nature of his crimes and the penalties attached. The court cautioned the petitioner, warning that although he had a constitutional right to proceed *pro se*, self-representation was not the best form of defense.
>
> The petitioner, a thirty-five-year-old college graduate, never wavered in expressing his desire to relinquish the right to counsel and to exercise his constitutional right to proceed *pro se*. . . .

EXHIBIT 16.24

Appellate Brief—Summary of the Argument (Excerpt)

SUMMARY OF THE ARGUMENT (Excerpt)

The Second Circuit correctly affirmed the district court's finding of a knowing and intelligent waiver of counsel. To exercise the right to self-representation, a defendant must voluntarily make the decision and be fully informed of its possible consequences. The circuit courts have split in their interpretation of what constitutes a knowing and intelligent waiver of counsel. There are three approaches. Two approaches are adopted by four circuits, and the other approach is adopted by three circuits. The three approaches are (1) the minimum-inquiry approach, (2) the middle-inquiry approach, and (3) the searching-inquiry approach.

The district court's inquiry and the record as a whole satisfy all three approaches. The inquiry held by the court covered what was essential in evaluating petitioner's understanding: the right being waived, the criminal charges, and the maximum penalties. Additionally, petitioner knowingly and intelligently waived counsel. He is a mature, intelligent adult and a graduate of a four-year college.

No mistreatment or coercion influenced his decision to waive counsel. He made a deliberate choice to represent himself, filing the motion to proceed *pro se* three weeks before trial. Throughout the court's inquiry, petitioner unequivocally expressed his desire to waive counsel . . . .

EXHIBIT 16.25

Appellate Brief—Argument (Excerpt)

I. The circuits have split three ways in establishing the level of inquiry necessary for a waiver of counsel to be knowing and intelligent.

   A. This court has never set out a specific line of inquiry for a trial judge to conduct when attempting to determine whether a defendant has knowingly and intelligently waived counsel.

      In <u>Faretta v. California</u>, this Court held that a defendant in a criminal trial has a constitutional right to proceed without counsel. 422 U.S. 806 (1975). However, the decision to proceed *pro se* must be the product of an "informed free will." <u>Id.</u> at 835. The Court in <u>Faretta</u> did not establish the level of inquiry a trial judge must make in determining that a defendant has knowingly and intelligently waived counsel:

> Although a defendant need not himself have the skill and experience of a lawyer in order competently and intelligently to choose self-representation, he should be made aware of the dangers and disadvantages of self-representation, so that the record will establish that "he knows what he is doing and his choice is made with his eyes open."

<u>Id.</u> (quoting <u>Adams v. United States ex. rel. McCann</u>, 317 U.S. 269, 279 (1942).

      Exactly what the record must reflect and what constitutes a choice made with "eyes open" has been disputed. The circuits are divided three ways in their interpretation of the standard set forth in <u>Faretta</u> . . . .

The Body of the Argument. The *body of the argument* develops the reasons why the court should decide in favor of the client. Detailed arguments are set forth in this section. Each argument must thoroughly analyze the legal and factual aspects of the case. Additionally, attorneys and paralegals must address only those issues and facts relevant to the case on appeal. The arguments in this section must be well organized and fully supported by law. Essential sources should be cited and relevant concepts discussed.

CONCLUSION. The *conclusion*, which follows the argument, is a very brief statement. It is not a summary of the argument but a claim for relief based on the arguments. In an appellant's brief, the conclusion asks the court to reverse the earlier decision of the trial court. In a appellee's brief, the conclusion requests that the earlier decision be upheld. The claim for relief is followed by a closing, typically in the form of "Respectfully submitted," and the name and address of the attorney responsible for the brief. This format is illustrated in Exhibit 16.26.

EXHIBIT 16.26
Appellate Brief—Conclusion

CONCLUSION

For the reasons stated above, the middle-inquiry approach is the standard that this court should adopt. The Second Circuit's inquiry standard for the determination of a knowing and intelligent waiver of counsel is sufficient, and therefore appellee respectfully requests that judgment be affirmed.

Respectfully submitted,

Joseph P. McCaffrey

Joseph P. McCaffrey
U.S. Attorney for the District of Nita

Today's Professional Paralegal

Preparing the Internal Memorandum

Ken Lawson, a legal assistant, works for Rhonda Mulhaven. Rhonda is representing the defendant, the Gourmet House Restaurant, in a slip-and-fall case. Ken is surprised that the plaintiff filed suit, because the plaintiff admitted that she saw water on the floor but walked through it anyway, apparently so that she could get to the telephone. Ken knows that there are several defenses available, including contributory or comparative negligence and assumption of risk.

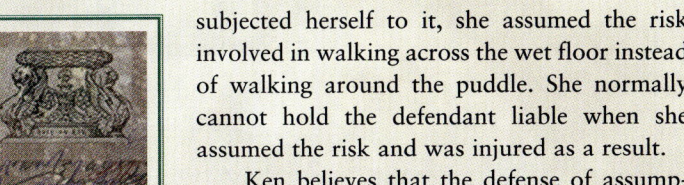

Researching and Analyzing Case Law

Ken looks in a legal encyclopedia, which defines assumption of risk as follows:

> The plaintiff knew that the situation was dangerous and, despite her knowledge of the danger involved, voluntarily subjected herself to the danger or risk. When a plaintiff has assumed the risk of danger, then the plaintiff cannot recover from the defendant for her injuries.

Ken often uses the IRAC method to analyze legal problems. First, he states the issue. Second, he states the rule of law. Third, he applies the rule to the client's facts. And fourth, he reaches a conclusion. Ken has found this method useful because it helps him to think through all aspects of the problem and to apply the law to the facts to reach a conclusion. He decides to apply the IRAC method to the case on which he is working to determine whether the defense of assumption of risk could be successfully applied.

Applying the IRAC Method

First, Ken identifies the issue in the case: Did the plaintiff assume the risk of falling when she walked across the wet floor? Next, Ken notes the applicable rule of law, as stated in the encyclopedia: a plaintiff who knows of a dangerous condition and voluntarily subjects himself or herself to it has assumed the risk and cannot hold a defendant liable. Ken then applies the rule of law to the facts of the case: the plaintiff knew of the dangerous condition, because she knew that the floor was wet. She voluntarily subjected herself to the danger by walking across the wet floor to get to the telephone. Ken then forms a conclusion: because the plaintiff knew of the dangerous condition and voluntarily subjected herself to it, she assumed the risk involved in walking across the wet floor instead of walking around the puddle. She normally cannot hold the defendant liable when she assumed the risk and was injured as a result.

Ken believes that the defense of assumption of risk might be appropriate in the client's case. He decides to continue researching case law and looks through a state digest. There he finds several cases that contain a definition of assumption of risk similar to the one he read in the encyclopedia. He reviews the cases and then uses KeyCite to check each case on Westlaw® to make sure that it is still current law.

Creating the Legal Memorandum

Ken sits down at his computer and prepares the following outline for a memorandum to Rhonda:

I. Statement of the Facts—A chronological statement of the events that led to the injury.
II. Question Presented—Did the plaintiff assume the risk of falling when she walked across the wet floor?
III. Brief Conclusion—Yes.
IV. Discussion
   A. Did the plaintiff assume the risk of falling when she walked across the wet floor?
   B. Check the encyclopedia's definition of assumption-of-risk defense and state case law supporting this definition.
   C. Apply the rules in B above to the facts in this case.
V. Conclusion—Based on the results of C above.

Having outlined the memo, Ken writes a first draft, edits and revises it, proofreads it carefully, and delivers it to Rhonda. The next day, she comes into his office and tells him that she is impressed with the quality and organization of his memo and with his analytical skills. She says that based on his research and the memorandum, she has been able to settle the case by convincing the plaintiff's attorney that his client has a weak case.

Key Terms and Concepts

address block 606
amicus curiae brief 621
appellant 621
appellant's brief 621
appellate brief 620
appellee 621
appellee's brief 621
briefing a case 590
chronologically 598
closing 608
confirmation letter 610
demand letter 611
dicta 589
holding 589
informative letter 609
opinion (advisory) letter 610
plain-meaning rule 594
point heading 626
reference line 607
reply brief 621
rules of construction 594
salutation 608

Chapter Summary

1. Paralegals who undertake legal research and writing need to be able to analyze the applicable case law, which they will find in reporters. Reporters use somewhat different formats in presenting cases. Typically, though, case formats include the following components: the title (name, or style), citation, and docket number of the case; the dates on which the case was argued and decided, and the name of the court deciding the case; a syllabus and headnotes; the names of counsel; the names of the judge or justice who authored the opinion; the opinion (the court's own words on the matter being litigated); and the court's decision (ruling, or holding) on the matter.

2. In analyzing case law, it is essential to understand the significance of the various components of a case. Legal professionals often use a technique called case briefing to reduce the content of the case to its essentials. Knowing how to read, analyze, and summarize cases makes it easier to compare and synthesize research results accurately and efficiently.

3. Reading and analyzing statutory language is often difficult. In reading statutory law, you should first note the statute's provisions concerning its coverage and effective date to ensure that it applies to the case or claim being researched. You should also note the definitions given in the statute and determine the relationships among subsections within the statute. In interpreting statutory law, the paralegal can turn to several helpful guidelines: the statutory rules of construction; the plain-meaning rule; previous judicial interpretations of the statute, if any exist; and the legislative history of the statute.

4. On receiving a writing assignment, the paralegal should make sure that he or she clearly understands the nature of the assignment, when the assignment should be completed, and what approach (objective versus adversarial, for example) should be used.

5. Good writing skills are essential for creating legal documents. The writing should be well organized and aimed at the intended audience. It should avoid legalese, when possible, be brief and to the point, present well-constructed sentences and paragraphs, use effective transitions, use gender-neutral language, and be free of typographical errors, misspelled words, and other flaws.

6. Much legal writing consists of documents relating to litigation procedures, such as pleadings and discovery documents. These important forms of legal writing were discussed in Chapters 10 and 11.

7. Paralegals frequently are responsible for maintaining correspondence files and writing legal letters. Most firms have a preferred format for legal correspondence, and the paralegal should become familiar with it. Paralegals commonly draft the following types of letters: informative letters (to notify clients or others of some action or procedure or to transmit documents), confirmation letters (to confirm an oral transaction or agreement), opinion letters (to convey to a client or other party a formal legal opinion or advice on an issue), and demand letters (to advance the client's cause by demanding something from an adversarial party on the client's behalf).

8. The internal legal memorandum is a thoroughly

researched and objectively written summation of the facts, issues, and applicable law relating to a particular legal claim. The purpose of the memo is to inform the attorney for whom the document is written of the strengths and weaknesses of the client's position. Generally, the legal memo is presented in a format that includes the following sections: heading, statement of the facts, questions presented, brief conclusion, discussion and analysis of the facts and the applicable law, and conclusion.

9. When a case is appealed to a higher court, attorneys for both sides file appellate briefs with the court of appeals. The purpose of an appellate brief is to convince the appellate court of the merits of a client's position on appeal. A persuasive and forceful writing approach is therefore used.

10. There are four types of appellate briefs: the appellant's brief (filed on behalf of the party appealing the lower court's decision), the appellee's brief (filed on behalf of the party against whom the appeal is being brought), the reply brief (filed by the appellant in response to the appellee's brief), and the *amicus curiae* brief (filed by a "friend of the court" on behalf of one of the parties to the case in the interest of a broadly held public concern).

11. Most courts require that appellate briefs be presented in a format that includes the following sections: title page, table of contents, table of authorities, statement of jurisdiction, questions presented, statement of the claim, summary of the argument, argument, and conclusion.

Questions for Review

1. List and briefly describe the components of a reported case. What is the syllabus, and how is it helpful to the legal researcher?

2. How do you brief a case? What is the purpose of briefing a case?

3. What are some points to consider when reading and interpreting statutory law?

4. List and describe some of the traditional guidelines used by the courts in interpreting statutory law.

5. What factors should you consider before undertaking a legal-writing assignment?

6. List and describe each of the guidelines for effective writing. What is meant by the statement "You should write to your audience"?

7. List the component parts of a typical legal letter. What is the function of each type of letter discussed in this chapter?

8. How is an internal memorandum organized? List and describe its components.

9. What must you know and understand before you begin to prepare a legal memorandum?

10. What is the purpose of an appellate brief?

Ethical Questions

1. Lynette Bennett, a paralegal, works as a clerk for a judge in the county circuit court. She has just finished reviewing the plaintiff's and defendant's briefs in an auto-accident case. The plaintiff's brief described the injury as follows:

    > The plaintiff was struck by the defendant's car as she crossed Lincoln Avenue at the crosswalk. She sustained serious injuries to her left knee, for which she had surgery. She also experiences pain and discomfort in her back and neck.

    The defendant's brief described the injury as follows:

    > The plaintiff was struck when she suddenly stepped in front of the defendant's vehicle. The defendant's vehicle was traveling at a speed of five miles per hour. In her lawsuit against the defendant, the plaintiff claims that she sustained significant injuries from this minor accident.

    Lynette is disturbed by the disparity in the two descriptions of the plaintiff's injuries. It sounds to Lynette as if someone is lying. What do you think? What impact would falsifying the facts have on the writer's credibility?

2. Bill Richardson, a legal assistant, has been asked by his supervising attorney to prepare an internal memorandum analyzing a client's claim. When Bill reviews the facts, he realizes that the client has a very weak case and will probably lose. But Bill thinks that the client was taken advantage of and that she should be given a chance to try to recover at least something. He

knows that his supervisor will not take a losing case to court, so he writes the memo in such a way as to favor the client's position as much as possible. He is not objective in analyzing the potential pitfalls of the case. Is what Bill has done ethical? Is it professional? How should he have handled the situation?

3. David Thomas, a paralegal, is sending out a letter to a client. It is an informative letter advising the client of the status of her case and explaining what the next step in the litigation process will be. David signs the letter without including his title. He mails the letter to the client. The client has questions, and she calls David, thinking that he is the attorney. How should David handle this situation? What should he have done to prevent it?

4. Ken Hall, a legal assistant, is handling all of his supervising attorney's mail while she is out of town on business for the week. The supervising attorney only wants to be contacted if absolutely necessary. She receives a letter marked "personal and confidential." Ken does not recognize the return address on the letter. How should Ken handle the situation?

Practice Questions and Assignments

1. Obtain a copy of *Ward v. K-Mart Corp.*, 136 Ill.2d 132, 554 N.E.2d 223 (1990). Using the material presented in the chapter, answer the following questions about the case.

   a. What is the docket number?

   b. What court rendered the decision in the case?

   c. What are the names of the attorneys who were involved in the case?

   d. What does headnote number 4 say?

   e. What is the name of the justice who authored the opinion?

   f. What does the synopsis of the case say?

2. Using the case presented in the chapter, *Bragdon v. Abbott*, ____ U.S. ____, 118 S.Ct. 2196, 141 L.Ed.2d 540 (1998), answer the following questions.

   a. How does the Americans with Disabilities Act (ADA) define the term *disability*?

   b. What disease was the United States Supreme Court reviewing to determine whether it was a disability under the ADA?

   c. What did the Court decide regarding whether the disease was a disability under the ADA?

   d. How did the Court apply the statutory definition of disability to the disease?

   e. Did the Court determine whether the disease constituted a "physical impairment"? If so, how did the Court reach this conclusion?

3. Clip an article out of the newspaper or a news journal. Then follow the instructions and answer the questions given below:

   a. Underline all of the active verbs and circle all of the passive verbs. Did the writer use more active verbs than passive verbs in writing the article?

   b. Count the number of words in each sentence. What is the average sentence length? Do short sentences predominate?

   c. Locate the topic sentence in each paragraph. Is the writer's paragraph construction effective?

   d. Notice how the author uses transitional sentences when moving from one paragraph to the next. Underline the key transitional words or phrases.

4. Analyze the construction of the following paragraphs. How could they be improved?

   > The first is knowing of the danger. The second is voluntarily subjecting oneself to the danger. The defense of assumption of risk has two elements.
   >
   > She did not voluntarily subject herself to the danger when the stadium assigned seats to season-ticket holders. She knew that balls were often hit into the stands. The plaintiff knew of the danger involved in attending a baseball game.

5. Proofread the following paragraph, circling all of the mistakes. Then rewrite the paragraph.

   > The defendent was aressted and chrge with drunk driving. Blood alcohol level of .15. He refused to take a breahalyzer test at first. After the police explained to him that he would loose his lisense if he did not take it, he concented. He also has ablood test to verify the results of the breathalyzer.

6. Review the *Practice Questions and Assignments* at the end of Chapter 14. If you did the research required by those questions, use the lemon law and the cases that you found to prepare an internal memorandum analyzing Mr. Consumer's problem and whether the lemon law in your state will help him. Be sure to include your opinion of the strength of his case.

7. Using the research results from question 5 in the *Practice Questions and Assignments* at the end of Chapter 14, draft an opinion letter from your supervising attorney to Mr. Consumer, advising him as to how the state's lemon law applies to his case and what type of relief he can expect.

8. Using the material presented in this chapter, prepare an informative letter to a client using the following facts:

   The client, Dr. Brown, is being sued for medical malpractice and is going to be deposed on January 15, 1999, at 1:00 P.M. The deposition will take place at the law offices of Callaghan & Young. The offices are located at 151 East Jefferson Avenue, Cincinnati, Ohio. The client needs to call your supervising attorney's office to set up an appointment, so that the attorney can prepare Dr. Brown for the deposition.

9. Review Exhibit 16.4, *Excerpt from the Americans with Disabilities Act of 1990*. Summarize sections (a) and (b) in two to three paragraphs. In your own words, write one paragraph explaining what sections (a) and (b) mean.

QUESTIONS FOR CRITICAL ANALYSIS

1. Review the hypothetical case discussed in Chapter 14 involving a lawsuit brought by Trent Hoffman against Better Homes Store for negligence. If possible, obtain a copy of the following case (on which that hypothetical is based): *Ward v. K-Mart Corp.*, 136 Ill. 2d 132, 554 N.E.2d 223 (1990). Read through the court's opinion and then do the following:
   a. Find at least one statement made by the court that constitutes *dicta*.
   b. Brief the case.

2. The Americans with Disabilities Act (ADA) of 1990 does not require employers to accommodate persons with disabilities if those persons pose a direct threat to the health and safety of others. Read the following case annotations and synthesize the annotations into the rule of law regarding the type of threat that is required to prevent employment under the "direct threat" provision of the ADA:
   a. Orthopedic surgeon posed a direct threat to the health of his patients as a result of his HIV-positive status, and thus, hospitals did not violate ADA by prohibiting the surgeon from performing surgery without patient consent given patients' knowledge of surgeon's HIV status; although current knowledge about HIV transmission from surgeon to patient is uncertain, because there is no known cure, the duration of risk posed by a surgeon in a surgical setting was permanent and the severity of the harm was that the disease was, at present, fatal in most cases. *Scoles v. Mercy Health Corp.*, 887 F.Supp. 765 (E.D.Pa.1994).
   b. Employers' executive director's inability to drive did not pose significant risk of substantial harm to health and safety of director or others that could not be eliminated or reduced by reasonable accommodation, as required to support employer's direct threat defense; driving was not an essential function of executive director's position, and providing the executive director with an alternative mode of transportation was a reasonable accommodation. *Equal Employment Opportunity Commission v. AIC Security Investigation, Ltd.*, 820 F.Supp. 1060 (N.D.Ill. 1993).
   c. Even if Georgia Ports Authority police officer had timely complained of his "benign esssential tremor" disability which caused him to fail a firearms proficiency test and had requested an accommodation, the officer failed to show how this could be done so as to prevail on his ADA claim; GPA police officer who could not shoot straight posed an unacceptable risk to others and the officer did not show how his deficiency, and the direct threat to the health of others that it represented, could be reasonably accommodated. *Fussell v. Georgia Ports Authority*, 906 F.Supp. 1561 (S.D.Ga. 1995).
   d. Neurologist with attention deficit disorder (ADD) which affected his short-term memory and led to mistakes on patients' charts and in dispensing of medicine to patients posed a direct threat to the health and safety of others, and thus, the employer was not required under the ADA to accommodate his disability. *Robertson v. Neuromedical Center*, 983 F.Supp. 669 (M.D.La. 1997).

3. Why is statutory language often difficult to read and understand? What factors must legislators consider when drafting statutes?

4. Why is it important to write to your audience? To what audience should legislators write when drafting legislation?

5. Using the material presented in the chapter, analyze the following hypothetical by applying the IRAC method:

   Mr. Damien is a teacher at the Wabash Academy, a private boarding school. He has a twenty-one-year-old son who has bipolar affective disorder, formerly called manic-depressive psychosis, a mood disorder. When visiting Mr. Damien, his son has repeatedly threatened members of the school community. On one occasion, Mr. Damien's son abducted the headmaster's sixteen-year-old daughter and attempted to have the teenager admitted to a psychiatric hospital. Mr. Damien's son also made threatening phone calls to the headmaster. In one such call, he claimed to have drained several quarts of his own blood from his body because he was not permitted to communicate with the headmaster's sixteen-year-old daughter. Mr. and Mrs. Damien refuse to prevent their son from visiting their home on the school's campus. As a result, Mr. Damien claims that such termination violates the Americans with Disabilities Act (ADA) of 1990.

   The case law interpreting the ADA does not require employment of an individual with disabilities if that individual, or that individual's disabled relative or associate, poses a direct threat to the health and safety of others.

PROJECTS

1. Compare Microsoft's *Word* and Corel's *WordPerfect* word-processing software. Write a one-page paper summarizing which you prefer and why. Be sure to note the legal applications each software package has available.

2. If possible, find a copy of a business letter. Identify its component parts. How does it differ from the sample legal letter presented in Exhibit 16.7? How is it similar?

3. Contact the court of appeals in your state. Ask if the court gives tours, has any programs available for college students, or allows observation of oral arguments. If so, arrange to take a tour and observe an oral argument. If available, it would be helpful if you could obtain a copy of each side's brief and read it prior to the oral argument. Check with your instructor for any special directions prior to contacting the court. Write a one-page paper summarizing your visit to the court of appeals.

4. Review your state's court rules that apply to the preparation of documents—such as pleadings, motions, and appellate briefs—to be filed with the courts. Are there any specific instructions for the format of these documents, such as page limits, double-spacing, or separately numbered paragraphs or allegations? Make a list of the rules and summarize the requirements. Your list and accompanying summary should not exceed two typewritten pages.

USING INTERNET RESOURCES

1. Access the Securities and Exchange Commission's "Handbook of Plain English" at the following site:

   www.sec.gov/consumer/plaine.htm#A3

   Scroll through the handbook to find answers to the following questions:

   a. Describe the "unoriginal but useful" writing tip given in the handbook's preface. Why did the writer of the preface find the tip useful?

   b. How does Chapter 1 of the handbook describe a "plain English" document?

   c. Browse through Chapter 6, titled "The Principles of Plain English." Write down two "before and after" examples showing how the use of plain English improved the writing.

   d. What is a nominalization? Write a sentence including a nominalization (not one of those listed in Chapter 6), and then rewrite the sentence to make the nominalization the main verb of the sentence.

2. The American Bar Association's (ABA's) Web site contains a helpful section on legal writing. Access the Web site at **www.abanet.org/lpm/writing**.

   a. Click on the "Writing" button. What topics are listed? Which might be helpful?

   b. Click on the "Style" button. What resources are available? Where are these resources available? Click on "Style Manuals." Give the names of the first two style manuals listed. Click on "Dictionaries." How does the Web site of Webster's Dictionary work? Access both the "Grammar" and "Miscellany" buttons and review the contents as well.

   c. Click on the "Labs" button. What is accessible from this Web page? What information is accessible from the "Handouts" Web site? How might a student use this information? What is accessible from Purdue Lab? How might a student use this information?

APPENDIX A

NALA's Code of Ethics and Professional Responsibility

A legal assistant must adhere strictly to the accepted standards of legal ethics and to the general principles of proper conduct. The performance of the duties of the legal assistant shall be governed by specific canons as defined herein so that justice will be served and goals of the profession attained. (See Model Standards and Guidelines for Utilization of Legal Assistants, Section II.)

The canons of ethics set forth hereafter are adopted by the National Association of Legal Assistants, Inc., as a general guide intended to aid legal assistants and attorneys. The enumeration of these rules does not mean there are not others of equal importance although not specifically mentioned. Court rules, agency rules, and statutes must be taken into consideration when interpreting the canons.

Definition: Legal assistants, also known as paralegals, are a distinguishable group of persons who assist attorneys in the delivery of legal services. Through formal education, training, and experience, legal assistants have knowledge and expertise regarding the legal system and substantive and procedural law which qualify them to do work of a legal nature under the supervision of an attorney.

Canon 1

A legal assistant must not perform any of the duties that attorneys only may perform nor take any actions that attorneys may not take.

Canon 2

A legal assistant may perform any task which is properly delegated and supervised by an attorney, as long as the attorney is ultimately responsible to the client, maintains a direct relationship with the client, and assumes professional responsibility for the work product.

Canon 3

A legal assistant must not: (a) engage in, encourage, or contribute to any act which could constitute the unauthorized practice of law; and (b) establish attorney-client relationships, set fees, give legal opinions or advice, or represent a client before a court or agency unless so authorized by that court or agency; and (c) engage in conduct or take any action which would assist or involve the attorney in a violation of professional ethics or give the appearance of professional impropriety.

Canon 4

A legal assistant must use discretion and professional judgment commensurate with knowledge and experience but must not render independent legal judgment in place of an attorney. The services of an attorney are essential in the public interest whenever such legal judgment is required.

Canon 5

A legal assistant must disclose his or her status as a legal assistant at the outset of any professional relationship with a client, attorney, a court or administrative agency, or personnel thereof, or a member of the general public. A legal assistant must act prudently in determining the extent to which a client may be assisted without the presence of an attorney.

Canon 6

A legal assistant must strive to maintain integrity and a high degree of competency through education and training with respect to professional responsibility, local rules and practice, and through continuing education in substantive areas of law to better assist the legal profession in fulfilling its duty to provide legal service.

Canon 7

A legal assistant must protect the confidences of a client and must not violate any rule or statute now in effect or hereafter enacted controlling privileged communications.

Canon 8

A legal assistant must do all other things incidental, necessary, or expedient for the attainment of the ethics and responsibilities as defined by statute or rule of court.

Canon 9

A legal assistant's conduct is guided by bar associations' codes of professional responsibility and rules of professional conduct.

© Copyright 1998 NALA.

APPENDIX B

NALA's Model Standards and Guidelines for the Utilization of Legal Assistants

NALA's study of the professional responsibility and ethical considerations of legal assistants is ongoing. This research led to the development of the NALA Model Standards and Guidelines for Utilization of Legal Assistants. This guide summarizes case law, guidelines, and ethical opinions of the various states affecting legal assistants. It provides an outline of minimum qualifications and standards necessary for legal assistant professionals to assure the public and the legal profession that they are, indeed, qualified. The following is a listing of the standards and guidelines.

The annotated version of the Model was revised extensively in 1997. It is online (NALA Model Standards and Guidelines) and may be ordered through NALA headquarters.

Introduction

Proper utilization of the services of legal assistants affects the efficient delivery of legal services. Legal assistants and the legal profession should be assured that some measures exist for identifying legal assistants and their role in assisting attorneys in the delivery of legal services. Therefore, the National Association of Legal Assistants, Inc., hereby adopts these Model Standards and Guidelines as an educational document for the benefit of legal assistants and the legal profession.

STANDARDS

A legal assistant should meet certain minimum qualifications. The following standards may be used to determine an individual's qualifications as a legal assistant:

1. Successful completion of the Certified Legal Assistant (CLA) certifying examination of the National Association of Legal Assistants, Inc.;
2. Graduation from an ABA-approved program of study for legal assistants;
3. Graduation from a course of study for legal assistants which is institutionally accredited but not ABA approved, and which requires not less than the equivalent of sixty semester hours of classroom study;
4. Graduation from a course of study for legal assistants, other than those set forth in (2) and (3) above, plus not less than six months of in-house training as a legal assistant;
5. A baccalaureate degree in any field, plus not less than six months in-house training as a legal assistant;
6. A minimum of three years of law-related experience under the supervision of an attorney, including at least six months of in-house training as a legal assistant; or
7. Two years of in-house training as a legal assistant.

For purposes of these Standards, "in-house training as a legal assistant" means attorney education of the employee concerning legal assistant duties and these Guidelines. In addition to review and analysis of assignments, the legal assistant should receive a reasonable amount of instruction directly related to the duties and obligations of the legal assistant.

GUIDELINES

These Guidelines relating to standards of performance and professional responsibility are intended to aid legal assistants and attorneys. The responsibility rests with an attorney who employs legal assistants to educate them with respect to the duties they are assigned and to supervise the manner in which such duties are accomplished.

Guideline 1

Legal assistants should:

1. Disclose their status as legal assistants at the outset of any professional relationship with a client, other attorneys, a court or administrative agency or personnel thereof, or members of the general public;
2. Preserve the confidences and secrets of all clients; and
3. Understand the attorney's Code of Professional Responsibility and these guidelines in order to avoid any action which would involve the attorney in a violation of that Code, or give the appearance of professional impropriety.

Guideline 2

Legal assistants should not:

1. Establish attorney-client relationships; set legal fees, give legal opinions or advice; or represent a client before a court; nor

2. Engage in, encourage, or contribute to any act which could constitute the unauthorized practice of law.

Guideline 3

Legal assistants may perform services for an attorney in the representation of a client, provided:

1. The services performed by the legal assistant do not require the exercise of independent professional legal judgment;
2. The attorney maintains a direct relationship with the client and maintains control of all client matters;
3. The attorney supervises the legal assistant;
4. The attorney remains professionally responsible for all work on behalf of the client, including any actions taken or not taken by the legal assistant in connection therewith; and
5. The services performed supplement, merge with, and become the attorney's work product.

Guideline 4

In the supervision of a legal assistant, consideration should be given to:

1. Designating work assignments that correspond to the legal assistant's abilities, knowledge, training, and experience.
2. Educating and training the legal assistant with respect to professional responsibility, local rules and practices, and firm policies;
3. Monitoring the work and professional conduct of the legal assistant to ensure that the work is substantially correct and timely performed;
4. Providing continuing education for the legal assistant in substantive matters through courses, institutes, workshops, seminars, and in-house training; and
5. Encouraging and supporting membership and active participation in professional organizations.

Guideline 5

Except as otherwise provided by statute, court rule or decision, administrative rule or regulation, or the attorney's Code of Professional Responsibility and within the preceding parameters and proscriptions, a legal assistant may perform any function delegated by an attorney, including but not limited to the following:

1. Conduct client interviews and maintain general contact with the client after the establishment of the attorney-client relationship, so long as the client is aware of the status and function of the legal assistant, and the client contact is under the supervision of the attorney.
2. Locate and interview witnesses, so long as the witnesses are aware of the status and function of the legal assistant.
3. Conduct investigations and statistical and documentary research for review by the attorney.
4. Conduct legal research for review by the attorney.
5. Draft legal documents for review by the attorney.

6. Draft correspondence and pleadings for review by and signature of the attorney.
7. Summarize depositions, interrogatories, and testimony for review by the attorney.
8. Attend executions of wills, real estate closings, depositions, court or administrative hearings and trials with the attorney.
9. Author and sign letters provided the legal assistant's status is clearly indicated and the correspondence does not contain independent legal opinions or legal advice.

The notes to accompany the NALA Model Standards and Guidelines for Utilization of Legal Assistants are updated regularly by the NALA Professional Development Committee. The standards and guidelines are adopted by the NALA membership, and changes to these provisions must be brought before NALA members during their annual meeting in July.

© Copyright 1998 NALA, All rights reserved.
Last Update: 01/11/99

APPENDIX C

NFPA's Model Code of Ethics and Professional Responsibility and Guidelines for Enforcement

Preamble

The National Federation of Paralegal Associations, Inc. ("NFPA") is a professional organization comprised of paralegal associations and individual paralegals throughout the United States and Canada. Members of NFPA have varying backgrounds, experiences, education, and job responsibilities that reflect the diversity of the paralegal profession. NFPA promotes the growth, development, and recognition of the paralegal profession as an integral partner in the delivery of legal services.

In May 1993 NFPA adopted its Model Code of Ethics and Professional Responsibility ("Model Code") to delineate the principles for ethics and conduct to which every paralegal should aspire.

Many paralegal associations throughout the United States have endorsed the concept and content of NFPA's Model Code through the adoption of their own ethical codes. In doing so, paralegals have confirmed the profession's commitment to increase the quality and efficiency of legal services, as well as recognized its responsibilities to the public, the legal community, and colleagues.

Paralegals have recognized, and will continue to recognize, that the profession must continue to evolve to enhance their roles in the delivery of legal services. With increased levels of responsibility comes the need to define and enforce mandatory rules of professional conduct. Enforcement of codes of paralegal conduct is a logical and necessary step to enhance and ensure the confidence of the legal community and the public in the integrity and professional responsibility of paralegals.

In April 1997 NFPA adopted the Model Disciplinary Rules ("Model Rules") to make possible the enforcement of the Canons and Ethical Considerations contained in the NFPA Model Code. A concurrent determination was made that the Model Code of Ethics and Professional Responsibility, formerly aspirational in nature, should be recognized as setting forth the enforceable obligations of all paralegals.

The Model Code and Model Rules offer a framework for professional discipline, either voluntarily or through formal regulatory programs.

§1. NFPA Model Disciplinary Rules and Ethical Considerations

1.1 A Paralegal Shall Achieve and Maintain a High Level of Competence.

ETHICAL CONSIDERATIONS

EC–1.1(a) A paralegal shall achieve competency through education, training, and work experience.

EC–1.1(b) A paralegal shall participate in continuing education to keep informed of current legal, technical, and general developments.

EC–1.1(c) A paralegal shall perform all assignments promptly and efficiently.

1.2 A Paralegal Shall Maintain a High Level of Personal and Professional Integrity.

ETHICAL CONSIDERATIONS

EC–1.2(a) A paralegal shall not engage in any *ex parte* communications involving the courts or any other adjudicatory body in an attempt to exert undue influence or to obtain advantage or the benefit of only one party.

EC–1.2(b) A paralegal shall not communicate, or cause another to communicate, with a party the paralegal knows to be represented by a lawyer in a pending matter without the prior consent of the lawyer representing such other party.

EC–1.2(c) A paralegal shall ensure that all timekeeping and billing records prepared by the paralegal are thorough, accurate, honest, and complete.

EC–1.2(d) A paralegal shall not knowingly engage in fraudulent billing practices. Such practices may include, but are not limited to: inflation of hours billed to a client or employer; misrepresentation of the nature of tasks performed; and/or submission of fraudulent expense and disbursement documentation.

EC–1.2(e) A paralegal shall be scrupulous, thorough, and honest in the identification and maintenance of all funds, securities, and other assets of a client and shall provide accurate accounting as appropriate.

EC–1.2(f) A paralegal shall advise the proper authority of nonconfidential knowledge of any dishonest or fraudulent acts by any person pertaining to the handling of the funds, securities, or other assets of a client. The authority to whom the report is made shall depend on the nature and circumstances of the possible misconduct (e.g., ethics committees of law firms, corporations and/or paralegal associations, local or state bar associations, local prosecutors, administrative agencies, etc.). Failure to report such knowledge is in itself misconduct and shall be treated as such under these rules.

1.3 A Paralegal Shall Maintain a High Standard of Professional Conduct.

ETHICAL CONSIDERATIONS

EC–1.3(a) A paralegal shall refrain from engaging in any conduct that offends the dignity and decorum of proceedings before a court or other adjudicatory body and shall be respectful of all rules and procedures.

EC–1.3(b) A paralegal shall avoid impropriety and the appearance of impropriety and shall not engage in any conduct that would adversely affect his/her fitness to practice. Such conduct may include, but is not limited to: violence, dishonesty, interference with the administration of justice, and/or abuse of a professional position or public office.

EC–1.3(c) Should a paralegal's fitness to practice be compromised by physical or mental illness, causing that paralegal to commit an act that is in direct violation of the Model Code/Model Rules and/or the rules and/or laws governing the jurisdiction in which the paralegal practices, that paralegal may be protected from sanction upon review of the nature and circumstances of that illness.

EC–1.3(d) A paralegal shall advise the proper authority of nonconfidential knowledge of any action of another legal professional that clearly demonstrates fraud, deceit, dishonesty, or misrepresentation. The authority to whom the report is made shall depend on the nature and circumstances of the possible misconduct, (e.g., ethics committees of law firms, corporations and/or paralegal associations, local or state bar associations, local prosecutors, administrative agencies, etc.). Failure to report such knowledge is in itself misconduct and shall be treated as such under these rules.

EC–1.3(e) A paralegal shall not knowingly assist any individual with the commission of an act that is in direct violation of the Model Code/Model Rules and/or the rules and/or laws governing the jurisdiction in which the paralegal practices.

EC–1.3(f) If a paralegal possesses knowledge of future criminal activity, that knowledge must be reported to the appropriate authority immediately.

1.4 A Paralegal Shall Serve the Public Interest by Contributing to the Delivery of Quality Legal Services and the Improvement of the Legal System.

ETHICAL CONSIDERATIONS

EC–1.4(a) A paralegal shall be sensitive to the legal needs of the public and shall promote the development and implementation of programs that address those needs.

EC–1.4(b) A paralegal shall support bona fide efforts to meet the need for legal services by those unable to pay reasonable or customary fees; for example, participation in *pro bono* projects and volunteer work.

EC–1.4(c) A paralegal shall support efforts to improve the legal system and access thereto and shall assist in making changes.

1.5 A Paralegal Shall Preserve All Confidential Information Provided by the Client or Acquired from Other Sources before, during, and after the Course of the Professional Relationship.

ETHICAL CONSIDERATIONS

EC–1.5(a) A paralegal shall be aware of and abide by all legal authority governing confidential information in the jurisdiction in which the paralegal practices.

EC–1.5(b) A paralegal shall not use confidential information to the disadvantage of the client.

EC–1.5(c) A paralegal shall not use confidential information to the advantage of the paralegal or of a third person.

EC–1.5(d) A paralegal may reveal confidential information only after full disclosure and with the client's written consent; or, when required by law or court order; or, when necessary to prevent the client from committing an act which could result in death or serious bodily harm.

EC–1.5(e) A paralegal shall keep those individuals responsible for the legal representation of a client fully informed of any confidential information the paralegal may have pertaining to that client.

EC–1.5(f) A paralegal shall not engage in any indiscreet communications concerning clients.

1.6 A Paralegal Shall Avoid Conflicts of Interest and Shall Disclose Any Possible Conflict to the Employer or Client, as Well as to the Prospective Employers or Clients.

ETHICAL CONSIDERATIONS

EC–1.6(a) A paralegal shall act within the bounds of the law, solely for the benefit of the client, and shall be free of compromising influences and loyalties. Neither the paralegal's personal or business interest, nor those of other clients or third persons, should compromise the paralegal's professional judgment and loyalty to the client.

EC–1.6(b) A paralegal shall avoid conflicts of interest which may arise from previous assignments whether for a present or past employer or client.

EC–1.6(c) A paralegal shall avoid conflicts of interest which may arise from family relationships and from personal and business interests.

EC–1.6(d) In order to be able to determine whether an actual or potential conflict of interest exists a paralegal shall create and maintain an effective record-keeping system that identifies clients, matters, and parties with which the paralegal has worked.

EC–1.6(e) A paralegal shall reveal sufficient nonconfidential information about a client or former client to reasonably ascertain if an actual or potential conflict of interest exists.

EC–1.6(f) A paralegal shall not participate in or conduct work on any matter where a conflict of interest has been identified.

EC–1.6(g) In matters where a conflict of interest has been identified and the client consents to continued representation, a paralegal shall comply fully with the implementation and maintenance of an Ethical Wall.

1.7 A Paralegal's Title Shall Be Fully Disclosed.

ETHICAL CONSIDERATIONS

EC–1.7(a) A paralegal's title shall clearly indicate the individual's status and shall be disclosed in all business and professional communications to avoid misunderstandings and misconceptions about the paralegal's role and responsibilities.

EC–1.7(b) A paralegal's title shall be included if the paralegal's name appears on business cards, letterhead, brochures, directories, and advertisements.

EC–1.7(c) A paralegal shall not use letterhead, business cards, or other promotional materials to create a fraudulent impression of his/her status or ability to practice in the jurisdiction in which the paralegal practices.

EC–1.7(d) A paralegal shall not practice under color of any record, diploma, or certificate that has been illegally or fraudulently obtained or issued or which is misrepresentative in any way.

EC–1.7(e) A paralegal shall not participate in the creation, issuance, or dissemination of fraudulent records, diplomas, or certificates.

1.8 A Paralegal Shall Not Engage in the Unauthorized Practice of Law.

ETHICAL CONSIDERATIONS

EC–1.8(a) A paralegal shall comply with the applicable legal authority governing the unauthorized practice of law in the jurisdiction in which the paralegal practices.

§2. NFPA GUIDELINES FOR THE ENFORCEMENT OF THE MODEL CODE OF ETHICS AND PROFESSIONAL RESPONSIBILITY

2.1 Basis for Discipline

2.1(a) Disciplinary investigations and proceedings brought under authority of the Rules shall be conducted in accord with obligations imposed on the paralegal professional by the Model Code of Ethics and Professional Responsibility.

2.2 Structure of Disciplinary Committee

2.2(a) The Disciplinary Committee ("Committee") shall be made up of nine (9) members including the Chair.

2.2(b) Each member of the Committee, including any temporary replacement members, shall have demonstrated working knowledge of ethics/professional responsibility–related issues and activities.

2.2(c) The Committee shall represent a cross section of practice areas and work experience. The following recommendations are made regarding the members of the Committee.

1. At least one paralegal with one to three years of law-related work experience.
2. At least one paralegal with five to seven years of law-related work experience.
3. At least one paralegal with over ten years of law-related work experience.
4. One paralegal educator with five to seven years of work experience; preferably in the area of ethics/professional responsibility.
5. One paralegal manager.
6. One lawyer with five to seven years of law-related work experience.
7. One lay member.

2.2(d) The Chair of the Committee shall be appointed within thirty (30) days of its members' induction. The Chair shall have no fewer than ten (10) years of law-related work experience.

2.2(e) The terms of all members of the Committee shall be staggered. Of those members initially appointed, a simple majority plus one shall be appointed to a term of one year, and the remaining members shall be appointed to a term of two years. Thereafter, all members of the Committee shall be appointed to terms of two years.

2.2(f) If for any reason the terms of a majority of the Committee will expire at the same time, members may be appointed to terms of one year to maintain continuity of the Committee.

2.2(g) The Committee shall organize from its members a three-tiered structure to investigate, prosecute, and/or adjudicate charges of misconduct. The members shall be rotated among the tiers.

2.3 Operation of Committee

2.3(a) The Committee shall meet on an as-needed basis to discuss, investigate, and/or adjudicate alleged violations of the Model Code/Model Rules.

2.3(b) A majority of the members of the Committee present at a meeting shall constitute a quorum.

2.3(c) A Recording Secretary shall be designated to maintain complete and accurate minutes of all Committee meetings. All such minutes shall be kept confidential until a decision has been made that the matter will be set for hearing as set forth in Section 6.1 below.

2.3(d) If any member of the Committee has a conflict of interest with the Charging Party, the Responding Party, or the allegations of misconduct, that member shall not take part in any hearing or deliberations concerning those allegations. If the absence of that member creates a lack of a quorum for the Committee, then a temporary replacement for the member shall be appointed.

2.3(e) Either the Charging Party or the Responding Party may request that, for good cause shown, any member of the Committee not participate in a hearing or deliberation. All such requests shall be honored. If the absence of a Committee member under those circumstances creates a lack of a quorum for the Committee, then a temporary replacement for that member shall be appointed.

2.3(f) All discussions and correspondence of the Committee shall be kept confidential until a decision has been made that the matter will be set for hearing as set forth in Section 6.1 below.

2.3(g) All correspondence from the Committee to the Responding Party regarding any charge of misconduct and any decisions made regarding the charge shall be mailed certified mail, return receipt requested, to the Responding Party's last known address and shall be clearly marked with a "Confidential" designation.

2.4 Procedure for the Reporting of Alleged Violations of the Model Code/Disciplinary Rules

2.4(a) An individual or entity in possession of nonconfidential knowledge or information concerning possible instances of misconduct shall make a confidential written report to the Committee within thirty (30) days of obtaining same. This report shall include all details of the alleged misconduct.

2.4(b) The Committee so notified shall inform the Responding Party of the allegation(s) of misconduct no later than ten (10) business days after receiving the confidential written report from the Charging Party.

2.4(c) Notification to the Responding Party shall include the identity of the Charging Party, unless, for good cause shown, the Charging Party requests anonymity.

2.4(d) The Responding Party shall reply to the allegations within ten (10) business days of notification.

2.5 Procedure for the Investigation of a Charge of Misconduct

2.5(a) Upon receipt of a Charge of Misconduct ("Charge"), or on its own initiative, the Committee shall initiate an investigation.

2.5(b) If, upon initial or preliminary review, the Committee makes a determination that the charges are either without basis in fact or, if proven, would not constitute professional misconduct, the Committee shall dismiss the allegations of misconduct. If such determination of dismissal cannot be made, a formal investigation shall be initiated.

2.5(c) Upon the decision to conduct a formal investigation, the Committee shall:

1. mail to the Charging and Responding Parties within three (3) business days of that decision notice of the commencement of a formal investigation. That notification shall be in writing and shall contain a complete explanation of all Charge(s), as well as the reasons for a formal investigation and shall cite the applicable codes and rules;
2. allow the Responding Party thirty (30) days to prepare and submit a confidential response to the Committee, which response shall address each charge specifically and shall be in writing; and
3. upon receipt of the response to the notification, have thirty (30) days to investigate the Charge(s). If an extension of time is deemed necessary, that extension shall not exceed ninety (90) days.

2.5(d) Upon conclusion of the investigation, the Committee may:

1. dismiss the Charge upon the finding that it has no basis in fact;
2. dismiss the Charge upon the finding that, if proven, the Charge would not constitute Misconduct;
3. refer the matter for hearing by the Tribunal; or
4. in the case of criminal activity, refer the Charge(s) and all investigation results to the appropriate authority.

2.6 Procedure for a Misconduct Hearing before a Tribunal

2.6(a) Upon the decision by the Committee that a matter should be heard, all parties shall be notified and a hearing date shall be set. The hearing shall take place no more than thirty (30) days from the conclusion of the formal investigation.

2.6(b) The Responding Party shall have the right to counsel. The parties and the Tribunal shall have the right to call any witnesses and introduce any documentation that they believe will lead to the fair and reasonable resolution of the matter.

2.6(c) Upon completion of the hearing, the Tribunal shall deliberate and present a written decision to the parties in accordance with procedures as set forth by the Tribunal.

2.6(d) Notice of the decision of the Tribunal shall be appropriately published.

2.7 Sanctions

2.7(a) Upon a finding of the Tribunal that misconduct has occurred, any of the following sanctions, or others as may be deemed appropriate, may be imposed upon the Responding Party, either singularly or in combination:

1. letter of reprimand to the Responding Party; counseling;
2. attendance at an ethics course approved by the Tribunal; probation;
3. suspension of license/authority to practice; revocation of license/authority to practice;
4. imposition of a fine; assessment of costs; or
5. in the instance of criminal activity, referral to the appropriate authority.

2.7(b) Upon the expiration of any period of probation, suspension, or revocation, the Responding Party may make application for reinstatement. With the application for reinstatement, the Responding Party must show proof of having complied with all aspects of the sanctions imposed by the Tribunal.

2.8 Appellate Procedures

2.8(a) The parties shall have the right to appeal the decision of the Tribunal in accordance with the procedure as set forth by the Tribunal.

DEFINITIONS

APPELLATE BODY means a body established to adjudicate an appeal to any decision made by a Tribunal or other decision-making body with respect to formally heard Charges of Misconduct.

CHARGE OF MISCONDUCT means a written submission by any individual or entity to an ethics committee, paralegal association, bar association, law enforcement agency, judicial body, government agency, or other appropriate body or entity, that sets forth nonconfidential information regarding any instance of alleged misconduct by an individual paralegal or paralegal entity.

CHARGING PARTY means any individual or entity who submits a Charge of Misconduct against an individual paralegal or paralegal entity.

COMPETENCY means the demonstration of: diligence, education, skill, and mental, emotional, and physical fitness reasonably necessary for the performance of paralegal services.

CONFIDENTIAL INFORMATION means information relating to a client, whatever its source, that is not public knowledge nor available to the public. ("Nonconfidential Information" would generally include the name of the client and the identity of the matter for which the paralegal provided services.)

DISCIPLINARY HEARING means the confidential proceeding conducted by a committee or other designated body or entity concerning any instance of alleged misconduct by an individual paralegal or paralegal entity.

DISCIPLINARY COMMITTEE means any committee that has been established by an entity such as a paralegal association, bar association, judicial body, or government agency to: (a) identify, define, and investigate general ethical considerations and concerns with respect to paralegal practice; (b) administer and enforce the Model Code and Model Rules and; (c) discipline any individual paralegal or paralegal entity found to be in violation of same.

DISCLOSE   means communication of information reasonably sufficient to permit identification of the significance of the matter in question.

ETHICAL WALL   means the screening method implemented in order to protect a client from a conflict of interest. An Ethical Wall generally includes, but is not limited to, the following elements: (1) prohibit the paralegal from having any connection with the matter; (2) ban discussions with or the transfer of documents to or from the paralegal; (3) restrict access to files; and (4) educate all members of the firm, corporation, or entity as to the separation of the paralegal (both organizationally and physically) from the pending matter. For more information regarding the Ethical Wall, see the NFPA publication entitled "The Ethical Wall—Its Application to Paralegals."

EX PARTE   means actions or communications conducted at the instance and for the benefit of one party only, and without notice to, or contestation by, any person adversely interested.

INVESTIGATION   means the investigation of any charge(s) of misconduct filed against an individual paralegal or paralegal entity by a Committee.

LETTER OF REPRIMAND   means a written notice of formal censure or severe reproof administered to an individual paralegal or paralegal entity for unethical or improper conduct.

MISCONDUCT   means the knowing or unknowing commission of an act that is in direct violation of those Canons and Ethical Considerations of any and all applicable codes and/or rules of conduct.

PARALEGAL   is synonymous with "Legal Assistant" and is defined as a person qualified through education, training, or work experience to perform substantive legal work that requires knowledge of legal concepts and is customarily, but not exclusively performed by a lawyer. This person may be retained or employed by a lawyer, law office, governmental agency, or other entity or may be authorized by administrative, statutory, or court authority to perform this work.

PROPER AUTHORITY   means the local paralegal association, the local or state bar association, Committee(s) of the local paralegal or bar association(s), local prosecutor, administrative agency, or other tribunal empowered to investigate or act upon an instance of alleged misconduct.

RESPONDING PARTY   means an individual paralegal or paralegal entity against whom a Charge of Misconduct has been submitted.

REVOCATION   means the rescission of the license, certificate, or other authority to practice of an individual paralegal or paralegal entity found in violation of those Canons and Ethical Considerations of any and all applicable codes and/or rules of conduct.

SUSPENSION   means the suspension of the license, certificate, or other authority to practice of an individual paralegal or paralegal entity found in violation of those Canons and Ethical Considerations of any and all applicable codes and/or rules of conduct.

TRIBUNAL   means the body designated to adjudicate allegations of misconduct.

APPENDIX D

THE ABA'S MODEL GUIDELINES FOR THE UTILIZATION OF LEGAL ASSISTANT SERVICES

PREAMBLE

State courts, bar associations, or bar committees in at least seventeen states have prepared recommendations[1] for the utilization of legal assistant services.[2] While their content varies, their purpose appears uniform: to provide lawyers with a reliable basis for delegating responsibility for performing a portion of the lawyer's tasks to legal assistants. The purpose of preparing model guidelines is not to contradict the guidelines already adopted or to suggest that other guidelines may be more appropriate in a particular jurisdiction. It is the view of the Standing Committee on Legal Assistants of the American Bar Association [ABA], however, that a model set of guidelines for the utilization of legal assistant services may assist many states in adopting or revising such guidelines. The Standing Committee is of the view that guidelines will encourage lawyers to utilize legal assistant services

---

1. An appendix identifies the guidelines, court rules, and recommendations that were reviewed in drafting these Model Guidelines. [This appendix is not included in *West's Paralegal Today*.]
2. On February 6, 1986, the ABA Board of Governors approved the following definition of the term "legal assistant":

    A legal assistant is a person, qualified through education, training, or work experience, who is employed or retained by a lawyer, law office, governmental agency, or other entity in a capacity or function which involves the performance, under the ultimate direction and supervision of an attorney, of specifically delegated substantive legal work, which work, for the most part, requires a sufficient knowledge of legal concepts that, absent such assistant, the attorney would perform the task. In some contexts, the term "paralegal" is used interchangeably with the term legal assistant. {Note: The ABA has since modified this decision. See Chapter 1.]

effectively and promote the growth of the legal assistant profession.[3] In undertaking this project, the Standing Committee has attempted to state guidelines that conform with the American Bar Association's Model Rules of Professional Conduct, decided authority, and contemporary practice. Lawyers, of course, are to be first directed by Rule 5.3 of the Model Rules in the utilization of legal assistant services, and nothing contained in these guidelines is intended to be inconsistent with that rule. Specific ethical considerations in particular states, however, may require modification of these guidelines before their adoption. In the commentary after each guideline, we have attempted to identify the basis for the guideline and any issues of which we are aware that the guideline may present; those drafting such guidelines may wish to take them into account.

Guideline 1

A lawyer is responsible for all of the professional actions of a legal assistant performing legal assistant services at the lawyer's direction and should take reasonable measures to ensure that the legal assistant's conduct is consistent with the lawyer's obligations under the ABA Model Rules of Professional Conduct.

COMMENT TO GUIDELINE 1. An attorney who utilizes a legal assistant's services is responsible for determining that the legal assistant is competent to perform the tasks assigned, based on the legal assistant's education, training, and experience, and for ensuring that the legal assistant is familiar with the responsibilities of attorneys and legal assistants under the applicable rules governing professional conduct.[4]

Under principles of agency law and rules governing the conduct of attorneys, lawyers are responsible for the actions and the work product of the non-lawyers they employ. Rule 5.3 of the Model Rules[5] requires that partners and supervising attorneys ensure that the conduct of non-lawyer assistants is compatible with the lawyer's professional obligations. Several state guidelines have adopted this language. E.g., Commentary to Illinois Recommendation (A), Kansas Guideline III(a), New Hampshire Rule 35, Sub-Rule 9, and North Carolina Guideline 4. Ethical Consideration 3–6 of the Model Code encouraged lawyers to delegate tasks to legal assistants provided the lawyer maintained a direct relationship with the client, supervised appropriately, and had complete responsibility for the work

---

3. While necessarily mentioning legal assistant conduct, lawyers are the intended audience of these Guidelines. The Guidelines, therefore, are addressed to lawyer conduct and not directly to the conduct of the legal assistant. Both the National Association of Legal Assistants (NALA) and the National Federation of Paralegal Associations (NFPA) have adopted guidelines of conduct that are directed to legal assistants. See NALA, "Code of Ethics and Professional Responsibility of the National Association of Legal Assistants, Inc." (adopted May 1975, revised November 1979 and September 1988); NFPA, "Affirmation of Responsibility" (adopted 1977, revised 1981).
4. Attorneys, of course, are not liable for violation of the ABA Model Rules of Professional Conduct ("Model Rules") unless the Model Rules have been adopted as the code of professional conduct in a jurisdiction in which the lawyer practices. They are referenced in this model guideline for illustrative purposes; if the guideline is to be adopted, the reference should be modified to the jurisdiction's rules of professional conduct.
5. The Model Rules were first adopted by the ABA House of Delegates in August of 1983. Since that time many states have adopted the Model Rules to govern the professional conduct of lawyers licensed in those states. Since a number of states still utilize a version of the Model Code of Professional Responsibility ("Model Code"), which was adopted by the House of Delegates in August of 1969, however, these comments will refer to both the Model Rules and the predecessor Model Code (and to the Ethical Considerations and Disciplinary Rules found under the canons in the Model Code).

product. The adoption of Rule 5.3, which incorporates these principles, implicitly reaffirms this encouragement.

Several states have addressed the issue of the lawyer's ultimate responsibility for work performed by subordinates. For example, Colorado Guideline 1.c, Kentucky Supreme Court Rule 3.700, Sub-Rule 2.C, and Michigan Guideline I provide: "The lawyer remains responsible for the actions of the legal assistant to the same extent as if such representation had been furnished entirely by the lawyer and such actions were those of the lawyer." New Mexico Guideline X states "[the] lawyer maintains ultimate responsibility for and has an ongoing duty to actively supervise the legal assistant's work performance, conduct and product." Connecticut Recommendation 2 and Rhode Island Guideline III state specifically that lawyers are liable for malpractice for the mistakes and omissions of their legal assistants.

Finally, the lawyer should ensure that legal assistants supervised by the lawyer are familiar with the rules governing attorney conduct and that they follow those rules. See Comment to Model Rule 5.3; Illinois Recommendation (A)(5), New Hampshire Supreme Court Rule 35, Sub-Rule 9, and New Mexico, Statement of Purpose; see also NALA's Model Standards and Guidelines for the Utilization of Legal Assistants, guidelines IV, V, and VIII (1985, revised 1990) (hereafter "NALA Guidelines").

The Standing Committee and several of those who have commented upon these Guidelines regard Guideline 1 as a comprehensive statement of general principle governing lawyers who utilize legal assistant services in the practice of law. As such it, in effect, is a part of each of the remaining Guidelines.

Guideline 2

Provided the lawyer maintains responsibility for the work product, a lawyer may delegate to a legal assistant any task normally performed by the lawyer except those tasks proscribed to one not licensed as a lawyer by statute, court rule, administrative rule or regulation, controlling authority, the ABA Model Rules of Professional Conduct, or these Guidelines.

COMMENT TO GUIDELINE 2. The essence of the definition of the term legal assistant adopted by the ABA Board of Governors in 1986 is that, so long as appropriate supervision is maintained, many tasks normally performed by lawyers may be delegated to legal assistants. Of course, Rule 5.5 of the Model Rules, DR 3–101 of the Model Code, and most states specifically prohibit lawyers from assisting or aiding a non-lawyer in the unauthorized practice of law. Thus, while appropriate delegation of tasks to legal assistants is encouraged, the lawyer may not permit the legal assistant to engage in the "practice of law." Neither the Model Rules nor the Model Code define the "practice of law." EC 3–5 under the Model Code gave some guidance by equating the practice of law to the application of the professional judgment of the lawyer in solving clients' legal problems. Further, ABA Opinion 316 (1967) states: "A lawyer can employ lay secretaries, lay investigators, lay detectives, lay researchers, accountants, lay scriveners, nonlawyer draftsmen or nonlawyer researchers. In fact, he may employ nonlawyers to do any task for him except counsel clients about law matters, engage directly in the practice of law, appear in court or appear in formal proceedings as part of the judicial process, so long as it is he who takes the work and vouches for it to the client and becomes responsible for it to the client."

Most state guidelines specify that legal assistants may not appear before courts, administrative tribunals, or other adjudicatory bodies unless their rules authorize such appearances; may not conduct depositions; and may not give legal advice to clients. E.g., Connecticut Recommendation 4; Florida EC 3–6 (327 So.2d at 16); and Michigan Guideline II. Also see NALA Guidelines IV and VI. But it is also important to note that, as some guidelines have recognized, pursuant to federal or state statute legal assistants are permitted to provide direct client representation in certain administrative proceedings. E.g., South Carolina Guideline II. While this does not obviate the attorney's responsibility for the legal assistant's work, it does change the nature of the attorney supervision of the legal assistant. The opportunity to use such legal assistant services has particular benefits to legal services programs and does not violate Guideline 2. See generally ABA Standards for Providers of Civil Legal Services to the Poor, Std. 6.3, at 6.17–6.18 (1986).

The Model Rules emphasize the importance of appropriate delegation. The key to appropriate delegation is proper supervision, which includes adequate instruction when assigning projects, monitoring of the project, and review of the completed project. The Supreme Court of Virginia upheld a malpractice verdict against a lawyer based in part on negligent actions of a legal assistant in performing tasks that evidently were properly delegable. *Musselman v. Willoughby Corp.,* 230 Va. 337, 337 S.E.2d 724 (1985). See also C. Wolfram, *Modern Legal Ethics* (1986), at 236, 896. All state guidelines refer to the requirement that the lawyer "supervise" legal assistants in the performance of their duties. Lawyers should also take care in hiring and choosing a legal assistant to work on a specific project to ensure that the legal assistant has the education, knowledge, and ability necessary to perform the delegated tasks competently. See Connecticut Recommendation 14, Kansas Standards I, II, and III, and New Mexico Guideline VIII. Finally, some states describe appropriate delegation and review in terms of the delegated work losing its identity and becoming "merged" into the work product of the attorney. See Florida EC 3–6 (327 So.2d at 16).

Legal assistants often play an important role in improving communication between the attorney and the client. EC 3–6 under the Model Code mentioned three specific kinds of tasks that legal assistants may perform under appropriate lawyer supervision: factual investigation and research, legal research, and the preparation of legal documents. Some states delineate more specific tasks in their guidelines, such as attending client conferences, corresponding with and obtaining information from clients, handling witness execution of documents, preparing transmittal letters, maintaining estate/guardianship trust accounts, etc. See, e.g., Colorado (lists of specialized functions in several areas follow guidelines); Michigan, Comment to Definition of Legal Assistant; New York, Specialized Skills of Legal Assistants; Rhode Island Guideline II; and NALA Guideline IX. The two-volume *Working with Legal Assistants,* published by the Standing Committee in 1982, attempted to provide a general description of the types of tasks that may be delegated to legal assistants in various practice areas.

There are tasks that have been specifically prohibited in some states, but that may be delegated in others. For example, legal assistants may not supervise will executions or represent clients at real estate closings in some jurisdictions, but may in others. Compare Connecticut Recommendation 7 and Illinois State Bar Association Position Paper on Use of Attorney Assistants in Real Estate Transactions (May 16, 1984), which proscribe legal assistants conducting real estate closings, with Georgia "real estate job description," Florida Professional Ethics Committee Advisory Opinion 89–5 (1989), and Missouri, Comment to Guideline I, which permit legal assistants to conduct real estate closings. Also compare Connecticut Recommendation 8 (prohibiting attorneys from authorizing legal assistants to supervise will executions) with Colorado "estate planning job description," Georgia "estate, trusts, and wills job description," Missouri, Comment to Guideline I, and Rhode Island Guideline II (suggesting that legal assistants may supervise the execution of wills, trusts, and other documents).

Guideline 3

A lawyer may not delegate to a legal assistant:

(a) Responsibility for establishing an attorney-client relationship.
(b) Responsibility for establishing the amount of a fee to be charged for a legal service.
(c) Responsibility for a legal opinion rendered to a client.

COMMENTS TO GUIDELINE 3. The Model Rules and most state codes require that lawyers communicate with their clients in order for clients to make well-informed decisions about their representation and resolution of legal issues. Model Rule 1.4. Ethical Consideration 3–6 under the Model Code emphasized that "delegation [of legal tasks to nonlawyers] is proper if the lawyer *maintains a direct relationship with his client,* supervises the delegated work and has complete professional responsibility for the work product." (Emphasis added.) Accordingly, most state guidelines also stress the importance of a direct attorney-client relationship. See Colorado Guideline 1, Florida EC 3–6, Illinois Recommendation (A)(1), Iowa EC 3–6(2), and New Mexico Guideline IV. The direct personal relationship between client and lawyer is necessary to the exercise of the lawyer's trained professional judgment.

An essential aspect of the lawyer-client relationship is the agreement to undertake representation and the related fee arrangement. The Model Rules and most states require that fee arrangements be agreed upon early on and be communicated to the client by the lawyer, in some circumstances in writing. Model Rule 1.5 and Comments. Many state guidelines prohibit legal assistants from "setting fees" or "accepting cases." See, e.g., Colorado Guideline 1 and NALA Guideline VI. Connecticut recommends that legal assistants be prohibited from accepting or rejecting cases or setting fees "if these tasks entail any discretion on the part of the paralegals." Connecticut Recommendation 9.

EC 3–5 states: "[T]he essence of the professional judgment of the lawyer is his educated ability to relate the general body and philosophy of law to a specific legal problem of a client; and thus, the public interest will be better served if only lawyers are permitted to act in matters involving professional judgment." Clients are entitled to their lawyers' professional judgment and opinion. Legal assistants may, however, be authorized to communicate legal advice so long as they do not interpret or expand on that advice. Typically, state guidelines phrase this prohibition in terms of legal assistants being forbidden from "giving legal advice" or "counseling clients about legal matters." See, e.g., Colorado Guideline 2, Connecticut Recommendation 6, Florida DR 3–104, Iowa EC 3–6(3), Kansas Guideline I, Kentucky Sub-Rule 2, New Hampshire Rule 35, Sub-Rule 1, Texas Guideline I, and NALA Guideline VI. Some states have more expansive wording that prohibits legal assistants from engaging in any activity that would require the exercise of independent legal judgment. Nevertheless, it is clear that all states, as well as the Model Rules, encourage direct communication between clients and a legal assistant insofar as the legal assistant is performing a task properly delegated by a lawyer. It should be noted that a lawyer who permits a legal assistant to assist in establishing the attorney-client relationship, communicating a fee, or preparing a legal opinion is not delegating responsibility for those matters and, therefore, may be complying with this guideline.

Guideline 4

It is the lawyer's responsibility to take reasonable measures to ensure that clients, courts, and other lawyers are aware that a legal assistant, whose services are utilized by the lawyer in performing legal services, is not licensed to practice law.

COMMENT TO GUIDELINE 4. Since, in most instances, a legal assistant is not licensed as a lawyer, it is important that those with whom the legal assistant deals are aware of that fact. Several state guidelines impose on the lawyer responsibility for instructing a legal assistant whose services are utilized by the lawyer to disclose the legal assistant's status in any dealings with a third party. See, e.g., Michigan Guideline III, part 5, New Hampshire Rule 35, Sub-Rule 8, and NALA Guideline V. While requiring the legal assistant to make such disclosure is one way in which the attorney's responsibility to third parties may be discharged, the Standing Committee is of the view that it is desirable to emphasize the lawyer's responsibility for the disclosure and leave to the lawyer the discretion to decide whether the lawyer will discharge that responsibility by direct communication with the client, by requiring the legal assistant to make the disclosure, by a written memorandum, or by some other means. Although in most initial engagements by a client it may be prudent for the attorney to discharge the responsibility with a writing, the guideline requires only that the lawyer recognize the responsibility and ensure that it is discharged. Clearly, when a client has been adequately informed of the lawyer's utilization of legal assistant services, it is unnecessary to make additional formalistic disclosures as the client retains the lawyer for other services.

Most state guidelines specifically endorse legal assistants signing correspondence so long as their status as a legal assistant is indicated by an appropriate title. E.g., Colorado Guideline 2; Kansas, Comment to Guideline IX; and North Carolina Guideline 9; also see ABA Informal Opinion 1367 (1976). The comment to New Mexico Guideline XI warns against the use of the title "associate" since it may be construed to mean associate-attorney.

Guideline 5

A lawyer may identify legal assistants by name and title on the lawyer's letterhead and on business cards identifying the lawyer's firm.

COMMENT TO GUIDELINE 5. Under Guideline 4, above, an attorney who employs a legal assistant has an obligation to ensure that the status of the legal assistant as a non-lawyer is fully disclosed. The primary purpose of this disclosure is to avoid confusion that might lead someone to believe that the legal assistant is a lawyer. The identification suggested by this guideline is consistent with that objective, while also affording the legal assistant recognition as an important part of the legal services team.

Recent ABA Informal Opinion 1527 (1989) provides that non-lawyer support personnel, including legal assistants, may be listed on a law firm's letterhead and reiterates previous opinions that approve of legal assistants having business cards. See also ABA Informal Opinion 1185 (1971). The listing must not be false or misleading and "must make it clear that the support personnel who are listed are not lawyers."

Nearly all state guidelines approve of business cards for legal assistants, but some prescribe the contents and format of the card. E.g., Iowa Guideline 4 and Texas Guideline VIII. All agree the legal assistant's status must be clearly indicated and the card may not be used in a deceptive way. New Hampshire Supreme Court

Rule 7 approves the use of business cards so long as the card is not used for unethical solicitation.

Some states do not permit attorneys to list legal assistants on their letterhead. E.g., Kansas Guideline VIII, Michigan Guideline III, New Hampshire Rule 35, Sub-Rule 7, New Mexico Guideline XI, and North Carolina Guideline 9. Several of these states rely on earlier ABA Informal Opinion 619 (1962), 845 (1965), and 1000 (1977), all of which were expressly withdrawn by ABA Informal Opinion 1527. These earlier opinions interpreted the predecessor Model Code and DR 2–102(A), which, prior to *Bates v. State Bar of Arizona*, 433 U.S. 350 (1977), had strict limitations on the information that could be listed on letterheads. States which do permit attorneys to list names of legal assistants on their stationery, if the listing is not deceptive and the legal assistant's status is clearly identified, include: Arizona Committee on Rules of Professional Conduct Formal Opinion 3/90 (1990); Connecticut Recommendation 12; Florida Professional Ethics Committee Advisory Opinion 86-4 (1986); Hawaii, Formal Opinion 78-8-19 (1978, as revised 1984); Illinois State Bar Association Advisory Opinion 87-1 (1987); Kentucky Sub-Rule 6; Mississippi State Bar Ethics Committee Opinion 93 (1984); Missouri Guideline IV; New York State Bar Association Committee on Professional Ethics Opinion 500 (1978); Oregon, Ethical Opinion No. 349 (1977); and Texas, Ethics Committee Opinion 436 (1983). In light of the United States Supreme Court opinion in *Peel v. Attorney Registration and Disciplinary Commission of Illinois*, 496 U.S. 91, 110 S.Ct. 2281 (1990), it may be that a restriction on letterhead identification of legal assistants that is not deceptive and clearly identifies the legal assistant's status violates the First Amendment rights of the lawyer.

Guideline 6

It is the responsibility of a lawyer to take reasonable measures to ensure that all client confidences are preserved by a legal assistant.

COMMENT TO GUIDELINE 6. A fundamental principle underlying the free exchange of information in a lawyer-client relationship is that the lawyer maintain the confidentiality of information relating to the representation. "It is a matter of common knowledge that the normal operation of a law office exposes confidential professional information to non-lawyer employees of the office. This obligates a lawyer to exercise care in selecting and training his employees so that the sanctity of all confidences and secrets of his clients may be preserved." EC 4–2, Model Code.

Rule 5.3 of the Model Rules requires "a lawyer who has direct supervisory authority over the nonlawyer [to] make reasonable efforts to ensure that the person's conduct is compatible with the professional obligations of the lawyer." The Comment to Rule 5.3 makes it clear that lawyers should give legal assistants "appropriate instruction and supervision concerning the ethical aspects of their employment, particularly regarding the obligation not to disclose information relating to the representation of the client." DR 4–101(D) under the Model Code provides that: "A lawyer shall exercise reasonable care to prevent his employees, associates and others whose services are utilized by him from discharging or using confidences or secrets of a client. . . ."

It is particularly important that the lawyer ensure that the legal assistant understands that *all* information concerning the client, even the mere fact that a person is a client of the firm, may be strictly confidential. Rule 1.6 of the Model Rules expanded the definition of confidential information ". . . not merely to matters communicated in confidence by the client but also to all information relating to the representation, whatever its source."[6] It is therefore the lawyer's obligation to instruct clearly and to take reasonable steps to ensure the legal assistant's preservation of client confidences. Nearly all states that have guidelines for the utilization of legal assistants require the lawyer "to instruct legal assistants concerning client confidences" and "to exercise care to ensure that legal assistants comply" with the Code in this regard. Even if the client consents to divulging information, this information must not be used to the disadvantage of the client. See, e.g., Connecticut Recommendation 3: New Hampshire Rule 35, Sub-Rule 4; NALA Guideline V.

Guideline 7

A lawyer should take reasonable measures to prevent conflicts of interest resulting from a legal assistant's other employment or interests insofar as such other employment or interests would present a conflict of interest if it were that of the lawyer.

COMMENT TO GUIDELINE 7. A lawyer must make "reasonable efforts to ensure that [a] legal assistant's conduct is compatible with the professional obligations of the lawyer." Model Rule 5.3. These professional obligations include the duty to exercise independent professional judgment on behalf of a client, "free of compromising influences and loyalties." ABA Model Rules 1.7 through 1.13. Therefore, legal assistants should be instructed to inform the supervising attorney of any interest that could result in a conflict of interest or even give the appearance of a conflict. The guideline intentionally speaks to other employment rather than only past employment, since there are instances where legal assistants are employed by more than one law firm at the same time. The guideline's reference to "other interests" is intended to include personal relationships as well as instances where a legal assistant may have a financial interest (i.e., as stockholder, trust beneficiary or trustee, etc.) that would conflict with the client's in the matter in which the lawyer has been employed.

"Imputed Disqualification Arising from Change in Employment by Nonlawyer Employee," ABA Informal Opinion 1526 (1988), defines the duties of both the present and former employing lawyers and reasons that the restrictions on legal assistants' employment should be kept to "the minimum necessary to protect confidentiality" in order to prevent legal assistants from being forced to leave their careers, which "would disserve clients as well as the legal profession." The Opinion describes the attorney's obligations (1) to caution the legal assistant not to disclose any information and (2) to prevent the legal assistant from working on any matter on which the legal assistant worked for a prior employer or respecting which the employee has confidential information.

If a conflict is discovered, it may be possible to "wall" the legal assistant from the conflict area so that the entire firm need not be disqualified and the legal assis-

---

6. Rule 1.05 of the Texas Disciplinary Rules of Professional Conduct (1990) provides a different formulation, which is equally expansive:

"Confidential information" includes both "privileged information" and "unprivileged client information." "Privileged information" refers to the information of a client protected by the lawyer-client privilege of Rule 503 of the Texas Rules of Evidence or the Rule 503 of the Texas Rules of Criminal Evidence or by the principles of attorney-client privilege governed by Rule 501 of the Federal Rules of Evidence for United States Courts and Magistrates. "Unprivileged client information" means all information relating to a client or furnished by the client, other than privileged information, acquired by the lawyer during the course of or by reason of the representation of the client.

tant is effectively screened from information concerning the matter. The American Bar Association has taken the position that what historically has been described as a "Chinese wall" will allow non-lawyer personnel (including legal assistants) who are in possession of confidential client information to accept employment with a law firm opposing the former client so long as the wall is observed and effectively screens the non-lawyer from confidential information. ABA Informal Opinion 1526 (1988). See also Tennessee Formal Ethics Opinion 89–F–118 (March 10, 1989). The implication of this Informal Opinion is that if a wall is not in place, the employer may be disqualified from representing either party to the controversy. One court has so held. *In re: Complex Asbestos Litigation,* No. 828684 (San Francisco Superior Court, September 19, 1989).

It is not clear that a wall will prevent disqualification in the case of a lawyer employed to work for a law firm representing a client with an adverse interest to a client of the lawyer's former employer. Under Model Rule 1.10, when a lawyer moves to a firm that represents an adverse party in a matter in which the lawyer's former firm was involved, absent a waiver by the client, the new firm's representation may continue only if the newly employed lawyer acquired no protected information and did not work directly on the matter in the former employment. The new Rules of Professional Conduct in Kentucky and Texas (both effective January 1, 1990) specifically provide for disqualification. Rule 1.10(b) in the District of Columbia, which became effective January 1, 1991, does so as well. The Sixth Circuit, however, has held that the wall will effectively insulate the new firm from disqualification if it prevents the new lawyer-employee from access to information concerning the client with the adverse interest. *Manning v. Waring, Cox, James, Sklar & Allen,* 849 F.2d 222 (6th Cir. 1988). [As a result of the Sixth Circuit opinion, Tennessee revised its formal ethics opinion, which is cited above, and now applies the same rule to lawyers, legal assistants, law clerks, and legal secretaries.] See generally NFPA, "The Chinese Wall—Its Application to Paralegals" (1990).

The states that have guidelines that address the legal assistant conflict of interest refer to the lawyer's responsibility to ensure against personal, business or social interests of the legal assistant that would conflict with the representation of the client or impinge on the services rendered to the client. E.g., Kansas Guideline X, New Mexico Guideline VI, and North Carolina Guideline 7. Florida Professional Ethics Opinion 86–5 (1986) discusses a legal assistant's move from one firm to another and the obligations of each not to disclose confidences. See also Vermont Ethics Opinion 85–8 (1985) (a legal assistant is not bound by the Code of Professional Responsibility and, absent an absolute waiver by the client, the new firm should not represent client if legal assistant possessed confidential information from old firm).

Guideline 8

A lawyer may include a charge for the work performed by a legal assistant in setting a charge for legal services.

COMMENT TO GUIDELINE 8. The U.S. Supreme Court in *Missouri v. Jenkins,* 491 U.S. 274 (1989), held that in setting a reasonable attorney's fee under 28 U.S.C. §1988, a legal fee may include a charge for legal assistant services at "market rates" rather than "actual cost" to the attorneys. This decision should resolve any question concerning the propriety of setting a charge for legal services based on work performed by a legal assistant. Its rationale favors setting a charge based on the "market" rate for such services, rather than their direct cost to the lawyer. This result was recognized by Connecticut Recommendation 11, Illinois

Recommendation D, and Texas Guideline V prior to the Supreme Court decision. See also Fla.Stat.Ann. §57.104 (1991 Supp.) (adopted in 1987 and permitting consideration of legal assistant services in computing attorney's fees) and Fla.Stat.Ann. §744.108 (1991 Supp.) (adopted in 1989 and permitting recovery of "customary and reasonable charges for work performed by legal assistants" as fees for legal services in guardianship matters).

It is important to note, however, that *Missouri v. Jenkins* does not abrogate the attorney's responsibilities under Model Rule 1.5 to set a reasonable fee for legal services and it follows that those considerations apply to a fee that includes a fee for legal assistant services. Accordingly, the effect of combining a market rate charge for the services of lawyers and legal assistants should, in most instances, result in a lower total cost for the legal service than if the lawyer had performed the service alone.

Guideline 9

A lawyer may not split legal fees with a legal assistant nor pay a legal assistant for the referral of legal business. A lawyer may compensate a legal assistant based on the quantity and quality of the legal assistant's work and the value of that work to a law practice, but the legal assistant's compensation may not be contingent, by advance agreement, upon the probability of the lawyer's practice.

COMMENT TO GUIDELINE 9.
Model Rule 5.4 and DR 3–102(A) and 3–103(A) under the Model Code clearly prohibit fee "splitting" with legal assistants, whether characterized by splitting of contingent fees, "forwarding" fees, or other sharing of legal fees. Virtually all guidelines adopted by state bar associations have continued this prohibition in one form or another.[7] It appears clear that a legal assistant may not be compensated on a contingent basis for a particular case or paid for "signing up" clients for a legal practice.

Having stated this prohibition, however, the guideline attempts to deal with the practical consideration of how a legal assistant properly may be compensated by an attorney or law firm. The linchpin of the prohibition seems to be the advance agreement of the lawyer to "split" a fee based on a pre-existing contingent agreement.[8] There is no general prohibition against a lawyer who enjoys a particularly profitable period recognizing the contribution of the legal assistant to that profitability with a discretionary bonus. Likewise, a lawyer engaged in a particularly profitable specialty of legal practice is not prohibited from compensating the legal assistant who aids materially in that practice more handsomely than the compensation generally awarded to legal assistants in that geographic area who work in law practices that are less lucrative. Indeed, any effort to fix a compensation level for legal assistants and prohibit greater compensation would appear to violate the federal antitrust laws. See, e.g., *Goldfarb v. Virginia State Bar*, 421 U.S. 773 (1975).

---

7. Connecticut Recommendation 10; Illinois Recommendation D; Kansas Guideline VI; Kentucky Supreme Court Rule 3.700, Sub-rule 5; Michigan Guideline III, part 2; Missouri Guideline II; New Hampshire Rule 35, Sub-Rules 5 and 6; New Mexico Guideline IX; Rhode Island Guideline VIII and IX; South Carolina Guideline V; Texas Guideline V.
8. In its Rule 5.4, which [became] effective on January 1, 1991, the District of Columbia will permit lawyers to form legal service partnerships that include non-lawyer participants. Comments 5 and 6 to that rule, however, state that the term "non-lawyer participants" should not be confused with the term "non-lawyer assistants" and that "[n]on-lawyer assistants under Rule 5.3 do not have managerial authority or financial interests in the organization."

Guideline 10

A lawyer who employs a legal assistant should facilitate the legal assistant's participation in appropriate continuing education and *pro bono publico* activities.

COMMENT TO GUIDELINE 10. While Guideline 10 does not appear to have been adopted in the guidelines of any state bar association, the Standing Committee on Legal Assistants believes that its adoption would be appropriate.[9] For many years the Standing Committee on Legal Assistants has advocated that the improvement of formal legal assistant education will generally improve the legal services rendered by lawyers employing legal assistants and provide a more satisfying professional atmosphere in which legal assistants may work. See, e.g., ABA Board of Governors, Policy on Legal Assistant Licensure and/or Certification, Statement 4 (February 6, 1986); ABA, Standing Committee on Legal Assistants, "Position Paper on the Question of Legal Assistant Licensure or Certification" (December 10, 1985), at 6 and Conclusion 3. Recognition of the employing lawyer's obligation to facilitate the legal assistant's continuing professional education is, therefore, appropriate because of the benefits to both the law practice and the legal assistant and is consistent with the lawyer's own responsibility to maintain professional competence under Model Rule 1.1. See also EC 6–2 of the Model Code.

The Standing Committee is of the view that similar benefits will accrue to the lawyer and legal assistant if the legal assistant is included in the *pro bono publico* legal services that a lawyer has a clear obligation to provide under Model Rule 6.1 and, where appropriate, the legal assistant is encouraged to provide such services independently. The ability of a law firm to provide more *pro bono publico* services will be enhanced if legal assistants are included. Recognition of the legal assistant's role in such services is consistent with the role of the legal assistant in the contemporary delivery of legal services generally and is consistent with the lawyer's duty to the legal profession under Canon 2 of the Model Code.

THE STANDING COMMITTEE ON LEGAL ASSISTANTS
OF THE AMERICAN BAR ASSOCIATION
May 1991

ADOPTED BY ABA HOUSE OF DELEGATES
August 1991

---

9. While no state has apparently adopted a guideline similar to Model Guideline 10, parts 4 and 5 of NALA Guideline VIII suggest similar requirements. Sections III and V of NFPA's "Affirmation of Professional Responsibility" recognize a legal assistant's obligations to "maintain a high level of competence" (which "is achieved through continuing education") and to "serve the public interest." NFPA has also published a guide to assist legal assistant groups in developing public service projects. See NFPA, "*Pro Bono Publico* (For the Good of the People)" (1987).

APPENDIX E

Paralegal Ethics and Regulation:

How to Find State-Specific Information

NALANet

One resource for finding state-specific information is NALANet. This is an online information service for the legal-assistant profession. NALANet reports on relevant topics such as ethics, guidelines, membership, case law updates, legislative activities, bar activities, significant research projects, and articles about the utilization of legal assistants on a state-by-state basis. The Florida example, shown below, illustrates the type of information provided for each state. NALANet is available to members of NALA. For further information, contact NALA at (918) 587-6828, or visit its Web site at www.nala.org.

Florida

Ethics

FL Opinion 86-4 8/1/86
(business cards, letterhead)

FL Opinion 88-15
(solicitation of clients, confidentiality, attorneys' fees)

FL Opinion 89-4 8/29/90
(nonlawyers, attorneys' fees, solicitation of clients, business cards)

FL Advisory Opinion 74479
(unauthorized practice of law)

FL Bar Re Advisory Opinion Hrs Non-Lawyer Counselor FLA Sup Ct No 70615 5/25/89
(nonlawyers)

FL Ethics Guide for Legal Assistants 86
(definitions, attorneys' fees, business cards, supervision, unauthorized practice of law, letterhead, ethics, qualifications)

FL Opinion 88-6 4/15/88
(initial interview, supervision, nonlawyers)

FL Opinion 87-11
Signing Lawyer Name/Pleadings & Notices
(nonlawyers, unauthorized practice of law, supervision)

FL Bar Advisory Opinion Non-Lawyer Pre of Living Trusts FL Supreme Court Case No. 78358
(nonlawyers, unauthorized practice of law)

FL Supreme Court Review of Opinion Unauthorized Practice of Law Comm Re Non-Lawyer Prep of Pension Plans 11/29/90
(nonlawyers, unauthorized practice of law)

FL Advisory Opinion 74479 Undated
(unauthorized practice of law)

FL Opinion 86-5 8/1/86
(conflict of interest, confidentiality)

FL Opinion 88-6 4/15/88
(supervision, unauthorized practice of law, work product)

FL Opinion 89-5
(real property, nonlawyers)

Rule 10-1.1(B), Rules Regulating Florida Bar (6/20/91) Forms Approved for Use by Lawyers/Non-Lawyers

FL Opinion 92-3 (10/1/92)
(nonlawyers, attorneys' fees, solicitation of clients)

Guidelines

FL Ethics Guide for Legal Assistants 86
(definitions, attorneys' fees, business cards, supervision, unauthorized practice of law, letterhead, ethics, qualifications)

Membership

FL Family Law Section Florida Bar
(certification, American Bar Association Approved School, experience)

FL Orange County Bar
(affiliate membership)

FL General Practice Section Florida Bar
(certification, American Bar Association Approved School, experience)

FL Local Government Section Florida Bar
(certification, Florida member)

FL Health Law Section Florida Bar
(open)

FL Practice Management & Technology Florida Bar
(certification, American Bar Association Approved School, experience)

FL Real Property Probate & Trust Section
(certification, American Bar Association Approved School, experience)

FL Trial Lawyers Section Florida Bar
(certification, American Bar Association Approved School, experience)

FL Environmental & Land Use Section
(open)

FL Broward County Bar

Cases

The Celotex Corp-Mid Dist. FL 90-10016-8B1 and 90-10017-8B1
(bankruptcy, attorneys' fees)

FL Bar v. Mitchell, 569 So. 2d 424 (FLA Sup. Ct. 1990)
(nonlawyers, supervision by lawyer)

Florida Bar v. Carter, 502 So. 2d 904 (FLA Sup. Ct. 1987)
(supervision)

FL Bar Re Advisory Opinion Hrs Nonlawyer Counselor FLA Sup. Ct. No. 70615 5/25/89
(nonlawyers)

FL Bar Advisory Opinion Nonlawyer Prep of Living Trusts FL Supreme Court Case No. 78358
(nonlawyers, unauthorized practice of law)

FL Supreme Court Review of Opinion UPL Comm Re Nonlawyer Prep of Pension Plans 11/29/90
(nonlawyers, unauthorized practice of law)

FL Advisory Opinion 73306 6/1/89
(forms, representation, unauthorized practice of law)

In Re Christopher Backmann, BR 1990 (Bkrtcy S.D. FL, No. 88-94588-BKC-AJC, 3/30/90)
(unauthorized practice of law, supervision, bankruptcy, forms)

Security First Fed. v. Broom et al., DCA No 89-01814, 4/18/90
(qualifications, regulation, real property)

Florida Bar v. Brumbaugh, No. 48803 S.Ct. Florida
(unauthorized practice of law, forms, constitutional law)

Florida Bar v. Furman, No. 51226 S.Ct. Florida
(unauthorized practice of law, constitutional law, nonlawyers, forms)

Std Guaranty Ins. v. Brenda L. Quanstrom, No 72100 Sup. Ct. of Florida 1/11/90
(fees, Missouri)

Town of Windermere v. Isleworth Golf & CC, Circuit Ct. 9th Judicial District, Orange County Florida, CI 87-2677
(attorneys' fees)

Ray v. Cutter Labs, 746 F. Supp. (MD FLA 1990)
(privilege waived, unintentional act, privilege)

Corn v. City of Lauderdale Lakes, 794 F. Supp. 364 (S.D. Fla. 1992)
(attorneys' fees, market rate fees if prevailing practice)

The Florida Bar v. Daniel E. Shramek, Case No 77,871
(nonlawyers, unauthorized practice of law)

Ippolito v. Florida, Case No. 92-880-Civ.T-99
(nonlawyers, unauthorized practice of law, legal technicians)

Ibanez v. Florida Dept of Bus. & Prof. Regulation, 114 S.Ct. 2084 (1994) 7/18/94
(professional designation)

Legislation

FL Statute 57.104 Computation of Attorney Fee
(definitions, attorneys' fees)

FL Senate Bill 2770 10/1/90 Passed Public Law Paralegal Fees in Guardianship Law
(attorneys' fees, supervision)

Articles

Amendment to Rule 4-6.1 of Rules Regulating the Florida Bar, Fla Sup. Ct., No 74,538 2/20/92 Pro Bono (*pro bono*)

Florida Legal Technician Committee 6/1/92 Preliminary Report Summary (legal technicians, unauthorized practice of law, regulation)

Rule 10-1.1(B), Rules Regulating Florida Bar (6/20/91) Forms Approved for Use by Lawyers/Nonlawyers (nonlawyers, forms)

What's in a Name? 8/1/94 Outlines Difference between Legal Assistant & Technician—Bar News Article Tech (definitions, certification)

Other

Florida Legal Technician Committee 6/1/92 Preliminary Report Summary (legal technicians, unauthorized practice of law, regulations)

APPENDIX F

Paralegal Associations

Paralegal Associations

NFPA Associations

Region I

Alaska Association of Legal Assistants
P.O. Box 101956
Anchorage, AK 99510-1956

Arizona Association of Professional
 Paralegals, Inc.
P.O. Box 430
Phoenix, AZ 85001

California Association of Independent
 Paralegals
39120 Argonaut Way, #114
Fremont, CA 94538

Hawaii Association of Legal Assistants
P.O. Box 674
Honolulu, HI 96809

Los Angeles Paralegal Association
P.O. Box 7803
Van Nuys, CA 91409
818/347-1001

Oregon Legal Assistants Association
P.O. Box 8523
Portland, OR 97207
503/796-1671

Sacramento Association of Legal
 Assistants
P.O. Box 453
Sacramento, CA 95812-0453
916/763-7851

San Diego Association of Legal
 Assistants
P.O. Box 87449
San Diego, CA 92138-7449
619/491-1994

San Francisco Paralegal Association
P.O. Box 2110
San Francisco, CA 94126-2110

Washington State Paralegal
 Association
P.O. Box 48153
Burieu, WA 98148
800/288-WSPA

Region II

Dallas Area Paralegal Association
P.O. Box 12533
Dallas, TX 75225
972/991-0853

Illinois Paralegal Association
P.O. Box 8089
Bartlett, IL 60103-8089
630/837-8088

Kansas City Paralegal Association
8826 Santa Fe Drive, Suite 208
Overland Park, KS 66212
913/381-4458

Kansas Paralegal Association
P.O. Box 1675
Topeka, KS 66601

Legal Assistants of New Mexico
P.O. Box 1113
Albuquerque, NM
87103-1113
515/260-7104

Manitoba Association of Legal
 Assistants, Inc.
22-81 Tyndall Avenue
Winnipeg, Manitoba R2X 2W2

Minnesota Paralegal Association
1711 W. County Rd. B, #300N
Roseville, MN 55113
612/633-2778

New Orleans Paralegal Association
P.O. Box 30604

New Orleans, LA 70190
504/467-3136

Northwest Missouri Paralegal
  Association
Box 7013
St. Joseph, MO 64507

Paralegal Association of
  Wisconsin, Inc.
P.O. Box 510892
Milwaukee, WI 53203-0151
414/272-7168

Rocky Mountain Paralegal Association
P.O. Box 481864
Denver, CO 80248
303/370-9444

REGION III

Baltimore Association of Legal
  Assistants
P.O. Box 13244
Baltimore, MD 21203
301/567-BALA

Cincinnati Paralegal Association
P.O. Box 1515
Cincinnati, OH 45201
513/244-1266

Cleveland Association of Paralegals
P.O. Box 14517
Cleveland, OH 44114
216/556-5437

Georgia Association of Paralegals, Inc.
1199 Euclid Avenue, NE
Atlanta, GA 30307
404/522-1457

Greater Dayton Paralegal Association
P.O. Box 515
Mid-City Station
Dayton, OH 45402

Greater Lexington Paralegal
  Association, Inc.
P.O. Box 574
Lexington, KY 40586

Indiana Paralegal Association
P.O. Box 44518
Indianapolis, IN 46204

Legal Assistants of Central Ohio
P.O. Box 15182
Columbus, OH 43215-0182
614/224-9700

Louisville Association of Paralegals
P.O. Box 962
Louisville, KY 40201

Maryland Association of Paralegals
P.O. Box 13244
Baltimore, MD 21203
410/576-2252

Memphis Paralegal Association
P.O. Box 3646
Memphis, TN 38173-0646

Michiana Paralegal Association
P.O. Box 11458
South Bend, IN 46634

Mobile Association of Legal Assistants
P.O. Box 1852
Mobile, AL 36633

National Capital Area Paralegal
  Association
P.O. Box 27607
Washington, DC 20038-7607
202/659-0243

Northeast Indiana Paralegal
  Association, Inc.
P.O. Box 13646
Fort Wayne, IN 46865

Northeastern Ohio Paralegal
  Association
P.O. Box 80068
Akron, OH 44308-0068

Palmetto Paralegal Association
P.O. Box 11634
Columbia, SC 29211-1634

Roanoke Valley Paralegal Association
P.O. Box 1505
Roanoke, VA 24007

REGION IV

Central Connecticut Paralegal
  Assoc., Inc.
P.O. Box 230594
Hartford, CT 06123-0594

Central Massachusetts Paralegal
  Association
P.O. Box 444
Worcester, MA 01614

Central Pennsylvania Paralegal
  Association
P.O. Box 11814
Harrisburg, PA 17108

Chester County Paralegal Association
P.O. Box 295
West Chester, PA 19381-0295

Connecticut Association of
  Paralegals, Inc.
(Fairfield County)

P.O. Box 134
Bridgeport, CT 06601-0134

Delaware Paralegal Association
P.O. Box 1362
Wilmington, DE 19899

Long Island Paralegal Association
1877 Bly Road
East Meadow, NY 11554-1158

Manhattan Paralegal Association, Inc.
521 Fifth Avenue, 17th Floor
New York, NY 10175
212/330-8213

Massachusetts Paralegal Association
c/o Offtech Management Services
99 Summer Street, Suite L-150
Boston, MA 02110
800/637-4311

Paralegal Association of Rochester, Inc.
P.O. Box 40567
Rochester, NY 14604
716/234-5923

Philadelphia Association of Paralegals
P.O. Box 59179
Philadelphia, PA 19102-9179
610/825-6504

Pittsburgh Paralegal Association
P.O. Box 2845
Pittsburgh, PA 15230
412/344-3904

Prudential Insurance Company of
  America—Paralegal Council
751 Broad Street
Newark, NJ 07102

Rhode Island Paralegal Association
P.O. Box 1003
Providence, RI 02901

South Jersey Paralegal Association
P.O. Box 355
Haddonfield, NJ 08033

Southern Tier Association
  of Paralegals
P.O. Box 2555
Binghamton, NY 13902

Vermont Paralegal Organization
P.O. Box 6238
Rutland, VT 05702

West/Rock Paralegal Association
P.O. Box 668
New City, NY 10956

Western Massachusetts Paralegal
  Association

P.O. Box 30005
Springfield, MA 01103

Western New York Paralegal
  Association, Inc.
P.O. Box 207
Niagara Square Station
Buffalo, NY 14201
716/635-8250

NALA State and Local Affiliates

Alabama

Alabama Association of Legal
  Assistants
P.O. Box 55921
Birmingham, AL 35255

Legal Assistant Society of Southern
  Institute/PJC
Birmingham, AL

Legal Society of Virginia College
Dept. of Paralegal Studies
800 28th Avenue, South
Birmingham, AL 35209
205/802-1596

Sanford Paralegal Association
Birmingham, AL

Alaska

Fairbanks Association of Legal
  Assistants
P.O. Box 73503
Fairbanks, AK 99707

Arizona

Arizona Paralegal Association
2700 N. Central Avenue, #1400
Phoenix, AZ 85004-1122
602/285-4400

Legal Assistants of Metropolitan
  Phoenix
Maricopa County Attorney's Office
301-W Jefferson, 9th Floor
Phoenix, AZ 85003

Tucson Association of Legal Assistants
W. J. Harrison & Associates
3561 E. Sunrise, Suite 201
Tucson, AZ 85718

Arkansas

Arkansas Association of Legal
  Assistants
P.O. Box 2162
Little Rock, AR 72203

California

Legal Assistants Association of Santa
  Barbara
P.O. Box 2695
Santa Barbara, CA 93120
805/965-7319

Orange County Paralegal Association
6 Hutton Centre Drive
Santa Ana, CA 92707

Palomar College Paralegal Studies Club
1140 W. Mission Road
San Marcos, CA 92069-1487

Paralegal Association of Santa Clara
  County
P.O. Box 26736
San Jose, CA 95159

San Joaquin Association of Legal
  Assistants
3729 N. Claremont
Fresno, CA 93727

Ventura County Association of Legal
  Assistants
P.O. Box 24229
Ventura, CA 93002

Colorado

Association of Legal Assistants of
  Colorado
105 E. Vermijo Avenue, Suite #415
Colorado Springs, CO 80903

Legal Assistants of the Western Slope
P.O. Box 1487
Montrose, CO 81402
970/249-2546

Florida

Central Florida Paralegal Association
1664 Wild Fox Drive
Casselberry, FL 32707

Dade Association of Legal Assistants
9100 S. Dadeland Blvd., Suite 404
Miami, FL 33156
305/670-2690

Florida Legal Assistants, Inc.
756 Beachland Blvd.
Vero Beach, FL 32963
407/774-7880

Gainesville Association of Legal
  Assistants
1110-C NW 8th Avenue
Gainesville, FL 32601
352/955-2260

Jacksonville Legal Assistants
1660 Prudential Drive, Suite 200
Jacksonville, FL 32207
904/346-3800

Legal Assistants of SW Florida, Inc.
1549 Ringling Blvd., Suite 600
Sarasota, FL 34236
941/365-0140

Pensacola Legal Assistants
220 W. Garden Street, Suite 801
Pensacola, FL 32501
850/434-6223

Phi Lambda Alpha Legal Assisting
  Society
2602 SE 23rd Avenue
Cape Coral, FL 33904
941/275-6659

Volusia Association of Legal Assistants
213 Silver Beach Avenue
Daytona Beach, FL 32118
904/254-2941

Georgia

Georgia Legal Assistants
1808 Seminole Trail
Waycross, GA 31501-4132
912/632-8693

Georgia Paralegal Association
P.O. Box 1802
Atlanta, GA 30301
707/433-5252

South Georgia Assn. of Legal
  Assistants
P.O. Box 25
Valdosta, GA 31603-0025
912/242-2211

Southeastern Assn. of Legal Assistants
  of Georgia
P.O. Box 9086
120 West Liberty
Savannah, GA 31401
912/232-6423

Idaho

Gem State Association of Legal
  Assistants
P.O. Box 1118
Burley, ID 83318-1118
208/678-9181

Illinois

Central Illinois Paralegal Association
One State Farm Plaza, E8
Bloomington, IL 61710

Heart of Illinois Paralegal Association
331 Fulton, Suite 704
Peoria, IL 61602
309/674-4222

Indiana

Indiana Legal Assistants
14669 Old State Road
Evansville, IN 47711-9408

Iowa

Iowa Association of Legal Assistants
410 Washington Street
Iowa City, IA 52240
319/356-5032

Nebraska Assn. of Legal Assistants
P.O. Box 1588
Council Bluffs, IA 51502

Kansas

Kansas Association of Legal Assistants
P.O. Box 2975
Wichita, KS 67201
316/828-8712

Kentucky

Western Kentucky Paralegals
P.O. Box 447
Benton, KY 42025
502/527-5500

Louisiana

Louisiana State Paralegal Association
306-B Windermere Place
Alexandria, LA 71303

Northwest Louisiana Paralegal Association
330 Marshall Street, Suite 1410
Shreveport, LA 71101
318/222-9100

Maine

Maine State Association of Legal Assistants
2211 Congress Street, Mail Stop M194
Portland, ME 04122
207/770-3229

Michigan

Legal Assistants Association of Michigan
P.O. Box 80857
Lansing, MI 48908-0857
517/886-7176

Mississippi

Mississippi Association of Legal Assistants
P.O. Box 22567
Jackson, MS 39225-2564
601/973-1499

USM Society for Paralegal Studies
P.O. Box 5108
Hattiesburg, MS 39406-5108

Missouri

Kansas Association of Legal Assistants
4420 Madison Avenue, Suite 150
Kansas City, MO 64111
816/753-3000

St. Louis Association of Legal Assistants
10 South Broadway, Suite 1500
St. Louis, MO 63102
314/241-6566

Montana

Montana Association of Legal Assistants
P.O. Box 9197
Missouri, MT 59807-9197
406/721-6655

Nebraska

Nebraska Assn. of Legal Assistants
1650 Farnam
Omaha, NE 68102
402/346-6000

Nevada

Clark Co. Org. of Legal Assistants, Inc.
302 East Carson, #1100
Las Vegas, NV 89101
702/385-3373

Sierra Nevada Association of Paralegals
290 S. Arlington Avenue, #200
Reno, NV 89501
702/322-3811

New Hampshire

Paralegal Association of New Hampshire
1819 Elm Street
Manchester, NH 03104
603/627-1819

New Jersey

Legal Assistants of New Jersey
P.O. Box 142
Caldwell, NJ 07006

New Mexico

Southwestern Assn. of Legal Assistants
49 FW/JA
490 First Street, Suite 1940
Hollomon AFB, NM 88330-8277
505/475-7217

North Carolina

Coastal Carolina Paralegal Club
444 Western Blvd.
Jacksonville, NC 28546-6877
910/958-6351

Metrolina Paralegal Association
2400 Yorkmont Road
Charlotte, NC 28217
704/329-4016

North Carolina Paralegal Association, Inc.
P.O. Box 130
Linvlle Falls, NC 28647-0130
828/765-8897

North Dakota

Red River Valley Legal Assistants
101 10th Street N., #110
Fargo, ND 58102
701/293-8425

Western Dakota Assn. of Legal Assistants
P.O. Box 1000
Minot, ND 58702-1000
701/852-0381

Ohio

Toledo Association of Legal Assistants
416 N. Erie Street, #500
Toledo, OH 43624

Oklahoma

City College Legal Association
1370 North Interstate Drive
Norman, OK 73072
405/329-5627

Oklahoma Paralegal Association
P.O. Box 1108
Enid, OK 73701
405/233-2020

TJC Student Association of Legal Assistants
909 South Boston, Room 416
Tulsa, OK 741919-2095
918/595-7317

Tulsa Association of Legal Assistants
525 S. Main Street, Suite 1000
Tulsa, OK 74103-4514
918/583-7129

Oregon

Pacific Northwest Legal Assistants
112 W. 4th
The Dalles, OR 97058
541/296-5424

Pennsylvania

Keystone Legal Assistant Association
60 W. Pomfret Street
Carlisle, PA 17013
717/249-2353

South Carolina

Central Carolina Tech. College
   Paralegal Assn.
506 N. Guignard Drive
Sumter, SC 29150-2499
803/778-7859

Charleston Association of Legal
   Assistants
P.O. Box 340
Charleston, SC 29402
803/720-4449

Grand Strand Paralegal Association
743 Hemlock Avenue
Myrtle Beach, SC 29577

Greenville Association of Legal
   Assistants
108 Whitsett Street
Greenville, SC 29601
802/298-0089

Tri-County Paralegal Association
P.O. Box 993
Charleston, SC 29402
803/724-6665

South Dakota

National American University Student
   Assn. of Legal Assistants
317 N. Dakota Street, Suite 834
Vermillion, SD 57069-2332

South Dakota Legal Assistants
   Association
P.O. Box 8108
Rapid City, SD 57709-8108
605/348-7516

Tennessee

Greater Memphis Legal
   Assistants, Inc.
80 North Front Street, Suite 850
Memphis, TN 38103

Tennessee Paralegal Association
124 East Court Square
Trenton, TN 38382
901/855-9584

Texas

Capital Area Paralegal Association
600 Congress Avenue, Suite 2700
Austin, TX 78701
512/495-8516

El Paso Association of Legal Assistants
11104 Paducah
El Paso, TX 79936
915/598-0067

Legal Assistants Association
400 West Illinois, Suite 1640
Midland, TX 79701
915/683-8844

Northeast Texas Assn. of Legal
   Assistants
2020 Bill Owens Parkway, Suite 200
Longview, TX 75604-6213
903/759-2020

Nueces County Assn. of Legal
   Assistants
711 N. Carancahua, #1508
Corpus Christi, TX 78475
512/883-5786

Southeast Texas Assn. of Legal
   Assistants
2380 Eastern Freeway Beaumont, TX
   77703
409/898-2123

Texarkana Association of Legal
   Assistants
P.O. Box 6671
Texarkana, TX 75505

Texas Panhandle Assn. of Legal
   Assistants
P.O. Box 9142
Amarillo, TX 79105
806/345-3107

Tyler Area Assn. of Legal Professionals
P.O. Box 2013
Tyler, TX 75710
903/595-3573

West Texas Association of Legal
   Assistants
P.O. Box 10104
Lubbock, TX 79408
806/763-3661

Utah

Legal Assistants Association of Utah
230 S. 500 E, Suite 460
Salt Lake City, UT 84102
801/521-6666

Virgin Islands

Virgin Islands Association of Legal
   Assistants
P.O. Box 70
St. Thomas, VI 00804
809/774-6680

Virginia

Peninsula Legal Assistants, Inc.
601 Thimble Shoals Blvd., Suite 202
Newport News, VA 23606
757/873-9425

Richmond Association of Legal
   Assistants
901 E. Cary Street
One James Center
Richmond, VA 23219-4030
804/775-7540

Tidewater Association of Legal
   Assistants
910 W. Mercury Blvd., Suite 2A
Hampton, VA 23666
757/825-0400

Washington

Association of Paralegals and Legal
   Assistants of Washington State
929 Sprague Avenue West
Spokane, WA 92204

West Virginia

Legal Assistants of
   West Virginia, Inc.
121 North Queen Street
Martinsburg, WV 25401
304/262-9300

Wisconsin

Madison Area Paralegal Association
P.O. Box 927
Madison, WI 53701-0927
608/257-9521

Wyoming

Legal Assistants of Wyoming
P.O. Box 8498
235 East Broadway
Jackson, WY 83002
307/733-8668

Other Law-Related Associations

American Association of Law Libraries (AALL)
53 West Jackson Boulevard, Suite 940
Chicago, IL 60604
312/939-4764

American Association for Paralegal Education (AafPE)
2965 Flowers Road S, Suite 105
Atlanta, GA 30342
404/367-4770

American Bar Association (ABA)
Standing Committee on Legal Assistants
750 North Lake Shore Drive
Chicago, IL 60611
312/988-5000

Association of Legal Administrators (ALA)
104 Wilmot Road, Suite 205
Deerfield, IL 60015-5195
312/940-9240

Legal Assistant Management Association (LAMA)
2965 Flowers Road S, Suite 105
Atlanta, GA 30341
404/367-4770

National Association for Independent Paralegals
585 5th St. W
Sonoma, CA 95476

National Paralegal Association
P.O. Box 406
Solebury, PA 18963
215/297-8333

APPENDIX G
State and Major Local Bar Associations

Alabama

Alabama State Bar
Founded 1879
P.O. Box 671
Montgomery, AL 36101
205/269-1515
fax: 205/261-6310

Birmingham Bar Assn.
Founded 1885
2021 2d Avenue N
Birmingham, AL 35203
205/251-8006
fax: 205/251-7193

Alaska

Alaska Bar Assn.
Founded 1955
P.O. Box 100279
Anchorage, AK 99510
907/272-7469
fax: 907/272-2932

Arizona

Maricopa County Bar Assn.
Founded 1914
303 E. Palm Lane
Phoenix, AZ 85004-1532
602/257-4200
fax: 602/257-0522

State Bar of Arizona
Founded 1933
111 W. Monroe Street
Phoenix, AZ 85003-1742
602/252-4804
fax: 602/271-4930

Arkansas

Arkansas Bar Assn.
Founded 1899
400 W. Markham
Little Rock, AZ 72201
501/375-4605
fax: 501/375-4901

California

Bar Assn. of San Francisco
Founded 1872
685 Market Street, Suite 700
San Francisco, CA 94105
415/267-0709
fax: 415/546-9223

Beverly Hills Bar Assn.
Founded 1931
300 S. Beverly Drive, #201
Beverly Hills, CA 90212
310/553-6644
fax: 310/284-8290

Eastern Alameda County Bar Assn.
Founded 1877
360 22nd Street, #800
Oakland, CA 94612
510/893-7160
fax: 510/893-3119

Lawyers' Club of Los Angeles
Founded 1930
601 W. 5th Street, #203
Los Angeles, CA 90017-2000
213/624-4223

Lawyers' Club of San Francisco
Founded 1946
685 Market Street, Suite 750
San Francisco, CA 94105
415/882-9150
fax: 415/882-7170

Los Angeles County Bar Assn.
Founded 1878
P.O. Box 55020
Los Angeles, CA 90055
213/896-6424
fax: 213/896-6500

Orange County Bar Assn.
601 Civic Center Drive W
Santa Ana, CA 92710-4002
714/541-6222
fax: 714/541-1482

673

Sacramento County Bar Assn.
Founded 1925
901 H. Street, Suite 101
Sacramento, CA 95814
916/448-1087
fax: 916/448-6930

San Diego County Bar Assn.
Founded 1920
1333 Seventh Avenue
San Diego, CA 92101
619/231-0781
fax: 619/338-0042

Santa Clara County Bar Assn.
Founded 1917
4 N. Second Street, Suite 400
San Jose, CA 95113
408/287-2557
fax: 408/287-6083

State Bar of California
Founded 1927
555 Franklin Street
San Francisco, CA 94012
415/561-8200
fax: 415/561-8305

Colorado

The Colorado Bar Assn.
Founded 1897
1900 Grant Street, #950
Denver, CO 80203
303/860-1115
fax: 303/894-0821

Denver Bar Assn.
Founded 1891
1900 Grant Street, #950
Denver, CO 80203-4309
303/860-1115
fax: 303/894-0821

Connecticut

Connecticut Bar Assn.
Founded 1875
101 Corporate Place
Rocky Hill, CT 06067
203/721-0025
fax: 203/257-4125

Hartford County Bar Assn.
Founded 1783
61 Hungerford Street
Hartford, CT 06106
203/525-8106
fax: 203/293-1345

Delaware

Delaware State Bar Assn.
Founded 1923
1225 King Street
Wilmington, DE 19801
302/658-5279
fax: 302/658-5212

District of Columbia

Bar Assn. of the Dist. of Columbia
Founded 1871
1819 H Street, NW, 12th Floor
Washington, DC 20006-3690
202/223-6600
fax: 202/293-3388

The District of Columbia Bar
Founded 1972
1250 H Street NW, 6th Floor
Washington, DC 20005-3908
202/737-4700
fax: 202/626-3473

Florida

Dade County Bar Assn.
Founded 1920
123 NW First Avenue, #214
Miami, FL 33128
305/371-2220
fax: 305/539-9749

The Florida Bar
Founded 1950
650 Apalachee Parkway
Tallahassee, FL 32399-2300
904/561-5600
fax: 904/561-5827

Hillsborough County Bar Assn.
Founded 1937
315 E. Madison, Suite 1010
Tampa, FL 33602
813/226-6431
fax: 813/223-3946

Orange County Bar Assn.
880 N. Orange Avenue, #100
Orlando, FL 32801
407/422-4551
fax: 407/843-3470

Georgia

Atlanta Bar Assn.
Founded 1888
2500 The Equitable Bldg.
100 Peachtree Street NW
Atlanta, GA 30303
404/521-0781
fax: 404/522-0269

State Bar of Georgia
Founded 1964
800 The Hurt Bldg.
50 Hurt Plaza
Atlanta, GA 30303
404/527-8755
fax: 404/527-8717

Hawaii

Hawaii State Bar Assn.
Founded 1899
Penthouse 1, 9th Floor
1136 Union Mall
Honolulu, HI 96813
808/537-1868
fax: 808/521-7936

Idaho

Idaho State Bar
Founded 1923
P.O. Box 895
Boise, ID 83701
208/334-4500
fax: 208/334-4515

Illinois

The Chicago Bar Assn.
Founded 1874
321 Plymouth Court
Chicago, IL 60604
313/554-2000
fax: 312-554-2054

Chicago Council of Lawyers
Founded 1969
220 S. State Street, Room 800
One Quincy Court
Chicago, IL 60604
312/427-0710
fax: 312/427-0181

Illinois State Bar Assn.
Founded 1877
424 S. Second Street
Springfield, IL 62701
217/525-1760
fax: 217/525-0712

Indiana

Indiana State Bar Assn.
Founded 1896
230 E. Ohio, 4th Floor
Indianapolis, IN 46204
317/639-5465
fax: 317/266-2588

Indianapolis Bar Assn.
Founded 1878
Market Tower,
10 W. Market, Suite 440
Indianapolis, IN 46204
317/269-2000
fax: 317/464-8118

Iowa

The Iowa State Bar Assn.
Founded 1874
521 E. Locust
Des Moines, IA 50309
515/243-3179
fax: 515/243-2511

Kansas

Kansas Bar Assn.
Founded 1882
P.O. Box 1037
Topeka, KS 66601-1037
913/234-5696
fax: 913/234-3813

Kentucky

Kentucky Bar Assn.
Founded 1871
514 West Main Street
Frankfort, KY 40601-1883
501/564-3795
fax: 502/564-3225

Louisville Bar Assn.
Founded 1900
717 W. Main Street
Louisville, KY 40202
502/583-5314
fax: 502/583-4113

Louisiana

Louisiana State Bar Assn.
Founded 1941
601 St. Charles Avenue
New Orleans, LA 70130
504/566-1600
fax: 504/566-0930

New Orleans Bar Assn.
Founded 1924
228 Saint Charles Avenue, Suite 1223
New Orleans, LA 70130
504/525-7453
fax: 504/525-6549

Maine

Maine State Bar Assn.
Founded 1891
P.O. Box 788
Augusta, ME 04332-0788
207/622-7523
fax: 207/623-0083

Maryland

Bar Assn. of Baltimore City
Founded 1880
111 N. Calvert Street, Suite 627
Baltimore, MD 21202
410/539-5936
fax: 401/685-3420

Bar Association of Montgomery County
Founded 1894
27 W. Jefferson Street
Rockville, MD 20850
301/424-3454
fax: 301/217-9327

Maryland State Bar Assn., Inc.
Founded 1896
520 W. Fayette Street
Baltimore, MD 20201
410/685-7878
fax: 410/837-0518

Massachusetts

Boston Bar Assn.
Founded 1761
16 Beacon Street
Boston, MA 02018
617/742-0615
fax: 617/523-0127

Massachusetts Bar Assn.
Founded 1911
20 West Street
Boston, MA 02111-1218
617/542-3602

Michigan

Detroit Bar Assn.
Founded 1836
2380 Penobscot Bldg.
Detroit, MI 48226
313/961-6120
fax: 313/965-0842

Oakland County Bar Assn.
Founded 1934
760 S. Telegraph, Suite 100
Bloomfield, MI 48302-0181
810/334-3400
fax: 810/334-7757

State Bar of Michigan
Founded 1936
306 Townsend Street
Lansing, MI 48933-2083
517/372-9030

Minnesota

Hennepin County Bar Assn.
Founded 1919
514 Nicollet Mall, #350
Minneapolis, MN 55402
612/340-0022
fax: 612/340-9518

Minnesota State Bar Assn.
Founded 1883
513 Nicollet Mall, #300
Minneapolis, MN 55402
612/333-1183
fax: 612/333-4927

Ramsey County Bar Assn.
Founded 1883
332 Minnesota Street, E-1312
St. Paul, MN 55101
612/222-0846
fax: 612/223-8344

Mississippi

Mississippi Bar
Founded 1905
P.O. Box 2168
Jackson, MS 39225-2168
601/948-4471
fax: 601/355-8635

Missouri

Bar Assn. of Metropolitan St. Louis
Founded 1874
One Metropolitan Square, Suite 1400
St. Louis, MO 63102
314/421-4134
fax: 314/421-0013

Kansas City Metropolitan Bar Association
Founded 1884
1125 Grand, Suite 400
Kansas City, MO 64106
816/474-4322
fax: 816/474-0103

The Missouri Bar
Founded 1944
P.O. Box 119
Jefferson City, MO 65102
314/635-4128
fax: 314/635-2811

Montana

State Bar of Montana
Founded 1975
P.O. Box 577
Helena, MT 59624
406/442-7660
fax: 406/442-7763

Nebraska

Nebraska State Bar Assn.
Founded 1877
P.O. Box 81809
Lincoln, NE 68501
402/475-7091
fax: 402/475-7098

Nevada

State Bar of Nevada
Founded 1928
201 Las Vegas Blvd., Suite 200
Las Vegas, NV 89101
702/383-2200
fax: 702/385-2878

New Hampshire

New Hampshire Bar Assn.
Founded 1873
112 Pleasant Street
Concord, NH 03301
603/224-6942
fax: 603/224-2910

New Jersey

Bergen County Bar
Founded 1898
61 Hudson Street
Hackensack, NJ 07601
201/488-0044
fax: 201/488-0073

Essex County Bar Assn.
Founded 1898
One Newark Center,
16th Floor
Newark, NJ 07102
201/622-6207
fax: 201/622-4341

New Jersey State Bar Assn.
Founded 1899
New Jersey Law Center
One Constitution Square
New Brunswick, NJ 08901-1500
908/249-5000
fax: 908/249-2815

New Mexico

State Bar of New Mexico
Founded 1886
P.O. Box 25883
Albuquerque, NM 87125
505/842-6132
fax: 505/843-8765

New York

The Assn. of the Bar of the City of
   New York
Founded 1871
42 W. 44th Street
New York, NY 10036
212/382-6620
fax: 212/302-8219

Bar Assn. of Erie County
Founded 1887
1450 Statler Towers
Buffalo, NY 14202
716/852-8687
fax: 716/856-7641

Bar Assn. of Nassau County, Inc.
Founded 1899
15th & West Streets
Mineola, NY 11501
516/747-4070
fax: 516/747-4147

Brooklyn Bar Assn.
Founded 1872
23 Remsen Street
Brooklyn, NY 11201-4212
718/624-0675
fax: 718/797-1713

Monroe County Bar Assn.
Founded 1892
One Exchange Street, 5th Floor
Rochester, NY 14614
716/546-1817
fax: 716/546-1807

New York County Lawyers Assn.
Founded 1908
14 Vesey Street
New York, NY 10007
212/267-6646
fax: 212/406-9252

New York State Bar Assn.
Founded 1876
One Elk Street
Albany, NY 12207
518/463-3200
fax: 518/463-4276

Queens County Bar Assn.
Founded 1876
90-35 148th Street
Jamaica, NY 11435
718/291-4500
fax: 718/657-1789

Suffolk County Bar Assn.
Founded 1908
560 Wheeler Road
Hauppauge, NY 11788-4357
516/234-5511
fax: 516/234-5899

Westchester County Bar Assn.
Founded 1896
300 Hamilton Avenue, Suite 400
White Plains, NY 10601
914/761-3707
fax: 914/761-9402

North Carolina

North Carolina Bar Assn.
Founded 1899
P.O. Box 12806
Raleigh, NC 27605
919/677-0561
fax: 919/677-0761

North Carolina State Bar
Founded 1933
208 Fayetteville Street Mall
P.O. Box 25908
Raleigh, NC 27605
919/828-4620
fax: 919/821-9168

10th Judicial District Bar Assn.
P.O. Box 10625
Raleigh, NC 27605
919/677-9903
fax: 919/677-0761

North Dakota

State Bar Assn. of North Dakota
Founded 1921
P.O. Box 2136
Bismark, ND 58502-2136
701/255-1404
fax: 701/224-1621

Ohio

Cincinnati Bar Assn.
Founded 1873
35 E. Seventh Street, 8th Floor
Cincinnati, OH 45202-2492
513/381-8213
fax: 513/381-0528

Cleveland Bar Assn.
Founded 1873
113 St. Clair Avenue NE
Cleveland, OH 44114-1253
216/696-3525
fax: 216/696-2413

Columbus Bar Assn.
Founded 1869
175 South 3rd Street
Columbus, OH 43215-5134
614/221-4112
fax: 614/221-4850

Cuyahoga County Bar Assn.
Founded 1928
500 The Terminal Tower
50 Public Square
Cleveland, OH 44113-2203
216/621-5112
fax: 216/523-2259

Ohio State Bar Assn.
Founded 1880
1700 Lake Shore Drive
Columbus, OH 43216-6562
614/487-2050
fax: 614/487-1008

Oklahoma

Oklahoma Bar Assn.
Founded 1939
1901 N. Lincoln
P.O. Box 53036
Oklahoma City, OK 73152
405/524-2365
fax: 405/524-1115

Oklahoma County Bar Assn.
Founded 1902
119 N. Robinson, Suite 240
Oklahoma, OK 73102
405/236-8421
fax: 405/232-2210

Tulsa County Bar Assn.
Founded 1903
1446 South Boston
Tulsa, OK 74119
916/584-5243
fax: 918/592-0208

Oregon

Multnomah Bar Assn.
Founded 1906
630 SW Fifth Avenue, Suite 200
Portland, OR 97204
503/222-3275
fax: 503/243-1881

Oregon State Bar
Founded 1890
P.O. Box 1689
Lake Oswego, OR 97035
503/620-0222
fax: 503/684-1366

Pennsylvania

Allegheny County Bar Assn.
Founded 1870
Kopper's Building, 4th Floor
Pittsburgh, PA 15219
412/261-6161
fax: 412/261-3622

Pennsylvania Bar Assn.
Founded 1895
P.O. Box 186
Harrisburg, PA 17108
717/238-6715
fax: 717/238-1204

Philadelphia Bar Assn.
Founded 1802
1101 Market Street, 11th Floor
Philadelphia, PA 19107-2911
215/238-6338
fax: 215/238-1267

Puerto Rico

Puerto Rico Bar Assn.
Founded 1840
P.O. Box 1900
San Juan, PR 00903
809/721-3358
fax: 809/725-0330

Rhode Island

Rhode Island Bar Assn.
Founded 1898
115 Cedar Street
Providence, RI 02903
401/421-5740
fax: 401/421-2703

South Carolina

South Carolina Bar
Founded 1975
950 Taylor Street
Columbia, SC 29202
803/799-6653
fax: 803/799-4118

South Dakota

State Bar of South Dakota
Founded 1931
222 E. Capitol
Pierre, SD 57501
605/224-7554
fax: 605/224-0282

Tennessee

Nashville Bar Assn.
Founded 1831
221 Fourth Avenue N, Suite 400
Nashville, TN 37129-2100
615/242-9272
fax: 615/255-3026

Tennessee Bar Assn.
Founded 1881
3622 West End Avenue
Nashville, TN 37205-2403
615/383-7421
fax: 615/297-8058

Texas

Dallas Bar Assn.
Founded 1873
2101 Ross Avenue
Dallas, TX 75201
214/969-7066
fax: 214/880-0807

Houston Bar Assn.
Founded 1870
1001 Fannin, Suite 1300
Houston, TX 77002-6708
713/759-1133
fax: 713/759-1710

San Antonio Bar Assn.
Founded 1916
Bexar County Courthouse, 5th Floor
San Antonio, TX 78205
210/227-8822
fax: 210-271-9614

State Bar of Texas
Founded 1939
P.O. Box 12487
Austin, TX 78711
512/463-1463 or
800/204-2222
fax: 512/463-7388

Utah

Utah State Bar
Founded 1931
645 S. 200 East, #310
Salt Lake City, UT 84111
801/531-9077
fax: 801/531-0660

Vermont

Vermont Bar Assn.
Founded 1878
P.O. Box 100
Montpelier, VT 05601
802/223-2020
fax: 802/223-1573

Virginia

Fairfax Bar Assn.
Founded 1935
4110 Chain Bridge Road, #303
Fairfax, VA 22030
703/246-2740
fax: 703/273-1274

Virginia Bar Assn.
Founded 1888
7th & Franklin Bldg.
701 E. Franklin Street, #1515
Richmond, VA 23219
804/644-0052

Virginia State Bar
Founded 1938

707 E. Main Street, Suite 1500
Richmond, VA 23219-2803
804/775-0500
fax: 804/775-0501

Washington

King County Bar Assn.
Founded 1906
The Bank of CA Bldg., Suite 600
900 4th Avenue
Seattle, WA 98164
206/624-9365
fax: 206/382-1270

Washington State Bar Assn.
Founded 1890
500 Westin Bldg.
2001 6th Avenue
Seattle, WA 98121-2599
206/727-8200
fax: 206/727-8320

West Virginia

West Virginia Bar Assn.
Founded 1886

904 Security Bldg.
101 Capitol Street
P.O. Box 346
Charleston, WV 23507
304/342-1474
fax: 304/345-5864

West Virginia State Bar
Founded 1947
2006 Kanawha Blvd. E
Charleston, WV 25311
304/558-2456
fax: 304/558-2567

Wisconsin

Milwaukee Bar Assn.
Founded 1858
533 East Wells Street
Milwaukee, WI 53202
414/274-6760
fax: 414/274-6765

Wyoming

Wyoming State Bar
Founded 1915

P.O. Box 109
Cheyenne, WY 82003-0109
307/632-9061
fax: 307/632-3737

Guam

Guam Bar Assn.
259 Martyr Street, Suite 101
Agana, Guam 96910
011/671/472-6848
fax: 011/671/472-1246

Northern Mariana Islands Bar Assn.
Founded 1985

Virgin Islands

Virgin Islands Bar Assn.
Founded 1921
P.O. Box 4108
Christiansted, VI 00822
809/778-7497
fax: 809/773-5060

APPENDIX H

Information on NALA's CLA and CLAS Examinations

Background and Numbers

Established in 1976, the Certified Legal Assistant program has enabled the profession to develop a strong and responsive self-regulatory program offering a nationwide credential for legal assistants. The Certified Legal Assistant program establishes and serves as a:

- National professional standard for legal assistants
- Means of identifying those who have reached this standard
- Credentialing program responsive to the needs of legal assistants and responsive to the fact that this form of self-regulation is necessary to strengthen and expand development of this career field
- Positive, ongoing, voluntary program to encourage the growth of the legal-assistant profession, attesting to and encouraging a high level of achievement.

As of January 1999, there are 9,594 Certified Legal Assistants and over 700 Certified Legal Assistant Specialists in the United States. Approximately 19,000 legal assistants have participated in this program. The distribution of CLAs is as follows:

CLA EXAMINATION DATA
STATES REPRESENTED AT TIME OF
CERTIFICATION AS OF JANUARY 22, 1999

State	Count	State	Count	State	Count
Alabama	117	Louisiana	133	Oklahoma	398
Alaska	78	Maine	47	Oregon	97
Arizona	715	Maryland	8	Pennsylvania	61
Arkansas	58	Massachusetts	14	Puerto Rico	1
California	442	Michigan	114	Rhode Island	4
Colorado	181	Minnesota	16	South Carolina	78
Connecticut	4	Mississippi	104	South Dakota	86
Delaware	1	Missouri	77	Tennessee	159
District of Columbia	2	Montana	49	Texas	1,993
Florida	2,577	Nebraska	89	Utah	99
Georgia	127	Nevada	175	Vermont	2
Hawaii	2	New Hampshire	45	Virginia	184
Idaho	37	New Jersey	45	Virgin Islands	24
Illinois	40	New Mexico	154	Washington	45
Indiana	39	New York	43	West Virginia	49
Iowa	99	North Carolina	221	Wisconsin	27
Kansas	175	North Dakota	87	Wyoming	78
Kentucky	16	Ohio	76		

On December 31, 1990, 3,974 legal assistants had achieved the CLA designation. As of the December 1998 testing session, there were 9,594 Certified Legal Assistants. This represents an increase of over 100 percent in the number of Certified Legal Assistants in the last eight years. Since the examination was first administered in 1976, over 19,000 legal assistants have participated in this program.

In order to pass, a legal assistant must successfully complete the seven sections of the CLA examination. Approximately 48 percent of the examinees pass all seven sections on the first sitting; over 90 percent of the examinees pass four or more sections of the examination on the first sitting.

Use of the CLA credential signifies that a legal assistant is capable of providing superior services to firms and corporations. National surveys consistently show Certified Legal Assistants are better paid and better utilized in a field where attorneys are looking for a credible, dependable way to measure ability. The credential has been recognized by the American Bar Association as a designation which marks a high level of professional achievement. The CLA credential has also been recognized by over forty-seven legal-assistant organizations and numerous bar associations.

For information concerning standards of professional credentialing programs, see the article "The Certified Legal Assistant Program and the United States Supreme Court Decision in *Peel v. Attorney Registration and Disciplinary Committee of Illinois*." In this case, the United States Supreme Court addressed the issue concerning the utilization of professional credentials awarded by private organizations. In *Peel v. Attorney Registration and Disciplinary Committee of Illinois*, 110 S.Ct. 2281 (1990), the Court suggested that a claim of certification is truthful and not misleading if it meets certain standards. This article details those standards in terms of the standards of the NALA Certified Legal Assistant Program.

CLA and CLA Specialist are certification marks duly registered with the U.S. Patent and Trademark Office (No. 113199 and No. 1751731 respectively). Any unauthorized use of these credentials is strictly forbidden.

ADMINISTRATION

The Certifying Board for Legal Assistants is responsible for content, standards, and administration of the Certified Legal Assistant Program. It is composed of legal assistants who have received a CLA Specialist designation, attorneys, and legal-assistant educators. In the technical areas of statistical analyses, examination construction, reliability, and validity tests, the Board contracts with a professional consulting firm offering expertise in these areas as well as in occupational research. Technical analyses of the CLA examination are conducted on an ongoing basis to ensure the integrity of the examination. Content analyses of the test design, accuracy of questions, and topic/subject mix for each exam section are ongoing processes of the Certifying Board. The Board also utilizes the occupational data available through surveys of legal assistants and other means, including review of textbooks and research within the field of legal-assistant education. Through these analyses and procedures, the Board is assured that the examination reflects and responds to workplace realities and demands.

THE EXAMINATION—ELIGIBILITY REQUIREMENTS

To be eligible for the CLA examination, a legal assistant must meet one of the following alternate requirements:

1. Graduation from a legal-assistant program that is:
   - Approved by the American Bar Association; or
   - An associate degree program; or
   - A postbaccalaureate certificate program in legal-assistant studies; or
   - A bachelor's degree program in legal-assistant studies; or
   - A legal-assistant program which consists of a minimum of 60 semester hours (900 clock hours or 225 quarter hours) of which at least 15 semester hours (90 clock hours or 22.5 quarter hours) are substantive legal courses.

2. A bachelor's degree in any field plus one year's experience as a legal assistant. Successful completion of at least 15 semester hours (or 22.5 quarter hours or 225 clock hours) of substantive legal courses will be considered equivalent to one year's experience as a legal assistant.

3. A high school diploma or equivalent plus seven (7) years' experience as a legal assistant under the supervision of a member of the Bar, plus evidence of a minimum of twenty (20) hours of continuing legal education credit to have been completed within a two (2) year period prior to the examination date.

EXAMINATION SUBJECTS

The Certified Legal Assistant examination is a two-day comprehensive examination based on federal law and procedure. The major subject areas of the examination are:

- Communications
- Ethics
- Legal Research
- Human Relations and Interviewing Techniques
- Judgment and Analytical Ability
- Legal Terminology

Substantive Law—This section consists of five mini-examinations covering (1) the American Legal System and four (4) of the areas listed below as selected by examinees:

- Administrative Law
- Bankruptcy
- Business Organizations/Corporations
- Contracts
- Family Law
- Criminal Law and Procedure
- Litigation
- Probate and Estate Planning
- Real Estate

CLA Specialty Examinations

Those who have achieved the CLA credential may seek advanced certification in specialty practice areas. Specialty certification examinations are available in the areas of Bankruptcy, Civil Litigation, Corporations/Business Law, Criminal Law and Procedure, Intellectual Property, Estate Planning and Probate, and Real Estate. Each of these is a four-hour examination written to test specialized knowledge of the practice area.

The CLA Specialty program began in 1982 with the examinations for those working in the areas of Civil Litigation and Probate and Estate Planning. In 1984, the Corporations/Business and Criminal Law and Procedure examinations were offered. A Real Estate specialty examination was offered for the first time in 1987; Bankruptcy in 1992; and Intellectual Property in 1995. As of the December 1998 CLA Specialty examinations, 771 CLAs have received a CLA Specialist designation, as follows:

Bankruptcy	36
Civil Litigation	402
Corporate/Business	39
Criminal Law and Procedure	35
Intellectual Property	13
Probate and Estates	87
Real Estate	159

NALA is also working with individual states to established advanced specialty certification programs designed to test knowledge of state law and procedures. State certification programs are available to legal assistants in California, Florida, and Louisiana.

Maintaining Professional Certification

The Certified Legal Assistant credential is awarded for a period of five years. To maintain Certified Legal Assistant status, legal assistants must submit proof of participation in a minimum of fifty hours of continuing legal education programs or individual study programs. Credit is also awarded for significant achievement in the area of continuing legal-assistant education such as successful completion of a state certification test, completion of a CLA Specialty examination, or teaching in a legal-assistant program.

REVOCATION OF THE CLA CREDENTIAL

The Certified Legal Assistant designation may be revoked for any one of the following reasons:

1. Falsification of information on the application form.
2. Subsequent conviction of the unauthorized practice of law.
3. Failure to meet educational and other recertification requirements.
4. Divulging the contents of any examination question or questions.
5. Subsequent conviction of a felony.
6. Violation of the NALA Code of Ethics and Professional Responsibility.

DATES AND DEADLINES AND TESTING CENTERS AND FEES

The CLA examination is offered three times a year: March/April (depending on the holiday schedule); July, and December. Application forms and the requisite fees must be received by the published filing dates. Filing deadline dates are January 15 for the March/April examination, May 15 for the July examination, and October 1 for the December examination session.

Many schools, universities, and junior colleges serve as testing centers through an arrangement with NALA. In cities in which a school testing center is not already established, NALA will establish a testing center where ten or more legal assistants apply. All testing center locations are subject to minimum registration.

The fee for the CLA examination is $225 for NALA members and $250 for nonmembers of NALA. Retake fees are $50 per section. CLA Specialty examination fees are $100 for NALA members and $125 for nonmembers.

STUDY MATERIALS

The CLA Review Manual is available from West Publishing Company, an imprint of Delmar Publishers, and International Thomson Publishing Company. Delmar Publishers also publishes the NALA CLA Study Guide and Mock Examination, a 250-page guide consisting of outlines for a nine-week study program with practice tests and a mock examination. The CLA Study Guide and Mock Examination is available from NALA Headquarters at a cost of $18 to NALA members, $21 to nonmembers. Study material is also available online at **NALA Campus.com.**

A series of study guides for those preparing for a CLA Specialty Examination were published through 1997 and 1998. The first, Real Estate Law Review Manual, is now available from West Legal Studies.

CALIFORNIA ADVANCED SPECIALIZATION CERTIFICATION FOR PARALEGALS

Established in 1995, the California Advanced Specialist (CAS) Certification was created for California paralegals who have achieved the national CLA (Certified Legal Assistant) credential and want to demonstrate advanced knowledge of California law and procedure. To qualify for the California Advanced Examination, these legal assistants have successfully completed a two-day examination covering general skills and knowledge required of legal assistants, and have demonstrated proficiency in the specialty practice area. Specialty certification in California is available in the areas of Civil Litigation, Business Organizations/Business Law, Real Estate, Estates and Trusts, and Family Law. As of July 1997, there are thirteen legal assistants in California who have achieved the CAS credential. For further details about the program, contact NALA Headquarters or the Commission for Advanced California Paralegal Specialization, Inc., P.O. Box 22433, Santa Barbara, California 93121.

Application Deadline Date	January 15, 1999
Examination Date	March 27, 1999
July 24, 1999	May 15, 1999
December 4, 1999	October 1, 1999

Florida Certification Programs

In 1980, Florida Legal Assistants, Inc. (FLA, Inc.), established its Certification Program to complement NALA's CLA program. Its purpose is to provide a standard for measurement of advanced skills and knowledge in Florida law of those persons who have already achieved the national CLA certification. FLA, Inc., began administering the CFLA exam in 1983. Florida, through FLA, Inc., was the first state to administer such an exam. As of December 1996, there were eighty-four CFLAs in the state of Florida.

The CFLA examination is administered through the Certifying Board of FLA, Inc., in conjunction with the FLA, Inc., midyear meeting in the spring and the annual meeting in September. A two-day CFLA review course has been established and is offered prior to the midyear and annual meetings.

FLA, Inc., has developed a CFLA study guide which is available from FLA, Inc., headquarters at a cost of $37.50 plus shipping.

The exam takes three hours and is limited to Florida law. The first part of the exam covers ethics and general Florida law which includes the Florida court system and terminology. All questions must be answered. Part Two covers seven substantive areas:

(1) real estate law
(2) civil litigation
(3) criminal law
(4) family law
(5) probate and estate planning
(6) corporate and business law, and
(7) contract law

There are three questions from each of the substantive areas. An examinee must answer a total of six questions and may select any combination of questions from the substantive areas. The examinee may not answer more than six questions. Only the first six questions answered are graded.

The test comprises true/false questions, short-answer essay questions, and multiple-choice questions.

Upon successful completion of the CFLA examination, a legal assistant becomes authorized to use the designation "CLA, CFLA."

CFLAs are required to have thirty hours of continuing legal education credit over a five-year period to maintain their CFLA certification which must be directly applicable to Florida law. Proof of continuing legal education must be submitted to and is maintained by the Certifying Board.

Information regarding the dates of the next study course and examination may be obtained from the headquarters office of FLA, Inc., as follows:

Florida Legal Assistants, Inc.
11812-A North 56th Street
Tampa, Florida 33617
Tel: 813-985-2044
800-433-4FLA (4352)
Fax: 813-988-5837

Louisiana Certified Paralegal Program

At its 1992 annual meeting, the members of the Louisiana State Paralegal Association (LSPA) passed a resolution which endorsed voluntary certification as a means of establishing professional standards and promoting recognition of the paralegal profession. Subsequently, the LSPA determined a state voluntary certification credential should be developed and made available to all Louisiana paralegals who desire to demonstrate comprehensive knowledge, a high degree of proficiency in Louisiana law, and adherence to a Code of Ethics to enhance the quality of paralegal services available to the Louisiana legal community and to the public it serves.

The resulting certification program requires the candidate to sit for both the LCP (Louisiana Certified Paralegal) and CLA (Certified Legal Assistant) examinations. The LCP examination is designed to test the examinee's knowledge and understanding of the Louisiana legal and judicial system, Louisiana general law, ethics, civil procedure, and four areas of Louisiana substantive law. The CLA examination offered by the National Association of Legal Assistants tests the core paralegal skills, knowledge of the American legal and judicial system, and four areas of substantive law based on federal law and common law principles.

To qualify for the examination, one must either have a valid CLA credential or meet one of the alternate eligibility requirements of the CLA examination.

Testing Sessions

The examination will be offered twice a year, in October and in the spring (March or April).

Subjects

As a state-specific examination, the LCP examination is designed to test a paralegal's knowledge and comprehension of the law in the state of Louisiana. Each examinee will be required to take the general law, ethics, and civil procedures sections and must select four law topics, from a list of eight, that will comprise the substantive law section of that examinee's test. The substantive law areas are:

- Business Organizations
- Contracts/Obligations
- Criminal Law and Procedure
- Wills/Probate/Successions/Trusts
- Family Law
- Property
- Torts
- Evidence

Preparation

Those individuals who have not had formal substantive law paralegal courses in Louisiana would benefit from study of a current textbook covering the topics selected for the substantive law section. Much of the material covered in this section of the examination is acquired through experience in the legal field.

The LSPA will offer a review course once a year to assist interested parties in preparing for the examination. Written materials and a videotape of the seminar sessions are available from the Louisiana State Paralegal Association in care of NALA Headquarters, 1516 S. Boston, #200, Tulsa, OK 74119, (918) 587-6828.

APPENDIX I

Information on NFPA's PACE Examination

Introduction

The legal service industry is facing great change. While containing costs, it is trying to respond to an increased number of pending cases, rapid changes in technology, and increased demands from consumers for a higher level of client service.

The paralegal profession is facing possible regulation through certification, licensing, or other means.

The National Federation of Paralegal Associations, Inc., a grass-roots organization, is addressing this issue. During the NFPA's 1994 midyear meeting, the membership voted to develop an exam to test the competency level of experienced paralegals.

> **PACE = Paralegal Advanced Competency Exam**
>
> Offering experienced paralegals an option to
>
> - validate their experience and job skills;
> - establish credentials; and
> - increase their value to their organizations and clients.
>
> The only exam of its kind, PACE
>
> - was developed by a professional testing firm;
> - is administered by an independent test administration company;
> - provides results across practice areas, and when available, for state-specific laws;
> - offers the profession a national standard of evaluation; and
> - is offered at multiple locations on numerous dates and at various times.
>
> **PACE = Personal Advancement for the Experienced Paralegal**

The development of this exam is a conscientious effort by paralegals to direct the future of the paralegal profession and acknowledges the vital role of paralegals within the legal service industry. It is a direct response to states that are considering regulation of the paralegal profession and are seeking a method to measure job competency. While the NFPA believes in the criteria established by its members to take this exam, it recognizes that any state may adopt the exam and modify the criteria.

The Paralegal Advanced Competency Exam (PACE) will be developed in two stages, identified as tiers. Tier I, comprising general and ethics questions, is available; state-specific modules will be developed within particular jurisdictions as the need arises. Tier II will comprise specialty sections.

Paralegals receive two major benefits by taking PACE. The exam

- provides a fair evaluation of the competencies of paralegals across practice areas; and
- creates a professional level of expertise by which all paralegals can be evaluated.

EXPERIENCE AND EDUCATION

Requirements for a paralegal to take either tier of PACE include work experience and education. The paralegal cannot have been convicted of a felony nor be under suspension, termination, or revocation of a certificate, registration, or license by any entity. PACE has generated a great deal of interest since the resolution to develop it was passed. Based on this interest, and the number of paralegals who may apply to take the exam (a number reported by the U.S. Department of Labor to exceed 113,000), a need exists for global grandparenting.

The global grandparenting period for paralegals to apply to take the exam expires December 31, 2000. Paralegals who intend to substitute work experience for the educational requirements must apply to take the test by December 31, 2000.

During the grandparenting period, paralegals have time to learn about PACE and understand the option of substituting extensive work experience for the educational requirements. After December 31, 2000, the educational standards originally established for PACE will be mandatory.

Requirements for Tier I

- a minimum of four years' work experience as a paralegal if application is made within the global grandparenting period, or
- a bachelor's degree, and completion of a paralegal program within an institutionally accredited school (which may be embodied in the bachelor's degree), and a minimum of two years' work experience as a paralegal.

Requirements for Tier II

- successful completion of Tier I, and one of the following
- a minimum of six years' work experience as a paralegal, if application is made within the global grandparenting period, or
- a bachelor's degree, and completion of a paralegal program within an institutionally accredited school (which may be embodied in the bachelor's degree), and a minimum of four years' work experience as a paralegal.

INDEPENDENCE AND FAIRNESS

The NFPA strongly believes PACE must produce legitimate and verifiable results and consistently pass only paralegals who demonstrate an established level of knowledge, skills, and competency. PACE was developed in cooperation with the independent test development firm, Professional Examination Service (PES).

PES was selected through an extensive proposal process and a personal interview with the NFPA Board of Directors. PES has developed professional exams for more than fifty years for groups such as the Federal Reserve System, the National Association of Securities Dealers, Inc., the Environmental Protection Agency, and the Emergency Medical Technicians and Paramedics Association. PES currently works with more than seventy-five professional associations and more than three hundred licensing boards in sixty-two jurisdictions in the United States and Canada.

PES does not work alone. An independent task force of paralegals, paralegal educators, attorneys, and other content specialists are assisting in every step, from the preparation of the job analysis for paralegals through creation of the initial exam and ongoing revisions.

To ensure test results are valid, the test is administered by PES, an independent firm.

All profits received from the exam will be passed to the "Foundation for the Advancement of the Paralegal Profession," an independent foundation, and will be used to further the entire paralegal profession.

CREDENTIAL

Those who pass PACE and maintain the continuing education requirement may use the designation "PACE–Registered Paralegal" or "RP."

HOW TO PREPARE AND REGISTER

To prepare for the exam, paralegals may use any of the following options:

- a study manual
- a practice diskette
- seminars sponsored by local paralegal associations and the NFPA;

- a video of an "Overview for PACE" seminar; or
- study information provided through the Internet.

To register to take the exam (details on application process), send $15 to NFPA, P.O. Box 33108, Kansas City, MO 64114-0108, for a Candidate Handbook, which includes an application, information on exam content, sample exam questions, and logistical information on taking the exam. The $15 fee will be applied to the overall examination fee of $225. Once the application has been approved, the exam must be taken within ninety days.

PACE is a four-hour, computer-generated test and is offered at more than two hundred Sylvan Technology Centers throughout the country. Once approved, each applicant can schedule the date and time to take the test at his or her convenience on any day except Sundays and holidays.

To maintain the RP credential, twelve hours of continuing legal or specialty education is required every two years, with at least one hour in legal ethics.

Preparing for the Future

The PACE exam provides hard facts about the competency of experienced paralegals. While PACE does not address all the issues of regulation, including certification and licensing, it does provide the legal service industry with an option to evaluate the competency level of experienced paralegals.

As members of a self-directed profession, all paralegals should consider the vital role the profession performs within the legal service industry. PACE is independently monitored and well structured. PACE provides test results across practice areas.

The NFPA is committed to ensuring that the paralegal profession responds to the changing needs of the public and legal service industry.

The NFPA's Role

First organized in 1974, the NFPA was created to provide a communications network and develop channels to expand the role of the paralegal profession. In addition, the NFPA has assisted the profession in evaluating educational standards and responding to organizations and entities interested in regulating the profession.

NFPA membership has significantly increased since its inception. In 1998, it included fifty-four associations located throughout the United States, with more than 17,000 members.

APPENDIX J

THE CONSTITUTION OF THE UNITED STATES

Preamble

We the People of the United States, in Order to form a more perfect Union, establish Justice, insure domestic Tranquility, provide for the common defence, promote the general Welfare, and secure the Blessings of Liberty to ourselves and our Posterity, do ordain and establish this Constitution for the United States of America.

Article I

SECTION 1.   All legislative Powers herein granted shall be vested in a Congress of the United States, which shall consist of a Senate and House of Representatives.

SECTION 2.   The House of Representatives shall be composed of Members chosen every second Year by the People of the several States, and the Electors in each State shall have the Qualifications requisite for Electors of the most numerous Branch of the State Legislature.

No Person shall be a Representative who shall not have attained to the Age of twenty five Years, and been seven Years a Citizen of the United States, and who shall not, when elected, be an Inhabitant of that State in which he shall be chosen.

Representatives and direct Taxes shall be apportioned among the several States which may be included within this Union, according to their respective Numbers, which shall be determined by adding to the whole Number of free Persons, including those bound to Service for a Term of Years, and excluding Indians not taxed, three fifths of all other Persons. The actual Enumeration shall be made within three Years after the first Meeting of the Congress of the United States, and within every subsequent Term of ten Years, in such Manner as they shall by Law direct. The Number of Representatives shall not exceed one for every thirty Thousand, but each State shall have at Least one Representative; and until such enumeration shall be made, the State of New Hampshire shall be entitled to chuse three, Massachusetts eight, Rhode Island and Providence Plantations one, Connecticut five, New York six, New Jersey four, Pennsylvania eight, Delaware one, Maryland six, Virginia ten, North Carolina five, South Carolina five, and Georgia three.

When vacancies happen in the Representation from any State, the Executive Authority thereof shall issue Writs of Election to fill such Vacancies.

The House of Representatives shall chuse their Speaker and other Officers; and shall have the sole Power of Impeachment.

SECTION 3. The Senate of the United States shall be composed of two Senators from each State, chosen by the Legislature thereof, for six Years; and each Senator shall have one Vote.

Immediately after they shall be assembled in Consequence of the first Election, they shall be divided as equally as may be into three Classes. The Seats of the Senators of the first Class shall be vacated at the Expiration of the second Year, of the second Class at the Expiration of the fourth Year, and of the third Class at the Expiration of the sixth Year, so that one third may be chosen every second Year; and if Vacancies happen by Resignation, or otherwise, during the Recess of the Legislature of any State, the Executive thereof may make temporary Appointments until the next Meeting of the Legislature, which shall then fill such Vacancies.

No Person shall be a Senator who shall not have attained to the Age of thirty Years, and been nine Years a Citizen of the United States, and who shall not, when elected, be an Inhabitant of that State for which he shall be chosen.

The Vice President of the United States shall be President of the Senate, but shall have no Vote, unless they be equally divided.

The Senate shall chuse their other Officers, and also a President pro tempore, in the Absence of the Vice President, or when he shall exercise the Office of President of the United States.

The Senate shall have the sole Power to try all Impeachments. When sitting for that Purpose, they shall be on Oath or Affirmation. When the President of the United States is tried, the Chief Justice shall preside: And no Person shall be convicted without the Concurrence of two thirds of the Members present.

Judgment in Cases of Impeachment shall not extend further than to removal from Office, and disqualification to hold and enjoy any Office of honor, Trust, or Profit under the United States: but the Party convicted shall nevertheless be liable and subject to Indictment, Trial, Judgment, and Punishment, according to Law.

SECTION 4. The Times, Places and Manner of holding Elections for Senators and Representatives, shall be prescribed in each State by the Legislature thereof; but the Congress may at any time by Law make or alter such Regulations, except as to the Places of chusing Senators.

The Congress shall assemble at least once in every Year, and such Meeting shall be on the first Monday in December, unless they shall by Law appoint a different Day.

SECTION 5. Each House shall be the Judge of the Elections, Returns, and Qualifications of its own Members, and a Majority of each shall constitute a Quorum to do Business; but a smaller Number may adjourn from day to day, and may be authorized to compel the Attendance of absent Members, in such Manner, and under such Penalties as each House may provide.

Each House may determine the Rules of its Proceedings, punish its Members for disorderly Behavior, and, with the Concurrence of two thirds, expel a Member.

Each House shall keep a Journal of its Proceedings, and from time to time publish the same, excepting such Parts as may in their Judgment require Secrecy; and the Yeas and Nays of the Members of either House on any question shall, at the Desire of one fifth of those Present, be entered on the Journal.

Neither House, during the Session of Congress, shall, without the Consent of the other, adjourn for more than three days, nor to any other Place than that in which the two Houses shall be sitting.

SECTION 6. The Senators and Representatives shall receive a Compensation for their Services, to be ascertained by Law, and paid out of the Treasury of the United States. They shall in all Cases, except Treason, Felony and Breach of the Peace, be privileged from Arrest during their Attendance at the Session of their respective Houses, and in going to and returning from the same; and for any Speech or Debate in either House, they shall not be questioned in any other Place.

No Senator or Representative shall, during the Time for which he was elected, be appointed to any civil Office under the Authority of the United States, which shall have been created, or the Emoluments whereof shall have been increased during such time; and no Person holding any Office under the United States, shall be a Member of either House during his Continuance in Office.

SECTION 7. All Bills for raising Revenue shall originate in the House of Representatives; but the Senate may propose or concur with Amendments as on other Bills.

Every Bill which shall have passed the House of Representatives and the Senate, shall, before it become a Law, be presented to the President of the United States; If he approve he shall sign it, but if not he shall return it, with his Objections to the House in which it shall have originated, who shall enter the Objections at large on their Journal, and proceed to reconsider it. If after such Reconsideration two thirds of that House shall agree to pass the Bill, it shall be sent together with the Objections, to the other House, by which it shall likewise be reconsidered, and if approved by two thirds of that House, it shall become a Law. But in all such Cases the Votes of both Houses shall be determined by Yeas and Nays, and the Names of the Persons voting for and against the Bill shall be entered on the Journal of each House respectively. If any Bill shall not be returned by the President within ten Days (Sundays excepted) after it shall have been presented to him, the Same shall be a Law, in like Manner as if he had signed it, unless the Congress by their Adjournment prevent its Return in which Case it shall not be a Law.

Every Order, Resolution, or Vote, to which the Concurrence of the Senate and House of Representatives may be necessary (except on a question of Adjournment) shall be presented to the President of the United States; and before the Same shall take Effect, shall be approved by him, or being disapproved by him, shall be repassed by two thirds of the Senate and House of Representatives, according to the Rules and Limitations prescribed in the Case of a Bill.

SECTION 8. The Congress shall have Power To lay and collect Taxes, Duties, Imposts and Excises, to pay the Debts and provide for the common Defence and general Welfare of the United States; but all Duties, Imposts and Excises shall be uniform throughout the United States;

To borrow Money on the credit of the United States;

To regulate Commerce with foreign Nations, and among the several States, and with the Indian Tribes;

To establish an uniform Rule of Naturalization, and uniform Laws on the subject of Bankruptcies throughout the United States;

To coin Money, regulate the Value thereof, and of foreign Coin, and fix the Standard of Weights and Measures;

To provide for the Punishment of counterfeiting the Securities and current Coin of the United States;

To establish Post Offices and post Roads;

To promote the Progress of Science and useful Arts, by securing for limited Times to Authors and Inventors the exclusive Right to their respective Writings and Discoveries;

To constitute Tribunals inferior to the supreme Court;

To define and punish Piracies and Felonies committed on the high Seas, and Offenses against the Law of Nations;

To declare War, grant Letters of Marque and Reprisal, and make Rules concerning Captures on Land and Water;

To raise and support Armies, but no Appropriation of Money to that Use shall be for a longer Term than two Years;

To provide and maintain a Navy;

To make Rules for the Government and Regulation of the land and naval Forces;

To provide for calling forth the Militia to execute the Laws of the Union, suppress Insurrections and repel Invasions;

To provide for organizing, arming, and disciplining, the Militia, and for governing such Part of them as may be employed in the Service of the United States, reserving to the States respectively, the Appointment of the Officers, and the Authority of training the Militia according to the discipline prescribed by Congress;

To exercise exclusive Legislation in all Cases whatsoever, over such District (not exceeding ten Miles square) as may, by Cession of particular States, and the Acceptance of Congress, become the Seat of the Government of the United States, and to exercise like Authority over all Places purchased by the Consent of the Legislature of the State in which the Same shall be, for the Erection of Forts, Magazines, Arsenals, dock-Yards, and other needful Buildings;—And

To make all Laws which shall be necessary and proper for carrying into Execution the foregoing Powers, and all other Powers vested by this Constitution in the Government of the United States, or in any Department or Officer thereof.

SECTION 9. The Migration or Importation of such Persons as any of the States now existing shall think proper to admit, shall not be prohibited by the Congress prior to the Year one thousand eight hundred and eight, but a Tax or duty may be imposed on such Importation, not exceeding ten dollars for each Person.

The privilege of the Writ of Habeas Corpus shall not be suspended, unless when in Cases of Rebellion or Invasion the public Safety may require it.

No Bill of Attainder or ex post facto Law shall be passed.

No Capitation, or other direct, Tax shall be laid, unless in Proportion to the Census or Enumeration herein before directed to be taken.

No Tax or Duty shall be laid on Articles exported from any State.

No Preference shall be given by any Regulation of Commerce or Revenue to the Ports of one State over those of another: nor shall Vessels bound to, or from, one State be obliged to enter, clear, or pay Duties in another.

No Money shall be drawn from the Treasury, but in Consequence of Appropriations made by Law; and a regular Statement and Account of the Receipts and Expenditures of all public Money shall be published from time to time.

No Title of Nobility shall be granted by the United States: And no Person holding any Office of Profit or Trust under them, shall, without the Consent of the Congress, accept of any present, Emolument, Office, or Title, of any kind whatever, from any King, Prince, or foreign State.

SECTION 10. No State shall enter into any Treaty, Alliance, or Confederation; grant Letters of Marque and Reprisal; coin Money; emit Bills of Credit; make any Thing but gold and silver Coin a Tender in Payment of Debts; pass any Bill of Attainder, ex post facto Law, or Law impairing the Obligation of Contracts, or grant any Title of Nobility.

No State shall, without the Consent of the Congress, lay any Imposts or Duties on Imports or Exports, except what may be absolutely necessary for executing its inspection Laws: and the net Produce of all Duties and Imposts, laid by any State on Imports or Exports, shall be for the Use of the Treasury of the United States; and all such Laws shall be subject to the Revision and Controul of the Congress.

No State shall, without the Consent of Congress, lay any Duty of Tonnage, keep Troops, or Ships of War in time of Peace, enter into any Agreement or Compact with another State, or with a foreign Power, or engage in War, unless actually invaded, or in such imminent Danger as will not admit of delay.

Article II

SECTION 1. The executive Power shall be vested in a President of the United States of America. He shall hold his Office during the Term of four Years, and, together with the Vice President, chosen for the same Term, be elected, as follows:

Each State shall appoint, in such Manner as the Legislature thereof may direct, a Number of Electors, equal to the whole Number of Senators and Representatives to which the State may be entitled in the Congress; but no Senator or Representative, or Person holding an Office of Trust or Profit under the United States, shall be appointed an Elector.

The Electors shall meet in their respective States, and vote by Ballot for two Persons, of whom one at least shall not be an Inhabitant of the same State with themselves. And they shall make a List of all the Persons voted for, and of the Number of Votes for each; which List they shall sign and certify, and transmit sealed to the Seat of the Government of the United States, directed to the President of the Senate. The President of the Senate shall, in the Presence of the Senate and House of Representatives, open all the Certificates, and the Votes shall then be counted. The Person having the greatest Number of Votes shall be the President, if such Number be a Majority of the whole Number of Electors appointed; and if there be more than one who have such Majority, and have an equal Number of Votes, then the House of Representatives shall immediately chuse by Ballot one of them for President; and if no Person have a Majority, then from the five highest on the List the said House shall in like Manner chuse the President. But in chusing the President, the Votes shall be taken by States, the Representation from each State having one Vote; A quorum for this Purpose shall consist of a Member or Members from two thirds of the States, and a Majority of all the States shall be necessary to a Choice. In every Case, after the Choice of the President, the Person having the greater Number of Votes of the Electors shall be the Vice President. But if there should remain two or more who have equal Votes, the Senate shall chuse from them by Ballot the Vice President.

The Congress may determine the Time of chusing the Electors, and the Day on which they shall give their Votes; which Day shall be the same throughout the United States.

No person except a natural born Citizen, or a Citizen of the United States, at the time of the Adoption of this Constitution, shall be eligible to the Office of President; neither shall any Person be eligible to that Office who shall not have attained to the Age of thirty five Years, and been fourteen Years a Resident within the United States.

In Case of the Removal of the President from Office, or of his Death, Resignation or Inability to discharge the Powers and Duties of the said Office, the same shall devolve on the Vice President, and the Congress may by Law provide for the Case of Removal, Death, Resignation or Inability, both of the President and Vice President, declaring what Officer shall then act as President, and such Officer shall act accordingly, until the Disability be removed, or a President shall be elected.

The President shall, at stated Times, receive for his Services, a Compensation, which shall neither be increased nor diminished during the Period for which he shall have been elected, and he shall not receive within that Period any other Emolument from the United States, or any of them.

Before he enter on the Execution of his Office, he shall take the following Oath or Affirmation: "I do solemnly swear (or affirm) that I will faithfully execute the Office of President of the United States, and will to the best of my Ability, preserve, protect and defend the Constitution of the United States."

SECTION 2. The President shall be Commander in Chief of the Army and Navy of the United States, and of the Militia of the several States, when called into the actual Service of the United States; he may require the Opinion, in writing, of the principal Officer in each of the executive Departments, upon any Subject relating to the Duties of their respective Offices, and he shall have Power to grant Reprieves and Pardons for Offenses against the United States, except in Cases of Impeachment.

He shall have Power, by and with the Advice and Consent of the Senate to make Treaties, provided two thirds of the Senators present concur; and he shall nominate, and by and with the Advice and Consent of the Senate, shall appoint Ambassadors, other public Ministers and Consuls, Judges of the supreme Court, and all other Officers of the United States, whose Appointments are not herein otherwise provided for, and which shall be established by Law; but the Congress may by Law vest the Appointment of such inferior Officers, as they think proper, in the President alone, in the Courts of Law, or in the Heads of Departments.

The President shall have Power to fill up all Vacancies that may happen during the Recess of the Senate, by granting Commissions which shall expire at the End of their next Session.

SECTION 3. He shall from time to time give to the Congress Information of the State of the Union, and recommend to their Consideration such Measures as he shall judge necessary and expedient; he may, on extraordinary Occasions, convene both Houses, or either of them, and in Case of Disagreement between them, with Respect to the Time of Adjournment, he may adjourn them to such Time as he shall think proper; he shall receive Ambassadors and other public Ministers; he shall take Care that the Laws be faithfully executed, and shall Commission all the Officers of the United States.

SECTION 4. The President, Vice President and all civil Officers of the United States, shall be removed from Office on Impeachment for, and Conviction of, Treason, Bribery, or other high Crimes and Misdemeanors.

Article III

SECTION 1. The judicial Power of the United States, shall be vested in one supreme Court, and in such inferior Courts as the Congress may from time to time ordain and establish. The Judges, both of the supreme and inferior Courts, shall hold their Offices during good Behaviour, and shall, at stated Times, receive for their Services a Compensation, which shall not be diminished during their Continuance in Office.

SECTION 2. The judicial Power shall extend to all Cases, in Law and Equity, arising under this Constitution, the Laws of the United States, and Treaties made, or which shall be made, under their Authority;—to all Cases affecting Ambassadors, other public Ministers and Consuls;—to all Cases of admiralty and maritime Jurisdiction;—to Controversies to which the United States shall be a Party;—to Controversies between two or more States;—between a State and Citizens of another State;—between Citizens of different States;—between Citizens of the same State claiming Lands under Grants of different States, and between a State, or the Citizens thereof, and foreign States, Citizens or Subjects.

In all Cases affecting Ambassadors, other public Ministers and Consuls, and those in which a State shall be a Party, the supreme Court shall have original Jurisdiction. In all the other Cases before mentioned, the supreme Court shall have appellate Jurisdiction, both as to Law and Fact, with such Exceptions, and under such Regulations as the Congress shall make.

The Trial of all Crimes, except in Cases of Impeachment, shall be by Jury; and such Trial shall be held in the State where the said Crimes shall have been committed; but when not committed within any State, the Trial shall be at such Place or Places as the Congress may by Law have directed.

SECTION 3. Treason against the United States, shall consist only in levying War against them, or, in adhering to their Enemies, giving them Aid and Comfort. No Person shall be convicted of Treason unless on the Testimony of two Witnesses to the same overt Act, or on Confession in open Court.

The Congress shall have Power to declare the Punishment of Treason, but no Attainder of Treason shall work Corruption of Blood, or Forfeiture except during the Life of the Person attainted.

Article IV

SECTION 1. Full Faith and Credit shall be given in each State to the public Acts, Records, and judicial Proceedings of every other State. And the Congress may by general Laws prescribe the Manner in which such Acts, Records and Proceedings shall be proved, and the Effect thereof.

SECTION 2. The Citizens of each State shall be entitled to all Privileges and Immunities of Citizens in the several States.

A Person charged in any State with Treason, Felony, or other Crime, who shall flee from Justice, and be found in another State, shall on Demand of the executive Authority of the State from which he fled, be delivered up, to be removed to the State having Jurisdiction of the Crime.

No Person held to Service or Labour in one State, under the Laws thereof, escaping into another, shall, in Consequence of any Law or Regulation therein, be discharged from such Service or Labour, but shall be delivered up on Claim of the Party to whom such Service or Labour may be due.

SECTION 3. New States may be admitted by the Congress into this Union; but no new State shall be formed or erected within the Jurisdiction of any other State; nor any State be formed by the Junction of two or more States, or Parts of States, without the Consent of the Legislatures of the States concerned as well as of the Congress.

The Congress shall have Power to dispose of and make all needful Rules and Regulations respecting the Territory or other Property belonging to the United States; and nothing in this Constitution shall be so construed as to Prejudice any Claims of the United States, or of any particular State.

SECTION 4. United States shall guarantee to every State in this Union a Republican Form of Government, and shall protect each of them against Invasion; and on Application of the Legislature, or of the Executive (when the Legislature cannot be convened) against domestic Violence.

Article V

The Congress, whenever two thirds of both Houses shall deem it necessary, shall propose Amendments to this Constitution, or, on the Application of the Legislatures of two thirds of the several States, shall call a Convention for proposing Amendments, which, in either Case, shall be valid to all Intents and Purposes, as part of this Constitution, when ratified by the Legislatures of three fourths of the several States, or by Conventions in three fourths thereof, as the one or the other Mode of Ratification may be proposed by the Congress; Provided that no Amendment which may be made prior to the Year One thousand eight hundred and eight shall in any Manner affect the first and fourth Clauses in the Ninth Section of the first Article; and that no State, without its Consent, shall be deprived of its equal Suffrage in the Senate.

Article VI

All Debts contracted and Engagements entered into, before the Adoption of this Constitution shall be as valid against the United States under this Constitution, as under the Confederation.

This Constitution, and the Laws of the United States which shall be made in Pursuance thereof; and all Treaties made, or which shall be made, under the Authority of the United States, shall be the supreme Law of the Land; and the Judges in every State shall be bound thereby, any Thing in the Constitution or Laws of any State to the Contrary notwithstanding.

The Senators and Representatives before mentioned, and the Members of the several State Legislatures, and all executive and judicial Officers, both of the United States and of the several States, shall be bound by Oath or Affirmation, to support this Constitution; but no religious Test shall ever be required as a Qualification to any Office or public Trust under the United States.

Article VII

The Ratification of the Conventions of nine States shall be sufficient for the Establishment of this Constitution between the States so ratifying the Same.

Amendment I [1791]

Congress shall make no law respecting an establishment of religion, or prohibiting the free exercise thereof; or abridging the freedom of speech, or of the press; or the right of the people peaceably to assembly, and to petition the Government for a redress of grievances.

Amendment II [1791]

A well regulated Militia, being necessary to the security of a free State, the right of the people to keep and bear Arms, shall not be infringed.

Amendment III [1791]

No Soldier shall, in time of peace be quartered in any house, without the consent of the Owner, nor in time of war, but in a manner to be prescribed by law.

Amendment IV [1791]

The right of the people to be secure in their persons, houses, papers, and effects, against unreasonable searches and seizures, shall not be violated, and no Warrants shall issue, but upon probable cause, supported by Oath or affirmation, and particularly describing the place to be searched, and the persons or things to be seized.

Amendment V [1791]

No person shall be held to answer for a capital, or otherwise infamous crime, unless on a presentment or indictment of a Grand Jury, except in cases arising in the land or naval forces, or in the Militia, when in actual service in time of War or public danger; nor shall any person be subject for the same offence to be twice put in jeopardy of life or limb; nor shall be compelled in any criminal case to be a witness against himself, nor be deprived of life, liberty, or property, without due process of law; nor shall private property be taken for public use, without just compensation.

Amendment VI [1791]

In all criminal prosecutions, the accused shall enjoy the right to a speedy and public trial, by an impartial jury of the State and district wherein the crime shall have been committed, which district shall have been previously ascertained by law, and to be informed of the nature and cause of the accusation; to be confronted with the witnesses against him; to have compulsory process for obtaining witnesses in his favor, and to have the Assistance of Counsel for his defence.

Amendment VII [1791]

In Suits at common law, where the value in controversy shall exceed twenty dollars, the right of trial by jury shall be preserved, and no fact tried by jury, shall be otherwise re-examined in any Court of the United States, than according to the rules of the common law.

Amendment VIII [1791]

Excessive bail shall not be required, nor excessive fines imposed, nor cruel and unusual punishments inflicted.

Amendment IX [1791]

The enumeration in the Constitution, of certain rights, shall not be construed to deny or disparage others retained by the people.

Amendment X [1791]

The powers not delegated to the United States by the Constitution, nor prohibited by it to the States, are reserved to the States respectively, or to the people.

Amendment XI [1798]

The Judicial power of the United States shall not be construed to extend to any suit in law or equity, commenced or prosecuted against one of the United States by Citizens of another State, or by Citizens or Subjects of any Foreign State.

Amendment XII [1804]

The Electors shall meet in their respective states, and vote by ballot for President and Vice-President, one of whom, at least, shall not be an inhabitant of the same state with themselves; they shall name in their ballots the person voted for as President, and in distinct ballots the person voted for as Vice-President, and they shall make distinct lists of all persons voted for as President, and of all persons voted for as Vice-President, and of the number of votes for each, which lists they shall sign and certify, and transmit sealed to the seat of the government of the United States, directed to the President of the Senate;—The President of the Senate shall, in the presence of the Senate and House of Representatives, open all the certificates and the votes shall then be counted;—The person having the greatest number of votes for President, shall be the President, if such number be a majority of the whole number of Electors appointed; and if no person have such majority, then from the persons having the highest numbers not exceeding three on the list of those voted for as President, the House of Representatives shall choose immediately, by ballot, the President. But in choosing the President, the votes shall be taken by states, the representation from each state having one vote; a quorum for this purpose shall consist of a member or members from two-thirds of the states, and a majority of all states shall be necessary to a choice. And if the House of Representatives shall not choose a President whenever the right of choice shall devolve upon them, before the fourth day of March next following, then the Vice-President shall act as President, as in the case of the death or other constitutional disability of the President.—The person having the greatest number of votes as Vice-President, shall be the Vice-President, if such number be a majority of the whole number of Electors appointed, and if no person have a majority, then from the two highest numbers on the list, the Senate shall choose the Vice-President; a quorum for the purpose shall consist of two-thirds of the whole number of Senators, and a majority of the whole number shall be necessary to a choice. But no person constitutionally ineligible to the office of President shall be eligible to that of Vice-President of the United States.

Amendment XIII [1865]

SECTION 1. Neither slavery nor involuntary servitude, except as a punishment for crime whereof the party shall have been duly convicted, shall exist within the United States, or any place subject to their jurisdiction.

SECTION 2. Congress shall have power to enforce this article by appropriate legislation.

Amendment XIV [1868]

SECTION 1. All persons born or naturalized in the United States, and subject to the jurisdiction thereof, are citizens of the United States and of the State wherein they reside. No State shall make or enforce any law which shall abridge the privileges or immunities of citizens of the United States; nor shall any State deprive any person of life, liberty, or property, without due process of law; nor deny to any person within its jurisdiction the equal protection of the laws.

SECTION 2. Representatives shall be apportioned among the several States according to their respective numbers, counting the whole number of persons in each State, excluding Indians not taxed. But when the right to vote at any election for the choice of electors for President and Vice President of the United States, Representatives in Congress, the Executive and Judicial officers of a State, or the members of the Legislature thereof, is denied to any of the male inhabitants of such State, being twenty-one years of age, and citizens of the United States, or in any way abridged, except for participation in rebellion, or other crime, the basis of representation therein shall be reduced in the proportion which the number of such male citizens shall bear to the whole number of male citizens twenty-one years of age in such State.

SECTION 3. No person shall be a Senator or Representative in Congress, or elector of President and Vice President, or hold any office, civil or military, under the United States, or under any State, who having previously taken an oath, as a member of Congress, or as an officer of the United States, or as a member of any State legislature, or as an executive or judicial officer of any State, to support the Constitution of the United States, shall have engaged in insurrection or rebellion against the same, or given aid or comfort to the enemies thereof. But Congress may by a vote of two-thirds of each House, remove such disability.

SECTION 4. The validity of the public debt of the United States, authorized by law, including debts incurred for payment of pensions and bounties for services in suppressing insurrection or rebellion, shall not be questioned. But neither the United States nor any State shall assume or pay any debt or obligation incurred in aid of insurrection or rebellion against the United States, or any claim for the loss or emancipation of any slave; but all such debts, obligations and claims shall be held illegal and void.

SECTION 5. The Congress shall have power to enforce, by appropriate legislation, the provisions of this article.

Amendment XV [1870]

SECTION 1. The right of citizens of the United States to vote shall not be denied or abridged by the United States or by any State on account of race, color, or previous condition of servitude.

SECTION 2. The Congress shall have power to enforce this article by appropriate legislation.

Amendment XVI [1913]

The Congress shall have power to lay and collect taxes on incomes, from whatever source derived, without apportionment among the several States, and without regard to any census or enumeration.

Amendment XVII [1913]

SECTION 1. The Senate of the United States shall be composed of two Senators from each State, elected by the people thereof, for six years; and each Senator shall have one vote. The electors in each State shall have the qualifications requisite for electors of the most numerous branch of the State legislatures.

SECTION 2. When vacancies happen in the representation of any State in the Senate, the executive authority of such State shall issue writs of election to fill such vacancies: *Provided*, That the legislature of any State may empower the executive thereof to make temporary appointments until the people fill the vacancies by election as the legislature may direct.

SECTION 3. This amendment shall not be so construed as to affect the election or term of any Senator chosen before it becomes valid as part of the Constitution.

Amendment XVIII [1919]

SECTION 1. After one year from the ratification of this article the manufacture, sale, or transportation of intoxicating liquors within, the importation thereof into, or the exportation thereof from the United States and all territory subject to the jurisdiction thereof for beverage purposes is hereby prohibited.

SECTION 2. The Congress and the several States shall have concurrent power to enforce this article by appropriate legislation.

SECTION 3. This article shall be inoperative unless it shall have been ratified as an amendment to the Constitution by the legislatures of the several States, as provided in the Constitution, within seven years from the date of the submission hereof to the States by the Congress.

Amendment XIX [1920]

SECTION 1. The right of citizens of the United States to vote shall not be denied or abridged by the United States or by any State on account of sex.

SECTION 2. Congress shall have power to enforce this article by appropriate legislation.

Amendment XX [1933]

SECTION 1. The terms of the President and Vice President shall end at noon on the 20th day of January, and the terms of Senators and Representatives at noon on the 3d day of January, of the years in which such terms would have ended if this article had not been ratified; and the terms of their successors shall then begin.

SECTION 2. The Congress shall assemble at least once in every year, and such meeting shall begin at noon on the 3d day of January, unless they shall by law appoint a different day.

SECTION 3. If, at the time fixed for the beginning of the term of the President, the President elect shall have died, the Vice President elect shall become President.

If the President shall not have been chosen before the time fixed for the beginning of his term, or if the President elect shall have failed to qualify, then the Vice President elect shall act as President until a President shall have qualified; and the Congress may by law provide for the case wherein neither a President elect nor a Vice President elect shall have qualified, declaring who shall then act as President, or the manner in which one who is to act shall be selected, and such person shall act accordingly until a President or Vice President shall have qualified.

SECTION 4. The Congress may by law provide for the case of the death of any of the persons from whom the House of Representatives may choose a President whenever the right of choice shall have devolved upon them, and for the case of the death of any of the persons from whom the Senate may choose a Vice President whenever the right of choice shall have devolved upon them.

SECTION 5. Sections 1 and 2 shall take effect on the 15th day of October following the ratification of this article.

SECTION 6. This article shall be inoperative unless it shall have been ratified as an amendment to the Constitution by the legislatures of three-fourths of the several States within seven years from the date of its submission.

Amendment XXI [1933]

SECTION 1. The eighteenth article of amendment to the Constitution of the United States is hereby repealed.

SECTION 2. The transportation or importation into any State, Territory, or possession of the United States for delivery or use therein of intoxicating liquors, in violation of the laws thereof, is hereby prohibited.

SECTION 3. This article shall be inoperative unless it shall have been ratified as an amendment to the Constitution by conventions in the several States, as provided in the Constitution, within seven years from the date of the submission hereof to the States by the Congress.

Amendment XXII [1951]

SECTION 1. No person shall be elected to the office of the President more than twice, and no person who has held the office of President, or acted as President, for more than two years of a term to which some other person was elected President shall be elected to the office of President more than once. But this Article shall not apply to any person holding the office of President when this Article was proposed by the Congress, and shall not prevent any person who may be holding the office of President, or acting as President, during the term within which this Article becomes operative from holding the office of President or acting as President during the remainder of such term.

SECTION 2. This article shall be inoperative unless it shall have been ratified as an amendment to the Constitution by the legislatures of three-fourths of the several States within seven years from the date of its submission to the States by the Congress.

Amendment XXIII [1961]

SECTION 1. The District constituting the seat of Government of the United States shall appoint in such manner as the Congress may direct:

A number of electors of President and Vice President equal to the whole number of Senators and Representatives in Congress to which the District would be entitled if it were a State, but in no event more than the least populous state; they shall be in addition to those appointed by the states, but they shall be considered, for the purposes of the election of President and Vice President, to be electors appointed by a state; and they shall meet in the District and perform such duties as provided by the twelfth article of amendment.

SECTION 2. The Congress shall have power to enforce this article by appropriate legislation.

Amendment XXIV [1964]

SECTION 1. The right of citizens of the United States to vote in any primary or other election for President or Vice President, for electors for President or Vice President, or for Senator or Representative in Congress, shall not be denied or abridged by the United States, or any State by reason of failure to pay any poll tax or other tax.

SECTION 2. The Congress shall have power to enforce this article by appropriate legislation.

Amendment XXV [1967]

SECTION 1. In case of the removal of the President from office or of his death or resignation, the Vice President shall become President.

SECTION 2. Whenever there is a vacancy in the office of the Vice President, the President shall nominate a Vice President who shall take office upon confirmation by a majority vote of both Houses of Congress.

SECTION 3. Whenever the President transmits to the President pro tempore of the Senate and the Speaker of the House of Representatives his written declaration that he is unable to discharge the powers and duties of his office, and until he transmits to them a written declaration to the contrary, such powers and duties shall be discharged by the Vice President as Acting President.

SECTION 4. Whenever the Vice President and a majority of either the principal officers of the executive departments or of such other body as Congress may by law provide, transmit to the President pro tempore of the Senate and the Speaker of the House of Representatives their written declaration that the President is unable to discharge the powers and duties of his office, the Vice President shall immediately assume the powers and duties of the office as Acting President.

Thereafter, when the President transmits to the President pro tempore of the Senate and the Speaker of the House of Representatives his written declaration that no inability exists, he shall resume the powers and duties of his office unless the Vice President and a majority of either the principal officers of the executive department or of such other body as Congress may by law provide, transmit within four days to the President pro tempore of the Senate and the Speaker of the House of Representatives their written declaration that the President is unable to discharge the powers and duties of his office. Thereupon Congress shall decide the issue, assembling within forty-eight hours for that purpose if not in session. If the Congress, within twenty-one days after receipt of the latter written declaration, or, if Congress is not in session, within twenty-one days after Congress is required to assemble, determines by two-thirds vote of both Houses that the President is unable to discharge the powers and duties of his office, the Vice President shall continue to discharge the same as Acting President; otherwise, the President shall resume the powers and duties of his office.

Amendment XXVI [1971]

SECTION 1. The right of citizens of the United States, who are eighteen years of age or older, to vote shall not be denied or abridged by the United States or by any State on account of age.

SECTION 2. The Congress shall have power to enforce this article by appropriate legislation.

Amendment XXVII [1992]

No law, varying the compensation for the services of the Senators and Representatives, shall take effect, until an election of Representatives shall have intervened.

APPENDIX K

Spanish Equivalents for Important Legal Terms in English

Abandoned property: bienes abandonados
Acceptance: aceptación; consentimiento; acuerdo
Acceptor: aceptante
Accession: toma de posesión; aumento; accesión
Accommodation indorser: avalista de favor
Accommodation party: firmante de favor
Accord: acuerdo; convenio; arreglo
Accord and satisfaction: transacción ejecutada
Act of state doctrine: doctrina de acto de gobierno
Administrative law: derecho administrativo
Administrative process: procedimiento o metódo administrativo
Administrator: administrador (-a)
Adverse possession: posesión de hecho susceptible de proscripción adquisitiva

Affirmative action: acción afirmativa
Affirmative defense: defensa afirmativa
After-acquired property: bienes adquiridos con posterioridad a un hecho dado
Agency: mandato; agencia
Agent: mandatorio; agente; representante
Agreement: convenio; acuerdo; contrato
Alien corporation: empresa extranjera
Allonge: hojas adicionales de endosos
Answer: contestación de la demande; alegato
Anticipatory repudiation: anuncio previo de las partes de su imposibilidad de cumplir con el contrato
Appeal: apelación; recurso de apelación

Appellate jurisdiction: jurisdicción de apelaciones
Appraisal right: derecho de valuación
Arbitration: arbitraje
Arson: incendio intencional
Articles of partnership: contrato social
Artisan's lien: derecho de retención que ejerce al artesano
Assault: asalto; ataque; agresión
Assignment of rights: transmisión; transferencia; cesión
Assumption of risk: no resarcimiento por exposición voluntaria al peligro
Attachment: auto judicial que autoriza el embargo; embargo

Bailee: depositario
Bailment: depósito; constitución en depósito
Bailor: depositante
Bankruptcy trustee: síndico de la quiebra

Battery: agresión; física
Bearer: portador; tenedor
Bearer instrument: documento al portador
Bequest or legacy: legado (de bienes muebles)
Bilateral contract: contrato bilateral
Bill of lading: conocimiento de embarque; carta de porte
Bill of Rights: declaración de derechos
Binder: póliza de seguro provisoria; recibo de pago a cuenta del precio
Blank indorsement: endoso en blanco
Blue sky laws: leyes reguladoras del comercio bursátil
Bond: título de crédito; garantía; caución
Bond indenture: contrato de emisión de bonos; contrato del empréstito
Breach of contract: incumplimiento de contrato
Brief: escrito; resumen; informe
Burglary: violación de domicilio
Business judgment rule: regla de juicio comercial
Business tort: agravio comercial

Case law: ley de casos; derecho casuístico
Cashier's check: cheque de caja
Causation in fact: causalidad en realidad
Cease-and-desist order: orden para cesar y desistir
Certificate of deposit: certificado de depósito
Certified check: cheque certificado
Charitable trust: fideicomiso para fines benéficos
Chattel: bien mueble
Check: cheque
Chose in action: derecho inmaterial; derecho de acción
Civil law: derecho civil

Close corporation: sociedad de un solo accionista o de un grupo restringido de accionistas
Closed shop: taller agremiado (emplea solamente a miembros de un gremio)
Closing argument: argumento al final
Codicil: codicilo
Collateral: guarantía; bien objeto de la guarantía real
Comity: cortesía; cortesía entre naciones
Commercial paper: instrumentos negociables; documentos a valores commerciales
Common law: derecho consuetudinario; derecho común; ley común
Common stock: acción ordinaria
Comparative negligence: negligencia comparada
Compensatory damages: daños y perjuicios reales o compensatorios
Concurrent conditions: condiciones concurrentes
Concurrent jurisdiction: competencia concurrente de varios tribunales para entender en una misma causa
Concurring opinion: opinión concurrente
Condition: condición
Condition precedent: condición suspensiva
Condition subsequent: condición resolutoria
Confiscation: confiscación
Confusion: confusión; fusión
Conglomerate merger: fusión de firmas que operan en distintos mercados
Consent decree: acuerdo entre las partes aprobado por un tribunal
Consequential damages: daños y perjuicios indirectos
Consideration: consideración; motivo; contraprestación
Consolidation: consolidación
Constructive delivery: entrega simbólica
Constructive trust: fideicomiso creado por aplicación de la ley

Consumer-protection law: ley para proteger el consumidor
Contract: contrato
Contract under seal: contrato formal o sellado
Contributory negligence: negligencia de la parte actora
Conversion: usurpación; conversión de valores
Copyright: derecho de autor
Corporation: sociedad anómina; corporación; persona juridica
Co-sureties: cogarantes
Counterclaim: reconvención; contrademanda
Counteroffer: contraoferta
Course of dealing: curso de transacciones
Course of performance: curso de cumplimiento
Covenant: pacto; garantía; contrato
Covenant not to sue: pacto or contrato a no demandar
Covenant of quiet enjoyment: garantía del uso y goce pacífico del inmueble
Creditors' composition agreement: concordato preventivo
Crime: crimen; delito; contravención
Criminal law: derecho penal
Cross-examination: contrainterrogatorio
Cure: cura; cuidado; derecho de remediar un vicio contractual
Customs receipts: recibos de derechos aduaneros

Damages: daños; indemnización por daños y perjuicios
Debit card: tarjeta de débito
Debtor: deudor
Debt securities: seguridades de deuda
Deceptive advertising: publicidad engañosa
Deed: escritura; título; acta translativa de domino
Defamation: difamación
Delegation of duties: delegación de obligaciones

Demand deposit: depósito a la vista
Depositions: declaración de un testigo fuera del tribunal
Devise: legado; deposición testamentaria (bienes inmuebles)
Directed verdict: veredicto según orden del juez y sin participación activa del jurado
Direct examination: interrogatorio directo; primer interrogatorio
Disaffirmance: repudiación; renuncia; anulación
Discharge: descargo; liberación; cumplimiento
Disclosed principal: mandante revelado
Discovery: descubrimiento; producción de la prueba
Dissenting opinion: opinión disidente
Dissolution: disolución; terminación
Diversity of citizenship: competencia de los tribunales federales para entender en causas cuyas partes intervinientes son cuidadanos de distintos estados
Divestiture: extinción premature de derechos reales
Dividend: dividendo
Docket: orden del día; lista de causas pendientes
Domestic corporation: sociedad local
Draft: orden de pago; letrade cambio
Drawee: girado; beneficiario
Drawer: librador
Duress: coacción; violencia

Easement: servidumbre
Embezzlement: desfalco; malversación
Eminent domain: poder de expropiación
Employment discrimination: discriminación en el empleo
Entrepreneur: empresario
Environmental law: ley ambiental

Equal dignity rule: regla de dignidad egual
Equity security: tipo de participación en una sociedad
Estate: propiedad; patrimonio; derecho
Estop: impedir; prevenir
Ethical issue: cuestión ética
Exclusive jurisdiction: competencia exclusiva
Exculpatory clause: cláusula eximente
Executed contract: contrato ejecutado
Execution: ejecución; cumplimiento
Executor: albacea
Executory contract: contrato aún no completamente consumado
Executory interest: derecho futuro
Express contract: contrato expreso
Expropriation: expropiación

Federal question: caso federal
Fee simple: pleno dominio; dominio absoluto
Fee simple absolute: dominio absoluto
Fee simple defeasible: dominio sujeta a una condición resolutoria
Felony: crimen; delito grave
Fictitious payee: beneficiario ficticio
Fiduciary: fiduciaro
Firm offer: oferta en firme
Fixture: inmueble por destino, incorporación a anexación
Floating lien: gravamen continuado
Foreign corporation: sociedad extranjera; U.S. sociedad constituída en otro estado
Forgery: falso; falsificación
Formal contract: contrato formal
Franchise: privilegio; franquicia; concesión
Franchisee: persona que recibe una concesión
Franchisor: persona que vende una concesión

Fraud: fraude; dolo; engaño
Future interest: bien futuro

Garnishment: embargo de derechos
General partner: socio comanditario
General warranty deed: escritura translativa de domino con garantía de título
Gift: donación
Gift *causa mortis*: donación por causa de muerte
Gift *inter vivos*: donación entre vivos
Good faith: buena fe
Good-faith purchaser: comprador de buena fe

Holder: tenedor por contraprestación
Holder in due course: tenedor legítimo
Holographic will: testamento ológrafico
Homestead exemption laws: leyes que exceptúan las casas de familia de ejecución por duedas generales
Horizontal merger: fusión horizontal

Identification: identificación
Implied-in-fact contract: contrato implícito en realidad
Implied warranty: guarantía implícita
Implied warranty of merchantability: garantía implícita de vendibilidad
Impossibility of performance: imposibilidad de cumplir un contrato
Imposter: imposter
Incidental beneficiary: beneficiario incidental; beneficiario secundario
Incidental damages: daños incidentales
Indictment: auto de acusación; acusación

Indorsee: endorsatario
Indorsement: endoso
Indorser: endosante
Informal contract: contrato no formal; contrato verbal
Information: acusación hecha por el ministerio público
Injunction: mandamiento; orden de no innovar
Innkeeper's lien: derecho de retención que ejerce el posadero
Installment contract: contrato de pago en cuotas
Insurable interest: interés asegurable
Intended beneficiary: beneficiario destinado
Intentional tort: agravio; cuasi-delito intenciónal
International law: derecho internaciónal
Interrogatories: preguntas escritas sometidas por una parte a la otra o a un testigo
Inter vivos **trust:** fideicomiso entre vivos
Intestacy laws: leyes de la condición de morir intestado
Intestate: intestado
Investment company: compañia de inversiones
Issue: emisión

Joint tenancy: derechos conjuntos en un bien inmueble en favor del beneficiario sobreviviente
Judgment *n.o.v.***:** juicio no obstante veredicto
Judgment rate of interest: interés de juicio
Judicial process: acto de procedimiento; proceso jurídico
Judicial review: revisión judicial
Jurisdiction: jurisdicción

Larceny: robo; hurto
Law: derecho; ley; jurisprudencia
Lease: contrato de locación; contrato de alquiler
Leasehold estate: bienes forales

Legal rate of interest: interés legal
Legatee: legatario
Letter of credit: carta de crédito
Levy: embargo; comiso
Libel: libelo; difamación escrita
Life estate: usufructo
Limited partner: comanditario
Limited partnership: sociedad en comandita
Liquidation: liquidación; realización
Lost property: objetos perdidos

Majority opinion: opinión de la mayoría
Maker: persona que realiza u ordena; librador
Mechanic's lien: gravamen de constructor
Mediation: mediación; intervención
Merger: fusión
Mirror image rule: fallo de reflejo
Misdemeanor: infracción; contravención
Mislaid property: bienes extraviados
Mitigation of damages: reducción de daños
Mortgage: hypoteca
Motion to dismiss: excepción parentoria
Mutual fund: fondo mutual

Negotiable instrument: instrumento negociable
Negotiation: negociación
Nominal damages: daños y perjuicios nominales
Novation: novación
Nuncupative will: testamento nuncupativo

Objective theory of contracts: teoria objetiva de contratos
Offer: oferta
Offeree: persona que recibe una oferta

Offeror: oferente
Order instrument: instrumento o documento a la orden
Original jurisdiction: jurisdicción de primera instancia
Output contract: contrato de producción

Parol evidence rule: regla relativa a la prueba oral
Partially disclosed principal: mandante revelado en parte
Partnership: sociedad colectiva; asociación; asociación de participación
Past consideration: causa o contraprestación anterior
Patent: patente; privilegio
Pattern or practice: muestra o práctica
Payee: beneficiario de un pago
Penalty: pena; penalidad
Per capita: por cabeza
Perfection: perfeción
Performance: cumplimiento; ejecución
Personal defenses: excepciones personales
Personal property: bienes muebles
Per stirpes: por estirpe
Plea bargaining: regateo por un alegato
Pleadings: alegatos
Pledge: prenda
Police powers: poderes de policia y de prevención del crimen
Policy: póliza
Positive law: derecho positivo; ley positiva
Possibility of reverter: posibilidad de reversión
Precedent: precedente
Preemptive right: derecho de prelación
Preferred stock: acciones preferidas
Premium: recompensa; prima
Presentment warranty: garantía de presentación
Price discrimination: discriminación en los precios

Principal: mandante; principal
Privity: nexo jurídico
Privity of contract: relación contractual
Probable cause: causa probable
Probate: verificación; verificación del testamento
Probate court: tribunal de sucesiones y tutelas
Proceeds: resultados; ingresos
Profit: beneficio; utilidad; lucro
Promise: promesa
Promisee: beneficiario de una promesa
Promisor: promtente
Promissory estoppel: impedimento promisorio
Promissory note: pagaré; nota de pago
Promoter: promotor; fundador
Proximate cause: causa inmediata o próxima
Proxy: apoderado; poder
Punitive, or exemplary, damages: daños y perjuicios punitivos o ejemplares

Qualified indorsement: endoso con reservas
Quasi contract: contrato tácito o implícito
Quitclaim deed: acto de transferencia de una propiedad por finiquito, pero sin ninguna garantía sobre la validez del título transferido

Ratification: ratificación
Real property: bienes inmuebles
Reasonable doubt: duda razonable
Rebuttal: refutación
Recognizance: promesa; compromiso; reconocimiento
Recording statutes: leyes estatales sobre registros oficiales
Redress: reporacíon
Reformation: rectificación; reforma; corrección
Rejoinder: dúplica; contrarréplica

Release: liberación; renuncia a un derecho
Remainder: substitución; reversión
Remedy: recurso; remedio; reparación
Replevin: acción reivindicatoria; reivindicación
Reply: réplica
Requirements contract: contrato de suministro
Rescission: rescisión
Res judicata: cosa juzgada; res judicata
Respondeat superior: responsabilidad del mandante o del maestro
Restitution: restitución
Restrictive indorsement: endoso restrictivo
Resulting trust: fideicomiso implícito
Reversion: reversión; sustitución
Revocation: revocación; derogación
Right of contribution: derecho de contribución
Right of reimbursement: derecho de reembolso
Right of subrogation: derecho de subrogación
Right-to-work law: ley de libertad de trabajo
Robbery: robo
Rule 10b-5: Regla 10b-5

Sale: venta; contrato de compreventa
Sale on approval: venta a ensayo; venta sujeta a la aprobación del comprador
Sale or return: venta con derecho de devolución
Sales contract: contrato de compraventa; boleto de compraventa
Satisfaction: satisfacción; pago
Scienter: a sabiendas
S corporation: S corporación
Secured party: acreedor garantizado

Secured transaction: transacción garantizada
Securities: volares; titulos; seguridades
Security agreement: convenio de seguridad
Security interest: interés en un bien dado en garantía que permite a quien lo detenta venderlo en caso de incumplimiento
Service mark: marca de identificación de servicios
Shareholder's derivative suit: acción judicial entablada por un accionista en nombre de la sociedad
Signature: firma; rúbrica
Slander: difamación oral; calumnia
Sovereign immunity: immunidad soberana
Special indorsement: endoso especial; endoso a la orden de una person en particular
Specific performance: ejecución precisa, según los términos del contrato
Spendthrift trust: fideicomiso para pródigos
Stale check: cheque vencido
Stare decisis: acatar las decisiones, observar los precedentes
Statutory law: derecho estatutario; derecho legislado; derecho escrito
Stock: acciones
Stock warrant: certificado para la compra de acciones
Stop-payment order: orden de suspensión del pago de un cheque dada por el librador del mismo
Strict liability: responsabilidad uncondicional
Summary judgment: fallo sumario

Tangible property: bienes corpóreos
Tenancy at will: inguilino por tiempo indeterminado (según la voluntad del propietario)
Tenancy by sufferance: posesión por tolerancia

Tenancy by the entirety: locación conyugal conjunta
Tenancy for years: inguilino por un término fijo
Tenancy in common: specie de copropiedad indivisa
Tender: oferta de pago; oferta de ejecución
Testamentary trust: fideicomiso testamentario
Testator: testador (-a)
Third party beneficiary contract: contrato para el beneficio del tercero-beneficiario
Tort: agravio; cuasi-delito
Totten trust: fideicomiso creado por un depósito bancario
Trade acceptance: letra de cambio aceptada
Trademark: marca registrada
Trade name: nombre comercial; razón social
Traveler's check: cheque del viajero
Trespass to land: ingreso no authorizado a las tierras de otro
Trespass to personal property: violación de los derechos posesorios de un tercero con respecto a bienes muebles
Trust: fideicomiso; trust

Ultra vires: ultra vires; fuera de la facultad (de una sociedad anónima)
Unanimous opinion: opinión unámine
Unconscionable contract or clause: contrato leonino; cláusula leonino
Underwriter: subscriptor; asegurador
Unenforceable contract: contrato que no se puede hacer cumplir
Unilateral contract: contrato unilateral
Union shop: taller agremiado; empresa en la que todos los empleados son miembros del gremio o sindicato
Universal defenses: defensas legitimas o legales
Usage of trade: uso comercial
Usury: usura

Valid contract: contrato válido
Venue: lugar; sede del proceso
Vertical merger: fusión vertical de empresas
Voidable contract: contrato anulable

Void contract: contrato nulo; contrato inválido, sin fuerza legal
Voir dire: examen preliminar de un testigo a jurado por el tribunal para determinar su competencia
Voting trust: fideicomiso para ejercer el derecho de voto

Waiver: renuncia; abandono
Warranty of habitability: garantía de habitabilidad
Watered stock: acciones diluídos; capital inflado
White-collar crime: crimen administrativo
Writ of attachment: mandamiento de ejecución; mandamiento de embargo
Writ of *certiorari*: auto de avocación; auto de certiorari
Writ of execution: auto ejecutivo; mandamiento de ejecutión
Writ of mandamus: auto de mandamus; mandamiento; orden judicial

Glossary

ABA-Approved Program A legal or paralegal educational program that satisfies the standards for paralegal training set forth by the American Bar Association.

Acceptance In contract law, the offeree's indication to the offeror that the offeree agrees to be bound by the terms of the offeror's offer, or proposal to form a contract.

Acquittal A certification or declaration following a trial that the individual accused of a crime is innocent, or free from guilt, in the eyes of the law and is thus absolved of the charges.

Active Listening The act of listening attentively to the speaker's verbal or nonverbal messages and responding to those messages by giving appropriate feedback.

Actus Reus A guilty (prohibited) act. The commission of a prohibited act is one of the two essential elements required for criminal liability; the other element is the intent to commit a crime.

Address Block That part of a letter that indicates to whom the letter is addressed. The address block is placed in the upper left-hand portion of the letter, above the salutation (or reference line, if one is included).

Adjudication The act of resolving a controversy and rendering an order or decision based on a review of the evidence presented.

Administrative Agency A federal or state government agency established to perform a specific function. Administrative agencies are authorized by legislative acts to make and enforce rules relating to the purpose for which they were established.

Administrative Law A body of law created by administrative agencies in the form of rules, regulations, orders, and decisions in order to carry out their duties and responsibilities.

Administrative Law Judge (ALJ) One who presides over an administrative agency hearing and who has the power to administer oaths, take testimony, rule on questions of evidence, and make determinations otherwise authorized by law.

Administrative Process The procedure used by administrative agencies in the administration of law.

Administrator A person appointed by a court to serve as a personal representative for a person who died intestate (without a valid will) or if the executor named in the will cannot serve.

Affidavit A written statement of facts, confirmed by the oath or affirmation of the party making it and made before a person having the authority to administer the oath or affirmation.

Affiliate An entity that is connected (or affiliated) with another entity. State and local branches of national or regional paralegal associations are often referred to as affiliates.

Affirm An appellate court's decision to uphold the trial court's judgment in a case.

Affirmative Defense A response to a plaintiff's claim that does not deny the plaintiff's facts but attacks the plaintiff's legal right to bring an action.

Agency A relationship between two persons in which one person (the agent) represents or acts in the place of another (the principal).

Agent A person who is authorized to act for or in the place of another person (the principal).

Agreement A meeting of the minds, and a requirement for a valid contract. Agreement involves two distinct events: an offer to form a contract and the acceptance of that offer by the offeree.

Allegation A party's statement, claim, or assertion made in a pleading to the court. The allegation sets forth the issue that the party expects to prove.

Alternative Dispute Resolution (ADR) The resolution of disputes in ways other than those involved in the traditional judicial process. Mediation and arbitration are forms of ADR.

American Arbitration Association (AAA) The major organization offering arbitration services in the United States.

American Association for Paralegal Education (AAfPE) A national organization of paralegal educators; the AAfPE was established in 1981 to promote high standards for paralegal education.

American Bar Association (ABA) A voluntary national association of attorneys. The ABA plays an active role in developing educational and ethical standards for attorneys and in pursuing improvements in the administration of justice.

***Amicus Curiae* Brief** A brief filed with the court by a third party (that is, a party not directly involved in the lawsuit) that is concerned about the outcome of the litigation. The purpose of such a brief is to convince the court to rule in favor of one of the parties because not to do so would affect a broad interest of society. (*Amicus curiae* is Latin for "friend of the court.")

Annotation A brief comment, an explanation of a legal point, or a case summary found in a case digest or other legal source.

Answer A defendant's response to a plaintiff's complaint.

Appeal The process of seeking a higher court's review of a lower court's decision for the purpose of correcting or changing the lower court's judgment or decision.

Appellant The party who takes an appeal from one court to another; sometimes referred to as the petitioner.

Appellant's Brief An appellate brief that argues in favor of the appellant's position. This brief will try to convince the court that the lower court's decision was erroneous.

Appellate Brief A document submitted to an appellate court setting forth legal arguments and supporting law in favor of the appellant or the appellee.

Appellate Court A court that reviews decisions made by lower courts, such as trial courts; a court of appeals.

Appellate Jurisdiction The power of a court to hear and decide an appeal; that is, the power and authority of a court to review cases that already have been tried in a lower court and the power to make decisions about them without actually holding a trial. This process is called appellate review.

Appellee The party against whom an appeal is taken—that is, the party who opposes setting aside or reversing the judgment; sometimes referred to as the respondent.

Appellee's Brief An appellate brief that argues in favor of the appellee's position. This brief will attempt to rebut (counter) any arguments in the appellant's brief and will emphasize the accuracy of the earlier judgment rendered in its favor.

Arbitration The settling of a dispute by submitting it to a disinterested third party (other than a court), who renders a decision that may or may not be legally binding.

Arbitration Clause A clause in a contract that provides that, in case of a dispute, the parties will determine their rights by arbitration rather than through the judicial system.

Arraignment A court proceeding in which the suspect is formally charged with the criminal offense stated in the indictment. The suspect then enters a plea (guilty, not guilty, or *nolo contendere*) in response.

Arrest Warrant A written order, based on probable cause and issued by a judge or public official (magistrate), commanding that the person named on the warrant be arrested by the police.

Arrest To take into custody a person suspected of criminal activity.

Articles of Incorporation The document filed with the appropriate governmental agency, usually the secretary of state's office, when a business is incorporated. State statutes usually prescribe what kind of information must be contained in the articles of incorporation.

Assault Any word or action intended to make another person fearful of immediate physical harm; a reasonably believable threat.

Associate's Degree An academic degree signifying the completion of a two-year course of study, normally at a community college.

Attorney-Client Privilege A rule of evidence requiring that confidential communications between a client and his or her attorney (relating to their professional relationship) be kept confidential, unless the client consents to disclosure.

Authentication Establishing the genuineness of an item that is to be introduced as evidence in a trial.

Auto-Cite An aid to legal research developed by the editors of Lexis(r). On Lexis(r), Auto-Cite can be used to find the history of a case, to verify whether the case is still good law, and to perform other functions.

Award In the context of ADR, the decision rendered by an arbitrator.

Bachelor's Degree An academic degree signifying the completion of a four-year course of study at a college or university.

Bail The amount of money or conditions set by the court to assure that an individual accused of a crime will appear for further criminal proceedings. If the accused person provides bail, whether in cash or by means of a bail bond, then the person is released from jail.

Bankruptcy Court A federal court of limited jurisdiction that hears only bankruptcy proceedings.

Bankruptcy Law The body of federal law that governs bankruptcy proceedings. The twin goals of bankruptcy law are (1) to protect a debtor by giving him or her a fresh start, free from creditors' claims; and (2) to ensure that creditors who are competing for a debtor's assets are treated fairly.

Battery The unprivileged, intentional touching of another.

Beyond a Reasonable Doubt The standard used to determine the guilt or innocence of a person charged with a crime. To be guilty of a crime, a suspect must be proved guilty "beyond and to the exclusion of every reasonable doubt."

Bill of Rights The first ten amendments to the Constitution.

Billable Hours Hours or fractions of hours that attorneys and paralegals spend in work that requires legal expertise and that can be billed directly to clients.

Binding Mediation A form of ADR in which a mediator attempts to facilitate agreement between the parties, but if no agreement is reached the mediator issues a legally binding decision.

Bonus An end-of-the-year payment to a salaried employee in appreciation for that employee's overtime work, work quality, diligence, or dedication to the firm.

Booking The process of entering a suspect's name, offense, and arrival time into the police log (blotter) following his or her arrest.

Breach To violate a legal duty by an act or a failure to act.

Breach of Contract The failure of a contractual party to perform the obligations assumed in a contract.

Briefing a Case Summarizing a case. A typical case brief will indicate the case title and citation and then briefly state the factual background and procedural history of the case, the issue or issues raised in the case, the court's decision, the applicable rule of law and the legal reasoning upon which the decision is based, and conclusions or notes concerning the case made by the one briefing it.

Business Invitee A person, such as a customer or client, who is invited onto business premises by the owner of those premises for business purposes.

Case Law Rules of law announced in court decisions.

Case of First Impression A case presenting a legal issue that has not yet been addressed by a court in a particular jurisdiction.

Case on "All Fours" A case in which all four elements of a case (the parties, the circumstances, the legal issues involved, and the remedies sought by the plaintiff) are very similar.

Case on Point A case involving factual circumstances and issues that are similar to a case before the court.

Certificate of Incorporation (Corporate Charter) The document issued by a state official (usually the secretary of state) granting a corporation legal existence and the right to function.

Certification Formal recognition by a private group or a state agency that an individual has satisfied the group's standards of proficiency, knowledge, and competence; ordinarily accomplished through the taking of an examination.

Certified Legal Assistant (CLA) A legal assistant whose legal competency has been certified by the National Association of Legal Assistants (NALA) following an examination that tests the legal assistant's knowledge and skills.

Certified Legal Assistant Specialist (CLAS) A legal assistant whose competency in a legal specialty has been certified by the National Association of Legal Assistants (NALA) following an examination of the legal assistant's knowledge and skills in the specialty area.

Challenge An attorney's objection, during *voir dire,* to the inclusion of a particular person on the jury.

Challenge for Cause A *voir dire* challenge for which an attorney states the reason why a prospective juror should not be included in the jury.

Chancellor An adviser to the king in medieval England. Individuals petitioned the king for relief when they could not obtain an adequate remedy in a court of law, and these petitions were decided by the chancellor.

Charge The judge's instruction to the jury, following the attorneys' closing arguments, setting forth the rules of law that the jury must apply in reaching its decision, or verdict.

Chronologically In a time sequence; naming or listing events in the time order in which they occurred.

Circumstantial Evidence Indirect evidence that is offered to establish, by inference, the likelihood of a fact that is in question.

Citation In case law, a reference to the volume number, name, and page number of the reporter in which a case can be found. In statutory and administrative law, a reference to the title number, name, and section of the code in which a statute or regulation can be found. In criminal procedure, an order for a defendant to appear in court or indicating that a person has violated a legal rule.

Citator A book or online service that provides the subsequent history and interpretation of a statute, regulation, or court decision and a list of the cases, statutes, and regulations that have interpreted, applied, or modified a statute or regulation.

Civil Law The branch of law dealing with the definition and enforcement of all private or public rights, as opposed to criminal matters.

Civil Law System A system of law derived from that of the Roman Empire and based on a code rather than case law; the predominant system of law in the nations of continental Europe and the nations that were once their colonies.

Closed-Ended Question A question that is phrased in such a way that it elicits a simple "yes" or "no" answer.

Closing A final comment to a letter that is placed above the signature, such as "Very truly yours."

Closing Argument An argument made by each side's attorney after the cases for the plaintiff and defendant have been presented. Closing arguments are made prior to the jury charge.

Code A systematic and logical presentation of laws, rules, or regulations.

Codify To collect and organize systematically and logically a body of concepts, principles, decisions, or doctrines.

Commercial Online Services Internet service providers that, for a fee, allow their subscribers access to resources that are otherwise restricted.

Common Law A body of law developed from custom or judicial decisions in English and U.S. courts and not attributable to a legislature.

Complaint The pleading made by a plaintiff or a charge made by the state alleging wrongdoing on the part of the defendant.

Computer-Assisted Legal Research (CALR) Any legal research conducted with the assistance of computers. CALR includes the use of CD-ROMs, fee-based legal-services providers such as Westlaw(r) and Lexis(r), and the Internet.

Concurrent Jurisdiction Jurisdiction that exists when two different courts have the power to hear a case. For example, some cases can be heard in either a federal or a state court.

Confirmation Letter A letter that states the substance of a previously conducted verbal discussion to provide a permanent record of the oral conversation.

Conflict of Interest A situation in which two or more duties or interests come into conflict, as when an attorney attempts to represent opposing parties in a legal dispute.

Conflicts Check A procedure for determining whether an agreement to represent a potential client will result in a conflict of interest.

Consideration Something of value, such as money or the performance of an action not otherwise required, that motivates the formation of a contract. Each party must give consideration for the contract to be binding.

Consolidation A process in which two or more corporations join to become a completely new corporation. The original corporations cease to exist.

Consumer An individual who purchases products and services for personal or household use.

Consumer Law Statutes, agency rules, and judicial decisions protecting consumers of goods and services from dangerous manufacturing techniques, mislabeling, unfair credit practices, deceptive advertising, and so on. Consumer laws provide remedies and protections that are not ordinarily available to merchants or to businesses.

Contempt of Court The intentional obstruction or frustration of the court's attempt to administer justice. A party to a lawsuit may be held in contempt of court (punishable by a fine or jail sentence) for refusing to comply with a court's order.

Contingency Fee A legal fee that consists of a specified percentage (such as 30 percent) of the amount the plaintiff recovers in a civil lawsuit. The fee must be paid only if the plaintiff prevails in the lawsuit (recovers damages).

Contract An agreement or bargain struck between parties, in which each party assumes a legal duty to the other party. The requirements for a valid contract are agreement, consideration, contractual capacity, and legality.

Contractual Capacity The threshold mental capacity required by law for a party who enters into a contract to be bound by that contract.

Copyright The exclusive right of an author to publish, print, or sell an intellectual production for a statutory period of time.

Corporate Law Law that governs the formation, financing, merger and acquisition, and termination of corporations, as well as the rights and duties of those who own and run the corporation.

Counterclaim A claim made by a defendant in a civil lawsuit against the plaintiff; in effect, a counterclaiming defendant is suing the plaintiff.

Court of Equity A court that decides controversies and administers justice according to the rules, principles, and precedents of equity.

Court of Law A court in which the only remedies that could be granted were things of value, such as money damages. In early England, courts of law were distinct from courts of equity.

Crime A broad term for violations of law that are punishable by the state and are codified by legislatures. The objective of criminal law is to protect the public.

Criminal Law The branch of law that governs and defines those actions that are crimes and that subjects persons convicted of crimes to punishment imposed by the government.

Cross-Examination The questioning of an opposing witness during the trial.

Damages Money sought as a remedy for a civil wrong, such as a breach of contract or a tortious act.

Deceptive Advertising Advertising that misleads consumers, either by unjustified claims concerning a product's performance or by the failure to disclose relevant information concerning the product's composition or performance.

Deed A document by which title to property is transferred from one party to another.

Default Judgment A judgment entered by a clerk or court against a party who has failed to appear in court to answer or defend against a claim that has been brought against him or her by another party.

Defendant A party against whom a lawsuit is brought.

Defense A legally acceptable reason, raised by a defendant, as to why the plaintiff should not be granted whatever it is the plaintiff is seeking.

Defense of Others The use of reasonable force to protect others from harm.

Defense of Property The use of reasonable force to protect one's property from the harm threatened by another. The use of deadly force in defending one's property is seldom justified.

Delegation Doctrine A doctrine that authorizes Congress to delegate some of its lawmaking authority to administrative agencies. The doctrine is implied by Article I of the U.S. Constitution, which grants specific powers to Congress to enact and oversee the implementation of laws.

Demand Letter An adversarial letter that attempts to persuade the reader that he or she should accept a position that is favorable to the writer's client—that is, demanding that the reader do or not do a certain thing.

Deponent A party or witness who testifies under oath during a deposition.

Deposition A pretrial question-and-answer proceeding, usually conducted orally, in which an a party or witness answers an attorney's questions. The answers are given under oath, and the session is recorded.

Deposition Transcript The official transcription of the recording taken during a deposition.

Dicta A Latin term referring to nonbinding (nonprecedential) judicial statements that are not directly related to the facts or issues presented in the case and thus not essential to the holding.

Digest A compilation in which brief summaries of court cases are arranged by subject and subdivided by jurisdiction and court.

Direct Evidence Evidence establishing the existence of a fact that is in question without relying on inferences.

Direct Examination The examination of a witness by the attorney who calls the witness to the stand to testify on behalf of the attorney's client.

Director A person elected by the shareholders to direct corporate affairs.

Disbarment A severe disciplinary sanction in which an attorney's license to practice law in the state is revoked because of unethical or illegal conduct.

Discovery Formal investigation prior to trial. During discovery, opposing parties use various methods, such as interrogatories and depositions, to obtain information from each other and from witnesses to prepare for trial.

Discovery Plan A plan formed by the attorneys litigating a lawsuit, on behalf of their clients, that indicates the types of information that will be disclosed by each party to the other prior to trial, the testimony and evidence that each party will or may introduce at trial, and the general schedule for pretrial disclosures and events.

Dissolution The formal disbanding of a partnership or a corporation.

Diversion Program In some jurisdictions, an alternative to prosecution that is offered to certain felony suspects to deter them from future unlawful acts.

Diversity of Citizenship Under Article III, Section 2, of the Constitution, a basis for federal court jurisdiction over certain disputes, including disputes between citizens of different states.

Dividend A distribution of profits to corporate shareholders, disbursed in proportion to the number of shares held.

Docket The list of cases entered on a court's calendar and thus scheduled to be heard by the court.

Double Billing Billing more than one client for the same billable time period.

Double Jeopardy To place at risk (jeopardize) a person's life or liberty twice. The Fifth Amendment to the Constitution prohibits a second prosecution for the same criminal offense in all but a few circumstances.

Due Process of Law The Fifth Amendment to the U.S. Constitution prohibits the deprivation of "life, liberty, or property without due process of law," meaning that fair, reasonable, and standard procedures must be used by the government in any legal action against a citizen.

Early Neutral Case Evaluation A form of ADR in which a neutral third party evaluates the strengths and weaknesses of the disputing parties' positions; the evaluator's opinion forms the basis for negotiating a settlement.

Elder Law A term used to describe a relatively new legal specialty that involves servicing the needs of older clients, such as estate planning and making arrangements for long-term care.

Eminent Domain The power of a government to take land for public use from private citizens for just compensation.

Employment at Will A common law doctrine under which employment is considered to be "at will"—that is, either party may terminate the employment relationship at any time and for any reason, unless a contract specifies otherwise.

Employment Manual A firm's handbook or written statement that specifies the policies and procedures that govern the firm's employees and employer-employee relationships.

Enabling Legislation A statute enacted by a legislature that authorizes the creation of an administrative agency and specifies the name, purpose, composition, and powers of the agency being created.

Environmental Impact Statement (EIS) A statement required by the National Environmental Policy Act for any major federal action that will significantly affect the quality of the environment. The statement must analyze the action's impact on the environment and explore alternative actions that might be taken.

Environmental Law All state and federal laws or regulations enacted or issued to protect the environment and preserve environmental resources.

Equitable Principles and Maxims Propositions or general statements of rules of law that are frequently involved in equity jurisdiction.

Estate Administration The process in which a decedent's personal representative settles the affairs of the decedent's estate (collects assets, pays debts and taxes, and distributes the remaining assets to heirs); the process is usually overseen by a probate court.

Estate Planning Making arrangements, during a person's lifetime, for the transfer of that person's property or obligations to others on the person's death. Estate planning often involves executing a will, establishing a trust fund, or taking out a life insurance policy to provide for others, such as a spouse or children, on one's death.

Ethical Wall A term that refers to the procedures used to create a screen around a legal employee to shield him or her from information about a case in which there is a conflict of interest.

Evidence Anything that is used to prove the existence or nonexistence of a fact.

Exclusionary Rule In criminal procedure, a rule under which any evidence that is obtained in violation of the accused's constitutional rights guaranteed by the Fourth, Fifth, and Sixth Amendments, as well as any evidence derived from illegally obtained evidence, will not be admissible in court.

Exclusive Jurisdiction Jurisdiction that exists when a case can be heard only in a particular court, such as a federal court.

Executive Agency A type of administrative agency that is either a cabinet department or a subagency within a cabinet department. Executive agencies fall under the authority of the president, who has the power to appoint and remove federal officers.

Executor A person appointed by a testator to serve as a personal representative on the testator's death.

Expense Slip A slip of paper on which any expense, or cost, that is incurred on behalf of a client (such as the payment of court fees or long-distance telephone charges) is recorded.

Expert Witness A witness with professional training or substantial experience qualifying him or her to testify on a particular subject.

Eyewitness A witness who testifies about an event that he or she observed or has experienced firsthand.

Family Law Law relating to family matters, such as marriage, divorce, child support, and child custody.

Family Limited Liability Partnership (FLLP) A limited liability partnership (LLP) in which the majority of the partners are persons related to each other or persons acting in a fiduciary capacity for persons so related. All partners must be natural persons.

Federal Question A question that pertains to the U.S. Constitution, acts of Congress, or treaties. A federal question provides a basis for jurisdiction by the federal courts. This jurisdiction is authorized by Article III, Section 2, of the Constitution.

Federal Rules of Civil Procedure (FRCP) The rules controlling all procedural matters in civil trials brought before the federal district courts.

Fee Simple Ownership rights entitling the holder to use, possess, or dispose of the property however he or she chooses during his or her lifetime.

Felony A crime—such as arson, murder, rape, or robbery—that carries the most severe sanctions. Sanctions range from one year in a state or federal prison to life imprisonment or (in some states) the death penalty.

Fiduciary Relationship A relationship involving a high degree of trust and confidence.

File Transfer Protocol (FTP) An interface program that connects one computer to another over the Internet to copy files.

Fixed Fee A fee paid to the attorney by his or her client for having rendered a specified legal service, such as the creation of a simple will.

Forms File A reference file containing copies of the firm's commonly used legal documents and informational forms. The documents in the forms file serve as a model for drafting new documents.

Freelance Paralegal A paralegal who operates his or her own business and provides services to attorneys on a contractual basis. A freelance paralegal works under the supervision of an attorney, who assumes responsibility for the paralegal's work product.

Friendly Witness A witness who gives voluntary testimony at an attorney's request on behalf of the attorney's client; a witness who is prejudiced against the client's adversary.

Garnishment A proceeding in which a creditor legally seizes a portion of a debtor's property (such as wages) that is in the possession of a third party (such as an employer).

General Licensing A type of licensing in which all individuals within a specific profession or group (such as paralegals) must meet licensing requirements imposed by the state before they may legally practice their profession.

Grand Jury The group of citizens called to decide whether probable cause exists to believe that a suspect committed the crime with which he or she has been charged.

Headnote A note near the beginning of a reported case summarizing the court's ruling on an issue.

Hearsay An oral or written statement made by an out-of-court declarant that is later offered in court by a witness (not the declarant) concerning a matter before the court. Hearsay is generally not admissible as evidence.

Holding The binding legal principle, or precedent, that is drown from the court's decision in a case.

Home Page The main page of a Web site. Often, the home page serves as a table of contents to other pages at the site.

Hornbook A secondary source presented as a single-volume scholarly discussion, or treatise, on a particular legal subject (such as property law).

Hostile Witness A witness for the opposing side in a lawsuit or other legal proceeding; an adverse witness.

Hung Jury A jury whose members are so irreconcilably divided in their opinions that they cannot reach a verdict. The judge in this situation may order a new trial.

Hypertext Transfer Protocol (http) An interface program that enables computers to communicate. Hypertext is a database system by which distinct objects, such as text and graphics, can be linked. Protocol is a system of formats and rules, such as the speed of a transmission.

Hypothetical Question A question based on hypothesis, conjecture, or fiction.

Immigration Law All laws that set forth the requirements that persons must meet if they wish to visit or immigrate to the United States.

Impeach To call into question the credibility of a witness by challenging the truth or accuracy of his or her trial statement.

Independent Paralegal A paralegal who offers services directly to the public, normally for a fee, without attorney supervision. Independent paralegals assist consumers by supplying them with forms and procedural knowledge relating to simple or routine legal procedures.

Independent Regulatory Agency A type of administrative agency that is more independent of presidential control than an executive agency. Officials of independent regulatory agencies cannot be removed without cause.

Indictment A charge or written accusation, issued by a grand jury, that probable cause exists to believe that a named person has committed a crime.

Information A formal accusation or complaint, usually issued by a prosecuting attorney, against a criminal suspect. The information initiates the criminal litigation process.

Informative Letter A letter that conveys certain information to a client, a witness, an adversary's counsel, or other person regarding some legal matter (such as the date, time, place, and purpose of a meeting).

Injunction A court decree ordering a person to do or refrain from doing a certain act or activity.

Intellectual Property Property resulting from intellectual, creative processes—the products of an individual's mind. Examples of intellectual property are patents, trademarks, copyrights, and trade secrets.

Intentional Tort A wrongful act knowingly committed that interferes with the interests of another in a way not permitted by law.

International Law The law that governs relations among nations. International customs and treaties are generally considered to be two of the most important sources of inter-national law.

Internet Service Provider (ISP) a company that provides dedicated access to the Internet, generally through a local phone number.

Interrogatories A series of written questions for which written answers are prepared and then signed under oath by a party to a lawsuit (the plaintiff or the defendant).

Interviewee The person who is being interviewed.

Inter Vivos **Trust** A trust created by the grantor (settlor) and effective during the grantor's lifetime—that is, a trust not established by a will.

Intestacy Laws State statutes that specify how property will be distributed when a person dies intestate (without a valid will).

Intestate The state of having died without a valid will.

Investigation Plan A plan that lists each step involved in obtaining and verifying the facts and information that are relevant to the legal problem being investigated.

Joint and Several Liability In partnership law, joint and several liability means that a third party may sue one or more of the partners separately or all of them together. This is true even if one of the partners sued did not participate or know about whatever gave rise to the cause of action.

Joint Liability Shared liability. In partnership law, partners incur joint liability for partnership obligations and debts.

Joint Tenancy The joint ownership of property by two or more co-owners in which each co-owner owns an undivided portion of the property. On the death of one of the joint tenants, his or her interest automatically passes to the surviving joint tenant or tenants.

Judgment Creditor A creditor who is legally entitled, by a court's judgment, to collect the amount of the judgment from a debtor.

Judgment The court's final decision regarding the rights and claims of the parties to a lawsuit.

Jurisdiction The authority of a court to hear and decide a specific action.

Justiciable Controversy A controversy that is real and substantial, as opposed to hypothetical or academic.

Key Number A number (accompanied by the symbol of a key) corresponding to a specific topic within West's key-number system to facilitate legal research of case law.

KeyCite An aid to legal research developed by the editors of Westlaw(r). On Westlaw(r), KeyCite can trace case history, retrieve secondary sources, categorize legal citations by legal issue, and perform other functions.

Laches The equitable doctrine that bars a party's right to legal action if the party has neglected for an unreasonable length of time to act on his or her rights.

Law Clerk In the context of law-office work, a law student who works as an apprentice, during the summer or part-time during the school year, with an attorney or a law firm to gain practical legal experience.

Law A body of rules of conduct with legal force and effect, prescribed by the controlling authority (the government) of a society.

Lay Witness A witness who can truthfully and accurately testify on a fact in question without having specialized training or knowledge; an ordinary witness.

Leading Question A question that suggests, or "leads to," a desired answer. Generally, in court leading questions may be asked only of hostile witnesses. A question that suggests, or "leads to," a desired answer. Interviewers may use leading questions to elicit responses from witnesses who otherwise would not be forthcoming.

Lease In real-property law, a contract by which the owner of real property (the landlord) grants to a person (the tenant) an exclusive right to use and possess the property, usually for a specified period of time, in return for rent or some other form of payment.

Legal Administrator An administrative employee of a law firm who manages the day-to-day operations of the firm. In smaller law firms, legal administrators are usually called office managers.

Legal-Assistant Manager An employee in a law firm who is responsible for overseeing the paralegal staff and paralegal professional development.

Legal Nurse Consultant (LNC) A nurse who consults with legal professionals and others about medical aspects of legal claims or issues. Legal nurse consultants normally must have at least a bachelor's degree in nursing and a significant amount of nursing experience.

Legislative Rule A rule created by an administrative agency that is as legally binding as a law enacted by a legislature.

Licensing A government's official act of granting permission to an individual, such as an attorney, to do something that would be illegal in the absence of such permission.

Limited Liability Company (LLC) A hybrid form of business organization authorized by a state in which the owners of the business have limited liability and taxes on profits are passed through the business entity to the owners.

Limited Liability Limited Partnership (LLLP) A type of limited partnership in which the general partner has the same liability as the limited partner. In other words, the liability of all partners is limited to the amount of their investments in the firm.

Limited Liability Partnership (LLP) A hybrid form of business organization authorized by a state that allows professionals to enjoy the tax benefits of a partnership while limiting in some way the normal joint and several liability of partners.

Limited Licensing A type of licensing in which a limited number of individuals within a specific profession or group (such as independent paralegals within the paralegal profession) must meet licensing requirements imposed by the state before those individuals may legally practice their profession.

Limited Partnership A partnership consisting of one or more general partners (who manage the business and are liable to the full extent of their personal assets for debts of the partnership) and of one or more limited partners (who contribute only assets and are liable only up to the amount of their contributions).

Liquidation In regard to corporations, the process by which corporate assets are converted into cash and distributed among creditors and shareholders according to specific rules of preference.

Listserv List A list of e-mail addresses of persons who have agreed to receive e-mail about a particular topic.

Litigation Paralegals Paralegals who specialize in assisting attorneys in the litigation process.

Litigation The process of working a lawsuit through the court system.

Long Arm Statute A state statute that permits a state to obtain jurisdiction over nonresident individuals and corporations. Individuals or corporations, however, must have certain "minimum contacts" with that state for the statute to apply.

Magistrate A public civil officer or official with limited judicial authority, such as the authority to issue an arrest warrant.

Malpractice Professional misconduct or negligence—the failure to exercise due care—on the part of a professional, such as an attorney or a physician.

Managing Partner The partner in a law firm who makes decisions relating to the firm's policies and procedures and who generally oversees the business operations of the firm.

Mandatory Authority Any source of law that a court must follow when deciding a case. Mandatory authorities include constitutions, statutes, and regulations that govern the issue before the court, and court decisions made by a superior court in the jurisdiction.

Mediation A method of settling disputes outside of court by using the services of a neutral third party, who acts as a communicating agent between the parties; a method of dispute settlement that is less formal than arbitration.

Mediation Arbitration (Med-Arb) A form of ADR in which an arbitrator attempts first to help the parties reach an agreement, just as a mediator would. If no agreement is reached, then formal arbitration is undertaken, and the arbitrator issues a legally binding decision.

Memorandum of Law A document (known as a brief in some states) that delineates the legal theories, statutes, and cases on which a motion is based.

Mens Rea A wrongful mental state, or intent. A wrongful mental state is a requirement for criminal liability. What constitutes a wrongful mental state varies according to the nature of the crime. For the crime of murder to exist, for example, the required *mens rea* is the intent to take another person's life.

Merger A process in which one corporation (the surviving corporation) acquires all of the assets and liabilities of another corporation (the merged corporation).

Mini-Trial A private proceeding that assists disputing parties in determining whether to take their case to court. During the proceeding, each party's attorney briefly argues the party's case before the other party and (usually) a neutral third party, who acts as an adviser. If the parties fail to reach an agreement, the adviser renders an opinion as to how a court would likely decide the issue.

***Miranda* Rights** The constitutional rights of accused persons taken into custody by law enforcement officials. Following the United States Supreme Court's decision in *Miranda v. Arizona*, on taking an accused person into custody, the arresting officer must inform the person of certain constitutional rights, such as the suspect's right to remain silent or right to counsel.

Mirror Site A Web site that duplicates an already existing site. A mirror site is used to improve the availability of access to a site that receives a lot of traffic or is distant from some users.

Misdemeanor A less serious crime than a felony, punishable by a fine or incarceration for up to one year in jail (not a state or federal penitentiary).

Mortgage A written instrument giving a creditor an interest in the debtor's property as security for a debt.

Motion A procedural request or application presented by an attorney to the court on behalf of a client.

Motion *in Limine* A motion requesting that certain evidence not be brought out at the trial, such as prejudicial, irrelevant, or legally inadmissible evidence.

Motion Challenging the Sufficiency of the Indictment A motion claiming that the evidence submitted by the prosecutor was insufficient to establish probable cause that the defendant committed the crime with which he or she has been charged.

Motion for a Change of Venue A motion requesting that a trial be moved to a different location to ensure a fair and impartial proceeding, for the convenience of the parties, or for some other acceptable reason.

Motion for a Directed Verdict (Motion for Judgment as a Matter of Law) A motion requesting that the court grant a judgment in favor of the party making the motion on the ground that the other party has not produced sufficient evidence to support his or her claim.

Motion for a New Trial A motion asserting that the trial was so fundamentally flawed (because of error, newly discovered evidence, prejudice, or other reason) that a new trial is needed to prevent a miscarriage of justice.

Motion for Discovery and Inspection A motion requesting permission from the court to obtain evidence in the adversary's possession.

Motion for Judgment Notwithstanding the Verdict A motion (also referred to as a motion for judgment as a matter of law in federal courts) requesting that the court grant judgment in favor of the party making the motion on the ground that the jury verdict against him or her was unreasonable or erroneous.

Motion for Judgment on the Pleadings A motion, which can be brought by either party to a lawsuit after the pleadings are closed, for the court to decide the issue without proceeding to trial. The motion will be granted only if no facts are in dispute and the only issue concerns how the law applies to a set of undisputed facts.

Motion for Summary Judgment A motion requesting the court to enter a judgment without proceeding to trial. The motion can be based on evidence outside the pleadings and will be granted only if no facts are in dispute and the only issue concerns how the law applies to a set of undisputed facts.

Motion to Dismiss A pleading in which a defendant admits the facts as alleged by the plaintiff but asserts that the plaintiff's claim fails to state a cause of action (that is, has no basis in law) or that there are other grounds on which a suit should be dismissed.

Motion to Reduce the Amount of Bail A motion requesting that the bail needed to release the defendant be lowered because it is unreasonably high under the circumstances and may violate the Eighth Amendment's prohibition against excessive bail.

Motion to Suppress Evidence A motion requesting that certain evidence be excluded from consideration during the trial.

National Association of Legal Assistants (NALA) One of the two largest national paralegal associations in the United States; formed in 1975. NALA is actively involved in paralegal professional development.

National Federation of Paralegal Associations (NFPA) One of the two largest national paralegal associations in the United States; formed in 1974. NFPA is actively involved in paralegal professional development.

National Law Law that pertains to a particular nation (as opposed to international law).

Negligence The failure to exercise the standard of care that a reasonable person would exercise in similar circumstances.

Negotiation A method of alternative dispute resolution in which disputing parties, with or without the assistance of their attorneys, meet informally to resolve the dispute out of court.

Networking Making personal connections and cultivating relationships with people in a certain field, profession, or area of interest.

Newsgroup (usenet group) An online bulletin board service (BBS), also known as a usenet group. A newsgroup, or BBS, is a forum, or discussion group, that usually focuses on a particular topic.

Nolo Contendere Latin for "I will not contest it." A criminal defendant's plea in which he or she chooses not to challenge, or contest, the charges brought by the government. Although the defendant may still be sentenced or fined, the plea neither admits nor denies guilt.

Offer A promise to do something in return for something of value.

Office Manager An administrative employee who manages the day-to-day operations of a business firm. In larger law firms, office managers are usually called legal administrators.

Officer A person hired by corporate directors to assist in the management of the day-to-day operations of the corporation. Corporate officers include the corporate president, vice president, secretary, treasurer, and possibly others, such as a chief financial officer and chief executive officer. Corporate officers are employees of the corporation and subject to employment contracts.

Open-Ended Question A question that is phrased in such a way that it elicits a relatively detailed discussion of an experience or event.

Opening Statement An attorney's statement to the jury at the beginning of the trial. The attorney briefly outlines the evidence that will be offered during the trial and the legal theory that will be pursued.

Opinion A statement by the court setting forth the applicable law and the reasons for its decision in a case.

Opinion (Advisory) Letter A letter from an attorney to a client containing a legal opinion on an issue raised by the client's question or legal claim. The opinion is based on a detailed analysis of the law.

Ordinance An order, rule, or law enacted by a municipal or county government to govern a local matter unaddressed by state or federal legislation.

Original Jurisdiction The power of a court to take a case, try it, and decide it.

Overtime Wages Wages paid to workers who are paid an hourly wage rate to compensate them for overtime work (hours worked beyond forty hours per week). Under federal law, overtime wages are at least one and a half times the regular hourly wage rate.

Paralegal (or Legal Assistant) A person sufficiently trained or experienced in the law and legal procedures to assist attorneys in the delivery of legal services to the public or to perform legal work as otherwise authorized by law.

Paralegal Certificate A certificate awarded to an individual with a high school diploma or its equivalent who has successfully completed a paralegal program of study at a private, for-profit business school, trade school, or college.

Parallel Citation A second (or third) citation to another case reporter in which a case has been published. When a case is published in more than one reporter, each citation is a parallel citation to the other(s).

Partner A person who has undertaken to operate a business jointly with one or more other persons. Each partner is a co-owner of the business firm.

Partnership An association of two or more persons to carry on, as co-owners, a business for profit.

Party With respect to lawsuits, the plaintiff or the defendant. Some cases involve multiple parties (more than one plaintiff or defendant).

Patent A government grant that gives an inventor the exclusive right or privilege to make, use, or sell his or her invention for a limited time period.

Peremptory Challenge A *voir dire* challenge to exclude a potential juror from serving on the jury without any supporting reason or cause. Peremptory challenges based on racial or gender criteria are illegal.

Personal Liability An individual's personal responsibility for debts or obligations. The owners of sole proprietorships and partnerships are personally liable for the debts and obligations incurred by their business firms. If their firms go bankrupt or cannot meet debts as they become due, the owners will be personally responsible for paying the debts.

Personal Property Any property that is not real property. Generally, any property that is movable or intangible is classified as personal property.

Persuasive Authority Any legal authority, or source of law, that a court may look to for guidance but on which it need not rely in making its decision. Persuasive authorities include cases from other jurisdictions and secondary sources of law, such as scholarly treatises.

Petty Offense In criminal law, the least serious kind of wrong, such as a traffic or building-code violation.

Plain-Meaning Rule A rule of statutory interpretation. If the meaning of a statute is clear on its face, then that is the interpretation the court will give to it; inquiry into the legislative history of the statute will not be undertaken.

Plaintiff A party who initiates a lawsuit.

Plea Bargaining The process by which the accused and the prosecutor in a criminal case work out a mutually satisfactory disposition of the case, subject to court approval. Usually, plea bargaining involves the defendant's pleading guilty to a lesser offense in return for a lighter sentence.

Pleadings Statements by the plaintiff and the defendant that detail the facts, charges, and defenses involved in the litigation.

Pocket Part A separate pamphlet containing recent cases or changes in the law that is used to update hornbooks, legal encyclopedias, and other legal authorities. It is called a "pocket part" because it slips into a sleeve, or pocket, in the front or back binder of the volume.

Point Heading A brief recapitulation of the point being made in a section of an appellate brief. Point headings separate the text into logical sections and make the argument easier to follow.

Post-Degree Certificate Post-Degree Certificate A certificate awarded by a college or university to an individual who, having already completed an associate's degree or bachelor's degree program, successfully completes a paralegal program of study.

Potentially Responsible Party (PRP) A party who may be liable under the Comprehensive Environmental Response, Compensation, and Liability Act, or Superfund. Any person who generated hazardous waste, imported hazardous waste, owned or operated a waste site at the time of disposal, or currently owns or operates a site may be responsible for some or all of the clean-up costs involved in removing the hazardous chemicals.

Prayer for Relief A statement at the end of the complaint requesting that the court grant relief to the plaintiff.

Precedent A court decision that furnishes an example or authority for deciding subsequent cases in which identical or similar facts are presented.

Preliminary Hearing An initial hearing in which a magistrate decides if there is probable cause to believe that the defendant committed the crime for which he or she is charged.

Pressure Question A question intended to make the interviewee feel uncomfortable and respond emotionally. Pressure questions are sometimes used by interviewers to elicit answers from interviewees who may otherwise be unresponsive.

Pretrial Conference A conference prior to trial in which the judge and the attorneys litigating the suit discuss settlement possibilities, clarify the issues in dispute, and schedule forthcoming trial-related events.

Primary Source In legal research, a document that establishes the law on a particular issue, such as a case decision, legislative act, administrative rule, or presidential order.

Principal In agency law, a person who, by agreement or otherwise, authorizes another person (the agent) to act on the principal's behalf in such a way that the acts of the agent become binding on the principal.

Privileged Information Confidential communications between certain individuals, such as an attorney and his or her client, that are protected from disclosure except under court order.

Probable Cause Reasonable grounds to believe the existence of facts warranting certain actions, such as the search or arrest of a person.

Probate To prove and validate a will. The process of proving and validating a will and the settling of matters pertaining to the administration of a decedent's estate, guardianship of a decedent's children, and similar matters.

Probate Court A court having jurisdiction over proceedings concerning the settlement of a person's estate.

Procedural Law Rules that define the manner in which the rights and duties of individuals may be enforced.

Product Liability The legal liability of manufacturers and sellers to buyers, users, and bystanders for injuries or damages suffered because of defects in goods purchased. Liability arises when a product has a defective condition that makes it unreasonably dangerous to the user or consumer.

Professional Corporation (P.C.) A firm that is owned by shareholders, who purchase the corporations stock, or shares. The liability of shareholders is often limited to the amount of their investments.

Professional Portfolio A job applicant's collection of selected personal documents (such as school transcripts, writing samples, and certificates) for presentation to a potential employer.

Prospectus A document that discloses relevant facts about a company and its operations so that those who wish to purchase stock (invest) in the corporation have the basis for making an informed decision.

Proximate Cause Legal cause. Proximate cause exists when the connection between an act and an injury is strong enough to justify imposing liability.

Public Defender A court-appointed attorney who is paid by the state to represent a criminal defendant who is unable to hire private counsel.

Public Law Number An identification number that has been assigned to a specific statute, or public law, following the legislative process.

Public Policy A governmental policy based on widely held societal values.

Public Prosecutor An individual, acting as a trial lawyer, who initiates and conducts criminal cases in the government's name and on behalf of the people.

Punitive Damages Damages that are awarded in a civil lawsuit to punish the wrongdoer. Punitive damages are usually awarded only in cases involving willful or malicious misconduct.

Real Estate Land and things permanently attached to the land, such as houses, buildings, and trees and foliage.

Real Property Immovable property consisting of land and the buildings and plant life thereon.

Reasonable Person Standard The standard of behavior expected of a hypothetical "reasonable person." The standard against which negligence is measured and that must be observed to avoid liability for negligence.

Record on Appeal The items submitted during the trial (pleadings, motions, briefs, and exhibits) and the transcript of the trial proceedings that are forwarded to the appellate court for review when a case is appealed.

Recross-Examination The questioning of an opposing witness following the adverse party's redirect examination.

Redirect Examination The questioning of a witness following the adverse party's cross-examination.

Reference Line The portion of the letter that indicates the matter to be discussed in the letter, such as "RE: Summary of Cases Applying the Family and Medical Leave Act of 1993." The reference line is placed just below the address block and above the salutation.

Reformation An equitable remedy granted by a court to correct, or "reform," a written contract so that it reflects the true intentions of the parties.

Relevant Evidence Evidence tending to make a fact in question more or less probable than it would be without the evidence. Only relevant evidence is admissible in court.

Remand An appellate court's decision to send a case back to the trial court for further proceedings.

Remedy at Law A remedy available in a court of law. Money damages are awarded as a remedy at law.

Remedy in Equity A remedy allowed by courts in situations where remedies at law are not appropriate. Remedies in equity are based on settled rules of fairness, justice, and honesty.

Reply Brief An appellate brief filed by the appellant to rebut (counter) arguments made by the appellee in the appellee's brief.

Reporter A publication in which court cases are published, or reported.

Reprimand A disciplinary sanction in which an attorney is rebuked for his or her misbehavior. Although a reprimand is the mildest sanction for attorney misconduct, it is nonetheless a serious one and may significantly damage the attorney's reputation in the legal community.

Rescission A remedy whereby a contract is terminated and the parties are returned to the positions they occupied before the contract was made.

Respondeat Superior A doctrine in agency law under which a principal-employer may be held liable for the wrongful acts committed by agents or employees while acting within the scope of their agency or employment.

Restitution An equitable remedy under which a person is restored to his or her original position prior to loss or injury, or placed in the position that he or she would have been in had the breach not occurred.

Retainer An advance payment made by a client to a law firm to cover part of the legal fees and/or costs that will need to be incurred on that client's behalf.

Retainer Agreement A signed document stating that the attorney or the law firm has been hired by the client to provide certain legal services and that the client agrees to pay for those services in accordance with the terms set forth in the retainer agreement.

Return-of-Service Form A document signed by a process server and submitted to the court to prove that a defendant received a summons.

Reverse An appellate court's decision that is contrary to the judgment of the trial court.

Rule of Four A rule of the United States Supreme Court under which the Court will not issue a writ of certiorari unless at least four justices approve of the decision to issue the writ.

Rulemaking The actions undertaken by administrative agencies when formally adopting new regulations or amending old ones.

Rules of Construction The rules that control the judicial interpretation of statutes.

Rules of Evidence Rules governing the admissibility of evidence in trial courts.

Sales Contract A contract for the sale of goods, as opposed to a contract for the sale of services, real property, or intangible property. Sales contracts are governed by Article 2 of the Uniform Commercial Code.

Salutation The formal greeting to the addressee of the letter. The salutation is placed just below the reference line.

Search Warrant A written order, based on probable cause and issued by a judge or public official (magistrate), commanding that police officers or criminal investigators search a specific person, place, or property to obtain evidence.

Secondary Source In legal research, any publication that indexes, summarizes, or interprets the law, such as a legal encyclopedia, a treatise, or an article in a law review.

Self-Defense The legally recognized privilege to protect oneself or one's property against injury by another. The privilege of self-defense only protects acts that are reasonably necessary to protect oneself or one's property.

Self-Incrimination The act of giving testimony that implicates one's own guilt or participation in criminal wrongdoing. The Fifth Amendment to the Constitution states that no person "shall be compelled in any criminal case to be a witness against himself."

Self-Regulation The regulation of the conduct of a professional group by members of the group themselves. Self-regulation usually involves the establishment of ethical or professional standards of behavior with which members of the group must comply.

Sentence The punishment, or penalty, ordered by the court to be inflicted on a person convicted of a crime.

Service of Process The delivery of the summons and the complaint to a defendant.

Session Laws Statutes passed by legislators that are officially published chronologically, by order of legislative session, in a multivolume set.

Settlement Agreement An out-of-court resolution to a legal dispute, which is agreed to by the parties in writing. A settlement agreement may be reached at any time prior to or during a trial.

Sexual Harassment In the employment context, the hiring or granting of job promotions or other benefits in return for sexual favors (*quid pro quo* harassment) or language or conduct that is so sexually offensive that it creates a hostile working environment (hostile-environment harassment).

Share A unit of stock; a measure of ownership interest in a corporation.

Shareholder One who purchases corporate stock, or shares, and who thus becomes an owner of the corporation.

Slip Law The first official publication of a statute that comes out shortly after the legislation is passed (presented as a single sheet or pamphlet).

Slip Opinion A judicial opinion published shortly after the decision is made and not yet included in a case reporter or advance sheets.

Sole Proprietorship The simplest form of business, in which the owner is the business. Anyone who does business without creating a formal business entity has a sole proprietorship.

Specific Performance An equitable remedy requiring exactly the performance that was specified in a contract; usually granted only when money damages would be an inadequate remedy and the subject matter of the contract is unique (for example, real property).

Staff Attorney An attorney who is hired by a law firm as an employee and who has no ownership rights in the firm.

Standing to Sue The requirement that an individual must have a sufficient stake in a controversy before he or she can bring a lawsuit. The plaintiff must demonstrate that he or she either has been injured or threatened with injury.

Stare Decisis A flexible doctrine of the courts, recognizing the value of following prior decisions (precedents) in cases similar to the one before the court; the courts' practice of being consistent with prior decisions based on similar facts.

State Bar Association An association of attorneys within a state. Membership in the state bar association is mandatory in over two-thirds of the states—that is, before an attorney can practice law in a state, he or she must be admitted to that state's bar association.

Statute A written law enacted by a legislature under its constitutional lawmaking authority.

Statute of Frauds A state statute that requires certain types of contracts to be in writing to be enforceable.

Statute of Limitations A statute setting the maximum time period within which certain actions can be brought or rights enforced. After the period of time has run, no legal action can be brought.

Statutory Law Laws enacted by a legislative body.

Strict Liability Liability regardless of fault. In tort law, strict liability may be imposed on those who engage in abnormally dangerous activities that cause harm to others, on merchants who introduce into commerce goods that are unreasonably dangerous, and in certain other situations.

Submission Agreement A written agreement to submit a legal dispute to an arbitrator or arbitrating panel for resolution.

Subpoena A document commanding a person to appear at a certain time and place to give testimony concerning a certain matter.

Substantive Law Law that defines the rights and duties of individuals with respect to each other, as opposed to procedural law, which defines the manner in which these rights and duties may be enforced.

Summary Jury Trial (SJT) A method of settling disputes (used in some federal courts) in which a trial is held but the jury's verdict is not binding. The verdict only acts as a guide to both sides in reaching an agreement during the mandatory negotiations that immediately follow the trial. If a settlement is not reached, both sides have the right to a full trial later.

Summons A document served on a defendant in a lawsuit informing the defendant that a legal action has been commenced against him or her and that the defendant must appear in court on a certain date to answer the plaintiff's complaint.

Support Personnel Those employees who provide clerical, secretarial, or other support to the legal, paralegal, and administrative staff of a law firm.

Supporting Affidavit An affidavit accompanying a motion that is filed by an attorney on behalf of his or her client. The sworn statements in the affidavit provide a factual basis for the motion.

Supremacy Clause The provision in Article VI of the U.S. Constitution that provides that the Constitution, laws, and treaties of the United States are "the supreme Law of the Land." Under this clause, state and local laws that directly conflict with federal law will be rendered invalid.

Suspension A serious disciplinary sanction in which an attorney who has violated an ethical rule or a law is prohibited from practicing law in the state for a specified or an indefinite period of time.

Syllabus A brief summary of the holding and legal principles involved in a reported case, which is followed by the court's official opinion.

Table of Cases An alphabetical list of the cases that have been cited or reproduced in a legal text, case digest, or other legal source.

Tenancy in Common A form of co-ownership of property in which each party owns an undivided interest that passes to his or her heirs at death.

Testamentary Trust A trust that is created by will and that does not take effect until the death of the testator.

Testate The condition of having died with a valid will.

Testator One who makes a valid will.

Third Parties Persons or entities that are not directly involved in an agreement (such as a contract), legal proceeding (such as a lawsuit), or relationship (such as an attorney-client relationship).

Time Slip A record documenting, for billing purposes, the hours (or fractions of hours) that an attorney or a paralegal worked for each client, the date on which the work was done, and the type of work that was undertaken.

Tort A civil (as opposed to a criminal) wrong not arising from a breach of contract. A breach of a legal duty, owed by the defendant to the plaintiff, that caused the plaintiff to suffer harm.

Toxic Tort A wrongful act (tort) that occurs when a person or business fails to properly use or clean up toxic chemicals that cause harm to a person or to society.

Trade Journal A newsletter, magazine, or other periodical that provides a certain trade or profession with information (products, trends, or developments) relating to that trade or profession.

Trade Secret Information or a process that gives a business an advantage over competitors who do not know the information or process.

Trademark A distinctive mark or motto that a manufacturer affixes to the goods it produces to distinguish the goods from goods produced by other manufacturers.

Treatise In legal research, a text that provides a systematic, detailed, and scholarly review of a particular legal subject.

Treaty An agreement, or compact, formed between two independent nations.

Trial Court A court in which most cases usually begin and in which questions of fact are examined.

Trial Notebook A binder that contains copies of all of the documents and information that an attorney will need to have at hand during the trial.

Trust An arrangement in which property is transferred by one person (the grantor, or settlor) to another (the trustee) for the benefit of a third party (the beneficiary).

Trust Account A bank or escrow account in which one party (the trustee, such as an attorney) holds funds belonging to another person (such as a client); a bank account into which funds advanced to a law firm by a client are deposited.

Unathorized Practice of Law (UPL) The act of engaging in actions defined by a legal authority, such as a state legislature, as constituting the "practice of law" without legal authorization to do so.

Unconscionable Contract A contract so unfair, oppressive, or one sided that it "shocks the conscience" of the court. If a court deems a contract to be unconscionable, the court will not enforce it.

Uniform Commercial Code (UCC) A uniform code of laws governing commercial transactions that has been adopted in part or in its entirety by all of the states. Article 2 of the UCC governs contracts for the sale of goods.

Venue The geographical district in which an action is tried and from which the jury is selected.

Verdict A formal decision made by a jury.

Vicarious Liability Legal responsibility placed on one person for the acts of another.

Voir Dire A proceeding in which attorneys for the plaintiff and the defendant ask prospective jurors questions to determine whether potential jury members are biased or have any connection with a party to the action or with a prospective witness.

Warranty An express or implied promise by a seller that specific goods to be sold meet certain criteria, or standards of performance, on which the buyer may rely.

Will A document directing how and to whom the maker's property and obligations are to be transferred on his or her death.

Winding Up The process of winding up all business affairs (collecting and distributing the firm's assets) after a partnership or corporation has been dissolved.

Witness A person who is asked to testify under oath at a trial.

Witness Statement The written transcription of a statement made by the witness during an interview and signed by the witness.

Work Product An attorney's mental impressions, conclusions, and legal theories regarding a case being prepared on behalf of a client. Work product normally is regarded as privileged information.

Workers' Compensation Laws State statutes that establish an administrative procedure for compensating workers for injuries that arise out of or in the course of their employment, regardless of fault.

World Wide Web a hypertext-based system through which specially formatted documents are accessible on the Internet.

Writ of *Certiorari* A writ from a higher court asking the lower court for the record of a case for review.

Writ of Execution A writ that puts in force a court's decree or judgment.

INDEX

A

AAA (American Arbitration Association), 200, 203
AAfPE. *See* American Association for Paralegal Education
ABA. *See* American Bar Association
ABA-approved programs, 11
Abstract, 238
Acceptance, 223–224, 233
Acquisition, 272
Acquittal, 441
Active listening, 459–460
Actus reus (guilty act), 417
ADA. *See* Americans with Disabilities Act
Address block, 606–607
Adjudication by administrative agencies, 294, 297–298
Administrative agency(ies)
   adjudication by, 294, 297–298
   administrative process and, 295–298
   creation and function of, 155
   defined, 153
   as employer, 32
   enabling legislation and, 155, 290, 294
   enforcement by, 294, 296–298
   examples of, 156
   executive agency as, 290–291
   hearing before, 297, 298
   independent regulatory agency as, 291
   investigation by, 296–297
   paralegal practice before, 100, 290, 299–300
   powers of, 293–295
   rulemaking by, 294, 295–296
   state, 298
   types of, 290–292
   See also Administrative law
Administrative law, 153, 155–156, 290–301
   defined, 153, 290
   finding tools for, 526
   and the paralegal, 155–156, 300–301
   researching, 525–526
   Shepard's Code of Federal Regulations Citations and, 530–532
   See also Administrative agency(ies)
Administrative law judge (ALJ), 297, 298
Administrative Procedure Act (APA)(1946), 295, 299–300
Administrative process, 295–298
Administrator, 39, 245
ADR. *See* Alternative dispute resolution
Advertising, deceptive, 302–303
Advisory (opinion) letters, 610–611, 612
Affidavit
   defined, 245, 341
   supporting, 352
Affiliates, 7
Affirmation of judgment, 404, 588
Affirmative defenses, 349, 352
Age
   credit discrimination on basis of, 305
   employment discrimination on basis of, 123, 202, 319
Age Discrimination in Employment Act (1967), 202, 319
Agency law, 259–261
   the paralegal and, 260–261
Agency relationship(s)
   defined, 259
   third parties and, 259–260
Agent(s)
   defined, 259
   escrow, 233–235, 238
   paralegal as, 260
   real-estate, 250
   subagent and, 260
Agreement(s)
   bilateral, 171
   contractual, 222–224
   family settlement, 246
   multilateral, 171
   retainer, 128–129
   settlement, 196, 197
      family, 246
   submission, 201–202
Ahalt, Arthur, 195
Air pollution, 310
ALI. *See* American Law Institute
Alibi, 420
ALJ (administrative law judge), 297, 298
All In One Search, 553
Almanacs, 571
AltaVista, 552
Alternate jurors, 393–394
Alternative dispute resolution (ADR), 194–207
   arbitration as. *See* Arbitration
   early neutral case evaluation and, 202

729

mediation as. *See* Mediation
mini-trial, 202
negotiation as. *See* Negotiation
the paralegal and, 205–207
providers of services in, 203–205
summary jury trial (SJT) as, 203
American Arbitration Association (AAA), 200, 203
American Association for Paralegal Education (AAfPE)
  defined, 3
  functions of, 8
  paralegal defined by, 4
  regulation of paralegals and, 106, 108
American Association of Legal Nurse Consultants, 45
American Bar Association (ABA)
  approved program of, 11
  "Associate Member" category of, for legal assistants, 7
  attorney regulation and, 73
  Canons of Ethics of, 75
  defined, 3
  double billing and, 137
  ethical opinions issued by, 572
  Model Code of Professional Responsibility of. *See* Model Code
  Model Guidelines for the Utilization of Legal Assistant Services of, 96
    disclosure of paralegal status and, 100–101
    illustrated, 97
  Model Rules of Professional Conduct of. *See* Model Rules
  paralegal defined by, 4
  professional status of paralegals recognized by, 7
  role of, in paralegal education, 10–11
  Standing Committee of, on Legal Assistants, 7, 96
  Uniform Probate Code (UPC) approved by, 245
American Civil Liberties Union, 621
American Digest System (West Group), 500–501, 526
  excerpt from, illustrated, 502
  illustrated, 501

American Journalism Review Web site, 576
American Jurisprudence, Second Edition *(Am.Jur.2d.)*(West Group), 493, 503, 523
  excerpt from, illustrated, 494
  illustrated, 493
American Law Institute (ALI), 162, 225, 416n, 503–505
  Web site of, 512
American Law Reports (A.L.R.) (West Group), 501–503, 523
  annotations from, 502–503
    illustrated, 505
  Blue Book of Supplemental Decisions of, 503
    page from, illustrated, 506
  Federal Quick Index of, 502
    excerpt from, illustrated, 504
    illustrated, 503
  Later Case Service of, 503
    page from, illustrated, 507
  Shepard's Citations and, 530
  Statutes Edition of Shepard's United States Citations and, 530
  updating supplements to, 503
American Medical Association (AMA), Web site of, 474, 558
American Paralegal Association, 8
American system of justice, 179–186
  the paralegal and, 184–186
Americans with Disabilities Act (ADA)(1990), 319–320
  excerpt from, illustrated, 593
  reading, 592–594
Amicus curiae brief, 621
AMLaw Tech, 569
Analysis
  of case law, 583–592, 629
  of cases, 589
    for specific performance, 161
  defined, 14
  IRAC method of, 618, 619, 629
  objective, 597
  of statutory law, 592–595
Analytical skills, 14
And, or *versus,* 594
Annotation(s), 495, 502–503
Answer, 349–352
  affirmative defenses and, 349, 352

counterclaim and, 352
defined, 79, 349
illustrated, 350–351
Antitrust law, 153
APA (Administrative Procedure Act)(1946), 295, 299–300
Appeal(s)
  court of. *See* Appellate court(s)
  criminal, 446
  defined, 403
  notice of, 404
  record on, 404
  of verdict, 403–405, 446
Appellant
  brief of, 621
  defined, 404, 621
Appellate brief(s), 404, 620–628
  defined, 583, 620
  effective, writing, 621–628
  sections of, 622–628
  types of, 621
Appellate court(s)
  decisions of, 491–492
    on a case, 588–589
    reporting of. *See* Case reporting system
  defined, 181
  federal, 191, 192
  options of, 404–405
  oral arguments before, 404
  state
    highest (supreme), 188–189, 491
    intermediate, 188
Appellate jurisdiction, 180–181
Appellee
  brief of, 621
  defined, 404, 621
Appraisals, 250
Arbitration, 200–202, 203
  award in, 201
  clause requiring, 200
  of commercial contracts, 205
  defined, 200
  mediation (med-arb), 202
  potential problems with, ethics and, 201
  process of, 200–202
    courts' role in, 201–202
Arbitration clause, 200
Area codes, 571
Arraignment, 435–436
Arrest, 426, 428–429

defined, 426
  investigation after, 431–432
Arrest warrant, 429
Articles
  of consolidation, 271
  of incorporation
    defined, 267
    illustrated, 268
    information generally
      included in, 269
    preparing, 282
  of merger, 271
  of organization, 273
Assault, 216
Assets, locating, 406
"Assisted negotiation," 202
Associate's degree, 10
Association Web sites, 574
Assumption of risk, 218
Attorney(s)
  attorney-client privilege and. *See*
    Attorney-client privilege
  city, 415
  county, 415
  deponent's, role of, 366–368
  disbarment of, 75
  discipline board and, 109
  district, 415
  in England, 172
  ethical codes and rules of,
    paralegal practice and,
    77–89
  confidentiality and attorney-
    client privilege and,
    83–86. *See also* Attorney-
    client privilege
  confidentiality of information
    and, 79–83
    violations of, 81–83
  conflict of interest and,
    86–89. *See also*
    Conflict(s) of interest
  duty of competence and,
    77–79. *See also* Duty(ies)
    of competence
  See also Model Code; Model
    Rules
  fees and. *See* Fee(s)
  as law clerk, 6n
  licensing of. *See also* Licensing
  malpractice and, 77, 81,
    166, 218
  name of, on case, 588

personal liability of, 117
prosecuting, 415
regulation of, 72–77
  licensing requirements and,
    74. *See also* Licensing
  participants in, 73–74
  self-, 72
reprimand of, 75
as sole (solo) practitioner, 117
staff, 6
suspension of, 75
work product and, 85, 127–128
Attorney-client privilege
  arising of, 85
  confidentiality and, 83–86
  defined, 83
  duration of, 85–86
  nature of information subject to,
    84–85
Australia, common law system in,
  169
Authentication of evidence, 479
Auto-Cite, 544
Award, arbitration, 201

B
Baby M, In re, 158n
Bachelor's degree, 10
Bail, 434
Bail bondsperson, 434
Bankruptcy Citations, 532
Bankruptcy court, 180
Bankruptcy Digest (West
  Group), 497
Bankruptcy law, 37
Bankruptcy Reporter (West
  Group), 514
Bar associations
  attorney regulation and, 73
  unauthorized practice of law
    and, 103–104
  See also American Bar
    Association
Bargaining
  collective, 317
  plea, 436, 437
Baroudi, Carol, 558
Bates v. State Bar of Arizona,
  73–74
Batson v. Kentucky, 393n
Battery, 216
Beneficiary, 39, 246
Benefits, 46

Beyond a reasonable doubt,
  442–443
Bilateral agreements, 171
Bill, 519
Bill of Rights
  defined, 150, 151
  safeguards under, to protect
    persons accused of crimes,
    421–423, 426
  summarized, 150
Billable hours
  defined, 133
  nonbillable hours *versus,*
    134–136
Billing procedures, 132–136
Binding mediation, 202
"Blank" stock, 275
Blotter, 430
*The Bluebook: A Uniform System
  of Citation* (Harvard Law
  Review Association), 514,
  571, 619
Boling, Anna Durham, 462–463
Bonus, 47
Booking, 430–431
Bragdon v. Abbott, 585–587
Breach
  of contract. *See* Contract(s),
    breach of
  defined, 78
  of duty of care, 217
Brief(s)
  amicus curiae, 621
  appellant's, 621
  appellate. *See* Appellate brief(s)
  appellee's, 621
  of case, 589–590, 591
  legal, case brief *versus,* 590n
  reply, 621
Briefing a case, 589–590, 591
*Brown v. Board of Education of
  Topeka,* 157–158
Business invitee, 490
Business Law Partner (Quicken),
  230
Business organization(s)
  corporation as. *See*
    Corporation(s)
  family limited liability
    partnership (FLLP) as, 276
  forms of, 261–278
  limited liability company (LLC)
    as, 273, 275

limited liability limited
  partnership (LLLP) as,
  275, 276
limited liability partnership
  (LLP) as, 273, 275, 276
limited partnership as, 266
the paralegal and, 276, 278
partnership as. *See*
  Partnership(s)
sole proprietorship as. *See* Sole
  proprietorship(s)

C
CALR. *See* Computer-assisted legal
  research
Canada
  common law system in, 169
  North American Free Trade
    Agreement and, 171
Cancellation of contract, 226
CancerWEB, 474
Capacity
  contractual, 224
  testamentary, 245
Career(s), 27–70
  creating opportunities in, 65–66
  paths of, 65
  planning, 48–49
    checklist for, 54
  reevaluating, 65–67
Case(s)
  on "all fours," 490–491, 583
  analyzing, 589
    for specific performance, 161
  briefing, 589–590, 591
  citation of, 163
  components of, 583–589
  criminal, major procedural steps
    in, summarized, 427
  defendant's, during trial, 399
  disposition of, 588–589
  early neutral evaluation of, 202
  of first impression, 158–159, 492
  flowchart of, illustrated, 332
  as mandatory authority,
    491–492
  parties in, 163
  as persuasive authority, 492
  plaintiff's, during trial, 396–398
  on point, 490–491, 583
  remandment of, 404, 589
  reporting of. *See* Case reporting
    system

summarizing, 589–590
table of, 501
titles of, 163, 587
See also Lawsuit(s)
Case citator. *See* Citator(s)
Case digests, 495–501
Case law(s)
  analyzing, 583–592, 629
  common law tradition and,
    156–167
  defined, 156
  primary source of. *See* Case
    reporting system
  researching, 489–518, 629
    defining the issue and,
      489–490, 491
    goals of, determining,
      490–492
    preliminary steps in, 489–492
    secondary sources and,
      492–511
  secondary sources of, 492–511
  terminology of, 163–164
Case reporting system, 511–518
  citations to. *See* Citation(s)
  federal court decisions in, 514
  state court decisions in,
    511–514
  state reporters and, 511–513
  United States Supreme Court
    decisions in, 514, 515–518
  West's National Reporter System
    and, 513–514, 515, 529
Causation, 217
CD-ROMs, 541–542
Cease-and-desist order, 302–303
Cellular phones, confidentiality
  and, 82
Center for Information Law and
  Policy, 418
Central Intelligence Agency,
  Factbook of, 167
CERCLA (Comprehensive
  Environmental Response,
  Compensation, and Liability
  Act)(Superfund)(1980), 313
Certificate(s)
  of consolidation, 271
  of incorporation (corporate
    charter), 267
  of limited partnership, 266
  of merger, 271
Certification

defined, 11
  by NALA, 11
  state, 12
Certified Legal Assistant (CLA), 11
Certified Legal Assistant Specialist
  (CLAS), 11
Certiorari, writ of, 192, 555
Challenge(s)
  for cause, 393
  defined, 392
  peremptory, 393
  during *voir dire,* 392–394
Chancellor, 159
Charge
  defined, 401
  illustrated, 403
Charitable trust, 247
Charles-Hampton, Charisse A., 356
Chasen, Andrea Nager, 198–199
Checks and balances, 294
Chicago Manual of Style, 597
Child custody, 44
Chronological structure, 598
Circumstantial evidence, 478
Cirrincione v. Johnson, 514
Citation(s)
  case, 587
    guide to, 571
    how to read, 516–517
    understanding, 518
  in criminal procedure, 426
  defined, 163, 514
  format of, 514
  parallel, 514
Citator(s)
  case, 529
  defined, 529
  learning to use, 529–532
  online, 532
  See also Shepard's Citations
City attorney, 415
City directories, 475
Civil cover sheet, illustrated, 344
Civil law
  codified law *versus,* 169–170
  criminal law *versus,* 35
  defined, 35
Civil law system, 169, 170
Civil litigation
  appealing verdict and, 403–405
  discovery in, 356–376
  enforcing judgment and,
    405–406

file of, creating, 334–335
jury selection and, 389–394
pleadings and. *See* Pleadings
posttrial motions and, 402–403, 405
preliminaries of, 333–335
preparing for trial in, 383–388
   checklist for, 384
pretrial conference and, 388–389
pretrial motions and, 353–356
procedural requirements and, 332
before the trial, 330–381
trial notebook and. *See* Trial notebook
trial procedures and, 382–413
See also Trial(s)
Civil Rights Act (1964), Title VII of, 193, 318–319
Civil Rights Commission, 293
CLA (Certified Legal Assistant), 11
CLAS (Certified Legal Assistant Specialist), 11
CLE (Continuing Legal Education) programs, 8, 12–13
Clean Air Acts (1963, 1970), 310
Clean Water Act (1972), 311
Client(s)
  attorney-client privilege and. *See* Attorney-client privilege
  bereaved, interests of, ethics and, 40
  billing of, 132–137
    client complaint regarding, 137
  communicating with, 137–139, 466
  conflict of interest and, 86–89. *See also* Conflict(s) of interest
  consent of, to disclose confidential information, 80–81
  deposition of, preparing for, 366
  disclosure of paralegal status to, 100–101
  documents from
    handling, ethics and, 464
    tips for collecting, 166
  files and. *See* Client file(s)
  following up with, 166, 461
  former, 87, 88
  gifts from, 87–88

intent of, to commit harmful or illegal act, 81, 82
interests of, ethics and, 295
interview of. *See* Client interview(s)
legal action brought by, for malpractice, 81, 218
questions of, about fees, 130
trust accounts and, 131–132
unauthorized practice of law by paralegals and. *See* Unauthorized practice of law
writing to, 611
Client file(s), 123–128
  adding subfiles to, 125
  closing, 125
  confidentiality and, 124
  new, opening, 124
  old, destroying, 125–127
Client interview(s), 18, 460–464, 480
  informational, 462–463
  initial, 333–334, 460
  subsequent, 460–461
Close corporation, 269
Closed-ended questions, 458
Closely held corporation, 269
Closing
  of client file, 125
  of letter, 608
  of sale of real property, 42, 238–239, 243
Closing arguments, 399–401
Closing costs, 238–239
CNN Web site, 565
Code(s)
  area, 571
  defined, 520
  federal, 520–523
    unofficial versions of, 521–523
  state, 525
  zip, 573
Code of Federal Regulations (C.F.R.), 296, 526
  on the Internet, 556, 574
  List of C.F.R. Sections Affected of, 526
    illustrated, 528
  Shepard's Code of Federal Regulations Citations and, 530–532

  subdivisions of titles and provisions in, illustrated, 527
Co-defendants, 163
Codified law, 169–170
Codify (codification), 162–163
Collective bargaining, 317
Color
  credit discrimination on basis of, 305
  employment discrimination on basis of, 193, 318
Commercial online services, 550–551
Commitment, 19–20
Committee reports, 524
Common law
  defined, 157
  in England, 149, 156–157, 169, 309
  environmental remedies and, 309
  paralegal and, 166–167
  precedent and. *See* Precedent
  statutory law and, 162–163
  today, 162
  tradition of, case law and, 156–167
Communication(s)
  client, 137–139, 466
  cyberspace. *See* Electronic communications
  electronic. *See* Electronic communications
  e-mail. *See* Electronic communications
  ex parte, 401
  skills in. *See* Communication skill(s)
Communication skill(s), 15–19
  client communication and, 138
  listening and, 18–19
  reading and, 18
  speaking and, 18
  tips for effective communication and, 16–17
  writing and, 19, 138
Comparative negligence, 218, 352
Complaint
  body of, 340–341
  criminal
    filing, 432–433
    illustrated, 433
  defined, 79, 335

drafting, 337, 340–341
  checklist for, 342
  filing, 341–342, 432–433
  illustrated, 338–339, 433
  serving, 345
Comprehensive Environmental Response, Compensation, and Liability Act (CERCLA)(Superfund) (1980), 313
Computer skills, 14
Computer-assisted legal research (CALR)
  cutting cost of, ethics and, 546
  defined, 541
  See also Lexis©; Westlaw©
Concurrent jurisdiction, 182
Concurrent ownership, 231
Concurring opinion, 164, 588
Confidentiality
  ability to keep confidences and, 21
  administrative practice and, 301
  client files and, 124
  of correspondence, ethics and, 608
  electronic communications and, 82–83, 84
  of information, 79–83, 357
  social events and, 83
Confirmation letters, 610
Conflict(s)
  of interest, 86–89
    checks for, 89
    defined, 86
    former clients and, 87
    simultaneous representation and, 86–87
    walling-off procedures and, 87, 88
  in the workplace, managing, 139
Conflicts check, 89
Congressional Information Service (C.I.S.), 525, 526
Congressional Record, 524–525
  on the Internet, 574
Consideration, 224
Consolidation
  defined, 271
  illustrated, 272
Constitution(s)
  state, 151
  United States. *See* United States Constitution
The Constitution of the United States of America, 526, 528
Constitutional law, 149–152
  courts and, 150–151
  defined, 149
  finding, 526, 528, 530
  nature of, 151
  paralegal and, 151–152
  Shepard's Citations and, 530
  See also United States Constitution
Consumer(s)
  defined, 301
  laws protecting. *See* Consumer law(s)
Consumer Credit Protection Act (1974), 305, 306
Consumer law(s), 301–308
  consumer credit protection and, 305–307
  consumer health and safety and, 304–305
  deceptive advertising and, 302–303
  defined, 153, 302
  and the paralegal, 307
Consumer Product Safety Act (1972), 305
Consumer Product Safety Commission (CPSC), 305, 525
  Web site of, 568
Contempt of court, 104
Contingency fee, 131
Continuing Legal Education (CLE) programs, 8, 12–13
Contract(s), 221–230
  acceptance in, 223–224, 233
  agreement in, 222–224
  breach of, 221–222
    defined, 221
    remedies for, 226–227
  cancellation of, 226
  capacity in, 224
  commercial, arbitration of, 205
  consideration in, 224
  defined, 221
  disaffirmance of, 224
  enforceability of, defenses to, 224–225
  forms for, 230
  legality of, 224
  offer in, 222–224, 230
  paralegals and, 227, 230
  reformation and, 226
  requirements of, 222–224
  rescission of, 226
  restitution and, 226
  review of, 227
  for sale of goods. *See* Sales contract(s)
  for sale of real property, 233
  sales. *See* Sales contract(s)
  unconscionable, 225
Contract paralegals, 33–34
Contractual capacity, 224
Contributory negligence, 218, 352
Conversations overheard by others, 81–82
Conversion, 278
Copyright, 281
Copyright Act, 281
Copyright law, 40, 153, 281
Corporate charter (certificate of incorporation), 267
Corporate law, 153
  defined, 36
  as paralegal specialty, 36–37
Corporation(s), 266–272
  classification of, 268–270
  close, 269
  closely held, 269
  consolidation and, 271–272
  as defendant
    finding, 345
    serving, 345
  directors of, 266–267, 270–271
  dividend of, 270
  as employer, 31
  formation of, 267–268
  for-profit, 269
  incorporation of. *See* Incorporation
  liquidation of, 272
  merger and, 271–272
  name of, reserving, 270
  nonprofit, 269
  not-for-profit, 269
  officers of, 267, 270–271
  private, 268
  professional (P.C.), 118, 270
  public, 268
  publicly held, 268

S, 270, 271
service (S.C.), 118, 270
shareholders of, 266, 271
taxation and, 271
termination of, 272
Corpus Juris Secundum (C.J.S.)(West Group), 493–494, 533
excerpt from, illustrated, 496
illustrated, 495
Counteradvertising, 303
Counterclaim, 352
Counteroffer, 223
County attorney, 415
Court(s)
alternative dispute resolution (ADR) and, 201–203
of appeal. *See* Appellate court(s)
appellate. *See* Appellate court(s)
bankruptcy, 180
choice of, 183
constitutional law and, 150–151
contempt of, 104
decisions of, 164, 491–492
reporting of. *See* Case reporting system
docket and, 337
electronic filing of documents in, 195
employment with, 33
of equity, 159–161
federal. *See* Federal court system
holding of, 589
Islamic, civil law system and, 170
jurisdiction of. *See* Jurisdiction
king's *(curiae regis)*, 157
of law, 159–161
opinion of, 164, 588
probate, 39, 180
procedures in, 184
reviewing. *See* Appellate court(s)
state. *See* State court system(s)
supreme
state, 188–189
attorney regulation and, 73
United States. *See* United States Supreme Court
trial. *See* Trial court(s)
venue and, 182–183
Cover letter, 56–58
sample, illustrated, 57

CPSC. *See* Consumer Product Safety Commission
Credit cards, consumer protection and, 305
Credit discrimination, 305
Creditor(s)
judgment, 406
laws protecting, 305–307
real-estate paralegal and, 279
Crime(s)
classifications of, 416–417
client intends to commit, 81, 82
criminal act and, 417
cyber, 418
defined, 415–416
on the Internet, 418
liability for. *See* Criminal liability
prosecution of. *See* Prosecution
state of mind *(mens rea)* and, 418, 419
variety of, 417
Criminal act *(actus reus)*, 417
Criminal defendant(s)
constitutional safeguards protecting, 421–423, 426
innocence of, presumption of, 441–442
See also Person(s), accused of crimes
Criminal law, 414–451
civil law *versus*, 35
criminal procedures and. *See* Criminal procedures
defined, 35
as paralegal specialty, 35–36, 420–421, 424–425
Criminal liability
defenses to, 419–420
elements of, 417–420
Criminal procedures
beginning of prosecution and, 432–437
discovery and, 437, 443
pretrial motions and, 436–437
prior to prosecution, 426–432
major steps in, summarized, 427
trial and. *See* Criminal trial(s)
Criminal trial(s), 437–444, 446
appeal following, 446
jury's role in, 441

rules of evidence and, 443
sentencing and, 444
standard of proof in, 442–443
Cross-examination, 397–398
Cumulative Later Case and Statutory Service, 523
Curiae regis (king's courts), 157
Current Legal Index, 508, 511
Cyber crimes, 418
Cyberspace communications. *See* Electronic communications

D
Damages
defined, 77
punitive, 215
DEA (Drug Enforcement Administration), 292–293
Deadlines
meeting, ethics and, 186, 278, 354
missing, 78, 79
Deadly force, 419
Debt collection, consumer laws regarding, 306
Debtor, real-estate paralegal and, 279
Deceptive advertising, 302–303
Deed(s)
defined, 238
preparation of, 42
sample, illustrated, 240
Deen, Kirtrena S., 476
Defamation, 216
Default judgment, 79, 349
Defendant(s)
case of, during trial, 399
co-, 163
corporate, serving, 345
criminal. *See* Criminal defendant(s)
defined, 34
response of, 349–353
Defense(s)
affirmative, 349, 352
to contract enforceability, 224–225
to criminal liability, 419–420
defined, 216
to negligence, 218
of others, 419
of property, 419

self-, 419
year-and-a-day, 422
Delegation doctrine, 294
DeLeo, John D., 222–223
Demand letters, 611–612, 614
Deponent
　attorney of, role of, 366–368
　defined, 365
Deposition(s), 360, 365–370
　defined, 360
　notice of taking, illustrated, 365
　preparing client for, 366
　questions for
　　drafting, 366
　　illustrated, 367
　transcript of
　　defined, 368
　　illustrated, 369
　　indexing, 369–370, 371
　　summarizing, 368, 369–370
　　　illustrated, 370
Dicta, 589
Dictionaries, 571
　legal, 571
　multiple, 572
　specialized, 572
Digest(s)
　case, 495–501
　defined, 495
　federal (West Group), 495–497
　state and regional (West Group), 498
　West's *American Digest System* and, 500–501, 502
Direct evidence, 478
Direct examination, 396–397
Direct regulation, 72n
Director, corporate, 266–267, 270–271
Directory(ies)
　city, 475
　Martindale-Hubbell Law Directory and, 50
　media, 576
　online, 552, 571
　telephone, 475, 572
　West Law Directory and, 50
　West's Legal Directory and, 565
Disability, employment discrimination on basis of, 319–320
Disaffirmance, 224

Disbarment, 75
Discovery, 356–376
　in criminal procedure, 437, 443
　defined, 356
　disclosures in
　　initial, 372–373
　　subsequent, 373–374, 376
　plan of, 373
　writing in, 604
Discovery plan, 373
Discrimination
　credit, 305
　employment. *See* Employment discrimination
Dissenting opinion, 164, 588
Dissolution of partnership, 266
District attorney, 415
Diversion programs, 432
Diversity jurisdiction, 181–182, 337
Dividend, 270
Docket, 337
Docket number, 337, 587
Document(s)
　client
　　handling, ethics and, 464
　　tips for collecting, 166
　electronic filing of, 195
DOJ. *See* United States Department of Justice
Double billing
　ABA's response to, 137
　defined, 136
Double jeopardy, 422
Drinking water, 311
Drug Enforcement Administration (DEA), 292–293
Due process of law, 422
Dunn, Karen, 154
Duty(ies)
　of care, 216
　　breach of, 217
　of competence, 77–79
　　breach of
　　　defined, 78
　　　inadequate supervision and, 78–79, 80
　　　missed deadlines and, 78, 79, 354
　　real-estate sales, ethics and, 233
　　statute of limitations, ethics and, 162

fiduciary, 259, 270–271
　of partners, 264
Dye, Dora, 43

E
Early neutral case evaluation, 202
Earnest money, 233
Easement, 231
ECOA (Equal Credit Opportunity Act)(1974), 305
Education Law Digest (West Group), 497
EEOC (Equal Employment Opportunity Commission), 38, 156, 293, 301, 319, 321
Eighth Amendment, 150, 422, 434, 436
Elder law, 44
Electronic communications
　with client, 138
　confidentiality and, 82–83, 84
　defined, 549
　E-mail addresses and, 571
Electronic filing of documents, 195
Elements of Style (Strunk and White), 597
E-mail. *See* Electronic communications
E-mail addresses, 571
Emergency in trial, 188
Eminent domain, 231
Emotional distress, intentional infliction of, 216
Employee(s)
　with disability, reasonable accommodations and, 319, 593
　key, 317
Employer(s)
　attorney discipline board as, 109
　corporation as, 31
　freelance paralegals and, 33–34
　government as, 32–33, 292–293
　independent paralegals and, 34
　law firms and. *See* Law firm(s)
　legal aid office as, 33
　potential, locating, 49–50
　public defender as, 33, 36
　public prosecutor as, 33
　types of, 28–34
　United States district court as, 445

Employment
  relationships regarding, 316–321
    paralegal and, 320–321
  at will, 122–123
  See also Employment law(s)
Employment discrimination, 122–123, 193, 202, 318–320
  on basis of
    age, 123, 202, 319
    color, 193, 318
    disability, 319–320
    gender, 123, 193, 318
    national origin, 193, 318
    pregnancy, 318
    race, 123, 193, 318
    religion, 193, 318
  sexual harassment and. See Sexual harassment
Employment law(s), 153, 316–321
  as paralegal specialty, 37–39
  See also Employment
Employment manual, 121
Employment records, obtaining, 471–472
Employment termination, 122
Enabling legislation, 155, 290, 294
Encyclopedias
  legal, 492–495
  nonlegal, 571
Enforcement
  by administrative agencies, 294, 296–298
  of judgment, 405–406
England
  common law in, 149, 156–157, 169, 309
  legal and paralegal practice in, 172
Environmental coordinator, 41
Environmental impact statements, 309–310
Environmental law(s), 41–42, 309–316
  air pollution and, 310
  common law actions and, 309
  defined, 41
  federal, 309–310
  and the paralegal, 314–316
  state and local, 313–314
  toxic chemicals and, 312–313
  water pollution and, 310–312

Environmental Protection Agency (EPA), 41, 155, 298, 310, 311, 313, 315
  creation of, 309
EPA. See Environmental Protection Agency
Equal Credit Opportunity Act (ECOA)(1974), 305
Equal Employment Opportunity Commission (EEOC), 38, 156, 293, 301, 319, 321
Equitable principles and maxims, 159–160
Equity
  courts of, 159–161
  merging of law and, 161
  remedies in, 159–161
Escrow agent, 233–235, 238
Estate administration, 243, 248
  the paralegal and, 248–250
Estate planning, 243–250
  defined, 39
  as paralegal specialty, 39–40
Ethical wall, 87, 88
Ethics
  accurate paperwork, sale of real estate and, 239
  agency hearings and, 298
  arbitration and, 201
  backing up work and, 136
  citing sources and, 519
  client billing practices and, 136–137
  "confidential" correspondence and, 608
  confidentiality and, 357
    administrative practice and, 301
    at social events and, 83
  cutting cost of legal research and, 546
  deadlines and, 79, 186, 278, 354
  effective utilization of paralegals and, 9
  efficiency in research and, 489
  ex parte communication with jurors and, 401
  finding ethical opinions on the web on, 572
  good record keeping and, 444
  handling client documents and, 464

  handling clients' questions about fees and, 130
  issuing subpoenas to friendly witnesses and, 386
  keeping client informed and, 466
  legal
    codes and rules pertaining to, 74–77
    on the Internet, 572
  legal research, *stare decisis* and, 158
  malpractice lawsuits and, 218
  objectivity, legal memorandum and, 619
  paralegal and
    ethical codes and, 89–90, 92–95
    ten tips regarding, 90–91
  paralegal as agent and subagent and, 260
  paralegal as apparent partner and, 265
  paralegal expertise and legal advice and, 5
  personal, professional ethics *versus*, 85
  plagiarism and, 511
  of plea bargaining, 437
  preparing exhibits for trial and, 442
  private justice and, 203
  professional, personal ethics *versus*, 85
  putting client's interests first and, 295
  questions about child custody and, 44
  real-estate sales, duties of competence and diligence and, 233
  serving interests of bereaved clients and, 40
  statute of limitations, duty of competence and, 162
  surfing the Web and, 562
  telling supervising attorney what you know about prospective juror and, 393
  time management and, 603
  trust accounts and, 132
  unauthorized practice of law and, 5, 105, 334, 465

letters and, 613
  and what to do when someone asks about remedies, 164
European Union, 171
Evidence
  authentication of, 479
  circumstantial, 478
  direct, 478
  hearsay and, 479, 481
  log of, 472
  motion to suppress, 436, 438–439
  "preponderance of," 442
  relevant, 479
  rules of, 477, 479
    in criminal process, 443
    investigation and, 477–479, 481
Evidence log, 472
Ex parte communications, 401
Examination
  cross-, 397–398
  direct, 396–397
  recross-, 398
  redirect, 398
  title, 42, 66, 237–238
Excite, 552
Exclusionary rule, 423
Exclusive jurisdiction, 182
Execution, writ of, 406
Executive agency, 290–291
Executor, 245
Exempt property, 406
Expense slip
  defined, 134
  illustrated, 135
Expenses, documenting, 133–134
Expert witnesses, 373–374
  consulting with, 407
  defined, 465
  locating, 386
  on the Internet, 565, 567
Express warranty, 226
Exxon Valdez, 311
Eyewitnesses, 465–466

F

FAA (Federal Arbitration Act), 200
Fact pleading, 340n
Factbook (Central Intelligence Agency), 167

Fair Credit Reporting Act (FCRA) (1970), 306
Fair Debt-Collection Practices Act (1977), 306
Fair Labor Standards Act (FLSA) (Wage-Hour Law) (1938), 47, 317
Fair Packaging and Labeling Act (1966), 303
False imprisonment, 216
Family and Medical Leave Act (FMLA)(1993), 317–318
Family law, 42, 44
Family limited liability partnership (FLLP), 276
Family settlement agreements, 246
Fax, confidentiality and, 82
FCRA (Fair Credit Reporting Act)(1970), 306
FDA. *See* Food and Drug Administration
Federal Arbitration Act (FAA), 200
Federal Bureau of Investigation, 298
Federal civil cover sheet, illustrated, 344
Federal court system, 190–194
  constitutional authority of, 179, 181
  decisions of, 514
  judges of, lifetime appointments of, 190
  jurisdiction of, 181–182, 194
  organization of, illustrated, 190
  the paralegal and, 192–194
  trial courts of, 181, 190–191, 445
  United States courts of appeals of, 191, 192
  United States district courts of, 181, 190
    illustrated, 191
    working for, 445
  United States Supreme Court of. *See* United States Supreme Court
Federal Deposit Insurance Corporation, 293
Federal Digest (West Group), 495
Federal Energy Law Citations, 532
Federal Food, Drug and Cosmetic Act (1938), 304

Federal Insecticide, Fungicide, and Rodenticide Act (1947), 312
Federal Law Citations in Selected Law Reviews, 532
Federal Maritime Commission, 299
Federal Practice Digest 2d (West Group), 495
Federal Practice Digest 3d (West Group), 495
Federal Practice Digest 4th (West Group), 495–496
  excerpt from, illustrated, 499
Federal questions, 181, 337
Federal Register, 295–296, 526
  on the Internet, 574
  List of C.F.R. Parts Affected of, 526
  monitoring, 314, 315
Federal Reporter (F., F.2d, or F.3d) (West Group), 496, 514, 518
  Shepard's Federal Reporter Citations and, 529
  Statutes Edition of Shepard's United States Citations and, 530
Federal Rules Decisions (West Group), 496
Federal Rules of Civil Procedure (FRCP), 184, 193, 342
  defined, 332
  discovery guidelines and, 357
  notice and waiver of service under, 346–348
  on posttrial motions, 402n
  revised discovery procedures under, 371–374, 376
  revision of, 367–368, 370, 371–372
Federal Rules of Evidence, 477, 479
Federal Supplement (F.Supp.) (West Group), 496, 514
Federal Trade Commission (FTC), 155, 291, 294, 301, 525
  deceptive advertising and, 302–303
  Internet fraud and, 304
  labeling and packaging laws and, 303
Federal Trade Commission Act (1914), 294, 302, 525

Federal Water Pollution Control Act (FWPCA)(1948), 311
Fee(s), 128–131
　alternative arrangements regarding, 131
　clients' questions about, 130
　contingency, 131
　fixed, 130
　hourly, 130
　retainer agreement and, 128–129
　splitting of, prohibition against, 132
Fee simple, 231
Felony, 416
Fiduciary relationship
　corporate directors and officers, corporation and, 270–271
　defined, 259
Fifth Amendment, 150, 422, 432, 433, 435, 443
File transfer protocol (FTP), 549
Filing, 124
　adding subfiles and, 125
　client files and. *See* Client file(s)
　closing a file and, 125
　creating and maintaining efficiently, ten tips for, 126–127
　destroying old files and, 125–127
　of documents, electronically, 195
　electronic, of documents, 195
　file use and, 125
　forms file and, 128
　opening a file and, 124
　procedures regarding, 123–128
　of reference materials, 127–128
　storage and, 125
　of work product, 127–128
Finding tools
　for administrative law, 526
　defined, 488
　See also Secondary source(s)
FindLaw, 167, 418
　home page for, illustrated, 552
FindLaw Legal News, 565
First Amendment, 73–74, 150, 151
Fitness, implied warranty of, 226
Fixed fee, 130
Flammable Fabrics Act (1953), 305

FLLP (family limited liability partnership), 276
The Florida Bar v. Brumbaugh, 103–104
The Florida Bar v. Furman, 104
FLSA (Fair Labor Standards Act)(Wage-Hour Law)(1938), 47, 317
FMLA (Family and Medical Leave Act)(1993), 317–318
FOIA (Freedom of Information Act), 477, 478
Follow-up letter
　to client, sample, illustrated, 461
　to prospective employer, 62
　sample, illustrated, 63
Food and Drug Administration (FDA), 155, 156, 303, 304, 309
　Web site of, 474
Ford, Henry, 259
Foreclosure, 66
Form(s)
　contract, 230, 234–237
　file of, 128
　purchase and sale agreement, sample of, illustrated, 234–237
　release, 334
　return-of-service, 345, 346
Forms file, 128
For-profit corporation, 269
Fourth Amendment, 150, 422, 423, 428–429, 433, 533
France, civil law system in, 170
Fraud, Internet, 304
Fraudulent misrepresentation, 216
FRCP. *See* Federal Rules of Civil Procedure
Free commercial Web sites, 575–576
Freedom of Information Act (FOIA), 477, 478
Freedom of speech, 150–151
Freelance paralegals, 33–34, 101–103
Friendly witnesses, 385
　defined, 466
　issuing subpoenas for, 386
FTC. *See* Federal Trade Commission
FTP (file transfer protocol), 549

Fuld & Company, 568
Future interests, 232
FWPCA (Federal Water Pollution Control Act) (1948), 311

G
Gaige, Michael, 615
Gallo, Diane S., 296
Garnishment, 306–307
Gender
　credit discrimination on basis of, 305
　employment discrimination on basis of, 123, 193, 318
General jurisdiction, 180
General licensing
　defined, 105
　limited licensing *versus,* 105–106
General partners, 266
General partnerships, 266
Goals
　long-term, defining, 48
　short-term, job realities and, 48–49
Goods, sale of, contract for. *See* Sales contract(s)
Government(s)
　administrative agencies of. *See* Administrative agency(ies)
　as employer, 32–33
　information from, accessing, 475, 477, 478
　paralegal positions in, 292–293
　regulation by. *See* Regulation of the United States, illustrated, 291
　Web sites of, 573, 574
Grand jury, 434–435
Grantor, 246
Great Britain, former colonies of, common law heritage of, 169. *See also* England
Guardian ad litem, 577
Guardians, locating, 577
Guides, online, 552
Guilty act *(actus reus),* 417

H
Hazardous wastes, 312–313
Heading, point, 626
Headnote, 495, 587–588

HealthGate, 474
Hearing
  administrative, 297, 298
  arbitration, 201
  preliminary, 434
Hearsay, 479, 481
Herbicides, 312
Hieros Gamos, 560
Hinkel, Daniel F., 168–169
Hiring Standards for Paralegals, 292
Holding, 589
Holding facility, 430
Hollier, Carol D., 241–242
Home page, 549
Hoover's Online, 568
Hornbook
  defined, 503
  page from, illustrated, 508
Hostile witness, 396–397, 466–467
Hostile-environment harassment, 319
HotBot, 552
Hourly fees, 130
http (hypertext transfer protocol), 549
Hung jury, 441
Hypertext transfer protocol (http), 549
Hypothetical questions, 458

I
IDG Books Worldwide, Inc., 558
Immigration and Naturalization Service, 293
Immigration law, 44–45
Impeachment, 368–369
Implied warranty
  of fitness for a particular purpose, 226
  of merchantability, 226
In personam jurisdiction, 179–180
In re Baby M, 158n
In rem jurisdiction, 180
In the Matter of Totten, 247n
Incorporation
  articles of
    defined, 267
    illustrated, 268
    information generally included in, 269
    preparing, 282

Independent contractors, 33–34
Independent paralegal(s)
  defined, 34
  unauthorized practice of law and, 103–105
Independent regulatory agency, 291
Index to Legal Periodicals, 508, 511
  entries in, illustrated, 513
  illustrated, 511
India, common law system in, 169
Indictment
  defined, 435
  illustrated, 435
  motion challenging sufficiency of, 436
Information, in criminal procedure, 434
Informational interview, 462–463
Informative letters, 609–610
Infoseek, 552
Infringement, 41
Injunction, 104
Injury, as requirement for negligence, 217
Inspection of premises, 236–237
Insurance, title, 237–238
Insurance company, contacting, 473–474
Insurance paralegal, 476
Intangible personal property, 231
Intellectual property, 278, 280–281, 283
  conversion and, 278
  defined, 278
  forms of, 280–281, 283
  and the paralegal, 283
Intellectual-property law
  defined, 40
  as paralegal specialty, 40–41
Intent
  of client, to commit harmful or illegal act, 81, 82
  legislative, 595
  as requirement for offer, 223
  torts and, 215–216
Intentional infliction of emotional distress, 216
Intentional tort, 215–216
Inter vivos (living) trust, 246–247, 248
Internal memorandum. *See* Legal memorandum

Internal Revenue Code, Subchapter S of, 270, 271
Internal Revenue Service (IRS), 66, 156, 298
  approval to practice before, 299
International law, 170–171
  defined, 170
  national law and, 167–172
  paralegal and, 171
Internet
  accessing, 550–551
  basics of, 548–553
  browsers and, 551
  commercial online services and, 550–551
  confidentiality and, 83, 84
  crimes on, 418
  defined, 548
  fraud on, consumer protection and, 304
  guides and directories and, 552, 571
  Internet service provider (ISP) and, 550, 551
  investigating companies on, 567–568
  locating people on, 565, 567
  medical research on, 474, 558
  mirror site on, 562
  navigating, 551–553
  research on
    best legal-resource sites for, 568, 571–576
    browsing the links and, 562
    conducting, 553–565
    creative searching and, 561
    discovering available resources and, 560–561
    effectiveness of, 554–557
    investigating companies and, 567–568
    locating people and, 565, 567
    narrowing focus and, 562–563
    planning ahead and, 557–558
    results of
      evaluating, 563–564
      updating, 564–565
    starting points and, 558–560
  search engines and, 552–553
    meta, 553
  search tools and, 571
  tools of, 548–550

INDEX

United States Supreme Court decisions on, 517
See also World Wide Web
The Internet for Dummies (Levine, Baroudi & Young), 558
Internet Law Library of the United States House of Representatives, 167, 556
    page from, illustrated, 557
Internet Network Information Center (InterNIC), 550
Internet service provider (ISP), 550, 551, 571
InterNIC (Internet Network Information Center), 550
Interpersonal skills, 14–15, 457
Interrogatories, 357–360
    answering, 360
    defined, 357
    drafting, 360
        ten tips for, 358–359
    sample, illustrated, 361–364
Interview(s)
    of client. *See* Client interview(s)
    conducting
        skills in, 456–460
        ten tips for, 462–463
    informational, 462–463
    planning, 453–456
    questions during, 457–459
        closed-ended, 458
        hypothetical, 458
        leading, 458–459
        open-ended, 457–458
        pressure, 458
    recording, 453–456
    of witnesses, 464–468, 471
Interviewee, 453
Intestacy laws, 245
Intestate death, 245
Invasion of privacy, 216
Investigation(s)
    by administrative agencies, 296–297
    after arrest, 431–432
    beginning, 469–470
    of companies on the Internet, 567–568
    conclusions of, 481
    investigation plan and, 470–474
    planning and conducting, 468–481
    preliminary, 334
    by professional investigator, 474
    recommendations based on, 481
    results of, summarizing, 481
    rules of evidence and, 477–479, 481
Investigation plan
    creating, 470–474
    illustrated, 470–471
IRAC (issue, rule, application, and conclusion) method, 618, 619, 629
Ireland, common law system in, 169
Irrevocable living trust, 247
IRS. *See* Internal Revenue Service
Islamic courts, civil law system and, 170
ISP (Internet service provider), 550, 551
Issue, defining, 489–490, 491
Issue, rule, application, and conclusion (IRAC) method, 618, 619, 629

J

JAMS/Endispute, 204
Japan, civil law system in, 170
J.E.B. v. Alabama ex rel. T.B., 393n
Job interview, 59–62
    at, 60–61
    before, 59–60
    after, 61–62
    follow-up letter after, 62, 63
    objectionable or illegal questions from interviewer, 61
    questions you might want to ask of interviewer, 62
Job search
    application process of, 54–59
    cover letter and, 56–58
    finding available jobs and, 49–50
    identifying possible employers and, 50
    interview and. *See* Job interview
    job-placement services and, 50, 52
    list of professional references and, 58
    maintaining files on, 62–63
    networking and, 49
    online, 51
    professional portfolio and, 58–59
    résumé and. *See* Résumé
    salary negotiations and, 63–65
Job-placement services, 50, 52
Joint and several liability, 265
Joint liability, 265
Joint tenancy, 231
Journal of the American Medical Association, 474
Judge(s)
    administrative law (ALJ), 297, 298
    federal, lifetime appointments of, 190
    justice *versus*, 163–164
    law made by. *See* Case law(s)
    name of, on case, 588
Judge-made law. *See* Case law(s)
Judgment(s)
    affirmation of, 404, 588
    default, 79, 349
    defined, 331, 401–402
    enforcing, 405–406
    as a matter of law, 399, 400, 402, 405
    on the pleadings, 353–354
    reversal of, 404, 588
    summary, 354–356
Judgment creditor, 406
Judicial procedures, 184
Jurisdiction
    allegations of, in complaint, 337, 340
    appellate, 180–181
    concurrent, 182
    defined, 179
    diversity, 181–182, 337
    exclusive, 182
    of federal courts, 181–182, 194
    general, 180
    limited, 180
    minimum contacts and, 180
    original, 180–181
    over persons, 179–180
    over property, 180
    over subject matter, 180
    in personam, 179–180
    in rem, 180
    statement of, in appellate brief, 622, 625
    types of, 179–181

of United States Supreme
    Court, 192
Juror(s)
  alternate, 393–394
  ex parte communication with,
    ethics and, 401
  prospective
    challenges to. See Challenge(s)
    telling supervising attorney
      what you know about,
      ethics and, 393
  See also Jury
Jury
  charge to, 401, 403
  in criminal trial, role of, 441
  grand, 434–435
  hung, 441
  instructions to, 401
  selection of, 389–394
  trial by
    demand for, 341
    right to, 422, 440–441
      waiver of, 441
      illustrated, 442
  verdict of. See Verdict
  See also Juror(s)
Justice(s)
  American system of, 179–186
    the paralegal and, 184–186
  judge *versus*, 163–164
  name of, on case, 588
  private, ethics and, 203
Justice Department. See United
    States Department of Justice
Justiciable controversy, 184

K
Key employee, 317
Key number, 495
KeyCite, 544, 545, 629
King's courts (*curiae regis*), 157

L
Labeling and packaging laws, 303
Labor law(s), 153, 316–317
  as paralegal specialty, 37–39
Labor Management Services
    Administration (LMSA), 38
Labor unions, 316
Labor-Management Reporting and
    Disclosure Act (Landrum-
    Griffin Act)(1959), 521
Laches, 159

Land, trespass to, 216. See also
    Real property
Landrum-Griffin Act (Labor-
    Management Reporting and
    Disclosure Act)(1959), 521
Last clear chance doctrine, 218
Law(s)
  administrative. See
    Administrative law
  antitrust, 153
  bankruptcy, 37
  case. See Case law(s)
  civil. See Civil law
  codified, 169–170
  common. See Common law
  constitutional. See
    Constitutional law
  consumer. See Consumer law(s)
  contract. See Contract(s)
  copyright, 40, 153, 281
  corporate, 36–37, 153156
  courts of, 159–161
  criminal. See Criminal law
  defined, 149
  due process of, 422
  elder, 44
  employment. See Employment
    law(s)
  environmental. See
    Environmental law(s)
  family, 42, 44
  immigration, 44–45
  intellectual-property, 40–41
  intestacy, 245
  judge-made. See Case law(s)
  judgment as a matter of, 399,
    400, 402, 405
  labeling and packaging, 303
  labor. See Labor law(s)
  memorandum of, 352
  merging of equity and, 161
  national. See National law
  packaging and labeling, 303
  patent, 40, 153
  personal-injury, 35
  procedural, 10
  real-estate, 42, 43
  remedies at, 159–161
  sales transactions and, 303–304
  session, 520
  slip, 519–520
  sources of, primary and
    secondary, 488

  statutory. See Statutory law
  substantive, 10
  tort. See Tort(s)
  trademark, 40, 153, 280
  unauthorized practice of. See
    Unauthorized practice
    of law
  workers' compensation, 37, 318
  See also Statute(s)
Law clerk
  attorney as, 6n
  defined, 6
Law enforcement offices,
    employment with, 33
Law firm(s)
  culture of, 140
  employment policies of,
    121–123
  fees and. See Fee(s)
  finding job with, 50, 51
  large
    small firm *versus*, 28n
    working for, 30–31
  management of, 118–121
  organization of
    as partnership, 118, 119
    as professional corporation
      (P.C.), 118
    as sole proprietorship,
      117–118
    structure of, 117–118
  personnel of, 118–121
  politics in, 140
  procedures of
    billing and timekeeping,
      132–136
    filing, 123–128. See also
      Filing
    financial, 128–137. See also
      Fee(s)
  small
    large firm *versus*, 28n
    working for, 28–30
  Web home pages of, 51
Law office. See Law firm(s)
Law Office Technology, 569
Law-related discussion
    groups, 573
Lawsuit(s)
  hypothetical, 332–333
  malpractice, 166, 218
  parties to, 163
  personal-injury, 166, 220

intake sheet and, 454–455
product-liability, 166
standing to bring, 183–184
See also Case(s)
Lawyer. *See* Attorney(s)
Lawyers Cooperative Publishing Company. *See* West Group; entries beginning with West
Lawyers' Edition of the Digest of the Supreme Court Reports (West Group), 501
Lawyers' Edition of the Supreme Court Reports (West Group), 501, 516, 518
  Shepard's United States Citations and, 529
  Statutes Edition of Shepard's United States Citations and, 530
The Lawyer's PC, 569
Lay witnesses, 465
Leading questions, 396, 458–459
Lease
  defined, 239
  terms of, typical, 242
'Lectric Law Library, 230, 560
  home page of, 576
Legal administrator, 119
Legal aid office, as employer, 33
Legal analysis. *See* Analysis
Legal assistant. *See* Paralegal(s)
Legal Assistant Management Association, 8
Legal Assistant Today, 569
Legal dictionaries, 571
Legal encyclopedias, 492–495
Legal Information Institute, 549–550
  home page of, illustrated, 550
Legal letters. *See* Letter(s)
Legal memorandum
  conclusion of, 619, 620
    brief, 616, 618
  discussion and analysis section of, 617–619
  discussion in, 620
  heading of, 614, 616
  objectivity, ethics and, 619
  preparing, 629
  questions presented in, 616, 618
  statement of the facts in, 614, 616, 617
  writing, 613–620, 629

Legal nurse consultant (LNC), 45
Legal periodicals, 506–508, 511
Legal research. *See* Research
Legal technicians, 34
Legal writing, 595–629
  of appellate brief. *See* Appellate brief(s)
  approaches to, 597
  avoiding legalese in, 599
  being brief and to the point in, 599–600
  to clients, 611
  effective, ten tips for, 605–606
  efficient use of words in, 601
  flexibility and, 596
  of general legal correspondence, 604–613
    general format for, 604, 606–608
    See also Letter(s)
  importance of good skills in, 597–603
  of legal memorandum. *See* Legal memorandum
  online "plain English" guidelines for, 600
  organization of presentation and, 597–598
  outlining presentation and, 597–598
  paragraphs in, 601–602
  pleadings and, 604
  preliminaries of, 595–597
  proofreading and revision of, 603
  sentences in, 600–601
  sexist language and, 602–603
  time constraints and, 596
  transitions in, 601–602
  understanding the assignment in, 595
  to your audience, 598–599
Legal-assistant manager, 119, 120
Legalese, avoiding, 599
Legality of contract, 224
Legislative history, 523–525
Legislative intent, 595
Legislative offices, employment with, 33
Legislative rules, 294
Letter(s)
  address block on, 606–607
  to clients, 488, 611

closing of, 608
"confidential," ethics and, 608
confirmation, 610
cover, 56–58
demand, 611–612, 614
follow-up
  to client, 461
  to prospective employer, 62, 63
informative, 609–610
legal, types of, 609–612
opinion (advisory), 610–611, 612
reference line on, 607–608
salutation on, 608
unauthorized practice of law, ethics and, 613
Levine, John R., 558
Levine, Sonia, 279
Lexis©, 532, 541, 542–548, 575
  accessing, 543
  Auto-Cite citator and, 544
  browser enhancements and, 547–548
  checking a citation on, 544
  retrieving a document by citation on, 544
  searching database on, 545–547
    natural language method and, 546–547
    terms and connectors method and, 546
  selecting database on, 544–545
Liability(ies)
  criminal. *See* Criminal liability
  joint, 265
  joint and several, 265
  limited, 271
  of members of limited liability company (LLC), 273, 275
  of partners
    general, 264–265
    limited, 275, 276
  of sole proprietors, 117, 263
Liber, 66
Library catalogues, 572
Library of Congress, THOMAS site of, 563, 574
Licensing
  of attorneys, 74
  defined, 74
  general, 105–106
  limited, 105–106

of paralegals, 105–108
Liens, 66
Life estates, 231–232
Limited jurisdiction, 180
Limited liability, 271
Limited liability company (LLC), 273, 275
Limited liability limited partnership (LLLP), 275, 276
Limited liability partnership (LLP), 273, 275, 276
Limited Liability Partnership Act, 512
Limited licensing
  defined, 106
  general licensing *versus*, 105–106
Limited partners, 266
Limited partnerships, 266
Line-up, 432
Liquidation, 272
Listening, active, 459–460
Listening skills, 18–19, 459–460
Listserv list, 561
Litigation
  civil. *See* Civil litigation
  defined, 34
Litigation paralegals, 34–35, 206, 356, 394–395, 500, 566, 615
Living *(inter vivos)* trust, 246–247, 248
LLC (limited liability company), 273, 275
LLLP (limited liability limited partnership), 275, 276
LLP (limited liability partnership), 273, 275, 276
LMSA (Labor Management Services Administration), 38
LNC (legal nurse consultant), 45
Long, Judy A., 292–293
Long arm statute, 179–180
Loose-leaf services, 518
Lycos, 552

M

Magistrate, 430
Majority opinion, 164, 588
Malpractice, 77, 81, 166, 218
Malpractice lawsuits, 166, 218
Management
  of conflicts in the workplace, 139
  law-office, 118–121
  time, ethics and, 603
Managing partner, 118
Mandatory authority, 491–492
Maps, 572
Marine Protection, Research, and Sanctuaries Act (Ocean Dumping Act)(1983), 311
Marital status, credit discrimination on basis of, 305
Martin, Susan J., 20
Martindale-Hubbell Law Directory, 50
Martindale's Health Science Guide, 474
MBCA (Model Business Corporation Act), 267
McCord, James W. H., 358–359
McVeigh, Timothy, 183
Meat Inspection Act (1906), 304
Med-arb (mediation arbitration), 202
Media directory, 576
Mediation
  binding, 202
  as form of alternative dispute resolution (ADR), 196, 198–199
  the paralegal and, 198–199
Mediation arbitration (med-arb), 202
Medical records, obtaining, 471–472, 473
Medical research, online, 474, 558
Medicare, 290
MEDLINE, 474
Members of limited liability company (LLC), 273, 275
Memorandum
  internal. *See* Legal memorandum
  of law, 352
Mens rea (wrongful mental state), 418, 419
Mental state
  required, lack of, as defense to criminal liability, 419
  wrongful *(mens rea),* 418
Merchantability, implied warranty of, 226
Merger, 271–272
  defined, 271
  illustrated, 272
Meta search engines, 553
Metacrawler, 553
Mexico, North American Free Trade Agreement and, 168, 171
Microsoft Explorer, 551
Military Digest (West Group), 497
Minimum contacts, 180
Mini-trial, 202
Minnick v. Mississippi, 426
Miranda rights, 423
Miranda rule, 422–423, 426
Miranda v. Arizona, 423
Mirror site, 562
Misdemeanor, 416–417
Misrepresentation, fraudulent, 216
Mistaken identity, 419–420
Model Business Corporation Act (MBCA), 267
Model Code
  defined, 75
  on unauthorized practice of law, 98
Model Penal Code, 416n
Model Rules
  client communication and, 138
  defined, 75
  fee splitting and, 132
  gifts from clients and, 88
  headings of, illustrated, 76
  protecting the record and preserving professional integrity and, 298
  reasonableness of fees and, 128
  violations of, sanctions for, 75, 77
Mortgage, 235–236
Motion(s)
  challenging sufficiency of indictment, 436
  for change of venue, 436
  defined, 352
  for directed verdict, 399
  for discovery and inspection, 437, 440
  to dismiss
    defined, 352
    illustrated, 353
  for judgment
    as a matter of law, 399, 400, 402, 405
    notwithstanding the verdict, 402
    on the pleadings, 353–354

in limine, 389, 392, 436
  for new trial, 402–403, 405
  for order directing defendant to appear for arraignment, 436
  posttrial, 402–403, 405
  pretrial, 353–356, 436–437
  to reduce amount of bail, 434
  for summary judgment, 354–356
  to suppress evidence, 436, 438–439
Multilateral agreements, 171
Multimedia Medical Reference Library, 474
Multiple dictionaries, 572

N
Nader, Ralph, 301
Nakaahiki, Victorialei "Nohea," 394–395
NALA. *See* National Association of Legal Assistants
National Association for Independent Paralegals, 8
National Association of Legal Assistants (NALA)
  billing rate for paralegals and, 130
  Certified Legal Assistant (CLA) Certification Program of, 11, 12, 13
  Certified Legal Assistant Specialist (CLAS) Program of, 11, 13
  Code of Ethics and Professional Responsibility of, 89
    compliance with, 90
    illustrated, 95
  creation, membership and function of, 8
  defined, 3
  disclosure of paralegal status and, 100
  Model Standards and Guidelines for the Utilization of Legal Assistants of, 96
    on unauthorized practice of law, 99
  paralegal compensation survey (1998-99) conducted by, 47, 49, 130
  paralegal defined by, 4
  regulation of paralegals and, 106, 107–108
National Conference of Commissioners (NCC) on Uniform State Laws, 225, 245, 512
National Environmental Policy Act (NEPA)(1969), 309–310
National Federation of Paralegal Associations (NFPA)
  billing rate for paralegals and, 130
  creation, membership and function of, 7
  defined, 3
  Internet security concerns and, 84
  Model Code of Ethics and Professional Responsibility and Guidelines for Enforcement of, 89
    compliance with, 90
    disclosure of paralegal status and, 100
    preamble and Section 1 of, illustrated, 92–94
  Paralegal Advanced Competency Exam (PACE) of, 11
  paralegal defined by, 4
  regulation of paralegals and, 106–107, 108
National Institutes of Health, 474
National Labor Relations Act (NLRA)(1935), 316–317
National Labor Relations Board (NLRB), 38, 317, 320, 321
National law, 168–170
  defined, 168
  finding information about other nations' laws and, 167
  international law and, 167–172
National Law Journal, 512
National Library of Medicine, 474
National origin
  credit discrimination on basis of, 305
  employment discrimination on basis of, 193, 318
National weather service, contacting, 472
Natural Gas Pipeline Safety Act (1968), 152
Natural language method of searching a database, 546–547
Navigable waters, 311
NCC (National Conference of Commissioners) on Uniform State Laws, 225, 245, 512
Necessaries, 224
Negligence, 216–218
  of attorney, 77
  comparative, 218, 352
  contributory, 218, 352
  defenses to, 218
  defined, 35, 216
  elements of, 217
Negotiation
  "assisted," 202
  defined, 194
  as form of alternative dispute resolution (ADR), 194–196
NEPA (National Environmental Policy Act)(1969), 309–310
NET-LAWYERS, 573
Netscape Navigator, 551
Networking, 49
New York v. Quarles, 426n
New Zealand, common law system in, 169
Newsgroup (Usenet Group), 561
NFPA. *See* National Federation of Paralegal Associations
Nichols, Terry, 183
Ninth Amendment, 150
NLRA (National Labor Relations Act)(1935), 316–317
NLRB (National Labor Relations Board), 38, 317, 320, 321
Nolo contendere plea, 436
Nolo Press, 104
Nonlegal encyclopedias, 571
Nonprofit corporation, 269
Nonprofit organization Web sites, 575
No-par stock, 274
Norris-LaGuardia Act (1932), 316
North American Free Trade Agreement, 168, 171
Not-for-profit corporation, 269
Notice(s)
  of appeal, 404
  of service of process, 346–348
  of taking deposition, 365
Notice pleading, 340n

Nuclear Regulatory Commission, 298, 309

O

Objective analysis, 597
Objectivity, 20–21
   legal memorandum, ethics and, 619
Occupational Safety and Health Act (1970), 155, 295
Occupational Safety and Health Administration (OSHA), 38, 155, 290, 295, 301, 525
   Web site of, 568
Occupational Safety and Health Citations, 532
Ocean dumping, 311
Ocean Dumping Act (Marine Protection, Research, and Sanctuaries Act)(1983), 311
O'Driscoll v. Hercules, Inc., 518
Offer
   contractual, 222–224, 233
   revocation of, 224
Offeree, 222
Offeror
   defined, 222
   revocation of offer by, 224
Office manager, 119, 121
Office of Personnel Management (OPM), 292, 293
Office of the Solicitor General, 293
Officer, corporate, 267, 270–271
Official Draft of the Model Penal Code, 416n
Oil pollution, 311–312
Oil Pollution Act (1990), 311–312
Oklahoma City bombing, 183
Omnibus Crime Control and Safe Streets Act (1968), 423
Online citators, 532
Online directories, 552, 571
Online guides, 552
Open-ended questions, 457–458
Opening statement, 396
Opinion, 164, 588
Opinion (advisory) letters, 610–611, 612
OPM (Office of Personnel Management), 292, 293
Or, and *versus*, 594
Oral arguments, 404

Ordinance, 152
Oregon State Bar v. Smith, 104
Organization Web sites, 575
Organizational skills, 13
Original jurisdiction, 180–181
OSHA. *See* Occupational Safety and Health Administration
Overtime wages, 47

P

P.A. (professional association), 270
PACE (Paralegal Advanced Competency Exam), 11
Packaging and labeling laws, 303
Paige, Lee A., 206
Paralegal(s)
   administrative law and, 155–156, 300–301
   agency law and, 260–261
   alternative dispute resolution (ADR) and, 205–207
   American system of justice and, 184–186
   as apparent partner, ethics and, 265
   associations of, 7–8
   business organizations and, 276, 278
   certification of. *See* Certification
   common law and, 166–167
   compensation of. *See* Paralegal compensation
   constitutional law and, 151–152
   consumer law and, 307
   contract, 33–34
   contract law and, 227, 230
   defined, 3–5
   education of. *See* Paralegal education
   effective utilization of, ethics and, 9
   employers of. *See* Employer(s)
   in England, 172
   environmental law and, 314–316
   estate administration and, 248–250
   federal court system and, 192–194
   freelance, 33–34, 101–103
   functions of, 5–6
   independent, 34

   as independent contractor, 33–34
   insurance, 476
   intellectual property and, 283
   international law and, 171
   job hunting by. *See* Job search
   legal nurse consultant (LNC) and, 45
   licensing of, 9, 105–108
   litigation, 34–35, 206, 356, 394–395, 500, 566, 615
   mediation and, 198–199
   performance evaluations and, 121–122
   personal attributes of, 19–21
   practice by
      before administrative agencies, 100, 290, 299–300
      attorney ethics and. *See* Attorney(s), ethical codes and rules of, paralegal practice and
   pro bono for, 168–169
   product-liability, 219
   as a profession. *See* Paralegal profession
   property law and, 240–243
   real-estate, 241–242, 279
   regulation of
      direct, 106–108
      indirect, 89–98
         guidelines for utilization of paralegals and, 91, 96
         increasing scope of paralegal responsibilities and, 96–98
         paralegal ethical codes and, 89–90, 92–95
   skills of. *See* Paralegal skill(s)
   specialties of. *See* Paralegal specialty(ies)
   state court systems and, 189
   statutory law and, 153
   supervision of, 119, 120
      inadequate, 78–79, 80
   technology and, 15
   termination of, 122
   tort law and, 219–220
   trusts and, 248–250
   utilization of, guidelines for, 91, 96

wills and, 248–250
Paralegal Advanced Competency Exam (PACE), 11
Paralegal certificate, 10
Paralegal compensation, 29–30, 45–47
  bonuses and, 47
  job benefits and, 46
  negotiating, 63–65
  overtime pay, federal law and, 47
  salaries *versus* hourly wages and, 46–47
  survey(s) of, 45–46
    by state, 46
    summary of, 30
Paralegal education, 8–13
  ABA-approved programs and, 11
  ABA's role in, 10–11
  certificate programs and, 9–10
  continuing, 12–13
  curriculum and, 10
  degree programs and, 10
Paralegal profession
  economics and, 8
  evolution of, 7
  formation of paralegal associations and, 7–8
  future of, 21, 23
  history of, 6–8
  personal attributes of paralegal and, 19–21
Paralegal skill(s), 13–19
  analytical, 14
  CLA exam preparation and, 12
  communication. *See* Communication skill(s)
  computer, 14
  interpersonal, 14–15, 457
  interviewing, 456–460
  listening, 18–19, 459–460
  marketing of, 53–65
  organizational, 13
  questioning, 457–459
  reading, 18
  speaking, 18
  writing, 19
    good, importance of, 597–603
Paralegal specialty(ies), 34–45
  bankruptcy law as, 37
  corporate law as, 36–37

criminal law as, 35–36, 420–421, 424–425
elder law as, 44
emerging areas of, 44
employment and labor law as, 37–39
environmental law as, 41–42
estate planning and probate administration as, 39–40
family law as, 42, 44
immigration law as, 44–45
intellectual-property law as, 40–41
legal nurse consultant (LNC) and, 45
litigation assistance as, 34–35, 206
personal-injury law as, 35
real-estate law as, 42, 43
Parallel citation, 514
Partner(s), 263
  defined, 118
  general, 266
  limited, 266
  rights and duties of, 264
  See also Partnership(s)
Partnership(s), 263–266
  defined, 118
  dissolution of, 266
  formation of, 264
  general, 266
  law, organizational chart of, illustrated, 119
  limited, 266
  limited liability (LLP), 273, 275, 276
  taxation of, 265
  termination of, 266
  winding up of, 266
  See also Partner(s)
Party(ies)
  defined, 163
  to a lawsuit, 163
  planning meeting of, report of, illustrated, 374
  potentially responsible (PRP), 313
  third. *See* Third parties
Par-value stock, 274
Patent and Trademark Office, 41n, 280, 283
  home page of, 574
Patent law, 40, 153

P.C. (professional corporation), 118, 270
Pearcy, Lloyd G., 274–275
Pener, Michael A., 90–91
Pennsylvania v. Muniz, 426n
Peremptory challenge, 393
The Perfect Lawyer, 569
Performance evaluations, 121–122
Periodicals, legal, 506–508, 511
Person(s)
  accused of crimes
    constitutional safeguards to protect, 421–423, 426
    initial appearance of, 433–434
    See also Criminal defendant(s); Criminal procedures
  jurisdiction over, 179–180
  other, defense of, 419
Personal liability, 117, 263
Personal property
  defined, 231
  intangible, 231
  tangible, 231
Personal representative, 39, 245
Personal-injury law, 35
Personal-injury lawsuits, 166, 220
  intake sheet and, 454–455
Persuasive authority, 492
Pesticides, 312
Petty offenses, 417
PLA (Professional Legal Assistants, Inc.), 8
Plagiarism, avoiding, ethics and, 511
Plain-meaning rule, 594–595
Plaintiff
  case of, during trial, 396–398
  defined, 34
Plea bargaining
  defined, 436
  ethics of, 437
Plea of *nolo contendere,* 436
Pleadings, 335–353
  amending, 353
  defined, 335
  fact, 340n
  judgment on, 353–354
  notice, 340n
  types of, 336
  writing, 604
Plessy v. Ferguson, 158n

Pocket part, 493
Point heading, 626
Police department, contacting, 471
Politics, law-office, 140
Pollution
    air, 310
    oil, 311–312
    water, 310–312
Post-degree certificate, 9
Posttrial motions, 402–403, 405
Potentially responsible party (PRP), 313
Prayer for relief, 341
Precedent
    absence of, 158, 492
    conflicting, 158
    defined, 157
    departures from, 157–158
Preemption, 152
Pregnancy, employment discrimination on basis of, 318
Pregnancy Discrimination Act (1978), 318
Preliminary hearing, 434
Preliminary investigation, 334
"Preponderance of the evidence," 442
Pressure questions, 458
Pretrial conference, 388–389
Pretrial motions, 353–356
Pretrial settlements, 331
Primary source, 488. See also Case reporting system
Principal, 259
Privacy, invasion of, 216
Private corporation, 268
Private justice, ethics and, 203
Privilege
    attorney-client. See Attorney-client privilege
    against self-incrimination, 423, 443
Privileged information, 357
Pro bono work, 168–169
Probable cause, 426, 428–429
Probate court, 39, 180
Probate of will, 39, 153, 245–246
Procedural law, 10
Product liability
    defined, 219
    lawsuits based on, 166
    strict, 219

Professional association (P.A.), 270
Professional corporation (P.C.), 118, 270
Professional investigator, 474
Professional Legal Assistants, Inc. (PLA), 8
Professional organization Web sites, 575
Professional portfolio, 58–59
Professional references, list of, 58
Promoters, 267
Proofreading, 603
Property
    defense of, 419
    exempt, 406
    intellectual. See Intellectual property
    jurisdiction over, 180
    ownership rights in, 231–232
    personal. See Personal property
    real. See Real property
    testamentary disposition of, 245. See also Will(s)
Prosecuting attorney, 415
Prosecution
    beginning of, 432–437
    criminal procedures prior to, 426–432
    trial and. See Criminal trial(s)
Prospectus, 267
Prosser and Keeton on the Law of Torts, Fifth Edition, 503
    page from, illustrated, 508
Proximate cause, 217
PRP (potentially responsible party), 313
Public corporation, 268
Public defender
    defined, 415
    employment with, 33, 36
Public law (P.L.) number, 520
Public policy, 158
Public prosecutor
    defined, 415
    employment with, 33
    office of, warrant division of, 441
Public trial, 422, 440–441
Publicly held corporation, 268
Puerto Rico, civil law system in, 170
Punitive damages, 215
Purchase and sale agreement,

sample of, illustrated, 234–237
Pure Food and Drug Act (1906), 304

Q
Québec, civil law system in, 170
Questioning skills, 457–459
Quicken's *Business Law Partner,* 230
Quid pro quo harassment, 319

R
Race
    credit discrimination on basis of, 305
    employment discrimination on basis of, 123, 193, 318
Raybourn, Pamela Jo, 500
RCRA (Resource Conversation and Recovery Act)(1976), 312–313
Reading skills, 18
Real estate, 42. See also Real property
Real Estate Settlement Procedures Act (1976), 239
Real property, 230–243, 244
    appraisals and, 250
    defined, 230
    law of, the paralegal and, 240–243
    lease of, 239
    ownership rights in, 231–232
    transfer and sale of, 232–239
        accurate paperwork, ethics and, 239
        appraisals and, 250
        closing of, 42, 238–239, 243
        contract formation and, 233
        duties of competence and diligence, ethics and, 233
        escrow agent and, 233–235, 238
        financing and, 235–236
        inspection of premises and, 236–237
        insurance and, 237–238
        steps involved in, summarized, 232
        title examination and, 42, 66, 237–238
Real-estate agent, 250

Real-estate law, 42, 43
Real-estate paralegal, 241–242, 279
Reasonable accommodations, 319, 593
Reasonable person standard, 217
Record(s)
  on appeal, 404
  employment, obtaining, 471–472
  good, keeping, ethics and, 444
  medical, obtaining, 471–472, 473
  vehicle title and registration, obtaining, 473
Recording an interview, 453–456
Re-cross examination, 398
Redirect examination, 398
Reference line, 607–608
Reference materials, filing of, 127–128
References, professional, list of, 58
Reformation, 226
Regulation(s)
  of attorneys. *See* Attorney(s), regulation of
  direct, 72n, 106–108
  federal
    of environment, 309–310
    state regulation *versus,* 152
  indirect, of paralegals. *See* Paralegal(s), indirect regulation of
  local, of environment, 313–314
  self-, 72
  state
    of environment, 313–314
    federal regulation *versus,* 152
  See also Administrative law
Release forms, 334
Relevant evidence, 479
Reliability, 19
Religion
  credit discrimination on basis of, 305
  employment discrimination on basis of, 193, 318
Relocation assistance, 250
Remandment of case, 404, 589
Remedy(ies)
  equitable, 160–161
  in equity
    defined, 159

remedies at law *versus,* 159–161
at law
  defined, 159
  remedies in equity *versus,* 159–161
what to do when someone asks about, ethics and, 164
Reply brief, 621
Reporting Services Digest (West Group), 497
Reports. *See* Case reporting system
Reprimand, 75
Rescission
  of contract, 226
  defined, 160
Research, 487–581
  of administrative law, 525–526
  of case law. *See* Case law(s), researching
  CD-ROMs and, 541–542
  computer-assisted. *See* Computer-assisted legal research
  of constitutional law, 526, 528, 530
  effective, ten tips for, 509–510
  efficiency in, ethics and, 489
  finding tools and. *See* Finding tools
  goals of, determining, 490–492
  on the Internet, 553–565. *See also* Internet, research on
  of legislative history, 523–525
  medical, online, 474, 558
  online, 553–565. *See also* Internet, research on
  results of, synthesizing, 590–592
  sources of
    citing
      ethics and, 519
      See also Citation(s)
    primary, 488. *See also* Case reporting system
    secondary. *See* Secondary source(s)
  stare decisis and, 158
  of statutory law, 519–525, 530
  strategy for, mapping out, 533
  updating the law and, 529–532
  using citators and, 529–532
Resource Conversation and

Recovery Act (RCRA) (1976), 312–313
Respondeat superior, 260, 261, 262
Responsibility, 19
Restatements of the Law, 162, 503–506, 512
  illustrated, 511
Restitution, 160, 226
Résumé, 54–56
  cover letter and, 56–58
  posting online, 51
  proofreading, 56
  sample, illustrated, 55
  what not to include in, 56
  what to include in, 54–56
Retainer, 131
Retainer agreement, 128–129
  defined, 128
  sample, illustrated, 129
Return-of-service form
  defined, 345
  illustrated, 346
Reuters Health Information Services, 474
Reversal of judgment, 404, 588
Reviewing courts. *See* Appellate court(s)
Revised Model Business Corporation Act (RMBCA), 267
Revised Uniform Partnership Act (RUPA), 264
Revocable living trust, 247
Revocation, 224
Richmond, Jan, 569–570
Risk, assumption of, 218
Rivers and Harbors Appropriations Act (1899), 310–311
RMBCA (Revised Model Business Corporation Act), 267
Rome, civil law ("code law") of, 169
Rule(s)
  of civil procedure. *See* Federal Rules of Civil Procedure
  of construction, 594
  of evidence
    in criminal process, 443
    defined, 477
    Federal, 477, 479
    investigation and, 477–479, 481

of four, 192
Rulemaking by administrative agencies, 294, 295–296
RUPA (Revised Uniform Partnership Act), 264

S
S corporation, 270, 271
Safe Drinking Water Act (1974), 311
Sale(s)
  consumer laws and, 303–304
  of goods, contract for. See Sales contract(s)
  of real estate. See Real property, transfer and sale of
Sales contract(s), 225–226
  consumer laws and, 303–304
  defined, 225
Salutation, 608
San Juan, Vitonio F., 390–391
S.C. (service corporation), 270
Scheduling order, 342
Scotland, civil law system in, 170
Search engines, 552–553
  meta, 553
  results of search using, illustrated, 554
Search query, 545
Search warrant
  defined, 429
  illustrated, 430–431
SEC. See Securities and Exchange Commission
Secol, Dorothy, 102–103
Second Amendment, 150
Secondary source(s)
  of case law, 492–511
  defined, 488
  See also Finding tools
Securities and Exchange Commission (SEC), 156, 291, 293, 525
  Electronic Data Gathering, Analysis, and Retrieval (EDGAR) database of, 563, 568, 574
  page from, illustrated, 564
  "Plain English Handbook" of, 600
Self-defense, 419
Self-incrimination, 423, 443
Self-regulation, 72

Sentencing, 444
"Separate-but-equal doctrine," 158n
Service corporation (S.C.), 270
Service of process, 343–348
  defined, 343
  notice and waiver of, 346–348
Session laws, 520
Settlement, pretrial, 331
Settlement agreement
  defined, 196
  family, 246
  sample, illustrated, 197
Settlor, 246
Seventh Amendment, 150, 341, 440–441
Sexual harassment
  defined, 319
  developing policy on, 321
Share(s)
  defined, 266
  "in series," 275
  See also Stock
Shareholders, 266, 271
Shepard's Citations, 307, 510, 533, 544
  abbreviations used in, 531–532
  illustrated, 529
  organization of, 529
  types of information provided by, 530
  See also entries beginning with Shepard's
Shepard's Federal Reporter Citations, 529
Shepard's Law Review Citations, 532
Shepard's United States Citations, 529
Signature on complaint, 341
Sixth Amendment, 150, 422, 423, 433, 441
SJT (summary jury trial), 203
Slip laws, 519–520
Smith, Robin, 104
Social Security Administration (SSA), 298
  hearing before, 297
  obtaining information from, 475
  paralegals' representation of clients before, 100, 290, 299
Sole (solo) practitioner, 117

Sole proprietorship(s), 117–118, 261–263
  advantages and disadvantages of, 263
  defined, 117
  formation of, 262–263
  taxation and, 263
  termination of, 263
South Africa, civil law system in, 170
Speaking skills, 18
Specialized dictionaries, 572
Specific performance, 226
  analyzing a case for, 161
  defined, 160
Speedy trial, 422, 440–441
Spendthrift trust, 247
SSA. See Social Security Administration
Staff attorney, 6
Standard of proof, 442–443
Standing to sue, 183–184
Stare decisis, 157–159, 166, 170
  defined, 157
  legal research and, 158
State(s)
  administrative agencies of, 298
  certification by, 12
  codes of, 525
  constitutions of, 151
  courts of. See State court system(s)
  governments of, as employers, 293
  guidelines of, for utilization of paralegals, 96
  legislatures of, attorney regulation and, 73
  paralegal compensation by, 46
  statutes of limitations of, 126–127
State bar associations, 7
State court system(s), 186–189
  decisions of, 511–514. See also Case reporting system
  illustrated, 187
  the paralegal and, 189
  trial courts of, 186–188
State prosecutor, 415
State reporters, 511–513
Statute(s)
  defined, 152
  federal, publication of, 519–523

interpreting, 596
of limitations. *See* Statute of limitations
long arm, 179–180
workers' compensation, 37, 318
See also Law(s)
Statute of Frauds, 224–225
Statute of limitations, 126–127, 159–160
as defense to criminal liability, 419
defined, 126, 159
duty of competence, ethics and, 162
Statutes Edition of Shepard's United States Citations, 530
Statutory law, 152–153
analyzing, 592–595
common law and, 162–163
expanding scope of, 152–153
interpreting, 523, 594–595, 596
legislative history and, 519, 523–525
paralegal and, 153
reading, 592–594
researching, 519–525, 530
Shepard's Citations and, 530
Stock
"blank," 274
no-par, 274
par-value, 274
See also Share(s)
Strict liability, 215, 218–219
Strike, 316
Subagent, 260
Subchapter S of Internal Revenue Code, 270, 271
Subject matter, jurisdiction over, 180
Submission agreement, 201–202
Subpoena(s)
defined, 384
illustrated, 385
issuing, 384–385, 386
Subscribers, 267
Substantive law, 10
Summary judgment, 354–356
Summary jury trial (SJT), 203
Summons
defined, 343
illustrated, 343
notice and waiver of service and, 346–348

serving, 345
Superfund (Comprehensive Environmental Response, Compensation, and Liability Act)(CERCLA)(1980), 313
Supervision, inadequate, 78–79, 80
Support personnel, 121
Supporting affidavit, 352
Supremacy clause, 149–150, 298
Supreme court(s)
state, 188–189
attorney regulation and, 73
United States. *See* United States Supreme Court
Supreme Court Bulletin (CCH, Inc.), 518
Supreme Court Reporter (S.Ct.) (West Group), 496, 514, 518
Shepard's United States Citations and, 529
Suspension, 75
Syllabus, 518, 587

T
Table of cases, 501
Tangible personal property, 231
Tax liens, 66
Taxation
corporations and, 271
limited liability company (LLC) and, 273, 275
limited liability partnership (LLP) and, 276
of partnerships, 265
sole proprietorships and, 263
Telephone directories, 475, 572
Templeton, Denise, 52–53
Tenancy
in common, 231
by the entirety, 231
joint, 231
Tentative trust, 247
Tenth Amendment, 150, 151
Terms and connectors method of searching a database, 546
Terry, Richard M., 605–606
Testamentary capacity, 245
Testamentary disposition of property, 245. *See also* Will(s)
Testamentary trust, 247
Testate death, 245
Testator
defined, 244

testamentary capacity and, 245
Thesauri, 573
Third Amendment, 150
Third parties
agency relationships and, 259–260
conversations overheard by, 81–82
defined, 82
TILA (Truth-in-Lending Act)(1974), 305
Time
constraints on, 596
documenting, 133–134
flexibility and, 596
management of, ethics and, 603
Time slip
defined, 133
illustrated, 135
Timekeeping procedures, 132–136
Title examinations, 42, 66, 237–238
Title insurance, 237–238
Tort(s), 215–221
defined, 215
intentional, 215–216
lawsuits involving, 166
paralegals and, 219–220
toxic, 309
Totten, In the Matter of, 247n
Totten trust, 247
Towne, V. Sheri, 566
Toxic chemicals, 312–313
Toxic substances, 312
Toxic Substances Control Act (1976), 312
Toxic torts, 309
Trade journals, job listings in, 49–50
Trade secret, 281, 283
Trademark, 280
Trademark law, 40, 154, 280
Treatises, 503
Treaty, 171
Trespass to land, 216
Trial(s)
appealing verdict and, 403–405
civil litigation and. *See* Civil litigation
closing arguments and, 399–401
criminal. *See* Criminal trial(s)
defendant's case and, 399
emergency in, 188

exhibits and displays for, 387, 388, 389, 442
by jury
demand for, 341
right to, 422, 440–441
jury selection and, 389–394
mini-, 202
new, motion for, 402–403, 405
notebook for. *See* Trial notebook
opening statement and, 396
plaintiff's case and, 396–398
posttrial motions and, 402–403, 405
preparing for, 383–388
checklist for, 384
presentation technology and, 388
pretrial conference and, 388–389
procedures during, 382–413
speedy and public, 422, 440–441
summary jury (SJT), 203
trial support and, 389
Trial court(s)
defined, 181
emergency in, 188
federal, 181, 190–191, 445
state, 186–188
Trial notebook, 387–388
defined, 387
ten tips for preparing, 390–391
True bill, 435
Trust(s), 243, 246–248, 249
charitable, 247
defined, 39, 246
living *(inter vivos)*, 246–247, 248
the paralegal and, 248–250
spendthrift, 247
tentative, 247
testamentary, 247
Totten, 247
Trust account(s), 131–132
creating, 133
defined, 131
ethics and, 132
Trustee, 39, 246
Truth-in-Lending Act (TILA)(1974), 305
Twenty-seventh Amendment, 150n

U

UCC. *See* Uniform Commercial Code
Unanimous opinion, 164, 588
Unauthorized practice of law (UPL), 98–105
avoiding problems with, 101
defined, 74
disclosure of paralegal status and, 100–101
ethics and, 5, 105, 334, 465
letters and, 613
giving legal opinions and advice and, 5, 99–100
independent paralegals and, 103–105
paralegals freelancing for attorneys and, 101–103
representing clients in court and, 100
Unconscionable contract, 225
Uniform Commercial Code (UCC)
Article 2 of, 232, 512
scope of, 225
leases under, 239
revisions of, 512
warranties under, 226
Uniform Electronic Transactions Act, 512
Uniform Partnership Act (UPA), 264
Uniform Probate Code (UPC), 39, 153, 245
Uniform resource locator (URL), 548–549
Unions, labor, 316. *See also* Labor law(s)
United Nations, General Assembly of, 171
United States
common law system in, 169
government of, illustrated, 291
North American Free Trade Agreement and, 168, 171
United States Claims Digest (West Group), 497
United States Code (U.S.C.), 520–521
on the Internet, 556, 574
link to, 550
Statutes Edition of Shepard's United States Citations and, 530
titles of, 520, 526
illustrated, 521
United States Code Annotated (U.S.C.A.) (West Group), 522–523, 528
on CD-ROM, 542
excerpt from, illustrated, 522
researching, 524
Statutes Edition of Shepard's United States Citations and, 530
United States Code Congressional and Administrative News (U.S.C.C.A.N.), 520, 525
illustrated, 525
United States Code Service (U.S.C.S.) (West Group), 520, 523, 528
Cumulative Later Case and Statutory Service of, 523
Statutes Edition of Shepard's United States Citations and, 530
United States Constitution
amendments to. *See* Bill of Rights *specific amendments*
delegation doctrine of, 294
federal court system's authority under, 179, 181
jury trials guaranteed by, 341
link to, 550
safeguards under, to protect persons accused of crimes, 421–423, 426
Statutes Edition of Shepard's United States Citations and, 530
supremacy clause of, 149–150, 298
treaty ratification under, 171
United States Supreme Court's jurisdiction under, 192
United States Copyright Office, 41n, 281, 283
United States courts of appeals, 191, 192
United States Department of Defense, 309
United States Department of the Interior, 309

United States Department of Justice (DOJ), 292–293
   Web site of, 418
United States Department of Labor, 309
   Bureau of Labor Statistics of, 23
   Occupational Safety and Health Administration of. *See* Occupational Safety and Health Administration
   Wage and Appeals Board of, 299
United States Department of Labor v. Page & Addison, P.C., 47
United States Department of Transportation, 293
United States district courts, 181, 190
   illustrated, 191
   working for, 445
United States Government Depository Library, 520
United States Government Manual, 32
   on the Internet, 574
United States Government Printing Office, 524
   online database of, 574
United States House of Representatives, Internet Law Library of, 167, 556
   page from, illustrated, 557
United States Law Week (Bureau of National Affairs), 518
United States Patent and Trademark Office, 41n, 280, 283
   home page of, 574
United States Postal Service, 293, 298
United States Reports (U.S.), 514, 516–517
   Shepard's United States Citations and, 529
United States Statutes at Large, 520, 521
   Statutes Edition of Shepard's United States Citations and, 530
United States Supreme Court
   attorney regulation and, 73–74
   constitutional authority of, 190
   decisions of, 491, 492
      reporting of, 514, 515–518
   how cases reach, 192
   jurisdiction of, 192
   justices of, 163–164
      lifetime appointment of, 190
   rule of four of, 192
   types of cases reviewed by, 192
   writ of *certiorari* and, 192, 555
United States Supreme Court Digest (West Group), 497
The University of Chicago Manual of Legal Citation, 514
University Web sites, 573
Unsafe at Any Speed (Nader), 301
UPA (Uniform Partnership Act), 264
UPC (Uniform Probate Code), 39, 153, 245
UPL. *See* Unauthorized practice of law
URL (uniform resource locator), 548–549
Usenet Group (Newsgroup), 561

V

Vehicle title and registration records, obtaining, 473
Venue, 182–183
   defined, 182
   motion for change of, 436
Verdict, 401–402
   acquittal and, 441
   appealing, 403–405, 446
   defined, 401
   directed, 399
   judgment notwithstanding, motion for, 402
   not-guilty, 446
Vicarious liability, 260
Voir dire, 390–394
   challenges during, 392–394
   defined, 391
   questions for, drafting, 407

W

Wage-Hour Law (Fair Labor Standards Act)(FLSA)(1938), 47, 317
Waiver
   of right to trial by jury, 441
   illustrated, 442
   of service of process, 346–348
Want ads, online, 51
Wards, locating, 577
Warrant(s)
   arrest, 429
   prosecutor's office and, 441
   search, 429, 430–431
Warranty(ies)
   express, 226
   implied, 226
   sales contracts and, 225–226
   under UCC, 226
Water(s)
   drinking, 311
   navigable, 311
   ocean dumping and, 311
   pollution of, 310–312
Water Quality Act (1987), 311
Web site(s)
   designer of, 566
   evaluations of, 574
   See also World Wide Web
the Web. *See* World Wide Web
Weber, Pamela Poole, 424–425
West Group
   annotations of, 501–503
   digests of, 495–501
   hornbooks of, 503
   publications of, 493. *See also entries beginning with West*
   reporters of. *See* Case reporting system
West key-number system, 495
West Law Directory, 50
Westlaw©, 532, 541, 542–548, 575
   accessing, 543
   browser enhancements and, 547–548
   checking a citation on, 544, 545
   KeyCite citator service and, 544, 545, 629
   opening page of, illustrated, 543
   retrieving a document by citation on, 544
   searching database on, 545–547
      natural language method and, 546–547
      results of, illustrated, 547
      terms and connectors method and, 546

selecting database on, 544–545
West's Bankruptcy Digest, 497
West's federal digests, 495–497
West's Legal Directory, 565
West's National Reporter System, 513–514
   illustrated, 515
   Shepard's Citations and, 529
Will(s), 243, 244–246, 249
   defined, 39
   drafting of, 246
   laws governing, 245
   the paralegal and, 248–250
   probate of, 39, 153, 245–246
   statutory law and, 153
   valid, requirements for, 245
William the Conqueror, 156
Winding up, 266
Witness(es)
   contacting, 383–385, 471
   coordination of, 375
   defined, 331
   examination of
      cross-, 397–398
      direct, 396–397
      recross-, 398
      redirect, 398
   expert, 373–374
      consulting with, 407
      defined, 465
      locating, 386
      on the Internet, 565, 567
   eyewitnesses and, 465–466
   friendly, 385
      defined, 466
      issuing subpoenas for, 386
   hostile, 396–397, 466–467
   impeachment of, 368–369
   interviewing, 464–468, 471
   issuing subpoenas for, 384–385, 386
   lay, 465
   locating, 386, 474–475
   preparing for trial, 383–384, 385–387
   qualifications of, checking, 467–468
   questioning, 467
   to signing of will, 245
   statement of, 468, 469
Witness statements, 468, 469
Words and Phrases (West Group), 493, 494–495
   excerpt from, illustrated, 497
Work product
   defined, 85
   files of, 127–128
Workers' compensation statutes, 37, 318
World Wide Web (the Web), 549–550
   browsers and, 551
   defined, 549
   ethical opinions on, finding, 572
   guides and directories and, 552, 571
   mirror site on, 562
   search engines and, 552–553
      meta, 553
   site designer on, 566
   surfing, ethics and, 562
   See also Internet
Writ(s)
   of *certiorari,* 192, 555
   of execution, 406
Writing, legal. *See* Legal writing
Writing skills, 19
   good, importance of, 597–603

Y

Yahoo Company Information Web site, 558, 568
   pages from, illustrated, 559, 560
Year Books, 157
Year-and-a-day defense, 422
Yellow pages, 50
Yera, E. J., 509–510
Young, Margaret Levine, 558

Z

Zip codes, 573